'MY HAREM, IT'S AN EXPENSIVE GAME'

A. A. Rouse, the Blazing Car Murder 1930 and Inter-War Criminal Justice and Society

GERRY RUBIN and TONY MILLAN

Mango Books

First edition published 2019
Softcover 2020

The right of Gerry Rubin and Tony Millan to be identified as
the authors of this work has been asserted in accordance
with the Copyright, Designs & Patents Act 1988.

Illustrations from the authors' collections except the following:
3, 14: National Justice Museum
10, 17: National Archives

ISBN: 978-1-911273-80-6 (hardcover)
ISBN: 978-1-911273-96-7 (softcover)
Also available in Kindle format

Published by

Mango Books
18 Soho Square
London W1D 3QL

www.MangoBooks.co.uk

'MY HAREM, IT'S AN EXPENSIVE GAME'

A. A. Rouse, the Blazing Car Murder 1930
and Inter-War Criminal Justice and Society

'MY HAREM, IT'S AN EXPENSIVE GAME'

Preface.. i

Section A: Mise-en-Scène

Chapter One: Police Search For Hatless Stranger 1

Chapter Two: "Bonfire They Won't Forget"................................22

Chapter Three: The Waitress With A Wedding Ring 35

Chapter Four: Police Search In Strange Riddle............................54

Chapter Five: Public Prosecutor Takes Action 66

Chapter Six: Re-Examination Behind Locked Doors........................91

Chapter Seven: Who Was The Man In Rouse's Car? 102

Chapter Eight: Further Amazing Disclosures At Today's Hearing.......... 126

Section B: Trial and Post-Trial

Chapter Nine: Crown K.C.: "Expert Will Say It Was Not Accidental"........ 157

Chapter Ten: Law's Cruel Kindness; Putting Accused Man In Box 186

Chapter Eleven: Mr. Justice Talbot On Rouse's Lies 216

Chapter Twelve: My Hectic Life Of Love And Deceit....................... 226

Chapter Thirteen: Murderer Hears His Fate Unmoved 237

Chapter Fourteen: My Prison Talks With Rouse - By His Wife 266

Chapter Fifteen: "My Peep Into The Condemned Cell" 299

Chapter Sixteen: How Rouse Spent His Last Days......................... 307

Section C: Rouse, Women and Society

Chapter Seventeen: A 1914 Man 353

Chapter Eighteen: Jekyll & Hyde Life: Unknown To Wife For Years 369

Chapter Nineteen: The Sheik In A Car 380

Chapter Twenty: Amazing Entanglements With Women 396

Chapter Twenty-One: Rouse And 3 Weeping Women 414

Chapter Twenty-Two: "So They Are Not Married?" 443

Section D: Miscarriage of Justice?

Chapter Twenty-Three: Faked Thefts Of Cars............................ 457

Chapter Twenty-Four: Wounded In The War 478

Chapter Twenty-Five: Would You Have Hanged Alfred Arthur Rouse?...... 507

Bibliography 535

Index 559

PREFACE

The authors of this book, each with separate connections to the University of Kent, perhaps form an 'odd couple' in jointly writing this study of the inter-war murder case of Alfred Arthur Rouse, an event widely known as the 'Blazing Car' mystery. One author is a seasoned academic researcher in the field of criminal justice and its history. The other is an experienced actor and scriptwriter. The former wished to give expression to a newly emerging academic *genre* of true crime writing, one that seeks to place the dramatic events surrounding murder *causes célèbres* within their social, economic and cultural milieux. Thus, to cite recent previous examples, how can one adequately understand the Crippen case without reference to the smug life in the emerging London suburbs; or the 'Brides in the Bath' case without reference to the plight of spinsters who believed that they risked being left on the shelf; the tragedy of the Thompson-Bywaters case without observing contemporary judgmental views on the 'New Woman' and marital infidelity; or to the fate of Ruth Ellis without reference to 'respectable' views on the practice of motherhood? By the same token one aim of this book is to locate the life, loves and misdemeanours (or worse) of Arthur Rouse within his contemporary post-Great War surroundings of ambiguous sexual behaviour, and increasing prosperity, consumerism and mobility, at least in the south coast and London suburbia of Rouse's existence.

The latter author, at home with fictional narratives written for television, was initially fascinated by the extensive reporting and dramatising both in the local press of his native Northamptonshire and also in the national press, of what were then described as the 'sensational' details of the Rouse case. Its features were intriguing. An incinerated corpse, unidentified to this day, found in a burnt-out car in a lonely country road near Northampton in the early hours of November 6, 1930, the commercial traveller driver, assumed to have been the victim, next turning up in an impressive cottage in rural south Wales where he had been assumed by the owners, in their ignorance, to be their son-in-law, then the unraveling of his story, when the police closed in, revealing him (at best) as a serial philanderer, legally married to one woman, bigamously married to another (and that apart from the supposed Welsh marital connection), and the father of two daughters by yet another woman who called herself Mrs. Rouse. It was as if one could not make it up. Thus for the second joint author of this book, the raw material for a drama more closely tied to the events of 1930-31 was promising.

We are grateful to all those who assisted us in offering advice, in affording us access to research materials in various archives, and in facilitating our research in other ways. We are particularly grateful to Richard Cowley, archivist at Northamptonshire Police archives who sadly died during the preparation of this book; to Bev Baker at the Nottingham Galleries of Justice (now the National Justice Museum); to Dr John Bond and Dr Lisa Smith of Leicester University who advised us on DNA sampling in regard to the Rouse case; to Eric Musgrave, men's fashion expert (now of Northumberland and formerly a frighteningly rugged midfield colleague of one of the present authors); to Gordon Pringle, fellow season ticket holder (Edinburgh); and to David Mills (Cardiff) of the Gelligaer Historical Society. We hope that this monograph, the joint effort of professional academic and professional scriptwriter, respectively, is a useful addition to the literature, not just of famous murder *causes célèbres*, but of aspects regarding inter-war criminal justice and society.

The present volume is dedicated to our wives (but not in Rouse's sense of 'wives').

GRR
TM

August 2018

SECTION A
Mise-en-Scène

CHAPTER ONE

POLICE SEARCH FOR HATLESS STRANGER

DAILY MAIL, November 7, 1930

How had it come to this? How was it that Alfred Arthur Rouse, a handsome and smartly dressed resident of suburban Friern Barnet, was walking along a moonlit Northamptonshire country lane in the early hours after Bonfire Night, looking dishevelled and panic-stricken?

How was it that he now found himself in the most dangerous and frightening situation he had ever known since his time in the First World War trenches? Then, he had witnessed an aeroplane, hit by gunfire and bursting into flames, crash near him on the Western Front. Now he had seen his own car devoured in a blaze, with flames shooting fifteen feet into the night sky, turning his world upside down. He was hurrying away from that inferno. Trying to put some distance between himself and the burning car. Trying to find time to think.

He had never been in such a perilous position before. Yes, he'd been a bit of a rascal. But these had only been minor brushes with the law; a bit of insurance fraud here; a speeding fine there; a summons still pending from another alleged motoring offence. And then there was his colourful life with women. The pleasures of the flesh were his biography, his provenance. But he'd always managed to keep one step ahead of the game. Was his life story entering a final chapter or could he still fashion more adventures by putting the incident of the previous half-hour behind him and by reconstructing himself far away from his immediate awful surroundings?

As he walked nervously along the country road his unkempt appearance was striking. He was in a suit, wearing a mackintosh and carrying an *attaché* case, but crucially he was not wearing a hat. That was highly unusual at that time, for Arthur was keen on style and headgear, and convention required that men be seen in public wearing hats, or flat caps if working-class. Indeed public reaction to anyone lacking headgear was almost akin to noticing the perverse image of the Emperor's new clothes.

"'Hats', [Engels] wrote, are the universal head covering in England, even for working men, hats of the most diverse forms, round, high, broad-brimmed, or without brim—only the younger men in factory towns wearing caps.... Those brave spirits who in the years before World War I dared to stroll bare headed in the open gave rise to a jeering urchin cry that swept the land: 'No 'at brigade'".[1]

Thus wrote Robert Roberts, the chronicler of Salford in the early twentieth century, in recalling the words of the mid-nineteenth century Manchester factory owner (and collaborator of Karl Marx), Frederick Engels[2]. As one writer has recently observed,

> "Roberts....suggested a concern with sartorial respectability and [with] the recognition of social hierarchies and appropriate models of manly behaviour that puts in doubt claims that the lower middle classes retained sole custody over clothing etiquette. Indeed, proof of competitive clothing practices in working-class areas heightens the sense that clerks and lower-status white-collar workers literally embraced aspirational stereotypes as a means of distancing their fashion choices from the models established by neighbouring artisanal communities."[3]

The late Denis Healey, commenting on more recent trends, put it in simple terms. 'When I started in politics, working-class people wore cloth caps, middle-class people wore trilbies or occasionally bowler hats and the toffs wore top hats'.[4] One could tell a lot about a man by his hat, particularly his position in the class system. John Galsworthy, for one, possessed an acute appreciation of the subtleties surrounding the disporting of headgear. Commenting on his novel, *The Man of Property*, the social historian, Laura Ugolini, has recently observed that,

> "....Galsworthy used the image of a hat, 'a soft grey hat, not even a new one—a dusty thing with a shapeless crown', to symbolize the difference between Philip Bossiney, the hat's owner, and his fiancée's family, the upper-middle-class Forsytes. It was this 'significant trifle' that to the Forsytes provided 'the detail in which was embedded the meaning of the whole matter'. Bossiney's insistence on wearing a shapeless old hat not only encapsulated the problem of the young man's uncertain status as a struggling architect, but also raised suspicions concerning his moral and psychological make-up."[5]

Rouse's favourite hat was his Stetson but it was his trilby that he wore when he set out on his fateful car journey. Now the trilby was nowhere to be seen. However,

1   Robert Roberts, *The Classic Slum: Salford Life in the First Quarter of the Century*, Penguin, 1971, pp. 39-40. Interestingly, the Prince of Wales, later Edward VIII, rebelled for a time against wearing any headgear on his travels. While his father, George V, remonstrated with him, the hat industry complained that the prince's habit was affecting sales. He apologised and agreed to wear more hats in the future, even promoting the straw boater in 1932 to boost employment among the Luton hatters. See Diana de Marly, *Fashion for Men: An Illustrated History*, Batsford, 1985, p. 121. A similar complaint that John F. Kennedy had single-handedly damaged the American hat industry by appearing bare-headed at his inauguration in 1961 is wrong on many counts, not least because he wore a silk top hat throughout most of the ceremony. See, for example, www.jfklibrary. org photograph KN17136.
2   Frederick Engels, *The Condition of the Working Class in England*, (introduction by Eric Hobsbawm), Panther, 1969; first published in Great Britain in 1892.
3   Christopher Breward, *The Hidden Consumer: Masculinities, Fashion and City Life, 1860-1914*, Manchester University Press, Manchester, 1999, p. 94. For a detailed analysis of more modern times, see Tim Edwards, *Men in the Mirror: Men's Fashions, Masculinity and Consumer Society*, Cassell, 1997.
4   Cited in the *Observer*, October 4, 2015
5   Laura Ugolini, "Men, Masculinities and Menswear Advertising, c. 1890-1914", in John Benson and Laura Ugolini (eds), *A Nation of Shopkeepers: Five Centuries of British Retailing*, I. B. Tauris, 2003, pp. 80-104, at p. 80. For a recent overview see Nicholas Storey, *History of Men's Fashion*, Pen & Sword, 2015.

sharply outlined against the dark sky were the flames from a fire behind him, shooting high into the air. He had just clambered out of a ditch at the side of the metalled road and was walking apprehensively towards the crossroads, maybe some hundred or so yards away, where the left turn took one in the London direction and the right turn to Northampton, just a mile or two away. Unseen so far by man or beast, he was now very close to the main road from where he could take stock regarding his next move.

But suddenly and alarmingly, in the crisp moonlight, he spotted them and they spotted him. For, as he made his way towards the crossroads, there they were, coming in the other direction at that unearthly hour, two young cousins, Alfred Brown, a cask repairer, and William Bailey, a shoe operative, coming back to the village from a Guy Fawkes dance at Northampton (which was, of course, the centre of the shoe manufacturing trade in England). And as they passed each other in silence, the physical features of all three were sharply illuminated, making the cousins' description of Rouse that they offered later to the police that night both vivid and accurate. A few steps further on, and Rouse's high-pitched voice was heard, calling back to them something like, 'It looks like they've had a bonfire up there', before he moved on more quickly towards the junction. The cousins turned round in the direction of the voice and watched as Rouse reached the crossroads where he paused for a moment or two, turned to the right in the Northampton direction, paused again and then moved off in the London direction. Perhaps he had originally planned to disappear unseen to Scotland after the blaze,[6] which might explain why he initially turned right in a northwards direction. However the chance meeting with Brown and Bailey seemed to have ruined everything, requiring him quickly to invent a Plan B. If this were the case then it presumably entailed a return to London, then a period of lying low in rural South Wales where he had, as we shall see, some intriguing connections.

As to Brown and Bailey, they were clearly puzzled as to why he was walking *away* from Hardingstone and showing none of the curiosity about the fierce blaze (at that very late hour) that gripped the cousins almost immediately after they had spotted the glow, and after being addressed by Rouse in such a casual manner. The matter, of course, became clearer some days later when they next saw and recognised him again, in the dock at Northampton police court. As they subsequently told a journalist, 'In the country we are in the habit of saying good-night but this man said nothing.'[7] Indeed at the police court one of the cousins remarked that it was not every day that one saw a well-dressed hatless man, carrying an *attaché* case, emerge from a ditch in a lonely country road at 1:45 in the morning. No wonder their recollection of him was vivid.

Meanwhile, alerted by the roaring flames shooting high into the air, the cousins made off round a bend towards the source of the fire where they discovered a small car burning fiercely at the side of the road. They rushed on to Hardingstone village to rouse the parish constable (actually Bailey's father) and the local Northamptonshire County policeman, PC Harry Copping. By the time of their return to the car, the flames had in fact subsided from fifteen feet to about five feet.

6   The blaze was described as Rouse's 'chemical experiment' by biographers of the famous pathologist, Sir Bernard Spilsbury, who became involved in the case. See Douglas G. Browne and E. V. Tullett, *Bernard Spilsbury: His Life and Cases*, Companion Book Club, 1952, p. 330
7   *Daily Mail*, November 7, 1930.

But what especially struck those present was that when Brown's torch shone onto the inside of the vehicle, they could just make out the outlines of what appeared to be a bundle like a large ball surrounded by the flames. The men organised buckets of water from nearby houses which eventually put out the fire to reveal not a large unidentifiable bundle of material but a charred corpse slumped over the front seats.

Copping instructed William Bailey Snr. to make his way to Northampton to summon a more senior policeman from the county force's police station. But that mission was dogged by misadventure before the message got through to the county force that a serious road accident had apparently occurred at Hardingstone. For when Bailey reached the Angel Lane police station before 3:00 am to ask for more senior police assistance in view of the grisly finding in the burnt-out vehicle, he rang the bell to be admitted to the closed building but no-one answered. Eventually giving up waiting for a response, he went off to the Northampton Borough Central police station where he did get an answer to his knocking and ringing and where he told his story of the vehicle blaze and of the dead body at Hardingstone. The borough force sensibly telephoned the county police office right away. Probationer Neasham answered and was requested immediately to contact Inspector James Lawrence of the county force (a policeman whom the press would go on to describe as 'tall, blonde and imperturbable'[8]). Bailey then made his way back to Angel Lane and in due course he, together with Lawrence and PC Robert Valentine, drove to the scene of the incident.

Perhaps out of courtesy, or else to enlist as much support as possible, Valentine of the county force telephoned the borough police at 4.05 am from Far Cotton police box to say that a Morris Minor, index number MU 1468, had been found burnt out in Hardingstone Lane and that the body of a woman had been found in the car. Disclosure of this last item of information had been prompted by the discovery of the heel of a lady's shoe at the scene. However, it would prove to be a red herring so far as the victim's identity was concerned. Indeed the county force, in charge of the investigation, would subsequently spend a fruitless day checking Northampton hotels for any missing female guests. Valentine also added that at 2:15 am a man with the following description, whom the police were anxious to trace, had been seen 100 yards from where the destroyed vehicle was found. He was described as,

> "....age 30 to 35 years; 5 ft. 10 ins.-6 feet in height; well built; full face; dark curly hair; dressed in a very light new pattern mackintosh with belt; dark trousers; no hat; appeared rather strange and was carrying a small brown attaché case".

Valentine requested that the borough police telephone those particulars to Newport Pagnell police so that an eye could be kept out for him at the train station and at bus stops. The latter then passed on the same message to the forces at Stony Stratford, Dunstable and Bletchley, as well as to all divisions of the Northampton borough police. With due courtesy the county chief constable later

8   Cited in Andrew Rose, *Lethal Witness: Sir Bernard Spilsbury, Honorary Pathologist*, Sutton Publishing, Stroud, 2007, p. 189.

sent his written thanks to Chief Constable Williamson of the borough police for the assistance the latter's men had provided.

Meanwhile, at the scene of the incident, their initial inspection suggested to Inspector Lawrence and PC Valentine that they were dealing merely with a tragic accident, not with a potentially criminal homicide. From the headlights of the police car it could be seen that the burnt-out vehicle had suffered severe damage. While some of the front section was not wholly destroyed, with one wire-rimmed tyre still more or less intact and the front number plate also clearly visible and readable, most of the rest of the car was reduced to a fragile charred wreck. Indeed portions of the vehicle, made from wood, linoleum and canvas, had collapsed in on themselves though the square shape of the small car was still visible. Thus items of wreckage were found higgledy-piggledy within a confined space, including the steering wheel, bits of mudguard and what remained of a damaged petrol can lacking its handle and screw top. During the search Copping also found small items such as a buckle, braces clips, buttons and the petrol can's screw lid. With the bonnet found open Valentine looked into the petrol tank which, in those models, was strapped to the side of the bulkhead nearest the front seats, and not in the engine compartment itself. With his torch shining on the petrol tank, the policeman removed the top of the petrol filler pipe and could see that the tank was, in fact, empty. Yet there was no sign of a leak or fracture at that location. The car was at the side of the road on the near-side, standing on a slightly south-leaning camber about 150 yards from, and facing away from, the village. There were no skid marks to be found on the frosty metalled road, which might otherwise have suggested an emergency stop. Indeed there was nothing to indicate other than that the car had been stopped normally, though it was in second gear. For if the car had caught fire while being driven it could not, in the opinion of the police, have been so skilfully and expertly drawn up at the side of the road.

But, of course, there was the charred body, with the exploded head face-down on the driver's seat, and with the rest of the torso slumped over the two front seats, so unrecognisable that the whole could easily have been taken for a burnt tree trunk. Apart from the torso and the collapsed head, there was one extended right arm, burnt off at the elbow, and stretched upward over the back of the seats (the other was twisted behind the body). There were also the partial remains of a right leg, burnt off somewhere below the knee (three policemen later differed in court as to how much of the right leg escaped being consumed by the fierce flames). The left leg was closely drawn up to the torso in an awkward and unnatural posture which challenged Lawrence to wonder how anyone still conscious could manoeuvre themselves into such a position. It was soon established that the wind had been blowing from the offside rear of the car in a diagonal direction, reinforcing the belief that the fire had started at the back of the car, where most destruction had occurred but where there was no longer flammable material. While the back cushions might have blazed up, the spread of the fire to the front would have been steady, not rapid, which would normally allow a front-seat occupant ample opportunity to escape.[9] As the *Evening News* would pose on November 7, after the

9   *The Times*, November 8, 1930.

sex of the victim had been determined,

> This gives rise to the question: Why did the man in the car not get out? If he
> was uninjured he would have had ample time to get clear before the flames
> spread to the front of the car and the petrol tank.

And the petrol tank itself, to the surprise of the onlookers, had not been damaged. Clearly it could be speculated that the victim had somehow been disabled before the flames had reached him. But if he had been, what had happened? Second, how could a fire start in the rear of the car where both mechanical parts vulnerable to ease of igniting, and also flammable material were not present? Was the fire therefore deliberately started in the rear and, if so, how? Was the empty petrol can a damning pointer? Then there was the evidence for the intensity of the fire as the flames roared to fifteen feet. What fed such a fierce conflagration? The technical evidence adduced at the trial would offer different explanations for this, one view attributing the fierceness of the blaze to human intervention, while another analysis offered a more innocent explanation.

One of the most shocking features of the initial police investigation, however, was the failure by Lawrence and his colleagues to take photographs of the scene during the night, or even to make written notes as to the position of the corpse and of the other items present, such as the location of the steering wheel after the fire had been extinguished. This failure presumably makes understandable the differences of opinion about the actual state of the protruding leg (the car door obviously being open at that point). More damning still, shortly before 4.00 am the remains of the corpse were wrapped in sacking and taken to the garage of the Crown Inn and then, at around 4:15 am, the vehicle was man-handled onto the grass verge at the side of the road resting, according to a *Daily Mail* report on November 8, next to a telegraph pole. This exercise was, almost unbelievably, conducted before a proper inspection in daylight could be carried out, and with what further damage to the integrity of the vehicle would never become known thereafter. To add to the confusion, while the policemen present at this time later stated the car's removal to the grass verge around 4:15 to 5:40 in the morning, another policeman, Sergeant Joe Harris, who arrived later in the morning, testified that the car had been moved after his arrival. Even more disconcerting, despite the *Evening News* of November 7 having reported that, 'All through the night police guarded the wreckage of the burned car at the side of the road....', no police guard had in fact been left at the site to prevent casual passers-by or 'sight-seers' from interfering with the charred wreckage, picking up items, moving vehicle parts to other areas of the chassis, unscrewing parts of the engine, or even taking away burnt parts as souvenirs; the precipitate removal to the verge simply to ensure that the morning commuter buses, following five different routes, were able to pass back and forth along Hardingstone Lane (which was about 18 feet in width).

Around 8:15 am in the morning a local chemist from Far Cotton, Arthur Ashford, arrived with his camera and took four photographs of the scene with a view to selling them to the press. Indeed reporters were already beginning to arrive and mill around at the scene. Yet it was clear from the sequence of photographs produced at the trial that Ashford and his assistant, Edgar Tipplestone, who had taken nine photographs at the site, had actually interfered with the debris to make the pictures more suitable, as he thought, for publication. Thus he carefully moved the steering wheel from where it had fallen during the blaze to replace it on the steering column, a more 'natural' position for it, he presumably reasoned.

The freedom of Ashford and other curious onlookers to rummage through the debris in the morning after the blaze would later prompt the trial judge, Mr. Justice Talbot, to be scathing about the police's failure to prevent unauthorised (or any) interference with the scene. Perhaps the only excuse for this deficiency was, as noted above, that most of the policemen on the spot during the night had been under the impression that the incident had been a mere tragic road accident and not a possible crime scene. Inspector Lawrence did, however, later claim (was it an afterthought or an attempt to excuse himself?) that he considered that there were some 'suspicious circumstances' surrounding the incident, though it is not clear whether he had shared his suspicions with his colleagues at the time when inspecting the vehicle. Nor had he been disposed to preserve the site carefully for a proper forensic inspection.

Moreover, that the investigation was a purely Northamptonshire affair, apart from, as we shall see, a lesser role for different elements of the Metropolitan Police, no doubt also concerned Talbot in retrospect. For the calling in of Scotland Yard ('Calling in the Met') to investigate difficult crime beyond the resources or ingenuity of local forces, conscious of the need not to contaminate or damage a crime scene before proper forensic investigation, was sometimes consented to by provincial forces.[10] But not in this case.

By some quirk of fate the car's number plate had survived more or less intact and it was quickly discovered that the registered owner of the burnt-out Morris Minor MU 1468 was one A. A. Rouse, a commercial traveller from Friern Barnet in north London. The *Evening News* on November 6, in the first newspaper reporting of the event, printed as its main headlines, 'Hatless Man Near a Blazing Car' and '"They Must Have Been Having a Bonfire"'. But it also printed as sub-headlines 'Driver Dead at the Wheel' and 'Believed to Have Been a Woman'. In reporting that the number plate indicated that the car was registered to Arthur Rouse of North Finchley, it added erroneously that Rouse had been seen in Northampton the previous afternoon some time before 5pm. It was only one of a number of misleading press reports to emanate from the incident. Perhaps what had happened was that a local journalist had quickly picked up from the police both the account of the cousins' statements about encountering Rouse and also some feverish rumours doing the rounds, and had fed them all to Fleet Street.

Naturally the police were interested in the whereabouts of this Mr. Rouse since they were still under the impression that the victim had been female. So at 11:30 am on November 6, Northamptonshire police sent a message to Whetstone police station (which was the nearest to Friern Barnet) that, '...it has now been ascertained that the body found in the car is that of a woman'.[11] They went on to request that Mrs. Rouse be questioned on their behalf as to whether the cousins' description of the strange man in Hardingstone Lane tallied with that of her husband, though if they had entertained some initial thoughts that the victim

10   G. R. Rubin, "Calling in the Met: Serious Crime Investigation Involving Scotland Yard and Provincial Police Forces in England and Wales, 1906-1939", *Legal Studies*, Vol. 31 (3), 2011, pp. 411-41.
11   MEPO3/1660, November 8, 1930.

might have been Mrs Rouse herself, they do not appear to have made any mention of this in their message to Whetstone police station.

Lawrence was actually under the impression that at that moment Rouse was on the 10:55 am train from Bletchley, due to stop at Willesden, which was close to Friern Barnet, before it terminated at Euston, and that the missing hatless man had travelled from Hardingstone to Leighton Buzzard from where he had caught a bus to Bletchley. Presumably they had hoped to reach Rouse when he returned home. But they were misinformed. His alleged movements were the product of someone's imagination and wholly without foundation.

In the next few days they would be given other misleading pieces of information. For example, on Monday November 10, Mr. Henry Damerel, a commercial traveller from Maida Vale, went to Scotland Yard with a strange story.[12] He stated that the week previously he had been staying at the Great Eastern Hotel, Northampton, when he entered into conversation with other salesmen in the hotel's 'commercial room' at about 10:30 pm on that Monday night (November 3). One of the men resembled the description of Rouse that Brown and Bailey had supplied. This man gave Damerel the impression that he had a 'baby' car which was cramped. The discussion then turned to the disposal of vehicles and the man surprised the listeners by suggesting that the best way to do so was by setting it alight, adding that, 'It would be damned funny if it happened to mine tomorrow'. Damerel then noticed that just after those comments had been made the man became uneasy and began to joke about what he had just said. He briefly greeted the man the next morning before he, Damerel, left the hotel. Then, on reading about the car blaze a couple of days later, he decided to approach the police about the mystery gentleman, though why he waited a few days before doing so he did not explain. With hindsight, it was clearly a false lead. It would have been impossible for Rouse to have been in a Northampton hotel on the night of November 3-4. For it is known that on the 4th, he had been making commercial calls in various Kent coastal towns, including Broadstairs and Herne Bay.

Late in the morning of November 6 Dr. Eric Shaw, the Northampton General Hospital pathologist, conducted a post-mortem in the garage of the Crown Inn. He found a prostate gland, confirming that the body was in fact male. In the light of this finding the Northamptonshire police, surely prematurely since steps formally to identify the corpse had not commenced, advised the Met some twelve hours after the blaze that they need no longer keep 14 Buxted Road under observation in case Rouse returned. Did this point to the Northamptonshire police now believing that Rouse had indeed been the victim, notwithstanding the cousins' statements? If so, then it represented yet another provincial police shortcoming in the investigation. Indeed, two local plain clothed Metropolitan policemen, one of whom was previously acquainted with Mrs. Rouse, arrived at the neat semi-detached house, presumably on Inspector Lawrence's instructions, to break the news to her that her husband's body was thought to have been found burnt to death in a car blaze in Northamptonshire the previous night. Would she be prepared to travel up to attend the inquest fixed for 12 noon on November 8 (though other versions insist that she had been called upon to visit the morgue in Northampton for identification purposes)? Shocked, she agreed to make the

12   *Ibid.*, November 10, 1930.

journey as soon as possible. But she had to arrange some domestic matters first. This entailed ensuring that the young boy staying with her and her husband was taken to the home of reliable neighbours, to be looked after while she was away. Who was this boy, given that Mr. and Mrs. Rouse had no children of their own?

Dr. Shaw's work had not been easy, given the shrivelled and almost carbonised state of the corpse. But he did ascertain that the cause of death was shock following burning and that the corpse was undoubtedly male. For while the genitals had been destroyed and the chest wall had collapsed, there was clear evidence of that prostate gland. Whether he was able to draw conclusions from the pelvic bones, which differ between men and women, was not stated. And, of course, a 'bachelor's' button that fastened men's suspenders, and a man's buckle and metal clips from men's braces, were also found in the wreckage.

So Rouse was feared dead and Lily, his wife, travelled to Northampton to assist the police in resolving the issue of identity. The received account is that she never saw the corpse because it was burnt beyond recognition. Therefore rather than upset her unnecessarily by exposing her to the traumatic sight of the charred body of her husband, the local police merely showed her items recovered from the body, that is, the buckles and belts that she thought *looked* like her husband's. However, her own story, as told to the press, was that when she got to Angel Lane police station she was given 'different information from that which she had received earlier', the purport of which was, presumably, that the police now thought her husband was still alive but missing. She did not, therefore, view the corpse but told the *Daily Telegraph* that, 'I do hope my husband is safe. This is a terribly worrying business and a complete mystery to me'. To the *Daily Mail* she stated that,

> "I am so terribly worried. The first thing I heard from the police was that my husband had been killed, and I planned to catch a motor coach soon after five o'clock [on the afternoon of the 6th] to Northampton. Then I was stopped and told by another police officer that it is not my husband after all. I don't know what to make of it."[13]

Perhaps her confusion was further complicated by her vague sleepy recollection of Rouse's return to Buxted Road at some unearthly time during the early hours of the Friday.

The police were therefore not yet prepared to stamp the file 'case closed' and to archive it as a tragic car accident that had consumed the poor driver, unable to escape from the burning vehicle. For one thing, if Rouse's charred corpse was now lying on a mortuary slab who, then, was the man spotted by the cousins, Brown and Bailey? Further, their description of the slightly harassed looking man resembled, in some respects, Rouse himself. And if the descriptions matched, then surely there was a strong possibility that the body in the burnt-out car could not be Rouse's? And if it was not Rouse's, then who was the victim? Moreover, where *was* Rouse? According to the press, Scotland Yard detectives (rather than Whetstone) were now once more requested on the 7th to wait outside Rouse's house in Friern Barnet in case he returned home and might be able to shed light

---

13   *Daily Mail*, November 7, 1930; *Daily Telegraph*, November 7, 1930.

on the affair. As the *Evening News* reported on November 7, 'The blinds of the Rouses' house are drawn to-day, and the house is locked up. A neighbour told [a journalist] that Mrs. Rouse had gone to Northampton'.

Though the *Evening News* reported that the Northamptonshire force was contemplating calling in Scotland Yard to take over the investigation, implying that the crime was proving especially challenging for a provincial force to solve, no such official request was made by the Northamptonshire police Chief Constable, the long-serving James Kellie-MacCallum. Divisions of the Metropolitan police, including Scotland Yard and local Hammersmith police detectives did, however, assist the Northamptonshire Constabulary in various ways. We have already noted the request made to Whetstone police to conduct inquiries with Mrs. Rouse at 14 Buxted Road regarding her husband's whereabouts. It reported back that Lily had said that her husband had left at 4 pm the previous day for an unknown destination and had not yet returned. She did not know the details of his car number plate. Later revelations suggested, however, that she was being economical with the truth. For while she might not have known his immediate destination in the late afternoon of November 5 (which was the City Road Maternity Hospital), she was, according to one account, aware that her husband had returned to the house in the evening of November 5 for a short while to collect his overnight things. This account also alleges that his soon-to-expire passenger was waiting in the car outside before the pair set off towards Leicester. The episode reinforces the view that one has to be very cautious about what Lily said about the affair.

The morning papers on November 7 were able to give their readers a fuller account of the mystery. The sub-headlines in the *Daily Telegraph* of that day announced, 'Police Search in Strange Riddle', 'Motor Belonging to London Man' and 'Detectives Wait at House'. The same day's *Daily Mail*, complete with photograph of the burnt out vehicle, and with steering wheel hanging from the dashboard, referred to 'Lonely Road Mystery' and to 'Police Search for Hatless Stranger'. The newspaper suggested that, from the position of the corpse, the victim had made some effort to escape from the car before death had occurred. This was, of course, mere speculation.

So where *was* Rouse? One newspaper that day, which named Rouse and which also published the familiar photograph of the burnt out vehicle and its prominent number plate, would, unwittingly or otherwise, play a far more dramatic role in the case than any other of Fleet Street's finest. This was the *Daily Sketch* of November 7th, whose crime journalist, J. C. Cannell, popped up at different intervals to put his own imprint on the proceedings. The significance of the *Daily Sketch* was due not only to Cannell's dogged pursuit of the complicated background to the incident, but also to events occurring at the Jenkins family home in the remote village of Gellygaer in Monmouthshire, South Wales.

The last sighting the cousins had of Rouse had been his indecisive movements at the junction between Hardingstone Lane and the main road, before he turned left in the direction of London. As he disappeared from view, the two young men then rushed off towards the blaze which was roaring some 400 yards from where they had encountered the hatless man. Their next sighting of him, as noted earlier, would be when he appeared in the dock at the local police court.

Rouse had endeavoured to wave down any passing vehicle going in the London direction. The first vehicle was a lorry that did not stop for him. This was unlikely to have been the vehicle whose driver, claiming to be travelling from Nottingham to London, had contacted the police on the Friday (November 7) to say that he had seen a hatless man jump out of a hedge near the road junction at the time of the blaze. The driver added that the man had appeared to signal to him to stop, then hesitated, apparently changing his mind, and finally turned and walked in the opposite direction.[14] But since the opposite direction was towards Northampton, this witness may well have been confused. Moreover he could hardly have seen Rouse emerge from the ditch in Hardingstone Lane (before the latter was spotted by the cousins) if he was driving along the main road south from Northampton to Stony Stratford. .

What is certain is that Rouse flagged down a lorry on the main road that was travelling to London, having commenced its journey in Mansfield. It stopped and the driver, Henry Turner, asked him what the matter was. Rouse, said Turner later, replied that he had been to Northampton and was due to be picked by a returning mate in a Bentley, but that somehow they had missed each other. Could the driver take him to London? Turner told him to climb in beside his chum, Pitt. So Rouse clambered into the cab, still clutching his attaché case. It is, perhaps, symptomatic of Rouse's *faux* snobbery that he later challenged Turner's account by insisting that he would never have used the term 'mate' to describe the elusive Bentley driver.

Later Rouse recounted how, within five minutes of clambering aboard, he had remarked to Turner that it had been a good idea of the driver's to have lifted up the floorboards of the cab to warm the lorry. For the lorry's exhaust was red hot and was keeping the cab cosy. He then commented on how noisy was the engine, suggesting that the silencer was defective. It was rather old and over-worked, replied the driver. Rouse then recalled talking about the engine and about cars generally and also working the headlights and dipped lights. If Rouse's matter-of-fact description of his conversation with Turner in the lorry is accurate, was he really in a state of panic just a short time previously?

At length he was dropped off at Tally Ho Corner, probably at around 5:30 am. In his police statement after his arrest, he said that he made his way straight to the Strand where he bought a new hat. Then he went to the Embankment where he intended to get on a coach to Wales to see the Jenkins family in Gellygaer. He claimed that his intention had always been to stay there, from the Thursday (November 6) to the following Monday, a routine he had previously followed. However, the lorry driver, Turner, in his police statement at Bow Street, explained that Rouse had earlier asked, during the journey to London, 'Do you touch Finchley?' 'Yes', replied the driver, 'What part do you want?' 'Tally Ho Corner' came the passenger's reply. So, after the lorry reached the Corner and had pulled up at its junction with Stanhope Road, a turning off the Great North Road, Rouse climbed out of the cab. This was his neck of the woods.

Turner briefly watched as Rouse 'hurried down the road but did not run'. A short walk along Stanhope Road and Friern Park would bring him to... where else but Buxted Road and the temporary sanctuary of home. Why otherwise would he alight from the lorry at this point?

14   *Ibid.*, November 8, 1930.

Let us leave to one side whether or not he *did* return to Buxted Road at this point. The full story regarding this brief episode did not emerge until the trial. What we do know is that Rouse, *sans chapeau*, was soon wandering along the Embankment 'in a bit of a stew', and looking for a coach to Wales. He was spotted there by George Smith, a kind of scout and porter acting for the Thames Transport Company, and whose job it was to steer confused travellers to the company's booking office in Villiers Street. Approached by Smith, Rouse must have seemed just the sort of mark that the former was looking for, as Rouse poured out his story of losing his car and of his need to get to Wales. So Smith led him to the Villiers Street ticket office which was, in fact, merely an agent for more than sixty different motor companies. The booking clerk, James Swetman, began to ring round to see if he could fix Rouse up with a ticket and while he was thus engaged, Rouse chatted to the office manager, Eric Farmer, repeating to this new sympathetic ear that his car had been stolen while he was at a coffee stall. As Rouse recounted on this occasion, there had been some lorry drivers parked up by the stall, but none of them knew anything about the car being stolen. He added to his story that he had even lost his Stetson hat. Indeed to Farmer it seemed Rouse had been more concerned about the loss of his hat than of his car. Now Rouse wondered whether it was possible to get from South Wales to Leicester directly, without coming back to London. There was a map on the ticket office wall and Farmer showed him that there was a route, using Black and White coaches. Rouse made a joke, asking him if he was not talking about Black and White whisky. With the route settled, the clerk found him a seat for the Wales journey and Rouse asked how long the coach would take. Farmer reckoned it would be about eight hours. Rouse scoffed. It would only take about three hours in his Wolseley Hornet (which his vehicle had now miraculously become). But he took the seat in any case, ticket No. 60033, on a South Wales Express Coach leaving from Bush House in the Strand.

The coach did not leave until 9.45 am, so Rouse had time to do a bit of shopping. He found an outfitter's open on the Strand and purchased, no surprise, a brand new hat. But what style of hat ought he to choose? Style was an important consideration. As a memoir-writing London policeman once observed,

> "Hats are an awful give-away of character. In my [pre-police] days every hat I wore immediately went limp and sloppy however firm and manly it had looked in the shop. I was told this was because I fiddled with my hats, but I stopped fiddling and got the same result. After being depressed for years at my reflection in shop windows, I decided to go hatless—which was considered eccentric."

But after embarking on the training course to become a policeman, he realised that recruits were not permitted to salute if hatless, and since 'civvies' were often worn at pay parade, he purchased a trilby.[15]

---

15   Harry Daley, *This Small Cloud: A Personal Memoir*, Weidenfeld & Nicolson, 1986, p. 122. Another policeman had a more conventional professional experience with hats. Ex-Detective Assistant Commissioner at Scotland Yard, John du Rose, recorded that, "Until I joined the police force [in 1931] I had never worn a hat, and when I appeared at classes bareheaded as usual, I was peremptorily ordered to obtain headgear forthwith. This I forgot to do and when the following day I arrived still hatless I was taken before the commanding officer, who warned me that if I didn't get a hat I would be expelled." See John du Rose, *Murder Was My Business*, Mayflower, 1973, p. 15.

Rouse did not buy a trilby to replace the one he had worn when setting out on his fateful car journey and which was now presumably lost in the blaze. Nor did he purchase his favourite hat, a Stetson, sometimes known as a Baden-Powell, a high-crowned and wide-brimmed felt hat originally created by the American firm, the John B. Stetson Hat Company, in 1865. Instead he opted for something fashionable and flamboyant. In all likelihood this was the hat he wore when photographed by the prison authorities following his committal to prison after being charged on Saturday November 8 with the murder of an unknown man. The hat in the prison photograph appears to be a 'snap brim' felt hat, almost certainly a Regent-style fedora, with a brim that could be turned down at the front and up at the back, possibly originating from the Italian firm of Borsalina in the nineteenth century. Trilbies had smaller brims that did not bend down at the front, but neither would they be curled up in the fashion of homburgs, as shown in a familiar photograph of the Dusseldorf mass-murderer, Peter Kürten, who wore a style of hat popularised by Edward VII who had taken a liking to it when visiting Bad Homburg.[16]

Sporting his new purchase, Rouse made his way to the coach pick-up point. The driver, George Bell, could not find the seat reservation on his booking chart, but then that had been made up the night before and Rouse was a latecomer. Rouse took his seat, up front, just behind the driver on the left of the coach. He told the same tale of his misadventures, with some embellishments, to Bell. He would have done the journey by car but it had been stolen when he had gone for a cup of coffee in a small roadside café near St. Albans. He would have to go back to Leicester the next day (November 7), but before then he wanted to see his wife who was living in a small town near Cardiff. Now, what was it called? Bell suggested Caerphilly. Or was it Yetradmynach (probably meaning Ystrad Mynach)? Yes, Yetradmynach, that was probably it. He explained that he had not been married long and his mother-in law was not keen on his wife being away from home, which would surely strike some listeners as odd. Nonetheless, Bell and Rouse chatted happily during the course of the journey. Most of their conversation was about cars and the tribulations of motoring. Bell told him one story about repairing a dent in his rear wing. He had used a wooden mallet and taken a swing at the dent. By an amazing fluke the mallet had glanced off the tyre and hit the dent spot on, knocking it out perfectly. Rouse said he also kept a mallet for that very purpose. But later Bell could not remember whether Rouse had said that he had the mallet in his possession (presumably kept in his garage) or whether he always carried it in the car.

Even if he could not remember where his 'new wife' lived, Rouse knew how to get there. He turned up at Primrose Cottage, or Primrose Villa as the Jenkins family preferred, in Gellygaer, at about 8.00 pm on that Thursday evening. Did he knock and walk straight in or did he wait for the door to be answered? William Jenkins, giving a statement three days after the event, recalled that he had answered the door and had said to his 'son-in-law', 'Good gracious, where is the car?' Rouse replied that, 'I have had the car stolen, Dad, it was stolen last night.

---

16   We are grateful to the author of *Sharp Suits* (Anova Books, 2013), Eric Musgrave, for guidance as to headgear. For men's hat styles see www.lockhatters.co.uk/fedoras-homburgs.html; Alan Mansfield and Phillis Cunnington, *Handbook of English Costume in the Twentieth Century, 1900-1950*, Faber and Faber, 1973, pp. 289-91, 335-6; Nicholas Storey, *History of Men's Fashion: What the Well Dressed Man is Wearing*, Remember When/Pen & Sword, Barnsley, 2015, chapter 8.

It has taken me 24 hours to come here, it was stolen in Northampton.' On the other hand, Thomas Reakes, a collier friend of Jenkins who had come round for a chat and was sitting in the front room, recalled that Rouse had come straight into the house. When he was interviewed by police some three weeks later, Reakes' version of what Rouse had said was somewhat fuller. 'Oh, Dad, I have been a long time coming from Northampton, about 18 hours on the road. I would have been here before but I lost my car. I went to have a cup of tea. I left my bag and hat in the car. When I came out it was gone, but I got it insured, but I don't want that. I want my car.' Perhaps Jenkins and Reakes took a little time to get their stories straight. For when Jenkins later testified at the police court, his recollection was that Rouse had knocked twice on the door and had indeed then walked in. Moreover, his version of what Rouse had said on arrival was now much closer to the dramatic version offered by Reakes. For this time Jenkins testified that Rouse had actually exclaimed, 'Oh, Dad, I've been a long time coming, almost 18 hours. I had my car stolen in Northampton.'

Rouse then asked if he might go up and see Ivy who was ill in bed and as he went upstairs, Reakes took his leave. 'Dad' set about getting some food together for supper. Up in the bedroom, Rouse explained to Ivy, or Paddy as she was known within the family, that his car had been stolen outside London. He asked what was wrong with her and coyly she said he had better ask her mother; well, that is what she told the police she had said. Of course Rouse was well aware that she was pregnant. Had he not brought her back home because she *was* pregnant? And they had spun her parents a story that they had got married on her twenty-first birthday. So he was entitled to call William Jenkins, 'Dad', wasn't he?

By the time the police interviewed Ivy ten days after Arthur's flying visit, when she recalled the exchange between supposed husband and wife, she had had time to 'recover....her thoughts'. Remarkably, she now remembered that when he had come to her bedside his clothes had smelt strongly of petrol. And she remembered that, 'His eyelashes appeared shorter than usual as if they had been singed by fire'. He was also very untidy and appeared to be very excited. But none of this would be revealed in court. Ivy was simply too ill to attend.

When Reakes returned to his home nearby, he found a copy of the evening newspaper for that November 6, the *South Wales Echo*, or perhaps it was the *Evening Express*. He later wasn't sure. There was a prominent account of the Northampton blaze and Reakes felt obliged to rush back to the Jenkins household. Not a person to resist a dramatic flourish, he waved the paper in front of Rouse who was now sitting at the kitchen table eating his supper. 'Is this your car? If it is, you will see it no more,' he shouted out. Glancing at the paper, and probably astonished to realise that even in this backwater of civilisation the news of a blazing car in Northamptonshire had penetrated rural South Wales, his initial shock led to instant denial. He was either in a state of cognitive dissonance or, more likely, knew that the game was up and that he must play for time in order to think what to do next. So he replied, 'That is not my car'. Presumably Rouse did not enjoy the sleep of the just that night.

The next morning, Friday November 7, Fleet Street (even if not the police just yet) closed in on Alfred Arthur Rouse. The newspaper boy called early at Primrose Cottage and delivered the *Daily Sketch*. This edition was destined to be Exhibit

21 in the case of *Rex* v. *Rouse*. The front page delivered the bad news. Phyllis, Ivy's sister, grabbed it first, took one look at it and showed it to Rouse, helpfully (though no doubt gleefully) pointing out that, 'There is a picture of your car, burnt, in the paper.' 'How do you know?' he asked. She did not need to be a detective to reply, 'Your name is underneath.' And it was. For overnight it had emerged that the car belonged to a Mr. A. A. Rouse of Buxted Road, North Finchley. The sex and identity of the charred body found inside the car had not yet been established but the police were anxious to interview a man seen near the car at the time of the accident. That very man was getting more anxious by the second. He didn't give the paper back to Phyllis. Instead he asked if he could keep it and he pocketed it. It was hardly surprising. Indeed on page three, alongside an account of the tragedy and a description of the man the police were looking for, was an article headlined 'What Wife of Motor-Car Driver Told Neighbour'. This wife wasn't Ivy who was still in bed upstairs. This wife was in Finchley where, 'Mr. and Mrs. Rouse had no children but adopted a boy some months ago'.[17]

Meanwhile, Ivy's brother Trevor was in the garage next to the cottage talking to a salesman about the purchase of a new lorry to haul coal. Jenkins senior was there too. Oddly, they both thought that they were talking to a man called 'Mr. Cook', from the firm of Cook and Bassett in Cardiff. William Jenkins persisted in calling the salesman 'Mr. Cook' even when it became known that his name was Hendell Brownhill. Rouse came from the house to join the group. Was Brownhill going back to Cardiff? He was. Then would he give Rouse a lift there? Brownhill agreed and Rouse went back to the house to get ready. The family quickly filled Brownhill in on the press reports of Rouse's car. Brownhill returned to the front of Primrose Cottage where he was parked. Rouse was saying his goodbyes to Mrs. Jenkins and to Phyllis, Ivy still being confined to bed. Naturally curious, and possibly sounding out a potential customer, Brownhill commiserated with his passenger on the loss of his car and asked if he had reported it to the police. Rouse said he had already done so, though he did not volunteer where or to whom he had reported the loss. Brownhill next asked if he, Rouse, was insured and being told that he was, said that, in that case, Rouse had nothing to worry about. A further question, the import of which is obvious, was fended off. It was, said Rouse, too complicated and lengthy a story to go into.

Brownhill had another customer to call on that morning, David Morris, publican of the Cooper's Arms Hotel in Ystrad Mynach. It was on the road to Cardiff so Brownhill stopped off and Rouse went into the pub with him. The landlord had just been reading the *Daily Express* which also carried the story of the burnt out car in Northampton. Brownhill introduced Rouse as the gentleman to whom the car had belonged and Rouse immediately became the centre of attention. The landlord wanted to know how it had happened. Rouse said he had gone into a restaurant in London and when he came out the car was missing. Morris thought that in the telling Rouse had appeared worried and upset and offered him a brandy which Rouse declined. A butcher's boy, also called Morris, Idwal Morris, came into the pub on his delivery round and, hearing the conversation, chipped in that the charred remains of a lady had been found in the wreckage (though by this time the press had confirmed the gender of the victim as male). This conversation was all too much for Rouse who immediately walked out of the room. According to Idwal, he had muttered, 'Oh dear, dear. I can't bear to hear anything about it.'

Now back in the car, Brownhill and Rouse resumed the journey to Cardiff. As they drove into the city, Rouse asked if he could be dropped off at a depot where he could get a bus to London. Brownhill drove him round to North Morgan Street where the Great Western coach service started out. On the way they passed the Glamorgan County Police headquarters, easily recognised by the large sign outside saying 'County Police'. For some (obvious but unspoken) reason, when they got to North Morgan Street, Rouse was unhappy with the Great Western Services, saying that he had used them on the journey down to Wales (this was not actually the case) and that their buses were not nice to ride in, too jerky or jumpy. So the obliging Mr. Brownhill drove him into Waldron Street, then into Neville Street and dropped him off at Lower Cathedral Road, directing him to Messrs. Hinton and Britton's in Castle Street. It was now 11:20 am.

Later in the day, Brownhill read a description in another newspaper of the man the police were anxious to question, a description which, of course, tallied with his passenger of that morning. Whom should he tell? For some reason he opted to approach a journalist initially rather than the police. So he went to the nearest newspaper office, the *South Wales Echo*, where a reporter called Yates whom he possibly knew (the evidence, while not conclusive, points in this direction) listened to, and no doubt recorded for publication, his story. The pair then went to the police station where the information was transmitted to an Inspector Hodges.

Right away, Hodges went to Hinton and Britton's garage where he obtained confirmation that a man resembling Rouse had taken the 12:15 pm coach to London, due to arrive at Hammersmith at 9:15 pm. At 8:53 pm he telephoned this information to Scotland Yard. He thought that the Northamptonshire police would be interested in his report and requested it also be sent on to them. And thus the plan was laid to intercept Rouse as soon as he arrived back in London.

The coach taking Rouse to London had actually left Cardiff at noon (not 12:15) and stopped at Cheltenham for three-quarters of an hour before reaching Hammersmith around 9 pm. The driver then reported to the company booking office. He was approached by two plain-clothes policemen from Hammersmith police station, Detective Sergeant Skelly and Detective Constable Holland, who asked about his passengers. The three then went towards the coach and the driver approached Rouse, telling him that the policemen would like to speak to him. He immediately acknowledged his identity, got up from his seat, collected his case and left the coach in the company of Skelly and his colleague.[18]

It should be made clear that at this point Rouse was merely voluntarily agreeing to 'help the police with their inquiries', which in fact meant the Northamptonshire constabulary through the agency of the Met. He was not under arrest and was free to decline to be interviewed. However, if Inspector Lawrence and his superior, Superintendent Brumby, were harbouring suspicions of foul play by Rouse, then they ought to have (if they had not done so) apprised Skelly of that fact, so that a

---

18   *Daily Mail*, November 8, 1930.

timely caution might be administered to Rouse on disembarking from the coach that he had the right to remain silent and was not obliged to say anything but that if he did say anything it would be taken down and could be used as evidence against him, a form of wording that has been amended over time. As it happened, and before such an opportunity to administer a caution had presented itself to the detectives, and whether or not they had been told by their county colleagues that Rouse was wanted in connection with a serious crime, the latter had already embarked upon one of his self-harming loquacious excesses. For as soon as he disembarked from the coach, his expressions of relief rapidly cascaded from his lips like a waterfall. And they were clearly heart-felt, unforced and spontaneous which, it is suspected, no amount of cautioning by the police would have stemmed.

The moment he got off the coach, right there on the pavement, and after confirming his name, and after being asked to accompany the detectives to the police station, he started talking. 'Very well', he said. 'I'm glad it is all over. I was going to Scotland Yard about it. I am responsible. I am very glad it is over. I have had no sleep.'

On arrival at the police station, he was told that he was being detained until officers from Northampton had arrived. But instead of complaining that 'being detained' meant that he was being unlawfully held unless he gave consent (for how was he to know the law?), he started talking again without any hint of a caution having been administered. And he talked and talked and talked.

> "I suppose they wish to see me about it. I don't know what happened exactly. I picked the man up on the Great North Road. He asked me for a lift. He seemed a respectable man and said he was going to the Midlands. I gave him a lift. It was just this side of St. Albans. He got in and I drove off and after going some distance I lost my way. A policeman spoke to me about my lights. I did not know anything about the man and I thought I saw his hand on my case, which was in the back of the car. I later became sleepy and could hardly keep awake. The engine started to spit and I thought I was running out of petrol. I pulled in to the side of the road. I wanted to relieve myself and said to the man 'There is petrol in the can, you can empty it into the tank while I am gone', and lifted up the bonnet and showed him where to put it in. He said, 'What about a smoke?' I said, 'I have given you all my cigarettes as it is.' I then went some distance along the road and had just got my trousers down when I noticed a big flame from behind. I pulled my trousers up quickly and ran towards the car which was in flames. I then began to tremble violently, I was all of a shake. I didn't know what to do and I ran as hard as I could along the road where I saw two men. I felt responsible for what happened. I lost my head and didn't know what to do and really don't know what I have done since."

That is what he *said*. Had he been concocting this story, rehearsing it in his head during that nine-hour coach trip? Was this what he would have said to Scotland Yard or to the first policeman to stop him in the street? Was he really going to Scotland Yard? Next stop for the coach was in Victoria, a short walk to Scotland Yard. He had obviously decided, at breakfast that morning in Gellygaer, to abandon plans he might have had for travelling across country from Wales to Leicester. Why had he decided to tell them that it was the body of a man? Yes, the *Daily Sketch* had reported that a 'pathological examination' had determined it was a man. But the butcher's boy had said it was a woman, which he had found distressing. Was he concerned that Lily might think his passenger had been female? He made a point of mentioning the policeman (that is, PC Lilley) who had ticked him off about his lights. They could easily check up on that. He had told them that he had left the man to play around with the petrol can; that the man was a smoker. He had told them that he had been caught with his trousers down. No one would, no one *could*, make up a story like that.

That is what he *said*. Or rather, that is what *Sergeant Skelly* had said he had said. For the detective had not written down any of the statement at the time. Rather, it was some time later when he jotted down, with remarkable memory recall, what Rouse had earlier said. In Skelly's notebook it came across as quite a coherent narrative. Indeed, he apparently learned it by heart so that he could recite it when giving evidence in court. Was that because Rouse had deliberately fed it to him, given that it was such a vigorously exculpatory account? If so, how irritating that Skelly had misheard him in the traffic at Hammersmith, taking him to say, 'I am responsible'. Luckily he, Rouse, now had a second chance to give his story to Skelly and to stress at the police station that he '*felt* responsible'. It was important to make the distinction.

Actually a slightly different version of events at the police station was recorded by a Metropolitan policeman, Harry Daley, on duty at Hammersmith that night. According to Daley, a colourful and gay police sergeant whose portrait was later painted by Duncan Grant, Rouse was being looked after by him and his colleague at the station for a short time,

'...before the big detectives arrived from the Yard [*sic*]. The ordinary-looking little man chatted away, telling me several times he was innocent, and recklessly I chatted back. Though I was only being friendly to a man in trouble, his lawyer could have alleged later, as they do when they have a weak defence, that I had questioned him without giving the necessary caution.'[19]

Daley was unaware at this point that the case would quickly become a *cause célèbre*. But he soon found a horde of reporters descending upon the station, and who were 'pretending to speak as friends of Mrs Rouse, even imitating her voice, in an attempt to get information an hour or two before the official announcement from the Press Bureau at the Yard'. The importance of the 'visitor' to the station was reinforced by the 'big shots' at the Yard instructing Daley not to use the station crockery with which to offer Rouse tea, but to 'pop along to the A.B.C. and ask if they'll lend you one of their best cups'. The detail in Daley's account was slightly inaccurate with its reference to senior Scotland Yard detectives, but the sense of the local Hammersmith uniforms basking in reflected glory lends an amusing gloss to the proceedings.

Superintendent Brumby and Inspector Lawrence eventually reached Hammersmith police station from Northampton at 1.15 am on the morning of Saturday November 8. At this point, before formally making a statement, Rouse was at last cautioned. Sergeant Skelly was the man with the pen and Rouse was choosing his words carefully or, perhaps, it is more accurate to say he was

19   Daley, *op. cit*, p. 132.

amending his words carefully. The statement took four hours to complete. Brumby observed that Rouse had a high-pitched voice and spoke so quickly that Skelly had difficulty keeping up with him. Each page was corrected by Rouse and alterations initialled by each of them. The observation that Rouse's passenger's breath 'smelt strongly of drink', for example, had the word 'strongly' excised. Perhaps Rouse was thinking that he might be overplaying his hand; that if he thought the man's breath had smelt strongly of drink he should have thought twice about giving him a lift. Each of the thirteen pages of the statement was signed by Rouse and witnessed by Brumby. It concluded with a correction. 'I now believe it was 8 o'clock in the evening of Wednesday 5th November 1930 that I last saw my wife and not 4 pm as I stated before.' For he had spent time at City Road Maternity Hospital in the early evening. Also there would be the suggestion, never proved, that Rouse had picked up the stranger at the Swan and Pyramids in Whetstone by prior arrangement, after leaving the maternity home but before calling at home. There, with his passenger in the car, he had grabbed some food and his overnight things, prior to setting off for Leicester.

Brumby and Lawrence took Rouse back to Northampton after interviewing him at Hammersmith, setting off from London in the early morning that Saturday. They arrived at Angel Lane police station around mid-morning. He was then detained in Lawrence's office and finally given some breakfast. Perhaps a little restored, Rouse started to talk again. Maybe he thought this was 'off the record'. He became quite confidential, perhaps a bit eager to please, before becoming positively (and, in the event, damagingly) sentimental. He asked Lawrence when the inquest would take place. He was told it would be at 12 noon. Would his wife be present, he wanted to know. Lawrence did not know. Could he see his wife now? Lawrence told him he could see her later. Rouse, with his addiction to the sound of his own voice, then immediately came out with some astonishing confidences that were to haunt him, define the public perception of him and probably prejudice his case to the extent that he was putting the noose around his own neck. Lily, he said,

> "....is really too good for me. I don't ever remember my wife sitting on my knee, but otherwise she is a good wife. I'm very friendly with several women, but it's an expensive game. I hadn't any money on Wednesday and was on my way to Leicester when this happened, to hand my slips in on Thursday morning, so that I could draw some money from the firm. I was then going to Wales for the week-end. My harem takes me to several places and I am not home a great deal, but my wife doesn't ask questions now. I was arranging to sell my house and furniture. I was then going to make an allowance to the wife. I think I should get from £100 to £150 clear from the sale."

It was an astonishing indiscretion to reveal at any time. But while being held in custody and being aware of police suspicions regarding the blaze and the corpse, he had either taken leave of his senses, had a deficiency of sensible judgment or else his outspokenness seemed like a mentally induced irresistible impulse. Indeed, when the statement was read out by the DPP's assistant solicitor, Gerald Paling, at the police court and dutifully reported under banner headlines in the press, the whole world and his dog would be taken aback and gripped by Rouse's amazing revelations of his sexual conquests and of his double-edged appreciation for his wife. What precisely occurred in the police station after that outburst is not clear. We may assume that Lawrence and Brumby went off to confer with their chief constable and with the deputy chief constable, Superintendent Tebbey. They presumably would also have been in touch with the DPP's office in London for guidance as to whether, and if so with what offence or offences, to charge Rouse, and how to frame the charge in those unusual circumstances. They probably would have had further telephone discussions with Skelly and, possibly, with Scotland Yard and Whetstone, the police station nearest Buxted Road. Thus at 4 o'clock in the afternoon, Rouse was charged with 'THE WILFUL MURDER OF SOME MALE PERSON AT PRESENT UNKNOWN'. And then he was allowed to see Lily. A touching scene ensued, a picture of marital harmony. Rouse told Lily that he had been charged with the murder of a man, but that he was innocent. She replied reassuringly, 'I know you are, my dear, you would not harm anyone. You are too tender-hearted to do a thing like that. I know that you are innocent and I will stick to you. Everything will turn out alright in the end.' It was almost as if she too had been rehearsing.

On Sunday November 9 Brumby informed Scotland Yard that Rouse had now been charged with the murder of an unknown man in Hardingstone Lane on the 6th inst. Found in Rouse's possession was an application by him, as from 1 Gillingham Street, Victoria, and dated October 30 1930, to search the marriage registers of 1924 or 1925 for the purpose of finding a 'marriage' between himself and a certain Helen Campbell. Brumby added that Rouse was also friendly with one Nellie Tucker, daughter of a Mrs. Nellie Stevens of Greenwich. When Mrs. Stevens had read in the press that the body in the car was thought to have been female, she immediately went to Blackheath Road police station and made a statement there. It was, however, quickly ascertained that Nellie had just given birth to a daughter at the City Road Maternity Hospital (where Rouse had visited her a few hours before the blaze). Brumby therefore requested the assistance of Scotland Yard in investigating Rouse's marriage search form (which was probably filled out in the name of 'Rowse'), and also the Victoria address. Could they also obtain a statement from Nellie Tucker about her relationship with Rouse? For, whoever the victim might have been (and it was probably the heel from Nellie's shoe that was recovered from the site), it was certainly not Nellie.

The police had at last found their 'Hatless Stranger'. Rouse, now charged with murder, was remanded in custody at Bedford Prison on November 10 for eight days. His fingerprints were taken but since he had no previous convictions there were no matches within Scotland Yard's Criminal Record Office. But, of course, he was no longer 'Hatless', as his highly presentable and impressive prison photograph would very soon confirm. His recently-acquired Fedora reaffirmed in his mind his middle-class identity and, ironically in the event, his perceived moral probity. There are other examples of murderers seeking the respectability and social standing conferred by a hat. Young Freddie Bywaters, 22 years old, was pictured wearing an almost outsize black homburg hat, as he was transported from police station to prison while investigations were continuing into the death by stabbing of Percy Thompson as the latter was walking home to Ilford with his wife, Edith, in October 1922. The lovers, Bywaters and Edith Thompson, were hanged in separate prisons in January 1923. The familiar picture of Patrick Mahon, the salesman and killer of Emily Kaye at the Eastbourne Crumbles bungalow in 1924, shows him wearing a large cream-coloured hat. The widely issued police photograph of Guy Frederick Browne in his bowler hat (he of the PC Gutteridge murder in 1927) perhaps reminds us that the simple dichotomy of cloth cap versus hat did not always indicate a sharp class divide,[20] for the bowler hat could also signify long artisanal experience or shop steward or foreman status at the works. It was, however, a form of headgear that King George V detested as a 'ratcatcher's hat', unless worn in the country.[21]

On November 12 Rouse's newly appointed solicitor, George Lee-Roberts, applied to the Home Office for permission to have his client's photograph taken, 'in the interests of Justice'.[22] Clearly his client would need to appear as an upright and respectable member of society....and so Alfred Arthur Rouse wore a hat.[23]

20 For Bywaters see the photographs in Ernest Dudley, *Bywaters and Mrs. Thompson*, Odhams Press, 1953. For Mahon, Browne and Kennedy, see photographs in Gordon Honeycombe, *The Murders in the Black Museum, 1870-1970*, Arrow, 1991.
21 De Marly, *op. cit.*, p. 119.
22 Lee-Roberts argued that if the photograph could be seen by the public, witnesses recognising the face might come forward to support Rouse's defence, though in what way was not made clear. The Home Office suspected that Lee-Roberts simply had the commercial aim in mind of selling the photograph to the press. In the event it was normal procedure for photographs of prisoners to be taken for internal purposes and not released to the public (till its transfer to the National Archives). Rouse's photograph was indeed taken but that had nothing to do with Lee-Roberts' request.
23 PCOM9/289, The Bedford Gaol photograph.

CHAPTER TWO

"BONFIRE" THEY WON'T FORGET

NORTHAMPTON INDEPENDENT, November 4, 1955

The Rouse Case as a *Cause Célèbre*

In 1994 an American academic wrote that, 'The genuine crime story is simply a branch of history and should be treated as such..... [T]hey contribute to the stock of historical knowledge in ways not necessarily related to crime, because they give intimate glimpses into people's lives..... [Yet] while they do not lack historical meaning, it is seldom the kind that can be readily generalized.'[24] However recent work on specific murder *causes célèbres* in Britain by academic writers such as Angus McLaren, Frank Mort, Martin Wiener, Ginger Frost, Lucy Bland, Anette Ballinger, Shani D'Cruze, Matt Houlbrook, John Carter Wood and others have cast serious doubt on such claims, as any examination of their writings would reveal.[25] Our knowledge of the wider significance of British murder *causes célèbres* is being enhanced today in a fashion not hitherto seen within historical writing. But that begs the question of what is, or is not, a murder *cause célèbre*. To begin to explore this question we start with a newspaper publication from half a decade

---

24   James Hitchcock, "Murder as One of the Liberal Arts", *American Scholar*, Vol. 63(1), March 1994, pp. 277-85.
25   Angus McLaren, *A Prescription for Murder: The Victorian Serial Killings of Dr Thomas Neill Cream*, Chicago University Press, Chicago, 1995; Frank Mort, *Capital Affairs: London and the Making of the Permissive Society*, Yale University Press, New Haven and London, 2010, pp. 104-25; Martin J. Wiener, "The Sad Story of George Hall: Adultery, Murder and the Politics of Mercy in Mid-Victorian England", *Social History*, Vol. 24 (2), 1999, pp. 176-95; Lucy Bland, *Modern Women on Trial: Sexual Transgression in the Age of the Flapper*, Manchester University Press, Manchester, 2013; Anette Ballinger, *Dead Woman Walking: Executed Women in England and Wales, 1900-1955*, Ashgate, Aldershot, 2000; Shani D'Cruze, "Intimacy, Professionalism and Domestic Homicide in Interwar Britain: The Case of Dr Buck Ruxton", *Women's History Review*, Vol. 16 (5), 2007, pp. 701-22; John Carter Wood, *The Most Remarkable Woman in England: Poison, Celebrity and the Trials of Beatrice Pace*, Manchester University Press, Manchester, 2012. In addition other non-academic studies of famous murder cases have contributed to a modest extent to our understanding of important historical themes surrounding those cases. The status of spinsterhood in the Edwardian period, the gothic imagination and the 'all-seeing' Scotland Yard detective in the 1860s, and the link between railway growth and fear of criminality in enclosed railway carriages from the 1870s have been explored in, respectively, Jane Robins, *The Magnificent Spilsbury and the Case of the Brides in the Bath*, John Murray, 2010; Kate Summerscale, *The Suspicions of Mr Whicher: Or, The Murder at Road Hill House*, Bloomsbury, 2009; Kate Colquhoun, *Mr Briggs' Hat*, Little, Brown, 2011. In contrast, works such as Andrew Rose, *The Prince, the Princess and the Perfect Murder*, Coronet 2013 (on the Fahmy case in 1923) and René Weis, *Criminal Justice: The True Story of Edith Thompson*, Hamish Hamilton, 1988 (on the 1922-23 case), while relying on contemporary records, perhaps cannot be viewed, and may not be intended to be viewed, as springboards into an understanding of the social history of the period.

ago. On April 20, 2013 the *Guardian Weekend* colour supplement published an article entitled 'Murder Most Ordinary', with an introduction by the celebrated author, Blake Morrison. The strap line was, 'We think of murder scenes as grisly, haunting places. But then the flowers fade and life moves on'. There follows a checklist of a number of homicides, mostly in London, that had occurred in 2011 and 2012, the victims being Negus McClean aged 15, Kunaliny Alagaratnam (42) and Santhirapathy Tharmalingam (59), David Petch (55), Sashana Roberts (24), Umesh Chaudhary (41), Colin Hammond (65), Michael Dye (44), Evaldas Svolkinas (34), and Jonathan Barnes (20). As for the assailants, some had been convicted of murder, some convicted of manslaughter, some were awaiting trials for murder, and in one case no-one had been charged. Around the same time the present authors were perusing, in the forlorn hope for inspiration, a book about murders committed in Manchester during the last century.[26] It contained a list of 28 persons hanged for murder in that city. However to our shame we realised that we knew only one of the cases listed, that of Walter Rowland in 1947 who some believe had been a victim of a miscarriage of justice.[27] Of the remaining 27 we had vaguely heard of just one of those listed but could not recall any details. As a coroner's officer, PC Goodwin, contacting the well-known pathologist, Dr. Keith Simpson, during the last war, explained over the phone, 'Not much of a murder, sir, just a husband run a sword through his wife'.[28]

The point of both these digressions is to acknowledge that subsequent generations' recollections of past murders, and present-day memory of recent killings are likely to be thin, to the point of total forgetfulness. Yet once in a while murder cases emerge that leave a lasting impression on both contemporaries and on later generations. In recent years the collective memory of cases such as the Moors Murderers, the Yorkshire Ripper, Dr Shipman, Rosemary and Fred West, Thompson and Venables, the murder of Jill Dando, and the killing of Milly Dowler by Levi Bellfield may dim but the horrors attached to those cases will ensure their longevity in the annals of modern murder. Similarly there are murder cases committed more than 100 years ago that will never be forgotten, and whose memory is constantly revived through film, documentaries and plays. Think of Jack the Ripper, Dr. Crippen and the Brides in the Bath killer, George Joseph Smith. Why is it, then, that the cases listed in the first paragraph (above) have left virtually no trace in the canon of famous crimes, while those cited in this paragraph have lived on? Naturally the grainy image, caught on CCTV, of two ten-year olds walking three-year old James Bulger to his death in Bootle in 1993 was an horrific unforgettable spectacle. Yet as the late John Archer noted in a crime history book published in 2011, the murder of a young child by two other boys who were scarcely older than the victim had occurred in Liverpool in 1891 when nine-year old Samuel Crawford and eight-year old Robert Shearon (or Sheeran) had drowned eight-year old David Eccles in a water-filled pit on a building site, apparently in order to steal his clothes. As Archer noted, 'The general reaction to the news of the killing within the city appears to have been more one of sadness

---

26   John Eddleston, *Murderous Manchester: The Executed of the Twentieth Century,* Breedon Books, Derby, 1997.
27   Bob Woffinden, *Miscarriages of Justice,* Coronet Books, 1988, Ch. 2.
28   Cited in Molly Lefebure, *Murder on the Home Front: The Unique Wartime Memoirs of a Pathologist's Secretary,* Grafton, 1990, p. 25.

than of outrage. This was, of course, a contrast with the outpouring of grief, shock, introspection and outrage following the Bulger murder'.[29] But it is probably safe to claim that apart from specialist criminal or local historians, the general public will have no knowledge whatever of this 1891 case (and a similar one in 1855) of child-on-child murder in Liverpool, though the memorable cases of Madeleine Smith and of Dr. Neill Cream, widely written about, had occurred within the close time frames of 1857 and 1892, respectively.

So what is it that renders a murder case 'notable' and therefore entitled to inclusion in the distinguished 'Notable British Trials' series published by the Edinburgh firm of William Hodge & Co from 1905 until its last volume in 1959, before being partially reprinted by Penguin Books in more recent times, and then resurrected by the publishers of the present volume, Mango Books?[30] Horror, itself, will not suffice. For many cases of wife-murder over the past two hundred years, where the victim has suffered horrific injuries, have (sadly) been quickly forgotten, especially in a working-class context where drunkenness or financial strains were significant factors. Instead,

> 'The classic murder is the one that satisfies us as a complete drama. It can be tragic or comic. It may horrify or baffle. It often raises important legal or moral issues. But above all it encapsulates time and place and personality in a self-contained story.'

These are the words of Robert Meadley when writing about murder cases that will not only remain long in the memory but also become iconic. Obvious twentieth-century examples that he mentions include the cases of Dr. Crippen, George Joseph Smith, James Hanratty, and Patrick Mahon (the Eastbourne 'Crumbles' killer in 1924).[31]

Meadley's point is, therefore, that a classic murder could easily be read as a gripping and high quality novel. It would possess atmosphere such as creaking doors, endless passages, secret or otherwise, stairs and corridors, sinister manoeuvrings, doppelgangers, coincidences, missing items, lock-fast places and rooms, locked jewellery boxes, incriminating love letters, and missing wills; all beautifully depicted in a variety of gripping sources ranging from Mrs. Rochester's 'prison' in Charlotte Bronte's *Jane Eyre*, to Krook's bottle and junk shop in *Bleak House*, to Kate Summerscale's *The Suspicions of Mr Whicher*, on the Constance Kent case in 1860, and to the aged Marion Gilchrist's family secrets and lies, and

---

29   John E. Archer, *The Monster Evil: Policing and Violence in Victorian Liverpool*, Liverpool University Press, Liverpool, 2011, pp. 176-7. The author noted an earlier case in 1855 when two nine-year olds, John Breen and Alfred Fitz, struck seven-year old James Fleeson on the head before throwing him into Stanley Dock some distance away, where his father found him two and a half days later. See ibid., p. 175.

30   The Israel Lipski, Louise Masset and Percy Lefroy Mapleton volumes of the new Notable British Trials (NBT) series have been published in 2017, 2018 and 2019 respectively, while others are currently in preparation. For a recent assessment of the original NBT series and of its objective in seeking to combine erudition, education, entertainment and puzzle solving, see Lindsay Farmer, "Notable Trials and the Criminal Law in Scotland and England, 1750-1950", in Philippe Chassaigne and Jean-Philippe Genet (eds), *Droit et Société en France et en Grande-Bretagne (XIIe-XXe siecles)*. Publications de la Sorbonne, Paris, 2003, pp. 149-70; see also Shani D'Cruze, "'The Damn'd Place Was Haunted': The Gothic, Middlebrow Culture and Inter-War 'Notable British Trials,'" *Literature and History*, Vol. 15 (1), 2006, pp. 37-58.

31   Robert Meadley, *Classics in Murder*, Xanadu, 1984, cited on back cover and in 'Introduction: Crippen, or, Is the Reader Sinister?'

documents, in the Oscar Slater case in Glasgow, 1909-10.

As well as the 'gothic' elements that one can detect in such cases (but especially in the 'grave robbers' case of Burke and Hare in pre-Victorian Edinburgh), there is, as Brian Marriner has pointed out, a desperation on the part of some murderers that the homicide of their victims should bring in its wake a positive magical transformation in the life chances of the killers. Marriner suggests that, [32]

> "....there is a close affinity between the criminal and the artist. Both are dissatisfied with life as it is, and seek to create change. Both seek to create order out of chaos. They demand that life should adapt to their terms. One thinks of Dostoyevsky's Raskolnikov [the killer of the old woman in *Crime and Punishment*] in the moment when he cries out through gritted teeth, 'I will not *live* like this anymore!'"

Marriner continues that, 'There is a real sense in which both art and crime can be viewed as acts of magic'. Magic uses ritual practices to bring about improvement, perhaps to eliminate disease or drought. In a similar fashion the act of murder can be perceived as a step to beneficial change in the mind of the practitioner. With sex-obsessed offenders such as Jack the Ripper, Dr. Neill Cream or the Yorkshire Ripper it might be to remove prostitutes from society, the latter perceived by the killers as pollutants of the body politic. Other murderers might more prosaically seek to remove direct obstacles to a better life, barriers such as the burdensome Cora Crippen, or the awkwardly clinging Emily Kaye and Elsie Cameron, intruding on the lives of Patrick Mahon and Norman Thorne, respectively, in the early 1920s. To remove such obstacles is, for the killer, to engage in a metaphorical magical practice that will, cathartically, result in a better life for the magician (and possibly for any constituent of his such as Dr. Crippen's Ethel Le Neve). That to commit murder is to effect improvement is, of course, both irony and paradox given the fate befalling the murdered victims as well as the likely vengeance society would wreak on the 'new man' (or woman) in due course.

For Marriner Rouse's case is a fine illustration of his point regarding the flawed belief in a magical transformation of life chances through homicide. Like others before and after him Rouse saw it as essential (if we are to accept the dominant narrative) to re-invent himself under a new identity in order to escape the spider's web of financial and relational commitments from which he was finding it increasingly difficult to extricate himself. Thus the murder and burning beyond recognition within the enclosed space of his burnt-out Morris Minor of an unidentified body, whom he described as a 'down-and-out, the sort of man no one would miss', could be seen by him as a magical means to transform his fortunes for the better. The magic, we know, was a snare and a delusion (there *was* no magic and all magic is, in any case, a delusion).[33]

At the end of her introduction to the Notable British Trials volume on the Rouse case, Helena Normanton noted that when Rouse was travelling back to England, after having been evacuated as a casualty from the Western Front in 1915, he regained consciousness just as his hospital train was passing through Bedford

---

32   Brian Marriner, *Forensic Clues to Murder*, Arrow, 1991, pp. 18-19.
33   Is it not ironic that the journalist most associated with the Rouse case, the *Daily Sketch*'s J. C. Cannell, also practised as a magician? See later in this volume.

station. Were the gods exerting their malign magic on him, given that his life was to end on the gallows of Bedford Jail some fifteen years later? Sensibly Normanton merely viewed the events as a 'curious coincidence'; which is undoubtedly what one might also say of the fact that the motor engineer who had carried out a repair on Rouse's car not long before the fateful journey to Hardingstone Lane was James Berry, the same name as one of England's most famous hangmen who had carried out his distasteful tasks between 1883 and 1891.[34]

But classic murders did not only reveal the narrow delusions of their perpetrators as they sought to re-invent themselves through their deeds. *Causes célèbres* can also offer a window into time and place, such as the tensions generated among the supercilious intellectual classes as they watched the expanding Edwardian north London suburbs, desired by and then occupied by the growing lower middle classes of bank clerks, office workers using new technology such as typewriters and the telephone, Prudential Insurance collectors and modestly earning quack homeopathic doctors and 'dentists'. Indeed this comfortable image for some (and appalling prospect for others) can be represented by Crippen and by his female office typist companion and lover, Ethel Le Neve, while Cora Crippen adds to the picture with her Pooteresque preoccupation with trivia, appearances, little social 'triumphs' and respectability, that is, characteristics that all combine in her case to exaggerate her tasteless gaucheness.[35] While horror, as previously suggested, is not a necessary, let alone a sufficient, element in a murder case, the idea of the 'mild murderer', Crippen, cutting up his wife's body, or of Samuel Dougal casually disposing of Camille Holland's body in the moat-dominated heavy clay soil of Moat Tree Farm in Essex in 1899, of Norman Thorne thoughtfully distributing the remains of Elsie Cameron in his chicken run on his small-holding in Crowborough in 1925, of Neville Heath committing unspeakable violent obscenities upon the bodies of Margery Gardner and Doreen Marshall in 1946, or of Donald Hume tossing the torso of Stanley Setty out of his light aircraft over the English Channel in 1949, there is a heightened sense of the dramatic prompted by the combination of the bizarrely hypnotic, possibly even admirable in a few cases, and the grotesquely horrific. For Crippen's gentleness, even his 'feminine' side, scarcely equate with his butchering of his wife's corpse. Heath's suaveness and sophisticated RAF manners hardly prepare for his sado-masochistic psychopathic behaviour. Norman Thorne's somewhat bucolic regard for his chickens is at odds with his disregard for, and indignity towards, his former lover, Elsie Cameron, irrespective of whether he had, indeed, been a victim of 'Spilsburyism', when the jury accepted the damning testimony of the renowned pathologist, Sir Bernard Spilsbury in preference to that of the more numerous pathologists whose evidence supported Thorne's innocent theory of the case.[36]

The drama of a murder can, of course, be found in the manner in which it 'baffles' the public or the authorities, and none more so than the Jack the Ripper

---

34   Brian Bailey, *Hangman: From Ketch to Pierrepoint*, True Crime, 1993, pp. 107-33.
35   Julie English Early, "Keeping Ourselves to Ourselves: Violence in the Edwardian Suburb", in Shani D'Cruze (ed.), *Everyday Violence in Britain, 1850-1950*, Pearson, 2000, Ch. 10; *ibid.*, "A New Man for a New Century: Dr Crippen and the Principles of Masculinity", in George Robb and Nancy Erber (eds.), *Disorder in Court: Trials and Sexual Conflict at the Turn of the Century*, Macmillan, 1999, Ch. 11.
36   The sources for these cases are too numerous to cite. They are all extensively covered in 'encyclopaedias' of murder and in the *Notable British Trials* series.

events. But in the scandalous case against Oscar Slater in 1909-10, it was not only the frame-up against him, nor the under-current of Presbyterian anti-Semitism in Scotland, nor the closing of ranks of the Scottish legal and professional establishment and the hounding of those few honourable policemen and lawyers who knew something rotten was afoot. It was the mystery surrounding the life story of the elderly victim, Marion Gilchrist, hiding her family secrets, that is surely one of the case's most alluring qualities. Slater was released in 1927 and his conviction (grudgingly) quashed in 1928 after years of campaigning by Arthur Conan Doyle and by various journalists. But if the murderer was not he, then who? And here the mystery of Marion Gilchrist opens up like an Agatha Christie reprise of a murder victim's earlier life, such as that of the unpleasant paterfamilias, Simeon Lee, in *Hercule Poirot's Christmas*. For it was the wicked killing of his gold prospecting partner in South Africa in his younger days that, in the Christie story, came back to haunt the master of Gorston Hall in his old age and which led, through circuitous family connections, to his own brutal murder. Tracking down the actual killer or killers of Marion Gilchrist would entail a similarly convoluted exploration of family 'secrets and lies', a 'Who Do You Think You Are?' exploration that cannot but engross the reader today but which, through an elite conspiracy of silence at the time, had little purchase for influential contemporaries.[37] One might leave aside for the moment, from Robert Meadley's list, 'important legal issues' such as whether William Joyce (Lord Haw-Haw), an American citizen with a falsely acquired British passport, *did* legally owe allegiance to the United Kingdom; or more pertinently, whether Ronald True, the killer of Olive Young (also known as Gertrude Yates) in 1922, or Neville Heath, or Reg Christie of 10 Rillington Place, or John George Haigh, the 'Acid-Bath' killer in 1949, were all 'as mad as a hatter', and who therefore ought to have been found guilty but insane.[38] What *are* important for the purpose of identifying certain murders as classics are, as Meadley indicates, whether the 'moral issues' raised in a case and the character and personalities of the leading actors contribute to the narrative as a 'self-contained story' possessing the qualities of a 'complete drama'. Nowhere are these features better articulated than in the Thompson-Bywaters Greek tragedy tale of inevitable doom of 1922-23, and in the Rattenbury and Stoner drama of 1935. Like Crippen, the Brides in the Bath killer and Jack the Ripper the previous cases have given rise, variously, to books, novels, films and plays. Jill Dawson's recent novel on the Thompson-Bywaters case, *Fred & Edie*, has received awards and praise, the criminologist F. Tennyson Jesse's 1934 novel based on it, *A Pin to See the Peep Show*, has stood the test of time, while the Rattenbury case attracted the attention of the playwright, Terence Rattigan, whose play, *Cause Célèbre*,

---

37   For Slater, see especially Thomas Toughill, *Oscar Slater: The 'Immortal' Case of Sir Arthur Conan Doyle*, Sutton Publishing, Stroud, 2006; Ben Braber, "The Trial of Oscar Slater (1909) and Anti-Jewish Prejudices in Edwardian Glasgow", *History*, Vol. 88, 2003, pp. 262-79. A comparable mystery concerned the killing of Julia Wallace in 1931. The case involved, inter alia, a chess club, a non-existent Liverpool address, a never-to-be-traced phone caller ('R. M. Qualtrough'), the conviction of the victim's seemingly inoffensive middle-aged husband (a 'man from the Pru') followed by the quashing of his conviction and then his sudden death within two years. Finally there was the revelation in a Liverpool radio station programme in 1981 of the name of the possible murderer, a 'spiv-like' character, all features that may fulfil many of the qualities of the classic, memorable murder *cause célèbre*. The most recent analysis is Ronald Bartle, *The Telephone Murder: The Mysterious Death of Julia Wallace*, Wildy, Simmonds and Hill Publishing, 2012.

38   See note 13, above. 'Not guilty by reason of insanity' is the current formula if cases ever reach that stage.

graced West End audiences (as well as BBC radio listeners) in 2011 with Anne-Marie Duff in the lead as the tragic Alma Rattenbury.

Central to those accounts were the issue of transgressive sex across age gaps (the woman was considerably older, more experienced and more sophisticated than the young man), across classes, and in breach of the code of marital loyalty. The general public were apparently shocked by the uncontrolled sexual energy of the older married woman with her much younger lover. The reading out in court of extracts from Edith's suburban letters to Fred on his voyages as a ship's writer, and candidly writing about the ecstasy of their sexual congress and of the gloom of satisfying her unloved husband provided sensational copy for a press caught between the need to be both censorious and titillating. When Alma and 18-year old George Stoner made love in the same bedroom as Alma's sleeping child, disgust was the publicly expressed emotion, but voyeurism might have been a more truthful sentiment. In other words the 'double standard' was not confined to married men's punishment-free sexual dalliances while their wives were expected to abandon chasteness only for their husbands.

But it is in the *character* of the two women in question that the fascination of those above cases really resides, especially in respect of Edith Thompson. Much of the controversy surrounding her execution on January 9, 1923 was the belief, shared by her distinguished counsel, Sir Henry Curtis-Bennett, himself no social critic, that she had been 'hanged for adultery'. She had taken no part in the physical attack on her husband by Bywaters that had resulted in Percy Thompson's death as the married couple neared their home in Ilford after a night out to the theatre. But Edith's amazing letters to Freddie were produced in court. They ranged over many topics, in particular, the middle-brow novels that Edith was reading. She constantly sought Freddie's opinion of the characters in the stories and of the plots. She referred to matters that had been raised in some of the books, such as Robert Hichens' 1909 desert romance, *Bella Donna*, a story of a wife poisoning her husband to take up a new life with a (supposedly) Arabian sheikh. Edith imagined how she might act in the context of the novels. She talked of crushed up glass from light bulbs, of her husband eating the 'wrong porridge' and of his complaining of 'bitter' tea. That the explanation might not have been the sinister one of her attempting to poison her husband, but possibly related to Edith's attempting to take abortifacients, did not save her from the gallows. But commentators have sought to 'get into the mind' of this troubled woman in order to offer an innocent explanation for the apparently damning evidence in her preserved letters. For her counsel, Curtis-Bennett, she was an innocuous romantic fantasist caught up in a loveless marriage and animated by her affair with the masculine young Freddie with whom she had become besotted. A more recent writer has claimed that her letters, in fact, manifested a search for self-identity or 'self-hood'. Rather than fantasising about living the life of the imaginary Bella Donna (or 42-year old Mrs. Ruby Chepstow in Hichens' novel) and being swept off her feet by a sultry Rudolph Valentino desert character on an Arab steed, Edith is on a mission, through the novels, to find her real self. It is not the fantasy of the gangster's moll which later captured the mind of 18-year old Elizabeth Jones from the Welsh valleys during the Second World War after she had met 'Lieutenant Ricky Allen' (actually the deserter, US Private Karl Hulten) in a depressing London cafe, when he charmed her with his tales of having 'run with the Mob in Chicago'. Desperate for a slice of excitement to transport her from her dull wartime reality, she then proceeded to go with him on a crime spree which culminated in the murder of a taxi driver in London in 1944. Edith's search for selfhood was not the escapism that Elizabeth Maude Jones, who took to calling herself Georgina Grayson, had sought, nor was it a fantasy existence that she had in mind. It was, rather, her seeking to fashion a life style representing her own strengths and achievements and character. Her literary imagination, her modernity in terms of pursuing a career as a milliner's buyer, entailing frequent trips to Paris and expressing herself in French despite having left school early (and earning more than her husband who had been discharged from the Army in 1916 with a weak heart), her competitive dancing skills and trophies for the foxtrot (an activity in which Percy Thompson did not participate), her modern hair style, her dress sense, her childlessness (at least with Percy); they all attested to the 'New Woman', the modern woman who did not see her place as confined to rearing children at home while her husband was the breadwinner, even if marriages from the start of the twentieth century were moving towards the more 'companionate' and away from the 'patriarchal'. But it was her sexuality, and talking about it in her letters that, above all else, shocked observers (the contemporaneous activities of Dr. Marie Stopes and her advocacy of birth control significantly referred to 'Married Love' [italics added]). In short one cannot understand the Thompson-Bywaters case without understanding Edith's character and how it appeared to jar with dominant contemporary sentiments, including those notoriously expressed by the high-minded muscular Christian judge in the case, Mr. Justice Shearman (though his summing up regarding the legal principles of joint criminal enterprise liability was fair to Edith).

While 'drama ...time, place and personality' were, for Meadley, central elements of the classic murder cause célèbre, social historians have also found much material to excavate from such episodes. As Richard Cobb wrote in 1969, 'Murder trials light up the years and give a more precise sense of period than the reigns of monarchs or the terms of office of presidents'.[39] More expansively the criminologist, Howard Engel, has written that,

> "The study of crime offers a special tool to the social historian. Through a study of the offenses that societies, throughout history, have chosen to criminalize, prosecute and, at the end of the process, punish, we get some notion of how people behave in extremis. When the heat is on. Here is society caught at a disadvantage, with its hair in curlers, still in its bathrobe at eleven o'clock in the morning. The study of crime cuts a trench into the tumulus of human existence. Here we can learn about the structure of the society, the classes, the power base and the mentality of not only the offenders, but also of those who judge them. Just as the archaeologist digs a trench into a mound to turn up a slice of an ancient civilization, the study of a particular crime allows the criminologist and anyone else interested in looking to see a slice of a micro-civilization that existed surrounding a peculiar group of circumstances. Such an investigation interrupts a series of events and exposes a drama that would otherwise be hidden from us".[40]

---

39   Cited in McLaren, *op. cit.*, whose stimulating study of the case of Dr. Neill Cream in 1891 has significantly influenced the shape and approach of the present study.
40   Howard Engel, *Crimes of Passion*, Robson Books, 2002, pp. 15-16.

In a sense this approach to analysing murder *causes célèbres* mirrors the rise of the 'history from below' movement of the 1960s and 1970s which saw in the 'Making of the English Working Class' (to invoke the title of E. P. Thompson's magisterial work from 1963) a more authentic, grass-roots and 'experiential' way of looking at the totality of social, economic and cultural (indeed, also, of political) history. It was not just a change of focus from the study of kings, queens, international wars and high politics. It also refined, in a much more sophisticated and conceptual manner, one's analysis of how the elite engaged with the lower classes.

However 'history from below' is not so prominent in murder *causes célèbres*. For such cases have tended to be located within middle-class contexts (and more rarely in cross-class contexts, as in the 1903 case of the working-class Kitty Byron, a former prostitute, who murdered her middle-class stockbroker lover).[41] Perhaps the more famous crime writers in the 'Notable British Trials' canon, such as H. B. Irving (son of the more famous Sir Henry Irving), the writer and criminologist, F. Tennyson Jesse, the Edinburgh master of the genre, William Roughead, and the Glasgow-born barrister and *Times* journalist, Donald Carswell, saw little of keen interest in a working-class 'domestic' involving male drunkenness, a paucity of income, poor housing conditions, domestic violence and wife-murder. In truth few writers have 'unpacked' such allegedly grubby and tedious cases in detail in order to offer a novel-length 'complete drama', possibly because the bias, as with earlier conceptions of 'social history' (which might mean the history of manners, of aristocratic households, their country mansions, and their field sports and culinary innovations, or their styles of dress) before the 1960s, meant that such working-class episodes were perceived as of such common currency that there would be nothing of historical or social significance to be extracted from a full-length study. As one of the characters remarked in Agatha Christie's *Towards Zero* (1944), 'I have had a fairly wide experience of criminal cases. Only a few of them have held any real interest. Most murderers have been lamentably uninteresting and very short-sighted'. Indeed who can admit to having heard of, let alone recall, the domestic killing of Eliza Range by her live-in lover, Charles Whittaker, in 1903, or that of Catherine Hartigan by her husband, Edward, in 1906, or the murder of Lilian Charlton by her partner, Charles Patterson, in 1907, or the killing of Ellen Ballington by her husband, Frederick, in 1908; and of the many hundreds, if not thousands, of 'working-class' killings at a time when the annual average of homicides, including infanticide and suicide pacts in England and Wales, from about 1870 to 1970 with occasional short-term spikes, was around 350?[42] However future writers who seek to open up such working-class glimpses of life and death may well succeed, to paraphrase E. P. Thompson again, in rescuing the working-class victim and killer 'from the enormous condescension of posterity'. For just as the unpacking of the lives of Dr. Neill Cream, Kitty Byron, Oscar Slater, Dr. Crippen, Ronald True, Edith Thompson and others may shed light on the

---

41   Ginger Frost, "'She is But a Woman': Kitty Byron and the Edwardian Criminal Justice System", *Gender and History*, Vol. 16 (3), 2004, pp. 538-60.

42   The four examples between 1903 and 1907 are taken from Eddleston, *Murderous Manchester*, *op. cit.*, pp. 9-33. The vast majority of the remaining 27 cases listed in the book could just as easily have been cited. For the statistics, see Barry S. Godfrey Chris A. Williams and Paul Lawrence, *Crime and Justice, 1750-1950*, Willan, Cullompton, Devon, 2006, for accessible statistics.

criss-crossing paths of the working- and middle-class worlds of their day, so also the re-imagining of a 'nasty little domestic murder' within the rough, twilit and alcohol-ridden world of the labouring or unemployed poor may yet reveal something of the complexity and tensions, whether sexual, medical, economic or otherwise, of the contemporary world inhabited by the deceased and defendant. 'Only connect!' as E. M. Forster famously stated in *Howards End*, is both one of the shortest, and yet one of the most profound, injunctions, urging us to look deeper into our lives. It was what J. B. Priestley memorably prompted us to do in his *An Inspector Calls*, written as a wartime reminder in 1944-45 that (unlike more unconvincing invocations by a recent Chancellor of the Exchequer to 'restore the public finances' in the wake of the financial crash of 2008) we were, indeed, 'all in this together', embracing both the suicide victim, Eva Smith, and the wealthy, self-satisfied and sanctimonious Birling family whose fates, secrets and thoughtless conduct were inexorably linked to Eva and to society, as well as to each other[43].

The Blazing Car Murder, for the most part, is mostly preoccupied with a lower middle-class way of life, and one where cross-class linkages are more limited. To excavate the case will not expose a 'holistic' view of inter-war social life, cutting across class, racial, sexual and cultural boundaries. But it will, it is hoped, offer an insight into significant episodes in the social history of the inter-war years. For it will engage issues such as sexual morality, and perceptions of masculinity and of illegitimate births, the way the press, in its efforts to sensationalise stories and to maximise sales, might operate prejudicially against a murder suspect, the degree of fairness or of unfairness of the inter-war criminal justice system, the potential longer-term consequences of war wounds, the reverence reposed in some trial 'experts' but not in others, the manner in which the Home Secretary exercised, or failed to exercise, clemency towards the condemned man, the life of the commercial traveller during this period and the growth of motoring, clothing styles (particularly the importance of men's hats), the literary and cultural legacy of the case in plays and novels (albeit only briefly covered here) and, not least, the respect, evidenced by the authorities' determination to pursue Rouse to the gallows, accorded to an unidentified corpse by a nation which had, a decade earlier, honoured at the highest level the Great War's Unknown Warrior.

So why ought the Blazing Car case to be classed as a murder *cause célèbre*?

As defence counsel asseverated in their petition for clemency for Rouse,

> "We believe this case to be unique in our criminal justice history. The victim remained unknown and unidentified to the end of the trial. No motive of any kind ever appeared in evidence [note the tantalising qualification 'in evidence'] from start to finish. The whole of the evidence against the prisoner remained circumstantial, depending partly on his own foolish conduct, and partly on highly debatable deductions drawn on highly technical matters. We are not aware of any case in our history where a man has been hanged on purely circumstantial evidence which failed to include any sort of evidence to indicate a motive or reason for the alleged crime."

---

43   If criminal proceedings ensue in the wake of the Grenfell Fire disaster in London in 2017, it may reveal deep connections similar to those unearthed in *An Inspector Calls*.

First it may be noted that counsel was mistaken in claiming that the case was unique on the ground that the victim was never identified. As we shall see when we address the issue of the victim's identity in chapter seven, there had been a famous precedent in 1786 when the identity of a seafarer murdered on the London-Portsmouth road was never discovered. Yet his killers, also sailors, were hanged. That aside, it might be claimed that the somewhat hyperbolic submission by defence counsel, Donald Finnemore (who, as Mr. Justice Finnemore, later sentenced to death in 1953 the serial killer of 10 Rillington Place, Reg Christie) and his junior, A. P. Marshall, was encouraged by their being too closely involved with the defendant and his desperate plight to offer a balanced assessment of the significance of the case in the annals of murder. None of these points can be gainsaid to question why the 'Blazing Car Murder' should not occupy a place in the canon of murder *causes célèbres*. For while it has scarcely attracted the amount of attention focussed upon, say, Dr. Crippen, or George Joseph Smith of 'Brides in the Bath' notoriety, or Thompson and Bywaters, or upon the three post-war psychopaths, Heath, Haigh and Christie, yet the case still fascinates in the way that thousands of murders over the years to 1970 have failed to do.[44] Apart from its inevitable inclusion in 'encyclopaedias' of murder, it still features in many selective murder 'collections'.[45] It is also discussed at length in different lawyers' biographies and autobiographies, including those concerning Sir Patrick Hastings, Norman Birkett and Lord Chief Justice Hewart, who were all involved in the case.[46] In addition it appeared in the Penguin reprint series of *Notable British Trials*,[47] as well as in two editions (1931 and 1952) of the Helena Normanton volume of the trial in that series. Moreover, no biography of the pathologist, Sir Bernard Spilsbury, was complete without description of his involvement in the case.[48] Finally, and apart from its being borrowed for literary purposes by the detective writers Dorothy L. Sayers and P. D. James, by the graphic novelist and comic writer, Alan Moore, and by the playwright, Dennis Potter,[49] it has even been cross-referred in an article entitled 'Man-Hunters: The 'German Rouse Cases,'' which appeared in a classic murder collection.[50]

Perhaps the view of a near-contemporary, introducing the Geoffrey Bles rival to

---

44 In the 100 years between 1870 and 1970, actual murder figures for England and Wales tended to hover between 120 and 180 per annum. Nearly all of those cases have been forgotten except by the most assiduous collectors of murder data.

45 They include Dorothy Sayers and Others, *Great Unsolved Crimes*, Hutchinson, 1938 (contribution by Ex-Superintendent John Prothero, "The Blazing Car Murder", pp. 173-79); Geoffrey de C. Parmiter, *Reasonable Doubt*, Arthur Barker, 1938, Ch. 2; Edgar Lustgarten, *The Judges and the Judged*, Odhams Press, 1951, pp. 83-8; Leonard Gribble, *Famous Judges and Their Trials: A Century of Justice*, John Long, 1957, Ch. XV; and James McClure, *Killers*, Fontana, 1976, Ch. III.

46 Sir Patrick Hastings, *Cases in Court*, Pan Books, 1955, pp. 191-201; H. Montgomery Hyde, *Norman Birkett: The Life of Lord Birkett of Ulverston*, Reprint Society, 1965, pp. 297-310; Dennis Bardens, *Lord Justice Birkett*, Robert Hale, 1962, pp. 150-64; and Robert Jackson, *The Chief: The Biography of Gordon Hewart, Lord Chief Justice of England, 1922-40*, Harrap, 1959.

47 James H. Hodge (ed), *Famous Trials 8*, Penguin, 1963.

48 Andrew Rose, *Lethal Witness: Sir Bernard Spilsbury, Honorary Pathologist*, Sutton Publishing, Stroud, 2007, Ch. 16; Colin Evans, *The Father of Forensics: How Sir Bernard Spilsbury Invented CSI*, Icon Books, 2009, pp. 219-42; D. G. Browne and E. V. Tullett, *Bernard Spilsbury: His Life and Cases*, Companion Book Club, 1952, pp. 327-42.

49 Gerry R. Rubin, "Dennis, Alan and Arthur x 3: Literary Legacies of the 'Blazing Car Murder' of 1930", *Law and Humanities*, Vol. 9 (2), 2015, pp. 1-34.

50 F. A. Beaumont, in J. M. Parrish and John R. Crossland (eds), *The Fifty Most Amazing Crimes of the Last 100 Years*, Odhams Press, 1936. Beaumont separately devotes a chapter to the Rouse case itself.

the William Hodge Notable British Trials series, captured just a part of the classic essence of the case when it referred to Rouse's 'personality'.[51] Thus the journalist and author, Sydney Tremayne, wrote that,

> "'The Blazing Car Mystery' provided one of the most sensational murder trials of this century. The circumstances of the crime, so gruesome, ingenious, and unusual—one might almost say original; the personality of the man accused of murder; the mystery surrounding the identity of the victim and the method of and motive for the murder, combined to excite public imagination to an unexampled extent. There were, additionally, certain aspects of the legal procedure which evoked criticism: the legality of the verdict itself was called in question and the subsequent controversy reached such a pitch that, even after the sentence had been carried out, the newspapers contained 'news' about Rouse and questions were actually asked of the Home Secretary in the House of Commons about Rouse's alleged confession which was published in certain newspapers."

Such an opening quote is helpful so far as it goes. It refers to the horror of the killing, its almost unique quality, the search for the character of Rouse, the unidentified corpse, the legal controversy, newspaper sensationalism, even the political dimension to the case. These are crucially relevant. However, and to conclude this chapter, there are other concepts that may characterise this work, concepts that may even appear contradictory. First we may borrow from a fairly recent analysis of the most famous unsolved murder in American crime history, the mutilation of Elizabeth Short, soon anointed in death as the 'Black Dahlia' (a borrowing from the 1946 thriller, *The Blue Dahlia*, starring Alan Ladd and Veronica Lake). As Russell Miller notes,

> "In its uniquely haunting way, Elizabeth Short's story is a play about randomness—the most profoundly disturbing and frightening play ever written about the consequences of Chance. By naïve, dumb chance, Elizabeth Short's path crossed that of a murderer. And from that point on, a shortly wound clock was ticking towards her macabre murder. It's a harrowing, *noir*-take on the worn-out Creation vs Evolution argument: was all this *created*, or did it happen by *chance*?"[52]

The story of Rouse and his unknown victim may likewise suggest a moral about the ambiguity of randomness and its fatal results, about the difficulty, perhaps impossibility, of separating chance from creation. Did Rouse 'create' a murderous

51 Sydney Tremayne, *Trial of Alfred Arthur Rouse*, Geoffrey Bles, 1931, p. 9. The volume was published in May 1931, two months after Rouse's execution, whereas the Hodge volume, edited by the barrister and feminist, Helena Normanton, was published in June 1931. Normanton had been refused permission to use prison photographs of Rouse in her volume. They are presumably those reproduced in this book. It is not clear whether Tremayne had sought such permission which, presumably, would also have been refused. Called to the bar in 1922, she was the first woman to have been briefed in the High Court and the Old Bailey. She may have been a feminist but she was also effusively admiring of the Office of Lord Mayor (that 'Stupendous Being') of the City of London and its associated Aldermen, Sheriffs and Under-Sheriffs, among whom women (and, of course, working-class representatives) would have been notable by their absence at the time she was writing. See Helena Normanton, 'A Note on the Old Bailey', in C. E. Bechhofer Roberts (ed.), *The Trial of Mrs. Duncan*, Jarrolds, 1945, pp. 349-52.
52 Russell Miller, "The Obsession with the Black Dahlia", in Roger Wilkes (ed), *The Mammoth Book of Unsolved Crimes*, Robinson, 1999, p. 179.

scheme or did his domestic life create an inevitable trajectory towards a burning blaze? Was it 'chance' rather than creation whereby the unknown man was supposedly 'selected' days before the event and then collected outside the Swan and Pyramids pub? Or, on the alternative basis of their paths crossing each other at a different venue, was it chance, or either the tramp's or Rouse's own 'creation', which resulted in the victim's being picked up at Tally Ho Corner apparently, on one interpretation, as a random hitch-hiker? Was it chance or was it fated that the cousins, William Bailey and Alfred Brown, would stroll back to Hardingstone Lane on a moonlit night from a Guy Fawkes dance at such an ungodly hour just at the very moment when Rouse suddenly emerged from the ditch? Of all the country lanes in all the towns in all the world, they walk into mine, Rouse might have ruefully paraphrased had he lived to see *Casablanca*.

*

But whether we are referring to creation or to chance, they did occur *somewhere* and at *some time*. Therefore what we are seeking to do in this account of the case is, in addition, to project a sense of both 'time' and 'place', not only in regard to the then rural Hardingstone Lane on a moonlit night in early November 1930, but also to the world of the commercial traveller, of suburban Buxted Road, and of the lives of Rouse's women. This approach, it is hoped, will provide the necessary atmosphere to transform a 'work-a-day' (so to speak) murder story into Robert Meadley's 'complete drama'; or even to justify, though perhaps not in the sense that he intended, Sir Thomas de Quincey's celebration in 1827 of 'Murder Considered as One of the Fine Arts'.

CHAPTER THREE

THE WAITRESS WITH A WEDDING RING

EVENING NEWS, December 12, 1930

Prelude to Disaster

Let us go back a few days in time before the evening of Guy Fawkes Night. It was 9 am on November 1, 1930 when a strange man walked into St Mary's Church in Islington. He asked to speak to the church clerk, Walter Frederick Turner. He explained that his brother, A. A. Rowse (note the spelling), described as a 31-year old bachelor of 284 Liverpool Road, Islington, London N.1, had been married in that very church in July 1924. He claimed that he was not certain what Christian names his brother had used for the ceremony. Nonetheless, his 'brother's' bride, staying at the same Liverpool Road address, had been a 24-year old spinster, Helen Dora Cambull (again, note the spelling), but tragically, the strange man recounted, his brother, Arthur Alec Rowse, had just been burned to death in a car accident. The dead man's widow lived in London but as the victim's brother, the visitor to the church had taken it upon himself to attend to the legal formalities accompanying the death of a relative. To this end, and as the original marriage certificate had been lost, he now sought a copy of his brother's, the supposedly deceased A. A. Rowse's, marriage licence. Mr. Turner exercised his brain in trying to recall the wedding ceremonies that had taken place some six years previously. But it was not an especially difficult matter to recall such events. For it was in 1924 that he had recently assumed the office of clerk, and his memories of the first few ceremonies in which he had officially participated had not faded. As he later told the police, he distinctly remembered that notice of the wedding had been given in the usual way and that the banns had been published. Indeed, during the evening of November 21, 1924, the day before the wedding, the groom had called upon Mr. Turner to ask whether the clerk and his wife would consent to witness the ceremony as they were keeping it secret and no friends were attending. Mr. Turner had inquired about the secrecy and particularly recalled the groom saying that his betrothed's father was a tea planter in South Africa (though Helen's father was accurately described as a lithographic artist in the marriage certificate), and that as he, 'Rowse', was not doing well in business, her father had cabled him to marry Helen and take her to South Africa before Christmas, even though his ('Rowse's') family disagreed with the plan. Turner was convinced by the explanation and he therefore agreed to witness the marriage, along with his wife, of Arthur 'Rowse' to

Helen 'Cambull'. But now, meeting 'Rowse's' 'brother' six years later, Turner was struck by how closely the man standing in front of him looked like the bridegroom in the second (or was it the third?) marriage ceremony conducted in the church after he had assumed his new duties.

The visitor, no doubt shifting uneasily, hurriedly replied that there had indeed been a close resemblance between the two brothers. However the deceased had in fact been the slightly older of the two. What made a lasting impression on Turner was the bridegroom's elegant and handsome appearance, his delicately trimmed moustache, his groomed hair and the cut of his suit. So, yes, the church clerk did vividly recall the marriage ceremony and would be pleased to furnish the deceased A. A. Rowse's brother with a copy of the certificate of marriage between Arthur Alec Rowse and Helen Dora Cambull. How soon, asked the visitor, would the certificate be ready. The earliest, he was told, would be 6:30 pm. 'Well', replied the 'brother', 'There is no immediate hurry, [and] that will do nicely. I can give it to her tomorrow'. Returning later that day, the visitor was handed the copy, signed and verified by the Rev. Hugh R. Gough, Curate. He eagerly read it, exclaimed 'Arthur Alec, that's it', paid the fee and then disappeared into the crowds.

But the visitor was not the dead man's brother. There *was* no dead man called A. A. Rowse at that point and there was no brother. However, there *was* an A. A. *Rouse*, actually Alfred Arthur Rouse, who had lost an infant brother decades previously and who had indeed gone through a form of marriage ceremony with Helen *Campbell* (not Cambull) at St Mary's Church in 1924. The problem was that it was bigamous, a situation of which Helen was to remain unaware for a few years. Indeed at the age of 21 Arthur Rouse had legally married 23-year old Lily (or Lilly in the marriage certificate) Watkins at St Saviour's Church in St Albans, near where his military unit was training, on November 29, 1914 more than three months before he was sent to the fighting on the Western Front the following March. Therefore, when he signed the register in Islington in 1924, he obviously, 'introduced a certain alteration into his name and signature', as the *Daily Sketch* journalist, J. C. Cannell, later observed.[53] Cannell did not indicate what that alteration was, but as we have seen, it involved changing the spelling of 'Rouse' to 'Rowse', and, more crudely, changing 'Campbell' to 'Cambull'.

Why did alarm bells not start ringing with poor deluded Helen when, after the ceremony at St Mary's, Islington, in December 1924, she received her marriage 'lines', complete with unfamiliar spellings of both her and her 'husband's' name (which, some years later, she proudly waved before Lily Rouse, née Watkins, before the truth suddenly dawned on her)? Or, what of the further opportunity to interrogate Rouse when little Arthur Jnr.'s birth was registered on July 28, 1925 and the birth certificate was riddled with inaccuracies? Perhaps she was scared of what she might discover. But it is more probable that she was simply besotted with Rouse and believed his story that Lily, a much plainer and older woman than she, was Rouse's aunt, not his wife of at least ten years standing. What is simpler to comprehend is Rouse's own motivation in pulling the wool over her (and over the registrar's) eyes. For if Rouse were able to alter the parties' names on the certificates, there would be less likelihood of his being caught for bigamy. The

53   J. C. Cannell, *New Light on the Rouse Case*, John Long Ltd, n.d. [1931], p. 14, for this and subsequent details.

names Arthur A. Rouse and Helen Campbell were undoubtedly shared by many in the registers of births and marriages, whereas the revised spellings were unusual and, possibly in Helen's case, unique.

So what do we know of the background of Alfred Arthur Rouse? He was born on April 6, 1894 at the family home at 202 Milkwood Road, Herne Hill (or Brixton in the 1911 Census return) in south London, and claimed Irish extraction on his mother's side. According to that Census he was living in 1911 as a sixteen year-old warehouseman with his Greenwich-born father, Walter Edward Rouse, and two much older sisters, Edith and Alice, 39 and 37 respectively. Edith had also been born in Greenwich and Alice in Islington. Walter was stated to be a hosiery manager while Rouse's sisters were listed as needle workers, perhaps with the same firm as their father. At some point in time Walter's employer had been Messrs Peter Abbott, Outfitters, 510, Central Market, Smithfield. As well as his father, Rouse's paternal grandfather was still alive at the time of the trial, while one of his sisters had become Mrs. Dockree by then and was living at 13, Topham Square, Lordship Lane, Tottenham. Confusingly, she was known by then as Ada, but presumably was the Alice listed on the Census return. She told the police that she knew little about him after he had left school. She knew about his Army career and referred to a serious motor cycle accident that he had suffered in 1917 away from London. As to Edith Rouse there is no further information and Rouse himself does not appear to have made reference to her at any point. Rouse also had a brother who had died while still a toddler. In 1900 his parents' marriage broke up and his mother later emigrated to Australia, having no further contact with Arthur. Arthur and his sister were then looked after by their paternal aunt, though his sister took on an increasingly important role in bringing him up. He went to the local council school and showed promise as a bright, enthusiastic and sporting child. After he left school at the age of fourteen, he dabbled in carpentry and went to evening classes to learn the piano, mandolin and violin. He had a decent baritone voice (he was elsewhere described as a tenor), though his speaking voice was noticeably high-pitched and somewhat unattractive.

He first worked as an office boy in an estate agent's for two years, then worked for five years as the warehouseman listed in the Census until 1914 at a soft-furnishings depot, Messrs Allistons of Friday Street, E C, a company that no longer existed by 1930. During this time he met Lily Watkins, the daughter of Leonard Watkins, a bookbinder from Clerkenwell. She was three years his senior, and they had met at a social function organised by her employer, the Post Office. They were obviously taken with each other despite the difference in age. He was slim and handsome, if a later studio photograph of him in Army uniform is any guide, while Lily was plainer-looking, and certainly not a raving beauty. Their relationship clearly blossomed and three months after he enlisted in the Army in mid-August 1914, they decided to get married in St Albans where his unit was training (his address was put down in the certificate of marriage as '1, Sandpit Lane'). This was just under four months before his deployment to France in March 1915.

As previously noted, the marriage took place at St Saviour's Church, St. Albans on November 29, 1914 and the witnesses listed in the certificate were Annie May Stableford and Phyllis Stableford. Police inquiries after the Hardingstone blaze elicited that Phyllis, sixteen at the time, was now Mrs. Phyllis Barnes of 54, Moat

Drive, Pinner View, Harrow, and that Annie May was presumably Phyllis's late mother who had died in January 1930 and whose real name was Annie Mary (she never signed her name May). Phyllis's police statement of January 6, 1931 declared that she had no recollection of being present at Rouse's wedding, or of signing the register as a witness. She did remember, however, that a number of soldiers had been billeted with her and her parents at Heath Road, St Albans, from August 1914. One of the soldiers was called Charlie Pye. He brought along to the house a friend of his, Arthur Rouse, who would often visit in the evening. Rouse also brought with him his intended, whose name was 'Lilly', and who he introduced to the household. Phyllis admitted that, due to various illnesses since 1922, her memory was not sharp, which might explain the gap in her recollection of Rouse's marriage. She could not remember how long Rouse remained in St Albans, would not recognise him again, and never saw him again after he left St Albans. In view of the various charades surrounding the subsequent 'weddings' that he contracted with Helen Campbell and Ivy Jenkins, leaving aside his altering of the 'certificate of marriage' between himself and Helen, in order to facilitate Nellie Tucker's confinement, we are entitled to be sceptical about the circumstances surrounding Rouse's marriage to Lily. Certainly the names given as the witnesses were challenged sixteen years later by Phyllis, who denied being there. So, conceivably, she was never there and therefore her and her mother's signatures had been forged. If that were the case, and if the ceremony had, indeed, been conducted by the Rev. L. S. Westall, the parish priest listed on the certificate, then who were the female witnesses? Were they a couple of the soldiers' acquaintances? Why was Charlie Pye not a witness? Was he not granted leave to attend the ceremony? Lily herself harboured no doubts regarding the genuineness of her marriage ceremony (but she would, wouldn't she?), as she waved her marriage lines in front of an incredulous Helen, at some point in 1929 or 1930, when the latter realised that her marriage to Rouse had been a sham. Whatever the truth behind the ceremony at St Saviour's Church, Rouse and Lily could manage only a short time together before he had to return to his Army camp, continue his infantry training and prepare himself for the Western Front once the static war commenced as the winter of 1914 set in. As to his time in France, we will examine this experience in chapter 17.

Following demobilisation and a lengthy recovery from serious injury, initially assessed by medical officers at 100% disability for pension purposes before it was gradually reduced to zero, Rouse set about pursuing a post-war career. After all a wife had to be provided for and a home to be found and paid for. From 1922 to 1927 Rouse was employed as a commercial traveller for Messrs Mark Green & Co., Tailors, 66 Carter Lane. The company secretary, Mr. Moss Green, later described Rouse as of good character but of an excitable disposition. He was at least half-right. There was also an uneventful four-month spell as a commercial traveller with Messrs Boodson & Woodford, 33, Old Change, EC. Neither employer 'noticed anything abnormal about Rouse', observed the police report of January 17, 1931.

The dilemmas Rouse faced, as the lawful husband of Lily Watkins, when confronted with Helen Campbell's marital desires and subsequently her pregnancies in 1924 and 1925, respectively, might have explained his fraudulent behaviour at that time. But it does not explain his conduct at St Mary's Church,

Islington, on November 1, 1930 and why he requested a copy marriage certificate from the clerk. The immediate answer was that another of his 'women', the very pregnant Nellie Tucker, had arrived with her 'husband', Rouse, at 6:50 pm on October 29, 1930, at the City Road Maternity Hospital to give birth to Rouse's second child by her. She gave her name as Mrs Nellie Rouse of 1, Gillingham Street, Victoria, London SW which was actually just an accommodation address, a tobacconist's and newsagent's shop, used by Rouse to pick up post occasionally sent to him there.[54] She was taken straight to the ward and delivered of a girl. During the birth Sister Searle, later called to testify at the police court hearing, asked Nellie whether she was married. When she answered yes, she was asked where her marriage certificate was, to which she replied at Victoria. The sister later asked Rouse to produce the marriage certificate. When he told her that it was at Herne Bay (he had, it appears, been conducting business there that day), she pointed out that Nellie had said it was kept at Victoria. OK, he would bring it in the next morning (which could only have been October 30 or 31, not November 1 when he actually went to St Mary's).

The City Road Maternity Hospital was obviously not a hole and corner country retreat where young unmarried pregnant girls were hidden away from friends and family to give birth to their illegitimate child. Thus the respectability and reputation of the institution demanded that Nellie and Arthur produce their marriage 'lines'. But given that they were not married either lawfully or bigamously, Arthur had to opt for the convoluted subterfuge of obtaining his 'marriage' certificate to Helen (Lily's age on *her* 1914 marriage certificate would be more problematic if used for such purposes since Nellie could hardly pass for 39). And after due alteration, to accommodate Nellie's name (and a new marriage date?), it was presented to the maternity hospital.

On November 5, 1930 Mr. Frederick Bilby, registrar of births, deaths and marriages for the sub-district of Finsbury within the St Luke's registration district, called at the maternity hospital to register Nellie's baby as Patricia Jean, cautioning her of the penalties for providing false information. Despite the warning, for she must have known that some, at least, of the information she was about to furnish was wrong, the father was listed as Arthur Alex Rouse, india rubber goods commercial traveller, and the mother as Nellie Rouse, formerly Campbell (Rowse and Cambull had obviously been quickly forgotten). The relevant address given was 1, Gillingham Street.

But reflecting on Rouse's steps to obtain a false document, it is apparent that the procedure he chose was itself clumsy, if not thoughtless. For why should Rouse take the risk of going to St Mary's Church, Islington, pretending to be a close relative of a person seen at close quarters by the clerk some six years previously? Why also concoct and outline to that same clerk a cock and bull story of a burnt car accident victim, purporting to be A. A. Rowse, killed a short while before? It may be that Rouse had not yet formulated any plan reflecting such a scenario. We simply do not know. However, what we can be certain about is that within six or seven days the press would splash across their front pages an account of a

---

54 The shop manageress, Mrs. May Smith, told the police after the blaze that Rouse would tend to receive on average one letter a month. They bore various postmarks. The last one was received on November 6, 1930, postmarked 'Hengoed, Cardiff, 6:16 pm November 5, 1930'. The police took possession of it. Hengoed was near Gellygaer.

man burnt to death in a vehicle owned by one A. A. Rouse, with the police looking for a man of Rouse's build seen walking away from the blazing car. Any semi-alert person in the clerk's position would, at the very least, have found his recent meeting with A. A. 'Rowse's' 'brother' either a most astonishing coincidence, somewhat inexplicable or, more likely, highly sinister.

Yet the puzzle for us is to comprehend the elaborate charade that Rouse performed to obtain the certificate from the clerk. Why not simply order it from Somerset House? Rouse did in fact visit Somerset House and paid a shilling to inspect the register of marriages. But it appears that he did not order up a copy of the document, but simply left the premises. Maybe he feared that the officials at Somerset House would be more inquisitive of the applicant. Perhaps he could not recall the crucial false names or dates to back up his request (the old dictum that facts can be remembered but that liars can often forget which lies they had previously told springs to mind). Yet this appears implausible. It is more likely that Rouse, failing to think clearly on his feet, was in a muddle as to what to do regarding Nellie's confinement certificate, a dilemma he also faced immediately after the blazing car incident. For, as we shall consider, had he acted more intelligently on Guy Fawkes Night, he might never have gone to the gallows. But both instances simply underlined a critical truth about Rouse. He was not as clever as he thought.

Rouse's story might not have been remembered today as a 'solved' murder case that resulted in the gallows had he embarked on calm thinking at the time of the blaze so as to give more thought to the words that he spoke to the strangers he met on a moonlit Guy Fawkes night. Similarly had he eschewed less extravagant planning in seeking to resolve the Nellie confinement problem, then he might not have needed to undertake the convoluted steps, which he did take, to obtain a false marriage certificate. But the incident with the church clerk, as well as his dumb stupidity in neither ignoring, nor calling for help from, the cousins, was surely symptomatic of the social, economic and domestic turmoil enveloping Rouse, mangling his thought processes, prompting him to illogical steps, and driving him to bizarre and drastic remedies to seek an escape.

For Rouse was not a serial killer but a serial lover. And it was his amorous philanderings, then the financial consequences following his fathering of various illegitimate offspring (ironically, his marriage of sixteen years to Lily had produced no children) and, finally, the apparently never-ending complications of his life, as he juggled his overlapping sexual relationships, that seem to have over-ridden his calmness.

When criminal proceedings were commenced against him following the discovery of the incinerated corpse in the blazing car, stories abounded of his list of conquests and his legion of offspring. It was said that he had 'possessed' eighty women and had fathered numerous children. Rouse himself stated that there were ten offspring that he knew of. There appears to be widespread agreement that while serving with the Army in France in 1915, following his marriage to Lily in 1914, he formed a relationship with a local Frenchwoman and that a child, named Alfred after him, was born as a result. He corresponded with the mother after he left the Army, though it is likely that contact later ceased. Another child was born to a woman in Paris. A further child born somewhere in Britain is mentioned in some sources but no details were revealed.

According to the journalist, J. C. Cannell, Scotland Yard also had a statement from an attractive young lady, whose name never appeared in the press, and who seems to have had a 'lucky escape'. Her name was Phyllis Skinner,[55] a hairdresser who lived with her parents in Sudbury Hill, Wembley, in London and who, like Helen Campbell, was now represented by a London solicitor, Henry Flint of 23, Shoe Lane, EC, an arrangement made through the *Daily Sketch*, and undoubtedly to the financial advantage of Miss Skinner. Indeed the twenty-year old Phyllis had been instructed by the newspaper not to give information to anybody, including the police, but to refer inquiries to Mr. Flint. Consequently Inspector Collins of Scotland Yard interviewed her at Mr. Flint's office on January 10, 1931. From this interview it emerged that Rouse had met the girl on the evening of July 10, 1929 on London Road in Southampton. She was waiting to meet her young man who was working on board the *Mauretania*. Her *beau* was late so Rouse took advantage of the situation to invite her for a spin in his car, at that time an Essex saloon. They made their way along the Bournemouth road towards Totton where he stopped at a quiet spot and made an improper advance by putting his hand up her dress. She angrily repelled him. But he apologised profusely and quickly sought to ingratiate himself by saying how much he admired her moral probity. 'You are the first decent girl I have met'. But his next move was unexpected. Could she get to like him such that they could make a match of it? He was a single man (he said) who had been abandoned by his former fiancee of eight years standing when he was unable to get back to London in time for his wedding due to business commitments. This ex-fiancee was an ungrateful young lady on whom his father had already settled £250 and for whom he had purchased expensive furniture for the couple's new home. His new companion from Southampton, while remaining non-committal regarding his crude marriage proposal, was nonetheless smitten. But as he had to leave Southampton in order to make business calls elsewhere, she agreed to write to him at the address given on his business card, which was the accommodation address of 1, Gillingham Street, Victoria. This she did on more than one occasion but never received a reply. Her letter was later found among Rouse's belongings at home (though probably not by the Northamptonshire police who seem not to have requested Scotland Yard to execute a search warrant, undoubtedly a failing of professional standards). It may be that Rouse was rather indifferent to the risk of leaving aside love letters at his home where they could easily be found by his wife (unlike, possibly, the killer, Patrick Mahon, whose left-luggage ticket allowing the holder access to a holdall containing the bloody clothing of the missing Emily Kaye in 1924, was discovered by his wife where it was tucked down in his inside jacket pocket).[56] Perhaps, notwithstanding all the admiring opinions of Rouse by most of his womenfolk, his carelessness regarding old love letters was a sign of his genuine callousness and of the cruel pleasure he took in humiliating his ever-loyal Lily.[57]

---

55 Cannell does not name her. Her name is included in the Home Office papers on the case, HO144/19178-19185.

56 For Mahon see, inter alia, Robin Odell, *Landmarks in 20th Century Murder*, Headline, 1995, pp. 129-34. There are numerous accounts of this case and of many famous murders cited herein. In general, only one or a handful of such sources will be cited.

57 Cannell, *op. cit.*, pp. 83-4.

Another example of Rouse's insatiable appetite to conquer young women whom he met on his travels is recounted by the authors of a recent murder anthology, and concerns an incident in the spring of 1930 in the life of the authors' grandmother when she was a girl of 19 in Leicester. Hattie Jones worked in Rudkin & Laundon's garment factory where Rouse called on business. He had noticed her at work and later spotted her looking in a shop window. As bold as ever, he approached her and invited her to dine with him. Unfortunately, she replied, she had already eaten and her father would probably object in any case. Undeterred he promptly phoned Mr. Jones (presumably from a nearby phone box) and obtained his permission to take Hattie out in his car, promising to return her home directly. While he went for a meal, she preferred to stay in the car munching chocolates that Rouse had bought her. They then went for a drive where he 'behaved like a gentleman'. He drove her back home and she never set eyes on him again. Why he made no arrangement to see her on his subsequent visits to Leicester might point to the randomness of his many associations and perhaps to a feeling on his part that his amorous life was already a tangle by that point, or else that it was the chase that enthused him as much as any sexual conquest. He may have succeeded in the latter respect in about eighty cases, according to police estimates (though how reliable they could be is open to debate). But Hattie Jones was not one of them.[58]

But perhaps the most revealing illustration of his superficial character and cavalier attitude to women is to be found in a deposition made to Detective Sergeant Douglas Weir of the Metropolitan Police by Mrs Joan Jones, the widow of a railway worker who had died seven years previously. The statement was made on Sunday November 23, 1930 and referred to events that had taken place on November 3, that is, two days before Rouse's journey with the unknown man. Mrs Jones' age is not given, but it is likely that she was in her thirties or early forties. She had moved to London from Cheshire after the death of her husband, and after living in various furnished properties, had found a furnished room at 123 Scott Ellis Gardens, St John's Wood the previous year. She obtained work as a cook in various clubs and hotels. She explained that on November 3 she had been walking towards Oxford Circus but that just as she was crossing Portman Street she was nearly knocked down by a man driving a Morris Minor saloon. The man stopped, spoke to her regarding the near collision and got into conversation with her. When she told him she was going to the labour exchange in Great Marlborough Street, near Oxford Circus, to see if there were any job vacancies, he offered to drive her there and wait for her. However since the exchange was crowded she decided not to wait. She returned to the car and was driven to the City where the driver left the car, telling her that he had to call in at his office. Although she did not know where she was or where he went to, she nonetheless agreed to wait in the vehicle, and he soon returned after fifteen minutes.

They then drove to St Albans and had lunch at one o'clock in an eating place which she believed was called the Tudor, staying there an hour. 'We then drove about the country and returned to London', a narrative striking, of course, for its (deliberately?) uneventful description. She was dropped off near her accommodation. The driver had disclosed to her his name. It was, of course,

58   Damon and Rowan Wilson, *Murder Spree: Real-Life Stories of Twentieth Century Crime*, Magpie Books, 2011, pp. 125-6.

Arthur Rouse, who added that he lived in Gillingham Street, Victoria. She guessed that he was a commercial traveller in view of the samples in the car's back seats. Remarkably, though predictably, Rouse arranged to see her again two days later in St John's Wood Road, that is, at 9 am on November 5. But disappointingly he did not turn up. Perhaps his mind had moved on to more portentous matters concerning Guy Fawkes Night. Instead Joan went back to the labour exchange and obtained a position at 'Maison Lyons' where she was still employed. Although she had not given him her address, nonetheless, she appeared taken by him. So she wrote him a letter to which, unsurprisingly, he did not reply. That letter was recovered by the police from the Gillingham Street *post restante* and was subsequently shown to Joan who added that she had suspected the Victoria address was merely a collection point for letters. Indeed, 'I did not think anything of that as it is unusual for a casual acquaintance to give his proper address', she added. That he was familiar with St Albans had been made clear by him, as he explained that he had been stationed there in the military. Indeed, she remarked, with his waterproof overcoat, brown lounge suit and trilby hat, he had a military bearing.

Sergeant Weir, not surprisingly, possessed a suspicious mind regarding Mrs. Jones' 'acquaintances'. As he haughtily reported to his superior at St John's Wood police station,

> "From the conversation I had with Mrs. Jones I formed the opinion that she is a woman who is not averse to making the casual acquaintance of men with motor cars and although she stated that she received nothing from Rouse, I do not think she is the type of woman who would spend an afternoon with a man and again try and get in touch with him, merely for the pleasure of his company."

Perhaps that was the case, but perhaps not, since she was currently employed in her catering occupation. It was the newspaper accounts of the incident at Hardingstone and the press's description of Rouse that linked her to the case, though presumably the police had contacted her once they had collected his mail from Gillingham Street, rather than that she had approached them. Indeed it is remarkable to note that she still told Sergeant Weir that 'I do not think that [from the newspaper description] he can be the same Mr. Rouse that I was with, on Monday 3rd November.'

But of course he was. For it all fits with his *modus operandi*. An accidental encounter occurs (or maybe not so accidental). The location is within one of his stamping grounds (he picked up Nellie for the first time near Marble Arch). He offers a lift to a specific location. He is then able to persuade his female passenger to come for a drive in the country (though a veil may have been drawn over what transpired when the car was stopped in a secluded spot). Regarding his address and marital status, Rouse is coy about some details and is positively deceptive in respect of others. Arrangements are made to meet again, but reliability and commitment are not Arthur's strong points. Indeed the date arranged, November 5, was one of intense pressure on Rouse, what with Nellie's recent confinement, the money worries he was enduring, prompting him to travel to Leicester to pick up his expenses, and the further financial burdens accompanying the birth of baby Patricia. Thus the encounter with Joan Jones, at the time when that encounter took place, and the way it fizzled out, seemed to embody much of Rouse's philosophy. Live for the moment. Enjoy it while you can. If it gets too big for you, then go into panic mode and cry off and pretend, or cast from one's mind, that there is no payback waiting as a consequence of over-indulgence. Don Giovanni he was not, but he acted like a distant cousin.

Helen Campbell

As noted previously Helen Campbell and Nellie Tucker not only shared the same lover for much of the time. They also became further linked (unknowingly, at least in Helen's case) by the forged marriage certificate issued on Rouse's 'marriage' to Helen, and which he then supplied, in a suitably amended form, to a suspicious sister at Nellie's maternity hospital. It had already been established that a search form for a Somerset House copy of that certificate had been found on Rouse on his arrest. In consequence Inspector Collins and Detective-Constable Mogford from Scotland Yard decided to make further inquiries regarding this bigamous ceremony which, unlike the fatal car blaze, had occurred within the Metropolitan Police area. They first called upon Mrs. Harriet Milton of 284 Liverpool Road, Islington which, it will be recalled, was the address listed by both Rouse and Helen on the 1924 marriage certificate. Mrs Milton, the widow of Tom Milton, a policeman serving in 'Y' Division (which included Tottenham, Edmonton, Southgate and Enfield), told the officers that she had lived at that address for 34 years and rented out rooms both furnished and unfurnished. Rouse and 'Mrs. Rouse' rented a furnished room from her from May 1923 until about January 1927 at ten shillings a week. Rouse, a commercial traveller, seldom stayed there at night and was always away at weekends. 'Mrs. Rouse' worked as a waitress at various restaurants, including Lyons and Slaters, during that time.

On July 22, 1925 Helen gave birth to a baby at the City Road Maternity Hospital (obviously *déjà vu* for Rouse, come Nellie's second confinement). The little boy, Arthur Alfred, was registered at the Liverpool Road register office (though the actual name on the certificate was different). But since Rouse did not support her, Helen continued working as a waitress. About 15 months later, Mrs. Milton heard the couple quarrelling. She went up to their room and heard Rouse call Helen a prostitute. Mrs. Milton then told them that they could no longer stay there as they were disturbing the other tenants, and it was then, she claimed, that Helen told her that she was not actually married to Rouse. However, whether the landlady's account of this 'admission' is correct is open to question given that when Helen later met Lily she appeared to have believed that the 1924 ceremony had constituted a valid marriage, though she was quickly disabused of this when Lily waved in front of her the latter's 1914 certificate of marriage to Rouse.

But in respect of Helen and Rouse, Mrs. Milton added that after the argument that she had overheard, the couple moved a month later to 38 Lonsdale Square, Islington, staying there for about a year (Helen stated that it was for three years). On one occasion Mrs. Milton was introduced by Helen to a man there called Fred who was holding the baby. She added that Fred was a restaurant proprietor who was looking after Helen and the child because Rouse had refused to do so (while Mrs. Milton did not mention it, it is obvious that Rouse and Helen had separated by then). Rouse had apparently taken exception to this relationship and, according to

Mrs. Milton, he had threatened to kill Helen and Fred and to take the baby away. Rouse did, indeed, take Arthur Jnr. away with him, presumably the first of the occasions when the boy stayed with Lily, and Helen did not see him or Rouse for a week when the boy was returned to her. It is certainly the case that Rouse was extremely jealous of Helen's association with Fred, though whether it was a perceived romantic or financial attachment, or both, that especially disturbed Rouse is unclear. It did not help their relationship that Helen had suggested to Rouse that she live in rooms above the restaurant to save on expenditure. But then Helen visited Mrs. Milton in September 1929, not only to tell her that she and Fred had opened 'Helen's Restaurant' at 30 Aldersgate Street, EC (apparently owned by Fred) that was doing well, but also to inform her that she was commencing proceedings against Rouse for non-payment of maintenance for Arthur Jnr. (though Helen agreed that Rouse had previously allowed her a £1 a week when they were staying in Lonsdale Square).

Subsequently Mrs. Milton received a letter from Helen's solicitors, Messrs Maitland, Peckham & Co, 17 Knightrider Street, EC (the firm later moved to Gordon Square in Bloomsbury), asking her to attend Guildhall police court on October 17 to give evidence for Helen to obtain a maintenance order in respect of Arthur Jnr. Arriving at court she then claimed (for a second time) that Helen was not in fact Mrs. Rouse though a sham marriage ceremony had been conducted in 1924 to enable Helen to gain admission to the City Road Maternity Hospital (Rouse apparently tore up the certificate as soon as Helen left the maternity home. No doubt it was a precipitate action, but perhaps not the most egregious of the mistakes he committed in his lifetime). Moreover Mrs Milton said that Helen had known that Rouse was married and that Helen had, indeed, visited Lily in North Finchley. It is obvious that Mrs. Milton's insistence that Helen had recognised that she and Rouse were not actually married to each other is inconsistent with Helen's later flaunting her marriage certificate in front of Lily. That could scarcely undermine Mrs Milton's credibility as a witness on behalf of Helen, as regards the maintenance claim. As she added in her police statement to Inspector Collins after the blaze, Mrs. Milton had not seen Helen or Rouse since the maintenance proceedings in the previous year, though Helen, still living at Aldersgate Street, had written to her on several occasions until six months previously. That was when she last saw Fred, described as 30 to 35, height 5 ft. 7, fair, clean-shaven, of medium build and of 'refined' appearance. She thought that he had a brother somewhere in the City of London. She also offered a description of Helen as about 27 years old, complexion and bobbed hair very dark, eyes black, prominent false teeth, slim build, always neatly dressed and spoke with a North Country accent (which we guess was a legacy of her formative years in Lancashire after her early years in Scotland). It is likely that Mrs. Milton's last contacts with Helen and Fred (his surname was apparently Johnson) coincided with the financial failure of 'Helen's Restaurant' around December 1929, when Fred disappeared from the scene. As to Rouse she said that he carried a large service revolver in a holster (Helen had also seen it in his car), which he had owned as an Army 'officer' and which she last saw just before Arthur Jnr. was born (that is, more than five years previously). It was usually kept in his *attaché* case, and Mrs. Milton recalled that Helen had once told her that he took it into the back yard for target practice, while Mrs. Milton's adult sons, Ernest and Harold, looked on. She had never, however, heard Rouse threatening anyone with the weapon.

Rouse did everything in his power to avoid paying the ten shillings week maintenance order that Helen had obtained in October 1929 at the Guildhall court, an order due to continue until the child was sixteen. For five weeks afterwards he refused to pay anything until an arrest warrant was issued against him on November 22, 1929, and three days later he was summonsed before the court where on payment of £5. 2. 0 to the court he was discharged by the magistrate, Alderman Isidore Jacobs. Thereafter, ten shilling postal orders were sent to Helen on an irregular basis, often accompanied by comments from Rouse about the boy's future. The financial obligation was yet another burden to wear him down and he took it in poor grace, on some occasions angrily making out the postal orders to Hell & Company, a play on Helen Campbell. At least this was an improvement on Helen's not receiving anything at all, which had previously been a regular occurrence (there is no record of any further legal proceedings by Helen against Rouse for maintenance payments). The whole affair makes her later decision to 'stand by' him, write to him affectionately and to visit him in prison even more puzzling. Was she a saint, a fool, or in love with him?

Helen's first baby by Rouse was a daughter born on October 21, 1921 who had died after five weeks (possibly through neglect by foster parents). While Rouse paid the maternity hospital fees, other details surrounding her confinement at the nursing home in Denmark Hill, Camberwell, are sketchy. But as she might have been only fourteen or fifteen at the time of conception (her year of birth is disputed; see chapter 21), it is possible that Rouse might have committed the offence of having unlawful carnal knowledge of a minor. She and Rouse had met around August 1920 when, by one account, she was only fourteen. Of Scottish background she had worked in the Lancashire cotton mills before travelling south to work as a domestic servant or nursemaid for friends of the Rouses who lived at Clarence House (obviously not the royal residence of that name), Green Lanes, north London. Rouse's roving eye spotted her and he set out to seduce her while she, for her part, imagined life as his wife. For, as far as she knew, her employers' visitors were simply aunt and nephew. By the age of sixteen (apparently) she had given birth to her first, ill-fated, child. But the baby's death did not dampen her relationship with Rouse. They remained an 'item' and, of course, went through the form of marriage at St Mary's Church in November 1924 described earlier, when she was in the early months of her second pregnancy by Rouse. However when Arthur Jnr. was born in July 1925, Rouse seemed to dote on him. Helen's nickname for her son was, somewhat unimaginatively, 'Sonny'. The couple lived together at various London addresses during this time but Rouse was frequently absent for prolonged periods. His job as a commercial traveller would obviously provide a convincing pretext for extended separations, but he also needed to find time to continue the appearance and reality of living with Lily at 14 Buxted Road. This was a semi-detached property of recent vintage in a lower middle-class suburb. The property provided a solid base for the pretensions of one who almost (but not quite) craved, more than anything else, respectability among the tennis club crowd and within Lily's circle of friends. And, of course, there was also Nellie from about 1928, already the mother of Pamelita, her first daughter by him.

In May or June 1930 Helen, now living at 89 Holloway Road, wrote to Rouse stating that if he could offer Arthur Jnr. a good education then she would be willing to allow him to have the boy so long as she could have access whenever she wanted. He called round one day in June and took the boy back to Buxted Road. It was on one of Helen's visits to his house around the end of September 1930 (she presumed that she had now been married to him for six years) that, after an argument with Lily regarding the surname that should appear in Arthur Jnr.'s school register (Lily presumably insisting that he was Arthur Campbell and Helen demanding that he be registered as Arthur Rouse Jnr.), she became apprised of Lily's real status vis-a-vis Rouse; not his aunt, as she supposed, but his wife. For in the course of this disagreement, as the two women confronted each other over Rouse himself, with Helen accused by Lily of stealing her husband, Helen insisted that she was not just Rouse's mistress but his wife. She even pulled out her supposed marriage certificate from her handbag to flaunt before Lily. The inevitable then occurred and Lily, in turn, took from a drawer her own 1914 marriage certificate to Rouse to wave it in front of Helen. The latter was naturally deflated and shocked. It would scarcely have endeared her further to Rouse. About two weeks later, around mid-October 1930, Helen called again at Buxted Road. Lily told her that Rouse had heard about the two women's quarrel and that he had told Lily to pack Arthur Jnr's things. Helen could now take him back on her next visit to Buxted Road (which had not taken place by November 5). Thus before the Guy Fawkes Night incident occurred, the separation of Helen and Rouse had long taken place. However even though they were meeting infrequently from June 1929, Rouse delighted in his son's company whenever the boy was with him, as he still was in early November. When Helen read about the car blaze in the press on November 7, she went to Buxted Road the next day but found no-one there. She was in a state of panic, knocking from door to door, asking the whereabouts of her son. In desperation she wrote to Lily who, to Helen's enormous relief, replied stating that Arthur Jnr. was staying with friends at 53 Percy Road, Finchley. Lily was now immersed in Rouse's tribulations at Northampton and Helen collected her son for the last time from Lily and her circle.

Nellie Tucker

On November 7 1930 Detective Inspector Andrews and Sergeant Smith of the Metropolitan Police No. 2 District 'S' Division which contained many police stations, including Golders Green, Whetstone, Hendon, Potters Bar and Elstree, called at the City Road Maternity Hospital. They were trying to trace the whereabouts of Arthur Rouse. They interviewed Nellie there and obtained a statement from her. She admitted that she was single and a domestic servant formerly of 49 Hendon Way, Hendon, a post that she had left on admission to hospital. She stated that she had met Rouse around 1925 (he had spotted her in the street near Marble Arch), and he had posed as a single man living at 1 Gillingham Street, Victoria. She was just sixteen at the time when he succeeded in offering her a lift in his car. They began courting, got engaged and on the promise of marriage she agreed to commence a sexual relationship with him, including staying in hotels (she had also visited his 'aunt's' house in Buxted Road, though whether intercourse between Nellie and Rouse took place there is not known). The couple's first child, Pamela or Pamelita (in the police report, Palma Elizabeth), was born on May 5, 1928, but as Rouse did not pay Nellie maintenance she obtained an affiliation order against him at North London police court around November 1928 with a view, somewhat optimistic as it turned out, to ensuring that he made regular maintenance payments of ten shillings a week for the child. Despite arrears building up she never summonsed him to court again. Nellie herself was paying foster parents twelve and sixpence a week so that she could continue working. And all the while she was still being taken out by Rouse in his car. Indeed on one occasion Arthur Jnr. was said to have been present and had asked her, 'Are you coming for a ride in my daddy's car?' In February 1930 she became pregnant by Rouse once again.

Her employer at Hendon Way was a Mr. de Leon who had telephoned Scotland Yard on November 7 after Rouse's name had appeared in the press. (The heel from one of Nellie's shoes had, of course, been found in the wreckage). He stated that Nellie was in his employment but that he thought (erroneously, of course) that she was currently in the Northern Hospital, Holloway. He believed that she was engaged to Rouse who had turned up at his house on the previous Sunday and had told him that Nellie had had a baby and that he, Rouse, had come to collect some of her clothes. Detective Inspector Andrews and Sergeant Smith then called upon Mrs. de Leon. Nellie had been employed by her as a general cook for about a month before October 29. Mrs. de Leon soon suspected that the girl was expecting and, on being asked, Nellie admitted that she was pregnant by Rouse. Taking the day off on October 29 (obviously to give birth), Nellie did not return to Hendon though Rouse turned up twice to collect some of her things and to let Mrs. de Leon know that the baby had been born.

Nellie's mother, Nellie Stevens, and her father, Frederick Tucker, were also interviewed by the police before Nellie was traced to the City Road Maternity Hospital and from where the story of the doubly forged marriage certificate emerged. Nellie Stevens of Greenwich, now married to a cable layer, Charles Stevens, turned up at Blackheath Road police station on the evening of November 6. They were accompanied by Mrs. Mary Game, wife of Joseph Game, a tailor's presser of 95 Royal Hill, Greenwich, and by Brian Lefevre Coles, a motor driver of 37 Ashburnham Grove, Greenwich. Mrs. Stevens was obviously concerned, having read the evening paper, that the victim in Rouse's car was thought at that time to be female. She knew that her daughter had been 'cohabiting' with Rouse, though she did not know exactly where they were living. Mrs. Stevens and Mrs. Game, though knowing each other, had not travelled to the police station together but had arrived independently. Nellie Tucker had, indeed, once lodged with Mrs. Game who, like Nellie's mother, had been worried when she, too, had read about the blaze in the evening paper. As to Brian Coles, he was married to Mrs. Game's sister, and knowing the link with Mrs. Stevens and her daughter, likewise became anxious on reading the newspaper story. Naturally Divisional Detective Cory considered that the above persons might be needed to identify a body. However after he had phoned Brumby at Northampton, it became clear that no identification of the victim would be possible. Mrs. Game later called at the police station that night with a photograph of Nellie and another of Nellie with Rouse. There is a photograph in the Northamptonshire police archive showing Rouse with a young woman. She could well be Nellie but the image is, unfortunately, too indistinct to be certain.

Further details about Nellie's employment history were provided a few days later by Mrs. Elizabeth Nicholson of 1, Ormonde Gate, Chelsea, S W, who gave a statement to police at Walton Street police station in 'B' Division. Mrs. Nicholson was the wife of Otho Nicholson MP. In August 1927 she began to employ Nellie as a kitchen maid at her previous address of 1 Onslow Crescent, South Kensington. Nellie, she recalled, had arrived recommended from the home of a Mrs. Hogarth of Lennox Gardens, SW. Her family home was, she thought, 106 Royal Hill, Greenwich and her mother's name was Stevens, but she, Nellie, told her employer that her address was 1 Gillingham Street. Mrs. Nicholson quickly discovered that Nellie was dating Rouse, who was then employed as a traveller by Dixon Millar & Co. of 35 Aldersgate EC (which is very near to where Helen would later open her soon-to-fail restaurant business at number 30).

In February 1928 Nellie told Mrs Nicholson that she was pregnant by Rouse. Mrs. Nicholson then affirmed in her police statement that the following month Nellie went into St Mary's Home for Mother and Baby, 153 Stamford Hill, giving birth in early May 1928 and remaining at the maternity home until, she declared (surely mistakenly), until March 1929 when she returned to her employment with Mrs. Nicholson. Meanwhile, as noted previously, a maintenance order (in the old demeaning terminology, a bastardy order) against Rouse had been obtained from the North London police court and around August 1929 Mrs. Nicholson realised that Nellie was again keeping company with Rouse. She noted the number plate of Rouse's Morris Minor and telephoned it through to the maternity home's mother superior, though it is not clear what role Mrs. Nicholson saw herself occupying. Was she a nosy parker or a social purity activist or a moral guardian? Was she a surrogate mother to Nellie, or a helpmeet, or one who considered that men were outrageous and must face up to their responsibilities in such cases? Nellie left her employment with Mrs. Nicholson in November 1929 without handing in her notice and Mrs. Nicholson never saw her again. She did, however, receive a letter from a gentleman subsequently who complained that he had employed Nellie on the basis of a false reference. She observed that her husband had spoken to Rouse once in February 1928 in respect of Nellie's condition, and that it was her husband who saw the photograph of the burnt vehicle in the press. The linkage was then made. Finally her former chauffeur, an ex-policeman called R. B. Copeland, had also seen Rouse and could give the police the address of Nellie's aunt, a Mrs. Raymond, who adopted Pamela for a while and who also knew Rouse.

Otho Nicholson (born 1891) was from a family of distillers. Educated at Harrow and Cambridge he became mayor of Finsbury, 1923-24 and then Conservative MP for Westminster (Abbey Division) from 1924 until 1932. In that year Mr. and Mrs. Nicholson, having married in 1927, went on to divorce. He had served in the Great War and in World War II he commanded the 40th Anti-Aircraft Brigade. One wonders whether he would have seen through Rouse's tall and self-aggrandising stories of his Cambridge and Army officer background. It might not have been difficult for Nicholson to judge Rouse a cad, at best.

It was, consequently, the impending birth in late October-early November 1930 of Nellie and Rouse's second child that, in the first instance, had prompted Rouse to search out the bogus marriage certificate between him and Helen, which he could then show, once it had been duly amended, to the City Road Maternity

Hospital in order to satisfy the hospital as to Nellie's entitlement to a bed. We have Nellie's (or a sub-editor's?) subsequent account of Rouse's appearance at her hospital bedside on November 5 a few days after she had given birth to Patricia Jean.

> "He entered slowly and hesitatingly. The air of jauntiness with which he had always carried himself since I first met him in 1925 had gone. He was worried... He took my hand and kissed, or, rather, pecked me. His hands were chilly, cold and trembling slightly. And as I gazed into his face I swear that he had been crying. His eyes were red and his eyelids swollen. He seemed to have shrunk. All his self-possession had vanished. There was something furtive in his manner as he glanced round the ward before opening his lips to speak... He kept wringing his hands, and now and then he would laugh—a nervous hysterical little laugh that frightened me. 'What is the matter?' I asked. 'Oh Nellie', he whispered, almost moaned. 'I'm worried, so worried'. His voice trailed off as though he were too weary to speak about his troubles. Suddenly he bent his head forward and cupped it in his hands... I said more gently, for his agitation was depressing. 'Are you worrying about me?' 'Yes, partly', he replied. 'But there are other things as well. I'm afraid I'm going to lose my job... I want to see about another job, and I have one in view'. That was all he would tell me then. He suddenly switched round the conversation. ...I told him that I expected to leave [hospital] in two days' time. For some reason or other he seemed annoyed... 'Why not stay on longer?' he said in a grumbling voice. 'I suppose', he said, 'that I'll have to look for another room for you'. Again came the nervous laugh. He jumped up from the chair as the clock struck eight. He looked like a highly-wound-up spring, taut and vibrant, and it struck me then that all the time he had been with me he had kept an anxious eye on the clock as though that night time was a vital matter for him. 'Are you meeting anyone?' I asked. He looked at me in a vacant way and said 'No'. 'Good-bye', he said. 'I'm in a hurry. I'll drop you a line and send some things for the baby".[59]

Unless this account was invented by a journalist Nellie's description of Rouse's demeanour was acute. She knew something extremely worrying was gnawing away at him, and it was not just the added cost of providing food, clothing and shelter for Nellie and the baby. He was distracted and impatient, distant and stressed, red-eyed and trembling and out of character, and was clutching what Nellie described as a 'dirty old felt hat'. There is nothing in Nellie's account about his admiring his new daughter or asking about her condition. In fact it was clear that he could not wait to get away although he had promised that he would return to see her on the following Monday.

Nellie was discharged from hospital on that Monday November 10 and was then taken by one of the sisters to the offices of Mr. Bilby, the registrar, further along City Road, presumably to have the details of Patricia's mother's name amended (from Helen's altered name) on her birth certificate. While Bilby told her that he would have to report the earlier deception to the registrar-general, no further steps seem to have been taken against Nellie, though she obviously was aware the marriage certificate was false. Inspector Collins of Scotland Yard noted that Nellie was thought to have returned to 49 Hendon Way after her confinement.

---

59   *Peg's Paper*, May 5, 1931, p. 16.

But we may assume that what was occupying Rouse's mind throughout his visit to the hospital was not the joy of celebrating with mother and baby but the car journey northwards that he was about to embark upon. We do not know for certain whether he was fearful of losing his job as a commercial traveller with W. B. Martin Ltd, the menswear manufacturers of Leicester, which he had mentioned to Nellie. But there is no independent evidence that his employment was at risk even if he, himself, was now facing even more financially straitened circumstances following both the birth of Patricia and the anticipated birth, in the next few months, of the baby he was soon to father with Ivy Jenkins in Wales. Or he may have been dwelling on what the future, in general, now held for him, as the messy and unsustainable reality of his complicated, perhaps disastrous, liaisons began to hit home. Or, finally, while half-engaging in mundane chit-chat with Nellie, he was in fact chomping at the bit to put into operation the plan he had already concocted to fake his death and to disappear from the social, economic and domestic troubles now engulfing him.

He could simply have sought to disappear from public view, as two thousand individuals contrived to do in 1930, some of whom possibly still carrying the psychological, respiratory (from gassing) or even the physical scars of the war years. But then who would he become and how would he be able to earn a living? Would life insurance cover this? Presumably only after a formal judicial declaration after seven years during which no information of his whereabouts was available. And, even then, only Lily would benefit. More promising, from the point of view of receiving an insurance pay-out, was that Rouse should unquestionably be assumed to be dead following some kind of plausible mishap, which *could* be a fierce car blaze, but might be some other 'tragedy'. For a simple and unexplained disappearance might not satisfy the police if Rouse's murky social and financial background were investigated. Nor might it convince the insurance company if a payment on the policy were soon sought.

However official acceptance of Rouse's death would normally require a body to 'prove' that Alfred Arthur Rouse was now deceased, and not just 'missing'. And the remains should possess at least a minimum level of bodily integrity, even if burned so badly that it resembled, as Rouse's victim did, the charred remains of a tree trunk with gnarled shapes and twists. Certainly, of the options available to Rouse, he could immediately discount that of transforming the victim's body into the acidized mush that, apart from the gall stones, false teeth and her rings, was all that would later remain of Mrs Olive Durand-Deacon in 1949 after John George Haigh had completed his acid-bath handiwork at his Crawley lock-up.[60] As to a burnt corpse, the journalist, J. C. Cannell, recounted a strange tale in his book where one individual insisted that a third party had obtained for Rouse a corpse that had previously been burnt to death in another fire. Were that to have been so then Rouse would not have been guilty of murdering the person whose charred remains were recovered from his Morris Minor. Indeed Helen Campbell had been questioned by an un-named individual as to whether there had been a fire at the house in Chatham where she took refuge for a period after the storm broke. She did understand the purport of the question and the issue melted away.[61]

---

60   See, eg, Jonathan Oates, *John George Haigh: The Acid-Bath Murderer*, Pen & Sword, Barnsley, 2014.
61   Cannell, *op. cit.*, pp. 102-3.

For it was an absurd proposition. In contemplating his options, perhaps Rouse reasoned that if his car were to be found at a cliff-top edge, a body would still be expected to be washed ashore. But there was always the risk that his passenger might be identified after being pulled from the sea or after recovery from the shore, either by relatives or through a finger-print match at Scotland Yard's Criminal Record Office (with or without the remarkable fingerprint-acquiring gifts of Superintendent Fred Cherrill that later enabled the police to identify the torso of the spiv and dodgy second-hand car dealer, Stanley Setty, washed up on the Essex Marshes in 1949 after being dumped in the English Channel by the flying killer and black market trader, Donald Hume[62]). For did not Rouse disclose that his unknown passenger had mentioned some trouble that the latter had previously been in with the police? Or what if Rouse's empty vehicle had been discovered abandoned up a remote forest track? Presumably he would be listed as missing, not dead, and police investigations would commence. If so, then the claim made by Rouse at St Mary's Church that he was A. A. Rowse's younger brother would simply not wash once the police, investigating an unexplained death or disappearance in relation to Rouse's car, had discovered that Rouse's 'younger brother', grieving for the loss of his 'older brother', did not actually exist and, indeed, that Rouse's younger (and only) brother had actually died while a very young child. It would not take an Einstein to conclude that the 'younger brother', suffering the tragic loss of his older brother, 'A. A. Rowse', was no such thing.

The upshot was that Arthur Rouse would have to assume a new persona *ab initio*. And, frankly, he was not prepared for this as he set out for Leicester shortly after leaving the maternity hospital. What plans had he made to disappear from society? Where exactly was he going, and was his arrival expected? What funds did he have to tide himself over, at least in the short term, if not for longer? What wardrobe did he carry with him? Did he change his appearance in any way? That he told Nellie that he would see her on the following Monday and that he was going to collect some commission from his employers in Leicester by themselves prove nothing as to whether he had or had not a plan to disappear. It has been claimed that Ivy Jenkins was his favourite woman and that he could well have travelled to South Wales from Leicester with a view to staying permanently in the then isolated and difficult-to-find hamlet of Gellygaer. But without bringing with him any considerable sum of money to invest in his new 'father-in-law's' small privately owned coal mine, such a scheme was implausible. In any event he was still A. A. Rouse so far as his new 'family' were concerned. Therefore the possibility of the local press in north London, let alone the national press, running a story that Mrs. Lily Rouse had reported her husband, Arthur, as missing, might just jog the memories of those of Ivy's former nursing colleagues at Highgate Hospital who had met him. His unmasking and discovery would presumably then only be a matter of time.

So we come back to two requirements. First, in order to disappear he must 'bring out the body' (to paraphrase Hilary Mantel), involving the acceptance by the authorities of some other corpse as that of Rouse. Second, he must assume

---

62   See, for example, Donald Thomas, *Villains' Paradise: Britain's Underworld from the Spivs to the Krays*, John Murray, 2006, Ch. 5. The chapter is entitled, 'My Victim's Body Had Followed Me Home'.

a completely new identity. As to the first, perhaps 'for want of a nail' in the form of a two-minute delay before the two young cousins happened upon him in Hardingstone Lane, that might have succeeded. As to the second, either he was too stupid to realise the degree of planning that was required to successfully bring it off; or, despite the overwhelming opinion of the authorities to the contrary, he actually had no such plan when he set off from Buxted Road to bump off another person, make it look as if the victim were himself, and then disappear into the arms of Ivy Jenkins and her family in the remote Welsh valleys (or somewhere else).

What *did* appeal to the authorities, though it did not come out at the trial, was that Rouse was actually thought to be in cahoots with *Lily* to pretend to be the burnt victim of a car accident and for the two somehow to share the insurance pay-outs. The plausibility of this theory will be considered later. But for the moment it is surely ironic to appreciate, with regard to this serial sexual cheat who let down his women so badly, that it was the supposed brutal attack on an unknown stranger and his burning to death in Rouse's Morris Minor that reignited (if one may forgive the pun) the love of three women for this vanity-ridden, selfish and irresponsible man. For at the end neither Helen nor Lily nor Nellie abandoned him. Indeed both Helen and Nellie and, separately, Helen and Lily, wept together at his conviction and execution. And it was only the intelligent but naive Paddy Jenkins, who later gave birth to his still-born child, who erased him completely from her life following his arrest.

CHAPTER FOUR

POLICE SEARCH IN STRANGE RIDDLE

DAILY TELEGRAPH, November 7, 1930

Rouse and the Police

It will be recalled that when the two cousins, William Bailey and Alfred Brown, rushed to Hardingstone village to seek help in putting out the car blaze, the first person they called upon was Bailey's father, Hedley, who was the parish constable for the village. The unpaid post of parish constable had been significant before the establishment of regular police forces in the nineteenth century. However its (often reluctant) occupant, 'volunteered' by the ratepayers, was frequently the butt of ridicule by writers and commentators, sceptical of his ability to suppress local crime, though historians have more recently sought to paint his record in a more favourable light.[63] By 1930 the parish constable had become almost a footnote in the roll-call of those charged with enforcing law and order. For unlike, say, the police community support officer (PCSO) today, his role had been more or less eclipsed by the local professional constabulary. But he was still a handy person to have around to offer a semblance of authority towards misdemeanants or, in this case, when being called to the scene of the blaze and, once the outlines of a body had been identified within the car, sent to Northampton to alert Inspector James Lawrence.

In fact this instruction to Hedley Bailey was issued by PC Harry Copping, a member of the Northamptonshire police force who also lived in the village. Alfred Brown had knocked on his door (presumably around 2 am) to inform him of the blaze 150 yards up the road, though at that time Brown had not observed a body in the blazing vehicle. Copping and Brown then ran to the car where Bailey, *père et fils*, had arrived before them. Exactly when the process began of the extinguishing of the flames with buckets of water obtained from the village is not clear, but with the flames now out, Copping was able to see the corpse spread over the front seats. It was at this point that he told Hedley Bailey to go to the Northamptonshire police station in Angel Lane, Northampton, and to summon Inspector Lawrence who Copping presumably knew was on duty that night.

And here the patchwork quality of policing in Britain before significant and

---

63   Elaine A. Reynolds, *Before the Bobbies: The Night Watch and Police Reform in Metropolitan London, 1720-1830*, Macmillan, 1998; Clive Emsley, T*he English Police: A Social and Political History*, Longman, 1996.

drastic twentieth century amalgamation commenced in the course of the Second World War becomes apparent. For in 1930 there were two police forces located in Northampton, the county police, under Chief Constable James Dalgleish Kellie-MacCallum, and the smaller borough force under the command of John Williamson, chief constable from 1924 to 1955. Copping, as noted, was with the former whose jurisdiction included Hardingstone. But when Copping's messenger arrived at Angel Lane at 3 am,[64] he could not rouse anyone from that office (and it later transpired that the door bell at Northamptonshire Police HQ was not working). Frustrated, he moved on to the headquarters of the smaller borough police, who opened their doors to him and to whom he was able to explain his mission. Sergeant Earl thereupon telephoned county police HQ where he spoke to a young probationer and instructed him to call Lawrence at once while he, Earl, would dispatch Bailey to Angel Lane. An hour later PC Valentine from the county force called Earl from Far Cotton police box, informing him of the existence of the burnt-out vehicle and of discovering a woman's body in the wreckage. Could Earl also let the police in Stony Stratford, Newport Pagnell, Bletchley and Dunstable (beyond the county boundary) know of the events? One can only marvel how such fragmentation of police forces within close proximity lasted for as long as it did before the borough force was absorbed into the county force on April Fool's Day 1966.

As a young man, the Edinburgh-born Kellie-MacCallum had been commissioned into the Queen's Own Cameron Highlanders. He had then been attached to the Black Watch when it suppressed the Ashanti Revolt of 1873 in West Africa, the native tribes objecting to paying levies to the British Empire. Eight years later, at the age of 36, he left the Army to take up his first and only post with the civilian police. And astonishingly he held that post, as Chief Constable of the Northamptonshire force, until 1931 when he retired at the age of 86. He died the following year.[65] Of course he left under something of a cloud, his ears no doubt ringing from the criticism levelled against his force during the Rouse investigations when the Hardingstone crime scene had not been secured. We shall say more about this aspect later.

When he arrived in 1881 the force was divided into six territorial divisions, comprising Brackley, Daventry, Oundle, Northampton (which included Hardingstone), Wellingborough and Thrapston. In 1900 the police station at Angel Lane, to where Rouse was taken on Saturday November 8, was built, and continued to be used as a police station until 1963 after which the force's prosecuting department took over (since 1986 prosecutions have been in the hands of the Crown Prosecution Service, not of the police). The size of the county force in 1930 is not clear. In 1900 it had 162 staff, including six superintendents, nine inspectors, 17 sergeants and 128 constables. In 1965, the year before the amalgamation, there was a staff of 458, including the same number of superintendents, 20 inspectors and chief inspectors, 61 sergeants and 370

---

64   Northamptonshire police files state that it was 'William Bailey' who arrived. Perhaps Copping was mistaken in stating that he had sent Hedley to Angel Lane. Alternatively, Hedley's son volunteered to make the journey. A third possibility is that Hedley was also known as William.

65   For this, and other information regarding the Northamptonshire and Northampton forces, the authors have relied upon Richard Cowley, *Policing Northamptonshire, 1836-1986*, Brewin Books, Studely, Warwickshire, 1986.

constables. So perhaps in 1930 the figures were somewhere in the middle.

The initial embarrassment suffered by the county police when Bailey had to request help from the borough force during the night was, perhaps, a pointer towards further inadequacies, not to say incompetence, on the part of the Northamptonshire police in the Rouse case. Even the normally calm and measured judge, Mr. Justice Talbot, felt it appropriate to comment during the trial on the force's shortcomings (in those distant decades before CSI) to preserve the crime scene from interference or contamination by the public. Thus the revelation at the trial that no police were on duty at the scene of the blaze on the morning of Thursday November 6 when a freelance photographer, Arthur Ashford, was able to replace the fallen steering wheel onto the steering column in order to offer a better picture (there were other photographic discrepancies) was disturbing. 'It is quite obvious', complained Talbot, 'that there is no security [i.e., certainty] either that the car was left alone when the police went or that it remained as this gentleman [Ashford] found it until he left'. Thus, '....anything may have been moved between the time he [Ashford] got there and when he left.' Indeed there had been a few people milling around at the scene at the time though it seems that the photographer had not been paying any attention to them.

The implication was clear. Anyone could have interfered with parts of the burnt-out vehicle and its surroundings, moving objects about. No doubt Rouse's counsel (and the judge) even wondered whether the loosening of a fuel pipe nut (which, by releasing petrol, would increase the intensity of the blaze), allegedly discovered as damning evidence against Rouse by an expert witness for the Crown, might have been carried out by any one of those curious spectators at the scene that morning, marvelling at the destruction wrought by the blaze. So there was an obvious failure to secure the surrounding area with a permanent police presence. In its defence the force insisted that despite discovering the body in the middle of the night, those on the scene did not yet think that they were dealing with a murder inquiry. On the other hand, is it likely at the time of the blaze or, especially, immediately following the corpse's discovery, that neither Brown nor Bailey would have said anything to PC Copping or to Bailey Snr. regarding their encounter with the hatless man, and that this strange occurrence and exchange were only mentioned by them when they later gave their official police statements? In fact Copping himself stated at the trial that after Lawrence, Valentine and Bailey Snr. had removed the body from the vehicle just before 4 am, he took down Brown and William Bailey's statements. Brown's account did, indeed, state that, 'I saw a man come out of the hedge on the right hand side of the Hardingstone Lane, we walked past this man, *thinking that he looked suspicious we watched him*' [original punctuation but italics added], before Brown made reference to the strange monologue that followed.

Now, according to Copping's trial testimony, he had remained with the car after the blaze had been extinguished and was still there when Lawrence and Valentine arrived from Northampton about 3:10 am, and also during the time they 'made a search: then I went away and came back again. I got back about twenty minutes to five, I should think, in the morning. Inspector Lawrence and Police Constable Valentine were still there. I left about a quarter to six'. It seems clear that when Copping 'went away' he did so in order to take the brief one-page statements from Brown and Bailey which contained their references to the suspicious-looking man walking away from the blaze. But by the time that he returned to the burnt-out vehicle it had been moved from the road to the grass verge. Indeed their trial testimony suggests that the removal of the debris had probably been carried out by Valentine and Lawrence at around 3:40 am immediately after the body had been extracted from the wreckage and taken to the Crown Inn garage. However just as with Ashford's tampering with the steering wheel, the removal of the car to the verge was also carried out in a manner which showed little regard for preserving the crime scene. Indeed the cross-examination of Lawrence by Finnemore on the second day of the trial brings this out clearly.

> "[Lawrence] With regard to the position of articles, I found the can [of petrol] immediately behind the driver's seat. At that place the whole of the floor had been burned away and had collapsed on to the road. The seat had all been burned and had collapsed except the springs.
>
> [Finnemore] When you moved the vehicle did you take that [presumably the can] out first, or did it just fall on to the road as you lifted the motor car?
>
> [Lawrence] It was taken out first, before moving it. I cannot quite say who took it out. It was replaced after the car had been moved—in the same place as near as possible.
>
> [Finnemore] A great many things had to be moved like that separately?
>
> [Lawrence] Yes.
>
> [Finnemore] There was no attempt made to put any of the other things into any particular place?
>
> [Lawrence] The only other part that I remember being moved was the rear mudguard."

Obviously there is some confusion in Lawrence's testimony in that while he admitted that a 'great many things had to be moved...separately", he could only remember the rear mudguard in that regard.

So the situation was that Copping was taking statements from Brown and Bailey which referred to the earlier sight of an inexplicable blaze up ahead, a hatless man emerging from a hedge and acting strangely, indeed standing out like a sore thumb, this stranger calling back 'very shakily' to the cousins *after* the parties had passed each other, and continuing to walk away from the scene. The statements ended with the tackling of the blaze and then the finding of the dead body slumped across the front seats of the burnt-out vehicle. At the same time Lawrence and Valentine are cavalierly moving the wrecked car and its strewn bits and pieces on to the grass verge, placing loose bits of debris within the burnt-out chassis. Now it may be that Copping, when taking the statements, could be excused for not rushing out to his colleagues (presumably he and the two cousins were in his house) to inform them of the highly suspicious circumstances as narrated by the cousins if, that is, he was under the impression that the car was still *in situ* and might remain there for the foreseeable future. But if he was already aware that, on his departure from the scene to take down the statements, Lawrence and Valentine were about to shift the vehicle on to the verge in anticipation of the morning commuter traffic along Hardingstone Lane with its five bus routes, then he was remiss in not immediately informing his colleagues of what Brown and Bailey were telling him as soon as he had heard it; *a fortiori* if the cousins' suspicions regarding the hatless man had already been conveyed to him as they were trying to extinguish the blaze.

As to Valentine and Lawrence, perhaps it was the case that at 4 am, as they were inspecting the scene, they had not yet been told of the hatless man, a situation continuing as the body was removed to the Crown Inn and the car moved on to the grass verge at about 4:40 am. Yet is it likely that none of the others had mentioned the strange sight of the hatless man disappearing into the distance? If such an omission to impart this information to a detective on the spot were unlikely (as seems a reasonable proposition), then Lawrence and Valentine were even more remiss than Copping. If, on the other hand, Lawrence and Valentine had indeed been unaware at that point of the mysterious stranger with an attaché case, then it looks like a case of the left hand not knowing what the right hand is doing (and we are scarcely talking about crossed messages within a huge bureaucracy or about the fog of war).[66]

Moreover, it is clear that immediately following the blaze, neither a police doctor nor a police photographer was called out (it can hardly be claimed that flash-bulb photography for night-time shots was unknown in 1930), while not even those police including Lawrence and Valentine who were at the scene took written notes of what they had found regarding the position of the corpse, particularly the state of the right leg and of what remained of it. Thus the slightly inconsistent testimony of the police witnesses at the trial regarding this point might be explained, at least in part. Clearly, therefore, operational shortcomings were spectacularly evident and the procedures expected to be followed by detectives at incidents (perhaps even if not yet identified as 'crime scenes' in modern terminology) were found wanting.

What, therefore, might be expected of the professionalism of inter-war detectives in such circumstances? Those such as senior Scotland Yard officer, George Hatherill, whose report on dockside thefts of British Expeditionary Force supplies in France before the Dunkirk evacuation in 1940 led to the creation of the Royal Military Police detective organisation, the Special Investigation Branch, and whose last major assignment involved tracking down the Great Train Robbers in 1963,[67] knew that detective skills were not simply a matter of having a nose for clues, or of possessing an alertness for other people's shifty behaviour or for their dissembling or evasive answers to enquiries. For detective skills required investigators to be acquainted both with scientific techniques and also with correct legal procedures when questioning witnesses or interviewing suspects. Detectives would be expected to have some familiarity with the 'Judges' Rules' on questioning suspects in order, for example, to avoid the risk of any resultant confession being later thrown out at trial on the ground that it was unfairly obtained and not voluntary.[68] They would be alert to the evidential limitations of, say, hearsay statements, or to the danger of contaminating witness statements

---

66   It may be noted that Sergeant Joe Harris, the discoverer of the mallet some six hours later, claimed that he had assisted in the removal of the car to the grass verge at 11 am.
67   George Hatherill, *A Detective's Story*, Andre Deutsch, 1971.
68   R v *Ibrahim* [1914] AC 599.

with their own or others' comments. Moreover, while it was 'difficult to draw a line between the duties of detective officers and those of the uniformed police',[69] and while at least one chief constable (of Bedfordshire) was of the view that 'the role of detective was the duty of every uniformed man',[70] there was also a corpus of knowledge that was distinctive to the detective's craft, but which members of the Northamptonshire detective branch appeared not to have followed.[71]

Indeed Metropolitan Police Orders going back at least to the first decade of the twentieth century had laid down instructions for any 'officer engaged on an investigation'. Thus the officer attending the occurrence, whether a minor offence or a serious incident such as a robbery or murder, was directed to 'attentively survey surroundings and take stock of the situation', and then to endeavour to find persons, whether relatives or others, best placed to furnish the information he required regarding the essential facts. He should then protect the scene from third parties and ensure nothing was touched or moved from the *locus delicti* before it was examined, in order to preserve the clues *in situ*. Accurate measurement and note taking should then follow, and should record such items as footprints, tool marks, impressions, finger-prints, bloodstains and articles such as clothing found at the scene. Moreover, apart from searching obvious places such as safes, cupboards, stores, chimneys and beds, the investigator should examine less obvious places like the stuffing of cushions, folds of a newspaper, between floorboards, the hole of an old key or the lining of a picture frame. For something otherwise insignificant might provide the opening to the mystery, such as a small piece of flannel cut from a petticoat that had been lit as the wick of a lantern used in carrying out a recent murder.[72] It is a moot point whether the above instructions could be deemed to be detective doctrine inasmuch as they seemed directed as much to beat constables discovering a crime scene as to detectives subsequently called in. The issue is, therefore, what corpus of knowledge could be specifically recognised as detective 'doctrine' that stood beyond the boundaries of ordinary, or 'beat', police work? There is, of course, a plethora of memoirs and reminiscences of former detectives in which the qualities necessary in an effective detective (qualities invariably found in abundance in the author in question) are postulated.[73] An eye for detail, powers of observation, logical thinking (both inductive and deductive), ability to assess suspects' and witnesses' body language, local knowledge, contacts and informants, undercover work and covert surveillance, and knowledge of the criminal *modus operandi*, were part of the canon. At the same time, the possession of such qualities in a detective was

---

69   Sir Edward Troup, *The Home Office*, Putnam's Ltd, 1925, p. 107.

70   Clive Emsley, *The Great British Bobby*, Quercus, 2010, p. 233. Before the war one of his constables was sent on a course to London to obtain the Metropolitan Criminal Investigation Certificate. See *ibid*.

71   For this and subsequent information see Colin M. Moore and Gerry R. Rubin, "Civilian Detective Doctrine in the1930s and its Transmission to the Military Police in 1940-42", *Law, Crime and History*, Vol. 4 (3), 2014, pp. 1-30.

72   HO45/19921, cited in circular from Troup to chief constables, July 2, 1909. Troup was permanent secretary at the Home Office at this time.

73   For policing memoirs see Paul Lawrence, ""Scoundrels and Scallywags and Some Honest Men...." Memoirs and the Self-Image of French and English Policemen, c.1870-1939", in Barry Godfrey, Clive Emsley and Graeme Dunstall (eds), *Comparative Histories of Crime*, Willan Publishing, Cullompton, Devon, 2003, Ch. 7; Philip Rawlings, "True Crime", in Jon Vagg and Tim Newburn (eds.), *The British Criminological Conferences: Selected Proceedings, Vol. 1: Emerging Themes in Criminology*, Loughborough University, Loughborough, 1998.

taken by some to be a gift of nature or, at the very least, qualities that could only be acquired on the job; and certainly not those that could be formally taught.

As one retired Scotland Yard detective put it, 'The Universities may save beginners in many professions years of going through the mill, but Scotland Yard has only one University, with Experience as its best professor. Detection is a profession, or perhaps I should say a craft, in which no amount of book learning or theoretical exposition can take the place of actual practice'.[74] Other writers, such as the Metropolitan Police Commissioner between 1945 and 1953, Sir Harold Scott, would argue for the triumph of perspiration over inspiration and luck.[75] Much earlier, in 1922, one chief constable had proposed that junior detectives should gain experience by working with more senior colleagues in neighbouring forces and that clearing houses of detective expertise should be established in three regions of the country. Such clearing houses, staffed by junior detective officers, would operate as central schools of detective instruction. Nothing seems to have come of the suggestion at the time.[76] Indeed formal course training for young detectives in the 1920s seems to have been restricted to a five weeks' course on criminal law and procedure while home-spun philosophies regarding the detective's 'knack' and 'instinct' can be traced through numerous histories of police detection going back to the creation of the Detective Department of the Metropolitan Police in 1842 (which became the CID in 1878).[77]

However, it was a Home Office committee on detective work that sat between 1933 and 1938, too late for the Rouse investigation, of course,[78] that laid down a formal syllabus of instruction for aspiring detectives to complement the informal and individualistic methods of on-the-job learning hitherto the officially preferred method of training for detectives. Indeed by the time the committee had

---

74   Cecil Bishop, *From Information Received*, Hutchinson, 1932, p. 15. See also Ex-Chief Superintendent Peter Beveridge, *Inside the CID*, Evans Brothers, 1957.

75   Sir Harold Scott, *Scotland Yard*, Penguin, 1957, p. 129. The author did, however, also state, at p. 124, that 'The CID itself is very like a university...'

76   Some sources suggest earlier dates. The 'Friends of the Metropolitan Police Historical Collection' website, while noting that the Peel House Training School in Regent Street, London, was opened in October 1907, also claims that a Metropolitan Police detective school had commenced in August 1901. See www.fomphc.org.uk/faq. According to another source, a detective training school was established in 1913. See Tom Tullett, *Murder Squad*, Grafton Books, 1996, p. 31. It does seem clear that training programmes for Metropolitan Police recruits commenced in 1905. The definitive volume, *The Official Encyclopedia of Scotland Yard*, edited by Martin Fido and Keith Skinner, Virgin, 1999, p. 68, states that, 'The world's first specialised training programme for detectives was offered in 1936' at the Hendon Police College estate (also known as the Peel Centre), formerly the London Aerodrome owned by Claude Grahame-White, and now housing the RAF Museum.

77   In the 1930s Scotland Yard offered courses of various lengths to other forces on single fingerprint identification. See MEPO2/5036.

78   See HO45/25052 for this and subsequent information. In fact only two of the five volumes of the report were to be made available to the general public on the ground that it was not desirable that the technical information in the other three volumes be disclosed. Volumes dealing with the selection and training of detectives, criminal records, and communications were therefore kept within police and government circles or otherwise available only to those with a legitimate interest in such matters. The public could have sight of the report's findings on the police system in England and Wales and the state of crime, and of its review of detective work (all in volume 1), as well as its findings on the application of science, on miscellaneous questions and its summary and conclusions (volume 5). See standard police histories including T. A. Critchley, *A History of Police in England and Wales*, Constable, new ed., 1979; David Ascoli, *The Queen's Peace: The Origins and Development of the Metropolitan Police, 1829-1979*, Hamish Hamilton, 1979; Begg and Skinner, *Scotland Yard Files: 150 Years of the CID, 1842-1992*, Headline, 1992; Moss and Skinner, *op. cit*; Guy R. Williams, *The Hidden World of Scotland Yard*, Hutchinson, 1972; H. Paul Jeffers, *Bloody Business: An Anecdotal History of Scotland Yard*, Pharos Books, New York, 1992.

completed its deliberations in mid-1938, and before publication of its findings in September of that year, many of its recommendations, including the institution of detective training courses, had already been implemented. Thus eight-week courses on detective training for constables hoping to join the non-uniformed branch[79] were already taking place at Hendon Police College, at the headquarters of the West Riding force at Wakefield, and most recently in Birmingham where detectives from other forces also attended. Additionally, a six-week course for senior detectives was also organised.

What did such courses comprise? First, a syllabus for general police duties was put forward. It covered 42 topics including sections on offences and on the Judges' Rules, prisoners' rights, the *modus operandi* of offenders, informants, cooperating with detectives, questioning persons, keeping observation on suspects and premises, bloodstains, fingerprints, footprints, scientific aids, communications and police publications, and practical demonstrations.[80] This was followed by the syllabus for detective training. The first two topics listed were, in fact, 'Advice to Young Detectives' and 'Dealings with the Press [and the] Confidential Nature of Detective Work', appropriately suggestive, perhaps, of induction to the secretive world of the masons.

This was followed by an extensive range of topics divided into 192 sections that built upon, but considerably expanded, the scope and depth of the topics taught in the general police duties syllabus provided for all police recruits. Certain areas of detective work clearly attracted comprehensive coverage otherwise lacking in the police duties course. Obvious examples would be examination of the scene of a crime and searching persons and places for clues, methods of identification, including identity parades, the application of the Judges' Rules on questioning suspects to ensure evidence was admissible at trial, and the correct way to take statements. Such topics would receive limited coverage in the police duties course (PC Copping, of course, took the initial statements from Brown and Bailey) but would receive extensive treatment in the detective course. To give one detailed example, under the heading of 'Keeping observation on suspected persons and premises', the general police course merely laid down that the topic would 'Deal with the ability to observe and memorise the personal descriptions of wanted or suspected persons'. By contrast the detective course, under the heading 'Keeping observation on suspected persons, premises and property', would 'Deal with the ability to observe and memorise the personal description of wanted or suspected persons, points of vantage, disguise etc'. The necessity for different types of officer for the different kinds of work falling under this heading was emphasised.

There then followed the further headings of 'Persons', 'Shadowing', 'Premises' and 'Property', under each of which sub-heading were yet more divisions. For example, 'Persons' included receivers of stolen property, possessors of stolen property, coiners, street pilferers, pickpockets and prostitutes. Under 'Premises' were listed licensed premises, brothels, shebeens, gaming houses, places of public

---

79 It should not be thought that every beat constable aspired to become a detective. Hours were longer and more unpredictable and promotion prospects were fewer. See Emsley, *The Great British Bobby*, op. cit., p. 246.

80 *Committee on Detective Work, op. cit.*, Vol. 2, Appendix 5.

entertainment, gold and silver dealers, and motor car breakers.[81] Thus by the time of the establishment of a dedicated Detective Training School in the following decade it became routine for trainee detectives to attend courses on forensic medicine, scientific aids, ballistics, firearms, footprints, fingerprints, photography, accountancy, falsification of accounts, banking, police communications, poisons, ballistics, explosives, precious metals, gems, antiques, cars, and many other subjects (apart from more detailed coverage of criminal law, evidence and procedure, and international cooperation).[82] The problem was, of course, that such courses had not yet been established for provincial forces by the time of the Rouse case.

Yet notwithstanding the virtual absence of provision of formal training in detective 'doctrine' for provincial police forces until the 1930s, it is difficult not to concur with the view of Mr. Justice Talbot that the policemen on the scene at Hardingstone Lane displayed lamentable levels of incompetence in regard to the exhibits during the initial investigation into the blaze. For it beggars belief to think that Brown and Bailey had not quickly passed on to the policemen in attendance, as they were dousing the blaze, the puzzling sight of the strangely attired man walking off into the distance just minutes before. Thus initiative and a curious mind from the outset seem to have been lacking, even on the part of the most senior police officer present, when dealing with the initially mysterious event of a car burning fiercely along the side of a deserted country road and with no indications of a crash or collision having taken place. Indeed what innocent explanation might have occurred to those arriving quickly at the scene? Could it have been an electrical fault or petrol igniting? Yet the flames were so high and so fierce that accident could not have been the only possibility.

However, while there may have been operational failings on the ground, there was also another aspect regarding the Northamptonshire police which scarcely helped matters (though, to be fair, it may not necessarily have made solving the crime more difficult). This was, in fact, the sensitive issue of whether and, if so, when a provincial chief constable should call in Scotland Yard to take over from the local force the investigation of a serious crime, particularly murder, in circumstances where that offence was not quickly cleared up and the case passed to the Crown to prosecute. In other words, was a further deficiency on the part of the Northamptonshire police exposed by their (ultimately, the chief constable's) decision to investigate the crime in-house, and by their deploying the more limited detective resources and experience of the force than would be found at New Scotland Yard? For though the Metropolitan Police were involved in the Rouse case, this was primarily confined to Inspector Collins of New Scotland Yard interviewing witnesses such as Rouse's women and their circle on instructions from Northamptonshire, and to Sergeant Skelly of Hammersmith police station inviting Rouse to leave the coach at Hammersmith Bridge so that he could ask some questions and take a voluntary statement, also as requested by Brumby and Lawrence. Thus at no time was the Met technically involved in investigating the crime itself. Indeed unless arrested by Skelly at the request of Inspector Lawrence, Rouse was free to decline the invitation to leave the coach; in fact free to decline

81 *Id.*, Appendix 6.
82 Hatherill, *op. cit.*, pp. 40-41.

to 'help the police with their inquiries' and to leave Hammersmith police station whenever he liked. Every exchange that he had with the Met was his own free choice, even if he was unaware of this himself, and the Met itself was only acting at the request of, and on behalf of, the Northamptonshire police. It had no executive role in this investigation. That remained exclusively within the province and jurisdiction of Northamptonshire. Only if the latter had officially 'called in the Met' would the jurisdictional situation have been different. But the provincial force had not done so, and it was up to it how it proceeded in the investigation. And we know that its exercise of 'police powers' of detention only occurred once Rouse had accompanied Lawrence and Brumby back to Northampton. Indeed it appears that given Rouse's cooperation with his questioners and given the voluntary statement he then made at Angel Lane police station, it is not even clear that he was under arrest at any time before he was actually charged with the murder of the unknown man. Once charged, of course, he was detained in custody. Thus while the Met had offered its assistance at Hammersmith and elsewhere in London (though a warrant to search Buxted Road was never sought by any police), the investigation was a Northamptonshire affair, albeit only by virtue of the fact that the death had occurred fortuitously (so to speak) in Hardingstone Lane rather than, say, where Rouse lived or where he had picked up his victim.

But compared with the Met, endowed as it was with the detective resources of New Scotland Yard, Northamptonshire was a poor provincial cousin. And the apparent weakness of provincial police when it came to investigating difficult-to-solve serious crimes had already attracted the attention of parliament by the time of the Rouse case. In 1925, for example, the Home Secretary was asked whether steps were being contemplated to give Scotland Yard full control of investigations into murder cases that were occurring throughout the country, and also whether any opposition was being shown by local forces to the employment of 'these specially trained officers'.[83] Three years later the Home Secretary was questioned on whether he would make it compulsory for provincial forces immediately to call upon Scotland Yard whenever any murder or murders became known and where the persons responsible had escaped detection and arrest.[84] In both instances the questioners were given discouraging replies. There were no plans to transfer police powers from the provinces to the Metropolis to investigate murders. Instead, only permissive powers to call in the Met were to remain, an arrangement that maintained the constitutional principle of local police autonomy. Thus the decision whether to call in the Met was left to the discretion of the provincial chief constable,[85] and where the provincial chief constable remained firm (or stubborn), criticism of his decision might be heard, not only locally, such as in the cases of Northumberland (the Evelyn Foster killing in January 1931) and Monmouthshire (Iris Watkins, 1926), but also from the Metropolis, which the DPP, Sir Archibald Bodkin, angered by the refusal of the Surrey chief constable to call in Scotland Yard to investigate the Vaquier case in 1924, wished to assume investigatory control.[86]

---

83   H. C. Deb., Vol. 184, June 10, 1925, col. 1980, Colonel Harry Day to Godfrey Locker-Lampson, Under-Secretary of State, Home Office.
84   *Ibid.*, Vol. 215, March 22, 1928, col. 571, John S. Potts to William Joynson-Hicks, Home Secretary.
85   There were minor exceptions permitting the DPP to be proactive in certain cases.
86   For these examples see G. R. Rubin, "Calling in the Met: Serious Crime Investigation Involving Scotland Yard and Provincial Police Forces in England and Wales, 1906-1939, *Legal Studies*,

It should be stressed that there is no compelling evidence that cooperation between provincial and metropolitan police forces in investigating serious crimes committed within provincial territory did not operate smoothly in most instances. However, as the above examples show, from time to time Scotland Yard, politicians and the press would imply that the investigation of some cases of provincial murder was being thwarted or being rendered more difficult because of the refusal or, perhaps, because of the delayed and grudging request, of local chief constables to call in the Met. Such reluctance could be attributed to jealousy of Scotland Yard deriving from a sense of local pride and from a refusal by some provincial chief constables to contemplate their forces' shortcomings in investigating complex violent deaths. Thus when critics such as the parliamentarians, above, were calling for drastic changes in the approach to investigating as yet unsolved murders outside London in the 1920s, they were, whether consciously or not, touching a raw nerve in respect of the organisational structure of British policing. For they were challenging the conventional constitutional wisdom which eschewed anything in the nature of a national police force, a wisdom that continued to celebrate the principle of local police autonomy from central direction.

Thus for the first half of the twentieth century, with the qualified exception of the war years, the drastic step of central direction of local police forces in the day-to-day conduct of their duties was never taken. There was, of course, some chipping away at laissez-faire for the avowed purpose, among others, of attaining those minimum standards of service,[87] and of securing, as far as practicable, common terms and conditions of employment. And, indeed, the distribution to local forces of Home Office circulars of 'best practice' and the encouragement to those forces to call in the Met when appropriate, reflect a similar development. But while central control was anathema to all bar a small minority of observers, there were from the 1930s, as noted earlier, the creation by the Metropolitan Police of both Hendon police training school and a dedicated detective training school to which officers from different forces could attend; in effect, involving the transmission of detective doctrine of national application. There was also, finally, a growth in inter-force deployment to prevent public disorder arising from major strikes, while schemes of cooperation, such as the 'Agility' scheme, to tackle and interdict 'motor bandits', who took to driving across country in fast cars, moving from one police jurisdiction to another, and taking with them with the proceeds of their robberies, were instituted.

Indeed organizational improvements, such as better police communications and deployment of fast cars, had already received a boost in the wake of the PC Gutteridge murder which had occurred in a country lane in Essex in the early hours of the morning on September 27, 1927.[88] For, although Scotland Yard became

Vol. 31 (3), September 2011, pp. 411-41, at pp. 430-1. Tensions between the local Wiltshire force and Scotland Yard's Jonathan Whicher, investigating the Constance Kent case in 1860, is well documented. See Kate Summerscale, *The Suspicions of Mr Whicher, or The Murder at Road Hill House*, Bloomsbury, 2009, esp. pp. 142, 156, 177, 179-80, 202-3, 238.

87   For example, the denial of Exchequer grants to smaller forces to compel them to amalgamate under the terms of the Local Government Act 1888. See Sir Edward Troup, "Police Administration, Local and National", *Police Journal*, Vol. 1, 1928.

88   The murder of Gutteridge by Browne and Kennedy, both of whom were subsequently hanged in May 1928, is an extensively covered case. Among many sources, see Macdonald Hastings, *The Other Mr Churchill*, Harrap, 1963, pp. 131-7; Robert Jackson, *The Chief: The Biography of Gordon Hewart, Lord Chief Justice of England, 1922-40*, Harrap, 1959, pp. 205-6; Stanley Jackson, *Mr*

involved, the *Daily Express* launched a strong campaign, exactly one week after the killing, to draw attention to the police's 'Out-of-Date Plans to Crush Crime'. It claimed that the recent outrage had emphasized the 'need for reorganising the police forces of Great Britain so that they are better equipped for the task of crushing criminals using all modern resources',[89] though statistics from a small sample of just over forty provincial cases suggested that when Scotland Yard had been brought in, it had been able to solve just over half of those cases (which had, of course, perplexed the local forces).[90]

We may be tempted to conclude that the Northamptonshire police's initial shortcomings at the crime scene in the Rouse inquiry served to highlight why calling in the Met might have been advantageous in certain serious crime investigations. But it also, paradoxically, should have reminded police officials of an increasing organizational trend towards greater mutual police cooperation between metropolis and province. At one end of the spectrum this was reflected in the matter of Northamptonshire requesting the Hammersmith police to 'invite' Rouse off the coach, to request that he answer some questions and to invite him to make a statement pending the arrival of Brumby and Lawrence from Northampton. In this respect localism co-existed with mutual cooperation, though the former remained the dominant element. At the other end of the spectrum might have been, had this occurred, the spectacle of Northamptonshire handing over the whole investigation to New Scotland Yard. This of course, did not happen. Indeed while the continuing sense of localism among provincial forces in other cases did not necessarily mean a *failure* to solve particular crimes, nonetheless, success might be achieved, as it was (controversially?) in the Rouse case, despite rather than because of the local force's efforts. Unity, not unification, was clearly the rallying cry, and the Northamptonshire detective element, despite the blip, should keep calm and carry on. Indeed, the limited reliance of provincial police on the resources of Scotland Yard might well attest to the ease with which borough and county forces could clear up most murders occurring within their territories. But it also spoke to the proud tradition of local policing that some chief constables, jealous of their autonomy, sought to uphold, even at the cost (though it was a small risk) of bungled murder inquiries. It is not clear whether Chief Constable Kellie-MacCallum, rather than Brumby, was directing the Rouse inquiry. Presumably, however, he had faith in his own detectives that this particular murder would be solved without his formally having to call in the Met. Whether he was acceptably provincial in outlook or unacceptably parochial is open to debate, but detective 'doctrine' was certainly found wanting among Northamptonshire police's finest in the Rouse case.

Justice Avory, Gollancz, 1935, pp. 334-49; Sir Travers Humphreys, *A Book of Trials*, Heinemann, 1953, pp. 184-94; Douglas G. Browne, *Sir Travers Humphreys: A Biography*, George G. Harrap, 1960, pp. 252-67; Christopher Berry-Dee and Robin Odell, *The Long Drop: Two Were Hanged—One Was Innocent*, True Crime, 1993 (the authors suggest that the principal, Browne, was innocent). Scotland Yard were involved from an early stage since the car used by Browne and Kennedy during the murder had been stolen from a doctor not far away in Billericay and was then discovered the next morning abandoned in the Brixton-Camberwell area. A spent cartridge and blood on the running board were found. However it was not until January 1928 that Browne was arrested by Chief Detective-Inspector James Berrett of Scotland Yard. For a brief description of Berrett see Ex-Deputy Commander William Rawlings, *A Case for the Yard*, John Long, 1961, pp. 57-8.

89   *Daily Express*, October 4, 1927.
90   MEPO3/2970. The years covered were 1919 to 1928.

CHAPTER FIVE

PUBLIC PROSECUTOR TAKES ACTION

NORTHAMPTON CHRONICLE & ECHO, November 18, 1930

Legal Personnel and the Criminal Justice System

Apart from the police, there were many elements of the criminal justice system with which Rouse necessarily became involved. They included representatives of the Director of Public Prosecutions (DPP); his own solicitors and barristers; the coroner inquiring into the cause of death of the unknown victim; indeed, the coroner presiding over the inquest into Rouse's own demise after execution (discussed in chapter 16); officials and members of the police court where the committal proceedings were conducted; those involved in the provision of state legal aid for his defence; counsel for the prosecution at his trial; the judge, officials and members of the jury at the assizes court; members of the Court of Criminal Appeal; prison officials including the governor and chaplain at Bedford jail; the Home Office officials involved in post-conviction matters concerning Rouse and whether he should be reprieved; and the judicial executioner. Other important personnel such as the honorary Home Office pathologist, Sir Bernard Spilsbury, also played a prominent role as expert witnesses. Some of the above are deserving of attention because of their crucial roles in the determination of the outcome of the proceedings from the initial Crown application before the magistrates to put Rouse on trial, to the final determination, in the chilling phrase of the Home Office signaling no reprieve, that 'the law must take its course'. Thus we shall give some biographical consideration to those criminal justice personnel whose roles in the Rouse case were particularly significant, such as leading Crown counsel, Norman Birkett, leading defence counsel, Donald Finnemore, the trial judge, Mr. Justice Talbot, the senior appeal court judge, Lord Chief Justice Hewart, and the senior Home Office official, Sir Ernley Blackwell, whose advice to the Home Secretary, J. R. Clynes, as to whether a reprieve should be granted to Rouse was decisive.[91] The approach to be adopted is loosely chronological, commencing with Rouse's appearance at the police court where the committal proceedings were undertaken to determine whether he should face his trial at the Northampton Assizes.

It is perhaps surprising to learn that until 1986 the vast majority of criminal

---

91 Legally the prerogative of mercy, if agreed upon, was exercised by the monarch. In practice the Home Secretary decided the matter on the advice of his officials, which advice was hardly ever rejected by him. See chapter fourteen.

proceedings in England and Wales were technically private prosecutions. Thus before the creation of the Crown Prosecution Service in 1985, whenever defendants appeared before the magistrates to answer, for example, a speeding charge or a complaint of common assault, the prosecutor was invariably conducting what was technically a private prosecution, even though the prosecution was in the name of the Crown which obviously had a public interest in seeking to uphold the criminal law. Indeed this would be the case whether the person actually prosecuting was the local police inspector, a private solicitor or barrister instructed by the police, or a 'staff' prosecutor such as Mervyn Pugh, Solicitor to the City of Birmingham from 1924 to 1958.[92] Needless to say, 'proper' Crown prosecutions were conducted in the most serious cases including murder, under the auspices of the DPP, an office going back only to 1879 and to the Prosecution of Offences Act of that year, though the DPP might still employ a local 'agent' and not a staff official to conduct the case.

Under that Act the duty of the DPP, appointed by the Home Secretary but answerable to parliament through the Attorney-General, was to,

> "....institute, undertake or carry on such proceedings [*not* investigations], and to give such advice and assistance [cf., 'instructions'] to chief officers of police, clerks to justices and other persons, as may be for the time being prescribed by Regulations under this Act or as may be directed in a special case by the Attorney-General."

The regulations essentially imposed on the DPP the duty to undertake cases which appeared to him 'to be of importance or difficulty' or where 'special circumstances' appeared to justify his involvement. It is clear that cases of importance would include, inter alia, homicide cases such as that involving Rouse.

It may, of course, be noted from the above that despite his title the DPP had no power to *direct* or instruct police to conduct criminal investigations. Nor was it the practice for him personally to appear in court to lead the prosecution in the serious or important cases that fell within his prosecuting jurisdiction, though he would perhaps be present in the well of the court as part of the prosecution team. Instead it was common for the Crown to be led in court by Treasury counsel, a small group of senior barristers permanently retained to conduct Crown prosecutions and who fell within the aegis of the Treasury Solicitor which, before the advent of the DPP's office, had assumed responsibility for 'Crown' prosecutions, sometimes known as 'State trials'. Among such Treasury counsel in the early twentieth century were Horace Avory and Sir Travers Humphreys who later in their careers were two of the appeal judges, along with Hewart, who would reject Rouse's appeal.

But it was not invariably the case that Treasury counsel would conduct serious or important prosecutions. For on other occasions the Crown would instruct independent barristers, both Queen's (or King's) Counsel and juniors, to act on its behalf. And obviously this would be necessary where all of the Treasury counsel team were tied up with other cases, usually at the Old Bailey or in the barristers' Home and South-east circuits which embraced the Home Counties. It is not clear

92   Allen Andrews, *The Prosecutor: The Life of M. P. Pugh*, Harrap, 1968.

whether this was the position in the Rouse case where the prosecution was conducted by Norman Birkett QC, assisted by his junior, Richard Elwes. It is more likely that since the case fell within the territory of the Midland circuit, the DPP instructed counsel from that circuit.

Given that the case involved murder, the DPP had primacy in the conducting of the case as a 'state' prosecution, though a refusal by him to take the matter to court (for he might consider the evidence insufficient to mount a specific prosecution) could still allow others to conduct a 'private' prosecution in such cases. The DPP at the time of Rouse's trial was E. H. Tindal Atkinson. Born in 1878 he was the son of Henry Tindal Atkinson, a former county court judge, and in March 1930 he succeeded the highly controversial Sir Archibald Bodkin who had held the post for almost ten years. The first Recorder of Southend-on-Sea, 1929-30, Tindal Atkinson had been a member of the Air Section of the British delegation to the Versailles Peace Conference in 1919, and while he retained the post of DPP until 1944, he generally maintained a low profile. Indeed, according to one author, Tindal Atkinson's period of office was described in an internal history as being 'one of the least contentious in the history of the department', and when he retired he made way to a successor, Sir Theobald Mathew, who was 'much more interesting'.[93] Tindal Atkinson was, indeed, far removed from his predecessor, Bodkin, in his reluctance to court publicity and controversy. For, as we shall see shortly, the latter, during *his* tenure, had attracted adverse attention by some of his actions in the pursuit of his duties which even contributed in one instance to the establishment of a royal commission into police powers and procedure which reported in 1929. His retirement shortly thereafter was probably timely, and was followed by Tindal Atkinson's distinctly unostentatious approach.[94]

A fierce critic of Bodkin was one Cecil Baines (whom we shall meet later in the story), with a colourful back story, who condemned the perceived 'miscarriage of justice' suffered by Rouse. Baines was correct in pointing to Bodkin's regime, when the latter was the 'state prosecutor', as being controversial at various times regarding the alleged manipulation of the criminal justice system in order to favour the prosecution. Tindal Atkinson, by contrast, had been in office only since March 1930, eight months before the Rouse case burst onto the scene the following November. Moreover, Bodkin's predecessor, Sir Charles Mathews (of whom Baines evidently approved), has been judged rather kindly by historians. He has been described as an 'easy-going man', perhaps verging on the complacent, given that he had to be pressed by public opinion to act in the wake of a major banking fraud that had led to the Charing Cross Bank collapse in October 1910 (Cora and Dr Crippen had had a joint account in the Charing Cross Bank). But Mathews' organization of the prosecutions of Dr Crippen (1910) and of another poisoner, Frederick Seddon (1911-12), attracted praise. In the Crippen case he sought to ensure that an experienced but fair trial judge (Lord Alverstone, the Lord Chief Justice) would preside over the trial, given the bad odour in which Crippen was at that time being held. In the Seddon case Mathews had immediately transmitted to Scotland Yard a letter received from a relative of Miss Eliza Barrow,

93   Joshua Rozenberg, *The Case for the Crown: The Inside Story of the Director of Public Prosecutions*, Equation, 1978, pp. 25-6.
94   On Bodkin see Robert Jackson, *Case for the Prosecution: A Biography of Sir Archibald Bodkin*, Arthur Barker Ltd, 1962.

a tenant of Seddon's, whose sudden death and hasty burial, without notification to the relative, had alarmed the letter-writer when he discovered the events. For Miss Barrow had only recently transferred her wealth to her landlord, Seddon, in exchange for an annuity payable to her weekly, a relatively modest financial commitment on Seddon's part that obviously expired on her early death.[95]

The office of DPP was therefore somewhat peculiar as an oasis, until 1985, of public prosecutors in a sea of private prosecutors, even if the latter conducted proceedings in the name of the Crown (as in *R v Smith* where *R* stands for *Rex* [King] or *Regina* [Queen]), and even when conducted by state officials such as the lowly local police inspector prosecuting in the name of the Crown a traffic violation. In the case of serious offences, regulations dating back to 1886 and under the Prosecution of Offences Act 1908 laid down that the DPP had primacy to take over the conduct of a case such as murder (which might also involve some ambiguous and preliminary police-like investigation by him of cases that were required to be reported to his office). As noted earlier, while he himself, as a matter of practice, never conducted a case in court but instead left it to his assistants, if his office did decline to prosecute, the refusal might leave the way open for a relative or even for a third party to undertake a more recognisable 'private' prosecution. But such latter cases were unusual and public officials, whether the Law Officers, that is, the Attorney-General and the Solicitor-General, the DPP, the police or their own solicitors, or counsel on behalf of the police, or even local authority solicitors, or specialist department prosecutors working for the Post Office or Customs and Excise, or even for bodies such as the RSPCA could conduct what were technically still private prosecutions.[96]

In respect of Bodkin, a thorough critical examination of his record as DPP has yet to be conducted but even the somewhat hagiographic biography of him by Robert Jackson reveals areas of disquiet with some of his actions which unfortunately implicated his assistant, Gerald Paling, who would go on to conduct the prosecution case against Rouse at the pre-trial committal hearing in late 1930.[97] Thus Jackson recounts Bodkin's controversial role in the investigation into the case of the Frenchman, Jean-Pierre Vaquier, tried in 1924 for the murder by poisoning of Alfred Jones, his lover's husband and the landlord of the Blue Anchor Hotel in Byfleet in Surrey (briefly mentioned in chapter four). Bodkin had been irritated by the prolonged refusal of the chief constable of the county to bring in Scotland Yard to conduct the inquiry which was making little progress

---

95   Rozenberg, *op. cit.*; Sidney Theodore Felstead, *Sir Richard Muir: The Memoirs of a Public Prosecutor*, John Lane, Bodley Head, 1926, *passim*. The Crippen and Seddon cases are widely discussed. See, for example, Robin Odell, *Landmarks in 20th Century Murder*, Headline, 1995, pp. 63-8, 81-5. There are numerous studies of the Crippen case.

96   State trials 'proper', such as the trials of Sir Walter Raleigh, Guy Fawkes and the 'regicides', tended to be more political, trying alleged offences such as treason and sedition. They range in time from the Elizabethan age to the time of the Chartists, and would be reported in the *State Trials* series of law reports.

97   Modern DPPs do, from time to time, attract controversy, one recent example being in relation to the decision of the DPP, Alison Saunders, not to charge the then 86-year old former MP, Lord Janner, with serious child abuse offences, on the ground of his dementia. Following widespread protests, that decision was reversed to enable merely a 'trial of the facts' involving Janner, which entails 'no trial, no conviction, no penalty'. That he undoubtedly lacked mental capacity to instruct counsel seems to be glossed over in such circumstances, as the claims of justice for victims of abuse are vigorously advanced. For differing views see *The Times*, June 30, 2015; *Guardian*, ibid. Janner died, aged 87, in December 2015, leaving uncertain whether a 'trial of the facts' would eventually take place.

in determining the mysterious death by strychnine poisoning of Jones. So, without informing the chief constable, he simply instructed Paling to travel to Byfleet to interview Mrs. Jones. This placed Paling in an awkward position. As noted previously, the DPP's office prosecuted but did not investigate serious crime, nor could the DPP actually 'direct' anyone outside his office. He could only invite police to conduct investigations. Paling saw the constitutional risk in his appearing to be conducting an investigation as if he were a detective. For, if so, he might be required to testify in the witness box as to what Mrs. Jones had told him; which would be somewhat anomalous if he were also part of the prosecution, as he would be. As Jackson noted,[98]

> "Paling demurred. He was a lawyer, not a detective. 'It would not be right,' he said. 'It might result in me being called into the witness-box'. Bodkin shifted his ground but only a little. 'I see the point', he said. 'But see her all the same. You can have a detective with you who can prove the statement in court but on my strict instructions, he is to be there only on condition that he does not open his mouth.'"

Whether the direction to the detective to remain silent owed more to Bodkin's desire to obtain an uncontaminated statement from Mrs. Jones, or whether he was sensitive not to intrude egregiously upon the Surrey chief constable's jurisdictional autonomy is not clear. But the subterfuge apparently worked. Mrs. Jones testified in court to her statement to Paling, and Vaquier was convicted and hanged. Yet ironically, nothing of this particular incident appears in the Vaquier papers in the National Archives.[99]

In fact Bodkin was questioned about the matter at a hearing of the Royal Commission on Police Powers and Procedure in 1928, itself set up to repair some of the damage caused by the DPP's heavily criticized action in the Irene Savidge affair (note 99, below). He blandly explained that while the police, and not he, were charged with investigating crimes, it was sometimes 'more appropriate' for the DPP to take a statement when there arose scientific, technical or medical questions or financial issues involving accountancy, wills, trusts and bank accounts. Yet according to Bodkin's biographer, '....it did not escape the notice of the members of the Commission that in her [Mrs. Jones'] case no questions which were beyond the experience of the police had arisen'. Bodkin then proceeded to tell the commission that it had taken Paling eleven hours to take Mrs. Jones'

---

98   Jackson, op. cit., p. 195.
99   For further possible subterfuge by Bodkin in the Vaquier case see G. R. Rubin, "Calling in the Met: Serious Crime Investigation Involving Scotland Yard and Provincial Police Forces in England and Wales, 1906-1939", Legal Studies, Vol. 31 (3), 2011, pp. 411-41, note 92. For his controversial and aggressive role in the Irene Savidge/Sir Leo Chiozza Money alleged scandal in 1928 that added pressure to the demand for the creation of the Royal Commission on Police Powers and Procedure in the same year, see ibid., note 98 and sources cited therein; H. Montgomery Hyde, A Tangled Web: Sex Scandals in British Politics and Society, Constable, 1986, pp. 185-202. Norman Birkett represented the Metropolitan Police in the Savidge/Chiozza Money inquiry, set up on parliamentary instructions, while Sir Patrick Hastings appeared for Savidge. Both counsel were later involved in the Rouse case. Vaquier had been successfully prosecuted by Hastings who, at the time of the trial, had been the Attorney-General in the first (minority) Labour government (we shall look briefly at Hastings' career in chapter thirteen). It was Hastings's only prosecution (since defence was his métier), and it was undertaken by him due to the convention that either the Attorney-General or the Solicitor-General usually led in poisoning cases (in this case Hastings led Sir Edward Marshall Hall). It was Sir Patrick who later unsuccessfully represented Rouse at the Court of Criminal Appeal.

statement, though it now appeared that rather than Paling going to Byfleet with a silent Scotland Yard detective, as explained previously, Mrs. Jones had gone to the DPP's office to give her statement and, to the astonishment of the commission members, had stayed there from 11 am to 10:30 pm. But, Bodkin reassured the commissioners, the grieving widow did enjoy breaks for lunch and tea.

It was clearly a marginally improper arrangement which must have caused Paling some professional disquiet but not enough discomfort to impel him boldly to resist Bodkin's instructions.[100] It was certainly unlike the position with, say, the procurator-fiscal (a Crown prosecutor) in Scotland who can indeed direct police inquiries and can participate in crime investigations (as he notoriously did in browbeating a crucial and impressionable young female witness, Mary Barrowman, to give mistaken evidence that helped to convict Oscar Slater of murder in 1909 in the most outrageous miscarriage of justice in Scottish legal history in the past two hundred years)[101]. By March 1930 Bodkin was gone from office, leaving behind him a trail of further controversies ranging from his aggressive interviewing of Irene Savidge in 1928 arising from two constables' allegations that indecency had occurred between her and a former MP, Sir Leo Chiozza Money, in Hyde Park in 1928,[102] his combative defence, before the Royal Commissioners on Police Powers and Procedure in the same year, regarding his role in the Vaquier case, his 'moral purity' prosecutions for indecency of such literary works as Radclyffe Hall's lesbian novel, *The Well of Loneliness* in 1928, and his campaign of literary censorship directed at, for example, D. H. Lawrence's collection of poems, *Pansies*, in 1929.[103] But Paling who, eight months later would be facing Rouse in the police court, still had far to climb up the greasy pole.

Paling's career after the Rouse case was solid, methodical and reliable without its hitting the heights (and controversies, in some cases) of departmental prosecutors or Treasury counsel such as Avory, Humphreys and Sir Richard Muir in earlier days. In any case he had qualified as a solicitor, not as a barrister, with the

---

100   To some extent this was a grey area. Bodkin, of course, insisted that the DPP's office could conduct interviews of witnesses on technical matters such as accounting practices in a fraud case, though in the Vaquier case Mrs. Jones was evidently not privy to any relevant technical knowledge. Tindal Atkinson himself, without expressly agreeing with Bodkin on this alleged power, later conceded that the DPP could 'instruct' the police to interview witnesses on technical issues. See Sir Thomas Hetherington, *Prosecution and the Public Interest*, Waterlow Publishers, 1989, p. 23. The doctrine therefore appeared to state that the DPP could not control a police investigation; except, that is, when he could, which seemed to be when the DPP considered that the investigation involved 'technical' matters.

101   Thomas Toughill, *Oscar Slater: The 'Immortal' Case of Sir Arthur Conan Doyle*, Sutton Publishing, Stroud, 2006.

102   Inspector Collins of Scotland Yard, who would later conduct inquiries and interviews on behalf of Superintendent Brumby in the Rouse case, had also been involved in intensive, perhaps oppressive, interviewing of Irene Savidge.

103   See Jackson, *op. cit.*, pp. 218-27 on the Savidge affair. For the obscenity trial involving Radclyffe Hall's novel, *The Well of Loneliness*, see Diana Souhami, *The Trials of Radclyffe Hall*, Weidenfeld & Nicolson, 1998, chs. 19-24. Hall's publisher, Jonathan Cape, retained Norman Birkett for the Bow Street Magistrates Court hearing. For Lawrence see Christopher Pollnitz, "The Censorship and Transmission of D. H. Lawrence's Pansies: The Home Office and the 'Foul-Mouthed Fellow'", *Journal of Modern Literature*, Vol. 28 (3), 2005, pp. 44-71. Some of Lawrence's paintings were seized by the police from a gallery in 1929. For details, see Christopher Hilliard, "'Is it a Book that You Would Even Wish Your Wife or Your Servants to Read?' Obscenity Law and the Politics of Reading in Modern England", *American Historical Review*, Vol. 118 (3), 2013, pp. 653-78. The quote in the title refers to Mervyn Griffith-Jones' memorable and foolish question to the jury in the *Lady Chatterley's Lover* prosecution of Penguin Books in 1960. Tindal Atkinson himself published a 32-page pamphlet, *Obscene Literature in Law and Practice*, Christophers, in 1936.

consequence that he had no right of audience in courts other than the magistrates court. Indeed his career ended soon after he had to defend his department in 1957 during a Scotland Yard investigation led by George Hatherill, Commander of the CID, into a notorious police corruption case in Brighton in which Chief Constable William Ridge was implicated. Thus the press published a copy of a letter from Paling, as Deputy DPP, to the Brighton Watch Committee, that is, to the local police authority, which had reassured that body that his department had not been responsible for leaks to the newspapers regarding the on-going bribery investigation.[104]

So what of Bodkin's, and then Tindal Atkinson's, assistant DPP, Paling, who conducted the prosecution of Rouse at the committal hearing? The information we have on him is limited. He was born in 1895 and his *Who's Who* entry shows that he was 34 during the Rouse proceedings. Married with a daughter, he had served in the Army during the war, suffering a wound in France in 1916. He was then admitted as a solicitor in 1918 and joined the DPP's department as a legal assistant in the same year. His rise was slow, he becoming Assistant DPP in 1944 and then Deputy DPP five years later. He died in Brighton in 1966.

His first significant role was when he appeared before the magistrates at Hay-on-Wye to represent the DPP at the police court proceedings against Major Herbert Rowse Armstrong, the solicitor eventually convicted and hanged for poisoning his wife.[105] Thereafter, apart from his uncomfortable role in the Vaquier prosecution in 1924, above, Paling also featured with Bodkin in many other celebrated prosecutions. For example, his role in the prosecution of Mrs. Beatrice Pace at Gloucester in 1928 for the poisoning of her husband (she was acquitted) has been recently described in a stimulating monograph on the case,[106] while his involvement in many other *causes célèbres* frequently, but not always, in the role of representing the DPP at the committal hearings before the magistrate, is a matter of record. One example is his involvement in the committal proceedings in the celebrated case of Dr. Buck Ruxton in 1936. His presence in those proceedings prevented his appearing for the DPP, held at the same time, at the committal hearing in the case of Charlotte Bryant, later hanged for poisoning her husband. He had, however, been closely involved in discussions in the DPP's office to institute proceedings against her after an inquest had failed to identify her as being responsible for her husband's death.

He was also involved the previous year in preparations that culminated in the leading House of Lords decision in *Woolmington v DPP* [1935] A C 462.[107] Here, a farm labourer had been convicted of murder after admitting shooting his estranged 17-year old wife. He had claimed her death had been an accident. However, at the time of the trial, it was believed that in such circumstances, where the accused had admitted causing a death without admitting to the particular

---

104 *The Times*, October 10, 1957. For brief details of the Brighton police saga see Rupert Furneaux, *Famous Criminal Cases V*, Allan Wingate, 1958, chapter VII.

105 Robin Odell, *Exhumation of a Murderer: The Life and Trial of Major Armstrong*, Souvenir Press, 1988, p. 67.

106 John Carter Wood, 'The Most Remarkable Woman in England': Poison, Celebrity and the Trials of Beatrice Pace, Manchester University Press, Manchester, 2012, *passim*.

107 See also J. D. Casswell QC., *A Lance for Liberty*, Harrap, 1961, ch. 7. Casswell was Woolmington's counsel. He later unsuccessfully defended, among others, George Stoner in the Rattenbury case, the husband-poisoner, Mrs Bryant, and Neville Heath.

charge, the burden of proof was on the defendant, on the balance of probabilities, to prove his innocence. On this basis he was convicted and an appeal dismissed. In the House of Lords, however, the Lord Chancellor, Viscount Sankey, resolutely insisted that this legal doctrine regarding burden of proof was wrong. For, ever since Magna Carta, the presumption of innocence (with a limited number of exceptions which did *not* include Reg Woolmington's circumstances) prevailed. It was thus for the prosecution, throughout, to prove guilt beyond reasonable doubt, which included its proving beyond reasonable that death had not been accidental. Poor Reg had blamed his mother-in-law's interference for the collapse of his brief six-week marriage when his wife went back to her mother with the couple's baby. Reg, distraught, turned up at his in-law's door and pleaded with his wife to return to him. Otherwise he would shoot himself. At which point, when he opened up his coat to reveal a shotgun tied round his waist in order to show his seriousness of purpose, it went off and killed young Violet. It should, of course, be pointed out that in regard to Rouse, since he had never claimed responsibility for his passenger's accidental death (indeed, the victim, according to Arthur, had brought about his own death), then the pre-*Woolmington* doctrine imposing a burden of proof on the accused did not apply in Rouse's case.

But before his involvement with Bryant, Woolmington and Ruxton, Paling was a particular target of the social critic, Cecil Baines', bile. Indeed, it was as if Baines was implying that Paling had inherited, or had been infected with, much of the moral guardian role that Bodkin had assumed for himself. The latter, it may be inferred from his record, above, was undoubtedly overbearing, pompous and prone to making wrong moves on occasions, and was identified by critical observers as representing much that was wrong with the personnel in charge of the criminal justice system at the time. Indeed, the cavalier manner in which, according to Baines, Paling had presented the case against Rouse at the latter's committal hearing (below), was of a piece with his former superior, Bodkin's, ruthless manner.

Thus, with Baines suitably angered by the outcome of the Rouse case itself, and displaying either *chutzpah* or the sensitivity of a rhinoceros, he wrote to Tindal Atkinson inquiring whether the latter would now wish to 'express an opinion, as I should like to be assured that you are not a party to this irregular procedure'? This was in fact a reference to Paling's presentation of the case against Rouse at the police court in an allegedly unfair manner (see chapters eight and thirteen) when he appeared to blacken Rouse's reputation by adducing at the committal hearing the testimony of Rouse's lovers, Helen and Nellie, and by raising at the same hearing the accused's 'harem' outburst at Angel Lane police station. Nonetheless, the thrust of Cecil Baines' complaint against Paling, that the latter was considered among the 'dregs' of the Bar (Paling was, of course, a solicitor), is more problematic. For whereas Baines' complaint against Paling was based on the former's view of the criminal justice system as always being institutionally conspiratorial against the interests of prisoners, especially against the majority poor prisoners, Paling, as we shall see, sought to justify his exposure of Rouse's immorality at the police court as bearing on the prisoner's motive to disappear, which lay behind the accused's alleged intent to commit murder. And, indeed, while evidence appearing to speak to the prisoner's 'bad character' as a thoroughly immoral individual was at the time (and still is, to a lesser extent) *ordinarily* not admissible in criminal proceedings (for the accused should be tried for the current alleged crime, not for his previous reprehensible behaviour), the issue was (and is), arguably, not legally clear-cut, as we will note when later examining the police court and Court of Appeal proceedings.

Opposing Paling at the police court was the experienced barrister, Donald Finnemore (see later), instructed by Rouse's solicitor, George Lee-Roberts, whose principal office was in fact in Wolverhampton. But as a sole practitioner who realized that this serious case was rapidly becoming more complex, especially in respect of expert testimony, Lee-Roberts was later assisted by the Northampton firm of solicitors, Darnell & Price. It is almost certain that Rouse was assigned his solicitor by the magistrates at the first police court hearing on November 9, 1930 in view of the shortage of funds available to him to appoint his own legal representatives. As we know from his 'harem' revelation to Inspector Lawrence at Angel Lane police station, he was anticipating being in funds on the sale of Buxted Road, but the amounts actually realised were disappointing. Indeed he notably told the police court that whatever the outcome of the proceedings he was not a wealthy man and that by the end of the case he would have 'lost his all'; which he probably did not think referred to his life. As to the composition of the magistrates' bench hearing the committal proceedings, we consider this in chapter eight.

Rouse was a beneficiary of the Poor Prisoners' Defence Act 1930 under which those charged with murder were offered financial aid to pay for their legal representation. At the committal stage of proceedings, however, the Act made no provision for defence counsel to receive his fee from that fund. Indeed, those prisoners responsible for funding their own defence might refrain from retaining, and paying for, counsel at this stage, on the premise that it might not strictly be necessary to be represented by counsel since the Crown were only expected to submit a prima facie case to the magistrates that a committal to trial should be ordered, at which point the full force of the defence would be deployed. In Rouse's case, legal fees were eventually charged to him, even though part of the total bill was paid for out of public funds. Thus he did partially benefit from paid legal assistance, but only because he was a man of very little means who was facing a murder trial. For unlike other accused and despite the hopes reposed in the Act's drafters that it would enable poor prisoners to receive proper legal representation, the overwhelming majority of those tried before the magistrates, even where a plausible or strong defence existed, were denied legal aid. Section 2 of the Act actually provided that,

> "If it appears to a Court of Summary Jurisdiction or examining magistrates that the means of a person charged before them with any offence are insufficient to enable him to obtain legal aid and that by reason of the gravity of the charge or of exceptional circumstances it is desirable in the interests of justice that he should have free legal aid in the preparation and conduct of his defence, the court or justices may grant in respect of him a certificate called a legal aid certificate."

In Rouse's case he was appearing before the 'examining magistrates' who would determine whether he should be committed for trial for murder at the next assizes. In such cases it would be unthinkable that the grant of a legal aid certificate to a near impoverished defendant facing a murder charge would not be in the interests of justice. However were a penniless defendant to be tried by the magistrates for offences such as malicious wounding, indecent assault, housebreaking, breaking into a shop, larceny, false pretences, receiving or forgery by a 'court of summary jurisdiction', his chances of obtaining legal aid were minimal. Thus as one writer noted, the 1,044 magistrates courts in 1935 granted 336 certificates, 363 the following year, and 315 in 1937. But the numbers convicted of all offences in those courts were 752,596 in 1935, 817,873 in 1936 and 807,688 in 1937.[108] In respect of those tried for 'either way' offences, that is, for crimes triable either on indictment before a jury, or before the magistrates sitting without a jury, the number of certificates granted between 1931 and 1934 inclusive was, respectively, 58,317, 62,103, 61,264 and 65,056.[109] Presumably such cases where certificates were granted were overwhelmingly tried before a jury whether at assizes or at quarter sessions. Thus it seems probable that legal aid in the jury-less magistrates court, payable from the local rates, was rarely granted. Unsurprisingly, however, there were no cases between 1931 and 1934 inclusive where the examining magistrates, when no juries sat, refused to accede to defence applications for a certificate in murder cases. Indeed in a number of cases the magistrates themselves offered certificates where no applications had been submitted by the prisoner (three murder charge defendants actually refused the offers; perhaps they intended to plead guilty despite the mandatory death sentence, reject the possibility of a mitigating plea from counsel which might go to influence a reprieve, and face execution). However in non-murder trials on indictment at assizes or first instance quarter sessions where a jury sat, committing magistrates during this period would refuse around a third of applications for certificates. These refusals might be remedied by the judges of assize in some cases, while a handful of applications for legal aid in murder cases would also be granted by assize court judges (though it is not clear if or why these murder cases escaped earlier consideration).[110]

Rouse therefore was granted a legal aid certificate in order that he could be legally represented by counsel at his trial for murder. Yet as the anonymous solicitor who authored the Pelican Books volume on *English Justice*, first published in 1932, pointed out, the funding available to Rouse was considerably less than the resources devoted to the case by the prosecution whose costs amounted to about £2,500. This meant, according to 'Solicitor', that, if financial resources had been equal, '.....important expert evidence to rebut the testimony given for the prosecution would have been available at the trial [of Rouse], instead of which it was too late'. In fact, while the defence team might have been inhibited by financial constraints in commissioning expert testimony to challenge Crown evidence that the blaze had been started deliberately by the accused, defence counsel may also

---

108   'Solicitor', *English Justice*, Pelican Books, 1941, p. 52.
109   'A Barrister', *Justice in England*, Victor Gollancz Ltd, 1938, p. 206. The author of this Left Book Club volume seems to have been the left-wing barrister and Labour MP (and later Communist), D. N. Pritt. See Nick Blake and Harry Rajak, *Wigs and Workers: A History of the Haldane Society of Socialist Lawyers, 1930-1980*, Haldane Society, 1980, p. 15.
110   'A Barrister', *op. cit.*, pp. 196-7.

initially have been less than proactive in seeking out their own experts. For in general the latter experts had approached the defence team with the offer of relevant technical information, rather than vice-versa. Yet the point regarding inequality of resources was well made.[111] It is, however, worth pointing out that not all defendants denied legal aid certificates were left to their own devices. Some legal representatives might not charge for their services in individual cases. Moreover, funding for the defence could be raised through appeals or donations, through the voluntary or charitable work of 'poor men's lawyers', or through the defendants' trade unions,[112] while the 'dock brief' arrangement (below) still existed.

But who were the counsel who actually appeared at the assizes when Rouse went on trial? As noted above the prisoner was represented by Donald Finnemore who also appeared on his behalf at the police court hearings. But at the trial itself Finnemore was assisted by his junior, A. P. Marshall, while appearing for the Crown was the formidable Norman Birkett KC, MP whose junior was Richard Elwes. Finally, in presiding over the trial was Mr. Justice Talbot, an unostentatious, solid and fair judge who, perhaps because of those very qualities, was not a household name among the judiciary of the day unlike, say, Travers Humphreys, Horace Avory, Jimmy Cassels, Rigby Swift or Gordon Hewart, all of whom have attracted full-length biographies (not cited here).

There are many theories of what is expected of an advocate defending his client in a criminal trial. The hoariest question often put is how could a barrister defend a client whom he knows is guilty, to which the straightforward answer is that it is for the Crown to prove guilt, not for counsel to prove innocence. And, in any case, unless counsel actually witnessed the unprovoked and intended criminal act by one whom he *knew* was not legally insane, or if he, today, reposes total faith in the damning DNA evidence, he can never be certain of his client's guilt, according to the legal standard of proof. The only qualification is that counsel, where he is privy to his client's admission of guilt, must not set out to claim that the defendant is innocent. He must either refuse the brief if the client, having admitted his guilt in conference, instructs counsel to run, as his defence, what the latter now knows is a cock-and-bull story. Or counsel can run a simple defence of not guilty, placing the burden on the Crown to prove guilt beyond reasonable doubt or, if not wholly implausible on the circumstances, he can raise issues such as accident or absence of the required *mens rea* (guilty mind), whether intention, recklessness or gross negligence, necessary for the offence charged. For to run a knowingly false alibi by counsel would be a breach of his duty to the court and to his profession and would be dishonest. It is for that reason that many leading counsel would refuse to meet their clients in the cells or prison before a trial. They would thereby ensure that they avoided the risk or actuality of hearing from the accused an admission that might scupper or compromise the defence to be put forward. It is an approach with which counsel for Christopher Craig, in the 'Craig and Bentley' case in 1952-

111 'Solicitor' also alluded to, though did not expressly cite, the Julia Wallace case in Liverpool in 1931 where the husband's conviction was overturned by the Court of Criminal Appeal. Yet the husband, a man of modest means, had to bear his own legal costs of £1,526 11s 6d. Indeed in parliament, the Home Secretary, Clynes, confirmed that no compensation would be paid to him.
112 See Blake and Rajak, *op. cit.* Also see Diana Leat, "The Rise and Role of the Poor Man's Lawyer", *British Journal of Law and Society*, Vol. 2, 1975, pp. 166-81.

53, John Parris, strongly disagreed.[113] Advocacy was not a 'science' which was subject to detached analysis by counsel and where meeting one's client prior to the trial would be unnecessary since the accused's solicitor would previously have furnished counsel with the depositions and other essential items. Advocacy was an 'art' where the meeting of counsel and client before trial could inform the former of the character traits of the prisoner, which aspects to emphasis and which to ignore, and how the accused might perform in the witness box, if called to testify (a tactical decision partly shaped by counsel's impressions of their pre-trial meetings in prison or in the cells below the assize court). Criminal trials, more than civil proceedings, might well turn on these personality aspects, and prior consultations between counsel and client might enable the former to advise the latter on trial court deportment which might appeal to a jury. But advice might be ignored, as the Edith Thompson trial tragically demonstrated where her counsel, Curtis-Bennett, had vainly pleaded with Edith not to enter the witness box. Or the advice to the accused to be restrained while testifying in the witness box might fall on deaf ears. Probably this applied in Rouse's case.

There are also the obvious pieces of advice offered to counsel as they embark upon their careers. G. D. ('Khaki') Roberts lists seven golden rules, commencing with 'be prepared'. So do not appear in a racecourse or bookmaking or cheating at cards case unless you know that 'NH rules' have no connection with the National Health Service, that you know what the totaliser is, and that you know that roulette is *not* a game played with cards (all examples from notable counsel showing their ignorance). Voice projection is important in ensuring that the jury does not fall asleep as you press your points. Especially in relation to prosecuting counsel, do not open a case with more detail or speculation or extraneous material than is necessary. For some information may be inadmissibly prejudicial and establish grounds for a valid defence objection on legal grounds, resulting in the jury being required to stand down, and a new one taking its place.

Linked to the above is another of Roberts' 'rules', that to 'let well alone'. That is, once a vital piece of evidence, admission, corroboration etc has been obtained from the witness, do not gild the lily. For follow-up questions may not only be superfluous, they may be inadmissible or damaging to counsel's own case and spoil the positive gain already secured. Thus they may indicate that the accused has not actually committed the offence with which he is charged, for example, handling stolen property, but a different offence with which he has not been charged, for example, theft (or larceny in older terminology). The rule to 'Be discreet' was illustrated by Roberts in one case in 1920 when a music-hall agent called Scranton, who was in dire financial straits, had been summonsed to Bow Street magistrates' court for fraudulent conversion. The prosecutor, Sir Ernest Wild, was cross-examining Scranton about his financial involvement with one Moey Tarsh. 'A moneylender?' asked Wild, followed by 'A Jew, I suppose?' 'Yes, I think he is a Hebrew'. Sadly for Wild, when the appeal against conviction came before the Court of Criminal Appeal, the Lord Chief Justice, Rufus Isaacs, himself a proud Jew, asked Wild what did he mean by the question, 'A Jew, I suppose'? What inference was Wild going to ask the jury to draw from that fact, if it were, indeed, established? Wild grew redder and redder but no answer there came,

113   John Parris, *Most of My Murders*, Frederick Muller, 1960, pp. 36-7.

while Isaacs pointedly emphasized that he had asked his judicial brethren sitting with him on the appeal who had agreed that Wild's question was intended to elicit an unfavourable view of Moey Tarsh, and therefore of Scranton. The conviction was quashed because the evidence was 'so finely balanced'. [114] So, given all the caveats and warnings, does the 'art of the advocate', that is, the 'art of persuasion', come down to the proposition that it is the 'art of misleading an audience with telling lies?' These were the words of Cyril Harvey QC, cited by Roberts, who remained frankly uncertain whether or not they were spoken with tongue in cheek. Certainly Roberts disagreed vigorously with the sentiment, but when we explore prosecuting counsel, Birkett's, cross-examining tactics in the Rouse case, it would be well to recall Harvey's words.

Donald Finnemore, a prominent member of the Midland circuit, and based in Birmingham, was in fact an old friend of Birkett's and shared with the latter a commitment to Liberal Party politics and support for the Boys' Brigade movement. Though not as outstanding as the latter in terms of presenting a calm but devastating authority as a court advocate, he would also, like Birkett, eventually take his seat in due course on the judicial bench. Indeed, due to the lay-out of the court at the Old Bailey, he was the only person present in the court many years later who could gaze upon the reptilian features of that tearful but unconvincing actor, the multiple killer of Ten Rillington Place, John Reginald Christie, whom he sentenced to death in 1953.[115] Born in 1889, Finnemore was called to the bar in 1914 and, of Baptist persuasion, served in France as a British Red Cross officer from 1916 to 1919. The Rouse trial was probably the most notable case in which he appeared, sandwiched as it was between various fruitless efforts to enter parliament for the Liberal cause. But it was during World War II that he gained greater official recognition. Apart from wartime committee appointments, he sat as a county court judge in the Midlands from 1940 to 1947, before promotion to the High Court where he presided over many trials, including Christie's, until retirement in 1964. He died ten years later.

Finnemore's junior, Archie Pellow Marshall, was ten years younger than Finnemore. Born in Cornwall he had served with the Royal Navy from 1914 to 1920, experiencing active service in the North Sea, the Mediterranean and in South Russia. President of the Cambridge Union in 1924 he joined the Midland circuit the following year and practised in Birmingham between 1927 and 1947 when he was appointed King's Counsel. Like Finnemore and Birkett he sought to enter parliament as a Liberal MP and in his case was unsuccessful on three occasions between 1929 and 1945. He became deputy chairman of the Northamptonshire bench of magistrates from 1947, chairman of Cornwall quarter sessions from 1957 and Recorder of Warwick (1949-51) and of Coventry (1952-59). Appointed a judge (commissioner) of Assize on the Oxford circuit in 1959, he was finally elevated to the bench in 1961, sitting in the Queen's Bench where, inter alia, he would preside over criminal trials, including the controversial trial of Stephen Ward in 1963, probably framed by Scotland Yard and MI5 in the wake of the

---

114 G. D. Roberts, QC, *Law and Life*, W. H. Allen, 1964, Ch. 2; *R. v Scranton* (1921) 15 Cr. App. Rep. 104. For later civil proceedings see *Scranton's Trustee v Pearse* [1922] 2 Ch. 87.
115 See Duncan Webb, *Deadline for Crime*, Muller, 1955, p. 209. Like Norman Rae, who testified at Rouse's trial, Webb was considered one of the doyens of newspaper crime reporting.

Profumo affair.[116] What is remarkable, of course, is how his political and legal career seemed to follow closely that of Finnemore. Indeed they also appeared to have shared a deep belief in Rouse's innocence of the murder charge.

But undoubtedly the most notable counsel at Rouse's trial was Norman Birkett, the subject of at least two biographies and of an anthology of his famous cases.[117] Particular attention will be given in a later chapter to his characteristic advocacy style in court where his twiddling of his gold propelling pencil while cross-examining Rouse could be taken as a metaphor for the striking home of a thin stiletto knife into the heart of the prisoner's defence.

Birkett was born in the Lake District in 1883 to a comfortable but not wealthy Wesleyan family, his father owning two drapery shops and serving as a local councillor. Travelling daily by train from his home in Ulverston to his grammar school in Barrow, he also cultivated a love of cricket and of hill walking. One biographer noted that, 'From the age of eighteen to twenty-four Birkett was subject to a recurrent emotional crisis',[118] though it seems that he was simply lonely as he plodded away, assisting in his father's business and attending night school from which he matriculated in 1907. Somewhat gaunt, if not exactly painfully thin, he went to Cambridge University where he enthusiastically embraced and participated in the debates at the Cambridge Union, whose president he became in 1910. It was, indeed, in that environment where his debating skills, so useful in a court setting, were honed, and where he apparently presented himself as a 'Liberal in politics and a Tory in matters of taste', as a student newspaper described his demeanour.[119] Graduating in 1911 he was called to the bar in 1913, but unlike his contemporaries his career was not disrupted by war since he was declared medically unfit in 1914. In fact he had been suffering from tuberculosis.

His early days on the Midland circuit (he was thirty when called), which included appearing at Northampton assizes, were marked by considerable nervousness, though not by courtroom inadequacy or by any hints of being tongue-tied. Indeed his eloquence, allied to humility, was marked. He first worked with one of the leading juniors on the circuit, J. G. Hurst. But it was the clerk of assize of the Midland circuit, George Pleydell Bancroft, who went on to sit as clerk to the assize at Rouse's trial, who launched Birkett on an illustrious career as a defence barrister whose sympathies for the poor who ended up in the dock never left him (which probably made Rouse's experience of being cross-examined in a deadly fashion by *prosecuting* counsel, Norman Birkett, even more painful and galling). For notwithstanding that it was an especially onerous task, even for barristers long in the tooth, to represent a client in one case on a charge of murdering his wife, Bancroft nonetheless decided to nominate the inexperienced tyro from Ulverston (as Bancroft would also do in respect of Finnemore), 'solely upon the strength of his conversational powers'.[120] This was Birkett's first case to be legally aided under the Poor Prisoners' Defence Act 1903, the predecessor of the slightly

116 Geoffrey Robertson, *Stephen Ward Was Innocent, OK*, Biteback, 2013.
117 See H. Montgomery Hyde, *Norman Birkett: The Life of Lord Birkett of Ulverston*, Reprint Society edition, 1964; Dennis Bardens, *Lord Justice Birkett*, Robert Hale, 1962; *ibid.*, *Famous Cases of Norman Birkett, K.C.*, Robert Hale, 1963.
118 Bardens, *Lord Justice Birkett, op. cit.*, p 31.
119 *Ibid.*, p. 36.
120 *Ibid*, p. 44.

more generous 1930 Act whose provisions ensured that Rouse was properly represented at his trial. It was also undoubtedly Birkett's first murder trial and one, it appears, where he undertook the defence on his own, and without a leader, despite the gravity of the charge.

Neither of Birkett's biographers cites the case by name but it seems likely that it was that of 42 year-old William Reeve, tried at Bedford Assizes in October 1915 for murdering his wife by shooting her at Leighton Buzzard. In the event Birkett, matched against two prosecuting counsel, failed to persuade the jury that the gun had gone off by accident (until *Woolmington*, of course, it was accepted ever since the later eighteenth century that the burden of proof was on the accused if he proposed to plead accidental death). As a result Reeve was convicted. However, Bancroft noted that the trial judge, Mr. Justice Shearman (who would later preside controversially over the Thompson-Bywaters trial in 1922), went out of his way to pay tribute in his summing up to the efforts of Birkett on behalf of his client. Reeve appealed to the Court of Criminal Appeal where the same three counsel appeared. But Birkett's submissions on his client's behalf were rejected by the appeal court and Reeve was executed at Bedford Gaol on November 16, 1915. Nonetheless, it was a remarkable achievement for such a novice at the bar to be appearing on his own before the Court of Criminal Appeal just two years into his career.

*

It is clear that Bancroft, in choosing Birkett, was a good judge of court advocacy. Indeed public performances were part of the fabric of Bancroft's life as he outlined in his autobiography, written in 1939.[121] For his parents, Sir Squire Bancroft and Marie Wilton, had been notable stage and society personalities, while he himself had been in the diplomatic service and had dabbled with the theatre, both writing and acting, before turning to the law where, as clerk of assize from 1913 to 1946, his manner was said to put most participants in the legal process at their ease.[122] As H. Montgomery Hyde, one of Birkett's biographers, also noted, in the early stages of the latter's career at the bar, he had

> ".... had his fair share of 'dock briefs'. By long-established custom, a prisoner who has been charged and is in the dock may pick out any barrister who happens to be in court and robed at the time to defend him, and by the etiquette of the Bar the barrister must accept the brief for the fee of £1 3s 6d, which sum must be paid in cash on the spot."[123]

In October 1915 he also appeared at West Bromwich county court to defend 32 Smethwick tenants from eviction proceedings. They had taken part in one of the many rent strikes throughout Britain, protesting against landlords' exploitation of housing shortages as workers from other parts of the country were drafted into munitions factories.[124] Though these were not exactly criminal proceedings

---

121 George Pleydell Bancroft, *Stage and Bar: Recollections of George Pleydell Bancroft*, Faber and Faber, 1939. It included a preface written by Norman Birkett couched in the usual praiseworthy terms.
122 *Ibid.*, pp. 43-4; James McClure, *Killers*, Fontana, 1976, p. 104; Montgomery Hyde, *op. cit.*, p. 71. See also Bancroft's autobiography at note 121, above.
123 Montgomery Hyde, *op. cit.*, p. 72.
124 David Englander, *Landlord and Tenant in Britain, 1838-1918*, Clarendon Press, Oxford, 1983, p. 209. Almost certainly some of the defendants were either war widows or wives whose husbands were serving abroad in the armed forces.

Birkett's court appearances in such cases confirmed that sympathy for the underdog thus remained a *leitmotif* of his career, though it is doubtful whether he would have placed Rouse in this category of underdog. With his career flourishing at the local bar in the Midlands, he made a great impression in 1919 in appearing with the redoutable Sir Edward Marshall Hall, then at the height of his illustrious career at the bar, in the 'Green Bicycle' trial of Ronald Light, spectacularly acquitted of murdering a young female cyclist, when Marshall Hall sought to argue (and obviously convinced the jury on the balance of probabilities) that the shooting had been accidental, the target, he satisfactorily argued, being not the victim but a crow found with bullet wounds near the location of the victim's death. Following the trial Marshall Hall invited Birkett to join his chambers in London in 1920, after which Birkett's career at the bar (and his earnings) advanced rapidly.

Appointed King's Counsel in 1924 he appeared in a number of sensational civil and criminal cases between the wars. They included defending in 1929 the well-known firm of solicitors, Withers, accused of negligence by their former wealthy client, Hayley Morriss, whom they had previously represented in domestic financial negotiations over a period of 6 years with his ex-wife. Morriss himself had also been sentenced to two years' imprisonment in 1925 for sexual procurement offences committed at his private mansion, Pippingford Park, deep in the Ashdown Forest in Sussex. Other high-profile civil cases in which Birkett took part included a defamation case involving the author and critic, James Agate, another such case involving the amateur golf champion, Cyril Tolley, who found himself depicted, without his permission, in an advertising cartoon endorsing Fry's chocolate; a breach of promise of marriage case involving Rupert Baring, who had recently succeeded to the title of Lord Revelstoke; and a divorce petition in 1936, listed simply as *Simpson* v *Simpson*. His client was an America lady known as Mrs. Wallis Simpson, though it is doubtful whether any other undefended divorce application case has had as much constitutional significance as did that hearing.

Among his major criminal cases might be listed the Brighton Trunk murder in 1934 when he succeeded in securing the acquittal of Tony Mancini for the murder and mutilation of Violette Kaye, only for Mancini to admit his guilt in an article in the *News of the World* in 1976. Other defence 'triumphs' included that of Mrs. Harriet Crouch, acquitted of murdering her 'faithless and bullying' husband, Frank, at Summerhouse Farm, Clacton, in 1926, and the case of the 'tragic widow', Mrs. Beatrice Pace (mentioned previously), acquitted in 1928 of poisoning her husband, Harry, in the Forest of Dean. Not every defence in a *cause célèbre* was a triumph, however, as the outcome of the sensational Dr. Buck Ruxton case illustrated, though even here the prisoner, before his execution, wrote to Birkett, thanking him for his efforts and leaving to his barrister a legacy of a set of fish knives and forks. Birkett declined them. Sir Patrick Hastings summed up well Birkett's qualities as a defence advocate.

> "His love of defending murderers made him a terror to the police, and a danger to all law and order. If ever it had been my lot to take a lady for a stray week-end, and at the conclusion of the entertainment I had decided to cut her into small pieces and place her in a suitcase—a form of procedure by no means unknown to him—[presumably a reference to a combination of the Patrick Mahon and John Robinson cases] I should unhesitatingly have placed

my future in Norman's hands, relying confidently upon his ability to satisfy a country jury (a) that I was not there, (b) that I had not cut up the lady, (c) and that if I had she thoroughly deserved it."[125]

While Birkett undoubtedly preferred to defend, we also know from the Rouse trial that he could be a formidable prosecutor if briefed to appear for the Crown in a murder trial. Thus he was able to repeat the success of the 'Blazing Car' case when obtaining a guilty verdict against Frederick Nodder for the murder of ten year-old Mona Tinsley at Nottingham Assizes in 1937 some months after the prisoner had received seven years at Warwick Assizes for the girl's abduction, her body not having been discovered at the time of the earlier trial. Birkett prosecuted in both cases. A year before these two trials, he had also secured the conviction of Nurse Dorothea Waddingham for the murder of 50 year-old Ada Baguley in a Nottingham nursing home in 1936, some months after the sudden death in the same care home of her elderly mother. Morphine poisoning was detected and Waddingham, the mother of several children, including a four month-old baby, was hanged despite the jury's recommendation to mercy. The case still invites questions regarding a possible miscarriage of justice.

Nonetheless, within two months, Birkett was back where he tended to excel, securing the acquittal of a prisoner, this time a sixty-nine year-old confectioner, Albert Hadfield, charged with the murder of Mrs. Laura Chapman in Twickenham. Birkett made capital out of the police admission that they had failed to check forensically whether two postcards from Hadfield to Chapman, found in her house, and which appeared to bear bloody thumb-prints that were too smudged to identify, were in fact formed with blood. An acquittal followed. What, we might ask, would have been the outcome of the Rouse trial had Birkett, if he had been defending rather than prosecuting the prisoner, sought to exploit the Northamptonshire police mishandling of the crime scene and to challenge and seek to refute the Crown's incriminating explanation that the blaze had been deliberately fed by human manipulation of the car's petrol union joint?

As an accomplished performer, Birkett was recruited for public service in 1937 to chair an inter-departmental committee on abortion and the law applicable thereto. The following year he was appointed commissioner of Assize, a part-time judicial post, and following the outbreak of war he chaired the committee that advised the Home Secretary on cases of detention under the notorious Defence Regulation 18B under which fascist sympathizers such as Oswald Mosley were detained without trial.[126] He was also recruited by the BBC to broadcast a weekly riposte to Lord Haw-Haw, William Joyce's, 'Jairmany Calling.... Jairmany Calling' Nazi propaganda programmes during the phoney war in 1940. But with the Bar Council objecting to lawyers using their own names in broadcasts (forbidden as a form of advertising), Birkett delivered his biting *Once a Week* broadcasts under the pseudonym, 'Mr X'. [127] At last, in 1941 he was elevated to the bench some months after being knighted (he had actually turned down the offer of a

125   Sir Patrick Hastings, *The Autobiography of Sir Patrick Hastings*, Heinemann, 1948, p. 130.
126   A. W. Brian Simpson, *In the Highest Degree Odious: Detention Without Trial in Wartime Britain*, Clarendon Press, Oxford, 1992, esp. Chapters 5 and 13.
127   Roy Bainton, "Battle of the Airwaves", *Saga Magazine*, February 2000, pp. 64-5.

judgeship in 1928, preferring to enjoy life at the bar at that time). But he was not especially suited to the dispassionate and adjudicatory role demanded of King's Bench; even less to the erudite atmosphere of the Court of Appeal bench to which he was elevated in 1950. Being despatched to the Nuremberg trials in 1945 only as an alternate to the British nominee, Lord Justice Lawrence, despite support from Prime Minister Attlee and Lord Chancellor Jowitt that he be appointed the principal British judge, must have rankled, especially since he was not accorded any subsequent honour in recognition of his performing such difficult duties. Birkett was a clinical assassin *par excellence* when prosecuting for the Crown, and both a destroyer of prosecution clarity and provider of an alternative and plausible narrative when in defending mode. Rouse was, in effect, assassinated by him.

Birkett's advocacy style, to which we referred earlier, was probably honed by his unostentatious and precise northern Methodist origins. He was not a flamboyant orator and did not seek to emulate in this regard the most notable practitioner of this art (or tomfoolery, depending upon one's point of view), Sir Edward Marshall Hall, whose career flourished between the 1890s and the late 1920s. Marshall Hall always gave the impression of disdaining legal expertise in his court room performances (he would never have been suitable for the higher bench, though until shortly before his death he had occupied the post of Recorder of Guildford, where most cases turned on matters of fact, not law,). 'There is some law in this', he would say to his junior. 'You take this point'. Instead, Marshall Hall, the 'Great Defender', would place heavy reliance on his appeals to the jury's emotions. 'God never gave this woman a chance. Will you?', he beseeched in 1894 to the jury trying Marie Hermann, a 43-year old prostitute with three children, one of them disabled, when she was charged with murdering a lecherous 70-year old client. Manslaughter, it was. Or when he purported to play out the scene in the corridor of the Savoy Hotel in 1923 as the French-born beauty, Mme. Fahmy, supposedly faced her younger Egyptian playboy husband who, 'crouching like an oriental', was allegedly about to spring on her. Fearful for her life (Marshall Hall claimed) she pulled the trigger of an apparently unfamiliar revolver and he fell. '*Qu'est-ce que j'ai fait, mon cher?*', she moaned as he lay dying. And having played out this almost wholly imaginary scene for the jury, Marshall Hall, who spoke impeccable French, paused, and let the gun fall from his hand with a dramatic clatter. That her husband had died of gunshot wounds to his back and that she was in the habit of keeping a gun under her pillow seemed of no consequence. She was acquitted to widespread acclaim, and the horrible danger of miscegenation with an oriental was providentially averted, and the cheering erupted. But even that performance paled against the familiar spectacle of Marshall Hall's acting out the scales of justice by holding out his arms, tipping one way then the other in sequence in order to influence the jury's deliberation on the prisoner's guilt. Were the scales evenly balanced, as he held his arms out in a horizontal line? Then he *demanded* that his client (whether the artist Robert Wood in 1907 or Harold Greenwood, the Kidwelly solicitor in 1920, or Ronald Light in the 'Green Bicycle' case the same year, or John Derham in the 'Stella Maris' old-Etonian love triangle case at Tankerton, near Whitstable in 1926, which was Marshall Hall's last murder trial before he died) be acquitted as tears rolled down his eyes and as those of the jury welled up.[128] As a court room opponent, in a deflating put-down, disarmingly told a jury when appearing against the 'Great Defender', it almost moved him to tears, '....every time I hear it'. Or, as Mr. Justice Shearman (one of the founders of the Amateur Athletics Association in the late nineteenth century) affectionately described Marshall Hall's court room theatrics, 'I am always pleased when Sir Edward Marshall Hall refers to his well-known blindfold figure of Justice [with the scales swaying first one way then the other], because it means that he has come to the end of his speech...'[129]

Similarly, Birkett (and Marshall Hall) could be contrasted with the highly cerebral and 'brilliant' advocate, Rufus Isaacs, later Lord Reading, Lord Chief Justice. The latter possessed such mastery of commerce that he could disarm the most calculating of fraudsters like Whitaker Wright in 1904, and enjoyed a gift for fair (or at least not unfair) but deadly cross-examination questions: 'Mr. Seddon, did Miss Barrow live with you from July 1910 till September 1911 [when she died of arsenic poisoning]?' 'Yes'. 'Did you like her?' Since Frederick Seddon, the grasping and miserly insurance company supervisor, was charged with the murder of this eccentric and somewhat unappealing spinster whom he had arranged to be buried in a pauper's grave after her death and before her relatives were aware of her demise, Isaacs in effect offered up to the prisoner a poisoned chalice of an answer. If yes, why bury her in such an appallingly insensitive manner? If no, who then could doubt that Seddon, having admitted his dislike, would not at least lack remorse at her passing, thus impliedly inviting the jury to look favourably upon prosecution evidence suggestive of his having chosen to do away with her for her money? A killer question, it perhaps was, but unlike Birkett's cross-examination of another Mr. Isaacs in the Rouse case (chapter ten), it was surely a fair, and not a trick, question.[130]

Both the flamboyance and showmanship of Marshall Hall, and the eloquence, supreme intelligence and forensically clever cross-examination of Rufus Isaacs could themselves be contrasted with another court room opponent (albeit a friend) of Birkett's, who also featured in the Rouse case. This was Sir Patrick Hastings who disliked appearing in homicide cases. Indeed his appearances for Rouse in the Court of Appeal and for Elvira Barney, tried for murder at the Old Bailey, both in 1931, were untypical of a man more at home with celebrity divorces and libel actions. But his style was forensically sharp. His questions to those in the witness box were invariably brief, concise and to the point, in a manner which the jury would quickly grasp. Not for him the 'over-the-top' emotional theatrics of Marshall Hall or the brilliant, even oratorical, questions of Rufus Isaacs. But

128   The cases are discussed in, inter alia, Edward Marjoribanks, *Famous Trials of Marshall Hall*, Penguin, 1950 (first pub. 1929) and Nina Warner Hooke and Gil Thomas, *Marshall Hall: A Biography*, Arthur Barker, 1966. See also Sally Smith, *Marshall Hall: A Law unto Himself*, Wildy & Sons, 2016. Marjoribanks, a young Conservative MP and stepson of Attorney-General, Sir Douglas Hogg, later the first Lord Hailsham who subsequently served as a Conservative Lord Chancellor, shot himself in 1932. Politically hugely ambitious, he was twice unlucky in love.
129   Cited in Roberts, *op. cit*,. p. 52. Roberts was always known in the profession as 'Khaki '.
130   Interestingly, when, in a famous wartime case of 1942, Harry Dobkin was being tried for murdering his wife, he had been asked a similar question by counsel. However since he was estranged from her and had withheld maintenance payments from her, as a result of which he had served terms of imprisonment, he could scarcely answer other than 'No'. See Molly Lefebure, *Murder on the Home Front: The Unique Wartime Memoirs of a Pathologist's Secretary*, Grafton, 1990, p. 84. For the lasting forensic significance of the Dobkin case, see Alan Moss and Keith Skinner, *The Scotland Yard Files: Milestones in Crime Detection*, National Archives, 2006, ch. 11.

nor was he inclined to the cool, careful, passionless, almost sleep-inducing probing of Treasury Counsel, Sir Richard Muir (who also occasionally took on defence duties). Instead, his was a 'rat-a-tat-tat' approach to breaking down the opponent's witness, using six words in cross-examination where others might use twenty-six, and eschewing flowery or literary language. It was not an *obviously* brilliant style, but it was brilliantly effective. As Birkett, his admirer, described him in one case where a Liberal MP, Handel Booth, during the Great War had taken advantage of an interned German engineer called Gruban to milk the latter's business of funds, Hastings' hugely successful cross-examination of Booth (that 'rogue' and 'swindler') was 'relentless, ruthless, eager, vehement, scornful, satirical, contemptuous by turns'; and all achieved without resort to vigorous hand gestures that characterized other counsel.[131]

It is arguable, therefore, that of the above prominent counsel, Birkett is closer to Hastings in style than to Marshall Hall and Isaacs. Indeed, the age of court room theatrics and of emotional outpourings by counsel probably died along with Marshall Hall in 1927, while the intellectual 'brilliance' of Rufus Isaacs, Sir Edward Carson and F. E. Smith (later Lord Birkenhead), and the forcefulness and intelligence of Sir Henry Curtis-Bennett (notwithstanding his doomed defence of Edith Thompson), would not be matched in the future. Along with Rudolf Valentino, Marlene Dietrich, Mary Pickford, Charlie Chaplin, Gloria Swanson, Douglas Fairbanks, Greta Garbo and many others, they were the 'celebrities' of the age. Birkett was admired but scarcely a celebrity (though Spilsbury might have slipped into that category). Instead, he embodied a style of advocacy that preached sharpness, precision and relative conciseness. It was 'spare' in character, much like Birkett's own physical appearance. Indeed the gold propelling pencil with which he twiddled in court could, as suggested earlier, be a metaphor for the assassin's dagger plunging into the heart of the prosecution case (or, in the rare prosecution that he himself conducted, into the prisoner's heart). Yet, ironically, when we consider Hastings, his friend and opponent, the latter, unlike Birkett,

> "....had none of those irritating little habits such as fiddling with the tape on the brief or things of that kind. Serjeant Sullivan, I remember, used to drive his opponents to despair during a protracted trial by constantly tying and untying the tape on his brief or, what was much worse, by jingling the coins in his trouser pocket incessantly."[132]

Clearly, for Birkett, it was 'horses for courses'. Indeed, notwithstanding the brilliance of his forensic reputation which resulted in his being elevated to the Bench before the outbreak of the Second World War (an elevation he may have regretted with hindsight), the like of those 'celebrity' barristers would not last

---

131   Lord Birkett, *Six Great Advocates*, Penguin, 1961, pp. 25-29. Birkett discusses Marshall Hall, Rufus Isaacs and Hastings, among others.
132   *Ibid.*, p. 30. For counsel listed in the text, see also Majoribanks, *op. cit*; Andrew Rose, *Scandal at the Savoy*, Bloomsbury, 1991, p. 70; René Weis, *Criminal Justice*, Hamish Hamilton, 1988; Ronald Wild and Derek Curtis-Bennett, *'Curtis': The Life of Sir Henry Curtis-Bennett*, Cassell, 1937; Edward Grice, *Great Cases of Sir Henry Curtis-Bennett*, Hutchinson, 1937; Derek Walker-Smith, *Lord Reading and His Cases: The Study of a Great Career*, Chapman & Hall, 1934; Stanley Jackson, *Rufus Isaacs: First Marquess of Reading*, Cassell, 1936; R. F. V. Heuston, *Lives of the Lord Chancellors, 1885-1940*, Clarendon Press, Oxford, 1964, pp. 353-402 [on Birkenhead]; John Campbell, *F E Smith: First Earl of Birkenhead*, Pimlico, 1991.

the post-war era, though some distinguished barristers (who never became High Court or other superior court judges), including 'Khaki' Roberts, Derek Curtis-Bennett (son of Sir Henry), Anthony Hawke, Russell Vick, Richard O'Sullivan, Hartley Shawcross, J. D. Casswell, D. N. Pritt and John Platts-Mills, still attracted press and public attention after 1945. As another barrister, Richard Du Cann, well-known for his classic analysis of the 'Art of the Advocate' wrote in 1964,

> "It is, however, no use ignoring the fact that the status of the advocate both in the public eye and in the courts has diminished in recent years, and that it will probably continue to do so. Few corners of any profession are now free from public inquiry, and much of the mystique of the Bar has been subjected to considerable and almost universally adverse publicity. At the same time, the rival attractions of film and television, unknown in the days of [Carson, Marshall Hall, Rufus Isaacs, Patrick Hastings, Birkett etc], have been able to fulfil for the public that craving for public idols which previously the Bar and the stage almost equally used to meet. In this the diminution in the quantity of press reports of trials has played its part, while the more factual approach of the courts to the cases coming before them has tended to discourage idiosyncrasies in the practitioner which the public found so attractive."[133]

Perhaps more modern equivalents of the personalities of Dr. Crippen, George Joseph Smith, Thompson and Bywaters, even of Rouse, might be identified (though we doubt it). But it is difficult to imagine a combination of 1923's Mme. Fahmy and Marshall Hall in the same 'team' today. Arguably, Hastings' defence of the 'socialite', Elvira Barney, in 1931 represented the end of an era of '*matineé idol*' barristers. For, if we look to those defending comparable female murder accused, the defence of the 'glamorous' Alma Rattenbury in 1936 was committed to the more 'sober' hands of the less inspirational Terence O'Connor. Nonetheless, it could be argued that counsel defending the 'peroxide blonde' and nightclub hostess, Ruth Ellis, charged in 1955 with murdering her playboy racing-car driver, David Blakely, was of a similar stamp to the earlier 'heroes' of the court room. For her counsel, Melford Stevenson, was wont to making unrestrained observations on other personalities and events, which suggested an outspokenness bordering on the rude and reckless and a maverick streak, and which probably delayed his elevation to the bench. He had begun to carve out his reputation when prosecuting war criminals. For example, he successfully conducted the *Peleus* trial in October 1945 when he secured the conviction of Captain Eck of U-852 and of five members of his crew (three, including Eck, were subsequently hanged) for the murder of survivors of the sinking by the U-boat of a Greek merchant ship in 1944 by shooting them in the water. Yet while Melford Stevenson unsuccessfully raised, at Ruth's trial, an important legal point about 'slow-burn' provocation (which anticipated law reform in 2009), the rest of his defence of his client was strangely muted and, to observers, half-hearted. Could one ever say that of the 'giants' of the previous generation of barristers?[134]

---

133 Richard Du Cann, *The Art of the Advocate*, Penguin, 1964, p. 25.
134 See his *Oxford DNB* entry. The large house in which he lived in Winchelsea, near Rye, Sussex, was called 'Truncheons'. There are of course numerous accounts of the Ruth Ellis case. For one of the more recent see Carol Ann Lee, *A Fine Day For a Hanging: The Real Ruth Ellis Story*, Mainstream, 2012. For academic analysis of the case, see Sue Tweg, "Not the Full Story: Representing Ruth Ellis", *Biography*, Vol. 23 (1), Winter, 2000, pp. 1-28; Anette Ballinger, "The

Admittedly, in recent years there have been barristers verging on the 'celebrity', including George Carman, Anthony Scrivener, Michael Mansfield, Geoffrey Robertson and Helena Kennedy. They are well-known, if not necessarily household, names. But these practitioners were very unlike their predecessors in the first three decades of the twentieth century and, indeed, unlike the post-war barrister and Nuremberg war crimes prosecutor, Mervyn Griffith-Jones, who in the 1960 prosecution for obscenity of Penguin Books, the publisher of D. H. Lawrence's *Lady Chatterley's Lover*, innocently asked the jury 'Is it a book that you would even wish your wife or your servants to read?' Thus it is admiration rather than adoration or adulation that attaches to those more modern practitioners from the 1970s onwards, named above, who became distinguished for their court room advocacy. They were not (or are not) popular 'stars'. But Birkett was, just.

Before examining the judge at the trial, Mr. Justice Talbot, it remains to mention two other barristers present at Rouse's trial. The first was Birkett's junior, Richard Elwes, from a prominent Northamptonshire family. The son of Gervase Elwes, a noted English tenor at the start of the twentieth century, he was called to the bar in 1925. A Territorial Army officer, he served in various adjutant-general posts during the Second World War. After the war he became recorder of Northampton (1946-58) before being appointed to the High Court bench. One of his children from his marriage to the elder daughter of Sir Mark Sykes of Sledmere, the politician and diplomat and joint author of the Sykes-Picot Agreement of 1917 carving up Western influence in parts of the Middle East, was Polly Elwes, a well-known television broadcaster with the 'Tonight' programme in the 1960s (she died in 1987) who married the fellow BBC broadcast and sports presenter, Peter Dimmock, who died in November 2015. The choice of Elwes as junior to Birkett would have been noted by the local press since his family featured frequently in the newspapers' society and gossip columns. Moreover no-one in court or on the jury would have been unaware of his local connections.

The other barrister in court was a former journalist, Sidney Campion, who was retained by Harry Flint, the solicitor of the 'mystery veiled woman', Helen Campbell, to maintain a watching brief on the proceedings on behalf of his client. Campion, of course, took no direct part in the proceedings and his voice was never heard in court. Perhaps that was an augury of things to come for him. He had joined the legal profession late, as did Rouse's prosecutor, Birkett, who himself had been thwarted in his pursuit of a career as a journalist after graduation. Indeed so had Rouse's leading counsel at his appeal, Sir Patrick Hastings, between 1902 and 1903, as well as the presiding judge at Rouse's appeal, Gordon Hewart, who had also spent a number of years as a journalist before entering the law. But unlike Birkett, Hastings and Hewart, Campion did not stay the legal course and after a couple of years at the bar reverted to his previous occupation as a journalist.

But during the Rouse proceedings Birkett had shown kindness towards Campion in the latter's new choice of career. As Bardens, another biographer of Birkett, explained, the press had homed in on this 40-year-old new addition to

Guilt of the Innocent and the Innocence of the Guilty: The Cases of Marie Fahmy and Ruth Ellis", in Alice Myers and Sarah Wight (eds), *No Angels: Women Who Commit Violence*, Pandora Press, 1996, pp. 1-28; Lizzie Seal, "Ruth Ellis and Public Contestation of the Death Penalty", *Howard Journal of Criminal Justice*, Vol. 50 (1), 2007, pp. 173-96.

the profession. 'Newspaper seller to barrister', announced a headline. As Bardens recounted Campion's explanation,

> ".... it was not surprising that Norman Birkett was curious about me. He took my arm and led me aside for a private chat, saying that he was interested in me coming to the Bar so late in life, although he knew two others who had made a success of it even later.[135] Did I, he asked, intend forsaking Fleet Street? Or would I run in double harness? If so, was it a wise move? It might be if I were in the twenties, but in the forties, ah! That was another matter. Unless I had private resources I would find it terribly difficult to make a living during the first few years." [136]

Campion spoke warmly of Birkett's 'eagerness to help' and of his being 'cordial without being effusive, friendly without being patronising'. In his autobiography,[137] Campion explained his difficult passage through life which encompassed, inter alia, newspaper boy, local reporter, airman during the Great War, publisher of poems, Poor Law guardian and town councillor in Chorley, member of the Independent Labour Party, failed Labour candidate for Oswestry in the 1923 general election (he stood against W. C. Bridgeman, the Home Secretary who refused to reprieve Edith Thompson from the gallows), schoolmaster, then member of the editorial staff of the *Daily News* by 1926. Perhaps he was a polymath but soon thereafter he resolved to become either a doctor or a lawyer in his spare time. Financial constraints certainly precluded the former. And while the latter also posed financial challenges (as Birkett made clear to him), at least he had wide journalistic experience of the whole gamut of criminal courts from which to draw guidance. Yet despite failing a number of bar exams first time round (he was, of course, studying only in his limited spare time), and anxious about the economic turbulence sweeping through Fleet Street which forced the shocked closure of the *Daily Chronicle*, he was called to the bar. The date was November 17, 1930, the very day when Helen Campbell's solicitor, Henry Flint, was announcing at Rouse's police court hearing that he (Flint) was representing an unnamed woman concerned in the case.[138] As Campion ruefully noted, his initial foray into court advocacy, which involved the Rouse case and another at the Old Bailey concerning a woman charged with murdering her child but who was detained on grounds of insanity, amounted to '....interesting experiences. They brought me a certain amount of fame but no fortune'.[139] So he returned to journalism though he remained determined also to succeed as an author, in which endeavour he achieved modest recognition.[140] At the end of his career he was a civil servant

135 This presumably referred both to Hewart and to Sir Patrick Hastings, Rouse's counsel at his appeal.
136 Bardens, *op. cit.*, p. 153.
137 Sidney R. Campion, *Only the Stars Remain*, Rich & Cowan, 1946, *passim*.
138 *Evening News*, November 18, 1930. As noted earlier, Flint appointed Campion as Helen's watching brief. From 1933 until 1940 Campion was chief of Allied (Kemsley) Newspapers parliamentary staff, then became chief press and broadcasting officer for the Post Office, holding the post until retirement in 1957.
139 Campion, *op, cit.*, p. 125.
140 In 1939 he claimed to have spotted Victor Grayson, the former Independent Socialist MP for Colne Valley (1907-10), getting on a tube train with a female companion at Sloane Square. This was many years after Grayson's mysterious and unsolved disappearance in 1920. Campion, however, had had no opportunity to approach him before the couple suddenly left the train at Westminster station just after the supposed Grayson had remarked to his companion, 'Ah, the old Firm!'. A

working for the wartime government, applying his 'special journalistic abilities to assist the General Post Office in educating the public on its many services'.[141]

Finally, we must explore the career of Mr. Justice Talbot. Sir George John Talbot (1861-1938) was 69 when he presided over Rouse's trial. The son of a former Conservative member of parliament, public school and Oxford educated, and descended from eminent judges traceable on both his and his wife's side, he was a predictable fit for the bar, unlike the drapers' sons, Birkett and Hewart. A late appointment to the bench at the age of 62 to replace, on the latter's retirement, the flamboyant and occasionally ridiculous Lord Darling in 1923 (who later contributed to the Lords' debate on the Rouse case in 1931) probably precluded his promotion to the higher courts, though he did sometimes sit in the Court of Criminal Appeal alongside two other judicial colleagues. For example, he gave the leading speech in 1930 in the appeal of an American, James Achew, against conviction for murdering his mistress, Sybil da Costa, in north London in November 1929. The prisoner's plea of insanity had been rejected by the jury at his trial, presided over by Mr. Justice Avory. The appeal judges held that while the accused had harboured 'insane' delusions of da Costa's unfaithfulness, that in itself did not amount to insanity for legal purposes under the restrictive McNaghten rules. Thus Achew had been properly convicted.[142] What came over in Talbot's judicial performances, perhaps reflecting his ascetic approach to life (his love of country walking and his daily cold baths) were a sense of dignity, application, seriousness but not pomposity, patience and courtesy; and it is difficult to argue with this assessment in the way in which he conducted the Rouse trial. For he was eminently fair towards the prisoner, allowing Rouse a degree of latitude during the latter's vain, tetchy and verbose exchanges with his interlocutors (it would be grossly unfair but deliciously rewarding to suggest that the judge's indulgence was his 'cunning plan' to ensure that a despicable individual would condemn himself out of his own mouth; but such a strategy would presumably have been unworthy of such a devout Christian). In passing, it might be observed that one possible consequence of Talbot's restrained judicial style was that, as stated in his Oxford DNB entry, "....(although he tried at least one sensational murder case) his name was unknown to the readers of the popular newspapers". Or, as his admirer and fellow-judge (and no judicial slouch), Sir Frank MacKinnon, wrote, following the latter's promotion to the Court of Appeal, 'With a taste for epigram one might be tempted to say that he is the best judge whose name is known to the fewest readers of the *Daily Mail*. On that, or on any other test, Talbot was the best judge I have known'.[143]

Of course, apart from those noted above, there were other legal personnel involved in the Rouse case. There was, for example, the clerk to the magistrates, and also the local coroner who conducted the inquest into the sudden death of the unknown victim. However their roles were modest and limited. On the other hand,

---

journalistic scoop thus slipped through Campion's fingers. See Hyde, *A Tangled Web, op. cit.,* pp. 212-15. The fullest account of the enigmatic Grayson is David Clark, *Victor Grayson: Labour's Lost Leader,* Quartet, 1985. Lord Clark of Windermere is a former Labour MP and was a shadow Defence Minister in the 1980s.

141   Campion, *op. cit.,* pp. 208-9.
142   Gordon Lang, *Mr. Justice Avory,* Herbert Jenkins Ltd, 1935, pp. 136-40.
143   Sir Frank MacKinnon, *On Circuit, 1924-1937,* Cambridge University Press, Cambridge, 1940. MacKinnon alludes only briefly to Talbot's involvement in the Rouse case. See *ibid.,* p. 188.

when we address Rouse's unsuccessful appeal in chapter thirteen, we shall note the professional careers and reputations of the judges before whom he appeared, Lord Chief Justice Hewart and Avory and Humphreys JJ., and also Rouse's new leading counsel at the hearing, the former Attorney-General, Sir Patrick Hastings. Whether the choice of appeal judges, in particular, Hewart, reinforced the belief by some that what was witnessed was a miscarriage of justice will be considered at that point.

CHAPTER SIX

RE-EXAMINATION BEHIND LOCKED DOORS

NORTHAMPTON CHRONICLE & ECHO, November 10, 1930

Inquest, Post-Mortems and Burial

On Friday November 7, Mrs. Rouse was requested by Northamptonshire police to attend the inquest on the corpse recovered from the burnt out Morris Minor. At that time it had not been conclusively established that the victim was *not* Rouse (who was probably travelling in the coach from Cardiff to London at the same time as Mrs. Rouse was asked to come to Northampton). In the event, and following Rouse's arrival at Hammersmith that evening, there was no longer a need for Mrs. Rouse to visit the mortuary. By this time, Saturday November 8, Rouse was himself in custody at Angel Lane police station where, among his torrent of self-incriminating pronouncements, he casually asked when the inquest was going to be conducted. The reason for his question was not immediately obvious. Perhaps it was to suggest that he was a concerned citizen bothered about the dreadful fate of his erstwhile passenger. In any event, Rouse was not present at the inquest held at noon that Saturday, but was, at that moment, putting together his last police statement before trial.

Thus after the debris of the car had been removed to police headquarters, an inquest on the body of the unidentified corpse opened at the Crown Inn, Hardingstone. As the *News of the World* described the event, 'Little outside interest appeared to be taken in the assembly, and the proceedings were formal in the extreme'.[144] Since its recovery the body had lain in the inn's garage where it had been initially examined by Dr. Eric Shaw, consultant pathologist at Northampton General Hospital, before its removal to the hospital where, due to its fragile state, it had been preserved in a tank filled with formaline. The coroner was C. H. Davies, coroner for the Midland Division of Northamptonshire. Under the Coroners (Amendment) Act 1926, a coroner appointed after the passing of the Act had to have held legal or medical qualifications for a period of at least five years. Indeed, some coroners, such as Sir Bentley Purchase in London, possessed both qualifications, and as he already had ten years experience as a deputy coroner in London, he was a shoe-in to be appointed by London County Council in 1930 as coroner for the metropolitan boroughs of Finsbury, Hampstead, Holborn,

---

144 *News of the World*, November 9, 1930.

Islington, St Pancras and the City of London.[145]

Whether Davies had dual qualifications is not known, but one effect of the 1926 Act was to limit the power of coroners effectively to usurp police criminal charges arising from violent, sudden or unexpected deaths when criminal investigations were being conducted. Indeed, the wings of nineteenth-century coroners, who previously could stand for election for the remunerative post as if they were parliamentary candidates, had already been clipped by parliament in mid-century. This followed campaigns involving Charles Dickens and the humanitarian founder of the *Lancet*, Dr. Thomas Wakley, who had exposed major failings, employer bias and gross medical ignorance on the part of coroners investigating sudden deaths.[146] After the passing of the 1926 Act, they could still issue warrants for murder, manslaughter or infanticide, as could magistrates, but section 20(5) of the 1926 Act now provided that

> "If on an inquest before verdict the coroner is informed that some person has been charged before examining magistrates with the murder, manslaughter or infanticide of the deceased, he shall, in the absence of reason to the contrary, adjourn the inquest until after the conclusion of the criminal proceedings. It shall be the duty of the clerk to the examining magistrates before whom a person is so charged to inform the coroner of the making of the charge and of the committal for trial or discharge as the case may be, of the person charged."

Eventually, the coroner would receive a notification from the clerk of assize of the outcome of any subsequent assizes trial arising out of the sudden death inquiry that he had been obliged to adjourn *sine die* (indeed, he might or might not have also later conducted the inquest into the executed man).

The provisions of section 20(5) therefore would obviously affect the scope of the Northamptonshire inquiry. Thus, swearing in his coroner's jury, Davies explained that while the inquiry was into the death of a person 'whose sex is unknown', he proceeded to announce that he did not propose to call any evidence that day and, instead, would adjourn the inquest *sine die*. Whenever the inquest was to be re-convened the jurors would receive three days notice to that effect. In explaining his action, he indicated that, 'Certain developments have occurred, and after consultation with the county police, I have come to the conclusion that it would not be proper that I should call any evidence today, or pursue the inquest further'.

Obviously he was aware that criminal investigations were continuing with the result that his own inquiry would be significantly constrained in eliciting cause of death and in indicting the person responsible. Thus had Rouse been present at the inquest (he was not), he would undoubtedly have been advised by the coroner not to answer incriminating questions. Indeed it is probable that, at that very moment, Rouse was making his infamous statement to Inspector Lawrence regarding his

---

145   Robert Jackson, *Coroner: The Biography of Sir Bentley Purchase*, Harrap, 1963, pp. 49-50.
146   Mary Beth Emmerichs, "Getting Away with Murder? Homicide and the Coroners in Nineteenth-Century London", *Social Science History*, Vol. 25 (1), Spring 2001, pp. 93-100; Joe Sim and Tony Ward, "The Magistrate of the Poor? Coroners and Deaths in Custody in Nineteenth-Century England", in Michael Clark and Catherine Crawford (eds.), *Legal Medicine in History*, Cambridge University Press, Cambridge, 1994, pp. 245-67.

expensive harem shortly before being charged by Superintendent Brumby around 4:00 pm with the murder of the unknown man.

But then a slightly farcical moment occurred just after the coroner had discharged the jury. For he immediately corrected himself by stating that, following post-mortems conducted by Dr. Shaw on November 6, it was realized that the body was actually male, rather than of indeterminate gender. It may be recalled that the police had at first suspected that the body was female in view, inter alia, of the discovery of a heel from a woman's shoe (probably Nellie Tucker's) in the wreckage. However, Dr. Shaw had not only found no evidence for the existence of female 'regenerative' organs in the corpse, but the size and shape of the pelvic bones clearly suggested a male body. Moreover he had located a stump which he took to be the remains of the victim's penis and, the clincher, he found what appeared to be a prostate gland which, when cut through, released seminal fluid.

On the adjournment of the inquest Brumby and Superintendent Tebbey held a conference with Shaw and with other medical staff in a corridor of the inn, after which Shaw conducted a second post-mortem behind the locked doors of the Crown Inn's garage. According to press reports, this was to explore whether there was any trace of a bullet wound on the body. Indeed, Brumby and Tebbey, with a number of constables, set off for the crime scene some 159 yards away to carry out a thorough search for any bullets among the debris. A handful of villagers looked on while Brumby, with a rake, and another officer searched the charred ground. They went over the ground in a most minute fashion, picking up small items only to discard them again. No bullets were found, but no doubt the search had been prompted by the revelation from Rouse's acquaintances that he had been in possession of a revolver and had shown it to his women in the past. When the policemen returned empty-handed to the inn, Dr. Shaw once more examined the corpse for nearly two hours, removing some of the organs for further investigation in his pathology laboratory.[147] In the event the inquest was never resumed and the inquiry was, in fact, formally terminated by the coroner some months later, after Rouse's execution. So an order for the burial of the unidentified body was issued by him, which burial took place on March 20, 1931. The jurors' and witnesses' fees were duly paid on April 2, 1931.[148]

The burial itself is worth examining for what it might suggest as to attitudes to the death of unknown persons in 1931. The respect shown to the unknown victim ('whom no one would miss', Rouse had reflected) is striking. He was laid to rest in the graveyard at Hardingstone Church. Perhaps some minds went back to the post-Great War period when an article in *The Times* on January 12, 1920 remarked, surely surprisingly, that the war had given respectability to the tramp (assuming Rouse's victim could be labelled thus). For such a character was imbued with patriotism and had done 'his bit' during the war, thereby demonstrating that he 'would work if he got it' as, perhaps, would Rouse's victim had he reached Leicester.[149] Thus on March 18, 1931, Brumby spoke to

147   *Evening News*, November 8, 1930; *The Times*, November 10, 1930.
148   NPA, Brumby to Chief Constable, April 10, 1931.
149   The authors are grateful to Douglas Commaille, a former postgraduate student at Kent University, for this reference to *The Times*.

the chairman of Hardingstone parish council, Mr. Tickler, regarding the unknown man's burial. They both then called upon the local vicar and it was agreed to hold the burial as soon as possible thereafter. Tickler suggested that Brumby should now call upon Mr. Tye, of W. G. Ward, Undertakers, Northampton, about making the coffin and other arrangements. The tramp's burial at last took place at six o'clock on the morning of Friday March 20, some ten days after Rouse's execution. The authorities had decided that the event should be conducted in secret, perhaps to ensure that the morbidly curious should be denied the opportunity to relish what some might enjoy as a ghoulish experience. Indeed even the grave-digger had been kept ignorant of the burial until late the previous evening.[150]

The charred remains had been taken the previous night from Northampton General Hospital where they had been preserved for five months and formally handed over by Dr. Shaw's laboratory assistant to the custody of the divisional police represented by Brumby. The remains were placed in a plain elm coffin and passed over to the undertaker for the night. As it set off in a motor hearse for Hardingstone early the next morning, it converged with a police car near Angel Lane police station which was carrying Brumby, Lawrence and PC Valentine as 'official mourners' and witnesses at the burial. At the graveyard they were joined by Sergeant Harris and PC Copping. All five had given evidence at Rouse's trial and just as the church clock struck six o'clock, the cortege reached the graveyard where the Hardingstone Church minister, the Rev. J. D. Massey, was to take the full burial service. The coffin was, of course, lighter than normal for an adult male.

As the coffin, placed on a bier, was being taken into the church, Brumby stepped forward to place on it a large and expensive wreath of lilies, red carnations and other flowers. It bore the inscription, 'With deepest sympathy, from the Officers and Constables of the Northampton and Daventry Divisions of the Northamptonshire Constabulary'. It was the only floral tribute to the unknown man. The coffin itself was of superior quality with brass fittings (contrast this with the cheapest plain deal coffins that Seddon and George Joseph Smith chose for their victims), and was inscribed, 'An Unknown Man. Died 6th November, 1930'. As the *Northampton Herald* put it,[151]

> "The funeral service was conducted by the Vicar with solemnity and dignity, and it was a very moving scene, heightened by the effect of the unusually early hour. Although the villagers even [sic] were unaware of what was transpiring, there were one or two people, apart from the police, who were present in the church and at the graveside....At the graveside the Vicar read the committal sentences, and the impressive silence of the early morning scene could almost be felt. It was indeed a memorable scene with the dawn just breaking. Towards the East the sky was tinged with the rising sun, giving promise of another glorious Spring day. In the trees the birds were commencing their morning salutations. The police officers stood in a small group with bared heads, and heard the words of the committal prayer pronounced by the Vicar."

The rector placed more flowers on the grave later in the day, and for the next two days crowds of people visited the graveside, with a constable on duty

---

150   *Daily Mail*, March 21, 1931.
151   *Northampton Herald*, March 20, 1931.

to ensure, reported Brumby, that 'no damage was done'. A wooden cross now marks the grave where the body lies, though it is not in fact the original position of the burial, which was nearer the church wall than the current location. On the cross is written simply, 'In Memory of an Unknown Man, Died November 6, 1930', with no further elaboration of the circumstances. The grave is not difficult to find and at least the wording is legible, unlike many of the inscriptions on stone tombstones to be found in any churchyard today. The cross's starkness and simplicity, however, fail to capture the genuine sense of community 'ownership' of the corpse which those participating at the burial service undoubtedly felt. As one writer, Byron Rogers, noted when visiting the grave, '....it is not just a personal loss. These places were part of our heritage. It was possible in living memory to go into a graveyard in Banbury and see the grave of Lemuel Gulliver, where once Jonathan Swift paused, just as Beatrix Potter paused in a London cemetery and found a tombstone to the Nutkin family'.[152] It is said that on the anniversary of the un-named victim's death, an unknown visitor lays flowers on his grave.

Regarding the burial at Hardingstone, those present (all were men except Mrs. Massey, wife of the vicar) were surely witness to solemnity, dignity, a 'moving scene', and the word 'glorious'; to an unknown and unrecognizable body that was formerly someone's son, or brother, or husband; to dawn breaking, sun beginning to glint, and heads bowed, but with birdsong starting to rise triumphantly from the solitude. It could almost have been the last burial of an Unknown British Soldier before the guns fell silent on November 11, 1918, or the prelude to an equally reverential ceremony of interment of the Unknown Warrior at Westminster Abbey exactly two years later.

> "The Lord Knoweth Them That Are His,
> Greater Love Hath No Man Than This
> Unknown and Yet Well Known, Dying and Behold We Live
> In Christ Shall All Be Made Alive".

Sentiments of patriotism reflected in Rupert Brooke's poem, *Dulce et Decorum Est Pro Patria Mori* [How Sweet and Beautiful It is to Die for One's Homeland], had already received their debunking at the pen of Wilfred Owen before he, himself, fell silent just days before the Armistice. And whether Rouse's unknown victim was, like him, a non-believer, may only be known if identification were ever to be established. But that is not the point. The point was one of respect and dignity, to challenge the throwaway remark of his killer that here was a man whom no-one would miss. The Unknown Warrior of Westminster Abbey might well have been a symbol for all the tragic losses in Britain during the First World War. But the Unknown Man of 1930 embodied a symbol of the eternal element of bereavement, mourning, community and the banishment of indifference. The two, the Unknown Warrior and the Unknown Victim of Hardingstone, were not very far apart in spiritual terms.

Why that was so, and why the latter received such respectful cherishing at

---

152 *Daily Telegraph*, April 20, 2002. Sinister examples can be found in the identity theft of a name from a tombstone described in Frederick Forsyth's *The Day of the Jackal* and, more recently, in the actions of undercover policemen borrowing the identities of dead children as part of their schemes to infiltrate environmental protest groups.

his graveside can, perhaps, be better understood when we briefly consider contemporary attitudes to death, especially premature decease, on the part of British men and women, especially in the light of the First World War experience. After a Victorian era of fatalism towards early deaths, manifested in private and secluded grief, attention would turn to what was the appropriate public space in which to mourn. The burials of the Unknown British Warrior of the Great War and of the unknown victim of Guy Fawkes Night pointed to a different ritual from the past. For previously, it was accepted that premature deaths were almost as routine, and to be forgotten as quickly as possible, as was living to a ripe old age. But after the slaughter of the Western Front and the Armistice, loss became more precious, more regretted, indeed, if possible, 'reversible' through the activities of spiritualists, mediums and *séances* as families sought to maintain 'contact' with their deceased loved ones, a kind of cognitive dissonance, and as society collectively commemorated loss through the interment of the Unknown Soldier in different nations.[153] Meanwhile, as if to emphasise or symbolise the 'eternal' qualities of Rouse's victim, a metal box containing newspaper accounts of Rouse's trial was buried with the charred remains in his coffin. And for a number of years thereafter, children from Hardingstone would put flowers on his grave every November, a practice that ended some time during the Second World War. Of course, he is not forgotten. Indeed the vibrancy of his story emerges in a striking fashion through literature, through further accounts of the case which may add new analyses of the events, or through more and more hopeful scientific breakthroughs. Metaphorically, his vitality is still with us, even if his name eludes us. We will note in the next chapter, when exploring the list of possible victims of the blaze in 1930, the thwarted hopes of hundreds at the time. But even today, we can feel the frustration of the Briggs family who in 2013 were unsuccessful, in seeking through DNA testing to reclaim the long-deceased victim as one of theirs. Indeed, in recent years the press mentioned the name of a Mr. Pepper, 'Briefly a hit-man for Al Capone, who told his girlfriend he was being given a lift to Leicester on November 5', and that of the uncle ("Bill") of a Mrs. Townsend of Rugby, an uncle who had always come home for Christmas but did not do so in 1930, nor did so ever again.[154] Perhaps, like the Unknown Warrior, the Unknown Tramp should rest in peace, unknown.

The Post-Mortems

As previously noted, Dr. Eric Shaw had carried out post-mortems, three in fact, at the garage of the Crown Inn, on November 6, November 8 and November 10 to ascertain, inter alia, the gender of the victim, the cause of death and any identifying features. The last-named post-mortem was conducted jointly with Sir Bernard Spilsbury both at the garage and later at the hospital. Cause of death was quickly discovered (shock caused by burning), while the size of the victim's

---

153   For illustrative material, see Pat Jalland, *Death in the Victorian Family*, Oxford University Press, Oxford, 1996; *Ibid., Death in War and Peace: A History of Loss and Grief in England, 1914-1970*, Oxford University Press, Oxford, 2010; Jay Winter, *Sites of Memory, Sites of Mourning: The Great War in European Cultural History*, Cambridge University Press, Cambridge, 1995; Neil Hanson, *The Unknown Soldier: The Story of the Missing of the Great War*, Corgi, 2007; Juliet Nicolson, *The Great Silence 1918-1920: Living in the Shadow of the Great War*, John Murray, 2009.
154   *Daily Telegraph*, April 20, 2002.

pelvis and the discovery of fragments of a diseased prostate gland confirmed that the body was not, after, all female. But as to identity, there was puzzlement. The police believed only at that stage that the victim had been 'of a good station in life, fairly well built, and about 5ft. 7in. or 5ft. 8in. in height'.[155] It is unnecessary to recount in full the graphic descriptions, as found by the pathologists, of the gruesome destruction wrought on the corpse by the intense heat of the blaze. A few examples will suffice. Thus the 'brain appeared as a pulped and desiccated mass'. The 'muscles of the face were burnt and separated from the zygoma on either side'. The 'right foot was found on the running board of the car, separated from the limb and badly charred and shrunken'. The 'whole of the vault of the skull was missing'. Most vividly,

> "...the external organs of generation were missing except for a stump representing the penis. The anus was destroyed and the rectum exposed with soft faeces occupying the opening. The skin was completely burnt off the rest of the body and no hair was found anywhere".

Much attention was focused on the position of the corpse and, in particular, on the legs and arms, as recalled by the policemen at the scene. For the pathologists believed that the awkward and unusual position in which the corpse was found was consistent with the body having been roughly thrown across the front seats by another (which, of course, was not proof that that was what had actually occurred). The state of the victim's clothing and, in particular, the piece of moist clothing smelling of petrol found in the fork between the legs was, it might be inferred, suggestive of both the corpse having been doused with petrol before ignition, and also of the pulled up position of the left leg protecting that sliver of cloth from the flames. Yet, 'There was no sign of fracture of the skull itself', a finding that could have benefited the prisoner by refuting any suggestion that Rouse had attacked the victim with, specifically, his mallet. As Shaw concluded after one of his preliminary examinations,

> "....the following explanation of the mode of death is possible. From the position of the body when found, suggestive of struggle, from the marked presence of the pink staining of the viscera, suggesting absorption of carbon monoxide, from the presence of black fragments of mucous [sic] in the mouth and bronchi, it seems probable that the man moved and breathed after the fire started."

While he added that further examination would be required before those findings could be confirmed, Shaw did not observe any wounds on the remains or, as just noted, any direct evidence of violence to the skull. However, the smell of petrol on the recovered piece of cloth might, he thought, suggest that the body had first been soaked in petrol and, possibly, rendered unconscious before the blaze had started.

In broad terms this was the prosecution's theory of the case, including how the corpse ended up in the stretched-out posture which the pathologist assumed to be its position in the car. But Shaw had not, of course, seen the victim *in situ*, no

---

155   *The Times*, November 10, 1930.

photographs had been taken of the cadaver before its removal from the car, and not two but three policemen offered slightly different descriptions of the condition of the corpse before it was bundled up in sacking (carefully or unceremoniously, we do not know) and transferred to the Crown Inn's garage. Needless to say, the criminal inferences from the pathology analyses would be disputed by the defence, as we shall see when we later turn to the court proceedings themselves.

According to one of his biographers, the Blazing Car Murder was 'probably the high watermark [sic] of Spilsbury's career'.[156] However, the famous pathologist's reports in the case are not free from criticism in that speculation still informed some of his judgments. Indeed, we know from Spilsbury's performance at the trial of the Crowborough chicken farmer, Norman Thorne, in 1925 that the prisoner, convicted and hanged for the murder of Elsie Cameron, whose dismembered and then buried body had been discovered in his chicken run, considered himself a 'martyr to Spilsburyism' when the jury, spurred on by the judge, Mr. Justice Finlay, chose to accept the single voice of Sir Bernard to the seven (yes, seven) defence medical experts whose testimony strongly raised the possibility that the victim had hanged herself. In the Rouse case Spilsbury was brought into the investigation four days after Shaw's initial examination. Another of Spilsbury's biographers suggests that this was symptomatic of a provincial police force's reluctance to cede its priority standing in a murder inquiry to Scotland Yard. But of course the victim's death was somewhat unusual and Spilsbury surely had more experience in investigating violent deaths (which the police, by now, suspected was the case) than most pathologists.[157] So Sir Bernard travelled to Northampton. As another of his biographers noted, the relevant questions were,

1. Did death occur prior to or after the commencement of the blaze?
2. Is the cause of death fire-related? If so, [what cause]....
   If not, what is the cause of death?
3. Why was the victim in the fire?
4. Why was the victim unable to escape the fire?[158]

The results of his examination of the corpse, which he characteristically scribbled on the spot in his case-cards before typing them up on November 25, did confirm Shaw's findings regarding the gender and physical condition of the corpse, the organic destruction, the presence of considerable amounts of carbon monoxide and of black deposits resembling particles of smoke. He agreed with Shaw's finding that there was no fracture in the skull caused by a blow or a weapon, as distinct from the skull collapsing in upon itself due to the intense heat. Indeed, Spilsbury could find no evidence to confirm that the victim had been rendered unconscious before death. He added, however, that a possible suggestion to this effect, albeit one disputed by the defence medical expert, Dr R. B. Harvey-Wyatt of Harley Street (who later became coroner for South London and, ironically, would

---

156 Andrew Rose, *Lethal Witness: Sir Bernard Spilsbury, Honorary Pathologist*, Sutton Publishing, Stroud, 2007, p. 185.
157 Colin Evans, *The Father of Forensics: How Sir Bernard Spilsbury Invented Modern CSI*, Icon Books, 2007, p. 229.
158 *Ibid.*, p.230.

jointly sit as coroner, with Sir Bentley Purchase, on the inquest into the suicide of Spilsbury in late 1947)[159], could be drawn from his (Spilsbury's) analysis of the workings of 'heat rigor' combined with the position in which the corpse was found.[160] And, of course, Spilsbury had estimated from the presence of carbon monoxide in the blood that the deceased had still been alive in the car for about thirty seconds before death ensued (though that is not, *per se*, inconsistent with the victim being conscious *or* unconscious when the fire started). As to Rouse's mallet, found fourteen yards in front of the wreckage, it had, in Shaw's opinion, at least one human hair attached to it and, according to Spilsbury, *appeared* to have (but no more than that) a human hair attached to it. Given this cautious finding, the pathologists could not directly link the mallet to the initial unconsciousness of the victim, even though Birkett, for the Crown, proceeded on the assumption that a blow on the head from the mallet had rendered the deceased insensate (the judge instructed the jury to ignore the mallet while a post-execution newspaper confession under Rouse's name stated that he had throttled the victim into unconsciousness). Indeed Birkett appeared to persist at the trial in ignoring his own expert witnesses' testimony when, for example, he asked the defence medical expert, Dr Harvey-Wyatt, 'What I am plainly suggesting is that an unconscious man was thrown into that posture. Dr Harvey-Wyatt: If the facts are as you say, yes'. We can readily appreciate that such an answer would be music to the ears of the Crown in that it was anything but a strong denial by Harvey-Wyatt that the victim had been unconscious when 'thrown' into the car (which would point to Rouse's criminal behavior rather than to accident). Harvey-Wyatt also failed to add in his reply that the victim's unconsciousness, if such indeed had been the case, could have stemmed from factors other than a blow on the head from the mallet. It was certainly permissible for Birkett to put leading questions to one's own expert witnesses (as well as in cross-examination to Harvey-Wyatt). But whether this paragon of a counsel proceeded to put inadmissible leading questions to the Crown's non-expert witnesses at other points on the trial, thus contributing to unease as to whether Rouse had received a fair trial, will be explored subsequently.

Regarding the victim's teeth, their condition suggested the victim had been aged around thirty and, given the destruction of the limbs, he could have been two or three inches shorter *or* taller than Shaw's estimate of 5ft. 7in. or 5ft. 8in. While the prostate disease was typical of middle-aged and older men, younger men could be affected in this way as a result of gonorrhea. The victim possessed small features, was neglectful of dental hygiene, perhaps suggestive of lower social status (contrary to early police conclusions) and, given the black deposits in the lungs, might have had connections with the mining industry. Yet Shaw also added that

159 Jackson, *Coroner, op. cit.*, p. 191. Perhaps Harvey-Wyatt's most famous inquest was into the death of Rachel Dobkin, whose skeletal remains were found 15 months after she was murdered in a heavily damaged church in Kennington in April 1941 by her estranged husband, Harry, subsequently hanged. The scientific aspects of the investigation were as memorable as in the Buck Ruxton case. See Molly Lefebure, *Murder on the Home Front: The Unique Memoirs of a Pathologist's Secretary*, Grafton, 1990, Ch. 10.
160 Douglas G. Browne and E. V. Tullett, *Bernard Spilsbury: His Life and Cases*, Companion Book Club, 1952, p. 337. See also Harold Dearden, *Some Cases of Sir Bernard Spilsbury and Others: Death Under the Microscope*, Hutchinson, 1948, pp. 35-42 (first published, 1934). Dearden's brief account has a number of shortcomings.

the black fragments, together with the oedema and haemorrhaging in the lung, were due to inhalation of smoke and of very hot air. In short, the victim might *not* have had mining connections, though he was certainly alive and continued to breathe for some time after the fire had started. However, Shaw estimated, from the absence of carbon monoxide in the blood, that this would have been for only a very short time, later fixed at thirty seconds, before the victim stopped breathing and died. This report of November 25 formed the basis of Shaw's evidence at the committal proceedings.

But it was Spilsbury's supplementary report of January 27, 1931, prepared the day before he testified at the trial itself, which would prove especially damaging for Rouse. For it focused not on the actual mechanical cause of death (that is, shock brought about by burns) but on Spilsbury's ideas of how the victim, whom he also had not seen *in situ*, had come to be found in such a puzzling position in the burnt-out car. Thus apart from commenting on the suspicious state of the recovered piece of cloth where the left leg had been pulled up to the abdomen, the January report (which his previous report had not done) put forward the famous pathologist's opinion that the corpse's position, found across the two front seats, was a result of his being 'pitched or....flung into the car from the near side [so that he] fell face downwards across the front seats', thus inviting the reader to infer a physical assault on the victim from behind (though, as noted earlier, this had also been raised as a possibility in Shaw's conclusions). As to the position of the arms and legs, Spilsbury stated that this was due to 'heat rigor' following the intense blaze. But the novel feature of the January report was Spilsbury's assertion, advanced at the trial (though not mentioned by Shaw), that at least the nearside door, if not both doors, had been open at the start of the fire, thus permitting the victim's right leg to protrude through it.

> "Mr Norman Birkett: What do you say about the projection of the right leg beyond where the door was, according to the evidence in the case?
>
> Sir Bernard Spilsbury: I think that clearly shows that the door must have been open....."

This meant that Spilsbury was rejecting Finnemore's suggestion for the defence that the victim, trapped in a car with the doors *closed*, had,

> ".....extended his legs through the passenger door in the act of attempting to kick open the door to escape the burning car. Spilsbury was emphatic. 'He would have been dead long before that happened'".[161]

That is, Spilsbury's view was that the position of the corpse was consistent with Rouse's having pitched the victim across the front seats with at least the nearside door open (Rouse insisting that when he got to the car after pulling up his trousers, the doors were closed and he could not get near to the vehicle to rescue the man, he (Rouse) having withdrawn a previous account stating that he had been unable to open the car doors, implying that he had at least been 'near' the vehicle). And, as Spilsbury replied to Birkett, after death the right leg would

---

161 Evans, *op. cit.*, p. 238.

not extend but would be stiffened by the intense heat (this was the 'heat rigor' process in action). Thus the right foot, found on the running board, had been burnt off from the right leg which was *already* protruding through an *open* car door. Indeed, if the door had been closed, the leg, due to heat rigor, could not have moved outwards after death once the closed door had burned away.

The car doors had in fact been made of fabric and therefore were destroyed in the blaze, leaving a large gap at each side of the vehicle. But had they been closed at the start of the fire, as Rouse insisted when claiming that the blaze had been accidentally caused by the victim's lit cigar igniting petrol vapour or dropping onto the petrol in the spare can inside the car, it would, according to Spilsbury, have been a 'most difficult position' for the legs to adopt in the confined space of a small saloon car. Indeed, one might have thought that the question of whether the doors had been open or not would have been straightforward. But PC Copping was the only one of the four witnesses to the blaze (Copping, Brown, Hedley Bailey and Brown's cousin, William Bailey, son of Hedley) who was asked at the trial about the position of the car doors (the heat was so intense that the four had to stand some yards away from the blaze). And his response was simply that because the flames were so intense at the time, and because the fire had been burning so fiercely, the car had been too badly destroyed to tell.[162]

The author, Andrew Rose, has opined that, 'Spilsbury was embellishing his evidence, putting a spin on the sketchy accounts of the police officers at the scene', and that 'many of his conclusions seem to argue certainties not soundly based on the forensic evidence'. He also wondered why Finnemore had *not* challenged the 'great man' at the trial as to why Spilsbury's new testimony had not been given at the committal hearings. The words in inverted commas ('great man') may explain it. As his biographer concludes, 'The effect of Spilsbury's evidence was not lost on Rouse who, once Spilsbury had left the witness-box, leaned over the dock and had a close consultation with Finnemore.[163] We can guess that Rouse was already envisaging himself as another 'martyr to Spilsburyism' after Norman Thorne. Together with some questionable and effective courtroom tactics employed by Birkett, some contentious and disputed technical evidence regarding the source of the blaze, and a climate, among the good citizens (and jurymen) of Northamptonshire, which was hostile to philanderers who casually made reference to their harems, the dice was loaded against Rouse.

---

162 After the trial, a potential 'expert' witness contacted the police. He was Robert Barnett from Hackney, East London, an insurance claims inspector and principal of the firm of Stretton and Smith, automobile engineers, 12 Woodstock Street, London W 1. While he primarily sought to offer evidence regarding the origins of the fire, an offer seemingly not followed up by either side, he also explained that, as a 'big heavy man' with some experience of Morris Minors, 'he always gets out of that type of car backwards'. Whether he was thereby suggesting that Rouse might have known of the practical difficulty for larger occupants to extricate themselves from a Morris Minor, or whether he was suggesting that the victim might have died because he got stuck getting out of the car the wrong way after accidentally starting the blaze is open to debate. No more from Mr. Barnett was apparently heard during the case. See MEPO3/1660, Inspector A. W. Beath to Chief Inspector, CID, New Scotland Yard, February 5, 1931.

163 Rose, *op. cit.*, pp. 195-6.

CHAPTER SEVEN

WHO WAS THE MAN IN ROUSE'S CAR?

DAILY MAIL, November 10, 1930

Who Was the Victim?

"I'm a lone wolf, unmarried, getting middle-aged, and not rich. I've been in jail more than once....both parents dead, no brothers or sisters, and when I get knocked off in a dark alley sometime, if it happens.... nobody will feel that the bottom has dropped out of his or her life".

It could easily have been a reflection on his sad life by Rouse's unknown victim. Indeed, Rouse himself had stated of the victim, 'He was the sort of man no-one would miss....' But in fact, it expressed the musing of Raymond Chandler's fictional and hard-boiled detective, Philip Marlowe, a man who believed that he would not be missed in the slightest.[164] But Rouse's 'down-and-out' was certainly missed if one can judge from the copious correspondence received by Northamptonshire police from members of the public, hoping against hope that their missing relative had now been located, albeit that he had now been transformed into a hideously shaped, virtually carbonised, cadaver.

Where a fresh corpse arising from sudden death is discovered, identification will usually be straightforward, with relatives coming forward or personal items discovered on the body. Rouse's victim's case was extremely rare in that the body was never identified. However Rouse himself was not unique in being convicted and hanged in Britain for the murder of an unknown person.[165] For in 1786 three sailors were hanged for the murder of another seafarer at Hindhead on the London-Portsmouth road. Yet the identity of the victim was never established, although one author has recently suggested that he was Edward Hardman born

---

164 See, for example, the preface to Chandler's *Farewell My Lovely*, Penguin Books, 2005 ed; first published in 1940.

165 There have been convictions in Britain for murder in cases where the bodies were never recovered such as the 'Porthole Case' in 1947, when a ship's steward, James Camb, was convicted of murdering a passenger, Gay Gibson, aboard the *Durban Castle*. The jury decided that she had been strangled by Camb after intercourse, as distinct from her dying of heart failure at the time. Camb admitted pushing her corpse through a cabin porthole. The body was never recovered. See Denis Herbstein, *The Porthole Murder Case*, Hodder & Stoughton, 1991. Similarly, the Hosein brothers who murdered a newspaper executive's wife, Muriel McKay, after kidnapping her for ransom on December 29, 1969, were convicted in 1970 despite there being no body. See Robin Odell, *Landmarks in 20th Century Murder*, Headline, 1995, pp. 361-9.

in Lambeth in 1732.[166] However, we can distinguish the 1786 case from that of Rouse since it is likely that all the sailors involved knew each other while no link of any kind, apart from the blaze itself, has been established between Rouse and his passenger. Certainly, many hundreds, if not thousands, of unidentified corpses have been discovered over the past two centuries which have displayed signs of a violent end, but which discoveries have not led to charges, let alone convictions. Among the best-known examples is the female corpse which featured in the Brighton Trunk Murder Number One case in 1934 when separate parts of the same torso were found in left-luggage offices at Brighton and King's Cross railway stations. As the head and arms remained missing, the body was never identified nor a suspect apprehended.[167]

Spilsbury's card index recorded numerous cases of unidentified and mutilated bodies, including some dredged from canals or the sea, and whose condition suggested foul play rather than, say, having been violently cut up by ships' propellers. In one case in 1935 a pair of human legs and feet were found under the seat of a railway carriage at Waterloo Station. These were linked to male human remains found a month later in the Grand Union Canal at Brentford. Dismemberment had been carried out by someone with anatomical knowledge, though actual cause of death, whether a head blow or other assault, was not discovered. Police investigations were undertaken from surrounding clues, including pages of newspapers which were used to wrap the body parts but the man's identity was never discovered and no-one was charged with his murder. As the early biographers of Spilsbury stated, 'The dead man, like Rouse's victim, very probably belonged to the homeless and friendless class. Lacking head and hands, he was never traced. Neither was his murderer'.[168]

On the other hand there are numerous examples involving the careful reconstruction of a dismembered torso or parts of it, or of the skeletal remains of a murder victim whose identity could be discovered. Notable examples include the discovery in 1910 of the sliver of skin containing an old operation scar belonging to Cora Crippen (despite recent alternative views that no female DNA was found); the skeleton of Mamie Stewart, a twenty-year old actress who went missing in 1919 and whose skeleton was discovered by cavers in 1961 in a disused Welsh mine and whose assumed murderer had died in 1958; the remains of Emily Kaye, dismembered and boiled by Patrick Mahon in the 'Crumbles' murder in Eastbourne in 1924; the skeleton of Rachel Dobkin found in a bombed-out church in London in 1942 some 15 months after her murder by her estranged husband; the tell-tale

---

166   Peter Moorey, *Who Was the Sailor Murdered at Hindhead 1786? A Search for his Identity*, Blackdown Press, Haslemere, Surrey, 2000. There are many literary allusions to the case including by Dickens in *Nicholas Nickleby*.

167   See Odell, *op. cit.*, pp. 203-4. Amazingly, police inquiries led to the discovery of the Brighton Trunk Murder Number Two case the same year, in which the corpse of Violette Kaye was discovered in a Brighton flat. Tony Mancini stood trial for her murder but was acquitted, only to confess his guilt in the *News of the World* some 40 years later. See Odell, op. cit., pp. 203-6.

168   D. G. Browne and E. V. Tullett, *Bernard Spilsbury: His Life and Cases*, Companion Book Club, 1952, pp. 323-4. Numerous other similar examples could be cited, such as the 'Torso Mystery'. See *ibid.*, pp. 324-5. As the head and hands were missing, the coroner's jury could not formally indentify the victim or how he died, but there was a clear suspicion as to his identification. Superintendent George Hatherill, who finished his career investigating the Great Train Robbery in 1963 and was the driving force in the creation of the detective branch of the Royal Military Police in 1940, cited similar cases in his autobiography. See George Hatherill, *A Detective's Story*, Andre Deutsch, 1971, Ch. 5.

gall stone and false teeth of Mrs Olive Durand-Deacon, which were virtually all that remained of the body after its immersion in John George Haigh's 'acid bath' in1949; and the headless and legless torso of Donald Hume's victim, Stanley Setty, washed ashore in the Essex Marshes the same year; as well as those previously mentioned, including the bodies of Elsie Cameron and Violette Kaye. In 1936 the imposition of outlines of the victims' skulls on to earlier photographs of them, together with the discovery of a local and limited-edition issue of a newspaper in which the bodies of his wife and housemaid had been wrapped, led the police to the door of the Lancaster doctor, Buck Ruxton.[169] There are even cases where, on the discovery of a skeleton, murder was suspected until forensic examination confirmed that the person in question had taken his own life. This applied in the case of a decomposed body found in an abandoned car in a remote part of a mid-Wales forest. The owner of the vehicle was traced to a retired senior Army officer from near London. The decayed skull had been separated from the rest of the body as a result of a gunshot wound, a Luger pistol being found under the body. Yet the Army officer had apparently been seen alive just three weeks earlier. Had he therefore murdered someone some months earlier and had then sought to have the body identified as his own in order that a relative, in cahoots with him, could make an insurance claim? In fact, the only means of identification were the corpse's teeth and they showed conclusively that the remains were, indeed, those of the officer. He *had* committed suicide and the climatic conditions in the forest had accelerated the process of decomposition. 'Memories of the Rouse case...... [had] made identification an urgent matter', commented the author discussing the incident.[170] But it was a false (criminal) alarm.

Of course, in the days before DNA testing, identifying a victim consumed in a fire from which virtually only ashes or teeth were recovered remained a challenge to the authorities unless dental records, as with Rachel Dobkin and the retired Army officer, above, could confirm identity. But one of the most remarkable cases early in the twentieth century was an American mystery involving one Wenzel Kabat. In 1906 he offered to buy a farm from Michael McCarthy in Wisconsin for $18,000 cash. The sale was completed and McCarthy proposed to move to town to stay with a girl friend there. In fact the girl friend was two-timing him, almost certainly in cahoots with Kabat. But she and Kabat, too, next fell out and she soon ran off with yet another man. Meanwhile, McCarthy was never seen again. Eventually the police were called in and interviewed Kabat who had been assiduously tidying up the farm for some time, burning brush piles and other rubbish that had accumulated for years. The district attorney wondered whether, as McCarthy had not been seen in months he or, rather, his body, might never have left the farm, leaving Kabat in a financially favourable position. Kabat was invited to police headquarters and another team of policemen moved onto the farm while he was away, and sifted through the ashes of the bonfire. They had just unearthed parts of bones, some teeth, buttons, a shoe heel and a belt buckle when

---

169 It had originally been thought that one of the disarticulated corpses cut up by Ruxton had been male. It will be recalled that Rouse's victim was initially thought to have been female. This and the other cases discussed above are to be found in Odell, *op. cit.*, and in standard encyclopaedias of murder. The Notable British Trials series includes nearly all those cases cited. Many encyclopaedias of unsolved murders also exist.

170 Bernard Picton, *Murder, Suicide or Accident: The Forensic Pathologist at Work*, Robert Hale, 1971, pp. 92-3.

Kabat returned. He denied the finds were McCarthy's, insisting that they were animal remains. He came up with an explanation for the buttons and heel but dodged the question regarding the teeth. Though he was arrested and taken into custody, the breakthrough only occurred when a handwriting expert established that McCarthy's signature on the deed of sale was a forgery. In addition laboratory tests showed that the bone fragments were indeed human. Kabat still denied they were McCarthy's, insisting that the missing man was living not far away and that the brush fire could not have consumed a body, including the skull. After months of no progress in their investigation, the authorities decided to experiment as to whether a 32-hour brush fire could, indeed, consume virtually all of a body. Acquiring an unidentified corpse found in a Chicago morgue, they placed it on top of a large brush fire similar to that previously set alight on the farm, and after 32 hours only fragments of bone, but no skull, together with teeth and buttons, were left. Kabat was tried for murder in June 1906, his former girl friend having been found dead with her new lover in a Buenos Aires hotel. They had apparently left suicide notes. At the trial Kabat's past record for forgery was revealed, but more damaging was the dramatic revelation of the scientific evidence regarding the experiment with the unidentified body. He was convicted and sentenced to life imprisonment. While ethical objections to the experiment can be mounted, and while the sudden springing of the scientific evidence on the defence without warning is likewise inadmissible today, relevant forensic knowledge was still in its infancy at the time and criminal trial procedure was in a constant state of refinement.[171]

Rouse's was, of course, different to this case since his victim, for whose killing he paid the ultimate penalty, was never identified. Moreover, as he himself was identified as the killer unlike, for example, the Brentford Canal murderer, above, he became the unfortunate exception that proved the rule that, absent war crimes prosecutions, no-one else has been convicted of murdering an unidentified victim in Britain since 1786. Nonetheless, the mystery surrounding the blazing car victim's identity has lasted for nearly 90 years, confounding the exhaustive efforts of the police for many decades to put a name to the charred body. Around 2,000 people went missing annually in Britain in 1930 when unemployment was widespread and men often went 'on the tramp' nineteenth century-style, as classically depicted in one of Eric Hobsbawm's charming essays.[172] Moreover, there was a clear belief on the part of the Crown that Rouse's victim had been deliberately chosen by him as a man with few personal contacts and no fixed abode. However, where he was actually picked up by Rouse remains a matter of dispute. Was it outside the Swan and Pyramids pub in Whetstone, or at 'Tally Ho Corner', or was it 'this side of St Albans', as Rouse had also claimed?

Almost a week after the blaze at Hardingstone detectives in cars drove the whole length of the main road from London to Northampton in order to put questions to the occupants of nearly all the lodging houses, inns and commercial hotels on the route. They also stopped at many coffee stalls and petrol stations. But

---

171 For the case see John Sanders, *Forensic Casebook of Crime*, True Crime Library, 2005, pp. 106-13, which also discusses Kabat's interesting fate after his release from prison.
172 E. J. Hobsbawm, "The Tramping Artisan", in E. J. Hobsbawm, *Labouring Men*, Weidenfeld & Nicolson, 1964.

regarding the unknown victim they drew a blank.[173] Similarly, St Albans cafes and hotels were visited by Hertfordshire police on behalf of Brumby.[174] As we know, journalists as well as the police were anxious to identify the body. Rouse, himself, in his prison confession made to the governor (chapter 16), had tantalisingly referred to the photograph of a man from Middlesbrough whom he identified as the victim. J. C. Cannell, the most assiduous of the newspaper reporters chasing the story, also devoted a chapter of his *New Light on the Rouse Case* to try to solve the mystery. Rumours abounded. Did Rouse know the man he had picked up? Was the victim a former colleague who had tried to blackmail Rouse over his sexual liaisons? Was the victim a rival for the affections of one of Rouse's lovers? Was he even the husband of one of Rouse's 'conquests'? The objection to some of these speculations is that if any of them were the case, then it is unlikely that identification would have been a problem, as the police probed Rouse's contacts. Moreover, Cannell believed that Rouse's own charm with women would have seen off any rivals without his resorting to drastic solutions. There was no 'eternal triangle', according to Mrs Rouse. The idea was 'mere nonsense', though perhaps such a belief was part of his wife's coping mechanism.

One blackmail theory did, however, possess some superficial purchase. According to this theory, Rouse knew the victim as a Welsh miner who lived near Ivy Jenkins. The man had possibly met Rouse locally in Gellygaer, found out that he was 'married' to Ivy, who was already pregnant, and had then travelled to London. There, he somehow discovered that Rouse was already legally married to Lily, so he threatened to disclose this information unless Rouse paid him hush money. Rouse then proposed to drive the man to Leicester where the bigamist could draw funds from his employer to pay off the blackmailer. Instead, the journey ended abruptly at Hardingstone. According to the *Sunday Dispatch*, published after Rouse's execution, 'This would explain, more than any theory which has yet been publicly put forward, why Rouse turned murderer, and only lack of definite corroboration prevented it being submitted by the Crown as the motive for the crime'.[175] The idea is intriguing, but surely fanciful. For the sudden disappearance of a Welsh miner from the Gellygaer district around the time of the blaze, a man acquainted with Rouse and Ivy Jenkins, would scarcely escape local notice and, presumably, communication of this fact to the local police.

Within ten days of the blaze, Superintendent Brumby of Northamptonshire police was already in receipt of 300 reports of missing persons, of which 50 required further investigation.[176] This haul of information included more than 200, mostly useless, letters concerning missing relatives and friends from all over the country.[177] Some of these had originally been sent to newspapers which, like the police, were being bombarded with unsolicited letters claiming to know the name of the victim. No doubt the prospect of a reward of £100 from the *Daily Sketch* if an informant were able to identify the victim correctly increased the flow of letters. There were those who claimed a particular detective-like insight into

---

173 *Daily Mail*, November 12, 1930.
174 *Evening News* (London), November 13, 1930.
175 *Sunday Dispatch*, March 15, 1931.
176 *Evening News*, November 15, 1930.
177 *Ibid.*, November 13, 1930.

the mystery such as the anonymous letter-writer on December 5 who sent a press cutting to Scotland Yard with an accompanying note reading, 'I wrote before. Stick to IDA, wife of manager. Rose and Crown Hotel, Watford (They have not long been settled there) and you will get the right one.'[178] Moreover, the usual collection of deluded or fraudulent individuals in touch with the 'other world' was present among the letter writers, while one woman was hoping that the victim was her husband as this would save her the cost and effort of having to divorce him. Many letters referred to long-lost relatives but closer attention was being paid to those men thought to have gone missing around the time of the blaze.

Yet there was something sad or pathetic in a good proportion of the letters received by the authorities from those desperate for news of their missing menfolk or even of the need to accord them a decent burial if the news were to prove as grim as they feared. This was not an uncommon sensation among those hoping against hope that a miracle rehabilitation to the family bosom would be made or that the family's duty to their deceased kinsman had at last been done. After all, the carnage of the war was not yet a distant memory, and the ritual surrounding the burial at Westminster Abbey, followed by the yearly remembrance, of the Unknown Warrior, was as much personal for hundreds of thousands as it was collectively symbolic. For the British and Commonwealth families of the thousands of the Missing whose names were inscribed on the Menin Gate memorial, or the families of the 300,000 French soldiers whose bodies were never recovered for proper burial, their fate was of 'tormented limbo, unable to mourn and the madness of hope'. Indeed, four years after the war ended, the French authorities arranged for a photograph to appear in French newspapers, showing an unidentified amnesiac. He had been confined to an asylum after being repatriated on January 31, 1918 from Germany, where he had been a prisoner-of-war suffering from dementia praecox (schizophrenia). The man, who was unable to speak clearly, gave his French de-briefers a name that sounded like Anthelme Mangin. But no purported family members could be located until the newspaper photograph appeared. The response was immediate, with hundreds of families contacting the authorities in the hope of establishing that the unknown man was theirs. With so many competing claims to 'Mangin' from bereaved widows and mothers, the matter eventually went to the French courts as late as between 1937 and 1939. They upheld the claim of the Monjoin family that the amnesiac was Octave Monjoin. Yet with social disruption caused by the advent of World War Two, followed by the deaths of the two Monjoin protagonists before all the formalities for the amnesiac's release from asylum had been completed, Octave (or Anthelme) continued to languish in his protected and controlled environment until his death in April 1948. In the end there were no pension or other benefits for the Monjoin family. But the significant point was that despite the Monjoin legal victory, the thwarted families, that is, the widows Mangin from St Brieuc and Nantes, respectively, Marthe Mazat Mangin, and Lucie Lemay Mangin, let alone the hundreds of other hopefuls, could yet look to the former soldier as, 'a body they could imagine belonged to them'.[179]

It might have been the same with some of those writing to the police about

178 MEPO3/1660, Collins to Chief Inspector, Scotland Yard, December 6, 1930.
179 Jean-Yves Le Naour, The Living Unknown Soldier, Heinemann, 2005.

Rouse's victim. Knowing that the possibility of the burned corpse being their missing relative was remote in the extreme, such correspondents, when receiving disappointing news, would nonetheless feel an indefinable affinity between their loss and that of the victim's actual family, wherever that latter family unit might be (and it would, indeed, be somewhere within these British shores).

One of the earliest communications after the incident involved the Glasgow CID writing to Northampton colleagues inquiring about a missing Jack Fulton Steel and seeking a sight of the preserved piece of cloth and teeth from the corpse. But when it became clear that Steel had worn false teeth, which Rouse's victim had not, the inquiry petered out.[180] A week later Frank Gray (1880-1935), a solicitor from Kidlington, Oxfordshire, wrote to the Northamptonshire force. He appreciated that the force had been bombarded with letters regarding the victim's identity. However, Gray pointed out that he was the former Member of Parliament for Oxford (in fact, he had been Liberal MP between 1922 and 1924) and had made a study of vagrancy in the UK and abroad. He had, further, recently given evidence to a departmental committee on the subject and was well-known in his area for 'rescue work done among young tramps in my house'. He did not, however, add that in order to study social conditions, he had disguised himself as an agricultural labourer, had toured Oxfordshire workhouses as a tramp, and had lived with the Warwickshire miners. However he did observe, perhaps surprisingly, that while it was extremely difficult for individuals to disappear or, when discovered, to remain long unidentified, it was quite easy for tramps to lose their identity by frequent changes of name and appearance. He suggested that the police compare the books of surrounding casual wards which might highlight missing men, although the practices of hitch-hiking and of alternately sleeping rough and sleeping in common lodging houses meant that tracking such tramps was more difficult. Some of his 'clients' he persuaded to join the Army or go to Canada. Ending in a morbid note, he wrote that, 'I need not touch upon the question of motive—always a perplexing one—but there are explanations, such as a mental lust for self-destruction which would explain the death of even a penniless tramp'.[181] Some of Gray's suggestions were clearly a tall order (the Army, Canada). Suicide was also highly improbable given the sighting of Rouse striding away from the blaze. Finally, the perusal of casual ward entries posed challenges of exactly what the police should be looking for. There is no evidence that Gray's ideas were acted upon. He received only the most cursory of acknowledgments.[182]

Yet by mid-November, Brumby's attention was now focussed on just six men missing from home in various parts of the country. The victim's dental features were also thought to offer a clue in that a dentist might have observed that the unknown man's jaw was smaller than the average, and that he had only 28 teeth in place rather than the usual 32.[183] At the same time it was reported that Scotland Yard detectives had begun a search of the records at Somerset House, an investigation described as 'of a very secret character'.[184] Yet it may be that they

---

180   Northamptonshire Police Archives [NPA], City of Glasgow Police to Chief Constable, Northampton Borough Police, and reply, November 13, 14, 1930.
181   NPA, Gray to Chief Constable, Northamptonshire, November 20, 1930.
182   Soon after he wrote to the chief constable he published a book entitled *The Tramp*, Dent, 1931.
183   *Daily Mail*, November 17, 1930.
184   *Evening News*, November 17, 1930.

were simply looking for Rouse's marriage records, with a view to proving his bigamous marriage in 1924 to Helen Campbell, than for information casting light on the victim's identity.

Particular interest was shown by the police and journalists in the case of Thomas Waite from Merthyr Tydfil in Wales. His mother had approached the local police (presumably not at the same Merthyr Vale police station where nearly 20 years later the tragic Timothy Evans would pour out his first incredible story about stuffing the body of his wife, Beryl, down a drain outside 10 Rillington Place). Waite's mother was anxious about his whereabouts as she had not heard from him since November 1 when he had left Brighton, where he had been living and where he had been working on sea defences since the previous April. Two men with whom he had been sharing his accommodation had told the Brighton police that the description obtained from the charred body appeared to coincide with that of Waite. He had £2 in his possession when they thought he had gone to London for the day. He usually sought lifts in cars that he had stopped on the road, and they considered it out of character that he had not contacted them.[185] Superintendent Taylor of Brighton CID went so far as to issue a statement that claimed that, 'Certain facts point to the conclusion that Waite was the man whose charred body was found in the car'. This included the strip of unburned cloth rescued from the debris, and which was similar to the cloth on Waite's suit.[186] That he had also previously been a miner for many years before seeking employment elsewhere, forced away by the depressed state of the industry, also chimed with Spilsbury's finding regarding the state of the victim's lungs. One discrepancy, however, was that the corpse, at five foot six or seven, was an inch or two taller than Waite.[187]

Cannell now got into the act by assiduously and 'altruistically' pursuing the case of the missing Welsh miner. At least that is the impression that he carefully crafted in his book.[188] Thus he states that he drove to South Wales to meet Mrs. Waite and that he was struck by the similarity between the mother's description of her son and the broad features of the burned corpse. He then recounted in his book the other known features of Waite, that is, the Welshman's time working and living in Brighton and his former employment down the pits. Readers would have been forgiven for believing that this information had been imparted to him by a distraught Mrs. Waite. But in fact, like the subtle journalist that he was, he did not actually say, though he certainly implied, that such details were the fruits of his overnight drive to Merthyr. In fact the information might have been culled from other sources, but it was a better story to imply that it came directly from the poor suffering mother.

---

185 *The Times*, December 1, 1930.

186 In fact, the quality of the cloth fragment recovered from the charred body, which suggested expensive and well-cut clothes, was one of the puzzling features if, as was widely believed, the unknown victim was a 'down-and-out'. Some correspondents insisted, however, that charitably-minded householders might well have donated a good suit to someone down on their luck. There is no indication that the police pursued this line of inquiry. They did, however, consult textile experts who microscopically and chemically examined the square of clothing. As a result they visited a number of tailoring firms in London, inquiring about a suit of that type that was distinctive to the City of London (presumably Savile Row). The suit was of the best quality and cut, with hand-sewn button-holes, and the jacket and trousers were of plum-coloured cashmere, with an almost invisible pin-stripe, and lined with fine black alpaca. See *Daily Mail*, November 14, 1930; *Evening News*, November 14, 1930.

187 *Daily Mail*, December 1, 1930.

188 J. C. Cannell, *New Light on the Rouse Case*, John Long, c. 1931, pp. 202-3.

When Waite's photograph then appeared in the press, a man told the police that he had seen someone at Tally Ho Corner on November 5 who looked like the missing Welshman. It is likely that this related to a statement issued by the police and reported in the press on November 13 to the effect that an informant had noticed a man of about 36, five foot seven in height (both descriptions strikingly matching Rouse's), wearing a well-cut suit and who was probably working-class (though according to other sources he might have been a clerk). This man had been heard asking a passing motorist at Tally Ho Corner for a lift as far north as possible since, being unemployed, he was looking for work.[189] Excitement rose. Superintendent Brumby travelled to an unidentified town 20 miles from Northampton (Markyate? Kettering?) where it was thought the man might be known, in order to make inquiries. Perhaps the man had originated from this un-named provincial town, had gone to London to look for work, had been unsuccessful in his quest and had sought to hitch a lift back to his home town when tragedy, in the shape of crossing paths with Rouse, eventually struck.[190]

But the *denouément* arrived within a fortnight. On December 2 the Nottingham police reported that they had received a postcard signed in the name of Thomas Waite, and which stated that he was well.[191] Then, suddenly, Waite himself arrived at Watford police station to announce his presence, and assuring everyone that reports of his death had been much exaggerated.

> "I left Brighton, where I worked on the seafront, three weeks or a month ago, and since then I have been tramping the country. I arrived in London last weekend, where I saw some friends. I then went to the Barnet workhouse, and on to Watford, where this morning I went into the public library. To my surprise I saw my name in the newspapers as the 'victim' of the Northampton mystery."[192]

If not Waite, what of the Middlesbrough lead? The police had a photograph of a missing young man from that town. The mother had had no contact with him for a year and when Cannell arrived on her doorstep, she delightedly announced that she had received a letter from him the previous night. Examining it Cannell saw that it had been dated November 23 but the 3 had been changed to a 5. This was puzzling, especially as the letter apparently had been written onboard an un-named ship *en route* to Australia and had been posted in Plymouth where the ship had called in. The handwriting was unmistakably that of the woman's son. As to the photograph in the possession of the police, Rouse had initially been shown the picture but had denied that it bore any resemblance to the dead man. However, as we shall see in a later chapter, his opinion changed after his conviction. It now looked like the man, he claimed; though presumably it could not have been him, in view of the Australian connection, so long as the Middlesbrough mother had accurately recognised her son's handwriting. Interestingly, Cannell's follow-up hunt, to confirm the man's presence in Australia, came to nought. Perhaps the quarry was continuing to work his passage, and perhaps he was contacted again

---

189   *Daily Mail*, November 13, 1930.
190   *Evening News*, November 13, 1930.
191   In fact, Waite had addressed it by mistake to Nottingham, rather than to Northampton. See *The Times*, December 3, 1930.
192   *Daily Mail*, December 4, 1930.

by the mother some time after Cannell's book appeared shortly after the trial and execution. In any event the Middlesbrough lead brought no definitive resolution.

Just like Cannell's futile efforts, even when about 20 other journalists inquired at the Swan and Pyramids public house in Whetstone, they failed to elicit from customers and staff any details that might identify the victim. He was not a regular customer, had little money and would not especially be noticed in a busy establishment when drinking with Rouse, the teetotaller, on one or two occasions.

Cannell was puzzled as why Rouse claimed he knew so little of the victim's background and family since the two of them had shared at least four hours together in a confined space. People such as the passenger, Cannell believed, tended, on such journeys, to talk about their experiences. Indeed in an experiment conducted by a friend of Cannell's, fifteen different men had stood on the roadside between Tally Ho Corner and Northampton seeking a lift. Five men were actually picked up at different intervals, and dropped a short distance away on some pretext. Without exception they all told the driver (presumably without prior prompting from Cannell's friend) a 'hard-luck story', presumably mentioning people, places and work, and all, no doubt, mixing truth with fantasy.

Rouse's more useful description of the man, below, only emerged slowly after his arrest. The Markyate policeman, PC Lilley, could scarcely be blamed for failing to provide a detailed description of the passenger, given that his conversation that night was with Rouse. So, before examining the available police and Home Office records on the man's identity, we are left with three possible descriptions, Rouse's, and the more detailed pathology reports by Spilsbury and the Northampton pathologist, Dr. Eric Shaw.

Rouse thought the victim was around 40, five foot six to eight, respectably dressed with a light overcoat. He had a slight 'brogue' and looked like a clerk. The tattoo on his right forearm was a boxing or sporting one. He wore London police-issue boots and carried a sports diary. While we shall have cause to refer in more detail, in the chapters dealing with the trial, to parts of the post-mortem findings, we may note at this stage that Spilsbury reckoned the deceased was nearer 30, possibly younger, with small features, a pronounced jaw (as against a smaller than average one, as reported in the press), a fairly prominent nose, and a long but not narrow (and therefore possibly oval) face. The state of the lungs suggested a mining background while marks on his teeth hinted at a severe illness in his youth. Finally, according to Shaw, the examination of the victim's teeth, which were irregular due to a prominent left canine tooth, were in good condition apart from molars missing in the upper and lower jaw. It is not clear, however, whether he therefore agreed on a total of 28 teeth being present, as the press had earlier disclosed, which would mean all four molars were missing.

Police and Home Office Information

The identity of the victim was therefore not known by the time of Rouse's trial despite the exhaustive investigations conducted before the proceedings by various police forces. Indeed, Inspector Collins of Scotland Yard, in writing to his chief inspector in mid-December 1930, listed another five missing men reported to him by relatives (see below). But none could be linked to the surviving features of Rouse's victim. Thus it would serve no good purpose even to submit these names to the Northamptonshire police.[193]

Nonetheless, following Rouse's execution, the search was not abandoned. 'Time after time the few trifling 'clues'—scorched braces, buckles, buttons and a little cloth from the victim's trousers—have been examined. Time after time the few known details about the dead man have been gone over until almost every man in the force knows them by heart', a journalist observed.[194]

By December 1932, the number of reports of missing persons who might have been the unknown victim had risen to more than 2,500. Missives had been sent in by grieving mothers and abandoned wives (no doubt some of the latter muttering 'Good riddance'). Several letters were sent from the Continent and 40 had arrived from spiritualists claiming to identify the victim. None matched the physical description of the body held by the police. Yet, 'A constant pilgrimage of tragic women has been wending its way for the past two years to the grave of an unknown man in the village churchyard at Hardingstone....'[195] It is not known whether Mrs. Mabel Reynolds, living with her mother in a tiny riverside cottage in Crookham, near Aldershot, was one of these women. But she had recently applied for relief to the Aldershot Public Assistance Committee, and when awarded the sum of seven and sixpence a week, told the relieving officer that her husband was Rouse's burned victim. Visited by journalists shortly afterwards, she felt certain from what she knew and heard that the victim was her husband, William Ernest Reynolds. The couple had married in 1919 when he had been discharged from the Royal Engineers and had lived together until 1924. After that time she heard very little from him, receiving only occasional letters. The last was in 1929 from Brighton where his mother lived. 'Later I heard indirectly that he was in London, and was playing in public houses along the North road, particularly in the Barnet district'.[196] To another journalist the story was slightly different. The missing husband would call into hotels throughout the country and offer his services as a pianist, while 'The little attaché case that was found near the burnt car was of the type that he would use'.[197] Of course, no attaché case was found near the car. Rouse had taken his briefcase with him and the gut feelings of this 'frail little woman sitting in her mother's riverside home in Crookham' were never to be confirmed.

Even before Mrs. Reynolds' story reached the newspapers, the police and the Home Office were examining a number of leads of whose existence the press were probably unaware. Given that Superintendent Brumby had referred to around 2,500 communications regarding the victim's identity, the existing papers in the Home Office and Metropolitan police files (leaving aside correspondence from Brighton or Hertfordshire police who assisted in the search) represent only the tip of the iceberg of reports. Whether the overwhelming majority had been disposed of as hopelessly misleading, such as the spiritualists' 'revelations', or as relating to persons who subsequently surfaced in rude good health, or for other

193 MEPO3/1660, Collins to Chief Inspector, Scotland Yard, December 15, 1930.
194 *Evening News*, December 10, 1932. Supposedly preserved 'with great care in a safe', according to the newspaper report, most of these artefacts in fact no longer exist among the Northamptonshire police archives, though two one-penny pieces thought to have belonged to the victim and also the mallet are still retained.
195 *Daily Mail*, December 12, 1932.
196 *Daily Express*, December 10, 1932.
197 *Daily Mail*, December 10, 1932.

reasons, we do not know. In particular the Northamptonshire police archives do not appear to have retained much in the way of original correspondence on the specific matter of identifying the victim, though other Northamptonshire police investigation material remains, as we shall see.

We are, however, able to examine a small surviving selection of unpublished Northamptonshire, Metropolitan police and Home Office papers concerned with the search to put a name to the body. Thus within a fortnight of the blaze, a prison officer at Maidstone Jail, J. C. Silvester, reported to his governor that the police description of the victim bore a strong resemblance to a prisoner released from Maidstone in November 1929. This was one E. C. Clarke, described by Silvester as sturdily built, aged 38, with a small mouth (*cf.*, the smaller than average jaw in another description), employed as a window dresser who had formerly worked for the London outfitters, Austin Reed. He had since travelled to the Midlands, obtaining work wherever he could, and had won an important prize for window dressing there. He was separated from his wife and was very particular about his personal appearance, especially his civilian clothing.

The report was then passed by the Prison Commissioners to a Home Office official, probably the barrister and Senior Clerk, Courtney Robinson, who himself later became acting chairman of the Prison Commission in 1939. He thought that Silvester's information was a 'long shot. Medical record says nothing about Clarke's teeth; but according to his description he had a deformed right little finger which might be identifiable if the burnt body is his'. The information was then forwarded to Northamptonshire police where it sat until the chief constable revealed after the New Year that he had received a report from the chief constable of Reading, stating that Clarke had been seen by his mother, who resided in Reading, on December 12, 1930. As the Prison Commission secretary tersely put it, 'this disposes of Officer Silvester's report'.[198]

On February 2, 1931 a person signing himself "Enery' wrote to Mrs. W. H. Simpson at 24 Denmark Hill, London. The letter bore a Cambridge postmark but was never delivered, the envelope being endorsed by the London postman with 'Addressee unknown'. In fact the address was that of a lock-up confectioners shop owned by the sweet manufacturers, Maynards, and had been in their occupation since 1901. The only assistant there had worked at the premises for 13 years, and above the shop were store rooms used by George Roberts, a saddler whose firm had been in business for over 100 years in the district. None of these people knew of a Mrs. Simpson. However what prompted the GPO to hand the letter to the police on February 5 was its contents, which referred to the Rouse case. It began,

"My dear Helen,

Of course Rouse is innocent of actual murder, as you well know, and I have the proof of his innocence with me all the time: What do you expect me to do about it? If you really want the papers you must write to me at my Northampton address before *Thursday* morning at the latest, as I have booked my passage to B.A. [presumably Buenos Aires] for Friday. As for Henry B...,Well, there's nobody now likely to be interested in him or his whereabouts. Let him remain anonymous and unidentified".

198   PCOM 9/289, January 17, 1931.

The writer was aware that the intended recipient might move in the meantime, which she had apparently threatened. So he hoped he still had the right address. He ended with, 'Lovingly yours, 'Enery. (Remember?).' The file was then presumably sent on to Northampton on the recommendation of Inspector Collins of the Metropolitan Police, who had checked out 24 Denmark Hill. What Superintendent Brumby made of it is not known but presumably it would not have been difficult to identify someone called Henry from Northampton or, possibly, from Cambridge, whose surname began with the letter B and who was about to embark for Buenos Aires. If such a search had been undertaken it seems reasonable to conclude that it drew a blank. Moreover, Somerset House might have revealed, albeit after an exhausting search, a marriage certificate for a (possibly) London-based Mrs. W. H. Simpson. Whether such an effort was expended is not known. It is more probable, however, that after initial inquiries in Northampton the letter was considered to be a hoax which would lead to a dead end.[199]

In the same month Inspector Collins, who was doing most of the running around in London on behalf of the Northamptonshire force investigating Rouse, reported on one of the ludicrous 'spirit messages' that gullible individuals, perhaps still mourning the loss of their loved ones during the Great War, believed held the key to the mystery. In this example of the maddening *genre*, a Mr. William Lenny from Walthamstow had called at his local police station where he handed in a letter said by him to be a copy of a 'spirit message' received during a private *séance* held at his home. Lenny had explained that as a spiritualist he occasionally held private *séances* at his house. On February 2 he was holding a session with his wife and two daughters when they heard a spirit moaning and crying out, apparently in great pain. 'Oh my burns, I'm dying. I can't get out. He's locked me in. I'm burning. Open that door. Oh my legs. Oh my head.' A member of the family, probably the nineteen-year old daughter, then said, 'You will be all right, friend. Who has locked you in?' The reply was 'Rouse has locked me in. I'm dying'. He said his name was Bradford, that he came from Montgomery and that he knew that he was in Northampton. The local police officer in Walthamstow, Inspector Henry Slaughter, explained that Lenny appeared to be 'quite a normal person' who believed his duty was to disclose the events at the *séance*. Naturally nothing further was heard about a missing man called Bradford from Montgomery (which was not, of course, all that far from Gellygaer).

Another possible lead came from a Mr. Frederick Pudney of Clapham. He reported to the police that on November 2 or 3 he had been visited by a big-boned man who was aged about 30, five foot seven, of 'muddy' complexion with brown hair, and dressed in a blue Burberry coat and belt and dark brown trousers. The man had called at Pudney's office at 66 Victoria Street looking for employment. The visitor explained that he had tried to obtain free travel aboard coaches to the North of England but had been unsuccessful. He therefore intended to try to get to the north by asking for lifts from cars and by walking. He said that he had been at sea and produced a Church Army Hostel bed ticket. Pudney gave him a shilling, sent him on his way and never heard from him again. Obviously the story does not stack up in that why seek work in central London if the apparent aim was to travel north? It was another story for the police to try to check out and clearly it

---

199   MEPO3/1660 for this and subsequent information unless otherwise indicated.

went nowhere.

On January 30, 1931 a commercial traveller from Hayes, Frank Hall, called into Harlesden police station. He gave a statement that, on his way to Plymouth about a year previously, he had picked up a hitch-hiker on the Great West Road near the Osterley Hotel. The man bore some similarity to Rouse's unknown victim and said that he was making his way to Southampton. He explained that he was hoping to get a boat to leave England as he had been in trouble with the police (Rouse had said something similar about *his* passenger). He had just come out of prison after serving a twelve month sentence for robbery. Indeed on being apprehended he had admitted that he had £200 10/- and some coppers in his possession, and on his release he was returned just the ten shillings and the pennies. Somewhat improbably, according to Hall's account of this hitch-hiker, the police had told the latter that if he did not get into any more trouble he could also recover the £200 if no-one else claimed ownership. He had said that he had a sibling in Leicester but did not go there because they were doing 'badly'. He had seemed to Hall to be a respectable working man who had explained that he had earned a few shillings doing gardening work following his release from prison.

Either the story was a none-too-clever flight of imagination or else the hitch-hiker, unsurprisingly no longer encumbered by £200 in banknotes, had a sudden change in plan. That is, he now decided not to get out at Southampton but to stay in the car until it reached Plymouth. There, Hall gave the man two shillings to find a bed and then checked into his own hotel. The next morning the man turned up at the hotel and proceeded to wash Hall's Buick saloon without being asked. Hall did not see him again in Plymouth. However in April or May 1930 Hall came across him again near Basingstoke when he stopped to pick up a hitch-hiker as he drove from Bournemouth to London. The man explained that he had found no work in Plymouth, or in Torquay, Exeter, Bristol and Southampton. So he now wanted to return to London. He had kept straight, albeit 'with a struggle'. After being supplied with cigarettes, he was dropped off at Hayes, and though he had told Hall his name, the latter could not remember it. On neither occasion had the man any money. Nor had he been in touch with his relatives for some time. Again there were some similarities with the Rouse victim's profile but once more nothing concrete seems to have materialised to solve the puzzle.

Then on January 31, 1931 Mrs. Joan White of Deptford Park reported that the description of the dead man given by Rouse in the witness box resembled that of H. C. Meads, last seen two years previously in Clements Inn in the West End of London. Formerly in the Royal Air Force, he was now believed by Mrs. White to be a down-and-out. He had no relatives in England but his mother was believed to be somewhere in America. He was in the habit of tramping and of asking motorists for lifts. While some of his features matched that of the corpse (he had some teeth missing from the back of the jaw) his height, at five foot ten, appears to have ruled him out.[200]

On February 3, 1931 a journalist from the *Daily Express*, T. C. Meaney, attended

---

200 The National Archives list a C. H. Mead (not H. C. Mead) as a merchant seaman in 1921 and C. H. Mead in receipt of a war disability pension (gunshot wound). See BT372/118/109 and PIN26/9842. Despite the difference in initials, it is always possible that they were one and the same person.

Scotland Yard and produced for Superintendent Nicholls an anonymous note received through the post in the newspaper offices that day. It named William Langford, 'who cadged drinks and begged his bread from door to door' as the man killed by Rouse. 'Ask Rouse, he knows him *well.*' Enquiries were being made in Finchley and Leytonstone, the postmark on the unfortunately discarded envelope indicating either the latter or Leicester. As well as all the information received by Scotland Yard being forwarded to Northampton (including hopeful and less hopeful details from informants too numerous to include here), a copy of the anonymous letter was also sent to the DPP.

Another doomed inquiry in January 1931 concerned Michael J. Barry wanted since April 1925 by the Irish police for embezzlement in Waterford. Barry had a sister married to a man named Rouse who, in turn, was believed to be a car-owning commercial traveller. Barry, thought to have been in London, was known to frequent racecourses in England. But the trail quickly petered out when the suspect, Barry, described as an ex-railway clerk, was said to be five foot ten in height and, in particular, when it was confirmed that Lily Rouse's maiden name was Watkins, not Barry, and that she was not Irish. Moreover 'Rouse' was a fairly common name in the Leicester district (and, indeed, throughout the country).

In November 1934 a Mrs. Rhoda Eastgate of Gainsborough wrote to the Northamptonshire police. Her husband, Harold Eastgate, had disappeared in February 1930 (she did not actually say from where) though she had in fact heard from him two weeks before the Rouse incident. However she had heard nothing from him since. She had been left with a new-born baby and two other children for whose welfare she was making this plea (there was no reference to life insurance). Her description of her husband was close to, but not identical with, that of the corpse. Thus Harold had good teeth (though one was missing), but he was only five foot four. Could she therefore inspect the remains (by which she presumably meant the remnants of his clothing which she had described in detail, including a Woolworths trouser belt) with a view to identification? In reply, she was told that 'nothing was left of the remains of the victim...with which it could be identified', and there was no information regarding her husband. In fact, we know that items such as belt and braces buckles were recovered, as well as the petrol-soaked square of clothing from the man's trousers. Perhaps by November 1934 these items had themselves been disposed of, but this seems somewhat improbable. It is more likely that Eastgate was discounted as a possibility on account of his height and that Mrs. Eastgate was being given a gentle rebuff to spare her further disappointment. The alternative interpretation was the cynical conclusion that the police could not be bothered investigating an extremely long shot. [201]

And so it went on in the weeks and year after the death of Rouse's passenger. More suspicions, more names, more dead ends. A letter from Mrs. Horace Booth of Westcliff-on-Sea, and reports and photographs of the following: Leigh Holcroft, missing since October 31, 1930; Charles Hart, missing since June 28, 1930; Walter George Baldock, missing since September 1930; William Charles Nelson, missing since October 26, 1930; and Thomas Thorne, missing since April 1930. There was even the usual crop of false confessions. For example, an insurance agent from 23,

201 NPA, Mrs. Eastgate to Northamptonshire police and reply, November 29, December 1, 1934.

Oxley Road in London, Ralph Mortimer Mayne, claimed in an undated confession that it was he who had caused the death of the victim found in a 'shockingly charred condition', which he clearly meant was the Hardingstone corpse.[202] His victim was named by Mayne as Thomas Paterson, another insurance agent, whom he had confessed to murdering because, as Mrs. Mayne had already admitted to her husband, he (Paterson) had been conducting an affair with her. Mayne, in his confession, explained that he had persuaded Paterson to come for a drive in his car. They stopped at some suitable quiet spot where Mayne jumped out of the car and asphyxiated his passenger with the aid of a bottle of chloroform. He then set Paterson's clothes alight, made for the nearest railway station and ended up in Plymouth where he was arrested by the police. Whatever the truth of the confession, it clearly bore no connection whatsoever to the Rouse case. The discrepancies were too obvious to need spelling out. However, presumably after some further investigation had dismissed the idea that there was yet another murderous vehicle arsonist, police record keeping no doubt required it to be put in the Met's Rouse file.

Such were the occupational hazards of the police attempting to solve mysterious deaths or to fix liability on a suspect. Members of the public who contacted the police were understandably hopeful of a resolution to the mysterious disappearance of friends and relatives. Others were always willing, with the deepest sincerity, to put in their uninformed tuppence ha'penny-worth in order to offer the most outlandish theories to solve criminal events. Another group might wish to cast suspicion on individuals against whom they held a grudge. Yet others would be suffering from mental disturbances impelling them to send poison pen letters or to offer up, unprompted, the most outrageous confessions. Most murder files contain a fair amount of such correspondence. But the problem for the police was to be certain that they were not missing a vital clue when dismissing correspondence from perceived cranks, exhibitionists or deluded souls. Even spiritualists were sometimes given the dubious benefit of not being entirely ignored by the authorities, especially in the aftermath of the Great War when the most eminent of British society, such as Rudyard Kipling, the grieving parent of his missing Irish Guards son, were desperate to 'contact' those family members missing in action. Many sceptics, of course, might detect no difference between asserted spiritualists' revelations and claimed spiritual revelations associated with established religion. But even the birth control pioneer and scientist, Dr. Marie Stopes, was not averse to invoking the inspiration of the divine during her famous libel trial against those accusing her of profiteering from the sale of contraceptives. Thus the 'art of contraception' had been revealed to her through a divine message while she was sitting 'beneath the old yews' in her garden in Leatherhead.[203] Of course, spiritualists might yet claim to have located buried bodies on wind-swept pebbly beaches but, like the discovery of the body of Irene Munro buried on the Eastbourne Crumbles in 1920 after her brutal murder

---

202 In fact, Oxley Road may not have existed. There was Oxhey Road in Watford, Oxleay Road in Harrow, and Oxleys Road in Dollis Hill. Perhaps he deliberately misled the reader of his hand-written confession.

203 Robert Graves and Alan Hodge, *The Long Weekend: A Social History of Great Britain, 1918-1939*, Hutchinson, 1985 (first pub. 1940), p. 106. For the libel trial, see June Rose, *Marie Stopes and the Sexual Revolution*, Faber, 1992, pp. 162-75.

by Field and Gray, such discoveries tended to be accidental. And in the case of Helen Duncan, the professed regurgitator of ectoplasm and supposed conveyor of messages sent by drowned sailors from HMS *Barham*, a warship whose sinking had not yet been officially announced (but whose loss was informally known to thousands); well, she was just a fraud, hiding many previous convictions before she became one of the last to be prosecuted and convicted during World War II under the Witchcraft Act of 1735.[204]

1935 Onwards

That the puzzle over the identity of Rouse's victim did not die a natural death can, of course, be attributed to police procedures that keep files open long after the event and, in some cases, long after convictions. This might be in anticipation of possible appeals or, as with the Rouse case, because of the possibility of new evidence emerging, whether from scientific advances or from conscience-stricken witnesses or from other serendipitous events. Moreover there is no legal limitation period in respect of homicides. Indeed, the execution of an innocent man would not preclude a new trial against a different defendant for the same murder. In any case, there is the feeling of lack of closure, or a refusal to let go, where no name can be put to the victim or, in other cases where, despite a murder conviction, there is lacking a body to be buried, as with Gay Gibson, the victim of the Porthole murder by James Camb in 1947 or the murder of Muriel McKay at the end of 1969 and the beginning of 1970, noted previously or, most famously, with Keith Bennett, as he rests in an undiscovered spot on Saddleworth Moor after his fatal encounter with Brady and Hindley (though they were never charged with his murder). Perhaps for the police involved, there pervades a sense of dissatisfaction, possibly bordering on failure, in an acknowledgement of unfinished business.

However, as discussed in respect of his burial, there may also have been something haunting and saddening about this unknown victim, as perceived by a post-Great War generation that venerated the Unknown Warrior. For the 1930 generation were not yet distanced from a post-war psyche that revolved around remembrance, grieving, permanent memorials, keeping the flame alive and, for the war poets at least, a sentiment of futility, filth, and contorted dead bodies. Perhaps the charred corpse of Hardingstone symbolically continued to exert a note of condemnation upon a society that had conscripted him to a life of poverty, unemployment, thwarted hopes and, finally, to sudden death. It is, admittedly, going too far to claim that institutional guilt caused the authorities to continue to pursue leads as to the corpse's identity in the following decades. For one cannot gainsay that the police were 'only doing their jobs'. But the cult of the unknown warrior may yet have informed the psyche of the police investigators seeking a 'decent burial' for their 'client' beneath an inscribed personalised tombstone. Such an outcome would not only give closure to the victim's relatives, whoever they were. It would perhaps also give a degree of satisfaction to a criminal law

---

204 Helena Normanton, who edited the Notable British Trials volume on the A. A. Rouse case, also co-edited the Jarrolds volume on the Helen Duncan trial. See Helen Duncan, C. E. Bechhofer Roberts, *The Trial of Mrs. Duncan (No. 3)*, Jarrolds, 1945. For later studies of Mrs. Duncan, see Nina Shandler, *The Strange Case of Hellish Nell: The Story of Helen Duncan and the Witch Trial of World War II*, Da Capo Press, Boston, 2007; Malcolm Gaskill, *Hellish Nell: Last of Britain's Witches*, Fourth Estate, 2001; Manfred Cassirer, *Medium on Trial: The Story of Helen Duncan and the Witchcraft Act*, PN Publishing, Stansted, Essex, 1997.

system that justice to the victim had at last been achieved.

So the search continued. In November 1935 a Mrs. Hayman of Sale in Cheshire contacted the police in the belief that her missing husband was Rouse's victim. The files tersely report, without further explanation, that the Northampton police were unable to help her. In January 1936 Walter Cope who lived near Clapham Common called at Scotland Yard to recount a story of stopping a car fifteen miles south of Northampton and of asking the driver to give his young 18-year old companion a lift to Northampton. The driver, he was sure, was Rouse. When he told the detective inspector that he thought that the event had occurred in April 1929, the interview was quickly terminated. In January 1938 Arthur Onions from Loughborough similarly believed he had vital information. Eventually seen by the now-promoted Superintendent Lawrence from the original inquiry, his information also proved to be useless in solving the mystery.

In July 1943 Harry Bright, a 67-year old café proprietor from Hungerford, called upon the Northamptonshire police. He said that before the outbreak of the Great War he had owned a café at Tally Ho Corner, assisted by his wife. He had two sons, John and Harry Jnr., who would now be 31 and 37 respectively. John was dead but his father had no knowledge of the whereabouts of his surviving son. Harry Snr. joined the Army in 1916, then discovered his wife had committed adultery while he was away. They separated but did not divorce. The café business closed in 1919 and Harry Jnr. went to live with his mother at an address unknown to Harry Snr. while John went to live with the latter. Harry Snr. had no more contact with his namesake son though he heard about him from friends and learned that he had stayed with his mother only for another couple of years. Harry Snr. thought that his son had been working in hotels, had good health and a good set of teeth and had never worked with coal. About a year after the Rouse case, he came across an old newspaper report of the case while he was managing a café in Bow, East London. The unknown man's description reminded him of his son. And since his son had spent his childhood in the Tally Ho Corner area, there was a possibility that he might have met Rouse. The father had approached the Northampton Borough police some eighteen months later but no-one was then available to see him. But now, as old age was creeping up, and as he had some money put aside, he was anxious to eliminate the possibility that his son was Rouse's victim so that he could once more try to find him and assist him financially. However, at an interview with Inspector Lee on July 14, 1943, Bright was informed about the corpse's particular teeth arrangement, that is, the missing first and second right molars and left first molar in the jaw, as well as other decayed teeth. Moreover, the evidence regarding possible coal deposits (a 'large amount of black pigment' in the lung, according to Spilsbury, and 'flecks of black mucous' in the bronchi, according to Dr. Shaw) and the belief that the victim had been about 30 seemed to rule out Harry Jnr. as the victim.[205] In May 1944 a conversation in the Prince of Wales pub in Whetstone had turned to the Rouse case. One man named Lovelock from East Barnet claimed to know the victim's identity. Detective Sergeant Clifford Smith from Whetstone police station was instructed to make discreet inquiries. These elicited from a reliable source that Lovelock was considered to be a 'very loquacious individual who is given to monopolising any conversation he joins in

---

205   NPA, Statement of Harry Bright, July 15, 1943.

and who has a reputation for exaggeration'. Smith also spoke to the pub landlord, Frederick Oxley, casually asking about Lovelock. The latter, he was told, was a 'great talker' and that he (Oxley) considered him wholly unreliable. According to Lovelock the man in question 'had been a worthless drunken individual, yet resided in a Convent at Finchley'. According to Smith, 'The various Convents in this and Finchley area are all Roman Catholic Convents occupied by women, and it is improbable that any male person, especially a drunken person would have resided in any one of them'.[206] On D-Day minus 1, Lovelock was eventually interviewed by Smith and Inspector Tapsell and denied any recollections of conversations about Rouse. Clearly he was yet another 'bull-shitter'.

The following month Northamptonshire police received a letter from Charles Astill of Leicester, inquiring about his missing brother-in-law, Alfred Phillips, who worked on ocean liners and fishing boats under the name of Arthur Taylor. About a month or so before the Rouse incident Arthur had written to his sister, Mrs. Astill, saying he was travelling up from London to see them. He gave no address, 'as', according to Charles, 'I do not expect he had one'. Arthur never arrived and was not heard of again. He may have had a musical instrument with him as he sometimes offered to play for money in pubs whenever he was short of cash. The details in Astill's letter were so scanty that it was inevitable that the police could not help.[207] Another rapidly determined dead end came in May 1946 from a firm of Yorkshire solicitors, H. Boocock & Son of Sowerby Bridge. They wrote to the Northamptonshire police seeking information on behalf of an American client. They explained that a Thomas Vardon of St Paul, Minnesota, had died in 1938 intestate. He had left a widow and two children, Stella and Leonard. The estate being divided equally among all three, both widow and daughter received one-third each but Leonard, in England in 1939, could not be traced and his share was being retained for the moment by the local Minnesota courts. The solicitors understood that Leonard had met with a fatal car accident somewhere in 'North England' around 1939-40. The Durham police had been unable to help which is why the solicitors were now approaching the Northamptonshire constabulary in the hope that the car accident might have been the famous Rouse case. Of course we can see immediately that Rouse's victim could not possibly have been Leonard Vardon which the most basic of searches regarding the date of the Hardingstone blaze would have quickly revealed. One wonders whether Boococks had the gall to charge their American clients for sending such an inquiry to Northampton, given that a quick consultation in the local library in 1946 of the index to *The Times* would have revealed that it was a wild goose chase.[208]

Around the same time a Mrs. O'Halloran from Tipperary approached the Salvation Army in London to help find her husband, John, whom she had last seen in October 1930 (which would fit with the murder timetable). But since her husband would now be 69 the Sally Army pointed out to her that he would have

206 Personal knowledge by one of the present authors of a now late-lamented, harmless, limping and often drunk and down-and-out fellow-Glaswegian,'Wullie', looked after by nuns in the former's current city until Wullie's death, suggests that exceptions do exist.
207 NPA, Astill to Northamptonshire police, July 11, 1944; Chief Constable, Northamptonshire to Chief Constable, Leicester, July 13, 1944.
208 NPA, Boococks, Solicitors, to Chief Constable, Northamptonshire police, and reply, May 20, 22, 1946.

been at least 23 years older than the victim and therefore could not possibly have been the unknown man. In June 1952 a London solicitor, Aidan Evans, with offices in Garrick Street, W.C.2, told Scotland Yard that his daily help, Mrs. Alice Roberts of Fulham Broadway, suspected she knew the victim. She had been widowed in the 1914-18 war and had subsequently married Arthur Charles Gilbert in 1927. This apparently was a bigamous marriage, the couple separated and Gilbert was prosecuted for bigamy. He was acquitted, however, due to a difficulty in proving his former marriage. On November 5, 1930, the day of Rouse's fateful journey with his passenger, Gilbert visited Mrs. Roberts to borrow money from her. He told her he was going to the Midlands but she had not heard from him since. His features were not dissimilar to Rouse's victim. He had four gold teeth in his upper jaw, mounted on a denture with gold bridgework. He left the denture with her, leaving a gap in his right upper jaw. This, however, did not correspond with Spilsbury's report that the dead man's teeth in his upper jaw were complete though there were missing teeth from the lower jaw. Mrs. Roberts said that she had recently read Dr. Eric Shaw's evidence at the Rouse trial (perhaps in Helena Normanton's 1950 edition in the *Notable British Trials* series) and thought that this might have pointed to the victim being Arthur Gilbert. But Shaw's evidence had suggested that two teeth were missing from each jaw which, again, did not square with Mrs. Roberts' statement. In any case the clincher was that she said that Gilbert had been born in 1887, and that would have made him too old to be the unknown corpse.

In September 1955 John Charles Butterfill from Plumstead in South London referred to an *Evening Standard* report of September 6, 1955 which resurrected the case. He thought that the victim might be his cousin, Leonard George Rumsey, whom he had not seen since the Rouse case. Unfortunately a photograph of Rumsey, identified by Butterfill, was in the Metropolitan Police Criminal Records Office (CRO) which showed that Rumsey had been sent to prison in 1933, ergo... The file added that Mr. Butterfill was not in fact the person with an identical name listed in another CRO file.

The final entry in the collection of National Archives reports on a possible name for Rouse's victim dates from 1957. Mrs. H. Davenport from Nelson in Lancashire had written to Scotland Yard about her husband, Tom, who had left her in 1930 when they were living in Burnley. In her letter she said that Tom had told her that he was going 'on the tramp'. She had been reminded of these events by a recent newspaper article on the case and recalled that her brother-in-law had told her at the time that he thought it was his brother (Tom) who had been burnt to death in the blaze. Again, Scotland Yard could not help (there was no CRO entry for Davenport) and the file was passed to Northampton where, once more, it led nowhere.

But perhaps the most intriguing correspondence in the Northamptonshire police files is a single letter from the Deputy Chief Constable (it is not stated whether he was still Tebbey). This indicated that in response to a telephone request from the East Midland Forensic Science Laboratory in Nottingham he was sending them Northamptonshire's complete file on the Rouse case. The letter concluded, 'I am afraid the file is now becoming a little dilapidated but....I hope [it is] of some help to you in any matter you have now in hand'. The letter is a carbon copy of the original, and unfortunately one cannot be certain of the date of dispatch, as the actual year is not typed in. The probability is that it was sent on February 2, 1942, but conceivably it might have been 1952, as only the number 2 appears on the copy (194- or 195- was obviously printed on the letterhead).

What was the involvement of the forensic laboratory? In the pre-DNA age, were there improved tests for the provenance of the cloth, or other tests for retained artefacts that had not previously been examined, or which had previously been examined using now-superseded tests? The letter is tantalisingly obscure and perhaps the successor, if any, to the Nottingham forensic science laboratory can produce an answer. For the Northamptonshire police files are silent on why the request was made and on the outcome of the request.

Recent Developments

On a Saturday night radio phone-in on March 15 2014, a programme broadcast on many local radio networks in the southern half of England, the presenter, Richard Spendlove, invited listeners to state which interesting characters were buried near the callers' places of residence. One listener phoned in from Hardingstone and related the story of the burial in the local churchyard of the unknown blazing car victim. He then went on to say that the victim's identity was now thought to have been discovered through DNA testing more than 80 years after his death. This referred back to a story that broke in the spring of 2012 when Northamptonshire police were approached by relatives of a Londoner, William Thomas Briggs (who does not, of course, feature in any of the above accounts), who had gone missing around the time of the Rouse episode. According to Briggs' great niece, Samantha Hall, it was known that he had left the family home in Kilburn, north London, to attend a doctor's appointment but was never seen or heard from again. When researching her family history, Samantha came across newspaper clippings and letters from 1957 written by a relative seeking to have William's disappearance re-investigated.[209] While the Northamptonshire police cold case review team would consider the case, sadly it was soon found that when DNA was extracted by Drs. John Bond and Lisa Smith of Leicester University from the sliver of prostate gland from the victim originally preserved by Spilsbury there was no DNA match with existing family members. As the *Northampton Herald* had written some eighty years earlier, at the time of the blaze, the identity of Rouse's victim 'would likely remain a mystery forever', a view also endorsed by Superintendent Brumby and Superintendent Tebbey at the time. Indeed, the latter stated that, 'There is now no likelihood of the murdered man's identity ever being established'.[210] Or, as the *Daily Mail* speculated on November 15, 1930, the deceased was either friendless or 'someone is hiding the truth'. The last possibility, that the victim's identity was indeed known in some circles, is certainly intriguing. However, despite the Home Office's, Sir Ernley Blackwell's, questionable conspiracy theory involving Mrs. Rouse (chapter 23), it is difficult to know who might wish to keep under wraps the burnt man's identity unless it were to keep hidden a family scandal or an illegitimate birth, or some completely separate joint criminal enterprise involving

209 www.bbc.co.uk/news/uk-england-northamptonshire-17899027; www.northants.police.uk/defa-ult.aspx?id=9655&datewant=ye
210 Cited in *Evening News*, December 10, 1932. See also *Daily Mail*, November 13, 1930.

the victim and those who could identify him.

The only other possible avenue, in the absence of further DNA testing, might be found in a currently closed Metropolitan Police file in the National Archives, MEPO3/1660/1—"Closed Extracts: Police report dated 7/2/1944". The Freedom of Information Act 2000, s. 40 exempts from disclosure personal information about a 'third party' (someone other than the requester), if revealing it would breach the terms of the Data Protection Act 1998 (DPA) which prevents disclosure on a number of grounds. In this case the file, more than 30 years old, of course, is retained by the department because it is stated to contain 'the sensitive personal data of living identifiable individuals; namely, references to their private lives... [and] classed as sensitive personal data' under s. 2 of the DPA. It is obviously a matter for speculation as to who is the 'third party'. It does, however, appear more likely to be someone related to Rouse than to the victim, the obvious candidate being Arthur Jnr. or his half-siblings. The file is currently closed until 2027.

That DNA profiling can, indeed, resolve many cold cases, is not disputed. However whether the most celebrated of age-old murder mysteries has been resolved by DNA testing, as has recently been claimed, may be questioned. Thus the apparent confirmation that DNA testing has recently 'proved' that Jack the Ripper was indeed the long-suspected Jewish immigrant, Aaron Kosminski, who died in Colney Hatch Lunatic Asylum (not far from Friern Barnet) in 1919 from gangrene is far from conclusive. Thus in September 2014 it was claimed that DNA testing of a shawl worn by one of the Ripper's victims, Catherine Eddowes, had revealed a DNA match with a female line descendant of Kosminski. The finding was yet to be subjected to peer review by other scientists, though doubts have already been expressed regarding the origin of the shawl and also that it had been handled by several people who might have shared the same mitochondrial profile linked to Kosminski's sister. Indeed, a respected Ripper expert, Donald Rumbelow, is unaware of any shawl listed by the police at the time as belonging to Eddowes.[211]

There is, perhaps, an analogy (in reverse) with a report issued by Michigan University that, after its forensic scientists had subjected Spilsbury's slides of flesh taken from the body found in Dr Crippen's cellar at 39 Hilldrop Crescent, they insisted that the remains that they had tested could not have come from his wife, Cora. For the DNA evidence pointed to the presence in the scar tissue of male chromosomes, not female.[212] Others disagree with the scientific findings, one critic claiming that there was no genealogical link between the alleged close relative of Cora who provided a DNA sample and Cora herself, a claim disputed by the Michigan University researchers. No clarification could come from a Criminal Cases Review Commission referral to the Court of Appeal since it refused in 2009 to refer the case on the ground that the applicant was too remote a relative from Dr. Crippen to have a sufficient interest.[213] We await scientific reactions to the Kosminski revelations while conscious that any new leads on Rouse's victim may

---

211 *Daily Mail*, September 7, 2014; *Independent*, September 7, 2014; Russell Edwards, *Naming Jack the Ripper*, Sidgwick & Jackson, 2014. It was Edwards, a self-employed businessman, who commissioned the DNA testing.
212 David R. Foran et al., "The Conviction of Dr Crippen: New Forensic Findings in a Century-Old Murder", *Journal of Forensic Sciences*, Vol. 56 (1), January 2011, pp. 233-40.
213 www.bbc.co.uk/news/magazine-10802059.

have to overcome further challenges to their credibility.

Profiles of Letter-writers

Borrowing (but not too closely) from the methodology of Matt Houlbrook's analysis of Edith Thompson's letters to Freddie Bywaters[214] and from John Carter Wood's analysis of the letters sent to Mrs. Pace during and immediately after her capital trial in 1928 for poisoning her husband (she was acquitted in a blaze of public relief and celebration),[215] what are we to make of the 30 or so surviving communications regarding the identity of Rouse's victim? What proportion, if ascertainable, was written by wives or parents? How many, if known, were from other persons or organisations? What was their tone (would they be pleased or disappointed with negative results?), and do they add to, or confirm, our existing understanding of social, economic and domestic conditions at the time? Moreover, in what respects, if at all, are the letters an attempt to make sense of a family that in one way or another has come apart in part or in whole? Do they, in fact, represent a search for, or an expression of, self-hood or self-identity which others might dismiss as mere fantasising, like Elizabeth Jones' romanticised quest to be a 'gangster's moll' when she hooked up with the US Army deserter, Karl Gustav Hulten, to commit the 'Cleft-chin murder' in 1944?[216] In other words, were some of the letter-writers pretending to be other than they were, that is, holding to the belief that they had been successful parents or wives rather than rejected ones whose nearest and dearest had simply walked out on them? To 'unpick' the stories of the letter-writers and how their situations might have linked with the Rouse affair, either directly or by analogy, would probably not only be a mammoth task but an impossible one. And while the work of Houlbrook and Carter Wood, above, on the letter-writing aspects of the Thompson-Bywaters and Mrs. Pace cases has been historically insightful, there is no certainty that a similar exercise in regard to the Rouse-victim letters would be as productive. But at least we gain a fleeting glimpse of the 'missing of the Depression years' whose mere existence would otherwise pass unrecorded.

Nonetheless, there remains a sad fascination with the 'missing', whether of the Somme, or of Saddleworth Moor, or of those who might or might not have been victims of the Wests or of Peter Tobin, irrespective of whether the last-named was Bible John of late 1960s Glasgow dance-hall notoriety before he moved to England where he carried out killings in Margate.[217] Thus consider the thousands of man-hours and the millions of dollars devoted to identifying victims of the 9/11

214 Matt Houlbrook, "A Pin to See the Peepshow: Culture, Fiction and Selfhood in Edith Thompson's Letters, 1921-1922", *Past and Present*, No. 207, 2010, pp. 215-49.
215 John Carter Wood, "Those Who Have Had Trouble Can Sympathise With You: Press Writing, Reader Responses and a Murder Trial in Interwar Britain", *Journal of Social History*, Vo. 43, 2009, pp. 439-62.
216 See C. E. Bechhofer Roberts (ed), *The Trial of Jones and Hulton*, Jarrolds, 1945.
217 For stimulating reflective observations, see, for example, Geoff Dyer, *The Missing of the Somme*, Phoenix, 2009; Andrew O'Hagan, *The Missing*, Picador, 1995; Blake Morrison, *And When Did You Last See Your Father?* Penguin,1994. As noted previously, there is extensive literature on 'remembrance' in the wake of the Great War. Apart from work by Jay Winter and Neil Hanson, noted elsewhere, see also Mark Connelly, *The Great War, Memory and Ritual: Commemoration in the City and East London, 1916-1939*, Boydell and Brewer/Royal Historical Society, 2015. For Bible John see, *inter alia*, David Leslie, *Bible John's Secret Daughter*, Mainstream, Edinburgh, 2007. For Tobin, see David Wilson and Paul Harrison, *The Lost British Serial Killer: Closing the Case on Peter Tobin and Bible John*, Sphere, 2010.

attacks in the years after 2001.[218] Obviously DNA identification of bone fragments would bring closure for families who had no integral body to bury. Moreover, as seen in the aftermath of the Great War, there were imperatives both to mourn and to memorialise the fallen, representing both the nation and the local community, and irrespective of whether society communed with the dead in a spiritual or in an emotional sense. But surely there is a profound sense of respect and dignity for humanity behind the challenging, painstaking, time-consuming and expensive efforts expended by those picking over the debris of the Twin Towers. We would be less of a civic body were we to discard bodies as dictators might do with their victims. Something of these sentiments surely informed the decisions to accord a noble burial to an Unknown Warrior and to the nameless victim of a blazing car outrage.

218   See, for example, "The Last Secrets of 9/11", Channel 5 television, August 14, 2014.

CHAPTER EIGHT

FURTHER AMAZING DISCLOSURES AT TODAY'S HEARING

NORTHAMPTON CHRONICLE & ECHO, December 16, 1930

Prison Remand and Police Court

Legal Representation

Once he had been remanded in Bedford Jail awaiting the committal proceedings, Rouse was granted the services of the Wolverhampton solicitor, George B. Lee-Roberts, who had a branch office in Northampton. The details of their meeting are not available but one can assume that the gist was Rouse's repeating to Lee-Roberts the story he had told to the police about the passenger being handed both the petrol can and a cigar while Rouse went off to relieve himself. For on November 12 Lee-Roberts, accompanied by Dr. Aubrey Telling, a local doctor, and by a photographer, went to view the charred body. Telling's medical assessment matched that of Dr. Shaw's and Sir Bernard Spilsbury's as expressed at the inquest (chapter six). But then the men undertook an inspection of the grass verge at a distance from the blaze site. They were looking for physical 'evidence', that is, human excreta, which could corroborate Rouse's account that the blaze had suddenly erupted, obliging him quickly to pull up his trousers and run towards it.

Apart from this issue, which was so indelicate to Rouse that he chose to make up a succession of lies about the loss of his car since he did not wish to embarrass the ladies present when asked about the event, there were pressing steps to be taken to build his defence. At the outset Lee-Roberts requested on behalf of his client that a photograph of Rouse suitable for publication should be taken as a matter of urgency, both 'in his [Rouse's] interests and in the interests of Justice.'[219] Naturally, the Home Office was cautious regarding 'publication', suspecting a money-raising venture on the part of Rouse and his solicitor. However Lee-Roberts subsequently explained that in order to check out Rouse's story of what had happened, then up-to-date and reliable photographs, rather than the existing but unsatisfactory snapshots of his client, were necessary to remind witnesses, such as PC Lilley at Markyate, of the incidents described by his client. It was therefore arranged that, assuming he consented, new portraits of Rouse would be

---

219   See HO144/19178, Lee-Roberts to Home Secretary, November 12, 1930.

taken by the prison authorities for use by the solicitor. If publication 'in the usual [commercial] sense' were to be contemplated, the Home Office warned, then a separate application to the department would be required. Thus was obtained the more flattering portrait of the handsome hatted Rouse that contrasted vividly with the wooden side-on portrait of the rather plumpish and round profile, with Hitler-style moustache, that has tended to dominate the portrayals of Rouse in the press and subsequently.

The following day the governor of Bedford Prison, F. W. Gwilliam, reported to the Prison Commissioners that he had had a conversation with the prisoner the previous evening. Rouse had told him that during a visit that morning, his solicitor, Lee-Roberts, had sold the copyright in the recently-taken photograph to a newspaper (this was presumably the *News of the World*) for £200. Furthermore, another newspaper had offered £500 for Rouse's life story, a sum that Lee-Roberts explained 'would prove useful in providing an adequate defence at the trial'. Rouse, Lee-Roberts urged, should therefore be permitted to start writing his account. Gwilliam was aware that facilities for Rouse to write his story were, of course, dependent upon Home Office approval and that both Lee-Roberts and his clerk had been obliged to sign forms 928 and 931 under the Prison Regulations regarding the confidentiality of discussions with their client during each visit.[220]

While the Poor Persons Procedure was available to fund elements of the defence, as noted in chapter five, money to pay the professional charges always bore a heavy weight on Rouse's thoughts. In fact he had written from prison on November 11 to his employer insisting that he was still owed £1.14.0 by them. He complained that,

"As a matter of fact, I would never have made the last journey to see you if you had sent a little more as promised. However, it is no use crying over what might have been but I do want you, if possible, to send my wife as much as you can as she is entirely without means. Myself, I do not mind so much, as, being without any kind of legal aid I am afraid it is somewhat hopeless for me, so am resigning myself to it and will let matters take their course."[221]

On November 22 he authorised his solicitor to take all necessary steps to sell his house, goods and effects to pay for his defence. Anything left over should go to his wife. However the sale of furniture from Buxted Road raised only £50. So the following month Lee-Roberts sought Home Office permission to sell the prison photographs to the press to further assist in paying for the defence. Defence costs would now have to stretch to paying for expert witnesses whose testimony had not originally been contemplated (the Home Office noted that Lee-Roberts had failed to mention that he had already had dealings with the press over the photograph and over Rouse's proposed life story). Thus if approval were to be given and since not all the furniture had been sold, Rouse could then look forward to a 'fresh start' after the trial, a remark that not surprisingly drew an exclamation

---

220 PCOM9/289, Gwilliam to Prison Commissioners, November 16, 1930.
221 He was, of course, not exactly 'without any kind of legal aid'. On February 27, 1931, after rejection of his appeal, Lily requested that the prison authorities ask Rouse if he would sign the blank cheque that she had sent them, as she wished to wind up his estate. What money, if any, remained in his Barclays account at that time is unclear. See PCOM9/289, Gwilliam to Prison Commissioners. It seems that he signed the cheque on March 2.

mark from the Home Office official reading Lee-Roberts' letter.[222]

Officials were quite clear, however, that Lee-Roberts was being disingenuous. For they considered that his object from the outset had been to sell the copyright, rather than to jog witnesses' memories. Indeed it was believed that one of the persons to be shown the prison photographs at this earlier stage for 'identification purposes' was a representative of the press. In consequence, and in keeping with an earlier decision by a previous Home Secretary, Sir John Simon, to refuse permission to George Joseph Smith, the Brides in the Bath murderer, to raise money for his defence by writing for the newspapers, Lee-Roberts' request was refused on January 2, 1931.

The solicitor was not easily fobbed off, however, so he asked the Home Secretary to reconsider. He pointed to the imbalance in resources between the Crown and the defendant, a problem exacerbated in this case by the medical and technical aspects of the case. In response, and stung by Lee-Roberts' complaint, the Home Office referred the matter to Tindal Atkinson, the DPP, for a considered reply which could effectively counter the argument that Rouse's defence was being unduly prejudiced by the decision regarding the photographs.

The DPP agreed that the sale of the photographs was out of the question, given that the reason why permission to photograph Rouse in prison had been granted was to enable the defence team to secure more witnesses who could possibly speak to Rouse's defence. As to Rouse's case being hampered in this endeavour as a result of the Home Office's decision, Tindal Atkinson stated, perhaps unconvincingly, that the authorities had always been willing to assist the defence in securing their witnesses. Moreover reasonable payment by defendants for witnesses as to fact, and also for expert witnesses in respect both of their fees and their trial expenses, was covered in the Costs in Criminal Cases Act 1908. And the possibility that professional and expert witnesses for the defence would decline to testify unless paid in advance, that is, before the defence solicitor had been granted local funding under the scheme, seemed improbable. Tindal Atkinson was correct regarding expert witnesses' fees under the Witnesses Allowances Regulations issued in accordance with the 1908 Act. But since it was for the court to consider what was a reasonable amount to be paid by the local ratepayers from county funds, 'having regard to the nature and difficulty of the case and the work necessarily involved', in the words of the regulations, there was always room for debate as to whether the defence was being hampered or short-changed.

Regarding the costs of legal representation, the DPP pointed out that it had been open to Rouse to apply for the necessary certificate under the Poor Prisoners' Defence Acts. The 1903 Act, in force at the time of the committal hearing in December 1930, had been replaced by the 1930 Act. And as we saw in chapter five, the latter contained more liberal allowances, including an allowance for two defending counsel. Of course, the financial limits in such provisions could have been perceived as inhibiting Lee-Roberts' conduct of Rouse's defence, thus dissuading him from applying for the certificate. However, since Rouse had already told the police court that 'I have lost all' (as Lee-Roberts himself reminded the Home Office), the DPP considered that it was not too late for the defence to make an application to the trial judge for financial assistance under the Poor Prisoners

---

222 HO144/19178, Lee-Roberts to Home Secretary, December 29, 1930.

scheme. This would also cover travelling and reasonable out-of-pocket expenses on a prescribed scale incurred by the solicitor or his clerk in the discharge of their duties to their client. But Tindal Atkinson made no reference to counsel's expenses.

It is, of course, possible that Rouse's vanity would have kicked against the suggestion that he should go cap in hand to the 'Poor Prisoners' Defence' fund, but in his position what alternative was there? Indeed even the DPP recognised that there was an inequality of resources available as between Crown and defendant. 'But that discrepancy is in practice discounted by the extreme care exercised, particularly in a case of this character, to see that every point which can reasonably tell in favour of a prisoner is given due weight at a trial'. Of course, whether this was always the case when the Poor Prisoners scheme had provided legal representation in a murder trial might or might not have been the case. The upshot, nonetheless, was that the Home Office wrote to Lee-Roberts informing him that it would not reconsider its decision to forbid the sale of the photographs.[223] Whether an application for a certificate was actually made is not confirmed from the sources but it would be almost unthinkable that no application had been made. As seen in chapter five, by the time of the trial Lee-Roberts had been joined by Messrs Darnell & Price, another firm of Northampton solicitors, and two counsel had been retained for the trial even though only one, Finnemore, had appeared for Rouse at the committal stage.

Medical Monitoring

Rouse had been held in custody at Bedford Prison since November 10, 1930 and was then kept under continuous observation. As Bresler notes,[224] every prisoner on a murder charge was medically examined by the prison doctor on his arrival in prison. He was then placed in the prison hospital and kept under permanent watch by a member of the hospital staff who reported regularly on his conduct and condition. In accordance with this protocol, the Bedford prison medical officer, Dr. G. Meredith Davies, had therefore interviewed and examined Rouse, compiling reports each time, and had seen both the witness depositions and copies of Rouse's Army record. He then reported on Rouse's physical and mental state to the DPP on January 22, 1931. This report, a copy of which was given to Rouse's solicitor, stated that Rouse had had a vague idea of once being told that his grandfather's brother had been insane but he knew no more details. His war wound at Festubert in May 1915, together with his hospitalisation, physical scars, medical discharge from the Army, degree of mobility and his disablement pension history were all recounted. While in prison, reported the medical officer, Rouse had conducted himself normally and had conversed rationally. He had been cheerful and confident, had slept and had taken his food well and had shown no sign of mental disorder. Consequently he was quite fit to plead at his trial.[225]

A further medical report was submitted by Dr. Hugh Grierson, senior medical officer at Brixton Prison, who had also examined Rouse in Bedford Jail (the defence were likewise entitled to instruct their own medical practitioner to examine

223   *Ibid.*, DPP to Home Office, January 8, 1931; Home Office to Lee-Roberts, January 10, 1931.
224   Fenton Bresler, *Reprieve: A Study of a System*, Harrap, 1965, p. 77.
225   PCOM9/289, Medical Officer, Bedford Jail, to DPP, January 22, 1931.

Rouse or to undertake any relevant medical inquiries, for example, to examine the corpse of the victim). According to Grierson, Rouse had once heard that the great-uncle had been detained in an asylum but that, so far as he knew, there was no history of insanity in his family. As to his war wound, which at the time had resulted in poor memory recall for a period, he had had no treatment to his head since 1920 when his pension had stopped. However about two years previously (that is, around 1929) he had complained of headaches, though 'glasses soon put that right'. When such very rare headaches were experienced, they were felt above his left eye. About ten years previously, around 1920, he had fallen off a bicycle and had required a two-week stay in hospital for a wound to the right side of his head. While he admitted being forgetful, he denied any loss of memory at any time. According to his wife he was generous and kind but temperamental, excitable and moody. However, he insisted that 'he used to be more excitable than he is now'.

In Grierson's view, Rouse appeared to be an 'easy-going man who outwardly shows no signs of anxiety and maintains a cheerful attitude'. He knew the purpose of the interview with, and examination by, Grierson and apparently cooperated fully. Talking openly and light-heartedly seemed to be Rouse's natural style, according to Grierson. There was certainly no sign of dementia or of disease of the central nervous system. In short, 'I can find no evidence of any mental disease, [whether] idiopathic or the result of his head wound'. Consequently Rouse was sane and fit to plead and stand his trial.[226] Indeed in a later report to the governor of Brixton Prison, Grierson noted that at the trial, which he had attended, no evidence had been called regarding Rouse's state of mind at the time of the event. However, the defence medical witness from Northampton, Dr. Aubrey Telling, who had examined the charred body on November 12 while it was still kept at Hardingstone, and who had then examined Rouse in Bedford Jail the following day, had agreed that Rouse was excitable and had a poor memory of the details of the alleged offence.[227]

Perhaps it is understandable that little consideration was given to the long-term effect of Rouse's wartime head injury on his mental processes. Conditions such as post-traumatic stress disorder, or combat stress reaction, were barely recognised before the Second World War. Shell-shock was thought to reduce sufferers to a state of imbecility rather than to work insidiously to affect thought processes or mental states such as empathy or psychopathy.[228] This is, admittedly, a speculative matter with more than a hint of *post-hoc* rationalisation. However, as Bresler suggested, the pre-World War Two regime of medical inspection of prisoners on their admission to prison before trial, while seeming to be comprehensive, was in fact woefully inadequate. Thus,[229]

"The prison doctor was the *only* doctor appointed by the State to inquire into the prisoner's medical condition on behalf of the prosecution, and most prison doctors at that time had no qualifications whatsoever in psychiatry:

226 HO144/19179, Senior Medical Officer, Brixton Prison, to DPP, January 21, 1931. Another copy is in HO144/19185.
227 *Ibid.*
228 On the effect of Rouse's war wounds see chapter twenty-four.
229 Bresler, *op. cit.*

some were not even full-time members of the prison medical service. One would have thought that if the State wished to have a truly reliable report on a prisoner's mental condition an experienced, full-time psychiatrist would at least have been one of the people to examine him."

It seems probable that Meredith Davies' medical qualifications did not extend to the specialism of psychiatry. Indeed even expertise in neurology would scarcely avail a prison medical doctor of a detailed understanding of mental illness, personality disorders, and the like. Moreover, it is unlikely, given the relatively modest size of Bedford Prison in 1930, that Davies occupied his post full-time. His assessment of Rouse's mental health must therefore be accepted with some caution.

Police Court Hearings

From the time when Alfred Arthur Rouse had left home at nine o'clock on Wednesday morning, November 5 until his appearance at Northampton magistrates' court five days later, he had 'walked 500 miles' to see three of his women (or, we ought to 'proclaim', he had travelled around 540 miles by car, lorry and coach) and had seen his life commence its descent into turmoil and purgatory, during which time he had snatched perhaps five hours sleep in 80 hours of wandering. By Saturday afternoon, November 8, he was at Angel Lane police station in Northampton. A local magistrate, F. H. Thornton, was asked to attend and just after 4 p.m., in Superintendent George Brumby's upstairs office, Rouse was charged with 'the wilful murder of some male person at present unknown.' As if adding an ironic comment, the Exchange Cinema, just a stone's throw from Angel Lane, was advertising R. C. Sheriff's Great War drama, 'Journey's End'.

The press were not privy to the moment when Rouse was charged. Their first glimpse of him came on Monday November 10 when he appeared before a special Northampton divisional police court. Sensing that the occasion would provoke considerable interest, the authorities opened up the assize court for this purpose. The *Northampton Daily Chronicle* the next day waxed lyrical about the venue, as if writing a tourist brochure. 'The court, with its centuries-old furniture and fittings, the judge's canopied throne, the high pew-like accommodation, and the dark panelled gallery in the background, made a memorable setting for the gravest charge which any man is ever called upon to answer.' Reporters from the London daily papers were seated on either side of the dock, while the local journalists took their customary places around a green baize table, right in front of the magistrates' clerk's desk. For once the local press had an advantage. They had the best view of the prisoner.

> "He wore a blue shirt open at the throat and was without a collar or tie. His coat and waistcoat of a blue-grey material was [sic] open, and the trousers were of a blue serge. He is a fresh-complexioned man of thirty-six, with dark hair well brushed back. He has a very slight auburn moustache, of the 'tooth-brush' pattern. He closely followed the brief proceedings and when he spoke in answer to the magistrates' clerk it was with a pleasant, cultivated voice."

In contrast, others present in court, even witnesses, did not have such a good view of the prisoner. At this point the proceedings on behalf of the Crown were being conducted by Superintendents Tebbey and Brumby prior to the direct involvement of the DPP. Indeed, it is likely that Tindal Atkinson's department knew nothing of the police court hearings until November 17 when the DPP wrote to the Northamptonshire chief constable.

> "My attention has been called to the reports in the Press in this case of murder in which the accused has already been arrested and remanded until, I believe, tomorrow and I shall be glad, therefore, if you can make your report under the Prosecution of Offences Act and Regulations thereunder at as early a date as possible" [230]

This, of course, was a reference to the primacy of the DPP in prosecuting serious offences as a 'state' public prosecutor. Two days later, the chief constable sent his apologies for the delay in furnishing the reports on the case. He explained that he had determined to wait until the accused had been 'further' remanded (which would have meant November 18 or possibly November 26: remands were generally for periods of eight days at a time). Thus he was awaiting Spilsbury's initial report, which had not yet been received, before sending the depositions to Tindal Atkinson. He now understood, however, that Spilsbury was sending a copy of the post-mortem report directly to the DPP and hoped that a representative of the DPP would be present at the next committal hearing, due to resume on November 27, to assume responsibility for conducting the prosecution. In fact the DPP's irritation was still boiling up after his initial letter to Northamptonshire on November 17, suggesting that copies of police reports had not yet arrived from Brumby. For five days later, Paling had telephoned Scotland Yard requesting copies of statements and reports[231] (presumably including Rouse's statements, items found on him, statements from coach personnel at the Embankment, and possibly statements from Nellie and Helen) already sent up by the Metropolitan Police to the Northamptonshire Constabulary. Was this another instance of provincial police shortcomings?

The chief constable, in his letter of November 19 to the DPP, also added that at the previous day's hearing on November 18, Rouse's counsel, Finnemore, had requested sight of the prisoner's statement made at Hammersmith police station on November 8 and witnessed by Brumby. This request, Kellie-MacCallum believed, was an 'unusual procedure' ('disclosure' of Crown evidence to the other side, especially that which might be helpful to the defence, was, indeed, unusual—and, on occasions, the withholding amounted to a travesty of justice--before the 1990s when administrative practice followed by the Criminal Procedure and Investigations Act 1996 restored some balance). Indeed, as we shall see later, the request had been refused at the time. Ironically, however, the DPP now intimated in reply that the defence *could* be supplied with a copy of that statement. What was agreed, however, was that Tebbey and Brumby would travel to London on November 24 for a conference on the case with the DPP, bringing with them a plan of the neighbourhood of the blaze, a drawing of which had been delayed due to illness in the county surveyor's office, and also some photographs connected with

---

230 NPA, Tindal Atkinson to Chief Constable, County Police, Northampton, November 17, 1930.
231 MEPO3/1660, Collins to Chief Inspector, Scotland Yard, December 6, 1930.

the case (obviously including pictures of the burnt-out vehicle).[232]

But before these events, the initial committal hearing on November 10 heard from William Bailey, the first to give evidence, who was asked to identify the man he had encountered in Hardingstone Lane. Bailey turned to the dock and said, 'I wish he would turn round.' Rouse obliged and Bailey, pointing melodramatically, exclaimed, 'That is the man!' The headline in the evening press wrote itself. The clerk to the magistrates, J. Faulkner Stops, reminded Rouse, who at that point was not legally represented, that he was entitled to ask questions at this stage but advised him not to. Rouse acquiesced. The police case was presented by Superintendent Tebbey, the Deputy Chief Constable. He was content to call only one other witness, not Bailey's cousin, Brown, whose own statement of the encounter with Rouse was being held in reserve, but Tebbey's colleague, Superintendent George Brumby, who merely recounted that he had charged Rouse with wilful murder at Angel Lane police station. Tebbey then declared that he was not proposing to bring any more evidence and asked the magistrates (Thornton had been joined by Major C. A. Markham) that the prisoner be remanded until Tuesday week, November 18. The clerk then asked Rouse if he had anything to say why he should not be remanded until Tuesday week. Showing, even at this stage, a propensity to say too much, Rouse replied, 'I seem to have no option, sir. While I am here, however, could I make myself a little more respectable before coming into public view? That is all I wish to ask now'. This referred to the fact that when his own clothes had been taken away by the police for examination, he had been supplied with ill-fitting replacements which evidently were not stylish enough for him. The clerk assured him that the police would do everything properly. And that was it. The proceedings had lasted less than ten minutes. Rouse was taken down by Inspector Lawrence and thence transported to Bedford Gaol.

The following morning the newspaper headlines were pre-occupied with a story that four elephants taking part in the Lord Mayor's Show in the City of London had stampeded on the Victoria Embankment, injuring thirty onlookers. Apparently the animals had been spooked by a banner bearing a lion's head. Pandemonium ensued as one of the elephants seized the banner with its trunk and cast it to the ground where its fellow pachyderms trampled on the offending image. The arrival of Sir Bernard Spilsbury in Northampton to examine the charred remains in the Crown Inn, Hardingstone, was relegated to the inside pages.

Superintendent George Brumby's relations with the press, already strained over the business of fending off journalists at the crime scene, were to turn decidedly more tetchy as the case progressed, but in the first few days of his investigation he was happy to give interviews. He needed all the help he could get.

"There must be someone who has missed a friend or relative since Wednesday, and I appeal for him to get in touch with me....I only wish the police had some clue as to the man's identity. That is the one thing we are waiting for... At present the segment of suiting which was adhering to the human remains is about the only thing which might possibly help from all that is left of the dead man in the Crown Inn garage." Indeed, he joked, "All the new and interesting information concerning this case that I get is from the newspapers. It is only

---

232 See correspondence on this matter in NPA; *Daily Mail*, November 24, 1930.

when I get home after a busy day's investigations, and commence to read the newspapers, that I really begin to learn things."

Rouse's next appearance on Tuesday November 18 was even shorter than the first. It lasted only five minutes. The magistrates (there were now three, Thornton and Markham having been joined by Colonel Eyre Coote, a long-serving JP and former honorary colonel of the Northamptonshire Yeomanry before the Great War) had barely taken their seats when Rouse lodged a protest. 'Before the proceedings start, I should be glad to have my own clothes. It would appear that the police want me to appear as disreputable as possible. Many times I have asked to be supplied with clothes from my home. I cannot even do my coat up. The sleeves of this jacket are much too short, and I want a change of clothing.' George Lee-Roberts had by now been appointed as Rouse's solicitor and, in turn, he had briefed Donald Finnemore as counsel. Finnemore's first utterance, having explained that he was instructed by the defence, was to reiterate Rouse's request for new clothes.

Superintendent Tebbey then reminded the magistrates that he had given them sufficient information to remand Rouse over the past week and as there were a great many investigations yet to be made, he was not prepared to provide any further evidence at that time. He therefore requested a further remand. In reply, and as we flagged up earlier, Finnemore stated that it appeared from his instructions and from reports that had appeared in the press that the prisoner had already made a long statement. He assumed that the defence would be given a copy of that statement. Indeed, that was the usual procedure, he said soothingly but perhaps not wholly accurately in respect of all hearings. Tebbey, prevaricating, replied that counsel would have it 'in due course' and it emerged that the case was about to be placed in the hands of the Director of Public Prosecutions. Rouse was then duly remanded to appear the following week. The press coverage might have been as cursory as the proceedings had not another ingredient to the story surfaced. A London solicitor got to his feet and told the magistrates, 'I am instructed to appear on behalf of a woman who may be concerned in this case, but at the moment I do not want to mention her name in court. I understand the chief constable has in his possession a statement voluntarily made by her in another district last night, and I think that might suffice at the moment.' The press spotted that while this exchange was being conducted Rouse had leaned forward with undisguised interest and had gripped the broad edge of the dock with both outstretched hands. It was now Superintendent Tebbey's turn to protest that her statement had not reached him yet. The clerk asked the newcomer who he was, to which the solicitor replied, 'My name is Henry Flint.'

Rouse may have only made a brief appearance before the magistrates but those five minutes changed the direction of the case irrevocably. Indeed Flint's intervention had fanned yet more vigorously the flames of press interest.

A WOMAN AND THE BLAZING CAR MYSTERY – *Evening News*
WOMAN AND THE CAR MYSTERY – HER NAME KEPT SECRET - *Daily Mail*
MOTOR CAR-MURDER CHARGE – A WOMAN'S STATEMENT – *The Times*
NEW TURN IN CAR DRAMA - WOMAN MAKES
STATEMENT- *Northampton Daily Chronicle*

When the reporter from the last-named newspaper had paid his customary morning visit to Angel Lane police station, he had found Superintendent Brumby inundated with enquiries concerning missing people or relatives. All inquiries required to be followed up but none of them had thrown any light on the identity of the man found dead in the car, and Brumby ruefully admitted that, 'The police are no nearer their objective than they were twelve days ago.' Therefore, perhaps he welcomed the vicarious arrival of a mystery woman who might divert the press from his own problems. He told the local paper that the woman had nothing to do with the charge being preferred against Rouse, but he could not say that the introduction of the woman in the case would not possibly have something to do with Rouse later on. Three days after that he was fanning those flames himself when he added that,

> "Of course some people would never be satisfied unless a woman was introduced into these sort of cases. I see that one daily paper states that altogether three 'mystery women' have been questioned in the course of police investigations. If the number had been given as thirty-three it would have been nearer the mark."

The morning of Thursday November 27 presented the police with a crowd-control problem with which they would become increasingly familiar. Large numbers, mostly women, queued for two hours hoping to gain admission to the assize court building where Rouse was making another appearance before the magistrates. Less than a third of the queue managed to get inside. About fifty of those admitted stood at the back of the court while forty or so of the more fortunate found seats in the gallery. This increased level of interest was not confined to the public. No less than seven magistrates now graced the Bench or wanted to be in on the act. They were John B. E. Campion (chair), Montagu Erskine, 6th Baron Erskine of Restormel Castle, Thornton, Colonel Coote, W. T. Elliott, W. B. Spokes and V. W. Wood. Major Markham, who had served with the Northamptonshire Regiment during the Great War[233] and who subsequently published in 1928 a charming volume with the enticing title, *The New Pewter Marks and Old Pewter Ware*, was not present but appeared at subsequent sittings. And eight witnesses were to be called. They sat to the right of the dock. The press were pleased to see that the 'intriguing figure' of Mr. Flint was again seated at the defence solicitors' table, alongside Donald Finnemore and George Lee-Roberts for the defence. Taking up the police case was someone new to the story, Gerald Paling, for the DPP. Paling would do his best to capture the headlines that day. But before this a new focus of attention now hove into sight as Lily Rouse became an object of curiosity.

> "To the women present the most attracting [sic] figure in court was Mrs. Rouse. The wife of the accused was accommodated to the left of the dock. She appeared perfectly composed, a neat, attractive fresh-complexioned woman, wearing a fashionable tricorn dark brown velour hat, and her brown jumper suit was worn underneath a heavily fur-collared and cuffed long out-door coat. A string of red beads gave a pleasing touch of colour to the costume."

233 See WO339/23310 for his Great War record.

Rouse himself also came under sartorial scrutiny. As the press reported,

> "His request had been granted, and Rouse now appeared in the suit he was wearing when first detained by the police, of smartly-cut, dark plum-coloured material, with neat soft collar and an artistically shaded brown and white tie. With his fresh colour, black hair, inclined to curl, and well brushed back, he made a striking figure in the dock. Rather above medium height, and well built, the accused stood firmly facing the magistrates with hands outstretched and resting on the ledge of the dock."

As one of the permanent London-based staff of the Director of Public Prosecutions, Paling opened the case for his superior, E. H. Tindal Atkinson, by offering, controversially one might think, a brief character sketch of the prisoner. Rouse was a commercial traveller working for a Leicester manufacturer of braces and garters. His salary was £4 a week plus expenses. He lived with his wife at Buxted Road, Finchley (Friern Barnet would have been more accurate), and was the owner of a Morris Minor, registration number MU 1468. On November 5 at seven o'clock in the evening or thereabouts he had called at the City of London Maternity Hospital in City Road where he saw a woman named Miss Nellie Tucker who had given birth to a baby girl on October 29, 'of which Rouse was the father'. Indeed, added Paling with relish, 'Incidentally, she had previously given birth to a child of whom Rouse was the father and he was paying her money in respect of that child'.[234] This information may well have been delivered as a cold, emotionless narrative. But respectable societal norms meant that the listeners present, including the press corps, on hearing the bare facts about Rouse's illegitimate children, were bound to have experienced a sharp intake of breath.

Paling continued by recounting the outlines of Rouse's car journey to Hardingstone, outside Northampton; of the prisoner, according to Rouse's account, picking up a man on the road who wanted a lift (at Tally Ho Corner, north London); of encountering a patrolling policeman at Markyate, north of St Albans, who investigated why the car had no lights on; of the car located on the road out of Hardingstone village, which was curious if Rouse was on his way to Leicester; of the flames which were some twelve feet high and inside the burned-out wreckage the body of a man who had been burned beyond all recognition. But what especially interested the prosecutor were Rouse's movements after the fire. He had been seen by Brown and Bailey stepping out of a ditch near the junction end of Hardingstone Lane. In passing the cousins at that lonely hour he had, without prompting, suggested to them that the blaze was a bonfire and he had then continued towards the junction with the main road going north and south, leaving the two young men to investigate the fire. By this time he had managed to stop a London-bound lorry and had clambered aboard to be driven south.

Moving swiftly on Paling described the scene at South Wales where the prisoner had called at the house of a Mr. Jenkins, whom he knew 'inasmuch as he [Rouse] had been paying court to Miss Jenkins, who at the moment was in a certain condition as a result of the prisoner's associations with her.' Rouse had promised to marry her and indeed she had told her family that they had already married and

234 *Northampton Daily Chronicle*, November 27, 1930; *Evening News*, November 27, 1930; *The Times*, November 28, 1930; *Daily Mail*, November 28, 1930.

that she was therefore now Mrs. Rouse. Although Rouse lived in 'Finchley', Mr. and Mrs. Jenkins thought that his address was in Gillingham Street, Victoria. But this in fact was merely an accommodation address occupied by a tobacconist's and newsagent's. These revelations of Ivy's pregnancy and of his pretended marriage to her must have had the scribes scribbling even more frantically in their press seats. Paling explained that Rouse had stayed the night with the Jenkins family (this would have been Thursday night and Friday morning, November 6 and 7). He had then been given a lift back to Cardiff and on the way had lied to the driver, Hendell Brownhill, an associate of Jenkins Snr., stating that his car had been stolen and that he had already reported the theft to the police and to his insurance company.

On his (Rouse's) arrival back in London on the Friday evening, Paling continued, police officers had approached him and had asked him to go with them to Hammersmith police station. Rouse had responded, 'Very well, I am glad it's all over. I was going to Scotland Yard about it. I am [sic] responsible and I am glad it is over as I have had no sleep.' Paling then recounted some comments that Rouse had made to Sergeant Skelly of the Metropolitan Police while waiting at Hammersmith police station for the arrival of the Northampton police; that the man he had picked up seemed respectable; that he [Rouse] had become sleepy and that the engine had begun to spit; that he had pulled up at the side of a country road after leaving a village he did not recognise and thought that he had told the man that there was petrol in the can; that he [Rouse] had wanted to relieve himself and that the man had asked him for a smoke; that, being some distance away from his vehicle while relieving himself, he had noticed the big flames coming from the car's direction; that he had run to the car and had tried to open the door, but could not because the vehicle was a mass of flames; that he had begun to tremble violently; that he had run as hard as he could along the road; and that he had lost his hat.

The statement which Rouse had made under caution when Superintendent Brumby and Inspector Lawrence arrived from Northampton, and which elaborated on the story he had recently told to Skelly, was then read out by Paling. This brought Donald Finnemore to his feet. He objected to certain passages being read since it would be not be fair to do so until there was a witness called who could speak to the words spoken and contemporaneously written down and who could also be cross-examined on what had occurred at the time. The upshot was that counsel agreed that just before the challenged passages were reached Finnemore would indicate the sections of the statement, obviously those which could be viewed by the defence as especially damaging admissions, to which he objected, and Paling would then refrain from reading out those particular extracts. Perhaps references to Rouse's mallet were, inter alia, what Finnemore had in mind at this point, though the more damaging statements made by Rouse were those, such as his 'harem' remark (below), that he would spontaneously make to Inspector Lawrence after reaching Angel Lane police station. Yet the objection and subsequent agreement seemed to fall on deaf ears insofar as Paling continued to read out during this opening statement a narrative of Rouse's Hammersmith statement which was faithfully reported by the press. Indeed, to add to the unfairness to the accused, such recitation could scarcely be considered 'evidence', unlike answers to questions put by either side to witnesses in the witness box.

Regarding Rouse's account of his departure from his home on the evening of November 5, and undeterred by the prosecutor's previous undertaking, Paling continued by reporting Rouse as having stated, 'My wife was in and packed my bags. I told her I was going up North. I only remained indoors about ten minutes or a quarter of an hour and made two other calls in London. One of the calls was in Holloway Road and the other I do not care to mention.' Paling, however, had no such inhibitions and, pre-empting any possible objection from Finnemore, added for the benefit of the court and the press, that 'That second call was possibly the call he made at the hospital upon Miss Nellie Tucker.' Having failed to prevent this damaging disclosure, Finnemore attempted to interrupt Paling's further recital of Rouse's remarks, including when the prisoner was taken off the coach at Hammersmith Broadway, and when he was kept at Hammersmith police station to await the Northampton police. But Paling continued to dish the dirt ('I'm glad it is all over'; 'I am responsible', and so on), as well as repeating Rouse's Hammersmith account of the events that fateful night, eventually taking up the story where Rouse had been conveyed to Angel Lane police station. Then at that point, with Rouse detained in the Northampton police station, came perhaps the most dramatic and shocking revelation, repeated by Paling, to pass Rouse's lips during the whole affair, at least as viewed from the perspective of 'respectable society'. For, as Paling continued (and, though already cited in chapter one, it is so central to understanding Rouse that it is worth repeating),

"Whilst there he [Rouse] spoke to Inspector Lawrence...... [the] defendant said his wife was really too good for him and added, 'I like women who make a fuss of me. I do not ever remember my wife sitting on my knee; otherwise she is a good wife. I am friendly with several women, but it is an expensive game. I had no money on Wednesday, and was on my way to Leicester to draw some money. My 'harem' takes me to several places, but my wife does not ask me any questions now.' He also said [continued Paling] he could sell his house and furniture, make an allowance to his wife, and clear £100 to £150 from the sale."

It is not possible to overstate the damaging significance of this passage for the image of Rouse thus projected and then publicised with glee by the press. The account of his 'harem' would dog Rouse for the remainder of his shortened life, mark him out as a serial philanderer with the morals of an alley cat (to mix the species), and render him completely untrustworthy when obliged to place himself before his peers at the Northamptonshire assizes. Indeed, since the case against Rouse was essentially circumstantial and contentious, many respectable souls at the time might have been prompted to conclude that the uncertainty and debatable nature of the prosecution's facts should not get in the way of the moral come-uppance that eventually befell Rouse. But that was yet to come.

For the moment, mention was made by Paling of the condition of the wreckage, the position of the body, the discovery of a mallet with hairs visibly attached to it and the post-mortem examination of the remains. Sir Bernard Spilsbury was of the opinion that the dead man might have been a coal miner because of certain stains found in the lungs. Both he and Dr. Eric Shaw were agreed that the victim must have been alive at the time the fire started. Without adducing the evidence, Paling suggested that, 'All these findings were consistent that this man, having been rendered unconscious, his body had been put into the vehicle then soaked with petrol and set alight intentionally.'

Following the revelations about Rouse's private life, the focus of the case shifted irrevocably from the identity of the dead man to the scandalous behaviour of the man in the dock. As to the motive, Paling stressed, probably because he believed that he was on weak ground in this regard, that it was not necessary in law for the Crown to prove motive. Notwithstanding, he pointed out, here was a man paying money to a number of women for child support on the orders of the courts. Indeed, the financial burden upon a father to maintain a daughter born out of wedlock only a few days previously was undoubtedly about to increase. In a devastating conclusion Paling reminded the court that the man in the dock 'was a married man who was paying court to more than one woman other than his wife and it might well be that he would have wished to disappear and so unburden himself of all those liabilities that were piled upon him.' Whether the magistrates on the Bench actually needed to be apprised of that speculative explanation for Rouse's alleged actions is moot. For the *prima facie* circumstantial evidence of late-night Guy Fawkes revellers strolling home in Hardingstone Lane, crime-scene photographers, county roads surveyors, lorry drivers and mates, and Leicester company secretaries adduced by the Crown, perfunctory though much of it was at this stage, together with the recorded accounts of Rouse's own verbal diarrhoea, probably justified the magistrates in sending the case to trial without the need for Paling to offer a plausible motive.

As the magistrates' clerk was looking through Alfred Brown's deposition which recounted his and his cousin, Bailey's, encounter with Rouse, the prisoner spoke up from the dock. 'Can anybody oblige me with an aspirin? I have got a bit of a headache.' He was holding his head in his hands. Lily Rouse hurriedly left the court room and ran to a nearby chemist shop. Rouse was given a glass of water and Lily swiftly returned with a bottle of aspirin tablets which were handed over to him. Pills were swallowed with water and no doubt the authorities breathed a sigh of relief that Rouse had not done a 'Whitaker Wright' on them (as the convicted fraudster had done in 1907, and as Slobodan Praljak, a Bosnian Croat general, convicted of war crimes in 2017, would also succeed in doing in a court room in The Hague) by swallowing poison and promptly dying before the criminal justice process could move to its next stage.

At last the proceedings that day came to an end when the Bench remanded Rouse in custody until the following Wednesday. But just before then, a smidgeon of levity had occurred when Finnemore asked the lorry driver's mate, Edwin Pitt, whether there had been much conversation between Rouse and the driver, Turner (the mate had remained silent during the journey from the junction at Hardingstone Lane to Tally Ho Corner). Pitt replied obscurely, 'Decent', to which Finnemore riposted, 'Yes, I hope it *was* decent'. Whether or not Pitt appreciated counsel's wit, the court appeared (or so feigned) to do so and the day closed with laughter.

Immediately, the prosecution's allegations about the character of the defendant were taken up with gusto by the press. While the *Evening News* story ran to five full pages, the *Daily Mail*'s to three, and *The Times*' story to two closely typed pages, the headlines screamed in bold type:

BURNING CAR: ASTONISHING DISCLOSURES
ALLEGED STATEMENT BY ROUSE ABOUT 'MY HAREM'
Prosecution suggests that Rouse Meant to Stage a 'Disappearance.'
Evening News, November 27, 1930.

BLAZING CAR MYSTERY
* Police Theory *
ROUSE STAGING A 'FADE OUT'
* Harem Story *
Daily Mail, November 28, 1930.

Somehow, the *Daily Mail* managed to print a photograph of Helen's watching solicitor, Flint, even though he had played no part in the proceedings. Pictures of various other interested parties also appeared, including those of Lily, photographed next to Lee-Roberts, Brown and Bailey and Paling. Many newspaper headlines similar to the above could be cited and the public's appetite for further lurid and insalubrious revelations was being carefully whetted. Indeed more was to come, even in the period after Rouse had been judicially executed the following March.

But returning to the police court hearings, the news that Sir Bernard Spilsbury had surmised that the dead man might have been a coal miner brought more enquiries to Superintendent Brumby's desk. As seen in chapter seven one concerned Thomas Waite, a thirty-year old miner from Merthyr Tydfil, but as with tens, indeed hundreds, of other cases noted in that chapter, it was either a false alarm or a lead that went nowhere. Stories such as Waite's did not assist Brumby. 'Up-to-date we have received over 500 reports of missing men, since the investigations in this case began,' he said, adding mischievously, 'and most of them were married men.' Waite, he believed, had all his teeth when he left home, whereas the dead man had only 14 in each of the upper and lower set, as compared with the usual 16. But that itself might not have been much of a clue. For, as Brumby confided to the reporter from the *Northampton Daily Chronicle*, 'I had only 14 original teeth in my top set, and plenty of people only have that number, instead of 16.' Too much information?

By the following Wednesday, December 3, the DPP had not yet been ready to offer further evidence. Thus it was public knowledge that Rouse's appearance, his fourth before the magistrates, would be a mere formality. However the public wanted to see him too. Crowds formed early. One woman was pushing a pram in which her small child sat, clearly hoping for a family day out. Neither Paling nor Finnemore was present and Rouse was represented by Mr. A. J. Darnell (of solicitors Darnell & Price) who was now working alongside George Lee-Roberts (the latter finding the work in defending Rouse too much for a sole partner). Lily Rouse was again in court and it was reported that she had taken employment the day before in a Northampton draper's shop to help defray the legal costs. Superintendent Tebbey told the Bench that by arrangement between the DPP and defence counsel, no evidence would be presented that day and that he now sought another remand. This was granted until the following Tuesday. Rouse nodded and made for the steps leading below without saying a word. Not much of a family day out, then.

The local journalists were much taken with the coincidence that another case of alleged murder had been brought before the magistrates on that same day. 'Could anyone remember the like?' they asked. But this was a case of a very different colour. A married woman, Mrs Emma Slater, was accused of the murder of a single girl who had died in hospital following a botched abortion. [235] She too was remanded for a week while, as noted elsewhere, further enquiries into the disappearance of Thomas Waite were suddenly abandoned when he walked into Watford police station and identified himself. Indeed that morning Brumby had received a letter-card previously sent to the Nottingham police, and purporting to be from Thomas Waite. 'Sir, I am not dead. I have my own reasons for not coming forward, but very much alive.' And, it would seem, very much travelled.

By Tuesday December 9, the DPP had still not gathered the technical and medical evidence thought to be needed to show that the blaze in Hardingstone Lane had not been accidental but had been deliberately ignited by Rouse. Instead Paling produced thirteen witnesses who would fill gaps in the narrative of Rouse's journeys and would, in effect, give further evidence of his dubious character. Rouse was said to be looking 'particularly well' when he stepped into the dock to face the magistrates. Five were on the Bench that morning, Campion (chairman), Lord Erskine, Major Markham, J. S. Smith, and Wood. Once the charge had been read again, the chairman told Rouse that he might sit down. Rouse accepted the offer. His demeanour was described as 'complacent' as he saw a succession of prosecution witnesses troop into the witness box one after the other to recount the events involving Rouse that we noted in the first chapter. Thus PC Lilley gave his account of speaking to Rouse at Markyate and noticing the car passenger. Then Hendell Brownhill recounted his story of driving Rouse to Cardiff and of his suspicions about his passenger's story and of the supposed reassurances that the vehicle loss had been reported to the police and insurers. Rouse's strange behaviour in the Cooper's Arms, also witnessed by the licensee, David Morris, when the butcher's boy, Idwal Morris, piped up about the charred female body in the car, prompting Rouse to exclaim, 'Oh, dear, dear, I cannot bear to hear anything about it. I don't want to hear anything about it', before removing himself, likewise stayed in the memory, while Rouse's decision not to travel to London with the bus company located beside Cardiff's main police station also struck Brownhill as odd.

The evidence of the Welsh contingent did not really electrify the court. Indeed one journalist was looking out of the window in search of inspiration. When in doubt, talk about the weather. As the *Evening News* that day reported, 'At this point in the hearing a heavy snowstorm broke over Northampton. Scores of people who were waiting outside the court to hear the latest scraps of information about the case were driven from the streets to the shelter of shop doorways and entries. The snow fell in huge flakes and within a few minutes it had covered the ground an inch deep.'

But Paling had a potential headline-grabber up his sleeve. For he now adduced as a witness Mary Teresa Casey, a sister at the City of London Maternity Hospital, who revealed that a Miss Nellie Tucker had been admitted as an emergency on

October 29 when she gave birth to a girl. At that time Nellie was calling herself Mrs. Rouse and, as Casey testified, Nellie had a visitor on the evening of November 5. The man from the *Evening News* pricked up his ears. This was what the journalist wanted to hear. And in due course the newspaper headline later that day ran, 'GIRL IN HOSPITAL AS 'MRS. ROUSE' – NURSE TELLS ABOUT A PATIENT AND HER VISITOR'. In fact, the fifty words that Sister Casey spoke at the hearing were not quite as incontrovertible as the man from the *Evening News* would have his readers suppose. Asked if the accused had visited her patient on November 5, the witness replied, 'A man visited her'. Asked who it was, she replied, 'I assume it was Mr. Rouse.' Finnemore rebuked her, 'It does not matter what you assume. You do not know who it was?' 'No, sir,' the sister replied. No matter. The reporter had his story, with a neat conclusion: 'After a consultation between Mr. Paling and Mr. Finnemore no further questions were put to this witness'. Perhaps Paling, prompted by Finnemore's undoubted discomfort as the examination of this modern angel with the lamp proceeded, recognised that he was encroaching upon dangerous ground by adducing what might be construed as the prisoner's potentially inadmissible 'bad character' at this stage. If in a hole, stop digging, Paling might have decided (even though it was 'unfortunate' that the bad odour from the hole had already begun to seep out).

Then there arrived a succession of disparate prosecution witnesses some of whom, at least, might have wondered why on earth they had travelled to Northampton to give evidence. For it transpired that they offered little, if anything, to the Crown case regarding the blazing car and the murder charge. There was Mrs. May Smith who ran the newsagent's and tobacconist's shop at 1, Gillingham Street, Victoria, London which Rouse (and many others) had used as an accommodation address for his correspondence with his lovers. There was the car salesman, the hire purchase company official and the insurance agent involved in Rouse's purchasing and insuring of MU 1468, the details of which, including that the car's tool kit did not contain a mallet, are covered subsequently. The court then adjourned for lunch, but as the public left the court room a queue immediately formed for re-admission.

On its resumption the court were entertained to the evidence of Thomas William Reakes, a collier, a neighbour of the Jenkins family and the most voluble witness of the day, with an unstoppable recollection for who said what, and to whom. *Da ni ddim yn gwybod os Reakes gallai o siarad Cymraeg*, but he sounded in the witness box as if he were about to recite in full flow the Anglesey village of Llanfair PG in all its 58-letter glory. He confirmed that when Rouse had arrived at the Jenkins home the prisoner had immediately explained, 'Oh Dad, I have been a long time coming, about 18 hours on the road. I lost my car around Northampton, I went in to have a cup of tea. When I came out my car was gone. My hat and bag were in the car, I have got her insured but I don't want that, I want my car.'

Reakes then went on to repeat what he had seen and heard in the Gellygaer house; about Rouse going upstairs to see Ivy just as he himself went home, of his returning with the evening paper with its picture of the burnt out car in Northampton and of Rouse denying that the car was his. Rouse, he agreed with Finnemore, had not been known to him previously, and his name was not in that evening's paper, though the point of Finnemore's questions here is unclear. PC

Copping next went into the witness box. This was the first time that the scene of the blaze and the position of the charred remains had been described in public, although we know that Copping had not made a note of his observations at the time and was reliant upon his memory. Indeed, he had not made a note of anything at the time. But he did testify to his helping put out the blaze, to rummaging through the wreckage looking for items such as buckles, braces, petrol can top etc, to assisting with the removal of the vehicle on to the verge and taking charge of the mallet found by Sergeant Harris the next morning. Another witness, Bowen Westbrooke, an advertising representative who had known Rouse for two and a half years, told the court that in the previous August he and his family had gone on a camping trip. Arthur and Lily Rouse with their little adopted son had joined them. Rouse had a wooden mallet in his car, similar to the one exhibited, which he made use of to hammer in the tent pegs. So there was a mallet. Rouse never denied it. So what?

The testimony of Sergeant Robert Skelly of the Metropolitan Police, based in Hammersmith, was obviously of vital importance to the prosecution's case, in particular, his repetition of Rouse's initial response to his, Skelly's, arrival: "Very well, I am glad it is all over. I was going to Scotland Yard about it. I am [*sic*] responsible. I am very glad it is all over. I have had no sleep." Similarly, Skelly told the court of Rouse's 'statement' to him at Hammersmith police station, before Brumby's arrival from Northampton, about picking up the man on the Great North Road. But Finnemore was quick to challenge this evidence. Skelly was reading from a notebook. Were these words supposed to amount to a signed statement? Rouse had not signed any such statement. Skelly acknowledged he had not written down at the time what Rouse had actually said but he had done so later. He also acknowledged that he could not arrest Rouse because he did not know with what to charge him (actually, he meant that he did not know which offence Rouse was *suspected* by the Northamptonshire police of having committed). He had just detained him. Finnemore protested, pointing out that 'The elementary rule of this country is when a man is being detained to see the officers he must be cautioned before any statement is taken from him. If this was written later it would not affect the validity of my objection [that no caution had been administered at the crucial time if he was actually being 'detained']. It may affect the officer's memory, but that would be a different point.'

What Finnemore was angling at was that, in law, Rouse had voluntarily accompanied Skelly to the police station in order, in the classic though ambiguous phrase, to 'help the police with their inquiries'. Thus he was *invited* as a witness, not as a suspect. If Skelly had suspicions about Rouse's involvement in criminality, then he ought to have cautioned him, advising him of his right to silence and of the risk, under the then applicable wording, that 'anything you say may be written down and used in evidence' against him. The problem for Finnemore was that it was always possible that Skelly was in the dark, though, in view of the wide newspaper coverage of the Hardingstone blaze and of the charred body, it would probably have been disingenuous of Skelly to deny knowledge of why he had been asked to intercept Rouse at the Hammersmith Broadway coach stop. On balance, we think that Finnemore raised a good point regarding admissibility of Rouse's spontaneous remarks at Hammersmith police station. On the other hand, Skelly might not easily have had an opportunity to administer the caution while Rouse was alighting from the coach before the latter commenced his 'I'm glad it is all over' statement. For this was not like the situation of those policeman who invite a 'person of interest' to accompany them in the police car to the police station and then drive the long, winding 'scenic route' to the destination in the hope that their passenger will offer up spontaneous incriminating 'verbals' during the journey that they recall or record for the trial. In any case, at this juncture in the police court proceedings, the magistrates' clerk interjected to point out that Paling had already read this account of Rouse's statements in full. But, undeterred, Finnemore countered that this 'full account' had been delivered in Paling's opening speech and technically had not been given as evidence. He was therefore formally objecting to this account being entered as evidence. The magistrates went into a huddle and eventually came to the conclusion that they would 'take note' of Finnemore's objection but would admit the 'statement', which hardly satisfied defence counsel, since the significance of 'taking note' might be zero.[236]

And so the rest of Rouse's narrative of the events surrounding the car passenger and the blaze was read out by Skelly, with every jot and tittle being carefully scrutinised by Finnemore for inaccuracy in its transcription. On one critical occasion it led to a vigorous challenge, with counsel claiming that Rouse had surely stated, 'I feel responsible', not 'I am responsible'. On another, Finnemore managed to elicit agreement from the witness that a man not under arrest (as Skelly had admitted) was entitled not to be searched but that Rouse's pockets had been emptied under instructions from the Northamptonshire Constabulary. It was a small victory for Rouse but only a minor set-back for the authorities as the prosecution managed to have the last word on this matter by getting Skelly to state that when 'prisoners are detained in this manner' they were always searched (for they might be hiding a revolver). Again, why let the facts get in the way of a good story. Rouse was not technically being 'detained' at that point and thus did *not* have (or enjoy) the accompanying status of a prisoner. Nor was he even a suspect under arrest, as Skelly himself had acknowledged in examination, nor kept in a police cell, even if he was 'not exactly' treated as a guest. No wonder, as seen in chapters five and twenty-five, Paling had been perceived by some, albeit untypical, critics of the criminal justice system as a malign influence.

At the conclusion of this exchange and after Skelly had stood down, Paling informed the Bench that he would require two more days' testimony before completing his case. So yet another adjournment was ordered until the following Monday. Finnemore's objection to Skelly's evidence received only limited attention in the press. The man from the *Evening News* must have departed early to file his copy. For his readers were treated to the image of the voluble Mr. Reakes in the kitchen of a Welsh cottage brandishing the newspaper picture of the burnt wreck, like the prominent-toothed, animated and bespectacled Private Cheeseman (the Welsh actor, Talfryn Thomas) in *Dad's Army*. The spurious suggestion that Rouse 'might have had a revolver' managed to make its way into the late editions of the local press. In fact we noted previously that Rouse *did* possess a revolver which he had occasionally practised with in the back yard when he had been living with

---

236 *Northampton Daily Chronicle*, December 9, 1930; *The Times*, December 11, 1930.

Helen Campbell in Liverpool Road, Islington (but that information was not yet in the public domain). As to the sensational revelation that Nellie Tucker had posed as 'Mrs. Rouse' in order to give birth to her second daughter by Rouse, that information had been disclosed sufficiently early in the day's proceedings for it to grab the evening paper's headlines. When *The Times* got round to publishing a more sober account of Skelly's evidence two days later, it noted that Paling had adduced the long statement which Rouse was alleged to have made under caution to the *Northampton* (not London) detectives at Hammersmith between 1 am and 5:30 am on Saturday November 8 and which extensively described, in fits and starts and with corrections and counter-corrections, Rouse's narrative of the events surrounding the blaze, and which he had signed before being driven to Northampton thereafter. However Paling had in fact deferred reading it and wished to reserve it until Superintendent Brumby went into the witness-box.

When the hearing resumed on Monday December 15 Lily was not present in court, which intrigued the sketch writers. But the prosaic explanation was that she had to be in London for the sale by auction of the house and furniture in Friern Barnet. Nonetheless, the press knew where the public appetite in the story lay. For that day the six headlines in the *Northampton Daily Chronicle*, in descending order of type face and therefore of presumed public interest, were:

NAME OF MYSTERY WOMAN DISCLOSED
ATTENDANCE AT COURT
CAR WITH DRAWN BLINDS
INTEREST IN ROUSE CASE
QUEUES AGAIN SEEK TO GAIN ADMISSION
TECHNICAL WITNESSES AT TODAY'S HEARINGS.

Indeed, the widespread belief that Henry Flint's mystery client was to be called to give evidence brought crowds tumbling on to the streets. Consequently, when the doors opened there was the usual surge of people at the front of the queue and the press reported that, '....stalwart policemen guarding the portals were surrounded by a pushing, jostling mob which resembled nothing more than a rugby football scrimmage. Women elbowed their way through the mass and it was the male who was threatened with being trampled underfoot.' Into this melée drove a car with blinds tightly drawn. The mystery woman had arrived. Despite the absence of at least three magistrates that morning, Colonel Coote, Smith and Spokes, there was also nearly a full house on the Bench with eight magistrates sitting, that is, Campion in the chair, Lord Erskine, Major Markham, Thornton, Wood and Elliott, with two newcomers, J. S. Walker and Major Geoffrey Elwes, who was the eldest brother of Richard Elwes, the barrister who would appear as Birkett's junior when the trial itself came on (if there had been an issue of judicial bias in view of this relationship it was not pursued by the defence. In any case Richard Elwes was not appearing before his brother at the committal stage). The Bench took their seats at 11.07 precisely, whereupon Flint rose and said that he understood that the woman whose interests he had been instructed to represent would be called (obviously not by him) as a witness. 'In order to prevent any misunderstanding, I want to disclose her name. It is Helen Campbell.' With hindsight it might have seemed that Flint had been manipulated by the

DPP, like other pieces of news management For Helen would *not* be called by Paling to testify that day. Indeed the latter must have known that his technical experts would dominate the day's proceedings. Certainly his list of automotive engineering witnesses would not have pulled in the crowds (though Spilsbury would obviously be an attraction later in the day) as they recounted their findings about, for example, the car being found in second gear (which was Rouse's habit in switching off the ignition and parking his car); or about the fused windscreen and badly burnt tyres; or about the loose petrol union joint, a leak from which, according to a Crown expert, Colonel Buckle, who had conducted an examination followed by a replicating test, an ordinary tumbler would be filled in one minute twenty seconds; all of which could imply that the ferocity of the fire had been due to its having been deliberately fed by petrol. Indeed, the major dispute over the cause of the intense blaze, a controversy joined at the trial itself, is covered in detail in chapter ten; which is more sensible since *defence* technical experts were notable by their absence from the police court hearing. In a similar fashion the medical evidence has primarily been addressed already in chapter six dealing with the post-mortem and inquest, and will also be touched on in chapters nine and ten covering the actual trial. It suffices here to note that prosecution medical evidence at the remand proceedings focussed on a handful of features. These included the burnt-off limbs, the conditions of which were relevant to identifying the position of the victim in the car and whether he had been placed there unconscious or whether, fully conscious, he had tried to scramble free from the burning vehicle which, according to Rouse, the victim had himself set alight. There was the issue of the hairs discovered on the mallet. Were they human, the residue of a blow to the head? There was the black mucus found in the bronchii and analysed by Spilsbury for traces of coal dust, smoke particles or of carbon monoxide. Was the victim a coal miner? Or was the black residue separate evidence that he had been alive and breathing for a short time before life was extinguished in the blaze? Was the triangular piece of petrol-soaked cloth retrieved from the victim's groin area especially significant in suggesting that Rouse had doused the unknown man with petrol before setting him (and the car) alight? These would all be debated in some detail at the trial itself.

It might have been assumed that Spilsbury would have been the star turn at the committal hearing that day. He usually was. For wherever he gave evidence his reputation preceded him. However his appearance in this hearing did not attract the usual attention. There were other factors at work, female factors. And when Paling proposed to call as his next witness Miss Nellie Tucker, Finnemore got to his feet to lodge an immediate objection to her giving evidence. He explained that he did so on the ground that it was a general and fundamental rule that only evidence in support of any charge was relevant to that charge. Yes, Nellie had borne Rouse's child and the prosecution was proposing to submit evidence that the accused's home and domestic life was not what it should have been. So how, on any principle of law, such disclosures could be evidence against this defendant on the charge of murdering an unknown man in a Northamptonshire country road by setting fire to him, he (Finnemore) did not know. In short, he failed to see what link there was between the (immoral) domestic life of the accused man and the alleged murder which had taken place on November 6. It would be as if the prosecution were to say, 'Here is a man of bad character with a criminal record and therefore we are going to show you the kind of man we're dealing with.' Nobody would dream of doing that. The law of the country was abundantly clear that evidence of that kind (bad character) could never be given against a man (which was not strictly true since limited exceptions did exist). Amplifying his point, he observed that the prosecution had already suggested that the accused had been living a somewhat irregular life and that he might be anxious to end it all. Indeed, the Crown were suggesting that Rouse 'did it by the extravagant method of picking up a perfectly unknown man, murder him in cold blood, and try to dispose of his body by burning in the hope that it might be mistaken for his own.' Addressing Paling directly, he insisted that, 'You cannot put to the court what I do not hesitate to say is a purely fantastic motive [falsely to appear to be dead] in order to prove [sic] any evidence [Nellie's testimony showing bad character] which obviously otherwise would not be admissible for one moment.' And with regard to the suggestion that the accused had wished to vanish, 'The whole evidence is absolutely to the contrary.' Quite apart from calling to the youths after they had walked past him, drawing attention to himself, he took a ride in a lorry back to London. He then journeyed in broad daylight, in a public vehicle, in his own name, carrying his suitcase with his own initials on it, to a place near Newport, where he was perfectly well known in his own name. It might be that there were things in the accused's married life that did not redound to his credit, but that was 'no matter to this court, on this charge'. Admittedly it was the responsibility of Paling at this preliminary stage to satisfy the Bench that he could (which meant as distinct from 'would') prove the charge. However, prosecuting counsel was not there with a roving commission into the past. Consequently, asserted Finnemore, he [Paling] was not entitled, because he had alleged a particular motive, to call evidence alluding to the prisoner's bad character which otherwise would obviously not be admissible. Indeed Finnemore also objected to Paling's having already alluded, in his opening speech, to Rouse's bad character by referring to his 'harem' as well as to his (Paling) having asserted that the victim had been intentionally murdered (actually intention is an essential ingredient in a murder charge, though as well as intention to kill, it might include intention to cause serious harm, from which death actually ensues). As to the latter claim regarding Rouse's alleged intent, the DPP official, at the commencement of the hearing, was merely (and fairly) outlining the case he was going to present, rather than presenting 'evidence' which, in fact, could only be spoken to by witnesses who could then be challenged on cross-examination. But his allusion in his opening remarks to Rouse's bad character was another matter. For if the 'bad character' of the accused was inadmissible, which was normally but not always the case, then Paling had evidently employed an underhand method to smuggle it in, even if not all the sleazy details had yet been aired in court.

So Paling's legal justification for calling Nellie (and Helen) to testify was that it was necessary for the prosecution ultimately (even if not immediately, he could have added) to prove Rouse's intent to kill the victim. But it is clear that for Paling to point to the motive on the part of Rouse as being to be rid of his domestic entanglements, notwithstanding that proving motive was not a legal requirement, would make the establishment of intent to murder the victim more plausible in the Bench's eyes, thereby justifying sending Rouse to the assizes. Thus the evidence to be given by Nellie and by other witnesses 'of a similar character', as Paling described Rouse's 'harem', would re-affirm Rouse's desperate situation and his need to employ drastic measures to escape from its net. Of course, Paling insisted, meeting the two men, Brown and Bailey, in Hardingstone Lane had upset the defendant's plan to disappear and to be assumed to have perished in the blaze. So, while momentarily wandering about on that night not really knowing what to do, Rouse improvised by opting to tell all and sundry whom he subsequently met, until he reached Hammersmith, either outright lies or half-truths regarding the car not being his (as he told Reakes and the Jenkins's in Gellygaer) or, alternatively, that it had been stolen (as he told to numerous others). That is, while Rouse's stories repudiated any hints of motive to disappear or of intent to murder, Paling sought to show otherwise. Thus by adducing the evidence of Rouse's women, Paling would not simply seek to demonstrate that Rouse was an immoral man (and to imply that immoral men were more likely to be of a criminal disposition), but to link his desperate sexual and financial circumstances to the motive behind his alleged plan to kill another and to disappear.

So was the evidence of Rouse's 'harem', to be adduced by Paling, inadmissible 'bad character' evidence or was it relevant evidence of motive that bore on intent? The responsibility for deciding this at the police court fell to Faulkner Stops, the magistrates' clerk who, as a legally qualified court official, was bound to advise the Bench as to the law. He asked Paling directly, 'Is it the serious suggestion on the part of the prosecution that the motive in this case was to suggest he [Rouse] had been burned in the car and that he meant to disappear?' to which Paling replied, 'That is so.' But despite the exchange raising no explicit link between Nellie's testimony, which would surely illuminate Rouse's immoral 'bad character' and the issue of motive, Finnemore remained seated, perhaps recalling that it had been Rouse himself who had spontaneously mentioned his 'harem' to Inspector Lawrence. So the magistrates retired to the justices' room to be advised on the law in private by their clerk. On their return, they allowed Nellie to testify in view of the motive suggested by the prosecution (though the question would remain whether motive was being adduced by the Crown in *evidence*, rather than just in Paling's opening speech?). Whether the direction to admit her testimony was legally correct or not is moot. It may have been wrong. It may have been right. Indeed, sometimes a ruling might be right, but for the wrong reason. Whatever the correct legal analysis,[237] the gentlemen of the press must have breathed a

---

237   The law on such questions was generally clear. But a lengthy digression may be in order. First, the 'bad character' of the accused was usually not admissible, especially where it took the form of previous convictions. For the prisoner ought to be tried on the current set of circumstances and not on his previous record. This would apply (certainly until 2003) even if charged with the type of offence with which he had previously been convicted. A number of exceptions to this rule existed but are mostly not relevant here. Second, 'relevance' means that the admissible evidence in question must make the 'facts-in-issue' more or less probable. In Rouse's case, the ultimate test would be whether the evidence in question, Nellie's testimony, would make his culpability for murder more or (from the defence standpoint) less probable. It is thus easy to see why Paling focussed on linking Rouse's sexual entanglements and their financial consequences with the motive to kill and disappear, while Finnemore stressed that the events should be confined to what happened in Hardingstone Lane. From the latter's point of view, Nellie's testimony would not only reveal Rouse's bad character as an immoral man but bad character which was irrelevant to making more or less probable Rouse's liability for an alleged murder occurring in a country road miles away from London. To take a hypothetical example, the previous sexually immoral but not unlawful behaviour by a priest should be irrelevant to whether he stole a box of chocolates from W. H. Smith. On the other hand a previous conviction for theft by the same priest, whether committed months previously, or years previously when he was a novitiate, may be considered relevant, since it was the same kind of offence, but nonetheless it would usually be inadmissible on the ground of its being more 'prejudicial than probative'. Indeed

collective sigh of relief. For what would they have been able to print without all these suggestive hints of sexual shenanigans? As to the defence, the sighs would have been of a different nature. Rouse's womanising in London and elsewhere (but not, apparently, in Northamptonshire) was now a central issue in the case of a burnt man found in a blazing car in a country village called Hardingstone.

And so Nellie Tucker gave evidence. All eyes in the courtroom turned to look at her as she entered, 'dressed in a blue helmet felt hat and a coat trimmed with a fur collar and cuffs'. She was allowed to sit in the witness box. She told the court that she had known Rouse for nearly five years. She had had a child by him in May 1928 and he had contributed to the maintenance of the child, but not regularly. The last time had been on November 1. She had taken out an order for maintenance against Rouse at the North London police court two years previously. On October 29 she had given birth to another child at the City of London Maternity Hospital. Asked who the father was, she whispered, 'Mr. Rouse.' She had last seen him on November 5 when he had visited her in the hospital. He had left at 8 o'clock in the evening, and that was her testimony completed. What did it signify for the prosecution? It reaffirmed not only Rouse's amorous entanglements but his fathering of not one but two 'bastard' children by Nellie; for whose provision he paid, and would otherwise have continued to pay dearly, had he not now fallen into the clutches of the law. It might also be inferred that his visits to Nellie were episodic rather than reflective of true and constant devotion (he had a wife, you know, as well as being 'friendly with several women'). Given that he was an obvious cad, was Nellie's testimony more or less persuasive as Crown evidence, on the basis of what had been disclosed already about his activities and about the lies that he had liberally disseminated from Hardingstone Lane to Hammersmith via the Embankment, Gellygaer and Cardiff, that a murder charge against him should be taken to the next stage? For the local elites comprising the Northamptonshire magistracy, presumably it was more than a case of there being no smoke without fire (which may, or may not, be an appropriate metaphor).

Then following Sergeant Harris's description of finding the mallet fourteen yards in front of the car, which was bound to lead to sinister speculation notwithstanding the ambiguity of this evidence, the court now adjourned at the late hour of 6.30 p.m. Rouse was seen to chat amiably with the policemen beside him in the dock, he exchanged a few words with Superintendent Tebbey, donned his coat and his hat before going down, and looked round the court smiling before

while his recent previous convictions of this nature might show his propensity to theft, it could not until 2003 normally be adduced by the Crown unless the criminal acts were accompanied by strikingly similar and unusual circumstances such as his being robed up like a bishop, or wearing an Indian head-dress when committing the crime. As to the theft committed by the priest many years previously, precisely because it had occurred so long ago then, for the Crown to drag it up again, would only taint the middle-aged or elderly accused for what had been a youthful excess, making the previous bad character more prejudicial than probative. Moreover, it could add very little, or nothing at all, to his state of mind at the time of the instant alleged theft, it would not demonstrate a fixed or distinctive *modus operandi* and, finally, would not add anything to reconstructing the event. Consequently, it would be inadmissible. Unfortunately, Rouse's case regarding admissibility was not straight-forward, as we have seen, with sexual misconduct (did this in fact constitute 'bad character' or was the phrase confined to previous convictions and the like?) apparently intertwined with motive and intent, added to which was Rouse's own unprompted admission to Inspector Lawrence about his expensive harem. Contemporary legal periodicals noted that the question was unclear in Rouse's case while the legal issue was not resolved at Rouse's appeal.

disappearing. It was as if he were taking a curtain call at the theatre. After all, whether theatre or court, performance matters.

Sadly for the evening press Nellie Tucker's appearance and testimony in court had occurred too late in the afternoon for printed reports to appear that day. Indeed, even Dr. Shaw's and Spilsbury's evidence failed to make the late editions. So, in their absence the evening headlines had to make do with Flint's early revelation of his client's identity.

'VEILED WOMAN IN BLAZING CAR CASE',
'TO COURT IN SALOON WITH DRAWN BLINDS',
'HELEN CAMPBELL'.

By the morning of Tuesday December 16, the *Daily Mail* had found a photograph of Helen Campbell, smiling wistfully into the camera and definitely not wearing a veil. However, the veil was back in place when she did arrive at court on foot, accompanied by Mr. Flint, after staying the night at the local Plough Hotel. But as soon as she entered the solicitors' room in the court building the veil was removed and she took a seat near the fire, where Walker, one of the magistrates, was warming himself. Mrs. Rouse was again not in court when the hearing resumed. After a brief re-appearance by Harris in the witness box where he had to correct a statement of his from the previous late afternoon, the moment that the crowds and press had all been waiting for now arrived. Wearing a wedding ring and a gold keeper, set with a diamond, Helen Campbell entered the witness box. Now staying at 21 Nelson Road, Chatham, she recounted her life with Rouse and the children who had resulted from that liaison. But for all the time that she was in the witness box it may have been significant of their acrimonious split that she did not look at Rouse, save for one brief glance in his direction when she named him as the father of her son. Pale and agitated, she gave her evidence almost in a whisper. As she signed her deposition, Rouse sat back in his chair with his arms folded. He smiled as she left the witness box but she did not look towards him.

And the assault upon Rouse's character continued. Next to give evidence were Ivy Jenkins's father and sister, William and Phyllis Jenkins from Gellygaer. As Inspector Evans from the Bargoed office of the Glamorgan police had reported on November 26, after interviewing the Jenkins family,

> "I might mention that William Jenkins is disgusted with the conduct of Rouse and states that he has ruined his daughter, and he together with all the members of the family appear most vindictive towards Rouse. They appear anxious to give evidence against him, and to render all possible assistance to the Police."

Thus William and Phyllis confirmed the account, noted in a previous chapter, of how Rouse had met and 'married' Ivy, of his arrival at Gellygaer on the evening of November 6, and of his stay, conversations and behaviour at their house, especially when confronted with the newspaper accounts of the blaze, until his departure for Cardiff the next morning. Such bizarre conduct on Rouse's part, especially in respect of the press reports from Northampton, must have suggested to the Bench a pronounced shiftiness associated with guilt.

After PC Valentine, next in the witness box, drew a verbal picture of the scene at Hardingstone Lane on his arrival there at 3:10 am on November 6, it was now Brumby's turn in the box to describe his confrontation with Rouse at Hammersmith police station in the early hours of Saturday, November 8. He had asked Rouse if he cared to say anything about the loss of his car or about his movements on the fateful night. Rouse had replied, 'Yes I will tell you about it.' He then cautioned Rouse before the latter commenced the prolonged and episodic statement that was patiently taken down by Sergeant Skelly between 1 am and 5:30 am that morning. At the end of the marathon exercise, Rouse had said it was correct and had signed it. At this point Paling proposed to read the long statement, but another legal wrangle ensued. Finnemore did not object to the statement being read because it was Rouse's defence up to the point at which the narrative ended. What he objected to being read out were Rouse's answers to a number of questions put to him *after* he had finished his statement. Thus Finnemore submitted that the Judges' Rules, the body of guidelines compiled by the judicial bench in 1912, and designed to protect suspects from overbearing or oppressive questioning by investigating policemen, laid down that once a suspect had finished his statement he ought not to be questioned or cross-examined about it, apart from the elucidation of a point which might not be clear.

In response, Paling quoted another of the Judges' Rules. 'When a police officer is endeavouring to discover the author of a crime there is no objection to him putting questions in respect thereof to any person or persons whether suspected or not from whom he thinks useful information can be obtained.' Of course, Paling's point was nonsense as the rule he quoted was simply a general introduction to police questioning of anyone, whether witness, suspect or other third party, and its application would obviously *precede* and permit the taking down and signing of *any* statement, whereas Finnemore's 'rule' was determinative and time-prescriptive: once the witness (or suspect) had made and signed his statement he could not *generally* be questioned again. So Paling proposed a curious compromise. 'I submit you should admit those questions and answers (put to Rouse *after* he signed his statement) as evidence, but that they should not be read in open court'. What precisely Paling meant by that proposal is unclear. If the additional questions and answers were not adduced in open court it is difficult to see how the Bench could take them into account on the central question of committal (though that is not to say that the content of the answers would necessarily be inadmissible under the rules of evidence at the trial itself). Nonetheless, once again the magistrates were obliged to retire to hear Faulkner Stops' legal guidance before making a ruling.

Meanwhile the press noticed that Lily had arrived opportunely. Rouse was keen to know the result of the auction sale of his house and furniture. He asked Superintendent Tebbey if he might talk to Lily. 'You can listen in if you want to,' said Rouse, 'I only want to ask her a personal question.' Tebbey told him he could see her afterwards but if he wanted to ask her anything now he could do so through his solicitor. So one or two papers were shown to Rouse, via Lee-Roberts. Apparently he was pleased. He smiled and nodded as he looked through the figures. It was a sham. Less had been raised from the sale than had been hoped.

The magistrates returned after ten minutes and agreed to adopt Paling's compromise, assuring the defence that the Bench would ignore that part of the statement objected to. The clerk then read from the signed statement a passage where Rouse explained that the mallet had never been used for anything other than knocking out dents in his motor. Brumby reiterated that Rouse, who had insisted that 'I am quite innocent', had been treated well by him and by Lawrence during his late-night and morning exchanges and interviews at Hammersmith and Angel Lane police stations, that Rouse had given his replies readily and voluntarily, and that there had been no threat or inducement held out to him. Indeed, there had been no need to threaten him. When the court adjourned for lunch, Rouse was able to have the promised earnest conversation with Lily, and Lee-Roberts had another consultation with his client in the cells below.

The afternoon resumption saw Inspector Lawrence in the witness box. But as he started talking about the conversation with Rouse that had taken place around noon on Saturday November 8 at Angel Lane, that is, after Rouse had been told by him that he could see Lily 'later', Finnemore objected once more to this evidence. For the prisoner's unprompted remarks about Lily being 'too good for me', of his being 'very friendly with several women' and of his 'harem' being an 'expensive game', were, argued counsel, matters bearing on the question of bad character, and not in respect of the events at Hardingstone Lane and beyond. Thus for Finnemore the evidence was inadmissible because it was not probative at all, in the sense that it was irrelevant to the 'matter-in-issue' (the murder charge). Indeed, even had counsel conceded its relevance, he would undoubtedly have claimed that its prejudicial character outweighed any probative element it might have possessed in relation to that charge. Unfortunately for his client, the Bench adhered to its previous view. The evidence was declared admissible insofar as it bore on motive. So Lawrence was free to tell the story of the 'harem' again and Rouse's dirty washing was going to get a further airing in public; and the press were free to print the story once more.

And with one final apology from Paling that Ivy Jenkins was too ill to travel to give evidence (and those present would have had a strong suspicion as to Rouse's role in causing her to be indisposed), he asked the Bench to commit the prisoner for trial at the next assizes in Northampton. But before the Bench finally decided on the question, Finnemore bobbed up again to remind them that the prosecution evidence tendered had to be clear and definite against any man who would next have to take his trial before a judge and jury. Indeed, it would, he continued, be difficult to think of a case where so grave an issue was at stake, but where the evidence was so flimsy, uncertain and insubstantial. 'You are asked in this case to fill a great gap in the evidence by assuming something happened [presumably, during the blaze]. What it was nobody can tell, and nobody has tried to tell you and you are asked to guess at it.' In other words, he was indicating that the focus should have been on the events causing and during the actual blaze, the evidence regarding which was virtually non-existent. Thus he insisted that the evidence of Rouse's women could not help the Bench to decide if there was a case of murder against the accused. Indeed, the Bench were being asked to send the case forward so that other people (the trial jury) might be asked to believe that Rouse had murdered in cold blood a complete stranger and had burned his body in the hope that people would think that he himself had vanished. Yet Rouse had not disappeared or hidden himself from a single person. As to the sinister-seeming mallet, no one could in fact state for certain how it came to be where it was found.

Furthermore, as to the one human hair, said to be a light one, identified on the mallet, there was also no evidence as to how *it* came to be attached to the exhibit. In sum, here was a man who sees his car in a mass of flames with a living man inside it. He cannot possibly assist. He becomes in his own terms panic-stricken and starts shouting, 'My God! My God!', and away he goes. It would surely not be right, fair or just to make that man take his trial. And with that appeal, he sat down.

It was ominous that the Bench did not even bother to retire to the magistrates' room. Instead, they consulted with each other in hushed terms in open court, with the chairman announcing that the Bench had agreed there was a *prima facie* case for the accused to answer. Rouse, who was now standing and leaning on the front of the dock, spoke in a slightly subdued voice. 'I am quite innocent of this charge. I have made this statement. In any case, not being a wealthy man, whether I am found guilty or not, my all is taken.' Was it in character that, faced with a trial on a capital offence which could result in his execution, the financial consequences of the proceedings remained one of his concerns; did his remarks speak forcefully to his *petit-bourgeois* modern consumerist suburban *mentalité*; or was he simply and calculatedly seeking sympathy and a fair response to any future request for legal aid, knowing that his house and goods were realising considerably less than he had hoped and anticipated? As ever, the last word went to the press. Even *The Times* succumbed to the temptation of an alluring headline:

ROUSE COMMITTED FOR TRIAL

MISS CAMPBELL'S EVIDENCE

Another stage in this compelling saga was completed and so the caravan moved on to the next round of revealing and titillating disclosures (or so the press hoped). Had Rouse been given a raw deal by the magistrates, insofar as they had admitted so much embarrassing material about his immoral life-style, some of it, of course, disclosed to Inspector Lawrence by the accused himself? For it must be remembered that the event being investigated was a suspected homicide occurring in a country road near Northampton, tens and hundreds of miles from the homes of wife or lovers. This was no crime of passion committed within the confines of the Villa Madeira in Bournemouth or on the approach road to Kensington Gardens (Ilford, that is), the scenes of the Rattenbury and Percy Thompson killings, respectively. So why bring in this questionable evidence about his tangled sexual affairs, if not to blacken his name? 'Motive' was the Crown's response, and motive it was that persuaded the Bench to hear Rouse's lovers testify. Just a pity that when the trial itself came round, 'motive' mysteriously (or not so mysteriously) disappeared from the Crown's agenda, and it was back to Hardingstone Lane and to Rouse's dissembling and obfuscations as to what had occurred there and elsewhere, and technical data about the causes of car blazes, that would preoccupy the assize court. But we are inclined to think that the Crown would have got their man irrespective of whether the police court disclosures about his sexual shenanigans had been admitted or excluded.[238]

---

238 It is not wholly clear that, had they been minded to do so, Rouse's defence team could have legally challenged the committal order on the basis of the alleged wrongful admission of the prejudicial evidence regarding Rouse's character. The hearing was not technically a 'trial'

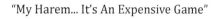

which might otherwise be challenged on appeal or by the process known as judicial review. Indeed the magistrates' 'legal bible', *Stone's Justices' Manual* which, since its first edition in 1842, has guided magistrates clerks and their magisterial benches almost to the present day as to the law (until recently 'usurped' by *Blackstone's Manual*), makes no reference to appeals against, or judicial review of, remand or committal orders. As will be noted subsequently, full oral committal hearings of the type conducted in Rouse's case generally no longer take place, while even further refinements, known as the 'allocation procedure', thereby shortening the pre-trial process, were introduced in May 2013.

SECTION B
Trial and Post-Trial

CHAPTER NINE

CROWN K.C.: "EXPERT WILL SAY IT WAS NOT ACCIDENTAL"

EVENING NEWS, January 26, 1931

Trial: The Prosecution Case

Summoned by the High Sheriff, the twelve members of the grand jury of the Northamptonshire Assizes gathered on Friday, January 23, 1931 to hear the trial judge, Mr. Justice Talbot, deliver his 'charge to the jury', the body that ritualistically determined whether the complainant had established a 'true' bill of indictment (a '*billa vera*') against the accused to answer at trial. Alternatively, it could determine that there was no criminal case for him to contest in court ('*ignoramus*'). In fact, since the Northamptonshire magistrates had already committed Rouse for trial in December 1930, the meeting of the grand jury the following month became merely a formal, ceremonial occasion.[239] Indeed, by 1931, the institution had almost run its course since the initial proceedings in the vast majority of prosecutions were now in the hands of professional lawyers or senior policemen conducting the Crown case at committal hearings at the police court. Thus with the increasing professionalisation of criminal prosecution and with the bulk of screening of indictments by magistrates, the grand jury was on its last legs, and indeed 'passed

239 Historically, the charge to the grand jury, a body composed of between twelve and twenty-three propertied men, was an opportunity for the justices in eyre, the itinerant judges visiting the monarch's far-flung regions of England and Wales, to spread the royal message of demanding loyalty from his lieges, the prohibition of tumult and criminality, the eschewing of immorality, and the injunction to pursue honest and God-fearing lives. The grand jury, like the 'petty' ('petit') jury, was seen as a bastion of English liberty. As the novelist and magistrate, Henry Fielding, in his charge to the grand jury at the City and Westminster Sessions, declaimed on June 29, 1749, "And of juries in general be so very signal a blessing to this nation....what, gentlemen, shall we say of the institution of Grand Juries, by which an Englishman, so far from being convicted, cannot be even tried, not even put upon his trial in any capital case at the suit of The Crown [which might nonetheless be an attempt at a private prosecution, perhaps by a local Association for the Prosecution of Felons], till twelve men at least have said on their oaths, that there is a probable cause for his accusation?" See Henry Fielding (Arthur Murphy, ed.), *The Works of Henry Fielding, Esq: Miscellaneous: Covent-Garden Journal, Essay on Nothing, Charge Delivered to the Grand Jury, 29th June, 1749....*, Nabu Press, Charleston, South Carolina, USA, 2014. The finding of ignoramus by a grand jury had not been uncommon before the mid-nineteenth century since many indictments would have been presented by aggrieved private individuals with their own proper or improper motives for commencing proceedings rather than, from around 1850, by experienced state prosecutors, primarily local senior police officers, acquainted with basic principles of criminal jurisprudence, evidence and procedure.

away' on September 1, 1933.[240]

Yet the solemnity and majesty of the law had to remain visible to ensure the appropriate level of deference and awe in a system still heavily weighted in the interests of the rich and powerful. Thus image and grand ceremony, that is, the semiotics of the occasion, must still prevail. Consequently, when addressing the Rouse case on the list, Mr. Justice Talbot, in what was effectively a superfluous homily, advised the grand jury that,

> "That case attracted a great deal of public attention, principally, I suppose, because of the very unusual and certainly surprising fact that it has been apparently impossible to say who the man whom the accused person is said to have murdered is [sic]. But of course that makes no difference to the legal aspect of the case, and I shall say no more about it except that after you have considered it, I think you will come to the conclusion that it is a case fit to be tried".[241]

Talbot's brief observation on the peculiarities of the case during this preliminary, essentially symbolic, hearing neatly identified two of the issues that would pre-occupy both prosecution and defence counsel throughout the trial. These were the huge public interest in the case, reflected in the continuing and extensive press coverage which had already devoted hundreds of column inches to Rouse's amorous adventures, and the puzzling anonymity of the victim. So, armed with the bill of indictment, the grand jury assembled to swear in and examine cursorily, needless to say, the prosecution witnesses due to line up for the expected trial itself. In the laconic words of the press, 'The jury found a true bill and the trial will begin on Monday'.[242] That the grand jury would have found otherwise would have been astonishing, given that the magistrates had already committed Rouse for trial after a much more extensive investigation into whether the Crown had established a *prima facie* case to be answered. But, presumably, despite its virtually redundant role, it still remained within its province, nonetheless, to have reported 'ignoramus'. Of course, it did not and from then on the press would lavish even more coverage on the trial itself, thereby adding colour to the sometimes dry, but occasionally dramatic, transcript of proceedings assiduously recorded for posterity by the court shorthand writers.

More than 1,200 applications for admission to the court room were received from members of the public. In response, the under-sheriff devised a ticketing system to ensure that those who had business before the court had a seat. These, notably, included Mrs. Rouse who, to much surprise, was not to be called as a witness by the defence (she could not, of course, be compelled to testify for the Crown against her husband). An architect was called in to take measurements of

240 The history of the grand jury from the eighteenth century has been explored by recent historians of crime and of the criminal law, such as John Beattie, *Crime and the Courts in England, 1660-1800*, Clarendon Press, Oxford, 1986; and John H. Langbein, *The Origins of Adversary Criminal Trial*, Clarendon Press, Oxford, 2005. But earlier brief accounts still possess value. See Pendleton Howard, *Criminal Justice in England*, Macmillan, 1931, pp. 352-4; Elizabeth Melling (ed.), *Kentish Sources: VI, Crime and Punishment*, Kent County Council, Maidstone, 1969, pp. 9-10.
241 *Evening News*, January 23, 1931.
242 *Ibid.* Indeed, there was another presentment against Rouse prepared for the grand jury, one for the offence of bigamy allegedly committed on November 22, 1924 when he had 'married' Helen Campbell. That presentment was left lying, pending the outcome of the murder trial. See HO144/19185, Presentment, January 22, 1931.

the small county hall court room and to determine its capacity. On the basis of his calculations sixty tickets were issued for each day. On the Saturday before the trial, a stream of applicants made last-minute efforts to gain admission by calling at the under-sheriff's office in person, but to no avail. Concerned that the level of public interest might prove disruptive, the judge, as his trial notes reveal, issued a strict instruction that there should be silence in the public area of the court room, and that any member of the public whispering or moving during the proceedings would be escorted by the police out of the building.

Perhaps his anxiety was justified. For, on the first day of the trial, 400 people seeking to gain entry queued from the early hours of a cold January morning amid the occasional flurry of snow. They were all hoping to witness what the press dubbed as, 'The most sensational trial ever held at the Northamptonshire Assize Court'. Most of those queuing were to be disappointed and most of those queuing were women. Were they factory girls or office typists lured by the spectacle of this handsome Lothario in the dock? Were they middle-class *Hausfrauen* outraged (or secretly excited) by the accounts of Rouse's philanderings and determined to witness his come-uppance or were they middle-class women enjoying 'sisterhood' together, and showing off their dress fashions while watching one of the greatest free entertainments offered to British people (now that executions were no longer conducted in public spaces)? Were they tired working-class housewives finding a break from domestic toil while the children were at school and the husband not due back home from work until much later? Or was it simply ghoulish curiosity? Historians, such as George Rudé,[243] have sought to analyse the social and political significance of the 'crowd in history', whether those engaged in seventeenth and eighteenth century food riots, the *tricoteuses* watching the French revolutionary guillotine coming down on aristocrats' necks, the 'rabble' witnessing the execution of Maria Manning (Dickens was present and Henry Mayhew interviewed spectators), or the Chartist 'rioters'. An analysis of women spectators at murder trials from, say, the time of Madeleine Smith in 1857 might well be a rewarding exercise in portraying an image of female interests, concerns, values and behaviour, and changes over time, from the mid-nineteenth to the mid-twentieth century.

Eventually, on Monday January 26, the doors of the court room were opened at 10:15 am, and the seats quickly and quietly filled. Lily, with her vivid red hair, had arrived early and took a place on the left of the dock. She wore a tight-fitting black coat, heavily trimmed with black fur at the collar and cuffs, a pale green felt hat (could that have been why Helen Campbell mischievously employed the *nom-de-plume*, Mrs. Green?), and a necklace of red jade beads. Beside her was an elderly grey-haired man, Rouse's father (his grandfather was also still alive). Governor Gwilliam of Bedford Prison entered the court and then accompanied Rouse's solicitor, Lee-Roberts, down the stairs to the cells for a last-minute interview with the prisoner.

Promptly at 10:30 a trumpet sounded outside the county hall and the court room fell silent as Mr. Justice Talbot, accompanied by his chaplain and the high sheriff, entered and settled himself into the comfortable judge's chair secured

---

243   George Rudé, *The Crowd in History: A Study of Popular Disturbances in France and England, 1730-1848,* John Wiley & Son, 1964.

on a raised dais. The clerk to the assize, the former actor and novelist, George Pleydell Bancroft, turned to the senior officer present and asked, 'Will you put up Alfred Arthur Rouse?' For some moments the silence was tense with expectation. Then Rouse appeared from the cells below, flanked by two prison warders. His sartorial vanity appeased, his request for new clothes had been granted by the prison authorities, and he wore a bespoke lounge suit in dark brown, with a stiff white collar, and a brown and cream striped tie. His smart appearance was complemented by a confident demeanour (which might not necessarily have pleased his defence team), though he appeared more drawn, while his face had lost some of its ruddy glow since his appearance at the police court. With hands spread wide, he gripped the front of the dock tightly.

The jury was summoned and the charge was put to Rouse: 'Alfred Arthur Rouse, you stand charged upon this indictment with the murder of a certain man whose name is unknown upon the sixth of November last. Are you guilty or not guilty?' Rouse replied in a quiet but firm voice, 'Not guilty, sir.' The clerk then advised that should he object to any of the jurors, the time to do so would be before they were sworn. This was the procedure of the now-abolished 'peremptory challenge' where no reasons for objection needed to be adduced. Rouse watched intently as the jurors entered the witness box. When the names of Mary Watson Penn and Ella Munday were called (women had been able to sit on juries following the passage of the Sex Disqualification (Removal) Act 1919, with the first murder trial with women on the jury being the 'Musical Milkman' trial of George Bailey in 1920),[244] they were challenged by Finnemore and these two ladies were therefore stood down. Clearly, Finnemore believed that women would be much more judgmental towards Rouse and his sexual incontinence than would men who might have been thought to be more tolerant of prisoners leading young women astray. Of course, evidence to justify those beliefs was (and possibly remains) elusive. Perhaps, therefore, it was simply gut instinct that, rightly or wrongly, prompted counsel's challenge. The jury that was finally empanelled was therefore composed of twelve men. Their names were published in the press, a practice that would today be considered a contempt of court since it subsequently came to be realized that publication might offer malevolent forces an opportunity for intimidation or corruption.[245]

After the jury members were sworn in, Rouse relaxed and glanced around the court room. He immediately spotted Lily sitting on the left of the dock. He was observed to mouth a question to her. She smiled and mouthed something back which the press, to their frustration, could not decipher. Then at 10:40 Norman Birkett rose to commence his opening address, outlining the Crown's case. He lost no time in confronting the problem that the corpse had not been identified.

> "I want to clear out of the way at the outset that you need not be troubled in this matter by the fact that the remains are not identified as those of any previous living person. It makes no difference in the law in this matter, but you

---

244 Anne Logan, *Feminism and Criminal Justice: A Historical Perspective*, Palgrave Macmillan, 2008, pp. 86-95; Quentin Falk, *The Musical Milkman Murder*, John Blake, 2012.
245 The Rouse jury comprised Cecil Armstrong, James Branson, William Gray, James Masters, Arthur Whiting, Harold Smith, Raymond Linnell, Oliver Tailby, John Wilford, George Loake, Albert Munn and Herbert Hornaby. No research into any of the individuals has been undertaken.

may regard it as a factor very important and most significant".[246]

Presumably he hoped by this remark to plant the notion that while it was not incumbent on the Crown to prove a motive for murder (which might be especially difficult with an unknown victim where only happenstance might appear to have formed a link, if any, with the accused), nonetheless the unrecognizable (and unrecognized) state of the victim might itself suggest the accused's motive to disappear and to be taken to have perished in the fierce blaze.

> "This grave charge of wilful murder, by the very nature of the case, is seldom committed when other human eyes behold it. Sometimes direct evidence is impossible or difficult to obtain and the evidence which is brought is termed circumstantial evidence. Circumstantial evidence may be of such a texture as to be superior almost to direct evidence."

Indeed, what he was suggesting is that whereas eye-witnesses offering direct evidence of the offence called upon to give police statements or to testify in court might be lying or be mistaken as to what they had seen, circumstantial evidence never lied (though it might be misinterpreted). Indeed except in the cases of many domestic murders and gang or pub fights resulting in homicide, most murders are not directly witnessed. Consequently most such convictions will depend on indirect circumstantial evidence or on forensic evidence. Birkett was therefore laying the ground for a case that consisted almost entirely of circumstantial evidence. Certainly, Rouse could be placed in Hardingstone Lane at the time of the incident, but not only was it a mystery as to who had died, the 'how', 'where' and 'when' of the murder, if murder it was, became a matter of informed conjecture. Indeed, the only direct evidence that Birkett could summon up and to which a number of witnesses could testify was Rouse's behaviour *following* the fire. And that behaviour related to the prisoner's alleged unwillingness to save his passenger as he passed the cousins, his failure to report the incident to the police, and the lies and deception practised on all those whom he encountered from the time of his march along Hardingstone Lane towards the junction, during his lorry journey to London, while travelling to Wales, in the course of his conversations in Gellygaer and during his subsequent return to London.

Birkett then proceeded to relate the train of events from the moment when the two young men on their way home from the dance and fireworks party in Northampton had chanced upon an unrecognized passer-by in Hardingstone Lane at such an unexpected hour. More unexpectedly was the stranger's spontaneous comment, as they passed each other, 'It looks like someone is having a bonfire up there'. These words, uttered when there was a terrible fire raging just 400 yards away, devouring not just the prisoner's car but an unidentifiable corpse, were such, said Birkett, that, 'The significance of it, the importance of it, cannot be over-emphasised'. Indeed the Crown would bring forward evidence indicating that the fire was 'designed and not accidental'. He then developed his account of the narrative of events, including Rouse's various explanations for having lost his

---

246 Transcripts of the proceedings are in HO144/19183 and HO144/19184. A list of exhibits is in HO144/19179. Pathologists' reports are in HO144/19185, which also contains the grand jury presentment. When reprinting counsel's opening and closing speeches, Normanton's Notable British Trials edition of the trial sometimes shifts from first to third person singular.

car, his apprehension by the detectives at Hammersmith (which was technically not an arrest), and the statements he made to the various police officers before being charged with murder.

Restating that, subject to any legal direction from the judge, the Crown need not adduce, let alone prove, motive, he added, nonetheless, that the jury might think that the circumstances pointed to the conclusion that,

> "....for some unknown reason the accused desired the charred remains of that unknown man to be taken for his and that when he had emerged out of that hedge at that hour in the morning and had been seen by two young men, the plan or design might have miscarried."

Counsel then concluded with a somewhat chilling rhetorical flourish which had echoes of his days as a Methodist preacher.

> "The springs of human conduct, members of the jury, are many times beyond all human divining, and are hidden far from that region where the human eye can see or the human mind can extend. You might think that there never could be an adequate motive for murder, but the question might be raised in your minds in the way I have indicated."

Concluding his speech with the familiar and standard concession that it was for the Crown to prove the prisoner's guilt beyond reasonable doubt, absent which, on the part of the jury, they were bound to acquit (a ritual statement of how fair the prosecution always supposedly were to the accused), Birkett sat down. The speech lasted two hours and at its conclusion the sun was streaming through the court room windows and shining directly into the prisoner's eyes. Rouse, who had been listening intently but with composure during the speech, lifted his hand to shield his eyes from the sunlight. At that moment the blinds of the court windows were drawn and preparations were made to call the first witness.

No doubt the public area was filled with excited anticipation at what was to come, though the journalists present were probably aware that initial witnesses for the Crown were invariably perfunctory functionaries, presenting maps, diagrams and photographs of the scene of the crime. And so it proved with the first witness, the photographer, Arthur Ashford, though his revelations regarding the chaotic and uncontrolled circumstances of his taking pictures of the wreckage did not quite fit the standard formula usually provided by police photographers and sketchers of the scenes of crimes. Nonetheless, it has to be said that over the next four days during which witness after witness trooped into court to testify, memorable highlights were, with one or two exceptions, in short supply. Of those exceptions, as we shall see, one of the most significant revolved around the demeanour and mode of testimony of Rouse himself. Then there was the questionable cross-examining by Birkett of the defence's engineering witnesses. But in respect of meaningful silences, there was the tantalizing presence in the court building of Helen and Nellie. 'Meaningful silences' because Birkett had decided, to avoid the legal trap of inadmissibly adducing the defendant's bad character, that Helen would not be called as a witness at all while Nellie would be called only to confirm that she had seen Rouse on the evening on November 5 in 'City Road' [sic], London, and that he had left her at 8 pm. Helen was therefore allowed to be present throughout the trial hearing while Nellie was not permitted to be present in the court room itself until she had testified in the brief and non-sensational manner indicated above. And no doubt that turn of events was to the intense disappointment of the press hordes whose anticipated headlines for the next day would have to be re-written. But even more intriguingly, in an echo of the dog that did not bark, was the absence of Lily Rouse from the witness box, but present in court throughout most of the trial, which we noted previously.

The first Crown witnesses called by Birkett (or, to be precise, by his junior, Richard Elwes), when the trial at last opened on Monday January 26 were Ashford, the photographer, and Edgar Tipplestone, his assistant, and we have noted the controversy surrounding the taking of the photographs. For, as well as the exhibits implying that the intensity of the blaze had suggested deliberate interference, the pictures could, on the other hand, also be to the advantage of the accused since who could say that, while it was not under police guard, the car had not been tampered with by an unknown third party? Then Reginald Tate, an assistant county surveyor, produced a scale plan of Hardingstone Lane as it came off the main road, with telegraph poles, the prominence of the finger post pointing to Hardingstone, the position of the hedges, the dimensions of the verges, the contours and bends on the road, the actual yardage from the first village house to the burnt-out vehicle, the car's resting place, and the distance from the car to the road junction, and so on. It was not suggested for a moment that the topographical details were inaccurate or would be admitted as being so from the witness box (the cases that come to mind in this regard being the Brixton taxi cab case of 1923 in which an outdated sketch map had been prepared by the police,[247] and the Robert Wood case in 1907 in which Marshall Hall had successfully challenged a policeman's evidence regarding the weather at the crucial time and the lighting up and street light extinguishing times[248]). But Birkett's insistence on locating precisely Hardingstone Lane in relation to Northampton drew the judge's irritation. 'I think we are wasting a great deal of time over this', as he called for a one-inch Ordnance Survey map to settle the issue, before announcing that the court would now move to its first lunchtime adjournment. As Talbot left his chair, Rouse looked across at the direction in which Lily had been sitting while making a gesture as if to brush away the two warders on either side of him. He craned his neck to try to pick her out but before alighting on her presence, he was quickly taken below.

On the trial's resumption after lunch, it was the turn of the cousins, Brown and Bailey, to testify to the strange tale of their unforgettable encounter with the hatless Rouse, an account which we have already recorded. 'When you go home at that time in the morning you do not usually see well-dressed men getting out of the ditch', Brown memorably recalled. And as for Rouse's voice sounding hysterical (since the accused had told the police that he had been in a panic), Bailey told Birkett that, 'I thought he did at the time, but since hearing his voice I think it was his natural voice'. They were followed by a succession of police witnesses, PC Copping from Hardingstone who took down the cousins' statements in the middle

---

247 For one account see E. S. Fay, *The Life of Mr Justice Swift*, Methuen, 1939, Chapter 10.
248 See, *inter alia*, Sir David Napley, *The Camden Town Murder*, Weidenfeld & Nicolson, 1987, pp. 90-91, 107.

of the night, and then PC Valentine who had arrived on the scene some time later, together with Inspector Lawrence from Angel Lane. Copping, having previously helped douse the flames, recounted his inspection of the scene, the location of the damaged petrol can, the state of the car bonnet, the fragments and scattered debris, some of it fused in the heat, and the position of the body, followed by the recovery of the latter and the moving of the vehicle onto the grass verge, as described in an earlier chapter. Of course, he had not been anticipating a murder inquiry at that point, so he may well have been blasé about securing the scene.

Valentine, arriving after the flames had been extinguished, also spoke to the position of the corpse and, with the aid of his police car headlights, noted the wheel marks in the gravel but also the significant absence of skid marks. He lifted the bonnet and observed that the fuel tank was empty though it appeared to be intact. Similarly blasé, it seems, he admitted to just chucking debris lying around into the middle of the wreck. Sergeant Joe Harris, based at Collingtree police station, told how, on his arrival at the scene the next morning before nine o'clock, the vehicle was still on the road (despite every other policeman disagreeing with him!) until it was moved, apparently by Harris with the help of Valentine, Lawrence and Superintendent Brumby, no doubt to the surprise of the last three-named when they heard his account. It was also Harris who had found the mallet some fourteen yards in front of the wreck, a discovery that no doubt told against Rouse despite the judge counseling the jury to ignore the item as evidence against the accused.

When Harris stepped down the court adjourned for the day and the judge asked counsel how long the case might last as he had an appointment in Leicester on the following Thursday January 29. But, 'On no account must the evidence be hurried', he quickly added. Richard Elwes, for the Crown, stated that not even the prosecution case would be completed by then (in fact the Crown case ended with the close of the previous day's proceedings), which caused Rouse to exchange looks with his wife, while Finnemore told the judge that quite frankly he could not see it ending by a reasonable hour on the Thursday. That was all that he needed to know, Talbot intimated. His Leicester appointment would have to be cancelled. When the judge rose from his raised dais for the day, Rouse stood smartly to attention. His father waved to him and he smiled back. Then Lily also gave him a little wave and Rouse lifted his fingers to his head in a form of salute.

Birkett made a swift exit since he was weighing up the prospect of voting in the Commons against a proposed Labour government Trade Disputes Bill. The measure was intended to overturn the vindictive provisions of the Trade Disputes and Trade Unions Act 1927 passed after the collapse of the General Strike the previous year, and which had severely curtailed trade union industrial action and trade union funding. So a period of intensive commuting between the Commons and Northampton was also on Birkett's agenda for that week. As to the Bill, the minority Labour government in 1931 could not hope to pass the measure in the face of a hostile Tory bench supported by right-leaning 'Orange Book' Liberal MPs. In fact, the measure completed its second reading in the Commons with some Liberal support. It was then sent 'upstairs' for its committee stage. During its progress through parliament Winston Churchill, hated by the South Wales miners since the Tonypandy shootings in 1911 when he was Home Secretary, had hoped that the Bill would 'have its dirty little throat cut by Liberal assassins'. Birkett was one of the Liberal Party 'assassins' whom Churchill had had in mind, but Birkett apparently preferred to see the measure suffer 'death by a thousand slices'. Thus he looked forward to its being rendered so ineffective in committee that it would have to be withdrawn, rather than that his party would have to oppose the Bill outright and thereby risk a general election. The tactic succeeded, the Bill was withdrawn and the repeal of the 1927 Act had to await the votes of the landslide Labour government and back-benchers in 1946. Was Rouse himself clinically dispatched by this Liberal 'assassin', this spare and cautious individual who, twirling his thin stiletto-like gold propelling pencil, metaphorically thrust it into the body of his prey when asking him the killer question why he had not called upon the cousins to help tackle the blaze? Or did the prisoner suffer 'death by a thousand slices' as he was done down by relentless questioning from Birkett about his reprehensible and callous behaviour in Hardingstone Lane, about his series of lies, about his stop-start and insincere police statements?

For some reason, perhaps linked to the chronology of events (though that is not wholly convincing), Birkett chose to call, as his last two witnesses on the third day of the trial, the remaining police witnesses, Skelly and Brumby (and Copping, recalled at the instance of Finnemore),[249] but only after the court had heard from the lorry driver and his mate, the coach company ticket-seller and drivers, members of the Welsh contingent, the medical experts and the Crown's automotive expert, Colonel Buckle. Skelly told the court of his meeting the Cardiff coach at Hammersmith Broadway, of Rouse's initial and cooperative actions, of the latter's expression of relief that it was 'all over' and that he was 'responsible', wording that Finnemore would contest (below). The exchanges conducted at Hammersmith police station which were *not* contemporaneously committed to writing, but which were written down by Skelly at a later stage (which could reduce their evidential significance or even hint at police collusion and fabrication), were adduced in court, as was Rouse's voluntary statement given to the now-arrived Brumby and Lawrence, which was recorded by Skelly at the time and signed by Rouse.

Finnemore naturally did he best to minimize the adverse impact of Skelly's testimony. The latter agreed that Rouse was travelling openly and not in disguise and that he had immediately confirmed his identity. The accused, having stepped down from the coach, had not been cautioned before he sighed, 'Very well. I am glad it is all over'. However, since this remark was not formally a statement but an example of unsigned 'police verbals', which are often uttered by the suspect as the police car takes him on the 'scenic route' to the police station, its admissibility might have been open to debate. Leaving that aside, Rouse further insisted that he was, anyway, going to Scotland Yard about the matter (the coach would, indeed,

---

249 In fact Birkett called his last witness, Sergeant Bertie Johnson of the Metropolitan Police, on the fourth day, with the leave of the judge, after the prosecution had already completed its case. Johnson testified that he had measured the distances from Tally Ho Corner to Buxted Road and from Tally Ho Corner to the White Flag Tearooms, Markyate, where PC Lilley had spoken to Rouse. The shortest distance of the former route (Tally Ho Corner to Buxted Road) was just under a mile and for the second it was nearly 24 miles via Barnet, Arkley and the Barnet by-pass, or 20 and a half miles if via Barnet, South Mimms, St Albans and Redbourne. The point of the evidence was, of course, to emphasise the unnaturally long time it took Rouse to travel those distances, implying that he was biding his time to await the dead of night and the onset of the victim's drunken stupor before carrying out his murderous assault.

travel on in that direction). Moreover, as Finnemore insisted, his client had stated, 'I *feel* responsible', not 'I am responsible', a suggestion with which Skelly strongly disagreed. Finally, in respect of the Hammersmith police station statement that Rouse *had* indeed signed after being interviewed by Brumby and Lawrence, although it had been erratically and lengthily delivered over many hours, with stops, starts, elisions and additions, the final version remained consistent throughout in its denial of knowledge of how the vehicle fire had actually started.

Brumby and Lawrence, as we know, then took Rouse back to Angel Lane police station in Northampton where the prisoner was finally charged on the Saturday afternoon with the murder of an unknown man. But it was Brumby who was responsible for perhaps the most awkward but amusing passage of the trial. That was when he self-consciously tried to explain his search for the 'evidence' that would support Rouse's claim that the latter had gone some distance to relieve himself when the fire had broken out.

> "What we were searching for was in consequence of what the accused said, that he left the car to ease himself [*sic*], and I went down to look to see if I could find where he had done this, but I could find no trace whatever. I mean that I went to look for what would have come from him [*sic*]. After searching the whole of the grass verge from the car to the road, we found nothing."

Of course, simply reading the passage gives no sense of the excruciating embarrassment that Brumby must have felt in groping for a form of words to describe defecation and faeces but without using those terms which would have been taboo to the non-medical lay middle class (Rouse himself, it will be recalled, claimed that he had made up the various stories about his car having been stolen so as not to embarrass ladies present in Gellygaer if he had indeed chosen to state that the blaze had started as he was pulling down his trousers in order to defecate). Finnemore, aware that one of his own expert witnesses, Dr. Telling, had indeed found some material which he had identified as faeces (though whether human or canine could no longer be determined) took up the point with Brumby.

> 'You did not find any excreta when you looked?' 'No, I did not'.
> 'You knew, of course, that a few days later Dr. Telling, who made a search, did find something which he thought was excreta?'
> 'I know that he found something. I saw him there, but I did not go to him to see what it was... A photograph was taken at the time... I saw the photograph'.
> 'I do not know whether you went across to examine yourself with them at that time or not?'
> 'No, not until they had gone away, until they had removed what was there [*sic*]'

What might Freud have made of Brumby's testimony? That he had not been properly potty-trained as a toddler? That he was emotionally repressed and uncomfortable in his own body? That he had an extremely low threshold of embarrassment? That words like faeces, excreta and defecation were like a dagger to his throat? At least it gave scope for some amusement in the public gallery as he squirmed to formulate acceptable and meaningful wording to describe that which he was seeking to find.

One other point of note from Brumby's cross-examination was when Finnemore raised the matter of a young *Evening Standard* journalist, Norman Rae, who would testify for the defence that he had found marks on the grass verge which he had pointed out to Brumby and which he had suggested were vehicle reverse marks, thereby challenging the Crown's claim that Rouse had deliberately stopped the car normally at a chosen point to fire it. Brumby denied speaking to Rae and complained that, 'There were so many press men talking all at the same time. [So] I was anxious to get away from them.' (Copping, on his recall to the witness box, also denied that Rae had raised the matter of reverse tyre marks with him). We shall address Rae's claim in the context of the defence case but we may note at this point that while Rae played a minor, perhaps even a discredited, role in the Rouse case he was later to emerge as one of the premier crime reporters of the 1940s and 1950s. Thus he became one of the celebrated 'murder gang' of national newspaper crime reporters who transformed the reporting of major murder cases in such a way that the journalists themselves became part of the murder story.

But this is to anticipate. The close of the first day's hearing ended with Sergeant Harris' testimony. For the second day, Tuesday January 27, the queue for admission to the public gallery was even larger than on the opening day. So once again hundreds were turned away. The police segregated the sexes, and first women, then men, were admitted four at a time, until the maximum number of sixty was reached. But despite the police presence, protests were lodged by several women who had lost out in the rush to get seats. An undignified scramble was not unusual at trial *causes célèbres*, with middle-class ladies sometimes complaining that girls of the shop assistant and shorthand typist class were taking seats that their betters should have been occupying. Several clergymen were also seated in the public gallery, while several girls who had waited patiently for two or three hours to gain admission managed to squeeze in, only to have to stand throughout. Lily again arrived early and passed the time chatting to a young lady sitting next to her.

When proceedings resumed the county assistant surveyor supplied the promised Ordnance Survey map of the area. But which route did Rouse take from Friern Barnet to the intended destination of Leicester? It seems clear that he took the old Great North Road out of Barnet, north London, via Tally Ho Corner towards St Albans. We know, also, that he stopped briefly at Markyate where PC Lilley spoke to him about his car lights. From there he would have picked up the A5 where he would have continued to Stony Stratford. Immediately after this he probably forked to the right towards Northampton along the A508 rather than continuing on the straight A5 road towards Daventry and Rugby, from which road, if he had taken it, he could have turned right onto the A43 at Towcester to reach Northampton by that route. But in sticking to the A508 towards Northampton, he would have driven through Wootton (now the location of Northamptonshire Police HQ) and passed the fork, midway between Wootton and Hardingstone, with the principal A-road that went south-east to Newport Pagnell (there were earlier B-roads forking to the right, offering an alternative route south-east to Newport Pagnell).

It was, in fact, just after that turn-off with the A-road south-east to Newport Pagnell that he turned right into the B-road (albeit one served by local buses) where the finger post on the bend of the main road indicated Hardingstone. When Finnemore questioned Tate, the latter agreed that the lights of Northampton would have been visible at night at that point. So was Rouse lost when he turned into Hardingstone Lane realizing, after a hectic and stressful day and a late start to his employers, that driving to Leicester should not have taken him close to Northampton? Or did he know of Hardingstone's existence and had decided that he would drive into the village, make a U-turn to face the junction and, some 159 yards from the nearest house in the village, carry out his nefarious plan (if murderous plan there was)?

In fact, it would not have been outlandish to travel to Leicester via Northampton. For today's A5199 is a straight but longer route from Northampton to Leicester. However, a more direct route for Rouse to take to Leicester was certainly to continue to Rugby on the A5 after leaving Stony Stratford. Presumably this would be the route that he would normally take when travelling to Leicester, but this did not come out in the trial. For if he *did* normally travel via Rugby, which was patrolled by AA men as far as Lutterworth, then the Northampton route (also patrolled by the AA) looked like a suspicious choice; unless he was, indeed, lost and had driven into Hardingstone Lane by mistake. [250]

Rouse's own explanation that he had ended up at Hardingstone in error (even if he had been making for the Northampton and Market Harborough route to Leicester rather than the Rugby route) is, of course, unconvincing. Certainly, as he later told his counsel in the witness box on the fourth day of the trial (Thursday, January 29), following his encounter with PC Lilley at Markyate,

"Some distance further on—I do not know, I have only been told near Northampton—I presume I was getting near Northampton—I noticed I was going through a village that I did not recognize. I said to my companion: 'I believe I am on the wrong road'. Then I believe I remembered a few moments previously bearing [*sic*] to the right. I could see Northampton, or the reflection of the lights, and it looked as if we were somewhere on the right road. I got to an obelisk or memorial, and I thought it would be better to go to the left [ie., to continue on the main road to Northampton] and I took the road to the right [presumably along Hardingstone Lane]."

Better to go to the left, but then instead take the road to the right? Surely a strange juxtaposition (see below). As to the obelisk, it was one of the series of twelve crosses erected by Edward I between 1291 and 1294 to commemorate the nightly resting places of the funeral procession for his late wife, Eleanor of Castile, as it made its way to her burial in London. Alan Moore, in his graphic novelette on the Rouse case, "I Travel in Suspenders", refers to the Cross (though he imagines Rouse formulating his supposed plan to bump off his passenger only as he approached Towcester which is on the A5, not the A508). [251] However, the confusing and contradictory nature of Rouse's recalled directions, above, is obvious. First, the obelisk itself is on the side of the A508, slightly north to the

---

250   See Automobile Association, *Handbook Supplement*, 1933, map at p. 13.
251   For diverse aspects concerning roads in Britain, see the Society for All British and Irish Road Enthusiasts, at www.sabre-roads.co.uk. For literary aspects of the Rouse case, see Gerry R. Rubin, "Dennis, Alan and Arthur x 3: Literary Legacies of the Blazing Car Murder of 1930", *Law and Humanities*, Vol. 9 (2), 2015, pp. 1-34.

B-road turn-off to Hardingstone. Moreover, while he had said that it was better to veer left (and thereby continue in the Northampton direction), he nonetheless added, '.....and I took the road to the right'. Had he indeed been able to think on his feet, as he patently thought he was capable of, he surely would have said to Finnemore, '*But* I took by mistake the road to the right'.

The county surveyor was later followed into the witness box by Inspector Lawrence. Described in the press as 'blond, tall and imperturbable', he spoke to the pre-charge events of Thursday November 6 to November 8. However, the startling 'harem' statement made by Rouse at around 11 am on the Saturday morning at Angel Lane police station, and previously adduced by Lawrence at the police court, following which it was gleefully splashed over all the newspapers, was perhaps surprisingly not explored in court. Maybe Birkett was wary of anticipating that the Court of Criminal Appeal might quash a jury conviction of Rouse on the ground that references at the trial to his harem were an inadmissible adduction of his bad character. So Birkett chose to avoid this risk, just as he decided against calling Helen Campbell or against asking Nellie more than a handful of perfunctory uncontroversial questions.

Regarding Lawrence, it was ascertained that his recollection of events during the night of the blaze was based on memory, not on contemporaneous note-taking, while he also conceded that the steering wheel (at least) must have been moved by someone after the blaze. He also agreed that his colleague, Brumby, and Metropolitan Police Inspector Welby had asked Rouse a number of questions at Hammersmith which he had answered 'readily, voluntarily, and eagerly'. Indeed Sergeant Skelly had written down the prisoner's replies at the same time. Lawrence then indicated that after Rouse had completed his long, protracted statement, he (Lawrence) began to doubt its veracity. This he attributed to Rouse's 'manner', which we take to mean the suspect's stilted, shifty and diversionary behaviour and his frequent alterations to his statement as each part was read back to him after he had delivered it. As Lawrence added, 'There was no need, in my opinion, if he was telling the truth to correct anything', and while he agreed with Finnemore that he, like other people, had made mistakes (by which he meant in communicating information or details at some points in his life), nonetheless, to correct the same passage numerous times struck him as suspicious. Lawrence himself had also asked Rouse a number of questions at Hammersmith police station as to how he could account for certain events. However, he agreed that his interview smacked more of cross-examination than of an inquiry, which Finnemore perhaps hoped would be perceived as oppressive questioning. On the other hand, that Rouse had suffered his war wound did not appear to Lawrence to have caused the accused any especial discomfort during his lengthy interviews with the police. It was decidedly not a 'formidable ordeal' that Rouse had faced nor, he insisted, had he been entrapped into making admissions.

It is one of the (not unexpected) ironies of Rouse's trial that the outcome was probably as much influenced by his own obnoxious character, his cold and unfeeling behaviour at the time of the blaze, and his repellent performance in the witness box, as it was by substantive, albeit circumstantial rather than direct, prosecution evidence. But when we come to the technical evidence as to how the fire had actually started in the car (introduced on Day 2 of the trial), we are confronted with the core issue which *ought* to have been the exclusive question in the jury's mind. Was it murder or accidental death (manslaughter did not seem to be a possibility at the trial, as far as the pleadings were concerned. But one of Rouse's alleged confessions did raise this possibility, as noted in a later chapter)?[252] We will see that the medical experts would address the state and position of the corpse after the blaze, and would argue over whether the victim, conscious or not, had been violently 'pitched' by Rouse onto the front seats or whether he had tripped, or whether he had negligently incinerated himself by carelessly waving around a lit cigar while stretching for, opening or replacing a can of petrol. But it was the technical experts on car fires who addressed how the blaze might have happened. Was it an accidental fire caused by some mechanical fault? Or did the technical evidence suggest that Rouse had tampered with the mechanical parts of the vehicle to ensure a constant flow of petrol to feed a car blaze that he had deliberated started, presumably with a match, either by spraying the victim with petrol (one may recall the recovered patch of petrol-soaked trouser cloth on the victim found by the pathologists) or by laying a trail of petrol in front of the car that he had ignited (or both)? This section introduces the evidence adduced by the prosecution expert witness, Colonel Buckle, regarding the technical causes of the fire and its intensity, and raises the possibility, to be elaborated when the views of technical witnesses for the defence are later heard, that at the very least a crucial element of Buckle's technical analysis was highly suspect, if not downright wrong.

Expert witnesses are often recruited from the ranks of surveyors, engineers, hand-writing experts, medical and medicine-related personnel, academics in various disciplines including foreign legal systems, history, entomology and linguistics, statisticians and, more and more frequently, child psychologists, psychotherapists and those specialising in memory recovery and its obverse, false memory syndrome. They are the only category of witness entitled to offer opinions on the evidence and on hypothetical scenarios, whereas other witnesses are questioned regarding what they saw (or, significantly, did not see), said, did, heard, felt, smelt etc. Expert witnesses, however, are debarred from testifying as to the actual culpability or otherwise of the accused. For they are not called in order to be advocates for one side or the other, but to explain the factual basis for their opinions and the assumptions underlying the expert evidence they present. Their evidence should, in appropriate cases, be grounded in verifiable, measureable and statistically sound research findings. However, in regard to DNA-type evidence they might indicate either the scientific impossibility of the accused being responsible for the crime charged or, subject to a valid theoretical and mathematical framework for analysis (upon which Professor Sir Roy Meadow recently notoriously failed the test in 'multiple cot-death' cases), the statistical chances of the prisoner *not* being the guilty party. Expert witnesses are expected to owe their highest duty to the court and to assist the court rather than the side that calls them, and this includes making clear the limits of their expertise, the qualifications and caveats to be attached to their findings, and any changes of opinion they might subsequently form in the light of other expert evidence heard

---

252 See generally, Thomas L. Bohan, *Crashes and Collapses*, Checkmark Books, New York, 2009, Ch. 5; Bernard Picton, *Murder, Suicide or Accident: The Forensic Pathologist at Work*, Robert Hale, 1971. Rouse is mentioned in *ibid.*, at pp. 75, 92 and 212.

(unlike other witnesses, experts are normally entitled to sit in the court to hear the proceedings before being called to testify). They must not, therefore, manipulate or tailor their findings, or be selective in their choice of expert evidence to adduce, in order deliberately to favour the side calling them. Moreover, while called as a defence or Crown witness in a criminal case (and usually paid a fee and expenses accordingly), they must maintain objectivity and independence and eschew improper influence.[253]

In the Rouse case, all the experts claimed to possess cognate engineering knowledge regarding the causes of car fires. Indeed engineering experts featured among the earliest of cases from the eighteenth century where such opinion providers were admitted as competent witnesses. In *Folkes v Chadd* (1782) 3 Doug K B 157, the father of modern lighthouse construction, the engineer John Smeaton (1724-1792), responsible for building one of the Eddystone lighthouses, testified as to whether the allegedly unauthorised construction of an embankment had caused the silting up of a harbour. Having studied canal and harbour construction in The Netherlands, he was permitted by the judge, Lord Mansfield, to offer his opinion in the instant case, thus expanding the range of expertise admissible in court from the then familiar category of hand-writing experts, conventionally called upon in cases where the validity of wills, negotiable instruments, deeds of transfer, mortgages and other documents was contested in both civil and criminal cases (where forgery was a capital offence). The Rouse engineering experts followed in the path of the earlier pioneering engineering expert, Smeaton.[254]

Colonel Buckle

The Crown's 'star' witness in the Rouse trial was their expert witness, Colonel Cuthbert Buckle CBE, CB, whose home address was St Aubin, Cross Lane, Gravesend, Kent. He was managing director of Ellis & Buckle Ltd, 9, Wallbrook, London, E.C. 4, fire assessors for insurance companies and for Lloyd's underwriters. He had served with the Royal Garrison Artillery during the Great War,[255] rising to the rank of half-colonel by 1920, and subsequently was a full colonel in the Army, in command of the 27th (London) Air Defence Territorial Brigade. He claimed 26 years experience as a fire loss assessor, having advised in 10,000 cases during that time. His firm had inspected 83 car fires in the four years prior to Rouse's trial while he himself had examined 56 cars during the same period. On December 4, 1930 (that is, a month after the blaze), he went to Hardingstone Lane, following a request by Inspector Collins of Scotland Yard, to inspect the site of the car fire and then travelled to Angel Lane police station where the remains of the Morris Minor were kept and where he examined the chassis, mechanical remains and debris. His report, submitted to the DPP the following day, sought to highlight the findings of fact following his inspection of the chassis, 'particularly any facts

253 See generally, *National Justice Compania Naviera SA v Prudential Assurance Co. Ltd.* [1993] 2 Lloyd's Rep. 68.
254 Leslie Blake, "The Tricks of the Trade: The Lot of an Expert Witness Under Cross-Examination is not a Happy One". *Estates Gazette*, January 27, 2001, pp. 136-8. The title refers to the situation of one expert witness in the Rouse case who was cross-examined 'as to credit' on the footing that he did not possess professional qualifications and lacked relevant theoretical knowledge. Whether the cross-examination by Birkett was proper in terms of the duties of counsel to conduct their cross-examination fairly is a moot point. See chapter 10.
255 W0372/3/153836.

favourable to the accused person'. Indeed, he found several points supportive of Rouse's claim as to what had happened. However there was one important finding that he made towards the end of his examination which forced him to a particular conclusion regarding the origin of the fire. Yet, in apparent contradiction, he also insisted that he had purposefully refrained from forming any theories as to how the blaze might have started. In fact his 'important finding' would relate to how the fire was fed and why it was so intense.

It is unnecessary to dwell on his written report of December 5. For his trial testimony (he was called to the witness box twice, on the second occasion to offer further evidence, and he had also testified at the police court) spelled out his findings in more detail, and offered a technical narrative that the prosecution argued would support its theory of the case and that Rouse had taken deliberate steps to incinerate his victim.

Buckle first explained that accidental fires in cars could be started due to a (petrol) inlet valve sticking in the open position. This would allow the 'fired charge' in a cylinder, that is, the compressed and ignited mix of petrol and air, to 'blow back' down the inlet manifold (a manifold being a pipe with multiple inlets and outlets) to the carburettor which on this vehicle model was shaped like, and was the size of, an old-fashioned steel-cased shaving set. The carburettor itself creates a fuel and air mixture that flows to the engine cylinders where the mix is compressed and ignited. Alternatively, a petrol leak might be ignited by flames blowing out of defective joints on the exhaust manifold or exhaust pipe, or an electric spark might ignite leaking petrol or the vapour from it. In the case of other possible causes of car fires due to defective electrical wiring or overheating in the ignition coil, or cigarette ends on the upholstery, the fires did not suddenly erupt and burn quickly. They were 'rather slow, smelly, smouldering fires in their early stages'. This implied that occupants would have warnings and could get out of the vehicle in time. The relevant point, of course, was that he found no evidence that the blaze had been caused by any of the above.

Instead the main thrusts of his findings, music to the ears of the prosecution, were as follows. First, the car was stationary and the engine turned off when the fire started (even though the car was in second gear). Second, the fire did not seem to have started in the engine compartment. As he explained at the trial, this opinion was reinforced by another finding. Thus,

> "From the fact that the gearbox casing had fused and the lugs had not fused I drew the conclusion that there had not been a fire sweeping through the engine space under the bonnet through to the body; otherwise, if there had been, the lugs would certainly have gone before the gearbox casing."

Third, he examined the petrol pipe which ran from the base of the petrol tank to the carburettor. But significantly, on this model, the petrol tank was actually strapped to the inside of the windscreen, nearer to the passengers, rather than sitting in the engine compartment, while the tank end of the petrol pipe and, more specifically, the petrol union joint itself, was exposed within the inside of the car, and could be touched by the foot of a passenger. As Normanton explained,[256]

256 Helena Normanton (ed.), *Trial of Alfred Arthur Rouse*, Notable British Trials Series, William Hodge & Co., Edinburgh, 1931, p. xxvii.

"The main petrol-tap [shaped on the outside like the handle of a water stop-cock] is just to the left hand of the centre of the extreme front sloping floorboard, and it is at the top of the sloping board so that it can just be touched by a passenger's right boot-toe if he pushed his foot forward, somewhat outward to his right....there are three places where direct contact may be made with the petrol in the car, not counting any loose cans carried....The second would be to unscrew the nut [not actually visible *in situ* to a passenger] when around the main petrol tap under the dash-board, so that petrol would weep or leak from around the joint on to the floorboards and mat, and around the gearbox and through the junctions of the boards on to the road".

In other words, a driver (or anyone else), while inside the car, could easily bend over to unscrew or loosen the petrol tap nut to release a flow of petrol. On examination of the pipe and of this joint in particular, Buckle found not only that the pipe inside the car had a bit of play. He also discovered that the nut at the petrol union joint was loose by one revolution. This would enable petrol to flow into the car from a position below the tank mounted, as noted above, on the inside of the windscreen and just below the level of the dashboard, directly onto the wooden floor of the car. This would, he told the assize court, create a 'great deal of fire underneath the car, where there is normally nothing to burn'. Moreover, it was 'very surprising to get a flame underneath the car like that in a roadside fire.' If the vehicle were stationary or was travelling with no fire present and the nut was loose, then the occupants would immediately smell the petrol fumes or even see the drip of petrol onto the floor on the passenger's side and, no doubt, deal with the leak. Indeed, if it were not dealt with, there would quickly be an explosive atmosphere inside the moving car. But if the vehicle were actually blazing, not only would the dripping petrol, ignited by the fire, cause the floor to be burnt through but the constant flow of petrol, burning at extremely high temperatures, what Buckle described in court as 'an unusually intense fire', would operate like a blow lamp cutting into and fusing the brass surround of the windscreen. To test the flow of petrol feeding the flames, he experimented on a police car built with a similar petrol union joint, loosened the nut by three-quarters of a turn, and found that an ordinary glass tumbler could be filled to the brim in one minute and twenty seconds. In the case of a car on fire, the rate of leakage would be even greater due to the pressure generated within the petrol tank. A central question, indeed, a central controversy, was how the nut had become loose. As his report to the DPP put it, when he found the pipe was loose, he had said to the police officers around him,

"'I expect that is because the nipple has become unsoldered: give me a spanner'. I then found the union nut one whole turn loose but still thought it might be due to the nipple coming unsoldered. I was surprised when I found on undoing the joint that the nipple was still in position on the end of the pipe. With fairly continuous motoring experience since 1910 on motor cycles, small motor cars and later large cars, I have never known a petrol union come unscrewed."

As he repeated in court, he agreed with Birkett that the 'joint' [presumably he meant the nut holding the joint in place] could not 'come a whole turn loose accidentally'. Indeed, the pipe itself,

> "....was fixed into the carburettor at the other end so that it cannot rotate in the plane in which you require rotation to unscrew that nut. It is not self-locking, but its natural tendency is to make these nuts not come loose in practice, and in my experience, as a motorist only [*sic*], they do not come loose".

He did, however, acknowledge that joints sometimes leaked slightly even if screwed up tightly. Notwithstanding, that clearly was not the case here, he insisted.

His principal findings thus impelled him to two inferences regarding the intensity of the fire underneath the car where there was normally nothing to burn.

> "I think [the fire] was fed continuously from the forward part of the body, in the vicinity of the petrol tank, and I think it was fed again, as it looks to me—I cannot be quite so certain as to this---from the back. I am quite certain it was fed from the front end. I am fairly certain it was fed from the back end also."

It seems beyond dispute that the loose nut at the petrol union joint caused the fire to be continuously fed and that this related to the 'forward part of the body, in the vicinity of the petrol tank' though, significantly, the petrol tank itself had 'stood the fire remarkably well'. But what about the claim that the blaze had also been fed from the back end? Buckle did not elaborate, though the full BP (British Petroleum) petrol can that was inside the car and possibly on the floor at the back of the car, may provide an explanation. (Because petrol stations were not as plentiful as today, drivers regularly kept cans of petrol in their cars.) In fact, after concluding his testimony, Buckle seemed to sense, from what he took were knowing glances from Rouse in the dock, that there was another possible explanation for the fire's intensity. It concerned the carburettor. But that was a supplementary matter that was raised later.

For the moment and, indeed, in regard to the crux of the matter, what was it that caused the fire to be fed continuously, causing flames to shoot upwards with ferocity and intense heat from underneath the car? For that was a rather unusual and normally baffling phenomenon. Buckle had already suggested from his examination of the wreckage that the fire had been continuously fed by a constant flow of petrol from the loose union joint. So the next question was: how did the nut releasing petrol become loose? Unless a passenger was especially 'fidgety', it was thought doubtful that a passenger, moving a foot in the footwell, could have struck the union joint so as to accidentally loosen the nut. There were, however, two other inferences. Either Rouse had deliberately interfered with the nut to ensure that the blaze he had allegedly started, or was about to start, was being continuously fed by the flow of petrol, in which case a murder conviction became more compelling. Alternatively, some other process, not attributable to Rouse's malevolent behaviour, had caused the nut to become loose. Buckle, as we saw from his quote above, had 'never known a petrol union come unscrewed'.

But he was mistaken. Indeed he seemed ignorant of the basic premise that when metal was exposed to extremely high temperatures and then was left to cool (and the petrol union nut had certainly cooled by December 4 when Buckle examined it!), one consequence was that very tightly screwed nuts could become loosened by the simple process of greater expansion in heat followed by lesser contraction on cooling. Moreover, it was not uncommon in such circumstances for the *threads* on which nuts were tightened to expand in the intense heat and to contract on subsequently cooling down, thus causing the nuts, whether or not they themselves had remained of the same diameter after heating and cooling, to be looser on the thread, and without a single rotation undertaken by hand. And this was the answer put by the defence at the trial to the Crown's allegation that Rouse, familiar with the mechanics of cars, had deliberately loosened the union joint nut. In other words, in car fires, despite Buckle's protestations, the defence insisted that such nuts could be loosened without direct human intervention. We will shortly examine how Birkett shamelessly and unfairly dealt with this challenge to the Crown's theory of the case. But before that, we can explore how Buckle fared at the capable hands of Donald Finnemore for the defence.

Cross-Examining Buckle

Perhaps Birkett's 'dirty tricks' aimed at the defence mechanical specialist, Arthur Isaacs (chapter 10), was prompted by the need to deflect attention from Buckle's 'shortcomings' as an expert witness, a credibility gap surely exposed (if not necessarily absorbed by the jury) in his, Buckle's, answer to Finnemore's first obvious question to the Crown witness:

"I am not an automobile engineer. I am certificated in electrical engineering. When I speak of 10,000 fires in 26 years, that includes fires of all sorts and conditions."

Forest fires, house fires, chip pan fires, who knows? Moreover, Buckle conceded that the number of car fires on which he had advised insurance companies regarding pay-outs was a 'comparatively small portion of the total' number of fires for which his advice was sought professionally. Indeed,

"Fabric bodies on cars [as with Rouse's vehicle] have only come in during the last two years or so. It is generally old cars that are burned. I have only seen half a dozen or less—four that I can remember."

He called himself an expert, but acknowledged that he had examined only four fires in fabric-bodied cars before Rouse's? Moreover, while his testimony certainly spoke to his familiarity with the mechanics of a vehicle, he admitted to only being 'certificated in electrical engineering', not in mechanical engineering. Did he have a university degree in the subject? Nothing was mentioned in that respect. Moreover, as we shall see, there seemed to be little evidence that his expertise had been deployed previously in vehicle workshops, repairing cars.

He certainly valiantly defended the position that it was the leakage of petrol and not the igniting of the petrol can or of the vapour expelled from it that had caused the damage to the brass windscreen or to the collapsed wooden floor. However, before fully damning the Crown witness, we may observe that even if the cause of the loosening of the nut were to be decided in favour of the defence, which we shall address soon, the defence theory of the case, focusing on the victim accidentally igniting the petrol can, would not necessarily be endorsed. For, as Buckle also testified,

"..... [a] petrol can does not go off with a big explosion. This [the actual conflagration] was a pressure explosion. Supposing the can was standing as it is now I would expect it to fall down. It would not go up with the pressure of that burst....It is not a violent explosion. It might fall over in the direction opposite from the burst."

In other words, even if Rouse had not loosened the joint and if the passenger had accidentally set light to the petrol can, the latter would merely have toppled over while the ferocity of the fire would still remain unexplained. Yet while Buckle had suggested that it was petrol vapour, combined with air, that had actually been ignited, he now claimed that when a car fire of that kind occurred, 'the flame is all over the car instantaneously'. Admittedly this is not identical to a 'violent explosion', but presumably for Buckle it was a distinction without a difference? Whichever, if the flame were to be 'all over the car instantaneously', this, of course, might mean that irrespective of a petrol can toppling over an occupant who had accidentally dropped his lit cigar in the closed environment of a small saloon car, especially with the car doors closed, would be so quickly overwhelmed by fire that he would have no opportunity to escape. To that extent, this testimony could yet favour the defence if the accident theory were to be accepted by the jury and if the loosened petrol union joint could be explained away innocently (which Buckle, it appears wrongly, was not prepared to countenance). A separate test was undertaken by him involving filling a can on the road, lightly screwing on the cap, and then lifting the container up to place it in the car. It was agreed that some light splashing of petrol from the top of the can onto the inside of the car might occur if the lifting had swished some of the petrol through the lightly screwed cap to the top of the can or had then dripped down its side, with more splashing if the container were to fall on its side. But Buckle avoided the issue of whether a combination of an accidental petrol leak and splashing from the can was 'dangerous' or would generate an 'extremely fierce fire', and was not pressed by Finnemore. Perhaps he should have been. Indeed, the question of the actual ignition was not mentioned at this point, while the possibility of spontaneous combustion was never raised.

Nonetheless, Finnemore did not hesitate to ram home one important point regarding the commencement, as distinct from the feeding, of the blaze. Thus, he put it to Buckle that, 'I take it that there is nothing that enables anybody to see with any *certainty* [italics added] what the primary fire was caused by or how it started?' To this Buckle replied, 'As to how it started, nothing at all' (though the Crown's theory was that a trail of petrol poured by Rouse in front of the car had allegedly been ignited by the prisoner with a match). Indeed, Buckle agreed, any one of a number of 'innocent' causes suggested by counsel could be identified, especially with petrol vapour in the atmosphere. Even an electric spark from a vehicle that was 'standing still' could set off a blaze (though it will be recalled that in his examination-in-chief Buckle had found no evidence for such explanations). While he did not expand on this point, he probably had in mind the operating of the 'self-starter' causing a charge through the live wire terminals linked to the coil and battery ignition system. However Buckle had found no fault in this system on Rouse's car, though he admitted that the wiring had been so damaged in the fire that he could not confirm that it had not previously been defective nor that a spark could not have been caused. But again Buckle avoided answering an important question directly when he was asked by counsel, 'I have no doubt that in your experience you have heard or read of cases of that sort?', referring to vapour being ignited by an electric spark while the vehicle was stationary. However, without providing chapter and verse, Buckle merely replied, 'I know it is possible'; which again might be seen as an admission of his limited expertise.

But the law of unintended consequences was in due course to rear its head. In his examination-in-chief Buckle had twice mentioned the carburettor in passing, noting that it had fallen off the engine block through the melting of the carburettor body. Finnemore returned to discussing this part of the engine, asking Buckle, in a further quest to explain the fire's ferocity,

> "If the top of the carburettor was blown off [as distinct from being pulled off by Rouse], that, of course, would spray petrol about the front part of the engine?—
>
> [Buckle] It would but I do not think that is at all likely to happen.
>
> [Finnemore] I am going to suggest to you that it probably did happen in the case...--
>
> [Buckle] No, I do not think that is probable. There is a more obvious cause [as to why, in this particular case, the water joints attached to the radiator were burnt].....I think [they have] been burned from the continuing [by which he meant the deliberately fed] fire. It is one of the facts which indicate the continuing fire from the open carburettor end of the petrol pipe [where the petrol union joint had allegedly been loosened]—after the carburettor had more or less disintegrated [sic], and its float and valve had ceased to function as such....
>
> [Finnemore] Is it not more reasonable [to explain the burnt water joints] that the carburettor burst [as distinct from its being forced off by Rouse to release more petrol] and the top flew off?
>
> [Buckle] No, I do not think that is anything like so reasonable."

This exchange was especially interesting on two levels. First, Finnemore was obviously seeking to explain why the fire was so intense and extensive, even though the engine itself had not been reduced to a fused mass. While the defence therefore insisted that the victim himself had accidentally brought about his own demise by his reckless behaviour in exposing petrol vapour around the petrol can to his lighted cigar, the destruction of the car was exacerbated by the release of petrol when the carburettor top blew off in the blaze. And as for the leak from the petrol union joint, that had not involved any deliberate human agency.

Moreover, so far as the carburettor was concerned, while the top had indeed melted and fallen off ('disintegrated'), Buckle did not accept the defence submission that it had been 'blown off' in the inferno, as a result of which more petrol would escape to feed the blaze. Yet while Buckle seemed to reject the idea of a violent, explosive separation of the top of the carburettor from its body, it is significant for Rouse's defence that *at that point in the proceedings* he also refrained from suggesting that the top had been pulled off manually (we return to this complex issue in chapter 14 where Rouse's reprieve petition is considered).

Thus for Buckle to conclude his testimony by agreeing that a leakage had occurred from the space *surrounding* the carburettor certainly implied nothing sinister on Rouse's part regarding the state of the carburettor. Yet there would very quickly be a twist to the tale. As Normanton remarked in her account of the trial,[257]

> "....all the while that this highly capable and astute [*sic*] witness had been testifying for the Crown, he had been watching the reactions of Rouse to his evidence, and from the fact that the prisoner seemed not too much disturbed by it, Colonel Buckle was led to ruminate critically upon his own chain of reasoning. *After he had left the box* [italics added] a further possibility occurred to his mind, namely, *that Rouse had deliberately removed the top......* [so that] the float chamber, deprived of the float which has come away with the top, rapidly fills, overflows, and continues to overflow whilst the supply of petrol lasts...."

This, of course, would provide a further source of fuel supply for the fire (which might also explain why the petrol tank itself remained relatively unscathed). Not surprisingly, therefore, Birkett ensured that the possibility of the carburettor *top*'s forceful removal by hand was put to Rouse in cross-examination as well as to one of the defence experts, Herbert Bamber, below. Interestingly, for tactical legal reasons, Buckle himself was not asked about this theory when he was recalled to the witness box by Birkett on the sixth day of the trial. For his re-examination by prosecuting counsel was, as we shall see, confined to answering a central claim by the defence experts that after a fierce car blaze, the nut on the petrol union joint found by Buckle a month after the blaze to be loose, was a predictable consequence of such fires rather than the result of deliberate human intervention.[258] As to the defence's mechanical experts who testified at the trial, we examine this in the next chapter.

The remaining Crown witness on the second day was Dr. Shaw. The latter's testimony repeated the post-mortem details covered previously in chapter six. Consequently, no further coverage of them in this chapter will be undertaken. There was, however, also brief prosecution evidence that day from an expert automobile engineer from Northampton, William Dickens, who stated that the car had been left in second gear. He did agree that it was possible that in a stationary vehicle like Rouse's (whose second and reverse gears required forward movements of the gear stick located between the two front seats), a driver's intention to engage reverse gear might nonetheless result in mistakenly engaging second, as a result of the cramped space caused by the presence of a passenger. Presumably the point of calling Dickens as a prosecution witness was to suggest that since the car had been found stationary in second gear, in which gear Rouse customarily left his vehicle when he switched it off, it was less likely that he had been suddenly engulfed in a car blaze prompting him to make a quick exit from the car while it was still in that driving mode. Thus it was surely implied that he had stopped the car normally, leaving it in second gear in order to carry out his

---

257 Helena Normanton, *Trial of Alfred Arthur Rouse*, Notable British Trials Series, William Hodge & Co., Edinburgh, 1931, p. xxx.
258 In his closing speech, Finnemore did remind the jury that the car had been left unattended for some hours after the blaze, though he did not explicitly raise the possibility of a curious on-looker fiddling with the nut, no doubt assuming, instead, that it had cooled down by the morning before the return of the police to guard the site.

attack. But these points were not spelt out by Birkett or Elwes for the Crown.

By the third day of the trial (Wednesday January 28), the crowds demanding admission were more canny and determined than on the previous days. Thus when the doors of the court building opened at 10 am, women rushed the barriers and scuffles broke out among the so-called gentler sex. A couple of women forced their way through the police lines while the latter were trying to keep them at bay, and a further twenty women skirted round the barrier and made a dash for the doors. Police reinforcements were called for from inside the building to 'drive them back', as one journalist recorded. Birkett arrived by car at 10:15 and the jury was in place by 10:25. Rouse was then brought up from the cells below and appeared refreshed as he entered the dock, giving a smile and a reassuring nod to his wife and father who were again sitting just to the left of the dock.

After Dr. Shaw had been briefly recalled to answer a couple of relatively inconsequential questions, the celebrated Spilsbury took the witness stand for the Crown. Again, his testimony has already been, in effect, considered at length in the post-mortem chapter. For his testimony did not vary from the report he had already submitted and which we have previously considered. After he had been examined and cross-examined for a considerably briefer period than that in respect of the car fire expert for the Crown, Colonel Buckle, but for a marginally longer length than Shaw's appearance in the witness box, a succession of Crown witnesses followed one after another that day. They included John Graham, the company secretary of Rouse's employer, W. B. Martin & Co., PC Lilley from Markyate, Henry Turner the lorry driver who had picked up Rouse at the junction with Hardingstone Lane, Edwin Pitt, Turner's companion on the lorry, George Smith and Eric Farmer who both worked for the transport company on the Thames Embankment that arranged long-distance coach tickets, and George Bell, the coach driver who had driven Rouse to Newport. There then followed various members of the Welsh contingent, including Ivy Jenkins' father and sister but not Ivy herself. Superintendent Brumby, PC Copping and Sergeant Skelly were also called, and finally (but not in order of appearance), and no doubt to the accompaniment of huge anticipation, Nellie Tucker was also called into the witness box. But her appearance in fact turned into the greatest anti-climax of the proceedings (below), as legal objections by the defence to her anticipated testimony meant that her appearance in the witness box was short and factual (though Birkett was probably already contemplating not bringing up Nellie's intimate relationship with Rouse).

Both sides had, indeed, probably harboured concerns about what Nellie might say and the jury was ordered out as the matter was resolved between counsel and judge. Finnemore's concern, of course, related not only to what her evidence might, or indeed would, imply about Rouse's unattractive traits regarding his sexually taking advantage of young women. It would also raise the matter of yet another maintenance obligation about to be imposed on Rouse to add to his existing financial woes, a further commitment that, to a receptive jury, might have caused him to concoct a violent solution perpetrated in Hardingstone Lane. Thus for the defence such evidence would be harmful and paint Rouse not only as an accused undeserving of any sympathy by the jury but as a possible killer. For Birkett such evidence could be perceived not only as affording a possible motive for murder but also as the Crown attempting to introduce Rouse's bad character where legal authority to do so did not exist (though it could be admissible if Rouse himself had attacked the character of Crown witnesses). If such bad character evidence had been admitted at trial and the prisoner was subsequently convicted, there would always be a risk, as Birkett was aware of in respect of adducing Rouse's 'harem' statement, that the Court of Criminal Appeal would quash the conviction because of this perceived flaw. The judge therefore advised Birkett to ask Nellie as little as possible, though 'The jury cannot help forming some conclusion', while Birkett now revealed, without having discussed the matter with Finnemore, that he was not proposing to call Helen or Ivy at all. At the police court, it will be recalled, Paling had referred to the women's evidence, in the light of Rouse's 'harem' statement, as pointing to motive. But now Birkett and Elwes concluded that the women's evidence would not be called, which Talbot recognized as an endeavour to exclude, as far as possible, evidence that might bear on the prisoner's bad character. Finnemore then requested that the judge instruct that the press should not report the discussion and the press gallery, present throughout, was directed accordingly. The jury then filed back in.

What was therefore reported the next day was that Nellie walked quickly into court when called. She wore a tailored tweed coat and a close-fitting brown hat. She had a large jade necklace round her neck and in answer to Birkett's questions stated that she had known Rouse for nearly five years and had last seen him on November 5 between ten past seven and eight o'clock in the evening. When the judge interceded with, 'You must get where it was', Birkett raised a hand in warning. 'Do *not* tell me the *precise place*. Perhaps I may lead about this [examiners-in-chief are rarely permitted to ask leading questions]. You saw him in London?' 'Yes', replied Nellie. 'Was it in City Road, London?' 'Yes', she replied. Finnemore who, as a cross-examiner, *was* unqualifiedly permitted to ask leading questions, asked, 'I think he was proposing to see you again the next week, was he not?' 'On the Monday', she responded. 'That would be the 10th, my Lord', Finnemore stressed so as to ram home the message that Rouse had *not* been planning to do a disappearing act. And that was Nellie's leading lady role in a public forum over almost before it had begun.

The evidence of PC Lilley from Markyate was notable only for his confirming that while he had not taken a note of the car's registration number, he distinctly recalled that the passenger had appeared to be about 35 to 40, small in stature and with an oval pale face. Both men in the car definitely wore trilby hats, despite Finnemore putting it to him that as a result of the war wound, Rouse never wore a hat while driving. Was Finnemore therefore suggesting that such an incident at Markyate at 11:15 pm (the time of which, for the Crown, indicated the deliberately slow pace of Rouse's driving) did not involve Rouse? Clearly, that was not a possibility given that Rouse himself had admitted that the discussion with a policeman had occurred, albeit that the prisoner had thought it took place 'outside St Albans'. More likely, Finnemore was simply suggesting that Lilley was not a very observant witness and that therefore his testimony should be ignored. Indeed a later witness, the coach company manager, Eric Farmer, told the court that while a coach ticket from the Embankment to Newport was being arranged on the morning of November 6, Rouse seemed more concerned about losing his *stetson* (not a trilby) hat than about his missing car, which did not square with Lilley's recollection.

Turning to the lorry and coach company witnesses themselves, their accounts in the witness box followed closely the statements they had given to the police and which we noted in an earlier chapter dealing with Rouse's flight to Wales. Again and again, the vivid and, for them, the unusual sight of a hatless man was fixed in the minds of those witnesses. So were their recollections of his explaining away the loss of his car and his jocular and calm nature, except in the case of George Smith, the Thames Transport Company porter. He thought Rouse 'seemed to be in a bit of a stew' as the latter stood around somewhat aimlessly at the Embankment. Approached by Smith as to his destination, Rouse at first said he was not sure and then confided that 'I am in a bit of a mess, and I lost my car or, rather, had it pinched', before indicating he wanted to travel to Newport, South Wales. Regarding the coach journey, the driver, George Bell, told the court that Rouse, sitting immediately behind the driver on the journey, had mentioned that he was travelling to see his wife in a place whose name he could not quite remember. Elwes then asked the witness whether Rouse had said anything about his married life, which question drew an objection from Finnemore (probably because, apart from issues of bad character, it might require Rouse in due course to make damning admissions about committing bigamy or to commit perjury when later cross-examined). The questioning was allowed. 'Did he [Rouse] say anything about his private affairs?' 'Yes'. Bell recalled Rouse telling him that his 'mother-in-law' would not allow her daughter to leave home just yet as the couple had only just married. What the jury thought of this supposed bizarre explanation by Rouse, as recounted by Bell, can only be imagined. By this time, of course, Rouse had purchased a replacement hat, a trilby that he wore when boarding the coach outside Bush House but which he doffed when he took his seat.

So what did the Crown hope that this evidence would convey to the jury? Was it to show Rouse's determination to get as far away from the scene of the blaze as possible, to suppress evidence of panic following his encounter with the cousins in Hardingstone Lane, an effort that broadly succeeded, as perceived by the above witnesses except Bell? Or were they all struck by the loquaciousness of this man who was talking nineteen to the dozen in a manner which suggested an excitable character or one who had, indeed, experienced some kind of shock? Was he looking for a refuge in South Wales after the trauma or was he affecting to act normally in visiting Ivy and her family (since he had previously arranged routinely to travel down to Gellygaer)? These men's testimony, in sum, was not obviously damning. It simply depended upon which inferences the jury chose to draw from it.

The evidence of the Welsh 'contingent' was probably more harmful to Rouse than that of the previous group of Crown witnesses. His different explanations and his dissembling regarding his missing car, his denial that the burnt-out car pictured in the evening paper, the *South Wales Echo*, was his, the charade the next morning over his acquisition (or expropriation) from Ivy's sister, Phyllis, of that day's *Daily Sketch*, with the details of the destroyed MU 1468 Morris Minor registered with one A. A. Rouse who lived at 14 Buxted Road, the testimony of Hendell Brownhill regarding the car journey to pick up a coach at Cardiff (so long as it was not too near Glamorgan County police headquarters), the discussion with Brownhill as to whether the car had been insured and whether Rouse had already reported, or was yet to report, the car's loss to the police, the brief stop at the hotel, *en route*, where Rouse did not want to hear any more from the butcher's boy about the female dead body supposedly found in the car's wreckage, even if they did not directly implicate him in the tramp's sudden demise, all pointed to Rouse's shiftiness and unreliability and to the impression that nothing that he said was capable of belief. All Finnemore could do was to peck ineffectively at the Crown evidence. Did not Rouse tell William Jenkins on the Friday morning that he was going to return to London right away to report his loss to the police (which prompted Jenkins to ask Brownhill to give Rouse a lift to Cardiff)? Surely this implied that Rouse was not being dishonest? Yes, but is there not a police station in Gellygaer itself, apart from the one in Cardiff, Birkett responded? To Thomas Reakes, a collier and fellow-resident of Gellygaer who had brought the evening paper to the Jenkins residence on the night of Rouse's arrival, Finnemore asked him whether it *was* the *South Wales Echo*, or could it have been the *Evening Express*? Was he certain as to the story's contents, and so on? In other words, did Reakes have a poor memory? The full contents of Rouse's obfuscations during his Welsh sojourn can, of course, be found earlier in the first chapter. However the précis, above, can just as well explain the antipathy towards Rouse reflected in the jury's verdict.

The final collection of Crown witnesses were all related to his employment and to his financial difficulties. John Graham was the company secretary to Rouse's Leicester employer, W. B. Martin & Co. Ltd. He explained that Rouse had a basic salary of £4 a week plus £1 for fixed expenses. The company also paid him his actual expenses and a commission on sales. Usually a cheque was sent to Rouse every Friday evening but occasionally he would himself call at the Leicester factory to pick up his wages. The last occasion was on October 24 when he was paid £8. 9s. 2d. Graham then produced a note that Rouse had sent from Herne Bay on October 29, saying that he had run out of money. The defendant was, as a result, sent a cheque the same day for £7 'against commission'. The cheque was produced as an exhibit. A further cheque was sent to him on October 31 for £6. 17. 10d. and he was not due to receive any more commission until November 21. An outstanding sum of £8. 6s. 5d, presumably his wages and fixed expenses up to November 6, was paid to his solicitor, Lee-Roberts. Birkett also asked about a sum of £10 paid to Rouse on account in September, as well as inquiring about the total amount of commission received by Rouse during his employment. Graham, however, could not oblige with these figures since he had only joined the firm in September. What it all meant for the Crown's case was not wholly clear. Presumably it was to stress Rouse's dire financial position and thus to imply that a motive to disappear existed. Yet notwithstanding the plea he had sent from Herne Bay, the amounts mentioned as paid to Rouse might not have struck too many people as suggesting impoverishment. But that, of course, took no account of his outgoings, including maintenance payments and presents to his women and son, hire purchase bills, mortgage payments and the cost of clothing for a man who took pride in his appearance. Certainly, Rouse's dealings with his firm after his arrest showed him pre-occupied with not being seen to be cheating his employer by retaining company samples at his home, or getting involved with the dubious

Reginald Bird, Lee-Roberts' soon-to-be dismissed clerk, or to cause Martin's business any embarrassment.

Finally, before the conclusion of the prosecution case, representatives of the relevant insurance companies, the hire purchase company and the car showroom gave testimony all with a view, once more, to emphasising Rouse's straightened financial circumstances as he struggled to keep up with his regular payments. Thus the representative from Chester & Cole Ltd., the hire purchase firm, pointed out that while Rouse's first two monthly payments of £6. 14s. 8d. for the new car were almost on time, the third payment, due on September 2, was actually made on September 26, while the fourth (and last) payment was made on October 7. The next instalment was due in the week of the blaze and therefore was never paid. Finally, Denis Kennedy, the underwriter of Rouse's 'Eclipse' comprehensive motor policy, the proposal form for which was misleadingly if not fraudulently completed by Rouse, recounted that the policy would pay out £1,000 in the event of the death of a passenger in the car, or of the owner if driving at the time (and the same or a lesser amount in the event of particular serious bodily injuries caused by an accident involving the insured vehicle).

So, again, the import of such evidence was to paint an image of a financially desperate (and fraudulent) Rouse who might be motivated either to pocket the £1,000 pay-out for the death of his passenger or for Rouse's executor to receive the payment on behalf of his beneficiaries if he himself had died in the blaze. There were, of course, obvious problems with such a scenario. If the passenger died, his identifiable beneficiaries would obtain payment, not Rouse, unless the passenger happened to be Lily (and Arthur Jnr.'s illegitimate status would exclude his inheriting). Second, if Rouse had died, or was presumed to have died, then only Lily would benefit, which would hardly improve Rouse's financial predicament—unless.....? (and here the senior Home Office official, Blackwell's, scent of a marital conspiracy began to take shape, as we shall see later).

Thus with the examination of Sergeant Skelly and Superintendent Brumby completing the list of Crown witnesses, discussed earlier, and in the absence of any police court testimony from Rouse himself that the prosecution might have desired to adduce at the trial, the Crown case closed.

It is often the case in criminal trials that, at this point, the defence lodge a submission that in view of the alleged weakness or paucity of evidence adduced by the Crown , there is simply no case for the defence to answer. When this submission is made (it is today known as a *Galbraith* plea after the case in 1981 where the legal issues surrounding such a plea were discussed in detail), the jury invariably is sent out of the court while counsel debate the matter with the judge. For if they were present when and if the judge ruled that the Crown *had* established that there was a case for the defence to answer, the jury might be influenced by this preliminary ruling by the judge to believe that there was more than simply a case to answer, but that the prosecution had established strong grounds for conviction (even before hearing the defence case). This is notwithstanding that the test for the judge is not whether the jury *would* convict on the evidence so far adduced, but whether the jury, properly directed by the judge as to law and guided as to salience, *could* reasonably convict. The judge's role is therefore not to trespass on the province of the jury as the triers of fact in order to assess the strength of the prosecution evidence, but to determine whether the Crown has established a *prima facie* case against the accused that he would be required to answer, or to determine whether it is so devoid of content that, taken at its most compelling, a properly directed jury could still not convict. In Rouse's time, the practical safeguard of removing the jury from the court while the plea is argued by counsel and decided by the judge was not in place. Finnemore therefore knew that if he were to submit such a plea at the conclusion of the Crown case and if that plea were to fail, his client might be in a less favourable position than he would have been had the plea not been submitted in the first place. It was a gamble, but Finnemore obviously believed it was a risk worth taking even if it were to prove unsuccessful. Which it did.

On what basis, therefore, did Finnemore argue that even before the defence case had opened there was simply insufficiently strong (as distinct from no) prosecution evidence to go to the jury? First he noted that no-one could say, or had even pretended to say, how the fire had started. Colonel Buckle, the Crown's technical expert, had admitted that the union nut from which petrol dripped under the car and which appeared to have fed the blaze, might have come loose by vibration or by the passenger's foot accidentally turning it. Moreover Buckle had agreed that there were a number of ways by which a spark might have ignited the petrol vapour accidentally. There were also a number of photographs which showed that some people had taken the opportunity to interfere with the wreckage, making it extremely difficult to say what had happened or how the fire had started. Additionally there was nothing to suggest a motive for the crime of murder. As counsel stressed,

> "One is faced here with such an extraordinary circumstance, the apparent victim being a man quite unknown, with no quarrel or grudge against the prisoner, or he against him, both of them utterly unknown one to the other, there being no evidence at all of his identity."

Consequently, there was a greater onus on the prosecution to prove beyond all doubt that, first of all, there was a crime and, second, that the prisoner had committed it. The only suggestion the Crown had made was that Rouse had wished the body to be mistaken for his own. But there was no evidence to support that proposition. On the contrary, after the incident, Rouse had made no attempt to hide or to conceal himself. Furthermore, there was no evidence that the car had been deliberately set on fire by the prisoner and also no evidence of injury of any kind done by him to the deceased. Indeed, the evidence as it currently stood was entirely consistent with the prisoner's innocence.

This was the submission that Mr. Justice Talbot had to consider, during all of which Birkett remained silent. But it may be observed right away that when Finnemore referred to the Crown's heavy burden of proving both a crime and the prisoner's responsibility for it, he was technically advancing the wrong test at this point. Not that it mattered. For on the basis of the correct *prima facie* test and whether the jury *could*, not *would*, convict on what the Crown had already adduced as evidence, the judge was clear and precise.

> "All these topics are matters which are very proper to be laid before the jury

on the question which they have to decide, and it is quite open to you, if you think fit, to go to the jury on the footing that [at the end of *all* the evidence] there is no case for you to answer as a matter of fact; but if you ask me to rule as a matter of law that there is no evidence to go to the jury [at *this* point], it is an impossible contention."

In other words, Talbot reminded the court that his ruling was on a question of law, not of fact (the 'could', not 'would', issue). Thus it might be recognized that there were clear weaknesses in the Crown case, in particular, the lack of direct evidence of Rouse's guilt (no eye-witnesses to the fire being deliberately started or to the prisoner loosening the petrol union joint or to his striking the victim, and no forensics linking Rouse to the crime). Second, the defence case had not yet been presented. However, there was circumstantial evidence adduced by the Crown which had been subjected, when Finnemore had so elected, to cross-examination. This included prosecution evidence regarding Rouse's behaviour when meeting the cousins in Hardingstone Lane, his troubled financial situation, his strange behaviour, dissembling and lying on his way to, during his stay at, and his return from, Gellygaer, that was *capable* of suggesting culpability, evidence that Rouse might or might not choose to, or be able to, answer in his own examination-in-chief. In other words the Crown had established that, *prima facie*, there was sufficient circumstantial but perhaps not totally irrefutable evidence already advanced, despite cross-examination, to suggest that the jury ought to hear how, if at all, the defence proposed to meet it by adducing their own evidence. Thus, rather than the judge withdrawing the case at this stage, it would in due course be for the jury to form its own judgment, once it had heard the case from *both* sides, whether that case had been established by the Crown beyond reasonable doubt. And no doubt any answers offered by Rouse to the Crown evidence would be taken into consideration by the jury in their deliberations on the central question. Thus Talbot J. ruled that the case was to continue and that Rouse was to remain in the dock. So the defence had no alternative but to proceed to the next stage, and to convince the jury, aided by its own witnesses, not least of whom was Rouse himself, not that their client was innocent (though that would be ideal), but that the Crown had failed to meet the legal standard of proof beyond reasonable doubt, which was the crucial ingredient necessary to convict.

The *Evening News* headline at the end of that day's proceedings was 'Rouse Trial: Girls Give Evidence'. Of course they did not; or, at least, Nellie made only a brief appearance in the witness box, disclosing no details at all about her steamy but sad relationship with Rouse. It is not surprising how the press could get it so wrong in their desperate endeavour to sensationalise with an immediacy that was still distant from today's 24/7 news feed. So the press coverage which had no doubt hoped to provide salacious detail after detail, but was thwarted in this regard by counsel's careful calibration of what evidence from Rouse's 'harem' was safe to adduce, had to make do with that other crime trial celebrity, Sir Bernard Spilsbury, as his every word and description of the corpse were dutifully reproduced for the avid reader.

CHAPTER TEN

LAW'S CRUEL KINDNESS; PUTTING ACCUSED MAN IN BOX

DAILY MAIL, February 2, 1931

The Trial: the Defence Case

It was half past three in the afternoon of Wednesday January 28 when Donald Finnemore opened the case for the defence, an event too late to be reported in the evening press. The jury, unlike the practice today, had just heard his failed submission to the judge that the Crown had adduced insufficiently strong evidence to continue the case. Therefore, his opening remarks outlining his argument may have seemed repetitive. He acknowledged right away that the jury 'must have heard or read something about the case before they came into court.' However, he exhorted them to 'put all that out of their minds'. Unfortunately, this ploy might just have served not to empty their minds but to remind themselves of their preconceptions. On the question of motive, Finnemore made reference to that which the prosecution had merely suggested, that is, that the prisoner may have wished to disappear. That, he insisted, was a proposition wholly devoid of substance. Indeed, as the judge himself confided in his notes, 'No evidence of any preparation for disappearance. Losing business [his job], where was he to go? No evidence of acute pecuniary difficulties. In fact no evidence of attempt to disappear, but contrary.' No doubt they were all getting tired, trying to maintain concentration. For after Finnemore had been speaking for an hour and had come to a stopping point, the judge decided it was time to adjourn for the day. It was 4.35 p.m.

On its resumption the next morning, Thursday January 29, the 'early birds' were out in force again, and on the opening of the court doors at 10.30 a.m. the usual rush of people trying to gain admission was repeated. Once more a police cordon was hastily set up to contain the crush, and the doors of the court room were in fact locked to prevent unauthorised intrusion. In the end more than fifty girls were bunched together in the restricted standing space under the galleries. The local press were diverted by the appearance of an elderly barrister, Mr. Walter Annis Attenborough. A veteran of the Midland circuit for over fifty years, Attenborough had appeared at Northampton in 1892, defending Andrew MacRae who had murdered and dismembered his lover, Annie Pritchard. Her head and arms were never discovered. However, in contrast to the Rouse case, patient police work had identified the victim and had secured MacRae's conviction. In his later years, Attenborough was still a familiar face in Northampton, giving a series of talks in the county hall, enlivened by a concert party, in which he himself played the cornet.

The gossip columnists had been investigating the local connections of another of the lawyers in court, Sidney Campion, whom we have met in chapter five. As a youngster Campion had run away from home in Leicester to try his fortune in London. Once upon the road, the columnists related, he found he had only one shilling in his pocket. Having stayed the night in lodgings in Market Harborough he was now left with just fourpence and by the time he reached Northampton he was penniless. By good fortune he had come across Mr. James Gribble, a philanthropic town councillor, whose generosity had enabled him to be sent on his way. Subsequently, Campion found work in journalism before being called to the Bar. Now he had returned to Northampton for his very first brief, acting for Helen Campbell. This was not too arduous. Helen Campbell had not been called by the Crown to give evidence and Campion took no part in the trial. However Miss Campbell did not need to worry about wasting her money. Her legal expenses were being paid for by the *Daily Sketch*.

Finnemore now resumed his opening speech and, referring to the position of the body, remarked that none of the policemen who had witnessed it *in situ* had thought it necessary to make any note of its position. He further suggested that if Rouse's intention had been to stage a disappearance, the obvious thing to do would have been to put the body in the driver's seat and not leave it slumped across the two front seats in such a way as to suggest it had entered or been pushed into the car from the passenger side. As to the mallet, he asserted that it had 'no significance at all as a possible weapon of attack.' While the defence did not dispute that one hair found upon it might be human, there was no sign of blood or skin or tissue. No-one knew why it had been found at a distance from the car but everyone now knew that the wreckage had been left unattended and had been interfered with by passers-by. If the prisoner had used the mallet in a murderous attack, surely the first thing he would have done with the wooden object would have been to put it in the car to be consumed by the fire. Finally he asked whether it was conceivable that anyone, intent upon murdering the man and burning the car, should choose a spot 159 yards from a village he had just driven through and set about the job in plain view of the nearby houses.

Now came perhaps the most dramatic part of the trial as he proposed to call his first witness, the prisoner himself, to tell his own story. He reminded the jury that Rouse was not obliged to give evidence, but the latter had chosen to do so. It was, indeed, a requirement that if an accused chose to testify (after non-binding advice in this regard from his defence team), then he or she would be the first defence witness to testify. However, from the moment that Rouse opened his mouth in the witness box, it was obvious that his decision would turn out to be a grave mistake.

As his name was called, Rouse pulled a handkerchief from his breast pocket, wiped his forehead and dabbed at his lips. He seemed to be bracing himself for the ordeal in the witness box. Once settled, he was taken through his evidence by Finnemore's junior, A. P. Marshall, a not unusual practice by counsel.

Problematically, however, Rouse's first few responses to the formal examination betrayed an obvious arrogance and flippancy. 'Do you live at 14, Buxted Road, Friern Barnet?' 'I *did.*' 'Are you thirty-six years of age at the moment?' 'I always understood I was thirty-six. I have no proof I am thirty-six.' Marshall then moved on to the prisoner's military record which might, of course, have induced some sympathy for him. However, even here Rouse did not help himself, with the friendly questions from his own counsel revealing not only that he was garrulous, which would be confirmed in spades during his time in the box, but also confused. 'Were you wounded in the war?' 'Yes.' (apochryphal advice has it that, certainly in cross-examination, prisoners should always confine their answers to 'Yes', 'No' and 'I can't remember'.) 'In what year were you wounded?' 'A few months after I joined up. I joined up on the 8th August, I think it was, and I was wounded on the 15th April; I believe it was February. 25th May, I think it was.' '1915?' 'Yes.' 'Where were you wounded?' 'In the body do you mean, or what part of France?'

When next asked about his movements on November 5 his account became rambling, even testing the patience of the judge. For example, after several exchanges as to whether Lily had given him any tea, who had packed his case and at what time he had finally set out for Leicester, Mr. Justice Talbot intervened: 'Is not the simplest way for him to give an estimate of when he left home?' His Lordship did not note Rouse's remark that it was Lily who had packed the attaché case. This, of course, might have been significant for the defence if the Crown were insistent that he had also packed his Army identity disc in order that it be found after the fire, placed round his 'victim's' neck (assuming no marital conspiracy to obtain insurance moneys). The mystery of that disc remains unresolved. The police claimed to have found it in his attaché case when he got off the coach at Hammersmith, implying that he had forgotten to leave it in the wreckage of the car or round the dead man's neck. But nothing more seems to have been heard of it.

There were intimations of Rouse's propensity constantly to qualify or amend everything he said (a mental manoeuvre which had perplexed Sergeant Skelly, trying to take down the Hammersmith statement) when he was describing his first encounter with the dead passenger. 'At about Tally Ho Corner--I should say anything between a mile and half a mile past-- a man stepped off the kerb, or not exactly stepped off the kerb, put his hand out from the kerb to stop me and I stopped.' Marshall asked Rouse what the man had requested. 'I believe his exact words were 'Can you give me a lift, Guv'nor?', or words to that effect.' This was an indication of how he would deliver his oral testimony. Thus he would repeatedly qualify phrases like 'exact words' with 'words to that effect'. Indeed, a combination of these phrases occurred seventeen times. His description of his passenger was equally unconvincing and vague. He pointed out that he had only a small light on the dashboard and when passing through areas lit by street lamps, he had not looked at his passenger. The man was of a similar build to himself, 'but not perhaps so meaty, perhaps not quite so stout.' He had not seen the colour of the man's hair as the latter wore a hat all the time. And as for his eyes, 'Naturally one man would not look at another man's eyes to tell the colour'. Was he implying that only men of a homosexual tendency might do so, and that he was decidedly not of that orientation?

Another feature which possibly grated with his listeners was that if he said something once, he considered it worth saying twice. As to his passenger, 'Very likely he was a country man. He spoke with a country accent', and, 'His breath smelt rather of drink. It was rather objectionable'. No doubt seeking to occupy the high moral ground, Rouse could not say whether that was due to beer or spirits. For he himself, he proudly announced, was a teetotaller. His passenger had talked of various things in which 'I really was not interested.....because I was not interested in him then and his breath certainly smelt very objectionably of drink.' As they neared Northampton, he continued in reply to questioning, 'I noticed I was going through a village [Hardingstone] that I did not recognise. I said to my companion, 'I believe I am on the wrong road'. Yes, I am certain I said to my companion, 'I believe I am on the wrong road'.' As this exchange affirmed, Rouse continually re-evaluated his recollection of events as if trying to find a more believable version. The jury may have found this very disconcerting, but more probably, very suspicious. His explanation of what part the mallet had played in the incident was particularly suspect. He seemed to be making it up as he went along. Marshall asked how he had unscrewed the cap of the petrol can.

> "I do not remember handling the mallet for that purpose; I have an idea that
> I did; but I cannot picture myself at the moment using it; but it was the only
> thing in the car I could use....As I no doubt remembered that I had a mallet in
> the back, very likely beside the petrol can for all I know...I do not remember it
> ...I no doubt used the handle of the mallet."

In continuing his narrative he went on to add that, 'I think it was about that time I heard my starter or self-starter go, or some mechanical noise of that description.' To make sense of this claim, we must note that by this point the prosecution expert, Colonel Buckle, had already insisted in his testimony (chapter 9) that an electrical spark could *not* have triggered the blaze. So was Rouse attempting to counter Buckle by implying that a technical mal-function could have been the innocent explanation as to why his car had caught fire? The problem for Rouse, however (and no doubt to the chagrin of Finnemore and Marshall, who must have been seething at their client's irrepressible compulsion towards verbosity) was that he had just told counsel that as he was relieving himself at some distance from the vehicle, he had noticed a reflection of light which had become brighter. So while he now conveniently recalled hearing the noise of a mal-functioning starter (which impliedly could bring about an accidental car blaze), it had somehow slipped his mind some minutes previously when recounting to the jury his sudden awareness, with his trousers down, of the ominous glow in the distance. At the very least this belated recall must have struck the jury as odd. At worst, it undermined Rouse's credibility regarding *anything* he might say in his defence. If only he had known when to shut up in the box (recalling the words of Sir Patrick Hastings). It was yet another instance of Rouse offering too much information for a sharp-eared jury to digest. Who needed the slim-line assassin, Birkett, when Rouse was risking *hara-kiri*?

Perhaps understandably, as he finished recounting the panic he had experienced when he ran to the blazing car, Rouse broke down in the witness box. He swayed slightly and one of the two warders moved to support him. His voice sank to a whisper, he sobbed and dabbed his eyes with his handkerchief. A glass of water was handed to him and the judge asked him if he would like to sit. In a faltering voice Rouse said he would prefer to stand. By now Lily was openly weeping. However he soon regained his composure and Marshall advised him to carry on quietly and carefully and to suit himself as to how he gave his story. Describing his encounter with Brown and Bailey, Rouse disputed their account of the words which he had exchanged with them, words whose significance Birkett had argued could not be over-emphasised. 'It looks as though someone is having a bonfire up there.' Claiming that his first thoughts were to get help from the two young men, Rouse said,

> "If I was going to speak to them, I do not know. Anyhow, I ran past them; thoughts must have struck me. Well, I do not know. I cannot account why I did not speak to them. I ran past them and I turned round, and I was going to run to them for help, but I did not. Whether I spoke to them or what I did I do not know."

He remembered that the conversations he had had with Henry Turner, from whom he had hitched his lift to London in the latter's lorry, were mostly about engines and mechanical matters. Indeed, he recalled telling Turner that there was a bad leak in the lorry's silencer which was blowing back. But his recollection of what excuse he had given for wanting a lift was less clear. 'When he stopped I do not remember exactly what I said to him. To be quite frank with you, I do not remember the exact words I used to him. No doubt he asked me why I wanted a lift; but I do not remember what I said, to be quite frank.'

Here was another of Rouse's verbal tics. Thus in the course of his evidence, he used the words 'frankly', 'to be frank' and 'to be quite frank' a total of eighteen times. Indeed, in her account of the trial in the Notable British Trials series Helena Normanton admitted that she wearied of counting the number of times Rouse used the expressions 'honestly', 'candidly', 'to be frank', and so on. They were '.... all so unnecessary when a man is really trying to be honest and remembering his oath.' Moreover, when he reached the point in his story where he was dropped off from the lorry at Tally Ho Corner and had then walked down to the Embankment, Rouse apparently made a colossal gaffe. It was a real Perry Mason moment. Asked by Marshall, 'Where did you go from Tally Ho Corner?' he replied, 'I went down to the Embankment, because I had made up my mind to go to Wales, and I knew I could get a charabanc from somewhere along the Embankment'. 'Did you go directly to the Embankment?' But now for the first time Rouse mentioned that he had not gone directly to catch a coach to Wales. 'To be honest no, I did not.' 'Where did you go first?' 'I first went home'. This, of course, was when Lily had previously stated to the police that she thought her husband had returned home about one o'clock in the morning, making his alleged death in the burning car near Northampton at 1:50 am somewhat improbable, and impossible if she knew he had actually returned at around 6:30 am. To Marshall, Rouse stated that he remained at home for between a quarter and half-an-hour.

But what he was doing during that time is not clear. If he changed his suit and burned it to remove traces of the petrol and of the burning, no-one seems to have noticed (it will be recalled that after he was charged the police removed his clothes for forensic testing, but if any incriminating evidence was discovered it was never revealed, and his suit was later returned to him). And he certainly did not change his stained shirt while at Buxted Road. Maybe he did return home briefly to reassure Lily, as he claimed. Maybe it was to collect more money, if he had any left, that is. For though it seems that he had less than a pound on him when he arrived at Hammersmith, he did buy a new hat and paid for his coach journey before travelling to Wales. Indeed, how he got from Newport to Gellygaer remains a mystery. He probably walked.

But let us go back to the Embankment question. *Was* it an unintended blunder when he first stated that he had gone straight to the Embankment from Tally Ho Corner, and then corrected himself (or changed his account) to admit returning first to his home? This was not actually news to the prosecution (whether it was news to the defence is another matter). Thus for two months the police, the DPP and, indeed, Helen Campbell and her journalist 'associate', J. C. Cannell, had known that, in all probability, Rouse had called in to see his wife as he passed through London. But the Crown did not introduce this evidence in court (it was, as noted above, revealed by Rouse in the witness box). Police knowledge of the visit had first emerged when, on December 1 1930, Cannell had interviewed Helen in the back of a car. Sitting on her knee was 'Little Arthur'. The five-year old had told Cannell that he had overheard his daddy arguing with his 'Auntie Lil' in the middle of the night on Bonfire Night. According to the boy, the argument had been about 'insurance' and a 'medal' (that is, Rouse's identity disc) which was not where it was supposed to be. Cannell realised this was something he could not keep as a press exclusive and arranged for the boy to repeat his story to Inspector Collins of Scotland Yard. The implication was that, whether Rouse had returned home at 1 am, as Lily had supposedly originally thought, or at the actual time of about 6:30 am, Lily was aware that her husband was very much alive when she agreed to a Northamptonshire police request to travel to Northampton with a view to identifying the charred remains recovered from the blaze. To the DPP and to Sir Ernley Blackwell at the Home Office, this confirmed their suspicions that Rouse had staged his own disappearance and that his wife was complicit in the plot. However because the source of the information was a small child, this was never produced as evidence (though early legal sources such as the eighteenth century *Bacon's Abridgement* laid down that the testimony of infants would not automatically be excluded if they had sufficient understanding of the sacredness of the oath on the Bible or, as might be expressed in modern times, the importance of telling the truth; and there is no reason to believe that Arthur Jnr. did not possess this understanding).

Perhaps Rouse and his defence team hoped to neutralise this potentially damaging omission from both his police statements and from his initial answer to Marshall about his short visit to his home by introducing it himself, rather than have it emerge under cross-examination. If so, it was a forlorn hope. Mr. Justice Talbot, of course, had not previously been aware that Rouse had been back to Buxted Road (the Bench are usually given sight of depositions before proceedings), and so was not previously alerted to the implications. He merely noted that Rouse now replied, 'I just went home, where I stayed not more than ½ hour.' His notebook was subsequently read and annotated at the Home Office where his brief comment was underlined four times in blue pencil and the above exchange between Marshall and Rouse was handwritten into the margin. Sir Ernley Blackwell was certain that there was more to the story than just Rouse's plan to feign death and disappear. Was that half-hour exchange with Lily the key to, and exposure of, a conspiracy?

Rouse then told the story of his flight to Wales, insisting that it had been his intention all along to go to Wales. He had promised to go, and he went. He would have travelled straight there from Leicester and then return to London by Monday (as Nellie Tucker had told the court that he had undertaken to do). But, 'All my plans were at a stand-still. I could not do anything without a car.' So when he did get back to London, he claimed it was with the intention of going straight to Scotland Yard to 'set things straight' (the coach he was travelling on from Cardiff, it had already been pointed out, would continue from Hammersmith, where he alighted with Sergeant Skelly, in the direction of Scotland Yard). Asked by his counsel if he had done anything wrong in Hardingstone Lane, Rouse replied,

> "Nothing criminal at all. I was wrong very likely, in running away, I ought perhaps to have helped, or tried to help, or endeavoured to help; but thinking of the whole of the circumstances I have come to the conclusion that it would have been impossible for me to have got anywhere inside the car, or near the car, or helped him out of the car. I could not get near him."

This was indeed consistent with his insisting that the car doors had been closed when he got to the burning vehicle (though he had initially told the police that he had tried unsuccessfully to open the car doors but had been driven back by the flames). Moreover, he excused all his subsequent lies concerning the loss of the car by claiming that he had given explanations which were 'most suitable at the moment'. This was particularly so in South Wales where there were ladies present (and who, he assumed, would be embarrassed about references to his relieving himself as he saw the blaze erupt). Asked if he now realised the difficulties that had arisen as a consequence, Rouse replied, 'It is very unfortunate; that is all I can say.' Final questions put to a prisoner by his own counsel are often intended to paint the accused nakedly white rather than black. And so it was with Marshall's concluding questions. 'Did you intend, or did you in fact do any harm or hurt to the man that you picked up as a passenger?' 'I have never done what I consider any harm to any one.' 'Do you know exactly just what happened that night?' 'Not in the car, no'.

And then Marshall sat down. Rouse had given evidence for fifty minutes. But sadly for him his performance in the witness box had surely done much to undermine his own defence. For, when Birkett next rose to cross-examine at 12.25 pm, a fundamental weakness in the defence case had already been exposed, that is, the unattractive personality of the prisoner. That might, of course, appear unfair since a person should be tried on what criminal act they were alleged to have done, and not on how they present themselves to the jury. But it is a fact that juries are often faced with the question, 'Whom do you believe regarding what was alleged to have happened? Are you more likely to believe the prosecution witnesses or the defendant as he told his story?', and *impressions* play a large part in influencing the jury's decision-making. Birkett was not one to throw away his advantage by getting the jury to focus on *him* (in the manner of Marshall Hall's flamboyant performances) rather than upon the garrulous and shifty-looking accused. His approach would be under-played controlled aggression. Thus, according to the *Daily Mail*,

> "Mr. Birkett faced him across a semi-circular table littered with plans, papers and photographs. Mr. Birkett's short, sharp, incisive questions came like tinkling ice compared with the swift torrent of the prisoner's answers. Counsel stabbed the air with a gold pencil, pointing ruthless questions."

He chose to pick up the story where Rouse had left off, that the lies told in Wales were 'unfortunate'. What did that mean? Rouse's reply to a jury which, as the defence acknowledged, had been well aware of his serial infidelities and deceptions, must have seemed preposterous.

"Well I think it is always best – I have always been noted for telling the truth the whole of my life; I am not used to telling lies. At the time I thought it was the best thing to do.....People seem to think I did tell lies, and I admit I did tell lies. My name has been clear up to now of lies."

The liar was now lying about telling lies. For what he no doubt *really* considered 'unfortunate' was that the lies had caught up with him. Pressing the point about the prisoner's mendacity, Birkett asked him whether an innocent man would not tell the truth. Rouse's response was quite frankly (to use Rouse's own terminology) pathetic. 'Yes, no doubt, to your way of thinking.' What on earth would the jury make of *that* reply? It was clear that Rouse might have been on a different planet of honesty to the rest of civilisation, so far as his responses were concerned. There was no contrite admission of, or apologies for, engaging in deliberate and serial untruths, nor of indulging in 'terminological inexactitudes'. Sure, he readily conceded (though obviously not his own words) that he had been 'economical with the truth' or had even been 'economical with the '*actualite*' (to plagiarise from more modern political events). But his justification ('there were ladies present') stretched credulity, given the seriousness of the situation.

Birkett now turned to Rouse's detention in Hammersmith. Were his first words to Sergeant Skelly, 'I am glad it is all over'? Rouse's reply was emphatic, or nearly so, 'Most decidedly. I did say words to that effect.' And had he said, 'I am responsible'? He did not remember the 'exact words' but had indeed said 'words to that effect'. But then he explained that he had always been told that the owner of the car was responsible for anything that happened to that car. Pressed as to what degree of responsibility he accepted for the fatal outcome, Rouse limited it to handing the man a cigar and asking him to fill up the car with petrol. And even that was admitting too much responsibility. He quickly added, 'Quite frankly [again!], he volunteered himself; I think quite frankly [and again!] he did; I am not certain.'

Something of a squabble ensued when Birkett asked why he had not tried to help his passenger when the car was alight. Rouse replied that, for one thing, he could not see that the man was there. Birkett reminded him that, in his first statement to the police, he had said that he had seen the man inside the car and had tried to open the door. Rouse did not remember saying that, so Birkett read out the relevant passage. In his response Rouse insisted that, 'It [what Rouse had told Skelly] was not true exactly; it was not true at all. I did not see the man.' Birkett was not deflected. He asked him again whether in his first statement he had said that he had seen the man inside and had tried to open the door. Rouse snapped back, 'If you will *think* for a moment, you must remember that the flames were 17 feet high, and how one can see through a mass of flames......' The judge quietly rebuked Rouse for this outburst, telling him that he must answer the question. But always needing to have the last word, Rouse replied petulantly, 'I want to answer.' Terrier-like in his pursuit, Birkett next asked Rouse to explain why Sergeant Skelly had recorded Rouse as stating that he had seen the man inside the car and had tried to open the door. By this time stung with exasperation, Rouse replied, 'I do not know. I can only infer that it was told [by Rouse to Skelly] since; it was some time after, and I was talking the whole time; he made no note until the time afterwards, and you are not going to tell me from the length of that statement...'

But before Rouse could finish his sentence the judge once more admonished him and told him not to argue but simply to state that he did not say what Skelly alleged he had said. Did the sudden appearance at this point of a black cat peering through a window of the court and looking straight at the witness box while the cross-examination was going hammer-and-tongs signify the presence of some hostile spirit? The *Daily Mail* told its readers that superstitious women in court were nudging each other, some seeing the cat as a good omen for the prisoner and others viewing it as a portent of doom. Meanwhile, Rouse stood his ground courteously when responding to Birkett's cross-examination about the mallet; how he might have used it to open the petrol can; what explanation there was for its having been found fourteen yards in front of the car; why he walked some two hundred yards away from the car before relieving himself, past gaps in the hedge that he claimed he had been looking for. Then Birkett asked him if he had a dog. Rouse replied that he had a fox terrier which sometimes travelled in the car with him. Leaving the jury to make their own deductions regarding the non-human hairs found on the mallet, Birkett then asked Rouse to account for the human hair which *was* identified as being present. The explanation that Rouse offered, though no doubt true to form, was both unexpected and far-fetched. His wife, he said, had trained as a hairdresser and though she had never gone into business, she occasionally cut neighbours' or friends' hair, sometimes his own. She would use his old shirts to cover her clients' clothing. Then these shirts would find their way into his garage as cleaning rags and it was possible that the rags might contain a few cut hairs. He thought it worth mentioning that a week or two prior to the incident he had knocked out some dents in a mudguard, following a bump on the Kingston by-pass, and had used a cloth to avoid damaging the enamel. Had not Sir Bernard Spilsbury given evidence that one of the hairs on the mallet had been flattened? Well, the action of the mallet on a hard substance would surely flatten it out. The whole account was somewhat implausible, and by trying to provide a clever rebuttal to the Crown's contention that the mallet had played a part in the death of the unknown passenger, Rouse only succeeded in giving it credence. At least the judge came to his rescue on this matter when he later directed the jury, in his summing-up, to pay no attention to the mallet. But he could hardly direct them to pay no attention to Rouse's overall performance in the witness box.

On being taken back by Birkett to the events in Hardingstone Lane, the prisoner could not remember uttering the words 'It looks as if someone has had a bonfire up there'. Three times he denied it. Indeed he could not remember saying anything to either of the two young men. He did not remember the 'exact' explanation he had given Henry Turner for needing a lift. He had offered some excuse but while conceding that it was not the truth, he could not remember what that supposed explanation was. Birkett reminded him that according to Turner's evidence he had claimed he was 'expecting a mate to pick me up with a Bentley'. One should not be surprised that Rouse took strong exception to Birkett's suggestion. For he, Rouse, 'should not use the word 'mate' in any event', though 'I might have said 'friend'', he added sniffily. 'In any case I should not use the word, 'mate''. So while he had no compunction about lying, he would never, ever, as a proud representative of lower middle-class suburban respectability, stoop to using working-class terminology!

Birkett then turned to Rouse's earlier admission, the 'Perry Mason' moment, when he disclosed that he had indeed ('To be honest') gone home and had spoken to his wife before catching the coach to Wales. This time the judge paid particular attention, asking, 'I do not understand this. Did he say, when he was asked a question as to where he went, 'To be honest, I went home'?' 'Yes, my Lord', Birkett replied. So, turning to the prisoner, Talbot asked Rouse directly, 'Why did you say 'To be honest'?' And the prisoner's predictable reply, no doubt inducing silent hollow laughs within the court, was that 'I wanted to be frank. In the previous statement I had not said a word about going home.' The purpose of the visit, Rouse explained, was to tell his wife not to be worried. He had stayed no more than half an hour. He had not eaten anything. He had not changed his clothes nor indeed donned another hat. Although his initial panic had gone he was very far from being composed. He was still 'very upset'. Perhaps he 'volunteered' this information to demonstrate that he was a considerate husband who had no intention of staging a disappearance. However, as Birkett quizzed him about his determination to continue with his planned trip to Wales, despite the 'horror' that had occurred, the question of why he had not gone straight to the police loomed large. Again, rather than justifying his actions, Rouse unconsciously created the impression that he had fled because he had something to hide.

He even managed to get into a wrangle with Mr. Justice Talbot. The judge had heard Rouse excuse the catalogue of lies that he had told to various witnesses by claiming that lying was 'the easiest course'. But surely, the judge came back, almost sympathetically, '....if you wanted to take the easiest way, the easiest thing would be not to tell different lies?....Do you not get into greater difficulties by giving different explanations than you would by telling the truth about the whole business?'

Rouse responded defensively that he was not trying to hide anything and that he was endeavouring to avoid giving long explanations. Indeed he snapped back petulantly, 'I was not considering being brought up before a jury to account for my actions'. Yet he could not have been more wrong. For he was in front of a jury *precisely* to account for his actions or, at least, to convince the jury that the Crown had failed to establish beyond reasonable doubt that the death of the unknown man had been due to any intentional criminal conduct on his part. But in furtherance of this object his explanations were becoming less and less convincing.

It was foolhardy to engage in discussions on the technical aspects of the Crown's case. But Rouse, vain man that he was, and who believed that he was technically gifted within certain limits, appeared quite willing to do so. He acknowledged that he had understood Colonel Buckle's evidence. He informed Birkett that a Morris Minor was the only make of car to have a petrol union nut in that particular position within the body of the car, and that he had once driven an Essex make of car which had a similar nozzle in the nut and which had leaked so badly that he had to turn off the petrol tap overnight so as not to lose fuel. However petrol would not gather in a pool from such a leak because they would drip through the cracks in the wooden floorboards which were covered, not by a cork linoleum mat as Birkett had supposed, but by a hair mat. 'Like a doormat?' inquired the judge. Not exactly, Rouse corrected him, as the hairs were only a quarter or an eighth of an inch long, a standard fitment on a Morris Minor. The cross-examination then descended into confusion as everyone joined in.

> "Mr. Birkett: Do you doubt yourself that the flame came from any other source than that joint?
>
> Rouse: That is rather a technical question.
>
> Mr. Finnemore: With all respect, is that a question for this witness?
>
> Mr. Justice Talbot: The witness is entitled to refuse to answer it, if he likes.
>
> Mr Finnemore: I understood the witness said it was a technical question.
>
> Mr. Justice Talbot: I did not hear that.
>
> Mr Finnemore: I did not hear it either. The witness must have been giving his answer as I made my objection.
>
> Rouse: Quite frankly, it is possible, but I would not like to say definitely.
>
> Mr Birkett: Leave it, Rouse."

This rather curt end to the exchange may have been a kindness to Rouse. But moments later he was at it again, claiming a degree of mechanical expertise that might not have played well with the jury. Thus 'You [Birkett] admit I have some knowledge of a car,' he preened to his interrogator.

> "To light petrol or petrol vapour you get a flash of a considerable degree, especially if you loosen a joint. You would have to wait a minute or so before you strike a light, and in that case you would get a flash, and in that case, being near it, striking the match, would be singed; and that is the first thing the police officers looked at, and I offered my hands in the first place."

With his vainglorious self-promotion, perhaps it was no longer for the jury a question of whether he had started the fire but of how he had got away with it; how the trick had been performed.

Yet worse was to come. For Rouse next chose to take issue with Birkett on how the corpse came to be lying across the front seats, using such a turn of phrase that probably left his own counsel quietly screaming in despair. Thus Birkett put it to him that he, Rouse, had first set about rendering his passenger, unconscious presumably outside the vehicle, and had then thrown him, face forward, into the car. Rouse's emphatic reply no doubt shocked the court out of its later afternoon

196

descent into weariness. He angrily riposted that he would not,

> "....throw a man....If I did a thing like that, I should not throw him down face forwards. I should think where I put him, I imagine.....If I had been going to do as you suggest, I should do a little more than that. I think I have a little more brains than that."

According to the *Daily Sketch* reporter, J. C. Cannell, at this point the whole court came alive on hearing this extraordinary statement. Indeed an audible gasp went round the room and the judge stiffened and turned in his seat. Was Rouse really arguing that it could not have been him because he would have made a better job of it? Birkett could not have chosen a better and more striking point at which to conclude his cross-examination and to sit down. For this was the moment when the carefully constructed edifice of Rouse's defence, that if his lying and dissembling could be explained away in a sincere manner he would be safe, looked on the point of collapse. 'I should not throw him face forward. I should think where I put him'. The scourge of self-inflicted 'too much information' now struck Rouse again.

Thus a difficult but not impossible task for the defence at the outset now looked grim and irremediable as Finnemore rose in re-examination, desperately hoping to rescue the situation and to attempt to mitigate the awful impression that his client had made. He did elicit an admission from Rouse that his actions had, indeed, been foolish throughout. Yes, 'Foolish but decidedly not criminal', he implied. Moreover, there was, Rouse believed, a document which could be produced, asking his customers to contact the company if their orders were not processed. This document would confirm that everyone knew he had a poor memory (and he notably never wore a watch). Moreover, there was his war wound (which he might have hoped the jury would link to his poor memory). Rouse had assumed that his discharge from the Army had been brought about because his wound would not enable him to wear a uniform cap. It was uncomfortable to wear a hat. He never wore a hat when in the car. The final comment in Mr. Justice Talbot's notebook, at the conclusion of Rouse's evidence, was, 'I never wore a hat when driving.' What was Finnemore trying to elicit here? First, that Rouse's shambolic performance in the witness box might be attributed to his poor memory, a result, of course, of his valiant war service and of the war wound that he had suffered in defence of his country. So perhaps Finnemore was simply touting for the sympathy vote at this point to explain away his client's *kamikaze* performance in the box. As to the evidence about not wearing a hat in the car, perhaps that was to compromise PC Lilley's evidence that both driver and passenger were wearing trilby hats when he had spoken to Rouse at Markyate.

Rouse finished his evidence at 4.30 pm. precisely. He returned to the dock, allegedly whispering to his prison warders, 'Only three more Sundays to go'. Perhaps he was indeed acutely conscious that he had 'blown' his opportunity and that his confident hopes at the outset had now evaporated. Or was he making another of his little jokes, confident in his ability to weather this major storm? It was probably the latter. He sat down and was immediately given a glass containing a 'brown-looking liquid'. He swirled the glass around as if to mix medicinal powders and then drank it eagerly. Perhaps he was optimistic (rather than suicidal). For, towards the end of his evidence he had confidently joined in an exchange with the judge about the need for caution when topping up a petrol tank from a can. Thus when Talbot had observed, 'It seems to me more reason why somebody should do it who understands it' (and therefore it should not have been left for the unknown man to carry out the task), Rouse added to Finnemore's 'Certainly', that 'I quite agree, my Lord'. But if Rouse thought he had performed well, others did not. J. C. Cannell suggested that when he stepped from the witness box to return to the dock, most of those who had previously felt that he had had a fighting chance of getting off now lost that hope. Birkett may have got the credit for the brilliance of his cross-examination but it was Rouse himself who had done the damage which could not be repaired.

As the clerk of assize, George Pleydell Bancroft, noted in his memoirs,[259] Rouse was an 'intriguing' character who 'through his vain volubility literally [*sic*] hanged himself', a view later shared by Sir Patrick Hastings, his counsel at the Appeal Court. Indeed, 'the volubility of the man was so pronounced that it was extremely difficult for his counsel to hide his despair'. It even reached the stage, concluded Bancroft, that with Rouse performing his stuff in the witness box those present in court became 'fearful that at any moment he might tell the jury exactly how he had done the crime!'

A bitterly cold wind with swirling snow brought relief to the police on the fifth day of the trial, Friday January 30. The numbers queuing for entry to the public gallery were this time entirely manageable. Besides, to those who had read the press reports it may have seemed to them that much of the drama had now gone out of the trial with the conclusion of Rouse's evidence. Indeed, the evidence that day was to be dominated by both the forensic evidence about the corpse and by the defence mechanical evidence exploring how the car had caught fire. However there were still some surprises in store. In a theatrical gesture (as Marshall Hall might have performed even more flamboyantly) Birkett had arranged for the mallet to be mounted on a stand and displayed beneath a magnifying glass. The jury were invited to step down into the well of the court and to view the collection of magnified hairs which were clinging to it, and on the conclusion of their inspection, Talbot himself decided to have a look before the defence's turn to take a peek. The apparatus was passed over and when all were satisfied that they had seen anything there was to be seen, the proceedings continued (Talbot, of course, decided that the matter of the hairs was too uncertain and ambiguous and therefore advised the jury to ignore the evidence concerning the mallet). In fact there was one other significant incident at the start of the day's proceedings that we shall mention below when introducing the defence engineering experts.

The first defence witness called that day was the gruff Aberdonian, Norman Rae, the emerging crime reporter of the *Evening Standard* who appeared for the third time in court. Previously he had been obliged to stand and be identified as the pressman to whom neither Superintendent Brumby nor PC Copping had wished to speak at the scene of the blaze. Now he was giving evidence for the defence that they did not want to hear. Rae had been to the scene of the burned out car on the morning of November 7 and again on the following day. He had seen tyre marks on the grass verge which, he said, could not have been made

---

259 George Pleydell Bancroft, *Stage and Bar: Recollections of George Pleydell Bancroft*, Faber and Faber, 1939, p. 309.

by the police car which had turned up when the wreckage was still on the road. Rae's description of where the tyre marks were and also what inference might be drawn from them were somewhat confusing. Birkett asked him to draw a diagram which he did. But that did not make it much clearer. Rae's rather off-the-wall theory, which he was unable to explain to the court, was in fact that the tyre marks indicated that Rouse's car had reversed slightly. This would account for the mallet having been found fourteen yards in front of the wreck and would be consistent with the passenger having pressed the self-starter, thus creating the spark which started the fire. Three weeks after the event, Rae had returned with a photographer and with a bag of flour. The intention was to find what remained of any tracks, sprinkle flour on them and photograph them for publication. It is small wonder that Mr. Justice Talbot commented, 'I really do not know how this is evidence'.

'Jock' Rae eventually became one of the members of the legendary 'murder gang' of crime reporters in the 1940s and 1950s, immersed in such notorious cases as those of Heath (the suave sadistic post-war killer), Thomas Ley (a former Australian state minister of justice!), Haigh (the acid-bath murderer) and Christie (of 10 Rillington Place notoriety). These were the crime reporters who became as much part of the murder investigation as they were the journalists reporting it (and thereby risked being indicted for contempt of court or of perverting the course of justice). Indeed to some extent it could be said that Cannell provided a model for this pattern with his involvement with Helen Campbell and with his investigation into Rouse's effort at St. Mary's Church, Islington to acquire a copy of the 'marriage certificate' between Helen and Rouse. So Rae's pathetic ploy with flour was, perhaps, an early effort on his part to be an element of the story as well as to report it. In the next two decades such efforts bore more fruit and newspaper circulation thrived accordingly. As one recent writer has noted, Norman Rae, by then with the *News of the World*, and Harry Procter of the *Daily Mail* and then of the *Sunday Pictorial*, stood out from the rest of their peers in chasing down (often with the aid of company chequebooks) the stories of murderers. Actually there were other outstanding practitioners of this particular journalistic art, including the *Sunday People's* Duncan Webb (who, to his shame, dated Haigh's ex-girlfriend in pursuit of his story, and who later married, though not out of professional duty, the killer, Donald Hume's, ex-wife), Stanley Firmin of the *Daily Telegraph*, and Hugh Brady of the *Daily Mail*. What was important was for such journalists actually to interview or to write personal accounts of meeting the murderers, preferably before they were arrested. Procter, for example, had met Neville Heath at least twice in Kensington pubs even before the killer had embarked on his sadistic killings in 1946. He had similarly interviewed both Haigh and Christie before their arrests. Conrad Phillips was another journalist who had had the 'pleasure' of meeting Heath, Haigh and Christie before their arrests. For example when Haigh knew that the game was up and the police were closing in, he arranged to meet Phillips in a Kensington tea shop (no doubt Haigh, like the other killers, was angling for the newspapers to pay his defence legal costs). Why choose this particular tea room to make a final pitch as a free man, asked Phillips. 'They put real butter on the scones', was the gratingly homely reply by the psychopathic acid-bath killer.

A few years after the Rouse case Rae had made contact with the fleeing Dr. Buck Ruxton in 1936 before the police had caught up with the fugitive wife-killer. His endeavours ensured that he secured the latter's story for the *News of the World*. However he endured the most frustrating of experiences in trying to get an exclusive interview with Reg Christie in 1953 while the latter was wandering around north and west London after vacating 10 Rillington Place and while police were out looking for him. He got a phone call in his office from Christie. For the price of a meal and shelter the starving, wet and dishevelled Christie would offer him his story before the inevitable arrest. A meeting outside Wood Green town hall, north-east London, is arranged for 1:30 in the morning. Rae is driven there and just as he looks round for Christie hiding in the bushes, a policeman appears on his regular beat. Christie is off with a rustle of the foliage, mistakenly thinking it is a trap, and Rae's scoop disappears in a flash. That was in 1953.

Of course, the prevailing culture of press involvement in crime investigation in the two decades after the Second World War, as epitomised by the careers of those journalists named above, would scarcely be tolerated by the CID today. Indeed, investigative crime journalists are more likely to be engrossed nowadays, not in pursuing current murder investigations, but in re-opening *old* cases suspected by them to have been miscarriages of justice (think of Ludovic Kennedy in respect of Bruno Hauptmann (the Lindbergh baby case), Timothy Evans and Patrick Meehan, among others or, in respect of Ruth Ellis, Tony van den Bergh and Laurence Marks (the latter before his career as a comedy scriptwriter in partnership with Maurice Gran, writing for, among others, Frankie Howerd and Rik Mayall). Other journalists and reporters such as David Yallop, Bob Woffinden, David Rose and Chris Mullin sought to re-open various cases such as those of Derek Bentley, Timothy Evans, Ruth Ellis, James Hanratty, and the Birmingham Six. Norman Rae was at the forefront of the post-war 'hot case' movement and, arguably, served part of his apprenticeship, perhaps inspired by Cannell, with his obscure and far-fetched 'flour of Scotland' experiment during the Rouse investigation.[260]

Next to enter the witness box for the defence were the two medical experts whose testimonies had first been aired at the police court hearing. Thus Dr. Telling, the local Northampton doctor instructed by Lee-Roberts, told the court that he had found what he believed to be excreta which had been lying *in situ* for some days (Superintendent Brumby's embarrassment regarding this search was described in chapter nine). Whether it was human or animal, as the next medical expert and

---

260   The principal sources for the above are Neil Root, *Frenzy: Heath, Haigh and Christie, the First Great Tabloid Murderers*, Preface Publishing, 2011; Donald Thomas, *Villains' Paradise: Britain's Underworld from the Spivs to the Krays*, John Murray, 2006, Ch. 6; Harry Procter, *The Street of Disillusion*, Revel Barker Publishing, Brighton, 2010; Duncan Campbell, 'The Man in the Mac', *Guardian Weekend*, September 5, 2009; Conrad Phillips, *Murderer's Moon*, Arthur Barker, 1956. Phillips (real name Horace Havord) also wrote detective novels. His son, also known as Conrad Phillips, was an actor best known for his role as William Tell in the ITV series (1958-59) of that name. In one of Ian Rankin's early *Rebus* novels, the Edinburgh journalist, Jim Stevens, endeavours to shape, or even to create, a crime story. For example, in hoping to expose the brother of Detective-Sergeant (as was) Rebus as a drug dealer, he dreams of the headline, 'Brothers in Law—Brothers in Crime!' See Ian Rankin, *Knots and Crosses*, Orion, 1998 (first published 1987), p. 98. For Rae's involvement in helping the police in 1951 to unmask a Nottingham killer, Herbert Mills, who had telephoned the journalist about printing a story of how the caller had 'discovered' a murder victim, Mabel Tattershaw, see Andy Owens and Chris Ellis, *Killer Catchers*, John Blake, 2008, Ch. 2. For a scholarly account of journalism and crime reporting see Judith Rowbotham, Kim Stevenson and Samantha Pegg, *Crime News in Modern Britain: Press Reporting and Responsibility, 1820-2010*, Palgrave Macmillan, 2013.

Bedfordshire County Hospital honorary pathologist, Dr. Harvey-Wyatt (who was probably surprised to have been called by the defence), had also observed, was now impossible to say, though Telling had originally formed a definite view at the time that it had, indeed, been human. The material had been found somewhere between 150 and 160 yards from the car. In fact it was just opposite a big gate at the side of the road and, Telling 'tellingly' added, where 'it was not possible to see the burned area from that point' (which might have reinforced Rouse's claim to have searched for a secluded spot for his ablutions). The material had been handed to Harvey-Wyatt. While the bulk of the latter's testimony concerned the condition of the corpse and, to a lesser extent, an analysis of the hairs found on the mallet, he did say that he had subsequently examined the sample of excreta. But given the delay between its being 'exuded' by someone or by some animal and the time of its being examined, it was now not possible to say for certain that the faecal material was human. No explanation for the delay in examining the organic matter was ever given (again, unfortunate timing was one of the worst enemies of the defendant who never wore a watch), nor was it indicated whether it could have been proved to be human excrement if it had been examined as soon as Telling had found it. As Birkett extracted from Harvey-Wyatt in cross-examination, the faeces recovered were dried up and shrivelled, and might have been from a dog.

But there was another possible piece of supportive evidence to back up at least this part of Rouse's story. For Telling had also handed Harvey-Wyatt the shirt that Rouse had apparently been wearing at the time of the blaze. There was a stain on the inside of the material that, on microscopic examination, was definitely faecal. However, the issue was quickly passed over during the trial as defence counsel, Finnemore, rapidly turned to Harvey-Wyatt's assessment of the condition of the corpse (Harvey-Wyatt later became coroner for Brixton). Yet if more had been made by counsel of the shirt's faecal stain (how old it was, where precisely it was found on the shirt, was its position consistent with Rouse's account of his suddenly seeing the conflagration and running towards it in a panic, while pulling up his trousers quickly and failing to clean himself first?), then that critical part of his story might have been viewed favourably by the jury. Indeed Birkett himself, in cross-examination, pointed to a possible lost opportunity for the defence when he asked Telling, 'Of course, whatever appears on the shirt, it is quite impossible to say when it got there?' To this the witness replied, 'One cannot say exactly when it got there, but one can come to a conclusion that it got there recently. It might have got there at any time when he went to the w.c. It means that if the man had not wiped himself properly, that mark might appear on his shirt, and it could happen at any time.' Of *course* it could have happened at any time, but the suggestion that Rouse went around with a shirt stained with faecal material either for a lengthy period of days (or weeks?) before Hardingstone Lane, or for a short period between leaving home at 9 pm on Guy Fawkes Night and *before* reaching Hardingstone lacks credibility. It is difficult to conclude that the prosecution succeeded in disproving this important part of Rouse's defence beyond reasonable doubt. But the final outcome must imply otherwise.

But it was the adduction of the three defence experts on automobile fires that held out the best hope for Rouse. In fact, their appearance in the witness box was preceded by what one newspaper called a 'minor sensation'. As the *Daily Mirror* reported,[261] a letter was handed by the judge to counsel, "....the contents of which were not revealed, but which apparently caused some excitement. 'It appears', said the Judge, 'to have been written by someone who knows a great deal about motor-cars, and I think that counsel on both sides ought to read it.'"

The letter consisted of three pages of closely written handwriting and was read by both Birkett and Finnemore. As the newspaper continued, "Mr. Finnemore, after reading the first page, turned round in a rather excited way to some experts who were sitting behind him, and who are assisting him in the defence. He handed them the first sheet of the letter, and three of the experts clustered around together while reading it."

This exchange was not reported in Normanton's account of the trial proceedings. However, Tremayne's narrative account[262] recorded Talbot as telling counsel at the start of that day's proceedings that he had received many letters about the trial, 'many of them written in good faith'. Why he produced just one for counsel's perusal, that is, the letter cited above, was not explained. Whether it was a delayed communication from one of the witnesses to be called that day by Finnemore is possible but not certain, but it presumably offered an alternative to the Crown's claim that Rouse had loosened the union joint. In any case, that would be thrust of the three defence experts' testimony.

Two of these engineers had offered their services to Finnemore after reading the evidence that Buckle had given at the police court, while the third engineer, Arthur Isaacs, came forward after Buckle had testified at the trial itself. Indeed the three men were so shocked at Buckle's claims, which they considered flawed and ignorant, that they offered their services *gratis* to the defence. Moreover, following Rouse's conviction, which had undoubtedly been influenced by Buckle's testimony, a whole phalanx of mechanical engineers from Britain and beyond would write to the defence team, offering to testify for Rouse at the Court of Criminal Appeal (chapter 13). And the core complaint of all these experts was that Buckle had misled the jury, perhaps not deliberately, by his claiming that the slightly loose nut holding the petrol union joint, through which there flowed a constant stream of petrol to feed the fire, could only have been turned one revolution deliberately. The defence experts, by contrast, including those who habitually repaired cars, were in no doubt that if the blaze had been started by other factors (whether innocent or otherwise), the intensity of the heat, followed by the cooling down of the metal, could cause the nut to loosen without human intervention. It was a simple case of expansion by intense heat, followed by contraction of the nut and/or the thread on cooling, thereby loosening the nut; as car mechanics regularly did with awkward or seized nuts in the garage, releasing them with the aid of a blow-lamp. We shall come to that shortly.

Finnemore's first technical witness was Herbert William Bamber, a consulting engineer, practising at 166, Piccadilly, London. His credentials were, on paper at least, even more impressive than Buckle's (who was, it will be recalled, a certificated electrical engineer). Bamber was a member of the Institution of Mechanical Engineers and of the Institute of Automotive Engineers, and also a

261 *Daily Mirror*, January 31, 1931.
262 Sydney Tremayne, *The Trial of Alfred Arthur Rouse*, Geoffrey Bles, 1931, p. 258.

Fellow of the Institute of Arbitrators. He frequently acted as a referee in motor cases in the London courts, and had formerly been works manager at Daimler's in Coventry. On January 7, 1931, he examined the remains of Rouse's car and told the court that he had not heard anything spoken in court to suggest that the blaze had been anything other than accidental. Leaving aside for the moment the substance of his observation, procedurally, his comment reminds us that expert witnesses are the only category of witness permitted to listen to the trial before they themselves are called upon to testify. There is sense in allowing of this exception since their evidence, while adduced on behalf of one side in the case, ought to offer not only a scientific analysis of raw data and a disinterested evidence-based interpretation, but an opportunity to challenge other scientific findings already presented to court. It will then be for the jury to decide which of the expert testimony, if any, is persuasive in regard to the Crown or the defence submissions.

Bamber's testimony runs to many pages in the Normanton transcript. But his central findings were that it was the presence of the two-gallon petrol can, with a considerable amount of petrol in it, together with the collapsing flammable fabric and wooden floor boards in the car, which had accounted for the intensity of the blaze under the vehicle. He noted that the top bar of the brass windscreen had been fused, but disputed that an intense flame, fed from the union joint, had been responsible. For, given that the joint was four to five inches underneath the tank, he could not envisage a flame, with the strength and intensity of a blowpipe, reaching from the joint to the top of the windscreen. Instead, he suggested that the windscreen had simply collapsed into the fire, perhaps where there was a concentrated source of fire on the top of the gearbox, and that it was there where the fusing had occurred.

As to the loose joint (he did not specifically refer to the nut at this point), it was conceivable that vibration could loosen it. However leaking petrol would either drip through the floorboards onto the road or be collected in a tray under the gearbox. Thus, 'In no circumstances in this case would there be a puddle of petrol in the car'. This suggested that if vibration *had* loosened the joint then, with no visible petrol around their feet, the occupants in the car would be unaware of anything untoward mechanically. Indeed, he added, assuming that the joint was finger-tight, then a fidgety passenger, sitting in a natural position, could still push the joint with his toe during the journey, though the leak would probably not be seen. However, if a passenger did this just as the car was stopping, a stream of petrol might then flow onto the floor below his feet. The witness did, nonetheless, observe that the coir mat on top of the cork linoleum covering the floor would operate as an absorbent, giving off petrol vapour, and rendering the space, whether or not the car was stationary, highly susceptible to a quick and violent flash fire from a spark. Admittedly, however, a weakness in his argument regarding the joint being accidentally loosened by a passenger's foot is that he made no mention of the smell of petrol or vapour, which might alert the occupants to a problem.

He noted that the door design of the Morris Minor was unusual, with the door opening from the front and with the hinge at the back. That might make exiting such a car on fire more challenging to those unfamiliar with its layout, assuming they were still conscious, of course. Another feature was that the tank filler cap must have been either loose or was off. Otherwise the tank would have bulged or burst. Moreover, Bamber thought that because no fire damage had been found under the engine itself, the tank would have had little petrol in it. Both points, of course, benefited the defence by raising the suggestion that once Rouse had allegedly set off to answer the call of nature, the passenger had, indeed, been in a closed car and was reaching for the petrol can to fill the tank, as instructed by Rouse who had already opened the bonnet. Moreover, the underside of the bonnet showed no evidence of the intense fire damage expected if it had been closed. Furthermore, if the petrol can's screw top were unscrewed a couple of turns or loosened a little by the mallet, it might still stay on but could yet leak, especially when the can was lifted up. Finnemore's final question adverted to the suggestion put by Birkett to Rouse in cross-examination the previous day, and vigorously denied by the accused, that Rouse had ignited petrol in the carburettor. In seeking to dismiss the suggestion, Bamber pointed out that if the offside bonnet on the petrol tank side had already been opened, which he was insistent was the case despite Crown witnesses having suggested otherwise, then it was not possible to open the other bonnet, that is, the nearside one above the carburettor, at the same time. Moreover, had that latter bonnet been open to allow access to the carburettor, then anyone closing the bonnet after igniting the petrol in the carburettor would suffer severe burns from the resulting flash, and Rouse had certainly not suffered in this way. (Whether Crown witnesses had found the nearside bonnet open, which Bamber had indicated would be impossible if the offside bonnet was already open, was not mentioned).

On cross-examination Birkett's first challenge to Bamber, after reminding the jury of the severity of the blaze (to which Bamber retorted that he had known plenty of car fires just as severe), was to question his experience in dealing specifically with car fires. 'Quite a number', Bamber replied, though he added that car collisions, crane accidents and 'all sorts of engineering matters' fell within his remit. But he acknowledged that fire assessors would have had more experience of car fires than he (which, of course, is neither here nor there if the fire assessor in question, leaving aside professional qualifications, lacked cognate knowledge to engage expertly with the specific technical challenge).

As to the controversial nut, Bamber accepted that it would be tight on a new car. But he added that the petrol pipe had to be taken off from time to time to be cleaned and might not have been screwed back sufficiently tightly thereafter. While vibration could then add to the looseness, he could not think of any other, presumably non-human, reason why the nut had been loose. While that answer would have delighted Birkett, Bamber quickly added that, 'I think I must go a little further than that. You [Birkett] say, 'No other cause'—No other cause *short of fire or something which expanded it*' [italics added].

So, in regard to the loose nut, he still abided by the heat transfer argument once the fire had reached a ferocious temperature. Moreover, he was still of the opinion that, as distinct from the case of a person striking a match to ignite petrol fumes present within a vehicle, a spark triggered by careless pressing of the self-starter could easily have ignited the vapour in the air around the floor carpet where petrol had spilled. He further indicated that if there were a loose terminal below the self-starter, where the 'live wire is fastened onto the self-starter, [that would be] an exceedingly dangerous thing, because you can get a spark very easily'. Indeed, he added crucially, the emergence of the vapour within the car might not be noticed by any occupants if it had occurred after the car had stopped (Rouse had previously told the police that just as he was relieving himself he thought he had heard the self-starter being operated). No, he told Birkett, he did not know whether the car's manufacturer, Sir William Morris, knew of this, referring to this dangerous design flaw. Moreover, he had never yet seen a self-starter switch which, on being pressed, generated an electrical current that did not give some sort of spark, despite the manufacturer's referring to the mechanism as a 'non-spark wipe pattern'. Of course, he agreed, a match might set off a violent flash if it was struck near the coir mat or the self-starter (but not if struck higher up). But the mat itself, of course, had been totally consumed. While such causes of the blaze were admittedly speculative, he denied that they fell within the 'extreme [outer] realms of possibility....Leave out the word 'extreme'', he retorted.

And as to Rouse having allegedly forced off the carburettor top to increase the petrol flow to the fire,

> "If I may, I think I must tell you why I do not think that this [presumably the top] was taken off and petrol allowed to run out there. Colonel Buckle tells us that there was no fire under the engine. If this had been taken off and petrol allowed to run out from the carburettor, at some time there must have been a fire right under the car [but there was not]."

He also observed that if the union joint had been one turn loose, fuel would *not* then flow into the 'topless' carburettor (which, to the non-expert, would seem to defeat any malevolent purpose behind the removal of the top). Or at least the fire's intensity would be less on the footing that the petrol was flowing downwards and not into the carburettor. Birkett's questioning therefore seemed premised on a choice of alternative sources of the blaze rather than on cumulative sources. This is puzzling since more than one supply of petrol to feed the fire was surely the Crown's position *after* Buckle had noted Rouse's apparently smug reaction to the expert Crown witness's failure to focus on the carburettor top in his testimony on the second day of the trial (Bamber was testifying on the fifth day). But even more puzzling was that despite what he had just explained to Birkett (and to Talbot who also put a related question to him), Bamber in fact went on to acknowledge that if the top had actually been prised off rather than blown off (and that was 'probable'), then there *would* be two sources of petrol to provide a continuous sustained flame. Was it the tension of a capital trial which caused even the most experienced of expert witnesses to contradict themselves on occasion?

Thus while Bamber's last admission was a positive result for the Crown, the question still remained whether it was Rouse (if anyone) who had removed the carburettor top in order to allow more petrol to feed the fire (the petrol tank itself, it may be recalled, was scarcely damaged). There are two points here. First, apart from the accused, no-one still alive was there to tell, though Colonel Buckle's further testimony the following day, highly suggestive of Rouse's culpability, as we shall see later, almost certainly impressed the jury as to Rouse's role vis-à-vis the carburettor top. But second, it should not be forgotten that the vehicle had been left unattended for a few hours in the early dawn and morning of November 6, with curious passers-by, possible souvenir hunters, unofficial photographers, all milling round the debris and possibly 'rearranging the furniture', as Arthur Vernon Ashford, the chemist and photographer, had admitted he had done. Who was to say that nobody had removed the carburettor top to see if any items could be salvaged or sold for scrap before the police arrived in the morning to protect the wreckage? Finnemore's only indirect probing of this possibility occurred when, on re-examination of his witness, he asked Bamber, 'It is now more than three months since it [damage to the carburettor] happened, and you naturally do not know what has happened to it in the meantime?' To which Bamber predictably answered, 'No'.

But this is to jump ahead a little. For Birkett had not yet finished with Bamber, though his final sally smacked more of desperation by endeavouring to challenge Bamber's credentials once more. And, of course, when the jury would come to consider their verdict, it would likely be the matter most easily recalled by them in respect of that particular exchange, both because it came at the end of the cross-examination and because it was not complicated by technical matters. Thus,

"[*Birkett*] It is not your main job to deal with fires?

[*Bamber*] No, it is not.

[*Birkett*] I daresay you put forward any views you have with considerable diffidence?

[Bamber] No, I do not. They are my views, otherwise I should not put them forward.

[Birkett] You do not put them forward with the surety that you would put them forward in a collision case?

[*Bamber*] I do. I think on my side I am as satisfied as I should like to be in a case of the sort you are setting up.

[*Birkett*] I think we can leave it like this: you do not profess to be an expert on fire?

[*Bamber*] No."

And at this point Birkett triumphantly sat down, obliging Finnemore, who immediately rose to rescue the situation, to ask his witness, 'You were described, when we first started, as an automobile engineer, a consulting engineer, particularly concerned with motor cars?' 'Yes', he replied emphatically. And once again, at Finnemore's prompting, the point was repeated that no-one could determine with any certainty how the fire had commenced or whether it had been started deliberately or accidentally. It is not actually certain that such questions should have been permitted by the judge if they were designed, not to clarify some confusion, but simply to remind the jury of the strong points made earlier by Bamber. A relevant example of clarification, by contrast, was Finnemore's very last question to his witness: 'Having regard to the petrol can inside, and the nature of the body, being a fabric saloon, is there anything in that which leads one at all to say what originally happened? [Bamber] No, nothing at all' (another instance of clarification rather than repetition might be when Bamber made clear that while it was a coincidence that a spark could ignite vapour, it was not an 'amazing' coincidence, as Birkett had previously suggested).

As with Buckle, it was an extensive examination and cross-examination of the technical expert. The opinions of the two witnesses differed, of course, as to whether the cause of the fire could be discovered with certainty and as to whether deliberate human intervention had taken place. But while both witnesses spent much of the time addressing the loose union nut, neither spent much, or any, time on the proposition that the heat of the blaze had caused the loosening. For Buckle his evidence pointed to Rouse having deliberately loosened the nut by one revolution to enable the fire that the prisoner had supposedly intentionally started to be continuously fed. For Bamber a careless car mechanic or the effects of vibration might have caused the loosening. But neither addressed their minds to the principles of heat expansion and contraction (or 'heat transfer'), or even to the simple practices of the workshop where a blowtorch might be used to ease off a seized nut on an engine component by heating it up and then leaving it to cool.

This simple process was, however, put forward by the next defence witness, Arthur Isaacs, as the obvious explanation for the loose petrol union joint found by Buckle (it should not be forgotten) nearly four weeks after the blaze, a length of time more than enough for any residual heat to have long departed. Isaacs' analysis, if accepted, could be critical. So how should the Crown seek to neutralize his potentially damaging testimony once he had been questioned about it in the witness box by Finnemore (and Birkett would have had a fair idea beforehand of what the defence experts were going to say)? Birkett could, of course, probe the scientific basis for Isaacs' theory with a view to challenging it. But suppose it was plausible, or even scientifically sound? Another tack in regard to expert witnesses was, of course, to question their standing as experts. It was to some extent a diversionary tactic, turning the focus onto the background of the witness rather than upon his expert knowledge. Indeed, some counsel might sail close to the wind, professionally, by appearing to ridicule an expert for the other side by questioning his formal qualifications or by posing a highly scientific and not particularly relevant question that the witness could not answer, and which was beyond the practical and *relevant* experience which the witness could bring to the case. Birkett did precisely this, as we shall see, undoubtedly causing lasting damage to Rouse's case. Yet it could be argued that Birkett's initial 'killer' question to the defence expert was unworthy of this otherwise Morrissey-like 'charming man' and polite counsel (he kindly told one defence witness at the trial who apologized for disagreeing with him that, 'You must maintain your opinion; do not express regret'). Moreover, not only was it grossly unfair and potentially in breach of Bar rules regarding cross-examination, but the question itself, in the form in which it was posed, was actually inept and meaningless. Thus what was tragic from Rouse's point of view was not only that Finnemore made no objection to the question at the time (which we shall consider shortly), nor that the judge did not disallow it on the ground of its unscientific nature (how would most lawyers know? They were not like the earlier House of Lords judge, Lord Fletcher Moulton FRS, whose scientific background made him an appropriate choice as Director of Explosives Supply at Lloyd George's Ministry of Munitions during the Great War). The tragedy for the accused was that the technical and mechanical expertise that the defence specialists in automotive engineering brought to the proceedings was lost behind the smoke and mirrors of Birkett's cheap and nasty shot. No wonder Isaacs was flummoxed at this initial flawed scientific question. Unless they were confident enough to tell counsel that his question, below, was nonsense, any half-decent metallurgist or physicist acquainted with the behaviour of metals would also find it confusing.

Perhaps Birkett viewed Isaacs, in particular, and the succeeding defence expert, Arthur Cotton, as fair prey, given that they were later described by Normanton[263] as 'the two most public-spirited volunteers....whose generous chivalry in coming forward merits every praise....'[264] But before examining Birkett's assault on Isaacs' credibility as an expert witness, the latter's examination-in-chief on behalf of the defence must first be considered. As Isaacs explained in his opening remarks in the witness box,

> "I am managing director of the Bramber Engineering Company Limited, of Cricklewood, London, manufacturers and specialists in the heat treatment of metals. I am an engineer and fire assessor, and I have acted for insurance companies in numerous cases for more than eighteen years. I have had a very vast experience of assessing damage in connection with fires to motor cars. I had nothing, however, to do with this case until two days ago, when I read a report of some of the proceedings, and I thought I had certain information and experience which I ought to bring before the Court."

Not beating about the bush, Finnemore next asked him, 'With regard to the finding of that nut a whole turn loose after the fire, what do you say?'

> "I say it is invariably found at all fires that have been very intense that these nuts are loose. As a matter of fact, I go so far as to say that in the last twenty-five cases that I have done, where the fire has been intense, these nuts have always been loose. By that I mean in consequence of the action of the fire; it might have been absolutely spanner-tight before the fire, or slightly loose, but over a long experience I have practically always found that as long as the fire has been round this particular nut you get that effect."

Indeed he had been investigating a similar case, along with the next defence expert, the consulting engineer, Arthur Cotton, when he read of the testimony in the Rouse case. As he explained to the court, the loosening of the nut was simply due to the heat expansion caused by the intense fire round the nut, which could also affect the thread, followed by the distortion of the metal in the cooling process. In such cases, the nut could be a quarter, half, or three-quarters of a turn loose. Indeed he added that even if the nut were tight it would still be possible to experience weeping. For there might be a 'bad seating on the taper', or if the nut, being a soft metal, had been previously replaced, even tightly, in a hurry, this might damage it, thus making the seating insecure. In the instant case, he did not think that such bad seating, as distinct from heat expansion and contraction, had happened here.

He averred that it was impossible to tell how the fire had started, and disagreed

---

263 Normanton, *op. cit.*, p. xxxi.
264 We can assume, therefore, that no consulting fees were paid by the cash-strapped defence to those witnesses.

with Buckle's proposition that the fusing of the windscreen frame had resulted from a fire jet from the union joint. For in order for the jet to navigate round the petrol tank while still maintaining sufficient intensity to fuse the brass, one would have to assume a forty-five degree trajectory followed by a right hand turn, before the jet could reach the frame. It was, instead, more likely that the windscreen had simply fallen into the car's burning body (which had been Bamber's suggestion), the unusual positioning of the petrol tank near the dashboard making this explanation more plausible.

With a handful of more questions about how the victim might have accidentally set the blaze himself while stretching for the petrol can on the driver's seat, the examination-in-chief concluded. Finnemore retired to his desk and Birkett rose, paused, and twiddled his gold propelling pencil. Then turning to Isaacs, he suddenly asked him, 'What is the co-efficient of the expansion of brass?' Clearly taken aback by the question, Isaacs drew in his breath, and paused to consider what Birkett was meaning. He obviously believed that the question as posed had some scientific significance but no matter how practical and experienced he was as an insurance assessor for car fires (and that experience was quite extensive), he did lack sufficient theoretical knowledge to proffer an answer.

"[*Isaacs*] I am afraid I cannot answer that question off-hand.

[*Birkett*] If you do not know, say so.....[265] I asked you: What is the co-efficient of the expansion of brass. Do you know what it means?

[*Isaacs*] Put that way, probably I do not. [*Birkett*] You are an engineer.

[*Isaacs*] I dare say I am.

[Birkett] Let me understand what you are. You are not a doctor?

[Isaacs] No.

[Birkett] Nor a crime investigator?

[Isaacs] No.

[Birkett] Nor an amateur detective?

[Isaacs] No.

[Birkett] But an engineer?

[Isaacs] Yes.

[Birkett] What is the co-efficient of brass? You do not know?"

The exchange certainly put Isaacs on the defensive, prompting him to offer only monosyllabic replies. And when he was able to be more expansive, he might just have reinforced Birkett's message to the jury that here was a defence so-called expert witness who was clearly a few bob short of the pound. For he went on to explain that his company dealt with the heat treating of metals and that it manufactured springs, including car laminated springs, forgings and 'all types of parts'. He did not possess any university degrees but had had training as a fire assessor, which prompted Birkett to ask, rather sarcastically, whether that meant that insurance companies went to a limited company 'engaged in spring

---

265 This was the form of words in the Normanton account. The actual transcript wording was slightly different but the difference is of no consequence.

manufacturing for fire assessing'?[266] Indeed insurance companies had regularly employed him to investigate the causes of fires as part of his firm's business since 1919 and he dealt with approximately 15-20 car fires a year, the majority of which were roadside fires. While he knew of no case where the fire had been *caused* by a loose union joint nut, in every car blaze he investigated involving intense heat (in due course followed by cooling down) a loose union joint had been found. While his reasoning is not easy to understand and his choice of wording would easily induce confusion (though a jury, doing its duty in a capital case, was surely obliged to follow his argument carefully), it seems to have boiled down to this. On cooling and contraction a nut, screwed in as part of the petrol union joint, would be expected to be slightly tighter than the thread of the cone (or taper) of the joint. But the nut would not necessarily be so tight on cooling as either to be lock-tight or to prevent a petrol leak from the union joint; or, as Isaacs put it, 'not necessarily tighter to pull the pipe up to its taper'. So the nut, and the joint itself, could be 'loose' once it had cooled after a fierce blaze, as Buckle had found it to be. Indeed, the degree of looseness would depend on different variables. Thus the female nut and male threaded cone would not necessarily expand or contract at the same rate, since the intensity of heat on the exposed nut would be different from the amount reaching the enclosed cone. Moreover, even though both parts were made of brass, they might not necessarily have had exactly the same composition, which might thereby differentially affect their reaction to heat.[267] The fire had emanated, according to Isaacs, not from the petrol union joint (which, on his reasoning, only became loose after the debris had cooled down) but from the well of the car, fed by petrol from both the can and from the tank which, he claimed, could no longer now hold petrol. Whether or not his reasoning was logical, his 'Not necessarily' remarks were not easy to follow. Allied to Birkett's opening salvo and Isaacs' consternation regarding the 'co-efficient of the expansion of brass', it may be suspected that the witness's nuanced analysis and practical experience counted for little in the jury room.

But bafflement at Birkett's question is understandable. For, as a more recent comment on the case from a technology specialist at the Open University, Dr. Ian Johnston, has noted,[268]

> "'What is the coefficient of brass' [though, as noted above, Birkett's flawed question was actually, 'What is the coefficient of the expansion of brass?'] is

---

266 It may be observed that the courts have long accepted in suitable cases the expert opinion of witnesses who did not possess formal qualifications on the subject on which they were proffering expert testimony. This has ranged from the solicitor in 1894 whose hobby was the private study of handwriting and who was allowed to testify in court on the samples provided, to the more recent instance of the Dutch policeman admitted to the witness box as an expert on different types of earprints, despite his having no relevant scientific or medical qualifications. What both experts possessed were thus not academic or professional qualifications in those fields but vast experience in classifying and analyzing handwriting and earprints, respectively. See *Silverlock* [1894] 2 Q B 766; *Dallagher* [2003] 1 Cr. App. Rep. 195. Isaacs' lack of formal qualifications should, therefore, have been weighed against his extensive practical experience regarding the causes of automobile fires.

267 Perhaps the contracted nut would also be looser, not tighter, because the *thread* was distorted even if the nut had contracted more than the thread. Isaacs did add that the nut would *expand* more than the thread, which might be one way for the thread to permit some play vis-à-vis the nut when both cooled down.

268 Ian Johnston [letter to the editor], *Herald* (Glasgow), March 26, 1998. An actual calculation of the coefficient in respect of brass is 0.0000189 per Centigrade or 0.00001058 per Fahrenheit. At twenty degrees Centigrade, the co-efficient of the linear temperature expansion of brass is 18.7.

a completely meaningless question and one which would almost certainly throw the most confident witness. Are we to assume that lawyers still make a habit of misleading juries as to the professional competence of experts in this way? Incidentally, a little research shows that if the question was meant to be 'What is the linear coefficient of thermal expansion of brass?' the answer would have been 'around twice that of iron or steel'. A brass nut on a steel tank will indeed get looser in heat."

This comment was in response to a newspaper article by journalist Robert Dickson in which he had lauded the deployment of forensic science in solving crimes such as the IRA bombing of Coventry in 1939 and the Great Train Robbery in 1963 (both mentioned elsewhere in this book). Dickson's article also referred to the Rouse case and remarked that,

"....the evidence given by a so-called expert was demolished by a single question posed by prosecuting counsel.....The assessor, Norman Isaac [*sic*], was clear in his evidence initially. Heat had caused the nut to expand and had resulted in the fuel pipe becoming free. There had in fact been no murder—only a tragic accident. As Birkett rose to cross-examine, the whole basis of the case against Rouse was at risk of being undermined. If the intensity of the fire could be a natural phenomenon, then there was support for the accused's story that while he had been out of the car a carelessly dropped cigarette had caused the fire which, after the nut became dislodged, led to the fatal blaze. 'What is the coefficient of brass?' [*sic*] inquired counsel. The inability of Mr. Isaac even to understand the question revealed that he knew little about the expansion of metal in heat. Rouse was rightly convicted and after his death a newspaper printed his confession to a callous crime committed to allow him to start a new life with a girlfriend."[269]

There are, of course, numerous errors in the above article (Dickson even managed to get the wording of Birkett's flawed question wrong, while Johnston's letter, as printed, also initially repeated Dickson's mis-quote word for word). More importantly, the journalist's conclusion regarding Rouse's guilt was one that the technology specialist, Ian Johnston, the following day did not share. But the fact that misconceptions about the forensic evidence in the Rouse case continue (almost) to the present day, and that wrongly posed scientific questions helped to hang the accused do, indeed, provide support for Johnston's claim that Dickson was 'taking pride in a miscarriage of justice caused by dishonest questioning' (though it may be objected that Birkett's question was recklessly ignorant rather than downright dishonest. In any event the consequences were dire for Rouse).

But after Birkett's below-the-belt question which left Isaacs hopelessly confused, any positive support that the latter's testimony might have offered the defence could not hope to be taken seriously by the jury. Indeed, much of his remaining testimony was couched in terms of possibilities, not certainties, and there are numerous examples in his answers to Birkett, before the latter sat down, which it would be tedious to repeat here.

With the authority and professional qualifications of Finnemore's witness assailed by Birkett's own unscientific question, defence counsel prompted Isaacs

---

269 Robert Dickson, 'Now Go Directly to Jail', *Ibid.*, March 25, 1998.

to remind the jury that even if he (the witness) could not advance a scientific or metallurgical explanation for the phenomenon, nonetheless, the science of observation should not be ignored. Thus, to the question why an intensely heated and tightly screwed nut became loose when cooled, Isaacs reiterated that that had been his experience, '....in every case I have had'. And with that Isaacs' gruelling exposure in the witness box was at last over.

He was followed by Arthur Cotton, an engineer from Manchester, with ten years experience as an assessor for numerous insurance companies, including the Atlas, London Insurance, Canada Fire, the Alliance, the Prudential and others. He obtained his practical engineering skills at the Daimler and Vulcan Works and dealt with approximately 1,000 cases a year for about 15 insurance firms. Five to seven per cent of such cases were fire-loss cases in respect of cars, or 50-60 a year (including one in conjunction with Isaacs the previous week). His evidence was brief, clear and concise, and he had no doubt about it. Where the fire was of the right intensity, that is, not sufficiently fierce to fuse metals, but hot enough to affect the distortion of the threads *more than* [italics added] the expansion and contraction of the nut (all these events occurring as a result of intense heat followed by cooling down, and during which time the nut would remain *in situ*), the nut itself would become looser. Indeed, even though the nut did not move in the sense of turning round, nonetheless it could become so 'loose' that the pipe itself would be in a 'jangling condition'. But, like Isaacs, he insisted that he was reporting his observations while a scientific explanation could only lie with a metallurgist. In the workshop, he told the judge, petrol surrounding a carburettor or a petrol pipe attached to a petrol tank would have a hardening effect upon the nut. Therefore it was common practice to use a blow-pipe, wherever it was safe, to loosen an exceptionally tight nut (oil splashes or oil leaks did not have the same hardening effect). Of course Cotton's suggestion that the nut 'was not moved from its position' might be contrasted with Buckle's having discovered the nut three-quarters of a turn loose, and with Isaacs' belief that such nuts were commonly found to be a quarter or half or three-quarters of a turn loose after a fierce car blaze. Dogmatism and certainty sat ill at ease with such conflicting views. Did the jury avoid addressing their minds to the conflicts of opinions when they retired to consider their verdict? Were they impressed by the metallurgical science or by their assessment of the character and status of the various expert witnesses? For the starkest choice facing the jury, none of whom presumably were automotive engineers themselves, surely involved deciding between a Great War colonel commissioned by Lloyds underwriters, on the one hand, and the owner of a Cricklewood factory making laminated springs who did not understand the 'co-efficient of the expansion of brass', on the other.[270]

---

270 Whether a solidly English name like Cuthbert Buckle was more appealing to the jury than the Jewish-sounding name, Isaacs, we will never know. For a critical view of how English judges discussed and depicted Jews and Jewishness in the twentieth century and beyond, see Didi Herman, *An Unfortunate Coincidence: Jews, Jewishness and English Law*, Oxford University Press, Oxford, 2011. See also Alyson Pendlebury, *Portraying 'the Jew' in First World War Britain*, Vallentine Mitchell, 2006. Of course, it cannot be assumed that Arthur Isaacs was in fact Jewish. Six men of that name are listed in the National Archives as having served in the Forces during the First World War while the British Jewry Book of Honour, 1914-1918, published in 1922, includes around fifty service personnel listed as 'A. Isaacs'. For his firm of Bramber Engineering, Cricklewood, see entry at www.gracesguide.co.uk/Bramber_Engineering_Co.

But to return to Arthur Cotton, one suspects that Birkett adjudged this witness's testimony in support of Rouse's defence as being rather more lucid, comprehensible and persuasive to the jury's ears than were Isaacs' efforts. So Plan B was adopted by Birkett. 'You know the co-efficient of the expansion of metal?' he asked, presumably hoping to flummox Cotton as he had done Isaacs. But Cotton was firm in his response (he had been in court when Isaacs had been cross-examined by Birkett). No, he did not know the co-efficient. He was not a metallurgist but an engineer, and though he possessed a standard engineer's diary which contained such information he had no need to consult it in his engineering practice. Perhaps an engineer in a melting works (where the latter might need to know about the scientific basis for the expansion and contraction of railway tracks in a very hot summer and in a very cold winter), might be acquainted with the value, but not this engineer. And with Cotton remaining resilient, Birkett's assault on the witness's credibility petered out, though his last question to Cotton served to remind the jury that the witness had been working with Isaacs on a car fire case the previous week. Was this an attempt at guilt by association with an apparently discredited witness? In fact when Cotton was re-examined by Finnemore after Birkett had sat down, he pointed out that the relevant nuts in that earlier case, which had involved a Sunbeam totally destroyed in a fire, were three-quarters of a turn loose, and finger-tight, respectively; *and* nine-and-a half gallons of petrol still remained in the tank. The inference was clear. No-one had fed that particular vehicle fire with a sustained flow of petrol, yet the car was a totally burnt-out loss. Moreover, there was nothing to indicate that the nuts had been loose before the blaze or had become loose other than through the operation of the intense heat of the fire. Apply that to the Rouse case, and an innocent conclusion, it might be inferred, could be drawn. Thus *nearly* endeth the technical lesson. But it was not the end of the technical controversy because Birkett and Buckle were determined to have the last word on the matter.

It will be recalled that when Buckle left the witness box he thought he had detected a hint of smugness or self-satisfaction on the face of Rouse as he passed him in the well of the court. This prompted Buckle into the re-evaluation of his evidence and to the realisation that he, Buckle, had not paid sufficient attention to the condition of the carburettor in seeking to explain the ferocity of the blaze. Thus far from its top having been blown off in the fire, he concluded after a period of reflection following the conclusion of his testimony that Rouse must have pulled it off (thereby explaining the bent float) to release more petrol into the conflagration.

At the court convened at the start of the sixth day, the judge had taken his place, and was studying a few sheets of paper handed to him by the clerk when the realisation dawned. Where was Rouse? He was not in the dock. The call went out and after a few seconds' hiatus, Rouse stepped briskly up the stairs and stood, pale and earnest, gripping the ledge of the dock. Outside the court wooden barriers had been erected along the street between the court and the judge's lodgings in anticipation of huge crowds wishing to be in at the finish. As people turned up they were advised by the police that it was pointless to queue for admission. The majority accepted this with good humour and after a short wait drifted away. It was estimated that, in total, more than 2,000 had congregated at one time or another before the proceedings commenced that morning. The local cafés did a roaring trade with waitresses running back and forth to serve coffee and sandwiches to the waiting crowds as they queued.

Back in the court, the significance of the documents Talbot was examining quickly became apparent. They were requests by jurors for further information or guidance. The first could be easily met. The jury wished to see a Morris Minor, identical to the one that had been burned. Finnemore could oblige. He had had one standing by throughout the trial. The next request was also settled easily enough. How long, asked the jury, had it taken, according to Buckle, for the blaze to fuse the windscreen (the possible significance of this is considered in a later chapter)? The judge could answer that from memory. Three to four minutes (did that mean time enough for the victim to escape this fire *if* he had not been rendered unconscious by Rouse?). Buckle, who was in court, confirmed the judge's recollection.

But then a juror, having heard the three automotive experts for the defence the previous day, wanted to know more about that petrol union nut. Had the colonel himself, who had testified on Day Two, experimented to see what the effect of heat on it was (that is, could it have been loosened to release petrol to feed the flames as a result of the heat and not by Rouse's fingers?). And would this allow the turning of the nut as had been described by the defence witnesses? Clearly Mr. Isaacs' journey to Northampton to testify for the defence had not been entirely in vain as at least one juror had paid attention to his testimony.

Mr. Justice Talbot was not sure what to do, that is, whether or not it was appropriate to recall Buckle to the witness box to give further evidence. Finnemore said he thought the jury had been given enough evidence to go on (presumably wishing that any doubts that they had on this matter would continue to linger). The judge agreed. It was better to leave things as they stood. But Birkett then interjected that Buckle had not been asked such specific questions (especially by Birkett; one wonders why not) and should be allowed to give his answer. This is interesting. For given that the consistent and largely unequivocal testimony of the defence experts on this question could be taken as damaging to the Crown's theory of the case, would not Birkett's adducing of Buckle to address the jury's questions on this question constitute a prosecution 'own goal'? But of course the classic advice to a barrister is only to ask his witnesses questions to which he knows his witnesses' answers beforehand. One therefore imagines that hasty discussions had taken place between Birkett and Buckle before the trial resumed on that Saturday morning prior to the latter's recall to the witness box.

So while Mr. Justice Talbot had agreed with Finnemore that the jury had been given plenty of technical evidence, he also agreed to Birkett's submission to hear further from Buckle. After all, Isaacs' evidence had been heard long after Buckle had given his testimony. There was, indeed, a further moment or two of dithering but Colonel Buckle was finally recalled to the witness box. Normally, if a witness is recalled to present new evidence, rather than simply to clear up any confusion regarding his previous evidence, then the other side can cross-examine, so that in this situation Finnemore would have had a further opportunity to cross-examine Buckle and to suggest how scientifically and empirically ridiculous were the witness's utterances. However, Mr. Justice Talbot took it upon himself to question the witness on this technical matter thus depriving Finnemore of putting a last cross-examining question to Buckle before the witness left the box. We can only speculate whether Rouse's fate would have been different had Finnemore got in that question regarding Buckle's cognate knowledge.

Mr. Justice Talbot's question to Buckle was direct, '....whether, in great heat, the expansion of the metal forming the nut and the thread on which the nut binds, and the subsequent cooling, will produce a loosened joint, assuming that it starts by being tight?' But instead of agreeing with the combined wisdom of the experienced Isaacs, Bamber and Cotton, Buckle's reply must have been startling to nearly all those present (but certainly not to Birkett). 'I can see no scientific or engineering reason why that should happen, why there should happen any looseness from contraction, or distortion of the thread due to contraction; but I can see a reason for it in some forms of this joint—not in this particular one.' As he sought to explain,

> "The two parts of the thread [*sic*; did he not mean the union joint?] would be expanding under heat in a fire like this more or less to the same temperature; so that they would expand together. There is a very small area of engagement of the thread, not more than a quarter of an inch deep. The lineal expansion of this would be very small. Both parts expand together, and, for all practical purposes, you have nothing like the looseness I found. There is no change in the relative positions of the parts at all."

No recognition here of potentially differential degrees of heat-exposed expansion (and cooling contraction) of the thread and nut, or of possible different metal compositions of each component affecting their respective amounts of expansion and contraction. Indeed, when reminded of Arthur Cotton's reference to standard workshop practice of using a blow-torch as part of the procedure for loosening a nut, Buckle was reduced to replying that, 'I cannot account for it if it is true....I cannot see any scientific explanation for it if it happened, and to the best of my knowledge and belief it does not happen.' He conceded that a rusted nut might react as the defence witnesses stated, because 'you would have expanded them [presumably he meant the nut, the thread and the pipe] at different rates in heating them up and broken [*sic*] the film of rust. I cannot understand it with a clean nut, or a brass fitting, where you do not get rust.' So whereas Norman Thorne had been 'Spilsburied' in 1924 when his experts were ignored or discounted by the jury in the Crowborough chicken farm case, we are tempted to claim, knowing the outcome, that Rouse had, indeed, been well and truly 'Buckled'.[271] And so the sparring and cut-and-thrust were over. The closing speeches and the judge's summing up were about to begin.

---

271 Finnemore actually called one more defence witness before the adjournment for the day, a press photographer, Roland Holloway. He testified to there being no police on duty guarding the remains of the car when he arrived on site after 9 am on November 6, though there were one or two people looking at the car. He took a photograph that was produced as an exhibit. It showed the petrol can at the back of the car. Finnemore was obviously seeking to press home the point that anyone could have tampered with *any* part of the car, especially the petrol union joint which the Crown insisted Rouse had deliberately tampered with, and that perhaps the victim had stretched over the back seat to grab the petrol can when his lighted cigar ignited the fumes.

CHAPTER ELEVEN

MR. JUSTICE TALBOT ON ROUSE'S LIES

DAILY MAIL, February 2, 1931

The Trial Ends

With all the witnesses having been heard, the closing sequences now commenced. First, defence counsel would make his closing speech on behalf of the prisoner, to be followed by Birkett's final appeal to the jury before the judge summed up the case (if Rouse had not testified then Finnemore would have had the final word before Talbot's summing-up. Nowadays defence counsel always have the final word before the judge sums up). Instead, Finnemore turned his efforts to his closing speech and to saving Rouse from the hangman.

He first compared the Crown's case to a work of fiction. Some authors, he said, could write so attractively and persuasively that they carried their readers from one improbability to another and it was only when the story was finished that the whole seemed so unlikely. He left the jury with five points which summed up the defence's case (though, of course, it was for the Crown to establish guilt, not for the defence to prove innocence). First, there was the unbelievable nature of the crime and the complete absence of any motive or reason for committing it. Second, there were the prisoner's story of panic and all the silly lies, which were more consistent with a man running away from an accident than with a planned murder. Third, there was the absence of any evidence of violence to the deceased, apart from the fire, and no evidence of the violent use of the mallet. Fourth, there was the inability of anyone to identify the source or cause of the fire. On this matter he reminded the jury that if his experts' practical experience regarding those troublesome loose nuts was to be recognised by the twelve jurymen as valid and significant, then, '..... they [the jury] were all left in complete ignorance of any single thing which the prisoner could have done to cause a deliberate fire' (innocent explanations being an electrical fault with the self-starter causing a spark which then ignited a fire, or the victim's own reckless behaviour in dropping a lighted cigar into or near the petrol can inside the car). And as to the carburettor having been ripped off by Rouse, not only was there no evidence to support this proposition (we recall that it was a suspicion belatedly harboured by Buckle on the basis, it seemed, of a perceived knowing smirk from Rouse as Buckle was leaving the witness box). Second, on the carburettor point, Bamber had testified that it was possible that the top could have been blown off. But third, it was surely pertinent that the carburettor theory was wholly inconsistent with the prosecution's central claim that Rouse had set fire to the vehicle by lighting a petrol trail in front of the car and loosening the petrol union joint. But the defence's fifth broad argument was the implausibility of the Crown's allegation that Rouse had supposedly stopped his car in order to carry out a deliberate murder just 159 yards from a village he had just driven through and within actual sight of its houses (he obviously did not see the need to remind the jury that there were at least another 400 yards of country road, with no buildings, before the junction with the main road).

In winding up his concluding speech, he reminded the jury of their responsibilities, and that each juror was obliged to come to his own separate conclusion, which meant that it required just one dissentient from a guilty verdict to result in an acquittal. But he also noted his own responsibility, in his capacity of representing Rouse on a capital charge against 'one of the most eminent members of the Bar leading for the Crown', as he put it a little disingenuously (since he had known and enjoyed a friendship with Birkett over many years). If he had fallen short in any way, then the blame was with him, he pleaded self-deprecatingly. It should not affect the prisoner. He closed his speech with the thought-provoking passage from Edward Fitzgerald's translation of *The Rubaiyat of Omar Khayyam*. 'The Moving Finger writes; and, having writ, Moves on'. That is, once they had given their verdict the jury could never call it back (though, of course, he refrained from mentioning that the Court of Criminal Appeal could do so, if legal grounds existed). At the back of the court women started to cry. As she listened to Finnemore's closing speech, Lily sat rigidly upright, eyes closed, face partially hidden in her large fur collar. As he finished she wiped tears from her eyes. According to the press Rouse sat easily in his chair in the dock, his hands in his pockets, his legs outstretched.

Birkett rose. Always the gentleman, he first told the jury that his opponent, Finnemore, had discharged his responsibilities not merely with ability, but with conspicuous and devoted care. With this fulsome compliment, Birkett moved on to the real business. Appealing to the 'unfailing logic of circumstance', which he somehow managed to avoid explaining, he insisted that the '....evidence conclusively, decisively, completely, beyond any human doubt, indicates that the accused in the early morning of 6th November, in that deserted lane, committed a deliberate, a calculated, and a horrible murder.' Then turning and pointing directly at Rouse, he declaimed that 'The motive, if motive there be, is locked in the accused's own heart, and there is no power under heaven which enables me to unlock it'. Not only did he sound, uncharacteristically, at that moment like an actor in a crude Victorian melodrama, he also eschewed putting his money where his mouth was by avoiding trying to prove that Rouse's motive was to fake his own death and to disappear, hopefully with a share of the insurance proceeds. Instead he fell back on the cowardly tactic of painting Rouse's motive as elusive and unreachable while simultaneously shifting to the jury the responsibility of concluding that it must both exist and undoubtedly be sinister. Why did the prisoner not simply do the decent thing and reveal it or admit it, Birkett seemed to suggest. 'Locked in the accused's own heart'? Rouse must surely be a blackguard of the first order. It was certainly an object lesson by Birkett in oratory but perhaps not in forensic enlightenment.

But Birkett did offer an original take on a familiar principle. The defence, he claimed, held that, 'It is better that a guilty man should go free than that an innocent man should suffer'. However in *his* book, 'The administration of justice fails if the guilty man goes free'. Indeed, instead of reviewing the evidence which the Crown had presented, Birkett chose to dwell upon the character of Rouse and his lack of credibility. 'He stands, not an innocent man speaking the truth, but the resourceful liar, escaping it at all costs' (though Birkett did not add that lying was not usually a crime). Why had Rouse omitted to say that he had gone home to reassure his wife? How could he know so little about the victim who had shared his car for five hours? Was not it remarkable that he had 'a complete explanation for the theory of an accident – namely, petrol and a match (others might have answered those questions with, 'Don't know', 'Why should he?' and 'Why should it be?')? Birkett did not remind the jury of the conflicting evidence about the hairs on the mallet (the judge, in any case, soon directed the jury to disregard it). Instead he chose to highlight Rouse's possible explanation. 'With regard to his suggestion as to how the hair got on the mallet, have you ever heard anything like it in your life?' he asked, referring to Lily's alleged hairdressing exploits. An innocent man might say, 'I really do not know', Birkett suggested. But Rouse had 'an ingenious explanation'. In an observation that the jury would have linked to Rouse's garrulous appearance in the witness box, counsel concluded that the prisoner '.... cannot resist the temptation to explain'. Again, an observer might query whether that in itself was a crime. Birkett's own 'scales of justice' moment, scarcely as practised and as melodramatic as Marshall Hall's, had now arrived. It was, he declared, the jury's plain, clear and compelling duty, as the keepers of that symbol (which was, of course, on top of the Old Bailey a long distance away), to return a verdict of guilty.

Yet far from reminding the jury of the Crown's theory of the cause of the blaze, which bore so heavily on the question of Rouse's guilt, Birkett's exact words on this crucial matter were, literally, restricted to, 'But, apart from the evidence as to the sustained and continuous fire, fed from the sources which have been indicated to you by Colonel Buckle....'. Indeed the words 'carburettor' and 'loose petrol union joint' never even passed his lips in that closing speech. Either he was so confident of the strength of Buckle's testimony that a reminder of Rouse's alleged tampering was unnecessary, or he was so fearful of the defence experts' analysis of how the union joint was loose that the least said on this matter the better. Was it thus a case of short and sweet becoming short and nasty, with Birkett's closing speech homing in on Rouse's unpleasant character, and not his conduct in Hardingstone Lane?

At least there was one more voice still to be heard which would oblige the jury to address their minds to every matter raised before them before they retired to consider their verdict. And that was to pay attention to the judge's summing up. 'Gentlemen, the case into which you have been inquiring in these five days is a most exceptional one,' Talbot's summing up began. Indeed, members of the all-male jury might have regarded this as something of an understatement. Thus the judge went on to say that one would have to go a long way back in legal history to find a case like it. For a start, it had been impossible to identify the 'unhappy man' and therefore, 'I say that in my opinion, there is no theory which is even plausible as to why this man did this murder – if he did it.' If the jury were satisfied that murder *was* done, it was not their business to enquire *why* it was done. Nevertheless, Mr. Justice Talbot was clearly troubled by the predicament and acknowledged that there was 'a very serious difficulty in bringing home the guilt of murder to this man, or to any man, if you are unable to give a reasonable explanation of why it was done.' For discovering no motive 'obviously deprives the Prosecution of what is ordinarily an important and, in many cases, perhaps a vital part of their case.' In default of a motive, Rouse's *behaviour* was described by the judge on that dreadful night. According to the prisoner's own account, repeated by the judge, when Rouse first saw the flames he was 150 to 200 yards from the car 'for the reason which he gives you', as Talbot delicately put it. He had tried to run back to the car, at the same time fastening his clothes. Then he ran towards the village shouting out 'My God!' before going back to the car again to see, he claimed, whether there was anything he could do. With Rouse presumably defeated by the flames, Talbot reminded the jury that Rouse had told the court that he had lost his head and had run 620 yards to the corner with the main road. Yet, noted the judge, there was no suggestion from the two witnesses who had seen him that he was out of breath. Continuing, Talbot noted that this sequence of events must have taken four or five minutes. The Crown's theory as to what had happened seemed to fit better because there was less time to be accounted for. The flames would only have started as Rouse left the car (though this seems rather imprecise). When the two witnesses reached the car the flames were still 12 to 15 feet high. In other words, what the judge appeared to be saying was that if, following Rouse's account, the prisoner *had* gone some distance to relieve himself and had then spotted the flames from where he was crouching, then the time spent in running back to the car, followed by the prisoner's running towards the village, and then returning to the car before walking off towards the main road would have taken much longer than four or five minutes. By contrast, if he had fired the vehicle and had moved from there, not to relieve himself but directly to pass the cousins near the junction, the shorter four to five minute time slot suggested by the Crown would be a better reconstruction of the event. And this would be so even taking into account that, according to Brown and Bailey, Rouse had not appeared to be out of breath when he passed them, in which state he was more likely to have been in had his version of events, involving his running back and forward in a panic, been true.

Talbot then turned to what he described as the 'improbabilities' of the defendant's account, a choice of wording which might not have been felicitous for Rouse's chances.

> "The whole notion of asking this total stranger to pour the petrol into the tank for him, when he had everything ready and had done everything except actually empty the can in, and at the same time give him a cigar, of all things in the world, and make sure he has a match to light it with, certainly sounds a very singular story."

There was the improbability of someone going 150 yards from the car to 'perform an operation of nature' in the dead of night, in order to be out of sight of another man, for reasons of 'delicacy'. Indeed that other man was, apparently, one in whom Rouse had no confidence, such that he took his attaché case with him. Yet he still chose to leave that same man whom he thought might be a thief in charge of the car whilst going to relieve himself.

As to the mallet on which the Crown placed some emphasis, his (the judge's) inspection of it, he had to say, had not impressed him. 'I do not know what you made of that mallet', he said to the jury, but having looked at it through the magnifying glass he thought the most conspicuous thing on the mallet was the mud, not a hair. This brought him to the scene of the crime, or accident, and provoked on his part a strong outburst on the conduct of the police. 'I could not have believed it, if I had not heard it admitted by the police officers, that upon the very morning of this catastrophe this car was left for long periods of time wholly without police supervision at all.'

Moving on, he noted that there were two propositions which the Crown claimed to have proved, '...first of all that it is impossible, or practically impossible, that this fire could have been an accident, and, secondly, that it is impossible that the dead man could have got into the position in which he died unless he had been placed there when unconscious.' As to the first proposition, the prosecution had relied upon Colonel Buckle's evidence; for the second it was the evidence of Sir Bernard Spilsbury.

Regarding the technical evidence, Mr. Justice Talbot adopted a becoming modesty. 'I am speaking to gentlemen who, I hope, know a great deal more about motor cars and their mechanism than I do.' He noted that all the mechanical experts had agreed that the fire had been fierce, continuously fed, sited under the vehicle and enhanced by the petrol can. However, while Buckle found the explanation in the deliberately loosened union joint and the vandalized carburettor top, the defence experts pointed to the accidental commencement of the blaze, probably from an electrical failure, and the flammable nature of the vehicle's upholstery collapsing into the body of the car, consistent with the fire being located at the bottom of the vehicle. Moreover, the carburettor top might simply have been blown off in the blaze. As to the petrol leak, all parties, including Rouse himself, appeared to agree that it had not occurred while the car was moving. For it would have been instantly noticed by the vehicle's occupants. Similarly, there was general consensus that it was unlikely that the loosening in this case had been caused by vibrations or by a 'fidgety' passenger.

When it came to the defence experts, a harsh degree of censure was reserved for the unfortunate Mr. Isaacs. 'I do not think anybody could say that Mr. Isaacs made a very brilliant appearance in the witness box. He assumed a scientific knowledge which he had not got. He appeared rather foolish when he was tackled as to what is the cause of this phenomenon.' Nonetheless, added the judge fairly, Isaacs' want of scientific knowledge 'does not mean that he is not telling you the truth about his experience'. Moreover, he acknowledged that the testimony of Arthur Cotton, who 'has the good sense to confine himself to what he does know,' actually supported Isaacs' view. Buckle, of course, had merely dismissed their evidence on how the nut had become loose as impossible. But this left the jury, as we noted earlier, with a stark choice whom to believe, though Talbot gave a perhaps-not-so-subtle hint of his own view when adding that,

"....[T]his fire could not have been the fire it was unless the leak was in existence at the beginning of the fire, and not as the result of the fire.....It is true that this leak, which is the main feeder, must have been in operation at any rate, from an early stage of the fire, and was essential to the fire being what it turned out to be."

But was this not a statement that merely assumed that which had yet to be proved, indeed, that which had *not* been proved, according to the testimony of Isaacs and Cotton? That is, *had* there been a leak from the joint at the beginning of the fire or, indeed, at *any* point during the blaze? For the defence's position was that the fire's ferocity had emanated from the flammable material in the body of the car, from the contents of the petrol can and, perhaps, from the flow of petrol escaping from the damaged carburettor (not from the union joint), with the trigger for the blaze either being a faulty self-starter or a careless, cigar-wielding passenger stretching for a petrol can. Yet Talbot did observe that while the petrol union joint was loose after the blaze, the carburettor joint was not. In other words, if cooling had loosened the union joint, why was the carburettor joint not affected in the same way, if heating and cooling would impact similarly on each joint? While he seemed to imply pointedly that the only variable therefore appeared to have been human intervention regarding the petrol joint nut, yet, that the metallic composition of the carburettor joint and its reaction to intense heating and cooling would be identical to those of the petrol joint seems, to his lordship, to have been assumed rather than proved.

Indeed, the tone of his remarks on the technical evidence distinctly favoured the prosecution's position. Thus he stressed that even Bamber for the defence felt that the existence of the bent float pin in the carburettor was more consistent with the carburettor top having been taken off rather than with having been blown off. Moreover, that the body of the carburettor, but not the top, had been fused had been taken as further reinforcement of this interpretation. It is true that Talbot did refer further not only to the 'existence of the leak' but also to 'the existence in the car of this petrol can with the top only screwed on a very short way'. Yet he drew specific attention to the 'fusing of the windscreen, which is a very striking fact' (by which he presumably meant that a flame intense enough to fuse the windscreen had been deliberately fed). Such statements were, of course, challengeable, as we have seen, or open to further qualification or explanation in a different kind of forum. However, if accepted at face value by the jury, then, at the very least, they scarcely pointed to Rouse's innocence. But whether they *confirmed* his guilt would surely involve a further leap of reasoning.

The technical evidence regarding the cause of the blaze (which might be said also to include the significance of the damp petrol patch found by Spilsbury on the victim's trousers) was, of course, only one aspect of the Crown's case against the prisoner, as Talbot reminded the jury. And while we do not know for certain what impact it had on the jury's deliberations, it would surely be astonishing if the lauding of Buckle and the ridiculing of Isaacs had not only captured their imagination but had also exerted a huge influence on their verdict. It was likely to be just another nail in Rouse's coffin (though we shall see that the technical controversies would not quite be over when the defence team later came to contemplate an appeal).

Regarding the medical evidence, the judge duly noted that neither the prosecution nor the defence medical experts had examined the remains of the body until a period of time after the event. 'Sir Bernard Spilsbury assumes, and you are asked to assume, that the police are substantially right as to the position of the body and particularly the legs,' though at this point the judge appeared to have set aside his stricture about police 'laxity' on that fatal morning. 'I should think you would feel, gentlemen, that it is almost impossible to doubt that this evidence [from the police] is anything but honest, and it is very, very difficult to believe that it is not accurate.' In reviewing the conflicting opinions of Sir Bernard Spilsbury and Dr Harvey-Wyatt, he came to a comforting conclusion. 'Then he [Harvey-Wyatt] is cross-examined. I think the result of the cross-examination – it is entirely for you to judge – was to bring these two eminent gentlemen into something near agreement as to the facts.' Comforting perhaps, but accurate?

And so to the most damning part of his summing up when Talbot turned to the character and admitted conduct of Rouse himself. 'Now a word [sic] about the defendant himself,' the judge began. While he claimed not to know what impression the prisoner had made upon the jury, nonetheless, if it had been unfavourable (which, of course, could hardly fail to have been the case), then they would have to make great allowances for the fact that Rouse was on trial for his life. Perhaps it was a 'cruel kindness of the law' that the prisoner was now allowed to go into the witness box to tell his story and be cross-examined. This oxymoronic phrase was a nod to the change in the law from 1898 which permitted an accused to testify on oath on his own behalf in the witness box. For previously it had been thought that, as an interested party, the accused's evidence might be unreliable, and that he might even be tempted to perjure himself. Moreover, it was for the prosecution to prove guilt, not for the Crown to rely upon the defendant to compromise his position by testifying, possibly recklessly. An unsworn statement from the dock was permitted to the accused before the 1898 Criminal Evidence Act (and continues to be so permitted). Indeed the option for the prisoner to deliver an unsworn statement from the dock had existed even before the Prisoners' Counsel Act 1836 granted the accused the right to legal representation, including counsel's right to examine and cross-examine witnesses (but not the prisoner himself), and to address the jury on behalf of the accused. For prior to 1836 counsel for the defence could only argue points of law for the prisoner and offer him advice as to which issues of fact to raise or to contest.[272]

In fact Talbot's reference to 'cruel kindness' was probably prompted by the memory of the arrogant and unpleasant Frederick Seddon talking himself to the gallows in 1912 under Rufus Isaacs' withering cross-examination. More significant and more recent was the memory of Edith Thompson's 'suicidal' and doomed effort, despite her counsel, Curtis-Bennett's, desperate plea that she keep well away from the witness box, as she struggled to explain to the jury the purity and innocence, and the flights of imagination, hope and desire contained in the love letters she had written to her lover, Bywaters. No doubt as confident as Seddon and Edith Thompson in their ability to 'sweet-talk' the jury but, unlike them, obliged to explain away his lies and obfuscations after the blaze, Rouse thus took his place in the witness box with, as we know (though Talbot did not know

272   John H. Langbein, *The Origins of Adversary Criminal Trial*, Clarendon Press, Oxford, 2005.

at that stage before verdict), the same disastrous outcome for the accused as in the Seddon and Thompson cases. In adverting to the prisoner's character, Talbot could scarcely avoid making the obvious remark that, by his own confession, Rouse was a most facile liar.

> "It is really not exaggerating the matter to say that from the moment when he got on to that lorry at the main road, a little south of Northampton, to the moment when he got out of the motor coach in London and saw Sergeant Skelly, he told lies about almost every conceivable matter and to almost every conceivable person he came across. It does not follow that because a man tells lies, thinking he is going to make his position better by telling some fictitious story, that he is guilty [a *Lucas* direction in such terms is issued by the judge to the jury nowadays]. A man may be innocent and yet be foolish enough to do that. It is far better to tell the truth; but a man is not to be convicted because he has been foolish or reckless."

But the most damaging point arising from Rouse's lies, in Talbot's judgment, was not just that 'most of these lies could have been perfectly easily refuted....' It was that,

> "....the excuse he gives for lying will not bear examination. He says that it would have to be a long and complicated story to go through. There is no complication about it. All he had to say was: I had given this man a lift; I left him for a minute or two, and when I looked round the car was ablaze; this wretched man by some folly must have set alight the whole thing. That is the whole thing. It is very difficult to see why he did tell these lies."

Like assault cases where no witnesses are present and no forensic (or, now, DNA evidence) can be produced, it will frequently come down to who the jury (or the magistrates) believe. Is it the victim and the Crown's other witnesses or the accused and his witnesses? Who sounds more believable (or who seems less untrustworthy)? In the instant case the victim could not speak, not even metaphorically through the vehicle of compelling forensic evidence against the accused. So was Rouse believable regarding the fire? The judge hardly needed to remind the jury that his record of lying was hardly a good pointer in his favour.

Talbot, in fairness, did conclude by noting the lack of evidence presented by the Crown regarding motive on Rouse's part. Thus, 'If he had an intention of disappearing, that intention was certainly abandoned, at the latest, when he got the seat in the coach which was going down to Wales, where he went straight to a house where he was well known.' Even the lorry driver had been told that he, Rouse, was on his way to Wales, as part of his commercial travelling duties. That, of course, was a point in favour of the accused, but we know that that might not have stopped the jury from believing that, assuming he had in fact set fire to the car with the victim inside, and before the cousins had appeared, he was indeed planning to fake his death and disappear. And while the jury were warned that, 'You cannot guess at things, even if you have the material here for forming what is even a plausible guess', it is a fair assumption that the jury ignored the judge's stricture. Concluding his summing up, he charged them with the task of considering their verdict but also added that if they desired to look at any of the exhibits, they should ask for them, while adding that, 'I think perhaps you would sooner get a little refreshment and then see the car.'

It was now 2.18 pm on that Saturday January 31, 1931 when the jury retired and it was anticipated by those intimately acquainted with such proceedings that they would not return until six or seven o'clock in the evening. In fact they came back into court just 75 minutes later. Having taken a light lunch and having inspected the Morris Minor supplied by the defence, they sat down to their deliberations at 3.20 p.m. At half past three (yes, ten minutes later) the trumpet sounded, announcing that Mr. Justice Talbot was taking his seat. Astonishingly for some, the jury had taken less than eight minutes to reach a verdict, the length of time some juries in the eighteenth century might have taken (in those rare cases where they considered that the verdict required deep reflection before agreement was reached!). The speed of their deliberations caught many people off guard. Again Rouse was missing from the dock and Pleydell Bancroft, the clerk of assize, was heard to whisper urgently, 'Why don't you bring him up?' Rouse appeared with a slight smile on his lips, which some interpreted as his foolishly believing that a swift return of the jury was a powerful indication in his favour. However, as the panel was called over and as each member answered to his name, none of them looked at the prisoner. To the knowing and experienced press this was an ominous sign. Pleydell Bancroft asked the foreman, 'How do you find the prisoner at the bar, Guilty or Not Guilty?' 'Guilty' was the firm reply. Rouse, standing up, gripped the ledge of the dock so tightly that his knuckles turned white.

Nellie Tucker, who had been seated on the right of the dock, shuddered and, with head bowed, burst into tears. Helen Campbell went deathly pale and collapsed in her chair. Lily Rouse was not in court but in a side room (another account claimed that she was in escapist mode, having tea with a friend in a nearby hotel, when the telephone rang and the dreadful news was then passed on to her by a waiter); on hearing the news she also collapsed. Rouse turned ashen grey as he stood staring in front of him, eyes unseeing. The clerk then asked him, 'Have you anything to say why judgment of death should not be pronounced upon you?' Rouse replied in a clear distinct voice, 'Only that I am innocent, sir.' The grim ritual took its course. With the black cap placed upon his head, Mr. Justice Talbot read the sentence.

> "You have been found guilty of that crime for which the law appoints one sentence and one sentence only. It is the sentence which I now pronounce upon you. It is that you be taken from hence to a place of lawful execution, and you will be there hanged by the neck until you be dead. And that your body be afterwards buried within the precincts of the prison in which you shall last have been confined. And may God have mercy on your soul."

Rouse was taken down, a ritual that was followed by the judge informing the jury that they were now exempt from jury service for ten years. Before the court rose, Norman Birkett had one more piece of business to conduct. 'My Lord, there was another indictment on the file. Would your Lordship's pleasure be that the indictment should remain on the file?' Mr. Justice Talbot agreed. This further charge would, of course, have been pursued had Rouse been acquitted on the charge of murder. For Birkett had already settled the indictment for another case against Rouse, that is, his (alleged) bigamous marriage to Helen Campbell in

1924... just in case.

One could speculate till Doomsday why the jury convicted when no eye-witnesses had been present to testify that they had actually seen him firing the vehicle with the victim inside, nor was there persuasive forensic evidence in the form of fingerprints, adequate hair samples or bloodstains on his clothing, nor any previous recorded history of violence. In reality we instinctively know why the jury convicted. It was because Rouse was a grossly undesirable, untruthful, dissolute and cocky individual whose projected image perceived by the jury was of one who simply could not have been believed, no matter what he said. But that may only be half the equation, if we leave aside Talbot's references, in his summing up, to Rouse's 'beyond belief' explanations for his own behaviour. The other half may be the (mostly elusive and unrecoverable) personal traits of the jury members. What were their backgrounds and life experiences? What was their knowledge of actual poverty or of sexual misbehaviour, or of petty crime? Did they have any empathetic personal experience of lives not so perfect, homely and secure? It is not just that they were all white, male, property-owning middle-class and, probably, middle-aged. What may also have mattered was that decision-making, whether judicial or by fact-deciding jurors, will often be influenced psychologically by tacit influences that are not reducible simply to issues of class, gender, age and wealth. The likelihood, though it is incapable of proof here, is that the jurors all shared common 'respectable' values on probity and morality (at least when their decision-making was on public display, a decision for which they would be held accountable), while Rouse's probity and morality occupied a different universe to theirs (though not necessarily to that of some of the rest of society; for generalisations on such matters can be misleading, as our later chapter engaging contemporary social and sexual mores will suggest). Thus what did for Rouse was 'character', or his perceived failings in that regard.[273] Mr. Justice McCardie, who ended up shooting himself in 1933, once said,

> "It may be asked which of the persons charged with an offence gives evidence in the coolest and most self-possessed manner? My answer is, it is the person charged with *murder*. I have tried many persons for murder, and in the majority of cases those accused have entered the witness-box. I recall but *few* [italics added] who have not given their testimony in a quiet, confident, almost dispassionate way with adroitness of reply, ingenuity of explanation and singular ease of manner. The ease of manner I have mentioned might perhaps be expected from those who have been guilty of deliberate and calculated murder. But, strangely enough, even in cases where the murder has been one of sudden passion or anger, the person accused when he enters the witness-box often displays a noticeable degree of self-possession and adroitness."[274]

Thus any observer claiming to have seen Rouse deliver his answers 'in a quiet, confident, almost dispassionate way' would have been imagining things. McCardie was right. Rouse was clearly one of the 'few'.

273   For a modern analysis of 'personal values' influencing judicial decision-making, and resulting in greater judicial diversity than one might anticipate from the profile of senior judges as predominantly white, male, middle-class and middle aged, see Rachel J. Cahill-O'Callaghan, "Reframing the Judicial Diversity Debate: Personal Values and Tacit Diversity", *Legal Studies*, Vol. 35, 2015, pp. 1-29.
274   George Pollock, *Mr. Justice McCardie: A Biography*, John Lane, The Bodley Head, 1934, p. 57.

CHAPTER TWELVE

MY HECTIC LIFE OF LOVE AND DECEIT

NEWS OF THE WORLD, February 1, 1931

The Press and Post-Trial Reporting

Following Rouse's conviction the authorities became particularly exercised by fears that somehow the press would get hold of salacious information about the prisoner from unauthorised sources. In particular, the possibility that either Rouse or those closely connected to him might sell sensational stories to the newspapers based on information smuggled out from prison, whether in the form of a confession, an account of his various amours, or a denial of his guilt, was a constant anxiety from before his conviction, becoming more acute as one moved nearer to the date of his execution and even beyond.

The flow of squalid, intimate and sometimes melodramatic press revelations appears to have commenced the day following his conviction on Saturday January 31, 1931. For, on the next morning, the *News of the World* published a long article under the headlines, 'Rouse's Own Life Story: A Sordid Tale of Love and Licence: A Sheik in a Car'. It was supposedly authored by Rouse himself in Bedford prison while awaiting trial.[275] Even the reference to a 'Sheik' was bound to raise salubrious, or even romantic, expectations among the newspaper's readership. The memory of both the Thompson-Bywaters trial in December 1922 and that of the exotic Madame Fahmy acquitted in September 1923 of shooting to death her husband, an Egyptian prince, in a corridor in the Savoy Hotel, both played up images of a brooding, if mythical, sheik as a major character in the murder drama.

For Edith Thompson, her literary escapism had embraced popular novels such as Robert Hichens' *Bella Donna* (1909), the story of a recently-married woman's infatuation with a dark, sultry Egyptian whom she and her husband had met while on honeymoon. Edith was an attractive, childless, but moderately successful businesswoman of 29, stuck in a rut with an unimaginative husband of modest ambition who, as a shipping clerk, earned less than she did at a time when popular culture, fed by a plethora of women's magazines, uncomplicatedly propagated the idea that a woman's place was in the home, cooking and caring for husband and children. Perhaps more significantly, Edith's husband, Percy, did not share her enthusiasms for middle-brow novels that prompted not just her flights

---

275　*News of the World*, February 1, 1931.

of fancy but her exploration of her own selfhood and identity. Perhaps, also, it was his shy personality, rather than limited competence, that prevented him from joining her on the dance floor during the many ballroom dancing competitions in which she excelled. Whichever explanation is correct, her emotional needs were met elsewhere in the arms of the much younger Freddie Bywaters, dark, handsome, virile and with exotic stories to tell of his adventures as a ship's clerk at ports throughout the world. It is thus easy to link many of the features of *Bella Donna* with Edith's own circumstances and imagination, with 'the novel's escapist locations, its illicit sexuality,.. the inscrutably passionate and sexually devious [Egyptian], the lilting rhythms of the East, the drugged pulse of life in the Delta of the Nile, and of course the poisoning of the husband'.[276]

Perhaps even less imagination is needed in respect of the Fahmy trial. For it involved the shooting to death by his wife, Marguerite, of Prince Ali Bey Fahmy, a genuine (albeit honorific) Egyptian prince of immense wealth and presence, with a sophisticated and cosmopolitan outlook, possessing a luxurious yacht on the Nile and a retinue of Nubian attendants, expensive vehicles, acquainted with international travel. When he died of gunshot wounds he was just twenty-two, and ten years younger than his lowly-born French wife who, at the age of sixteen, had given birth to an illegitimate daughter, who had previously worked as a 'high-class' prostitute, and who, according to a recent writer, had also had an affair with the future playboy king, Edward VIII. The marriage of Marguerite and Fahmy was tempestuous. Indeed one might say that it was nasty, brutish and short. But whereas Robert Hichens' portrayal of the East in *Bella Donna* could be a romantic image of Arabian Nights, Marguerite Fahmy's celebrated defence counsel, Sir Edward Marshall Hall, painted the victim and the East in general as an immoral, primitive society where women were kept to be 'trained' to fulfil their husbands' needs. The Eastern desert became a 'dark' place from which the jury, by a verdict of acquittal, should release this poor, suffering wife of an oriental 'beast' whose sexual indignities towards her merely exacerbated her painful unmentionable condition (which was common or garden haemorrhoids). Not a desert of hope or of promise, as Rudolf Valentino might have projected it, but a dreadful fate, not only befalling Western woman succumbing to the sexual predations of the East, but befalling the pure gene pool of the West, as it became contaminated by miscegenation. The negative image, depicting chaste Western womanhood falling into the unnatural clutches of men who kept harems, prevailed, no doubt to the relief of the British Royal Household watching the trial from afar, and perhaps even to the prosecution. Madame Fahmy was thus acquitted, to universal approval. Or, at least, to the universal approval of the British, but not of the overseas, press.[277]

Against this background of not-so-distant in time previous murder sensations that contained such imagery, phrases and sentences such as 'A Sheik in a Car' and 'My harem takes me to several places' (as Rouse volunteered to the Northamptonshire police on the morning of Saturday November 8, 1930) rendered it hardly surprising that in early 1931 the press were falling over themselves to

---

276 René J. A. Weis, *Criminal Justice: The True Story of Edith Thompson*, Hamish Hamilton, 1988, p. 140. Other references to the Thompson-Bywaters case are cited elsewhere in the present volume.

277 Andrew Rose, *The Prince, the Princess and the Perfect Murder*, Coronet, 2013 (first published as *Scandal at the Savoy: The Infamous 1920s Murder Case*, Bloomsbury, 1991). Again other references to the case are cited elsewhere in the present volume.

get the sensational story of this Lothario behind the 'Blazing Car Mystery'. As indicated above, first off the mark was the *News of the World* on February 1, 1931 with its account presumably written before Rouse's trial but published only after the verdict.

> "What a mess I have made of my life! Sitting in a cell in Bedford Gaol with a charge of murder hanging over my head, I have nothing to do but think and think and think of the past... If the verdict goes against me, well, I have lived my life—a short and hectic one--but I have lived it. There are women who may shed a few tears and bemoan my fate. Or they may not. I don't know, and I don't particularly care."

Being indifferent to one's own life is surely the mark of a depressive or of a heroic type or of a selfish individual. Whichever category the press would place Rouse within, Fleet Street's finest clearly believed it worth regaling the public with this anti-celebrity's (alleged) innermost thoughts. In particular, it must have been calculated, in determining print runs, that there was an avid readership just waiting to hear from a man who did not 'particularly care' what the attitude of his harem might be to his predicament. Here was the raw sexual masculinity of a bygone mediaeval age, the crude insensitivity of the predator knights of the past which surely coloured the reading of Rouse's account. Yet his narrative was within the eighteenth century tradition of dying speeches from the condemned as they addressed the raucous multitudes come to witness the awful spectacle of the public execution.[278] Here was the Rake's Progress for the modern age, the warning to errant youth to pursue a more uplifting life than the one followed by Yours Truly for whom the pleasures of the flesh had joyously deprived him of his moral compass.

> "I have had many love affairs, or so-called love affairs, but what have they brought for me? Some fleeting moments of happiness on the one hand, and on the other many hours of scheming and deceit, and now to the shadow of the scaffold".

But it was not quite the contrition required of those hoping that the Pearly Gates might yet find an opening for a sinner who genuinely repents. For, '...even if I wished to regret, it is too late. I've not worried so far, and I am not going to commence now'. Indeed, if he were to gain his acquittal (and he probably believed before the trial that he had a decent prospect of escaping), he scarcely seemed to worry about securing or retaining the sympathy of the clean-living newspaper reader. Thus if found not guilty, '....there are two women I shall turn to—neither of them my wife' [a reference to Helen Campbell and Nellie Tucker]. With massive presumptuousness he explained that,

> "I shall put the circumstances before them very plainly, and it will be for them to decide which will have me. I like [*sic*] both of them equally well, but I cannot myself decide which I should prefer to have as a mate",

---

278 Peter Linebaugh, *The London Hanged: Crime and Civil Society in the Eighteenth Century*, Penguin, 1991; V. A. C. Gattrell, *The Hanging Tree*, Oxford University Press, Oxford, 1996; Harry Potter, *Hanging in Judgment: Religion and the Death Penalty in England*, SCM Press, 1993.

where the term 'mate' presumably had a raw sexual connotation. It is as if, like the Bourbon monarchs, he had learned nothing and forgotten nothing. The revelation might well have disgusted many readers but it was bound, also, to have titillated thousands. For it would have made their Sunday reading as pleasurable as the sports pages and a diversion from the next morning's early rise to work and from the other diet of newspaper coverage of international crises and economic distress.

As the late John Mortimer acutely observed,

> "High among the great British contributions to world civilisation, the plays of Shakespeare, the full breakfast, the herbaceous border and the presumption of innocence, must rank our considerable achievement in having produced most of the best murder trials in the long history of crime.....Colour supplements devoted to *nouvelle cuisine* have failed to make any great change in the English Sunday, which goes with a joint in the oven, the all-pervading smell of boiled cabbage, and an account of charred remains found in a burnt-out Ford Popular as described in page one of the *News of the World*." [279]

Discounting the reference to a different make of car from that owned by Rouse, Mortimer shows why such stories were avidly lapped up in an age of radio. It was pure joy to read about such cruel events suitably leavened by the emotional accounts of those left behind. That the *News of the World* story was also accompanied by a gentle posed photograph of Helen Campbell and Nellie Tucker looking together at a magazine, with Helen's left arm languidly resting on Nellie's left shoulder, could only add to the 'human interest' angle. Indeed what is left unsaid is whether they considered themselves as joint victims of Rouse's amorous living, or whether they united together, as sisters in adversity standing in solidarity by their man, notwithstanding the unorthodox relationship linking the two. It was all so tantalising and intriguing. As George Orwell famously wrote in 1946,

> "It is Sunday afternoon, preferably before the war. The wife is already asleep in the armchair, and the children have been sent out for a nice long walk. You put your feet up on the sofa, settle your spectacles on your nose, and open the *News of the World*. Roast beef and Yorkshire, or roast pork and apple sauce, followed up by suet pudding and driven home, as it were, by a cup of mahogany-brown tea, have put you in just the right mood. Your pipe is drawing sweetly, the sofa cushions are soft underneath you, the fire is well alight, the air is warm and stagnant. In these blissful circumstances, what is it that you want to read about? Naturally, about a murder." [280]

As the novelist, Ursula Bloom, recalled about her youth, she was an enthusiastic reader of the *News of the World*. For '....it was my relaxation from the classics, and nothing could have enchanted me more'.[281] In regard to Orwell, it is true that he did not specifically refer to Rouse's case among the nine classic cases that, according

279 John Mortimer (intro.), *Famous Trials*, Penguin, 1984, p. 7.
280 George Orwell, "Decline of the English Murder", in George Orwell, *Decline of the English Murder and Other Essays*, Penguin, 1965 (first published in 1946), pp. 9-13.
281 Cited in Nicholas Connell, *Doctor Crippen: The Infamous London Cellar Murder of 1910*, Amberley, Stroud, 2013, p. 114. Bloom later claimed to have located Ethel Le Neve, the lover of Dr. Crippen, living quietly in the 1950s. See *ibid.*

to him, had stood the test of time during 'Our great period of murder', which he dated between 1850 and 1925. That scarcely matters since even within his own time scale he also failed to list such *causes célèbres* as the cases of Madeleine Smith, Constance Kent, Dr. Pritchard, Oscar Slater, Stinie Morrison, Ronald True, Field and Gray, and Patrick Mahon. The Blazing Car Mystery is certainly the equal of those cases in the canon of *causes célèbres*, as contemporaries such as Sir Patrick Hastings and the former newspaper editor, A. G. Gardiner (see later), recognised when writing about the trial. But in any case, the issue for the authorities was to prevent the appearance of material relating to Rouse emanating from unofficial sources that would feed the voracious and unhealthy appetite of contemporary newspaper readers.

The rest of Rouse's account of his 'Own Life Story' simply repeats most of the ground we have covered in earlier chapters, where his previous life and his first meetings with his various women are described. There was only one problem when the authorities set about investigating this 'leak' to the press just one day after his conviction and before any question of an appeal had been considered. Rouse had never written it. Thus following the appearance of the *News of the World* article the governor of Bedford prison, F. W. Gwilliam, sent a copy of the article to the Home Office. He explained that Rouse had been under close observation during the whole time that the prisoner had been in detention. He had not had, nor had requested, facilities for writing such an account, and certainly had had no opportunity to smuggle it out of prison. He added that Rouse's solicitor, Lee-Roberts, had vigorously denied any knowledge of the piece, as had Lee-Roberts' clerk, Reginald Bird. But since the latter had in fact left the solicitor's employment prior to Rouse's trial, it seems probable that Rouse's story in the *News of the World* was actually penned by Bird. Unfortunately, definitive proof of this and of any financial details, that is, who paid whom, and how much (and we can assume that filthy lucre changed hands), are lacking.

The Home Office then instructed Gwilliam to show Rouse the article and to ask him whether he had written it or whether he could otherwise account for it. When this was done, Rouse denied making any statements to anyone except his barrister, his solicitor and (significantly?) the latter's clerk. Only these people, he believed, were in possession of the kind of detail contained in the article, information that he had been assured had been necessary properly to prepare his defence. In fact the bulk of the article had contained statements of which he had been ignorant. It had been, he added, his own intention to publish his life story following his anticipated acquittal, 'with the view to making a little money'. In short the *News of the World* article was 'pure journalese'.

Given the prisoner's strict disavowal of responsibility, a senior Home Office official did conclude that it was probably Bird who had worked up the article from material obtained from Rouse during the lawyers' prison visits, or even (though less likely) that Rouse had dictated the contents to Bird during such visits. But it appears that, apart from considering the possibility of the department checking the background to the photos that accompanied the piece, no further investigation of the article took place.[282] In fact the Home Office would soon have more controversial newspaper articles to consider. For, apart from the sensitive

282   The details of a possible inquiry are contained in PCOM9/289.

issue of whether press publication of the police court revelations about Rouse's harem had prejudiced the fairness of his ensuing trial, there was another issue. That is, whether the alleged confession by Rouse, published after his execution, was genuine and, if so, how it had been obtained by the press.

Post-Conviction Published Reviews

Given the uniqueness and notoriety of the case, it is not surprising that it attracted the attention of a number of writers, anxious to express their views on the proceedings. One of the best known was the crime writer and journalist, Edgar Wallace. Writing in the *Daily Mail*[283] shortly after Rouse's conviction, he admitted that in his opinion Rouse had been guilty. Indeed, the prisoner's notorious comments regarding the women in his life which he (apparently) had published in the *News of the World* the day after his conviction (above) would more than justify hanging him. Yet Wallace affected to be 'a little shocked' that the jury's verdict was reached in only 25 minutes (which was not strictly accurate). What exercised him was that, 'It is becoming an increasingly simple matter for an innocent person to place himself in such a position that he is liable to suffer the extreme penalty of the law'. What he actually meant was that the killer's acts of folly *after* the victim's death transformed, in the minds of the jury, that which might have been an accidental death or, at most, non-capital manslaughter, into a verdict of murder. Thus it was the idiocy of the failed estate agent, John Robinson in 1927, who cut up the body of Minnie Bonati before stuffing her in a trunk to be taken away by taxi, which condemned him to death. For, according to Wallace, the death of the part-time prostitute, during a sexual encounter with Robinson in his now empty office, was manslaughter, not murder. In other words Robinson, who already had a criminal record, was hanged because he fell into a panic and dismembered Bonati's body in order to dispose of it after she had been unintentionally killed by her head banging on a hard surface.[284]

By the same token, Rouse was sentenced to death because of what he subsequently did—in a state of 'terrible shock' he had run away and then told countless lies *after* the body had been consumed by the flames. And who was to say definitively that the man had been rendered insensate by Rouse and that the firing of the car had been deliberate? The 'proof' of his guilt was, according to Wallace, merely inferred from Rouse's subsequent actions. To paraphrase the crime writer's point, such an inference might be 'proof' in a court of law but it was not 'proof' as a logical proposition. Thus, 'It does not matter a snap of the fingers whether Rouse is guilty or not' (and Wallace believed he was). It was the lack of 'unassailable proof' of that guilt that disconcerted the writer, a view obviously not shared by the Home Office official, presumably Blackwell, who saw fit to scribble an exclamation mark next to this line of the press cutting.[285] This

---

283   *Daily Mail*, February 4, 1931.
284   For one account of the Robinson case, see Robin Odell, *Landmarks in 20th Century Murder*, Headline, 1995, pp. 140-41.
285   The response to Wallace's article was considerable, with numerous correspondents writing to the *Daily Mail*. While we have no way of knowing the total number of letters received, the newspaper published eleven such communications some days later. See *Daily Mail*, February 6, 1931. Views were more or less equally divided. The following October Wallace stood unsuccessfully as an independent 'Lloyd George' Liberal candidate in Blackpool in the general election (he refused to stand as a National Liberal, viewing the proposed National Government

was followed in the *Sunday Dispatch*[286] by an article entitled 'My Doubts about Rouse Conviction', written by a 'Barrister-at-Law' who, the Home Office later suspected, was a recently retired Irish bar practitioner of little consequence. The author stated that he joined with other critics of the verdict, such as A. A. Milne, the creator of Winnie the Pooh, and Sir Philip Gibbs, the author and commentator. Focusing on the perceived improbability of the Crown's theory of Rouse having suddenly concocted the idea of passing off the victim as himself after picking him up (though the Home Office later seemed to accept Rouse's supposed confession of having planned to haul in the victim outside the Swan and Pyramids at Whetstone), the writer wondered, 'Why, if he wanted to fade away, should he not have done so, without taking the risk of a charge of murder and a criminal hue and cry?' For there was no suggestion that Rouse would gain financially by murdering an unknown man who was 'perhaps a tramp' and possibly epileptic, a proposition to which the department, suspicious of Mrs. Rouse's role in regard to a possible car insurance fraud, were sure they had an answer.

And as for his flight from the scene in Hardingstone Lane, followed by his stream of lies from the time of climbing aboard the lorry at the Hardingstone turn-off, via Tally-Ho Corner, Friern Barnet, the Embankment, Gellygaer, Newport and Cardiff, until he disembarked from the coach at Hammersmith, the 'Barrister-at-Law' opined that fear of a bigamy charge might have motivated him to avoid immediately contacting the police whose investigations into the 'accident' might have uncovered his murky past. The trial itself, the writer seemed to imply, was conducted in such a way that, with evidence regarding motive eschewed by the prosecution, the jury were predominantly confronted with the technical evidence. And the author smelled a rat. Whereas the Court of Criminal Appeal could invite a (presumably impartial) technical assessor to sit alongside them to advise the three members of the Bench, no such facility was available for a jury, where the technical experts were inevitably partisan, albeit not deliberately misleading, on one side or the other. The result, concluded our anonymous Barrister-at-Law, was that a jury, lacking an Einstein among its membership, 'may be fogged, and almost compelled to let the issue go by default, by reason of the weight of authorities, which they can grasp, rather than because of the weight of evidence, which they can't. That becomes trial by experts as much as trial by jury'. For they had '....no assessors to sit with them and to guide them through the mazes of the involved and intricate evidence of the experts; to expound to them the meaning and mystery of such things as 'the coefficient of the expansion of brass'' (which, as we saw in chapter 10, at least one expert today argues is, without more, a meaningless phrase). Thus their reception of the evidence was bound to be hazy, almost certainly prompting them to choose without understanding; a result which, the author hinted darkly, was Birkett's object all along, once the decision to omit the 'harem' evidence had been taken. That the Crown expert was *Colonel* Buckle, a Lloyd's assessor and veteran of the Great War, while the surname of the defence expert, floundering before Birkett's trick question on metal boiling points, was

---

as, effectively, a Conservative one). No details of the Rouse case are included in Margaret Lane, *Edgar Wallace: The Biography of a Phenomenon*, Hamish Hamilton, 1964 (first published in 1938). See also Neil Clark, *Stranger Than Fiction: The Life of Edgar Wallace, the Man Who Created King Kong*, History Press, Stroud, 2015.

286 *Sunday Dispatch*, February 8, 1931.

the Jewish-sounding Isaacs may not have been insignificant (see chapter 10).

Thus leaving aside the probable contamination of the scene of crime (or accident) consequent upon the ignorance, inexperience or incompetence (take your pick) of the Northamptonshire police in the first few hours after the blaze, we know today that 'experts', whether medical statisticians, medical researchers or forensic scientists, have been shown to be gravely fallible (see chapter 13). As the 'Barrister-at-Law' noted regarding contemporary experts,

> "A Continental criminologist made an interesting experiment in this connection. He conducted a group of scientific experts through a big hospital. He asked them if they had noticed a clock in the big ward. All of them had observed it, some of them thought they had noticed the time by it. There was no clock. What misled them was a barometer".[287]

The pressure was maintained in the *Daily Mail* on February 7 when a journalist rejoicing in the name of F. W. Memory commented acidly that, 'Belief in the equity of the British jury has received a rude shock during the past seven days during which verdicts which have been given in two criminal case have created much discussion and the taking of sides'. The first was the case of Evelyn Foster who had died of burns some hours after the taxi she owned and was driving at the time was set on fire by an unknown passenger in a remote stretch of countryside in Otterburn, Northumberland in early January 1931.[288] In this case what startled the journalist was the coroner's jury's refusal to follow the coroner's guidance when he challenged whether there were grounds to return a verdict of murder by an unknown assailant. Undeterred, this was indeed the verdict the jury returned (and while no-one ever stood trial for her homicide, it is now widely believed that she had been murdered by Ernest Brown, hanged at Armley Prison, Leeds, in 1934 for the murder of a former employer, an outcome that would ironically have vindicated the view of the stubborn coroner's jury).

But for Memory, the *Daily Mail* journalist, the Rouse case also demonstrated a divergence of views between judge and jury. For with Talbot J. questioning why a guilty Rouse would expose his presence to the two young men in Hardingstone Lane, instead of remaining hidden in the ditch till the coast were definitely clear, the jury was evidently recalcitrant towards this way of thinking (though it has to be said that Talbot, counter-intuitively in the light of that brief incident, came to believe that Rouse's guilt was confirmed when the Home Office told him about Lily and Rouse's insurance arrangements). Whether the two outcomes in the Foster and Rouse proceedings did indeed justify Memory's extreme headline, 'Shock to Faith in Juries', may be debatable. For even if Rouse's jury did convict on what the journalist clearly believed to be insufficient evidence, nonetheless, others might have commented that the verdicts represented victories for the independence of the jury (which harked back to the glorious principle in *Bushell's*

---

287 The criminologist was presumably a reference to Hans Gross and his *Criminal Investigation: A Practical Textbook*, Sweet & Maxwell, 1924 (first published in English in 1906). It is briefly discussed in Colin R. Moore and Gerry R. Rubin, "Civilian Detective Doctrine in the 1930s and Its Transmission to the Military Police in 1940-42", *Law, Crime and History*, Vol. 4 (3), 2014, pp. 1-30.
288 See Jonathan Goodman, *The Burning of Evelyn Foster*, Headline, 1977. For the obstructionism of the local chief constable in refusing to call upon Scotland Yard to solve the crime, see G. R. Rubin, "Calling in the Met: Serious Crime Investigation Involving Scotland Yard and Provincial Forces in England and Wales, 1906-1939", *Legal Studies*, Vol. 31 (3), 2011, pp. 411-41, at p. 430.

Case of 1670 when, despite being cowed and fined for contempt by the Bench, the Old Bailey jury refused to convict the Quaker, William Penn, of unlawful and tumultuous assembly when 'preaching in Gracechurch Street'). Whatever the correct interpretation, Memory's headline was sufficiently emotive to offer further ammunition for those who believed that a miscarriage of justice had occurred.

The Home Office's assessment of the post-trial press coverage was, however, that newspaper coverage had been temperate, though it observed that many publications felt that the evidence to convict could have been stronger. This latter opinion did not extend to the *Daily Express* where its chief reporter, Stanley Bishop, insisted that 'despite a great cleavage of public opinion, [and] that thousands of men and women expected that Rouse would be acquitted....never was a jury more abundantly justified in returning a verdict of 'guilty".[289] Apart from Rouse's arrogant demeanour in court (which, he suggested, those not attending the trial could not appreciate), Bishop also claimed that, 'Not all the facts in the possession of the prosecution were brought out. They could not be. Legal difficulties and the law of evidence forbade'. This presumably referred to Rouse's sexual 'bad character', but there were more matters that had come up before trial, some of which we have already noted. One, as yet unrevealed, aspect that he raised was the recent taking out of a further insurance policy on Rouse's life. Not only did Bishop consider this more than suspicious. We shall see later that the Home Office harboured suspicions that Rouse and Lily were in cahoots over an alleged insurance swindle which had led, intentionally or otherwise, to the victim's death. Rouse's Army identification disc was intended to play a role in this (and Lily to have packed it with his things as he set out for Leicester on November 5). Thus he had taken it with him on the journey, presumably with the view to its being found alongside or on the unrecognisable corpse in the burnt-out rubble. But according to Bishop that disc had never been found and perhaps he assumed that it had been lost in the flames (though we know that the Hammersmith police had found it in Rouse's attaché case, their possibly concluding that he had forgotten to leave it in the blazing car. The disc never surfaced again).

Then there was the matter of the alleged statement by five-year old Arthur Jnr., an account known to the authorities but not, of course, adduced in court. Bishop believed this suppressed evidence was also damning. Finally, the journalist concluded, the victim had not been picked up at random, but had been carefully selected beforehand by Rouse because he fulfilled the requirements of the friendless and relative-free 'vagabond-type'. While such a person would not be reported missing, Bishop was convinced that such a person *was* now missing from his usual haunts where he had previously scrounged for food, drink and coppers. So, even if the public might question whether the Crown, on the basis of the evidence adduced at the trial, had proved guilt beyond reasonable doubt, Bishop insisted that there had been more to the case than met the eye and that what had *not* been disclosed at the trial was conclusive as to Rouse's guilt. So *he* may have been convinced that no miscarriage of justice had occurred, but the inconvenient truth was that the test for guilt or acquittal had to be confined to what had been properly admitted as evidence at the trial, and to nothing else (though the criteria regarding an appeal against conviction or in respect of a

---

289 *Daily Express*, February 2, 1931.

reprieve might be different).

By contrast, the Communist Party's *Daily Worker* of the same date insisted that a prisoner was being sent to the scaffold on the most flimsy and circumstantial of evidence. Nothing, it protested, had been proved against Rouse, and it was only the brilliance of Norman Birkett that had persuaded the jury otherwise. Indeed, the paper reminded its readers that the trial judge had to correct Birkett who had told the jury that the question was whether Rouse had committed murder. For as Talbot J. pointed out, the actual question for the jury was whether the prosecution had established that Rouse was guilty of murder beyond reasonable doubt; a more nuanced and legally accurate question. Indeed, the capitalist press on the Sunday after the trial had run riot over stories of Rouse's relations with women, 'relations which in a Prince or Duke would only be matters of amused discussion among the bourgeoisie. It is obvious that these stories, rather than the evidence, influenced the jury in their verdict', a proposition which, of course, is plausible but also incapable of proof.

The conclusion of the *Daily Worker* was that, 'we unreservedly condemn the death sentence on Rouse'. Capital punishment in capitalist societies, it proclaimed, was targeted at those perceived as a menace to the established order, whereas they were victims of a rotten system of society. Rouse was, by inference, one such victim (though it is difficult to see how, apart from crude reductionist reasoning, it could be argued that this commercial traveller in garters and braces fell into the category of exploited wage slave from whom his employers extracted surplus capital). Under this system, 'someone has to be punished, and once an individual falls into the hands of the police, escape is often almost impossible, as the Podmore case showed'. Podmore's case was, however, a puzzling example for the *Daily Worker* to cite in support. For, since his conviction in 1930 there has been little or no questioning of the guilt of William Podmore, a convicted thief and fraudster, for the murder of his employer, Vivian Messiter, an oil company agent in charge of a depot in Southampton. Perhaps there was more mileage in its complaint that the pregnant Mrs. Wise was still in prison 'for a crime of poverty, kept there by Mr. J. R. Clynes' whose record as Home Secretary suggested to the paper that, 'Under the Labour Government the administration of capitalist justice is even more barbaric than under 'Jix'', that is, the right-wing and somewhat anti-semitic previous Home Secretary, William Joynson-Hicks.[290]

---

290   *Daily Worker*, February 2, 1931. On Podmore see, inter alia, Hugh Young, *My Forty Years at the Yard*, W. H. Allen, 1955, Chapter Five; Tom Tullett, *Murder Squad: Famous Cases of Scotland Yard's Murder Squad*, Grafton, 1996, pp. 88-94. For 'Jix' see David Cesarani, "The Anti-Jewish Career of Sir William Joynson-Hicks, Cabinet Minister", *Journal of Contemporary History*, Vol. 24 (3), 1989, pp. 461-82. Mrs. Olive Wise had been convicted on Christmas Eve 1930 of murdering her baby. The sentence was commuted to penal servitude for life and she soon gave birth to twins in prison in February 1931. For brief details see the *Straits Times* [Singapore] March 9, 1931. Her experience coincided with an attempt by Edith Picton-Turbervill MP to reform the law in the Sentence of Death (Expectant Mothers) Bill, which would allow such prisoners temporary release from prison to give birth elsewhere. The Home Secretary at that time had no power, apart from the provisions of the anti-suffragette 'Cat and Mouse' Act, to permit temporary release. There was in fact a maternity ward at Holloway and children born in prison were registered as having been born at a numbered property in Holloway Road. See letter by Picton-Turbervill in *The Times*, February 10, 1931. Mrs. Wise had been visited by Mrs. Clynes in Holloway Prison and this had inspired Mrs. Rouse to telephone Mrs. Clynes, seeking the latter's help to intercede with the Home Secretary on behalf Mrs. Rouse's husband. For this episode, see J. C. Cannell, *New Light on the Rouse Case*, John Long, c. 1931, pp. 146-7.

Interestingly, the newspaper's opposition to capital punishment was confined to capitalist societies. For in socialist societies the death penalty, imposed by a revolutionary working class which would have swept away the rotten remains of the old order, would only be inflicted as an act of 'social protection...where the anti-social deed threatens to undermine the Workers' State'. It was as if it had been written by Stalin's trusted advisers. Which one might suppose was, indeed, the case in the 1930s.

CHAPTER THIRTEEN

MURDERER HEARS HIS FATE UNMOVED

EVENING NEWS, February 23, 1931

The Court of Appeal

As soon as the outcome of the trial was published in the press, Rouse's legal team were once more approached by engineers concerned at Birkett's dismissive attitude towards Isaacs' testimony and, of course, at its presumed effect on the jury. Among the correspondence is a letter from John Chapman of Edgware, a member of the Institution of Mechanical Engineers, who wrote to Finnemore on January 29, 1931. His terse account stated,[291]

> "This petrol union evidence is wrong, as the heat would cause the loosening. When a union is tightened the metal (in this case brass or gun metal) is stressed. At approaching dull red heat this metal would stretch under the stress, and on cooling this stretch remains—and the nut is loose. With a steel or iron nut or bolt, the temperature would be red heat [sic] and the action would be masked by scale forming on the thread and joining the surfaces. There is almost no scaling with brass or gun metal".

Similarly, a Dutch engineer, H. de Wilde, wrote from The Hague on February 1 (though he erroneously wrote '1930' at the top of his letter). Referring to the report of the trial in the *Daily Mail* of January 31, he reiterated to Finnemore in confidence (as he did not 'want to be mixed up in this matter') that on the petrol union, while the nut and thread might expand identically with heat and then contract at the same rate on cooling down, thereby restoring the status quo, nonetheless, above a certain temperature, resulting in the components becoming red hot, distortion occurs and the nut is thus loosened.

Fred Price, the joint owner of Charles Price & Sons, a firm of engineers and boilermakers from Broadheath, near Manchester, was so concerned about the unfairness of the trial that he actually sent to Finnemore, on the following day, a typical brass union with three nuts which had been heated up and cooled. In every test conducted, he pointed out, the nuts had become loosened. However Price's explanation was slightly different to De Wilde's in that the masses of the metals were not equal. Moreover, since the nuts were of lighter weight than the union, the union, by reason of its greater mass, expanded more than the nuts on heating up. This forced the nut to expand '....over its elastic limit, forcing it to move slightly on the thread. When this cools again the nut is not able to go back to its original size, because it has been overstressed, and it is then found to be slack upon the thread.'

But despite their disagreement on the heat transfer process, they were both clear that the nut could become loose without direct human intervention after intense heating followed by cooling down.

Another communication came ten days later from W. S. Thompson in Dundee. He sent to Finnemore a sample piece of screwed rod fitted with two nuts, on which he had undertaken experiments. The nut that was heated to 700 degrees Centigrade before being allowed to cool was slack while the other (unheated) nut remained tight. He presumed that the nuts had originally been manufactured from bars that had been rolled to a hexagonal section, during which process the metal was compressed and in a state of internal stress. Following heating this metal would expand but would not return to its original size (on cooling). Again, it was an experimental finding that offered an alternative to the Crown's interpretation as to why the petrol union joint had been loose on Rouse's car.

J. P. Line from Gidea Park wrote an undated letter to A. P. Marshall in which he stated that after his own car had burnt out in July 1928 he, although not an engineer, found that 'ALL nuts etc were very loose on their bolts after the fire, though quite tight before'. The presence or absence of spring washers also made no difference to this finding, but most significantly, perhaps, was his revelation that it was Colonel Buckle's firm, Messrs Ellis & Buckle, that had inspected his vehicle for the insurance company. Did Line's letter therefore raise the implication that Buckle was being wilfully ignorant in his trial testimony, or careless? Or did it do nothing to invalidate the gallant colonel's evidence?

Another correspondent, S. H. Moorfield from Wigan, wrote to Rouse's solicitors on February 14. He was 'amazed' that the Crown's technical witness had been unable to offer a scientific explanation for the loose petrol union nut. He pointed out that when the whole union is screwed up tightly 'some parts of it are in tension, some in compression and the metal is slightly strained.' In this situation the nut would resist further tightening. However, when heated sufficiently to soften the metal, it is free to stretch and compress as required, and,

> "....thus all tensile and compressive stresses disappear. On cooling down, the resistance to further turning of the screw no longer exists and therefore further tightening is possible. How much it would be possible to turn the nut depends upon the pitch of the thread and the degree of heating".

Moreover, in his opinion, the finding of a slack nut in those circumstances was very poor evidence of its having been loosened deliberately since it was 'exceedingly common' for vibration to cause the slackening.

In Moorfield's case, it is not surprising that his correspondence did not reach the public domain, unlike that of the two following expert correspondents who contacted the defence team after the trial. For there was nothing in Moorfield's letter to indicate whether or not he could be counted as an expert. Moreover, what he had to say, though no doubt prompted by concern at Rouse's fate on the basis of what he clearly felt was inaccurate Crown testimony, did not actually offer anything to add to what Isaacs, Cotton and Bamber had already said in court.

But it was the expert evidence of H. S. Rowell of West London, and also the practical knowledge of Horace Carew who lived in the City of London area, that the defence team wished to adduce at the appeal hearing. And as indicated previously, the request by Sir Patrick Hastings to produce this additional evidence was peremptorily refused by the Court of Criminal Appeal on the ground that, if it were to be admitted, it would then be necessary to call expert Crown evidence to endeavour to refute it.[292] But although a man's life was at stake, the appeal judges were more concerned at the bother this might cause to the proceedings (or to their own private arrangements in the 'country'?). And in any case, said Lord Chief Justice Hewart, the jury had heard the expert evidence and had decided accordingly; which ignored the inconvenient truth that the defence were claiming that Buckle's evidence both defied common observation and also the scientific principles underpinning heat transfer.

Carew described himself as the former managing director of a car import business in Tokyo from 1910 to 1925. This had offered him wide practical experience both in the motor trade and as a motorist. After the Tokyo earthquake and fire of September 1, 1923 he had inspected hundreds of cars destroyed in the fire and, '...in every case, except where the metal had been entirely fused by the heat, it was noticeable that all oil and petrol union[s] were found loose.' He could not offer a scientific explanation for the phenomenon and also considered that vibration had to be a cause in other cases. Presumably Carew's experience regarding the intense nature of the post-earthquake fire (in a country with notoriously fragile building structures), together with his inspection of the large number of vehicles destroyed at the same time, were a tantalizing prospect for the defence team to exploit, if offered the opportunity.

Henry Rowell was a chartered civil and mechanical engineer with a further host of professional qualifications. He was, inter alia, a doctor of science from London University, a lecturer in engineering at Leeds University (1912-1914), an associate of the Royal College of Science (now Imperial College, London), a fellow of the Institute of Physics and a member of the Institution of Automobile Engineers (both of Britain and of New York). During the war he had served with the Royal Artillery, transferring to Woolwich Arsenal in 1916 to become Assistant Superintendent of its laboratory. In 1917 he was appointed Deputy Director of Armaments Production at the Admiralty with the rank of Honorary Captain, Royal Marines. This work earned him the OBE in January 1919. After the war he became manager of the light engineering department at the Elswick works of Sir W. G. Armstrong, Whitworth & Co (he had earlier been the recipient of a Whitworth Scholarship originally endowed in 1868 by the famous Manchester toolmaker and engineer, Sir Joseph Whitworth). Thereafter, for some years he had been a member of the Screw Threads Committee and the British Engineering Standards Association. He had taken out several patents on the locking of screw threads and had undertaken a study of the circumstances causing nuts to become loose. For nine years he had been director of the Research Association of British Motor

292   The two experts' evidence is reproduced in Normanton, *op. cit..* Appendix VI.

& Allied Manufacturers and was still a consultant to that body, and for eighteen months had been engineering director of the British Dardelet Threadlock Corporation and still remained a consultant to the company.[293]

On the day of the trial verdict, Rowell had telegraphed to Finnemore that the evidence given by Isaacs had been correct while that of Buckle was wrong. He followed this up with a letter on February 2 offering to testify 'in a scientific way' without any fee (only travel expenses) if an appeal were to be heard. While he was 'entirely indifferent about the final result', he found the technical evidence at Northampton 'wholly unsatisfactory'. In particular, he was '....very indignant in regard to Mr. Birkett's cross-examination on 'co-efficients of expansion''.

His short report to Finnemore dealt with both the loose nut and the carburettor. As to the former, he observed that, 'Even when nuts are quite tight they will work loose in many cases. There have been more inventions to attempt to correct this than in almost any other branch of engineering'. No doubt that included a number of patents taken out by Rowell himself from the 1920s.[294] He explained that with the application of ferocious heat to structures, intense vibrations would tend to follow due to distortion and to convection currents. Such vibrations could themselves loosen nuts. However, there were several further causes. For example, stressed metals yield and stretch, reflecting the state of internal strain within metals. With heating, the strains vanish. In industry this process was known as 'annealing'. Thus tightening a nut on a bolt would strain and stress the metal. But when heat is applied, the disappearance of these effects means that the parts 'are no longer gripping one another'. Post-fire, the discovery of a loose nut must be invariably attributed to the heat as there would be no evidence to prove prior human intervention (though no doubt anyone could envisage a malicious hand at play. But the evidence to prove it would presumably require to be direct, in the absence of overwhelmingly compelling circumstantial evidence).

Regarding the carburettor, Rowell explained that since the alloys used in casting the part were of a low melting point, it was therefore 'easily possible' that given the heat generated under the car during the fire, the weight of the copper piping combined with the softening of the metal would lead to fracture near the joint (though he did not amplify this explanation in lay terms). Petrol would then flow out from the float chamber, be ignited and flash back to the chamber, creating an explosive mix. Given the small vent hole in the carburettor lid, this mix would suffice to blow the lid and the needle out of the float chamber. The heat would be so intense that the rim of the float chamber would become fused. Convection would then tend to draw the rim inwards, thus locking in the float. While this might seem overly technical for the lay-person, Rowell ended by stating categorically that, 'In my opinion the state of the carburettor is quite consistent with the top having been blown off and not removed by hand. Experiments have since been made in my presence and confirm this opinion.'

So here was a top-class expert with a wealth of cognate theoretical and practical experience which could put Buckle's credentials in the shade. He was prepared

293 See his obituary published by the Institution of Mechanical Engineers, 1952, at www.gracesguide. co.uk. For his Admiralty service see ADM196/101/178.
294 See the Assignee Patent Directory at www.patent.ipexl.com/assignee/henry_snowden_rowell_1. html.

to come forward to help the defence, at only minimal cost, after being disgusted at reading what he clearly considered to be scientific nonsense spouted by the Crown's 'expert' during the trial itself. But perhaps the most astonishing feature of Rowell's offer was that it was made just two weeks before the death of his wife, Maud, at the tender age of 38. We do not know the cause of her death, whether it was sudden, an accident, or after a prolonged illness. But there is no evidence to suggest that the offer was withdrawn before the hearing of the appeal on February 23, exactly a week after Maud's death. Perhaps that is a measure of Rowell's sense of injustice meted out to Rouse by the jury's apparent acceptance of Buckle's evidence (for in no sense did Rowell have any sympathy for Rouse himself).

But there was one more technical witness who was *not*, so far as we can gather, on the list of experts whose testimony could help the defence. Indeed, the defence were probably unaware of this person's existence, though he was far closer to the events, both spatially and chronologically, than any of the other experts available to testify. He was, in fact the proprietor of the Augustine Garage in Commercial Street, Northampton but, more crucially, lived in High Street, Hardingstone. At eight o'clock on the morning of November 6 he, together with a friend, saw the burnt-out wreckage of the car as he made his way to work. This man, William Smethers (or Smeathers), actually gave a statement to PC Valentine on December 4 [295] explaining that he had stopped his journey to his garage, looked round the vehicle, and saw that the offside bonnet was up. He inspected the petrol tank, noticed that it was in a sound condition and 'remarked that it was funny the cap was on and I thought the tank would hold petrol if any was put in.' He next examined the cap,

> "....to see if I could see where the fire started and in my opinion it did not start near the petrol tank. If it had started near the petrol tank or at the engine the seams of the tank would have blown out. The fire in my opinion started at the rear of the car."

There are three highly significant points in the statement. First, the words 'rear of the car' had been underlined, though we do not, of course, know who underlined them. However the suspicion must be that it was a senior member of the Northamptonshire Constabulary such as Lawrence or Tebbey. Otherwise, it could have been Paling from the DPP's office, or Blackwell from the Home Office, as he reviewed the evidence regarding a reprieve. But the point is that someone on the Crown side knew of the statement whereas it is almost certain that if the defence had been aware of it, they would have been bound to call Smethers as a defence witness at the trial. Second, the substance of Smethers' statement surely supports the defence's interpretation that the fire had been started as a result of the carelessness of the victim when, with a lighted cigar in his hand, or mouth, he replaced the petrol can in, or pulled the can from, the back seat, that is, 'at the rear of the car', in Smethers' words. The witness made no mention of any loose petrol joint (or nut) or of petrol having soaked the passenger footwell, though evidence for these may not have been visible. Nonetheless, evidence *for* the Crown's interpretation is absent in this witness's account. But the third point

295 The document is in the Northamptonshire Police archives.

is why the defence remained in ignorance of this statement. Obviously it would hardly have been in the Crown's interest to 'put it in' and to call Smethers and given its potential support for the defence case, it was scarcely in the Crown's interest to let the defence know of its existence. This, in fact, was one of the scandals of criminal court procedure until radical changes were made from the 1990s (following the spate of miscarriages of justice, including many of the Irish terrorist cases, when Crown evidence supporting the defence case was not disclosed to the other side). In short, in 1930, the Crown were not obliged to disclose to the other side evidence in its possession that might vindicate the accused. So Smethers' evidence was almost certainly withheld from the defence. But that raises a further matter. If Carew, Rowell, Isaacs, Cotton and others came forward to offer their insights to the defence, why did not Smethers? We can never know the answer. But given that he was local and almost certainly knew Copping and Hedley Bailey, did he believe that his duty was to support his local policemen neighbours? Or was he, perhaps, pressurized by them and by Valentine not to contact Lee-Roberts and the defence team? Certainly there is a strong whiff of cover-up in respect of Smethers' evidence, made more pungent by the fact that, unlike Buckle, he had actually examined the car within twelve hours of the blaze. And while the inspection might not have been thorough (how could he have seen what was *under* the burnt-out chassis?), his conclusion was definite. The fire had started in the rear, just as the defence had insisted.

We have seen above that the appeal judges saw no need to hear further expert testimony for the defence. So the cogent arguments advanced by Rowell and others (and by Smethers and, possibly, by further Crown expert testimony in response) were not to be heard in court. The only audience left to hear about loose petrol union joints and carburettors (and possibly of a rear end fire) was thus the Home Secretary in subsequently contemplating a reprieve.

What Finnemore and Marshall personally felt about the trial verdict has not been recorded. But there seems little doubt that they were disappointed with the jury's verdict and had genuinely thought that Rouse had had, in the prisoner's own words, a 'sporting chance' of securing an acquittal. The trial outcome assuredly made them more determined to proceed to the appeal stage and to encourage Rouse to back their efforts. He himself had his own reservations as to whether his defence team had properly understood the technical and mechanical issues surrounding the car blaze (which assumes innocence on his part), and he would later express his frustration, before his execution, that counsel had chosen their approach to the issue in preference to his own 'take'. Leaving that aside, counsel now set about drafting their extensive grounds of appeal, which we shall examine below.

In anticipation of the hearing, Lily wrote to the Home Office on February 20, 1931 requesting that her husband be permitted to wear black morning coat and dark trousers at the Court of Criminal Appeal in London three days later when his appeal against conviction would be heard.[296] When that day arrived the three

---

296 Technically, as official court documentation showed, the procedure was that Rouse was applying for an extension of the time within which notice of appeal or application for leave to appeal might be given; for leave to appeal against conviction; for legal aid; for permission to be present during the actual appeal, as distinct from the application to appeal; for bail; and for leave to call further

judges took their places in the court, the 'doors of the court were locked against a struggling crowd of barristers and members of the public',[297] and the clerk of the court called out, 'The King against Alfred Arthur Rouse.' Then all eyes in the crowded court,

> "....turned towards a green curtain over in the corner, hiding a door..... The curtain was pulled back by an unseen hand and Rouse stepped through the opening. With two springy strides he was at the front of the dock, looking straight at the Lord Chief Justice. He wore black—a smart double-breasted black jacket and a black silk tie, with a stiff white collar. His rather wavy hair was neatly brushed back, and he looked just as spruce as he did during his trial. He was just as composed looking, too, though he seemed a little flushed as he stood absolutely still, waiting for Sir Patrick Hastings to make the last fight for his life."

Indeed, it was something of a *coup* for Rouse's solicitors to have secured the services of the former Attorney-General, a doyen among defence counsel and a worthy opponent for Norman Birkett who once again appeared on behalf of the Crown (Finnemore would be Hastings' junior on this occasion). While favoured with Hastings' presence, Rouse was, however, unfortunate in the choice of appeal judges who would listen to his counsel's argument why his conviction should be quashed. For presiding over the appeal was the Lord Chief Justice, Sir Gordon Hewart, himself a former Attorney-General and, like Hastings, a former journalist. Flanked by Hewart were the ascetic, severe and elderly Mr. Justice Avory and the more humane figure of Mr. Justice Humphreys, the former Crown prosecutor, Sir Travers Humphreys.

It is not for nothing that Hewart has the unenviable reputation of being considered one of the worst chief justices of the modern era. Even his appointment as chief justice in 1922 was a miserable political fix by Lloyd George, while his retirement was actually a forced resignation after a curt telephone call from Churchill at 10 Downing Street in 1940. As Robert Stevens in the *New Dictionary of National Biography* (2004) wrote of Hewart,

> "Unfortunately, his behaviour as a judge lacked many basic judicial qualities. He made up his mind early and was frequently boorish and rude to counsel. Out of court, he extended his discourtesy to fellow members of the bench and to the lord chancellor...."

Indeed his biographer, Robert Jackson, in an otherwise hagiographical study, found many instances of appeals when Hewart's impatience in hearing argument from counsel for which he obviously had no sympathy, shone starkly through the proceedings. And it must not be forgotten that the life of the appellant was at stake in those cases. Thus within a short span of time in 1922 he 'had dismissed almost contemptuously four appeals against sentence of death', involving the cases of Major Armstrong, Ronald True and Thompson and Bywaters.[298] Once

evidence. However, the substance was that it was his appeal against conviction. It is not giving away any secret prematurely to observe that all the applications failed, although he was present at the failed application for leave to appeal.

297 *Evening News*, February 23, 1931, for this and subsequent reporting, unless otherwise indicated.
298 Robert Jackson, *The Chief: The Biography of Gordon Hewart, Lord Chief Justice of England, 1922-*

again, Sir Patrick Hastings, with his perspicacity, captured the essence of Hewart on the bench. Thus, compared to what Hastings perceived as the courteousness, impartiality and desire for fair play evinced by a recent predecessor chief justice, Lord Reading (Sir Rufus Isaacs),

> "Lord Hewart was the direct antithesis, and it was a tragedy. At the Bar and in the House of Commons his career had been meteoric. He was a brilliant advocate, an astute politician, and as a man a charming and extremely delightful companion, but unfortunately it always appeared to me that he had no judicial sense whatsoever. I have no doubt that he equalled Lord Reading in his desire to see that justice should prevail in every Court over which he presided. Unfortunately the steps he took in order to achieve that result were those of an advocate and not of a judge. The moment he arrived at a conclusion as to which side should prevail, he appeared, whether he intended to or not, to strain every effort to bring about the verdict which he considered right. As a result, nobody was satisfied and the trial appeared one-sided from the outset."[299]

It is, however, only fair to point out both Hewart's distaste for trial judges imposing lengthy sentences of penal servitude for property offences, and also one of his more welcome lasting legacies. And that latter was his dictum in the Divisional Court case of 1924 when he quashed the conviction of a motorist because the magistrate's clerk worked for the same firm of solicitors that advised the prosecutor. As he declared, 'Justice must not only be done but should manifestly and undoubtedly be seen to be done'.[300] But this was one of the few noble exceptions, in a chief justice regime lasting 18 years, which merely proved the rule. For as with many of his trials, so with his Appeal Court hearings, with a succession of dismissive rejections to his name, and the cursory disappearance, often after a brief half-day appeal hearing, of the second-last hope of the condemned prisoner, to escape the gallows. Arthur Rouse's appeal was one such example where reasoned arguments for a reconsideration of his conviction, on the grounds of a prejudiced trial, of far from compelling circumstantial evidence against him, and of the existence of new expert technical evidence not available at the trial which would strongly challenge Colonel Buckle's prosecution testimony, were more or less cursorily swept aside. It is, however, important to add two points. First, Hewart did not sit alone in the appeal court. For both Avory and Humphreys concurred with Hewart that Rouse had been properly convicted. But it is still helpful to see how they formulated their conclusion. Second, it must be remembered that an appeal court hearing does not involve a rehearing of the case against the accused, for the jurors are the triers of fact. However, as noted later in this chapter, legal argument can be joined between counsel regarding the evidence that had been adduced at, commented upon by the judge during, or ruled inadmissible by him at the trial.

1940, Harrap, 1959, p. 155. Indeed in his subsequent biography of the London coroner, Sir Bentley Purchase, Jackson wrote that, '...in his later years [Hewart] had grown into an intolerant bully on the Bench. Hewart often did great disservice to English justice by his innumerable prejudices', often deciding cases according to whether or not he liked whichever counsel was present. See Robert Jackson, *Coroner: The Biography of Sir Bentley Purchase*, Harrap, 1963, p. 38.

299 Sir Patrick Hastings, *The Autobiography of Sir Patrick Hastings*, Heinemann, 1948, p. 135.
300 *R v Sussex Magistrates, ex parte McCarthy* [1924] 1 KB 256.

The senior puisne (that is, unpromoted) judge sitting with Hewart was the spare and gaunt figure of Horace Avory, often considered to be a 'hanging judge'. The tragic Mr. Justice McCardie (as noted previously, he later committed suicide) once told the story of a,

> "....certain impassive judge in an important criminal trial at the Northampton Assize Court. His hands never moved and his eyes never moved all the time the counsel spoke. Then, after an hour, the judge spoke and a little girl in the front of the gallery, sitting there with her father, jumped up, her voice thrilling with excitement as she called out: 'Why, daddy, it's alive!'"[301]

That judge could have been none other than Avory. Yet Rouse's new counsel, Hastings, who was not a dewy-eyed sycophantic type of barrister, but who had been a member of Avory's chambers before the latter's elevation to the Bench, considered him to be a 'great' judge.

> "His reputation for cold severity remained with him throughout the many years he sat upon the bench but it was quite undeserved; to a guilty criminal he was inflexible and his punishments, though just, were hard; but I am certain that no innocent person was ever convicted in a Court over which he presided. If I were guilty Horace Avory was not the Judge whom I would have selected for my case; but if I had been innocent I should have been overjoyed to feel that my future lay in his hands."[302]

According to Avory's entry in the *New Dictionary of National Biography* (2004) (which entry should be treated with caution since one of the present authors wrote it!), his career at the Bar had seen him involved in some of the most sensational prosecutions around the turn of the century. They ranged from the Cleveland Street male brothel scandal (1889-90) to the trials of Oscar Wilde (1895), the Jameson Raid plotters which involved Cecil Rhodes (1896), and the arch-fraudster, Horatio Bottomley (1909). Avory escaped condemnation for his role in the continued miscarriage of justice which kept the innocent Adolph Beck in prison long after the authorities knew he had been a victim of mistaken identity, one of the handful of cases which prompted the creation of the Court of Criminal Appeal in 1907. Appointed a judge in 1910 he went on to preside over major trials such as that of Sir Roger Casement (1916), Field and Gray who murdered Irene Munro on the 'Crumbles' at Eastbourne in 1920, Patrick Mahon, yet another 'Crumbles' murderer (1924) at whose trial the judge ordered the removal of women from the jury in case they might be distressed by the medical evidence, and Browne and Kennedy (1928), hanged for the murder of P C Gutteridge in rural Essex. Called upon by the government to chair numerous inquiries into various branches of the criminal law, he was small of stature and 'desiccated in appearance'.[303] Indeed 'it was said of him that he was spare of flesh and sparing of compliments, but never spared criminals'.[304] His fellow judge at Rouse's appeal, Mr. Justice Humphreys, once observed that any judge who saw the law both as his hobby and as his profession, as was the case with Avory, perhaps enjoyed a more

---

301 George Pollock, *Mr Justice McCardie: A Biography*, John Lane, The Bodley Head, 1934, p. 54.
302 Hastings, *op. cit.*, p. 124.
303 Jackson, *The Chief...*, *op. cit.*, p. 288.
304 D. G. Browne and E. V. Tullett, *Bernard Spilsbury: His Life and Cases*, Reprint Society, 1952, p. 277.

cloistered existence than others of his calling. The sense of lofty detachment in his court was total, though Hastings' panegyric cannot be wholly dismissed.

Travers Humphreys' career mirrored to some extent that of Avory's. As with the latter, criminal law was his *forté*, a less common specialism when, as today, commercial law was more financially rewarding for a practitioner. Humphreys first prosecuted for the Crown in London in 1905, appearing at the Old Bailey in 1908 as junior counsel, then from 1916 as senior Crown counsel. He was involved, sometimes accompanying Avory, in the prosecutions of Oscar Wilde, Crippen, Frederick Seddon, Roger Casement, Horatio Bottomley, the 'Brides in the Bath' murderer, George Joseph Smith, and Thompson and Bywaters. He became a judge in 1928, presiding over the trials of the socialite, Elvira Barney, Rattenbury and Stoner and, later in life, the 'Acid-Bath' killer, John George Haigh. Indeed, his son, Christmas Humphreys, often appeared before him prior to Humphreys Jnr.'s own elevation to the Bench in 1962, which resulted in the unusual spectacle of an English judge, professing the Buddhist faith, presiding over criminal trials. In the post-war period Humphreys Snr. would often sit alongside Lord Chief Justice Goddard to hear appeals against conviction. He probably considered it a more satisfying experience than sitting with Hewart whose judicial style was always grating. With Goddard there was almost a kindred spirit in their determination to uphold 'law and order' with firmness when violent youth gangs, previously undisciplined (it was believed) when their fathers were away in the Forces during the war, were perceived as the 'folk-devils' of the day (though Goddard's egregious displays of weaponry, for example, the knuckle-duster found on Derek Bentley, and which Goddard produced before the jury at the Craig and Bentley trial in 1953, may not have been to Humphreys' taste). In short, though no soft touch, Humphreys was a more balanced trial and appeal judge than were Hewart or Goddard. Colleagues, obituarists and biographers (there were three biographies of Humphreys) lauded his achievements. He was 'one of the most successful judges' in his field, a 'most competent judge', a 'first-class brain' (yet he obtained only a Pass degree!) and evinced 'scrupulous fairness'.[305]

Such judgments are, of course, frequently coloured by the personal knowledge of those passing those opinions within a tightly-knit Bar where conservatism, the upholding of superior class values, etiquette, *politesse*, and a rigid hierarchy where patronage tended to prevail, were crucial factors. Most studies of the lives and careers of judges of the pre-war period, leaving aside those that were autobiographical, verged on the hagiographical, including two 1930s studies of Avory, by Stanley Jackson and Gordon Lang, respectively. There have been significant studies in recent years of twentieth century judges, notably of lord chancellors who became more significant politically than legally, such as Neil Duxbury's recent work on David Maxwell-Fyfe, who became Lord Chancellor Kilmuir, Geoffrey Lewis' study of Quintin Hogg, the second Lord Hailsham, and John Campbell's study of F. E. Smith, Lord Birkenhead. However, with the possible exception of Professor R. F. V. Heuston's classic study of the lord chancellors between 1885 and 1940, it is only in recent years that we have begun to see more balanced academic studies of some of the prominent judges of the earlier twentieth century such as Foxton's recent study of Lord Justice Scrutton or

---

305   Douglas G. Browne, *Sir Travers Humphreys: A Biography*, Harrap, 1960, pp. 344-7.

Geoffrey Lewis' study of Lord Atkin. Even entries for twentieth century judges published from 2004 in the Oxford *New Dictionary of National Biography*, while generally more critical of their subjects than comparable entries in the earlier series some decades ago, are likely only to express provisional judgments pending fuller assessments (as one of the present authors well recognizes, having contributed entries on about a dozen such judges, including Avory, in the *New DNB*).[306]

One should therefore remain cautious about journalistic or 'popular' studies of famous twentieth century judges, often described as 'eminent' or 'distinguished', for critical distance must always be maintained. However this is not to say that (invariably positive) judgments on such public personages may not be valid or acute, but there has been a tendency in such works in the past to present an uncritically banal and favourable assessment of their subjects, perhaps due to deference or expectations or due to fears lest accusations of a form of *lesé-majesty* or a variant of contempt of court might be levelled against the authors.

As to Hastings, his early legal career under the tutelage of Horace Avory showed his strength in such branches of law as libel (he represented Marie Stopes in one such case). It did, of course, reflect his previous journalistic career, but he also practised in the financially rewarding branch of commercial law, especially defending insurance companies against false claims. He undertook a reasonable amount of criminal work, though was reluctant to appear in murder cases. Nonetheless, among his earliest murder cases was the defence, albeit unsuccessful, of George McKay, alias John Williams, convicted of shooting dead a policeman, Inspector Arthur Walls, during a burglary in Eastbourne in 1912.[307] No doubt assisted by being rejected, due to chronic asthma, for military service in the Great War, though he had spent two years with the Suffolk Yeomanry in the Boer War, he became a King's Counsel in 1919. Slightly to the left in politics, he became disillusioned with Lloyd George Liberalism and eventually became Labour MP for Wallsend from 1922. In January 1924 he was appointed Attorney-General in the first ever (minority) Labour government under Ramsay MacDonald. But some months later that government came to grief over the 'Campbell Case'.[308] The controversy erupted when Hastings announced in parliament that he was no longer planning to prosecute one J. R. Campbell, the acting editor of the *Workers' Weekly* (later re-named the *Daily Worker*, and now the *Morning Star*), for incitement to mutiny. Hastings' attention had originally been drawn by the DPP, Sir Archibald Bodkin, to an article by Campbell in the Communist Party's newspaper, calling upon soldiers not to fire upon strikers. Various questions had been put

306 Stanley Jackson, *Mr Justice Avory*, Gollancz, 1935; Gordon Lang, *Mr Justice Avory*, Jenkins, 1935; Neil Duxbury, *Lord Kilmuir: A Vignette*, Bloomsbury, 2015; Geoffrey Lewis, *Lord Hailsham: A Life*, Cape, 1997; John Campbell, *F E Smith: First Earl of Birkenhead*, Random House, 1992; R. F. V. Heuston, *Lives of the Lord Chancellors, 1885-1940*, Oxford University Press, Oxford, 1964; David Foxton, *The Life of Thomas E. Scrutton*, Cambridge University Press, 2013; Geoffrey Lewis, *Lord Atkin*, Butterworths, 1983.
307 Belton Cobb, *Murdered on Duty*, W. H. Allen, 1961, Ch. 9.
308 See N. D. Siederer, "The Campbell Case", *Journal of Contemporary History*, Vol. 9 (2), 1974, pp. 143-62; F. H. Newark, "The Campbell Case and the First Labour Government", *Northern Ireland Legal Quarterly*, Vol. 20, 1969, pp. 19-42; J. L. J. Edwards, *The Law Officers of the Crown: A Study of the Offices of the Attorney-General and Solicitor-General of England....*, Sweet & Maxwell, 1964, pp. 199-215; ibid., *The Attorney-General, Politics and the Public Interest*, Carswell, 1984, pp. 310-18. See also Thom Young (with Martin Kettle), *Incitement to Disaffection*, Cobden Trust, 1976, pp. 37-9.

in parliament about the affair. But when Hastings (and Travers Humphreys) examined the matter in more detail, they concluded that a prosecution under the Incitement to Disaffection Act 1797 would be unlikely to succeed. For, inter alia, the tone of the article, which was published, as Hastings was well aware, by a highly decorated injured Great War veteran, the possessor of the Military Medal, could reasonably be read as merely discouraging soldiers to stay out of, and not to take the employers' or government's side in, industrial disputes. And that could well be distinguished from an article 'inciting them to mutiny' (one wit reckoned that every Labour MP at the time would have been vulnerable to criminal proceedings if a prosecution of Campbell had succeeded. In fact if Campbell had indeed encouraged soldiers not to fire on fellow-members of the working class, would this have been a criminal offence of encouraging them to disobey lawful orders or encouraging them to disobey unlawful orders?).

In the event, and in the wake of much harrumphing in the right-wing press, it was widely perceived, correctly or otherwise, that Hastings had improperly allowed political considerations, that is, pressure from Labour ministers to uphold working-class interests, to interfere with his legal or quasi-judicial decision-making. However, the political damage for the government had been done despite Hastings' insisting in parliament that the decision to withdraw the prosecution was taken on legal grounds and was his alone. That may only have been partially true, for as one modern commentator, reviewing the convoluted story, concluded,

> "The position as I see it is that the cabinet asserted the right to interfere, and Hastings seems to have conceded that right. But in fact there was no political interference because the cabinet decided to adopt the course on which Hastings had already decided."[309]

In the end, few in the affair succeeded in covering themselves in glory. Bodkin's political prejudices may have influenced his initial approach to the Attorney-General, Hastings was lax throughout and inconsistent, the prime minister, Ramsay MacDonald, was duplicitous, and the opposition, as one might expect, were opportunist. The Labour government fell on a vote of confidence, even though the story of politicians instructing law officers as to what proceedings they must or must not take was not as black and white as the opposition painted it. The first MacDonald government was in due course voted out of office in the resultant general election. But its fall was undoubtedly aided following the publication in the *Daily Mail* of the forged Zinoviev letter a week before the election which suggested that the Labour government had been subservient to Moscow.[310] Hastings remained an MP for another two years, after which he

309 Newark, *op. cit.*, p. 40.
310 Today, we know that the Zinoviev letter, allegedly written on September 15, 1924 from Gregori Zinoviev, head of the Comintern, to the Communist Party of Great Britain, and which encouraged the CPGB to intensify 'agit-prop' among the armed forces and, generally, to prepare for the coming communist revolution, was a forgery. It was constructed by anti-Bolshevik White Russians and intercepted by MI6's Riga station. Thereafter, it went through the hands of MI5, Army commands, Scotland Yard and Conservative Central Office before being published in the *Daily Mail* on October 25, 1924, four days prior to the general election that returned a majority Conservative government. See Keith Jeffery, *MI6: The History of the Secret Intelligence Service, 1909-1949*, Bloomsbury, 2011, pp. 216-22; Christopher Andrew, *The Defence of the Realm: The Authorized History of MI5*, Penguin, 2010, pp. 148-52; ibid., *Her Majesty's Secret Service: The Making of the British Intelligence Community*, Penguin, 1987, pp. 301-16; Martin Pugh, *'Hurrah for the Blackshirts!': Fascists and Fascism in Britain Between the Wars*, Pimlico, 2006, pp. 87-8.

resigned his seat through ill health. He now resumed full-time court advocacy where, again, murder cases were a rarity.[311] His style was not showy. That had gone out of fashion with the death of Edward Marshall Hall in 1926. But Hastings was not averse to employing facial gestures of surprise, incredulity, even anger, to impress upon the jury, while the quick-fire delivery of his questions, especially in cross-examination, would often undermine the other side's witnesses to his own client's advantages. There was, indeed, a superficial similarity with Birkett's style, though the 'assassin' description that we conferred upon Birkett did not fit Hastings when confronting a witness.

So with the line-up settled for the appeal hearing, Rouse was due his second day in (a necessarily constrained) court. Interestingly, his application to appeal had stated that he had not been issued with a certificate from Mr. Justice Talbot confirming that his was a fit case for appeal. But that did not matter so long as the appeal judges consented to hearing his application to have his conviction and sentence set aside. It was also noted on the form that he did not desire the appeal court to assign him legal aid, which suggests that the legal aid certificate for his trial remained valid for his appeal. Accompanying the application was a statement prepared by his defence team outlining his grounds for appeal. In the normal course of events an appeal against conviction is not, as indicated earlier, an effort at having the case reheard by a differently composed tribunal. For the trial jury's verdict on the facts is normally final. They heard the evidence at first hand, they listened to the examination and cross-examination and viewed the demeanour of the witnesses, and were able to form their own judgments (which is what jury trial entails) of the evidence, of the veracity of the testimony, of counsel's speeches and of the judge's summing-up. So it is not a case of defence counsel telling the appeal judges that the jury was wrong in convicting the accused on the evidence they had heard. Indeed, it is a paradox that in the much-vaunted system of trial by jury in Britain the jury are *entitled* to go wrong, in the opinion of the judge, counsel and appeal judges. For the jury members are masters of the facts and judges are the masters of the law. Thus, so long as the jury have not 'taken leave of their senses' in convicting, the guilty verdict remains valid, even if wrong, unless a *legal* objection to the verdict, or the subsequent discovery of highly significant exculpating evidence not available at the time of the trial, were to find favour with the appeal court.

So the appeal judges' remit is a narrow one, as previously explained; which is not to say that no re-evaluation of the evidence at all could be considered by the appeal court. For the 'facts-in-issue' could intrude into the appeal court by a side-wind. Thus the defence might wish to argue that, on the basis of a deficiency of prosecution evidence, the trial judge had been wrong, at the close of the prosecution case and before the defence had been opened, in not directing the jury to acquit at that point (a ground of appeal raised by Rouse and now known as a *Galbraith* application). Alternatively the defence might claim that in the light

---

The title refers to a notorious *Daily Mail* headline of January 15, 1934 supporting the British Union of Fascists.

311   For a selection of his murder cases, including Rouse and Mrs. Barney, see Sir Patrick Hastings, *Cases in Court*, Pan, 1955, Ch. V. In accordance with the convention that one of the law officers was expected to prosecute in a poisoning case he successfully prosecuted the Frenchman, Vaquier, in 1924 when he was Attorney-General.

of all the evidence presented at the trial, no jury in their right mind could have convicted on that evidence. The defence might further seek to argue that the judge's direction during the trial on any matter of legal doctrine or of evidence or procedure was flawed, such as his admitting important evidence that ought to have been excluded on legal grounds, for example, that it was significant hearsay or, alternatively, his wrongfully refusing to admit important evidence that should have been allowed in. Or the defence might claim that the summing-up was unfair in over-emphasising certain incriminating or irrelevant matters and under-emphasising exculpatory factors, or that the trial judge interrupted counsel so frequently that the defence case could not be adequately put and grasped by the jury. Finally, the defence might seek to adduce evidence in its favour that, without fault on the part of the defence, was not available to the prisoner at the time of the trial. This might be, as in the Rouse appeal itself, expert testimony, not previously available, that rejects as scientifically unlikely the technical evidence advanced by the Crown at the trial which, as at least implied by Buckle, had been based on a deliberate tampering with the petrol union joint. Instead the defence could (and would) propose an alternative and compelling scientific interpretation based on further newly obtained scientific testimony to explain the accidentally brought about nature of the fierceness of the blaze (as distinct from explaining the blaze itself which Rouse had already attributed at the trial to his careless passenger). Thus in an appeal the defence might seek to adduce new scientific evidence that discredits the Crown's forensic case against the accused. One thinks, for example, of when the defence was eventually able to expose the shoddy laboratory work of Dr. Frank Skuse that had led to the wrongful conviction of the 'Birmingham Six'. For here the traces of nitro-glycerine found on the prisoners' hands had been wrongly interpreted as showing that they had been handling explosives, whereas the traces came from the coating on a pack of new playing cards that the men had been using on the train from Birmingham to Holyhead after they had attended the funeral of an IRA operative who had accidentally blown himself up. Or the defence might endeavour to expose on appeal the flawed statistical basis on which the Crown's expert witness, in this case Professor Sir Roy Meadow, had concluded that where more than one cot death had occurred in a family, foul play was the compelling interpretation. The recent cases in question were those of the tragic Sally Clark, Trupti Patel and Angela Cannings.[312]

So which line of attack did Rouse's defence take? Hastings' and Finnemore's grounds for appeal were in four over-lapping sections. First it was claimed that the conviction was against the weight of the evidence (the 'jury having taken leave of their senses' argument). This turned on Rouse's claim that the victim was a complete stranger whom he (Rouse) had had no reason to kill. Indeed no motive for the killing had been established, though the Crown had suggested a disappearing act (which Talbot J. had, of course, dismissed in the circumstances). Moreover there was no evidence of ante-mortem injury caused to the victim prior to the fire, thereby negating the suggestion that he had first been hit over the head with Rouse's mallet (again Talbot J. had directed the jury to ignore the mallet

312 More recently scientific testimony regarding the concept of 'shaken baby syndrome' has divided medical experts. See *New Scientist*, November 9, 2016 ('Shaken Baby Science Questioned'); *The Times*, October 9, 2015; *Guardian*, November 4, 2016 in respect of the work of neuropathologist, Dr. Waney Squier. There are a number of, primarily American, books on the question.

with its obscure hairs attached). Indeed it was again submitted that there was no evidence as to how or where the fire had started or that it was *not* accidental (raising the 'perverse' jury decision?). Thus, overall, the evidence pointed to death by accident rather than to death by malice. Moreover, though counsel did not specifically mention it at this point, the defence would wish, with permission, to submit new technical evidence not available at the time of the trial which would reinforce the claim that the victim's horrific death had been a ghastly accident. Indeed, that second ground of appeal, that is, accidental death, should have led, Hastings now insisted, to the trial judge withdrawing the case from the jury at the close of the prosecution case. Talbot J.'s failure to do so was therefore put forward as a solid ground for appeal.

The third head advanced on appeal was the whole business of prejudice, leading to an unfair trial, caused by the revelations at the police court of Rouse's extra-marital affairs and of his various illegitimate children. Even though such details were omitted from the trial itself, the damage to Rouse's reputation had already been done and in reaching their verdict the jury would have been unable to insulate themselves from those details in forming their conclusion as to his guilt. Fourthly and finally, counsel drew attention to evidence for the defence that was missing in the trial judge's summing-up (which would, of course, be the last thing a jury would hear before retiring to consider their verdict). First the position of the body across the front seats, which should have been mentioned in the summing-up, was as consistent with the victim falling onto that position accidentally as it was with the prosecution's claim that Rouse had pushed or thrown him down there. Second, assuming that the near-side door had been open (and Rouse claimed that it had been closed when, as he said, he returned to the car after relieving himself), that would still be as consistent with the victim's accidentally falling, as with a less innocent explanation. Third, the judge failed to point out a number of relevant features. They included no evidence offered explaining how the fire had started (though the prosecution had referred to a trail of petrol starting near where the mallet was found 14 yards in front of the car; no evidence regarding the splashing around of the petrol can inside the car; no evidence in respect of the loosening of the petrol joint; and none in regard to the alleged unscrewing or violent man-handling of the carburettor top.

Thus all four heads or over-lapping sections, it would be submitted, pointed to the fifth catch-all head, that is, that the trial judge had misdirected the jury in failing to direct them, or to direct them sufficiently, on Rouse's defence, especially with regard to his claim of accident. Indeed in law, the accused only required to raise such a defence in those circumstances. He was not obliged to prove such a submission on the balance of probabilities, let alone beyond reasonable doubt. It was, instead, for the Crown to disprove accident beyond reasonable doubt and to establish to the jury's satisfaction, again beyond reasonable doubt, the prisoner's homicidal act with 'malice aforethought'.

As it happened, even before the appeal hearing the Home Office were making arrangements for the new date of execution in the event of an unsuccessful appeal. For in response to a query by the magistrates' clerk and under-sheriff of Northamptonshire, J. Faulkner Stops, Sir Ernley Blackwell at the Home Office informed him on the day of the appeal that a final date for an execution should be fixed so as to allow an interval of not less than fourteen days and not more than eighteen clear days to elapse between the determination of the appeal and the date of execution. Thus if the appeal were to be dismissed that day, February 23, the execution could take place on any day between March 10 and March 14, and certainly not on March 6 as Faulkner Stops had first suggested. Thus either Tuesday March 10 or Wednesday March 11 would be a 'suitable day' (like the ironic 'suitable day for a hanging', as penned by the *Daily Mirror's* Cassandra when contemplating the dawning of the awful day of Ruth Ellis' execution in 1955).

Blackwell was, of course, correct in his prediction. As we shall see, the rejection of the appeal would prove to be almost a formality, the manner of its conducting undoubtedly puzzling to Rouse and to the spectators present. And when it was suddenly terminated without fanfare, the laypersons present, including Lily, Helen and Nellie, were no doubt bemused by the rapidity of its conclusion, and almost at a loss as to what to do next as the judges closed the file on Rouse. So how did the appeal proceed?

Apart from Finnemore and Marshall's lengthy draft of their grounds for appeal, Rouse himself had submitted a five-page memorandum to his solicitor, Lee-Roberts, prior to the appeal, setting out points that he felt had not been resolved at the trial. Most of it concerned Rouse's rejection of the Crown's claim that he had deliberately loosened the petrol joint nut in order to feed a fire that he had intentionally ignited. We will examine his claim in a later chapter. As to his other points, the first was to offer an explanation of how it might have appeared that he had been deliberately driving slowly from north London, presumably, implied the Crown, in order to commit the outrage in a lonely spot in the early hours of the morning when no-one would be about. Not so, he insisted. First he had left the maternity home at 8 pm (this was confirmed by Nellie's evidence) and could not have reached Buxted Road before 8:45 pm if he had been driving fast. Lily and Arthur Jnr. were not back yet so he waited 15 to 30 minutes outside the house (for some unexplained reason) awaiting their return. After their arrival Lily made him a meat tea and packed his belongings before he retrieved a can of petrol from the garage prior to setting off for Leicester. He never wore a watch and had a bad memory and therefore, in response to police questioning, he had merely guessed that he had left home around 8 pm, whereas he insisted in his memorandum that it could not have been before 10 pm. However if he had been driving at normal speed then it still seems slow progress to reach Markyate, a distance of 20 miles from his home in north London, at 11:15 pm when PC Lilley spoke to him regarding his car lights, unless there had been heavy north London traffic before he reached rural territory.

As for the stranger whom, he continued to insist in court, he had picked up somewhere near Tally Ho Corner (and before confessing in prison that he had actually picked him up at the Swan and Pyramids before going to Buxted Road to collect his things), he explained his ignorance regarding his passenger's identity by declaring that it was not usual to ask a hitch-hiker personal information, just as the lorry driver giving him a lift back to London had not asked him his name or other details. Instead he talked with the latter about vehicles and towns in the Eastern counties. Indeed the two men in the lorry had failed to pick out Rouse at an identity parade and only recognized him when all three were in court.

Presumably he was seeking to establish that he did not check out the background of his passenger to ensure that 'he would not be missed', thereby endeavouring to negate the suggestion that he had planned to find a suitable victim whose unrecognisable body would be assumed to be his.

In respect of Rouse's claim of ending up in Hardingstone Lane in error, he insisted that such a mistake, of veering off the main road, was easy to make. He was not wholly familiar with the route to Leicester and sometimes drove a different route, via Bedford. Moreover there were many deceptive bends en route, and thus it was just unfortunate that he found himself in Hardingstone Lane, a wide road lined with telegraph poles, he added (suggesting a major road?), with the engine spluttering and in need, as he thought, of more petrol.

Regarding an alleged plan to disappear, given how little money he had with him (about £4) when he left for Leicester, and at a time when he was clearing £10 a week, the idea was ludicrous. Indeed, he was expecting to receive £40 in expenses from his employer. So, if he *had* planned to disappear, it would have been sensible to wait until he had safely pocketed that amount. He further lamented that the excreta found by Dr. Telling, the local GP in Northampton, had not been laboratory tested by him nor, until too late definitively to determine its origin, by Dr. Harvey-Wyatt, the honorary pathologist at Bedford County Hospital. Yet he insisted that the finding of such material corroborated his story of relieving himself when he saw the blaze. He could have, but did not, mention that Harvey-Wyatt had confirmed that faecal material had also been found in a stain on the shirt worn by him (Rouse) at the time (the doctor did not add that it was of human origin, but neither did he say it might not have been).

Next, he referred to his hat. The sight of the hatless man emerging from the ditch had greatly surprised Brown and Bailey. And when, after they had asked each other what that bright glow was further up the road, and after Rouse had shouted back at them about its looking as if someone was 'having a bonfire up there', Brown had testified in court that '...what made us take more notice was to see a respectably dressed man with no hat on'. But that was precisely Rouse's point. Why draw attention to himself (even more) by not wearing his hat as he emerged from the ditch, if he had just been guilty of nefarious deeds? His answer was, obviously, that the hat had been lost in the accidental conflagration. Thus if he had deliberately set fire to the car with the man inside, surely he would have taken his hat with him? Instead when he went to relieve himself he left it behind in the car. Indeed he never wore it while driving, probably because it was not wholly comfortable when placed against the site of his war wound. He did, of course, take his *attaché* case with him (he thought that the passenger had earlier tried to rifle through it) as he searched for a secluded spot. The essence of his point was therefore that after the call of nature he was, of course, intending to return to the vehicle, containing his hat, and if he had truly intended foul play, then why emerge hatless from the ditch. The latter could only be explained as resulting from the accidental destruction of his vehicle with the hat in it, while he was away from the scene.

Most of these points had *something* to commend themselves. Were they therefore arguments that the prosecution would be obliged to meet during the appeal hearing? First, if previously addressed during the trial, then the jury would have been aware of them and their possible significance. Consequently, such issues could not be raised again on appeal. But in fact they were details that had *not* been raised by the defence at the trial. So could Finnemore *now* raise them at the appeal court? Sadly, this was not permitted since Rouse had been in a position to disclose all these matters to his counsel before the trial, thereby theoretically enabling them to raise the points during the trial itself. However, it appears that he had failed to do so (and Finnemore and Lee-Roberts were not sufficiently curious to tease out this information from Rouse). On the other hand, had he already revealed them to his defence team before his trial, then his lawyers presumably could have assumed that they had had instructions from him to raise them at trial, assuming that they had not warned him that such a move would be inadvisable. Notwithstanding, given Rouse's (or their) failure to bring the points out at trial, that failure could not subsequently be rectified by the appeal court. Moreover, even if the barristers' error, if error it was, had amounted to gross negligence on their part, counsel at that time enjoyed immunity from being sued by disgruntled clients (and it is difficult to think of clients more disgruntled than those about to lose their lives as a result of an incompetently conducted defence). It is thus fair to say that Finnemore and Marshall (and Lee-Roberts and Darnell & Price) could breathe freely in the knowledge that legal recriminations at the instance of Arthur Rouse for any actionable failings on their part in defending him was pie in the sky (similarly in respect of possible disciplinary steps against them by their professional bodies).

And so we turn to the appeal hearing itself. In his opening remarks Hastings made clear that, with one minor factual disagreement, he was taking no issue with Talbot J.'s summing up, which he described as 'unassailable' (thus giving a hostage to fortune in regard to which Hewart did not hesitate to remind him). He then turned to his central theme, flagged up earlier in Rouse's typed grounds for appeal that accompanied the prisoner's application. Thus apparently distilling all the detailed bases for the appeal, Hastings concluded that the two broad grounds for appeal were, first, that his client had been convicted on 'prejudice' and, second, damned on 'very grave suspicion'. The former referred, of course, to both the broadcasting at the police court of Helen and Nellie's testimonies about their relationship with Rouse and about their illegitimate children, and to the revelation by Paling at the same proceedings that Rouse was paying court to several women in addition to his wife and, in particular, the disclosure by the DPP solicitor of Rouse's statement to Inspector Lawrence that his 'harem' had taken him to 'several places'. How, asked Hastings, could the trial jury possibly put such matters out of their mind when judging Rouse's guilt, try as they might? Such information ought not to have been revealed at the police court, given that it amounted to 'bad character' evidence which could only prejudice the jury against him. As he continued, the prosecution had vigorously pressed their case from the very beginning so that,

> "....this man's character was blazoned abroad in such a way that to any person who had a high or even a moderate view of his duties as a private citizen in his private life must have regarded this man's whole career with utter horror."

Such pleading, verging on hyperbole, on behalf of one's client is to be expected.

But even the detached Helena Normanton later commented that,

> "From that moment the accused was accurately, but from the purposes of an unbiased trial unfairly, branded as a callously immoral man; one who, in the judgment of that man in the street who ultimately so often becomes the man in the jury box, richly deserved a hanging anyhow, and was just the sort of villain who could be relied upon to burn up his car and an out-of-work passenger in order to defraud insurance companies and stage his disappearance from his seduced victims".[313]

For Hastings all these sexual and adulterous revelations were 'absolutely dreadful matters' that ought not to have been disclosed in the court of a legal system that set great store by the suppression of evidence showing the accused's bad character. That principle, he claimed, was breached in this case with dire consequences. This alone would justify quashing the conviction. But to every legal submission there is invariably a reply, and in this case it was Mr. Justice Avory who pointed out that it was Rouse himself who had originally disclosed his bad character in his voluntary statement to Inspector Lawrence and which Paling had duly adduced before the magistrates in the presence of the press. How could the prosecution be blamed for repeating that which Rouse himself had freely chosen to disclose? After all, one does not always know the motive behind a prisoner's admission of bad character and he may, indeed, consider it would redound to his advantage by disclosing the same (the obvious example is the case of a prisoner with a record for dishonesty, which he discloses, when he is on trial for a violence offence that he denies and which he claims is not his 'style'). But the further riposte to the claim of damaging prejudice was that juries were commonly warned in sensational trials to ignore what they might have read in the press about the events prior to the trial. Indeed the following year, one of Rouse's appeal judges, Humphreys J., presiding over the trial of Elvira Barney who would be successfully defended by Hastings, would similarly warn the jury to ignore press reports of the shooting, adding that much of the printed detail was inaccurate. Indeed Humphreys would not read reports of police court hearings of cases that he might later be called on to try. His first acquaintance with the details would only emerge when he read the depositions days before the trial. In a similar fashion, a number of counsel, including Hastings, would not visit their clients for instructions prior to the trial, for fear that they might be told something by the prisoner that might compromise the defence that counsel was planning to run. For example, and irrespective of guilt or innocence, counsel would not be in a position to deny the prisoner's presence at the scene of a crime, nor even to suggest that his client had never been seen by any witnesses near the scene of the crime, thus implying that he had not been there, if the prisoner had already told him that he had actually been there. But as in the Rouse trial, the Bench insisted that juries in capital trials must not set about their task in a cavalier fashion. For knowing that another life was at stake, they were enjoined to reach their decision with due care and solemnity, conscious of the standard of proof, beyond reasonable doubt, that was required of the Crown. They should not be diverted by extraneous

---

313   Helena Normanton (ed.), *Trial of Alfred Arthur Rouse*, William Hodge & Company Limited, Edinburgh, 1931, p. xv.

considerations such as Rouse's life-style and immorality. Of course, the modern observer will respond, 'How does one know what the jury is thinking?', and we do not know. For it is an imponderable to ascertain whether the jury was biased against this Casanova from the outset, though many psychological experiments confirm levels of bias against individuals simply for what they look like, let alone for what they have done or for what they believe, or are perceived by the jury to believe. We will touch on this matter in a later chapter.

With this line of attack, that is, rank prejudice against the accused on the part of the supposedly morally upright jury, unable to make headway, Hastings focused on his second point which was, simply, that Rouse was convicted, not on the circumstantial evidence (there was no direct or even persuasive forensic evidence), which was insufficiently strong to convict, but on 'very grave suspicion' emanating from the string of stupid and unnecessary lies and bizarre behaviour that commenced as soon as he had passed Brown and Bailey in Hardingstone Lane while the blaze was at its height. Combined with his supercilious, arrogant and pedantic performance in the witness box, a spectacle that was bound to 'put the back up' of those prepared to listen fairly to his exculpatory explanations, Rouse was a master at alienating those upon whom he depended for his continued survival. As Hastings later commented, 'If Alfred Arthur Rouse had only kept his mouth shut, he would never have been hanged'.[314] What Hastings meant was that all of Rouse's *ex tempore* remarks, that is, those to Brown and Bailey, the lorry driver and his assistant, the two coach company staff at the Embankment, the coach driver to Wales, the Jenkins family, Brownhill and the Welsh coach people, and also his spontaneous remarks to various policemen were not, by themselves, incriminating, though they were shot through with lies, boasting and dissembling, and were repellent to many. Even his comment to Sergeant Skelly at Hammersmith Broadway at 9:30 pm on Friday November 7, that he was 'responsible' and 'glad that it is over', only meant that he *felt* responsible for the blaze and that he was relieved no longer to be running from pillar to post. And as far as his written police statements were concerned, then apart from minor discrepancies, his accounts exculpating himself were consistent (though he altered the narrative both at his trial and, more dramatically, in his various alleged 'confessions' after conviction and before execution). Overall, insisted Hastings, there was nothing in the prosecution's locker to justify Rouse's conviction (and his loquaciousness was scarcely criminal).

But it was not only that Rouse's own bombastic verbosity was, for Hastings, a

314 Hastings, *op. cit.*, p. 191. Rouse was not the only notable prisoner to talk himself to the gallows. Apart from the previously cited cases of the arrogant Frederick Seddon and of Edith Thompson, the latter having been vainly implored by her counsel not to enter the witness box, another significant example is the Lanarkshire serial killer, Peter Manuel. For further references to Seddon, see, for example, Adrian Vincent, *A Gallery of Poisoners*, Warner Books, 1993, pp. 1-21 (chapter entitled, 'The Man Who Hanged Himself'); Gerald Sparrow, *Vintage Victorian and Edwardian Murder*, Victorian (and Modern History) Book Club, Newton Abbot, 1972, Part Two, p. 37; for Manuel see, for example, Hector MacLeod and Malcolm McLeod, *Peter Manuel: Serial Killer*, Mainstream Publishing, Edinburgh, 2009. As the authors note, in choosing to testify, 'He [Manuel] is sure he will succeed. Over the years, in his imagination, he has created an image of himself as a master criminal, highly intelligent, able to out-think the police, able to out-argue the lawyers. Now he can speak for himself, tell his tale without interruption, talk directly to the jurors and triumphantly prove his innocence'. See *ibid.*, p. 279. As Rupert Furneaux put it, 'His self-esteem and bravado were enormous'. See Rupert Furneaux, *Famous Criminal Cases 5*, Allen Wingate, 1958, pp. 21-95, at p. 94.

red herring that duped the jury. Motive was lacking. As the grounds for appeal stressed, the victim was unknown to Rouse. Therefore what possible reason would Rouse have for killing an absolute stranger? And as for creating an unrecognizable corpse followed by Rouse's proposed 'disappearing act', the prisoner, down to his last £4 and carrying an *attaché* case containing only a handful of overnight things as he set off from London, was hardly equipped to pull off such a plan (even if his trip to the familiar surroundings of the Jenkins family could be explained by the prosecution as reflecting a sudden change of the plan to disappear after being spotted by Brown and Bailey). Arguably, all these points were questions of fact that were before, or should have been put before, the jury, and therefore not for the appeal judges to consider. However, Hastings insisted there was a point of law here. For he cited one of the most famous murder cases in the nineteenth century, that of the Wainwright brothers, reported in *The Times*, December 2, 1875. Thus he quoted from Lord Chief Justice Cockburn who stated that,

> "Where the case rests wholly or mainly on circumstantial evidence, it does, no doubt, become a matter of vast importance that the identity of the person alleged to have been killed should be established. In such a case the question of some motive to take the life of the person killed becomes an essential element of the inquiry."[315]

Hastings did not elaborate the point before quickly moving on to his next argument, presumably resting on the concluding words of Cockburn's statement ('essential element of the enquiry'), even if the phrase 'vast importance' is not quite the same as 'indispensable'. For his following argument was that given the interference with Rouse's car due to police inefficiency, prosecution evidence regarding anything to do with the vehicle must be unreliable. In particular, such interference with the car's remains by unofficial photographers or members of the public might invalidate any sinister theory as to how the blaze had started (the defence did not need to prove a benign theory). The Crown, of course, were adamant that, to a greater or lesser extent, the position and condition of, inter alia, the petrol can and mallet, the petrol union joint, and the exposed carburettor and its bent needle, pointed to the deliberate setting fire to the vehicle. But Hastings claimed (though not in so many words) that if curious visitors to the scene, let alone Arthur Ashford with his more photogenic re-arranging of the steering wheel, had been poking around the debris, how could one be certain that it was not a local Hardingstone or Northampton sight-seer who had pulled off the carburettor head or had loosened the petrol union nut. And that is without taking into account the further mass of expert evidence now available to the defence as to how the nut innocently became one turn loose (which even Buckle had conceded in cross-examination was a possibility). But in what was undoubtedly the most dramatic episode during the appeal hearing, the appeal court refused to hear the new scientific witnesses for the defence on the ground, Avory J. pleaded weakly, that if they were to be admitted, the court would have to allow expert rebuttal evidence for the Crown—as if this were such a burden when a man's

---

315   For the Wainwright case see Richard D. Altick, *Victorian Studies in Scarlet: Murders and Manners in the Age of Victoria*, J. M. Dent, 1970, Ch. 1; also reprinted in Jonathan Goodman (ed.), *Masterpieces of Murder*, Magpie Books, 2004, pp. 356-64.

life was at stake. In any case, said Hewart, all that business about loosened nuts had been before the jury. But had '*all* that business' been exposed, or only a scientifically flawed and misleading portion of it? For with his dismissal, the chief justice overlooked the adduction of a mass of compelling scientific proof, and not just tentative surmise among three trial witnesses, that was consistent with non-interference with the nut. And he also overlooked Birkett's trick question to the defence expert, Isaacs, regarding the 'co-efficient of the expansion of brass', which wrongly painted the latter as an ignoramus out of his depth. On the latter point, the reality was that the distinguished Birkett had engaged in a disreputable and unworthy (and mathematically flawed) attack on the witness's specific expertise by highlighting a technical deficiency of knowledge on Isaacs' part that bore not at all on the witness's wide experience of such matters. And, as a result, Birkett's 'low blow' effectively consigned Rouse to the gallows, a feature of this counsel's glittering career which his admirers would no doubt wish to gloss over. And even the evidence that the carburettor had been removed by hand, rather than having been blown off by the fire was difficult to credit, given that the item had not been seen since the time of the fire until its production in court. In other words, Hastings implied, without spelling it out (as he should have done), if the fact that the carburettor pin float was bent could be suggestive of the top having been removed manually, who was to say that its deliberate removal, perhaps causing the pin to bend, had not been done by a curious bystander on the morning of November 6, or even had occurred days or weeks after the blaze when Rouse was in custody?

Of course it is possible that the appeal court also concluded that the defence team should have commissioned mechanical experts as soon as Rouse had been committed for trial and that its failure to do so once more could not be rectified by the appeal court. Yet this is to ignore the financial constraints facing a defence team in 1930 which had to stretch out limited legal aid funds to cover many items of expenditure. Indeed, those vehicle engineers who testified at his trial and all those, around 200 correspondents, who indicated their willingness to testify at the appeal court seem to a man (literally) to have volunteered their services without any expectation of payment, clearly a sign of their disquiet, if not distress, at seeing a man due to hang on the basis of flawed science. Moreover it is not as if the defence knew of the technical challenges they would have to confront from the beginning (it appears that Finnemore first represented Rouse at the police court on Monday, November 18). For Colonel Buckle's examination of the vehicle and of the loosened nut, from which he inferred that the latter had been deliberately tampered with, occurred a month after the blaze.

The other features of the trial evidence that fell under Hastings' gaze, prompting him to raise them at appeal, included the position of the corpse as it was found by the three policemen. He did not seek to challenge their testimonies despite (or perhaps because of) the minor discrepancies in their evidence (it will be recalled that, inexcusably, no contemporary notes or photographs were taken of the scene), But he did insist that Spilsbury's testimony that the corpse's position was consistent with the man having pitched forward or been thrown face downwards from the nearside car door after being rendered insensate was also consistent with the man having fallen forward 'without being knocked unconscious at all'.

After all, the position and condition of the mallet did not support the Spilsbury interpretation (and the defence case was that it was the inebriated passenger's carelessness with the petrol can, while he was holding a lit cigar, which caused the petrol fumes to ignite and to set the car ablaze with him inside; though Hastings did not clarify whether, in this scenario, the doors were open or closed).

Such a defence 'theory of the case', claimed Hastings, left no scope for a finding of guilt (so Rouse's trial, he implied, was an illustration of a jury convicting in the face of clear evidence to the contrary). But even if, Hastings continued, the appeal court agreed that the position of the corpse *could* give rise to suspicion, the supportive evidence for guilt was only the poor impression that Rouse had made on the jury by his constant stream of unnecessary lies and his bizarre behaviour after the blaze. For Hastings, Rouse's 'performance' did not at all amount to substantive, let alone circumstantial, evidence against the prisoner, to which Hewart interjected that the jury had spent 75 minutes considering their verdict, prompting Hastings to remind Hewart, as if the latter did not know, that the bulk of that time was spent at lunch and at examining a similar Morris Minor to Rouse's. Indeed, how was anyone to know whether for the remainder of the time the jury were not simply discussing Rouse's private life (or the racing at Kempton Park), rather than the events at Hardingstone Lane?

So, in sum, Hastings' case was that Rouse had been convicted because, in the light of his almost congenital disposition to telling blatant lies, his exculpatory explanation as to why a burnt corpse had been found in his car was not considered satisfactory by the jury. For there was nothing else on which to base a conviction once it was accepted that Colonel Buckle's technical evidence was clearly challengeable, that traces of petrol on the victim's clothing might be explained innocently (as Hastings had endeavoured to do), that inferences favourable to the defence might be drawn from Spilsbury's evidence regarding the position of the body, especially when the mallet, as an offensive weapon, was taken out of the equation on the trial judge's direction, when the absence of evidence for intention, motive or planning was taken into account, and when the prejudicial evidence about Rouse's life style and immorality was discounted. Instead, Hastings submitted that there had been no evidence upon which a jury, properly directed, could have convicted, and that the case should have been withdrawn from the jury by the trial judge on the conclusion of the prosecution's case. As we know, Talbot J. had spurned Finnemore's submission and had indeed characterized it at the trial as 'an impossible contention', thereby obliging the latter to open the defence case that the jury would eventually reject.

Birkett's job in the appeal court scarcely needed to be forensic. All he was obliged to do was to remind Hewart and his colleagues of Talbot J.'s rejection of Finnemore's 'impossible contention' at the trial, to emphasise that the jury had heard 'evidence for five days...guided by the Judge in a summing-up which Sir Patrick Hastings himself had described as 'unassailable'', and that they had convicted after being directed as to the strict standard of proof beyond reasonable required for a conviction. Moreover, far from there being no, or no adequate, evidence to go to the jury, Birkett reeled off,

> "....the evidence of the journey; the time of the fire; the place of the fire; the
> fact that it was the appellant's car; that the dead man was a man whom it

was impossible to identify; that Rouse, when the fire occurred, was unable to render assistance; that he did not stay and report to the police."

The common denominator was, of course, Rouse's presence (and merely presence) either on the spot or as near as dammit. But added to this were all the inconsistent stories told by him, both to policemen (and to others) and to the trial court. As to the technical evidence it was impossible for the Crown to state categorically that, 'There [that is, at a particular location in the car] the light was applied' to the vehicle. However 'the sustained nature of the fire was one of the elements put forward by the prosecution to show design'. But this point carefully skated over the defence claim that even if the fire, melting the windscreen frame, had been fed by petrol from the leaking union joint, the nut at this joint had been loosened through expansion by the blaze and not by a deliberate hand. Indeed Birkett sought to reverse the onus of proof on this point by claiming there had been no evidence as to when it had become loose (though he still insisted that Rouse had loosened it). In fact the defence expert, Isaacs, had suggested at the trial that the blaze had caused the nut to expand, thus releasing petrol that fed the blaze. However, his credibility had been shot down by Birkett's disreputable tactic in asking the witness the scientifically inept question about the coefficient of the expansion of brass, a question, framed in such terms, which was impossible to answer.[316] Finally, as to the defence's suggestion of the carburettor having been blown off by the blaze, Birkett merely adduced the trial testimony of the defence expert, Bamber, that it was 'possible' that the top had been deliberately wrenched off to enable anyone to light petrol, which would flash down to the union joint, from outside the car. 'Possible'? Well, anything is possible, but hardly a firm foundation on which to send a man to the gallows.

What was unavoidable, of course, was reference to the 'elephant in the room', that is, the sordid business of the police court testimony of Helen, Nellie and Ivy (via her father), and Rouse's 'harem' speech, withheld from the trial itself. But this hardly troubled the Crown's case (or the Bench). For when Hewart observed, 'Is it not unfortunate that evidence as to character should be given at the police-court which cannot be given at the trial?', his choice of the word 'unfortunate' surely signified the chief justice's feelings on the matter. 'Oh dear, how sad, never mind', as the puff-cheeked and moustachioed Battery Sergeant-Major 'Shut Up' Williams (Windsor Davies) in It Ain't Half Hot, Mum would whisper somewhat volubly with a smirk on his face as another disappointment confronted his rabble of a Royal Artillery concert party in the Indian sub-continent in 1945. In other words, the harmful revelations regarding Rouse were no doubt to be regretted, Hewart seemed to think, but, hey, that's just the way it was. Birkett could scarcely contain his satisfaction. Thus given that Hewart had simply expressed regret, then he, Birkett, could not but agree with such a sentiment. However, for the avoidance of doubt (as lawyers would say), counsel also strove to press home the claim that the trial itself had not thereby been rendered unfair by the disclosure at the earlier committal hearing of Rouse's 'harem' speech. For he insisted that, '....I do not wish it to be thought that I accede to the proposition that statements made by

---

316 Hastings did not seem to argue, despite its having been raised at the trial, that the nut could have become loose accidentally during the journey.

a prisoner containing matter derogatory to himself are not evidence' (a situation which did not, of course, strictly apply to Rouse's trial itself). Indeed, as seen previously, Avory J. had pointed out that prisoners might well have good reasons to disclose their own bad character, but as Hastings riposted that did not address the three women's testimony at the pre-trial police court regarding Rouse's illegitimate children and the harm that that disclosure might have caused to the prisoner's chances of an acquittal at the trial itself. In other words, the parties remained sharply divided as to the legal effect of the police court revelations regarding Rouse's private life. And then, as quickly as it had begun in the appeal court, the talking suddenly stopped and the centre of attention fell onto the appeal judges. They could have adjourned to give deep thought to the legal issues underlying each side's submissions. Thus there was Hastings' central proposition that Rouse had been convicted on prejudice and on 'very grave suspicion' rather than on substantive evidence, and there was Birkett's insistence that the jury had heard a full case against the accused, had rejected his explanation and had decided upon guilt, which had to be presumed to have been established beyond reasonable doubt, so that any judicial interference at the appeal stage would be unfounded and an encroachment on the sovereignty of the jury. Instead, Hewart brought the other two judges into a huddle on the bench where they conferred for a short while in whispers. He then spoke.

He insisted that the only ground of appeal that the bench had to address was that there had been no case to answer and that the trial should not have proceeded once the prosecution case had closed. Hewart, however, agreed with the trial judge that that had been an 'impossible contention', and that since the jury had then convicted after hearing both sides, the appeal court must dismiss the appeal. Not a mention of the prejudicial police court hearing as tainting the trial, no accommodation of new, and previously unavailable, technical evidence about the fire's origins, nor observations regarding conviction on mere 'very grave suspicion' of Rouse's lying habits. It was as if Hastings had never raised those points. Indeed, a major part of Hewart's speech, which ran to a total of 35 lines (maybe just a smidgeon over half a book page), was devoted to that which Talbot J. had directed was irrelevant, that is, the mallet, which Hewart discussed in 13 lines, but only to draw attention to the inconsistent accounts by Rouse as whether he or the victim had used it to take off the petrol can stopper. And with those present having been reminded that Talbot J.'s summing up had been praised by Rouse's counsel himself as virtually 'unassailable', the hearing ended with Hewart tersely announcing that, 'We see no reason why this appeal should be allowed, and it is dismissed'. As an exercise in judicial reasoning it was sloppy and lazy. But no different from Hewart's style in similar appeal cases where his boredom shone through. As noted previously the role of the Criminal Appeal Court was to address primarily legal, not factual points (though fact and law could overlap, for example, in regard to admitting new evidence or determining whether a jury had acted perversely in convicting on the evidence adduced). But as to legal analysis of whether the prejudicial evidence at the police court had rendered the trial legally flawed, or whether the public's tampering with the burnt-out car had rendered the conviction unreasonable (the modern term is 'unsafe'), or what were the circumstances in which new evidence could be adduced at the appeal, or what were the guidelines as to when a defence plea of 'no case to answer' could or could not be upheld by a trial judge after the prosecution case had closed, there was nothing except a rehash of the inaccurate proposition that the jury had heard it all before and had disbelieved the accused. Superficiality and unreasoning in delivering verdicts on the part of appellate judges who ought to have tried harder to formulate intellectually respectable arguments for their decisions were not unique to Hewart. For example, many judgments of the House of Lords for the years 1979/80, subjected to close scrutiny by researchers, were revealed to be devoid of, or lacking, coherence, closure and reasoned bases that might, for example, have justified, on close legally grounded scrutiny, the exclusion of material as irrelevant or more prejudicial than probative or, indeed, have satisfactorily explained in legal (rather than in personal, political or empirical) terms the final decisions themselves.[317]

Unreasoned closure Hewart certainly gave to Rouse's appeal. But he also gave the impression that he could scarcely be bothered being present and would much rather be elsewhere (Avory was more civilized, but he had known Rouse's counsel, Hastings, intimately since the latter's early days at the Bar). Whatever one might think of Rouse and his guilt or otherwise, it was a disgraceful performance by a lord chief justice whose biographer stated that, 'The Chief viewed the case with distaste'.[318] Thus he displayed a mixture of irritation and impatience, interlaced with a sense of moral outrage. Such a potent brew would ensure that appellants before Hewart were short-changed too frequently for his record to be dismissed as a random outcome. Indeed no appellant prior to Rouse had had his conviction quashed in Hewart's court, and scarcely any accused thereafter.

The famous case of the Prudential insurance official, William Wallace, mentioned previously, who had been convicted of murdering his wife, Julia, in Liverpool in 1931 was one such exception. Yet how Hewart could distinguish the outcome of that appeal from Rouse's is forensically difficult to explain. Certainly, in quashing Wallace's conviction, and thereby apparently accepting the prisoner's elaborate story of the mysterious phone call to the chess club by the never-to-be discovered Qualtrough, followed by Wallace's fruitless visit to the non-existent Menlove Road East, Hewart concluded that the trial verdict could not be supported by the evidence. As he continued,

"The conclusion to which the Court has come is that the case against Wallace, which we have carefully and anxiously considered and discussed, was not proved with that certainty which is necessary to justify a verdict of guilty."[319]

'Carefully and anxiously considered and discussed'? Perhaps that was so in Wallace's case. But Hewart had obviously not extended this courtesy to the Rouse appeal. Indeed is it really obvious that Rouse's trial verdict possessed that degree of certainty of guilt that the chief justice agreed was lacking in Wallace's case? Both defence stories were elaborate and somewhat convoluted. Both men acted strangely immediately after the event (Wallace with apparent cool detachment and lack of emotion; perhaps he was autistic? Might Rouse have been?). There was some questionable forensic evidence in both cases (the origin of the car blaze

317 W. T. Murphy and R. W. Rawlings, "After the Ancien Régimé: The Writing of Judgments in the House of Lords 1979/80", *Modern Law Review*, Vol. 44 (6), 1981, pp. 617-59.
318 Jackson, *The Chief, op. cit.*, p. 288
319 See, for example, Roger Wilkes, *Wallace: The Final Verdict*, Grafton, 1985, p. 169.

in Rouse's case and the spot of blood in Wallace's bathroom). Of course Wallace's personal life was not salaciously exposed before his trial and he did not appear to have been an inveterate liar. But we know that in Rouse's case the appeal judges effectively claimed to have discounted those factors as the reasons for his conviction. For they preferred to conclude that the jury had condemned him because the twelve jurors chose to believe, on the basis of Colonel Buckle's 'dodgy dossier', the prosecution's theory of what had occurred at Hardingstone Lane rather than Rouse's account (which he had not, in law, been obliged to prove). Yet it is obvious that Rouse's admitted record of constant lying after the blaze must have inclined the jury to favour the Crown's version, whose narrative could only receive strong corroboration if one were to accept Colonel Buckle's contested testimony. For all the other prosecution witnesses in Rouse's case spoke only to the prisoner's behaviour after the blaze, or to the site of the blaze, or to the state of the body, or to the examination of the debris, or to more remote matters concerning Rouse's car insurance cover or his wages. They did not *directly* link him to the crime, much as the Crown could not link Wallace directly to the killing of his wife, if it be accepted that the blood-stained mackintosh belonging to the insurance agent was placed on Julia Wallace's body by the unknown killer. In short, why was Wallace released by Hewart and Rouse hanged? Could it simply be attributed to Hewart's personal disgust at what Rouse represented in relation to family values, whereas Wallace had pursued a morally unblemished existence? Academics have debated 'judicial values' for decades (if not longer), taking account of judges' class, educational, ethnic, religious, gender and gender-orientation characteristics, as well as attitudes to the role that judges should perform (whether abstentionist or interventionist in applying or interpreting the 'law'), and their political views in both a broader and narrower sense. Indeed we may note the emphasis in one study of the relevance of psychological theories of decision making resulting in tacit diversity among the Supreme Court judiciary in recent years which in turn can reflect diversity in judicial reasoning and in actual decisions. It is, indeed, arguable that, for many reasons, the tacit judicial diversity in the modern era detected by researchers was actually lacking among the senior judiciary in Hewart's time. If that were to prove to be the case, would it explain the divergence in the appeal outcomes in the Rouse and Wallace cases (that is, that all the appeal judges detested Rouse's sexual immorality and upheld Wallace's marital values), or should we remain puzzled regarding the specific difference in the outcomes of the two cases heard within a short time of each other?[320]

In the 'real' world Rouse heard his fate 'with no show of emotion whatsoever. After they [Hewart] had spoken he stood for just a second, then turned and was hidden to view by a curtain.'[321] Though he exited the court 'with his head thrown

---

320 Rachel J. Cahill-O'Callaghan, "Reframing the Judicial Diversity Debate: Personal Values and Tacit Diversity", *Legal Studies*, Vol. 35 (1), 2015, pp. 1-29. Important studies of judicial values include J. A. G. Griffith, *The Politics of the Judiciary*, 5th ed., Fontana, 1997; Alan Paterson, *Final Judgment: The Last Law Lords and the Supreme Court*, Hart Publishing, Oxford, 2013; J. Lee (ed), *From House of Lords to Supreme Court: Judges, Jurists and the Process of Judging*, Hart Publishing, Oxford, 2011. On the matter of judicial 'free speech', see Gerry R. Rubin, "Judicial Free Speech versus Judicial Neutrality in Mid-Twentieth Century England: The Last Hurrah for the Ancien Régime?", *Law and History Review*, Vol. 27, 2009, pp. 373-412.
321 *Evening News*, February, 23, 1931.

back defiantly'[322], he assuredly did not understand how the hearing had ended so peremptorily. Neither, of course, did those spectators unfamiliar with the quaint ways of the appeal courts which, in this respect at least, must have seemed like a Chancery hearing in *Bleak House*, with its irrational turns of events. One woman cried out, 'Oh! The poor wretch', but it was Rouse's women who felt the gloom most of all. During the hearing Lily had fixed her eyes intently on her husband until she received a smile in recognition. Then she gazed 'with an expression of mute misery'[323] as he disappeared behind the curtain, before she broke down in tears when the realization dawned of what had occurred. Rouse was driven back to Bedford Gaol in a car, arriving there about 4:30 pm to be greeted by a crowd of several hundred. They rushed towards the vehicle but he was quickly hustled through the gate and into the prison, to be locked up once more.

In the day after the hearing, a barrister, W. B. Franklin, who was clearly concerned at the outcome, wrote to *The Times*, urging that whenever a defence team objected unsuccessfully to the admissibility of Crown evidence on the basis that it was prejudicial, not probative, the bench could always order the press not to report the matter objected to, a power existing under the Indictable Offences Act 1848. Indeed, the correspondent added, the questionable evidence of the prisoner's immorality had been admitted at the Rouse committal hearing by a bench of magistrates who, while they had 'acted to the best of their ability.....are not trained lawyers' (which ignored the role of the legally trained magistrates' clerk).[324] On the same day, even the *Daily Telegraph* criticised the Crown for having previously brought forward the prejudicial material at the police court when it had not been prepared to do so at the trial itself, but merely aligned itself with Hewart's observation that the incident was 'unfortunate'. Not 'unfortunate' enough to taint the conviction, however. For the newspaper agreed that there had been ample evidence for a jury to convict.[325] The Attorney-General, Sir William Jowitt, evidently concurred. For although Rouse's legal advisers had initially hesitated about lodging a further appeal to the House of Lords, believing it to be futile, they later relented and sought the Attorney-General's authority, his *fiat*, to take the matter to the highest law court. However, on March 5, 1931 it was reported that he had refused to sanction a further appeal to the House of Lords against conviction. For he decided that the appeal court's decision had not involved a point of law of exceptional public importance nor that it was desirable in the public interest that a further appeal should be brought.[326] Thus Rouse's situation was not comparable to that of Charles Beard whose House of Lords appeal in 1920 concerned the legal effects of drunkenness on convictions for homicide, or Reg Woolmington's appeal in 1935 on the question of who bore the onus of proof when the accused claimed that the death of the victim at his hand was accidental, or whether, in the 1940 murder case of Tony 'Baby-face' Mancini (who was different from the Tony Mancini of the Brighton No. 2 Trunk murder in 1934), *any* claim of provocation, however minor, which had been raised by

---

322 *Daily Mirror*, February 24, 1931.
323 *Ibid.*
324 *The Times*, February 24, 1931.
325 *Daily Telegraph*, February 24, 1931.
326 *The Times*, March 5, 1931.

the defendant had to be put by the judge to the jury.[327] Rouse's fate now lay in the hands of the humane, but otherwise undistinguished, Home Secretary, J. R. Clynes and his principal Home Office adviser, Sir Ernley Blackwell, for whom sentimentality was a dirty word.

327 *DPP* v *Beard* [1920] A C 479; *Woolmington* v *DPP* [1935] A C 462; *Mancini* v *DPP* [1942] A C 1.

CHAPTER FOURTEEN

MY PRISON TALKS WITH ROUSE – BY HIS WIFE

DAILY EXPRESS, March 11, 1931

A Reprieve for Rouse?

While efforts were made by third parties to secure a reprieve for Rouse (see chapter 15), we concentrate in this chapter on the endeavours of his defence team to persuade the Secretary of State to spare the prisoner's life. Three separate sets of documents were created for the purpose. These were counsel's 'Opinion' to Rouse's solicitors for submission to the Home Secretary, the formal petition itself, beautifully drafted with exquisite calligraphy and couched in beseeching and humble terms seeking the Grace and Mercy of His Majesty. Finally, there was Rouse's own five-page compilation in his own hand-writing, which was separately submitted and which sought to offer a different technical (and innocent) explanation for the blaze. In fact, there were further documents in the shape of desperate letters sent to Clynes by Helen Campbell in the few days before the execution in which she endeavoured to express in her own words the exculpatory technical argument that Rouse himself had offered for the blaze and which differed from his own counsel's explanation.

Because the aim was to secure a reprieve and not a trial acquittal, the material adduced by counsel could range over a wider field than that strictly relevant at a trial. Finnemore and Marshall were, indeed, probably still of the view that the Crown had not proved its case beyond reasonable doubt. For in referring (below) to public disquiet at the verdict, they insisted there were solid grounds for unease at the verdict even though, as a matter of professional etiquette, they explicitly refrained from expressing their own opinion on Rouse's guilt or innocence. Rouse's futile appearance before Hewart had occurred because the Criminal Appeal Act 1907 permitted an appeal not only on a question of law, but also, with leave, on questions of fact or of mixed fact and law (an example at that time being whether angry, insulting or threatening words could amount to provocation in a murder case), or on 'any other ground which appears to the Court to be a sufficient ground of appeal'. Indeed section 4(1) of the Act also referred to the appeal court quashing a verdict not only if the jury's verdict was unreasonable or unsupported by the evidence at the trial, but also if, otherwise, there would be a miscarriage of justice. The appeal judges had, of course, been impatient with such pleading (though Finnemore had previously wrongly advised that appeals were limited to questions of law and to where, despite a conviction, there had been 'no evidence at all' to justify that decision). But with Finnemore now armed with stronger technical evidence for the defence, the appeal judges' rejection on February 23 was no bar to counsel's seeking to widen the debate in the reprieve petition by observing that,[328]

> "....there is a broader case of the very gravest importance to be submitted to the anxious consideration of the Secretary of State, in dealing with the question of proceeding to the extreme limit of the irrevocable penalty of death. From all parts of the country, and from all kinds and conditions of people, engineers, men of science, as well as ordinary citizens, we have received so many letters as to make it clear beyond question that there is widespread uneasiness in regard to the case, and very strong public feeling against the carrying out of the death sentence on the evidence adduced against the accused."

Indeed, this was the more remarkable given the unprepossessing character of the prisoner. Why a Secretary of State might have wished to advise the exercise of the royal prerogative of mercy at a time before capital punishment was abolished (effectively in 1965) will be discussed at length below but the formal role of the minister, like that of the appeal judges, was not to retry the case (though the Home Secretary could, in effect, be performing such a task behind the scenes). In this chapter much of our attention will focus on how the technical evidence acquired by the defence after Rouse's trial, and which the appeal judges had refused to hear, fared at the hands of the Home Office when considering Rouse's petition for a reprieve.

In Finnemore's Opinion for the Home Secretary he first observed that a major plank in the Crown's theory of the case that condemned Rouse was Buckle's testimony. Yet he reminded the Home Office that a previous Crown expert, William Dickens, an automobile engineer (which Buckle was not), who had examined the vehicle on November 14, long before Buckle had done, had not been asked in court to explain the cause of the fire. No doubt, Finnemore was implying, the Crown's failure to ask Dickens this question was suspicious and indicative of the weakness of Buckle's testimony. Would Dickens have answered differently from Buckle? Indeed might he have offered an innocent explanation for the blaze? Nor did Dickens refer to the loose petrol joint in his testimony, so central in Buckle's testimony to the Crown's case against Rouse. Of course, perhaps Dickens had not noticed it, but if he had done, might it have been the case that, unlike Buckle, he had not attached importance to it? And if not important, then so much for Rouse's tampering with it to feed petrol to the fire?

As to Buckle himself, counsel pointed out that this Crown expert had been recalled to testify on the sixth day of the trial after the court had heard the evidence of the defence witnesses, Cotton and Isaacs. They had both cited their own personal knowledge and experience of the effect of intense heat in loosening joints, though they could not explain the phenomenon scientifically. But Buckle, the fire-loss assessor, could likewise not offer a scientific interpretation. Indeed, he had flatly denied that, to the best of his knowledge, such a phenomenon had

---

328   As well as a typescript in HO144/19180, counsel's Opinion is reproduced in Normanton, *op. cit.*, Appendix VII.

occurred. However, as Finnemore and Marshall wrote, '....on this point he [Buckle] was clearly and demonstrably mistaken'. Indeed it would be 'impossible' for them to submit a 'tenth' of the letters they had received on this point. Instead the Secretary of State should be provided with a sample of letters from 'practical engineers' that would demonstrate and explain the scientific basis for the finding of the loose union joint after the blaze. Thus the letters from Line and Carew (chapter 13, where the additional technical evidence was discussed) would reflect the practical experience of Cotton and Isaacs, while the correspondence from Rowell, Moorfield, Chapman, de Wilde, Thompson and Price would furnish the theoretical and scientific foundation for the phenomenon. Given that the evidence of Isaacs and Cotton,

> "....might well have been discounted in the eyes of the jury by the cross-examination on theoretical matters, and by Colonel Buckle's statement already referred to, [w]e think it can be said to be truly impossible to base any theory of a deliberate loosening of the nut on the condition of that nut as found [by Buckle] on 4th December. If this is true, the prosecution case was wrong on this vital technical point...."

As to the carburettor, and the suggestion that Rouse had pulled its top off to increase the intensity of the fire, counsel first observed that defence testimony had suggested that the condition of the carburettor after the blaze had been equally consistent with its top having been blown off. Thus this particular question could not be carried further. But they also pointed out that this matter had not been raised at the police court and, crucially, it had not been adverted to at the trial by Buckle in the witness box either at first examination or on re-examination. Indeed, it was well known that he had only been alerted to this possibility when he saw Rouse's apparently smug face when he returned to his seat after testifying, after which he told the prosecution team of his suspicions. The legal and practical consequence, Finnemore pointed out, was that the defence could not cross-examine *him* on this theory. For the point had been put by Birkett only to Rouse himself and not to Buckle or to any other prosecution witnesses, with the result that, due to a technical rule of evidence, the Crown's star expert (unlike Isaacs) was not obliged to face a cross-examination aimed at embarrassing, indeed undermining, him and his scientific credentials.

Moreover, the Crown's theory regarding the carburettor did not square with Buckle's opinion, given at the police court and in his deposition, that since certain lugs on the fly-wheel casing were not fused, the fire could not have started in the bonnet of the car (where the carburettor was located to the right-hand bottom side of the engine block). Thus since prosecution evidence regarding the carburettor top was both new, inconsistent with other aspects of the Crown's technical case, and incapable of being challenged in cross-examination by defence experts during the trial itself, counsel believed that the evidence of Henry Rowell, in particular, should be read by the Home Secretary. Rowell, after all, had been willing and able to testify at the appeal but had been refused permission by the appeal court to do so (a fortnight after his wife had died, it will be recalled, though it is not clear whether counsel was aware of this). So if the Home Office were to pay attention to the *real* engineering experts, a terrible miscarriage of justice would not occur.

The department's principal adviser on the exercise of the Royal Prerogative of Mercy, and who effectively guided Clynes' decisions on whether condemned prisoners should live or die, was Sir Ernley Blackwell, the Legal Assistant, Under-Secretary of State, who had held that office in the department from 1913 until his retirement in 1933. He was, indeed, the unseen and unsung power, the *eminence grise*, behind the throne watching over every Home Secretary when the fateful decision had to be made. Blackwell certainly was highly influential and powerful within the Home Office. A barrister since 1892 he had joined the department in 1906 as an assistant under secretary of state, an appointment made in the wake of fierce criticism directed against the Home Office following exposure of its culpability in the prolonged Adolph Beck miscarriage of justice scandal. For not only did it inexcusably ignore evidence over many years clearly pointing to the prisoner's innocence (Horace Avory, one of Rouse's appeal judges in 1931, was Beck's prosecutor in 1896 and may also have borne some culpability). Its treatment of Beck's appeals for a review of his conviction was tainted by its want of legal skills within the department adequate to spot the miscarriage until it was officially acknowledged in 1904.[329]

Blackwell was involved as a legal adviser in many high-profile cases including that of Sir Roger Casement in 1916 when it was on his advice that, after the prisoner's conviction, and to pre-empt campaigns for his reprieve, extracts from Casement's 'black' diaries recounting his homosexual encounters in Africa, were circulated to journalists, politicians and the American ambassador. Blackwell wrote,

> "I see not the slightest objection to hanging Casement and afterwards giving as much publicity to the contents of his diary as decency permits, so that at any rate the public in America and elsewhere may know what sort of man they are inclined to make a martyr of".[330]

But not all his departmental duties revolved around the death penalty which, after all, constituted only a fraction of the Home Office Legal Department's case load. For example in 1941, presumably after being recalled from retirement to assist a depleted department during the Second World War, he drafted a memorandum, apparently dated 1941, on the technical matter of onus of proof in the wake of a major legal ruling in *Woolmington v DPP* [1935] AC 462, referred to previously. This was the case where the Lord Chancellor, Viscount Sankey, reasserted the golden thread of the common law which laid down that, apart from insanity or any contrary statutory provision (for example, relating to persons soon found in possession of stolen property), it was for the prosecution to establish guilt beyond reasonable doubt, not for the defence to establish innocence.[331]

---

329 [Anon], *The Strange Case of Adolph Beck*, The Stationery Office, 1999; N. W. Sibley, *Criminal Appeal and Evidence*, T. Fisher Unwin, 1908, pp. 52-8.

330 Surprisingly, there is no *Oxford DNB* entry for Blackwell. He is listed in Wikipedia. For his involvement in the Casement trial, see H. Montgomery Hyde, *Famous Trials 9: Roger Casement*, Penguin, 1964, passim. Most of the quote in the text is reproduced in Brian Inglis, *Roger Casement*, Coronet, 1974, p. 376.

331 G. R. Rubin, "Some Immediate Consequences of the Woolmington Ruling (1935): British Colonies and Irish Cattle", *Journal of Commonwealth Law and Legal Education*, Vol. 7, 2009, pp. 78-86. The memorandum no longer seems to exist. Moreover, since Blackwell died in September 1941, it is possible that the date is simply wrong. His obituary in *The Times*, September 23, 1941, makes no mention of wartime service.

But it is his role in capital cases that is most relevant for our purposes. An unusual instance concerns the Brixton taxi-cab murder case of 1923 when Alexander Campbell Mason had been sentenced to death for the shooting of a taxi driver, Jacob Dickey. The Home Secretary, W. C. Bridgeman, had expressed his own doubts as to the correctness of the jury's verdict, thus prompting a visit to the scene of the shooting by Blackwell, who accompanied the Director of Public Prosecutions, Sir Archibald Bodkin, and the prosecutor, Sir Richard Muir. Following the visit Muir was even more certain than previously that Mason was guilty (Mason had accused another robber, Eddie Vivian, of the killing). For the sketch map of the scene presented in court and prepared by the police had been based on an out-of-date Ordnance Survey map. Thus Mason's story adduced at his trial (though obviously not believed by the jury) of running away from the scene, scaling a wall and clambering over garden fences after Vivian, and not he, had allegedly killed the taxi-driver, did not fit with the *current* lay-out of the scene where the position of the fences had been altered. In this case, however, Bridgeman would not be shifted from his doubts regarding Mason's guilt. The jury had spoken but a reprieve was granted, almost certainly to Blackwell's dismay.[332]

The previous year an eighteen year-old pantry boy, Henry Jacoby, was about to hang for the murder of a hotel guest, Lady Alice White. Controversy had surrounded his conviction (with a recommendation to mercy) at the Old Bailey due to doubts as to his mental capacity. This concern became more intense, prior to his execution, because of the contemporaneous reprieve, on grounds of insanity, of the middle-class and financially privileged Ronald True who had battered to death a young prostitute of his acquaintance with whom he had been sleeping. But with no indication emerging from the Home Office regarding the pantry boy's plea for mercy, Jacoby's solicitor, Simon Burns, marched down to Whitehall, demanding to see the Home Secretary, Edward Shortt. He saw Blackwell instead.

> "I went into Blackwell's room, where he was sitting at a desk. Along a ledge running right the length of one wall I saw a whole lot of tin trays, each one containing a pile of papers and a murderer's name at the top. I saw, among others, Jacoby and True. This man was obviously reading them. It was quite obvious that he was the man who made the recommendation to the Home Secretary....He's the fellow who really decides. I said. 'Good morning, sir'. He said nothing. I sat down. He did not answer. I looked at him, and he looked at me. Eventually he said, 'What do you want?' I said, 'I've come to see you about the boy Jacoby. I'm his solicitor.' He still said nothing, so I went on, 'You realize, sir....' and put to him all I had to say about the lad's unfortunate background and every argument I could think of for not putting him to death. Blackwell said never a word from beginning to end. Finally I stopped. There was a pause, and he said, 'Is that all, Mr Burns?' and I said, 'Yes, sir', and he said, 'Very well, good morning', and I left".[333]

Burns initially thought the interview was 'very odd'. But he later comforted himself with the belief that Blackwell had no option at the time other than to

---

332   The Brixton taxi-cab case in discussed in numerous sources, for example, E. S. Fay, *The Life of Mr Justice Swift*, Methuen, 1939, Ch. 10; S. T. Felstead, *Sir Richard Muir: The Memoirs of a Public Prosecutor*, John Lane, The Bodley Head, 1926, pp. 51-7.

333   Fenton Bresler, *Reprieve: A Study of a System*, Harrap, 1965, p. 155.

remain non-committal. It is not difficult to ascertain Blackwell's advice. Jacoby was hanged some days later.

In the Edith Thompson case, whether Blackwell's view of her conduct influenced the Home Secretary, William Bridgeman, to refuse a reprieve, is open to debate. As Bridgeman's son subsequently stated, his father,

> "....was advised by Sir Ernley Blackwell, the Legal Assistant at the Home Office, and accepted the advice that her crime was as great as his [Bywaters']. If she had not instigated and incited Bywaters to kill her husband he would not have been murdered."

However, while the Home Secretary did not discuss such matters with his family, his son added that, '....he did refer to it later and this was most definitely his attitude: the husband would still have been alive if his wife had not plotted his death'.[334]

There can be no meeting of minds over the Edith Thompson affair. The likes of Hewart, Blackwell, and Bridgeman would read her letters literally as proof of murderous intent, even if the trial judge, Mr. Justice Shearman, was more circumspect in that regard. But all four would have been appalled at her perceived immorality which surely coloured their interpretation of her letters. Most modern commentators consider the outcome as an indictment of those men's moral bigotry and narrow-mindedness. As her counsel, the 'respectable' Sir Henry Curtis-Bennett, observed, Mrs. Thompson was hanged for adultery, and Blackwell played his role in this shameful tragedy.[335]

To return to the contents of the Rouse petition, Blackwell took issue with Finnemore on a couple of non-technical points. He disputed, for example, counsel's claim that there existed 'widespread unease' at the verdict. Nor did he agree that the 'prejudicial evidence' of Rouse's sexual liaisons given at the police court had been inadmissible (or 'unfortunate' as Hewart had commented in the Appeal Court). The justification for properly admitting Rouse's 'bad character' at the police court, he insisted, was to show Rouse's motive for the murder and, but for the cousins, for his plan to disappear. And Blackwell considered that he had a trump card up his sleeve to strengthen his belief, an ace that concerned Lily (below).

Going back to the new technical evidence from Rowell and the other engineers submitted to the Home Office in support of Rouse's petition, what did Blackwell make of it and how did he respond? The shocking, but not unpredictable, answer (given that, if persuasive, its import would suggest that an innocent man was about to be hanged), is that he simply refused to address the new evidence and considered the scientific evidence given at the trial to have been the last word on the matter. As he noted when sending copies of the petition to Hewart, to the DPP and to Clynes, 'I do not attempt to deal with the technical evidence as to deliberate or accidental fire. That must be held by HO to have been decided [obviously without the benefit of Rowell's compelling new evidence] by the verdict of the jury' (he also noted that at the police court hearing, Paling had referred to the

---

334 *Ibid.*, p. 175.
335 See, for example, Lucy Bland, *Modern Women on Trial: Sexual Transgression in the Age of the Flapper*, Manchester University Press, Manchester, 2013, Ch. 3.

removal of the carburettor top). At another point he did outline, albeit in the merest detail, the competing technical theories, but then added,

> "For a discussion on this technical question I would refer to the evidence itself and to Mr. Justice Talbot's summing up. It is much too intricate to discuss it in detail in this memorandum. The jury, as the Judge points out, took a very short time ....to arrive at their verdict of guilty. No doubt, they had discussed and considered the evidence night by night during the six days trial."

No doubt? He may have had a point. For at that time, when a jury trial adjourned for the night, the jurors would be accommodated together in a local hotel (in Old Bailey trials it was at the expensive Brown's Hotel or later, at the less plush Howard's Hotel, prompting mischievous suggestions that reaching a jury verdict was a deliberately long drawn-out process[336]).

Finally he did, admittedly, refer to the loosened petrol union joint but only to observe that he was not competent to comment and, more ominously for Rouse, that whatever its cause, '....it does not appear to me to conclude the matter'. For Rouse 'must have hit his passenger over the head with a mallet and then thrown his body across the front seats of the car' before, the official felt it unnecessary to add, setting fire to the car. Yet he would have been aware of the inconclusive matter of the hairs on the mallet and of Talbot's instruction to the jury to ignore it but, in advising Clynes, he chose not to refer to those inconvenient points for reasons which some might judge disreputable but which others might consider of little consequence.

The DPP, Tindal Atkinson, adopted a similar line to Blackwell's towards the technical evidence. As he wrote to the latter on March 4,

> "It is difficult for the Secretary of State after a careful trial and an unsuccessful Appeal to review evidence of this character. The difficulty of such a proceeding is illustrated by the points raised as to the carburettor.....These are matters of detail—no doubt detail of the utmost importance—occurring in a body of evidence dealing with the cause of the fire and its probable results. While I think it can be contended upon the physical remains of the car....as found that accidental fire was conceivably possible, there was in my opinion clear evidence [sic] upon which a Jury could act in finding that the fire was not accidental. But the contention in the last sentence [presumably a reference to an accidental cause of the fire] can in my opinion only be made tenable by treating a part of the case in—as it were—a watertight compartment and divorced from many surrounding circumstances in themselves not technical.... It can be said in favour of the prisoner in this aspect of the case that by reason of the destruction wrought by the fire the technical.....evidence was perforce dependent to a large extent on theoretical conclusions deduced from the remains which were open to criticism by other conclusions not wholly inconsistent with the condition of the remains [sic!]. But a discussion on this subject does not really amount to more than a re-weighing of the evidence which, while possibly within the prerogative, may not appear to you to be feasible."

---

336 *Guardian*, January 30, 2000 (Marcel Berlins). As from the Juries Act 1974, section 13, the judge had discretion to allow jurors to 'separate', which enabled them to return home each evening during overnight adjournments.

So Tindal Atkinson himself seemed to skip gingerly over, if he addressed it at all, the new evidence from the likes of Rowell. This much seems clear from his reference to a 're-hearing of the evidence'. He was in effect saying that the technical evidence (though it is not clear whether this extended to the post-trial material) could be viewed as indecisive one way or another, and therefore it was the broader picture of Rouse's deeds and words throughout the whole saga that ought to convince the minister of his [Rouse's] having been properly convicted. But is that not to say that Rouse was guilty because of his character faults, his irrational behaviour at critical moments and his reckless outspokenness when he would engage his mouth before engaging his brain? Second, did it not mean that the DPP refused to make a judgment as to which scientific theory was the more persuasive, given the legion of experts supporting the defence as against the sole voice of Colonel Buckle who, if his own testimony is to be believed, had apparently never come across the common workshop practice of heating up with a blow-lamp, and then allowing to cool, the most awkward of seized nuts? Perhaps similar to those who support the three per cent of scientists who do not accept human involvement in global warming compared to the 97% who do?

But as another official sardonically remarked in what some might think of as extreme callous indifference (it could have been Paling or the permanent secretary, Sir Alexander Maxwell, but the initials are illegible), 'What is there to worry about? Ignorance as to the identity of the corpse, absence of motive, conflict of expert testimony as to how the fire was caused, need not trouble us in view of the verdict of the jury'. However, it may also be noted that in respect of H. S. Rowell's suggestion, not reproduced in counsel's Opinion, that intense heat could have blown off the carburettor top, Blackwell did annotate, 'How long wd. it take for all this to happen?', the purpose of which question may be a matter of disagreement. Yet these departmental responses could hardly be said to amount to a refutation of the defence's scientific evidence, especially that concerning the loose petrol union nut. In the end, the apparent strength of that evidence counted for nothing in the effort to save Rouse's life.

Rouse's own analysis of the cause of the fire was contained in a section of his five-page statement in support of his reprieve application, and was completed on February 27 a few days after the rejection of his appeal. There was, of course, some public recognition of his possessing requisite knowledge, acquired through practice rather than through formal study and qualifications, of the workings of the internal combustion engine. The *Sunday Dispatch*,[337] for example, described him after his execution as having been an 'expert engineer' who 'knew how to set fire to that car. He was an engineer—a practical motor engineer—and there is no doubt that he devised a scheme which defied all the experts.'

Irrespective of the newspaper's judgment, it does appear that some tension existed between Rouse and his defence team as to how best to counter the Crown case that had claimed he had deliberately loosened the petrol union joint before setting fire to the vehicle. As he apparently told Helen Campbell during a prison visit by the latter,[338]

---

337 *Sunday Dispatch*, March 15, 1931.
338 HO 144/19181, cited in Campbell to Clynes, March 4, 1931.

"This [see below] was my theory and defence in the beginning but it was put aside by my solicitors and theirs was substituted and which failed miserably to my cost. At the last moment scientific tests were carried out to prove mine and were found correct but were not admitted at the Appeal so too late it was realized that I knew more than the experts".

Perhaps this was another instance of Rouse's unreconstructed hubris and of his air of superiority. But possibly he was making a valid point. The last-gasp tests he referred to, however, probably related to Isaacs' and Rowell's analyses and not to the technical points he raised in preparation for his petition. Thus while he did not refer to the scientific theory concerning heat transfer and the loosening of the petrol union joint, he did note that the two-way petrol tap facing the passenger seat (as noted previously, it is like a water stop-cock) was meant to be made leak-proof by a cork washer about the size of a penny. The washer was horizontal with the car, but it would quickly burn (once, that is, the passenger had supposedly, according to Rouse, set himself alight when he dropped his lit cigar into or near to the nearly-full petrol can). The contents of the can would, claimed Rouse, also splash over his passenger (which could explain the damp petrol patch on the victim's trouser that had been preserved from burning by the protective shape of the body and which was found in the groin area of the clothing item). Once the washer had burnt, there would be a blow-lamp type of flame across the front of the passenger's knee which, Rouse suggested, would account for the victim's severed feet. Moreover, this flame would continue until the tank was empty, further destroying the victim's limbs.

But more relevantly, according to Rouse, the flame would also cause the melting of the top of the windscreen which would fall into the car when its supports collapsed, especially on the nearside. For the steering column on the offside would hold up or prevent that side from falling onto the floor of the car. 'In the meantime', he added, 'the flames would have set the carburettor alight, melt it after a time [the alloys used for casting that particular part were of a low melting point], and would fall off from the cylinder block as when found'. So the carburettor damage, in this assessment, was a consequence of the initial fierce fire accidentally started by the victim.

But how did he explain the loose nut since he did not indicate any acquaintance with the scientific principles expressed by Rowell or the wide practical experience of burnt vehicles professed by Isaacs, Cotton and Carew? And here may be the area of disagreement as to what technical evidence should have been put in by the defence. In other words, it is possible that Rouse had already outlined the following theory to his defence team but that they chose to stick at the trial with the testimony of Bamber, Isaacs and Cotton, to Rouse's frustration. Whatever had occurred in that regard, Rouse claimed that in Buckle's evidence the latter had stated that only one washer had been fitted on the petrol pipe and one on the carburettor, but none on the petrol tank joint itself. Moreover, a complete new petrol pipe was produced at the trial as an exhibit and was stated to have only one washer fitted. However, it had not been examined by the defence experts. Yet, according to Rouse, all Morris Minor petrol pipes were fitted with two washers, one at either end. Indeed, MU 1468 still had two, one of them fixed by the heat in the hollow of the nut.

Where, then, was the other washer in the pipe exhibited by the prosecution? Had it been tampered with? If not, why was it not found? Crucially,

> "If this washer had been of a combustible material [presumably it was], and after being [sic] burnt, [this] would allow of the nut to be tightened up [he presumably meant 'to be able to be tightened up'] in the space normally or originally occupied by the washer. This would account for the union nut being a whole turn loose."

In other words the sinister interpretation put by the prosecution on the finding of the loose nut could be innocently explained away in terms of Rouse's theory (let alone in accordance with the views of Isaacs, Rowell et al.). Was it a credible theory that the burning of a washer would leave space resulting in a loosened nut? Or was it nonsense? No-one at the time, despite Rouse's mentioning the possibility on paper about ten days before his execution (he may previously have spoken to his solicitors about it), seems to have tested it.[339]

Finally, the reconciled and determined Helen Campbell kept up a barrage of correspondence with the Home Secretary right to the end. Part of that correspondence involved pressing, and pressing again, the technical argument supporting the accidental death theory. She had written to Clynes on March 4, March 8 and March 9 (Rouse was hanged the next morning). Her letter of March 4 had already referred to Rouse's theory of the victim starting the fire. In her letter of March 8, she wrote another hand-written letter to Clynes, stating that she had 'learned only today that a document was dictated in prison to Mrs. Rouse [who presumably mentioned it to Helen], by Arthur Rouse, giving important information regarding how the fire in his car could have been caused by accident'. Helen was most anxious to know that the document dictated to Lily had reached Clynes and, if not, that he should ensure that he obtain it.[340] This was because she understood that the governor had apparently refused to allow the document to be taken away by Lily. By the following day her desperation was acute, the execution being less than twenty-four hours away. So this time she typed a letter to Clynes repeating the technical information regarding the fire that Rouse had allegedly included in the document communicated to Lily. Whether this repetition by Helen was from memory or, indeed, from sight of the document, on the footing that it had been smuggled from prison by Lily, is unclear.

In any event the document (if it existed) in fact only contained Rouse's denial that he had pulled off the carburettor top in order to add further fuel to the flames. It did not, therefore, raise the issue of the missing and burnt washers

---

339 He had claimed (see his defence in chapter 10) that the petrol can had been full when it exploded, blowing parts of it, such as the brass filler cap, into small pieces. Thus if it had remained full, he could hardly have poured its contents over the car and over an allegedly unconscious victim, nor set a fourteen-yard trail of petrol towards the car which he had then allegedly lit. He himself would have been singed and his clothes reeking of petrol. These were not the cases, despite rumours of singed eyebrows. His suit had, of course, been taken away for examination after he was charged, but no more was heard of this examination. At one level the reason seems obvious. It did not smell of petrol. But after his execution a Sunday newspaper offered an alternative suggestion, that is, that when he went to London after the blaze, he changed his suit and destroyed the one he was wearing in Hardingstone Lane, as it would have smelt of petrol. See *Sunday Dispatch*, March 15, 1931. However, if this were the case (and neither he nor Lily had indicated that he had changed his clothes on his brief return to his home), one might well ask why he had not also changed his stained shirt.

340 HO144/19181, Campbell to Clynes, March 8, 1931.

and the connection of the latter to the loose petrol joint in order to explain the fire's intensity. One might cynically remark, in any case, that *any* technical claim by Rouse, no matter how convincing and scientifically grounded, would receive short shrift from the Home Office. Notwithstanding, Rouse made the following points. First, the carburettor top was slightly burnt, the inference presumably being that if a deliberate removal had occurred, obviously before the car caught fire, there would have been no signs of burning at all. He did, however, ignore the possible riposte that a removed top might have been placed or dropped by him somewhere within the body or engine compartment of the car where it might have been slightly burned. Certainly no evidence was ever given of the top having been found away from the car.

He also pointed out that the police apparently agreed that there had been no evidence of singeing on any part of his body. Was this decisive of his not having removed the top? Perhaps it was not, because it could point in opposite directions regarding guilt or innocence. Thus he might have deliberately pulled off the top *before* the blaze in order to increase its intensity, and had *then* fired the car, leaving no evidence of singeing. Alternatively, he might indeed have been relieving himself some good distance away from the engine compartment before the blaze started, thereby explaining the absence of singeing. Second, he insisted, the bend in the carburettor float needle (it was actually a valve) could only have been accounted for by the top having been blown off, not pulled off. As he sought to explain, the top was clipped down on one side of the carburettor chamber. Consequently, when an explosion occurred, the top would be blown off, but due to the presence of the retaining strip of metal holding down one side of the top, the top would be blown one-sided by the force. This in turn would cause the needle to bend while it was being forced through the centre float, whereas it could not have been bent to that extent if it had simply dropped off the carburettor after the top had been manually removed. For if the top had been removed by hand and if the carburettor had been fired by Rouse, the needle would have shot straight out without bending (presumably leading to its 'simply dropp[ing] off the carburettor'). Similarly, the float chamber itself would have been blown out of the carburettor on the mix being ignited by Rouse.

Moreover, he pointed out that the *body* of the carburettor had melted away from the cylinder block in the heat (presumably before the top blew off), whereas the float chamber remained nearly intact apart from a slight collapsing of the wall imprisoning the float. Indeed the float itself had been found undamaged in the well of the topless carburettor at the bottom of the component. His argument was therefore that if the top had been forcefully removed and the carburettor had then been fired explosively by a match, the fiercely ignited petrol would have lifted the float which would then have been expected to have melted in the intense heat of the flame, rather than be found later in an intact state. Alternatively (and this assumed the tramp's culpability with cigar and petrol can), a fierce blaze started by the petrol in the can and fed by the car's fabric padding would probably have reached the carburettor. On that premise (and leaving aside the loosening of the petrol union joint through heat expansion which would increase the petrol flow), and acknowledging that the separated carburettor top could have been blown off in the intense heat, then the diameter space at the top of the float chamber (presumably he meant the funnel where the float valve or needle was located to regulate the fuel intake) could well have imprisoned or wedged the float itself against the side of the chamber, such that it still retained its shape intact. So the bend in the float valve and the intact state of the float itself were evidence, he suggested, that the carburettor top had been blown off in the intense blaze. For if the top had been removed manually, then the sudden firing of the carburettor would have produced such an intense explosion of heat and fire that the valve would have shot straight out of the float chamber without being bent, while the float itself would have melted into nothing at that high temperature. And since the float still existed and the valve was bent, the inference was that, though the fire had reached the carburetor and might even have been fierce enough to blow off the top, a powerful explosion of the carburettor had not been engineered by human endeavour.

These are complex claims which for many (admittedly including the present writers) might not be easy to follow. The likelihood is, however, that those technical arguments had not been aired by Rouse before the trial commenced. For Rouse was notoriously slow to reveal features about the case, even to his legal advisers (his delayed revelation that he had called into his home in the early morning of November 6 before he set off for Wales is one startling example). But if his defence team *had* been apprised before the court proceedings of his theory regarding the carburetor (though the timing is unlikely), it is possible that they were still at that point rather lost as regards the technical evidence. For although they had been contacted by two engineers following Buckle's police court testimony, at least one of their technical experts had only made his presence known to counsel after the second day of the trial following Buckle's appearance in the witness box. It was therefore unfortunate for Rouse that the Home Office simply ignored his exculpatory mechanical explanations when his technical account reached the department days before his execution. 'Too late, chum' would have been their instinctive response if, that is, they had not already decided to ignore his points. In fact, it was just like the Court of Criminal Appeal in respect of the defence's line-up of technical witnesses.[341] As Blackwell minuted the day before the execution, 'The Govr. tells me that no statement has been dictated by pr[isoner] to Mrs. Rouse. There is nothing of importance within. Lay by'. The contested and problematic technical evidence, like Rouse himself, was thus tersely and briefly disposed of.

Yet as a recent lord chief justice, Lord Thomas of Cwmgiedd, observed in a public lecture in 2014, there remains the 'risk of a miscarriage of justice if the forensic science is wrong, or the expert presents or interprets it incorrectly....' Indeed he went on to remind his audience of the warning to Congress from the US National Academy of Sciences in 2009 that, '....with the exception of DNA analysis, no forensic method has been rigorously shown to have the capacity to consistently, and with a high degree of certainty, demonstrate a connection between evidence and a specific individual or source'. Moreover even fingerprint

---

341 Rouse's last-minute plea also insisted that if, as the Crown had alleged, the car doors had been open, how was it that the door handles and locks were found within the charred remains in the body of the car, rather than three feet away. This, claimed Rouse, surely supported his claim that the car doors had been closed. This, of course, would have prevented his attempting a rescue, and would also have cast doubt on the prosecution's allegation of his having 'pitched' the victim into the car.

and hair analysis, and ballistics and handwriting analysis, were based on 'tenuous and largely untested evidence', whereas analytically based disciplines were generally perceived by scientists to be more rigorous than those based on expert interpretation (presumably this being due to the former being more susceptible to the application of mathematical tests of probability such as Bayes' statistical theorem, which is now widely deployed in courts).[342] Unlike Norman Thorne, the Crowborough chicken farmer, Rouse may not have been a notable victim of 'Spilsburyism'. But he may have been the victim, not only of his own smug loquacity, but also of 'Buckleism', 'Birkettism' and even of an inverse 'Isaacsism'. For it is difficult to accept that the technical evidence for the Crown was impressive, let alone compelling. In fact the opposite might be a more accurate judgment. Of course the authorities contented themselves with the thought that, leaving aside the technical evidence regarding the cause of the fire, every other circumstantial factor (in their opinion) pointed to Rouse's guilt. It might therefore be argued that their belief in Buckle's testimony was more an article of faith than of persuasive science. But so too might it be claimed (despite a risk of our making a premature judgment) that their certainty of his guilt was, if not necessarily flimsily based (and he may well have bumped off his passenger), then hardly likely to be shared by a jury today.

As the department examined (cursorily, it appears), the contents of the petition, it may be useful to note common grounds for granting reprieves from the hangman (not, of course, acquittals). For the eighteenth and nineteenth centuries historians have ascertained clear patterns such as youth, good character, judicial recommendations, prospects for successful rehabilitation into society after transportation abroad and, possibly most importantly, the intercession of the respectable sort, especially the landed, the gentry and aristocracy, on behalf of the prisoner.[343] Yet comparable archival research has not, ironically, been conducted in respect of the twentieth century. Some guidance regarding the prerogative of mercy during and after Rouse's time was offered by the Home Office in its evidence to the Gowers Committee on Capital Punishment (1949-1953). It cited three definite grounds for a reprieve that had been adopted by the authorities. They were cases involving mercy killings, cases of survivors of genuine suicide pacts (where 'pity' ought to prevail) and previous cases that would now (by 1953) fall into the non-capital offence category of infanticide as a result of the Infanticide Acts 1922 and 1938. Indeed, no execution had been carried out, since 1849, of a mother for killing her child who had been under one, or, since 1899, of a mother for killing her child who had been over one.

The Home Office also provided a list of ten further grounds that were said to encourage close departmental scrutiny. They included whether the killing had been unpremeditated or whether it had been provoked (though not to the extent

---

342 Lord Thomas, "Expert Evidence: The Future of Forensic Science in Criminal Trials", October 14, 2014, at www.judiciary.gov.uk. For a brief overview of the application of Bayes' theorem in the courts see, inter alia, Roderick Munday, *Evidence*, 5th ed., Oxford University Press, Oxford, 2009, pp. 409-111. Recent findings also suggests that 60% of psychology research cannot be replicated, thus casting doubt on its universal validity. See *Guardian*, August 28, 2015.

343 See, for example, P. J. R. King, "Decision-makers and Decision-making in the English Criminal Law, 1750-1800", *Historical Journal*, Vol. 27, 1984, pp. 25-58; ibid., *Crime, Justice and Discretion: Law and Social Relations in England, 1740-1820*, Clarendon Press, Oxford, 2000; Roger Chadwick, *Bureaucratic Mercy: The Home Office and the Treatment of Capital Cases in Victorian Britain*, Garland, 1992.

that it rendered the prisoner guilty of non-capital voluntary manslaughter on grounds of provocation). Murders where it was proved that the prisoner had not intended to kill (though he was still guilty of murder since he had met the legal requirement for murder in that he had intended to cause at least serious harm to the victim who had died as a result) might be examined more closely in deciding upon reprieve petitions. So also might be cases where the prisoner, unless completely insensate, had been drunk when he had intended to kill or cause serious harm. For while his drunken state might arguably lessen his moral responsibility for the killing, he would still remain criminally liable for murder ('a drunken intent is still intent'). If, however, he had been so drunk that he was now completely unaware of his actions, with the result that his condition might be akin to automatism induced by alcohol, he would still be guilty of manslaughter. For, unlike cases of automatism due to, say, an unanticipated hyperglycaemic or hypoglycaemic episode, he had still been blameworthy in getting paralytically drunk in the first place. Another Home Office example that was listed and which might prompt a more sympathetic consideration of a reprieve application would be the situation of a group murder characterized by varying degrees of responsibility for planning or differing levels of involvement. And so also, of course, would youth (old age was not listed) and female gender.[344] But given that in each of the above categories, some prisoners were hanged and some reprieved, it is clear that the ten categories mentioned above should not be relied upon for their predictive qualities. As Arthur Koestler and C. H. Rolph pointed out in their study of 123 executions occurring between January 1949 and February 1961, nearly a quarter of the cases did involve, according to the authors, extenuating circumstances which they considered ought to have led, but did not lead, to a reprieve.[345]

Indeed the randomness of outcomes probably reflected the fact that, irrespective of apparently systematic civil service approaches to the issue and the possibility of referring to precedent books, the individualism of each prisoner and, possibly, the individualism of the deciding Home Secretary could never be discounted. Nonetheless, regarding the latter, it is probably true to say that the minister almost never overruled the officials' recommendation to reprieve the prisoner, though on some occasions the Home Secretaries interviewed by Bresler for his book published in 1965[346] did reject the recommendation of their officials that 'the law must take its course'. Similarly, a prison medical panel's finding that there were medical or mental health reasons for granting a reprieve was invariably followed, notwithstanding that many establishment figures would be highly sceptical of medical 'alienists'.

It remains the case, however, that in the absence of longitudinal archive-based research on departmental practice, we are left with impressionistic findings or predominantly anecdotal or unattributed accounts seeking to shed light on that bureaucratic practice during the last century. The picture that emerges consequently offers only outlines of departmental behaviour and snippets of information from which weak patterns might be inferred. Nonetheless, for the

344 *Report of Royal Commission on Capital Punishment, 1949-1953* (Ch., Sir Ernest Gowers), Cmd. 8932, HMSO, September 1953, esp. paras. 36-43.
345 Arthur Koestler and C. H. Rolph, *Hanged by the Neck*, Penguin, 1961.
346 Fenton Bresler, *Reprieve: A Study of a System*, Harrap, 1965.

purpose of putting Rouse's application for a reprieve into context, the material available for the twentieth century remains useful.

The first point to make, which might have been of some initial comfort to Rouse, is that the percentage of reprieves granted in the first fifty years of the twentieth century showed a steady increase. Indeed, the period from around 1930, when the Hardingstone tragedy unfolded, saw changes in Home Office practice in this area of its activities. For the percentage of reprieves increased from 38.9% in the 1920s to 53.3% in the1930s (falling slightly to 48.5% in 1949). The author and barrister, Fenton Bresler, believed that this reflected a greater preponderance of abolitionist views within the Home Office, with three Home Secretaries, J. R. Clynes (who nonetheless refused to reprieve Rouse), Sir Samuel Hoare (1937-39) and James Chuter Ede (1945-51) who declined to reprieve Timothy Evans, identified as abolitionists. Clynes and Chuter Ede were Labour Home Secretaries, while Hoare was a Conservative.

The Legal Principles

The principal means by which the royal prerogative of mercy could be exercised in favour of any prisoner in Rouse's day was by the grant by the Sovereign of a free pardon or of a conditional pardon.[347] Indeed, it could be granted in respect of *any* offence and not just in relation to a capital crime. Thus it was widely used, when an appeal hearing was not available, to 'set aside' (but see below) wrongful motoring convictions when, for example, it was subsequently discovered that speed limit signs had been missing or that the magistrate had not been properly qualified to sit on the case. Changes have inevitably been made to this regime since those days (leaving aside the abolition of capital punishment since 1965). For example, in capital cases, the Home Office introduced a practice after the Second World War of conducting 'informal' medical examinations of the condemned prisoner to determine whether he or she was suffering from any mental abnormality that fell short of legal insanity. If the panel of three doctors and psychiatrists found any such evidence, then they were in a position to inform the Home Secretary of the condition and the latter could then give consideration to their finding in his determining whether or not to recommend to the Sovereign to grant a reprieve in the form of a pardon conditional on the prisoner serving his life sentence with or without hard labour (after the Homicide Act 1957 a qualified defence of diminished responsibility could be raised at trial).[348] For Rouse, provision for such an examination came too late to offer him a possible escape from the gallows since the only psychiatric inquiry prior to execution in his day was whether the condemned prisoner, when examined in the days leading up to his execution, was insane under the terms of the Criminal Lunatics Act 1884 and not just mentally

---

347 According to *Halsbury's Laws of England*, Vol. 8 (2), para. 826, there also appears to be a power to commute or remit, partially or otherwise, a sentence, while other sources refer to a power to 'respite' or postpone (whether *sine die* or not is unclear) the execution of a sentence. See CAB21/5949 regarding the powers of colonial governors in 1944 in military cases. In *R v Secretary of State for the Home Department, ex parte Bentley* [1994] Q B 349, Lord Justice Watkins referred to a 'limited form of pardon'. This resulted in the Home Secretary, Kenneth Clarke, recommending the award of a posthumous 'pardon limited to sentence' to Derek Bentley, a form of wording that is probably just another term for a conditional pardon which can scarcely apply to the deceased grantee of a pardon

348 Bresler, *op. cit.*, pp. 75-6.

disordered or vulnerable; and despite his war wound to his head, he had been clearly certified as not falling within this category.

Another change from the 1960s was initiated by the decision of Home Secretary Roy Jenkins in 1966 to cut the Gordian knot tied by a conservative Home Office aimed at preventing procedural change when he recommended a posthumous pardon at common law to Timothy Evans, hanged in 1949; a decision followed more than twenty-five years later by the grant of a similar pardon to Derek Bentley, who had been hanged in 1953.[349] This latter 'award' to Bentley followed another change in the pardons regime in 1993 when the Divisional Court held in *R v Secretary of State for the Home Department, ex parte Bentley* [1994] Q B 349 that it possessed the power to review the legality of the Home Secretary's decisions on whether to recommend the exercise of the prerogative of mercy and also regarding the type of pardon in question. Today it is more common to grant posthumous pardons by statute, such as in the case of the 'Shot at Dawn' British soldiers of the First World War executed by firing squad for military offences such as desertion, cowardice, or sleeping on guard duty.[350] Another example is the posthumous pardon awarded to the celebrated mathematician and cryptanalyst, Alan Turing who, at the Bletchley Park Listening Station in the Second World War, broke German ciphers allowing other code breakers to crack the German Enigma codes. After the war, brutally chemically castrated in 1952 following his hounding and conviction for homosexual offences, he took his own life in 1954 by eating a cyanide-laced apple. Though the historical circumstances giving rise to it are a moral blight on the bigotry of opinion formers of a previous generation, the Alan Turing (Statutory Pardon) Act 2013 is the least that the country could seek to do to make amends.[351]

Returning to the regime in 1931, it should be noted that while the 'free' pardon would relieve the prisoner from all the consequences of a conviction (following a conditional pardon a condemned murderer would normally serve a life sentence thereafter), it would not itself amount to an acquittal. Thus the award of a free pardon to a prisoner might, perhaps, result in his release from prison; or result in the return of the fine to him. But it did not, according to a later Court of Appeal ruling,[352] constitute the quashing of a conviction. Only the *judges* could formally set aside a conviction and only where certain conditions, also confirmed subsequently in another case, had been met.[353] The reasoning was that in civilian cases the courts recognised the Crown's prerogative of mercy but not, ever since

---

349   G. R. Rubin, "Posthumous Pardons, the Home Office and the Timothy Evans Case", *Criminal Law Review*, January 2007, pp. 41-59.
350   Armed Forces Act 2006, s. 359.
351   It may be noted that posthumous statutory pardons had been common in previous centuries to ensure that the property of a prisoner executed for offences such as treason (he possibly backed the wrong horse at the time) was not subject to 'attainder'. For an Act of Attainder would have the effect of depriving his family of their inheritance which would then go to the Sovereign.
352   *Peace* [1976] Crim L R 119.
353   *Director of Public Prosecutions v Shannon* (1974) 59 Cr. App Rep 250, HL. For example, if there were no facts elicited at the trial which rendered a guilty plea unwarranted, then a quashing by the Court of Appeal was not available, even if a free pardon had previously been granted by the Crown. Note that an appeal to the superior courts is not available to those *pleading guilty* before the magistrates. Only legal defects such as a lack of jurisdiction on the part of the magistrates to try such a case might avail a prisoner seeking to overturn his own previous accepted plea of guilty before the justices.

the early seventeenth century, a Crown prerogative of *justice*.[354] Thus Derek Bentley's posthumous pardon in 1993 was not enough to render him not guilty. For that conclusion, the Court of Appeal would have to quash his conviction, which it did in 1998 when the appeal judges exercised the 'prerogative' of 'justice'.[355]

A conditional pardon, by contrast, 'substitutes for one punishment another, lesser sentence' where the serving of that sentence is the 'condition' for receipt of the pardon. In former days this commonly meant that if the Sovereign granted a conditional pardon to (that is, 'reprieved') the prisoner under sentence of death, the latter would instead be required to serve a sentence of imprisonment, usually for life, perhaps with hard labour, or of penal servitude (until 1948), sometimes for life, or to undergo branding (until 1779) or transportation to the colonies (until 1867). This, of course, was the possibility on which Rouse and his advisers pinned their hopes.

In advising the Sovereign whether to exercise the prerogative power, the Home Secretary enjoyed a personal jurisdiction in 'recommending' (which effectively means 'directing') the course of action which the monarch was to take. Indeed, according to a Cabinet Office document (presumably based on Home Office advice, and probably dating from 1961), whenever the Home Secretary was deciding on the matter and advising the Sovereign accordingly, his 'function [was] essentially judicial'.[356] Was this 'judicial' function, perhaps like that of magistrates, therefore reviewable by the courts (to ensure the power had been 'lawfully' exercised), long before the Divisional Court so held in *Bentley*'s case in 1993? The point remains moot.[357] However what is widely acknowledged, at least with respect to conditional pardons (see below), is the wide scope of the discretionary factors which the Home Secretary could take into account in coming to his decision on whether to intervene and, in respect of some of the cases discussed here, to save the prisoner's life. A former Home Secretary before the Great War, Herbert Gladstone, informed the Commons in 1907 of the operating principles when he sought to explain his decision to reprieve Horace Rayner, convicted of murdering the millionaire London store owner, William Whiteley.[358]

> "It would be neither desirable nor possible to lay down hard and fast rules as to the exercise of the prerogative of mercy. Numerous considerations—the motive, the degree of premeditation or deliberation, the amount of provocation, the state of mind of the prisoner, his physical condition, his character and antecedents, the recommendation or absence of recommendation from the jury, and many others--- have to be taken into account in every case: and the decision depends on a full review of a complex combination of circumstances, and often on the careful balancing of conflicting considerations."[359]

354 *Foster* [1985] Q B 115. For the complex issue of whether a different rule applies to court-martial cases, see Rubin, "Posthumous Pardons", *op. cit*, p. 45, note 22.
355 *Bentley (Deceased)* [1998] EWCA (Crim) 2516.
356 See CAB 21/5949, above.
357 A pre-1993 academic article suggested as much. See B. V. Harris, "Judicial Review of the Prerogative of Mercy", *Public Law*, 1991, p. 386.
358 Rayner believed that Whiteley, known as the 'Universal Provider', was his biological father but the latter had spurned Rayner's request for funds. For the case see Sidney Theodore Felstead, *Sir Richard Muir: A Memoir of A Public Prosecutor*, John Lane, The Bodley Head, 1927, pp. 225-33; Brian Lake, *The Murder Book of Days*, Headline, 1995, pp. 29-30.
359 Cited in Sir Edward Troup, *The Home Office*, Putnam, 1925, pp. 63-64.

Indeed the considerations which the Home Secretary would be free to take into account when deciding whether to recommend a conditional pardon could also include political factors. Thus when the minister was faced with the decision whether to recommend a reprieve (which amounted to a conditional pardon) in the cases of Sir Roger Casement in 1916 and of the Coventry IRA bombers in 1940 the Home Secretary in each case considered the perceived adverse political consequences which might flow from allowing the sentences of death to be carried out. Thus given that the United Kingdom was engaged in war with Germany on both occasions, the minister decided to consult with Cabinet colleagues as to whether public opinion in Ireland and in the United States might be inflamed against Britain if the executions were to be carried out. In both instances, the Home Secretary 'allowed the law to take its course'. Indeed the adverse consequences feared by some War Cabinet members, certainly in 1940, did not materialize after the executions of the IRA bombers, Peter Barnes and James Richards.[360]

No case is being presented here for a posthumous free pardon for Rouse, in the wake of those already granted to Evans, Bentley and others (conditional posthumous pardons are self-evidently oxymoronic). But the particular difficulties in awarding a posthumous 'free' pardon, raised by civil servants in past decades when addressing such scenarios, included questioning, since the proposed recipient was already dead, the practical value in granting such a pardon. But there was a further obstacle erected by departmental practice, that is, that the recipient of a pardon, whether dead or alive, should have 'clean hands', which meant being 'morally and technically innocent'. Thus, leaving aside Rouse's alleged bigamy, claims that deceased candidates such as Timothy Evans and Derek Bentley lacked these qualities (did not Evans conspire with Christie to procure his wife's abortion, and did not Bentley go armed with Craig to carry out a robbery?) complicated their cases for posthumous pardons. However, ministerial determination and family doggedness, together with non-capital examples from the early 1960s, one of which arose from the notorious Detective-Sergeant Harold Challenor affair, where pardons were issued after conviction, demonstrated that the clean hands principle was honoured as much in the breach as in the observance.[361] For Rouse (and probably for all now-deceased prisoners convicted of murder where convictions could be successfully challenged), these points are almost certainly now irrelevant. For even if the Criminal Cases Review Commission were to reopen Rouse's case today and to refer his case to the Court of Criminal Appeal with a view to quashing his conviction (which prospect we explore in the final chapter), the era of common law posthumous pardons is probably past. Thus today, the only routes to posthumous rectification appear to be the enactment of rare statutory pardons or carefully scrutinized and filtered references to the Court of Criminal Appeal for possible posthumous quashings of

---

360 CAB 21/5949. See also Letitia Fairfield (ed.), *Trial of Peter Barnes and Others*, William Hodge & Co., Edinburgh, 1953.

361 A full analysis of these points is in Rubin, "Posthumous Pardons", *op. cit.* For the Challenor case in 1964, see *Report of an Inquiry by Mr A E James QC etc.*, Cmnd. 2735, 1965; James Morton, *Bent Coppers*, Warner Books, 1994, pp. 117-120; Mary Grigg, *The Challenor Case*, Penguin, 1965; Dick Kirby, *The Scourge of Soho: The Controversial Career of SAS Hero Detective Sergeant Harry Challenor MM*, Pen & Sword, Barnsley, 2013. For the Grosvenor House Hotel conviction of students protesting against the Greek Junta, see *Report of Inquiry by Mr. W. L. Mars-Jones QC etc.*, Cmnd. 2526, 1964; Morton, *op. cit.*, pp. 108-114. Incriminating evidence had been planted on the accused by the police. Appeals in those cases were unavailable.

convictions.[362]

The Bresler Analysis

The exercise of the royal prerogative of mercy in the cases of Evans and Bentley was highly distinctive, given the posthumous character of the pardons and the issue of whether they were both 'technically and morally innocent'. However, the procedure in the cases of those still languishing in the condemned cell before abolition, and pinning their last hopes on the susceptibility of the Home Secretary to increasingly desperate arguments by the prisoner for a reprieve (until, of course, capital punishment was abolished), can be described. In his 1965 book, *Reprieve*, Fenton Bresler looked first at the practice of the Home Secretary in anticipation of the decision whether or not to reprieve. He next examined the practice in respect of the actual decision itself, before exploring 'Who really made the decision?'

He noted that it was extremely rare for murderers facing the death penalty to be reprieved without having gone to the Appeal Court first.[363] He also observed that following the rejection of an appeal, the prisoner tended to recover his composure as the hope of winning a reprieve took a hold on his mind. The latter's regime in the condemned cell did not alter. He was visited daily by the prison governor, twice a day by the medical officer, and sometimes more frequently by the prison chaplain. During the day outsiders such as family members could visit, if the prisoner were agreeable, with a maximum of three visitors at any time. They were, however, kept separate from the prisoner by a glass panel. The wardens were, of course, present at all times. Many condemned cell prisoners ate well and slept well, while most of them read books and newspapers (with items detailing their own case cut out). They also interacted with the 'death watch' guards, playing chess, cards, draughts and dominoes, and might discuss various topics and events (apart from that which had led to the prisoners' current predicament).

Meanwhile the Home Office began to collect relevant confidential information from the police, doctors and trial and appeal judges, and sometimes set in motion the steps for a medical inquiry. The prisoner's mental state and behaviour were constantly recorded in the days following the dismissal of his appeal. Indeed, relevant portions of the warders' observations of their charge, recorded in the occurrence book, would be transmitted by the governor to the Home Office to form part of the material considered by the department when reviewing the case for a reprieve. As noted previously, some prisoners cheered up as they waited in hope for the outcome of the reprieve petition. However, others became more depressed and distressed as the date fixed for their execution drew inexorably nearer. It simply depended on each prisoner's strength of character.

The formal request for a reprieve submitted by the prisoner's solicitor, whether in the form of a letter from the solicitor or from the prisoner himself, or in the

---

362   Following the statutory pardon for Turing, demands were made for pardons for the approximately 65,000 other men convicted of homosexual behaviour before decriminalisation in 1967. But the effort in listing all such cases for pardons must be enormous.

363   The last such case listed was that of Arthur Bosworth in 1958 whose solicitor explained to him that the circumstances of the killing indicated that any appeal would be hopeless. So the lawyer simply wrote directly to the Home Secretary in those terms seeking a reprieve, which was granted eleven days later.

form of a beautifully prepared calligraphic parchment (the latter two were employed in Rouse's case) would receive attention from the Home Office. But the department was generally not influenced by reprieve petitions in the form of thousands of names from the public. Thus the 832,104 signatures in favour of a reprieve for Freddie Bywaters availed him not at all in 1923 (Crippen attracted only 15,000 signatures). Nor, indeed, was the department influenced by a jury's recommendation, strong or otherwise, to mercy; unless, that is, it was endorsed by the trial judge. For the jury's recommendation, if not backed by the judge, might simply have been a compromise settlement to appease the one juror holding out for an acquittal, and not a reflection of the views of the other eleven.

But, as we saw in respect of the Casement and Peter Barnes cases, public opinion might still have a role to play. It therefore seemed, according to one of Bresler's sources, that in many cases before the execution had been due to take place, the police would try to gauge the reaction in the neighbourhood where the crime had taken place were a reprieve to be granted. A negative reaction would be unlikely to help the killer, though the Home Secretary could nonetheless take a different view. Moreover, while he might be prepared to meet the prisoner's constituency MP, ambassadors (if the prisoner was someone like the Frenchman, Vaquier, or the American, Dr. Crippen) or a bishop, he would never agree to meet family members pleading for a reprieve. For an emotional appeal, as distinct from one based on solid grounds, such as the prisoner's age, background, 'diminished' responsibility etc, was deemed inappropriate. Indeed, even the prisoner's lawyers could not expect to see the minister, though some did make strenuous efforts to contact the Home Secretary at his home. For example, Edith Thompson's solicitor, accompanied by a reporter, journeyed to the Home Secretary, William Bridgeman's, Shrewsbury home in January 1923 where he appealed to him in a last-ditch but vain effort to prevent her execution two days later. Home Office officials, however, would invariably be prepared to meet anyone, including relatives.

It will be recalled that until the post-war period, the medical inquiry into the prisoner's mental state could only determine his sanity under the Criminal Lunatics Act 1884. If insane, he was not to be hanged, though whether this insanity was confined to the somewhat artificial 'legal' insanity under the McNaghten Rules of 1843 is unclear. After 1948, on the initiative of the Home Office permanent secretary, Sir Frank Newsam who, in a more junior capacity, had himself been involved in considering the reprieve issue in the Rouse case, the procedure for a more wide-ranging inquiry into the prisoner's mental state was instituted. Thus a finding of mental instability short of insanity, as certified by the medical panel which included psychiatrists, could well lead to a reprieve. Such a finding could also relate to what may now fall within the scope of diminished responsibility under the Homicide Act 1957 as amended by the Coroners and Justice Act 2009. For this can cover a number of personality disorders, 'syndromes', neuroses and other conditions, extending from clinical alcoholism, schizophrenia, paranoia, clinical or manic depression, even severe pre-menstrual tension. But clearly a finding by the medical panel of a prisoner's mental instability did not lead to an automatic reprieve. After all, psychopaths such as the Scottish serial killer, Peter Manuel, in 1958 and Francis Wilkinson in 1953 went to the gallows.

However, armed with a portfolio of diverse information on the prisoner culled from various sources, the deputy under-secretary would collate the information, draft a summary, and then, subject to the permanent secretary's approval, present the department's advice to the Home Secretary as to what he should decide regarding the petition.

We know from his own published memoirs that J. R. Clynes opposed the death penalty. This apparently caused him anguish in wrestling with the decision whether to reprieve William Podmore, also in the fateful year of 1930. Podmore, mentioned previously, had apparently been working for Vivian Messiter, a sales agent for an oil company, and had been pocketing commission on the basis of false orders placed with the company. On the footing that Messiter had discovered the fraud, Podmore battered him to death. A few days before Podmore was due to hang, Clynes claimed that he had been visited at his home at midnight by a ghost-like character wishing to speak to him about the hammer used in the attack. Clynes advised the visitor to go to the Home Office the next morning where he would be willing to see the strange man. But no-one arrived and Podmore was hanged. 'Something like a ghost story comes into this record', reflected Clynes.[364]

Yet it was more common for the former trade union leader simply to leave the matter to his civil servants and to follow their advice which, indeed, was the case with Arthur Rouse. In fact, many Home Secretaries took refuge in the doctrine that they had to administer the law as they found it, usually applying the formula that 'the law must take its course'. Actually, as noted above, that was not always so. Discretion still resided with the Home Secretary. Thus it is clear that in a small number of cases ministers refused to follow their senior officials' advice to reject a reprieve, while Herbert Morrison, a policeman's son and Labour Home Secretary during the wartime coalition, admitted that he overrode the department's recommendation for mercy, '...if I thought the facts did not warrant it'.[365] Clearly, such intra-departmental disagreements were rare. Internal unanimity was the norm, but it was not always predictable, beforehand, what that unanimous decision would be. As we shall see, there was no question of Clynes overruling his officials on the question of Rouse's reprieve. And so to the prisoner's petition we now turn. There is little doubt that in Rouse's case it was Blackwell's 'advice' that ensured that Rouse would hang, irrespective of whether Clynes had harboured his own doubts as to whether an execution would be appropriate. Indeed, there is little evidence from the Home Office papers that Clynes himself had weighed up the decision with the degree of thoroughness that the enormity of such a decision would justify. That is not to assert that Clynes did not give the matter much thought, nor that it did not cause him acute concern (see below). It is, however, to claim that rather than pursue his own evaluation of the petition in all its infinite complexity, and to reach his own independent conclusion as to whether Rouse

364 J. R. Clynes, *Memoirs, 1924-1937*, Hutchinson, 1937, p. 140. He only briefly mentions the Rouse case, noting the numerous written appeals that were sent to the Home Office, mostly from women who 'make hysterical promises to keep the murderer straight, even by marrying him, if he is reprieved'. See *ibid.*, p. 145.
365 Bresler, *op. cit.*, p. 119. Morrison discusses some of his reprieve decisions in Lord Morrison of Lambeth, *Herbert Morrison: An Autobiography*, Odhams Press, 1960, pp. 226-29. He noted that the King would offer his opinion on reprieve applications (it was, after all, an exercise of the 'royal prerogative'), while accepting that the minister's decision prevailed in each case. Among the wartime cases, he reprieved Elizabeth Jones (in the 'Cleft-chin Murder' of 1944) while allowing her co-prisoner, Karl Hulten, the American GI, to hang. Churchill and the American ambassador disagreed with his decision. See *ibid.*, p. 228.

should live or die, he allowed himself, as most Home Secretaries probably did in those circumstances, to rely on the judgment of his officials to advise him of the 'correct' decision. Clynes himself, whose ministerial career began with the crucial post of Food Controller in Lloyd George's wartime coalition in 1918 (arguably Germany lost the war because it had been unsuccessful in feeding its nation[366]), was scarcely a man of political strength, though whether in 1931 he was one of the worst Home Secretaries in living memory, as 'Solicitor', the (Conservative) author of *English Justice*[367]asserted, would depend on the criteria employed.

Rouse's Further Points in his Hand-Written Petition

We have already drawn upon Rouse's own precise, though slightly ungainly, handwritten petition which revealed his frustration at his defence team's failure to pursue his own theory of the fire. Thus it will be recalled that he sought to offer, in a somewhat complex narrative, explanations for the intense fire, started by the victim's carelessness, which referred both to a burnt washer and to the carburettor top. The document reminds one of his concentrated body language, alternately showing approval and disapproval, when listening intently at his trial to the engineering experts' different explanations for the conflagration.

But he wanted to revisit and to rebut strongly the Crown's claim that the car's doors had been open during the blaze (he had, the prosecution had insisted, allegedly pitched his victim through the open door). He therefore first raised the matter of the heel, weighing one ounce, found a few inches away from the burnt-out chassis. Rouse's object in mentioning it here was to argue that although the item had been found outside the car, that fact could still be consistent with his claiming that the car doors had been closed when he reached the blazing car after relieving himself (the Crown had alleged, of course, that the doors had been left open after and, in effect, because he had attacked and then pitched the now-unconscious victim into the vehicle). Thus he suggested that where the intensity of the fire had caused the doors, made primarily of fabric, to swing open on their hinges (which was more plausible than suggesting that the villagers had pulled the car doors open to try to rescue the man), the heel could have been shifted outside the car by the force of the water thrown over the car by the villagers in their vain attempt to put out the flames. So the later inconvenient discovery of Nellie's shoe heel outside the car should not detract from his own story that the doors had been closed while he had been attending to his ablutions, and should not be taken as proof of the Crown's version that he had thrown his victim into the vehicle through an open door. Was the point raised a central one or a footnote quibble? It scarcely mattered in the end.

Rouse's next point was linked to the above in that one of the photographic exhibits showed both the car and part of the grass verge. However the latter betrayed no trace of burnt debris of wood or fabric. This, he implied, would support his argument that the car doors had not been open during the fire and that therefore the debris was necessarily confined within the vehicle by the closed doors and not found on the verge. Consequently, Rouse argued that this finding (the absence of fire detritus on the verge) proved he had not shoved the man in

366 *Cf.*, Avner Offer, *The First World War: An Agrarian Interpretation*, Oxford University Press, 1989.
367 'Solicitor', *English Justice*, Penguin, 1941 (first published in 1933), pp. 77, 186.

his unconscious or semi-conscious state onto the front seats of the car, with the victim's right leg supposedly protruding through the open passenger door. For the Home Office there was a simple explanation annotated on Rouse's petition. That is, that the car had been moved off the road (as we know it had been), where signs of burning still remained on the tarmac, and onto the undamaged grass verge.[368]What was not discussed, however, was whether the 'signs of burning' on the road were widespread and therefore consistent with open doors, or narrowly confined, and thus consistent with closed doors. The photograph reproduced in Normanton's NBT volume (Exhibit No. 4) is indeterminate on this question.

Finally, as he had previously forgotten to mention the point, he now claimed that the finding of the victim's arm (presumably with lit cigar in the other hand) over the driver's seat was explained by reference to the man's having thrown the petrol can to the back of the car, which action might also, due to splashing, have explained the presence of petrol on the man's clothing. In thus focusing on the position of the victim's arm, he now seemed to agree that the fire had not started when the cigar-wielding victim was pouring petrol from the can into the tank. 'All this', he insisted, 'has [sic] been my contentions from the beginning and not the absurd ones put forward by my defence and still referred to in the Court of Appeal and ridiculed by the judge'. In conclusion he insisted that he was 'absolutely innocent of this charge' and was the 'reverse of a quarrelling disposition'. He had never quarreled with any man in his life, and 'how anyone could think I would murder a man for no cause is inconceivable'. However, as we well know, his appearance in the witness box might have strongly suggested that a person with his unappealing traits would not have been averse to quarrelling with others.

So the aim of his own hand-written petition was not to persuade the Home Office that the account presented by his barristers at his trial explaining what had happened was correct, even though an explanation that an accident had occurred had been put forward by Rouse's team. Instead, Rouse was complaining that his *own* (and to his mind, the correct) explanation for the 'accident' had never been fully put to the jury due to his lawyers' incompetence (but *was* there such a wide divergence between the two defence accounts? For they both sought to blame the victim for the conflagration and to exculpate Rouse). The poor standard of defending by a prisoner's lawyers might, as a matter of principle, offer possible grounds for an appeal in extreme cases. For example, one might be able to construe the words of section 3(b) of the Criminal Appeal Act 1907 allowing an appeal on 'any other ground which appears to the [Appeal] Court to be a sufficient ground of appeal', as meaning that the Appeal Court could revisit questions of fact, law or mixed fact and law that had been grossly incompetently adduced (or omitted to be adduced) by counsel at trial. Even if this proposition lacked merit, the incompetence of the petitioner's legal representatives could certainly be a matter for the Home Secretary to take into account *after* the appeal stage had passed, given the *tabula rasa* approach to a petition, but only if there were any substance to the prisoner's complaint.

Blackwell purported to address the points in Rouse's hand-written petition

---

368   The annotator thought that Rouse was referring here to Exhibit 48 'which CCA had not sent'. It is not clear to what this refers. Blackwell thought it related to evidence regarding the victim's protruding right leg.

almost immediately, but his brief comments, for the most part, failed to engage the prisoner's arguments and, when they did, tended towards the dismissive. Moreover, he seemed to conflate the formal petition from the defence team with Rouse's own hand-written submission. For example, on the further expert testimony which the Court of Appeal had refused to hear (and that was in Finnemore's petition, not in Rouse's separate one), Blackwell merely observed that both the jury's and the Appeal Court's decision on the 'technical evidence' had to be taken as 'conclusive'. But there are grounds for arguing that significant evidence in the form of expert testimony, if for good reasons it was not available at the time of the trial, could well be heard by the Appeal Court, or at least could offer grounds for a re-trial. Perhaps the appeal judges mentally considered (because they gave no reasoned explanation why they refused to hear the new expert testimony, apart from inconvenience) that the evidence had previously been available, if only the defence had done their homework properly. But that does not explain why the issue could not be considered for the purposes of the *petition*, particularly since an irrevocable decision regarding a man's life was at stake. Moreover Blackwell's perspective that all this was 'technical evidence', and therefore raised merely questions of fact for the jury which, unlike the Court of Appeal or the Home Office, had actually tried the case, was an unduly narrow approach when the defendant's 'facts', rejected by the jury, could be proved to be scientifically valid. For later scientific findings have subsequently proved that the mediaeval 'fact' that the Earth is flat is arrant nonsense, and, as noted previously, that Sir Roy Meadow's trial testimony that innocent explanations for multiple cot deaths in one family are less than 1 in 75 million was wholly flawed. Thus whether the technical cause of the blaze in the fire was an incontrovertible (scientifically correct) 'fact' may be of a different and more compelling order from (sensory or impressionistic) 'facts' such as whether a witness was correct when he claimed to identify the accused in the gloom at the scene of the crime, or whether a non-expert witness's testimony was convincing or not.

Moreover, as we saw in chapter 10, more recent scientific comment suggests that Norman Birkett's devastating opening question to the defence witness, Arthur Isaacs ('What is the co-efficient of the expansion of brass?'), which he posed with a view to destroying the expert's credibility at the outset of the latter's cross-examination, should not have been permitted by Mr. Justice Talbot (though the latter was presumably also unaware of the scientific ineptness of the question). For it was either a technically illiterate question or else a trick question which, when put to the witness, may well have been both contrary to bar etiquette and a factor rendering the cross-examination unfair and whose effect on the jury might well have been considerable.

On the question of the heel found near the remains of the victim's foot outside the car, Blackwell considered that there 'seems to be little in the point...one way or another'. This may have been the case if one accepted the Crown's theory that Rouse had placed the helpless victim along the car front seats with the car doors open, a premise that Rouse, of course, rejected. Yet while Rouse's point, that the buckets of water had shifted the position of the heel, was designed to lend support to his thesis that the fire had started in a car with closed doors, the petitioner's point, it has to be acknowledged, remains somewhat speculative.[369]

Blackwell also referred to the victim's leg jutting out of the car as evidence to suggest that the fire had started while the car doors were open, contrary to Rouse's narrative that when he had got back to the car the doors had been closed, presumably pulled shut by the cigar-smoking victim, and perhaps just before he tried to replace the petrol can on the floor behind the front seats. Rouse, of course, had insisted all the time that the doors had been closed, and this was irrespective of which account by him he had finally endorsed, that is, whether he had tried unsuccessfully to open the doors or whether the intensity of the flames had kept him away from the doors. And as to the victim's right arm being found stretched over the backs of the two front seats, this 'by no means necessarily means' [sic], argued Blackwell, that the victim carelessly threw the petrol can into the back of the car while smoking the cigar. For the position of the arm could be just as consistent with *Rouse* having thrown the petrol can into the back of the car after sprinkling petrol over the prostrate victim. And that possibility was sufficient to reject this element of Rouse's petition. For the jury (not Blackwell) had heard the arguments and the Crown, in addressing the petition itself, was not required to prove beyond reasonable doubt its theory of how the body had been positioned. It was sufficient here to recognise that the jury had pronounced on the theory of the victim's carelessness or of the prisoner's malice. And for the purposes of the petition, this particular choice was now incapable of proof one way or another, as Blackwell himself expressed it (and he did not see the need to use the adjective 'incontrovertible').

To all intents and purposes, Paling at the DPP's office was of the same opinion as Blackwell regarding Rouse's points, which did not augur well for the prisoner's chances when his solicitor's more formal petition was submitted shortly afterwards. The only further information it contained was Paling's reference to the prisoner's explanation for his lack of curiosity in his passenger. That was because he (Rouse) tended not to 'talk much when driving as it is bad practice', surely another instance of our anti-hero projecting himself as a responsible citizen while at the same time seeming to contradict a previous remark of his that he often picked up hitch-hikers for company.

While the rest of Rouse's statement covered familiar (circumstantial) ground, and had been heard by the jury (and therefore ignored by the Appeal Court), perhaps its repeating might still appeal to the Home Secretary's sense of justice, though Lee-Roberts had clearly been doubtful in preparing the formal petition, writing plaintively to Rouse after the Appeal Court decision, 'Is there nothing more that you can tell me which would help you in the matter?' There was, indeed, no more for his defence team. So the formal undated petition (separate from Finnemore's accompanying Opinion and Rouse's hand-written document) was sent to the Home Office on March 2 by Darnell & Price. It declared,

---

369   Blackwell had also scribbled beside his comments that the remains were the victim's right heel. This may have been the case but other sources such as the prosecution's own exhibits list also identify a shoe heel, probably belonging to Nellie Tucker. In other words, a shoe heel and the remnants of a human heel were probably found outside the car.

"Petition for the Reprieve of Alfred Arthur Rouse.

To,

The Right Honourable John Robert Clynes MP., Secretary of State for Home Affairs.

We, the undersigned, hereby humbly Petition you as his Majesty's Principal Secretary of State for Home Affairs, that you will be pleased to recommend the case of Alfred Arthur Rouse, who was convicted of murder at the Northamptonshire Assizes and sentenced to death on the 31st January 1931, as a fit and proper case in which the Royal prerogative of mercy should be exercised and a Reprieve granted, on the following grounds:-"

There then followed familiar arguments, that neither the victim nor motive had been identified, that all the evidence had been circumstantial, that the medical evidence was consistent with innocence and, finally, that, 'The trial was conducted in an atmosphere of prejudice, evidence at the Police Court [sic] having been tendered, which was abandoned at the Assizes, but the prejudice remained'. All, including the last-named point which might have involved a question of law, not fact, had already been dismissed by Hewart at Rouse's appeal and would fare no better with the Home Office, despite the latter's broader remit (we will consider in a separate chapter whether rejection of the 'prejudice' argument meant that a miscarriage of justice had occurred when Rouse was executed).

As noted previously, a reprieve petition was designed only to highlight extenuating circumstances which might lessen the penalty without altering the guilt. Ordinarily at the conclusion of trials where the accused was found guilty, such points would be put by defending counsel (or by the police regarding previous, hopefully minor, convictions, if any) after verdict but before sentence, so that the punishment could be fixed to reflect any mitigating or aggravating factors. With a conviction for murder, however, there was only one sentence, with the result that no provision for defence counsel's plea in mitigation existed. And, as we have seen, even the jury's recommendation for mercy in a capital case might go nowhere at the petition stage if the trial judge did not express his concurrence with the recommendation.

As one newspaper editorial noted,[370] while the Appeal Court could not concern itself with whether the evidence was really strong enough to justify the jury's verdict, nonetheless, '...it does not follow that it will be ignored. The Home Secretary has full power to review all the facts: and if he has any reasonable doubt as a result of his examination of the justice [sic] of the verdict, he will, of course, allow the convicted man the benefit of it'. No doubt Clynes, a committed abolitionist, would have endorsed the sentiments of the eighteenth century French writer, Alain-René Lesage, that 'Justice is such a fine thing that we cannot pay too dearly for it'. Yet the list of ten factors, let alone the three compelling grounds for a reprieve, offered to the Gowers Committee on Capital Punishment in 1949-53, and noted previously, did not feature in the Home Office's consideration of Rouse's case which formed the basis for their recommendation to the minister. And for the most part, the reasons are obvious. For in his case no questions arose of the prisoner's youth, female gender, drunkenness, lesser degree of gang-member responsibility, judicial support for a reprieve etc. However, we will note that at some stage Rouse would, albeit unconvincingly, claim that the unknown man had provoked him so that he reacted by harming the unidentified victim. It was a claim that had never been made during the trial, and the truth of it will never be established.

What is especially interesting is that, apart from rehearsing the uniqueness of the case (unidentified victim etc), and the irrevocability of the punishment, the lawyers' petition included, inter alia, not just a copy of the technical evidence prepared by Rowell and Carew, unread by Court of Appeal, which they believed satisfactorily answered Buckle's evidence, but also a copy of the *Law Journal* for the week ending February 28, 1931 (considered in more detail in chapter 15). The solicitors explained that the legal periodical had expressed uneasiness at the outcome of the judicial proceedings and that this also reflected public opinion dissatisfied with the verdict. Indeed the defence team claimed they were daily receiving signatures for the public petition in support of Rouse, though in fact there were probably fewer than 5,000 signatories in favour of a pardon.

> "From all parts of the country and from all kinds and conditions of people; engineers and men of science, as well as ordinary citizens, we have received so many letters as to make it clear beyond question that there is wide-spread [*sic*] uneasiness in regard to the case, and very strong public feeling against the carrying out of the death sentence on the evidence adduced against the accused."

Indeed, they added that this unease, which they shared, was 'perhaps the more remarkable as Rouse's character necessarily negatives any feeling of sympathy in the ordinary sense'. 'We are not aware of any case in our history where a man has been hanged on purely circumstantial evidence which failed to include any sort of evidence to indicate a motive or reason for the alleged crime', added to which, 'it is gravely doubtful if this man would have been convicted without the knowledge of his character which must have been present in the minds of the jury'. Moreover, as to the motive suggested by the Crown at the police court (albeit abandoned at his trial), that Rouse had wished to swap places with the dead man and then disappear because of his immoral liaisons, there had not been a shred of evidence to support this theory and plenty of evidence to the contrary.

Moreover, the judge in his summing up had already noted (though his comments should be taken with a huge pinch of salt) that there had been 'no evidence at all that there was any crisis in his [Rouse's] affairs, no urgent need of money, or no difficulty of any kind', which might otherwise have suggested a motive to disappear. However, to this alleged absence of motive, Blackwell dismissively annotated, 'The Judge did not know then of Mrs. R's conduct [a suggestion that she had been financially implicated in his alleged plan to disappear: see below]. He does now and is greatly impressed by it'. Whether Mr. Justice Talbot *should* have been impressed by Blackwell's imaginative speculations as to motive (that the married couple were in cahoots to defraud the car insurer) will be examined in a later chapter.

The Home Office Response

In the first instance the documents in support of a reprieve were examined by Blackwell at the Home Office. What is surprising at the outset is that in commenting on Finnemore's acknowledgement that the Appeal Court had no jurisdiction to re-try the case, Blackwell himself had annotated on the barristers' report that section 4 (1) of the Criminal Appeal Act did actually permit the Appeal Court to set aside a conviction on any ground where there had been a miscarriage of justice. But not only had Hewart and his colleagues not found evidence for such a conclusion, the Attorney-General, as noted in chapter 13, had also refused his *fiat* for Finnemore to take the case to the Lords on the ground of an important point of law being at stake. But from then on, it was an uphill struggle for Rouse against Blackwell's pre-conceived notion of the case.

As with Rouse's hand-written petition, Blackwell refrained from commenting on the technical issue of whether the fire had been started deliberately or accidentally. 'That must be held by HO to have been decided by the verdict of the Jury', which in truth was only a partially accurate statement. However, as to the four summarized points beautifully drafted in the formal petition, Blackwell minuted,

> "(1) Victim has not been identified—but what of that?
>
> (2) Absence of motive—but his wife's conduct goes far to establish motive.
>
> (3) Evidence circumstantial—nothing in this.
>
> (4) Prejudice owing to evidence of women at P.S." [*sic*]

For the moment we will leave point (4) for separate consideration in chapter 25, apart from noting at this juncture that not only did Blackwell approve of Paling's disclosure of Rouse's bad character at the police court. He would even have gone further than Birkett by introducing it at the trial itself. For, suggested Blackwell, no jury would have been influenced against the prisoner by such disclosures when determining the accused's criminal liability which he, Blackwell, took as unarguable, though this fails to acknowledge that the question of guilt was not the only issue to be considered in a petition for mercy.

In addressing the three remaining points we will first look briefly at the issues of identification and of circumstantial evidence before addressing the more interesting question of motive. As to the absence of victim identification, Blackwell was correct in claiming that that there was nothing to it. But that only related to the formal legal position. For it was a requirement of the law of homicide only that the victim be a person in being at the time of death, not that the corpse be identified. We might, for example, ponder that the fact that thousands, if not millions, of Holocaust victims could not be positively and individually identified at the time hardly saved Nazi war criminals, such as Rudolf Hoess, Josef Kramer or Irma Grese from the gallows.

And the point regarding the existence only of circumstantial evidence was also, in Blackwell's opinion, inept. Proof in most murders did not turn on witnesses seeing the crime being committed or from the defendant's admission of guilt. Instead proof of guilt beyond reasonable doubt had to be inferred from the surrounding circumstances, whether scientific or otherwise, which the prosecution hoped would build up a compelling case against the prisoner.

That left the issue of motive at this stage. Finnemore had in fact sought to conjoin the issue of non-identification with that of motive to argue that since no-one knew who the victim had been then what possible motive could Rouse have had for murdering him? That is, the greater the 'emotional' or personal distance between the prisoner and the victim, the less likely would Rouse have had a reason to kill him. In one respect Finnemore's point was of no consequence because, properly speaking, the prosecution and the Home Office had been correct in claiming that identifying a motive for a killing was not a requisite to securing a conviction. There are many instances where the prosecution has been unable to discover a motive for a particular homicide. In recent years, for example, the killing by two young men in Sheffield of an organ player walking to church on Christmas Eve to play the organ at a midnight mass appears motiveless in terms of such headings as robbery, revenge, jealousy, drunkenness, provocation, or factors that could establish diminished responsibility. It was what would be widely classed (though not to many social analysts) as 'mindless violence', for which no psychiatric explanation was forthcoming at the trial. But the absence of an identifiable motive did not prevent the men's conviction, one for murder and one for manslaughter.[371]

In fact, as Blackwell had noted when summarizing the second point (above), a different motive could be ascertained by exploring *Mrs.* Rouse's conduct, to which brief reference was made above. In other words, the Home Office believed in the theory that Rouse *and his wife* had conspired to commit an insurance fraud in respect of the blazing car, though the department did not go so far as to believe that Arthur and Lily had jointly conspired to *murder*.[372] Nonetheless, the Home Office's assessment was that Lily Rouse's involvement in the affair was distinctly suspicious. This suspicion appears to have first arisen when the Metropolitan police arrived on her doorstep in the early afternoon of November 6 to tell her of the 'tragedy', which we may assume also implied that the dead body was that of her husband. At the same time she was invited to travel to Northampton later that day to identify the victim. In its charred state it was, of course, unrecognizable and she was spared this particular ordeal. However the police also asked her if she could identify items of men's clothing saved from the blaze. When she responded that the salvaged brace clips, belt buckles and buttons, including a 'batchelor' button, 'looked like' her husband's, there was nothing to sow the seeds of doubt about her non-involvement at that point. However, when it was subsequently discovered that Rouse had returned briefly to his home around 6:20 that morning before his trip to Wales, and that Lily had heard him come in, it became clear to the police that something was amiss, or even suspicious about her behaviour. For if the man had been burnt to death at 1:45 am, and Lily had heard her husband arriving home at about 6:20 am, then it would appear obvious that when Lily travelled to Northampton with a view to identifying her husband's body or, at least, items of his clothing, she would presumably know, as the police could easily deduce, that the corpse and, indeed, the recovered clothing items, could not have been her husband's. Therefore what was her purpose in travelling north to identify what

---

371   *Guardian*, July 19, 2013.
372   Technically a husband and wife cannot be charged with conspiracy to commit an offence, unless a third party is also involved. The qualified immunity of a spouse from being a compellable witness against their partner is the probable explanation.

was assumed to be the corpse of her husband or his items of clothing if she had heard him come home for a brief visit some four to five hours *after* the time of the fire (and he had not apparently changed his clothes during his brief stay)?[373] Was it a clumsy attempt to further a joint fraud on Rouse's insurers?

Mrs. Rouse's implausible explanation was that she had believed, due to the darkness and gloom at 6:20 am on a November morning, that the time was actually around 1 am when she heard Arthur returning home, and staying for about half-an-hour. Therefore, when the Metropolitan police called on her later that early afternoon to break the news of the fire, after which she travelled to Northampton, she might conceivably have believed that the incident had occurred some hours, perhaps at 6 am, *after* she had heard him return at what she thought was around 1 am (but which was actually about 6:20 am). Certainly this would have been plausible if the Metropolitan policemen had not actually told her the *time* of the conflagration. And perhaps they had not, for the evidence is unclear. But *had* they referred to the blaze having occurred at around 1:50 am, then Lily would have known that it would have been impossible for Rouse to have arrived home at 1 am, to have stayed for about 30 minutes, and then to have died near Northampton at 1:50 am. So, in this scenario, where the time of the incident had been disclosed to her, she would have known that Rouse's return to Buxted Road in the gloom could not have been at 1 am. But, as explained, the exact information given to her on the doorstep cannot be verified. Nonetheless, her explanation for confusing the time of Rouse's return home remains highly unconvincing. Thus it is difficult to believe that when she was travelling to Northampton to undertake what would normally be one of the most heart-wrenching tasks asked of family members, she was genuinely distraught rather than, say, puzzled or confused. As she told the *Daily Express* before she left for Northampton, 'I have had many conflicting messages, I do not know whether it is my husband who is dead in the car or not', while the following day she told the press that, '...she has had no word from her husband' (who was probably travelling back from Wales in a motor coach at that moment).[374] Her innocence and distress regarding this matter may well have been plausible. But given her unsatisfactory account regarding the time of her husband's return to Buxted Road during the night, the Home Office might well have been justified in harbouring suspicions about what was *really* in her mind as she travelled to Northampton many hours later.

For assuming both her misapprehension regarding the time of Rouse's return home (mistakenly thought to be one o'clock), and that she had been told by the policemen at her door the location and time (1:50 am) of the fatal fire, then she could scarcely believe, the Home Office might reasonably conclude, that her husband could have been in two places a hundred miles apart at the same time.

373 According to Rouse one purpose of his short stay at Buxted Road was to tell his wife 'not to be worried'. It is possible that Normanton and Tremayne were unaware of the subsequent claim by Cannell that Arthur Jnr. had overheard the alleged animated discussion between Lily and Rouse over insurance and his identity disc, and the police would not have been privy until possibly weeks later to this alleged exchange between the couple. For Rouse simply testified at his trial that when he returned home briefly around 6 am on November 6 his wife was in bed. No mention of a conversation with her appeared in either the Normanton or the Tremayne version of the trial. See Cannell, *New Light....*, op.cit., pp. 51-3 for the claim regarding the child's statement. See Normanton, *op. cit.*, pp. xii, 145, 181-3 and Tremayne, *op. cit.*, pp. 35, 188-9, 226, for trial references to Rouse's brief return to his home.
374 *Daily Express*, November 7, 1930.

Second, might not Blackwell consider it more likely, in the circumstances of Rouse returning to the house in darkness, and with Lily awakened by the noise, that she would instinctively look at a bedroom clock to check the time? Granted that Rouse did not appear to be in the habit of wearing a watch and that some writers[375] claimed he was indifferent to time. But, while Rouse's self-denying ordinance was certainly uncommon, and while we do not know for certain whether Lily was able to look at a clock in the bedroom, nonetheless, the absence of one would be unusual.

One can disregard the more outlandish conspiracy theory that Lily was implicated in those deeds of Rouse's that purported to envisage the murder of an unknown man followed by her husband's plan to disappear from the face of the Earth. For apart from any talk of a plan to commit murder, whether a solo effort by Rouse or a conspiracy between the two (either of which plans one might presume would horrify Lily), for what conceivable reason would Lily, who was hardly leading a double life with a lover, wish to see her husband disappear from her life? But this dismissal of a homicide plot is not to discount the possibility that she was involved in a £1,000 car insurance fraud attempt by Rouse, who had a track record of such schemes. Such a perspective certainly seemed to the Home Office to offer a motive for Rouse's setting fire to the car. And while this theory would appear to absolve Lily of any degree of responsibility for murder, there may well have remained suspicions regarding her precise role in the affair.[376]

Blackwell had accompanied Clynes to see Mr. Justice Talbot after the minister had written to the judge on February 27, explaining that 'the case is giving me some anxiety' and that Talbot's advice would assist him in reaching his decision on the petition. When the three met, the judge informed his guests that he had been 'quite satisfied' of Rouse's guilt and (theoretically a separate question) that the jury's verdict was correct upon the evidence. Yet he admitted that he had not expected a verdict of guilty (a view shared with many others, of course). Therefore he 'paid high tribute' to the (predominantly middle-class) jury for their 'courage in facing the facts and doing their duty'. Indeed in his post-trial hand-written letter to the Home Office on February 1, briefly stating the verdict and sentence, he had added that he 'judge[d] from the shortage [sic] of the time which the jury ultimately took for the consideration of the case, that they felt, after the long trial, no difficulty in deciding upon their verdict'. He must have been especially gratified when Blackwell now disclosed to him Lily's (alleged) role in the thwarted financial conspiracy with her husband to defraud his car insurers by firing the car and then disappearing for a time (which does not explain how she could have distanced herself from a plan that also required for its completion the dead body of someone other than her husband). Talbot, he recorded, had nonetheless been 'much impressed' by what the official had told him about Mrs. Rouse's role. Indeed Talbot had '....agreed that it went a long way towards dispelling the mystery which seemed to surround the question of motive' (though whether there was sufficient evidence to justify his being 'much impressed' is another matter).

Indeed Blackwell only conceded doubt regarding the Crown's case when it came

---

375 Tremayne, *op. cit.*, p. 37.
376 See also Chapter 23 regarding Lily's action on October 28, 1930 in taking out a Prudential 'LOA' policy on Rouse's life which did not require his knowledge of its existence.

to the question of whether the deceased had been plied with whisky by Rouse in order to render him drunk. This uncertainty was presumably because Spilsbury had previously found no trace of alcohol in the victim's stomach. Yet even this opaqueness was turned to Blackwell's advantage. For he pointed out that, 'This is curious because the prisoner made a point of saying that his passenger's breath smelt unpleasantly of drink when he got into the car'. So the famous pathologist's finding of the victim's apparently sober state (thereby challenging the Crown's claim that Rouse had deliberately got the victim drunk to murder him the more easily) merely reinforced the official's belief that Rouse was an inveterate liar whose protestation of innocence counted for little.[377] In any case, he implied, a mallet over the head could be just as effective in relation to a sober man as to a drunken one.

There was emphatic endorsement of Blackwell's advice by the permanent secretary, Sir Alexander Maxwell. Thus not only did Maxwell conclude that Rouse had condemned himself out of his own mouth. All the judges involved in the case had harboured no doubts as to his guilt. And, 'This takes no account of the very significant facts available to us but not to the jury or judges—respecting Mrs. Rouse's conduct'. Consequently, 'What then is there to worry about?' The various issues raised in the petition 'need not trouble us' of the victim's identity. Even the issue of prejudice was a 'technical' (by which he meant a legal) point. But as it had been dealt with by the Appeal Court, it 'ought not to influence the S of S'. Finally, despite some 'suspicion in a limited circle', public opinion would, overall, be satisfied if the execution were to proceed.

Similar views on the petition were expressed by the DPP, Tindal Atkinson, who also felt that Lily's journey to Northampton where she had 'identified' some of Rouse's clothing (in fact she had not been definite on that point) had been part of his disappearance ploy before it supposedly unraveled (but like Talbot and the other Crown officials, he did not pursue the logic of explaining how there could be an insurance pay-out of £1000 on an apparently dead Rouse found in a burnt-out car without there actually being evidence for Rouse's planning a long-term disappearance act). As to Rouse having endured a 'prejudicial' trial, the DPP acknowledged that, '...it is impossible to say ... [that] some bent might not have been given to the minds of some of them by prior information to the prisoner's prejudice'. However, the risk of an unfair trial had been theoretical, not practical. For the jury would have undertaken their heavy responsibility in a capital trial fairly and honourably, with the result, he declared confidently, that Rouse had not suffered prejudice (one wonders what became of Lord Hewart's dictum that 'Justice must not only be done, but should manifestly and undoubtedly be seen to be done', as noted in chapter 13? It may be observed that the courts have wrestled with issues such as this in other cases, most notably involving the trial of Rosemary West in 1995[378]).

The DPP did agree that while 'a re-weighing of the evidence…. [might] possibly [fall] within the prerogative [that is, that the Home Secretary could in effect reject

---

377 As noted previously, nowadays, when an accused has been shown at his trial to have lied, judges are required to issue to the jury a *Lucas* direction (1981) to the effect that it does not follow that he has lied on other matters. Indeed, there may be understandable non-criminal reasons for certain lies, such as a reluctance to admit adultery with the victim.

378 *Independent*, January 3, 1995; Tom Welsh and Walter Greenwood, *McNae's Essential Law for Journalists*, 16th ed., Butterworths, 2001, p. 159.

the jury's findings if he were so minded], [nonetheless it] may not appear to you to be feasible'. What he meant by 'feasible' was not, of course, articulated. Did it mean 'practicable'? Well, it remained 'practicable' to grant a reprieve. Most murderers were reprieved at that time, it will be recalled. Or did it mean 'acceptable'? If so, to whom was it acceptable? Was it to parliament, to the judges, to the police, or to the electorate? And what did 'acceptable' mean? Did it mean morally acceptable, or socially or empirically acceptable? In other words, what sort of judgment was Clynes expected to make? Was it one that would not be at odds with his Home Office civil servants and with the legal 'establishment' with whom he consulted? Was it one that sought to ensure that the 'punishment fitted the crime' according to contemporary standards or, alternatively, one that gave practical effect to his own conscience as an abolitionist? Undoubtedly he was not alone among Home Secretaries in agreeing with (did this mean deferring to?) his professional advisers. But why did he do so? To paraphrase Norman Birkett, describing Rouse in his closing speech, 'The motive, if motive there be, is locked in the [minister's] own heart, and there is no power under heaven which enables [us] to unlock it'. But we can make an informed guess. And that is that Jimmy Clynes did not have the strength of character or missionary zeal in office as was later possessed by Roy Jenkins. The Labour government at the time (1931) was weak and would only last a few more months, while the 'respectability' craved by Rouse in his outward appearances was paralleled by Clynes' pursuit of his own variant of governmental 'respectability'. So the 'system' prevailed by 'capturing' a minister who would not ruffle feathers in a wild pursuit of socialist or progressive 'justice'. Indeed, as against continuous government of the Sir Humphrey Appleby variety, Clynes could be put down as a minister who, in Sir Robin Day's memorable phrase some fifty years later, was 'here today and gone tomorrow'. Unsurprisingly, therefore, he showed no inclination to disagree with his advisers, to look beyond narrow legal issues, or even to give the time of day to the powerful expert views of Rowell, Carew and others. He merely inscribed a terse 'I agree. JRC' on the petition file, confirming that, short of a last-minute change of heart by him, there would be no escape route for Rouse who had been languishing in Bedford Prison awaiting execution.[379] And to add insult to injury, Rouse was at that moment suffering the further discomfort of a severe cold ever since after the Appeal Court's dismissal of his appeal.[380]

---

379 Only six others have been hanged at Bedford Prison. See chapter 16.
380 *Daily Mirror*, February 26, 1931.

CHAPTER FIFTEEN

"MY PEEP INTO THE CONDEMNED CELL"

DAILY EXPRESS, March 13, 1931

Last Efforts

Apart from the petitions submitted by Rouse and his defence team, efforts were made by various parties to influence the Home Secretary before his final decision was reached. Those persons included distinguished correspondents, public figures and journalists writing articles in the press or writing to the Home Office, automotive engineers sceptical of Colonel Buckle's explanations who offered their expertise at a late stage to the defence team, and finally members of Rouse's family and Helen Campbell who made desperate efforts by correspondence and by other means to prevent the trap door from opening. Many of the arguments, ranging from the juridical and scientific, right through to the emotional, sought to demonstrate why Rouse was innocent or, due to the effects of his war wounds, why he was not responsible for his actions.

In the first instance, Rouse's solicitors had forwarded various documents with the formal petition. One, as briefly mentioned in chapter 14, was an extract from a legal periodical, the *Law Journal* of February 28, 1931. '[F]or the benefit of those who in future years may wish to read about....one of the most remarkable cases of the present century', it set out the basic facts and the areas of sharp controversy. While it did not offer any new startling revelations which might have settled the disagreements one way or another, it did reflect unease felt within sections of the legal profession. There was the unpromising context of the trial which the Lord Chief Justice himself had stated was 'unfortunate' (to say the least) and, more importantly, there was the nagging feeling among some lawyers, at least, that the case against Rouse had not been proved to the legal standard of beyond reasonable doubt. Surely such anxiety and doubt must operate in favour of a prisoner for whom any future vindication would come too late?

Yet it is surprising that Rouse's solicitor, Lee-Roberts, did not bombard the Home Office with similarly expressed articles published elsewhere, which also cast doubt on the verdict and on the appeal's outcome. Perhaps he reasoned that the department's press-cutting service would have picked up the items. Thus there were newspaper editorials and other learned articles from legal periodicals taking issue with the decisions in Rouse's case. There were also contributions from authors and journalists as varied as a recently retired assistant commissioner at Scotland Yard and former senior Army officer, Sir Wyndham Childs, and the author and former editor of the *Daily News*, A. G. Gardiner. As we shall see, such prominent figures were sufficiently concerned to pen newspaper articles that questioned Rouse's guilt or questioned whether he had received a fair trial. For a vain man like Rouse, it must have been gratifyingly ironic that such attention from distinguished personages should have been showered upon him at this late stage as he counted down his days.

Another public figure was Dr. Joseph Hunter (1875-1935), the Liberal MP for Dumfriesshire and a former prison doctor. On March 2 he wrote to Clynes explaining that when he had previously been a member of the Commons Select Committee on Capital Punishment in 1930, which had led to the abolition of capital punishment for certain military offences, he had 'reluctantly' voted in favour of retention on being reassured by former Home Secretaries and judges that no man or woman had been executed in respect of whom there had been any shadow of a doubt as to their guilt. However, in Rouse's case he had no confidence that guilt had been proved. For not only did the 'how' and the 'why' of the death of the unknown man trouble him. More crucially was whether a murder had in fact been committed. As he pointed out, a medical witness for the defence, while agreeing that Spilsbury's testimony (presumably regarding strangulation) was plausible, had nonetheless insisted that it was impossible to tell from the state of the corpse whether the death had been murder or accident (and Hunter himself was also a former police surgeon). Indeed, he added that a Scottish 'not proven' verdict, had it been available, would have been appropriate. Thus if Rouse were to go to the gallows, he (Hunter) could not envisage being reassured by any future witnesses, 'however eminent', that only those absolutely proved guilty were hanged.

So when it came to Rouse's fate, sentimentality was certainly not pulling at the official's heart strings. Indeed, in regard to Dr. Hunter's letter (above) of March 2 sent to Clynes, Blackwell's advice of March 4 to the Home Secretary was laconic. 'I suppose', he wrote, 'that in regard to any man who has been hanged upon circumstantial evidence there are or have been some nervous people who have had misgivings based upon fanciful doubts such as juries are constantly warned not to entertain'. Such persons, he surmised, usually obtained their information on cases from the press which, in the Rouse trial, reported perhaps only one-fifth of the 600 pages of trial transcript. In Dr. Hunter's case, he clearly did not know of Mrs. Rouse's intentional deception (as Blackwell saw it) when she falsely identified the burnt body's belongings as her husband's (which Blackwell knew, or should have known, she had not, in those terms, actually done).

But no doubt to appease a former member of parliament, Blackwell saw Hunter on Clynes' instructions following Rouse's execution and acquainted him with the department's 'inside information' regarding Mrs. Rouse. The official reported proudly that Hunter had been 'much impressed' (the same phrase used by Blackwell to describe Talbot's reaction to the disclosure) by what he had learned about Rouse's wife, although the MP still lamented the unavailability of a 'not proven' verdict in this case. Blackwell's retort was to remind Dr. Hunter of the extensive press coverage of Rouse's own testimony at the trial and the unanimous jury verdict. As a postscript in his note to Clynes, he pointed out that 'proof' was a relative term and that, 'Proof to Dr. H. might not be 'proof' to me: but then neither of us was on the jury and it was for them to decide'. One suspects, indeed, that Hunter's expression of satisfaction with Blackwell's confidential revelation did not survive his journey home.

Another influential advocate for Rouse was Sir Wyndham Childs who wrote to the department on March 2. Childs was a former Director of Personal Services at the War Office during World War One. A major-general and subordinate to the Adjutant-General, he was closely involved in matters of military discipline including the sensitive issue of executions of soldiers shot by firing squad after conviction by court martial for capital offences such as desertion, cowardice or sleeping on post.[381] After the war he was employed by the Metropolitan Police as Assistant Commissioner between 1921 and 1928. In January 1929 he joined the staff of the popular magazine, *John Bull*, founded by the controversial Horatio Bottomley, and held the post of 'Chief Commissioner'. In that capacity he had published an article on the Rouse case shortly after the trial verdict.[382] In it he had first declared that, 'Of the jury's verdict I have no criticism to make'. But he then rehearsed the by-now familiar complaint at the perceived injustice to Rouse caused by the police court revelations of the prisoner's personal life and amours, details that he believed had been illegitimately adduced by the Crown at the pre-trial hearing. This was also a point made by A. G. Gardiner in the same periodical[383] three days before Rouse's execution. However, as we shall see later, the thrust of Gardiner's article was to seek to uphold the right of the press to comment responsibly on trial verdicts, a right that he believed had been threatened by the Lord Chief Justice's comments in the Appeal Court.

In respect of Childs, his own *John Bull* article had revealed him as one of the many who had wrongly claimed that Mr. Justice Talbot had refused to allow the bad character material to be adduced at the trial. But he also questioned why the evidence adduced by the prosecution regarding the £1,000 insurance cover for passengers killed in the car bore any relevance except prejudice against Rouse. For, as the former soldier and policeman queried, 'If Rouse were the dead man in the car, there was no passenger, and therefore no liability!' In fact under the insurance policy the car insurer would pay out £1000 in respect of the death of any passenger or of the death of the owner if driving at the time. Therefore, contrary to Childs' belief, the policy did cover the situation of Rouse dying in the car, even with no passenger. In that scenario, and although the policy wording was not wholly clear, the sum would be paid to Lily, assuming she was his heir.[384] Childs' misunderstanding, according to Blackwell, was therefore two-fold. Not only had he misread the insurance provisions. But, unlike the smug Home Office official, he had missed the plot in failing to grasp the devilish plan hatched by Lily and Rouse to defraud the Eclipse motor car insurer (we have noted that Blackwell himself had 'missed the plot' in that to effect a conspiracy between Lily and Rouse to secure an insurance pay-out for the death of her husband, the body of *someone* had to be found a prospect that asks us to believe that Lily would conspire with Rouse somehow to obtain a corpse. Was it to be a 1930 version of the 'Man Who

---

381 Sir Wyndham Childs, *Episodes and Reflections*, Cassell, 1930.
382 Idem., "Rouse--My Protest" *John Bull*, February 7, 1931.
383 *John Bull*, March 7, 1931.
384 See the evidence given by Denis Kennedy, Lloyd's underwriter, at the trial, reproduced in Helena Normanton (ed), *Trial of Alfred Arthur Rouse*, William Hodge & Co. Ltd., 1931, pp. 119-20.

Never Was'? This was part of an Allied disinformation campaign prior to the invasion of Sicily in 1943 and involved the daring case of a body, obtained from a London morgue after a fatal poisoning, which was 'transitioned' into Major Martin, RM. It was then floated from a British submarine off Huelva in southern Spain, together with attached briefcase containing false documents, and picked up by a Spanish fisherman whence it ended up in the hands of the Germans. Having read the false documents, the Germans were deceived into sending reinforcements to Greece and Sardinia, and the invasion of Sicily was successful.[385]

Nonetheless, any embarrassment felt by Childs on subsequently discovering his mistake regarding the reason for the non-adduction of the harem evidence at the trial proved no deterrent to his pleading Rouse's case directly with the department. His letter of March 2 repeated the important claim that the failure of the Crown to adduce the controversial evidence at the trial pointedly demonstrated that it 'should never have been before the magistrate', and that its withholding at the trial was simply too late. Indeed any pre-trial revelations of such material by the press, he insisted, would undoubtedly have been visited by contempt proceedings against the newspaper. Warming to his theme, he also took the Lord Chief Justice's reference during the appeal hearing to the 'unfortunate' revelations at the police court as an admission that their disclosure *had* prejudiced the jury's decision. Yet Childs failed to mention that it was Rouse himself who had originally and without prompting set the ball rolling with his lurid sexual boasting to Inspector Lawrence at Northampton police station in the early hours of November 8. Indeed, we have previously noted that Avory J., sitting alongside Hewart, later observed that prisoners might see some advantage in disclosing their bad character at an early stage. Yet unlike the case with Dr. Hunter there is no indication in the departmental files that Childs' letter was even discussed by the officials.

So, if the heavy hitters (it is a relative term) could make no headway in pleading for Rouse's life (and we saw in chapter twelve Edgar Wallace's doubts regarding the trial outcome), then 'ordinary' members of the public and those closer to the prisoner were unlikely to fare any better. Yet it was almost a ritual that emotion-driven members of the public and family members would write desperately to those who they thought might be able to exert influence of the decision-makers. One Alan Graham wrote to the King on March 6 (the letter was, of course, forwarded to the Home Office). He had seen in the *Bulletin*, a newspaper published in Glasgow on February 27, an extract from the *Law Journal* earlier that week that, as we noted previously, had concluded that the case against Rouse had not been proved to the legal standard.

> "Lord Derby and Lord Robert Cecil", he urged, "have both publicly stated that the Sovereign is the servant of the people; but the Legal Profession dominates Crown and people, and if the Sovereign power is thus to be in the Legal Profession and not in the Crown as representing the people, sooner or later there will be an upheaval".

---

385   See Ewen Montagu, *The Man Who Never Was*, Penguin, 1956; Ben Macintyre, *Operation Mincemeat*, Bloomsbury, 2010; Denis Smyth, *Deathly Deception: The Real Story of Operation Mincemeat*, Oxford University Press, 2010; Michael Howard (ed), *British Intelligence in the Second World War*, Vol. 5, HMSO, 1980, p. 89-92. 'Major Martin' was actually a 34 year-old unemployed labourer, Glyndwr Michael, living in London as a tramp, who killed himself by drinking rat poison. What stories might he and Rouse's passenger have been able to share!

Angered at the Appeal Court's decision to refuse to admit the new expert evidence of how the blaze might have started ('....those judges should be dismissed and receive no pension!'), and distressed at Mrs. Rouse's 'agony', the letter-writer also sent copies to the Prime Minister, Ramsay MacDonald, and to the Rev. James Barr, the Labour MP for Motherwell (presumably his own MP). Finally, he threatened to print and distribute copies of his letter in order to expose the 'shame' in hanging a possibly innocent man. Such a threat was presumably not carried out.

The following day a member of the British Legion living in Buckinghamshire, one Ladbroke Black, wrote to the general secretary of the charity, Colonel E. C. Heath. With three days to go before Rouse's execution, he urged the British Legion, 'without taking sides for or against Rouse', to ensure that the Home Secretary was seized of the information that the fact that the prisoner had been shot in the head during the war had not been brought out at his trial. Black (1877-1940) was in fact an established journalist, author, short-story writer and biographer (Delius and Nell Gwyn were among his subjects). During the Great War he had been commissioned into the Royal Garrison Artillery. Whether Heath had been impressed by Black's admission that he had been prompted to write to the British Legion after reading correspondence on the Rouse case in the Fabian-inclined *New Statesman* may be open to speculation (though it was a Labour government at the time).

Another plea to Clynes, following the failure of the appeal, came from Emmeline Pethick-Lawrence on February 25. Acknowledging that any representations by her must be trivial and unimportant compared to those made by 'influential people' like Childs, she nonetheless felt impelled to add her voice to those seeking a reprieve for Rouse. But she was not without her own influence. For she was, in fact, the author-wife of the Labour MP for West Leicester, Frederick Pethick-Lawrence (Eton and Trinity, Cambridge), a parliamentarian who held the post of Financial Secretary to the Treasury and was thus a colleague of the Home Secretary. So perhaps that was why, unlike with other correspondents, Emmeline was graced with a reply from Clynes who assured her, in true civil service-speak, that, '...at this stage, I can only say that the whole case will receive my most earnest consideration'.

But much correspondence, not surprisingly, emanated from the otherwise assured and business-like, but now clearly fearful, Helen Campbell who, in the circumstances, had struck an expedient reconciliation with Mrs. Rouse. The latter had already sent a desperate reply-paid telegram to Clynes at his home address in St John's Road, SW15 on February 23 following the rejection of Rouse's appeal. 'I make this last despairing appeal to you, the only man who can save my husband from the fate of a murderer. My husband is not guilty of this foul crime. He is innocent and the public conscience is uneasy. Please save him from the fearful punishment for a crime he did not commit.' Probably just before this she had also telephoned *Mrs.* Clynes from the Imperial Hotel in Russell Square before she left for Bedford. According to the *Daily Sketch* journalist, J. C. Cannell, when Mrs. Clynes answered the call, Mrs. Rouse had stated, 'Thank you, Madam, for speaking to me. This is Mrs. Rouse, and I want to know, as woman to woman, if you can do anything to save my husband'. As Cannell commented, while Mrs. Clynes 'spoke kindly to the wife of the condemned man, [she] naturally had to refer her to official sources'. It seems that Lily had been struck by Mrs. Clynes' concern for the female prisoner in Holloway, Mrs. Wise, who had given birth to twins while in prison. The Home Secretary's wife had visited the mother and babies in prison, thereby persuading Lily that 'Mrs. Clynes *must* be a good woman'. Indeed, when interviewed by the press the following day, Mrs. Clynes had expressed her sympathy for Rouse's long-suffering wife.[386]

At an earlier stage, shortly after the trial verdict, Rouse's grandfather also wrote to Clynes, his scratchy and fragile writing betraying his 83 years. As with similar correspondence, it rehearsed the victim's carelessness in accidentally causing the fire, the supposed absence of premeditation on Rouse's part (which somewhat contradicts the previous point), and Rouse's wartime patriotism and injuries (Arthur clearly was not one of General Plumer's Fifth Army 'worthless men', often Irish, whose executions by wartime firing squad for desertion would be 'no loss' to British society).[387] The letter also alluded to support for the abolitionist cause (which Clynes, of course, favoured). In the absence of correspondence from Rouse's mother who lived in Australia and who had not seen her son since he was five, her step-sister, Mrs. Lucy Gilbert, who had known Rouse since he was a child, and who had visited him in prison, wrote to Clynes, begging for mercy. The day before his execution she wrote again, stating that she had just received a letter from Rouse who once more protested his innocence. Surely that strongly suggested that his conscience was clear, she insisted? Another family member, Rouse's father, Walter, also wrote in, desperately suggesting that the prisoner was not 'quite to blame' for his 'amours'. For this had been the trait of a previous family member, going back some four generations. It was hardly a compelling plea.

But the most persistent correspondent was Helen Campbell. Thus four times between March 1 and March 10, the day when Rouse was executed, she wrote frantic letters to the Home Office. According to the *Daily Mirror*, the fact that she had written a personal appeal to the Home Secretary was a surprise to Mrs. Rouse, notwithstanding that they had established an alliance of sorts. Moreover, according to Rouse's solicitor, George Lee-Roberts, Helen had chosen to write entirely of her own initiative.[388] In her first letter she conceded that the petition seeking signatures for a reprieve had not attracted as much support as she had hoped. The time available had been short and she admitted that she had encountered hostility as well as sympathy in drumming up signatures. However, her plea for mercy, she added, was not for selfish reasons but to prevent her son being subsequently stigmatised, so far as the public were concerned, as the child of an executed murderer. Her next letter, dated March 4, sought to turn public indifference to Arthur's fate to his advantage, by claiming that it was the salacious stories of his sexual misdemeanours that prompted refusals to sign the reprieve petition ('What, sign for Rouse and his four women? Not likely', she quoted). From that point, it was compelling to suggest that the jury's verdict was shaped by such accounts, despite their 'inadmissibility' [sic] at trial, rather than by an objective assessment of the admissible evidence. Moreover, as we saw in chapter 14, she

386   J. C. Cannell, *New Light on the Rouse Case*, John Long, c. 1931, pp. 146-7.
387   Gerard Oram, *Worthless Men: Race, Eugenics and the Death Penalty in the British Army during the First World War*, Francis Boutle, 1998.
388   *Daily Mirror*, March 2, 1931.

claimed that Arthur's own theory for the fire had never been aired and that the document he had dictated to Lily might have been suppressed. Blackwell insisted that the governor had denied any such statement had been dictated. In any case, 'There is nothing of importance within'. Helen's prolonged correspondence was futile. Arthur was hanged the following morning.

Of course not all correspondents were pleading Rouse's case. Thus a John H. Cox, writing from Hamilton, Lanarkshire, sent the Home Office a press cutting from the *Glasgow Weekly News* of February 28, 1931 (it is now published nationally on Fridays as the *Weekly News*). It gives an account by Ivy Jenkins under the headline, 'Rouse's Last Visit: My Escape from Poisoning' and purports to suggest that her continued ill-health could be attributed to Rouse's attempts to poison her. As Cox wrote to Clynes, the enclosed 'eye-opener' story revealed 'the type of a man you are all dealing with'. In fact the department took a rather honourable view of the newspaper story. For Blackwell minuted that, 'This should form no part of the material on which consideration of the prisoner's case by S of S is based and I therefore do not send it forward [to Clynes]'. Indeed Blackwell only saw the item *after* he had drafted his recommendations opposing a reprieve. Tindal Atkinson, the DPP, played a straight bat. 'While the question of calling Ivy Jenkins as a witness was still under consideration, we were rather puzzled at her persistent ill-health, but whether that had any connection with the incidents described by her [in the newspaper] I cannot say'.

In the end, possibly the most decisive factor, apart from Blackwell's assessment, was the Lord Chief Justice's reply to Clynes' anxious letter seeking Hewart's view as to whether the 'evidence before the jury was sufficient to justify the conviction'. This, it should be noted, was not a question which the Appeal Court were entitled to address when sitting on an appeal (unless it pointed to the jury members having taken leave of their senses in condemning on no, or on virtually no, evidence, once the trial judge had wrongly allowed the case to proceed on the conclusion of the prosecution case, thus offering the defence a double bite of the same cherry in the Appeal Court). For in the trial context, that was solely for the jury to decide, on the footing that the trial judge was correct in determining that there was *some* evidence to go to the jury. So what Clynes was seeking was Hewart's *private* opinion as to whether he agreed with the jury's verdict. But Hewart refused to rise to the challenge, even at this stage where wider factors could be considered. Instead, the Lord Chief Justice kept to a tight script, replying that,

> "I have really nothing to add to the unanimous judgment of the Court of Criminal Appeal. We were clearly of the opinion (1) that there was ample evidence to go to the Jury and (2) that the summing up of the learned Judge was quite free from criticism. We therefore held that the conviction was right".

It was the kind of indifferent reply that characterised Hewart's approach to appeals from those prisoners he undoubtedly considered disreputable. For his point (1) is significant more for what it did not say than for what it did state. Thus no references were made by him to prejudice or to inadmissible evidence at the committal, nor mention made of the new scientific evidence unavailable at the time of the trial, that is, matters which could well be considered at the reprieve stage. Indeed, his treatment of Edith Thompson's appeal some years earlier had been just as terse and dismissive. Thus, as noted previously, it is not for nothing that he has been unflatteringly portrayed in the *New Oxford DNB* and elsewhere; indeed is considered by some as among the worst Lord Chief Justices of modern times, which is somewhat of an inverted accolade considering the reigns of successors such as Rayner Goddard and Lord Widgery whose reputations have been sullied by the injustices (Derek Bentley and the Bloody Sunday whitewash) associated with their names. It certainly put the last nail in the coffin for Rouse. The latter may indeed have been a rogue and a 'dirty dog'. But he might have expected better from the appeal judges.

CHAPTER SIXTEEN

HOW ROUSE SPENT HIS LAST DAYS

EVENING STANDARD, March 3, 1931

Execution and Confession

No last-minute reprieve was obtained. Helen and Lily's fight was over. The endorsed declaration of the under-sheriff of Northamptonshire, J. Faulkner Stops (who was also the magistrates' clerk), dated March 10, 1931, stated that the execution of Rouse had been carried out that day 'in a proper and competent manner'. The signed certificate of Bedford Gaol's prison surgeon, G. Meredith Davies, confirmed that Rouse had been certified dead after medical examination. The coroner's inquest into his cause of death was held at noon, presided over by the Bedfordshire county coroner, G. J. M. Whyley, with Superintendent R. Tingey of Bedfordshire Constabulary also in attendance.[389] Whyley explained to the twelve jurymen who had appointed Mr. H. Kishere as their foreman why he, the *county* coroner, was conducting the inquest even though the prison was in the *Borough* of Bedford. He next outlined the inquest jury's duties. Under the Coroners (Amendment) Act 1926 an inquest in such cases had to be conducted within 24 hours to determine the cause of death. In ascertaining this, the jury was not obliged to view the body but he thought that in this case it would be well that they did so. This the jurymen did and the first witness was called.

He was Gwilliam, the prison governor, who outlined the basic biographical details of the deceased, his time in prison, the dates and details of the various court proceedings and petition and the time of his execution that morning. He, Gwilliam, had been present at the execution, along with Meredith Davies and Faulkner Stops. The executioner, Pierrepoint, and his assistant, Phillips, were also obviously present but no press representatives were permitted to witness the grisly ritual. When Meredith Davies was called to testify, he informed the court that Rouse's death had been instantaneous and without a struggle, the whole ritual having been carried out expeditiously and humanely (and there was no-one who contradicted this statement). There were no other witnesses and the jury immediately proceeded to find, first,

> "...that the body of the said Alfred Arthur Rouse now lying dead is the identical body of the said offender who was so convicted and executed for the offence

---

389 *Bedford and District Daily Circular*, March 12, 1931.

aforesaid, and that at the time of his death he was a male person, of the age of 36, and a commercial traveller".

Second it found that the cause of death were the fatal injuries (described below), and that the sentence had been carried out expeditiously and properly in accordance with the law. For their trouble the jurymen were permitted to inspect the prison.

The prison register of executions recorded the weight and height of Rouse as 180 lbs. and 5 feet 7 and-a-half inches, respectively. The length of the drop before the execution had been measured at 6 feet 3 inches and, after execution, was measured at 6 feet 4 inches. Cause of death was fracture, dislocation of the cervical vertebrae and consequent injury to the spinal cord. The physical evidence showed merely a slight abrasion to the skin on the right side of the cheek. Combined together, these procedures constituted the legal formalities that signalled the judicial execution and decease of Alfred Arthur Rouse (1894-1931). In accordance with administrative practice he was buried within the precincts of the prison in which he had been executed. The record of his burial is in a Home Office register.[390] It shows that he would share the burial area with just six others, though some bodies have been removed for re-burial in outside cemeteries. The earliest was Arthur Covington, aged 27, hanged in December 1895 for the murder of his twenty-year old cousin, Effie Burgen. He was re-buried in 1969. Next was William Reeve, aged 42, hanged on November 16, 1915, for the murder by shooting of his wife, Harriet, in Leighton Buzzard. In July 1935 Walter Worthington was also hanged for shooting dead, in front of his teenage sons, his much younger wife at their home near St Ives, Huntingdonshire. In July 1940 William Cooper, aged 24, battered to death his employer, 68-year old John Harrison, a farmer at Thorney in Cambridgeshire. Cooper was hanged four months later. There was then a gap of more than twenty years before the last two executions at Bedford took place. Thus in March 1961 Jack Day, aged 31, was hanged for the murder of twenty-five year old Keith Arthur in Dunstable. Day, a car dealer probably suspicious regarding his wife's infidelity, arrived home one day to find Arthur talking with his, Day's, wife. Although a thirteen-year old girl was also in the room at the time, Day pulled out a revolver and shot dead Arthur. An unsuccessful attempt was made to prevent the execution when proceedings were taken against the *Spectator* magazine for having already published a letter stating that Day had been convicted and executed. Though his lawyers considered that such a premature statement had been libellous and imperilled the chance of a reprieve, there were no further legal steps to prevent the execution.

But apart from Rouse, the most notable occupant of the Bedford burial plot, until its removal to a cemetery near Bushey in Hertfordshire, was James Hanratty, hanged in April 1962 for the 'A6' murder of Michael Gregsten, shot dead at 'Deadman's Hill', Clophill, south of Bedford, as he was held captive, with his lover, Valerie Storie, in his car by Hanratty. She had also been shot five times, but survived, and had been raped by the assailant. The Hanratty hanging will continue to attract controversy for a number of reasons, not least that another man, Peter Alphon, claimed on a number of occasions after Hanratty's execution to have been the killer. While DNA results in 2001 appeared to confirm Hanratty's

---

390 HO324/1, Register of Prison Burials, 1834-1969.

responsibility, and while the Court of Criminal Appeal ruled in May 2002 that Hanratty's conviction had not been 'unsound', doubts remain regarding their reliability.[391] Nonetheless, that the small prison of Bedford, with just seven executions since 1895, has hosted the demise of the supposed killers in two of the country's twentieth-century murder *causes célèbres* where, indeed, residual doubts still remain regarding the outcome in both cases, is surely noteworthy (even if not exactly statistically significant).

In regard to Rouse, one immediate ritual, however, remained. That was the disposal of the physical property of Rouse's that had been kept within the prison confines. Thus on the day following his execution Lily, writing from 160 Howbury Street, Bedford, requested the governor to return her late husband's gloves, mackintosh and hat. She was obviously aware that the clothes he had been wearing when executed (even had she wanted them) had been destroyed as per prison regulations.[392]

The actual hanging had been carried out by Thomas Pierrepoint, then living at Clayton, near Bradford, assisted by Thomas Phillips from Farnworth, near Bolton. The former, the uncle of the better-known executioner, Albert Pierrepoint, had undertaken his first execution as principal hangman, launching into eternity John Coulson, killer of his wife and child, at Leeds Prison in 1910. Thomas' initial introduction to his unusual occupation had been when he had first assisted his brother, Henry Pierrepoint, at the execution of Harold Walters at Wakefield Prison in 1906, hanged for the murder of his mistress. In regard to Phillips, his first exposure to the deathly ritual was when he assisted Thomas Pierrepoint at Armley Prison, Leeds, in January 1923, at the execution of Lee Doon (Leong Lun), who had killed his laundry-owning employer, Sing Lee, the previous September. He then assisted Thomas on numerous occasions right through to the dispatch of the Coventry IRA bombers, Peter Barnes and James Richards, at Birmingham in 1940. Indeed Thomas Pierrepoint was still performing his grisly trade until mid-1945 when he executed an American serviceman, Ancieto Martinez, at the US military prison facility at Shepton Mallet. Martinez, a guard at a prisoner-of-war camp, had raped a 75-year old woman in Rugeley, Staffordshire, and thus became the last American serviceman to be hanged in the United Kingdom as well as the last person to be hanged for rape in Britain.[393] A year before he executed Rouse (the third of eight men Thomas would hang in 1931), Thomas Pierrepoint, aged 60 at the time and working at a foundry, expressed his view to a local newspaper in Yorkshire that capital punishment should be retained as a deterrent to murder. Indeed, he added, 'Why should a murderer be nursed for the rest of his life?' In fact, the financial rewards of the job probably played a part in shaping his opinion, at a time when the future of capital punishment was under scrutiny by a parliamentary select committee in 1930 and when a believer in abolition, Clynes, was at the Home Office.[394]

---

391 For the doubts, see *Guardian*, April 4, 2001. For a spirited argument that Hanratty had been wrongly hanged, see Bob Woffinden, *Hanratty: The Final Verdict*, Macmillan, 1997. See also Louis Blom-Cooper, *The A6 Murder, Regina v James Hanratty: The Semblance of Truth*, Penguin, 1963.
392 Her request at the end of the month for a copy of his death certificate is mentioned elsewhere.
393 For details of those hanged and the dates of executions, see John J. Eddleston, *The Encyclopaedia of Executions*, John Blake, 2004, *passim*.
394 Steve Fielding, *Pierrepoint: A Family of Executioners*, John Blake, 2008, pp. 123-4. Fielding briefly describes the Rouse case at pp. 125-6.

But was it another 'fine day for a hanging', as the *Daily Mirror*'s Cassandra would later write on the day of Ruth Ellis' execution in 1955? Five days before Rouse's execution, the Home Secretary was asked in parliament whether he would 'prevent further executions' being carried out in Bedford Gaol which had previously achieved notoriety in the writings of the late eighteenth and early nineteenth century prison reformer, John Howard, who had visited the gaol and had found it significantly wanting.[395] Now, the barrister and National Labour MP for Lichfield, James Lovat-Fraser, considered it undesirable that a 'special' prison that housed young offenders under the age of 21 serving sentences of more than three months should host such a disturbing event (perhaps the reference to 'undesirable' signified Lovat-Fraser's acceptance that Rouse's execution could not be moved elsewhere at this late stage). Similarly the veteran MP and former Labour Party leader, George Lansbury (grandfather of the actress Dame Angela Lansbury), had mentioned to Clynes that the young prisoners at Bedford were in a 'state of excitement' regarding the forthcoming deadly ritual. The problem was that the Sheriffs Act 1887 had bound the hands of the authorities by confining the choice of prison for execution purposes either to one in the county of trial, or to the prison where the prisoner had been detained prior to the trial. However, as Northampton prison no longer existed, Bedford was the default choice. In any case this was thought to be more convenient for Rouse's family, friends and legal team than the nearest alternative prison, which was Leicester Jail, to where Rouse would otherwise have had to be transferred after his committal for trial, in order, it was claimed puzzlingly, to comply with the 1887 Act. Indeed, even if he had been kept at Brixton before his trial, the normal venue for remand prisoners in London awaiting trial, he could not be returned there for execution, notwithstanding its convenience for his relatives, because executions were not carried out at that prison. And if he were removed for execution to another London prison, not only would it attract a larger crowd outside the prison (no doubt including the flamboyant Mrs. van der Elst[396]) than would be anticipated for Bedford. But it would have been even more inconvenient for the Sheriff of Northamptonshire, the official responsible for the execution, even if he had possessed the legal power to preside over the execution elsewhere than in his county goal or in Bedford Gaol, where the prisoner had been confined before trial.

But in any case, the prison governor reported to the chairman of the Prison Commission, Sir Alexander Maxwell (who would rejoin the Home Office the following year and become its permanent under-secretary in 1938), that there was in fact *no* excitement among the young prisoners. Moreover, there were no young 'mental defective' prisoners in Bedford. Indeed, young offenders in this category were kept at Wormwood Scrubs (along with those not so afflicted), pending transfer to institutions for criminal 'mental defectives'. If there *were* any such prisoners of a 'specially emotional or highly-strung type', they could be transferred elsewhere, but the removal of 50 young offenders in anticipation of

395 See, for example, D. L. Howard, *John Howard: Prison Reformer*, Christopher Johnson, 1958, pp. 40-1.
396 She was a wealthy and inveterate campaigner against capital punishment, driving to prisons on execution days in her Rolls-Royce. See Violet Van der Elst, *On the Gallows*, 2nd ed., privately published (London), 1939; Charles Neilson Gattey, *The Incredible Mrs. Van Der Elst*, Leslie Frewin, 1972; Lizzie Seal, "Violet van der Elst's Use of Spectacle and Militancy in her Campaign against the Death Penalty in England", *Law, Crime and History*, Vol. 3 (3), 2013, pp. 25-41.

Rouse's execution would itself generate the kind of 'excitement' and disturbance that should be suppressed. Let them just carry on with their normal routines, it was concluded. Nonetheless the Prison Commissioners felt that it might be better in future not to carry out executions in small prisons like Bedford which contained 150 prisoners, of whom 50 were young.

On March 7, three days before the execution, L. Stileman-Gibbard, JP, DL., the seventy-five-year old chairman of the Bedford Prison Visiting Committee, in a pre-emptive step, sent a letter (presumably to the governor) seeking guidance on whether he should send a draft letter, that he also enclosed, to the *Bedfordshire Times*. The draft was as follows:

"Re Alfred Arthur Rouse

Sir,

Now that this sad and tragic affair is over I think it right that the Public should know these two things.

1   Much that has got into the Press has been wilful and deliberate lying by persons who had no foundation whatever, except their own imagination, for what they wrote.

2   Although at first Rouse was inclined to be very suspicious and even resentful with his guards, officers whose painful duty it was to be continually with him, it was not long before he spoke to me very warmly of the kindness he was receiving on all hands and added, 'I couldn't have believed it'."

On March 13 a departmental official at the Prison Commission observed that those elements of the London and Bedford press which had reported calmly and without sensation that the actual execution and inquest had taken place, 'ought to have wider publicity!'[397] But he knew that he was being ironic. For in respect of Stileman-Gibbard's inquiry, normal practice had to prevail for a civil service whose informal motto was 'Never explain, never complain'. Of course it went without saying that the commissioners agreed with the writer's sentiments and deprecated any criticism of the fine prison staff. But even the disclosure of Rouse's suspicious demeanour and of his retreat from that position over time, although sounding 'harmless enough', bore on confidential matters which were not for the press. In sum the authorities would prefer that Stileman-Gibbard maintain the 'traditional prison policy of silence'. They hardly needed to add that termination of his Bedford Prison appointment was always available in the unlikely event of his recalcitrance.

Far more controversial were the issues of Rouse's last hours before execution and whether a confession published in the *Daily Sketch* of March 11, the day after his execution, had been genuine. As we shall see later in this chapter, the prison governor had already reported an off-the-record confession by Rouse to his prison wardens before his appeal. Now that the prisoner was dead, both his last hours and whether he had confessed were bound to excite a public interest stoked up by the press.

---

397   As to the local press, he was undoubtedly referring to the *Bedford and District Daily Circular*, March 12, 1931.

On the former matter, it had been widely reported that while awaiting trial Rouse had initially been pessimistic about the outcome and was exhibiting bouts of depression. These moods had begun to lift as he re-thought his situation, believing that he now had a 'fighting chance' of an acquittal. But when it seemed that his own explanation for the blaze would not be advanced by his defence team in evidence, for they proposed to adduce a somewhat different theory of accident, his mood once again darkened. Indeed despite his confident and ebullient appearance both in the dock and in the witness box; indeed, perhaps *because* of that impression, the verdict may not have been completely unanticipated by him (though he was bound to have been shocked by it), even though large swathes of the general public who had not attended the trial might have been surprised at the outcome. The heavy cold that he was suffering during the appeal hearing in London, at which he was seen frequently to be using a handkerchief, perhaps also deepened his gloom following the terse dismissal of his appeal.

And as he waited for the outcome of his reprieve application, there was speculation as to how he was coping in the condemned cell, and as to whether any creature comforts had been provided to ease his distress. It is, of course, what one would expect newspaper readers to devour as they veered from the crude voyeurism of wondering how a condemned man was spending his last days to looking for signs of bravery. At least it did not possess the added frisson of imagining the torments of a female prisoner such as Ruth Ellis in 1955 where the press seemed to compete with one another in portraying the glamorous Ruth alternately as brave, penitent, unrepentant or distraught.[398] Indeed when Rouse was informed by the prison governor on Saturday March 7 that the Home Secretary had directed that the law must take its course, the rumour mill regarding his behaviour went into overdrive. Was he in a state of collapse, did he fall into a deeper depression, did he become overly sentimental, or was he resignedly brave, maintaining a stiff upper lip? Leaving aside for the moment the issue of a purported confession from the condemned cell, questions in parliament were later raised on March 16, six days after his execution, about Rouse's last hours, a subject of intense newspaper speculation. Thus James Gardner, the Labour MP for North Hammersmith, asked whether newspaper reports were correct that Rouse had been provided with a gramophone during his last days, whether he had been doped or whether he had collapsed before being taken to the scaffold, and whether he had to be revived with brandy. In reply Clynes stated that where press statements did not relate to matters of ordinary routine, they were sheer fabrications, such as the story regarding a gramophone. He also rejected the idea that the law might be changed to prevent such disclosures similar to the legislative restrictions in section 41 of the Criminal Justice Act 1925 preventing publication of photographs of court proceedings. It is this rule, which is essentially still in force (subject to provision for television coverage of a small number of hearings), which obliges the press and media today to rely upon artists to sketch from memory, for subsequent illustration in news outlets, the principal actors in a trial drama.[399] But in respect of Clynes' parliamentary reply, what was left unstated

---

398 Lizzie Seal, "Ruth Ellis in the Condemned Cell", *Prison Service Journal*, No. 199, January 2012, pp. 17-19.
399 Gerry Rubin, "Seddon, Dell and Rock 'n' Roll; Investigating Alleged Breaches of the Ban on Publishing Photographs Taken Within Courts or Their Precincts, 1925-1967", *Criminal Law*

was the source of the alleged information about Rouse's last hours, the inference being that it must have come from Rouse's visitors, or from prison officials or, as the Home Secretary would have it, from the fevered imagination of journalists.

In fact the prison governor, as well as satisfying himself by interviewing his warders that no breaches of regulations had been committed by his staff, had also undertaken a trawl through the newspaper reports purporting to reveal the truth of those last hours. The reports 'are a curious mixture of truth and fiction, and it is reasonable to suppose that if the informant had been an official, a more consistently true statement of what occurred would have appeared'. Gwilliam's review took in the *Evening Standard* and the *Evening News*, published on the day of the execution, that is, March 10 (there were three London evening papers at this time, and as many as nine in 1900),[400] and the *Daily Herald* and *Daily Mail*, both from March 11, the day after the execution.

Gwilliam reported that it had been 'utterly false' for the *Evening Standard* to publish that Rouse had made a special appeal to the governor to have some music (his love of music and his fine baritone (or was it tenor?) voice were indeed recognised by the authorities), leading to supposed appeals to 'higher authority', and apparently resulting in the supply of a portable gramophone borrowed from a warder. Consequently stories of the supply of operatic records, including 'Poet and Peasant' and Handel's 'Largo', and of a box of record needles kept by the warders outside the cell were baseless. It was only partly true, despite the newspaper claim, that he had declined to play chess (in fact, the rival *Evening News* reported that he had spent several hours playing chess on his last night after his visitors had departed). However, he enjoyed beating opponents at three-handed bridge where the stakes were cigarettes. There was no truth in his alleged inability to concentrate at draughts, though he may have swept the pieces on to the floor on occasions and, 'running a nervous finger round the inside of the collar of his tunic, he would pace feverishly up and down the [hospital] ward'. He did not take a daily dose of aspirin, nor was occasionally given a sedative (we know that, towards the end, Edith Thompson had been heavily sedated throughout much of her ordeal), though he did smoke heavily. Nor was there any truth in the account that after his appeal had been rejected, he collapsed completely, broken in spirit and holding his head in his hands for hours on end. In fact there was still some optimism on his part and he may have given the impression to visitors that he expected the Home Secretary to intervene before his execution on the ground that the case had not been proved against him. According to the *Daily Mail* he had had very little rest on his last night, dozing fitfully and getting up every few minutes to ask the warders the time. But elsewhere it was stated that he had gone to sleep on that last night almost immediately, 'so convinced was Rouse', said the *Evening News* (as to which the governor was agnostic), 'that the morning would bring good news'.

Review, No. 11, 2008, pp. 874-87. In 1967 the Metropolitan Police, on the instructions of the DPP, investigated a possible breach of section 41 of the 1925 Act by, *inter alia*, *The Times* over the publication of photographs of Mick Jagger and Keith Richard outside Chichester Magistrates' Court where they were standing trial for drugs offences. The editor of the newspaper, William Rees-Mogg, was interviewed by the police under caution but no criminal proceedings were taken for breach of the provision. A better analogy regarding restrictions on the press might be those introduced in 1926 to prohibit the publication of salacious details in divorce hearings. See Gail Savage, "Erotic Stories and Public Decency: Newspaper Reporting of Divorce Proceedings in England", *Historical Journal*, Vol. 41, 1998, pp. 511-28.

400   John Montgomery, *The Twenties*, Allen & Unwin, 1970, p. 225.

The governor further denied that when Rouse awoke on the fateful morning he had asked whether there had been any messages, and on being told there had been none, 'his manner, which was of boastful confidence, completely changed'. It had certainly not been the case that a few minutes before six o'clock on the morning of his execution he had been taken from the hospital to the condemned cell twenty feet from the execution shed, nor that most of the prison staff were outside the door of the cell when Pierrepoint and his assistant entered just before 8 o'clock. The governor also denied that at that point Rouse had become hysterical, or had shouted long rambling sentences, or was in a fainting condition when the cell door opened, requiring him to be assisted to the scaffold, struggling all the while. It was *not* the case that, 'As his arms were pinioned behind his back, he struggled hysterically', as the *Evening News* had written. Nor had his nerve deserted him at the end, despite the *Daily Mail's* claim (the newspaper reported that Rouse had walked to the scaffold 'slowly and mechanically like a man who was oblivious to what was happening to him'). As the local newspaper, the *Bedford and District Daily Circular* noted on March 12, 1931, '...as all prison warders are pledged to secrecy it was strange to read in the London Press detailed—and varied—accounts of the actual hanging'. Indeed, even the suit Rouse wore at his execution became a matter of dispute between the national press and the governor. Although all these additional points were not needed by him, they were nonetheless made available to Clynes for potential use in parliament in the event of supplementary questions being put to him by Gardner or by another Labour MP who had given notice, Derwent Hall Caine.

There was, however, one activity undertaken by Rouse during his last days in prison which we are certain had occurred. For lurking at the bottom of a cardboard box in the Northamptonshire Police Archive is a most intriguing artefact. It is a piece of wood, approximately eleven inches long, an inch wide and half an inch thick. It is a stick. It has been shaped or whittled with a knife to suggest a figure with a waist, like some primitive figurine. On each side of the 'head' a small caricatured face has been drawn, wide-eyed and full mouthed.

On one side there are other small markings, including the initials, one supposes, of the artist who created it – AAR.

And on the reverse side there is an inscription:

Made in BEDFORD GAOL
By Arthur Ed [*sic*] Rouse
Subsequently hanged
For MURDER

Here is a tangible link with Rouse and with the time he spent in the condemned cell. But is it authentic?

The other contents of the box suggest it is. There is the mallet which the Crown unconvincingly suggested had been used to stun the victim before burning him in the car. Presumably this item was returned to the police for safe keeping after trial. There are two pennies (one a Victorian 'bun' penny) found in the victim's pocket after the fire. Actually, Dr. Shaw found three pennies in the victim's pocket when he performed the first post-mortem. Perhaps the third penny found its way into the safe keeping of a policeman's pocket, to be produced and gawped at on special occasions when the tale of the blazing car was recounted yet again. There is a 'tin-type' photograph of Arthur and one of his harem, seemingly enjoying a day out at the seaside. This last was not recorded as being in Rouse's possession when he was apprehended, so perhaps he received it as a gift to console him in his incarceration. The 'tin-type' as its name suggests was a method of printing a photographic image on a thin metal sheet. It was quick and easy to produce and therefore favoured by beach photographers, eager to supply the day tripper market. The image has been degraded over the years to the point where it is not possible with the naked eye to determine which member of the harem is accompanying Rouse. It would seem likely that the tin-type found its way into the cardboard box following the execution.

Once the sentence had been carried out the clothes worn by the prisoner were destroyed. There were strict regulations to that effect to prevent the distribution of ghoulish mementoes. It is not recorded whether Lily's request for Rouse's hat, gloves and mackintosh to be returned to her was granted. Other personal effects would have to be stored. Clearing out the condemned cell would seem the likely moment for the whittled stick to have been consigned to the cardboard box. The inscription was obviously written after the sentence had been carried out. The error in Rouse's name suggests that it was inscribed by someone not entirely familiar with him, though within Bedford Gaol and to prison officers Priest and Cockerell who guarded him in his final days, he would have been known as Arthur Rouse.

The most convincing argument for the authenticity of the whittled stick is that, had anyone fabricated it with a view to financial gain (and given the publicity that was surrounding the case there would undoubtedly have been a market for an item with such grim associations), that person would surely have tried to sell it. Thus it would not have been consigned, as it was, to a cardboard box, unnoticed, out of sight, in this provincial equivalent of the Black Museum.

But what can this curiosity tell us of Rouse's state of mind in the condemned cell? It would seem that Priest and Cockerell had sufficient confidence that Rouse would not self-harm, or indeed attack them, that they allowed him to use some sort of knife. It would only require a short bladed pocket or penknife to shave away the waisted portion, so perhaps they were not taking too many risks. The little grooves cut into side one suggest that Rouse was working out proportions for the figure, chin, shoulders, waist and knees. The small hole bored above the waist may perhaps represent the navel. So he was taking care with his creation, he was in control.

The faces and other decorations are drawn in pen and ink. The face on side one looks to the left, its wide eyes glancing at a companion or maybe alert to something coming from that direction or from behind. The face on side two looks straight ahead. Neither of them smiles. These are not reassuring faces. Side two appears to be female, the lips are filled in as if by lipstick, the eyes appear to be emphasised by make-up, the line of the jaw is softer and it would seem to have a dimpled chin. Side one has a more masculine square jaw. While the nostrils in both drawings are all that indicate a nose, the length of the nose in side two suggests more delicate features than the shorter nose in the beefier face on side one.

Though it is fanciful to interpret these faces, are we not looking directly at

Alfred Arthur Rouse's fancies? One interpretation is that both sides represent a single couple, Rouse and his true love, though can we be sure that as the end approached for him, it was, indeed, Lily, whom he now belatedly recognised as his true soul-mate? Or did it represent Ivy with whom he had been deeply smitten after Helen and Nellie, but who obviously detested the man. It is noticeable that none of the images were of children, whether Arthur Jnr. or Nellie's two. Perhaps that might strengthen a more prosaic interpretation of the images. Thus could side one depict Rouse himself shooting a sideways glance at a pretty woman, or at his travelling companion on that dreadful night, or indeed at his impending fate? And could the face on side two represent one of the women (but which one?) or, indeed, all of the women around whom his life had revolved? She (or they) stares back at him, with doll-like anonymity, showing no emotion. Rejected by her, rejected and discarded by society.

Finally, on the side of the stick is a detail which is the most chilling. No more than three quarters of an inch long, there is a tiny representation of a hanged man dangling from a gibbet. No matter what other thoughts, distractions or hopes might have been inhabiting the condemned cell, around the corner was the prospect of the rope. This little addendum to Rouse's artwork might indeed be considered the very essence of gallows humour.

Whatever the carved legacy signified, the crowds outside a prison that had not witnessed an execution since 1915 were wholly unaware of its existence. Special police had been on duty all night but there was, in truth, little for them to do as the intense cold had kept most people indoors (and there is no evidence that the campaigning abolitionist, Mrs. van der Elst, driving in her Rolls-Royce to protest at many executions, was present at Bedford).[401] A local newspaper reported that,[402]

> ".... by seven o'clock sunshine had pierced the dull and heavy clouds, and a keen wind was blowing. Two elderly ladies made their way along Dame Alice Street, and halted at the huge green gates of the Bedford Prison. A soft, sad, 'Good morning' to the policeman on guard, and they took up their stand near the guarded prison entrance where, within less than sixty minutes the finale of one of the most discussed murder cases in history would be enacted.....The minutes passed slowly by, and only the footsteps of the policemen on duty echoed across the frosted pavements and roadway. The time signals of the Bedford factories sounded 7:30—the condemned man had entered his last half-hour of his earthly life—and the crowd was barely 50 strong. Gradually the hands of the clock in the tower of Holy Trinity Church told the now rapidly increasing crowd of people that only a few minutes had to pass before the execution would take place."

In total a crowd of between 2,000 and 3,000 was present outside the prison by 8 am, according to the local newspaper and, as the *Daily Mail* expressed it,[403]

---

401 Intimidating correspondence to the Home Office regarding the Rouse case seemed to be at a premium. One anonymous letter (which has not survived), presumably threatening revenge if the execution were to go ahead, was transmitted, 'for what it is worth', from the prison governor to the Northamptonshire Police on Blackwell's instructions. Another five-page letter written in German and sent from Geneva, was a lengthy plea in favour of the abolition of capital punishment. See PCOM9/290/1.
402 *Bedford and District Daily Circular*, March 12, 1931.
403 *Daily Mail*, March 11, 1931.

'Never within living memory have so many babies in arms and children waited outside a prison while the law was demanding its penalty'. It is possible that the contrast in crowd profiles was because crowd scenes during executions tended to be photographed outside major prisons like Holloway or Pentonville or Strangeways in major cities where more mobile single men or women could attend. Women with young children were more likely to be able to be present at a smaller town prison, especially if taking their children to school at the time. Indeed, Bedford Gaol, on a busy road, was flanked by Bedford High School for Girls and by almshouses. As the *Daily Mail* observed, 'Babies in their mothers' arms struggled restlessly and cried in the cold wind. Girls between the ages of 10 and16 gathered in groups and laughed and tittered. Schoolboys on bicycles rode about, indulging in trick-riding 'stunts''. And all this was happening, complained the newspaper, just a minute or two before Rouse was due to go to the scaffold. Before this moment the assembled crowd had seen the arrival of the 'dignitaries' and their admission to the prison. Gwilliam had arrived from his nearby home, the prison doctor, G. Meredith Davies, reached his destination by car, followed by the Under-Sheriff of Northamptonshire, Faulkner Stops. Moreover, as the clock of the nearby Holy Trinity Church struck eight o'clock, a motor-coach nosed its way through the crowds. 'Signs of reverence there were none. Not a hat was doffed, not a head was bowed', observed the *Daily Mail* journalist, with not a little sanctimonious piety. But the crowd's capacity, alternately to impress and to shock, duly manifested itself. 'A woman dressed in black fell to her knees in prayer, and the murmurings of the crowd ceased, and that strange silence that one experiences on an Armistice Observance Day was felt', reported the local *Daily Circular*.

> "Then", according to the *Daily Mail*, "a cry rang out. It came from a man who had been walking backwards and forwards outside the prison walls since 3 am. 'May the Lord have mercy on his soul'. The effect was instant. Most of the men took off their hats and mothers tried to muffle the cries of their babies."

'A crow, its black feathers glistening in the sunlight, passed over the dark prison building, while a flight of pigeons whirled around the roofs', noted a local reporter. He went on, "I had in the last minute or two taken up a position, with less than a dozen others, in Adelaide Square, with but the prison wall dividing us from the execution shed. We heard no sound of the approach of the chaplain, executioner, or condemned man to the scaffold, but fully ten seconds before the larger crowd in Bromham Road, the fringe of which was within our view, gave any indication that the end was imminent, we had heard the thud, and the echo of the thud, as the drop fell, and we knew that the soul of Alfred Arthur Rouse had taken wing."

The more cynical *Daily Mail*, however, was less reverent.

> "But that silence which is usually observed on such a solemn occasion was absent. Within a minute of the execution the crowd were moving about casually. Boys on their bicycles rode recklessly among them; girls laughed as if in their playground game. The women with babies gathered together and gossiped."

They waited ten minutes till the official notice of the carrying out of the execution had been pinned to the prison gates. 'People surged round the door, read the notice and stared at it in morbid curiosity', while an amateur photographer took a picture of it with a pocket camera. Perhaps we should not think that we, of the twenty-first century, are any more morally superior to that previous generation simply because we have abolished capital punishment. For why should the present generation be especially immune from the 'morbid curiosity' that appeared to grip those disparate groupings congregating outside the prison?

Certainly, the spectacle of such crowds was distasteful to some. F. H. Lyon, writing to *The Times* from the Athenaeum Club, offered the draconian suggestion that it should become a criminal offence to publish 'any matter relating to an execution beyond the bare announcement that it has been properly carried out'.[404] Following its appearance in the correspondence columns, George V's secretary, Sir Clive Wigram, wrote to the Home Office, stating that the King 'entirely agrees' with that letter's sentiments. In response, an official sent a reply couched in the predictable civil service format of (we paraphrase) 'It's a good idea, really desired by ministers, but it won't wash with parliament ....' Perhaps the suggestion of T. W. G. Acland that the notice of execution should be pinned elsewhere than on the prison gates, say, at the Old Bailey, would quash the onlookers' 'morbid curiosity' and remove a meeting place for 'undesirable crowds'.[405]

Such correspondents did not, of course, question the efficacy or, indeed, the morality of the gallows ritual, whether behind prison walls or not. Perhaps, however, there is at least one respect in which we can claim that abolition was undoubtedly an enlightened step.

> "'Today Ruth Ellis was hanged', began a letter sent in to the *Islington Gazette* by a teacher at a school close to Holloway Gaol:
>
> 'Not only myself, but many of my colleagues were faced with the effect of this upon the boys and girls we teach. The school was in a ferment. There were some children who had waited outside the prison gates; some claimed to have seen the execution from their windows; others spoke with a fascinated horror about the technique of hanging a female..... not only was Ruth Ellis hanged today, hundreds of children were a little corrupted.'"[406]

We do not know whether the children of Bedford had been corrupted by the execution of Arthur Rouse, though it is clear that after abolition in 1965 no more schoolchildren would be corrupted in such a manner (politicians and others would, of course, find plenty of other perceived baleful influences on the young). But it certainly appears that the governor of Bedford Prison and others believed that the press had (further?) corrupted itself with its sensational and often conflicting accounts of Rouse's last hours. Yet, despite the governor's forensically filleting newspaper reports for their fabricated contents, only a small portion of his correctives were actually released to the public. 'Never complain, never

---

404 *The Times*, March 14, 1931. The writer may have been Francis Hamilton Lyon (1886-1964) who translated many foreign works of literature, including Thor Heyerdahl's *The Kon-Tiki Expedition* (1948), into English.

405 *The Times*, March 17, 1931. The writer was probably Theodore Dyke Gull Acland, son of a distinguished physician and governor of a number of London hospitals, and grandson of Sir William Gull, Queen Victoria's physician and another of the numerous Jack the Ripper suspects.

406 Carol Ann Lee, *A Fine Day for a Hanging: The Real Ruth Ellis Story*, Mainstream, 2012, p. 15. The teacher saw the effect on the children as a good argument in favour of abolition.

explain', as noted earlier, continued to prevail as the civil service's *leitmotif*.

But the supposed revelation that Rouse had 'confessed' to the murder was the most explosive issue which had the press falling over each other in an endeavour to publish the 'definitive' account of his admission of guilt. It was the *Daily Sketch* and its intrepid journalist, J. C. Cannell, who immediately made the biggest waves by publishing Rouse's 'genuine' confession on March 11, the day after his execution. But was it genuine? Of course Cannell insisted that it was. Indeed, apart from insisting in his book, *New Light on the Rouse Case*, that it had been obtained from 'an informant' (whom he declined to name, and who may not have heard it at first hand, but see below), he also published in the following year *When Fleet Street Calls*,[407] an account of journalists' involvement in many of the classic murder cases of the period. Cannell's role in the Rouse case is briefly mentioned, and he continued to claim that Rouse's confession in the *Daily Sketch* had been genuine. On the other hand, not for nothing was he also a practitioner of the art of prestidigitation, publishing *The Master Book of Magic* in 1935 and *The Secrets of Houdini* some years later.[408]

Thus whether it amounted to a magic trick or whether it was, indeed, authentic, on the day after his execution Rouse's 'full murder confession' appeared in Cannell's newspaper. It seemed from the published account that the now-executed prisoner had at last admitted (though to whom was not stated) that he had strangled the unknown man who had been 'half-intoxicated' at the time, and that he, Rouse, had started the blaze with a trail of petrol. Indeed he had met the victim, a 'loafer', two or three times previously and had carefully planned the murder.

Rouse explained, according to the story, that the idea had come from his reading of the case of Agnes Kesson, the previous June, which he believed had shown 'that it was possible to beat the police if you were careful enough' (the Kesson case and other contemporary German 'precedents' will be examined in a later chapter). He recounted his impending fatherhood difficulties involving Nellie Tucker and 'Paddy' Jenkins, as well as other, presumably financial, difficulties. 'I was fed up. I wanted to start afresh'. Meeting the 'down and out' outside the Swan and Pyramids in Whetstone High Road the previous autumn, talking to him in the pub to discover that his fruitless search for work had already taken him to Peterborough, Norwich, Hull and other places, meeting him again on a subsequent occasion, not being told his name but learning that he had no relations (compare this with the claims, in chapter 7, of relatives seeking to claim the victim as one of their own), all these disclosures had given him, Rouse, the idea of murder. Searching out the man in the familiar territory of the Swan and Pyramids on November 2 or 3, Rouse supposedly put his plan into effect on Guy Fawkes Night.

According to the confession's sequence of events, they left the pub that evening, drove to Buxted Road for Rouse to collect his belongings for the proposed journey to Leicester, and set off on the stop-start fateful journey that ended for the half-intoxicated passenger at Hardingstone where Rouse strangled him, made a 10-yard (not 14-yard) trail of petrol in front of the car, poured more petrol over him,

---

407   J. C. Cannell, *New Light on the Rouse Case*, John Long, c. 1931, p. 191; ibid., *When Fleet Street Calls*, Jarrolds, 1932.
408   See *idem.*, *The Master Book of Magic*, Quaker Oats, 1935. He also wrote *The Secrets of Houdini*, Dover Publications, USA, 1973.

loosened the petrol union joint, took the top off the carburettor, and set the car ablaze.[409] Brief details of his onward journey to Wales and thence to London and his arrest filled in the remainder of the story, though nothing was said about first having arrived back at Buxted Road before he journeyed to Gellygaer. Nor did he state, despite what he had said at his trial, that he had picked up the hitch-hiker at Tally Ho Corner. According to Cannell, the newspaper confession was corroborated by the statement, made some time previously, of a business acquaintance of Rouse's who had seen him on more than one occasion speaking to a stranger outside the Swan and Pyramids. In one instance the man had been spotted by the acquaintance leaning into Rouse's car and speaking to Rouse who was in the driver's seat at the time. Inquiries at the pub suggested that the stranger was actually from the Finchley area but could otherwise not be identified by customers.

What was the reaction to the *Daily Sketch* confession? It has to be remembered that the inter-war press were in a constant circulation war where murder stories were valued for their interest to the public (as distinct from being in the 'public interest' as more recent critiques would put it) and for their ability to generate sales. While journalists would not wish to be exposed as fabricators of the truth, the general public in 1931 might have short memories if facts were subsequently shown to be otherwise. Moreover, the reading public, as George Orwell later implied, enjoyed being entertained by such confessions, irrespective of whether they harboured scepticism of what they were avidly reading; and, in any case, as Pontius Pilate once asked, 'What is truth?'

One of Rouse's solicitors, A. P. Price of Darnell & Price, told the Press Association that he had no knowledge of any such confession as recounted in the newspaper. The report was 'startling news' to him and its source was also unknown to the lawyer.[410] Closer to home, on the same day that the *Daily Sketch* published Rouse's 'confession', the [London] *Evening News* reported Mrs. Rouse as stating that it was untrue that Rouse had confessed before he died. And again, despite his trial testimony to the contrary, Mrs. Rouse insisted that her husband had not driven to Buxted Road with the stranger before setting off to Leicester. Yet this denial by Mrs. Rouse was itself inconsistent both with a statement attributed to her and reported in the *Daily Sketch* of February 5, and also with a brief *News of the World* report on March 8, that is, two days before his execution, that Rouse had confessed (whether to his wife or to another is not stated) that the jury's verdict had been the correct one. Indeed, according to Cannell, Mrs. Rouse herself had been the source of his rival, the *News of the World*'s, story.[411] On March 12 the *Daily Sketch*

---

409 Cannell stated that a pub landlord in St Albans had claimed that the half-bottle of whisky had been bought at his premises by a man whom he identified as Rouse and who was accompanied by another man. An acquaintance of the landlord, present at the time, disputed the identification of Rouse, claiming that the purchaser was half-an-inch shorter than Rouse, whose description and photograph had been widely disseminated by then. The police considered the acquaintance to be a more reliable witness than the publican. The latter had previously picked out Rouse in an identity parade but had probably seen a photograph of him beforehand. See Cannell, *When Fleet Street Calls*, pp. 183-4. The scandalous and notorious way in which the flawed identification of Oscar Slater had been carried out in both Glasgow and in New York, the latter conducted under instructions from the Glasgow police in 1909, perhaps made the police in 1930 more wary. For Slater see Thomas Toughill, *Oscar Slater: The 'Immortal' Case of Sir Arthur Conan Doyle*, Sutton, 2006, chs. 5 and 6.

410 *Daily Sketch*, March 12, 1931.

411 Cannell, *New Light*, p. 167.

published further details of his 'informal confession' which, it was explained, he had made before his execution in order to 'get it off his chest' (in the familiar apologetic terminology).[412] Yet Mrs. Rouse, despite (or, perhaps, because of) her understandably distressed and exhausted state, now vehemently refused to accept the truth of the previous day's *Daily Sketch* exclusive, notwithstanding her apparently having supplied the *News of the World* with the opposite information. Thus, interviewed by a Press Association journalist, she told him that she had sent a telegram to Helen Campbell stating, 'I am flatly denying the confession, and await your reply', to which Helen had responded by concurring.

But according to the *Daily Sketch* on March 12, all that Mrs. Rouse and Helen Campbell were denying was that Rouse had made any confession to either of *them*, which was different from claiming that he had not confessed at all. Indeed the newspaper surmised that Rouse was likely to have protested his innocence to both women in order to spare them the horrible truth about him. Moreover the newspaper's scepticism of Mrs. Rouse's denial that he had confessed was deepened when she claimed not to have seen her husband, his car and his passenger 'that night', which presumably related to the *evening* of November 5 before the two men set off towards the Midlands. For in a previous statement by her published in Cannell's newspaper on February 5, she had admitted seeing and speaking to her husband that day in Friern Barnet. She had agreed to be home by about 8 or 8:30 pm in anticipation of his departure for Leicester, but she had only returned home at about 9 pm. Rouse was waiting for her, they had a row, he then grabbed a meal and packed his bag before driving off. This account does, of course, vary in detail but perhaps not in substance from Rouse's narrative of driving *with his passenger* to Buxted Road. For in his account, he still went indoors and spoke with his wife, while the passenger remained in the car. Whether she did or did not see another person in the car (and Rouse had stated at some point that he had intended that she should see that he had a passenger with him who was not female), remains unclear. Indeed, to add to the newspaper's scepticism regarding Lily's more recent denial of a confession, it may be recalled that Mrs. Rouse had also given one statement, not read in court, to the effect that her husband had returned home for a short time in the early hours of November 6 before he travelled on to Wales, but that she improbably (and therefore dishonestly?) thought it was about 1 am, whereas it had to have been about 6 am.

However, the *Daily Mail* on March 12, irked by the previous day's *Daily Sketch* scoop, declared that it was sceptical about any confession, obviously miffed that it had not secured its own version first. In subjecting the *Daily Sketch* 'confession' to scrutiny, the *Daily Mail* sought to query whether the 'down-and-out' could have worn good quality clothing, which Rouse had noticed (a strange challenge since a patch of trouser cloth *had* been recovered from the corpse). It also pointed out that Rouse's claim to have stopped for a rest in St Albans was mistaken, since the incident over the car lights had occurred further away in Markyate. There were further alleged inconsistencies in the *Daily Sketch* 'confession' regarding the victim's 'fuzzled' state as a consequence of drinking from the whisky bottle. For Spilsbury had found no evidence for large quantities of alcohol present in

---

412 Soon after his arrest he was reported to have stated, 'I know I shall swing. Anyhow, I have been a dirty dog, and I know I shall have to pay the penalty'. See *ibid.*, p. 181.

the corpse's stomach. Moreover apart from the physical difficulty, as the *Daily Mail* saw it, of Rouse leaning over from the driver's seat and strangling the victim to death with his right hand, according to the *Daily Sketch* confession, Spilsbury had testified in court that carbon deposits in the victim's lungs indicated that the deceased had still been breathing when the car had been set alight, implying that Rouse's confession account of strangling the victim to death *inside* the vehicle before it was set on fire simply could not have been true..

Finally, objected the *Daily Mail*, the confession, if it existed, could presumably only have been made after the Home Secretary had rejected Rouse's appeal for clemency, that is, on Saturday March 7, a timetable based on the argument that he would not compromise his chances of a reprieve by revealing to a third party how he had planned the whole thing callously. And it was superfluous for the newspaper to add that the identity of Rouse's *confidant* had not been revealed by its daily rival. Moreover, between March 7 and his execution three days later, claimed the *Mail*, his every move and writing had been monitored by the prison warders. It would therefore have been impossible for a confession to have been smuggled out of the condemned cell. Therefore any such confession would have to have been made even before he went on trial, a timetable that the *Daily Mail* had already discounted (though we suspect that Reginald Bird, Lee-Roberts' former clerk, may well have had a hand in its early drafting). Indeed Rouse's legal advisers knew nothing about such a confession (with Lee-Roberts no doubt wishing to write Bird out of history). Therefore, the possibilities were that, unknown to the *Daily Mail*, an unidentified third party had heard Rouse confessing and had made a note of it, or Rouse had handed him or her his written confession, and in either case the recipient had suppressed it until disclosing it to the *Daily Sketch*, which might fit with Reginald Bird's behaviour. Alternatively, the *Daily Mail* 'ha[d] good grounds for saying' that there had been no confession and that its newspaper rival, the *Daily Sketch,* had been making it up.[413]In fact it is more likely that it was a third party who made it up (and Reginald Bird's name again comes to mind) and then sold it to Cannell to publish in his newspaper.

The attack by the *Daily Mail* on the *Sketch*'s exclusive did not deter the latter. On both March 13 and March 14 further details of Rouse's published 'confession' were revealed under Cannell's by-line. First there were descriptions of three previous car frauds perpetrated by and admitted by Rouse, to which he made reference in the supposed confession. He mentioned a successful fabricated theft of a motor-cycle and side-car in 1921 when the insurance company agreed to pay out, and a purported theft of Rouse's car from outside the Golders Green Empire in about 1925 (Rouse had hidden the motor-cycle and car in a lock-up garage, and had cannibalised them for repairs). A third attempt to cheat the insurers by reporting the theft of his car from outside a Finchley mortuary failed when a dealer reported to the police that a car had been offered to him for £2. The owner, Rouse, was traced and, to his chagrin, the car returned to him.

The same newspaper edition also sought to dispose 'easily' of its rival's attack on its exclusive of March 11. Cannell wrote in response that it was perfectly feasible for a 'down-and-out' to wear a good cut suit.[414] For it would probably have been

---

413   *Ibid.*, pp. 175-6.
414   See *ibid.*, pp. 174-7 for the *Daily Mail* view and for Cannell's *Daily Sketch* response.

handed to him as an act of charity. As to confusing St Albans with Markyate as the place where Rouse had stopped his car temporarily, Cannell noted that Arthur's lengthy police statement, read out by Paling at the magistrates' court hearing, had also referred to St Albans, which is where he *believed* he had been spoken to by PC Lilley. And as to the Spilsbury testimony, Rouse had in fact admitted in his supposed confession to having strangled the victim (which was perfectly possible with his right hand) either rendering him dead or unconscious. If the latter, then the victim could well have been breathing in carbon deposits once inside the burning car, and even laymen might question whether a pathologist could establish death by strangulation in a body nearly carbonised by a fire of such intensity. As to Spilsbury's finding no evidence of alcohol in the victim's system, Cannell defended the confession by claiming, somewhat unconvincingly, that Rouse had not stated that the victim had drunk a *large* volume of whisky. It is clear, however, that this explanation does not account for Spilsbury's failure to find *any* remains of alcohol in the victim's stomach. Nor does it square with Rouse's description of the man being in a 'fuzzled' condition.

So was the *Daily Sketch* confession genuine? Indeed the question has continued to excite interest decades after Rouse's execution. Thus in the *Glasgow Herald*, correspondents again debated the issue in 1992. One writer, in a discussion on capital punishment, opined that there remained the 'gravest doubt' as to whether Rouse had been guilty of murder.[415] In reply, another correspondent remarked that the view 'that Rouse was innocent is quite preposterous...The man confessed', pointing to the *Daily Sketch* account, and adding that, 'There is hardly more convincing proof than that'.[416] But this, of course, simply invited the first correspondent to respond by stating that, 'Mr. Haines is correct to point out that Arthur Rouse did indeed leave behind him a confession...What he fails to recognise is that the confession was even less believable than his [Rouse's] protestations of innocence'. This was especially the case given that the two pathologists, including Spilsbury, had found no evidence of strangulation on the corpse (no doubt due to its incinerated state), despite Rouse's having allegedly confessed to have strangled the stranger.[417]

Psychologists and criminologists are familiar with the phenomenon of false confessions and have conducted and reported upon experiments to establish the ease with which police authorities can extract false confessions without resort to violence or torture. Some individuals may, indeed, be fantasists and derive pleasure from confessing to crimes that are puzzling the police. In February 1907, for example, Alfred Land, a twenty-year old clerk in Essen, Germany, went up to a policeman to confess the murder of a young British woman, Madeleine Lake, on September 30, 1906. He explained that he and two others had attacked Madeleine in order to commit a sexual assault and had then fled to Belgium after murdering her. In fact no evidence of sexual interference had been discovered, nor any trace of the two other men. At his trial he did not withdraw his claim to have attacked

---

415 The *Herald* [Glasgow], September 5, 1992. Whether the writer believed that Rouse was, nonetheless, guilty of manslaughter is not clear.
416 *Ibid.*, September 9, 1992.
417 *Ibid.*, September 12, 1992. The writer, Ted Ramsey, believed that the victim died as a result of a massive stroke and not from shock occasioned by his extensive burns. What triggered the stroke is not stated.

the victim though he admitted to having made up the story of the two men. Luckily, the defence were able to adduce a last-minute witness, a café owner in Essen who, corroborated by her daughters and by an account book entry, testified that Land had been in her café at the crucial time. Land's sister told the court that her brother had previously attempted suicide and was an alcoholic who had been to prison previously for fraud. Though he continued to insist he was guilty, he was acquitted, his confession later being attributed to his passionate desire for notoriety. [418]

Undoubtedly this can explain why many individuals admitted to being Jack the Ripper or to being the killers of countless victims, including the 'Black Dahlia', Elizabeth Short, in Los Angeles in 1947. They simply sought to draw attention to themselves. Indeed the authorities in Sweden are aware of at least 130 confessions to the murder of the then Prime Minister, Olof Palme, in 1986. Others may have false confessions extracted from them by a process of interviews which may employ brow-beating or even fiercer tactics as with the Birmingham Six, the Guildford Four and so on. For others, subtle suggestiveness, especially in respect of those with mild learning difficulties or with other cognitive syndromes such as Stefan Kiszko, wrongly convicted for the rape and murder of eleven-year old Lesley Molseed, may lead to the detainee confessing to something they had not done. Perhaps most striking was the case of Timothy Evans confessing to the killing of his wife and baby (actually murdered by Reg Christie at 10 Rillington Place). The pathos is apparent when he reportedly stated that 'all the people [police] were very nice' and was surely prompted to intone the formula (if, indeed, he ever said it) that he was 'glad to get it off his chest'.

But death-bed confessions or those made before execution do not share, to the same extent, the self-serving features associated with the above. Why would Rouse confess if all hope of a reprieve had been lost? There may, of course, be a religious angle where the prisoner is hoping to gain God's forgiveness and reach the Kingdom of Heaven rather than be plunged into Dante's Inferno (perhaps Rouse's last hope, as we shall see). Eighteenth and early nineteenth century prisoners on the scaffold would entreat the watching crowds at their public executions to beware the Rake's Progress and a life of the basest irreligious iniquity, lest they, the crowd, find themselves in a similar place. In more modern times, there may also have been a money angle, that is, that the prisoner's relatives might benefit financially from a published confession, with the business details possibly having been previously hammered out pending the trial outcome. In some cases, such as with George Joseph Smith, the 'Brides in the Bath' murderer, the thwarted hope was that a newspaper deal would pay for the prisoner's legal costs.

But if none of these factors were present, was it likely that a published confession made by a prisoner shortly before his execution was truthful? Cannell reported that after Helen Campbell had read Rouse's confession in his newspaper, she had told him that,

> "If Rouse had confessed to me or to Mrs. Rouse I would not have believed him. I do not care how strong is the proof you have of his confession. I could not believe Arthur capable of such a thing. Though it is true that he did act cruelly

418 Colin Wilson, *World Famous Murders*, Magpie Books, 2005, pp. 116-7.

and viciously towards me when we quarrelled, it was not in a physical sense. I admit that although he did not confess to me, he did come into contact with a number of other people".[419]

If it was not exactly a ringing endorsement by her of Rouse's innocence, it was more a case of a half-hearted acceptance that despite her knowledge of him, he *might* have confessed to others.

On March 14 the *Daily Sketch* published a further admission apparently emanating from Rouse. He explained that after the blaze and in endeavouring to get away unseen from the scene, he had looked through a gap in the roadside hedge which ran along the road's verge and ditch parallel to an adjoining field. If he went into the field through the gap, he would be hidden from the road and could then make his way in comparative safety, shielded by the hedge, to the junction at the end of Hardingstone Lane. However, he ruefully acknowledged, he made the fatal mistake of misreading the contours of the field in the bright moonlight and assumed that it had been ploughed. So to avoid leaving footprints in what he wrongly thought was a muddy field, as he made his way from the burning car to the main road north and south, he opted to stick to Hardingstone Lane, not for one moment imagining that anyone else would be about at that unearthly hour. And so he was spotted by the two young men returning from the dance at 1:45 am and ended up in the condemned cell. Indeed, the newspaper reported, Rouse had earlier requested, while in prison, that someone should check whether the field in question had in fact been ploughed up. He gave no reason for his request but when the information came back that the field was still a meadow, he reputedly exclaimed, 'What a fool I was! I might have saved myself'. Indeed, he also sadly recognised that he might have escaped punishment had he asked the two young men for help rather than engage in the peculiar charade that had actually occurred when he saw them.[420]

On March 15, five days after his execution, the Sunday press had a field day discussing the veracity or otherwise of the confession, given that the *Daily Sketch* had appeared to have stolen a march on its Fleet Street rivals with its scoop on March 11. The *Sunday Dispatch* pointed out that there had been 'no *official evidence* of any kind' that Rouse had confessed, and that the question would remain a debatable issue in the absence of such an announcement (did it really expect a Home Office confirmation or did it simply want the story to run and run?). It observed that 'competent lawyers' (whatever that meant) had advised the public to remain cautious about all confession stories, no matter how circumstantial (did the 'lawyers' *really* mean 'circumstantial'?) they claimed to be. Yet to add to the murkiness, the Sunday newspaper also reported at the same time that the prison chaplain, the Rev. Walter Musgrave's, last words to the prisoner before his slow walk to the execution shed, were, 'Well, at least, Rouse, I am glad you have made your peace with your Maker'. It continued that, 'The two men, one a murderer and the other a minister of the Gospel, stood alone for a brief space [in fact, for ten minutes], the one soon to die, the other appointed to read the burial service. What they said to each other no man knows', a strange remark by a newspaper

---

419 *Daily Sketch*, March 13, 1931. Elsewhere Helen revealed that he had occasionally threatened violence against her when relations were strained.
420 See also Cannell, *New Light*, pp. 182-4.

purportedly reporting Musgrave's last words to Rouse. And needless to say, the newspaper had failed to identify the source of its information. Was it Musgrave himself? Had Musgrave told a third party who had then disclosed the details to the press? If so, who was the third party? Was it the prison governor, warders, the Home Office? Or was the whole thing regarding Musgrave a fabrication?

Musgrave himself was distressed about the story. On March 15 he wrote to Gwilliam, complaining that the *Sunday Dispatch* story was wholly fictitious and that he was looking to the Prison Commissioners to offer him protection from the slur on his integrity that was implied by the newspaper report.[421] 'An execution is not easy work', he commented, especially in a small prison like Bedford where the condemned cell was 'right in our centre'. Moreover, 'the prisoner's visitors etc have done their best to embarass [*sic*] us' in this case, while the 'intolerable press campaign' was unlikely to show any let-up. Indeed, he predicted, 'So far as I can see there is nothing to prevent a Sunday paper next week from publishing a dying statement from Rouse, and suggesting myself as the authority for it'. Gwilliam then contacted the Prison Commissioners' chairman, Sir Alexander Maxwell, on the matter. The governor noted that,

> "It is not nearly so terrible as I thought from the Chaplain's conversation with me, but it does bear the implication which the Chaplain so much—and so properly—resents. If the S of S wd. agree to reply to an arranged question that the statement is entirely fictitious, it wd. seem to be the only way in wh. the Chaplain cd. be afforded the protection wh. he claims."[422]

Maxwell's subsequent reply to Musgrave expressed the Commissioners' sympathy and referred to Clynes' statement in parliament on March 16 (in response to James Gardner MP) when the Home Secretary had told the House that such supposed conversations reported in the press were 'sheer fabrications'. Indeed (and obviously without the knowledge of the press) the prison governor wrote to Blackwell on March 26 describing the ministrations accorded to Rouse by the chaplain. The 'young and keen' man of religion had spoken with Gwilliam a few days before the execution regarding the conditions that would entitle the prisoner to have Holy Communion. Gwilliam 'suggested that, inter alia, a confession of his guilt—either free or under the seal of the confessional—appeared to be essential, and the chaplain agreed'. The governor went on to suggest to Blackwell that if a confession had, indeed, been made, it was likely to have been in similar terms (see below) to that already transmitted by Gwilliam to the Home Office (again, without Fleet Street's knowledge); an admission which was certainly not a confession to the passenger's murder. Nonetheless, Holy Communion was administered to Rouse at 5:30 in the morning of his execution after Musgrave had spent 'some considerable time' with him, although Blackwell later noted on April 1 that, according to Gwilliam, Rouse had told the chaplain that when he, Rouse, had slammed the door of the blazing car, with the passenger inside, he had uttered,

---

421 PCOM9/290/1. A newspaper cutting dated March 15, 1931 is closed for public inspection under a Freedom of Information Act exemption. One can only speculate that a third party had written on the cutting something entitled to be withheld under the Public Records Acts. Otherwise, the legal basis for withholding the cutting should be scrutinised..

422 Indeed 1931 was not all doom and gloom for the Rev. Musgrave. For in that year he married the daughter of Walter Ellis, verger of St Paul's Church, Bedford, where he had previously been the curate. See *Bedfordshire Times and Independent*, January 8, 1932.

'Damn you! That will finish you'. As Blackwell concluded, 'It appears, therefore, that any 'confession' that preceded the administration of the Communion was on the lines of Rouse's statement to the Govr. [see later] —with the above addition [that is, the imprecation 'Damn you!]'. And presumably that concluding curse was taken by Blackwell as evidence proving Rouse's murderous intent.

In fact there appear to have been a number of different confessions. There is the one printed by the *Daily Sketch*, and discussed at length above, which had been obtained via an unidentified source, whether a prison visitor such as a family member or friend, or one of Rouse's legal team (or Reginald Bird), or some other visitor, or none of the above. But there is also one made to Nellie (below), which she thought had been overheard by his prison warders when Rouse was being visited by her after the Home Office had rejected his plea for mercy. Then there was an alleged exchange between him and his warders which was transmitted to the governor who, in turn, then heard Rouse's account directly. There was, furthermore, the one confided to the prison chaplain which appears to be similar to the one overheard by the warders, but with the additional curse of 'Damn you!' uttered by Rouse. There are also the ones reported by (but also later denied by) Mrs. Rouse, including a letter written by her in which Rouse had admitted his guilt to her and which appeared in facsimile form in the *News of the World* on March 15 (see next paragraph). Some of the versions of the confession, whether (supposedly) from the horse's mouth or second-hand, offer competing glosses on how the actual death of the victim had occurred and, in so doing, similarly invite different legal analyses of the event. For it is possible to read the different confessions as raising differing legal consequences for Rouse in regard to the victim's gruesome demise. In short, the offence could have been murder or it could have been non-capital involuntary manslaughter. Or he might have been guilty but insane in the light of his wartime head injury. Indeed, there might not have been an offence at all. For leaving aside Rouse's claim of accident, the death might well have amounted to justifiable homicide where Rouse had been acting in legitimate self-defence if facing what he had honestly and reasonably perceived at the time as a significant threat to his life from his passenger. In short, what is clear is that where the evidence for what had occurred was confusing or ambiguous, and where 'confessions' varied in detail, the legal line between life and death for the accused could have been fine.

With public excitement at a high pitch in relation to the Rouse case and to a possible confession by him, both the *News of the World* and the *People*, not wishing to be outdone by press rivals, weighed into the debate on March 15. The former published the facsimile of Mrs Rouse's supposed admission, written a week earlier, that Rouse had, indeed, confessed to her. It went,

> "March 7, 1931--- I have fought to the last ditch to save my husband's life. But alas! I have failed and the law will take its course. Those who knew him well knew the good that was in Arthur. I did, and so do others. But I knew I was fighting a lost cause: for before he went to the Court of Criminal Appeal he had told me that the jury's verdict was the correct one, and he was guilty. My own opinion is that he was not in his right mind on November 5.
>
> Lily May Rouse".

Leaving aside whether the writing style was genuinely Lily's, if the last sentence was a plea to recognise that he had been temporarily insane at the time of the killing, there was, of course, no psychiatric evidence adduced to support the case (which, if submitted, would only require to have been proved by the defence to the legal standard of the balance of probabilities, rather than beyond reasonable doubt). Whether, however, his war injuries resulted in some cerebral or intellectual impairment of reasoning, so that he might invoke what is currently called 'diminished responsibility' as the basis for a *reprieve* (as distinct from reducing the offence of murder to voluntary manslaughter which was only introduced in England by the Homicide Act 1957, as amended in 2009), will be considered in a later chapter when issues arising from World War I 'shell-shock' will be considered.

But Mrs. Rouse was not the only woman in his life who spoke to the press about his apparently confessing to the crime. Thus in the *People* of March 15, Nellie Tucker, who had been visited by Rouse at the maternity hospital on the early evening of November 5, revealed that on her last visit to him in prison after his plea for clemency had been turned down on Saturday March 7, Rouse had finally confessed that the prospect of securing the insurance moneys had driven him to murder. As Nellie recounted to the newspaper, her last interview with Rouse had left her 'without the slightest doubt as to his guilt'. She added,

> "I knew Rouse so well. If he had been innocent he would have been storming and fuming against the injustice of it all. He would have passionately protested his innocence---all restraint would have left him; he would have sobbed and raved alternately. [Instead] I found Arthur fully self-possessed and overflowing with an infectious sort of gaiety and banter that was entirely typical and didn't seem in the least forced."

She said that he had only expressed anger once, and that was directed at an un-named business acquaintance who had let him down over some business arrangement, and which, it was implied, had forced him into the more drastic homicide measure in order to obtain insurance funds. Seeking clarification from Rouse, Nellie then saw him make a sign to keep silent since the warders might overhear the conversation. As we shall see below, however, the prison authorities had no doubt that no such whispered confession had been made. Indeed the actual conversation between Rouse and Tucker, overheard by the warders, was described as being 'rather silly' which, perhaps, sounds more likely.

With this welter of press coverage, the matter of whether Rouse had indeed genuinely confessed and, if he had done, to whom, and under what circumstances, were all matters of intense public interest. Indeed, how had the press got hold of the alleged detailed confession published in the *Daily Sketch*? From the standpoint of the Home Office, the smuggling out of a confession would, of course, have been an outrageous impropriety, almost certainly involving breaches of prison regulations, perhaps even an infringement of the Official Secrets Act 1911, though this was not mentioned at the time. But there was also the wider policy issue of how the Home Office should ordinarily deal with alleged condemned cell confessions when rumours, very often grotesquely false, were swirling about.

The day before Rouse's execution, Lord Knutsford, a barrister and chairman of the London Hospital, had written to Frank Newsam at the Home Office to urge that the department should publish the confessions of murderers who had acknowledged their guilt. In one of his last engagements with public affairs (he died in July 1931), Knutsford believed that, 'It would give great relief to many and might tend to show to themselves what asses these sentimental people are who get up petitions whenever a man is sentenced to death'. Moreover, members of a jury who felt 'over-persuaded' to convict would likewise feel relieved and the public would be satisfied. He was partially brushed off with the put-down reply that, '...there are many sound arguments against adopting the course proposed by you which may not perhaps have been present to your mind'. With a view to reassuring him of what *was* appropriate regarding this matter, he was also encouraged to read the *Daily Telegraph* editorial of March 11 (see below) and to call on Blackwell, no doubt for 'proper' enlightenment. Yet this 'fussy old man', as he described himself, left a final suggestion that the Home Office should announce that a prisoner, before his execution, had admitted the 'justice of his sentence' (presumably he meant only where the condemned person had expressed sentiments of this nature). In noting this proposal Blackwell could not, however, resist observing that, '... where the prisoner accuses the innocent [as Rouse had done, according to the governor's story, below, when the former had suggested that his victim had initiated the violence] he does *not* admit to the justice of the sentence!' Indeed, as Blackwell wrote elsewhere, what if the prisoner had solemnly asserted his innocence to his relatives on their very last visit and he had then confessed verbally to the governor twenty minutes before his execution? There might be no time to reduce the confession to writing and, if there was, the prisoner might refuse to sign it, meaning that the status of the confession might still be in doubt (with his denial to his relatives of his responsibility still ringing in their ears, Blackwell might have added). Confessions made to prison chaplains might only be disclosed to the authorities in confidence, and if made to Catholic priests, the admissions might remain locked within the priest's breast. So, once again, its existence would be open to debate. Moreover, what if the confession, especially a verbal one, were ambiguous? For some, it might be a confession. For others it might not be. Moreover some confessions, as with the one supposedly made by Rouse to the prison governor, might be admissions to manslaughter, not to murder. Should *they* be disclosed? Or should the Home Office, albeit misleadingly, disclose that no confession, or even no confession to murder, had been made prior to the prisoner's execution? The publication of detailed confessions was clearly out of the question. They might disclose only a part of the truth. They might incriminate others. They might be defamatory towards a living person, which would be grossly unfair to the person libelled, especially if the fact that it had been made before the prisoner was executed was somehow seen by the public as a vindication of its truth. But the most compelling reason to withhold even the fact that a confession had been made, let alone its details, was that where the conviction had been essentially based on circumstantial evidence, and if the practice had been changed to disclose confessions, the absence of a confession might strengthen the public view that the prisoner had been wrongly convicted, or convicted on insufficient evidence, even though there might be no possible doubt as to his guilt.

The particular case of Thomas Allaway, hanged on August 19, 1922, was cited by Blackwell as raising some of the issues surrounding the problem of whether to publish or not. Allaway was the Bournemouth chauffeur who, by means of both a *Morning Post* advert offering an employment position and a mis-spelled telegram, had lured a young woman, Irene Watkins, from London to her death at his hands. Thus, on August 27, more than a week after his execution, the Home Office announced that he had, indeed, confessed to the murder.[423] In fact, the prisoner had made a verbal confession to the governor just before his execution. But the Home Office believed that were the department to have immediately thereafter published his actual confession, then a controversy would certainly have arisen on the part of those who doubted whether he had confessed at all, with critics likely to suspect (and suggest) that the announcement merely reflected the officials' insecurity regarding the correctness of the conviction. The Home Office was also aware that Allaway had requested that his confession should not be made public. For he had said, 'I did it all right but I don't want my wife to know'. Indeed he had forbidden the governor to disclose his admission of guilt even though the governor explained to him that his wife probably already knew of his guilt. However, due to a verbal slip by the prison chaplain at the following Sunday's prison service, conducted a few days after the execution, the press, via a discharged prisoner's disclosure that Allaway had 'owned up', had learned of the confession. 'There must be rejoicings in Heaven that day', the unfortunate prelate had intoned, 'over at least one person who has repented of his sins'. Thus had it not been for the chaplain's over-exuberance in contemplating a saved soul on the Sunday following Allaway's execution, the authorities would have felt bound to respect the condemned man's request. But in the new circumstances, it was now decided to 'come clean' and to issue an official press release, published eight days after the execution, which disclosed not the actual words but the fact that a confession had been made.

But as to Rouse, and despite (or because of) a clear Home Office bias against publishing confessions notwithstanding the Allaway precedent, the *Sunday News*, on March 15, 1931, reported that Derwent Hall Caine, the Labour MP for Liverpool Everton (1929-1931), had expressed his determination to extract from the Home Office, which up to this time had remained silent on the issue of Rouse's confession, a statement on the matter. Hall Caine , the actor and younger brother of Gordon Hall Caine, Conservative MP for East Dorset, 1922-1929 and 1931-1945 (and so they did not overlap in parliament), was the son of the famous novelist, biographer, playwright and secretary to Dante Gabriel Rossetti, Sir Hall Caine (who in 1912 had agreed to bring up, with his wife, one of Derwent's illegitimate children, Elin, as their own).[424] A previous parliamentary question on what, if anything, Rouse had said in prison, had been turned down by the Speaker. However Hall Caine would press on by moving a motion on March 16 to reduce the Home Secretary's salary by £10, a parliamentary device enabling the mover to

---

423 *The Times*, August 28, 1922.
424 Hall Caine Snr. had had associations, allegedly sexual, with Francis Tumblety, another Jack the Ripper candidate. Bram Stoker, author of *Dracula*, dedicated his book to Hall Caine ('Hommy-Beg'). See Nicholas Rance, "'Jonathan's Great Knife': Dracula Meets Jack the Ripper", in Alexandra Warwick and Martin Willis (eds.,), *Jack the Ripper: Media, Culture, History*, Manchester University Press, Manchester, 2007, Ch. 8; for the inter-linking of the stories of Hall Caine, Tumblety and Stoker, see Neil R. Storey, *The Dracula Secrets: Jack the Ripper and the Darkest Sources of Bram Stoker*, History Press, Stroud, 2012.

prompt a debate on matters within the minister's remit. The MP felt strongly that where, in this case, a large section of the population was of the view that Rouse had been convicted on insufficient evidence, the question of any confession by him would be in the public interest. It was also important for the jury and judges in the case to know that a confession had been made. Thus 'I can see no reason why a confession should be kept secret' (though the Home Office certainly had identified reasons). Similarly, James Gardner MP, who had asked a parliamentary question about Rouse's last hours, as we saw earlier, also wished to raise the issue of any confession.[425]

The Home Office was prepared. Thus when notice of Gardner's forthcoming question about Rouse's confession was received, the long-serving senior clerk at the department, A. Locke, minuted on March 12 that the question referred to the *Daily Sketch*'s 'yarn', that is, to the detailed 'confession' by Rouse published on the previous day. A few days later, Locke added that fellow journalists, 'on the strength of internal evidence' (was that a reference to a whisper from the Home Office, to the forensic evidence in the case, or to jealousy, or to dismissive views of Cannell's journalistic talents?), appeared to concur in the view that the *Daily Sketch* exclusive of March 11 was fake news. For the newspaper's 'confession' had differed both from what Rouse had said *at any time* [italics added], which presumably related to his police statements and trial testimony, and from the inherent probabilities regarding the facts. After all, the official reasoned, why would Rouse leave such explosive (presumably meaning self-incriminating) material, a 'confession' to murder, for disposal by others while he was fighting to the last to establish his innocence? And if he *had* made that particular confession, why transmit it to 'friendly' visitors who then passed it on to a profit-seeking newspaper (presumably benefiting anyone *but* Rouse)? Moreover, its provisions did not square (though were they inconsistent?) with Mrs. Rouse's simple account, dated March 7 and published in the following Sunday's *News of the World*, of her husband's confession. These events implied, suggested Locke, that the *Daily Sketch* confession could not have been made by Rouse and certainly it could not have been passed out from his cell. The only remote possibility of its veracity, thought the official, might relate to Rouse's earlier confidential conversations with his legal team (which originally included Lee-Roberts' sacked clerk, Reginald Bird). But while this possibility could not absolutely be ruled out, it remained unlikely, probably leaving only the suggestion of a journalist's fevered imagination.

The upshot was that in parliament, on March 16, the Home Secretary told Gardner that after a searching inquiry he was satisfied that no confession had been passed out by any official and that it was very unlikely that 'any such document' had been sent out or passed out in any other way (presumably he meant via visitors). In answer to subsequent questions Clynes told the House that there were no, and were unlikely to be in the future, powers to curb the inventiveness of the press in such matters. To Edward Marjoribanks MP, Marshall Hall's biographer, Clynes intimated his refusal to introduce arrangements for the official publication of confessions. Indeed, there was a firmly established practice to the contrary. So while Clynes stopped short of expressly stating either that Rouse had confessed to prison officials or to third parties, or that the press had invented his confession, it

425 See also *Daily Sketch*, March 16, 1931.

was blatantly obvious that of these possibilities the House was expected to accept the last-named, even if that were not the full picture.

The following day, on March 17, the *Manchester Guardian* expressed approval for Clynes' stance. Alleged newspaper confessions were 'an extremely unedifying side of journalism'. Despite the uncertainty, however, the Home Office position, the newspaper asserted, was correct. The press could not be muzzled but 'official' releases of confessions were deemed inappropriate. Indeed, even though the newspaper surmised that most murderers did confess before their execution, 'what good purpose would be served by saying so?' For what of those cases where the condemned prisoner had *not* confessed? Would the public read into this that there had been a miscarriage of justice? Confessions were only legally relevant when an accused was pleading guilty, the editorial (somewhat inaccurately) noted, and the release of post-trial confessions might cast doubt on the reliability of the trial process where the circumstantial and other evidence had been tested. It did not explain its point. Did it refer to where the accused had been acquitted, as would later be the case with Tony Mancini in the Brighton No. 2 Trunk murder case of 1934 and where he subsequently confessed in the *News of the World* some forty-two years later? It noted, finally, that abolition of the death penalty, a matter of contemporary political interest at the time, might avoid the kind of newspaper exploitation which had occurred in this case, though there were other, more compelling, arguments for pursuing that significant shift in punishments.

The day after Rouse's execution a leader in the *Daily Telegraph* had encouraged the Home Secretary not to succumb to Hall Caine's parliamentary question and demand to reveal whether Rouse had confessed. The principle was that such a matter must remain an official secret. But it did concede that there had been rare occasions when information regarding a death cell confession had been released by the authorities. One was the case of Israel Lipski in 1887, hanged for the murder by poisoning of Mrs. Miriam Angel in the East End of London, before the Jack the Ripper series of gruesome killings began. In view of a 'more than usually irrational and emotional agitation against the conviction', as the newspaper coyly highlighted not-quite-British shows of excessive emotion on the part of the alien 'Other' in our midst, the authorities at the time had deemed it expedient to release to the press details of Lipski's 'full, though possibly not...accurate', confession the day before his execution. Its 'publication may be thought', the editorial added, to have been 'a crushing answer to the sentimentalists, but the policy must be condemned unhesitatingly'.[426] Lord Knutsford had also referred to the confession of the 'blackguard named Lipski'. But going further back in time he also cited the case of Franz Müller in '1868' (it was actually in 1864) who was hanged for committing the first railway murder. 'I think he [confessed] on the scaffold. '*Ich habe es gethan* [I did it].'"[427]

---

426   *Daily Telegraph*, March 11, 1931. For the Lipski case see Martin L. Friedland, *The Trials of Israel Lipski*, Macmillan, 1984. The author believes that Lipski was wrongly convicted but that he may not have been innocent. A recent revival of the Notable British Trials series includes M. W. Oldridge (ed.). *Trial of Israel Lipski*, Mango Books, 2017. Oldridge believes that Lipski had been 'justly convicted', and points to a contemporary suggestion that his confession had been an act of 'martyrdom' designed to spare the East End Jewish community from anti-Semitic reprisals for the murder. See *ibid.*, pp. 42-3.
427   For a recent full account see Kate Colquhoun, *Mr Briggs' Hat: A Sensational Account of Britain's First Railway Murder*, Little Brown, 2011. For the confession see pp. 268-9.

Another example discussed by the officials advising Clynes on how to respond to Hall Caine and Gardner's questions regarding Rouse's supposed confession was the case of John Lincoln, hanged in 1926. In fact, there were significant differences between the two cases, not least because a written confession by the accused had been adduced by the Crown at his trial. The common feature, however, were press disclosures of Lincoln's alleged prison communications with his girlfriend, which appeared to include the contents of their discussions in prison after his conviction. Lincoln, whose real name was Ignatius Emanuel Naphtali Trebitsch Lincoln, was the eldest son of a man whom his biographer's publishers colourfully described as the 'Member of Parliament, international spy, right-wing revolutionary, Buddhist monk [though of Jewish background]—and this [20th] century's most extraordinary con-man'.[428] A soldier with the Honourable Artillery Company, Lincoln had written to his girlfriend, while he was in prison awaiting trial, admitting to having fired the shots during a robbery that had killed Edward Richards, at the house where the victim was staying in Trowbridge, near to Lincoln's barracks. The particular letter was adduced in evidence by the prosecutor, Rayner Goddard, later Lord Chief Justice, at the trial and the jury duly convicted the prisoner. However, the accused's accomplice in the drunken robbery was acquitted of murder on the direction of Rouse's later trial judge, Mr. Justice Talbot. But following Lincoln's conviction, the press went on to publish some further communications arising from his girlfriend's prison visits (probably information obtained both before and after the trial), while the Home Office seemed to be aware of further information communicated to her by the now-condemned Lincoln which she had then disclosed to the press, though the latter had not yet got round to publishing it.

But what had already been published in the press probably led to public scenes of sympathy for Lincoln. A meeting was held in Trafalgar Square and 50,000 signatures (compared to the approximately 5,000 signatures for Rouse) which called for clemency for Lincoln were obtained. As a result of her indiscretions the girlfriend was required by the Home Office to undertake not to make any further communications to the press regarding her visits, nor to write letters to the press. Otherwise, no more prison correspondence would be permitted, nor visits to him allowed. In the event no reprieve came for Lincoln and he was hanged on March 2, 1926, aged 23, at Shepton Mallet. A newspaper report claimed to record the final moments.

> "Ignatius walked to the scaffold without visible emotion, standing rigidly at attention as the noose was adjusted. Until late last night he had waited in his death cell for his father's promised visit [trying to rush back to Britain from exile in Ceylon in time to see his son], and when told that it was impossible for him to arrive he [Ignatius] broke down and wept....Filled with remorse he [Trebitsch] is reported to have written to the son: 'My sins seem to have been visited on your head, and I pray you will forgive me before you die. If I had been a better father, this might not have happened, and I am filled with a terrible regret for my past.'"[429]

---

428   Bernard Wasserstein, *The Secret Lives of Trebitsch Lincoln*, Penguin, 1989, back cover.
429   Ibid., p. 260. His biographer doubted the sincerity of Trebitsch's remorse. See *ibid*.

In following up the Lincoln incident, Blackwell had asked the Prison Commissioners at the time whether all prisoners under sentence of death should not be warned that if any of their communications were to be used for press purposes, then they would be forbidden from sending or receiving further letters. The Commissioners' not wholly unambiguous reply was that one letter a day to and from friends and relatives should be permitted, while letters involving other persons should be a matter for individual decision (presumably by the governor) in each case. In particular, it was not desirable to warn such prisoners that if their correspondence were to be used by the press, then they would not be permitted to send or receive letters. Visitors were to be treated similarly.

Indeed at the same parliamentary session on March 16, Clynes told Colonel Harry Day, Labour MP for Southwark, that no pledges were ever demanded from relatives and friends visiting a condemned prisoner that they must not divulge or publish the results of interviews with such prisoners. Nor would he undertake to impose such obligations in the future. Such commitments would be difficult to enforce (even if desirable in principle, according to a senior Home Office official). More immediately pertinent, Clynes replied, was that 'nothing happened in the present [Rouse] case to suggest that the practice should be altered', thus skating over any question of whether information from Rouse had been smuggled out of his cell to the press.

Undaunted, the journalist, Cannell, continued to bask in the glory of his supposed *Daily Sketch* scoop of March 11. He had telegraphed Clynes at his home on March 14, asking for an appointment that weekend with the Home Secretary for his (Cannell's) informant, whose identity, whether Reginald Bird or not, was not, of course, disclosed. In passing over the telegram to Frank Newsam, his private secretary, Clynes made clear that he had no intention of seeing this un-named person. However, whether his officials might do so could be considered. Locke minuted that any such meeting should be undertaken with care. Otherwise, the interview might become the occasion for yet further publicity of a misleading kind (presumably meaning leaks to the press). Indeed, even if the informant were to consent to confidentiality, a public admission of the tantalisingly 'our lips are sealed' variety would be harmful (in the 1960s the House of Lords judge, Lord Reid, warned against the 'captious criticism' of government if restrictions on the disclosure of government documents in court proceedings were lifted. However, he failed to acknowledge that such 'captious criticism' might be stimulated if documents were *not* released). The line to take, therefore, was for Clynes to decline to see the gentleman (assumed to be male). However, Cannell was told on March 17, the same day on which the *Daily Sketch* announced that it had offered Clynes proof of the confession's authenticity, that officials might consent to an interview with the unnamed source only if further documents of significance, together with an indication of the nature of the information to be communicated by the informant, were submitted in the first instance. A week later, presumably realising he could not come up with the 'goods', Cannell tried to wriggle out with as little loss of face as possible. He now observed limply that the questions raised in parliament on the matter had been answered by Clynes without his (Cannell's) informant's assistance (but we know that the Home Secretary's answers in the Commons, while suggestive, were less than unambiguous). Moreover

Mrs. Rouse's more recent revelation in the *News of the World* of her husband's admitting, before the appeal hearing, the correctness of the jury's verdict, now rendered the informant's 'proof' of a confession 'superfluous'. As Locke finally noted, the informant and Cannell had made a 'mountain of the confession out of a mite of information'. So the *Daily Sketch*'s scoop was just so much rubbish. Of course, what was glossed over in this advice was that the reading public would probably still be captivated by such an artificial mountain of rubbish. What was not in any doubt for the Home Office was the question of Rouse's guilt. So it authorised Gwilliam on March 11 to post the five last letters the prisoner had written before his execution to their intended recipients. As Blackwell reassured himself, 'They contain no assertion of *innocence*'.[430] And presumably they did not contain an explicit confession to murder, either. For if they had done so Blackwell, we suppose, would have mentioned that.

In fact, days *before* Rouse's execution, the prison authorities at Bedford had been given further, and to the Home Office compelling, information about his criminal responsibility emanating, indeed, from Rouse himself. In other words, perhaps we are now getting nearer to Rouse's 'real' confession (if any). The stimulus to departmental discussion of this 'real' confession, considered by the officials a few days after Rouse's death, was of course the *Daily Sketch* 'confession' published the day after the execution. After its appearance the prison governor and the prison commissioners were asked, whether as a matter of routine or not is unclear, for their observations on the newspaper story. The governor, F. W. Gwilliam, replied to the Home Office on March 12, two days after the execution. He was obviously exercised by the question of Cannell's mysterious informant. So first he made clear that he had no reason to believe that any prison officer had communicated with the press concerning Rouse's innocence or guilt; let alone, he might have added, to have smuggled out an alleged confession, including that published by the *Daily Sketch*. In fact, wrote Gwilliam, throughout the time from Rouse's incarceration in Bedford until his execution, he had 'stoutly maintained his innocence' which, with hindsight (as we shall see below), we can take to mean innocence of murder. Indeed, in none of the reports maintained by the officer in charge of visits to Rouse had there been any references to the 'slightest admission of guilt'. Moreover the prison warders had been frequently reminded of their duty to bring to notice any such admission.

However, the governor then dropped a mini-bombshell by stating that late on Saturday March 7, after Rouse's plea for clemency had been rejected by the Home Secretary, the condemned man had sent for Gwilliam in order to make a statement.

> "I took this down at his dictation, and read it over to him. He signed it. I sent it to the Secretary of State by special messenger---in civilian clothing --- on Sunday morning. In this statement <u>no</u> [underlined by a Home Office official] essential particular agrees with the supposed confession as published in the 'Daily Sketch' of the 11th March. I feel assured that either:

---

430 PCOM9/290/1. The contents of some of these letters are alluded to in the accounts written by Rouse's 'women' in the magazine, *Peg's Paper*. See chapter twenty-one.

1   the [newspaper] 'confession' was made to a person---other than a prison officer---in the very early days of the case, or

2   it was never made [Home Office underlining]."

So what was clear to the governor was that the *Daily Sketch* confession involving the prisoner's elaborate scheme to murder the tramp, burn him beyond recognition so that he would be assumed to be Rouse himself, and thence to disappear, not only bore no relation to what Rouse had told him on that Saturday night (and what Rouse did have to say will be revealed shortly). But he also believed that, unless it had been disclosed to Rouse's legal team at a very early stage (which would be unlikely if Finnemore's instructions had been to insist upon Rouse's innocence), then the confession published on March 11 had probably never been made by Rouse (and had therefore probably been concocted by Cannell or by someone who had come into contact with Rouse). However, in the unlikely event that a scenario existed in which a confession *had* been smuggled out of jail, then Gwilliam attached for the Home Office a list of prison visitors to Rouse from among whom the recalcitrant might be found. They included his legal team, which 'in the very early days of the case' (above) probably would have included Lee-Roberts' disloyal clerk, Reginald Bird, as well as a doctor, motor experts (there are no further details of this fascinating disclosure), and a tailor (no doubt to remedy Rouse's early complaint at the police court of having to wear someone else's ill-fitting clothes). All such visits were within sight, but not within hearing, of the prison officer. Rouse was also visited by his wife, father and aunt, and by Helen Campbell and Nellie Tucker. For this category of visitor the warder remained within hearing distance, implying that he would have overheard any confession if it had been made by Rouse to his relatives or lovers (though Nellie Tucker's story, above, seemed to question the effectiveness of the supervision).

What, then, of Rouse's statement taken down by the governor at 10:30 pm on March 7? Before looking at its contents, the first observation to make is that, according to the governor, his statement to Gwilliam had not been the first statement made by Rouse to prison officials that night. For an hour earlier, around 9:30 pm he had, said Gwilliam, given a brief account regarding the crucial events to his two prison guards, Priest and Cockerell. This, in turn, was reported to the governor, presumably right away or, at any rate, in the short period before Gwilliam spoke to him at 10:30 pm. The account supposedly given by Rouse to the warders was typed out and transmitted to the Home Office, but also along with the longer statement, according to the governor, dictated by Rouse to Gwilliam an hour later. We shall consider them in chronological order. Thus in Priest and Cockerell's account, what Rouse had told the prison officers around 9:30 pm was that after he had stopped his car in Hardingstone Lane, he had asked the man he had picked up in London to fill the petrol tank while he, Rouse, went away to relieve himself.

> "When I came back the man was sitting in the car, with his left leg outside on the near side, and a cigar in his right hand alight. He may have had the Mallet in his left hand. He said that if I did not give him £5 he would go to the Police, and tell them that I had attempted an indecent action with him. We quarrelled for a little while, called me a rotten name and said his pals would make me

pay. I then hit him with my fist, he rolled on the seat, and knocked the can of petrol over which was on the seat. Having a lighted cigar in his hand, the car burst into flames. When the flames burst on to me I got the wind up and shut the door, and ran down the road where I met the two men".

He then added that the man burnt in the car was a person from Middlesbrough shown to him in a photograph (the puzzle of the victim's identity has been considered in chapter 7 where the Middlesbrough connection was discounted).

This version of Rouse's account of events, as told to his prison guards, certainly introduces not only a more plausible confession, albeit possibly not to murder, but also a new element to the mystery regarding his motive, though physical evidence that the 'flames [had] burst on to [him]' was, at least, ambiguous (would he not have been singed?). Yet what may be significant is that there is nothing here about Rouse's being 'fed up' with his marital situation and with the related problems surrounding his 'harem', nor about arranging an insurance fraud to relieve himself of his financial woes. Rather, it is about resisting a homosexual advance, which might have offended his masculinity and his heterosexual identity, or it is about his being angered at the crude attempt to blackmail him or to demand money with menaces. Certainly, there had been speculation in some quarters that the corpse was that of an acquaintance who had been aware not only of Rouse's various amours and offspring but also about his bigamous marriage to Helen Campbell and who had sought to blackmail him in exchange for not disclosing the offence to the authorities. There is, however, no evidence to support that particular (non-homosexuality) blackmail interpretation and, indeed, there is only Rouse's alleged statement to his warders on that Saturday night, days before his execution (and, significantly, *not* raised before or at his trial), that blackmail of another sort was behind the killing.[431]

Though we cannot be certain, it is probable that Rouse envisaged that his statement to the warders, if true, would be transmitted without delay to the Home Office for their last-minute consideration before the trapdoor fell. And he was probably even more confident that his account to Gwilliam, which purported to elaborate upon the points he had earlier made to the prison officers, Priest and Cockerell, would likewise wend its way to Whitehall. Thus specifically on the blackmail allegation, Gwilliam reported that Rouse, on his return to the car after relieving himself, had asked the man, seated in the passenger seat, whether he had filled up the tank,

"...but he started using foul language....Among his foul remarks he said, 'I want a fiver off you because I can bring proof to the Police that you have committed----', he meant, I think, buggery or sodomy. I then said to him 'You can't prove anything like that. Carry on.' He added he could bring his pals to stand by him and corroborate his tale, bloody fools like me were easy. The price came down to £2".

---

431   A newspaper article on the case in 1949 revisited the question of blackmail while failing to offer evidence in support. Thus it asked, 'Was Rouse being blackmailed by his unknown victim? If so, what was the knowledge which Rouse, who was certainly not averse to a reputation as a modern Casanova, never revealed, even in his confession [sic; which confession?] made just before he hanged?' See *Sunday Pictorial*, September 25, 1949. The author was a barrister, Anthony Worth.

As for supposedly striking the victim with his fist, Rouse claimed that the passenger, who 'smelt strongly of whisky', had 'made a movement as if to attack me through the open [passenger] door, and I struck him a second time with my fist under his jaw, as he continued to use foul language and to call me foul names.' Rouse was then said by Gwilliam to have described how the victim fell backwards, drawing his foot into the car and putting his knee on the seat (though this combined movement of position seems difficult to make). Whether the passenger then attempted to scramble out of the car through the driver's seat and door is unclear. However Rouse explained that at that moment the petrol can, with its top having been removed earlier by the mallet, was resting on the driver's seat. Thus it was actually forming an obstacle to any escape by the passenger through the driver's door unless he could move it. And while Rouse was considering his next step the whole car, in this account of events, suddenly burst into flames (which the reader would be expected to presume was a result of the cigar igniting the petrol). He jumped away from the car, slammed the passenger door shut (whether or not accompanied by, 'Damn you! That will finish you!'), picked up his *attaché* case from the grass verge, and ran off in a panic down the road. He added that he felt 'responsible' for the man's death but had had no intention of murdering him. However, he admitted that it was 'through hitting him that the car burst into flames' which presumably meant that the blow from Rouse's fist caused the victim to drop the lighted cigar into the open petrol can. He concluded, according to Gwilliam, by suggesting that if the man, whose photograph was in the possession of Rouse's solicitors (it cannot be found among the Rouse papers in the archives), could be identified through police records covering the West End, then he, Rouse, was certain that the man's character would support the above statement. Presumably by this Rouse meant that the victim would have had a police record for blackmail or attempted blackmail, especially in relation to homosexuality, or that he was a member of the queer community in the West End who might have come to the notice of the police in recent years.[432]

The statement, which Gwilliam said had taken 30 minutes to deliver and write down, was read over twice to Rouse to enable him to make minor changes (there were scarcely any). It was then signed by him as a voluntary and truthful account. But what are we to make of his particular admissions? In the first instance we note that Rouse accepted 'responsibility' for the man's death but not for his murder. 'Responsibility' here could mean moral responsibility to which no legal consequences attached, for example, in the case of an accident or of justifiable homicide, such as when a person acted honestly and proportionately in self-defence. It is possible that Rouse hoped that his 'anticipatory' self-defence, before 'genuinely' believing the man would strike him, would fit into this category, notwithstanding the tragic consequences. But 'responsibility' could also mean legal responsibility for unlawful conduct short of murder. In this case, Rouse insisted that he had not *intended* to murder the victim. If a jury were to accept this in light of the surrounding circumstances (and no issue of a homosexual

---

432   For the West End homosexual community during the relevant period see Matt Houlbrook, *Queer London: Perils and Pleasures in the Sexual Metropolis, 1918-1957*, University of Chicago Press, Chicago, 2005. For blackmail, see passim. See also Mike Hepworth, *Blackmail: Publicity and Secrecy in Everyday Life*, Routledge & Kegan Paul, 1975, Ch. 2. For the relationship between poverty and homosexual behaviour, see Houlbrook, *Queer London*, pp. 175-77.

approach by the victim or of an attempt to blackmail Rouse was raised at his trial), then a murder conviction could only be returned if the jury were certain that he had still intended serious harm to the victim. For the quaint term for murder, that is, 'unlawfully killing a reasonable creature who is in being and under the King's peace, with malice aforethought either express or implied, the death following within a year and a day',[433] embraced the centrality of the mental element of the prisoner's intention to kill or cause serious harm, a conception of individual responsibility that was the product of nineteenth century political thinking and criminal jurisprudence.[434] And in the absence of this mental element of intention to kill or cause grievous bodily harm, the unlawful homicide would be the non-capital offence of involuntary manslaughter (or, just possibly, non-capital voluntary manslaughter due to the victim's provocation if the latter had 'done' something to Rouse as well as 'saying' something to him). Did Rouse therefore only wish to 'fend off' the victim with minimum force (though he admitted hitting him with his fist) before seeing the unfortunate man lose balance, fall down inside the car and set the petrol can alight with his cigar? That is, was he claiming accident, or justifiable self-defence, or non-capital manslaughter, and without the incriminating parting words allegedly uttered by Rouse as he slammed the door shut and which had been mentioned by Musgrave, the prison chaplain? Or was the story another example of his *penchant* for elaborate lies, even if Gwilliam believed it and accurately reported its telling to the Home Office?

As noted earlier the governor had sent to the Home Office by special messenger on Sunday morning, March 8, Rouse's signed statement to him and an account of his statement to the warders made the previous night. The items arrived just after midday and Blackwell and the DPP, admirably conscientiously, discussed the matter fully between 2:30 pm and 4 o'clock. In a memorandum, presumably for Clynes' eyes, Blackwell suggested that the best 'general test' to apply to this last-minute submission by the condemned man was to ask: 'If it were true why is it only made now at the last moment?' For Rouse could have put those points to Sergeant Skelly of the Metropolitan Police when taken off the coach at Hammersmith on the evening of November 7. Instead he had declared, as he got off the coach, 'I am glad it is over. I was going to Scotland Yard about it. I am responsible'. Further, his subsequent account to Sergeant Skelly at Hammersmith police station had made no reference to his being blackmailed over his passenger's threatening to accuse him of sodomy or buggery. Instead, and devoid of such details, the story of the accidentally ignited blaze, caused by the cigar-smoking passenger's negligence while Rouse was relieving himself some distance away, had been narrated by the prisoner to Skelly. Moreover, his lengthy statement to Superintendent Brumby at Northampton similarly omitted reference to such 'shocking' details while, on being charged with murder, he had made no effort to offer the 'blackmail' explanation which he was now putting forward at the last minute.

Blackwell also considered that Rouse's failure to tell his wife of the alleged blackmail attempt and of its consequences when he had returned to Buxted Road between 6 and 7 am was significant. For if, indeed, such an assault had occurred,

---

433   For a contemporary legal analysis, see G. Godfrey Phillips (ed.), *Kenny's Outlines of Criminal Law*, 15th ed., Cambridge University Press, Cambridge, 1936, pp. 146-7.
434   See K. J. M. Smith, *Lawyers, Legislators and Theorists: Developments in English Criminal Jurisprudence, 1800-1957*, Clarendon Press, Oxford, 1998, esp. Ch. 7 on 'moral agency'.

why had Rouse not mentioned it to Lily at the time? It may be that Blackwell thought that his own dismissal of Rouse's new account was consistent with his belief in Mrs. Rouse's criminal role in the whole affair. We have already noted that she had admitted seeing her husband before dawn on November 6, though later claiming that she had thought it had been about 1 am. She had also broken down in tears at being told later that day that her husband had (presumably) died in the blaze some hours earlier around 1:45 am at Hardingstone. But if she still *believed* at that stage (and there is no conclusive evidence that she *knew* at that time that it was actually around 6 am) that she had heard him returning home at 1 am, just 45 minutes earlier than the first reported time of his death, and had been ready thereafter to travel to Northampton to identify 'her poor, dear husband', she must either have been hopelessly confused regarding the crucial times or, as Blackwell appeared to reason, have been up to no good.

As to the photograph of the man from Middlesbrough, Blackwell thought the most likely explanation was that Rouse' solicitors had acquired the photograph (possibly sent in by a desperate family), and that they had shown it to Rouse, indicating that it was of a person who had been convicted of an indecent assault in the West End. Inquiries in that district or elsewhere would be quite useless (presumably because Blackwell was certain that Rouse's new story was a tissue of lies). In any case, if Rouse had been faced with such a demand for £5 or £2, he could simply have forced the man from the car and driven off. In sum, it was just another fabrication by an inveterate liar in order to save his skin. Further discussion with Clynes and with the permanent under-secretary, Sir John Anderson, on Monday March 9, confirmed that the execution would go ahead the next morning.

Two days after Rouse's judicial hanging, Blackwell saw fit to add to his pre-execution memorandum by noting that the petrol can, as found by PC Copping after the blaze, was standing the right way up 'suspended' between the back of the front seat and the front of the rear seat. Thus it could not possibly have fallen to the floor of the car when Rouse allegedly punched the man with his fist. That punch, according to Rouse, had caused the victim to fall backwards and make a turning movement that involved drawing in his foot and putting his knee on the seat. In that position, Rouse had implied, the man had knocked over the can and the escaping petrol (or its vapour?) had been ignited by the man's lighted cigar. However, the position of the can, as found by PC Copping, disproved this wild and desperate account by Rouse unless 'it had jumped over the back of the driver's seat and landed in the position in which it was found!' Blackwell thus adhered to the view that Rouse had stunned his passenger (though because the 'hairs' evidence on the mallet was inconclusive, the judge had advised the jury to disregard the use of this tool for that purpose), had then thrown his body across the two front seats, probably splashed his clothes with petrol and, before setting alight the trail of petrol at the front of the car, had finished by 'throwing the empty can into the back of the car'. And though we might consider it remarkable that, thus discarded, the can had been found by Copping 'suspended' between the front and rear seats (had it also jumped and landed upright in Blackwell's narrative as well?), the dismissal of Rouse's last effort to escape the hangman was never in doubt.

After the execution Blackwell also sent to Mr. Justice Talbot a copy of Rouse's statement to Gwilliam. Reiterating the point about the position of the petrol can, he also noted that the statement differed from Rouse's testimony in court that he had only seen the car bursting into flames from a distance. In sum the last-minute submission appeared to Blackwell and to the DPP, Tindal Atkinson, to be an attempt (futile in their opinion) to confess, not to murder, but to an 'excusable' manslaughter. He added that the department had not yet decided whether to make a public announcement about Rouse's statement. For 'very good reasons' (noted earlier), the Home Office policy was normally to keep silent as to whether a confession had been made, though exceptionally it might be disclosed that a confession had been made in cases where there had been public unease. However the *contents* of a confession would never be officially revealed. As to Rouse's *Daily Sketch* confession to murdering the man in the way suggested by the prosecution at the trial, 'so far as we know, Rouse never made such a confession and we are inclined to regard it as a pure journalistic concoction', which is not to say that the victim had *not* been killed in the manner described by the newspaper on March 11. After all, Birkett's conducting of the prosecution had been premised on not too dissimilar a line.

In reply Talbot expressed his concurrence with Blackwell's views on the unreliability of Rouse's statement to Gwilliam, the public disclosure of which would be 'inexpedient'. Moreover, incredulous that the *Daily Sketch* confession, which he had read, could have been smuggled out of prison without detection, he considered it an 'ingenious fake'. Indeed, he wished something could be done to curb newspaper excesses in respect of condemned prisoners. 'The conduct of some newspapers in this regard is truly disgusting'.

Blackwell's reply to Talbot on March 19 drew attention to Mrs. Rouse's revelation of March 7, published in the *News of the World* on March 15, that Rouse had admitted to her that the jury's verdict had been correct. He also referred to Nellie Tucker's story in the *People* of the same date in which Rouse, while in prison, had allegedly told Nellie (apparently without the warders having heard it) that the motive for the killing was the prospect of obtaining the insurance money. While he (Blackwell) was also appalled by the press coverage, he remarked that there was little prospect of remedial legislation on this matter. However, the positive aspect was that those newspaper accounts (Lily's and Nellie's references to a confession) would go far to allay public anxieties that a miscarriage of justice had occurred. Finally, with regard to Rouse's conduct before his execution, Blackwell pondered whether discharged prisoners (perhaps exploiting prison chaplains' 'careless talk' during their Sunday sermons after an execution?) had been able to 'gull reporters anxious to get copy with such stories', or whether the reporters were quite capable of inventing such accounts themselves.

Going back to Mrs. Rouse's *News of the World* letter in which Rouse had supposedly confided to her that the jury had been correct, the Home Office official, Locke, expressed doubt as to its genuineness and, indeed, as to whether it had actually been written before Rouse's execution. After all, it was dated March 7 and Rouse still had three more days during which he was hoping for a reprieve, which perhaps lends support to Locke's claim. March 7 was, moreover, the very day when, learning that no reprieve would be granted, Rouse had, according to Gwilliam, told the prison governor that he had not *intended* murder (notwithstanding his alleged confirmation to Lily in February that the jury's decision had been correct), and therefore was possibly liable only for non-capital manslaughter. Third, despite the date of the letter three days *before* his execution, it was written in the past tense ("Those who knew Arthur...."), suggesting that it had been drafted *after* his execution. Indeed, surmised Locke, 'the wretched woman[435], having known all along that he was guilty, offered up corroboration of the *Daily Sketch*'s fabricated 'confession' by Rouse, in order to benefit financially. For Blackwell, her obviously contrived and opportunistic letter simply reinforced his opinion that when Rouse had returned home at 6 am on November 6 before departing for Gellygaer, he had indeed told his wife that he had murdered his passenger. Not surprisingly, Cannell remained undaunted, and in the *Daily Sketch* of March 16 reproduced the letter (discredited, as we have seen, in the Home Office's eyes) written in Mrs. Rouse's handwriting, and publishing it under the headline, 'Mrs. Rouse Proves That Her Husband Confessed'.[436]

While the Home Office no doubt suspected naked financial motives behind the rash of competing newspaper accounts provided by various *dramatis personae* in the case, at this stage it contented itself with an overview of the press coverage. As to the immediate post-trial period from Monday February 2, 1931, we noted in chapter 12 that the Home Office had assessed the generality of reports as being essentially temperate. However that did not prevent it from referring some of the coverage to the Attorney-General, Sir William Jowitt. For whether the defence would lodge an appeal had not yet been settled at that point, and recklessly or grossly adverse newspaper comment about Rouse, as distinct from fair comment and accurate *reportage*, might fall into that realm where the risk of contempt of court proceedings could not be discounted. However, when consulted, Jowitt cited the case of *R v The Editor and Publishers of the 'People', ex parte Hobbs* (1925) in which he himself had appeared for the editor and the publisher, Odham's Press.[437]

---

435 The terminology 'wretched' perhaps indicates the official's belief in his 'natural' moral superiority, rather than his empathy with her situation.

436 Though both newspapers were Conservative-inclined, they were not stable-mates under the same ownership.

437 We need not concern ourselves with the details of the complicated *Hobbs* case which arose from a 'honey trap' in 1925 that had ensnared a 'Mr. A.', in reality, a rich Indian prince, Sir Hari Singh. Hobbs was a dodgy lawyer's managing clerk in cahoots with a number of men, including Mr A.'s aide-de-camp, Captain Arthur, who set out to blackmail Mr. A. over his indiscretion with a Mrs. Robinson (long before *The Graduate*, of course) in a Paris hotel bedroom. Cheques for huge sums of money were written by Mr A. as hush money, but the plot unravelled and eventually Hobbs was imprisoned for two years by Mr. Justice Avory who bemoaned that other co-conspirators had not been charged. After Hobbs' conviction on March 9, 1925, the *People*, under the editorship of Henry Ainsworth, published on March 15 and on March 22 the first two of a projected series of articles on the trial. The prisoner was described therein as the 'wizard crook of the underworld'. He was accused of 'diabolical roguery, of being a master crook, and of having deserved a sentence of ten years' penal servitude'. However, the day following the appearance of the first article, Hobbs gave notice of appeal against conviction. That being so, the press would require to be careful in their further comments on the case. But the *People* ploughed on and published its second unflattering article about Hobbs on March 22. This ignited the ire of the Attorney-General, Sir Douglas Hogg, later the first Lord Hailsham. At his instigation a conditional order (a rule *nisi*) was obtained on behalf of Hobbs on March 27 requiring the newspaper (Odhams were in fact only the printers, not the publishers) to show the Divisional Court, presided over by former journalist, Lord Chief Justice Hewart, why a writ of attachment for contempt should not be issued against it. Hewart made clear that the single issue was whether the above press description of Hobbs before the appeal hearing constituted a contempt of court (whether the words were defamatory was moot and was a separate matter not contested there). Hewart's narrow test for this was simply whether the words used were *calculated* to prejudice the fair hearing of the appeal. This, of course, would be different from the broader test of whether they *could* or *might* prejudice it. It is, in fact, possible that the narrow and strict test of 'calculation' here, which arguably stresses the alleged contemnor's improper intention, was chosen by Hewart on the ground that criminal appeal judges were undoubtedly less

With that precedent in mind, he concluded it was unlikely that the High Court would hold the *Daily Express* (selected for this purpose) liable for contempt in revealing certain information about Rouse on February 2, that is, before any decision regarding an appeal had been taken by the defence. That information related to material that had been withheld from the trial due to unspecified 'legal difficulties and the law of evidence', that is, the 'shameful' material revealed in the police court concerning Rouse's affairs and his pre-trial admissions. It was arguable that there might have been substance regarding motive to be extrapolated from that material (but we do not know whether the *defence* would have found a way to use that material to Rouse's advantage, procedurally or substantively, in an appeal; though *prima facie* it would not redound to Rouse's credit). Nonetheless, Jowitt probably concluded that since Birkett himself had failed to adduce it at the trial, thereby suggesting that it was either irrelevant or inadmissible, then the newspaper disclosures immediately after the trial about Rouse's private life could now only bear on matters of taste. And since Hewart's ruling in *Hobbs* had made clear that matters of taste did not come within the scope of the law of contempt, Jowitt was probably wise in concluding that newspapers were unlikely to be held legally accountable for contempt of court for their comments about Rouse's private life immediately following his trial.[438]

However, that the exchange of money was believed to have been at the root of this newspaper evil was also the proverbial elephant in the room during a House of Lords debate on April 29 initiated by the eccentric and publicity-seeking retired judge, Lord Darling.[439] Though he skirted around the issue of newspapers paying informants to produce confessions allegedly disclosed to them by convicted prisoners, he nonetheless cited the view of the *Daily Mail* owner, Lord Rothermere who, in a letter to Darling, had deplored disreputable newspapers (which clearly did not include the later 'Hurrah for the Blackshirts' *Daily Mail*, as mentioned in a previous chapter) that chose to publish 'matters' to the detriment of convicted persons before the appeal process had been exhausted. This was a reference to the publication of various newspaper articles on the case, including that entitled 'My Doubts about Rouse Conviction. By a Barrister-at-Law' published, as we saw in chapter 12, in the *Sunday Dispatch* of February 8. Such timing was, indeed, improper, in Lord Darling's view. For the piece appeared the day after Rouse had entered notice to appeal, which appeal was then held on February 23. Such newspaper excesses constituted, he did not doubt, a contempt of court as Lord Chief Justice Hewart had surmised after the conclusion of Rouse's failed appeal. Indeed Hewart, in contrast with Jowitt's view regarding the immediate post-trial press coverage, seems to have been exercised by 'improper comment' in certain

impressionable than a lay jury. But his journalistic impulses were also deployed when he added that the 'views of a *censor morum* or tasteful critic about these articles' were not the issue.

438 Different considerations applied in the case of courts-martial. For the decisions of such tribunals were not completed, and therefore were *sub iudice* (and there was no Court-Martial Appeal Court until 1951) until the 'awards' had been confirmed, some time later, by the 'confirming officer', usually a divisional, corps or Army commander. There was also a subsequent 'review' process, looking at legal and other factors, which could lead to the quashing of the court-martial's finding against the accused. When newspapers in the later 1940s organised polls of readers' opinions on the outcome of some major courts martial, the newspapers were warned in parliament by the Attorney General, Sir Hartley Shawcross, about the dangers of contempt proceedings. See Gerry R. Rubin, *Murder, Mutiny and the Military: British Court-Martial Cases, 1940-1966*, Francis Boutle, 2005, p. 249.

439 H.L. Deb., 29 April 1931, Vol. 80, cols. 936-57.

newspaper after the trial and before a decision by the defence on any appeal, as he stated at the conclusion of the appeal. Among his targets was probably a *Daily Express* article of February 2, with its purported disclosure of the salacious evidence withheld from the trial. But, of course, nothing by way of proceedings for contempt against the newspaper came of it in view of Jowitt's stance.

Nonetheless, in his speech in the Lords, Darling cited the views of the Metropolitan Stipendiary Magistrate, Robert Mead, published in the *Justice of the Peace* on March 28, where the latter had written, '...in prosecutions of importance, application may be made to the justices that the proceedings should be private'. The aim was to exclude press reporting of prejudicial evidence (whatever that was; all evidence is prejudicial in some respect) that had been admitted before the magistrates but which might be ruled inadmissible at trial. The 'harem' evidence presented at the police court but not adduced by the prosecution at the assizes is the obvious example. In fact, until the Summary Procedure (Domestic Proceedings) Act 1937, whose title is self-explanatory, it is doubtful whether Mead's legal authorities at the time supported Lord Darling's view that it would be perfectly lawful, *without further qualification*, to exclude the press and public from attending pre-trial police court hearings. Most opinions, following the Rouse hearings, including that of Lord Hewart, believed it was simply 'unfortunate' that Rouse's sexual reputation had become a matter of notoriety once evidence of his mistresses had been admitted by the justices following legal advice from the justices' clerk in the case. The genie was out of the bottle, and effective non-draconian changes would take approximately another 35 years to be enacted following the Tucker Committee report of 1958 (presumably no relation to Nellie!). Responding to Darling, the Lord Chancellor, Viscount Sankey, a veteran of the public inquiry into coal miners' pay grievances after the Great War, observed that it was not for him to set down or formulate a code governing contempt of court.[440] In fact he seemed to agree with Jowitt that the articles complained of were unlikely to have amounted to a contempt of court. Moreover, in the majority of cases the press had exercised their powers both well and wisely. Nonetheless, future articles of a similar nature could be carefully scrutinised to ensure that this would remain the practice. While he welcomed the role of the press in the detection and prevention of crime, nonetheless, he (Sankey) did condemn the marketing of sensational stories connected with crime and encouraged editors and owners to consider the non-desirability of such newspaper items. But he might as well have been asking professional beer tasters to take the pledge.

In fact, it is clear from correspondence between Blackwell and the DPP that the Home Office had been in discussion with Darling over his proposed parliamentary intervention. Tindal Atkinson, for example, while probably envisaging that the decision in *Hobbs* had rendered any immediate contempt proceedings unlikely, nonetheless pondered 'whether the whole question as to the limits of newspaper comment pending an Appeal or a possible Appeal is one which might well come under review by a Court', especially if alleged confessions had been published pending an appeal (and if published after an execution a review might be focussed not on the press but on possible leaks by prison officials). The Home Office, in regard to Darling's strictures on the press, had opined, as noted previously, that

---

440   See also *News of the World*, May 3, 1931.

newspaper coverage of Rouse's case, after he had submitted his notice of appeal on February 6, was 'probably of a comparatively unobjectionable character'.

Yet despite Hewart's having previously found no grounds for contempt of court proceedings in *Hobbs* in 1925, the Lord Chief Justice did make some pointed remarks on this matter in dismissing Rouse's appeal on February 23, 1931. Thus he complained that there had been 'a great deal of improper comment in certain newspapers [regarding the Rouse case] and in letters to the members of the [Appeal] Court, including one from a person describing himself as a Member of Parliament. They would have to consider whether proceedings of that kind pending an appeal did not constitute a contempt of Court'. As the Home Office noted, this was a different Lord Hewart from that defender of the press who had presided in *Hobbs*. But perhaps the action of the *Daily Express* on February 2, 1931, in claiming to reveal that which had been hidden from the trial (though much of it had been previously disclosed at the police court), was perceived by the judge as over-stepping the boundaries of reasonable comment, given the uncertainty at that time of Rouse's next move. Indeed, the case against the press would have been stronger had newspapers published Rouse's alleged 'confessions', no matter their concocted quality, *pending* his appeal, as distinct from the various 'confessions' published after his execution. However, as a matter of legal doctrine it might have been difficult to uphold a finding of contempt without clear legislative, or even common law, guidance, which was lacking.

That still left unresolved the matter of reporting restrictions at the police court stage where Helen and Nellie's testimony and the prejudicial material regarding Rouse's 'harem' had been admitted. It is possible, however, that at that stage fairness towards the defendant did not weigh as heavily as the concern of certain parliamentarians to protect the public from the moral corruption of hearing about such shenanigans. Thus Sir Nicholas Grattan-Doyle MP once more voiced his concern at the press's descent into moral obloquy by asking in parliament on May 6, 1931 whether anything could be done to limit the opportunities for press reports of the preliminary stages of criminal proceedings in serious cases. Lord Darling had, in fact, suggested during the previous debate (above) that police court hearings might be held *in camera*, while Lord Chancellor Sankey, perhaps with a greater regard to the plight of the defendant, thought that the suggestion might apply in those circumstances where counsel had objected to certain evidence, as indeed had occurred in Rouse's police court hearing. In the event Clynes replied, first, that the matter was one for the courts whose attention, no doubt, was being directed to such issues as a result of Darling's initiative. Second he pointed out that magistrates did possess power to hear a case wholly or partially *in camera* if they thought fit (which was probably a legally imprecise statement).

It is highly probable, however, that the Home Office felt especially gratified when, on May 9, *John Bull* also sought to discredit the *Daily Sketch* confession of two months previously. The magazine's editor, H. Kingsley Long, had written to Clynes on April 29 enclosing a letter, which he believed genuine, received by the publication regarding the *Daily Sketch* 'scoop' of March 11. The letter was written on April 22 from 120 Howbury Street, Bedford, which is where Mrs. Rouse had been staying as a paying guest of the letter writer in Bedford since early January while she awaited Arthur's trial. The writer, H. Milton, who was probably the husband of Lily's landlady at Howbury Street, claimed that he was the 'only man outside the party [Rouse's family and women] who drew the money for them that know the lot [*sic*]'. He stated that he had been entreated by them not to communicate with the press to *deny* that any confession had been made, and that he had been the first person to hear Rouse's last letter read. This was possibly a reference to a letter apparently written by Rouse the night before his execution to his wife and published in the *Sunday Express* on March 15. In it he apologised to her 'for having brought this trouble on you' and seeking her forgiveness for all the worry he had caused her. 'I did not know until this happened what a priceless jewel of a wife I had....What I would like you to think of are the memories of when we were lovers. Do think kindly of me.' Yet despite her making common cause with Helen Campbell in their joint adversity, it is, however, questionable whether Mrs. Rouse appreciated his adding that, 'I have had passing passions. Helen Campbell was one of them, and she was really the second person who really counted in my life. She was the mother of my only [*sic*] son whom I cherished dearly'.

What is missing in the letter, it may be noted, is any express admission of guilt which might, of course, be read in a number of ways. It could mean, as Milton had claimed, that Rouse had not made the confession published in the *Daily Sketch*. Second, it might be consistent with Rouse's claim to innocence of murder (irrespective of possible liability for manslaughter). Third, it did not exclude the possibility (which the Home Office believed) that, while the *Daily Sketch* 'confession' was a concoction because it could not have been drafted by Rouse in the condemned cell under the eyes of the warders, nor smuggled out of prison, he had, nonetheless, verbally confessed to murder to others, such as to Nellie Tucker.

Regarding the *Daily Sketch* controversy, Milton was willing to be interviewed to set the record straight and to remove any lingering suspicion of impropriety on the part of the prison officials (a point underlined by the Home Official civil servant who considered the letter). 'There need be no fear, I have chapter and verse I think the World that reads should know how they were lied for money [*sic*].' Perish the thought that the writer of the letter had visions of pound signs, with the compliments of *John Bull*, flashing past his eyes.

Within the Home Office Locke's view was that such an exposure in the magazine would be worthwhile in order to reveal to the public not just the falsity of the confession in the *Daily Sketch* but also the 'whole machinery of [newspaper] concoction'. However, in the present circumstances, where the Home Office were aware that Rouse had made *a* confession, albeit 'practically of manslaughter', it might not be wise to encourage the magazine to 'demonstrate publicly' the falsity of the published confession and to expose the 'method' of concoction. Blackwell also took a cautious line on what the department should consider to be the most helpful angle it could recommend the magazine to adopt. That money had passed to Mrs. Rouse and to others was not in doubt, but it was not for the Home Office to prove that confessions (leaving aside the one made on the night of Saturday March 7 to the prison governor) were concocted. That was for *John Bull* to undertake if it so wished. Consequently the letter that wended its way from the Home Office to the magazine's editor merely reiterated Clynes' Commons statement that no prison official had passed out any confession and that it was unlikely that any such document had been sent out or smuggled out in any other way. The inference was that it was not willing to enter into discussion regarding other 'confessions' by Rouse, that *John Bull* was free to publish what it wished, and that the proposed publication could only redound to the advantage of the department by dampening newspaper sensationalism in such matters.

In the event the *John Bull* article appeared on May 9, 1931 under the headline, 'Rouse Confession: Startling New Facts'. The fact that publication appeared two months after his execution perhaps signifies the grip that the case still exerted on the public imagination. Clearly it had not become 'yesterday's news' but nor had the case yet become one appropriate for a journalistic 'retrospective', one, ten or twenty years down the line, when the passage of time would allow better judgments to be drawn on the characteristics, quality and contextual significance of the particular *oeuvre*, whether paintings, sculptures or, in this case, a murder *cause célèbre*.

The sanctimonious tone of the *John Bull* article ('the ignoble traffic in sensational stories of men in the shadow of the scaffold....must cease') is clear in the manner in which the magazine elided any distinction between stories, such as Lily's, of Rouse's alleged confession after he had been convicted and stories of his alleged confession published after his execution. Arguably, as Lord Darling had implied, the former was reprehensible in that it might prejudice a fair appeal hearing or a last-minute reprieve. In contrast the publishing of the latter, unless its provenance and terms of publication were beyond reproach, was surely regrettable if concocted by journalists, fabricated by money-grubbing friends or family, or if it amounted to an invasion of family privacy during an extremely raw time. But *John Bull* lumped all these possibilities together in condemning the orgy of press coverage of Rouse's 'admissions' (of course, it was surely its failure to find its own niche in the earlier mass publishing 'hysteria' that had prompted its *post hoc* 'party pooper' spoiler).

The magazine also reiterated the separate and contradictory statement of Mrs. Rouse, made two days before her husband's execution, to the effect that Rouse had *not* confessed, during which statement, as we saw previously, she had indicated that she would also telegraph Helen Campbell to support the denial. It further recounted the eve-of-execution visits to Rouse by his wife, and then by Helen Campbell, when every word that passed between prisoner and visitors could be heard by the three warders present. Yet it also referred to Mrs. Rouse's facsimile letter of March 7, reproduced in the *News of the World* a week later, in which it was stated that Rouse had acknowledged the correctness of the jury's verdict even before he had gone to the Court of Criminal Appeal. So, asked *John Bull*, 'Where, when and how did he confess? That is what the public is entitled to know'. Indeed, according to the magazine (which did not, of course, know of Rouse's qualified confession to the prison governor), his warders, his lawyers and the Home Secretary had denied that he had made any confession. It therefore urged the Home Office to break with practice (as the department had done in the Allaway case) and to issue a statement as to whether Rouse had indeed made a confession to the chaplain before his execution. For *John Bull*'s honourable aim all along, it pleaded, was to 'assist in preventing any further traffic in stories about men under the shadow of the scaffold who have no means of protecting themselves'. And, of course, the use of the word 'traffic' was clearly meant to convey that there had been a commercial purpose behind the confession revelations, much as trafficking in young girls for prostitution was also business for some. The actual phrase 'money changing hands' was, however, noticeable by its absence from the piece, perhaps for the eponymous 'legal reasons' (to avoid defamation proceedings), but the accusation against informants (although obviously not in relation to the blessed Mr. Milton of 120 Howbury Street, Bedford) was just below the surface. And as to its own journalistic standards, banish the thought that *John Bull* would itself ever engage in murky dealings to obtain a scoop. Heaven forefend that the brain-child publication of Horatio Bottomley, the convicted fraudster, ex-MP, xenophobe, hypocrite and all-round scoundrel, would stoop to such low cunning as it was accusing other rivals of doing.

What, then, are we to make of the whole farrago regarding a confession? A likely possibility was that Rouse, while in prison, *did* whisper a terse confession to his wife some time before the Court of Appeal hearing (perhaps even in the early hours of November 6 when he returned briefly to Buxted Road). This would appear more plausible if, as Blackwell believed, Mrs. Rouse had been privy to Rouse's scheme to disappear after finding a suitable victim to be burned beyond recognition, and had agreed to share the insurance money (Mrs. Rouse being the only person who could claim the insurance). But had Rouse been panicked both by the burning episode and by being spotted by the two young Hardingstone men, or just by the latter? If it were only Brown and Bailey, and not the fiery flames reminding him of the crashing aeroplane on the Western Front, then we might infer his murderous intent. But if also the former, then his apparently genuine qualified confession to the prison governor, where he spelled out a plausible, but still arguable, manslaughter scenario, could have had some purchase if his final flourish of 'Damn you! That will finish you', as he slammed shut the door of the blazing vehicle, could be explained away as Musgrave's figment of the imagination or as a despairing gesture of impotence and of fear for his future prospects.

We have already seen that following Rouse's execution and the flurry of newspaper articles purporting to record, or to attest to, his confession, a significant group of commentators and members of parliament continued to express concern regarding the correctness of the verdict. We have also noted that, given the perceived damning effect on the prisoner of public knowledge of his alleged sordid lifestyle and of references to his 'harem', suggestions were made to impose reporting restrictions on committal hearings. However, while such critics might have been uneasy at the outcome of the case, it is possible that they did not all share the view that a miscarriage of justice had occurred. For example the MP for St Albans, Colonel F. E. Fremantle, forwarded on February 4 1931 a constituent's letter to the Home Office. Couched in somewhat general terms, but clearly reflecting the Rouse proceedings, it complained that 'Press reports of alleged crimes' could have an unfortunate effect upon juries and therefore upon the interests of justice. Fremantle consequently sought from the department an undertaking that, in the immortal phrase, something must be done. In reply it was pointed out that the power of press censorship or control simply did not exist (whether this was strictly correct as a general proposition was open to debate given possible injunctive relief proceedings and laws against blasphemy, disclosure of official secrets, incitement to commit various offences etc). However, after proceedings had commenced, either the prosecution or defence could apply to the High Court to punish publishers of articles or comments that 'might tend to deflect the course of justice', in other words, to punish for contempt of court. Indeed, 'I understand that an application of this kind was in fact made in the case of Rouse'. The problem was (though this was not explained to Fremantle) that the legal precedents were distinctly unpromising. Moreover, this was probably why Sir Nicholas Grattan-Doyle's parliamentary question to Clynes on March 16, asking whether the Home Secretary 'will take steps to restrict the publication in newspapers of accounts of trials for murder' received a discouraging reply. 'It is a cardinal feature of our system,' the Home Secretary replied, 'that criminal trials should be public, and it is a matter of opinion how far the advantages of that system outweigh any possible disadvantages.'

A few days later, a different parliamentarian tried again. On March 19 the barrister and Labour MP for East Wolverhampton, Geoffrey Mander, asked,[441] 'Would the Attorney-General consider the possibility of introducing legislation to render possible an appeal in murder cases on grounds of wrongful admission of evidence at *any* [italics added] stage of the proceedings?' The reply by a junior Treasury minister, Wilfred Paling, a former colliery checkweighman (and therefore unlikely to have been related to Gerald Paling, whose tendering of Rouse's women at the police court had caused the ruckus in the first place), was familiarly dismissive. No change in the law was being considered. But it was an issue that would hang over the conduct of police court committal proceedings for many years, until the Tucker Committee on magistrates' court proceedings in 1958 recommended major changes which would ordinarily prevent the disclosure of damning material regarding the prisoner's guilt from being aired through examination and cross-examination of witnesses. Instead, as noted elsewhere, committal proceedings would many years later usually be based on prosecution documentation outlining a *prima facie* case against the accused, and the latter would normally reserve his defence until the trial itself, assuming that the magistrates decided to order the prisoner to stand trial at the next assizes. Such a reform would effectively remove the spectacle of the press reporting fully the case against the accused made at the police court. It would also mean that the trial jury, before the trial evidence was presented, would be less likely to have pre-conceived ideas regarding the prisoner's guilt than if they had read the press accounts of the Crown's police court evidence (where the magistrates clearly thought the evidence sufficient to justify sending the prisoner for trial). In fact it would take another decade after 1958 before such changes were introduced at the magistrates' courts, following the enactment of the Criminal Justice Act 1967, and nowadays, with even more changes implemented in 2013 to create 'allocation' hearings prior to Crown Court trials, preliminary proceedings are either formalistic or hugely technical affairs (though it will always be difficult to prevent lurid accounts of murders and of the state of play regarding the police investigations from exerting an influence on future jurors trying such cases).

---

441 During the Second World War he became parliamentary private secretary to the Secretary of State for War, Sir Archibald Sinclair.

1. The 1914 Man

Lily

Nellie

My Harem

Helen

Ivy

2. The Groom

3. The Morris Minor Fabric Saloon

The

**MORRIS
MINOR
FABRIC
SALOON**

PRICE
£140

Finish—Blue with Karbyde upholstery to match, chromium plating, Triplex glass windscreen and windows.

THE car offers ample comfort over long distances, and will as readily tackle a trip from Land's End to John o' Groats as a shopping expedition with the lady of the house.

The single-pane windscreen 'and sliding windows, all of Triplex glass, provide plenty of ventilation in warm weather, while the wide doors ensure ease of entry.

A virtue of the body design not to be overlooked by the family man is the safety of the rear seats, where small children can easily be accommodated with the certain knowledge that they are secure.

The equipment includes —

Four sliding windows, single-pane windscreen, speedometer, oil gauge, two-level petrol tap, automatic windscreen wiper, chassis lubricating pump, licence holder, calormeter and wings, driving mirror, progressive shock absorbers on all wheels, single bumpers (front and rear), Lucas Sparton electric horn, six-volt lighting, starting and coil ignition set, coil indicator light, five-lamp equipment, instrument festoon lamp, rear light, five detachable wire wheels, five Dunlop reinforced cord tyres, spare wheel carrier, complete tool kit.

The wide doors ensure ease of entry.

7

4. Exhibit 4 – Hardingstone Lane 8.15 am

5. Exhibit 3 – Hardingstone Lane 8.15 am
(before improvements by Arthur Vernon Ashford)

6. Exhibit 32 – The Mallet

DAILY SKETCH

INCORPORATING THE DAILY GRAPHIC

No. 6,727   FRIDAY, NOVEMBER 7, 1930.   ONE PENNY.

BODY FOUND IN A
BLAZING CAR

A GIANT BIRD IN FLIGHT

DEATH OF A
SOCIETY GIRL

---

7. Exhibit 21 – Daily Sketch 7th November 1930

8. Exhibit 1: Hardingstone Lane 8.20am (with steering wheel added, "to make a more effective photograph")

9. Exhibit 2: Hardingstone Lane 8.20am

10. Exhibit 48: Hardingstone Lane 9.15 am – Roland Holloway

11. "Mr Paling drew this for me" Talbot J
A sketch indicating the position of the corpse provided by
Mr G. R. Paling. Included in the Judge's notebook.

12. The Crown Inn, Hardingstone (2014)

13. Buxted Road (2014)

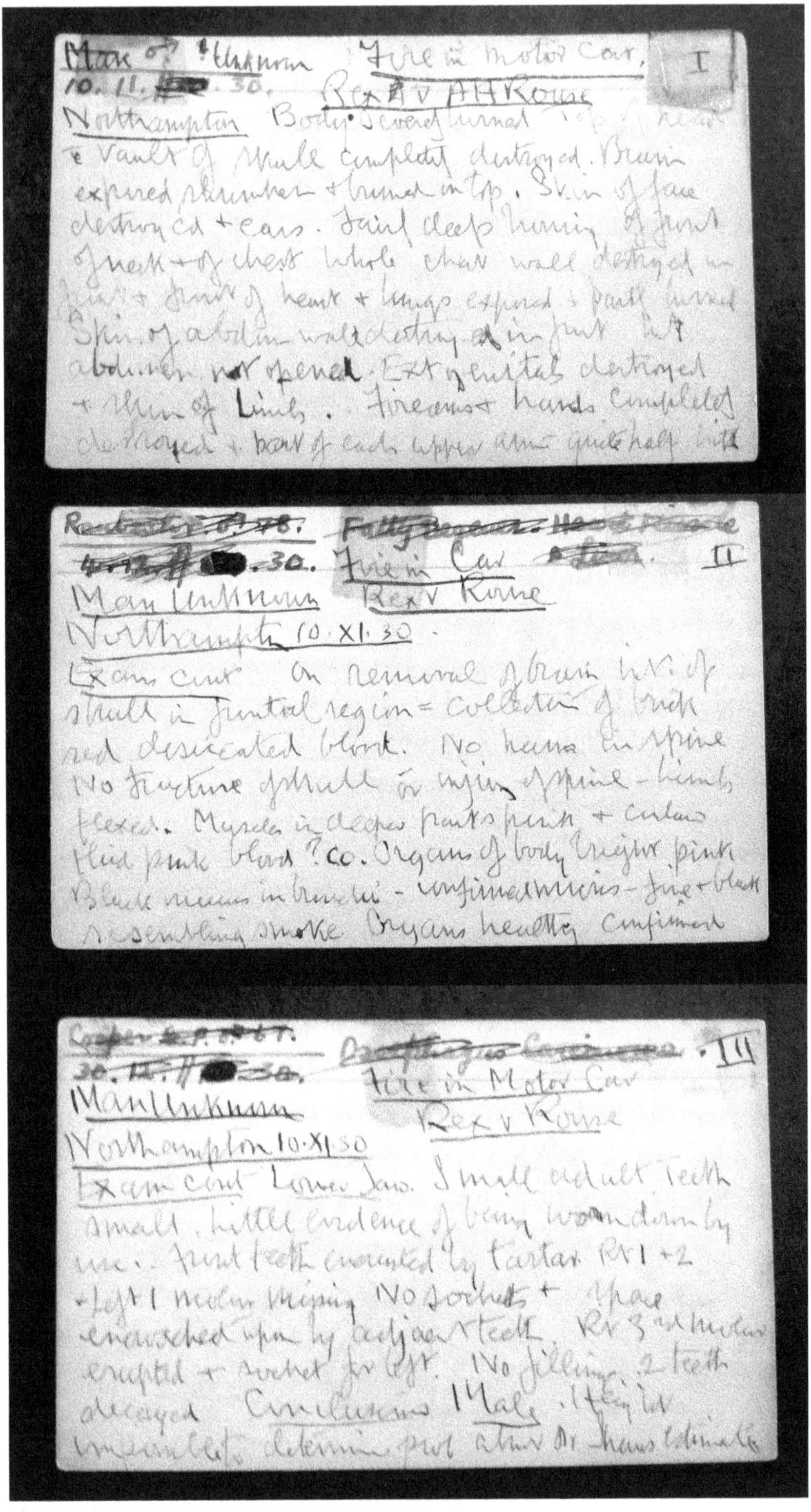

Man ? Unknown Fire in Motor Car, I
10.11.[redacted].30. Rex v A H Rouse
Northampton Body severely burned Top of head
& vault of skull completely destroyed. Brain
exposed shrunken & burned on top. Skin of face
destroyed & ears. Fairly deep burning of front
of neck & of chest. Whole chest wall destroyed in
front & front of heart & lungs exposed & partly burned
Skin of abdomen wall destroyed in front but
abdomen not opened. Ext genitals destroyed
& skin of limbs. Forearms & hands completely
destroyed & part of each upper arm quite half with

[illegible] [illegible] Fire in Car [illegible] II
Man Unknown Rex v Rouse
Northampton 10.XI.30.
Exam cont On removal of brain L.S. of
skull in frontal region = collection of brick
red desiccated blood. No haem in spine
No fracture of skull or injury of spine - limbs
flexed. Muscles in deeper parts pink & certain
fluid pink blood ? CO. Organs of body bright pink
Black mucus in bronchi - confirmed micro - fine & black
resembling smoke Organs healthy Confirmed

[illegible] [illegible] III
30.12.[redacted]30. Fire in Motor Car
Man Unknown Rex v Rouse
Northampton 10.XI.30
Exam cont Lower Jaw. Small adult teeth
small little evidence of being worn down by
use. Front teeth encrusted by tartar. Rt 1 + 2
+ Left 1 molar missing No sockets + space
encroached upon by adjacent teeth. Rt 3rd molar
erupted + socket for Left. No fillings. 2 teeth
decayed Conclusions Male. [illegible]
[illegible]

14. Spilsbury's Post-Mortem Notes

AT THE GRAVE OF THE UNKNOWN MAN.

16. Superintendent Brumby lays a wreath

17. Statement of Alfred Arthur Rouse, 22nd February 1931

Top:

Dear Mr. Lee Roberts,
It seems very late in the day to ask me to make further statements or comments on the mechanical side of the case as it seems too near the hearing of the appeal to be of any use and also as you know I have emphasized the following points before. However, I think the following facts must stand out with any reasoning man.

Bottom:

As I have for the last four three months considered the events of the fateful evening of November 5th, I come to the conclusion that this statement is, and must be, the only lucid solution to the problem. All other theory theories advanced lack substance and backing.

I request that a copy of this statement shall be sent to the Home Office as there has been a very grave miscarriage of justice. This shall be done by my solicitors after their perusal.

This Form is not to be pinned.

MALE.

C.R.O. No......../

Name in which charged. *Rouse Alfred Arthur*

Aliases ....

Classification No. ....

This space is reserved for use in the Finger Print Bureau.

RIGHT HAND.

1.—Right Thumb.	2.—R. Fore Finger.	3.—R. Middle Finger.	4.—R. Ring Finger.	5.—R. Little Finger.

(Fold)   (Fold)

Impressions to be so taken that the flexure of the last joint shall be immediately above the line marked (Fold). If the impression of any digit be defective a second print may be taken in the vacant space above it.

When a finger is missing or so injured that the impression cannot be obtained, or is deformed and yields a bad print, the fact should be noted under **Remarks**.

The "rolled" and "plain" impressions are to be obtained first, then the prisoner should sign his name, and lastly an imprint of the right forefinger is to be impressed on the back of the form.

LEFT HAND.

6.—L. Thumb.	7.—L. Fore Finger.	8.—L. Middle Finger.	9.—L. Ring Finger.	10.—L. Little Finger.

(Fold)   (Fold)

LEFT HAND.
Plain impressions of the four fingers taken simultaneously.

RIGHT HAND.
Plain impressions of the four fingers taken simultaneously.

Impressions taken by	*Butler*	Rank *Inspector*	Police Force } *Northants Constabulary*	Date *10-11-30*
Classified at Finger Print Bureau by			Date	
Tested at Finger Print Bureau by			Date	

M.P.-30-16302/10M   G58

[P.T.O.

18. Fingerprints

19. The Bedford Gaol Photograph

The Bedford Gaol Photograph

20. Left to right: Mr. Norman Birkett, K.C. M.P. / Mr. Justice Talbot / Mr. Donald L. Finnemore

Side One

Side Two

21. THE WHITTLED STICK

Side One   *Side Two*   *The Hanging Man*

22. Peg's Paper
Signed up Helen, Lily, Nellie... and Arthur

THOMSON'S WEEKLY NEWS, FEBRUARY 28, 1931.

Thomson's Weekly News

LATEST CERTIFIED CIRCULATION—658,565 COPIES WEEKLY.

NO. 3952 [REGISTERED AT THE GENERAL POST OFFICE AS A NEWSPAPER]   SATURDAY, FEBRUARY 28, 1931   (Established 1855)   PRICE TWOPENCE

Rouse's Last Visit.

MY ESCAPE FROM POISONING.

By MISS IVY JENKINS.

Continuing the story of her astounding love romance with Alfred Rouse, who was condemned to death for the blazing car murder, Miss Ivy Jenkins, of Gelligaer, South Wales, this week reveals the truth about a rumour which was broadcast about her and also describes a mysterious illness with which she was seized.

An innocent country girl, Miss Ivy Jenkins was being trained to be a nurse at a London hospital when she first met Rouse who, posing as a bachelor, immediately began to make love to her.

Rouse eventually lured her into a bogus marriage. Then followed on the part of the "husband" a life of the most unblushing deception until his arrest for murder.

NOW that the Court of Appeal has decided that Arthur Rouse is to die, I am at liberty to make plain many things I have had to keep to myself, including the truth about the statement made by Rouse that I was to become the mother of a child by him, and that my child was still-born.

This rumour has been passed from lip to lip until practically every person who has taken an interest in the mystery of the blazing car has come to believe it.

Before I tell it in all its detail, I want to put things in their proper sequence. Already I have tried to tell you something of Rouse's last visit to my home at Gelligaer, where he had been called by my father's telegram because of my illness. I have told you of the shock I had when I saw his filthy condition and of the anxiety created in my mind by his strange behaviour during our last evening together and the next morning when he said good-bye to me for the last time.

There was something about him on that Thursday evening that not only worried me but repelled me. I found myself shrinking at his touch, and all for the kisses which, on this occasion, he seemed too worried to give me. I was puzzled. I could not get out of my mind a feeling of coming tragedy.

But other things happened during the last night Rouse spent at my house which, had I known about them at the time, would have heightened my suspicions and increased my concern. I have learned about them since from Phyllis and my mother, and I have found that they, too, were filled with a sense of foreboding; they, too, had become convinced by Rouse's manner in the house that he was hiding from us the true story of his last visit to me, and that the story he had told on alighting of the car having been stolen while he was having a cup of tea somewhere was very far from the truth.

I had noticed that his right sleeve was torn, and that two buttons were missing from the cuff. Phyllis, who is never happier than when she is sewing, saw it, too, and offered to repair the rent and sew on the buttons before he started out on his sudden return journey to London.

Phyllis has told me since that she got her needle and cotton and was busy in the back kitchen sewing the rent, more as a joke than anything else, she repeated an old Welsh superstition which runs something like this:—

Sew on buttons,
Sew on sorrow,
Sew up rags,
A sad to-morrow.

At these words Rouse started as though he had been shot. He drew his arm roughly away from Phyllis and said "For God's sake stop. Leave it as it is. It doesn't matter."

A LOOK OF HAUNTING FEAR.

And Phyllis has told us all that she had never seen in Rouse's eyes before, or indeed in the eyes of any person, the look that came into them. It was, she says, an expression of haunting fear.

Then, without another word, he turned quickly and walked into the front room. When, a short time later, he left the sleeve there was partly repaired, just as Phyllis had left it, and the buttons were still missing from the cuff.

I think that I have told you that Phyllis and Arthur never really hit it off together. I don't mean to suggest that they were bad friends, but they were always finding something to squabble over. There was not a single subject on which they agreed. Yet, when he left Primrose Villa for the last time, Rouse seemed particularly anxious to have my sister's good will and good wishes.

As he went out of the door, Phyllis shouted "Good-bye, Rouse." She had always refused to call him by his Christian name, and this with him had seemed a very sore point. He thought he has been

was irresistible where women were concerned, and it hurt his vanity to find that, do what he could, my sister refused to fall for him.

Rouse turned back and held out his hand.

"Don't say good-bye, Phyllis," he pleaded with tears standing in his eyes. "Say Au revoir," and then as Phyllis repeated "Bye-bye, Rouse," he asked her very meekly to "Call me Arthur just this once."

Lying on my bed upstairs I heard the footsteps of my "husband" as he walked down the stone path to the little lane in which our home lies. If he had shouted to me I must have heard him through my open window, but he went away without another word, and left me with troubled thoughts and uneasy mind.

PLEADED WITH HIM TO UNBURDEN HIMSELF.

At that moment I knew very little of what had been in Arthur Rouse's mind during that unhappy night. He had kept his secret. Once, when I pleaded with him to unburden himself to me and tell me what was making him so miserable, I thought he was going to confide in me, but he thought better of it, and went away with no word of explanation.

Much of my bitterness against Rouse now arises from this refusal of his to play the man with me at that moment. Though I should never have forgiven him—surely he could never have expected that—I could now be thinking less hard of him than I do if from his own lips I had learned the secrets of his past which I was bound soon to know.

I can understand his silence about the death of the man in his car, but those other things—those other women of whose part in his life I had never dreamed—surely he could, and should have spoken.

He must have known as he sat by my bedside that night, and as he wished me good-bye the following morning, that the chances were that he would never have another opportunity to make his peace with me face to face. If only he had had the courage to do so I should feel now that beneath all that is bad in Rouse there is at least a spark of manliness.

Even if, after his arrest or after his conviction, he had been awakened by the loss awaiting him to a sense of the vile thing he did to me I would gladly accept even that as his credit. But there has been no word of regret and no appeal for forgiveness.

During recent weeks, at any rate, Rouse has been free to write as many letters as he chooses. Surely, after all that has happened, he might have spared the time and the thought for a few lines to me, knowing, as he must do, if he has any heart at all, that it would help me a little to bear the burden of grief and shame which he has put upon me.

Indeed, he has gone out of his way to widen the barrier between us. In the only statements he has made about me he has seemingly sought only to add to my pain and sorrow.

WRETCHED MEMORY.

It was from his lips that the world first learned the sad story which I want to tell you—that I was deceived into a mock marriage with a man who had a wife and a child, and that at a more terrible trial I gave birth to a baby that was still-born.

Before I publish for the first time what is the whole truth about what I want to tell you just how the first knowledge of it all I had been deceived came to me.

That Friday morning—the day I saw Rouse for the last time—will always be one of the most wretched memories of my life. Rouse had said when he arrived the previous evening that he would be staying the usual until the following Monday. As I was so ill, and he had been sent for specially on that account, this was only natural.

What caused him to change his plans and go off to Cardiff and London in a panic I will tell you. A newspaper was delivered at our house that morning. Phyllis took it up to his room, without knowing what it had in it. Then he saw the paper out of his hands. But then he began to read the newspaper without knowing anything more about it.

The first thought that came to me was, "What a blessing he came down here. What a fright I should have had if I had read that in the newspaper without knowing he was safe."

I don't know what I should have done, I told him, "if I had seen that in the news paper and you had been away. Why, I must have thought it was you. Wouldn't it have been terrible!"

WHAT MY PEOPLE DISCOVERED.

Rouse said something about that being one of the reasons for coming straight down to Wales.

Then my thoughts ran to his own people, and particularly to his father. "Then you had better let your father know you are safe," I asked him.

He lowered his eyes and confessed that he had not.

"Then you must do so at once," I said. "The poor old chap. He will be worried to death when he sees the papers this morning."

"I ought to have sent him a wire, Rouse said, "but the truth is I was thinking too much of you to worry about anybody else," Rouse said.

And he promised that he would send a telegram to his father to say that he was better immediately.

There were other things in that newspaper which Rouse was most eager that none of us should see, and while I cautioned him to make up his mind that Primrose Villa was no longer a healthy place for him.

In the report which the paper contained of the blazing car story on an inside page there was an interview with a woman who claimed to be the wife of Mr A. A. Rouse, the owner of the burnt-out car.

So Rouse kept the tell-tale newspaper in his pocket, and hid with the secret locked in his guilty heart.

Later that day my people bought another newspaper and read for themselves what he had hidden from their eyes. They saw then that if the statement made by the woman who claimed to be Mrs Rouse was true, he had been living a lie and cruelly deceiving them and me.

But they didn't believe it then. They couldn't believe it of Rouse. They knew Rouse as they did, and being convinced of the genuineness of his love for me, they could not bring themselves to believe that he could be guilty of a thing like that. Even Phyllis, who had never really trusted Rouse, hoped and believed at that time that a ghastly mistake had been made.

KEEPING TRUTH FROM ME.

For this reason they said nothing to me. In my bed upstairs I was a prey to all sorts of fears and doubts. The very fact that they roused my mother did not cause me to see a newspaper added to my suspicions. I imagined all sorts of things during the restless days and sleepless nights that followed, but the last thing I thought was that Arthur Rouse, my "husband," as I thought, had been untrue to me in thought, word, or deed.

My fears at that time were not for myself, but for him. I could not suppress the feeling that he was in deadly peril of some kind, and I could not drive out of my mind a premonition, so strong almost it amounted to certainty, that I had looked upon his face for the last time.

Far these whole days my people kept the truth from me. The revelations of the Saturday had convinced them that Arthur Rouse was not my husband. The news papers had made it perfectly clear that all the time I had known him he had been living with his wife. But they knew how it would break my heart if I learned the horrible truth at Buxted Road.

My mother has told me since what a desperately unhappy time they all had about it. They knew it was something that ought to be told, but they couldn't bring themselves to break the news. You see, I was very ill, and they quite naturally thought that such a shock might be very harmful to me indeed.

More than once my mother made up her mind to tell me the horrid truth, but when she got beside my bed and saw my whole worried face she changed her mind.

So, until the Monday evening, I remained in ignorance, which was far from blissful because, although the truth was being kept from me, I was tormented all the time by doubts which nothing could settle.

I remember calling my mother, but more than once, Mother! was the matter, mother? What does it all mean? Was anything happening to Arthur? What doesn't he write?

My mother did her best to pacify me by assuring me that everything would come right in the end, but there was that they down inside me which told me as plainly as though she herself had spoken that she was withholding something that it would hurt me to hear.

HOW I LEARNED THE WORST.

Then, on the Monday evening, Inspector Evans, an old friend of the family, came over from Bargoed and brought with him news about Rouse. I do not know the real reason for his visit, but the fact was he worse than to reveal to my father and mother at that time, but I know the the inspector had to say about how was far, far worse than anything they had ever dreamed.

Inspector Evans told my people he thought it ought to know something of the truth, but as was too kindhearted a man to take on the task of breaking the news himself. My mother asked him as though she herself had spoken that a old friend to do what they had shrunk from doing, but he could not face it.

Our picture shows a recent portrait of Ivy Jenkins; (centre) "Primrose Villa," Gelligaer, where Miss Jenkins now lives, and (inset) A. A. Rouse.

(Continued on Page Two.)

23. Thomson's Weekly made the most of Ivy's story

SECTION C
Rouse, Women and Society

CHAPTER SEVENTEEN

A 1914 MAN

EVENING NEWS, January 29, 1931

Rouse and the Military

Within four days of the outbreak of the war on August 4, 1914 Rouse had enlisted at the Southwark headquarters of the 24th (County of London) Battalion, the London Regiment (the Queen's) based at 73 New Street, Kennington, South-East London. The unit was a battalion of the Territorial Force and obliged enlistees to serve, as a minimum, four years in the United Kingdom. The London Regiment expanded to 88 battalions during the war and the 24th, formerly the 4th Volunteer Battalion, The Queen's (Royal West Surrey Regiment), and before that the 8th Surrey Rifle Volunteer Corps, became part of the 6th London Brigade. Rouse's number in his attestation certificate was 2011, and in it he was described as a warehouseman working for Alliston & Co., of Friday Street, London, EC1. His address was 77 Mildmay Park, London, N1 (near the Balls Pond Road), where he lived with his father. He was 21 and three months when he enlisted and was described as being five foot seven and a half inches, in good health and with good vision.[442] One may then presume that either he found his employment tedious, and sought an escape route or, more likely, he had been swept up by patriotic fervour in London following the declaration of war.[443] If the latter, then he would have been no different from thousands of other young men around him, but not necessarily throughout the country, who had not hitherto displayed any particular political opinions, nor had engaged with the peacetime Territorial Force.

It is not clear for how long he had been courting Lily Watkins, three years his senior, before August 1914. In any event, some three months after his enlistment, the couple married at St Saviour's Church, St Albans, on November 29. It is likely that Rouse had been training with his battalion at Hatfield at this time in preparation for its move abroad.[444] Thus on March 1, 1915, Rouse entrained with his colleagues at Harpenden for the journey to Southampton Docks (a location that he would later revisit on his prowls during his commercial travelling days). There he boarded the *Empress Queen* for the voyage to Le Havre, arriving at the

---

442 See HO144/19181. This file additionally contains copies of the medical reports of his war injuries. Extracts from his medical reports are also reproduced in Helena Normanton's Notable British Trials volume at Appendix I.
443 It is a myth that the whole country was united in war fever. See Adrian Gregory, *The Last Great War: British Society and the First World War*, Cambridge University Press, 2008, Chapter 1.
444 Details regarding the unit's training and deployment, its operations at the battle of Festubert, and the action at Givenchy are in the unit war diary for the period. See WO95/2744/2 and text below.

French port on March 16.

The battalion then made for Rest Camp No. 6 nearby, before boarding a train for St Omer and Arques. The unit proceeded to billets at the village of Blendecques from where, the next day, they joined up with other units of the 6th (London) Brigade. The brigade next moved on to the village of St Hilaire, a 'squalid' village compared with Blendecques, according to the compiler of the war diary, the battalion adjutant, Captain G. C. Maude. The marching was 'hard', the paving stones taking their toll on some of the men's feet. The weather was also cold, with snow and sleet. On March 21 it was recorded that a hostile aeroplane had dropped a bomb three miles away at Lillers, but there was no damage. The following day, the commander-in-chief, Sir John French, inspected the battalion.

Perhaps an early indication of the 'learning curve' experienced over time by the British Army in France and Flanders was the lecture given by Brigadier-General A. Montgomerie to the officers of the battalion on March 24 on the subject of 'Cooperation between the Artillery and the Infantry'. Three days later the unit, still in the reserve lines, moved to Lapugnoy where the billets were mercifully cleaner than those at St Hilaire. From then until the men moved up to the front lines in early May to a position near Festubert, it was a regular diet of training, digging, marching, working parties, firing practice, mock night attacks, making obstacles and more digging. The tedium was interrupted only by the occasional arrival overhead of enemy aeroplanes and by an inspection by the GOC, General Sir Douglas Haig, on April 15.

On the 19th the men moved up to the trenches at Richebourg St Vaast occupied by 1 South Wales Borderers and 2 Welsh Regiment, but only for familiarization purposes. The first taste of enemy shelling by 6-inch howitzers was experienced by C and D companies the next day, though without losses. The two companies were temporarily attached to 23 Field Company, Royal Engineers, and the Glosters, respectively. The unit's first battle casualty, one man wounded, was suffered that day and two days later, on April 21, the first fatal casualty of the battalion was recorded, the death of a private in C Company, by then occupying the trenches of the Welsh Regiment.

On April 24 HQ, A and B companies were relieved at Richebourg by two companies of the Northamptonshire Regiment and were then marched the short distance south to the village of Le Touret. Frustratingly, we do not know in which company Rouse was serving, but if it had been one of the three companies above, then the provenance of the relieving companies afforded a further ironic coincidence (or fatal tryst, if one preferred the more gothic interpretation) in the life of Arthur Rouse.

More deaths were suffered over the next few days, including that of Fusilier G. Davies who died of wounds at Béthune on May 1. These losses were mainly due to sniper fire coming from the enemy trenches. Meanwhile the battalion had been moved again, though still within the sector bounded by Essars, Givenchy, Festubert and Richebourg. It is an area now dotted with British war cemeteries containing the dead from the battles about to erupt.

Rouse and his fellow-soldiers endeavoured as best they could to settle into sectors DI (c) and (d), otherwise known as Dead Cow Farm, in order to relieve the 23rd London battalion.

A, B and C companies now occupied the trench firing and support lines, and carried out improvements to the structures. D Company was posted as Local Reserve but lost another man and two wounded while digging a communication trench to Brigade HQ.

Yet the general feeling of Captain Maude was that things were mostly quiet. Indeed on May 2, the battalion was ordered to move to the Divisional Reserve at Essars on the night of May 3-4. That day there had been heavier firing from the enemy which Maude attributed to a change-over of units in the German lines. The British retaliated with heavy shelling causing, it was believed, much damage to the enemy parapets. When the 24th did move the next day to Essars for rest and clean-up (and for baths in Bethune for B Company), it simply exchanged places temporarily with the 23rd London Battalion until it moved back to Dead Cow Farm the following day. Its billets at Essars were then taken over by the 60th Rifle Regiment (the prestigious King's Royal Rifle Corps). Very soon Rouse would be taking part in two major battles, commencing with his unit's support role in the failed assault at Aubers Ridge on Sunday, May 9, and then a more direct involvement in the battle of Festubert between May 15 and 27. In particular, the action at nearby Givenchy on May 25-26 led not only to bravery awards, including the Victoria Cross, to members of Rouse's battalion. It also resulted in the serious head, leg and thigh injuries suffered by him which ended his military service and which led to his evacuation to hospital in England within two days.

But perhaps the most puzzling aspect of the period before the 1/24 London Regiment went into battle was how Rouse managed, while in the reserve lines, to meet and impregnate a Frenchwoman from Paris, who later gave birth to his child. His unit and its component companies do not appear to have stayed in any one reserve position for long before being moved forward or backward as it exchanged places with other battalions. Nor is there any clear indication in the unit diary entries of Rouse and his fellow-soldiers being granted leave to visit towns or village estaminets where liaisons could be forged with the local women (let alone one from Paris unless she had travelled to the area), though soldiers' and officers' recourse to brothels in northern France is well documented. But when it came to young women Rouse was certainly resourceful. He clearly did manage some time off duties, and what he did with his leisure time (assuming that his account of fathering a child while in France can be believed) is not wholly surprising.

Meanwhile, it may be noted that in the British Army Order of Battle for Aubers Ridge (and for Festubert),[445] Rouse's was one of four battalions forming 142 Brigade, all London units under the impressively-named Brigadier-General C. S. Heathcote-Drummond-Willoughby.

The brigade was in turn part of the 47th (2nd London) Division under Major-General C. St. L. Barter. This was a component of I Corps under the command of Lieutenant-General Charles Monro, one of the three corps (together with the Indian Corps commanded by Lieutenant-General J. Willcocks and IV Corps under Sir Henry Rawlinson) forming Haig's First Army whose strategic role was, simply, to assist the French in pushing back the German armies from France and Belgium.

---

445 www.cgsc.edu/CARL/nafziger/915BXAC.pdf

A map at this time would show that the trenches separating the Allies from the Germans ran in a line, north to south, from just north of Nieuport in Belgium, east of Dixmude, then just west of Ypres, La Bassée and Lens. It continued south in a line just to the west of Vimy, then veered east of Arras. Thereafter it followed a line separating Albert in the west from Thiepval to the east. From there it swept across the Somme then swooped south-east, following the route of the River Aisne, before passing to the right of Rheims in the Champagne region.

Continuing east, it ran just north of Verdun, then took a dog-leg route at the Meuse, before proceeding south to Mulhouse and Switzerland, passing north of Nancy en route.

The 400-mile front line did, of course, shift to some extent between the spring of 1915 and the German spring offensive in 1918. Indeed, 'If a man served near Festubert [a very short distance from where Rouse was injured in battle] *after* 1915, ...the war passed him by.'[446]

Thus fighting between mid-1915 and March 1918 led to Allied gains in Flanders and to more substantial gains further south in a line from Lens to the Chemin des Dames, north of Laon. Yet ironically, the collapse of the German armies from the summer of 1918 occurred after their spring offensive had resulted in the Allies being pushed back, in most places, to lines further *east* than the latter had established in the spring of 1915. It is thus a sign both of the fluidity of the front lines over four years and of the dramatic and rapid nature of the German military collapse that would lead to the Armistice in November 1918.

As may be clear from the above, the 1/24 London Regiment was kept as a reserve battalion during the battle of Neuve Chapelle, located to the south of Aubers and east of Richebourg, and which commenced on March 10, 1915. The French, under Joffre and Foch, were unenthusiastic about taking the offensive at this point, but were keen for greater British involvement despite the British Expeditionary Force's (BEF's) relatively limited battle experience in France. For the French were recovering their energies after their exertions further south in Champagne where they had lost, on one estimate, 240,000 men. Haig, however, saw the prospect of enhancing British military prowess and therefore bowed to French wishes that the former relieve some of the pressure on the French. The British therefore embarked upon the battle of Neuve Chapelle after careful preparations. Rehearsals for infantry attacks were carried out, deception tactics were used, and light railways carried munitions to the front lines. Moreover, artillery bombardments, though puny by later standards, but organized according to strict timetables, preceded the infantry assaults, while aerial reconnaissance was employed to photograph the enemy trenches.[447] It was a template for the future, and shows early indications of the 'learning curve' (mentioned previously) which later military historians have identified as a refutation of the charge against the generals that they had scandalously sacrificed their men to be mown down by German machine guns in suicidal attacks across No Man's Land, that is, the 'lions led by donkeys' accusation.

Immediate gains by the British were recorded but then the attacks got bogged

---

446   Denis Winter, *Death's Men: Soldiers of the Great War*, Penguin, 1979, p. 82. Italics added.
447   See, for example, John Terraine, *The Great War, 1914-18*, Arrow, 1967, p. 82.

down, casualties increased and munitions ran short. After three days fighting the battle ended. The British lost 13,000 men, the Germans around the same, and the Allied gain was just one shattered village. A month later, heavy fighting further north at Ypres (Ieper) in Belgium in April 1915 took its huge toll of manpower on all sides (the Germans had envisaged Ypres only as a limited engagement to try out their new weapon of chlorine gas). The French then refocused on the Artois region further south between Armentières and Béthune. Although the British were stung by their failure to make progress at Neuve Chapelle, Foch called upon them again to assist, asking them to assault Aubers Ridge on May 9, just north of the previous bloody stalemate at Neuve Chapelle. This proved a further huge failure, with 11,500 British casualties. It also saw the commander-in-chief, General Sir John French, tactically complaining to a journalist friend, Colonel Repington of *The Times*, of a deadly shell shortage. It was the press reporting on May 14 of this 'scandal' that saw a new government department, the Ministry of Munitions, created in the same month, with Lloyd George installed as its first minister (which became a springboard for his premiership in December 1916).[448]

Rouse's battalion was not directly involved in the fighting at Neuve Chapelle and Aubers Ridge. However, we have already seen, in the account of his unit's activities since arriving in France, the creeping encroachment towards the grim reality of trench warfare at the sharp end in which it would soon become involved. There had, first, been a slow introduction to a military regime in the comfortable surroundings of a Home Counties camp, followed by the excitement of entraining to Southampton and boarding the troopship to Le Havre. The train to Arques might yet have been perceived as an adventure in a foreign land, but thereafter the men's journey on the march through dull villages in Northern France, and through driving rain and sleet, together with trying to sleep in crude and unpleasant billets, was scarcely a picture postcard scene to send the pulses racing among young men, most of whom were unlikely previously to have travelled far from home before being sent abroad. However, there was the opportunity to imagine and a chance to pretend to familiarity. As the late military historian, Richard Holmes, observed,[449]

> Men easily found familiar comparisons. The old hospital in Corbie [near Amiens] was 'something on the lines of St Cross in Winchester', the stream running through Lumbres [near St-Omer] would make 'an ideal trout stream, if only it was properly cared for'. Scottish infantry sitting about their billets in St-Omer made it seem like a Lanarkshire town, and Aubers Ridge looked just like the Hog's Back between Guildford and Farnham.

However the deflating realisation that the surroundings lacked the excitement of the new, the continental-style exotic, and the unfamiliar might compete for mental dominance with the patriotic fervour driving the men on to face the Hun. Indeed, the greater likelihood was that the strained (at most) appreciation for their new but gloomy surroundings could be a far more significant factor in determining unit morale than the positive drive to fight for King and country (though the men's

---

448 Arthur Marwick, *The Deluge: British Society and the First World War*, Macmillan, 1973, p. 59; Phillip Harding, *The British Shell Shortage of the First World War*, Fonthill, 2015.
449 Richard Holmes, *Tommy: The British Soldier on the Western Front*, Harper Perennial, 2005, p. 23.

resilience to fight for their mates or pals would generally trump all other factors). Yet the initial shelling, sightings of enemy aeroplanes and the sight of the first, albeit minor, casualties in the battalion, spoke to a new and forbidding reality, that one's mortality could be at stake as he faced the enemy across No Man's Land or ensconced in the villages and trenches of targets marked on his officers' maps.

On May 7 Rouse's battalion was finally readied to support the British attack, now scheduled for Sunday, May 9, at Aubers Ridge. The next day it moved up the line. Its initial task was to occupy an existing line of British trenches and to support by fire the advance of 2 Brigade, I Division, as the latter set out to capture a road junction. Unit commanders were under strict instructions to ensure that their firing did not mow down the advancing columns of 2 Brigade. Each NCO and private was to carry 200 rounds of ammunition (with another 200 rounds kept in trench stores to be used only for covering fire). Sandbags, entrenching tools, rations, and protection against gas (crude and dampened mufflers or cap comforters at that time) were to be carried. Reassuringly, so it was believed, 'Should belts of gas be encountered, units should charge quickly through them if advancing. If troops are stationary, rapid fire directed at the belt does much to dissipate the gas'. Other instructions and preparations concerned wearing apparel (no greatcoats were to be worn), the tasks for grenade throwers, and the direction that all available ladders were to be brought to the trench start points from Dead Cow Farm.

The battalion would hold its present position to cover a flank of the attack conducted by I Division, though it might later be called upon to relieve a part of the line at position P4, between La Quinque Rue and Rue de Marais, once the attackers had secured that target. Thus in anticipation of its potential involvement in a high-intensity battle, battalion HQ was moved from the position known as Rue du Bois to Dead Cow Farm at 4 am on the 9th, and a dressing station was set up at the old battalion HQ. Where non-fatal injuries were suffered, uninjured men were forbidden to accompany the wounded to the rear. The latter were to make their own way to the regimental aid post or await a stretcher party. A bombardment commenced at '5 pm' (clearly an error in the diary for 5 am), lasting 40 minutes, at the cessation of which the Northamptonshire Regiment and the 60th Rifles launched their assault on the German lines. At the same time, A, C and D companies of Rouse's battalion commenced rapid firing against the enemy to cover the attacking forces, each company being allotted a separate section of the enemy parapets as targets. However, as Captain Maude laconically noted, the attackers 'were stopped by uncut wire and MGs, losing heavily.'

Indeed the fire support companies themselves also came under heavy shrapnel fire for some time.

A second bombardment and attack were undertaken in the afternoon. A battalion of the Black Watch even managed to reach the enemy lines but was beaten back due to the lack of close support and to the deadly effect of German machine guns. That there had been some confusion during the battle was shown by the unplanned arrival of a company and a half of the 9th Liverpool Regiment in the 24th London lines. The latter lost the services of two junior officers, Lieutenants Truelove and Solomon, both injured, as well as four killed and 44 others wounded. The next two days, however, remained quiet and a number of senior officers from

7th Division, including General Hubert Gough, visited the battalion to reconnoitre the immediate front line. It must have been a disappointment when all units of the London Division were withdrawn *except* the 24th which was temporarily attached to 5 Brigade, 2nd Division.

Aubers Ridge was quickly followed by the Allied decision to assault the German lines at the village of Festubert, about 10 kilometres further to the south. The village had previously been held by the Indian Corps in December 1914 but was now in German hands. However, with the fighting at Aubers Ridge indecisive, and with the French under Joffre forced back at Vimy Ridge after initial gains, Festubert was seen as another chance, led by IV Corps under General Rawlinson, to assist the French to eject the Germans from Artois.

The battle commenced on May 15, 1915, with a huge artillery bombardment. The British initially gained 1,000 yards of a 2,000 yards front, forcing a limited German retreat on May 17. But 16,500 British soldiers became casualties in the process. With mounting losses, Allied progress had ground to a halt by May 24. German counter-attacks also failed, and although the British captured the frequently flooded German trenches in the village of Festubert itself, both sides dug in as the war of attrition took over. Within the higher command, Rawlinson was passed over for command of the newly-formed Third Army, and Monro, Rouse's corps commander, was appointed instead.[450]

But before the game of senior officer musical chairs was organized, the 1/24 London Regiment was ordered to attack the German trenches at nearby Givenchy. Thus on May 25 at 17:30 hours the battalion took over a section of the Scottish trenches in anticipation of the attack on the German lines in the village. Part of the attack required the battalion to capture a critical hill in German hands from which the enemy were pouring a constant stream of withering fire. The men were organized in company formation, with the assault over open ground to be led by A Company, bombers attacking the left of the hill and the bayonet soldiers attacking the right. The subsequent companies would follow in alphabetical order.

The machine guns were also readied. But despite the accompanying battalion, that is, the 1/23 London Regiment, not being completely ready to attack, the decision to go, fixed for 18:50 hours, was given since the timetable for the British artillery barrage could not be altered.

Thus A Company, in platoon order, now ventured forward over the top to secure the initial target, an enemy trench marked as position I.4 on the map. Platoon No. 1, together with a platoon of the 23rd battalion, reached the target first, and captured it 'without great loss'.

Both B Company and half of C Company soon arrived and provided close support. The rest of C Company followed ten minutes later, to be joined by D Company (it should only have been two platoons of D Company but the whole company was mistakenly sent forward).

At 18:56 hours the OC of B Company reported that his men could not go beyond their first objective at position I.4 and now was the time to prevent a German counter-attack from higher ground. They were in urgent need of more bombs and ammunition, and these quickly reached them. The rest of the time till 2100 hours

450   *Ibid.*, pp. 35-6; www.historyofwar.org/battles_festubert.html

on May 25 was spent in consolidating the limited gain of position I.4, during the whole of which time, the battalion was engaged in fierce bomb throwing exchanges with the enemy. In addition the anticipated German counter-attacks from open ground on the flank were repulsed. But the capture was at a heavy cost. Five officers were killed. They were Captain Gill and Lieutenants Morrison, Garner-Smith, Chance and Gaskell. Three officers were wounded, Captains Nadand and Wheater, and Lieutenant Mobberley. Garner-Smith, aged 23 from Hampstead, is buried at Le Touret war graves cemetery. The number of casualties among NCOs and other ranks arising from this action is not recorded in the war diary, though we can be sure that the numbers well exceeded the officer losses. As we know that the date of the injury suffered by Rouse was May 25, it is likely that it occurred while he was occupying the captured enemy trench after assaulting it as one of the bayonet wielding riflemen, rather than as one of the group of around seventy bombers in his unit.

After midnight on May 26 reinforcements arrived in the shape of one company from the 22nd battalion and a number of bombers from one of the Divisional Cyclist companies. The orders were now to push towards the next objective on the map, trench positions I.2 and I.9, while a communications trench was also being dug to link up with the start point. A group of 20 German soldiers was at this time captured by the combined actions of Lieutenant Morland of the 3rd London Field Company, R.E., and Lieutenant C. G. Davies of Rouse's battalion as the British party was excavating a mine. However half-an-hour later, the plans to move on were abandoned in view of the loss of too many bombers and because German forces were still occupying higher ground. Instead the orders were to consolidate position I.4 against heavy bomb attacks and sniping from the right flank. With no further attack ordered, D Company and two platoons of C Company were withdrawn to the Scottish trenches.

In the early morning Maude submitted a number of situation reports (SITREPS) to brigade HQ. Thus at 06:20 hours he reported that although it was quieter than previously, position I.4 was still under spasmodic attack from snipers and German bombers dug in on higher ground. Twenty battalion casualties were suffered in these exchanges. A request for artillery and mortar support was sent in, and also the assistance of rifle grenade help from the 18th battalion. An hour later little had changed. Indeed at 07:30 hours the enemy began a heavy shelling of the captured trench from an enfilading position on the right flank. It not only caused a large number of further casualties in the battalion, but to the loss of 237 killed in the 23rd Battalion, a quarter of its strength, including all its officers.[451] In consequence Captains Millner, Figg and Armstrong of the 24th were sent to take command of the remaining officer-less soldiers of the 23rd, and to order them to 'hold out at all costs'. The courage of those officers in rousing the men ensured that this section of the trench was not abandoned under the heavy enemy shelling.

Similarly the orders to the men of the 24th were couched in similar terms: 'Hang on at all costs'. The storm was weathered and while the captured trench remained under attack, the Germans made no effort during the day to recapture it by an assault. Indeed Maude reported at 11:15 hours that so long as the enemy guns on

---

451 According to Adrian Gregory the high casualties in those London regiments may have contributed to the anti-German riots in the Capital that month. See Gregory, *op. cit.*, p. 123.

the battalion's right flank were kept quiet, his men would 'possibly' continue to hold out. And so it proved. Eventually, at 18:30 hours on May 26 the battalion, still dug down at position I.4, was relieved by the 20th before it was later sent back to the reserve trenches at Windy Corner at 22:30 hours.

It had been an eventful time for the battalion, and the intense fighting over the 28 hours of the engagement had taken a heavy human toll. As well as the five officers killed (above), three others were injured. Early returns also suggested that of the other ranks, 52 had been killed, 252 injured and 96 missing. That would normally represent about one-half of the authorized battalion strength. The injured presumably included Rouse. As noted earlier, we do not know the immediate circumstances of Rouse's injury apart from his looking up to see a burning aeroplane crash to the ground; at which precise point in time he was struck by shrapnel from an exploding shell above his head. Exactly what advantage was gained by the battalion's success in capturing and holding the trench may be difficult to assess. In the larger scheme of things, the village of Festubert was captured by the British, although the bulk of the territorial gain of almost two miles into German-held territory was further north, between Neuve Chapelle and Aubers. Total British casualties at the battle of Festubert between May 15 and 25/26 were 16,648 men, with Rouse's 47th Division suffering 2,355 losses.[452]

In his summary of the events Captain Maude considered that the most significant feature was the retaining of the captured trench 'by a few exhausted and, in many cases, wounded men after very heavy enfiladed rifle fire from the enemy'. Bombers from the battalion and from a divisional cyclist company performed especially sterling work. He noted that of his 75 bombers in this group, there were only 17 left when this phase of the fighting ceased. The battalion stretcher bearers also performed valiantly all through the night. His report attracted the attention of higher authorities. Indeed the actions of one of the company of 75 bombers, Lance-Corporal Leonard Keyworth, were considered so outstanding that he was awarded the Victoria Cross for his bravery. The citation in the *London Gazette* of July 2, 1915 reads as follows:

> For most conspicuous bravery at Givenchy on the night of 25-26th May, 1915. After the assault on the German position by the 24th Battalion, London Regt., efforts were made by that Unit to follow up their success by a bomb attack, during the progress of which 58 men out of a total of 75 became casualties. During this very fierce encounter Lance-Cpl Keyworth stood fully exposed for two hours on the top of the enemy's parapet, and threw about 150 bombs amongst the Germans, who were only a few yards away."[453]

Keyworth, aged 22, had originally applied to join his county regiment, the Lincolnshires, on the outbreak of the war, but was turned down. However he managed to join the London Regiment on September 16, 1914 and was posted to the 24th Battalion. The battalion war diary recorded, '6.45-9 p.m. Captured trench being consolidated. A severe bomb fight taking place all the time on the right flank.' A member of No. 9 platoon, he later informed a reporter, 'I and my

---

452 Festubert, like Aubers Ridge, was a component of the Second Battle of Artois between May 3 and June 18, 1915. The French lost 102,533 men and the Germans 73,072.
453 His medal listing is in WO98/8/169.

chums had already been 'blooded' before we were engaged at Givenchy....for we
had previously been in the neighbourhood of Festubert in a pretty tight corner',
which was a reference to the Battle of Aubers Ridge on May 9. His description of
his actions at Givenchy, given in a letter to his sister, stated that,

> I can tell you we have had a very rough time. We entered the trenches at 6.30
> on May 25th, and were told to mount the trenches and commence straight
> away an attack on the German trenches about 250 yards away. This attack
> we made without our artillery's covering fire. Our lads went at it with great
> determination, and were soon successful. I was with the bombing party, and
> was the only one to come through without a scratch. I went along a ridge on
> my stomach and threw bombs into a German trench, my distance being about
> 15 yards. Men were shot down by my side. Still I continued, and came out safe.
> I was at once recommended to my officers who posted it to the colonel. It is
> supposed to be for bravery, but I cannot understand where it came in, as I was
> only doing my duty. But how I came out God only knows. Some of our men
> who were only slightly wounded, and who have come back, could not believe
> that I came out alive."[454]

On another occasion he told reporters that, 'I had my duty to do, which was to
throw bombs and do as much damage as I could....The bravery of my officers—
poor Lt. Chance died a glorious death, inspiring everyone with pluck—filled me
with a 'do or die' feeling'.[455]

Keyworth told the *South London Press*,

> When I was throwing the bombs, the other fellows kept on shouting to lie
> down. Now and then an effort would be made to bring sandbags up to serve
> as protection; every man who tried to do it was killed or wounded....To get the
> VC, as I am to get it, is fine, but do please say that every man who took part in
> that charge was as brave. I am proud to belong to the Queen's. You will grant
> that they have made a name for themselves.[456]

Indeed, the warnings from his colleagues to lie down reflected the fact that while
he was standing up to throw his bombs throughout this two-hour engagement, his
silhouette, outlined against the sky, was fully exposed to enemy shooting in spite
of the darkness. 'I did not realize that I was fully exposed, but I was conscious all
the while that I was being continually sniped at.[457] But Keyworth's actions were
central to the success achieved. As a fellow-soldier observed,

> Seeing that we were done for, Keyworth laid hold of all the bombs he could
> get, and springing on to the enemy parapet, kept pelting them with bombs just
> as if he were taking shots at an Aunt Sally. It was a mercy that he escaped, for
> all the time the Germans were shooting at him madly. He kept it up for over
> two hours, and his audacity paralysed the whole German counter-attack.[458]

454 Cited at www.itsaboutlincoln.co.uk
455 Peter Batchelor and Chris Matson, *VCs of the First World War: The Western Front 1915*, Sutton
     Publishing, 1997, p. 121. The most detailed account of Keyworth's life and legacy is in Paul
     Oldfield, *Victoria Crosses on the Western Front, April 1915-June 1916*, Pen & Sword, Barnsley, 2015,
     pp. 318-20. For the battle, where Keyworth is introduced by the author, see *ibid.*, pp. 60-5.
456 Cited in Neil Bright, "A Lad from Lincoln", 2005, at www.londonwfa.org.uk
457 Cited in G. A. Leask, *VC Heroes of the Great War*, Harrap, 1916, p. 222.
458 www.itsaboutlincoln.co.uk

Nonetheless, it is clear that his unit failed to move beyond position I.4. But that scarcely detracted from the bravery displayed. Nor did it prevent a British tactical gain. For we know that Festubert village did fall to the British, suggesting that even though Keyworth and his colleagues had made no further advances, they had not been obliged to withdraw in the face of rugged German resistance.

Keyworth received the Victoria Cross at a ceremony at Buckingham Palace in July 1915 and then visited Lincoln where he received a rapturous welcome on Bastille Day as he was accompanied through the streets by his fellow-soldiers. Yet sadly, but not uniquely for holders of the VC, he was later killed, dying in a hospital at Abbéville on October 19, 1915, four days after being struck in the head by a sniper's bullet near Hulluch, during the battle of Loos. His family received a last cheery letter from him three days after his death. His medal passed to his sister, Lily, who died in 1962. It is now on display at the Queen's Royal Surrey Regiment Museum in Guildford.[459] In the same engagement at Givenchy was a battalion officer, Captain Douglas Figg, who received the second highest bravery award, the Distinguished Service Order, for his actions during the trench struggle. Another significant individual in that particular exchange was Herbert Hodgson, a celebrated printer after the war who printed a rare subscribers' edition of T. E. Lawrence's *The Seven Pillars of Wisdom* in 1926. Later diagnosed with shell shock after injury in 1918, he carried out light duties until the Armistice.

On the day following the battle, Thursday May 27, the depleted battalion moved from the reserve trenches at Windy Corner to the north bank of La Bassée canal where the men could bathe. They next marched to Béthune via the village of Beuvry and were billeted at the tobacco factory in the town. 'The march there took on an aspect of a Roman Triumph, as the men were in great spirits, carrying spoils of war (German helmets, hat badges etc), and the locals showed considerable enthusiasm,' recorded Captain Maude in the unit war diary. The CO of 7 Division (presumably an error for 47 Division), Major-General Barter, and the GOC, First Army, Lieutenant-General Monro, congratulated the men on their 'good work'.

It is likely that by the time of the engagement at which Keyworth earned his VC Rouse had already become a casualty. Certainly, no evidence has been found where the latter mentions the incident in which a fellow-member of his battalion had been awarded the highest award for valour. It suggests that, although he was scarcely modest about his, often pretended, achievements, Rouse seems not to have basked in the reflected glory that recounting such a story to open-mouthed listeners might have brought. Assuming his non-participation in this particular incident, one should not belittle his particular efforts in the front line, however. His claim of having nightmares regarding the bayonet fight against the German enemy directly facing him may well have been based on his actual experience.

In any event, as to Rouse's injury itself, we know that when the battle of Festubert was grinding to a finish as the British at last captured the ruined village, he was cut down by an exploding shell burst at Givenchy on May 25.[460] In a short story, 'England, My England', published in 1922, D. H. Lawrence described a searing

---

459 www.victoriacross.org.uk
460 At his trial he twice got the date of his injury wrong before getting it right, suggesting problems with his memory. His memory loss might have pre-dated the war but arguably it became more problematic after his injury.

moment in the trenches experienced by the fiercely independent though dutifully uniformed Egbert. The German artillery had got their range and the British officer had ordered a tactical retreat. But just at that moment,

> A shell passed unnoticed in the rapidity of action. And then, into the silence, into the suspense where the soul brooded, finally crashed a noise and a darkness and a moment's flaming agony and horror. Ah, he had seen the dark bird flying towards him, flying home this time. In one instant life and eternity went up in a conflagration of agony, then there was a weight of darkness. When faintly something began to struggle in the darkness, a consciousness of himself, he was aware of a great load and a changing sound. To have known the moment of death! And to be forced, before dying, to review it. So, fate, even in death. There was a resounding of pain. It seemed to sound from the outside of his consciousness: like a loud bell clanging very near. Yet he knew it was himself. He must associate himself with it. After a lapse and a new effort, he identified a pain in his head, a large pain that clanged and resounded. So far he could identify himself with himself. Then there was a lapse.[461]

Egbert was not Rouse. Egbert was killed by the shell while Rouse survived. Yet while Lawrence offered an imagined and protracted account of Egbert's end, perhaps it was a metaphor for the long drawn-out, but ultimately futile efforts of a marginally effete, dull and self-satisfied gardening Englishman to transcend that characterization with noble martial deeds. To some extent, the death of Rouse, high-pitched of voice and self-satisfied, though not exactly dull, was even more long drawn-out but ultimately futile (albeit not in pursuit of a redeeming warrior status).

Accounts from survivors in the trenches might closely resemble the sentiments expressed by the literary character, Egbert, as well as the experience of Rouse. Thus writing in erratic and anxious fashion, one Devonshire Regiment soldier, Private Lucas, talked of, 'showers of lead flying about & big big shells, it's an unearthly sight to see them drop in amongst human beings. The cries are terrible, I escaped being hit but....got buried once that caused me to have fits....'[462]

In 'Rouse's Own Story' published in the *News of the World* on February 2, 1931 after his conviction, he explained that several times during the battle he had gone over the top. 'It was during a German counter-attack that a shell knocked me out—gave me a 'blighty' one, in fact.' The more familiar different account, noted above, was that as he was sheltering in a trench, he noticed above his head an aeroplane that was crashing in flames nearby. So he peered up, only to be struck by splinters exploding from the shell, thus causing severe injuries to his head, thigh and leg. His newspaper account continued that,

> I was hit in the left temple and knee, and remember running wildly about until I collapsed near some British soldiers who were coming towards me. I remember nothing more until I recovered consciousness in a hospital in Boulogne. I was being fed at the time, but I must have gone off again, as I

---

461   D. H. Lawrence, *England, My England*, Penguin, 1966 (first published 1922), pp. 38-9.
462   Cited in Joanna Bourke, "Effeminacy, Ethnicity and the End of Trauma: The Sufferings of 'Shell-shocked' Men in Great Britain and Ireland, 1914-39", *Journal of Contemporary History*, Vol. 35 (1), 2000, pp. 57-69, at p. 58.

do not remember anything until I heard a nurse telling me I was in Dover Harbour.

Rouse was not, of course, alone in suffering serious injury on May 25. As an anonymous nurse at a casualty clearing station, probably just three miles behind the front lines, recorded in her diary at Festubert the following day,[463]

*Wednesday, May 26*th

No time to write yesterday; had a typical Clearing Hospital Field Day. The left-out-in-the-field wounded (mostly Canadians) had at last been picked up and came pouring in. I had my Tent Section of eighty beds nearly full, and we coped in a broiling sun till we sweltered into little spots of grease, finishing up with five operations in the little operating tent. The poor exhausted Canadians were extraordinarily brave and uncomplaining. They are evacuated the same day or the next morning, such as can be got away to survive the journey, but some of the worst have to stay.

So what would have happened to Rouse once the British soldiers had reached him? If the experience of Mickey Chater, a Gordon Highlanders infantryman at the battle of Neuve Chapelle two months earlier, where Rouse's unit was kept in reserve, is anything to go by,[464] then the soldiers who arrived would probably have carried him back to the start point of the assault. From there the unit's stretcher bearers would have hoisted him onto a stretcher to carry him, if his condition was not obviously desperate, to the regimental aid post nearby (RAP), possibly in some abandoned farmhouse. The regimental medical officer (RMO), if Rouse were in luck compared to other casualties, would then attend to him to see whether he was so badly injured, and breathing with such difficulty in his unconscious state, that the effort to treat him would better be spent on another, less seriously injured, casualty. But assuming it was decided that he should receive treatment (and some battle casualties would be whisked straight into a waiting ambulance without an initial examination by the RMO to be taken to a casualty clearing station or even a base hospital), he might have morphine tablets inserted under his tongue, be splashed with water and then his wounds dressed. But it was, essentially, only first aid, for the RAP had no capacity to look after casualties after initial treatment. Stretcher bearers would therefore then carry him (or he would walk) to an advanced dressing station (ADS),[465] a tented or brick structure set up by the Field Ambulance unit, possibly around 400 yards behind the aid posts. Indeed, serious cases could be taken there directly, via collecting posts (CPs), thereby by-passing the RAP. But the ADS similarly had no holding capacity, so a casualty in need of further treatment might be sent back to a main dressing station (MDS) which had a store of horsed or motor transport. Only life-saving operations would be carried out at the MDS, with the casualty possibly remaining there, if necessary, for up to a week. Thereafter he would be sent on in the next available ambulance, more likely mechanized than horse-drawn,

463 Anon., *Diary of a Nursing Sister*, Amberley, Stroud, 2014, p. 187. For a senior nurse's diary account that commences in June 1915 see Richard Crewdson (ed.), *Dorothea's War: The Diary of a First World War Nurse*, Weidenfeld & Nicolson, 2013.
464 Emily Mayhew, *Wounded: The Long Journey Home from the Great War*, Vintage, 2014, ch. 6.
465 www.ramc-ww1.com/chain_of_evacuation.html for this and subsequent information.

to a casualty clearing station (CCS) containing doctors, surgeons, nurses and ancillary staff, and located in a large area of land. The CCS soon lost its character as a mere staging post for onward evacuation of patients onto hospital ships to become a fully-fledged medical facility when casualties quickly mounted. It could accommodate at least 50 beds and 150 stretchers for a minimum of 200 sick or injured men at any one time. The CCS would be located about 20 kilometres behind the front lines, and also near a main railway line or canal for ease of evacuation and patients would be accommodated there for a maximum of about a month. They would then be returned to their units or put on an ambulance train or canal transport to be sent to a base hospital, which would either be a general hospital or one for specialist treatment such as for gas victims or for shell-shock victims. These would be located in base areas, usually major ports and centres such as Etaples, Boulogne, Le Havre or Paris and would be organized similarly to a civilian hospital even though the building might have been a requisitioned hotel or casino. The casualty would remain in the base hospital until fit to be evacuated across the Channel and, once admitted to a British hospital would have at least a four in one chance of survival, after which they would be medically discharged or eventually returned to their unit.

In one respect, the casualty transported by ambulance would have been fortunate if he had remained unconscious during the journey. For, strapped down on his stretcher, he would otherwise have found the travelling slow, jarring and bumpy, added to which the crying and moaning of his fellow-casualties would not have made for an especially comfortable experience. His arrival at the CCS would have been overseen by a nurse, initially looking to check his moans and that a grey pallor had not descended onto his skin, a sure sign of an imminent fatal decline. For other casualties the journey itself would have finally done for them, the ambulance driver telling the reception team that it had all gone quiet in the back.

The nurse would then instruct stretcher bearers to carry the patient gently to the casualty ward, cautioning them to avoid bumping into or standing on patients already laid on the floor of the overcrowded ward. A doctor would arrive to examine him to ascertain whether immediate surgery was needed or whether an operation could be delayed either until life-and-death cases had been dealt with or until he was evacuated to England. In either case, he would be cleaned up by the nurse, his grubby, mud-caked and torn uniform removed, clean bed clothes provided and made as comfortable as possible in a sanitary environment.[466]

The documentation regarding Rouse's medical condition does not make clear whether he actually underwent surgery in France (almost certainly he did not). But we know that he was soon put on a hospital ship on May 28 and after a few days arrived back in England. From Dover he would have travelled by train either to Charing Cross or to Victoria station in London. There he would have been met off the train by nurses and orderlies of the London Ambulance Column (LAC), a group of volunteers who, in between meeting their patients at the London railway termini, would attend courses to learn basic and advanced nursing skills as they went along. The ambulances that they used did not belong to the relevant

466 Mayhew, *op. cit.*, ch. 1.

hospitals but had been donated to the Column by rich benefactors.[467] On his arrival in London, he was transported, probably by the LAC, to the 6th London Field Ambulance depot,[468] where he was examined and his shrapnel wounds recorded. The next day he was sent to the 13th General Hospital, also in London, before being transferred to the 2nd Northern General Hospital, Beckett's Park, Leeds, where he stayed for four months (it was surely during this train journey north that he awoke from intermittent unconsciousness in time to see the fateful name 'Bedford' on a station signboard as the train passed through). This was a Territorial Force hospital which could accommodate 60 officers and 2,039 other ranks. It also contained a 126-bed unit for limbless servicemen from Yorkshire and surrounding counties.[469]

It was presumably in Leeds where he underwent a neuro-surgical operation on the left side of his head. He was discharged from hospital to sick furlough, probably in Harrogate, on September 24, 1915, before spending six months recuperating at Harewood House, the stately home of the wealthy Lascelles family. According to Normanton, '....for several months he was a war-shattered invalid. As a patient he was brave, uncomplaining, and cheerful'.[470] During this time he was technically transferred from the 24th London Regiment to, ironically, the 108th Provost Battalion to continue his recovery at a private convalescent home in Clacton-on-Sea. The following year he was discharged from the Army on February 11, 1916 as being 'no longer physically fit for War Service', in accordance with King's Regulations, chapter XVI, para. 392. He had served one year and 188 days in the Army and his character had been recorded as 'Good'. [471] His medal card showed that he was entitled to the Victory, British and 1915 Star medals.[472] The card also noted that his 'invaliding disability' was a 'Wound of head. Left temporal region. Wound of left thigh lower 4th involving knee-joint.' At a medical board hearing on December 12, 1915, the finding was 'Wounded by shell explosion. Givenchy. Scar at lower 4th anterior surface of left thigh. Unable to bend the knee or to walk except with difficulty. Leg oedematous. Operation performed for removal of foreign bodies. Wound of head and left thigh due to service. Assessment— capacity reduced by three-quarters.'

Further details regarding his injuries are contained in his post-discharge medical reports. Thus under 'Head', the following was recorded on July 10, 1916: 'Healed scar at anterior end of temporo-parietal junction (left). Scar irritable— unable to wear hat of any kind. Memory very defective. Reading etc causes headache. Sleeps well unless excited in any way. Speech and writing unaffected (Assessment of disablement: 100%)'. On February 18, 1918 a further examination of his head confirmed an operation scar in the area described above. There was

---

467 *Ibid*, ch. 13.
468 See Frank Coleman, *A Brief Record of the 6th London Field Ambulance (47th London Division) During the War*, John Bale and Danielsson, 1924. Copy in Imperial War Museum
469 www.1914-1918.net/hospitals_uk.htm
470 Normanton, *op. cit.*, p. vii.
471 For this see HO144/19181 for extracts from his military medical records. Also Normanton, Appendix I; *News of the World*, February 1, 1931.
472 WO372/17. He is also listed in the 'WW1 Service Medal and Award Rolls, 1914-1920' and in the 'Silver War Badge Records, 1914-1920', accessible through .wwww.ancestry.co.uk. There were at least four other Arthur or Alfred Rouses serving in the Army during the war. Corporal Alfred A. Rouse of the Royal Army Service Corps died early in the war. Private Arthur B. Rouse of the 5th Royal Warwickshires was discharged due to sickness in July 1916 (he had possibly gone absent without leave prior to this as his card records that he had been 'Returned by Birmingham Police').

some irregularity of the bone with one small furrow, probably from the operation. Rouse reported no pulsation and the furrow was filling in and becoming harder. He suffered from pain whenever the weather changed and experienced dizziness and some loss of memory. He was 'talkative and laughs immoderately at times [we can clearly picture this], but he states that he always did so'. There was no paralysis and no loss of power. Indeed, he was 'improving somewhat' so that his head disability was now reduced to 80%. Seven months later a further assessment found him easily excited and talkative, having difficulty falling asleep and then sleeping badly when he did manage to fall asleep. He also complained of forgetting important matters such as orders related to his business. Perhaps significantly, the report noted that, '....he lives over again a bayonet attack and melee through which he went—when he missed his man and awaited momentarily enemy bayonet thrust'. He was back to 100% disability in respect of his head. Almost a year later, however, the head disability had disappeared, apart from the tell-tale scar.

Meanwhile the assessment of his leg and thigh disability had reduced from 75% in January 1917, to 30% at the end of July 1919, to less than 20% in August 1920 which included just two and a half per cent disability in his thigh. The consequence of these shifts was that his disability pension ranged from 20 shillings a week between February and August 1916, to 40 shillings for only two weeks in September 1919, to just 12 shillings a week from September 1919 to September 1920 when an allowance was also made for Lily. When disability payments stopped on September 15, 1920, a gratuity of £41.5.0 was awarded in final settlement of Rouse's entitlement.[473]

Though thousands, if not millions, of others underwent similar traumas, Rouse endured a frightening war experience involving fierce front-line combat during which a comrade earned the VC, he suffered a serious head injury, obtained a medical discharge from the Army after less than a year's service, and was registered war disabled from 1916 to 1920, living with various symptoms including dizziness and poor sleeping patterns and poor memory. But one crucial question for us to pose is whether they were of relevance in passing judgment on his more daunting challenge with the criminal justice system some 15 years later. As we shall see, his war-time experiences were of no consequence as far as the authorities were concerned on that later occasion. Whether they were right to ignore his brief but savage war will be considered in chapter 24.

---

473 HO144/19181; Normanton, *op. cit.*

CHAPTER EIGHTEEN

JEKYLL & HYDE LIFE : UNKNOWN TO WIFE FOR YEARS

DAILY MAIL, February 2, 1931

Rouse and the Suburbs

In a review in *The Times* of Philippa Lewis' book on residential dwellings,[474] it was observed that, 'At first glance, the image on the front—an unglamorous 1930s house set on a black background—would lead you to believe this was a *noirish* saga of suburban murder rather than a celebration of our nation's properties'.[475] Suburbia and, in particular, houses rather than Continental-style flats, might thus be associated with dark doings behind the lace curtains. Indeed, it was an image bolstered by memories of such earlier 20th century middle-class suburban murders as the Crippen, Seddon and Rattenbury cases, not forgetting Croydon's 1929 'Riddle of Birdhurst Rise'[476] Thus we should not be surprised that Rumpole of the Bailey's greatest success, albeit post-1945, was the astonishing acquittal of his apparently doomed client, the young Simon Jerold, in the case of the *Penge Bungalow Murders*. As Rumpole reminisced,

> I even remembered the street of bungalows [in Penge] which had sprung up in the 1930s to accommodate the growing population of the families of bank clerks, department store managers and commercial travellers who looked on Crystal Palace Park as their particular and privileged glimpse of the countryside".[477]

Suburbia and murder may thus be presented in some texts as enjoying a symbiotic

---

474 Philippa Lewis, *Everyman's Castle: The Story of Our Cottages, Country Houses, Terraces, Flats, Semis and Bungalows*, Frances Lincoln, 2014.

475 Anne Ashworth book review, *The Times*, August 2, 2014.

476 Richard Whittington-Egan, *The Riddle of Birdhurst Rise: The Croydon Poisoning Mystery*, Penguin, 1988.

477 John Mortimer, *Rumpole and the Penge Bungalow Murders*, Penguin Books, 2007, pp. 12-13. Rumpole's 'greatest triumph', endlessly recalled by him in Pommeroy's Wine Bar to whomever might be within hearing distance, is not to be confused with the real Penge *cause célèbre* of 1877, the murder by her husband and in-laws of Harriet Staunton who was effectively deliberately starved to death. See Judith Flanders, *The Invention of Murder*, Harper Press, 2011, pp. 343-50. For a full report of the trial, see www.oldbaileyonline.org/browse.jsp?path=sessionsPapers%2F18770917.xml. For a fictional account, see Elizabeth Jenkins, *Harriet*, Persephone Press, 2014; first published in 1934. For a study of the history of the suburb of Penge, see Martin Spence, *The Making of a London Suburb: Capital Comes to Penge*, Merlin Press, 2007.

relationship. An exaggeration, of course, but the classic *causes célèbres* of which George Orwell wrote possessed more than their fair share of suburban intrigue and mystery. Indeed recent studies of the Crippen case have sought to emphasise the centrality, albeit laced with complexity, of the suburban experience. As we shall note below, the immediate beneficiaries of late Victorian urban expansion, especially of the London suburbs, became a target of criticism by elite journalists such as Philip Gibbs, for the petty, trivial, 'uncultured' and *petit bourgeois* values that the new arrivals brought with them. Nowhere was this phenomenon better reflected than in the discursive writings of Charles Pooter, one of the head clerks at Mr. Perkupp's office in the City. Pooter began his *Diary of a Nobody* following his and his wife, Carrie's, move to a new six-roomed property, The Laurels, Brickfield Terrace, Holloway. Thus Pooter's scribblings on his insignificant day-to-day doings (one correspondent has suggested a similarity between the current trend of tweeting and Pooter's writings in that, 'Both describe the tedium of everyday life, but at least the latter is amusing rather than tedious.'[478]) embodied, 'the centre of the middlebrow, conformist, respectable uninspiring members of society who are quite content to potter around in their own rather limited world'.[479]

As Flint notes,[480] suburbia 'is a world which simultaneously inspires affection for its safe familiarity, and a desire to rise up against its imaginative limitations and its conservative complacency'. That is, there is a tension between the reassurance of the predictable and the knowable, what we tend to describe as our comfort zone, and the sense that we ought to break out from this dull conformity. For the most part the Pooterish character veers more towards the former than to the latter. But the suburbanite's respectability might yet necessitate 'doing something dangerous' (though not literally). For Pooter it might be 'painting the bath red'. Or, as Max Beerbohm observed, the suburban dweller might put on a show (literally), such as placing in a prominent position a bust of the goddess Minerva to be seen by passers-by through the front window. The only problem for Beerbohm was that the bust would be facing the wrong way, that is, outwards, not inwards as one would have expected. It thus simply represented the 'tragic symbol' of stunted, anxious lives. As Julie English Early noted, 'In the suburbs, life was not lived in the street, but behind the twitch of the window curtain.'[481] It was predominantly a woman's domain with her decorations adorning (or, as with the Minerva bust, or with Cora Crippen's garish pink ribbons tied round paintings on the wall of 39 Hilldrop Crescent, 'violating') the property. Thus 14 Buxted Road was Lily's home and castle. After all, Rouse himself was scarcely there for much of the time. Though perhaps not widespread, suburbanites might also, at the same time, be both stalwarts of local associations such as the tennis club (until Rouse's activities in that direction fell into a decline) and also an 'unknowable' and undifferentiated quantity so far as neighbours were concerned. Such people might indeed be content to 'keep themselves to themselves', as Julie Early, above, observed.

Edwardian suburbia certainly suffered a bad press so far as some writers,

---

478   Raj Kothari, *Independent*, October 5, 2013.
479   David Thorns, *Suburbia*, Paladin, 1973, cited in Kate Flint, 'Introduction' to George and Weedon Grossmith, *The Diary of a Nobody*, Oxford Classics ed., 2008, p. vii.
480   *Ibid.*
481   Julie English Early, "Keeping Ourselves to Ourselves: Violence in the Edwardian Suburb", in Shani D'Cruze (ed), *Everyday Violence in Britain, 1850-1950*, Pearson, 2000, p. 175.

journalists and social critics were concerned. Thus apart from Beerbohm, above, T. W. H. Crosland, writing of *The Suburbans* in 1905, 'was fascinated by the suburb, but had little sympathy with its 'pitiful people! Of its dead-level of dullness and weariness and meanness and hard-upness, who shall relieve it?"[482] The small-mindedness, the conservatism, and the need to keep up appearances, the last-named a particular affliction for Cora Crippen, which prompted the ridiculous display of inverted Minerva busts or the plaster-of-Paris stags' heads (or the flying ducks or luminescent lava lamps, or the turquoise portrait of Tretchikoff's 'Chinese Girl' in more recent times), drew contempt from the intellectual classes. Indeed what alarmed commentators even more than tastelessness was that the suburbs, with their expanding mix of classes, such as skilled manual workers living alongside lower-class clerks and insurance agents (or commercial travellers such as Rouse) were increasingly becoming 'unknowable' and, in consequence, unreliable.

This was particularly alarming when it was believed that the suburban home was essentially a feminized institution into which the male of the species had been co-opted. The traditional paterfamilias of the Victorian age had not only given way to a more equal and companionate marital arrangement where responsibilities in some spheres became more shared and where opportunities for married women (the 'New Woman' was not exclusively single) to become more fulfilled socially and economically were expanding. A corollary was the emergence of the 'New Man' at the turn of the century, a more gentle specimen than the 'Men of Blood' of the nineteenth century whose selfish perception of the role of women in their lives was crude, callous, violent and insensitive.[483] However, the New Man, according to Gibbs, writing in 1913, was also 'Suburban Man, 'a pathetic creature who had evolved in the last twenty-five years, and who would be woefully inadequate to the task soon at hand'. In other words, suburbia was tending to emasculate manhood, a terrible prospect in view of the looming conflict with Germany.[484]

The critics thus looked askance, if not actually regretting, that the replacement of the inner-city's overcrowded, insanitary and poorly-lit slums (the improvements ironically given a boost in East London by the activities of Jack the Ripper) did not lead to *intellectual* or 'manly' improvements. Instead, there seemed something bucolic and perennial in the labels given to later Victorian three-story houses, such as Charles Pooter's The Laurels. Numerous street names were no different. Thus we have Cora Crippen's 39 Hilldrop Crescent, Holloway (a street name of such banality as surely to appeal to Cora Crippen's sense of idyllic self-satisfaction), and Lily Rouse's 14 Buxted Road, named after a rural village in East Sussex.[485]

---

482   Cited in Flint, *op. cit.*, p. xii.
483   Martin J. Wiener, *Men of Blood: Violence, Manliness and Criminal Justice in Victorian England*, Cambridge University Press, Cambridge, 2004.
484   Early, *op. cit.*, pp. 178-9.
485   Buxted in Sussex had associations with Constance Kent. On her release from prison in 1885 for the murder of her half-brother, Savile, in 1860, she stayed at a convent in the village before emigrating to Australia the following year. See Kate Summerscale, *The Suspicions of Mr. Whicher: or The Murder at Road Hill House*, Bloomsbury, 2008, p. 288. Tollington, which hosted 63 Tollington Park, Islington, the massive semi-detached villa from the 1830s and 1840s, purchased as an investment, as well as living quarters, for the cold and calculating (in the literal sense) poisoner, Frederick Seddon, was listed in the Domesday Book. Thus Seddon's 'calculation' also referred to the insurance agent supervisor's working out the financial balance sheet on the life of his victim, Miss Barrow.

But in condemning the New Man for effeteness (the New Woman did not escape his critical eye) Gibbs was only half-right (if right at all). There are three strands to this argument. First, as the literary critic, D. J. Taylor, has recently observed,[486]

> There never was a British literary world that didn't believe itself to exist in a permanent state of flux. The 'serious writers' of the 1890s, grimly regarding developments in popular journalism, thought they were being deluged in trash. The columnists of the 1930s lamented the decline of the 'mid-list' (meritorious works with average sales) quite as feelingly as their modern day successors.... Times have always been hard, and from the travails of the impoverished hacks in George Gissing's *New Grub Street* (1891) onwards, conspectuses of literary life nearly always turn out to be jeremiads.

As with fiction, so with contemporary journalism and cultural commentary where 'flux', social change, indeed 'crisis' would always attract a good headline, even if others might prefer to dwell on the dictum, *plus ça change, plus c'est la même chose*. Second, recent research has suggested that the London suburbs should not simply be characterized as static and boring. Instead, their creation stimulated the growth of private means of transport, especially cars and motor cycles that enabled suburbanites to enjoy driving at speed on the new arterial roads springing up to absorb the increase in motorized traffic, to visit roadhouses for evenings of outrageous drinking and pleasure, and even to drive to local aerodromes to enjoy five shilling flights before they travelled home at speed to the suburbs. Of course speed on the roads came at a price, as we shall see when we explore in the next chapter Rouse's pre-occupation with the car.[487]

The third strand is the paradox that suburban conformity and gentleness could, at least in the cases of Crippen and Seddon, sit alongside the impulse to 'do something dangerous', as the rather pathetic 18-year old cinema usherette and failed strip-tease artiste, Elizabeth Jones, later explained to her new companion, Karl Gustav Hulten, the American army deserter in London in 1944.[488] Indeed, without resort to violence, suburbanites could yet be lauded as pioneers willing to vacate or abandon their secure late Victorian or Edwardian semis. They would be couples like Edith and Tom Baldwin, recently retired from his City clerk job, and both living in their Pooterish 'Grasmere', in St John's Wood, off the Edgware Road, the creations of R. C. Sherriff, better known for his wartime play, *Journey's End*. Tom is depressed since all the plans that he had had in mind following retirement had proved difficult to achieve, and now ensconced at home he is getting under Edith's feet, much to her irritation. One day on a country walk, they spy a new housing development under construction in Surrey, with the houses to be fitted out with all 1930s 'mod-cons'. They are 'up for it', a complete 'make-over'. They purchase

---

486   D. J. Taylor, *The Prose Factory: Literary Life in England Since 1918*, Chatto, 2016. The quote is from his article discussing his book. See *Guardian*, January 2, 2016.

487   Michael John Law, *The Experience of Suburban Modernity: How Private Transport Changed Interwar London*, Manchester University Press, Manchester, 2014.

488   See chapter two. This was the case that later became known as the 'Cleft-chin Murder' that George Orwell condemned for its crude American gangster-type killing and which represented the 'Decline of the English Murder'. As a perceived thoughtless, meaningless and random killing from the 'dance-hall' culture, it was far removed from the English *cause célèbre* that would well merit Thomas de Quincey's nineteenth century description of 'Murder Considered as One of the Fine Arts'.

their new home. But the paradox never goes away. They are praised as 'go-getters', as pursuers of modernity escaping their Pooterish existence. Yet they are likewise intellectually condemned. For where are they moving to? Yes, to a more rural environment than the Edgware Road. But, in fact, to an even more entrenched suburban housing estate, this time of 1930s vintage. However while their lives are thus altered, the transformation remains problematic with traditional issues of class, status, comfort and taste testifying to a resilient suburban cast of mind which undermines their project of modernity and re-invention. They remain, in essence, suburbanites and are not as ambitious or as brave as would be expected of 'pioneers'.[489]

Paradox, indeed, also manifests itself at the heart of suburbia's association with dark deeds. Thus the suburbs, as the film director, Mike Leigh, might have put it, hid 'secrets and lies' just as effectively as the nation's security services in those days. Crippen, it should not be forgotten, was a lower middle-class man of the suburbs. He was banal, boring, respectable, polite to all Cora's friends, and tolerant of Cora's domination. She not only appeared, metaphorically, to wear the trousers in their marriage, but she literally chose them for him. She even decided that his name, Hawley, was not manly enough. He should henceforth be known and addressed as Peter. But perhaps this was not so uncommon in similar relationships. Indeed it was the commonplace nature of that particular eternal triangle, underpinned by Ethel Le Neve's own mousy, tedious and unambitious character, which was that of the neurotic office typist whose stock reply to formulaic inquiries about her well-being was, typically, 'Not very well, thank you', that partly explains why the public were gripped by the Crippen case. It was the very ordinariness of the persons involved (possibly excepting the brash, blousy but perhaps warm-hearted Cora, desperate to record her little social triumphs among the music hall fraternity, whose performing standards she had not quite attained, as she undertook her compensatory charitable good deeds).

Yet that very ordinariness was mixed in with the paradoxical, even the oxymoronic, character of Crippen, the 'mild-mannered murderer'. For did not Crippen carefully administer the deadly drug, hyoscine, to his wife, after which he filleted her body, burying bits of flesh in his (almost gothic-sounding) 'North London Cellar', and disposing of the rest of the corpse through various, probably unprovable, means, such as dropping her severed head into the English Channel as he and Ethel sailed to the Continent? This killer was evidently callous, conniving, calculating, cruel, butcher-like, unfeeling, greedy, adulterous, shameless and flaunting of his new amour in the presence of Cora's worried friends (why waste the Music Hall Benevolent Fund Ball tickets which he had previously purchased when Cora was still alive?).

Yet this paradoxical man of both cruelty and suburban inoffensiveness displays a further confusing twist. For it was once said of him that, '....the very crime itself brought out in him high human qualities'.[490] That was surely a reference to his almost sacred and spiritual love for Ethel Le Neve which drove the gentle

---

489 R. C. Sherriff, *Greengates*, Persephone Press reprint (first published 1936), 2015. The modern terminology we have employed here, such as 'up for it', should not be taken as an anachronism, but as a reminder that *plus ca change, plus de la meme chose*.

490 Filson Young, 'Introduction', *Trial of Hawley Harvey Crippen*, Notable British Trials series, William Hodge & Co., Edinburgh, 1950, p. xxxiii.

homeopathic doctor, widely perceived to have been metaphorically emasculated by a domineering Cora Crippen, to end his torment with the ruthlessness of one possessing anatomical knowledge as he went about his dissecting business. Thus the *cause célèbre* quality of the murder is surely due, in this instance, to the three-dimensional character of its leading actor, first, his suburban ordinariness, second, his vicious deed, but third, his honourably-inspired motive and his dignified acceptance of his fate. Of course, that alternative views of the killing exist, especially those informed by feminist perspectives who view Cora as a woman maligned by male hegemonic values, is readily acknowledged.[491] But the affectionate judgment of Raymond Chandler that, 'You can't help liking the guy somehow', prevails over all else.[492]

But not all views of suburbia saw it in the apocalyptic terms of the social commentator, C. F. G. Masterman who in 1905 bemoaned the encroachment of bricks and mortar into green fields on the boundaries of London: 'North, East, South and West the aggregation is silently pushing outwards like some gigantic plasmodium: spreading slimy arms over the surrounding fields, heavily dragging after them the ruin of its desolation.'[493] Perhaps such commentators were simply intellectual snobs whose cultural world was the closed society of 'high' art, sculpture, classical architecture, chamber music, opera, poetry and literature. But as Flint acknowledges, emerging novelists, '….delineate the suburbs, and those who inhabit them, with understanding, even idealism, rather than standing back in a vantage point of implied superiority'.[494] Residents were 'making the best show we could. The brass knocker, the bay window, the dining and drawing rooms, establish the fact we had in view, the great suburban ideal of being superior to the people next door'.[495] It certainly reads as a back-handed compliment, and contains just a whiff of the echo of more recent politicians' admiration for 'strivers, not shirkers'. Perhaps the pre-1914 critics and the targets of their criticisms were *both* guilty of a degree of self-satisfaction that would soon be rudely interrupted by the coming Armageddon on the Western Front which almost did for Rouse.

Rouse had bought 14 Buxted Road, Friern Barnet, for £750 on mortgage in about 1927, paying a sum of £1.7.6d a week to his building society and, as he told his police interlocutors in Northampton, 'I was arranging to sell my house and furniture. I was then going to make an allowance to the wife [implying a separation?]. I think I should clear between £100 and £150 from the sale'. The outer London suburb of Friern Barnet, about seven miles north-west of Charing Cross, forms part of the larger suburb of North Finchley which is centred on Tally Ho Corner, a major junction from which roads lead to East Finchley, Church End, Friern Barnet and Whetstone (we recall that Tally Ho Corner was one of the places where Rouse had claimed his passenger had climbed into his car). By the

491 Julie English Early, "A New Man for a New Century: Dr. Crippen and the Principles of Masculinity", in George Robb and Nancy Erber (eds), *Disorder in the Court: Trials and Sexual Conflict at the Turn of the Century*, Macmillan, 1999, Ch. 11.
492 Chandler to James Sandoe, December 6, 1948, cited in Dorothy Gardiner and Kathrine Sorley Walker (eds), *Raymond Chandler Speaking*, University of California Press Ltd., 1997, p. 197.
493 Cited in Flint, *op. cit*, pp. xv-xvi. Perhaps the advance of the Martians' tripod warriors through the Surrey towns and villages, as depicted in H. G. Wells' *The War of the Worlds* conjures up similar images.
494 Flint, *op. cit.*, p. xviii.
495 Shan Bullock, *Robert Thorne*, T. Werner Laurie, 1907, cited in *ibid*.

1890s shops were lining part of the High Road from Tally Ho Corner to Avenue Road, with residential streets such as Friern Park accessed from the main drag. By the end of the 1900s North Finchley had a motor bus service and trams taking workers into London and encouraging shoppers to visit in the other direction. There were almost 20,000 people in the larger suburb by 1931 (7,392 in 1901). Art deco buildings such as Price's department store were constructed, and the Tally Ho pub was built to replace the nineteenth century Park Hotel. The old chapel was demolished in 1935 and was soon replaced by a cinema, now itself no longer standing.[496] In other words, here was an expanding and thriving district ('desirable' as estate agents would no doubt describe it), with good transport links, busy shopping areas, residential properties, quality buildings and social amenities. What not to like for men such as Rouse seeking to better themselves in an increasingly respectable and cosmopolitan environment where bricks and mortar were beginning to be perceived, though ever so slowly (see below), as a solid investment and not just as a home?

As to the sub-area of Friern Barnet itself, it emerged as a distinct area following the building of Colney Hatch pauper lunatic asylum in 1851 (which later housed Aaron Kosminski, one of the Jack the Ripper suspects, Solomon Beron, brother of Stinie Morrison's supposed victim, Leon Beron, killed on Clapham Common on New Year's Day, 1911 and, in more recent times, the serial 'railway' rapist, John Duffy). More importantly, the construction of mid-century railway stations on the Great Northern and Metropolitan Railways, and the extension of the electric tram line in 1909 boosted the growth of this outer London suburb. Typical large Victorian villas were built, followed by the later construction of numerous semi-detached and terraced houses in the Edwardian period.

When, exactly, 14 Buxted Road was constructed is not wholly certain. The current Land Registry entry for the property (MX 344525) refers to a conveyance dated January 13, 1910 between the British Land Company Ltd and Huggins & Co. Ltd., and containing (presumably standard for housing estates) restrictive covenants. As there was another conveyance with restrictive covenants dated April 27, 1926 between British Land and Alfred William Jones, it is possible that Huggins were the builders, Jones a house purchaser and mortgagor before Rouse, and British Land the original owners of the land and mortgagees. Rouse himself is not listed in the current entry for the property.

A map of the district shows residential streets of semi-detached and terraced properties running off Buxted Road, all sharing the names of Sussex villages and towns, such as Petworth, Horsham, Ashurst and Lewes. The area was thus not exactly *rus in urbe*, but it was not wholly urban either. As is well documented, the inter-war years witnessed growing affluence for many, especially in Southern England which was less dependent on the heavier industries and extractive industries that were particularly affected by trade cycles and economic depression than were the newer lighter industries. Household goods such as washing machines, cookers, and vacuum cleaners manufactured in new light and airy industrial estates proved popular among the rising middle-class which was already benefiting from falling family size and an increased surplus in real terms between income and expenditure.

---

496   See www.northfinchley.townwalk.co.uk/local/history.

Obvious manifestations of such increased wealth was the middle-class drive to own their own properties, albeit on mortgage. Yet the rental sector still continued to be a feature of both the upper class and the lower class, at a time when houses were not yet widely perceived as a financial asset or as an investment (though the middle class, such as Frederick Seddon and, possibly, Rouse himself viewed properties in this further and more rewarding light). Thus the better off would often take tenancies on comfortable, perhaps even on opulent, town houses, while the poor and working class would hope to benefit from the growth of municipal housing. Otherwise they faced paying rent to private landlords for properties that might be slum dwellings (or they did a 'midnight flit' to avoid payment). As Stevenson observes,

> The inter-war years saw the completion of two and a half million houses for private sale, reaching a peak in the middle and late thirties when more than 350,000 houses were being completed each year. New semi-detached houses with bathrooms and garage could be bought for as little as £450. Mortgages were available on easy terms, with an average interest rate of around four and a half per cent and repayments which came well within the range of most of the middle-classes and a significant portion of the better-off working classes.[497]

As Pugh notes, thirty-five per cent of all houses by 1938 were now owner-occupied,[498] with the London suburbs proving especially attractive. Thus, 'Between 1900 and 1914 new suburbs spread across North London in Ilford , Walthamstow, Wood Green, Edmonton, Wanstead, Enfield, Palmer's Green, New Southgate and Hendon', though the condescending pre-war tones of the likes of Gibbs, George Gissing and Masterman, whom we have encountered earlier, extended into the inter-war years. No wonder Edith Thompson from Kensington Gardens [sic], Ilford, was viewed disdainfully by critics of her reading habits when she came to trial in late 1922. As one commentator wrote in 1907, 'Ilford, albeit of mushroom growth, has a pretty conceit of itself'.[499]

It was, undoubtedly, a class thing. It was about 'getting on' and distancing oneself both physically and mentally from the lesser skilled working class who were liable to suffer unemployment more than any other category of employee. Suburbia signified respectability and achievement, the acquisition of a considerable financial asset which perhaps would be left to the children in due course. There was, indeed, an element of snobbery surrounding the suburbs, though perhaps not as much as would be found in the detective novels of the day written by Margery Allingham, Agatha Christie and Dorothy L. Sayers, where ponderous detectives are outflanked by well-spoken and cerebral upper-class or genteel men or women whose little grey cells can unwrap the murder mystery. *Snobbery with Violence: English Crime Stories and their Audience* is the pointed

---

497   John Stevenson, *British Society, 1914-45*, Penguin, 1990, pp. 129-30. See also Joseph Melling, 'Introduction', in Joseph Melling (ed.), *Housing, Social Policy and the State*, Croom Helm, 1980, pp. 9-36, esp. at pp. 25-26. The cost of labour and raw materials and competing returns from financial investment influenced the state of the house-building market.

498   Martin Pugh, *'We Danced All Night': A Social History of Britain Between the Wars*, Vintage, 2009, p. 63.

499   Cited in *ibid*, p. 65.

title given to a study of the genre by Colin Watson.[500]

But as was the case before the war, social commentators between the wars were not wholly enamoured. George Orwell, in his *Coming Up for Air*, written in 1939, saw suburban stasis as represented by, 'The stucco front, the creosoted gate, the privet hedge, the green front door. The Laurels, the Myrtles, the Hawthorns, Mon Abris, Mon Repos, Belle Vue'.[501] For his part J. B. Priestley claimed, with reference to property acquisition, that, 'You need money in this England, but you do not need much money. It is a large-scale, mass production job, with cut prices....'[502] These remarks, it must be acknowledged, were no different from those of the pre-war critics or, indeed, from the Grossmiths' gentle mocking of Charles Pooter's narrow suburban world.

This, then, was Arthur Rouse's recent existence. He lived in precisely that kind of environment which could combine a limited degree of civic engagement through tennis clubs or gardening societies, or preservation groups, or the local Conservative association, with a private enclosed world of a husband daily commuting and his wife maintaining her domain, using the new electric household aids, reading 'house-proud' and 'style' magazines of the day or, in some cases, surreptitiously watching what the neighbours were up to, through the twitching lace curtains. Perhaps, in Lily's case, this was somewhat of a caricature. For we do not know much of how her time was spent in the recent years and months before her familiar world was overturned. She certainly undertook shopping, occasionally seeing her husband in the district while she bought provisions. But did she entertain visitors or undertake paid work before she began working after Rouse's arrest?

With regard to Rouse himself, was *he* 'self-satisfied' in his suburban setting? Was *he* aspirational and upwardly mobile? Did *he* engage in local civic activities? We know of his membership of the local tennis club and of his relative skill in that sport, and we know that he latterly ceased to play. Of course, such disengagement was no doubt partly because he was 'away' a lot, even if only to stay at another part of North London, in Liverpool Road, with Helen Campbell. Did he have other social activities? It is presumed that, from his dealings with the unknown man at the Swan and Pyramids, he did not drink alcohol. But there is no independent proof of this. Nor, unlike the Acid-Bath murderer, John George Haigh, did he express any political views, so far as is known (Haigh was a strong Conservative critic of the post-war Labour government). However, rather than pottering away in his garden or his allotment, as so many suburban men did in the inter-war period, he pottered away in his garage. At least he did so when his lower-middle class occupation of commercial traveller or his string of lovers did not tear him away from the comforts of Friern Barnet. So, the ownership (on mortgage) of a semi-detached three bedroom-house in Buxted Road by a man earning more than the average wage for the time might be grounds for self-satisfaction. But perhaps this would not be the case where court-mandated affiliation commitments, apart from hire purchase (HP) payments on his car, had to be met.

500   Colin Watson, *Snobbery With Violence: English Crime Stories and Their Audience*, Eyre Methuen, 1971. See also Shani D'Cruze, '"The Damn'd Place Was Haunted': The Gothic, Middlebrow Culture and Inter-War 'Notable British Trials'", *Literature and History*, Vol. 15 (1), 2006, pp. 37-58.
501   Cited in Flint, *op. cit.*, p. xvii.
502   J. B. Priestley, *An English Journey* (1934), cited in Stevenson, *op. cit.*, p. 130.

As we know, Rouse was as much exercised by his financial difficulties as he was by his marital and relational ones. His very reason for journeying to Leicester on Guy Fawkes Night, he claimed, was to secure some needed payments from his employer (though the other circumstances of that evening might suggest that this explanation was merely a pretext). That he had been late with his September HP payment on his car is a matter of record. Was his mortgage payment the next to be delayed, let alone his payments for Arthur Jnr. and Pamelita (and what of paying for Nellie Tucker's new-born and of providing accommodation for them)? In other words, living in the suburbs did not insulate residents from financial distress. Indeed, joining the march of the hundreds of thousands in moving to the suburbs, and taking out a mortgage rather than paying council house rent, would have over-stretched countless home-owners. As one writer has noted,

> Behind the statistics were human tragedies. In 1935 a judge attached to a suburban county court told a journalist that credit was demoralizing the middle class, especially the 'small middle class' who took on debts they could never afford. He was astonished by the courage of men and women living on a 'narrow margin of security' without 'peace of mind'. Their misfortunes were aired in his court. There was an unemployed commercial traveller with a £1,400 mortgage and a maidservant who helped his invalid wife. He was in arrears in payments for his car, which, he argued, was vital for his work".[503]

In (presumably) a different case from 1933, a commercial traveller from near Leeds kept from his wife that he had lost his job but nonetheless purported to go out to work every morning (like Gerald, played by Tom Wilkinson, in the wonderful film, *The Full Monty*). Eventually, with mounting financial problems, he could not keep up the pretence and gassed himself at home. The inquest returned a verdict of 'Suicide during a fit of depression'.[504] Rouse might well have been a lesser version of the commercial traveller who had come unstuck in 1935, above. In short, suburbanites were being sneered at by some of the elite for being smug while at the same time being encouraged to better themselves. For the suburban dwellers themselves, the transition could be double-edged, launching them into a spiral of debt from which they could only seek to extricate themselves by drastic measures. One couple, a bank cashier and his wife, committed suicide in the wake of 'financial difficulties'. Others might declare themselves bankrupt, or await a summons from the county court. Rouse, of course, apparently chose a more drastic but futile stratagem. According to the writer, Lawrence James, the action of this killer (Rouse) from the middle-class suburbs was designed to 'avoid the repercussions of heavy debts'. By this James appears to mean that Rouse chose to pursue a homicidal path rather than be exposed as one who could not pay his bills. 'Suburbia was inextricably linked with traditional middle-class notions of

---

503   Sir Philip Gibbs, *England Speaks* (1935), cited in Lawrence James, *The Middle Class: A History*, Abacus, 2008, p. 528. For the role of the county courts in inveighing against working-class credit and the legal consequences of default see G. R. Rubin, "The County Courts and the Tally Trade, 1846-1914", in G. R. Rubin and David Sugarman (eds.), *Law, Economy and Society: Essays in the History of English Law, 1750-1914*, Professional Books, Abingdon, 1984, pp. 321-48. For the view that acquiring goods, even fripperies, on credit was respectable for the middle and upper classes but was shameful for the poor see Frank Trentmann, *The Empire of Things: How We Became a World of Consumers, from the Fifteenth Century to the Twenty-First*, Penguin, 2016.
504   *The Times*, July 9, 1933.

visible personal worth. Old snobberies took on new forms and a fresh lease of life in suburbia, inevitably since so many status-conscious middle-class families were in such close proximity.'[505]

But *was* Rouse a middle-class snob who would be too shame-faced to engage with neighbours, friends and colleagues if his debt-ridden status had become widely known? Perhaps we can leave aside the question of which particular stratum in the class structure should be accorded to him (though it was probably lower middle class in view of the non-industrial occupations he had followed, and despite his father's background as a hosier). But as to his sense of his own worth as perceived by others, we know that he was happy to tell listeners whom he might meet at random that he had been educated at Eton and Cambridge, and that he had served as an officer in the Army. We also know that he was appalled to appear at the first police court hearing in a suit that did not belong to him and which fitted badly (his own suit undergoing forensic testing at the time), that at his trial he turned up in a smart brown suit, wearing spats, and that he ostentatiously and carefully placed his gloves and hat on the edge of the dock while looking round the court-room gracefully and with a smile, as if drinking in the applause from family, friends and acquaintances.

To that extent he was a snob, but clearly not an intellectual snob (we only sketchily know his reading habits unlike those of, say, Edith Thompson, though he did play that most cerebral of games, like the chess-playing William Wallace, husband of the murdered Julia Wallace). On the other hand he liked nothing better (apart from the obvious) than tinkering with cars. Indeed, he was not, apparently, overly proud of his cars' appearances. Did not he use the notorious mallet to knock out dents on the mudguards or wings of his vehicles? It is therefore difficult to agree that it was shame at his financial predicament that drove him to murder. It is more likely, assuming he was guilty *as charged*, that it was simply his own misplaced vanity in believing that he could commit the perfect crime and get away both with it and with a large sum of insurance money that the authorities believed had driven him on. Sure, he was a product of the suburbs but he did not necessarily share the impetus to full 'respectability' that came with the territory. He was more on the 'self-satisfied', hedonistic, reckless and acquisitive, not to say hypocritical, point on the spectrum of what suburbia meant to its residents. It was those personal characteristics, and not shame or fear of what the neighbours might think of him, which led to his downfall.

505   James, *op. cit.*, p. 529.

CHAPTER NINETEEN

THE SHEIK IN A CAR

NEWS OF THE WORLD, February 1, 1931

Rouse, Cars and Commercial Travelling

Cars were, of course, central to Rouse's existence and to his identity. He had owned a number of vehicles before acquiring the soon-to-be nationally known MU 1468, and loved tinkering with engines in his richly fitted out garage in Buxted Road. He was said to have been an expert driver, whatever that actually meant in the world of private cars in the inter-war years. Perhaps cars *were* an extension of his sexual identity, though phallus-shaped sports cars were not part of his repertoire. But cars were clearly important to his philandering and to his chances of picking up young impressionable girls drawn from a class which would be unused to travelling by such a mode of transport.

The wider appeal of motoring after the Great War meant that the,

> .....lanes of Britain were full of motorists learning how to drive. On the wireless Grandma Buggins 'went for a spin' with the family, and became, like so many members of other families, a back-seat driver who knew all about everything. And on the stage, Harry Tate was still getting roars of laughter from audiences with his popular sketch, *Motoring*. It was a wonderful way of getting out of town at weekends. A Wolseley 'ten' two-seater carrying five fair bathers direct from their home to the beach at Hove, Sussex, was described in the *Illustrated London News* as a 'motor car eliminating the bathing machine'. Couples in little open cars sat out at night on Surrey commons, and planned the future. The coming of cheap cars had made it possible for whole families to move out of industrial areas".[506]

Indeed, as Juliet Gardiner points out, motorists could venture down country roads previously undiscovered by urban dwellers. She also notes that whereas Ordnance Survey maps for travellers depicted walkers, then cyclists, by 1935 the quarter-inch series was depicting motorists on its covers. This was an 'individualistic, particularly middle-class, form of penetration ...., one which G. K. Chesterton likened to the tanks of an invading army'. While she insists that hire purchase (see below) put the price of cars within the reach of most white-collar workers in the 1930s,[507] they were still not quite so cheap in the 1920s as the previous quote by Montgomery, above, appeared to imply.

506   John Montgomery, *The Twenties*, Allen & Unwin, 1970, p. 179.
507   Juliet Gardiner, *The Thirties: An Intimate History*, Harper Press, 2010, p. 245.

Cars offered mobility to the leisured classes. But it also offered opportunities for more criminal activities in the shape of the 'motor bandits' whose emergence was beginning to be noticed even as the First World War was grinding to a halt. Thus the origins of the Flying Squad in London could be traced to concerns among senior Metropolitan policemen such as the 'legendary' West Countryman, Superintendent Frederick Wensley, that motorized robbers were now carrying out successful raids on banks and post offices and escaping in fast, often stolen, cars.[508] The police had to react quickly and therefore needed their own powerful vehicles with which to compete with the eponymous motor bandits in the 1920s. Much anguished concern was expressed at this new(ish) phenomenon, as former policemen explained to newspaper readers how the authorities should respond to this menace. 'Can We Foil the Motor Bandit?' asked a former senior policeman in India, Sir Reginald Clarke,[509] while Wensley himself extolled his former colleagues in a piece entitled, 'Chased by the Flying Squad: Ex-Chief Constable Wensley discusses the century's greatest duel, Police v Motor-car Criminal.'[510] Inter-police force cooperation was expanded, as seen in chapter 4, through innovation such as the Agility scheme, while the savage killing of PC Gutteridge by Browne (assumedly) and Kennedy in their stolen vehicle led to changes in police patrolling and organization methods.

But with respect to Rouse, his motorized criminality was not an occupational choice, even if his actual chosen profession did require a motorized means of getting from town to town with his samples of select categories of menswear. Thus he might be tootling between the drapers' shops in the Kent seaside resorts of Cliftonville, next to Margate, and Herne Bay, as he did on the day before his rendezvous with Hardingstone Lane. Or he might be driving to his employers in Leicester, as was his stated intention on November 5. He might be picking up a young girl in London Road, Southampton, and 'trying it on' with her (partially unsuccessfully), or making his way to the remote location of Gellygaer every fortnight in his last year of life to stay with the Jenkins family. Possessing a motor car thus afforded him opportunities for his somewhat predatory (even if not violently predatory) behaviour. But being on the road might also afford anonymity. Any girl he picked up far from his home could be spun a tale (as with the Southampton episode), with a false history and a false name. Outside London, how could such a passenger be able to check the veracity of what she had just been told?

But being a knave (rather than a knight) of the road also implied a sense of rootlessness or of impatience with what he already possessed. There was disloyalty (obviously) to Lily, perhaps also to Helen and Nellie. It was not the freedom of the roads that one might associate with the visibly mobile (in the literal sense) 'Bright Young Things', as they drove down to the coast, Isadora Duncan-like (but without its tragic ending), in their powerful and fabulous open-topped sports cars, an image so beloved of Agatha Christie murder mysteries.

---

508   Neil Darbyshire and Brian Hilliard, *The Flying Squad*, Headline, 1994, Chs. 2-3.
509   [Birmingham] *Evening News*, January 15, 1927.
510   *Pearson's Weekly*, April 4, 1931. For a study of criminal 'mobility', see Alyson Brown, "Crime, Criminal Mobility and Serial Offenders in Early Twentieth Century Britain", *Contemporary British History*, Vol. 25 (4), December 2011, pp. 551-68; *idem.*, 'The Bobbed-Haired Bandit and the Smash-and-Grab Raider', in David S. Nash and Anne-Marie Kilday (eds.), *Fair and Unfair Trials*, Bloomsbury, forthcoming, 2019.

Arthur Rouse did not have 'freedom' in that sense. He was struggling financially and emotionally, trying to make a living as a commercial traveller in buckles, braces and men's suspenders, while endeavouring to satisfy his women-folk in an increasingly impossible juggling act.

We shall consider shortly the world of the commercial traveller which he had chosen to occupy. For the moment, we can observe the extent to which his obsession with and dependence on the motor car reflected the stage of development in the car industry at the time. The market for motor cars in the inter-war years was one of the defining features of the 'new consumerism' of the period which primarily benefited lower middle- and middle-class families. The expansion of electricity supply into the house, replacing total reliability on gas, was the most notable feature. For most families, it permitted electric lighting and the widespread acquisition of small vacuum cleaners, electric irons, radios and telephones which made domestic life more pleasant. For a smaller number of middle-class families, electricity in the home permitted the installation of refrigerators, electric cookers, and washing machines which made housework far more tolerable for housewives than for those of their mothers' generation. The third major growth was in the availability of the relatively inexpensive family-sized motor car as technological changes and greater demand and competition enabled manufacturers actually to reduce the price of smaller vehicles from the late 1920s. Cars did not come within the reach of the majority of the population until the 1960s. However annual numbers of cars on the road grew from 579,000 in 1924 to 2,045,400 in 1938. Of these one million were private cars, 600,000 were motor-cycles and 350,000 were commercial vans.[511] Indeed, during that period the numbers would increase annually by, very approximately, 100,000. It was a time when the market for cars had ceased to be only a luxury choice and was beginning to shift from a predominantly (middle-) middle-class market, to the early stirrings (but no more than that) of a mass market. The lower middle-class Rouse could easily fit into that transitional stage.

Indeed his situation regarding his vehicles was highly representative of his class. The move to the suburbs was giving a boost to vehicle purchase but the terms of such purchases were increasing favourable to new car owners because of the growth of the hire purchase system. Well-known finance companies like Bowmakers and United Dominions Trust (UDT) began to dominate this particular market (one of the present writers, recalling his legal studies in the 1960s of hire purchase laws, clearly recalls early 1960s cases involving Bowmakers and UDT). Rouse, of course, purchased his last two cars from a different finance house, no doubt one linked to the car showroom where he chose his vehicles. But nonetheless, the idea of purchasing outright would have been impossible for him.[512]

For vehicle manufacture in Britain it was not yet the age of mass production such as had been experienced in the United States where 70% of American households owned cars by 1939. Car production and car ownership were still on a smaller scale in the United Kingdom. Thus there was only one car for every

---

511   Noreen Branson and Margot Heinemann, *Britain in the Nineteen Thirties*, Panther, 1973, p. 261.
512   For much of the above see Sue Bowden, "The New Consumerism", in Paul Johnson (ed.), *Twentieth Century Britain: Economic, Social and Cultural Change*, Longman, 1996, Ch. 14.

44 Britons, and not one in ten families possessed a car.[513] Perhaps with this untapped market in mind, in 1928 the car manufacturer William Morris (later Lord Nuffield) announced that he would build a new 'baby' car to compete with the 'baby' Austin 7, launched in 1922 and being sold in 1928 at a relatively modest price of £165. Thus was created the Morris Minor, displayed at the 1928 London Motor Show, and to be purchased for £125 for the touring model and £135 for the fabric model.[514]

In fact the Morris cars catalogue for 1930 listed the convertible Morris Minor Tourer at £130, the Fabric Saloon at £140 (as paid by Rouse), and the Coach-built Saloon at £149, while one magazine columnist[515] reported that 'Morris Reduces Prices All Round'. Indeed the Morris Cowley folding-head coupe, the writer advised, was a 'useful commercial traveller's saloon' (at £199). The Morris Minor model purchased by Rouse was advertised as supplying 'ample comfort over long distances, and will as readily tackle a trip from John O'Groats to Land's End as a shopping expedition with the lady of the house'. Though the advert seemed to imply that only men were thought fit to drive such a car, a journalist writing elsewhere believed that a changed arrangement in the Morris Cowley chassis, enabling lubricants to be applied more easily to the grease-gun nipples, would be 'well appreciated by owner-drivers of both sexes'.[516] The Triplex windows and windscreen were said to offer good ventilation in warm weather, while the wide doors to the body of the car would ensure ease of entry, which one might cynically think suited Rouse's purpose admirably when, according to received wisdom, he set about bundling his unconscious passenger across the front seats. With a maximum speed of 55 mph, it was described in an advert in one motoring magazine[517] as 'Built on a small scale...to the exacting standards of a big car'. With road holding 'particularly good', it claimed to offer a driving experience that was 'exhilarating, satisfying—with safety and economy'. Anticipating later 1970s campaigns to save on national balance of payments deficits, the advert exhorted readers to 'Buy British and Be Proud of It'.

Fit for the purpose of trouble-free driving from John O'Groats to Land's End seemed a bold claim for the Morris Minor. But in fact the frequency of mechanical breakdown of vehicles had reduced considerably from the 1920s, while the AA and RAC were on hand to lend assistance, and for AA patrolmen perhaps self-consciously to salute those cars displaying the distinctive yellow badge of the Association (a military gesture which no doubt chimed with the later absorption of many AA patrolmen into the Corps of Military Police following the outbreak of war in 1939). Nonetheless, cars were regularly in need of repair or maintenance. Thus on October 20, 1930 Rouse had taken his car to the Tottenham High Road garage of Stewart & Ardern Ltd, the firm that had provided the vehicle from new. The differential was playing up, possibly making cornering more difficult. There

513 Branson and Heinemann, op. cit., p. 262.
514 Montgomery, op. cit., p. 177. According to Branson and Heinemann, op. cit., p. 261, in 1931 the Austin Seven cost £118 and the Morris Minor two-seater cost £100. The steel-bodied Morris Minor was introduced in 1930. Technical specifications are not provided here. For an interesting analysis see Simon Dentith, "From William Morris to Morris Minor: An Alternative Suburban History", in Roger Webster (ed), Expanding Suburbia: Reviewing Suburban Narratives, Berghahn, Oxford, 2001.
515 H. Thornton Rutter, "The Chronicle of the Car", Illustrated London News, September 13, 1930.
516 Ibid.
517 Light Car and Cyclecar, January 23, 1931.

was also minor collision damage to repair, including scratches and a missing wing lamp glass. It seems that the work was done the same day but no invoice of the cost appears to survive.[518]

Minor collision damage? Perhaps it arose from the incident on the Kingston by-pass that he had mentioned in passing during his police interviews. We also know that had it not been for the fact that he was appearing in the dock at Northampton police court for his committal hearing, Rouse would have been facing the Highgate magistrates on November 11, 1930, charged with exceeding the about-to-be-abolished speed limit of 20 miles an hour in Colney Hatch Lane, Muswell Hill. Unsurprisingly, the speeding case was adjourned indefinitely.[519]

What the above paragraph hints at is one of the downsides of the growth of the motor car, the increasing toll in deaths and injury of fellow-drivers, passengers and pedestrians in the inter-war years caused by collisions and dangerous driving.[520] The casualty figures for those years are, in absolute terms, scarcely different from present-day figures despite the huge expansion in the number of vehicles on the road today than in the inter-war years. Better-constructed roads, improved street lighting, safer motorways, strict driving tests and higher driving standards, improved medical care and, especially, far greater safety features in today's cars explain this apparent anomaly. Thus we know that between 1913 and 1935 the number of fatal and non-fatal road accidents in England and Wales caused by vehicles is as follows:

Year	Fatal	Non-fatal
1913	1,743	38,050
1916	2,393	46,090
1917	2,047	38,326
1918	1,852	31,604
1919	2,239	43,305
1920	2,386	49,317
1921	2,328	55,153
1922	2,441	62,504
1923	2,694	74,290
1924	3,269	87,867
1925	3,535	102,704
1926	4,236	108,846
1927	4,581	117,239
1928	5,358	129,199
1929	5,817	132,529
1930	6,317	136,077
1931	5,855	159,257

518 Documents concerning Rouse's car are among the papers on the Rouse case in the (formerly named) Nottingham Galleries of Justice archive.
519 *Evening News*, November 10, 1930.
520 See Sean O'Connell, "From Toad of Toad Hall to the 'Death Drivers' of Belfast", *British Journal of Criminology*, Vol. 46 (3), 2006, pp. 455-69. 'Toad' was a reference to slow, pondering 'road hog' drivers. For a wider perspective, see, ibid., *The Car and British Society: Class, Gender and Motoring, 1896-1939*, Manchester University Press, Manchester, 1998.

Year	Fatal	Non-fatal
1932	5,800	161,952
1933	6,321	169,417
1934	6,456	180,168
1935	5,690	172,864

Source; Clive Emsley, "'Mother, What *Did* Policemen Do When There Weren't Any Motors? The Law, the Police and the Regulation of Motor Traffic in England, 1900-1939", *Historical Journal*, Vol. 36 (2), 1993, pp. 357-81, Table 2.

As a comparison, figures for recent years show:

All Road Users	2005 -2009 Average	2009	2010	2011	2012	2013	% Change re 2005-00
Killed	2,816	2,222	1,850	1,901	1,754	1,713	-39
SeriouslyInjured	27,225	24,690	22,660	23,123	23,039	21,657	-20
K+SI	30,041	26,912	24,510	25,023	24,793	23,370	-22
Slightly Injured	216,010	195,234	184,138	178,927	170,930	160,300	-26
All Casualties	246,051	222,146	208,648	203,950	195,723	183,670	-25

Source: Government statistics, Table RAS300001, at www.gov.uk/government/statistical-data-sets/ras30-reported-casualties-in-road-accidents

It is therefore plain that fatal crashes were much more plentiful in the inter-war period than today, despite the far fewer motorized vehicles on the roads before World War Two compared with now. Indeed the number of private cars in 2013 was 27.7 million, a figure that excludes 'other' vehicles, goods vehicles, motor cycles etc, buses, 'other' commercial vehicles, and Crown and exempt vehicles which, if further added, would bring the total to 35 million.[521] The injury and death toll was indeed a matter of some concern before 1939, with one police chief before the Great War complaining that (lower class) chauffeurs and 'trade agents', which was surely a synonym for commercial travellers, were among the least law-abiding motorists.[522] However the debate had already been overlaid by claims of a new type of class war, in this instance, one between the police and middle-class drivers. Many of the latter resented being taken to task for speeding or for dangerous driving when the accusers were working-class policemen who (obviously) 'did not know their place' in the class structure of the period. This war of attrition led to the passing of the Road Transport Act 1930 which abolished the previous limit of 20 miles per hour (a restriction that Rouse had appeared to have breached) under the Motor Car Act of 1903.[523]

It was clearly a mistake to make the change as vehicle crash figures, together

521 For complete figures for Great Britain, see www.gov.uk/government/collections/vehicles-statistics, Table VEH0103, 'Licensed vehicles by tax class, Great Britain, annually: 1909 to 2013'.
522 Emsley, *op. cit.*, p. 371.
523 Local authorities could vary the limit where deemed appropriate. See Emsley, *op. cit*; Pugh, *op. cit.*, p. 246.

with human casualty numbers, soared. The Road Transport Act 1934 introduced a 30 mile-an-hour speed limit which had an immediate impact in reducing casualty figures for 1935 (above). It is not surprising, however, that press reporting of car accidents in the decade straddling Rouse's trial sometimes featured commercial travellers, either as errant drivers or as victims of other drivers' negligence. It is one of the peculiarities of the historical study of consumerism and retailing in the twentieth century that the role of the commercial traveller scarcely features in the academic literature. The history of the great stores such as Lipton's, Boots', Marks & Spencer, Lewis's, Selfridges, Whiteleys, has been more or less comprehensively explored. The history of shop advertising has similarly been studied in detail.[524] Even the activities of the travelling salesmen, the generally self-employed credit drapers or 'Scotch drapers' who went from door to door, selling household goods, especially to the poorer classes on weekly terms, have attracted the attention of historians, including one of the present writers.[525] According to Richard Mawrey QC in a relatively recent contribution, the door-to-door salesman was a,

> ….recognizable historical character…In the 1920s, the salesman, often a desperate unemployed Great War veteran, sold brushes and other cleaning materials; in the 1930s, smooth young men sold vacuum cleaners and the like; in the 1940s spivs in kipper ties flogged dubious black-market nylons; the 1950s and 1960s saw the encyclopaedists [sic], and the 1970s and 1980s, the vendors of double-glazing.[526]

But in respect of the commercial traveller, there is much less coverage. Perhaps that is because they might have been thought exclusively to be manufacturers' representatives and therefore would not come into direct contact with the consumer. However, this was not the case. Even if the credit drapers catered to the poorer classes of housewives in their own homes, the rise of more expensive consumer goods in the inter-war period, especially vacuum cleaners (as well as the ubiquitous *Encyclopaedia Britannica*) became a familiar item for door-to-door

---

524 *Cf.*, John Benson and Laura Ugolini (eds), *A Nation of Shopkeepers: Five Centuries of British Retailing*, I. B. Tauris, 2003 for references; W. Hamish Fraser, *The Coming of the Mass Market, 1850-1914*, Palgrave Macmillan, 1982.

525 Gerry R. Rubin, "From Packmen, Tallymen and 'Perambulating Scotchmen' to Credit Drapers' Associations, c. 1840-1914", *Business History*, Vol. 28 (2), 1986, pp. 206-25; Margot C. Finn, "Scotch Drapers and the Politics of Modernity: Gender, Class and National Identity in the Victorian Tally Trade", in Martin Daunton and Matthew Hilton (eds), *The Politics of Consumption: Material Culture and Citizenship in Europe and America*, Berg, Oxford, 2001. For earlier developments, see Hasia Diner, *Roads Taken: The Great Jewish Migrations to the New World and the Peddlers Who Forged the Way*, Yale University Press, New Haven, USA, 2015.

526 Richard Mawrey, QC., 'Consumer Credit Column', November 2011, at www.hendersonchambers. co.uk. It is not clear, however, why the author concluded that such a trade 'thrived, in the main, for [only] about 50 years' when its pedigree covered centuries. Similarly, whether the '1940s spivs' should be placed in the same category of trader may be historically problematic. For authoritative studies of the spivs, see Mark Roodhouse, *Black Market Britain, 1939-1955*, Oxford University Press, Oxford, 2014; Donald Thomas, *Villains' Paradise: Britain's Underworld from the Spivs to the Krays*, John Murray, 2006. For a more 'cultural' take, see Richard Hornsey, *The Spiv and the Architect: Unruly Life in Postwar London*, University of Minnesota Press, MN, USA, 2010. Hornsey discusses the classic post-war British gangster film, *The Blue Lamp* (1950). The author analyses the role in the film of Dirk Bogarde as the slightly effeminate young spiv/gangster, Tom Riley, who shoots dead PC George Dixon (Jack Warner) during a cinema box-office raid. Though the incidents differed, recollections of the then recent Charlotte Street shooting of Alec D'Antiquis in 1947 by the young Jenkins/Geraghty gang after a failed jewellers/pawnbrokers' shop armed robbery would still have been fresh. For the last-named see Paul Willetts, *North Soho 999: A True Story of Gangs and Gun-Crime in 1940s London*, Dewi Lewis Publishing, Stockport, 2007.

selling by commercial travellers. Indeed, one of the more gruesome murders in 1931 was committed by a commercial salesman of vacuum cleaners. A 54-year old widow, Louisa Kempson, described in the class-conscious terminology of the day as being 'highly respectable', had been murdered in her home in Oxford with 'unbridled ferocity', and the local chief constable quickly called in Scotland Yard.[527] Not only had a hammer been used on her but a chisel-like instrument had been rammed through her throat. She had been due to spend August Bank Holiday with relatives in London but had not arrived. Eventually police broke into her house to find her sprawled on the dining-room floor. Searching the house Chief Inspector John Horwell of Scotland Yard picked up a written receipt for an electric cleaner. Inquiries elsewhere in Oxford unearthed the information that two years earlier a Mrs. Andrews, who lived ten minutes away from Mrs. Kempson, had bought a vacuum cleaner from a man named Henry Seymour who called round on a few occasions thereafter to check that everything was all right with the machine. He then stopped coming until, that is, just before the recent August Bank Holiday when he turned up at her door with a hard luck story of having been robbed while bathing in the Thames, and could she lend him a few bob. He returned after three hours, claiming to have missed the last bus and persuaded her to let him stay in the spare room. In the morning she noticed a brown paper parcel on the hall stand, open at both ends, and containing what appeared to be a new hammer and chisel. After breakfast, he thanked her, put the (presumed) hammer and chisel in his coat pocket and left, though in which direction she was not sure. A few days later she received a thank-you letter posted in Hove from Seymour. He enclosed a postal order for 10/6d but did not provide an actual address. He ended by stating that he hoped to return and see her again in about ten days' time.

Mrs. Andrews had known that the murdered woman had also bought a vacuum cleaner from Seymour around the same time, and then more and more customers in Oxford came forward with a similar experience. One witness, Mrs. Collins, recalled talking to Seymour at a bus stop in Headington on the day of the murder. He told her he was going to London, and then to Brighton. But he seemed nervous and agitated and 'not his usual smooth-salesman self'. A check at the Criminal Records Office showed that Seymour had a string of convictions for serious assault. Moreover the same Seymour who had left Mrs. Andrews' house in a state of destitution was, just a few hours later, flush with funds, according to the landlord of the King's Arms at Wheatley who had served him drinks between 11:30 and 12:30 that morning. By then Mrs. Kempson had been dead for probably not more than two hours. Further clues implicating Seymour were found, including his suitcase which had been retained by an Aylesbury hotelier after Seymour had bilked him. When Seymour was eventually tracked down by Horwell, the former said to the detective that he supposed the latter wanted to talk to him about the 'Oxford murder'. Of course, Horwell had not mentioned the murder to Seymour but, yes, that was the purpose of his questioning.[528]

---

527 Tom Tullett, *Murder Squad: Famous Cases of Scotland Yard's Murder Squad*, Grafton, 1996, pp. 99-105.

528 Famously, Chief Inspector Wensley had believed he had caught out Steinie Morrison in January 1911 when the latter denied involvement in the Clapham Common murder before the detective had explained why Morrison was being arrested. However, the murder and the Sidney Street Siege were the talk of Whitechapel. It is a familiar trope in detective novels where the suspect

Seymour had been employed by the Tellus Company since 1927. His duties were to call on householders in order to demonstrate and sell the company's brand of vacuum cleaners.[529] He was described as the area manager of the firm and lived in Oxford with his wife and ten-year old son until he moved to furnished accommodation in Brighton in June 1931, leaving the others in Oxford. In Rouse's case, Arthur had claimed he had been owed money by his employer and was exercised by the fact that while in custody he still had possession of some of his firm's samples that he wished to be returned. But in the case of Seymour the latter admitted that he had failed to pass on to his employer sums of money that he had received in payment for vacuum cleaners that he had sold. At the police court Gerald Paling for the DPP had made much of Seymour's financial distress as offering a motive for Mrs. Kempson's murder (as he had done the previous year in respect of Rouse). At the trial itself defence counsel conceded that his client was dishonest (a tactical admission of the defendant's bad character) while seeking to persuade the jury that he was not a murderer. Counsel was not believed and Seymour was convicted of murder on October 25 and sentenced to death. An appeal failed and he was hanged at Oxford Prison on December 10, 1931. His criminal activities may have been unrepresentative of his fellow-commercial travellers, but the goods he was selling from door to door were typical of the new consumer tastes of the inter-war years, especially in the more affluent areas of Britain.

The Tellus vacuum cleaner was manufactured by a Danish firm, Nilfisk, a company established in 1906. It opened a British sales office in 1926 which marketed a new design of cleaner (shaped somewhat like a Thermos flask today) launched earlier in 1922. For the first time the household labour-saving device could be purchased on hire purchase, a method of payment that ensured wide sales for the product, especially among the middle class. Thus initially sales increased by 300% over the previous year when payment on instalment had not been available. In 1932 a new version was introduced which, in comparison with rival vacuum cleaners, was almost silent. It was consequently dubbed 'the Silent Dane'. In 2012 it was reported that a working Tellus vacuum cleaner, manufactured in 1955, had been donated to the firm by a Lancashire couple who had had it in the family for three generations. It was still functioning efficiently when handed over.[530] Though we cannot be certain, it is possible that the item could only be purchased directly through travelling salesmen and not from retail outlets. Moreover, while it might be possible to draw a distinction between a travelling salesman like Seymour and a commercial traveller like Rouse, it remains the case that in the newspaper reports of Seymour's trial (above), the prisoner had expressly been described as a commercial traveller.

We have already noted that there are few, if any, academic studies of the inter-war commercial traveller. Thus their numbers, economic significance, products

---

mentions something to the police, such as a weapon or a particular poison, to which information it was assumed that only the police and the guilty would be privy. It is likely that the murder of Mrs. Kempson was likewise widely known in Oxford.

529   *The Times*, September 10; October 26, 1931 for this and subsequent information.

530   See www.nilfisk.co.uk; www.nilfisk.com.au/Info/CompanyInfo....aspx. Some records of the Tellus Super Vacuum Cleaner Ltd, which had a factory in Slough in 1968, are kept in the London Metropolitan Archives under reference GB 0074 LMA/4568.

carried, average earnings, class and ethnic backgrounds, and life-styles remain elusive. Moreover, *The Salesman's Handbook*, the fictional *vade mecum* of the trade, frequently cited by Dorothy L. Sayers' Monty Egg during his deliberations, was more likely primarily to be the textbook for the retail salesman than for the commercial traveller, though genuine publications on the trade during this period, such as Murphy's *Modern Drapery....*, Cook and Cooper's *Drapery and Boot Management* and Ellison and Hill's *Salesmanship in the Drapery Department*, were also pitched at the wholesale trade.[531] What follows is therefore only a crude and limited attempt to picture the world of the commercial traveller as Rouse might have known it. Leaving aside the cases of Rouse and Seymour, there is no doubt that certain images of such men were generally not favourable. Yet the opinion of Lord Justice Scrutton in 1918 perhaps says more about elite expectations than about commercial travellers when he complained that as a result of the wartime government minister, the Food Controller's, directions, 'The judges were at first told by a subordinate official that they were in the same class as a commercial traveller and must get their meals at a hotel', rather than be privately waited upon by housekeeper-cooks at the lodgings set aside for the assize judges. A 'veritable outburst of judicial wrath' quickly persuaded the authorities that 'slumming' on the part of judges on circuit was simply 'not on', and that the level of hospitality should be on an ambassadorial scale for them.[532] To expect the judges of assize to be treated like commercial travellers, perish the thought. However Dorothy L. Sayers' Monty Egg, a commercial traveller in wines and spirits, who also turned his hand to occasional part-time sleuthing (presumably when Lord Peter Wimsey was not available), is a respectably pleasant and cheerful exception to the genre.

While there were approximately 35,000-40,000 commercial travellers in inter-war Britain, an unknown proportion were in fact women. Would women mainly offer samples of lingerie to fashion and clothes shops? Would they supply chemist shops with new brands of women's sanitary protection? Certainly, female family members would often work as credit drapers, though they might only be employed to collect the weekly payments, certainly among immigrant Jewish communities.[533] But as to unfavourable images of the (male) commercial traveller, it was even mentioned in more recent times by the celebrated broadcaster, Nicholas Parsons, that the BBC's *Green Book* had formerly banned jokes about such salesmen, holding them in the same prohibited and shameful category as

---

531 William S. Murphy (ed), *Modern Drapery and Allied Trades, Wholesale and Retail*, Gresham Publishing, 1914; T. D. Cook and E. W. Cooper, *Drapery and Boot Management*, Cooperative Union Ltd, Manchester 1925; T. Ellison and A. N. Hill, *Salesmanship in the Drapery Department*, Cooperative Union Ltd, Manchester, c. 1935. See also [Anon.] *The Random Recollections of a Commercial Traveller*, Sherrat & Hughes, Manchester 1909.

532 T. E. Scrutton, "The War and the Law", *Law Quarterly Review*, Vol. 34, 1918, pp. 116-133, at pp. 118-9. Whether the Food Controller at the time was Clynes or one of his two predecessors in the post is not clear. Scrutton insisted that as far as actual food availability was concerned, the judges and the rest of British society were 'all in it together', to coin a phrase used by a recent former Chancellor, George Osborne, in regard to government 'austerity' policy. Leaving aside post-2015 society after Osborne's remark, historical research suggests that civilian diets improved during the Great War. See P. E. Dewey, "Food Production and Policy in the United Kingdom, 1914-1918", *Transactions of the Royal Historical Society*, Fifth Series, Vol. 30, 1980, pp. 71-89.

533 For one example of a female commercial traveller, see *The Times*, March 8, 1930 on the rescission of a decree of divorce previously granted to the woman. For the murder of Elizabeth Benjamin, a 14-year old girl in Glasgow collecting payments for her credit draper father, see Donald M. Fraser, *The Book of Glasgow Murders*, Neil Wilson Publishing, Glasgow, 2009, Ch. 5.

prostitution, effeminacy among men, lodgers and lavatories.[534] Kenneth Williams was, indeed, later to refer to the 'awfully boring & hearty commercial traveller' whom he had met in lodgings in Norwich, where he was on tour, in the 1950s. This character 'became suddenly confidential. He took me aside in the kitchen, in a burst of confession, and explained that he was homosexual. I had to act deliberately nonchalant to cover my own dumbfoundedness, confusion and embarrassment. I practically fell over myself in the effort to be casual and burnt my fingers on the gas ring. Life holds so many surprises for us'.[535] Given our present-day knowledge of Kenneth Williams, his final remark does possess more than a hint of ambiguity about it, though the hostile climate towards gay men at the time might explain the actor's coyness.

Dennis Potter, in his 1970s production, *Pennies from Heaven*, which starred the late Bob Hoskins, Cheryl Campbell and Gemma Craven, certainly depicted commercial travellers in his script as one-track-minded, slightly sleazy, characters. Thus his leading character, Arthur Parker, loosely based on Arthur Rouse, would sometimes descend to uttering crude sexual remarks.[536] But away from fictional characters, when Mrs. Elizabeth Perfect became pregnant while her husband was abroad serving in the Army in 1917 (unlike Michael Morpurgo's imaginary creation, was he a genuine Private Perfect?), she claimed that a travelling draper who had called at her house in the course of his business (thus not, strictly speaking, a commercial traveller) had taken improper advantage of her. When she later sent a letter to him demanding money, thus implying his responsibility for her pregnancy, the draper was so outraged that he took out a private prosecution charging her with uttering a letter demanding money with menaces and without probable cause, contrary to the Larceny Act 1916. While the accusation against the traveller might not have been surprising (stories from the nineteenth century suggest that credit drapers were sometimes paid 'in kind'), the jury's decision to believe the prosecutor and not Mrs. Perfect, in the face of a summing-up in her favour by Mr. Justice Darling, was perhaps a matter of surprise.[537]

Commercial travellers, apart from Rouse and Seymour, might be identified as such in newspaper reports of arrests or trials for criminal activity. For example, in 1928 two men were arrested by Flying Squad officers in a residential road between Bickley and Chislehurst on the Kentish outskirts of London. The two men, Arthur Sherwood (49), a labourer from Dalston, and Richard Miller (37), a commercial traveller from Kennington, had been detained as 'suspected persons loitering with intent to commit a felony'.[538] At the end of October 1930, Joseph Schonberg (23), a watchmaker from Tottenham Court Road, and Louis Schiller (29), a commercial traveller from Cricklewood, were convicted of handling a stolen painting of Thomas Cranmer, the property of one Richard A. Loeb (not, of course, the Richard Loeb of Leopold and Loeb infamy in the United

---

534   BBC Radio 4 broadcast, Christmas Morning, 2008. Nonetheless, the inter-war assize judge who presided over the trial of Henry Seymour in the Oxford murder case liked to describe himself as a 'commercial traveller in justice'. See E. S. Fay, *The Life of Mr. Justice Swift*, Methuen, 1939, p. 152.
535   Cited in David Kynaston, *Family Britain, 1951-57*, Bloomsbury, 2009, p. 264.
536   The link between the Rouse case and literary depictions of it is discussed in Gerry R. Rubin, "Dennis, Alan and Arthur x 3: Literary Legacies of the 'Blazing Car Murder' of 1930", *Law and Humanities*, Vol. 9 (2), 2015, pp. 1-34. The article is available online at www.tandfonline.com/doi//full/10.1080/17521483.2015.1093302.
537   *The Times*, June 26, 1917 for her unsuccessful appeal against conviction.
538   *Sunday Times*, February 19, 1928.

States). Schonberg was fined £30 and Schiller was fined £15. The magistrate at Marlborough Street police court added that had they been professional receivers he would have sent them to jail.[539] A couple of months earlier, Louis Lesser (28), a commercial traveller of no fixed abode, and Alexander Goodstein of King's Cross, London, were charged at the Mansion House with evading Customs duty. This had been due on bales of wastepaper, which also contained tobacco, sent from Belgium and unloaded at West India Docks. Lesser pleaded guilty and Goodstein was found guilty. Both were heavily fined but Lesser was also sentenced to one year's prison with hard labour for the further offence of making a false customs declaration to which he had already pleaded guilty.[540] Finally, in the same court, an out-of-work commercial traveller, Frank Morgan, was fined £5 with three guineas costs for offering himself as a servant with false references written by himself. [541] One suspects that Miller, Schiller and Lesser used the term 'commercial traveller' rather loosely and that they were, unlike Morgan who probably *had* lost his job as a commercial traveller in the depression, merely semi-detached members of that fraternity. Indeed, they were more likely to have been 'wheelers and dealers' looking for the main chance in the style of Del-boy and Rodney Trotter rather than a sexual opportunist like Rouse.

Yet, just as low-class Scotch drapers who might require pedlars' licences from the police sought to transform themselves into respectable credit drapers' associations, so too did commercial travellers endeavour to establish their respectable, white-collar credentials, especially when representing well-known brands and driving impressive vehicles. And it must not be forgotten that Rouse himself was making a reasonable income of about £10 a week, which was considerably more than the average wage at the time (one of his problems being that his outlays were outstripping his income). Thus entries in the National Archives catalogue under the heading 'commercial travellers' include files for the Commercial Travellers Society Trust Fund, 1900-01 (TS18/874), identity cards for commercial travellers abroad, 1931 (BT11/44), and a reference to the National Union of Commercial Travellers, n.d., (LAB28/8). There was also a refusal of the title 'Royal' in respect of the Commercial Travellers' Benevolent Society, 1947-48 (HO45/22449), and of the Pinner Royal Commercial Travellers' School for Orphans and Necessitous Children, 1932-33 (ED27/8147). There were, similarly, commercial travellers' hotels though we know from the trial of the matricide, Sidney Harry Fox, in 1929 that a number of commercial travellers, including Henry Dickens Miller, Reginald Reed and a Mr. Hopkins, were staying at the Hotel Metropole in Margate when Fox set fire to a chair in the room in which he had already strangled his mother.[542] Of course, in Rouse's case, there may have been more welcoming sisters of mercy than anonymous hotels or boarding houses when his travels took him away from London if, that is, we can believe the tales of his 80 or so conquests. But hard facts in this regard are lacking.

The pursuit of respectability for the occupation might be seen in a Commons debate in 1925 on amending the Representation of the People Act 1918 which not only famously extended to women over thirty the right to vote in parliamentary

---

539   *The Times*, November 1, 1930.
540   *Ibid.*, August 30, 1930.
541   *Ibid.*, December 17, 1930.
542   James H. Hodge (ed.), *Famous Trials III*, Penguin, 1950, p. 64.

elections but also regulated other aspects of the voting process. Thus it was claimed that, along with fishermen and railwaymen, there were, under the 1918 Act, 35,000 commercial travellers who were at risk of being denied the opportunity to vote due to their peripatetic occupations. Many of these employees, it was claimed, were from London, including the Fulham constituency of the Unionist MP, Colonel Vaughan-Morgan, who contributed to the debate. The demand was for the names of such persons to be put on the 'absent voters' list, thereby permitting them a postal vote. But as the Home Secretary, William Joynson-Hicks, opposed the proposal, the amending Bill failed to advance.[543]

Another marker of respectability, as hinted above, was the existence of representative bodies in the trade, such as the United Commercial Travellers' Association. At its 1925 annual conference in Great Yarmouth, among more immediate concerns affecting employed members, it condemned the practices of employers who enforced 'secret agreements' not to employ commercial travellers previously employed by other businesses parties to the agreements, 'irrespective of whether the traveller had given satisfaction or not'.[544] Similarly, the conference also approved steps to secure from motor dealers and petrol stations preferential rates 'for commercial vehicles when used for business purposes'. This was probably meant to cover ordinary saloon-type cars such as Rouse drove for both business and leisure. Third, branches were advised to communicate with the 'proper authorities' so that commercial travellers be permitted to leave their cars for a reasonable period while conducting their business and, presumably, not be prosecuted for obstructing the highway. However, the conference also moved into civic mode and urged that special instruction be given to children in schools 'on the subject of motor traffic' (presumably meaning generating awareness of the danger that cars posed to children playing), and that children should be taught to regard the uniformed constable 'as their best friend'.[545] It is not clear whether the National Union of Commercial Travellers was separate from the United Association, above. But the former certainly sought to ingratiate itself with respectable society when, at its 1931 conference at Newcastle, its president, a Cornishman, told his listeners that, on the occasion of the Prince of Wales's visit to South America, '...if his Royal Highness turns out to be as good a commercial traveller as he is a landlord, his success is assured and he will have deserved well of his firm, British Commonwealth Limited'.[546]

Other bodies such as the Incorporated Sales Managers' Association included not only commercial travellers among their ranks but also indoor salesmen and their managers. It held an annual dinner in 1930 at the Cambridge Chamber of Commerce where its president, delivering a speech on 'Education for Commerce', encouraged its practitioners to embrace not only salesmanship but also the 'whole science and art of finding, catering for and developing markets for the products of our manufacturers'.[547] Two weeks earlier Sir Stanley Machin, president of the Commercial Travellers' Benevolent Institution, told the 81st festival dinner of the

---

543   *The Times*, May 9, 1925.
544   It is arguable that such agreements were illegal at common law as being in restraint of trade.
545   *The Times*, June 3, 1925. At the 1931 annual conference, one concern was to secure compensation when commercial travellers lost their jobs through mergers and amalgamations. See *ibid.*, May 27, 1931.
546   *Ibid.*, April 6, 1931.
547   *Ibid.*, April 25, 1930.

institution, held at Salters' Hall in London, that the 40,000 commercial travellers in Britain were the equal of those from other countries. All that they required at this time of economic depression were equal opportunities to show their worth. The Lord Mayor, in replying to the toast to the City of London, opined that the two qualities of the commercial traveller that led to success were perseverance and personality.[548] Whether Rouse possessed either or both those qualities may perhaps be debated endlessly.

We noted earlier that one chief constable had considered 'trade agents' before the Great War to be among the more reckless of drivers. Given their constant use of the roads on long journeys to demonstrate and deliver their samples to retailers throughout the country, it is no surprise that they featured quite regularly in reports of traffic accidents between the wars (when, as will be recalled, casualty rates were even higher than today). Thus John Mordechai (39), a commercial traveller from Llanishen, near Cardiff, was sentenced to penal servitude for three years and his licence suspended for 20 years after committing manslaughter while driving a van.[549] In another case Harry Ruebin, a commercial traveller from Birmingham, was ordered to pay £1,600 damages to a domestic servant, Lily Hatton (24). She was hurt when the commercial traveller's car collided with the motor-cycle on which she was riding pillion. Presumably his insurers paid the damages but whether he had also been prosecuted is not known.[550]

More commonly reported at this time, however, was the fate of commercial travellers as the *victims* of crime or of road accidents. Thus in September 1930 James License, a policeman in Rochester, Kent, was sent for trial at Margate Quarter Sessions, charged with the theft of a vehicle belonging to a commercial traveller, John Robinson from Strood. License owned a greyish-black 1925 Austin but was seen driving a 1930 brown Austin saloon. Robinson's car had gone missing while he was attending a Masonic meeting, on a night when License, also charged with possessing a number of skeleton keys and shop-breaking, was not on duty. When Robinson's car was recovered it had been painted a different colour and displayed the registration and number plates of License's 1925 vehicle.[551] Robinson's occupation had clearly not made him more vulnerable to theft, since the alleged crime had occurred in the general area where he lived. However, in another incident the car belonging to Herbert Barnett, a commercial traveller from Forest Gate in London, was stolen with 200,000 cigarettes inside. He had only left it for two minutes when two youths jumped into it and drove off.[552] In another case a commercial traveller, also from London, and working for an electrical supplies company, became the victim of an assault while on his rounds in Yorkshire. While travelling on a lonely stretch of road between Sheffield and Doncaster in 1932, Arthur Cunnington was flagged down by an apparently distressed female motorist whose car, it appeared, had broken down by the side of the road. He pulled up to help and got out of his car, whereupon two men jumped out of a hedge and attacked him.[553] Cunnington later described the incident to a newspaper reporter:

548 *Ibid.*, April 12, 1930.
549 *Ibid.*, November 20, 1930.
550 *Sunday Times*, June 25, 1933.
551 *The Times*, September 29, 1930.
552 *Ibid.*, September 5, 1930.
553 *Sunday Times*, October 2, 1932.

"I was punched in the stomach and fell to the ground helpless. Then one of the men put his hand in my trousers pockets and the other took my wallet from my coat pocket. They did not touch my car, but climbed into their own car, a yellow sports model, and made off at a fast speed."[554] In an echo of Rouse's complaint that his passenger had had his eye on Rouse's briefcase at some point during the journey to Hardingstone, David Steer (63) was sentenced by Brighton magistrates to one month's imprisonment with hard labour for stealing a commercial traveller's case (and a piece of meat).[555] In another instance a commercial traveller, John Allan from Isleworth, West London, had been defrauded by a stockbroker from Chelsea, William Sidney (64), whose office was in Cornhill in the City of London. Sidney had been instructed by Allan to buy 100 shares in a South African gold mine and had received a cheque for £112.15.6d for the purchase. While Sidney bought the shares as instructed, he did not pay for them and Allan's cheque went straight into Sidney's bank account. On settlement day (after further time to pay had been granted to the broker), Sidney defaulted and informed Allan that he had been 'hammered' on the Stock Exchange. He was sent for trial at the Old Bailey.[556]

The above are examples of commercial travellers as victims of crime (even if the Allan case is untypical and is suggestive of a commercial traveller with more resources than Rouse possessed). The following, however, are examples of the vulnerability of commercial travellers to serious traffic accidents (Rouse's collisions seemed mild by comparison as he wielded his mallet to smooth out dents on his car's bodywork). Thus in May 1930, William Campbell, a commercial traveller, was injured and his passenger, a hotel manager, was killed when Campbell's car overturned near Dunfermline, Fife.[557] Three months later Robert Davies (20), a commercial traveller from Stamford Hill, North London, died from his injuries in St Albans Hospital after his car had collided with a lorry in Watling Street, outside St Albans on August 2, 1930 (St Albans, of course, featured in the Rouse saga).[558] Finally, T. J. Sumner, a commercial traveller from Leeds, died in Hull Royal Infirmary from injuries when his car overturned after he had managed to avoid knocking down a boy.[559]

Given what little historians know about the world of the commercial traveller between the wars, a partial picture, such as that painted above, is better than no picture at all, with which to illustrate facets of Rouse's career. Rouse, as we know, was a representative for the Leicester firm of W. B. Martin & Co., manufacturers of selected types of menswear, especially garters and braces.[560] Thus his last calls on behalf of his employer on November 4 1930 were to drapers' shops on the Kent coast. The Man's Shop of 62 High Street, Broadstairs, received a dozen larger garters, a dozen smaller ones and a dozen braces, while A. J. Bartlett of

---

554 *Sheffield Daily Telegraph*, October 3, 1932.
555 *The Times*, February 10, 1931.
556 *Ibid.*, September 11, 1931.
557 *Ibid.*, May 23, 1930.
558 *Ibid.*, August 11, 1930.
559 *Ibid.*, September 9, 1930.
560 Little is known of the firm based in Meynell Road. There seems to be no national archive listing. The firm is briefly mentioned in a Board of Trade file at BT365/21/7 regarding modest compensation for loss of goods in the post in 1918. No doubt local records relating to Leicester and the local press would be more revealing. Interestingly, the factory of W. B. Martin & Co. was partially destroyed by fire in November 1927, although it is not suggested that Rouse was in any way responsible for the blaze. See *Sheffield Daily Telegraph*, November 11, 1927.

177 Northdown Road, Cliftonville, took possession of a dozen braces and a dozen smaller garters. The shops would be invoiced from the Leicester premises in due course. Rouse himself was usually paid by cheque from the company's bank account held at the Granby Street, Leicester, branch of the Midland Bank, and would pay in the cheques into his own bank, Barclays, at their Friern Barnet branch. Thus the most recent payments before his arrest appear to have been two cheques, one for £6.17.10d, dated October 31, 1930, and another for £7 dated two days earlier. The latter, at least, appears to have been in response to a telegram sent by Rouse on October 29 from Herne Bay to Mr. Graham at W. B. Martin, complaining that he had not been paid the £7 he was owed. 'Not yet received cheque so have to leave journey half done, as have no more money. Will wait in London for it', he telegraphed. He evidently did not have to wait too long as the sum was credited to his account on November 4.

For some reason Rouse was particularly animated when in custody at Bedford Prison by the prospect of not returning to his employer the company's samples that were still in his possession at Buxted Road. Thus he made a statement, probably written about January 26, 1931, in which he wrote that he had contacted his employer, Mr. Martin, around November 14, 1930, asking him to collect the company's samples from his home. He had not received a reply but had asked his wife to telephone the London office of the firm with the same message. Doing everything by the book? Or more smoke and mirrors?

The world of the inter-war commercial traveller is, admittedly, barely captured by the above account of new car sales, new household products, commercial travellers' hotels, their representative organizations and attendant propaganda, expressions of loyalty and trumpet-blowing, their dodgy dealings, traffic accidents and road casualties both caused and suffered by them. But then, again, it is scarcely fully represented by the fictional Arthur Parker (or Arthur Miller's later Willie Loman in his *Death of a Salesman*) or by the murdering vacuum cleaner salesman, Henry Seymour. On the other hand, cumulatively, we hope that we have obtained an impression, albeit a partial one, of the commercial employment world of Arthur Rouse.

CHAPTER TWENTY

AMAZING ENTANGLEMENTS WITH WOMEN

NEWS OF THE WORLD, February 1, 1931

Rouse, Sex and Inter-War Society

'My harem....it's an expensive game', Rouse notoriously confided in a spontaneous and somewhat regretful boast to Inspector Lawrence on their arrival at Northampton police station on the morning of Saturday November 8. The remarks were not, of course, repeated at the trial, but the press had already pounced on them following their disclosure at the earlier police court hearing, together with reference to his children by the unmarried Nellie and to Miss Jenkins' 'indisposed' state. The defence had made much of how prejudicial such disclosures by the prosecution had been to the fairness of the actual trial, while even the normally cantankerous and impatient Lord Chief Justice Hewart, in the Court of Criminal Appeal, had observed that the police court revelations had been 'unfortunate'.

The Crown, for its part, insisted that Rouse had been tried fairly and that it was not believed that the assize jury had been swayed in their verdict by their awareness of Rouse's earlier ambiguous triumph of multiple sexual conquests involving pliant females. For the circumstantial evidence, in both the prosecution's and Home Office's view, was sufficient to damn the prisoner (though no doubt the Crown would not have been surprised that, given Rouse's immoral record, the jury would still have convicted had the circumstantial evidence not been as damning as the prosecution actually believed). Like Edith Thompson, he might indeed have been convicted because of his adultery, notwithstanding the Crown's less than compelling case. But is this comment not, in itself, an unfair stereotyping by the present writers of the beliefs and values of Rouse's jurors?

The aim of this chapter is to explore public attitudes towards sexual behaviour in the inter-war period. We would thereby hope to ascertain whether, in fact, a 'typical' jury during this period would hold that sexual incontinence, the conducting of extra-marital affairs, and the fathering of illegitimate children were a matter for such unequivocal condemnation that the accused should not expect to benefit from reasonable doubt as to his guilt. Indeed a more extreme version of this belief had previously been notoriously expressed by Lord Guthrie during the trial of Oscar Slater in Edinburgh in 1909.

About his own character.... [he] has maintained himself by the ruin of men and on the ruin of women, and he has lived a life that many blackguards would scorn to live......a man of that kind has not the presumption of innocence in his favour. Which is not the form in the case of every man, but is a reality in the case of the ordinary man. Not only is every man presumed to be innocent, but the ordinary man has a strong presumption in his favour".[561]

Slater, however, was not an 'ordinary' man. He was a pimp, he managed a gambling house, he was an immigrant, a Jew whose real surname was Leschziner. Well, the last three were true. But maintaining himself 'on the ruin of women' was assumed, never proved. Not that that mattered to Lord Guthrie (or, perhaps, to the jury). Slater was convicted and the biggest conspiracy in modern Scottish legal history, designed to protect the real killers of Marion Gilchrist, that is, the 'respectable' but financially greedy Charteris brothers distantly related to the victim, proved successful.[562]

Rouse was not a pimp, nor a gambler, nor an immigrant, nor a Jew. He professed no religion (though he may have been comforted by the prison chaplain as the end drew near) and his name 'Rouse' was a long-standing one in different parts of England. Although the familiar press photographs of him are unflattering, the police photograph shows a man of remarkably handsome features with a moustache slightly thicker than the pencil type displayed by film stars like Ronald Colman, Clark Gable or Errol Flynn. He did, in fact, look like a film star and undoubtedly had an appeal and presence for certain women. He might, indeed, have been the embodiment of a handsome Lothario. He was certainly not constrained in his sexual behaviour and his sexual liaisons. In the dock did he therefore automatically invite feelings of disgust towards himself from onlookers? More relevantly, was this the sensation felt by the all-male jury, the two women originally selected having been stood down following defence counsel's peremptory challenge, either on the footing that their outrage would be greater than the men's or, less likely, that Donald Finnemore considered the details of the case would be too delicate for a woman? Or might there have been indifference as to his private life and his sexual complications?

For some, judgments on sexual matters outside marriage were unremittingly unforgiving and shaming. For example, when the former suffragette and then campaigning socialist, Sylvia Pankhurst, gave birth to a baby outside marriage in 1928, Sylvia's mother, the redoubtable Mrs. Emmeline Pankhurst, read about her daughter's 'shame' in the News of the World. 'She wept uncontrollably, and said she would abandon politics and never speak in public again. She would never see nor forgive Sylvia. Already in poor health, she deteriorated.'[563] Perhaps Mrs.

---

561 William Roughead (ed.), *Trial of Oscar Slater*, Notable Scottish Trial Series, William Hodge & Company, Edinburgh, 1910, pp. 285-6.

562 Thomas Toughill, *Oscar Slater: The 'Immortal' Case of Sir Arthur Conan Doyle*, Sutton Publishing, Stroud, 2006, p. 116. One brother was Professor of Law at Glasgow University. The other subsequently became Professor of Medicine at St Andrews University. An uninvolved third brother, Major-General Sir John Charteris, was Haig's chief of intelligence during the Great War before being sacked. He later became a Conservative MP, no doubt shifting uneasily on his seat in parliament when the House considered the matter of Slater's eventual release in 1927. Toughill's portrayal of the various links among the Scottish professional (especially Presbyterian) 'establishment' in furthering the cover-up is a remarkable revelation.

563 Melanie Phillips, *The Ascent of Woman: A History of the Suffragette Movement and the Ideas Behind It*, Abacus, 2003, p. 313.

Pankhurst was of a similar cast to the fictional character of Lady Chalford in Nancy Mitford's *Wigs on the Green*, first published in 1935. The comic novel was a thinly disguised portrayal, relentlessly emphasising the absurdity of Nancy's Nazi-sympathising sisters, Diana and Unity, and of Diana's husband, Sir Oswald Mosley and his Blackshirts. For Lady Chalford, whose character was modelled on Nancy's mother, Lady Redesdale, the divorce of her son, Lord Malmains, from his wife was a greater tragedy in her life than his death in 1920 from war wounds suffered the day before the Armistice. Her grand-daughter, Eugenia Malmains (aka Unity Mitford), the teenage village organiser of the Union Jackshirts, was damned by her because she (Eugenia) 'had the tainted blood of an adulteress in her veins' rather than because she professed Nazi race superiority. Indeed her provenance had cast such a shadow of disgrace over the Chalford dynasty, plunging Lady Chalford into the deepest slough of shame, that the dowager never set foot outside her park gate again.[564]

Mrs. Pankhurst and Lady Chalford probably embodied elite values regarding sexual mores (Mrs. Pankhurst had been adopted in 1927 as a Conservative candidate for parliament, impelling Sylvia, in turn, to a bout of weeping). But were such strict views on adultery so widely shared that in the case of Rouse he was universally perceived as a social outcast irrespective of his guilt regarding the death of the unknown stranger? In an age following the publication of Marie Stopes' *Married Love* (the adjective was probably considered essential) which first appeared in 1918, how widespread was sexual knowledge among both married and unmarried young persons and adults? How vital was respectability for both males and females, married or single, in setting boundaries to sexual behaviour? How much extra-marital sex took place? Was it widely considered shameful? Were 'affairs' with 'eternal triangles' considered more acceptable than 'one-night stands', or vice-versa? What was expected of virile young (and not so young) men? What, indeed, was expected of wives in relation to their husbands' sexual appetites? Did masculinity imply only marital sexual conduct or did masculinity embrace Lotharios or Don Juans? Crippen, for example, conducted his affair with Ethel Le Neve for seven years, the last four years sexual, before the death of his wife, Cora.

Yet, even at the time, Hawley Crippen's adultery was viewed ambiguously. Partly this was due to Cora's unattractive features, her buxom and over-weight image, her garrulous style, her tasteless home decorations, her flaunting of expensive gowns, her name-dropping and social climbing among the successful achievers of the music hall profession, her slovenly housekeeping and her continual undermining of her husband's manhood. But partly it was because many observers recognised a spiritual dimension to his relationship with Ethel. Their love was 'sacred' and precious. Both essentially weak personalities needing each other, they were symbiotically strong and honourable, with Crippen lauded in some intellectual quarters, as noted in chapter 18.

564 Nancy Mitford, *Wigs on the Green*, Penguin, 2010, p. 72. Mitford wrote the book only a year before Edward VIII abdicated in order to marry the divorcee, Mrs. Simpson. What Lady Chalford would have made of the event defies imagination. What Eugenia would have made of Mrs. Simpson, whose second husband, Ernest Simpson, had Jewish parentage (Solomon), is also tantalising. The Queen Mother's hostile attitude to Wallis Simpson is well known. Imagine if the latter had been called Wallis Solomon.

Thus moral judgments on adultery could be expressed in ambiguous terms even twenty years before Rouse's trial. Indeed, sociological and historical literature on adultery and pre-marital sex in the first half of the twentieth century suggests that the condemnation of Rouse's behaviour might contain not a little whiff of hypocrisy (though we know that Rouse himself was a rank hypocrite on matters of sex and infidelity).

In his favour it might be said that prevailing male values as to suitable marriage partners seemed to stress that a wife 'had to be young, pretty, domesticated ('all the men insist on that'), blond and interested in sport'.[565] Today, such views would be condemned as demeaning and chauvinist and as failing to identify such crucial features as personality, love, mutual commitment and compatibility.[566] Rouse, himself, had notoriously admitted to Inspector Lawrence that Lily was 'really too good for me', before spoiling this apparently sincere expression of appreciation. For he then, as we know, gratuitously added that, 'I like a woman who will make a fuss of me. I don't ever remember my wife sitting on my knee, but otherwise she is a good wife', before really sticking in the knife (which came back to stab him in turn) with his 'I am very friendly with several women but it is a very expensive game'. Dennis Potter, in *Pennies from Heaven*, did in fact seek to make the extremely strait-laced and respectable Mrs. Arthur Parker rethink her prudishness, verging on fatalism, towards sex as the fictional Arthur Parker's interest in her was noticeably waning. Thus imagining what would sexually excite her husband, she sought to apply lipstick to her nipples before exposing her breasts to him in the bedroom. His reaction was utter disgust, though we can imagine that had it been another woman with whom he was conducting an affair, his reaction would have been wholly different. But that dramatic scene, whether viewed as pathos or bathos, captured the essence of Rouse's own hypocrisy towards sex at a time when there was an excess of eligible women over men in the marriage market. Indeed in 1897, 'Mrs. Humphry', in *Manners for Women*, had reminded her readers that 'Brides' were 'Two a Penny'. Thus, 'The tragedy of this disparity!'; 'Alas! for the plain girl'; 'Nowadays one is first a woman'; 'She must shine on nothing a year'; and 'Be sympathetic so long as his pocket is not touched'.[567]

But perhaps that does not adequately explain the appeal that Rouse had for the single females, Helen Campbell, Nellie Tucker and Ivy Jenkins and, indeed, for many of the other, approximately 75, women allegedly featuring at some time or another in Rouse's love life, and whose names have been lost to history (unless hitherto undiscovered police files reveal the extent of his conquests). For none of the significant trio were older than 19 when meeting Rouse for the first time. Therefore not for them the nagging feeling that the marriage scrap heap awaited them unless a Prince Charming suddenly materialised in front of their eyes. For this haunting prospect undoubtedly spurred at least two of the 'Brides in the

---

565 Martin Pugh, *We Danced All Night: A Social History of Britain Between the Wars*, Vintage, 2009, p. 124, referring to the views of marriage bureau founders, Heather Jenner and Mary Oliver in 1939. See also H. G. Cocks, *Classified: The Secret History of the Personal Column*, Arrow Books, 2010, Ch. 7.

566 For other examples of similarly worded chauvinistic adverts to those listed in *ibid.*, see Jane Robins, *The Magnificent Spilsbury and the Case of the Brides in the Bath*, John Murray, 2010, pp. 2-3.

567 'Mrs. Humphry' ('Madge' of 'Truth'), *Manners for Women* (1897), reissued by Pryor Publications, Whitstable, 1993, pp. 52-3; 58-9.

Bath' victims, Bessie Munday and Margaret Lofty, to throw caution to the winds and to allow themselves to be swept off their feet by the apparently worldly-wise George Joseph Smith. Statistics for the ratio of eligible males to females suggest what Bessie and Margaret, both in their 30s, were up against. Thus in 1911 the figures show:

Table 1: Unmarried Males and Females x 1000 in 1911

Age	Male	Female
20-24	1,502	1,673
25-34	1,822	3,125
35-44	2,336	2,509

Source: Katherine Holden, *The Shadow of Marriage: Singleness in England, 1914-1960*, Manchester University Press, Manchester, 2007, p. 27.

Thus we can see that the imbalance is especially pronounced in the age range 25-34, and after the Great War it would, of course, have been greater. Jane Lewis presents more detailed statistics, as follows:

Table 2: Selected Demographic Characteristics, England and Wales, 1911-1931

Percentage of Women Ever Married			Sex Ratio (F/M x 100)		'Excess' Women (F/M '000s)	
Year	Age15+	Age 45-49	All Ages	15-44	All Ages	15-44
1911	61.0	83.5	106.8	108.0	1178	664
1921	63.2	83.2	109.6	114.2	1736	1,174
1931	64.6	83.2	108.8	109.4	1686	842

Source: Jane Lewis, *Women in England, 1870-1950: Sexual Divisions and Social Change*, Wheatsheaf Books, Sussex, 1984, Table 1, p. 3.

We can see that over those three decades almost one third of women over 15 never married, though more than four-fifths of those between 45 and 49 had done so. Moreover in the crucial age range of 15-44 there was a considerable excess of eligible women over men, especially noticeable in 1921 after the Great War. Indeed there were over a million more such women than men in the 1921 census year, though that excess had fallen to 842,000 by 1931 (in 1951 the excess was only 290,000). It thus seems at the statistical level that the challenge facing women between the wars to find a marriage partner was greater than the choices facing men. The classified ad and Heather Jenner's marriage bureau, offering the prospect to clients of obtaining a marriage partner, emerged as two consequences of this demographic imbalance. It has to be said that men were as likely to advertise for a wife as vice-versa, but the terms seemed unfairly weighted against those women who did not possess funds nor saw themselves as other than dutiful housewives with domestic skills. Holden's figures for 1911 do, of course, make the obvious point that younger women were in a more favourable position in this regard than those women a few years older. So Rouse was given a favourable playing field because demography was working in his favour even though Helen, Nellie and Ivy were scarcely harbouring increasing pessimism (as almost certainly had troubled Bessie Munday and Margaret Lofty before they met Smith) as to their future marriage prospects. [568]

On November 25, 1928, the *News of the World* splashed across its front page a 'special' item headed, 'Curtain Falls on Intrigue: Shooting of a Nurse and Married Man'.[569] It was not an imaginary account of what the future might hold for Arthur Rouse and the nurse, Ivy Jenkins (if only because Rouse was not the dramatic type who would be plunged into suicidal despair over a romance whose future was doomed). But some, albeit not all, of the other similarities were striking. As the newspaper almost poetically revealed,

> Behind the locked doors of a good-class home in Peckham Rye, a married man and a pretty hospital nurse passed to swift and silent death from revolver bullets through the brain. They had been firm, fast friends for many months secure in their intrigue by the knowledge that the breadth of the metropolis lay between the married man's home and their nightly meeting place. That they were on exceedingly affectionate terms was common knowledge amongst the nurse's colleagues, but, on the other hand, friends and acquaintances of the man were amazed to learn last night that he had any other 'interest' apart from his work and home.

A clandestine tragic affair, as if penned by Graham Greene in *The Heart of the Matter*, but without the colonial and Catholic over-lay, was not uncommon fare for the Sunday press in the inter-war years. But were such affairs commonplace, or were such challenges to what passed for contemporary moral values unusual events? In recent studies aimed at the general reader, Steve Humphries has sought to pull back the curtain on the perceived taboo of pre-marital or adulterous sex in the first half of the twentieth century. He noted that, apart from the sensational press, there was little publicity given to such affairs. The Church's teachings preached moral rectitude, the BBC under Lord Reith would not transmit material that hinted at smut or immorality, nor would it employ those who had been divorced. Rumours of scandal surrounding married employees could threaten their jobs. Also, sanctimonious bodies seeking to uphold 'moral hygiene' continued to lobby and preach against sexual sin, having already demonstrated their influence during the Great War. For they had encouraged the creation of female vigilance police forces to try to prevent any hanky-panky between soldiers and girls working in munitions factories far from home. Apart from anything

---

568   Today within western societies a more balanced female to male ratio among those considered of marriageable age is masking a female to male imbalance in respect of higher education qualifications, with 'educated women....struggling to meet their match'. See Jon Birger, *Date-onomics: How Dating Became a Lopsided Numbers Game*, Workman Publishing, New York, 2015.
569   Cited in Steve Humphries and Pamela Gordon, *Forbidden Britain: Our Secret Past, 1900-1960*, BBC Books, 1994, p. 51.

else, the ravages of venereal disease would impact on military efficiency and on munitions output.[570] Indeed the nightmares of syphilis and of gonorrhoea featured in propaganda films of the 1930s that received the approval of bodies such as the Social Purity and Hygiene Movement.[571] According to Humphries[572] it was widely assumed that the number of extra-marital affairs was increasing in the inter-war period, as evidenced by the rise in the number of divorces from around 500 per annum in the 1900s to around 7,500 annually by the late 1930s. But the increasing numbers probably fail to reflect how widely adulterous affairs were conducted. This is because divorce was not only an expensive procedure for most people until legal aid was introduced in 1949. It also remained a significant stigmatising event until recent decades, which greatly inhibited many parties' resort to the divorce courts. Of course, it became almost institutionalised among middle- and upper-class circles for husbands, whether the 'guilty' party or not, to go through the charade of booking a bedroom in a hotel in Brighton or Hastings for a platonic evening with an unnamed woman, and where the chambermaid would see the couple the next morning, A whole cast of celebrities conspired accordingly. Thus the husbands of Wallis Simpson and Diana Mitford agreed to do the 'honourable' thing in order to enable their wives to obtain divorces and then marry the abdicating Edward VIII and Sir Oswald Mosley, respectively. Gracie Fields similarly obtained her divorce through this simultaneously clandestine but very public manipulation of the then unsatisfactory divorce law.[573]

In the 1930s there was a school of thought that men's biological needs were responsible for the increase in affairs. In one book published in 1932, it was stated that, 'Men, being more polygamously inclined than women, have claimed for themselves the right to change their sexual partners whenever the fancy takes them as the opportunity arises'.[574] The passage could have been written for Arthur Rouse though it does not adequately explain why it was thought that affairs suddenly increased from the 1930s. At the time the increase was attributed to a decline in the number of prostitutes to whom married men previously resorted for extra-marital sex. Thus if the number of prostitutes had declined from the nineteenth century (vague figures of around 50,000 prostitutes in London during the previous century had been bandied about), then married men's heterosexual energies outside marriage would have to be satisfied in affairs. The only problem is that recent research by Stefan Slater has suggested that the number of prostitutes, at least in London, was *not* in decline in the inter-war period.[575] Consequently, we are still in a position where the number of extra-marital affairs during this period

570 See, for example, Philippa Levine, "'Walking the Streets in a Way No Decent Woman Should': Women Police in World War I", in Chris A. Williams (ed,), *Police and Policing in the Twentieth Century*, Ashgate, Aldershot, 2011; Lucy Bland, "'In the Name of Protection': The Policing of Women in the First World War", in Julia Brophy and Carol Smart (eds.), *Women-in-Law: Explorations in Law, Family and Sexuality*, Routledge, 1985, Ch. 2; Alison Woodeson, "The First Women Police: A Force for Equality or Infringement?", *Women's History Review*, Vol. 2 (2), 1993, pp. 217-32. For a photograph of the first female police constable, Edith Smith, based in Grantham, who drew up lists of 'frivolous and wayward girls' engaged in 'unseemly conduct' with soldiers in the town, see *Guardian*, December 2, 2015.
571 Humphries, *op. cit.*, p. 55.
572 *Ibid.*, p. 52.
573 Pugh, *op. cit.*, pp. 136, 139, 142.
574 A. Buschke and F. Jacobsohn, *Introduction to Sexual Hygiene*, Routledge, 1932, cited in Humphries, *op. cit.*, pp. 52-4. Buschke, a Jewish dermatologist, was murdered by the Nazis in the Holocaust.
575 Stefan Slater, "Containment: Managing Street Prostitution in London, 1918-1939", *Journal of British Studies*, Vol. 49 (2), April 2010, pp. 332-57.

remains a dark figure, like the number of crimes not reported at the time.

So, if the number of affairs was increasing, was it, perhaps, because *women* felt more sexually liberated? Stopes' *Married Love* (1918) may well have been intended to be targeted at a 'respectable' audience of matrimonial couples. Yet the wider availability of contraception in the generations prior to the 'Pill' may not have been the trigger. For the condoms and mechanical methods of that era lacked the increased reliability of products in much later decades, and may yet have proved a disincentive to some women to conducting an adulterous affair.[576] Nonetheless it is clear that the average size of families was falling in this period. It is possible that some women took advantage of this to conduct 'Brief Encounters', even if the childless Lily Rouse apparently did not. But it also meant fewer paternal commitments and ties binding the man to his household.

The 1920s were seen by some as spawning a generation of the 'new woman'. To a greater or lesser extent, depending on the individual, she was independent in thought and in finance, she pursued a career, she was interested in politics, culture, dancing, jazz, smoking, fashionable clothes and hair styles, and having an occasional flutter on the horses. Importantly, her horizons were not determined by house, home and duty towards husband and children. In this regard, she was sexually liberated without being sexually promiscuous. There were various models, both attractive and repellent. They might be the 'dope girls' like Billie Carleton and Freda Kempton (sometimes rendered as Kempson), in the immediate post-Great War period, who fell victim to drugs overdoses.[577] They could be the film stars and actresses like the American silent screen star, Theda Bara, in her sultry and mysterious Hollywood roles. They could be like Clara Bow, the original 'It' girl of the early 1930s, with her sex appeal. Or they could be like Edith Thompson who, like Madeleine Smith in the nineteenth century (according to F. Tennyson Jesse's *Notable British Trials* portrait), was 'born before her time'.[578]

What seems clear from an understanding of inter-war affairs is that they stereotypically involved the eternal triangle, with a married party, usually the husband, conducting an affair with a single woman behind his wife's back (though in Rouse's case, it seems that Lily may well have long since resigned herself to her husband's philandering). What also seems to have been quite widespread, and especially noticeable in working-class circles, was the practice of couples living together 'in sin' between the wars where one, at least, of the parties was already married to, but not divorced from, a third party. No doubt there were also examples involving couples living together without marrying, though free to do so, though its prevalence is unknown. Indeed, we tend to get glimpses of such relationships only through news reporting of scandals or killings, such as the case

---

576 There are numerous accounts of earlier twentieth century birth control and contraception methods. See, for example, Lucy Bland, *Banishing the Beast: English Feminism and Sexual Morality, 1885-1914*, Penguin, 1995, esp. Ch. 5; Cate Haste, *Rules of Desire: Sex in Britain, World War I to the Present*, Pimlico, 1994, esp. Ch. 4; Sheila Jeffreys, *The Spinster and Her Enemies: Feminism and Sexuality, 1880-1930*, Pandora, 1985, esp. Chs. 2 and 8; Ruth Brandon, *The New Women and the Old Men: Love, Sex and the Woman Question*, W. W. Norton, New York, 1990, *passim*.

577 Marek Kohn, *Dope Girls: The Birth of the British Drug Underground*, Granta, 1992.

578 F. Tennyson Jesse, "Introduction" to *The Trial of Madeleine Smith*, in John Mortimer (compiler), *Famous Trials*, Penguin, 1984, p. 139. For Edith Thompson's 'modernity' see Lucy Bland, *Modern Women on Trial: Sexual Transgression in the Age of the Flapper*, Manchester University Press, Manchester, 2013, Ch. 3; for Madeleine Smith's 'modernity' see Eleanor Gordon and Gwyneth Nair, *Murder and Morality in Victorian Britain: The Story of Madeleine Smith*, Manchester University Press, Manchester, 2009, *passim*.

of the rich and spoilt Elvira Barney, luckily acquitted (and fortunately represented at the Old Bailey by Sir Patrick Hastings) for the murder by shooting of her 'live-in' wastrel-lover, Michael Scott Stephen, at their fashionable Knightsbridge mews property in 1932.[579]

In rural communities before the Great War, when a young couple 'walked out' together on a regular basis this could be perceived as a *de facto* engagement, which in due course would result in marriage. Indeed pre-marital sex was widely acknowledged, for 'it was accounted no shame... for a child to be begotten out of wedlock—the shame was when there was no wedding to follow. That was something almost unknown—something that didn't stand thinking about.' Indeed in earlier generations, the man might well wish to know that his betrothed was fertile. There was an economic rationale regarding support for old age, and no doubt family assistance with rural occupations. Pregnancy, advanced or not, did not matter. Marriage did, even hours before the birth.[580]

With all these cross-currents, it is arguable that Rouse's perceived domestic situation and its relationship to his sexual liaisons are well captured in the words of a near contemporary, the British sociologist, philosopher and eugenicist (and thoroughly unattractive personality), Anthony Ludovici,

> Human courtship and the subsequent union of the sexes to which it leads is full of the excitement, the doubt, the anxiety and the final triumph of the huntsman. Beside this however, the steady hum-drum routine of married life can at best only be a flat parody. ...children are obviously a source of variety in the home. Each child in its turn, gives the home a different aspect, a different outlook, a different responsibility. Children moreover, give the family unity a superior aim and purpose, which increases in importance with the number of offspring. In this sense alone, therefore, a state of childlessness or of family limitation constitutes a dangerous state from the standpoint of connubial stability.[581]

Perhaps it was the case, especially in light of his string of illegitimate children, that the 'dangerous state' of his domestic childlessness was the spur to his extra-marital liaisons, though we are inclined to the more prosaic view that he was just a sexual predator. What is clear is that much of the evidence regarding the extent, or otherwise, of extra-marital relations in inter-war Britain is necessarily impressionistic and partial (apart, that is, from the unreliable indications to be inferred from illegitimacy rates and from divorce figures). In one respect this is not surprising given the nature of the inquiry. For how many elderly female interviewees would discuss with researchers today their pre-marital sexual relations in the inter-war years? On the other hand, as the French 'post-modernist', Michel Foucault, once remarked, while sexuality was perceived in the nineteenth century as an 'unspeakable subject', the irony was that it nonetheless managed to

579 Peter Cotes (ed.), *Trial of Elvira Barney*, David & Charles, Newton Abbott, 1976.
580 John Burnett, 'Introduction' to Margaret Penn, *Manchester Fourteen Miles*, Futura, 1982 (first published 1947), p. xvii.
581 Anthony Ludovici, *Woman: A Vindication*, Constable, 1923, cited in Humphries, *op. cit.*, p. 56. According to Richard Overy, Ludovici believed that 'contraception was like weeding in the dark, randomly destructive of the best human stock, and unable to prevent the birth of the worst'. As a result he advocated that babies with abnormalities and 'incurable lunatics' should be 'painlessly put away'. See Richard Overy, *The Twilight Years: The Paradox of Britain Between the Wars*, Viking, 2009, p. 116.

inspire an enormous amount of discussion about the subject.[582] But apart from impressionistic accounts, the necessary evidence may also often be derived from biographical or autobiographical accounts that have the effect of sensationalising politics or upper-class society. Dorothy Macmillan's cuckolding of her husband, Harold, as she dallied with Bob Boothby is notorious. Similarly, the author of the Cazalet family saga, Elizabeth Jane Howard, described in her autobiography[583] how she regularly jumped into bed with various men in the 1940s and 50s during her marriages. Her extra-marital affairs may have been designed 'to shock the bourgeoisie' (*pour épater les bourgeois*). But they probably already knew.

Within working-class communities, though less so in rural communities (above), there were prevailing, though sometimes ignored, taboos against sex outside marriage, whether emanating from the Church, one's parents, broader strict socialization, moral hygiene organisations, or film and radio. Cate Haste claims that, 'The young were still closely controlled. Fear of pregnancy and the premium placed on female chastity regulated sexual activity'.[584] Moreover the long arm of the law, through the agency of the Mental Deficiency Act 1913, could cruelly label unmarried mothers as 'feeble-minded' and suitable only for institutionalisation in an asylum or home for unmarried mothers, where thereafter they would lead a life of involuntary, laundry-linked drudgery and permanent separation from their babies, and where they would be expected symbolically to wash away their sins (as recent films such as *Philomena* and *The Magdalene Sisters* remind us).[585] The abandonment of a baby in the deepest forest, employed not wholly as a fictional device in *Grimm's Fairy Tales* or, as better documented, depositing the child anonymously at a foundling hospital in France or Italy or, during the institution's earlier years, at the Thomas Coram Foundation in London, were other despairing steps taken by young mothers in distress.[586] Hovering above all this, the cultural memory of an unreformed New Poor Law emanating from 1834 which effectively penalised financially those mothers producing illegitimate children would take decades to dissolve.[587] Yet illegitimacy was a widespread phenomenon, as Jane Robinson's recent study demonstrates,[588] though it did not always generate the predictable community response of condemnation of the mother. For Robinson shows that while societal expectations were that unmarried mothers would (and should) experience shame and humiliation, and many pregnant teenagers did so, there were also different reactions. Thus in some instances the young mother

---

582   *Cf.*, Nicola Lacey, "Unspeakable Subjects, Impossible Rights: Sexuality, Integrity and Criminal Law", *Canadian Journal of Law and Jurisprudence*, Vol. 11 (1), 1998, pp. 47-68, at p. 47.

583   Elizabeth Jane Howard, *Slipstream*, Pan, 2002. Bed-hopping among the married *literati* and *literatae* is well documented, and often involved bi-sexual notables. Obvious cases include members of the Bloomsbury Group, below, Vita Sackville-West and her husband, Harold Nicolson, and Iris Murdoch.

584   Haste, *op. cit.*, p. 70.

585   For a study of the Magadalene system, see Rebecca Lea McCarthy, *Origins of the Magdalene Laundries: An Analytical History*, McFarland & Co., Inc, USA, 2010. For a personal account see Angela Patrick and Lynne Barrett-Lee, *The Baby Laundry for Unmarried Mothers*, Simon & Schuster Ltd, 2012. For one account of bringing up an illegitimate child as an unmarried mother in the 1950s, see Sheila Tofield, *The Unmarried Mother*, Penguin, 2013.

586   Katherine O'Donovan, "*Enfants Trouvés*, Anonymous Mothers, and Children's Identity Rights", in Katherine O'Donovan and Gerry R. Rubin (eds), *Human Rights and Legal History: Essays in Honour of Brian Simpson*, Oxford University Press, 2000, Ch. 3

587   Jo Pearman, "This Tribe of Ogres: Exploiting the Infant Child", chapter in Ph.D., University of Kent, 2017.

588   Jane Robinson, *In the Family Way: Illegitimacy Between the Great War and the Swinging Sixties*, Penguin, 2015.

would be supported by friends and relatives in bringing up a 'love-child' which was doted upon. Not for that baby the experience of being put out for adoption as quickly as possible as soon as the mother returned from an extended 'visit' to some previously unknown 'aunt' in a distant part of the country, with the tragic consequence that the mother would live to regret her decision (or, more precisely, the decision forced upon her by family or church authorities) to her dying day. Indeed Margaret Penn, the author of the 'disguised' autobiography, *Manchester Fourteen Miles*, above, where she features as Hilda Winstanley, was herself illegitimate, the daughter of a woman 'led astray' by a 'gentleman' who promptly eschewed his responsibility for fatherhood. The mother died in childbirth after a convenient marriage to a former admirer whose passage to Canada was paid for following his new wife's death giving birth to Hilda. But Hilda was cheerfully taken in by the Winstanleys in the village (Moss Ferry in the book, Hollins Green in actuality) and brought up 'like one of our own', and 'given perhaps even more affection than the other children by her husband. The village knew, but didn't care, that she was not their flesh and blood.'[589] Perhaps we can see how simple humanity, transcending 'respectable' attitudes to illegitimacy and to 'bastards', was extended to Arthur Jnr., Pamelita and new-born Patricia (indeed, towards their mothers), irrespective of widespread views regarding their father.

Returning to the oral history stories regarding pre-marital sex recorded by Steve Humphries, some of his upper-class respondents spoke to 'intimacy' and to 'heavy petting' at weekend parties, with the delights of actual intercourse being forgone for the sake of 'female chastity'. Lower down the class structure, 'proprieties had to be observed' at dances. Couples might be prevented by the event organisers from dancing too close to each other (did Bailey and Brown face this difficulty with their respective dance partners before returning to Hardingstone?). Young women feared 'loss of respect' if they yielded too easily (obviously not a fear inhibiting the young girl who later coined the phrase 'Reggie No Dick' to describe Reg Christie's embarrassing non-performance as a teenager in Halifax's 'Monkey Walk'), while one male respondent observed that, 'When you got the right girl you decided that no matter how hard you tried you would never get sex and that was a good thing....'[590]

A more nuanced finding was that made by Judy Giles in 1992 following her interviews with working-class women from Birmingham and York who had married in the inter-war period.[591] Her thesis is that such women, while adhering to prevailing ideologies of respectability regarding sexual behaviour before marriage (thus the concept of 'playing hard to get'), were asserting their own distinctive form of personal identity, rather than 'saving themselves' for their societally ascribed roles as housewives and mothers. Their stances thus represented a resistance to the accusations of sexual promiscuity *or* of being financial 'gold diggers' which would follow if they had offered themselves for pre-marital sex. In other words Giles presents such respondents as asserting their own version of (perhaps quasi-feminist) power in a harsh economic climate. Their views were, indeed, far from the ideology of marriage encapsulating romantic love and

589 Penn, *op. cit.*
590 Haste, *op. cit.*, p. 71.
591 Judy Giles, "'Playing Hard to Get': Working-Class Women, Sexuality and Respectability in Britain, 1919-1940", *Women's History Review*, Vol. 1 (2), 1992, pp. 239-55.

femininity, and as propagated in *Woman's Weekly* and other similar magazines. For such magazines (including *Peg's Paper* which serialised Helen's, Nellie's and Lily's stories) did not trade exclusively in reality but to a significant extent in fairy-tale. Female sexuality, indeed, was conceived, for such readership, as 'bourgeois, latent and passive', requiring 'the patience and goodwill of an ardent lover' (male) to prepare for the 'full submission' required of femininity.[592]

It was not that all such women were morally offended by the idea of pre-marital sex (though at least one respondent was morally judgmental). It was just that those who engaged in such behaviour displayed 'silliness' which could lead to future regret and to a poor choice of long-term partner. Nonetheless, one of Giles' respondents was in no doubt that, '...there was quite a lot of it [sex] around in the nineteen twenties but it was very much more discreet and it was a very private thing---you didn't make it so public', which we must take to refer to pre-marital, as well as to marital, sex.

But for most of Giles' working-class respondents, sexual activity or inactivity were not the defining feature. It was the women's *control* over their relationships that defined their (scarcely denied) 'femininity' as non-passive. 'Playing hard to get', while sustaining 'respectability', was power play which might be contrasted with middle-class 'lady-like' behaviour where a coy demeanour and fluttering eye-lash were more likely to repel than to attract suitable men.

Yet despite the findings cited above (and leaving aside such obvious indicators as illegitimacy rates in the inter-war period), Humphries and Haste themselves, as well as a number of other writers,[593] went on to cite conflicting evidence culled from the results of various surveys into sexual behaviour conducted in the 1940s but relating to behaviour in the earlier period, including the inter-war years. The most notable survey, the results of which must nonetheless be interpreted cautiously, and which involved completing anonymous questionnaires, was that conducted by the well-known 'sexologist', Dr. Eustace Chesser, which questioned 6,000 women in 1956. Another survey was conducted by the creator of the Mass-Observation organisation, Tom Harrisson, in 1949. A third survey by Mass-Observation questioned 200 working-class couples in London in the 1940s, while a fourth investigation in the 1950s questioned 5,000 readers of the *People*.

A summary of the findings, albeit weighted towards middle-class respondents, suggests that more and more people were engaging in pre-marital sex from the turn of the twentieth century than was thought to be the case for the previous century,[594] though if one young (male) murder suspect during the last war is any

---

592 R. Edynbury, *Real Life Problems and their Solution*, Odhams, 1938, p. 193, cited in Giles, *op. cit.*, p. 248.

593 See, for example, Jeffrey Weeks, *Sex, Politics and Society: The Regulation of Sexuality since 1800*, Longman, 1st ed., 1981, pp. 208-9.

594 These figures would presumably relate to consensual sex. In February 2015 *The Times* reported an academic study suggesting that two out of five teenage girls in England between 13 and 17 had been 'coerced' into sex by their boyfriends. *The Times*, February 11, 2015. No figure was given for the pervasiveness of consensual sex on the part of girls within that age range. For the broader research project within which these findings were made, see Christine Barter, 'Safeguarding Teenage Intimate Relationships: Connecting Online and Offline Contexts and Risks', *Policy Hub Scotland*, November 30, 2015; Nicky Stanley, Christine Barter et al, 'Pornography, Sexual Coercion and Abuse and Sexting in Young People's Intimate Relationships: A European Study', *Journal of Interpersonal Violence*, 2016, pp. 1-26. Cf., Sara E Thomas, '"What Should I Do?" Young Women's Reported Dilemmas with Nude Photographs', *Sexuality Research Social Policy*, Vol. 15, 2018, pp. 192-207.

guide, the language used to describe pre-marital sex was coy and almost biblical. 'I first met Rosy [the victim] four years ago. We first had connection about five months ago and her father had suspicions about it.....Rosy's parents had always tried to guide our lives. I was determined they were not going to part us.' So he killed her.[595]

According to Chesser 19% of married women born before 1904 engaged in pre-marital sex, while the figure rose to 36% for those born between 1904 and 1914. It then rose in the next ten years to 39%, finally increasing to 43% between 1924 and 1934. In regard to single female respondents (that is, presumably, those still single at interview), the proportion of such respondents shifted from 18% for those born before 1904, to 32% for those born in the decade, before falling to 30% for those born between 1914 and 1924. As Humphries points out, one must be careful in interpreting these figures. As suggested above, there was possibly a bias in the responses towards middle-class liberal views. Yet given the continuing stigma against pre-marital sex at the time of the surveys (it was before the 'Pill' and the 'Swinging Sixties', even if that particular period of 'Free Love' has itself been hyped up), perhaps the figures were even under-stated. Thus the Mass Observation survey in 1949 of the 200 working-class London couples interviewed raised suspicions that some of their respondents had been too embarrassed to admit to such behaviour in their younger days. So even though that particular survey reported that 58% of the male and 34% of the female respondents had disclosed their pre-marital sexual experience, the researchers thought that the correct figures were more like 75% for men and 50% for women, notwithstanding that the bulk of the surveys were *not* primarily interested in the respondents' sexual behaviour before marriage.[596]

Further research,[597] while not addressing survey returns, has nonetheless suggested that women's sexual subjectivity was enhanced after the Great War by the publication of a number of widely read sex manuals. These included Marie Stopes' *Married Love* (1918), G. Courtenay Beale's *Wise Wedlock* (1922) and Isabel Hutton's *The Hygiene of Marriage* (1923), the titles of which, at least, paid homage to 'respectable' relationships. Together with E. M. Hull's sexually charged (and apparently racially transgressive) desert novel, *The Sheik* (1919), which was later made available to wider audiences through the cinematic version starring Rudolph Valentino in 1921, women's widening sexual knowledge and their own subjective agency in respect of sexual conduct can be taken as a corrective to popular beliefs that sex and drugs arrived only in the era of rock 'n' roll or, as Philip Larkin famously declared (with tongue in cheek), that 'Sexual intercourse began in nineteen sixty-three/ (which was rather late for me)....'[598] Indeed, whether Helen or Nellie or Ivy (or even Lily) had read any of the above works (or had seen the Valentino film) is not known.

Of course, it does not follow that a causal link exists between the appearance of such manuals and changing sexual behaviour among young unmarried women

595   Cited in Molly Lefebure, *Murder on the Home Front: The Unique Wartime Memoirs of a Pathologist's Secretary*, Grafton, 1990, p. 35.
596   For details, see Steve Humphries, *A Secret World of Sex: Forbidden Fruit, The British Experience, 1900-1950*, Sidgwick & Jackson, 1988, pp. 32-4.
597   Karen Chow, "Popular Sexual Knowledges and Women's Agency in 1920s England", *Feminist Review*, No. 63, Autumn 1999, pp. 64-87.
598   Philip Larkin, '*Annus Mirabilis*'.

(the link is more strongly inferred than proved in Chow's account). For even if we accept that women's sexual knowledge deepened after the Great War and that pre-marital sex (leaving aside same-sex relationships) became more common among young women, we still await conclusive qualitative evidence on this issue, as distinct from limited interview or anecdotal evidence, or from questionnaire-type quantitative evidence or from figures and rates of illegitimate births.

More academic studies have also attempted to reassess the effectiveness of the prevailing ideology in the inter-war years that respectability and femininity were paramount qualities to which young women should aspire. As Sheila Jeffreys has shown, married heterosexuality for women was expected by articulate society to be the only acceptable framework for sexual behaviour, with lesbians, 'frigid' women and the celibate woman perceived as abnormal.[599] Thus when asked by Jaspar Aspect in Nancy Mitford's *Wigs on the Green*, above, why she had made such an unsuitable marriage with her husband, Anthony, Poppy St Julien was taken aback. 'How stupid you are. A girl must marry once, you can't go on being called Miss—Miss all your life, it sounds too idiotic'.

Open marriages and 'uncommon arrangements' were likewise seen as deviant (except by their practitioners), though they tended to be indulged in by those in literary and philosophical circles, including members of the Bloomsbury Group, Vita Sackville-West and Harold Nicolson, and Dora and Bertrand Russell.[600]

But for working-class women between the wars, the options were more limited due, no doubt, to their more confined horizons and to their assumptions being shaped by the less favourable economic and social environment that chance had thrown at them. Nonetheless, as Judy Giles explains, such women were able to adapt and transform the prevailing ideology of respectability in sexual affairs to their own experiences. Like the eighteenth and early nineteenth century pre-industrial sharecroppers, weavers and labourers whose struggles led to the 'making' of the English working class of the Industrial Revolution, such working-class women of the inter-war years 'made' their own 'sexual' class that did not necessarily conform to the hegemony of the respectable (whose male component may well have continued to uphold the double standard of the previous century; perhaps now even practising a triple standard by condemning immorality, which their nineteenth century predecessors might not have been expected to do, while simultaneously engaging in it).

So, given the above knowledge, can it still be claimed that Rouse's transgressive sexual intrigues outside marriage, both with the working-class Helen and Nellie and also with the lower middle-class Ivy (which in due course produced four illegitimate births and one miscarriage), did, indeed, shock suburban society? Was polite society not so used to witnessing such 'immoral' behaviour that the conduct in question soon lost its power to shock or to invite more than ritual condemnation from the usual social purity and women's institute suspects? Had society not yet reached a stage where, despite public utterances of disgust, the reality of non-marital or of extra-marital coupling, with its potential consequential results of adding to population statistics, was privately accepted as a permanent if

---

599 Jeffreys, *op. cit.* See also Holden, *op. cit.*
600 For examples, see Katie Roiphe, *Uncommon Arrangements: Seven Portraits of Married Life in London Literary Circles, 1910-1939*, Virago, London, 2008.

regrettable (for practical reasons) feature of life?

Indeed, for the earlier period of later Victorian London, Charles Booth had noted that, 'With the lowest classes premarital relations are very common, perhaps even usual....I believe it to constitute one of the clearest lines of demarcation between upper and lower in the working class', while the 'sexologist', Havelock Ellis, added that women in such communities recognised numerous advantages for themselves in such 'free sexual unions'.[601] In other words, courtship practices were perceived not through the prism of morality but through custom and culture. It is the perennial tension between dogma and relativism where social power to determine the terms of a particular agenda may not be evenly distributed throughout society or may shift over time. Thus church and state may exert little or no influence in local communities where more pragmatic and rational values may prevail.

The world of Rouse's women between the wars was certainly no Alsatia where the King's writ did not run. But it was a world where the injunction to female chastity, propounded by the influential institutions of the day, both formal and inchoate (such as 'family values'), clearly had a lesser impact on sexual behaviour than might be inferred from the constant rhetoric of respectability. Thus it is reasonable to believe that the findings and figures cited previously might suggest that the revelations regarding Helen Campbell's, Nellie Turner's and Ivy Jenkins' sexual experiences (let alone Rouse's) ought not to have been remarkably shocking so far as the general perception of such matters was concerned. For the proposition that society could be outraged by the disclosure of Rouse's promiscuity and of his string of 'conquests' has to be measured against what is known of prevailing sexual practice at the time. Nonetheless, while unmarried sexual practice was one thing, the *acknowledgement* by 'respectable' society (and by juries) that such conduct was, if not normative, then at least widespread, was another. And this is where the whiff of hypocrisy might be smelt if, as was probably the case, the jury might affect to be outraged by Rouse's sexual record while at the same time presumably scandalized by the very suggestion that they might have been swayed by it in reaching their guilty verdict.

It might be thought that in murder cases defendant women perceived as morally upright were more likely to obtain acquittals than those portrayed as promiscuous or unfaithful or, even worse, as 'vamps' preying on weaker, especially younger, males. The contrast would be with those women on whom damning moral judgments might not easily be divorced from legal judgments, including the obvious case of Edith Thompson (as above), but also embracing the later cases of Ruth Ellis and Charlotte Bryant, the last-named hanged in 1936 for poisoning her husband.[602] All these women were perceived as sexually promiscuous, lacking the 'essential' female qualities of reticence, devotion to children and duty, sexual fidelity to their lawful partners, compassion, contrition for their 'sins' and feminine weakness in the dock and witness box.

By contrast the portrayal of Mrs. Beatrice Pace in 1928 at her trial for the

601 See Weeks, *op. cit.*, p. 60, for these references.
602 For Bryant, see, for example, Anette Ballinger, *Dead Woman Walking: Executed Women in England and Wales, 1900-1955*, Ashgate, Aldershot, 2000, pp. 277-92. There are, of course, numerous accounts of the Ruth Ellis case, with differing perspectives advanced. Some references are given elsewhere in this work.

poisoning of her husband was one where the conscientious fulfilment of her maternal duties was emphasised whereas she was constantly 'put upon' by her ignorant brute of a husband in the rural community of the Forest of Dean.[603] Indeed even the exaggerated display of femininity when flaunted by the woman in the dock facing a murder charge would go some way to explaining the acquittal of Madame Marguerite Fahmy in 1923. Thus her fragile appearance and simpering manner, swoons and tears in the witness box may well have melted the hearts of the jury as they listened to her tales of woe at the hands of her allegedly brutalizing and sodomising oriental playboy husband in 1922. However, not a whiff was uttered in court regarding her former career as a high-class French prostitute who had also, as an unmarried 16-year old, given birth to a daughter before she embarked on a secretive love affair with the Prince of Wales (later Edward VIII) during the Great War.[604]

Yet that sexual promiscuity or 'waywardness' might not in all such cases condemn the accused woman to the death penalty can be shown by the example of the glamorous and strong Alma Rattenbury. For despite her portrayal as an older sexual 'vamp', she was nonetheless acquitted, unlike the confident Edith Thompson in *her* trial, of the murder of her ailing elderly husband, a distinguished retired Canadian architect, at the 'Villa Madeira' in Bournemouth in 1935. However Alma's young lover, the teenage George Stoner, *was* convicted although, unlike Edith's lover, Freddie Bywaters, was soon reprieved from the death penalty. Stoner had been hired by Alma the previous year as a chauffeur and handyman following her insertion of the notorious advert in the *Bournemouth Daily Echo* of September 25 1934, seeking 'Daily willing lad, 14-18, for housework. Scout-trained preferred'. Very soon they were lovers, but at their joint trial it is arguable that her devotion to her children (Edith had none) swayed the jury in her favour.[605]

A similar reassessment might have occurred in respect of the fortuitously acquitted Elvira Barney (see above) who initially would have appeared to trial spectators (and perhaps to the jury) as a thoroughly spoilt rich young woman of the post-'flapper' era. But once in the witness box she quickly comprehended the unattractiveness to the watching audience of her indulgent life-style. Now she came over as a restrained character, not given to over-emotional responses, and one who was perhaps to be pitied rather than condemned, and who had learned her lesson the hard way. So it was fortunate for her that Hastings' court room skills succeeded in imprinting this new version of Elvira Barney on the jury's mind, a portrayal that seemed to negate malicious intent and which, indeed, did result in her acquittal.[606]

---

603 John Carter Wood, 'The Most Remarkable Woman in England': Poison, Celebrity and the Trials of Beatrice Pace, Manchester University Press, Manchester, 2012. For sympathetic letters from the public to her, see esp. Ch. 9. Her portrayal in the press was, however, only a partial one, for there is some speculation, perhaps falling short of hard evidence, of her 'straying' before and during her marriage.

604 Anette Ballinger, "The Guilt of the Innocent and the Innocence of the Guilty: The Cases of Marie Fahmy and Ruth Ellis", in Alice Myers and Sarah Wight (eds.), No Angels: Women Who Commit Violence, Pandora Press, 1996, pp. 1-28; Andrew Rose, The Prince, the Princess and the Perfect Murder, Coronet, London, 2013.

605 For the Rattenbury case, see The Rt. Hon. The Lord Havers, Peter Shankland and Anthony Barrett, The Rattenbury Case, Penguin, 1989; J. D. Casswell, A Lance for Liberty, Harrap, 1961, pp. 99-118; Sir David Napley, Murder at the Villa Madeira, Souvenir Press, Weidenfeld and Nicolson, 1990; Terry Reksten, Rattenbury, 2nd ed., Sono Nis Press, Vancouver, Canada, 1998.

606 Cotes, op. cit; Sir Patrick Hastings, Cases in Court, Pan Books, 1953, pp. 202-13. Unaccountably,

In contrast, however (and as if to show the complexity and individuality of each case), for Ruth Ellis no such pleading could avail a working-class woman widely perceived as an artificially made-up peroxide blonde and tainted woman, who stepped out of her class to run drinking clubs for the middle- and upper classes late into the night. That she also apparently slept with customers, neglected her offspring, including one born to a married Canadian soldier when she was just 18, and refused to show either contrition for the death of her wealthy playboy lover, or any *lack* of intent to kill when she shot him five times outside the Magdala Arms in Hampstead in 1955, earned her no sympathy.[607]

Sexual waywardness on the part of female defendants facing a capital charge was no secure guide to the outcome of a trial as the Rattenbury and Barney trial outcomes showed. However, the idea of femininity itself, as embodying 'respectability' and restraint in regard to sexual behaviour, was secure on its pedestal.

By contrast, men's 'masculinity' could be ambiguous in public perception. On the one hand it might be perceived as a positive trait of the 'new man', fulfilling his responsibilities within the context of the mutually supportive and loving companionate marriage that had been firmly and socially established in a suburban setting in the inter-war years. But, on the other hand, there remained certain other expectations as to the meaning of masculinity and as to the boundaries of acceptable manhood, even where marriage had already intruded. For example, even by the 1930s expectations remained of young men 'sowing their oats' being viewed sympathetically, or even admiringly, while young women should preserve their virginity until marriage (a combination of factors not easy to square with one other). Thus adulterous men might not attract as much opprobrium as adulterous women in a working-class or lower middle-class environment (the double standard still proving resistant to eradication). In short, 'respectability' remained an elastic concept, no more so than in the white-collar milieu of the commercial traveller whose reputation went before him. For, as Dennis Potter in *Pennies from Heaven* cleverly reveals round the breakfast table of the bed and breakfast guest house, fellow commercial travellers (obviously also married) thought nothing of ribbing Arthur Parker about his and their sexual adventures encountered during their travels.[608] Yet their suburban domestic milieu would affect shock and horror at such behaviour while probably well aware (at least in more working-class environments) of sexual secrets and lies. Indeed, such hidden lives could possibly be even closer to them than they would care to confess to their priest. Thus sexual transgression may have been more pervasive in Britain before the Second World War than respectable society would be willing to recognise. Arthur Rouse may therefore have been iconic in this regard rather than a complete misfit. One of his tragedies was that no-one was prepared to attack respectable society's sexual hypocrisy (though Cecil Baines would attack the class hypocrisy of the criminal

no alternative charge of manslaughter was put forward by the Crown, though the judge, Travers Humphreys, directed the jury that such a verdict remained open to them. See Douglas G Browne, *Sir Travers Humphreys: A Biography*, Harrap, 1960, p. 296.

607 Ballinger, "Guilt of the Innocent....", *op. cit*; Carol Ann Lee, *A Fine Day for a Hanging: The Real Ruth Ellis Story*, Mainstream, Edinburgh, 2012. Sadly the Magdala Arms closed down in early 2016, no longer being an ideal place of pilgrimage for the thirst-driven morbid or curious.

608 Gerry R. Rubin, "Dennis, Alan and Arthur x 3: Literary Legacies of the 'Blazing Car Murder' of 1930, *Law and Humanities*, Vol. 9 (2), 2015, pp. 1-34.

justice system), no matter how adamant were the authorities regarding what happened in Hardingstone Lane.

Among Arthur Rouse's main challenges (and the crisis that eventually led to his violent demise) was to address his own masculinity and to reconcile his different social roles: as husband, suburbanite, a travelling salesman, a man constantly in debt but who has to keep up appearances and who has to be in two (or more) places at the same time, a lover of cars, a lover to three (or more) single young women, father of Arthur Jnr, and father to Nellie's little ones. In exploring the complex character of Arthur Rouse, we will hit upon what, fundamentally, brought about his undoing. For him there was indeed a crisis of masculinity. And in searching in the last chapter for the real Arthur Rouse, we will come face-to-face with the demons that eventually caught up with him.

CHAPTER TWENTY-ONE

ROUSE AND
3 WEEPING WOMEN

DAILY MAIL, February 2, 1931

His Women's Stories

Feminist historians have often complained that the record of women's voices in the past has been suppressed or 'hidden from history'.[609] Whether or not this was part of a male chauvinistic plot to silence the other sex, the voices of the women in Rouse's life did not remain silent after his conviction or, more especially, after his execution. For their stories found outlets in the popular press and periodicals. However, and it is an important caveat, we should not take what was written under their names as expressive of their own words to the journalists recording their stories. The likelihood is that their stories were 'ghosted', edited and improved by professional staff writers to match the latter's agenda for publication. One result is that the published accounts, no doubt to comply with and meet social convention and 'respectable' expectations at the time, still managed to project a female viewpoint that reflected a subordinate position of women (of that class) in inter-war society. Perhaps this is especially so in the case of Rouse's wife, Lily. For not only was the portrait of his long-suffering spouse, as depicted in the press throughout the legal ordeal, an unflattering one in the sense that she was invariably portrayed as a meek and loyal marriage partner who stuck to her man through thick and thin despite the appalling disregard and contempt for her that he evidently displayed in the ten years before his execution. But her own newspaper accounts of her life with Arthur did little to dispel that negative impression, or to suggest that she was now, after his death, sufficiently fired up and animated after her years of subordination to Arthur's selfish whims that no man whom she might encounter in the future (whether romantically or otherwise) would be able to exert such power over her.

Similarly, the images projected of Helen Campbell and Nellie Tucker in their own accounts were that they had been loyal partners to the love of their life and had cheerfully assumed the mantle of motherhood for him. Not for them was the role of teasing and exotic sexual playthings, an objectification that might otherwise be inferred from Rouse's notorious reference to his 'harem'. On the other hand

---

609 A pioneering example from the 1970s is Sheila Rowbotham, *Hidden from History*, Pluto Press, 1974.

Nellie's story, in particular, was balanced by the suggestion that in due course she became conscious of his shallowness of character, while Helen likewise homed in on his jealousy. In regard to Ivy Jenkins, however, what comes over is the voice of righteous contempt for a man who used and abused her and whose capacity to 'get away with it' for so long (leaving her to pick up the tab of shame) was an object lesson for gullible young single women everywhere.

One should not, therefore, hold one's breath in anticipation of a feminist critique by Lily, Helen, Nellie and Ivy of male sexual and social domination in the inter-war years. Feminism was surely an alien concept to those women. However, while the tone of Nellie and Helen's stories was moralistic and mildly minatory, and designed to draw in the reader to empathise with their plight, when they were left 'holding the baby', redemption was on the horizon as new beginnings beckoned or were hinted at for the 'wronged' women. The key word was resilience, a feature of their personality acquired in the wake of all the slings and arrows thrown at them by Fate. Indeed, a similar description of inner strength might also apply to the cultivation of Lily's image, as a counter-balance to the picture of a sad and grievously misled loving wife offering a tear-jerking account of their last endearing parting. Our point here is that the images that jump out from the printed page are simultaneously simple, yet they still manage to convey a nuanced, multi-faceted, even contradictory portrait. They are the product not so much of the inner thoughts of the women in question, but of the literary imagination of the journalists who knew their audiences. No doubt much of what was written under the names of Lily, Helen and Nellie *was* true, but much was invented or subtly re-ordered for public consumption. Whether the same is true regarding Ivy's angry outburst against profound immorality, a charge that was coupled with a more serious criminal accusation against Rouse (below) is more problematic. Her tone was consistently vicious and uncompromising, she was clearly of a much higher intellectual level than the others, and her account was not written for a popular young women's magazine.

In short one cannot avoid the strong suspicion that Lily, Helen and Nellie had little to do with drafting the final accounts that appeared under their names. They possibly OK'd the final galleys and may well have added some further detail to their stories than was already in the public record. When one digests those published accounts below, especially in relation to Lily's story, one must therefore remain conscious, first, of the subtle mix of truth and fiction woven through the wording, second, of the character of the target audience, as to which the journalists were the experts and, third, of the essentially non-radical viewpoints that the women espoused. That is not to say that they would not have railed at being described as part of his 'harem'. Indeed the invocation of the term 'harem' by a struggling commercial traveller from Friern Barnet tells us more about that particular Englishman's vanity and self-projection and about the disrespect for, and the image he conjured up of, his lovers than about any glamorous and *louche* life-style in which he might have hoped to indulge.

We have previously adverted to the views of his 'loved ones' as expressed in the period between his arrest and execution (though the term 'loved ones' was probably as phoney as was much of his life, notwithstanding that having latterly met Ivy Jenkins, he would protest that he had now found the love of his life). While his women's fearful pressing thoughts at this time might be revealed in their correspondence with Rouse, especially in respect of Helen Campbell, the passage of time after his execution might have allowed for deeper reflection on their part as they faced up to the prospect of recording their views for the newspaper and magazine reader. And while the actual financial details of what the press had paid for the 'women's stories' are not available, we can be sure that payment was indeed made. So it is clear that we must approach such accounts with caution, if not with deep scepticism, in the same manner in which Rouse's 'confessions' need to be treated. That being said, the women's accounts of life with and after Rouse do contain insights into what certain female audiences enjoyed reading about in 1931, that is, to obtain glimpses of what domestic life, marriage, affairs and children born out of wedlock meant to working-class and lower middle-class women in the later 1920s. In other words, the discourse was conservative and defensive and certainly not feminist. Instead, here were accounts of how difficult it was to ensure, without a man in the house even on an erratic basis, a proper upbringing for Rouse's children on the part of women who had been bewitched, bothered and bewildered by the swirl of events that had suddenly swept them from total anonymity to notoriety or, at least, to public notice.

The bulk of these accounts of Rouse's women appeared in a magazine, *Peg's Paper*. This was the first of the weekly pulp fiction magazines (commencing in 1919) which provided 'entertainment' for poor and working-class women. Its items were thus not specifically aimed, as did many magazines such as *Woman's Friend* (1924) and *Woman's Companion* (1927), at household style, tips and improvements. Its first editorial breathlessly exclaimed,

> It is going to be your weekly pal, girls. My name is Peg, and my one aim in life is to give you a really cheery paper like nothing you've ever read before. Not so very long ago, I was a mill-girl too. Because I've been a worker like you, I know what girls like, and I'm going to give you a paper you'll enjoy...Look upon me as a real friend and helper.

Here was a firm desire to strike a strong rapport with the working-class girl. It was an endeavour that apparently succeeded, given that it had one of the largest readerships among working-class women, a fact that no doubt justified the editorial decision to devote weeks of the paper to publishing the reflections of the *dramatis personae* in the Rouse affair. Indeed, *Peg's Paper*, unlike some of its rivals, continued to publish until the Second World War.[610]

As another writer has observed of the items published by *Peg's Paper*,

> Printed on the cheapest paper and melodramatically, if smudgily, illustrated, they contained lurid tales of love, crime and adventure.The word 'revenge' figures frequently in the titles of stories in *Peg's Paper* as do 'passion' and 'jealousy'. Readers of that paper could read 'A rich girl's revenge', 'Her mad jealousy', 'In passion's coils'.[611]

---

610   Cynthia L White, *Women's Magazines, 1693-1968*, Michael Joseph, London, 1970, pp. 97-8, 118.
611   Deirdre Beddoe, *Back to Home and Duty: Women Between the Wars, 1918-1939*, Pandora, 1989, pp. 15-16. In 1930 the magazine told working-class girls that the famous 'It-Girl', Clara Bow, went hatless in order to save on clothing expenditure. See *ibid.*, p. 22. Presumably they, of limited means, were encouraged to emulate her.

It also boasted, not an Agony Aunt column, but a 'Between Ourselves' column where correspondents could share confidences (with millions of other young female readers) on a 'best pals' basis. Dinah from Leeds, for example, was distressed that her boy friend suddenly dropped her for another girl. What should she do? To this Peg replied that she should not 'cheapen' herself by clinging to him and trying to drag him back. 'Pansy Eyes' from Southampton (the geographical spread was clearly wide, assuming for the moment that the letters were genuine) was concerned that her boy friend might be showing more interest in her female pal who, at 'Pansy Eyes" invitation, had accompanied the couple on outings since she had no other friends. Finally, 'Blonde' from Eastbourne asked Peg 'rather a difficult question which I cannot well answer here'. Instead she was advised to consult a doctor, though 'I do not think you have need to worry', Peg added.[612]

So what are we expecting to discover about Rouse and about Lily, Nellie and Helen from these *Peg's Paper* reminiscences by his 'women'?[613] Are they savage in their indictment of a two-timing cad? Are they full of self-pity? Do they show compassionate feelings about the now-executed Rouse? Do they continue to express passionate love, devotion and forgiveness towards him? Do Campbell and Tucker fret about their offspring that were a result of their coupling with Rouse? More broadly, do they confirm or refute what we already know about love, sex, marriage and adultery within the working-class and the lower middle-class in the inter-war years? For it may be recalled from the previous chapter that subsequent questionnaire surveys strongly suggested that sexuality and sexual practices in the inter-war years did not conform to the presumed image of 'respectability', of sexual restraint, and of girls consciously and conscientiously 'saving themselves' for marriage to their ideal husbands. Thus the widespread practice of non-marital and pre-marital sex, particularly among the upper class and the working class, and despite moralising lectures from the church, the medical profession, and 'family purity' organisations, is now widely recognised to have occurred. Expressions of shock and shame might abound in the wake of the revelations of how Rouse 'took advantage' of young women such as Helen, Nellie and Ivy. It is interesting, therefore, to consider the extent to which the 'objects' of Rouse's 'conquests' spoke this language of shame and of victimhood at the hands of a scheming and older Lothario, even if they did not express more 'advanced' views as autonomous subjects, not objects. We shall start with Lily's story, bearing in mind the need to 'read' her (and the others') account with a critical eye.

Lily's Story

Lily had already published three articles for the *Daily Express* which appeared on consecutive days between March 11, the day after Rouse's execution, and March 13, 1931. According to the newspaper they were based on her diary entries recounting her visits from February 10 to see her husband in Bedford Gaol. The diary, readers were told, '...gives in simple language a vivid insight into

---

612   *Peg's Paper*, June 30, 1931. A final inquiry from 'Maureen' in Knaresborough wanted to know what it meant to dream of seeing fire. The reply was that it usually indicated sudden good news, but it occasionally meant a serious quarrel. See *ibid*. At least there is a good 150 miles from Hardingstone to Knaresborough!
613   Ivy published her 'story' only in *Thomson's Weekly News*, while Lily also wrote for the *Daily Express* as well as in *Peg's Paper*. See *infra*.

the humdrum life which a condemned man leads, hoping against hope that he will be spared from the scaffold'. Actually (and it could scarcely be Lily's fault), the one thing that her accounts lacked was, indeed, a sense of vividness. For 'the humdrum' routine imposed on her husband for the most part characterised her descriptions of her visits. There were the little jokes exchanged; the remarks on how his suit now hung down from his body; the quality of the prison fare; his exercise regime in the snow; the board games he played with his jailers; Sir Malcolm Campbell's *Bluebird* reaching 245 mph; the re-opening of the White City; a recent tennis tournament in the French Riviera ('Who won the mixed doubles?', asked Rouse).

More sensitive matters were also broached, such as the friends he had not heard from, the letter that she (Lily) had received from Helen, and the well-being of Arthur Jnr. Lily wrote of her pleasure that Rouse had received a photograph of the boy. For, 'At a time like this,' she added honourably, 'one cannot bear malice about such a trifle, because I loved the little chap when I had him with me. They are all God's children.' He told her that he had not been visited by 'N.T.' but Lily would not have minded had Nellie turned up since she (Lily) was interested in how Nellie and her children were faring. Not one to bear a grudge, especially against the innocent, then. Yet there were times when she was aware that she had exhausted her store of conversation. Nonetheless, the diary entry recorded that the prospect of the forthcoming appeal on February 23 had encouraged the couple, especially Rouse. For the latter now set about putting together the technical evidence of those motor engineers who disputed Colonel Buckle's accusation, given at the trial, that Rouse had deliberately loosened the petrol union nut. But the optimism soon dissipated and she wrote of her emotional desolation following Hewart's contemptuous dismissal of the appeal, together with her sudden realisation that the appeal was over almost before it had begun.

While her tearful collapse at court was publicly observed, she invariably sought to maintain a stiff upper lip and to confine her tears to her private moments. For example, she maintained a pleasant demeanour when seeing Rouse's solicitor, Lee-Roberts. Thus he asked her what she thought of the people of Bedford (they were 'fairly decent to me with regard to 'not staring', as they did in other places I had been in'). There were, however, other occasions when emotions spilled into the open, such as on February 16 when the couple apparently had an argument and Lily broke down. It probably related to Ivy Jenkins who, in the same month, was serialising in four episodes in *Thomson's Weekly News* her own story entitled 'My Life as Rouse's Secret 'Wife'' (which we will examine later). Apparently, and probably unaware of Ivy's publishing plans, Rouse had been conducting an exchange of letters (presumably with Ivy or her sister), against which Lily had warned him. Then the correspondence was revealed in the press, to the anguish of both. However, the incident quickly blew over as (in this case literally) she and Rouse obviously felt that life was too short.

It was especially stressful for her on her visit to the prison after the unsuccessful appeal. The prison staff had told her that Rouse, further encumbered with his heavy cold, was feeling particularly depressed, so they hoped that she would make him smile. 'What a joke,' I said to myself. 'I am not supposed to be needing courage.' Yet the following day he appeared much better as she encouraged him to be more cheerful in view of the emerging campaign for signatures supporting a reprieve. Yet on her visit on March 3, a week before his execution, he seemed unimpressed with her news that 5,000 signatures had already been obtained. Perhaps he knew that almost a million people had signed the petition to reprieve Bywaters in early 1923, and that that had not saved Edith Thompson's young lover. Indeed, Lily told her readers that Rouse had suffered 'terrible distress' when news of the Home Secretary's refusal to interfere was received on March 7, the same day he was also visited by both Helen and Nellie. Lily, herself, was heartbroken. The last diary entries were, naturally, poignant (though they could hardly be described as vivid). Little could be said between the pair. News of Helen Campbell's arrival was then received but Rouse insisted that Lily should be the last of his women to see him, so she went to the chaplain's office for twenty minutes until Helen departed.

> Then I was taken back. He asked me to take my hat off so that he could see my hair. He said I looked wonderful. I have never seen him looking so handsome. I did not know what to do....and at the end I had to say good-bye. I cannot write any more.[614]

Let us assume that this exchange did occur and was not mere journalistic 'puff'. Was his compliment regarding Lily just another of his lies? Alternatively, did he always genuinely feel this emotional attachment to Lily? Or, third, was he sincere at that parting moment? The answer is probably yes to the third question. However the nagging suspicion remains that his sincerity was only because one usually does not know what one values and appreciates until one loses it.

It is difficult to view the above articles by Lily as other than a confirmation of her deep loyalty to her husband and of her belief in his innocence. That he had betrayed her was never made explicit, but the regular references to Helen, Nellie and Arthur Jnr. cannot surely be read as unproblematic for her. Thus one cannot help thinking either that she was an angel or else that through gritted teeth she must bear the emotional burden of cooperating with his mistresses if that was the price to pay in a last-ditch effort to save his life. Her sense of victimhood was, indeed, confined to her own sadness at the impending violent termination of their marriage. That Lily, a childless wife, was the real victim of his egregious affairs, she probably quietly ignored. In any case she was scarcely the strong woman, though she was clearly resilient in her own way. Perhaps her newspaper articles demonstrated this very quality. And that she undoubtedly received payment for them in no way diminishes, perhaps it even enhances, this attribute.[615]

Indeed the instalments in the *Daily Express* were not the only extended accounts of Lily's tortuous last few years with Rouse. She also contributed a series of articles about her marriage to the popular young women's magazine, *Peg's*

---

614 *Daily Express*, March 13, 1931.
615 How inter-war feminists might have viewed Lily's plight can only be a matter for speculation. Certainly those like Cicely Hamilton before the Great War, who perceived 'marriage as a trade', that is, a relationship that reduced married women to the status of men's property (thereby discounting limited legal improvements in the status of married women since the 1880s), might have had their views vindicated. See Cicely Hamilton (introduction by Jane Lewis), *Marriage as a Trade*, Women's Press, 1981, first published in 1909. The literature on the status of women in the inter-war period is vast. For examples see Pamela Horn, *Women in the 1920s*, Amberley, Stroud, 2010; Elizabeth Roberts, *A Woman's Place: An Oral History of Working-Class Women, 1890-1940*, Blackwell, Oxford, 1985; Jane Lewis, *Women in England, 1870-1950*, Wheatsheaf, Brighton, 1984.

Paper, over the course of April 1931. The first article appeared on April 7, three weeks after Rouse's execution, and at a time when the events were still bound to be extremely raw. Yet while the tone might be said to have been set by the same headline accompanying each episode, which declared 'How I Found Out and Why I Forgave', what is immediately apparent assuming once again the genuineness of its authorship, is the greater sense of brutal candour, though not extending to feistiness, with which Lily's position was explained.

> I have been described as the most talked of woman in the country. I sometimes feel as if I could describe myself as the most unhappy woman in the world. Have you ever wondered, you women who live in security, what you would feel like if the eyes of the world suddenly turned on you? And if they saw you as a dupe, as someone living in a fool's paradise, a deceived and deserted wife who thought she was happily married all the time?"[616]

Yet, surely pathetically (or inevitably?), she still loved her husband, 'as we have all loved him, myself and....the others.' As she sought to explain, 'He has the gift for keeping women's affection'. Undoubtedly he had, and the target readership of *Peg's Paper* probably had more empathy with the defensive sentiments expressed by this cheated wife than with the harsh judgments of the hardened unforgiving woman of strength and independence. For the young female reader of the magazine was surely of the type who still ached for a love story, albeit that in this instance the complex romance was heavily compromised. It does, indeed, beggar belief that Lily protested that Rouse was 'in many ways the perfect husband' who was kind and considerate 'to a degree'. Indeed Rouse 'was regarded by my married friends as all that their own husbands failed to be in the way of matrimonial courtesy and thoughtfulness'. She recalled the 'many small sacrifices' he had made before the war to provide her with a home and garden where she could plant penny packets of seeds and make a rockery. Here was a (now post-war) image of suburban domestic bliss for which the young readers of *Peg's Paper* would plan once they had met Mr. Right. And, Lily seemed to imply, he could well be someone like Rouse Mark I. For her husband, she wrote, was certainly no 'heartless seducer'. Maybe out of loyalty she took exception to the adjectives that others might have used in describing her husband. Perhaps the most poignant illustration of her delusions regarding her husband was that she was not ashamed to tell her readers that Rouse had 'bestowed upon me the absurd title of 'Toffee-Nose" which was the insulting term Rouse had used to describe her (as his aunt) to Helen.[617]

Somehow, the article continued, it was just his handsome face, 'devastating attraction', and charming manner that had induced other women to fall in love with him, even in Lily's presence, and without any encouragement on his part. So that was all right, then. Arthur was not at fault. Or so she convinced herself. And, in any case, the war had changed him mentally, she concluded. So, once again, he could not be to blame, so far as she was concerned. Moreover, his travelling job did lead to further enticements for which, naturally, he could not be blamed.

---

616 *Peg's Paper*, April 7, 1931.
617 In his book Cannell had actually cited the phrase 'Old Toffy Face'. See J. C. Cannell, *New Light on the Rouse Case*, John Long, c.1931, p. 33.

After all, the majority of men were not faithful to their wives 'in thought and action' and temptation was often put in his way. So when Helen Campbell's first baby was born, and a letter arrived at the Rouse home addressed to 'Miss Helen Campbell Rouse' regarding a position for Helen, was Lily's faith in his innocence now shattered? Were the 'early days of love and real comradeship' now gone and every memory poisoned, as she feared? Confronted, Arthur sobbed bitterly and, so the account continued, Lily walked out of the house, trudging alone with her thoughts and anguish through the wind and rain. On her return, however, Arthur's practised lies persuaded her that the baby was not his, but that of a male friend. He, Rouse, had just wanted to help Helen. And it was this good intention that, he insisted, had explained the name on the letter that had arrived. It is, indeed, difficult to know if Lily could have been that naive, or whether she simply allowed the copywriter free rein at this point.

But despite his denial of paternity (which denial *does* sound like Rouse), it was apparent to Lily that Rouse had been unfaithful with Helen. He had probably boasted having had sex with the young girl though Lily refrained from actually stating that he had explicitly made such a confession. Indeed, numbed by the shocking revelations, and having, she wrote, uttered threats of suicide, she 'could not look upon him as my husband', though his subsequent efforts to be 'penitent' and to make her happy did cause her to forget the business on occasions. During those times, of course, he was getting deeper and deeper into his relationship with Helen, a complex liaison that Lily eventually learned about in 1928.

On its disclosure Lily alleged that Rouse had threatened to leave. But if made at all, it was a threat that we should take with a huge pinch of salt, given that, apart from financial troubles, Rouse was sitting pretty with mistresses here and there, and 'owned' a not undesirable suburban semi-detached property. The truth was that Lily 'could not let him go: I felt I would rather have him unfaithful, faulty--anything rather than lose him. Many unfortunate wives have made the same decision'. *This* was probably the genuine voice of Lily Rouse, not the cringe-worthy protestations of how wonderful and thoughtful a husband he had been. Married women were often tightly locked into an unsatisfactory marital relationship from which it was extraordinarily difficult to extricate themselves. The shame of separation, let alone of divorce (and the requirement, admittedly not too difficult in this case, to establish grounds, even after some relaxation of the law in 1923), the costs involved, the loss of a 'breadwinner', all militated against divorce *a vinculo matrimonii*. And if children were involved (as they obviously were not, in respect of Arthur and Lily), the practical difficulties were multiplied for those other than the upper classes.[618] As one study of inter-war working-class marriage points out,

Flushing out the character and complexities of husband-wife relations remains a difficult task....[thereby] challenging easy assumptions about

618 For divorce law controversies in the 1920s, see D. M. Stetson, *A Woman's Issue: The Politics of Family Law Reform in England*, Greenwood Press, New York, 1982; Gail Savage, "'The Magistrates Are Men': Working-Class Marital Conflict and Appeals from the Magistrates' Court to the Divorce Court after 1895", in George Robb and Nancy Erber (eds), *Disorder in Court: Trials and Sexual Conflict at the Turn of the Century*, Macmillan, 1999, Ch. 2; George Behlmer, "'A Whiff of Stale Debauch': Summary Justice and Working-Class Marriage in England, 1870-1940", *Law and History Review*, Vol. 12, 1994, pp. 229-75.

intimacy, partnership and adult heterosexual commitments. The absence of marital violence, for instance, does not mean that there were no profound tensions; nor does its presence mean that a relationship was in danger of collapsing.[619]

The Rouse marriage was, of course, a lower middle-class one, but the issues raised above may be applicable, to a greater or lesser degree, across most classes. In particular, 'flushing out the character and complexities' of the Rouse relationship must be at least as challenging as in the working-class marriages discussed by the above authors. While we might consider Lily to be either delusional or saintly in regard to Rouse's behaviour, it is apparent that the revelations of his 'true' character prompted her to search for a coping strategy which kept her within her own comfort zone, stressful though it undoubtedly was. And perhaps one should not be judgmental about her responses to Rouse's parallel lives. For Lily was in a better position than anyone else to make a decision regarding her marriage. Anyway, as her article affirmed with determination, 'He was my husband. Why should I allow another woman to steal him from me?' But this hardly addressed the real problem, which was Arthur, not 'another woman'. Indeed, in a defensive concession, she did recognise that 'a marriage ceremony does not bind a man to a woman for life'. So she made the various pathetic allowances for Arthur's behaviour that were noted above. Indeed, she had anticipated middle age (with Rouse) not as a tragedy but as a haven and harbour, and a time when men 'settle[d] down to find pleasure in the companionship of the dull wife they have not appreciated for years', while the 'women grew more philosophical with every wrinkle' (though Lily as philosopher may be too much of a stretch). Moreover, she insisted that she was 'not wrong in refusing later to have children [with Rouse] with illegitimate half-brothers'. This speaks more generally, of course, to the popular stigma attached to the status of illegitimacy between the wars, which we will consider later in this chapter in respect of Helen and Nellie's children.

Why Lily also recounted Rouse's frankly provocative action, around 1928, in putting a sketch of Nellie's baby, Pamelita (as she later discovered), on the piano alongside other family photographs, including that of Arthur Jnr., is puzzling (or maybe the journalists added it for dramatic effect?). Incredibly, he even apparently told her he did not know whose baby it was and believed that a nun had drawn it. There is, indeed, a hint of masochism in Lily's story expounding and, in some respects, excusing her husband's extra-marital frolics and their consequences. However the reader was expected to 'feel her pain' when, about to attend the second house alone at the Wood Green Empire (since Arthur was 'busy' that day), she actually came face-to-face with Arthur as he and Nellie were leaving the first house performance of 'Murder on the Second Floor'.[620] She stared

619 Pat Ayers and Jan Lambertz, "Marriage Relations, Money and Domestic Violence in Working-Class Liverpool, 1919-39", in Jane Lewis (ed.), *Labour and Love: Women's Experience of Home and Family, 1850-1940*, Blackwell, Oxford, 1986, pp. 195-216, at p. 195.

620 *Murder on the Second Floor*, where a novelist imagines the murder of fellow tenants in his boarding house, was written by the British actor and playwright, Frank Vosper, in 1929, and made into a film in 1932 directed by William McGann and starring John Longden (Vosper also wrote the play, *People Like Us*, based on the Thompson-Bywaters case. It had been banned in 1929 by the Lord Chamberlain after a performance starring Atholl Fleming at the Strand Theatre, but was revived at Wyndham's Theatre in 1948, starring Miles Malleson and Robert Flemyng). *Murder on the Second Floor* was one of the plays put on for the local population by Alien Pioneer Corps companies

him in the face, he carried on walking out with Nellie before turning back to grasp Lily's arm. 'Come along and be introduced, dear,' he said brazenly (the seeming domestic calm of the previous two years as his relationship with Helen died away was obviously now rent asunder). Her self-respect naturally would not permit such an introduction, so she continued into the auditorium but cried throughout the performance, oblivious to the plot and tormented by the sight of the happy couples round about her. This does, at least, sound like genuine turmoil.

But the next stage was predictable. Arthur was waiting for her in the foyer after the show to drive her home (as he earlier promised he would do). '"No, Arthur, I'm through. I cannot stand it any longer,' I cried. 'His smiling face, his utter indifference to my pain, the absence of any apology—all made me feel that I never wanted to see him again. Yet....again he triumphed.'" Her resolution to leave him had failed and they drove home together where a 'terrible scene' then ensued. She could never live with him again under those conditions. Arthur did promise to explain the next day. 'But I [still] went to bed a defeated woman.' Unsurprisingly, he did not explain on the following day, and the story of Nellie and Pamelita was only drawn from him some days later. And if Lily chose to make an issue of it, then he would simply move out to live with Nellie, his relationship with Helen, he told Lily, having previously ended.

Yet she still continued to live in the marital home at 14 Buxted Road at this time. In practice, for a wife in her situation, an alternative was impracticable unless she could find employment, as she later did in Bedford in order to make her prison visits easier (the Friern Barnet house and contents would have to be sold to pay the legal bills). But under the blanket of hatred that she felt for him probably lay the intense love of a wife for whom the marriage ceremony was sacred in reflecting an indissoluble bond of emotional commitment (obviously only on one side, in this case). 'It colours one's whole life, it is sewn into every stitch, it helps to dust the parlour, to baste the Sunday joint.' Perhaps the feminist of the day would say that such an appeal was fine if the 'one' to which reference was made was female *or* male.

Like Britain at war they continued to 'muddle through', the arrival of Arthur Jnr. and her generous reception to him, after initial resentment, offering Lily a diversion from her dark thoughts. And, she admitted, it might mean that Arthur (Snr.) might be at home more often. So no more quarrels.....until, that is, the photograph of Ivy Jenkins was found by Lily in his jacket pocket some two months later. It was *déjà vu*, with further accusations arrowed at him, pleas from her that he should honour his previous promises of fidelity, and more bluster from Arthur. '[T]he girl was nothing to him and I need not bother my head about the photograph.' So, on this deceptively positive note she made her Christmas plans towards the end of 1930 to decorate the house and buy presents for Rouse and Arthur Jnr. before the latter was due to be handed back to his mother. It was, according to Lily, a transfer insisted upon by Rouse, and to the disappointment of Lily, after Helen had met her to complain that Lily had registered the boy at school as her own, and not as

at No. 3 Training Centre, Ilfracombe, from 1940. The British Army companies were composed of (in British legal eyes) enemy aliens, mostly German and Austrian Jews who had fled the Nazis. The latter had stripped Jews of their nationality. Coco the Clown (Nicolai Poliakoff) was one of the artistic organisers. See Helen Fry, *The King's Most Loyal Enemy Aliens: Germans Who Fought for Britain in the Second World War*, Sutton Publishing, Stroud, 2007, p. 15.

Helen's, child. This followed the two women's clash over who actually possessed the valid certificate of marriage to Rouse.

The closing passages of Lily's 'story', involving difficult coach trips to and from Northampton, certainly piled on the emotional syrup, a style surely designed to prompt her readers to visualise themselves making the same stressful journeys. 'Then the blow fell', the account commenced, as soon as the policeman, with tears in his eyes (for he knew the Rouses) called on November 6 with news of the Hardingstone Lane blaze, of the body recovered from the scene, and of the request that Lily should travel to Northampton for identification purposes. A roller-coaster of emotions on Lily's part then burst forth. First she learned of his death. Then she experienced joy unconfined at hearing that he had been 'found', as shouted out by the Northampton newsboy as she made her way to the police station (which did not exactly tally with the earlier account in p. 9). And finally there was the shock on being told that her husband was now being detained at Northampton police station. 'I will not dwell on the closing scene of that dramatic meeting. I kissed him fondly when I left—the last kiss I was allowed to give him before the hard machinery of the law was put in motion', after which such intimacies were to be no more. For Lily a difficult and tortuous coach trip back to London 'wound its way through dark lanes and wind-swept roads'. Indeed the protracted journey no doubt increased her anguish mirroring, perhaps, the long trip back from Cardiff to Hammersmith Bridge endured by her husband some time previously. Whether it was her intention that one should feel sympathy towards Rouse or only towards Lily may not have been spelled out. But the notion of that last kiss, of Rabbie Burns' 'Ae fond kiss and then we sever!' was a sentimental touch in her narrative, undoubtedly appealing to her younger romantic readers, irrespective of whether it ever occurred (it probably did).

The final part of Lily's story to appear in *Peg's Paper* recounted her agonising trip back to London when she felt that she 'hated' her fellow-coach passengers and harboured her own death wish.[621] But she knew that, while in a state of semi-collapse as the coach arrived at its destination, she was being unkind to those who would undoubtedly have rallied round had she in fact fainted during that awful journey. She avoided Friern Barnet for the next few days, choosing to stay with friends in between her trips to Northampton. At length returning to Buxted Road she found, among the pile of letters and bills on the mat, a short note from Helen Campbell sympathising with her situation. It moved her, she wrote, to express forgiveness towards Helen.

On her next visit to prison she observed a definite deterioration in Arthur's appearance and demeanour, which made more urgent the need to raise money to conduct a proper defence. Buxted Road and its contents, many of them of sentimental value, were auctioned off, raising less money than was hoped, while Lily herself obtained a job as an assistant in a draper's shop near the police court in Northampton, and stayed in a rented single room in the town. While she and not Arthur thus became the curio and the object of attention, that itself did not upset her, though there were a few who caused her great pain and suffering. At the police court she was able to sit close to him in the dock and to reach over and squeeze his hand occasionally. She even rushed out to buy aspirin when she thought he looked so ill that he might faint. The magistrates' clerk did, of course,

621 *Peg's Paper*, April 28, 1931.

have to check the pills, even if the memory of Whitaker Wright's suicide in the dock (chapter 8) was too distant. In any case the idea that Lily would give poison to a husband whom she knew to be innocent was absurd. She wondered, the narrative continued, about what Helen, Nellie and Ivy were thinking about Arthur, the man who had ruined their lives. Indeed, what were they themselves thinking about the fourth wronged woman, Lily herself? But choosing not to answer those questions, she instead wound up her story by describing the scene at the assizes where hope would vie with despair for dominance. She wrote no more (or no more was written under her name). It was as if she had exhausted herself. And given that she had already published in the *Daily Express* (above) the details of her last visits to Arthur before his execution, she probably had.

Her story was a curious mix of indignation at her husband's continued infidelity until his arrest brought it to a halt; disdain, if not hostility, towards his lovers, albeit tempered by a recognition that they themselves were for the most part victims and, for most of the time, unaware of his lies, deceptions and deviousness; a sense of victimhood herself; and, on the other hand, a spirited determination not only to shield him from the rancour of society but to defend him, and to make sacrifices on his behalf, as a wife should. It was a complicated and cleverly crafted story, full of conflicting sentiments, justifications and recriminations. In the end does she come over more pathetic than noble, or vice-versa? It is a difficult call.

Helen Campbell

In seven episodes from June 9 to July 21, 1931, Helen Campbell 'revealed' her 'life story' to the readers of *Peg's Paper*. It was prefaced by the magazine's own introduction which referred to the now-executed Rouse as having been the 'possessor of a fascinating personality [who] proved an irresistible lover to other girls besides his wife'. It reminded its readers that not only Helen but also Nellie and Lily were distraught when the death sentence was passed on Arthur while, it added ambiguously, Rouse's fourth young 'wife', Ivy, 'lay prostrate in bed' in Wales. Helen would explain to her readers that from the time when she fell 'victim' to her seduction by Rouse at the age of 15 until the present day, twelve years after, she still loved him, and would expect to continue to do so for the rest of her life. The strange combination of victim and lover was scarcely in the Stockholm syndrome league. However it does speak to considerable reserves of loyalty (whether laudable or pathetic) on her part, given that in the year leading up to the Hardingstone incident the couple had effectively been living separate lives, but more especially in light of the discoveries she would make in due course regarding the existence of Lily, Nellie, Ivy and, indeed, of numerous other un-named girls.

She defended her position vis-a-vis Rouse by setting aside his negative character in order to highlight his perceived good qualities, that is, 'the kind and gentle lover and husband, and devoted father to our little son, whom he idolised' (and whose photograph appeared in the magazine alongside Helen on numerous occasions). In her column she expressed pity for him rather than any bitterness at having been betrayed by him. Indeed he represented the happiest years of her life. Yet from the outset when he and Lily, whom she presumed to be brother and sister, would visit her employers on a social call (Helen was employed as a live-in domestic servant), she acknowledged not just Rouse's charm but his conceit, his vanity and pride in his appearance. As a naive 15 year-old she was not dissuaded, however, from accepting an invitation from him, on one occasion when the Rouses were visiting, for a surreptitious half-hour ride in his car, just the two of them, when he assured her that they would not be missed. How was she to know the true relationship between him and Lily at the time? The details of that first outing, and of the numerous subsequent trysts in his car, were coyly hidden behind a screen of (inferred mutual and rapturous) love and manly gentleness. Even her first pregnancy, during which period she became 17 (she said), did not horrify her, fortified as she was by Arthur's vague hints of marriage which, he nonetheless affected to regret, might be difficult to arrange in the short term (no doubt he alluded principally to financial obstacles). Once more there was presented a sweet and sour account of their relationship, of both his betrayal of her youthful trust, and of his irresistible appeal. Was Helen herself capable of writing with such ambiguity?

The narrative went on to explain how her confinement in 'one of those nursing homes where unfortunate girls are cared for and tended in similar circumstances' necessitated her not disclosing the father's name since, as she was not yet seventeen when she had become pregnant, such disclosure could get Rouse into 'serious trouble'. In fact she was mistaken on this point of law, for under the Criminal Law Amendment Act 1922, section 1, which was in force at the time, it was a 'child' *under* 16 who could not give consent to sexual intercourse (although if the prisoner charged with unlawful carnal knowledge of a girl between the ages of 13 and 16 was himself aged 23 or under, he could argue that he had reasonable cause to believe she was 16 or over, a qualification not applicable to the then 26-year old Rouse). So if she were 'not yet seventeen', we may reasonably infer that she was suggesting that she was already sixteen when made pregnant by Rouse; which would not be a breach on his part of the 1922 statute.

But the picture was a tad more confused. First, in her *Peg's Paper* column, it was stated that Helen had been fifteen when she and Rouse had first met. While this does not, per se, imply sexual intercourse had taken place before her sixteenth birthday, our instincts tell us something different. She also referred to love letters passing between them which dated from 1919. So how old *was* she, either in 1919, or when they first had sexual relations, or when she became pregnant with her first child? This seems to be shrouded in mystery. Contemporary reports during Rouse's trial suggested that she was about 27 by then (and therefore born around 1904), but on her sham marriage certificate to Rouse in 1924 her age was stated to be 24 (making her birth year about 1900). According to Normanton, however,

> In 1920 a fourteen-year-old Edinburgh girl named Helen Campbell had become a member of a household where Rouse was a frequent visitor, and by the time the girl was fifteen she had borne a child to him in a home for unmarried mothers. That child was born on 21st October 1921, but unfortunately died when only five weeks old....[622]

---

622 Helena Normanton (ed.), *Trial of Alfred Arthur Rouse*, William Hodge & Son, Edinburgh, p. viii. Yet even this passage may be inaccurate for, in a letter from Helen to Rouse while he was awaiting execution, she referred to 'those old love letters of 1919' that the couple had previously exchanged. See *Peg's Paper*, July 7, 1931.

This would suggest that Helen had been born around 1906 (Arthur Jnr's birth certificate of 1925 does not state her age). That year, indeed, seems to be confirmed by her own magazine account where she stated that she had been fifteen when she and Rouse had met and that given the baby's birth in October 1921, she and Rouse would have first engaged in sexual intercourse in January 1921 when she was almost certainly still fifteen and he was nearly 27. Indeed the journalist, J. C. Cannell, also stated that, 'Helen Campbell first met Rouse when she was a mere child; she was only 14, and before she was 16 she was a mother of a child by Rouse'.[623] Rouse would therefore have been liable for prosecution under the 1922 Act (a provision which remained in similar form until 2003). Consequently, Helen's fiddling of the dates is understandable if the aim was not to blacken Rouse's record further, or even if it were to imply that moral disapprobation of Helen herself might be less where her sexual experience had commenced at the age of 15 rather than at 14. She took pains to point out how solicitous Rouse was to her during this period, smuggling in love letters to her in the unmarried mothers' home (for his identity could not be revealed to the matron lest he be pursued to pay the costs of Helen's confinement). And following the death of little Iris after five weeks (it seems that the foster-carer neglected to provide adequate care to the baby as Helen returned to work after the birth), she wrote that Rouse never forgot to bring her a bunch of irises on the sad anniversary each year, nor failed to buy tickets for dances (though he himself did not dance) held in aid of the hospital which had tried valiantly to save her infant in 1921.

The article stated that she was extremely satisfied by his ready supply of 'real love letters' sent to her when he was on the road, by his little gifts of flowers, cigarettes or even a bottle of wine on his return to 'our little home' (which at one point was a rather dingy flat in Liverpool Road, Islington, before she later moved to Lewisham), and by the care and attention that she claimed he lavished on her. Indeed, according to this version, she had no complaints at all about his conduct towards her. While they remained 'unmarried' for about four years, which did not distress her because they were 'in love', the subsequent 'marriage' at St Mary's Church, Islington, in 1924 left her overjoyed and buoyed with the prospect of presenting Arthur with a son.

Her chance discovery of letters from Lily to Arthur did little, it was stated, to extinguish her love for him once he had convinced her that Lily, explained away as an acquaintance and not as his wife, meant nothing to him. His indulging Arthur Jnr. in toys and treats also undoubtedly reassured Helen of Rouse's devotion to this small family group. But even her subsequent realisation of his intrigues with other women appeared to prompt no bitterness against him. It was his war injuries, you see. And even their parting, when Rouse, unable to increase maintenance payments for Arthur Jnr., could not stomach the idea of Helen pursuing a business partnership with another man to run a restaurant, a venture that soon failed, was explained in terms of his vaunted vanity rather than in terms of selfishness or callousness. So, she implied, he remained basically good, not basically bad, while all the time (though not to her knowledge) he was carrying on with other women such as Nellie Tucker. But it was plainly not his fault, but the war's, or so she (or her ghost writer) reasoned.

623 Cannell, *op. cit.*, p. 96.

Indeed his good-hearted nature was reaffirmed for Helen when, around June 1929, she persuaded him to take Arthur Jnr. into his and Lily's home at Buxted Road while she (Helen) took a job as a demonstrator of vacuum cleaners at a coastal venue (perhaps it was in Chatham where she later stayed for some time after the furore of November 1930 had erupted). Such a commitment by Rouse was surely evidence of his wonderful nature, Helen appeared to reason. Yet her handing over of 'Sonny' was portrayed as the saddest day of her life. The maternal trope was strongly emphasised and *Peg's Paper*'s readers' heart strings were to be pulled as tightly as they would go. 'Then I returned to my lodgings, flung myself down on the bed, and wept as I have only wept once before or since that sad parting'. It was a scene that could have been lifted from the silent movies.

It was about six weeks before the Hardingstone incident that Helen discovered, during an altercation with Lily over a schooling matter, as noted earlier, that Rouse had been deceiving her for all those years regarding his relationship to Lily. Obviously emotionally shattered by the revelation, nonetheless, true to form Helen rationalised Rouse's lies and deceptions as an effort on her part to lessen the hurt he was causing her during his double or triple life. Indeed, according to the magazine's narrative, though it appears to conflict with other accounts, she held back from waving her own 'marriage' lines at Lily on the ground that had she done so not only would such behaviour harm the man she loved but also because Lily herself was a fellow-victim. In short, whatever anguish Rouse had caused to her and Lily, the roads he had travelled (literally, in his case) were still paved with good intentions.

It was only when the newspaper headlines during the trial screamed 'ROUSE AND HIS HAREM' that Helen's sense of shame was laced with bitterness. For this was the 'cruellest blow of all'. Or so it seemed for, true to form, 'the spasm of anger passed, and once again I knew that I would do anything to save Arthur from peril.' Here was another dollop of betrayal, redemption and reconciliation ladled on to excess. Helen's desperate endeavour to obtain signatures to the petition for a reprieve for Rouse has been mentioned in chapter 15. But she preferred to share with *Peg's Paper*'s readers how her love for Rouse had deepened every time Arthur Jnr. called for his father, and of her successful effort in persuading Rouse to allow her to visit him in jail after his sentence. That 'man of mine was wonderfully brave', she commented when she eventually saw him through the glass partition. And when she mentioned little Arthur to him, she 'saw the love light in his eyes' (clearly predating Eric Clapton's employment of those striking words in 'Wonderful Tonight'!). She affected to have been convinced by Rouse's protestations of innocence and that a 'terrible mistake' had been made. Yet what perturbed her during her visits was that Rouse himself never spontaneously asked about Arthur Jnr., which clashes with other evidence regarding this father-son relationship. When she later wrote to him pointing this out, his acknowledgement of his failure, in the letter he sent back, could at best speak to his choosing to put the youngster out of his mind as a coping mechanism. It is more likely, however, that his omission to mention Arthur Jnr. in conversation with Helen spoke once more to his endemic self-centredness (though perhaps more understandable in the particular circumstances of the moment). Certainly the relevant letter to Helen, reproduced in *Peg's Paper* of July 7, 1931, was strangely unenthusiastic (though not outright discouraging) at the prospect of Helen's visiting him once more in Bedford Gaol. He did, however, later recall to her an incident with a paint box made by an acquaintance, a Mr. Bailey, which had excited Arthur Jnr., but he remembered it only when prompted by Helen's further letters.

Perhaps Rouse himself became more acutely aware of the broadly one-way nature of the correspondence between Helen and himself. For, as the date of execution drew inexorably nearer, his responses to her became more sentimental and filled with concern over Arthur Jnr. In a perverse way, of course, this was what Helen wanted to hear, though quite what she made of his disclosure that 'Sonny's' photograph was placed between that of herself and of 'Lil' on the mantelpiece in his death cell is not recorded.

The final episode of her magazine account, published on July 21, 1931, was simply a reproduction of Rouse's last two letters to her, written on the afternoon before his execution. One was addressed to her and the other to Arthur Jnr. The tone of the first was dignified and resigned. It alluded to Kipling's poem, 'If', to which he had previously been introduced by Helen. It recalled for him the joyful times they had had together, it recognised Helen's 'true worth' and it expressed reassurance that young Arthur would be well looked after. But what was lacking was any affirmation of love for Helen. While Helen loyally (rather than venally) reproduced Rouse's last letter in her piece (and there is no evidence that the letter was not genuine), did that omission regarding true love on his part not sum him up perfectly?

Nellie Tucker

Nellie Tucker soon put her past behind her when she (as Ellen E. Tucker) married a widower, Mirza Knott, in Bath, towards the end of 1931. In the previous April it had been reported that Nellie had broken off her engagement to Knott but her fiancé explained that this was 'only a subterfuge to avoid publicity', given her previous association with Rouse.[624] But the explanation scarcely squares with the publicity-seeking account of Nellie's 'story' published in three episodes in *Peg's Paper* the following month[625] (which was in addition to the interview she had previously given to the *People* five days after Rouse's execution).

In that earlier account which the popular Sunday newspaper had published on March 15, 1931, it will be recalled that Nellie had told her readers of her last visit to Rouse on March 7 (at his and not at her request, she had made clear) just a few hours after the Home Secretary had refused to grant him a reprieve. Rouse's calm and self-possessed demeanour when she saw him, she said, confirmed for her that he was indeed guilty. For an innocent man, she reasoned, would have been storming and fuming at the news, rather than spreading an 'infectious sort of gaiety' which she believed was genuine. Indeed, 'He seemed almost without a care in the world' apart from the one instance when he expressed anger at the person who had 'let him down'. Although it was a conversation which the Home Office, as we saw in chapter 16, concluded had never taken place, nonetheless, if Nellie is to be believed (notwithstanding the officials' vigorous denial), it must have been a

624 *Sunday Times*, April 5, 1931. Knott, originally from Lincolnshire, died aged 56 in June 1942.
625 *Peg's Paper*, May 5, 12, 19, 1931.

reference to Ivy's family, as we also surmised previously. Thus when he allegedly told Nellie that, 'It was the insurance money I was after, partly to help him', the 'him' in question had to be Ivy's father to whom Rouse had proposed investing money in Mr. Jenkins' modest colliery business, the Old Mill Colliery in Gellygaer.

But in a hint of what was yet to come in her *Peg's Paper* account, she could not resist drawing attention to Rouse's vanity when the matter of her and Rouse's older daughter, Pamelita, was raised.

> You know, she's a handsome kid, Nellie. People who've seen her photographs say she's just like me. 'While that child's alive you won't be dead', they've told me. Of course she takes after me, Nellie, doesn't she—beautiful kiddie".

As Nellie recorded, '....Arthur showed that whatever his fate he was keeping his conceit to the last—there's no doubt he thought a great deal of himself'. And as they parted his fixation with flirting could not be suppressed. 'You've got a long journey—be careful. Are you sure you haven't got anyone outside waiting for you? Don't I wish this barrier wasn't here. I'D BE AFTER YOU!' It set the tone for Nellie's next foray into print when, two months later, she published the 'story' of her life with Rouse.

In suitably dramatic style she began by recounting in *Peg's Paper* Rouse's last visit to see her in the maternity hospital in November 1930 before he set off with his doomed passenger. She noted his distractedness and his apparent indifference towards her, his grubby appearance and the old felt hat (and not his usual smart fedora) that he was fingering nervously, his trembling and his wringing of his hands. He never asked her how she was. Indeed she sensed that he had been crying and he definitely did not present the picture of a proud father, husband or even ardent lover. In fact she herself no longer cared for him but only for her children. What was the matter, she asked. Was he worrying about her? Yes, he whispered, almost moaned. That was partly the issue. But he also told her that he feared losing his job and was setting about finding a new one. And then he quickly changed the subject, asking when she would be leaving the hospital. When she replied that it would be in two days time, the news clearly disappointed him. Could she not stay longer? He would have to look for a suitable room for her (though Nellie did not mention any comment by him regarding the additional expense that this might entail). And then he jumped up to set off as the ward clock struck eight o'clock. No, he wasn't meeting anyone, he said vacantly. 'Goodbye, I'm in a hurry. I'll drop you a line and send some things for the baby.' Disappearing from the ward, he was back a minute later to ask what she was going to do on the following Monday (which would be five, not two, days hence). 'I'll wait here for you,' she replied. It would, of course, have been a long wait had she done so, though she could hardly have anticipated the events that would unfold that night after he then told her that he was about to drive north on business.

She was clearly concerned about where she stood in the scheme of things involving Rouse. His money troubles were mentioned, while she needed to know what arrangements he was making to accommodate her and her daughters. She herself needed to be employed, but he told her he would 'see to that' and that somehow he would manage despite his money worries. She did, however, wonder how someone earning £500 a year (which was considerably more than the national average) had financial cares. On that disturbing note he departed for the second time, while the other mothers in the ward looked on puzzled and curious at his strange behaviour. Nellie herself knew that he had been holding something back.

And then the account harked back to their first meeting in 1925 when their paths had crossed in Oxford Street as she was taking a stroll and he was emerging looking dashing, in her judgment, from a restaurant. He made his introduction and, after some persuasion, she agreed to go for a spin in his car. Driving away from the busy roads, he alarmed her when he moved his left arm round her and kissed her. His lies soon began to flow, commencing with his declared single status and then his flat near Victoria. During his business trips he would send her telegrams, express letters and ordinary letters, often more than one a day. He would explain to her face his loneliness when away and at last persuaded her to accompany him on journeys not too far from London. They presumably became lovers during one of those trips while she broached the question of marriage. To this, and to other inquisitive questions about him, his friends, his earnings and interests, he merely fended her off by referring to the difficult economic climate (in respect of marriage) or simply by promising to tell her at a later date. It was, indeed, her infatuation towards him that prevented her from pressing such matters.

During a vacation on the Isle of Wight he slipped a gold ring on her wedding finger, declaring that she was now his. At their holiday accommodation she got the impression that Rouse was known there, and while she was introduced by him as his wife, she was addressed on one occasion there as Miss Rouse. Though she corrected the person by stating 'Mrs., please', she had an uneasy feeling about the otherwise trivial incident. Other visits were made to Brighton, Eastbourne and, again, to the Isle of Wight. A road incident with another car in Eastbourne revealed to Nellie a display of anger, and a glimpse of violence, on Rouse's part as he emerged from the altercation satisfied (and muttering the fashionable phrase of the time, 'road hog') at the other driver's discomfiture after they had stopped their vehicles and had squared up to each other. That was most unlike the polite and gentle Rouse whom she knew, though she would later become the target of his stormy temper.

Indeed she herself continued in the article to vent her anger at him and at his deceptions and lies, a disgust that increased daily as the trial proceeded. Any love that she had felt for him was dead (she did not, however, stress the point by making reference to her new relationship). And as for Rouse himself apparently stating in a newspaper interview that on release he would decide whether to spend his future with Ivy Jenkins or with herself, Nellie had only contempt for the man. But most damningly, even were circumstances such that he would in due course be in a position to plead forgiveness and to seek a resumption of their relationship, she could never contemplate such a prospect. For what he had done was to ensure that her daughters were now stigmatised, not only as illegitimate but also as the children of a murderer. 'What woman—and mother—would not weep?'

She was, with the wisdom of hindsight, now able to assess his character. She found him well-groomed, he tipped waiters generously, seemed to be popular with the female managers and staff in the hotels where he and Nellie were staying, offered to buy drinks rounds though he himself was an abstainer (indeed, without the air of moral superiority attaching to temperance devotees), and appeared comfortable in the company of other men. It was a world into which Nellie felt that she did not fit and which suggested to her that their relationship was doomed. He also, on occasions, wore a diamond ring and diamond tie-pin which he would ostentatiously display in her company. 'Presents from people', he would remark, and say no more about it, maintaining secrecy to the end. When she later remarked that she had not seen him wearing those items for some time he visibly bristled and became evasive. But when pressed again he eventually mumbled something about business being bad. It was a precursor to a proper fall-out when his maintenance money for Pamelita dried up.

His 'bad' side was now becoming clearer. He was undoubtedly melodramatic, presenting himself to Nellie (though at what point is not clear) as a much misunderstood and martyred husband (presumably to Nellie, in a symbolic sense). She now saw him as a jealous and all-demanding lover who insisted on knowing about all of Nellie's movements. He would try to get hold of her handbag to search for letters to her from other men, all the while 'making false love to other women'. No wonder, she concluded, that he did not appear to trust her. Indeed he often referred to other women who were 'pestering him with their attentions....I had a letter today from Helen. She is still in love with me, but I am through with her', he would tell Nellie, seemingly quoting from the correspondence but never allowing Nellie to see the letter itself (which might, or might not, have told a different story). When she was out with him, his eyes would be forever wandering, looking closely at the passing girls or at the waitresses in the tea shops that they frequented (a previous brief fling had apparently taken place with one of those waitresses before he met Nellie).

His whole life, indeed, was a study in being two-faced and in making himself become the centre of attention. Thus he had to be the principal actor in little cameos. He had to be recognised as the 'lady-killer' *par excellence*, the wonderful lover and wooer. But that deception would also include staged displays of emotional commitment. This was exemplified by the occasion when, with an elaborate but gentle flourish, he presented Nellie with a diamond engagement ring. 'What a piece of mockery! An engagement ring from a man who had been married for nearly twenty years!'

But as with Lily's and Helen's judgments, Nellie could not dismiss what she perceived as Rouse's good points. He was never harsh or cruel, and he never threatened her or struck her. While modern observers might consider that the absence of such features was a *sine qua non* to any companionable or loving relationship, the inter-war years were still an era, as seen previously, when the 'unwritten rule' of marital chastisement or, to be more precise, domestic violence, remained problematic in many (though more commonly in working-class) marriages. In the end Nellie informed her readers that Rouse was 'gentleness itself in some of his moods, and his love of children was real and sincere'. In fact she believed him when he told her that '....he had in him a natural love of children possessed by few men indeed'. To which we might respond, in a famous paraphrase, 'He would say that, wouldn't he?'

So the same combination of the good, the bad and the downright ugly can be perceived in Nellie's account, a subtle mix of different character traits, some designed to appeal to the dreamy nature of *Peg's Paper* readers and others aimed as a warning to the young and innocent. Again, was Nellie sufficiently talented to paint a complex picture such as this in her own words, but also in a manner that would be gripping and understood by a typical nineteen-year old girl? It is probably doubtful but Nellie was not stupid.

Ivy Jenkins

Ivy was a different proposition altogether. She was venomous in her condemnation of Rouse and unlike Lily, Helen and Nellie she chose to heap not one iota of praise for any residual qualities that he might have possessed hidden under his despicable character. Ivy's 'story' was told in the pages of *Thomson's Weekly News* (and also in its Glasgow version, the *Glasgow Weekly News*) in four episodes published in February 1931, that is, while Rouse was still alive. The newspaper, which in its current embodiment is published nationally on Fridays as the *Weekly News*, is from the Dundee stable of D. C. Thomson & Co (with a strong history of anti-trade unionism) and is, of course, better known for publishing *The Beano* and *The Dandy*. It is also home to the best-selling Scottish Sunday newspaper, the *Sunday Post*, featuring those valiant Scots cartoon characters, Oor Wullie and the Broons, whose appeal is to a broader age range than in the case of Dennis the Menace and Desperate Dan.

But light-heartedness was most definitely not a theme of Ivy's narrative. Indeed her fourth and last episode in the newspaper (a planned episode in the issue on March 7 never appeared) was headlined 'My Escape from Poisoning'. In the first article, published on February 7, 1931, the 21-year old trainee nurse from the valleys explains that she is not writing out of vindictiveness, though methinks she probably protested too much in this respect. For she declared that even '....if I loved him once, I hate him now as bitterly as it is possible for a woman to hate a man'. Indeed she vowed that she would not lift a finger to save him (though how she could have done is not stated), and that he was not deserving of any sympathy.

She recounts her shame at being labelled one of Rouse's 'harem' and his 'secret wife' and although she was pleased that illness had prevented her appearing at the police court hearing at Northampton alongside Helen and Nellie, for whom she expressed sympathy, she urgently felt the need to tell her story. Why that was so may be a matter of speculation. Perhaps a remote village in the Welsh valleys was not remote enough in which to hide away in shame. Perhaps she chose to ignore the dictum of 'Least said, soonest mended'. Perhaps parental pressure was exerted in an attempt to uphold the good name of the Jenkins family. Perhaps a hoped-for career in nursing was now a pipe-dream, and so the promise of payment for her story became more attractive than it might otherwise have been to a relatively comfortably-off young woman. But the most compelling explanation is surely her sense of outrage, felt by a woman who had not exactly been scorned but who had definitely been made a fool of and whose marriage prospects, she probably believed, were now severely diminished. It was even worse, for she believed that she had been targeted for poisoning by the monster, Rouse. Thus the series of articles she was now penning.

She freely admitted her vulnerability at the time she met him in London when she was feeling sad and lonely. And she also recognised her naivety in not asking the crucial questions about Rouse's father and his 'aunt' (that is, Lily),[626] nor why he had not taken her to see them. Moreover, while he told her that he lived in a flat in Gillingham Street, Victoria, paying 30 shillings a week (double what Ivy was earning at the hospital where she enjoyed board and lodgings), it is plain that she was never taken to visit it (it was, after all, a tobacconist and newsagent shop), nor did she propose to him that she should visit it. As to the Buxted Road address which was supposedly his father's house on this occasion, Rouse did, indeed, take Ivy there once when his father was 'out' and where she was introduced to his 'aunt'. Who this lady was Ivy never found out but she was almost certainly not Lily, who would be hardly likely to agree to such a deception. It was one of many elaborate ruses in Rouse's repertoire, with his forthcoming 'marriage' to Ivy soon to provide another example (below).

She was impressed by his professed and outspoken (but, unknown to her, his obviously hypocritical) moral standards and by his teetotal stance. Yet she culpably failed to ask herself why a handsome 32-year old man (as he told her), driving around the country as a commercial traveller, did not appear to have any women in his life. However, while they were courting he spun her a yarn about his having been jilted two days before he was due to marry another girl twelve years previously after he had left the Army. Not only that, but the girl in question had later tried to renew their relationship, only for Rouse to reject her and to feign distrust for the female sex; until now, that is.

In emphasising that she was a person of upright character, Ivy told her readers that she had firmly declined, after being pressed by him, to go away on holiday as a couple except as his wife (his awkward response to her angry refusal being to say that he had only been joking). She added that,

> Had Arthur Rouse been content with my friendship only, I would not now be so bitter towards him. But he was not. When he found out that I was a respectable girl with what some people may regard as old-fashioned ideas, he got over the difficulty by tricking me into what I now know to have been a bogus marriage.

She described how it had been conducted on her 21st birthday (June 12, 1930) by a kindly-looking elderly man with a white beard. But the venue was surprisingly bland, an anonymous room in an office block in the Victoria district of London (though she did not doubt, even then, that it was a register office). Yet although Ivy was obliged to return to her hospital duties immediately afterwards, with the honeymoon postponed till her three-week annual holiday at the end of the month (and Rouse even managed to change *that* arrangement when competing plans arose), she could not have been happier. Thus was Rouse able (without committing bigamy on this occasion) to overcome the 'difficulty' of which she spoke and regarding which she was too coy to spell out for her readers. It is also clear that Ivy quickly became pregnant shortly after the 'ceremony', after which she moved back with her parents in Gellygaer to await her baby and her 'husband's' arrival every fortnight at her parents' large cottage, Primrose Villa.

---

626 The heavy and apparently unflattering jumper that he was wearing as they travelled on a day trip to Leicester was, he said, knitted by his 'aunt', though in this instance it was actually made by Nellie.

Indeed, today, the road where the cottage (now divided into two) is situated is known locally as Rouse's Lane, though the actual location is in Trosnant Crescent which joins the main road, Penallta Road, in Gellygaer.[627]

Seventy years previously, in the Cotswold village of Fairford, 37-year old Sarah Thomas, the owner of Milton House, kept a diary. At that time unmarried, her first diary entry on January 19, 1860 noted that she had greeted the return of her younger sister, Kate, who had arrived home from Bath with an acquaintance, Sarah Wassell. Miss Wassell was accompanied by her fiancé, John Roberts. In her diary Sarah Thomas wrote that, 'My first impressions of John Roberts were not prepossessing'. Indeed she added, 'Was surprised to notice John Roberts so attentive to my dear Kate, much more so than to his Sarah'. Three days later she confided that, 'John Roberts is more familiar with us than I like and is more attentive to us than to Sarah, so was pleased when he received a letter this morning hastening him back to Bath. He is most sadly disappointed but not we'.[628] The above trivia, relating to a fiancé in 1860, could well have been written by Ivy's sister, Phyllis, in 1930 as she analysed Rouse in a manner that saw through the facade of politeness on the part of this male visitor to reveal less admirable features about him while being hosted by his supposed 'in-laws'. Indeed, on his first visit to Gellygaer, on the weekend before the couple could get away for a week's (and no longer a three-week) honeymoon, Rouse had struggled to impress the men-folk in Ivy's house. Nor did Ivy's sister, Phyllis, take to him (there are hints that he may have tried to take advantage of her, also). Only Ivy's mother seemed to approve of her daughter's choice. The general feeling was that he talked too much, usually about himself, while he came over as very opinionated, especially in his vehement rejection of religion. This he attributed to the spectacle, when he had been a choir boy, of seeing the local clergyman take a young girl into the vestry and kiss her, at which point he, Rouse, claimed that he went straight out of the church. In her newspaper article Ivy did not set much store by the story which was supposed to emphasise Rouse's hatred of hypocrisy. What her siblings thought of it was probably even more dismissive.

Setting off on honeymoon at last they travelled, via London, to the south coast, stopping first in Herne Bay (where George Joseph Smith had drowned his bride, Bessie Munday, in the bath in 1912). At the Kent resort they stayed at one of the best hotels there before travelling on to Hastings, Eastbourne, Brighton and Bournemouth. Ivy thus enjoyed five glorious days in the summer sun before night-shift duties at last called her back for her final stint at the hospital before her employment there was due to end in September when she was to take her final nursing exam (after which, she believed, the detached villa in Kingston, Surrey, to be shared with her husband, beckoned).

At some stage in her story she reflected on her earlier life in Gellygaer: how she had learned shorthand typing in Cardiff and had then worked as a book-keeper with her father, William (apparently known locally as Tal), and brothers in the family's nearby Old Mill Colliery (or, as others knew it, Pottery Colliery).

---

627 David Mills, "A Murderer Visits Gelligaer", *Gelligaer*, Vol. 14, 2004, pp. 47-8, published by the Gelligaer Historical Society. The village's name was spelt 'Gellygaer' at the time. We are grateful to David Mills for providing further information about Gellygaer and the Jenkins family.
628 June Lewis-Jones (ed), *The Secret Diary of Sarah Thomas: Life in a Cotswold Market Town, 1860-1865*, Nonsuch Publishing, Stroud, 2007, pp. 19-20.

The colliery had possibly been run by the Glyngaer Colliery Company at one time in the 1920s, and was linked underground to two other local collieries. Ivy then interested herself in working the equipment at the pit including, according to elderly locals who remember hearing stories about her during their childhood, and who were questioned recently, working the haulage engine while wearing un-lady-like jodhpurs or trousers. She also set out to acquire a degree of knowledge of mining engineering. This continued until the pit flooded shortly after the General Strike of 1926. It is probable that the site of the colliery is now overgrown and located in a heavily wooded area known as Cefn Hengoed.[629]

It was after the flooding of the colliery that Ivy obtained the post of probationer nurse at the Holborn and Finsbury Hospital, Highgate, where she was to live during her training. Although initially daunted by the busy city she eventually settled down after being befriended by another trainee, Nurse Jones, who lived in Richmond. She then described how, two years later, in November 1929, Rouse first inveigled himself into her life. He had spotted her looking out of a hospital window as he drove by, and in typical fashion slowed down, tipped his hat and smiled at her. He persisted in driving past the same spot on successive days and she, struck with curiosity, actually waited at the window for his car to arrive. Then, one day, she went out the hospital gate with a companion just as the car drew up. Introductions were made and an invitation was extended to both girls to go for a spin. Rouse talked non-stop and at pace during the journey, piling on one lie after another about his alleged single situation. Ivy was hooked, she readily agreed to meet him again and romance blossomed. Indeed she was captivated by his sparkling eyes, his handsome appearance and by the thought that such a man was genuinely interested in her. It was not just his 'dreamy' quality. There was some indefinable and strange appeal that he possessed and which drew her in (whether it was similar to the hypnotic appeal that the Brides in the Bath killer, George Joseph Smith, allegedly exerted over his victims is moot). Whatever it was it led her to 'marriage' the following June and then to pregnancy.

Only a small number of his love letters to her apparently survived her bonfire of vengeful destruction. One of them, sent from a hotel in Bournemouth and dated October 13, 1930, commenced with 'My Own Darling Wife' (and thus could well have been written for Helen or even for Nellie). In it he charmed Ivy with glowing references to her parents (whom he refers to as 'mother' and 'father') and mentioned samples of men's suspenders and belts that he was sending on for her brothers. Finally he stressed how hard he was working to provide for the new home that she and he would soon occupy (this referred to the non-existent property in Kingston-upon-Thames that he had promised her).

By this time Ivy was confessing in her account that Rouse, when he was away on trips, was not featuring in her thoughts as animatedly as before. This may well have been a self-serving admission to suggest that she was not irremediably naive, but it probably spoke to her beginning to use her head and not just her heart to guide her. It certainly does not compel us to the conclusion that the whole account was a journalist's creation. Though she was delighted with Rouse's presence she was slowly beginning to perceive that there was no real depth to him. He talked a lot but in a manner inclined to get on one's nerves. Indeed when

---

629   If using Google Earth, the postcode is CF82 7DQ.

she was near to completing her nursing training after three years, and when the purchase of the home in Kingston, which was to cost £1,250, was no nearer realisation, she was pleased to return to her parents in Wales for a break. While Rouse tried to persuade her not to travel to Gellygaer, she replied that it would only be for a 'few weeks' and he could, of course, join her there at weekends. But such a reassurance from a newly-wed bride, in a fully committed relationship, would surely be unusual, to say the least. Yet she conceded that, leaving aside his visits to Gellygaer, he never failed to keep to any arrangement that they had previously agreed upon. She did surmise, however, that that might have been due to her having replaced a previous occupant of his 'harem', a word she obviously detested and found demeaning. Helen would have been the obvious candidate to make way for Ivy.

She was especially embarrassed by his outburst of sobbing, witnessed by fellow-travellers in her compartment, just before her train at Paddington Station departed for South Wales, a story which it would be difficult to fabricate. Indeed she found it discomfiting when he shed tears in her presence on other occasions, such as when she commented, in a moderately critical manner, on his appearance. She attributed it simply to his being an emotional person who had been spoiled in life, but she made no reference to his wartime experience which might have been a factor.

She then moved on to discuss the last phase of their relationship. This included his weekend visits to Gellygaer in September and October 1930 during which they examined furniture catalogues that he had brought with him. For, as a man earning the ample sum, he claimed, of £12 a week, he was keen to encourage her to make plans to furnish the Kingston house. Expensive items of bedroom, dining room and drawing room furniture, an electric cooker, a wireless and gramophone player were not too good for Rouse's 'wife', he reassured her. Phyllis could stay with them in Kingston for three months once they moved there, while he told Ivy that he did not expect her (Ivy) to make any financial contribution to the household bills.

But then her un-named illness, presumably a threatened miscarriage, struck, and her condition soon became worse. Her father sent a telegram to Rouse, who was supposedly on his travels, to try to come down on the Thursday (that would be November 6) earlier than planned. He did, of course, arrive that night but in a haggard, dirty and unkempt state, spinning the story of his car having been stolen outside a cafe and failing to improve Ivy's morale as he sat by her bed crying and looking despairing. Indeed she was amazed that the atheist, Rouse, would join in the hymn singing, including 'Nearer My God to Thee', with the rest of the family downstairs while otherwise exchanging nary a word with anyone in the house during that visit. Although, with hindsight, she hardly needed to spell out the significance of this empty 'conversion', in the short term she was cheered by what she had heard from downstairs and called Rouse up to her bedroom where she thought she might be able to spread her uplifted spirits to her 'husband'. But there was no religious epiphany. Rouse had not felt like singing his usual favourites such as the 'Trumpeter' and 'If I Might Only Come to You'. So he joined in the singing of the hymns since he knew that her mother would like to hear him singing them. That explanation was not exactly what Ivy wanted to hear, so she turned away from him and suggested he might want to go back downstairs. The next morning he came up to see her and whispered that he was going to make his way back to London. He kissed her and asked her to wish him luck. But she was so choked and in an emotional turmoil that three such requests by him were followed by silence on her part. 'Goodbye' was all she could manage within his hearing as he left the room. 'Good luck' was whispered by her only after the bedroom door was closed and when Rouse could not hear. They scarcely saw each other again. It sounds melodramatic but only two persons were present at the time and one of them probably had more things on his mind than the need to verify or refute what was written.

Ivy's last article on February 28, dramatically entitled 'My Escape from Poisoning', made great play of the almost surreal atmosphere in the Jenkins household on that last Thursday before Rouse set off for captivity the next morning. His haunted look, his fearful appearance, and his sensitivity while Phyllis tried to mend his torn shirt were all palpable. But so was his troubled reticence to come clean to Ivy, at least about the other women even if not about the dead tramp. This she clearly resented subsequently, for it was obvious that it would all come out in due course. Yet he lacked the courage to 'make his peace with me face to face'. He even compounded matters the next morning when he left without saying goodbye to Ivy thus, in her eyes, failing the manliness test. But on his departure he was still anxious to gain Phyllis's approval, pleading with her to call him Arthur, not Rouse. She refused to budge. Rouse it was as he trudged off.

So for the next three days Ivy remained in ignorance of the real Rouse and of the existence of Lily. While the latter's interviews with the press had been published and read by the rest of the Jenkins family, they remained too worried about Ivy's medical condition to disclose those shattering details to her until the following Monday evening after the arrival of local police Inspector Evans, an old friend of the family, who supplied fresh news about Rouse. And even then her father told her only about the existence of another Mrs. Rouse and not the even more unpleasant details about him. But that limited information was itself enough to propel Ivy into a collapse from which she did not wake for some hours. Not surprisingly she expressed bitterness (a mild word in the circumstances) towards Rouse, and revealed to her readers that not even the daunting prospect of impending execution had prompted him to write to her apologising for the heartbreak, grief and shame he had caused her.

But her next revelation was astonishing. For whereas she had initially assumed that her illness had been due to a difficult pregnancy eventually resulting in a miscarriage, instead Ivy offered to her readers a completely different interpretation. Her condition, she now believed, was not because, 'married' to Rouse, she 'had been called by fate to play the role of motherhood', a prospect that had thrilled her initially. It was because, as she was not getting better, she believed that, far from being pregnant, she was actually being poisoned by Rouse. As she explained, the exposure of his empty commitment to carrying her across the threshold of the £1,250 house in Kingston was drawing inexorably nearer. So to escape the inevitable *denouement*, he now resorted, she convinced herself, to the drastic solution of doing away with her. Thus on the evening of Monday, October 27, after Rouse had returned to London, she became violently sick and experienced pains in the back of her neck. She went straight to bed but still felt very ill the next morning. She recalled that at supper during the previous Sunday evening,

> ....Rouse was in one of his playful moods....The thing I have in mind happened when we reached the pudding stage. We had apple sponge, I remember. Rouse, still play-acting as we thought then, took my plate from me, and left the table carrying it in his hand . He went to the door, behind which his coat was hanging, and pretended to be looking for his handkerchief. He was laughing gaily at the time, and when he came back to the table he handed my plate back to me with a funny remark. I ate the apple sponge but I didn't like the taste of it. 'Whatever have you done to the pudding, Phyllis?' I asked my sister, who had done the cooking. 'Nothing, Paddy', she answered. 'Why?' 'It is terribly bitter', I explained, at which the others laughed. 'It must be my fancy', they told me. My illness developed the next day, as I have described, and I have never been well since.

She then described unusual happenings during Rouse's last visit before his arrest. When he came up to her bedroom he finished off a glass of water beside a jug that was near her bedside. He then told her that she was looking flushed and ought herself to drink a large glass of water which he then poured from the jug. She drank only a few sips at the time but finished the glass during the night. The next morning her mother was in the room and topped up the glass. But then she gave out a cry. She held up the jug and said to Ivy, 'Look at this. Whatever is the matter with the water?' She lifted the jug and Ivy could plainly see traces of sediment containing white crystal at the bottom. She emptied the jug and, presumably having rinsed it out, refilled it with fresh water.

Ivy added that she now recalled that the water that Rouse had given her the previous night did have a peculiar taste but that she had been too ill to mention it to him. And then she remembered that on the Saturday, October 25, Phyllis had drunk a cup of tea that had been poured out for Ivy. A 'tea party' for the family and for Rouse had been arranged. 'Mother' was pouring and stated who was to get which cup. Ivy had been late arriving at the table but Rouse had placed Ivy's cup beside his own. Phyllis now picked up Ivy's cup by mistake, took one sip from it and realised that it was her sister's. Rouse, it appeared to Ivy, was keen that his 'wife' should appropriate 'her' cup. But Ivy said it didn't matter and that Phyllis should just keep that cup, which she did. Two hours later Phyllis became extremely sick and fainted three times, while Rouse expressed great concern for her. And when she went into the garden for fresh air, Rouse was anxious to join her there.

While nothing more was said by Ivy in her newspaper account about the incident, she did add that when she and Rouse had been on honeymoon in Brighton and Eastbourne there were two occasions when she had fallen ill, although not as seriously, in a similar manner to her illness in Gellygaer. In both instances it followed her drinking coffee with Rouse the previous evening. She insisted to her readers that she would not have mentioned such episodes had Rouse not made critical comments about her (see later). Indeed she added that Rouse had told her and her family that he had taken out a £500 life insurance policy on her, though she did not know whether there was any truth in his claim. Obviously, if such a policy had existed, there would be a further motive for a financially hard-pressed Rouse to be rid of her, especially since it has been claimed by another source that he had already been paying her £2 per week housekeeping.[630]

The obvious difficulty with Ivy's account is the lack of proof. There is no indication that either she or Phyllis was medically examined for symptoms of poisoning, bodily fluids were not laboratory-tested, the apple sponge was not preserved for analysis, and the white crystal sediment was presumably flushed down the sink. Moreover, it is arguable that the highly respectable Ivy might have preferred to explain her distress as due to poisoning than to a miscarriage. Yet this argument is complicated by her insisting that for a young 'married' woman to bear a child with her 'husband' would be a fulfilment for her. And it is difficult to imagine that to suffer a miscarriage in such assumed marital circumstances would have been shameful to her. On the other hand she was, of course, now writing with hindsight.

So what are we to make of her allegation? In the absence of scientific evidence we can reject her claim outright. Yet we may surmise that the idea of poisoning her was not beyond Rouse's mindset, given the circumstantial (even if not incontrovertible) evidence that he had planned to do away with, and did murder, the unknown tramp. But perhaps it was something in between. As with the case of Edith Thompson, was there not the possibility that what was being administered to Ivy was an abortifacient, though in the latter instance without Ivy's knowledge? In Thompson's case there remains the suspicion that the bitter taste of the tea drunk by her husband, Percy, was the abortifacient Edith was attempting to take (but Percy had picked up the wrong cup) in order to procure the abortion of the child she might have been expecting with Bywaters. Indeed the horrific spectacle at her execution when her 'insides fell out' is interpreted by some as reinforcing this theory. So might the tampered coffee, water and apple sponge consumed by Ivy (and the bitter tea tasted by Phyllis) have signified Rouse's attempt to relieve himself of at least one additional financial burden, the need to pay maintenance for his child by Ivy?[631] It is a possibility but obviously not provable. Indeed the complication regarding this theory is that even if Ivy did miscarry, once Rouse's promises regarding the Kingston house had been exposed as empty, as would shortly occur, the whole unravelling of his relationship with Ivy was bound, in any case, to take place.

It seems more probable that in her vengeful frame of mind Ivy was clutching at straws in attempting to paint Rouse even blacker than was the case (which was black enough). Indeed one should bear in the mind that when the story of poisoning was published Rouse was still awaiting execution and his only hope was the Royal Prerogative of Mercy. Perhaps, therefore, Ivy was to be believed

---

630 Mills, *op. cit.*, p. 47.
631 His action might have constituted the still extant offence of administering a poison or other noxious thing so as thereby to endanger life or inflict grievous bodily harm on the victim, contrary to section 23 of the Offences Against the Person Act 1861. An offence against the Infant Life (Preservation) Act 1929, still in force with minor amendments, would not have been committed as Ivy's baby would not have been capable of independent existence outside the womb at that time. It is still an offence under section 58 of the 1861 Act for a mother to bring about the abortion of her unborn child or for another person unlawfully (that is, outside the protection of the Abortion Act 1967) to procure the mother's miscarriage (as Vera Drake, played memorably by Imelda Staunton in the Mike Leigh film of that name, discovered to her cost).

when she stated that she would not lift a finger to save him from the gallows, Indeed it looked as if she were twisting the knife.

She certainly had good reason. For Rouse had signally failed to express remorse for his treatment of her when he, himself (or the journalists in question), was afforded an opportunity to speak to the public. Thus as noted previously Rouse had published his story in the *News of the World* on February 1, 1931,[632] on the day following Lord Hewart's peremptory rejection of his appeal against conviction.

While his account of his first meeting with Ivy differs only in detail from her explanation of how they meet, there is a chasm of difference regarding their intimate relations. Thus Ivy's account made clear that she insisted that sexual relations could only, and in the event did, take place once they had 'married', whereas Rouse stated that,

> After going about with her for a couple of months or so, I began to realise that further trouble was in store for me. 'Paddy' then confessed to me that she was in trouble, and some days later, when I called at the hospital to see her, I was told that she had left and had returned to her home in Wales.

It will be recalled that far from being courted by him 'for a couple of months or so' before, according to Rouse, she allegedly became pregnant, Ivy's account indicated that they had actually undergone the 'marriage ceremony' on June 12, 1930, some six and-a-half months after they first met meeting in late November 1929. Second, Rouse's reference to Ivy's 'confessing' to him that she was 'in trouble' is a million miles away from how Ivy would have broken the news to her 'spouse'. For, rather than confiding shameful information, Ivy was surely assuming that she was sharing wonderful news with her husband.[633] No wonder she resented his portrayal of her as a young woman with loose morals, with the implication that she had engaged in pre-marital sex, until at last she was able to challenge that portrayal later that month (and after his character assassination of her had been in the public domain for a period of time).[634]

Rouse's views on the other principal women in the case, Lily, Helen and Nellie, have only been glimpsed in the above accounts, and where his opinions had been expressed in the months before his execution their sincerity must obviously be questioned. But what was the nature of his personality problems? Was he suffering an identity crisis for some time before November 1930, or confronting an early mid-life crisis? Was his sense of masculinity being challenged so that he had to prove his sexual prowess (indeed, sexuality) time and again? Was he a sexual predator who could not resist a pretty face, was he simply lonely on his travels throughout the country and then found that he could not extricate himself

---

632 It was reprinted in *Peg's Paper* on May 26 and June 2, 1931, two and a half months after his execution, perhaps indicating the persistent interest among readers in his fate.

633 There are similar passages in his account where he implies that Ivy became pregnant even before they had 'married'. For example he stated that, 'I had in mind the fact that 'Paddy' was in trouble, and I did not want her to incur the anger of her parents'. Thus the subsequent disclosure to her parents of their 'marriage'. He added that he later learned that she had given birth to a still-born child a few days before his trial began.

634 Before his recounting of her 'confession' Rouse had stated that after their initial meeting, '...we became on intimate terms, and I continued to see her two or three times a week'. It is probable that 'intimate terms' implied for Rouse (though obviously not for Ivy) sexual relations at this point.

from those relations, was he a product of his age, or was he, indeed, a victim of his war wounds? These thoughts may be considered in our concluding chapter. For there we will attempt to sum up the 'real' Arthur Rouse and decide whether the press's view was spot-on or simplistic, whether Ivy was closer to the 'truth' about him than were Lily, Helen and (possibly) Nellie and, finally, the extent to which, if at all, Rouse, despite his label for posterity as an executed murderer, was nonetheless a creature of his time.

More immediately, however, it is proposed to analyse in the next chapter the wider social significance of the 'stories' presented by the four women, Lily, Helen, Nellie and Ivy (though the situation of the last-named is probably *sui generis*). In particular what do the cases of Helen and Nellie tell us of the way that inter-war society and the media portrayed unmarried women who gave birth to babies during this period or, indeed, how such 'bastard' children were presented? For the sympathetic press portrayal of Helen, Nellie, Arthur Jnr., Pamelita and newly-born Patricia seems to challenge the stereotypical negative image of such 'outsiders', cut off from the desirable nexus of the socially approved nuclear family which itself is bonded together through parental marriage. To this and related issues we turn in the next chapter.

CHAPTER TWENTY-TWO

"SO THEY ARE NOT MARRIED?"

EVENING NEWS, December 12, 1930

Rouse, Single Mothers and Society

In 1998 an academic study of lone motherhood observed that,

> During the 1990s the polemical literature on lone mothers, which is often fiercely part political, has been vast. '[T]hink tanks' have produced a stream of material deploring the 'end of the family'.....[and] the end of stable working-class communities.[635]

Similarly, newspapers regularly inveighed against single mothers who were perceived as anti-social and as a drain on the state. For such women were commonly depicted as 'hooked' on benefits with the result that it was the taxpayer who, it seemed, was paying for the upkeep of their illegitimate children. Moreover, such 'abuse' of state largesse might be portrayed as inter-generational, with caricatures of overweight grandmothers and mothers looking adoringly at the newly arrived baby daughter. The image was not just of such mothers as a social problem but also as a social threat. For they were threatening to undermine the moral foundations of society embodied in the concept of the nuclear ('hard-working') family comprising husband, wife and children of the marriage. Any other arrangement and, in particular, that of the single unmarried mother and her child, was economically, socially and morally unacceptable. Indeed after the summer riots in England in 2011 following the police shooting of Mark Duggan, the Prime Minister at the time, David Cameron, perceived 'Children without fathers' and, by implication, single mothers, as culpable. One popular newspaper complained that '....we have bred feckless, lawless males who pass on to their own children the same mistakes' (so much for absent fathers abandoning single mothers).[636] Of course, it may be that such harsh judgments come out of the woodwork at times of crisis. However, it is probable that in general, 'different' kinds of relationship, including the challenge of the single mother bringing up her child on her own rather than choosing to be tied to a 'feckless' and possibly violent male partner, are more widely accepted.

---

635 Kathleen Kiernan, Hilary Land and Jane Lewis, *Lone Motherhood in Twentieth-Century Britain*, Clarendon Press, Oxford, 1998, p. 1.
636 Cited in Owen Jones, *Chavs: The Demonization of the Working Class*, Verso, 2012, p. xix.

443

Yet the discourse of the ideal family structure, bonded together by marriage and fidelity, was still the dominant trope when addressing family life before and after the Second World War. In particular, women's magazines during this period hailed the image of the 'modern' wife and mother as the domestic goddess of her age.[637] For it was she who conscientiously catered for all her husband's domestic needs, who kept the home clean and tidy, and who knitted and sewed to perfection. And it was she who brought up the children to be polite and responsible and to share the domestic enthusiasms and hobbies of mother and father respectively, as the portrayal of the Ladybird book characters, Peter and Jane, so vividly (and almost sickeningly) demonstrated.

The picture is, of course, a very middle-class one, unlike that of the children of poor parents living in damp, overcrowded accommodation in rows of terraced houses in the industrial districts, and where the grubby children, outside school hours, play on makeshift wooden bogey-carts, hammered together with a few nails and discarded pram wheels, in the streets outside their cramped houses. Nonetheless, there are still recognisable family units in such images, even if the wife is exhausted through worry, ill-health, lack of money, overwork in the house and having given birth to a succession of children. While this picture of working-class domestic life may appear caricaturist, the documented experiences of wives and mothers in such communities only reinforce such images, as published research from Maud Pember Reeves' *Round About a Pound a Week* (1911), to Margery Spring Rice's *Working-Class Wives* (1939), to modern historians' findings, such as Elizabeth Roberts' *A Woman's Place* testify.[638] For the most part research on working-class women before the 1960s has focussed on married women (sometimes including widowed or separated women). But our preoccupation here is with single mothers before the modern period, the predecessors of the category who were lambasted by politicians and the press in the 1990s (above). For that was the status occupied by Helen and Nellie (at least for part of their lives). And it might have been the status to be ascribed to Ivy had she not miscarried (as seems probable she did, despite her obfuscations).

Were we to project back in time the highly condemnatory views of unmarried mothers in the 1990s uncovered by Kiernan *et al.* (above), then we might expect similar critical judgments to be made regarding Helen and Nellie (it will be recalled that Nellie never 'married' Rouse but had two children by him, and that Helen, who had already lost a five-week old child by Rouse, 'married' him only after she later became pregnant with Arthur Jnr.). In the case of Ivy, however, her readers could readily absolve her of any moral irresponsibility (but not, perhaps, of naivety or impetuosity) in view of the crass deception that was the 'marriage ceremony' (which she insisted upon before she allowed intimacy) that she and Rouse underwent. What strikes one as somewhat surprising, however, is that despite the vituperation by 'respectable' society directed against single mothers between the wars, with the churches and other religious bodies adding their

637   See M. Ferguson, *Forever Feminine: Women's Magazines and the Cult of Femininity*, Heinemann, 1983.
638   Maud Pember Reeves, *Round About a Pound a Week*, Virago reprint, 1979 (first published 1913); Margery Spring Rice, *Working-Class Wives: Their Health and Conditions*, Virago reprint, 1981 (first published 1939); Elizabeth Roberts, *A Woman's Place: An Oral History of Working-Class Women, 1890-1940*, Blackwell, Oxford, 1984.

hostile voices to those of the press and politicians, *Peg's Paper* chose to offer a platform to (and presumably paid) a couple of unmarried mothers who recounted their affairs in such a manner that they did not express shame but, rather, pride in producing their illegitimate children.

Of course the magazine might justify its serialisation of their stories by citing it as a cautionary tale for its working-class female readers. It would thereby be performing a service to its young and impressionable readers by alerting them to the dangers of the silver-tongued, snappily dressed and (apparently) sophisticated white-collar salesmen driving round the country in almost-new cars. Or, more likely, it was simply cashing in on the notoriety of Arthur Rouse and his self-destructive references to his 'harem'. In other words the particular circumstances of the case unlike, say, that of the 'cerebral' murder of Julia Wallace shortly afterwards, offered an editor's dream 'true life' story, told by young women with whom the readers of *Peg's Paper* would readily identify. For not only was it a case of thwarted love on the one hand, and the 'love cheat' on the other. The women in the case were themselves essentially working class (as was the principal readership of the magazine), even if not *industrial* working class. Thus both Helen (originally from Glasgow, then later living in Edinburgh) and Nellie (from Greenwich) had worked as domestic helpers in the homes of those higher up the class structure,[639] while Helen, whose father was a printer, had previously undertaken factory work in Lancashire. Given the above, it may well be appreciated why a normally censorious tone found elsewhere and directed towards unmarried mothers was hidden from the readers of *Peg's Paper*. To that extent the publication deserves recognition and praise at a time when unmarried motherhood was condemned in 'respectable' circles even if the real motivation of the magazine was probably to sell copies in abundance.

So how were single mothers perceived and portrayed at the time (or how might Helen and Nellie have been viewed as the unmarried mothers of children, had they not presented themselves as 'victims' of Rouse)? Historically, unmarried mothers were scarcely popular in official discourse. For as an Act of 1773 had expressed it, 'Great Inconveniences have been found to arise from single women pregnant with children likely to be born bastards'.[640] This referred to the economic 'inconvenience' borne by the parish worthies whose rates funded local provision of welfare under the Poor Law, including taking in for shelter unmarried mothers with nowhere else to go. At least the law required the local Poor Law guardians to track down, if possible, the father, and to get him to pay up for the child. But failing this search, mother and baby would become another financial burden to be confined within the workhouse.

But even apart from the Poor Law stigma, unmarried mothers generally tended to be viewed widely (if not universally), in more urban settled environments in particular, as suspect, women who had rejected the civilised norms of society by their loose morals and, by becoming pregnant, who had thereby entrapped sturdy

---

639 Cannell claimed that the 14-year old Helen worked as a 'nurse or governess'. This seems a somewhat lofty description for a girl of that age. See J. C. Cannell, *New Light on the Rouse Case*, John Long, c. 1931, p. 30.

640 An Act for the Better Regulation of Lying-In Hospitals etc, cited in Jo Pearman, "The Tribe of Ogres that Fatten on Little Children: Legal Responses to Baby Farming in the Late Nineteenth Century", University of Kent Ph.D, unpublished, 2017.

young men (who may already have been married to another), causing them or the parish further financial misery. That such an analysis tended to be a grotesque caricature of the respective positions of the parties involved had little purchase among the judgmental authorities. But it has to be conceded that the 'norms of society' did privilege marriage as a status to which young women strove. Thus between the wars young unmarried interviewees in working-class Liverpool overwhelmingly told researchers that their ambition in life was to get married.[641] In setting out this aim they consciously ignored the greater opportunities for employment and higher wages offered in the new consumer industries which were now supplying items and products designed to enhance the quality of life within the home, on the roads, or in the pursuit of leisure. Their mothers had to endure 'the double burden of paid work and unpaid domesticity', which invariably also involved bringing up a number of children in crowded and unwholesome accommodation on very limited income. But the interviewees themselves envisaged a more romantic and contented notion of married and family life

Single motherhood did not, of course, fit into this vision. But single motherhood could not be willed away. Indeed some mothers consciously chose, on intellectual or ideological grounds, not to forge a co-habiting relationship with men, while others who entered into a permanent relationship with a male partner resisted the lure of a formal marriage. But such examples (see below) were rare. Single motherhood sometimes meant the mother living on her own with her child, and not sharing accommodation with the father, as was the case with Nellie. But it was probably more common for the urban or semi-urban single mother to leave her familiar surroundings while still pregnant, give birth in some distant nursing home, give up her child for adoption soon afterwards and return 'home', explaining her absence as due to some temporary employment elsewhere that had now come to an end. And the reason for that elaborate ploy was, of course, to deflect the shame and opprobrium that would attach to the local girl exposed as an unmarried mother.

Yet to what extent is it the case that public opinion was overwhelmingly hostile to the unmarried mother? We have already noted the ambiguity surrounding Margaret Penn's mother in rural Lancashire before the Great War. Pre-marital pregnancy was only a 'problem' if marriage did not follow. In those circumstances was the 'problem' of stigma becoming worse or becoming reduced between the wars? And what do the accounts of Helen and Nellie in *Peg's Paper* tell us about popular attitudes to unmarried motherhood during this period (or were their cases untypical because they could be 'excused' as 'victims' of Rouse's sexual incontinence and of his lies)?

From the 1840s to 1940 the rate and ratio of illegitimate births are shown below, where the rate refers to the number of live illegitimate births per 1,000 unmarried women aged 15-44, and the ratio is the number of live illegitimate births per 1,000 total live births:

---

641   Judy Giles. "'Playing Hard to Get': Working-Class Women, Sexuality and Respectability in Britain, 1918-1940", *Women's History Review*, Vol. 1 (2), 1992, pp. 239-55, at p. 241.

Period	Rate	Ratio
1851-60	18.3	65
1861-70	18.2	61
1871-80	15.1	50
1881-90	12.6	47
1891-00	9.6	42
1901-05	8.4	39
1906-10	8.1	40
1911-15	7.9	43
1916-20	8.4	54
1921-25	6.7	43
1926-30	6.0	45
1931-35	5.5	43
1936-40	5.6	42
1938	5.8	42
1939	5.7	42
1940	5.9	43

Source: Shirley M. Hartley, "The Amazing Rise of Illegitimacy in Great Britain", *Social Forces*, Vol. 44 (4), 1966, pp. 533-45, at p. 537.

The table shows that, in respect of ratios, there had been a gradual fall in numbers from an average of 65 illegitimate births per 1,000 births per annum in the 1850s to an average of 40 in 1906-10. Thereafter the ratio remained more or less stable at around 42-43 per annum, apart from the war years (from 1947 to 1962 it hovered around 48 to 52 per annum, apart from the Second World War years, before the 'permissive society' allegedly arrived). As to the rate, which represents the number of illegitimate births per annum per 1,000 unmarried women of child-bearing age, there was a significant fall throughout the second half of the nineteenth century (from 18.3 to 9.6) which continued, though in less dramatic fashion, from 1900 to 1940. A minor spike occurred during World War One and the rate gradually increased from 1941 until by 1962 the figure had even exceeded the figure of 18.3 which had obtained during the decade of the 1850s. While we can venture broad explanations for these variations (and the 'rate' figures from the 1950s might suggest a decline in the popularity of marriage compared to previously), our particular interest relates to the inter-war years. Thus the rates for the two five-year periods between 1921 to 1930 (6.7 and 6.0 respectively) suggest that when Helen and Nellie were bearing Rouse's children, the numbers of illegitimate births per 1,000 unmarried women aged 15-44 had fallen significantly from previous decades (averaging 8.2 per annum) and from the even higher figures for the second half of the nineteenth century. Thus unmarried mothers were becoming less common among this very large cohort, and they would become even less common until 1940.

As to the ratio of illegitimate births per annum to every 1,000 live births during the 1920s, the figures, at an annual average of 44, remained relatively static during this decade, though slightly higher than in the 15 years from 1901 to 1915 (the war years witnessed a spike, as noted previously). It is difficult to interpret these figures. First, since most live births during this decade were presumably born to married women, it may be that the stable figures show a persistence of illegitimate births at a time when advice on birth-control methods was being expressly targeted by Marie Stopes and others at married women. Indeed some family doctors remained reluctant to offer even married women advice on contraception or to prescribe contraception.[642] Or it could be that better health facilities were available to unmarried mothers during their confinement than in the past when mortality rates for unmarried mothers and their babies were higher (better midwifery provision would also obviously benefit married expectant mothers). That the figures increased significantly during the war years is, of course, suggestive of a more lax attitude to non-marital sex, the intensity of which presumably weakened once the peculiar circumstances of the war had ended (and long before the supposed 'permissive' age of Aquarius in the 1960s had dawned).

The upshot from analysing the figures is, perhaps, that the circumstances of Helen and Nellie vis-a-vis other unmarried women were becoming slightly less common (and therefore they might have been more easily singled out for condemnation). But they were not in a noticeably uncommon situation, though at least some maternity homes, as we have seen in regard to Nellie, were insistent that marriage lines be produced before an expectant mother could be admitted for her confinement.

Did the vilification of single mothers in the 1990s, noted at the start of this chapter, reflect a similar pattern earlier in the twentieth century when Helen and Nellie were in the public eye? There was a broad assumption that women were primarily responsible in the event of pregnancy. Indeed that may well have been true in many cases where the newly-wed wife planned to become pregnant shortly after marriage or, less commonly, where the woman, while choosing to remain unmarried as an expression of her feminist credentials, was not inhibited from producing children. One such example was the late Victorian university graduate and activist, Edith Lanchester, who went on to live for fifty years with her partner, James Sullivan, and her two illegitimate children.[643] But while the assumption of maternal responsibility might apply in numerous cases, this might overlook inconvenient truths in other examples. Most obviously the woman might be the victim of a rape, especially by males who could feel 'entitled' to exert power over them while the latter were employed in domestic service (though the girl's own 'culpability' might still be raised). More commonly she might permit sexual intercourse to occur following a marriage proposal, only for the ceremony not to take place subsequently for a variety of reasons. So even if her 'moral culpability' might be lessened by such factors, she remained nonetheless stigmatised as an unmarried mother who, in the nineteenth century at least, was still expected to apply herself primarily to work rather than to full-time motherhood. By contrast, welfare assumptions by the twentieth century tended to perceive the wife as the

642 Janet Fink, "Natural Mothers, Putative Fathers and Innocent Children: The Definition and Regulation of Parental Relationships Outside Marriage in England, 1945-1959", *Journal of Family History*, Vol. 25 (2), 2000, pp. 178-95.
643 Jane Robinson, *In the Family Way: Illegitimacy Between the Great War and the Swinging Sixties*, Viking, 2015, p. 28-29.

home-maker rather than a factory worker who, certainly after the introduction of family allowances (as distinct from child benefit) later in the century, enjoyed access to family-oriented state benefits denied to single mothers.[644]

As Robinson has recently suggested, 'It has traditionally been assumed that unmarried mothers must all be promiscuous, feckless, daft, or far too easily taken in'.[645] The belief was one of the driving forces behind many of the 'purity' movements of the later nineteenth and earlier twentieth century such as the Social Purity and Hygiene Movement, the Association of Moral and Social Hygiene and the National Vigilance Association which sought to expose the evil works of prostitutes, irresponsible girls with lax morals (who obviously embraced unmarried mothers), and pornographers and those 'addicted' to masturbation.[646] Some lower-level judges might inveigh against the immorality of unmarried mothers and view their efforts to obtain maintenance payments from alleged errant fathers as a form of blackmail (the more modern version was for certain politicians to accuse single mothers of deliberately becoming pregnant in order to jump the queue to obtain a council house). Not surprisingly senior representatives of the Church were in the van of such moral crusades, some of them seeking to exclude from their charitable ministrations those young girls who fell pregnant without a wedding ring. To be fair, however, other senior prelates adopted a more 'Christian' attitude towards this category of the poor and needy. And there were, of course, a number of charitable organisations offering confinement facilities, some verging on the benign, such as the Salvation Army, as well as harsh and almost inhumane charitable regimes, such as some of the notorious Magdalene homes in Ireland. But were one to assert that the lack of sex education in the home or at school might have had something to do with unmarried pregnancy, or that some members of the medical profession were abandoning their responsibilities by failing young women in respect of contraception or contraceptive advice, one could imagine the bristling and angry response that such suggestions might have provoked.

A familiar consequence of illegitimate birth was that the child (where abortion, miscarriage, still birth or infanticide had not occurred) would be expected to be taken in by grandparents, foster or adoptive parents, or placed in the workhouse while the mother would be expected to return to work. Indeed the confinement, as noted above, would often be a somewhat shady process, taking place in a lying-in house at a distance from the girl's home. And the child itself would be as stigmatised and as harshly dealt with in the future as the mother. And if this were to be the mother's second or further illegitimate birth, she might find herself detained as a moral imbecile under the Mental Deficiency Act 1913 before this vicious arrangement was formally (but not in reality) abolished in 1959.[647] Such cruel detention was the most obvious way in which an unmarried mother might be hidden from view, while the smooth transition from expectant single mother,

---

644   *Cf.*, Fink, *op. cit.*, p. 179.
645   See Robinson, *op. cit.*, p.53, for this and subsequent detail.
646   For the latter two organisations see Helen J. Self, *Prostitution, Women and Misuse of the Law: The Fallen Daughters of Eve*, Frank Cass, 2003.
647   Ginger Frost, "'The Black Lamb of the Black Sheep': Illegitimacy in the English Working Class, 1850-1939", *Journal of Social History*, Vol. 37(2), 2003, pp. 293-322. This paper, like many other sources, offers numerous examples of the verbal and physical cruelty suffered by children merely because they were born illegitimate.

sent away for her confinement, to a return to her familiar surroundings minus her (adopted or fostered) child was another. Where Helen and Nellie differed from this construction was in their high visibility as single mothers. Their photographs and those of their children adorned their articles in *Peg's Paper*. Nasty comments about Nellie's Pamelita and Patricia may not have been expressed or, at least, not publicly documented (and presumably Nellie's fiancé, Mirza Knott, was willing to provide for them as components of a new nuclear family). But in respect of Arthur Jnr., he seems, if we are to believe J. C. Cannell's account in his story of Rouse, to have captured the imagination of many of the journalists who met the young boy when they were interviewing his mother. For gifts and Christmas presents seem to have been heaped upon him after 'whip-rounds' had been arranged by Cannell and his colleagues. Indeed the photographs of Arthur Jnr., sitting or standing alongside his mother, are charming and warm portraits of a smiling young lad with a cheeky grin on his face. In an official sense the little boy was a 'bastard', a word weighted with negativity, shame, contempt and lack of compassion. He was even legally unrelated to his biological father (except to the extent that Helen could claim maintenance for him from Rouse). For 'It was marriage, not insemination, that legitimated a man's status as a father.'[648] And while a pompous and wilfully ignorant legal writer in the 1890s might insist that such offspring, '....will [probably] inherit the moral flabbiness, the uncontrollable impulse, the selfishness, and the lack of self-respect which usually characterises one or both of the parents of illegitimate children',[649] the picture of this happy and contented five-year old illegitimate child of Helen Campbell challenged everything undesirable about the status of the stigmatised 'outsider'. Yet he could neither be legally adopted by his own mother nor, under the Legitimacy Act 1926, be legitimated were Rouse to have married Helen since Rouse had been married to Lily at the time of his son's birth (a provision not repealed until 1959). Although not an H. M. Stanley ('Dr Livingstone, I presume'), nor Ramsay MacDonald, nor Catherine Cookson, who all suffered degrees of discrimination in their younger years because of their status, but whose subsequent fame suggests that not every 'bastard' was doomed to outcast status, Arthur Jnr. could well have been a bright and endearing 'poster boy' for a new approach, away from stigmatised illegitimacy. Of course being the acknowledged illegitimate child of Rouse was scarcely the ideal start to public acclaim. On the other hand the very fact that his father had been convicted and hanged as a murderer (and who apparently loved Arthur Jnr.) might, counter-intuitively, have increased sympathy for the little boy. Not simply an illegitimate child but yet another victim, to join the list with the unknown tramp and Rouse's duped wife and lovers. Thus little Arthur should be accorded support, not contumely. Indeed, journalists such as Cannell might well have concluded that never had it been less seemly to apply to Arthur Jnr. the dismissive injunction that the 'sins of the fathers are to be visited on the sons'.

It might be suggested that Helen and Nellie (and their children) seem to have boldly confronted those narrow-minded and judgmental voices, often within officialdom, who painted any deviation from sexual normalcy and the nuclear family as a threat to the very foundations of civilised society. There was certainly

---

648 Fink, *op. cit.*, p. 181.
649 Cited in Robinson, *op. cit.*, p. 35.

no shortage of such censorious voices targeting single mothers. Yet the sky did not fall when Helen and Nellie threw off the cloaks of anonymity that had enshrouded them at the police court hearings when they were described in the press as 'mystery women' with veiled faces. Given the climate of the time and the dominance of 'respectable' opinion, Helen and Nellie struck a blow for single motherhood, not in the sense of making political or ideological statements but in asserting their right to be heard as mothers. It was a perspective, together with an emphasis on the importance of psychological and emotional bonding between mother and child, that some pressure groups, such as the British Medical Association and the National Council for One-Parent Families (or its earlier incarnation), facing criticism that they were condoning immorality, later highlighted when furthering the interests of illegitimate children.[650]

Admittedly there was undoubtedly a money payment from the magazine involved, especially in respect of Helen (for Nellie could look forward to a forthcoming marriage to Mirza Knott). Moreover, there is a strong though unprovable suspicion that the actual writing was done *for* them, rather than *by* them. But it is probably uncharitable to believe that financial reward was the only, or even prime, motive for the women to tell their stories. Their endeavour to paint themselves as collateral though ambiguous victims of Arthur Rouse was more likely to have been the driving force, though their financial situations could hardly have been rosy. For the niggardly sums of ten shillings a week for each child (half the maximum allowable per child) that Rouse had been ordered by the magistrates to pay in maintenance for Arthur Jnr. and for Pamelita (that is, when he deigned to pass over the sums), hardly ensured financial security for the two mothers. Even foster mothers could receive from local authorities up to £1 7s 9d a week as maintenance payments for foster children in their care.[651] And with the exhaustion of Rouse's funds to pay for his defence, which was later followed by his execution, the erratic payments ceased altogether.

The abiding significance, therefore, to be drawn from Helen and Nellie's stories was the boldness with which it appeared that they faced down the moral guardians of the day, and celebrated their illegitimate children with a maternal pride not in the least diluted by the circumstances of the little ones' conception. They were fighting back, or at least it strongly appeared so from the articles, and they were moving on (though in which direction, in Helen's case, would not be clear). Their children, they seemed to be urging, were as entitled to feature in (albeit more attenuated) family portraits published in the press, as any other children. The children were well dressed and turned out, healthy and smiling. If they were stigmatised, then that was others' problem, not theirs or Helen's or Nellie's. Indeed, though neither Helen nor Nellie stated as much, if any stigma could be raised, it derived not from the circumstances of their birth but from the separate matter of their father's murderous actions. To be sure, that was shameful, like a father being sent to prison for larceny or experiencing bankruptcy or suffering a sexually transmitted disease (or supporting an extremist political party). But that was the *father*, not the child, and if any shame were to be felt, surely it attached to those pious souls whose predilections towards judgmental attitudes

650   Fink, *op. cit.*, p. 181.
651   *Ibid.*, p. 183.

blinded themselves to their own double standards. And while neither Helen nor Nellie aspired to anything beyond immediate post-elementary schooling, we cannot discount, in the absence of conflicting evidence, that their celebration of motherhood and of their bastard children was not a genuine and conscious riposte to the sexual and family hypocrisy of the day, rather than the scandal-mongering of press journalists. Indeed we positively aver that that was their motive

There is, therefore, more than simply the 'rehabilitation' of these particular illegitimate children into a 'mainstream' where distinctions of status (over which Rouse's children self-evidently had no control) would be of no account. For what was being heard was women's voices publicly challenging serious misconduct perpetrated against them (the politically loaded term 'oppression' may be an over-statement here) by a dominating male who, it is acknowledged, eventually over-reached himself. Here were female voices being raised, not exactly in unison, but with a similar refrain of being beguiled and cheated by a man consumed with his own vanity and with what he believed was his 'lady-killer' charm. It is interesting, for example, that one obvious feature of the series of articles by the different women published in *Peg's Paper* is that in each of the accounts there appear photographs not just of the writer in question and of Rouse but of all the women involved. No doubt that might satisfy the curiosity of the reader but perhaps it signified a degree of solidarity on the part of Rouse's 'women', in that their experiences united them more than they divided them (friendly meetings, accompanied by soft photos, were reported). A kind of inchoate 'sisterhood in adversity' was formed, even if it only remained temporary until events moved on. But perhaps we should not make too much of these points. Certainly, these women were now to be found in the 'public' sphere or 'thoroughfare', albeit in a writing capacity, a *habitus* (to use sociological jargon) from which women had tended to be excluded (thus 'hidden from history' in Sheila Rowbotham's distinctive phrase[652]). For the 'public sphere', and not the confines (literally and metaphorically) of the home, was where men were to be seen, thereby emphasising their superior importance, such as in employment, the pub, the racecourse, and in politics. Yet while Lily *et al.* were now occupying 'public space' with their writings, old assumptions still prevailed. For their accounts tended to stress domesticity, raising families, and expectations of, and flowing from, marriage, suggestive of the female-dominated private sphere. But in their writing for the public, these women nonetheless signified a cross-over from private to public that ordinary women without more than standard school education, let alone university experience, could actually achieve. For they were neither novelists, professional lawyers or doctors or politicians, unlike, say, Agatha Christie, Dorothy L. Sayers, Virginia Woolf, Vita Sackville-West, Vera Brittain, Winifred Holtby, Nancy Astor, Eleanor Rathbone, Margaret Bondfield or even Helena Normanton. Instead, the three Rouse women were venturing beyond their comfort zones or the familiar terrain expected of them. Gender boundaries were becoming more fluid, albeit not in a pronounced way, as far as they were concerned (indeed, we will consider in the concluding chapter whether Rouse himself was facing a crisis of masculinity, as the demands of domestication in respect of men became more noticeable).

---

652   Sheila Rowbotham, *Hidden from History: 300 Years of Women's Oppression and the Fight Against It*, Pluto Press, 1974.

Yet, as mentioned above, the transformation can be exaggerated. After all, Lily, Helen and Nellie were writing in a *women's* magazine, and not in, say, a national newspaper or in a middle- or high-brow 'non-gender' periodical. Whether the words published under the names of 'Rouse's women' were their own or were the creations of journalists, one cannot help feeling that, in the cases of Helen and Nellie, they sought to ensure that their children were projected as their pride and joy despite, or perhaps because of, their stigmatised legal status. Second, in respect of Lily and Ivy the strong message among the dross of love and betrayal was female resilience. But only in third place was the mixed message targeted at the young female readers of *Peg's Paper*, which was that romantic idealism is a fine trait to possess (after all, it was the currency of *Peg's Paper*), but be careful what you wish for. However packaged or whoever were the actual authors, the achievement of 'Rouse's women' was not just that their messy stories (and the 'celebration' of Helen and Nellie's children) were transmitted, but that, as a warning to other young women, they also consented to run the risk of exposure to ridicule as silly, naive women. That was bold. That was brave.

It was slightly different in the case of Ivy Jenkins. For her publishing outlet was not a specifically women's magazine but the more general *Thomson's Weekly News*, liable to be read by at least some men and not exclusively targeted at women readers. Her writing was also couched in more analytical terms with greater depth of detail of her background, her family and her professional aspirations. Moreover, it raised a new perspective on the case which was that Rouse was attempting to poison her in order to extricate himself from the couple's impending fateful trip with Phyllis to their 'new house' in Kingston, a ghost journey that was looming nearer and nearer. It was strongly suggested previously that the story of poisoning seemed implausible and that it was more comforting to Ivy to offer this explanation for her severe illness, rather than her attributing her bed-ridden condition to a miscarriage or even to extreme morning sickness. She did, of course, refer in her story to widespread talk of pregnancy and to a still birth but, interestingly, she neither admitted nor denied that such events had occurred. Given the wording of her article, we might have had to leave this particular issue in an uncertain state, with two rival interpretations for her illness. While the heart might encourage us to embrace the poisoning story, not only the head but also the statement of her medical practitioner, Dr. E. L. Phillips, given at Ystrad Mynach police station on December 26, 1930, makes clear that when he examined her on November 12 she was five months pregnant. He added that due to her severe state of nervous exhaustion, she would not be fit to travel to Northampton for the committal proceedings. Indeed he did not expect her to recover until after her confinement which was yet two months away (as is known she miscarried before her due date).

But apart from this startling accusation, her account was also more consciously moralistic, painting her as the most respectable of young women pained not just by Rouse's duplicity but by his immorality and hypocrisy, especially in respect of religion. For the latter surely played a much greater role in her life (given the traditions of Welsh Non-Conformism) than can be found in the lives of Lily, Helen and Nellie. The treachery on the part of one who disdained religion but who then joined in with her family to sing hymns lustily as the enormity of his situation sank in would thus have been felt keenly in Ivy's case Yet the idea of Christian forgiveness, given that she declared that she would 'not lift a finger' to save Rouse, was not to be found. Could anyone really blame her?

Thus the written testimonies of the four women most directly affected by Rouse's callous excesses offer, first, a slightly skewed glimpse of the travails of the single mother between the wars. For what does *not* come through clearly, with regard to Helen and Nellie, is a picture of poverty, degradation and shame which we might instinctively associate with the fate of the single abandoned unmarried mother, especially in an urban setting, between the wars. This is not to say that the two young women did not suffer financially and emotionally as a result of giving birth to Rouse's children while enduring a tentative, erratic and insecure life with him. Yet while their stories would undoubtedly serve as a warning to other young women tempted by an older man who did not strike them as too good to be true, while he charmed his way into their affections and then into their beds, there was nonetheless a positive gloss to their stories as they sought to rebuild their lives with their darling children. Ivy's story is, of course, the most combative and the most outraged at Rouse's conduct. Yet one might still harbour the thought that by referring to the alleged poisoning, the lady rather clumsily sought (unless she thought her readers exceedingly naive) to deflect attention from the enduring shame she undoubtedly felt as a 'tainted' young woman who could no longer walk down the aisle in the future as a virginal bride. Perhaps Lily's story is, however, the saddest of the four (pipping at the post Ivy's experience in the sadness stakes). For what emerges is the stoicism that Lily, married to Rouse for sixteen years, continued to manifest as revelation followed revelation about her husband's philandering, followed by his succession of empty promises to reform and never to contact the 'other women' again. For that attitude was grounded in her traditional belief in love and in a lifelong commitment to one's marriage partner. He may have been a (metaphorical) bastard but she clearly was insistent that he was *her* bastard (to paraphrase General Patton). And that is how it continued via his imprisonment, trial and execution, right through to her final words in *Peg's Paper* in a series perhaps significantly entitled 'How I Found Out and Why I Forgave'.

SECTION D
Miscarriage of Justice?

CHAPTER TWENTY-THREE

FAKED THEFTS OF CARS

DAILY SKETCH, March 13, 1931

Rouse's Insurance Frauds?

This first chapter in the section headed 'Miscarriage of Justice?' seeks to examine the evidence that the Home Office, and Sir Ernley Blackwell, in particular, believed had proved that the killing of the tramp was part of a plot by Rouse to disappear and to benefit himself financially through insurance fraud. Indeed Blackwell was convinced that Lily was herself a party to the financial arrangement, even if he gave no strong indication that he believed she had been party to her husband's plan to do away with a third party whose corpse would be assumed to be her husband's (but on the other hand, Blackwell does not seem to have questioned how Lily could *not* have been privy, before the police arrived at her door, to the essential component of the plot, that is, how to acquire or create a dead body that would not be her husband's? For how could one claim on the insurance if there was no body? Was *all* trace of it to disappear, as the 'Acid-Bath' killer, John Haigh, later foolishly thought was possible?).

It will be recalled that at the outset of Rouse's trial, prosecuting counsel, Norman Birkett, explained to the jury in outlining his case against the accused that he did not propose to offer a motive as to why Rouse had murdered the unknown victim. As a matter of law, it was (and still is) unnecessary for the Crown to establish proof of motive when it sought to persuade the jury to return a murder conviction. It was *mens rea* ('guilty mind') or malice aforethought (the latter a somewhat misleading and old-fashioned phrase, inasmuch as premeditation is not a requirement for the criminal mental state) that the Crown required to prove beyond reasonable doubt. Together with the 'criminal act', that is, the *actus reus*, here were the two prongs on which a prosecution had to proceed.[653]

Of course there had been intense speculation as to what *was* Rouse's motive, with most views believing that he had got himself into such a mess with his women, illegitimate children and, possibly, other sundry financial commitments relating to the hire purchase on his car and the mortgage on 14 Buxted Road, that a 'Reggie Perrin' or a John Stonehouse-type disappearing act was the driving force. It is unlikely that he had gained his inspiration from reading H. G. Wells' *The History of Mr Polly* published in 1910, and in which the gentlemen's outfitter

---

653 Today, intention to kill the victim or to cause him or her serious harm (from which death ensues, and no longer bound by the 'year and a day' rule) is preferred to the term 'malice aforethought'.

of the title suffered a mid-life crisis in the provincial town of Fishbourne. Facing bankruptcy and hating his wife, his neighbours and not least himself, he imagined his only escape was by burning his shop down and committing suicide. The first task was incompetently and incompletely carried out and the second was flunked. In desperation he goes 'on the tramp', finds his inner self and ends up in peaceful enjoyment at a Sussex country pub.

While Mr Polly's financial problems had been caused by bad luck rather than by recklessness or by dodgy transactions, fraudulent dealings in the keeping of accounts were, in other cases, reasons prompting a person to disappear. This was why a Welsh solicitor, John Wagstaffe, decided in 1938 to abandon his family and his familiar identity in order to become John Watson, helping to crew the vessel of one 'Potato' Jones who shipped supplies to the Republican side in the Spanish Civil War. Watson then enjoyed a varied wartime career with the French Foreign Legion, being captured by the Germans and marrying a Polish woman undertaking forced labour for the Nazis, and with whom he had two children. After the war he obtained employment with the British Embassy in Paris. Meanwhile the local police in Newport had discovered the reason for Wagstaffe's sudden pre-war disappearance and still had an outstanding warrant for his arrest. After a 'cold case'-type review in 1957, a connection was made between Wagstaffe and Watson after the police checked old rugby club records for South Wales. But it was too late. Wagstaffe (or Watson) had died in 1954 and the police finally requested the justices, almost 20 years after Wagstaffe's disappearance, to dismiss the warrant for his arrest.[654]

No-one died violently as a result of Wagstaffe's assuming a new *persona*, and if any insurance payout were to result, this would not benefit the disappeared. A more recent variant of this was the case of Mr. and Mrs. John Darwin from Hartlepool, Co. Durham. This was the couple who contrived a plot to swindle their insurance company by faking the husband's death in 2002 in a canoeing accident in the North Sea near their home. The company were taken in by Mrs. Darwin's tearful life insurance claim following her husband's tragic 'drowning', only for the plot to unravel when there appeared photographs of the smiling couple posing with an estate agent in a flat in Panama City, images taken after the husband's alleged demise at sea.[655]

However in the Rouse case the DPP and the Crown were certain that Rouse's scheme was an insurance fraud to benefit both him and Lily and, of course, involved the callous murder of an unrecognisable (and hopefully unlamented) man whose burnt corpse would be assumed to be that of Rouse himself. For both

654 Leonard Gribble, *Notorious Crimes*, Robert Hale, 1985, Ch. 10.
655 It was reported in mid-2014 that the husband, by this time separated from Mrs. Darwin, had only repaid £121 of the £679,000 fraudulently obtained and that he had now been ordered to repay £40,000, the proceeds of two maturing pension policies. A confiscation order for the balance was still outstanding at the time of writing. Mrs. Darwin had previously repaid £500,000 with £177,000 still outstanding. See *Guardian*, May 29, 2014. At the couple's trial in 2008 Mrs. Darwin had unsuccessfully pleaded the defence of 'marital coercion', like that unconvincingly advanced by Vicky Pryce, ex-wife of former Energy and Climate Change minister, Chris Huhne (though arising from different circumstances). See Gerry Rubin, "Pre-dating Vicky Pryce: the Peel Case (1922) and the Origins of the Marital Coercion Statutory Defence", *Legal Studies*, Vol. 34 (4), 2014, pp. 631-59. In August 2014 the press reported the case of Andrew Biddle in New Jersey, suspected of faking his own death in a powerboat crash in order to flee fraud charges. A coastguard search had previously failed to locate his body. See *The Times*, August 6, 2014.

Paling and Blackwell were convinced that the key to the mystery (if not to the identity of the victim) lay in a plot by Rouse, in cahoots with his wife, to fake his death in the car blaze. The corpse would be mistaken for him, he would next lie low somewhere for a sensible period of time, Lily would then claim off the insurance company for the loss of her husband, and finally the couple would meet up again (whether as a couple or as a separated pair was not stated), and share the proceeds of the insurance hand-out. At first sight the imagined scenario seems far-fetched. For what if the victim had not been burnt to death and if relatives of the stranger could, indeed, confirm his identity beyond peradventure? Another unravelling would soon take place followed by criminal vengeance on both husband and wife.[656] In any case, just as no military plan survives first contact with the enemy, so Rouse's scheme was rent asunder as soon as he emerged from the ditch in Hardingstone Lane into the clear line of moonlit vision of the two young men returning from the Guy Fawkes Night dance.

What, then, was the reasoning of the authorities that drew them to claim that an insurance fraud was at the heart of the supposed murder? The first thing to note is that from 1930, when the Road Traffic Act of that year came into force, every motorist was obliged by law to take out car insurance to indemnify third parties suffering injury, death, loss or damage as a result of the driver's negligence (as legally conceived). While the Third Parties (Rights against Insurers) Act the same year protected road traffic victims where drivers had failed to take out compulsory insurance,[657] some critics remained dissatisfied. They included Mr. Justice Rigby Swift who had presided over a number of tort cases involving injury to young children harmed in car crashes.[658] For if the driver's action were found not to amount to 'negligence', the injured plaintiff (whether adult or child) would still be denied damages.[659]

In Rouse's case the car insurance picture is confusing (no surprise there, then). First, when he obtained delivery of MU 1468 on June 2, 1930 from Messrs Stewart & Ardern Ltd of New Bond Street,[660] the cover on his existing Dominion of Canada car insurance policy appears to have been transferred to his new car, although it seems that this policy, while insuring the value of the car (still partly 'owned' by the hire purchase company, Messrs Chester & Cole Ltd), did not include the compulsory indemnity element vis-a-vis third parties, presumably because the requirement in the 1930 Act had not yet come into force. However, that policy expired on July 18, 1930, at which point he replaced it with an 'Eclipse' motor policy (which he mistakenly believed was an 'Economic Insurance' policy) underwritten by Lloyd's. This comprehensive policy, costing £11 per annum, also

---

656 Not even a plea of marital coercion could avail Lily in such circumstances because, for the defence to apply, both parties have to be present when the crime is committed. And, in any case, the defence is not available in cases of murder or treason.

657 P. W. J. Bartrip, "Pedestrians, Motorists, and No-Fault Compensation for Road Accidents in 1930s Britain", *Journal of Legal History*, Vol. 31(1), April 2010, pp. 45-60, at p. 53.

658 E. S. Fay, *The Life of Mr. Justice Rigby Swift*, Methuen, 1939, pp. 216-7.

659 The indemnity requirements were subsequently strengthened beyond the driver's 'negligence' to include circumstances where careless driving could be established. Criminal proceedings were, of course, a separate matter, and could be instituted for offences such as causing death by dangerous driving or committing motor manslaughter (as his fellow peers in the House of Lords had found against Lord de Clifford in 1935 in the very last House of Lords trial by one's peers before the procedure was abolished). See, *ibid.*, pp. 239-41. Swift J. was one of the four justices who advised the lords spiritual and temporal on the law.

660 They had a branch and repair shop in Tottenham.

contained an endorsement (apparently for the additional sum of £2 a year), to the effect that the insurer would pay out £1,000 to the personal representatives of the passenger, whoever that might be, in the event of the latter's death in the vehicle, or £1,000 to Lily in the event of Rouse's loss of life.[661] To acquire the new vehicle Rouse paid a lump sum of £64.10.0 after receiving £92.10.0 trade-in for his previous vehicle, with the balance to be paid at £6.14. 8d. per month. As well as the vehicle, coloured blue, Rouse also received the car's new registration book issued by Middlesex County Council and dated May 30, 1930. He further had to pay road tax (at a rate of £8 per annum) of £4. 18s. 0d. This would cover the period up to December 31, 1930, by which time, of course, there was for Rouse no longer any vehicle, nor freedom to drive one.[662] However, as the total payable on the new Morris Minor was 4s. 6d a week more than his mortgage, we should not be surprised that, as revealed at the police court,[663] his September payment was more than three weeks late, being paid on September 26 instead of on the first of the month, as required.

It is noticeable that in his proposal form for his previous vehicle, MM 9043, he had declared that the car would be used only for 'private pleasure' purposes, a somewhat ironic, not to say partially dishonest, statement. He also declared that he had previously been insured with the Economic Motor Insurance Company, had suffered one previous vehicle loss involving the 'theft' outside the theatre in Golders Green in 1928, that he had been driving since 1909-10, and that he had one conviction, for breaking a ten miles an hour speed limit. According to an insurance underwriter, Denis Kennedy, giving similar evidence at the trial to that which had been adduced at the police court, the proposal form for the new Eclipse policy was also couched in similar, if not identical, terms. Thus Rouse had stated in the form that the vehicle would be used solely for 'private pleasure purposes', that he had held a licence for ten or twelve years, that he had once exceeded a twenty miles an hour speed limit but without his licence having been endorsed, that he wished to cover all accidents to passengers (though 'Never got any passengers, but yes'), that he would not bear any excess, that he was not then, nor had been, insured in respect of any vehicle (a puzzling statement since Kennedy was presumably aware of the Dominion policy), that he had had no accidents or claims in the previous two years, and that he had not previously been refused cover or been subject to an increased premium or to an excess requirement. Finally, there was the endorsement regarding the contingent pay outs of £1.000.

But it was this endorsement that struck Paling as particularly significant and as pointing to Rouse's criminal intent. For it had not appeared in the Dominion of Canada policy covering both MM 9043 and the first few weeks of MU 1468. As he noted in a memorandum of February 25, 1931, written two days after

---

661 It was not stated explicitly what would happen if both were to die in a car accident, though it might be inferred that the heirs such as Rouse's father (and which would probably exclude Rouse's illegitimate children), administrators or executors of both parties would receive £1,000 for each victim. Provision was also made for significant payments in the event of physical injury. The vehicle's Service Identification Plate No. 6800, made of solid brass and incorporating Rouse's signature, was attached to the car, probably on the offside of the dashboard. His previous vehicle, also a Morris, registration number MM 9043, had been bought by Rouse for £135 in July 1929.

662 The registration book is preserved in the (formerly-named) Nottingham Galleries of Justice archives.

663 *The Times*, December 11, 1930.

Rouse's unsuccessful appeal, 'The passenger's personal representatives would have received £1,000 if Rouse had reported his [*sic*] accidental death. Thus Rouse would have had full knowledge that his passenger was so covered'. For Paling this was highly suspicious and supported his theory of a marital conspiracy to defraud Rouse's insurers.

But what is puzzling is Paling's pre-occupation with a passenger. Clearly, the £1,000 cover would be of benefit to Lily in the event of Rouse's accidental death, or of Rouse in the event of Lily's accidental death if she were to be the unfortunate passenger. But if the deceased or badly injured passenger were a third party who, according to the policy, had to be between the ages of 15 and 65, then the endorsement provided that payment for injury was to be made to such person (or their heirs, administrators or executors if death ensued). How, then, could Rouse himself benefit financially from an arrangement to compensate for injury or death to a passenger other than Lily (apart from rendering unnecessary the need for such passengers or their representatives to sue him if he had been negligent in driving)? But, of course, such a pay out to a passenger would not *increase* Rouse's wealth and would only prevent any depletion. Thus there might have been a fraudulent advantage to Lily and Rouse only in the event of the unidentified corpse in the car, in reality a third party passenger, being mistaken for Rouse or Lily, as the case might be (but how on earth, notwithstanding the discovery of a woman's shoe heel among the debris, could an unknown *male* passenger be presumed to have been Lily, were she to have gone into hiding for a spell after the blaze, which she obviously had not done?). More crucially, it is difficult, on the other hand, to see what financial *gain* would accrue to Rouse or Lily in the event of a corpse, deemed to be a *passenger*, the focus of Paling's attention, above, being discovered in the burnt-out shell. Indeed, while the personal representatives of an identified victim, rather than Rouse or Lily, would receive the £1,000 (and identification might make a police investigation into a conspiracy easier if suspicions were aroused), the position would be different if the corpse were unidentified. For presumably no-one would be entitled to that sum, unless the body were presumed to have been a now-disappeared Rouse. For this was the premise on which Paling and Blackwell could only have built their conspiracy theory involving Lily and Rouse, with the latter disappearing off the face of the earth and the insurance proceeds, claimed by Lily, being divided between the two. But in this scenario there was no room for any passenger (except possibly Lily). So while Paling might well have advanced a possible, but surely far-fetched, theory involving a conspiracy by Rouse and Lily to profit from murdering and burning beyond recognition an unidentified passenger, he was surely wide of the mark if he had based his suspicions on a scenario in which the passenger's personal representatives would receive £1,000 in the event that 'Rouse had reported his accidental death', and where Rouse, according to Paling, 'would have had full knowledge that his passenger was so covered'. So Paling could theoretically have been right about a joint conspiracy, but surely for the wrong reason when he incorporated an insured third-party passenger into the plot (though we believe that he was wrong anyway). For could one reasonably envisage an arrangement that involved the otherwise law-abiding Lily conspiring with her husband to murder a third party (or to steal a corpse like Major Martin, *The Man Who Never Was*)? And the corpse that would be found in the wreckage of Rouse's burnt-out Morris Minor would also have to be so unrecognisable that, in order for the £1,000 insurance moneys to be paid out to her, it would have to be assumed to be Lily's husband rather than a separate insured passenger. Yet no homicide or, indeed, any other criminal proceedings were taken against Lily. Why not, if Paling of the DPP really was convinced of her involvement in a murderous (or even in just a fraudulent) conspiracy? Did not inaction in this regard speak a thousand words as to his deepest thoughts on the matter? Technically, the simple answer why she was left alone by the DPP, as noted earlier in this book, is because a conspiracy involving only a husband and wife is not a criminal offence (whether there were other possible offences against her, such as an attempt to defraud, was probably doubtful on the evidence).

But in respect of Rouse himself, the conspiracy theory arguably did much to ensure that he would not secure a reprieve, as the authorities congratulated themselves on bringing to justice a cunning, financially-driven killer, aided by his wife (as Talbot J. also later came to believe). But the theory was as illusionary as Cannell's magic tricks and as illusory as Rouse's own flights of fancy. Indeed the only other (surely implausible) possibility was that Rouse had been contemplating bumping off *Lily* herself for the money, or even disposing of Helen or Nellie, and thereby possibly controlling the insurance funds going to their, and his, children who would benefit as next-of-kin of the deceased mothers. Needless to say, there is no evidence whatsoever for this speculative whimsy.

Paling also observed that on October 16, 1930 Mrs. Rouse had phoned the head office of the Prudential at Holborn Bars, London, for particulars regarding the company's personal accident insurance scheme. (His account was based on statements taken from Prudential officials by Inspector W. Collins of Scotland Yard, acting on behalf of the Northamptonshire police.) Lily was very anxious to take out a personal accident insurance policy as soon as possible on the life of her husband. The 'Man from the Pru', Mr. S. P. White (not, indeed, the ill-fated Prudential representative, William Wallace),[664] called at once and explained the benefits of such a policy and added that the premium was £6 for £600 coverage. Rouse's own signature (he was not at home at the time) would be required on the proposal form. So an appointment was made with another agent, Mr. Alfred Cripps, to call at 3 pm the next day, as Mrs. Rouse had explained that her husband would be away for three weeks from the following Saturday. Cripps duly arrived but no-one answered. He called again on October 28 when he saw Lily but explained again the need for Rouse's signature. However this requirement seemed to disconcert Lily, so Cripps offered her an 'LOA' ('letter of assurance') policy that necessitated only her signature but not that of her husband, a product that Lily, perhaps over-eagerly, accepted. For a shilling a week Rouse would be covered for £73.4.0 payable to Lily in the event of his death after six months of the policy being executed, and half that amount if he died within the first six months. If, however, he died in an *accident* within the first six months, she would still receive the full amount. According to Collins, Lily had explained to Cripps that her husband was 'very erratic, fond of the ladies, very quick tempered and was likely to come home in a temper at any time, [and] threaten to sell up the house and disappear'. Undeterred by these revelations, the company agreed to provide cover and Mrs. Rouse made the first payment, the actual policy being delivered to

664   The intriguing Wallace case in Liverpool in 1931 has been mentioned in, inter alia, chapter two.

her only after Rouse's arrest some days later, Cripps remarked to his supervisor that, 'Isn't it strange that the man has disappeared. Mrs. Rouse had previously told me he might disappear'. Given that Rouse was already safely in custody when the agent made these remarks, the insurance man's observations hinted either at his suspicious nature, his gullibility or his ignorance of current events.

Blackwell, for his part, in considering the question of a reprieve on March 3, 1931, had also declared that,

> It is abundantly clear that at least up to the time when the prisoner left his wife on the morning of the 6th November between 6 and 7 am he and she both intended that that body should be identified as his body so that the £1,000 insurance money could be drawn by his wife and divided between them, or appropriated by the prisoner as the case may be.

It is likely that Blackwell's analysis of what, at least to him, was 'abundantly clear', was reinforced by the enigmatic evidence allegedly provided by five-year old Arthur Jnr, referred to at different intervals in the pre-trial proceedings but which was not disclosed at the court hearings. According to Inspector Collins of Scotland Yard, he had been summoned to a meeting on the evening of December 2 with Mr. Henry Flint, Helen Campbell's London solicitor, who had maintained a watching brief on her behalf at the police court hearings. The meeting took place at the Royal Hotel, Bloomsbury. Also present were Helen Cambell [*sic*], J. C. Cannell and W. E. Cameron-Waller, Cannell's colleague at the *Daily Sketch* whose interest in sensational disclosures depended greatly on persuading central characters to enter into exclusive deals. Flint then explained to Collins that he had just been told by Waller that Arthur Jnr. had said that he had seen his father at 14 Buxted Road on the morning after 'Fireworks night', and that he, Arthur Jnr., had heard his father and 'Auntie Lil' talking about insurance. In fact, according to Cannell, the 'tiny, keen-witted son of Rouse [had earlier] babbled out to me a story one night, the great importance of which I instantly recognised'.[665] Collins was even told that the little boy could be brought from his bed to speak to him, if required. However, a meeting was arranged with the boy and his mother for the next afternoon at Flint's office in Shoe Lane in the City of London. Paling instructed Collins to go ahead with the arrangement. Collins then learned of Helen's life since 1920, of her long association with Rouse, her 'marriage' and giving birth to her babies, and her shock at meeting Lily and discovering the truth of her and Rouse's marital status.

As to what Arthur Jnr. had allegedly heard regarding insurance on November 6, Helen had told Collins that she was in a car with her son and the two newspaper representatives on December 1 when her son started to talk about fireworks. He said he had not seen his father on Guy Fawkes Night but had seen him the next morning at Buxted Road. His father had been speaking in a loud voice with 'Auntie Lil' and he had heard them use the word 'insurance' several times. His father had also seemed quite cross about something and spoke of a medal (presumably Rouse's Army identity disc) which should have been in the car. Collins went on to explain that the child, who was in another office at the time, was then brought in and was sat on his mother's knee as she talked to him quietly. He continued,

665   J. C. Cannell, *When Fleet Street Calls*, Jarrolds. 1932, p. 182.

It was then obvious to me that he had either been present at many discussions of this case, or had been prompted by some interested party. He said nothing which would be of any material use, nor could this be expected from one so young. It is also significant that he has been silent for nearly a month. The fact that Rouse, when at Northampton, made a remark about his "harem" may also be taken into account, as this has made Miss Cambell [*sic*] very bitter.

What did this observation signify? First, the use of the term 'insurance' by a five-year old would appear to be odd in that such a term would be beyond a young child's conceptual awareness, though this is not to say that he did not overhear the word used in the early morning of November 6. Indeed, while there is no independent evidence that he was awake and could overhear conversations from another bedroom when Rouse returned home at about six o'clock on the morning after 'Fireworks night', every parent in the world is aware that young children have an inconsiderate habit of waking up far too early in the morning. But if the magic word 'insurance' *had* been heard on November 6 by Arthur Jnr., why was it that Helen had only mentioned it on December 1? Collins clearly believed that she had been motivated to raise it at this point as a reflection of her anger or hatred against Rouse (and Lily), following her 'betrayal' by him. Yet militating against this view is that by December 1 there is no clear evidence that she bore Rouse (or Lily) such ill-will that she would adduce damning evidence, via Arthur Jnr., that could send Rouse to the gallows. Second, Collins did not actually state that the boy had, in fact, used the term 'insurance' in his presence, only that Helen had said he had done so. But whichever view is taken of whether Arthur Jnr. had overheard a loud discussion between his father and Lily in the early morning of November 6, during which the word 'insurance' may or may not have been uttered, the boy's alleged testimony was never used in court. For Collins this was partly because the child was too young to give credible evidence (though children much younger than Arthur Jnr. have been able to testify under protective conditions in trials in recent years; for example in a rape case against Stephen Barker following the death of Peter Connelly ('Baby P') in 2010). But it was also because, as noted above, Collins had concluded that, probably as a result of coaching by his mother, the child had nothing material to say.

Yet to disregard Arthur Jnr.'s 'evidence' was not enough for Blackwell to discount the conspiracy theory that husband and wife had originally planned to commit an insurance fraud. On February 28 Blackwell had noted that on the afternoon of the previous November 6, Mrs. Rouse had telephoned Superintendent Brumby of Northamptonshire police, telling him that, 'I am Mrs. Rouse. I want to speak to you about my poor dear husband who has been burnt to death in his motor car at Northampton'. Brumby then replied that it was thought that the corpse was that of a woman (he was probably thinking at the time of the heel of Nellie Tucker's shoe found in the debris). According to Blackwell, however, Lily had broken down in tears when visited by Metropolitan policemen earlier that day who had told her of the destruction of Rouse's car in the early hours of that morning and of the corpse found in it. So when she responded to Brumby, she remained insistent that the corpse, far from being a woman's, was that of her husband. 'I had an awful dream about him last night. I cannot rest until I have seen him. I know it is no woman.' When she said she would travel to Northampton the next day, Friday November

7, to identify the body, Brumby advised her that it would be unrecognisable and that the only things belonging to Rouse were parts of the clothing and the metal parts of the braces; to which Lily replied, 'That will be all right; I shall know them as soon as I see them'. On her arrival at Northampton Brumby asked her if she had heard anything further about her husband, to which she replied, 'No, I never shall, he is dead'. On examining the clothing remnants she declared (at least according to the authorities), 'I can certainly swear that this [combination underwear] is what my husband was wearing when he left home'. As to the metal braces with 'Oxford' marked on them, she allegedly said, 'Yes, they are my husband's braces.' She also supposedly identified the buckle of a mackintosh belt, though Blackwell annotated that the prisoner's braces and buckle were quite unlike those found in the debris. She would not be able to view the corpse until the following day, so she stayed the night at a Northampton hotel. Of course Rouse had been detained at Hammersmith that evening and was being brought to Northampton the following morning, information that Lily would have learned that same morning. Indeed, she eventually saw her husband at 4 pm that afternoon, November 8, after he had been charged. But it had been clear to the authorities probably since around lunch-time on November 7, if not earlier that day when Rouse was aboard the coach going to London, that her husband had not been the blaze victim and that Lily's implied assertions to the contrary were untrue. As we have seen, Paling and Blackwell considered that her identification of the objects as Rouse's (though we know that other recollections suggest that she did not exactly claim this) placed Lily as a co-conspirator in an insurance fraud, even if not necessarily in a conspiracy to murder. In one respect Lily's rather far-fetched claim that she thought she had heard him return home some time after midnight, and not around 6 am when he had in fact arrived, would not necessarily be inconsistent with the DPP's conspiracy theory (though Rouse's 6 am return would obviously be more consistent with that theory). Thus, if her claim of his return 'after midnight' and of his subsequent supposed demise at 1:50 am were to be credited, then it would depend on two unlikely events having occurred. The first was that after he was apparently heard arriving home 'after midnight', he had then left the house again shortly afterwards, presumably to drive in the direction of Leicester. The second was that he was able to drive from Friern Barnet to Hardingstone in 80 or 90 minutes, a difficult feat to accomplish in his low-powered Morris Minor. Both events were, of course, highly improbable, verging on the impossible. Indeed, all the external evidence from the cousins and from the lorry driver and his mate, together with Rouse's own belated admission at his trial clearly confirmed his return home around 6 am before setting off again for the coach to Wales. But that hardly substantiated the theory that Lily had conspired with him to commit a fraud on the insurers for financial gain by destroying the car or, even worse, by destroying a human being who, it was allegedly planned, was meant to be mistaken for her husband.

However, Blackwell appeared to imply that Lily had compounded her deception when she eventually saw Rouse in Northampton police station on the afternoon of Saturday, November 8. Told by her husband that he had been charged with murder but that he was innocent, she reassured him with, 'I know you are, my dear, you are too tender-hearted to do a thing like that'. Yet this was the woman, wrote Blackwell, who had seen her husband for half-an-hour at 6 am on November

6 before he set off for Wales (her claim of his returning 'after midnight' being dismissed as hooey). In other words her protestation that it was impossible for Rouse to have committed such an offence in the very early hours of November 6 was despite the fact, according to Blackwell's reasoning, that she had been fast asleep at 1: 45 am and therefore could hardly vouch for his innocence at that time. Again that might have been so, but did it amount to evidence for a conspiracy?

The official, reflecting the belief of the DPP, Tindal Atkinson, further argued that Lily's decision to travel to Northampton on the supposed pretext of identifying Rouse's body or his clothing had followed her discussions with her husband on his return to Buxted Road at 6 am. Blackwell acknowledged that the conspiracy theory was inconsistent with Rouse's trip to see Ivy Jenkins in Gellygaer where he was obviously known. Nonetheless, he countered illogically, Lily's actions to travel to Northampton the following day were designed to create the strong impression of Rouse's tragic demise. Second, he concluded more persuasively that Rouse's flight to Wales represented a sudden change of plan by a man (what of the alleged 'co-conspirator' now?) who did not, or could not, keep his nerve in circumstances that he found more trying and psychologically disturbing than originally anticipated. Thus the Gellygaer visit was in the form of a respite cure, allowing him time to firm up the story he would recount to the detectives at Hammersmith in the early hours of November 8. But like a dog with a bone, Blackwell was still convinced that Lily had travelled to Northampton in order to 'identify' Rouse's remains, in accordance with instructions allegedly given to her by him when he had briefly returned home at 6 am on the morning of the blaze. No-one, of course, testified to this instruction having occurred. Indeed, apart from Arthur Jnr.'s alleged 'earwigging' about insurance and Rouse's 'medal', there is no evidence that Lily and her husband had exchanged a single word during his brief early-morning sojourn at Buxted Road.

Undaunted, Blackwell nonetheless concluded that a motive for killing the stranger lay in the £1,000 insurance moneys payable on Rouse's (or on a passenger's) death. The couple would then split the amount between themselves before going their separate ways. Indeed, for Blackwell, Lily's 'obvious' deviousness was further evidenced by her surreptitiously seeking to gain additional insurance cover on Rouse's life without her husband's knowledge, that is, the shilling a week policy paying out £73.4.0 on his death, whether accidental or natural. But presumably that policy reflected Lily's concern about her own future without Rouse rather than an evil cast of mind that would contemplate engaging in a homicidal conspiracy with him.

For Blackwell, in dwelling on the Eclipse policy, what had to be challenged were both the passage in Rouse's reprieve petition that had claimed there had been no evidence that he, Rouse, had wished to disappear, nor had made preparations to do so, and also the passage in Mr. Justice Talbot's summing up when he had stated,

> What possible grounds or theory can be put forward for [Rouse's] intention to disappear? There was no evidence at all that there was any crisis in his affairs, no urgent need of money, or no difficulty of any kind. What was he to do? Where was he to go? What was he to do? It is very difficult to see.

But for Blackwell that puzzlement on Talbot's part would simply not do. For the love of (insurance) money was clearly one of the routes, along with his sexual appetite, of all of Rouse's evil conduct. Thus in the light of the police court disclosures about insurance and about Rouse's assumed motive to disappear, Talbot's observation, above, appeared fanciful to Blackwell, especially since the brief evidence from Kennedy at the trial itself regarding the financially advantageous Eclipse policy endorsement for £1000 might have suggested a fruitful line of argument for the Crown to develop and which could link up with what had actually happened at Hardingstone Lane.

Indeed, by the time of the reprieve petition, the judge had been apprised by the Home Office of Mrs. Rouse's conduct in the affair (or, at least, of the department's interpretation of her behaviour) and its link with anticipated insurance pay-outs. Moreover, it was claimed that Lily 'undoubtedly took the first step' (whatever this meant) to securing Rouse's wish to disappear. Further, as Blackwell annotated regarding the judge's previous ignorance of Lily's supposed insurance machinations, 'He [Talbot] does now [know of her involvement], and is greatly impressed by it'. In the end, Lily's insurance claim amounted to £173 though she was advised by the prison governor at Bedford that she would first require to supply the Prudential with a copy of her husband's death certificate, obtainable from the registrar of births and deaths at Bedford, before the claim could be settled. How that figure was reached is not clear. The claim for £1,000 could scarcely be entertained since Rouse did not die in a traffic accident nor in the blaze, and as the victim's identity remained (and remains) unknown, his representatives could not benefit (is there a sum of money awaiting a descendant once DNA tests have established a claim?). Perhaps the figure of £173 represented the £73. 4s. 0d payable under the Prudential LOA policy and just under £100 payable on the Eclipse car policy. The situation with regard to the LOA policy is interesting since it was unclear whether life companies were obliged to pay out to dependants on the death by judicial execution of the insured. So we may suppose that the Prudential took a charitable view of Lily's situation rather than contest it. Indeed this legal conundrum on whether to pay out for the death by judicial execution of an assured had in the past led to litigation following the hangings of Dr. Crippen and the poisoner, Frederick Seddon.

There is certainly a long-standing legal rule based on public policy that no person may take a benefit arising from a death brought about by murder (or manslaughter) committed by him. Both the cases of Florence Maybrick[666] and of Dr. Crippen[667] confirmed this point. Thus any third party benefit under a life policy could not accrue to the third party who had unlawfully brought about the death, which meant that the widow (Mrs. Maybrick) and the widower (Dr. Crippen) could not receive insurance pay-outs on the loss of their spouses. Instead, in Florence's case, the insurance moneys went to her late husband, James Maybrick's, estate, ultimately to benefit the members of his family other than Florence. In Crippen's case, and depending on the precise terms of any will or insurance policy, Cora's immediate relatives would benefit, thus depriving Crippen of the opportunity of passing on the proceeds to Ethel Le Neve following his execution. Consequently, so far as Rouse was concerned, he could not have benefited to the tune of £1,000 provided under the Eclipse policy on the death of a passenger (if he were the next-

---

666 *Cleaver v Mutual Reserve Fund Life Association* [1892] 1 Q.B. 147.
667 *In re the Estate of Crippen* [1911] P. 108.

of-kin) since he himself had brought about the passenger's death. A variant on the theme concerns Mme. Fahmy, discussed in previous chapters, who had been acquitted of murdering her husband at the Savoy Hotel, London in 1923. For some years later she attempted to sue the Fahmy family in Cairo to recover enormous sums of money from their estate to which she claimed she was entitled. Under *sharia* law, as under English domestic law, a court would refuse to allow a woman to inherit from her husband's estate if she had been responsible for his death, which presumably referred to criminal responsibility. She had, of course, been acquitted of murder at the Old Bailey. But the *sharia* court in 1929 saw through the sham of the English justice system as manifested in Marguerite's trial six years earlier where a verdict of manslaughter (at least) would have been a proper finding. Consequently, she was given short shrift by the *sharia* court unimpressed by her earlier acquittal, an Old Bailey verdict no doubt influenced to some degree by racially-inspired motives whipped up by Marshall Hall, as we saw previously.[668]

In respect of Rouse's situation, we have already considered the position of Lily as a beneficiary, including the likelihood that she received just under £100 for the loss of the car. However, it is, in the alternative, possible that the insurance company also settled with the hire purchase firm (the legal car owners), Chester & Cole Ltd, for the loss of their written-off vehicle, the remains of which legally came into their possession (for what they were worth). And this notwithstanding that Rouse had paid hardly any of his monthly hire purchase payments. Indeed, the principal purpose of a driver taking out the policy was to insure the value of the car, so that the capitalised value of the hire-purchase payments could still be covered by the owners even if the car were to be lost.

But car insurance frauds were apparently not unfamiliar to Rouse even if his illegal practices were not as systematic as those of Frederick Guy Browne hanged, with William Kennedy in 1927, for the brutal murder of PC Gutteridge in a country road in Essex. For after the Great War and living near Southend, Browne would habitually steal and undertake changes to cars and then make fraudulent insurance claims on the altered vehicles. When caught in 1923 he was sentenced to four years at the Old Bailey.[669] As to Rouse the *Daily Sketch* cited three other instances of vehicle insurance fraud, alluded to elsewhere, whose perpetration it claimed he had admitted. Thus in 1921, in south-east London, Rouse conspired with another man to swindle an insurance company by arranging the 'theft' of a

668 Andrew Rose, *The Prince, the Princess and the Perfect Murder*, Coronet, 2013, p. 306. For the will of Frederick Seddon's victim, Eliza Barrow, which left her estate to two named individuals, see *The Times*, May 1, 1912; March 29, 1913. Seddon had been named as her executor but had, of course, been hanged before the will had been proven by a cousin of hers as administrator of an estate worth £650 which had managed to evade the clutches of Seddon. Under the Estates of Deceased Persons (Forfeiture Rules and Law of Succession) Act 2012 innocent parties deprived of an inheritance due to a mother or father, as the case might be, murdering the testator will no longer be excluded. For example, take the common case of a wife whose will leaves her estate to her husband and then to her son in the event that the husband predeceases her. The husband kills the wife but cannot inherit her estate due to the common law rule noted previously. However, until the 2012 Act removed doubts, it remained arguable that neither could the son since his father did not predecease his wife as required under her will. The alternative view would be that the murderous husband is 'struck out', there is no will and the son would inherit under intestacy rules rather than the estate going to the Crown as *bona vacantia*. See also *Re Callaway; Callaway v Treasury Solicitor* [1956] 3 W.L.R. 257.
669 W. Teignmouth Shore, "Browne and Kennedy, 1928", in James H. Hodge, *Famous Trials III*, Penguin, 1950, p. 17; Christopher Berry-Dee and Robin Odell, *The Long Drop: Two Were Hanged--One Was Innocent*, True Crime, 1993, p. 30.

motor-cycle and side-car. The vehicle did not belong to Rouse but he participated in the fraud which involved the machine being driven to hilly ground. The owner then jumped out and Rouse, springing from the side-car onto the driver's seat, turned the machine and disappeared quickly, as previously planned. The owner then reported the vehicle stolen, received an insurance pay-out and split it equally with Rouse. A similar fraud was committed around 1925, but this time involving a car belonging to Rouse (many cars passed through his hands during his adulthood). On that occasion he parked the car outside the Golders Green Empire and probably conspicuously got out of the car in full view of passers-by. Hanging around for a short while, he then waited until the coast was clear and drove off quickly when he thought that no-one was looking. The car was next hidden in a private lock-up after which Rouse returned to where he had first left the vehicle. Feigning shock and distress at the disappearance of the car, he reported its loss and later received another insurance payment. The money was used to purchase a better vehicle, the tyres and some parts of the hidden vehicle were kept as spares, and the engine was sold on.

On the third recorded occasion, Rouse chose to leave the car outside a mortuary in Finchley, walked away quickly and then reported it stolen. Unfortunately, a dealer reported to the police that the car had been offered to him for £2. The police then traced Rouse as the owner and, sadly for him, returned the car to him.[670] How grateful he was to receive it back is not, of course, recorded.

These efforts at putting one over the insurance companies were, however, hardly on a par with the magnificent efforts of Leopold Harris, the notorious insurance assessor whose speciality was to arrange with business owners the destruction by fire of their commercial premises, the causes of which would be certified in each case by Harris and his accomplices as due to some non-intentional conflagration, such as an electrical fault in the factory or warehouse. Known as the 'Great Arson Conspiracy', the individual incidents straddled the Rouse case, commencing in November 1927 and concluding with the trial of Harris and his 15 accomplices at the Old Bailey in July 1933. One bona fide investigator, a solicitor named William Crocker, even drew up an intricate 'map' of 29 linked fires that he presented as evidence to the Old Bailey under the heading, 'Willesden Junction' (obviously a more serious and pointed exercise than 'I'm Sorry I Haven't a Clue's' 'Mornington Crescent'). Not as impenetrable as the business structures of some globalised multinationals today that might seek to evade the proper gaze of the taxman, the complex diagram displayed lines drawn from one fire to another on the map, all of which conflagrations highlighted links with Leopold Harris or his associates.[671]

The 'Great Arson Conspiracy' was clearly not the inspiration for Rouse's scheme. Instead his post-execution *Daily Sketch* 'confession' on March 11, 1931 commenced with the admission that, 'It was the Agnes Kesson case at Epsom in June which first set me thinking. It showed that it was possible to beat the police if you were careful enough. Since I read about that case I kept thinking of various plans. I tried to hit on something new. I did not want to do murder just for the

---

670   For the incidents, see the *Daily Sketch*, March 13, 1931.
671   An extensive account is in Douglas G. Browne, *Sir Travers Humphreys: A Biography*, Harrap, 1960, pp. 303-19; Roland Wild, *Crimes & Cases of 1933*, Rich & Cowan Ltd, 1934, Ch. II. For a full account see Harold Dearden, *The Fire-Raisers*, Heinemann, 1934. For Crocker's own account see his autobiography, *Far From Humdrum*, Hutchinson, 1967, Chs. 16-21.

sake of it'. The reference to the Kesson case, however, is puzzling in that it did not involve an unidentified corpse pulled out of a burnt car. Indeed, as we shall see, there were then-recent German examples similar to his crime upon which he could have borrowed, had he known of them (which, presumably, he did not). Kesson was therefore significant only in the sense that it was a contemporary unsolved murder that had apparently caught Rouse's imagination, even though the *modus operandi* bore no relation to Rouse's presumed method.

Agnes Kesson was a 20-year old waitress from Falkirk (and therefore, coincidentally, born in the same Scottish burgh and around the same time as the mother of one of present writers). At the time of her death she had been employed by a Mr. Frederick Deats and his wife in their café, shop, garage and taxi service, known as The Nook, in Burgh Heath, near Epsom in Surrey. On Epsom Derby day, June 5, 1930, her body had been found in a nearby ditch by the side of the road between Epsom and Tolworth. This was two days after she had left her employment, having handed in her notice. Witnesses spoke of seeing her at the races with a young man, and rumours and counter-rumours swirled around as to whether she had been an honest or a dishonest employee at the café. Suspicion fell on Mr. Deats but he claimed as an alibi that a neighbour had asked him to collect a passenger at Sutton station. However no-one was there when he arrived in his taxi. Driving back from his wasted journey he picked up two fares and drove them to an address in Sutton before reaching home at 1.40 am. He attributed the wild goose chase to 'people in opposition to me around here'.[672]

As to Agnes she was engaged to a fellow café employee but was said to have had a roving eye for other admirers. When her body was discovered it was found that she had been strangled by a ligature, she was wearing only under-clothes and the rest of her clothes were missing. She had been badly beaten and bruised before her death, with evidence suggesting she had tried to resist the assault. She had not, however, been sexually assaulted. No-one was arrested in connection with her death and at one time the police speculated that two or more men had been involved in the assault and that they had sought to disguise the murder by endeavouring to leave her body hanging from a tree, thereby suggesting suicide. According to this theory, the idea was abandoned when the men remembered a similar case involving the death of 42-year old Mrs. Carrie Whitehouse whose body had been found by the roadside at Gatley in Cheshire some two weeks before Agnes Kesson's body had been discovered. Like Kesson, Whitehouse had been found partially clothed and Spilsbury, who also gave evidence at the Kesson inquest as to cause of death, testified at the Whitehouse inquest that the deceased had probably died of cocaine poisoning administered orally. Again, the suggestion that Whitehouse might have died by her own hand, whether deliberately or accidentally (thus diverting attention away from homicide), was canvassed, but the surrounding elements of the case were mysterious. These included the circumstances of her discovery in Cheshire, some distance from her home in Manchester, that she was naked from the waist down, the fact that she had a police record (probably for soliciting), that her real name was Carrie Wilkinson,

---

672   For the Agnes Kesson case, see MEPO3/1655; *Daily Mirror*, September 17, 1930; *Glasgow Herald*, July 4,7, 1930; *Brisbane Courier*, June 9, 1930; www.epsomandewellhistoryexplorer.org.uk/Kesson.html.

that she had never been married to her 'husband', Captain Bert Whitehouse, now living in the South of England and from whom she had been separated for years, and that letters found in her room both referred to a lover, Norman (probably another commercial traveller), and seemed to imply that she was exploring having an abortion even though Spilsbury could find 'no sign that she was in a certain condition'. [673]

This seems far away from Rouse and the mystery of the blazing car, which might suggest that it was *not* Rouse who had come across the Kesson case as his inspiration. In other words perhaps it was the *Daily Sketch* journalist, J. C. Cannell, who had floated the name upon which Rouse latched for journalistic effect. In any case, the whole purpose of the Rouse scheme (assuming he had planned it) was to find a victim who would not be missed or recognised after the car blaze. Neither the Kesson case, nor the Whitehouse case nor, indeed, the mystery of the 'Burning of Evelyn Foster' in her taxi in the open stretches of Otterburn in January 1931, mentioned in an earlier chapter, corresponded to the Rouse scenario. For all the victims were readily identifiable. The only common denominator, from Rouse's perspective, was that the crimes against the three women remained officially unsolved, though suspicions lingered. For example, as he was about to hang in 1934 for the murder of his employer committed some five years earlier in Huddersfield, did Ernest Brown, prompted by the chaplain to confess his sins, actually reply 'Otterburn', or did he say 'ought to burn'? Did either remark refer to Evelyn Foster? Bizarrely, like Rouse's victim, the charred body of Brown's employer, Frederick Morton, had been found in the latter's burnt-out car, parked in his garage, though the car keys and a ring had confirmed Morton's identity. But unlike Rouse's man, alive in the Morris Minor for perhaps thirty seconds before the flames took over, Morton was dead before being placed in the car, having been shot by Brown through the chest at close range.[674] In the Kesson case, likewise, suspicion remained for some years after the event with her employer, Frederick Deats (the surname probably anglicised from Dietz during the war). This was enhanced when he was convicted, three years later, of assaulting an eighteen-year old, Netta Jean Elmer, whom he had persuaded to climb into his car late at night following the offer of a lift home.[675] So if the Kesson case seems a puzzling precedent for Rouse and if the burning car episode involving Evelyn Foster likewise could not have inspired him, since it occurred in January 1931, two months *after* Rouse's conflagration in November 1930, then what events, if any, *might* have triggered the idea and the deed for which Rouse paid the full penalty? In her Notable British Trials account of the case Helena Normanton states that,[676]

> Another curious feature of this case was that its suggestion *may* have been due, more or less, to a war spy story published in the *Evening Standard* in January, 1929, or else that that work of fiction—"The W Plan" by Mr. Graham Seton—intelligently anticipated in certain ways what Mr. Rouse did with his car and his passenger. The crime of Rouse was also paralleled by those of two German murderers, both of whom killed motor car passengers to obtain

673 *The Times*, May 22, 28, June 5, 1930.
674 Robin Odell, *Landmarks in 20th Century Murder*, Headline, 1995, p. 173. See also, Jonathan Goodman, *The Burning of Evelyn Foster*, Headline, 1977, pp. 139-45.
675 *The Times*, January 25, 1933.
676 Normanton, *op. cit.*, p. xlii.

insurance money. The first, Karl Erich Telzner [*sic*; his name was actually Kurt Erich Tetzner], confessed to his crime and was executed at Regensburg, after expressing repentance, on 2nd May, 1931.

We shall return to the 'W Plan' shortly. But meanwhile we may note that, like Rouse, the Tetzner case involved another young commercial traveller accused of burning to death an unknown tramp whose body was meant to be taken as his own.[677] Kurt Erich Tetzner had been arrested over the border in Strasbourg on December 5, 1929 after his burnt-out vehicle had been found near the village of Ettershausen in Bavaria some eleven days earlier. A charred body had been found in the driving seat and, based on the circumstantial evidence found in the car, the police in Leipzig, Tetzner's home city, contacted Frau Tetzner who identified the body as that of her husband. Frau. Teztner, distraught and tearful, followed her husband's coffin in an elaborate funeral and then pocketed the insurance moneys of 145,000 marks (£7,250). But the insurance companies had their suspicions and requested the Leipzig police to keep their eye on Frau. Tetzner.

She had no telephone in her flat but on two occasions in the next few days she was summoned to a neighbour's house to take calls from a Herr Stranelli (or Stanelli), phoning from Strasbourg. The Leipzig police contacted their French counterparts in Strasbourg, provided a description of Tetzner, and asked them to take a close look at Stranelli. It was no surprise to discover they were one and the same person. A Leipzig detective flew to Strasbourg and took his quarry, already arrested by the French police, back to Germany. After lengthy delays, he eventually stood trial for murder in the town of Ratisbon shortly after Rouse had been executed in March 1931. Indeed, the public prosecutor referred to Rouse as being 'just a pupil of Tetzner'.

In outlining the case against Tetzner, the prosecutor explained that on his arrest the accused had confessed to murdering his passenger and to burning the body. The latter's corpse would then be assumed to be that of Tetzner so that Frau. Tetzner would receive the insurance moneys. However, he had later withdrawn his confession and now claimed that the victim had been a pedestrian whom he had accidentally run over and who had then died in the car after presumably being placed there by Tetzner in a bid to save him. So while he agreed that he had burnt the body as part of an insurance swindle, he denied murdering the victim. This was despite his admitting that he had previously discussed with his wife different methods of pretending that he had died in a car crash, and despite acknowledging two other unsuccessful attempts to lure young men to their deaths in his car, in furtherance of insurance frauds. Indeed one of the intended victims gave a horrifying account at Tetzner's trial of his dramatic escape from the prisoner's attack upon him with a hammer. But, according to Tetzner, on November 25, 1929, he did actually knock down a man near Bayreuth. He then placed him on the passenger seat where the man soon died. Later that night, Tetzner disclosed, he simulated a car accident by driving into a tree, sprinkling petrol around, and setting the vehicle alight. While the pathological evidence was conflicting as to

677 F. A. Beaumont, "Men-Hunters: The 'German Rouse Cases'", in J. M. Parrish and John R. Crossland (eds), *The Fifty Most Amazing Crimes of the Last 100 Years*, Odhams Press, 1936, pp. 624-34 for this and the Saffran case, below. Tetzner is also discussed in J. H. H. Gaute and Robin Odell, *Murder 'Whatdunit'*, Harrap, 1982, pp. 36-7; *Real-Life Crimes*, Vol. 3, No. 32, 1993, pp. 710-12.

whether the victim's body did display signs of being run over accidentally, it was agreed from internal examinations that, unlike Rouse's victim, Tetzner's had not been alive when the blaze started. The jury eventually convicted him of murder, probably persuaded by the fact that he had initially admitted to murdering the victim despite his subsequently withdrawing the confession. He was hanged at Regensberg on May 2, 1931, confessing to the murder before his execution. His account was that on November 25, 1929, he had picked up a young 21-year old journeyman, whose name he did not know. The man complained of the cold so Tetzner wrapped a heavy rug blanket around him, pinioning his arms. Then he strangled him with a piece of rope. Outside Ettershausen he crashed the car, opened the petrol tank, laid a petrol trail from the tank and over the mudguard and the right footboard to the back of the car, and set it alight with the young man inside. It is rather astonishing how closely the story matches Rouse's (and Lily's?), though there is no indication that the 'German Rouse' had been involved in the intricate romantic entanglements and financial burdens that proved to be the former's downfall.

Helena Normanton does not mention the name of the second German murderer whose deeds supposedly paralleled Rouse's. However, although it did not involve a car blaze the episode probably concerned Fritz Saffran and two other conspirators. For it was listed as the second of the German cases discussed in Beaumont's 1936 chapter (above) under the sub-title, 'The German Rouse Cases'.[678] Saffran was charged, with two associates, with murdering a randomly chosen man whose corpse, set alight in the furniture store that Saffran had been managing in Rastenburg, East Prussia, was intended to be mistaken for him. For he was desperately trying to cover up various fraudulent actions committed while manager, including creating false hire purchase contracts with non-existent customers (for which finance companies in Berlin and Koenigsberg would advance the capital to Saffran). But as the tide of claims against the store continued to mount up unbeknown to the store's owner, Herr Platz, who was also Saffran's father-in-law, and at a time of raging Weimar inflation, the plot to feign Saffran's death in a blaze by having a burnt and unrecognisable corpse mistaken for him was concocted.

On the evening of September 15, 1930 the Platz Furniture Store suffered a catastrophic fire after an explosion. It was believed that all those in the store at the time managed to escape as the building was razed to the ground. Yet the chief clerk, Erich Kipnik, rushed to Herr Platz's house. He frantically explained that Saffran had been drinking coffee with him in a nearby cafe when they suddenly spotted the blaze. Bravely the manager had rushed back to the store to save the ledgers but tragically died in the all-consuming fire. Indeed a charred corpse partially clothed in the remnants of a suit identified as Saffran's was later recovered from the site. Saffran's monogrammed watch and rings were also found on the unrecognisable body.

The story then shifts to a female employee of Saffran's, Ella Augustin, who had

---

678   The case was also listed in a Nazi-approved and rabidly anti-Semitic book, *The Jew as Criminal*, written by J. Keller and Hanns Andersen in 1937, with an introduction by the Nazi war criminal, Julius Streicher. It was translated into English in 2002. The unpleasant provenance of the translation can easily be imagined. 'Safran' is a Hebrew word meaning 'librarian'.

a crush on him which he, a married man, did not enthusiastically reciprocate. However, she had been in thrall to him and always desired to please him. Thus two days after the fire and after clear displays of grief on her part at the apparent loss of her *beau*, she hired a chauffeur named Reck ostensibly to drive her seriously ill mother to Koenigsberg. He would pick up mother and daughter from their house at 3 am. However it was a man, recognised by the driver as Saffran, and not the mother, who stepped out of the house and into the car. Reck, however, would only drive as far as the outskirts of the village of Gerdauen and refused to go further. Saffran got out and walked into Gerdauen while Reck drove back to Rastenburg. The chauffeur recounted this strange journey to a third party and the police soon became interested. Inquiries with former clerical staff at the furniture store revealed its surprisingly precarious financial situation when customers defaulted on their hire purchase payments (obliging Saffran to embark on his cover-up). Ella was arrested and put in prison. From there she smuggled out a letter to Saffran who was still at large, but it was intercepted by the authorities. They learned that he was staying with a relative of Ella's in Berlin, a poor carpenter. Saffran decided after a few weeks to steal the carpenter's papers and assume his identity in order to escape abroad by sailing from Hamburg to Brazil. An alert was put out by the police but Saffran thought he could escape detection by travelling by train to Hamburg via a quiet Berlin suburban station, Spandau (where Rudolf Hess would be imprisoned after the war). But Sod's Law intervened and his plan came unstuck when the railway official at Spandau recognised him since both men had previously served together in the Rastenburg Rifles. Though Saffran had already departed on the train, the police had been called and stopped him at the next station, Wittenberg, where he was waiting to change trains. He was arrested as also was Kipnik, the chief clerk, for helping to falsify the books.

While all this was happening, the pathologist was examining the burnt corpse. He first concluded that it must have lain in the earth for some weeks before being burnt in the store. However it was the corpse's dental records that led to its identification as Friedrich Dahl, a 25-year old dairyman from Wermsdorf, near Koenigsberg. He had been missing for several weeks after he had set off on his bicycle to look for work. His wife identified the remaining scraps of clothing salvaged from the body as similar to that worn by her husband (which admittedly clashes with the subsequent testimony regarding the clothing as belonging to Saffran).

On March 23, 1931, just days after Rouse's execution, the three, Saffran, Augustin and Kipnik, stood trial at Bartenstein, East Prussia, for offences ranging from murder to complicity in frauds. Not unexpectedly, cut-throat defences, where each blamed the others for the wrongdoing, were adduced. Ella, for example, testified that Saffran had come into the store one day, waving a newspaper, and announcing, 'Have you read the report about this man, Tetzner? That is how I will do our job, too'. For his part, Saffran explained that when he realised the scale of the firm's losses, he insured himself for 140,000 marks (£7,000), with the intention of committing suicide and thus benefiting Frau Saffran. Ella then apparently dissuaded him from taking such steps and Kipnik suggested that they obtain a body from somewhere and burn it in the store. Rejecting the idea of raiding a churchyard, they set up a 'murder camp' in the Nikolai Forest. A first attempted abduction failed when Ella panicked at seeing Kipnik strike a victim. In the commotion, the man managed to escape. A later attempt involving just the two men was claimed to be more successful when Kipnik got out of the car to strike down a pedestrian while Saffran drove on at speed, not wishing to witness the bloodshed. On his return shortly afterwards he said that he helped Kipnik put the body, wrapped in a carpet, in the car boot (actually, a 'dickey', a term exported from India). They drove back to Rastenberg, dressed the corpse in Saffran's clothes, putting his rings on its fingers, placed it in the store where they poured 25 gallons of petrol over it, and finally set it (and the store) alight.

Kipnik's account squarely placed the blame on Saffran who, he claimed, had shot the victim three times in the head. Moreover, said Kipnik, it was Saffran, not he, who had arranged the corpse for burning in the store. It is clear that each account was flawed inasmuch as the post-mortem findings regarding the burial of the body in the earth for several weeks before its removal to Rastenberg did not correspond with each defendant's testimony. What precisely happened can no longer be discovered but the two men were convicted of murdering Friedrich Dahl and sentenced to death, while Ella Augustin was sentenced to five years penal servitude. Yet surprisingly, both men were reprieved by the Prussian government, their sentences being commuted to penal servitude for life. Thus, while the episode lacked a blazing car, it did share a number of similarities with the Rouse case. For, if Ella Augustin is to be believed, it was inspired by the Tetzner case which *did* closely resemble Rouse. Moreover the store blaze in Rastenberg occurred on September 15, 1930. Is it possible that at this time, Rouse was beginning to formulate some ideas as to how he might extricate himself from his domestic mess?

Let us turn, now, to Graham Seton's 'W Plan' as a suggested inspiration for Rouse's scheme. Lt Col Graham Seton Hutchison (1890-1946) had served with distinction in the Argyll & Sutherland Highlanders during the First World War. He then turned to writing novels, especially spy novels, and some works of non-fiction. In the inter-war years he associated with fascist organisations. Surprisingly, as a Scot, he joined a bizarre group of 'authentically English' fascists in 1930, the English Mistery. This particular racist and fascist outfit sought a return to a pure, hierarchical and rural English 'idyll' (Anthony Ludovici, whom we have met elsewhere, was among its adherents). Perhaps because it was too theoretical for his tastes, Seton Hutchison soon left to become a member of Mosley's British Union of Fascists. However, not only discredited by his failure to raise supporting columns as he had promised, but finding the BUF insufficiently anti-Semitic, he founded the National Workers' Movement (later, the extreme pro-Nazi National Socialist Workers Party) in 1933.[679]

Meanwhile his fame as an author was undimmed. *The W Plan*[680] told the story of how British military intelligence in the Great War had sought to discover the

679   For details see Richard Griffiths, *Fellow Travellers of the Right: British Enthusiasts for Nazi Germany, 1933-9*, Oxford University Press, Oxford, 1983, pp. 101-4; Martin Pugh, *Hurrah for the Blackshirts! Fascists and Fascism in Britain Between the Wars*, Pimlico, 2006, pp. 71, 227. The most extensive discussion of Seton Hutchison is in Gavin Bowd, *Fascist Scotland: Caledonia and the Far Right*, Birlinn, Edinburgh, 2013, pp.49-60.

680   Graham Seton, *The W Plan*, Thornton Butterworth, 1929. It went through eight impressions between October 1929 and January 1930. A 'popular' edition was issued in May 1931.

details of what a captured and severely injured German engineers' regimental officer, Major Muller, had been deliriously referring to as the W Plan during his last hours of life in a British casualty clearing station. They sent Lt Col Duncan Grant, commanding officer of the 'Inverness Regiment' and a fluent German speaker, by aeroplane to infiltrate the area around Essen, Muller's home town. Here he pretended to be a fellow-engineering officer conveying bad tidings to Muller's wife, the underlying aim being to find out more about Muller and the details of the Germans' W Plan. Once the information had been obtained he would rendezvous back at the improvised landing strip with his British pilot ten days later. As fate would have it, Grant's pre-war German girl friend, Rosa, was staying with Frau. Muller when he turned up at the latter's house wearing an appropriate German officer's uniform. He conveniently found a copy of the plan on Frau. Muller's desk, and he copied it on to the back of a photograph of Rosa. At a cafe with Rosa he was asked by German officers to show his (in reality, Muller's) papers. Initially satisfied, the Germans later became suspicious of him. He had to flee and, after various hair-raising and life-threatening adventures, during which he, incredulously, became a German Army private sentenced to death for desertion before being reprieved, found himself, as a bi-lingual interpreter under threat of execution, with a party of British POWs tasked with assisting in the underground work which was integral to the W Plan. For the plan was to explode massive mines under Allied trenches and territory on the Western Front to secure a German military victory (Seton Hutchison probably recalled the huge British craters, Lochnagar and King's Crater, exploded under the German lines in 1917). Grant's sabotage of the plan was carried into effect and with one great bound he was free to join his beloved Rosa in Switzerland whence they traveled to Britain to be married. The novel was made into a film in 1930 featuring, as Grant, the actor Brian Aherne who had recently starred in *The Barretts of Wimpole Street* and, as Rosa, Madeleine Carroll who later achieved greater fame as Richard Hannay's fleeing companion in the first, Hitchcock, version of *The Thirty-Nine Steps*.

But what, in Helena Normanton's judgment, has that got to do with Arthur Rouse? The answer does not seem apparent, let alone obvious compared with, say, the 'German Rouse Cases'. For Colonel Grant's assumption of the identity of Major Muller, including carrying his documents and wearing his clothes, does not, in any way, correspond to the Rouse scenario. If anything it is closer to Operation Mincemeat and 'The Man Who Never Was', mentioned previously.[681] Rouse, of course, never assumed, nor had the chance to assume, the identity of the tramp. Indeed the objective was the opposite, that the tramp would be assumed to be Rouse. Yet even here, and despite Lily's claim that the surviving remnants of buckles and braces from the blaze 'looked like' her husband's, there is no evidence that Rouse had carried with him a complete change of clothing to don, once he had supposedly dressed up the deceased tramp in his own clothes before disposing of him in the conflagration. So *The W Plan* continues to retain its 'mystery' quality in

681 A fictional account, *Operation Heartbreak*, was written by Duff Cooper who had served as wartime Minister for Information. Rumours have more recently surfaced suggesting that, to improve authenticity, the body of the tramp had been substituted at the last moment by a sailor, recently killed when HMS *Dasher* controversially blew up while undergoing post-launch trials in the Firth of Clyde. See John and Noreen Steele, *HMS Dasher*, Argyll Publishing, Glendaruel, Argyll, 2004.

a manner that not even its unpleasant author would have imagined shortly after writing it.

So *was* Rouse's whole scheme a flawed attempt to carry out an insurance fraud? As to the compulsory car insurance element, since it was an indemnity policy for the hire purchase company that still legally owned the vehicle, there could clearly be no gain to Rouse or Lily in terms of that cover. Second, and in respect of the Prudential policy taken out by Lily, even if we leave aside the relatively paltry amount involved, it is not clear that Rouse himself knew of its existence. So that leaves the Eclipse £1,000 endorsement covering Rouse and any passenger accidentally killed in a car accident. Arguably such a sum of money (perhaps worth at least £50,000 today) was sufficient motivation to commit a murder, but it is plain that since Rouse could hardly claim for his own death, any criminal plot could only have succeeded had Lily been party to the deed. We know that Blackwell and Paling were in no doubt on this score, though Paling also confusingly referred to a third-party passenger. But is the evidence convincing? These officials obviously considered her account of her husband's return to Buxted Road after midnight on November 6 as decidedly dodgy. For did Lily *really* think it was only one o'clock in the morning when Rouse slipped back into the house, when in fact he had returned around six o'clock, albeit before dawn had broken on that dark winter's morning? Second, her phone call to Superintendent Brumby to arrange her trip to Northampton in order to 'identify' the body and her husband's belongings appeared too contrived for those officials. Rather, the phone call would seem to fit neatly into a plan whose aim was to defraud the insurers. Yet, on the other hand, can credence be attached to Arthur Jnr.'s supposed recollection of the Rouse couple animatedly discussing 'insurance' in the early morning of November 6? Moreover, how could Rouse have been party to an attempt to defraud the Prudential (not the Eclipse) policy, when it is probable that he was unaware of that policy's existence? Of course, this does not discount the possibility that Lily was seeking to gain a further sum from the 'conspiracy' above and beyond that which would secretly accrue to her husband, along with her share from the Eclipse policy. But the most puzzling aspect of the conspiracy theory is this. If Lily was indeed implicated in Rouse's plan to disappear and to claim on the life policies, did the DPP not consider, in the absence of conspiracy charges, whether she could be charged with any relevant fraud offence, or even an inchoate offence, for example, under the still extant Accessories and Abettors Act 1861? After all the adulteress, Edith Thompson, had been hanged in 1923 for less. But no hint of possible proceedings against Lily has been found in the case papers. Does this suggest that her involvement was pure speculation or imagination? Was Blackwell and Paling's conspiracy theory offered with the cosy benefit of hindsight, or were their post-trial outpourings just sound and fury, signifying nothing? Surely the latter is more credible than the former.

CHAPTER TWENTY-FOUR

WOUNDED IN THE WAR

THE TIMES, December 17, 1930

Rouse, Criminality and Shell Shock

According to James McClure, writing about Rouse, in the immediate period after the Great War 'A lesser man might have opted to become a permanent invalid, but there was good in Arthur, as Lily said'. Thus by September 1920 Rouse was 'entirely self-supporting'[682] and working hard as a commercial traveller to improve his domestic circumstances and his (and Lily's) home comforts, even if his philanderings had not ceased after his wartime service. But was there any long-lasting effect of his head injury upon his cognitive processes? Helena Normanton had no doubt that,[683]

> ....Rouse was a war product and a war tragedy. Some people are blessed with a faculty for seeing war as a moral purifier. That is a very limited facet of the truth. The war did not purify Rouse—it markedly helped his moral ruin. It broke his morals, and I consider that his wound broke his mental power and shattered his controls without lessening his conceit. [Thus] he was a good lad until he saw service in France. There he learned to kill at his country's behest, and later he applied that lesson in his own behalf. In France he suffered a severe head wound, from which it is probable that he never fully recovered.

Of course this passage begs more questions than it answers. Is Normanton offering a psychiatric assessment of Rouse's mental state, suggesting that he was clinically (or even legally) insane? Or was he, at least, suffering from such an abnormality of mind, as a result of his wartime experiences, that he was subject only to a diminished level of personal responsibility for his post-war actions; in particular, for the death of his car passenger in 1930? Or did the war simply brutalise his attitude to other human beings, so that he felt no moral qualms about using and abusing them emotionally? Or was he so brutalized by bayonet attacks that after the war he became indifferent to the sanctity of life? We know that elite opinion within government, police and the press was fearful of a violent crime wave emerging in the wake of demobilisation after the Armistice. Indeed the origins of the creation of Scotland Yard's Flying Squad in October 1918 (it

---

682   James McClure, *Killers*, Fontana, 1976, at p. 145.
683   Helena Normanton, *Trial of Alfred Arthur Rouse*, Notable British Trials Series, William Hodge & Co., Edinburgh, 1931, p. xliv.

became operational the following year) might be attributed to senior detectives' fears for law and order in the post-Armistice era. Especially if unemployment were to return, the war experiences of the 'usual suspect' crooks and villains, as well as of newcomers to crime, deprived of parental control, or who had been toughened up in the struggle to survive the harsh conditions of war, might pose a major challenge to a peaceable kingdom.[684] We also know that some serious crimes could be linked to war service, such as jealous revenge being exacted by a returning soldier on his wife or her lover when he arrived back from the Front, or emotionally damaged ex-servicemen committing violent acts, sometimes randomly, or post-war unemployment driving trained ex-soldiers to raid banks and post offices. But the findings of Emsley and Jon Lawrence for the most part deny the Doomsday scenario painted by the worried establishment as the war drew to a close.[685] Therefore the prospect of someone like Rouse returning from France, and then assuming a violent disposition in England, was always likely to be much rarer than the authorities feared.

So did Normanton have in mind the moral degradation that the war could bring about on the part of otherwise 'good lads' such as Rouse? We have seen elsewhere that moral standards in respect of sexual behaviour were perhaps not as straight-laced among the general population after the war as religious authorities and 'respectable' society might prefer to imagine. So the war might not necessarily have brought about a decline in moral standards, so much as a hastening of changing standards that were already occurring. Thus to bemoan Rouse's sexual immorality, or to blame the war for propelling it forward is, perhaps, to mistake the occasion for the cause: *post hoc, ergo propter hoc.*

The journalist, Sydney Tremayne, who edited the volume, *The Trial of Alfred Arthur Rouse*, published by Geoffrey Bles in May 1931 (the rival to Normanton's publication), was more certain that one could discount Rouse's war injury as a factor contributing to his conduct in 1930. For Tremayne,

> In connection with the head wound a famous mental specialist, in response to an inquiry which I ventured to address to him, said, 'That Rouse was to some degree abnormal seems clear.....I do not think that the wound in the temple sustained in the war can be in any way connected with his crime. We do not know what it amounted to, whether there was concussion or depression of the bone, but, in any case, it occurred some thirteen or fourteen years ago, and during those years he had been earning his living and going about without any suspicion of mental unsoundness attaching to him. We may be sure that he never sought medical advice for cerebral trouble at a hospital or of a private medical man, for if so the fact would have been brought out at the trial to explain his panic and confusion.'

Yet Tremayne speculated that although Rouse's wound, in his opinion, did not account for the planning and execution of the murder, nonetheless, '....it is conceivable that it was in some degree responsible for his instability, abnormal

684 Neil Darbyshire and Brian Hilliard, *The Flying Squad*, Headline, 1994, Ch. 2.
685 Clive Emsley, *Soldier, Sailor, Beggarman, Thief: Crime and the British Armed Services Since 1914*, Oxford University Press, Oxford, 2013, Ch. 8; Jon Lawrence, "Forging a Peaceable Kingdom: War, Violence and Fear of Brutalization in Post-First World War Britain", *Journal of Modern History*, Vol. 75, 2003, pp. 557-89.

physical propensities, and his extraordinary untruthfulness'.[686] In exploring this claim one would obviously ask in what respect Rouse displayed 'instability', apart from his behaviour in the immediate days following the burning of his car. According to his own account, he was initially gripped by panic as he paced backward and forward between Hardingstone and the burning vehicle. Perhaps having then composed himself, he at last emerged from the ditch only to be dumbstruck (once more?) at the sight of the two cousins, Bailey and Brown, at that unearthly hour after midnight. His subsequent stream of conversation with the lorry driver and his companion, with the coach company booking clerk, and then with the driver on the Cardiff-bound coach might simply evince the high degree of nervousness and trepidation he was experiencing as the ramifications of his actions began to sink in. It might have been instability, but it was surely specific to the incident.

As to his 'abnormal physical propensities', could they really be attributed to a clinical problem, perhaps triggered by the neurological injury suffered in the war? Or was Rouse simply a priapic commercial traveller, with an older, somewhat unglamorous, wife, and whose sexual appetite was constantly being whetted by the opportunities to pick up young women in his car while on his rounds away from Friern Barnet? For, as we have seen, the reputation of commercial travellers was such as to lead to Reithian instructions forbidding jokes on the BBC about their sexual exploits. To the extent (which is uncertain) that his war service in the reserve lines in France, before being sent to the Front, afforded opportunities for other sexual liaisons (which produced a child, as we know), perhaps he did cross the boundary into marital infidelity which he had not hitherto contemplated, and thus set a pattern for the future. But did that create, or release, 'abnormal physical propensities' previously absent, or did the shrapnel injuries to his head trigger his predatory sexual appetite? Arguably, even if there is a clinical connection between head traumas and heightened sexual drive, it is surely more probable that it was Rouse's choice to lift self-restraint in this department than that his behaviour reflected an irresistible impulse, over which he had no control, to make sexual conquests. And as to his 'extraordinary untruthfulness', was it indeed so extraordinary compared with that of those who loved to 'spin a yarn', like poor and inadequate Timothy Evans ('bull-shitters', in today's vernacular)? We know that Rouse's first recorded instances of criminality occurred around 1921 and involved a minor motor-cycle insurance fraud. But it is difficult to argue that this was evidence of wartime brutalization or of the delayed effect of his war wound. As Lily enigmatically once commented, Arthur did not like or trust insurance[687] (though he was obviously prepared to take fraudulent advantage of it). No doubt such a view of his was opinionated, like that of those opposed to wearing seat belts. But that speaks to narrow-minded arrogance or to cheap-skate beliefs, not to mental instability or to clinically-diagnosed personality defects.

But could Rouse's moral decline and fall, which Normanton claimed had been due to war service, be linked to the ex-soldier's perceived 'instability' which Tremayne suggested might have been a consequence of his war wound? Tremayne did, of course, cite the view of a contemporary 'mental specialist' who denied

---

686 Sydney Tremayne, *The Trial of Alfred Arthur Rouse*, Geoffrey Bles, 1931, p. 39.
687 *Daily Express*, March 11, 1931.

any connection between war wound and the murder. But is that too dismissive? That is, is there a case for arguing that Rouse had been suffering undiagnosed battle shock for years? There were, indeed, no familiar symptoms on his part of the condition between 1915 and 1930, such as significant shaking and trembling, mutism, alcoholism, or repeated flashbacks and nightmares. However, memory loss, obsessive sexual appetite, a compulsion to talk at length in a high-pitched voice and, perhaps, some loss of concentration were present on some occasions.

What do we know about the relationship between war traumas and crimes committed by servicemen and ex-servicemen during and after the Great War? There are a number of aspects of the First World War that have attracted the attention of historians in recent years and which provide a valuable corrective to the previous pre-occupation with the international causes of the outbreak of the war, the military history of the war, its literary and artistic legacy, and the impact of the war on capital, labour, gender, social class and welfare. Instead, much attention is focusing on the memorialisation of the war, on remembrance and on how grieving families, famous or otherwise, 'communed' with their lost sons or husbands; on comparative perspectives, such as how cities in different countries coped with total war; and, finally, on the concept and physical and cultural experience of shell shock. The literature on these topics is vast and has been growing enormously as the centenary of the outbreak of the war was reached in 1914.

For our purposes, the aim is to explore two issues. The first is to ask (albeit briefly) to what extent shell shock (or battle shock, post-traumatic stress disorder, or combat stress reaction) was a mental condition, whether identified from the outset or delayed in its manifestation for months or years, and which might be invoked on behalf of its sufferers in order to diminish or negate individual criminal responsibility. Thus with particular reference to Rouse, could his supposed murderous action in 1930 be linked to his being blown up and buried under the earth by an exploding German shell in May 1915? Second, how did shell shock feature in criminal cases whenever it was invoked by the defence? And, where it had not been raised during the trial, might it have possessed some significance in explaining, mitigating or excusing the accused's criminal conduct? This, of course, is to assume that shell shock could be a qualifying or excusing condition in determining the existence or otherwise of individual criminal responsibility, and not just a cultural trope invented to explain away (rather than to explain) unacceptable behaviour.[688]

Unlike Egbert in D. H. Lawrence's essay, 'England, My England', noted in chapter 17, the Devonshire Regiment soldier, Private Lucas, cited by Joanna Bourke,[689] had not died under the German barrage. But he had become 'prone to fits' after being buried under the earth thrown up by the exploding shell. He had undoubtedly experienced a traumatic event, even if it had not caused visible physical damage, nor (as some would believe) had it created shock waves which battered his neurological system. Had he suffered shell shock in the form of a clinical, rather

---

688 Jay Winter, "Shell-shock and the Cultural History of the Great War", *Journal of Contemporary History*, Vol. 35 (1), 2000, pp. 7-11.
689 Joanna Bourke, "Effeminacy, Ethnicity and the End of Trauma: The Sufferings of 'Shell-shocked' Men in Great Britain and Ireland, 1914-39", *ibid.*, pp. 57-69; cf., *ibid.*, *Dismembering the Male: Men's Bodies, Britain and the Great War*, Reaktion Books, 1999, p. 115.

than a cultural, condition? Modern analysis refers to soldiers' 'traumatic brain injury', frequently the result of the constant thud from high explosive projectiles. It is thought it could explain a former soldier's subsequent aggressive behaviour in later civilian life, particularly where the artillery barrage had affected his orbifrontal cortex, the part of the brain located just above the eyes.[690] Thus shelling might cause invisible injury to the brain, as well as visible injury to any part of the body. But arguably the vivid imagination of the soldier subjected to incessant shelling, even without its hitting its target, could induce such a morbid fear that the brain could no longer cope rationally.

"Hark! Thud, thud, thud,--quite soft....they never cease--
Those whispering guns—O Christ, I want to go out
And screech at them to stop--I'm going crazy;
I'm going stark, staring mad because of the guns."[691]

As one historian has written, this kind of industrialized warfare entailed a 'static struggle dominated by machines where the individual counted for little, [but which] contributed greatly to widespread mental illness after November 1914'.[692] Sassoon might well have written that, 'I'm going stark, staring mad because of the guns'. But the irony of that particular poem is that the narrator (Sassoon himself) is actually, after his earlier breakdown at the Front, recuperating in Kent to where the sounds of France and Flanders carried, and he cannot get the sounds of the guns out of his mind. How much more vexing for the soldiers crouching in their trenches as the incessant bombardments roar overhead?

Indeed, readers may be familiar with the shocking film clips from the Great War of soldiers shaking uncontrollably in hospital wards or gibbering maniacally while hiding under beds in hospitals far from the front lines (and irrespective of whether exposure to extremely fearful images do have the capacity to turn a young man's hair white overnight). While it is surely beyond argument that broken soldiers, displaying no physical bodily injuries, may yet have been suffering from shell shock, the same is just as likely to be the case with soldiers who *had* been wounded by a shell. In either situation the combatant's personality, dictated by his brain patterns, would be unable to cope. Thus his 'brain disorder', while in some cases invisible, was still 'physical', not 'mental', because it emanated from an external source. Its clinical treatment might differ from that accorded to familiar diseases such as cancer and diabetes. However, medical attention was surely the appropriate approach rather than the discarding of the patient as a malingerer or as 'lacking moral fibre', or even labeling him, like Ronald True, below, as being 'as mad as a hatter'.

In 1915 an article in the *British Medical Journal* described the condition of 'temporary nervous breakdown' among the troops as one that,

---

690 Emsley, *op. cit.*, p. 149.
691 Siegfried Sassoon, "Repression of War Experience" (1917), cited in Jean Moorcroft Wilson, *Siegfried Sassoon: The Making of a War Poet, A Biography, 1886-1918*, Duckworth, 1998, p. 378.
692 Ted Bogacz, "War Neurosis and Cultural Change in England, 1914-22: The Work of the War Office Committee of Enquiry into Shell-Shock", *Journal of Contemporary History*, Vol. 24, 1989, pp. 227-56, at p. 233.

...occurs in those who have been strong and well and is ascribed to a sudden or alarming physical cause, such as witnessing a ghastly sight or undergoing a harassing experience. As a result of such shock the patient becomes nervy, unduly emotional and shaky, and most typical of all, his sleep is disturbed by bad dreams of experiences he has passed, of shells bursting, of duels between aeroplanes, or the many harassing sights of war in the trenches."[693]

As Wendy Holden put it in her analysis of shell shock in the Great War,

The symptoms were wildly diverse, from total paralysis and blindness to loss of speech [Reg Christie of Ten Rillington Place infamy notoriously remained mute for months after a gas attack], vivid nightmares, hallucinations and memory loss. Some patients declined eventually into schizophrenia, chronic depression and even suicide. The medical consequences of severe trauma to the moral and mental state on the battle lines were, it seemed, unquantifiable."[694]

Most psychiatric practitioners believed that shell shock was more likely to precipitate autism, mutism or incapacity than criminality as manifested in, particularly, inter-personal violence committed by the afflicted.[695] Indeed this consequential condition has been described elsewhere as conversion hysteria or psychogenic or emotional illness suffered by the psychiatric casualty or the victim of battle shock (the latter two terms being preferred to that of shell shock).[696] However numerous military doctors during the Great War would have no truck with soldiers' claims of shell shock believing, in the case of soldiers tried for desertion or cowardice before capital courts martial, that executions were necessary to deter other soldiers deserting. Thus one author has quoted the 'authentic' opinion of a doctor, M. S. Esler, who had witnessed the execution of a deserter during the war.

I think that it was absolutely essential. It was setting a bad example to the men. They would have begun to feel that you only had to walk off during a battle and then come back afterwards and you escaped death or mutilation...I think it was a necessary punishment.[697]

---

693 Cited in Wendy Holden, *Shell Shock*, Channel 4 Books, 1998, p. 17. In the same year (1915) Captain Charles Myers RAMC published his seminal article on shell shock in the *Lancet*, February 13, 1915, pp. 316-20. His military superiors took a dim view of his publishing papers on the subject. His interest in the psychological underpinnings of shell shock clashed with colleagues' remit to remove physical ailments. See Ben Shephard, *A War of Nerves: Soldiers and Psychiatry, 1914-1994*, Jonathan Cape, 2000, p. 49. The case of David Greenwood is particularly interesting. Convicted of the rape and murder of Nellie Trew on Eltham Common in February 1918, Greenwood, a former soldier, had claimed at his trial that he had been suffering shell shock, having been buried alive by a shell explosion at Ypres during his war service. He was nonetheless convicted of murder though the Home Secretary commuted his death sentence to life imprisonment. See, inter alia, Terry Charman, *The First World War on the Home Front*, Andre Deutsch, 2014, pp. 128-9. His wartime experience bore some similarities with Rouse's time in the trenches.
694 Holden, *op. cit.*, p. 7.
695 Clive Emsley, "Violent Crime in England in 1919: Post-war Anxieties and Press Narratives", *Continuity and Change*, Vol. 23, 2008, pp. 173-95.
696 Frank Richardson, "Postscript", in Anthony Babington, *For the Sake of Example: Capital Courts Martial, 1914-1918*, Paladin, 1985, pp. 283-4. Richardson had been a senior Army psychiatrist during the Second World War.
697 Cathryn Corns, "'Shot at Dawn': Military Executions in the Great War", *Journal of the Royal United Services Institute*, Vol. 143 (1), 1998, pp. 53-5, at p. 55.

This may, indeed, have also been the 'authentic' voice of a wartime medical officer in the RAMC, writing many years later in 1970.[698] But some other unit medical officers might have possessed too rudimentary a knowledge of the issues, or they might simply have been too junior to challenge the more senior medical officers who took a robust view of soldiers' conduct. For the concept of a man's 'bank balance' of moral courage being overdrawn, as Lord Moran would later explain in his post-World War Two book, *The Anatomy of Courage*,[699] was not yet widely accepted. As Major-General Frank Richardson, an Army psychiatrist in World War Two, commented in respect of the cases examined by Judge Babington regarding the British soldiers shot for desertion in the Great War, '...reading between the lines in many of the cases described briefly by Judge Babington....malingering or shamming seem less likely than genuinely hysterical states, such as amnesia or fugues'.[700] Indeed Lord Southborough, who chaired a post-Great War enquiry into shell shock,[701] suggested in parliament that of the 346 British soldiers executed by firing squad during the war, a sizeable number could well have been suffering from 'war-induced mental illness and had been unjustly sentenced'.[702] Such an analysis, however, probably had only a limited number of medical adherents at the Front. Indeed the Southborough Committee contented itself with the lukewarm recommendation that the, 'system pursued in France in the late war, of obtaining the best possible expert advice when any medical question or doubt arose, before or at trials for serious military offences, or on subsequent review of the proceedings of the Court, should be followed in the future'. Most regimental medical officers at the Front were, of course, unacquainted with specialized branches of psychiatry and might, in any case, be sceptical of imported German theories. Moreover their preoccupation would be with the immediate tending to the physically wounded. But even where some psychiatric experience had been gained by doctors at the Front, the difficulty remained that, in the committee's own words, '....it is extremely difficult to distinguish cowardice from neurosis, since in both fear is the chief causal factor'.[703] Thus for doctors doubtful or dismissive of new concepts that sought to explain men's inability to cope under fire, the explanation for 'funk' was more likely to lie in those soldiers' character defects. Indeed it was believed that shell-shocked men were more prone than others to turn to crime, with one writer, T. W. Sandwell, penning an article in 1920 entitled, 'Are You a Potential Post-war Criminal?'[704] An article from April 1918 had already warned about the dangers from certain neurasthenics (sufferers from wartime hysteria and anxiety), declaring that,

> These patients easily get into trouble; they issue false cheques, are hopelessly unreliable and extravagant etc and yet are not sufficiently irresponsible

---

698 See also Babington, *op. cit.*, pp. 249-50.
699 Lord Moran, *The Anatomy of Courage*, Constable, 1945, p. x.
700 Babington, *op. cit.*, p. 245.
701 *Report of the War Office Committee of Enquiry into 'Shell-Shock'* (Southborough Committee), Cmd. 1734, 1922, reprinted in 2014 by the Naval and Military Press Ltd and the Imperial War Museum.
702 HL Deb., 5th Series, Vol. 39, col. 1105, cited in Douglas Commaille, "An Assessment of Causes, Responses and Attitudes to Insanity in Capital Cases in Post-World War One England", LL.M. extended essay, Kent University, September 2014.
703 Southborough Committee, *op. cit.*, pp. 192-3.
704 Cited in Fiona Reid, "Distinguishing Between Shell-shocked Veterans and Pauper Lunatics: The Ex-Services' Welfare Society and Mentally Wounded Veterans After the Great War", *War in History*, Vol. 14 (3), 2007, pp. 347-71, at p. 355.

always to justify confinement. Moreover they have such a poor make up that psychological treatment is very difficult. All psychological treatment depends upon the essential moral worth of the individual".[705]

Presumably, therefore, the morally upstanding could be cured while the morally reprobate could not (though whether they should simply be punished like reprobates elsewhere was not stated).

As to the feared explosion of criminality caused by a brutalized soldiery demobilized on the cessation of hostilities, there was no shortage of dire warnings. For example the Metropolitan Police Commissioner in May 1919 referred to returning soldiers as 'men grown callous after four years' experience of killing', while the commentator, Sir Philip Gibbs, observed that such men had been exposed to an 'intensive culture of violence'. The Labour-inclined *Daily Herald* on July 19, 1919 observed that 'Human life has never reached such a low valuation as today', and that '....the atmosphere of blood and violence necessary for the perpetration of war of the kind we have just survived....has gradually altered the moral aspect of the country at large and sown such seeds of perversion and lust for violence that the crop will be heavy and bitter'. Finally, *The Times* on January 2, 1920 condemned the 'disregard for human life ...inevitably created and fostered in thousands of uncontrolled minds by the war'.[706]

But the expected deluge of violent criminality after the war simply did not occur in the numbers feared.[707] Indeed this was despite a growth in domestic upheavals and a sense of grievance, bitterness, disorientation, hopelessness, loss and emasculation both physical and emotional among many of the returning troops. True, they had quickly learned, when they disembarked on British soil from the troopships, that the politicians' promises of a 'land fit for heroes'[708] was a delusion, even though employment prospects had been initially favourable as the women were kicked out of their wartime jobs.[709] However when ex-servicemen *did* commit violent acts, there was in some circles an understanding of the unnatural existence they had previously endured for so long. Thus the *Sheffield Mail*, commenting on December 2, 1920 on the conviction for murder of demobbed soldiers, noted that, '...where a man is placed upon a pedestal for the greater the number of lives taken by him, it is not easy, indeed it is not sensible, to expect to bring him back to the adequate appreciation of the standards compatible with order and civilization'. Less sympathetic judicial views were not, however, dulled. For example Mr. Justice Avory would afford no sympathy to Major Robert Ferguson, charged with fraudulent dealings. For the latter's gallant war service,

---

705   Cited in *ibid.*, pp. 355-6.
706   Cited in Commaille, *op. cit.*
707   Recent studies today do, however, suggest that former soldiers under the age of 30, such as those who had served in Iraq and Afghanistan, were three times more likely to commit violent offences on their return to the UK than their civilian peers. See Deirdre MacManus et *al.*, "Violent Offending by UK Military Personnel Deployed to Iraq and Afghanistan: a Data Linkage Cohort Study", *Lancet*, Vol. 381, No. 9870, March 16, 2013, pp. 907-17. The experiences of almost 14,000 soldiers and ex-soldiers were studied.
708   P. B. Johnson, *Land Fit for Heroes: The Planning of British Reconstruction, 1916-1919*, University of Chicago Press, Chicago, 1968.
709   For the relevant legislation which sought to restore male skilled workers' job privileges against female wartime encroachment, see Gerry R. Rubin, "Law as a Bargaining Weapon: British Labour and the Restoration of Pre-War Practices Act 1919", *Historical Journal*, Vol. 32 (4), 1989, pp. 925-45.

including repeated concussion and injuries to the head, failed to move the solemn, stern and unbending Avory to leniency. 'A man's service in the war was not to be taken as any excuse or justification for subsequent crime committed by him.' Ferguson's war wounds were thus brushed aside, as would be Rouse's a decade or so later.[710]

Yet while crime statistics, overall, showed no perceptible increases in violent crime after 1918, the newspapers were quick to publicise individual cases involving ex-soldiers which the press thought would interest their readers. Perhaps, as the former Army general and now Metropolitan Police Commissioner, Sir Nevil Macready, suggested, 'What was happening now was that directly a crime [committed by ex-servicemen] occurred, a great deal more than usual was made of it.'[711] Prominent among the press reports were cases where the accused appeared to be carrying the traumatic legacy and mental scars of the trenches. The leading crime historian, Clive Emsley,[712] identifies reports for a number of such cases. Perhaps the most well-known involved Colonel Rutherford, RAMC, found guilty but insane of murdering Major Miles Seton in January 1919. Since it was shown at the trial that Rutherford had decided that Seton was an evil influence on his family, the invocation of shell shock by the accused was, perhaps, easier for the jury to accept in upholding the defence of insanity.

Of course insanity in law was, and remains, a carefully circumscribed concept that psychiatrists today would scarcely recognize. The legal definition derives from the trial of the delusional Daniel McNaghten in 1843, who suffered from a persecution mania, being pursued at different intervals by the Church of Rome, the new police founded by Sir Robert Peel, and Tory politicians held responsible for his failings in life (he was, after all, from Glasgow, one of the present writers' city of birth). After he had been charged with shooting dead the prime minister's secretary, Drummond (Peel, the prime minister, had been the intended target), on January 20, 1843, the jury returned the 'special verdict' meaning that McNaghten had been incapable of distinguishing between right and wrong. The verdict was received with shock, prompting parliament to press the judges to clarify where sanity ended and madness began. It was, nonetheless, a procedure which is of dubious authority since they were being asked hypothetical questions. Notwithstanding, it resulted in the McNaghten Rules. More accurately regarded as (more or less) binding guidelines, they were framed by a panel of 13 judges (with one dissentient) who 'ruled' that insanity referred to a 'disease of the mind', leading to a 'defect of reason' as a result of which the prisoner does not know the nature and quality of his act or, if he does know its nature and quality, he does not know that it is wrong.

It is important to stress that the accused's 'not knowing' that his act is 'wrong' must be proved by him, on the balance of probabilities, to have derived from a clinical 'disease' of the mind 'leading to' (or causing) 'his defect of reason', resulting in his inability to perceive anything wrong, both morally *and* legally, in his action, and the Crown is not required to prove the accused's sanity. Thus the

---

710   See Commaille, *op. cit.*, for the Sheffield and Ferguson cases. The Sheffield soldiers appear to have been reprieved.
711   *Manchester Guardian*, January 20, 1920, cited in *ibid*.
712   Emsley, 'Violent Crime', *op. cit.*

assassin who believes it is morally right to shoot dead the leader of a death cult or a country's president or monarch could not claim McNaghten insanity if, in the absence of a 'disease of the mind' affecting his cognitive reasoning, he knows that murder is illegal.[713] In a similar vein, foreigners who come to Britain on a motoring holiday and drive on the right hand side could not avoid conviction by setting out to prove that they did not know that the act, of whose nature or quality they were aware, was legally wrong. For the dictum of *ignorantia iuris neminem excusat* would apply here unless the visitor could indeed show that he was suffering from a 'disease of the mind' which would result in a 'defect of reason' to explain his not 'knowing' his act was 'wrong' (and some, including drivers, causing harm while suffering epileptic fits or experiencing diabetic hyperglycaemic episodes, thereby causing them to black out, have in the past been deemed legally insane[714]). Thus inasmuch as Colonel Rutherford, above, was delusional (suffering from a disease of the mind) regarding Seton's conduct towards his wife, resulting in nonsensical reasoning, so that he did not know that he was committing a wrongful act in a moral (and legal) sense, then a special verdict of insanity could be returned.[715]

Another ex-officer, Lieutenant Redfern from the Devonshires, had shot dead a bank manager in Leeds while carrying out a robbery. Yet while the officer had been severely wounded during the war, was partially paralysed and still had a bullet lodged in his spine, four doctors could not agree on his mental state. Two believed that his hysteria, which the newspaper reader would have assumed, in the absence of an expressed explicit link in the report, had derived from his war traumas, meant that he lacked 'moral responsibility' for his actions. By this the experts probably implied that he was *McNaghten* insane. However, the other two doctors considered that any hysteria present at the time of the shooting was not such as to render Redfern legally insane. That is, for those clinicians, his hysteria did not amount to a 'disease of the mind' affecting his reasoning processes. In the end the jury, free to accept or to reject any, some or, indeed, all of the medical testimony, convicted the prisoner, although their recommendation to mercy was heeded.[716] While *Redfern* would not have been a useful case for Rouse to cite at his trial in 1931, had the issue of linking war trauma to possible insanity been pursued, the reprieve of the officer hinted at what might have been for Rouse.

Emsley also cites the case of Henry Parry (alias Beckett), charged with murdering a couple and their two children in Forest Gate, London. Formerly with the Army Veterinary Corps, he claimed shell shock in that he had been wounded in the head by shrapnel, had been blown up by high explosive and had been flogged and put in a dungeon while a prisoner-of-war of the Turks. Moreover 'voices' had told him to commit murder. He was not believed and was convicted. His long record of previous convictions probably ensured that he went to the gallows. Similarly,

---

713   Nigel Walker, *Crime and Insanity in England, One: Historical Perspectives*, Edinburgh University Press, Edinburgh, 1968, Ch. 5. Only if he were acting in self- or in 'public' defence or was acting under the laws of armed conflict while himself a lawful combatant could criminal liability be avoided.
714   *Sullivan* [1984] 1 A C 156; *Bingham* [1991] Crim L R 433.
715   Mrs. Rutherford's divorce from her husband after a decree nisi had been granted to her in 1921 on grounds of cruelty and adultery was rescinded by the Court of Appeal (her adultery evidence being successfully challenged). The rescission was upheld in the House of Lords. See *The Times*, November 4, 1922. Mrs. Rutherford shortly after wrote to the newspaper on the more enlightened and more equal Divorce Reform Bill then going through parliament. See *ibid*, November 13, 1922.
716   *The Times*, March 18, 1920.

Mr. Justice Darling gave short shrift to the plea from the congenitally syphilitic George Lucas, charged with the murder of his baby, that he had been gassed at Vimy Ridge in July 1916 and had experienced pains in his chest and head. Further, he had no recollection of having previously attacked his parents. Neither judge nor jury was impressed. While it is not clear whether the defence tendered psychiatric evidence for insanity, the Home Office approved a commutation of the death sentence. Presumably in the case of Parry, the psychiatrists examining him, or even the jury itself, concluded that his accounts of delusions were fabricated, while in respect of Lucas, the incontrovertible medical evidence regarding his congenital syphilitic condition counted for something when the Home Office finally determined his fate. For Rouse the distant memory of insanity on the part of a previous generation of the family counted for nothing.

While Emsley suggests that the public could find comfort in shell shock as an explanation for ungentlemanly violence by officers such as Colonel Rutherford, and return a verdict of guilty but insane accordingly, he recognizes that other ranks' behaviour could similarly be attributed to shell shock.[717] But this could still result in a conviction, as in Parry and Lucas, above, if the test for insanity in the McNaghten Rules of 1843 had not been met. Yet a defence claim of shell shock in a capital case (or of gassing or war-induced paralysis and hysteria, as seen above), where an insanity finding was not returned, could still have an effect on disposal, post-conviction, when the Home Office, prompted by the prisoner, reviewed the death sentence.

Apart from Colonel Rutherford there were other murder *causes célèbres* after the war where the ex-service officer had pleaded insanity. They included the case of Lieutenant Frederick Holt. He had been called up as a Territorial officer in August 1914 and served in the trenches. However he was invalided out of the 4th Loyals (North Lancashire Regiment) suffering from amnesia and depression. When Holt was about to face trial for the murder of Kitty Breaks on the beach at Lytham St Annes in December 1919, his counsel, Marshall Hall, first claimed that Holt, harbouring a persecution mania, was unfit to plead, and called a number of doctors to testify that he was insane. However the jury rejected this preliminary plea, perhaps because the Attorney-General, the soon-to-be-appointed Lord Chief Justice, Gordon Hewart, asked a medical expert what Holt had first said to him when the psychiatrist came to assess his mental condition. 'He said he would like to see his solicitor first', which did not sound like the remark of an insane prisoner. Therefore Holt now stood trial before a different jury, during which hearing he appeared totally oblivious to his surroundings, even reading a newspaper upside down. If it was a ploy it did not succeed and he was found guilty despite Marshall Hall's claiming that his client had been 'unhinged' by the war. At his appeal additional evidence regarding his syphilis, contracted in Malaya, was admitted, the doctor who treated him also claiming that Holt appeared to be suffering from shell shock. But the Court of Criminal Appeal felt disposed not to interfere with the jury's verdict, especially since the trial judge, Mr. Justice Greer, had left it to the jury to decide whether to acquit on the ground of irresistible impulse, which they had obviously declined to do, and which he presumably (or charitably) had deemed to be evidence for *McNaghten* insanity. As Lord Reading, the Lord Chief

---

717   Emsley, 'Violent Crime', *op. cit.*

Justice, pointed out, irresistible impulse was not actually covered by *McNaghten* (the reason being that a prisoner subject to such an impulse knew the nature or quality of the act, a fact that would disqualify him from pleading insanity).[718] Before Holt's execution the Home Secretary consulted a panel of psychiatrists regarding the prisoner's mental condition. Although they could in those circumstances apply tests for insanity that went beyond the artificial confines of *McNaghten*, they nonetheless found him to be sane notwithstanding insanity in his family. Thus his wartime amnesia and depression, his bizarre behaviour at his trial and his history of syphilis, not only failed the narrow McNaghten test, but those symptoms also failed to establish that he suffered from such a severe psychiatric illness that it would be wrong to execute him. He was hanged at Strangeways on April 13, 1920.[719] Rouse, of course, could not lay claim to those conditions which did not even avail Holt.

Perhaps even more notable was the case of Ronald True, the former Royal Flying Corps (RFC) pilot sent to Broadmoor following his brutal killing of Gertrude Yates in her flat in Fulham, London, in 1922. True had been born in Manchester in 1891 to an unmarried 16-year old. When she later married into money, she indulged him to excess. He had already shown signs of systematic mendacity and of cruelty to animals (like Donald Hume later on). Totally unreliable and self-obsessed, he was packed off abroad after boarding school at Bedford Grammar School (which was within walking distance from where Rouse would spend his final days), and was a consistent failure at whatever he turned his hand to, whether farming, ranching, trading or managing.

In 1915 the RFC took the ridiculous step of enlisting him in its officer-cadet ranks at Gosport with a view to his piloting aircraft. Two crashes followed in quick succession while he was still training in the United Kingdom. One occurred at Farnborough where he suffered severe concussion and unconsciousness for two days, and one a month later at Gosport where he suffered only cuts and bruises. While he frequently failed many simple examinations as part of his training programme, he somehow persuaded his commanders to award him his wings. His fellow-pilots nonetheless viewed him as an extreme oddity. As Donald Carswell's 'Introduction' to True's Notable British Trials volume put it, '....he was regarded as little removed from a madman. His general demeanour is described as feverish, nervous, and imbecile'.[720] His addiction to morphine obviously did not help and he was inevitably discharged. After a period spent in a Southsea clinic where he terrorized the staff with his outrageous and violent conduct, he successfully blagged himself into a post as a government pilot trainer at Yeovil early in 1917. Quickly shown the exit as his incompetence became immediately manifest (and where his delusional behaviour became more marked) he next turned up in New York and once more managed to pull the wool over the eyes of military recruiters, this time the United States War Department which offered him a post as an

718 It was only when the partial defence to murder of diminished responsibility was introduced by the Homicide Act 1957, section 2, that the plea of irresistible impulse could reduce the offence to voluntary manslaughter. The first major such case was that of Patrick Byrne, convicted of the manslaughter of Stephanie Baird in the Birmingham YWCA in 1961. See *R v Byrne* [1960] 3 All E R 1; Robert Church, *Accidents of Murder: Ten Cases Re-examined*, Robert Hale, 1989, Ch. 5.
719 For the Holt case see, for example, Edward Marjoribanks, *Famous Trials of Marshall Hall*, Penguin, 1951, pp. 316-28.
720 Donald Carswell (ed.), *Trial of Ronald True*, William Hodge and Company, Edinburgh, 1950, p. 3.

instructor at one of their flying schools which soon moved to Houston. By now married to an American actress on tour, his stay in Texas was, of course, short-lived. The war finally over, he was back at his mother's home in Britain with wife and baby in tow. But despite his obvious symptoms of severe mental disorder, he was left untreated and packed off abroad again on another futile posting (to the Gold Coast). Returning after a few months, he was admitted to a Brighton clinic where his addiction, and the steps taken to feed it, grew more alarming and violent.

The erratic nature of his existence, moving from clinic to clinic, staying with his wife some of the time, appearing in court on drug-related charges, becoming increasing dangerous as his psychotic condition worsened but avoiding the restraints and treatment that his family so badly desired for him, eventually culminated in his murder of Gertrude Yates (or Olive Young), a young woman who had once entertained him in her flat but who was reluctant to do so subsequently. She obviously had the measure of his mental instability, of his kleptomania and of his fixation with her. It did not save her, her blood-stained body being found by her maid after True had left her apartment on March 6, 1922. The story unfolding at his trial reveals the depth of his personality disorder, and his delusions regarding his supposed *doppelganger*. This was the 'other' Ronald True who, he claimed, had been signing dud cheques in the name of the 'real' Ronald True. Anticipating a reckoning, 'He would have to meet the other Ronald True one day, he declared, and then there would be a 'how d'ye do'.[721]

It is unnecessary to recount more lurid details of True's bizarre conduct. At his trial two psychiatrists for the defence agreed with the prison doctor that True was suffering from a congenital mental disorder, exacerbated by his drug-taking. The Crown, in contrast, offered up no medical experts but instead relied on cross-examining the defence experts to suggest that True was not wholly mad. As the jury returned a verdict of guilty they obviously took the view that although he had displayed clearly bizarre behaviour such as a madman might engage in, he himself was not a lunatic under the McNaghten Rules.

Indeed an account of what he did at the time of the murder suggests a complex and contradictory pattern of behaviour. Knowing that Gertrude Yates' cleaner, who was quite familiar with the polite 'Major True', would not arrive at the flat for another hour and a half, he clubbed Gertrude to death in the bedroom with a rolling pin after bringing in the morning tea that he had made. He ensured she was dead by also strangling her. But while he arranged pillows on the bed to simulate someone sleeping there, he actually dragged her body to the bathroom. He then took £8 from her handbag and stole her jewellery. But irrationally he stayed behind in the flat until the cleaner arrived, and told her not to disturb Gertrude in the bedroom as her mistress was fast asleep. He then left, tipping the cleaner for helping him on with his coat, and shortly thereafter the game was up as she found the body on the bathroom floor. The layperson might well understand a jury homing in on True's cold and calculating behaviour in the flat while refusing to view his reckless actions as proving his insanity. Indeed a subsequent appeal failed. However, as Donald Carswell pointed out, the fact was that,

721   *Ibid.*, p. 11.

Prima facie True's crime was prompted by a perfectly sane motive [robbery]. He needed money. Gertrude Yates had cash and valuables. He murdered her, took everything that was worth taking, lost no time in turning the jewellery into cash, and used every means that suggested itself in his mind [perhaps an important qualification] to escape detection. That was the sum and substance of the case against True; and the prosecution submitted that it not only did not support, but negatived the suggestion that the murderer of Gertrude Yates was a madman.....Nevertheless it was based on a fallacy, viz., that an act that might well be the act of a sane man cannot be the act of an insane one.

In other words the fact that Ronald True appeared to be rationally and calculatingly driven to murder Gertrude, even that he knew the morally and legally objectionable nature and quality of his act, did not mean that he was not suffering a congenital mental disorder. Although, arguably, he may not have been suffering from delusions in terms of the McNaghten Rules, nonetheless, in respect of his actions in killing Gertrude Yates, he was undoubtedly suffering from other delusions, making him mentally disordered. Indeed, the Home Secretary, Edward Shortt, was still bothered about the case after conviction. He ordered True to be examined by three more psychiatrists in Pentonville Prison where he was awaiting execution. They conveniently pronounced him insane. As Shortt explained to Cabinet on June 13, 1922, the Home Secretary possessed statutory power to establish a committee of investigation in such cases, and he, Shortt, had exercised it in this case in view of the numerous submissions from the doctors involved and from the trial judge regarding True's sanity. Crucially,

> The question of what was the state of the prisoner's mind at the time of the commission of the crime and/or of the trial, was not material to the action of the Home Secretary, as the Statute on which he had acted, and on which the expert examination had been based, related only to the period after conviction. It was a well-established legal doctrine that a murderer who was found to be mad after conviction was never hanged.[722]

Saved from the gallows True, 'as mad as a hatter' but not McNaghten insane, spent the rest of his life living happily in Broadmoor, and died there in 1951, aged 60.[723] Indeed the aircraft crashes that he experienced seemed almost

722 CAB23/30/2, June 13, 1922. The 'legal doctrine' (though it was in fact a practice) went back at least to 1840. The legislation was the Criminal Lunatics Act 1884, section 2. Bizarrely if, after conviction, a prisoner sentenced to death *then* became insane, he could yet be hanged after he had recovered sanity. For, on recovery, he might be in a position to submit grounds for a reprieve. See Courtney Stanhope Kenny, *Outlines of Criminal Law*, 4th edition, Cambridge University Press, Cambridge, 1936, p. 68; Sir Edward Troup, *The Home Office*, Putnam's, 1925, p. 69. It is very doubtful whether any executions in such circumstances were carried out from the Victorian era onwards. In August 1917 Thomas Cox, aged 59, cut his wife's throat in the bedroom in Ludlow that they shared with their children. At his trial his plea of insanity, based on his allegedly having previously attempted suicide, was rejected by the jury. On his appeal the Court of Criminal Appeal reiterated that when a full trial had already taken place, and where the issue of insanity had been raised at that trial, the Home Secretary was in a better position to investigate the matter than the appeal court which therefore dismissed his appeal. Though he was hanged at Shrewsbury in December 1917 it is not clear whether or not the Home Secretary ordered a prison medical board of inquiry. If he had in fact done so then the psychiatrists clearly found him not to be insane at the time they examined him. See *The Times*, December 4, 1917 for the appeal hearing, and John J. Eddleston, *The Encyclopaedia of Executions*, John Blake, 2004, p. 313.
723 The case was controversial because the Home Secretary had refused to intervene in the case of the teenaged Henry Jacoby, hanged for murdering Lady White in a London hotel where he had worked as a pantry boy. Jacoby and True had met each other in Brixton prison hospital. Class

incidental and not central to his emotional and mental state. On the other hand, it is conceivable that in Rouse's case, his frightening experience as the burning aeroplane crashed near him just before the shell explosion rendered him severely wounded and unconscious might have profoundly affected him psychologically.

Georges Codère was a lieutenant serving with the Canadian Royal Artillery in 1916. With a reputation as 'Fou Codère' among his colleagues, he had not been trusted by his superiors to exercise command in France. So he remained in England where he decided upon disposing of a Canadian sergeant, possibly for financial gain which would, of course, cast doubt on any insanity claim (though Ronald True's theft of Gertrude's money did not mean that he did not suffer a severe mental illness). Thwarted in his efforts to recruit help from fellow-officers, Codère managed to kill his victim with great brutality in the officers' mess, finishing off the deed by slitting his victim's throat. He then enlisted some junior ranks to clear up the mess and store the body in a stable. One servant cooperated, in gratitude for which assistance Codère accused him of the murder. Soon the actual train of events became clear and at his trial before Mr. Justice Darling his plea of insanity was rejected. Since he 'knew' the 'nature' of his act was a homicidal deed and, more importantly, that the killing was 'wrong' in the sense of being impermissible within wider society, he could not prove on the balance of probabilities that he did not 'know' that the nature and quality of his deed were 'wrong'. When he appealed the appeal judges affirmed that with reference to the moral 'quality' of the act, which the trial judge had had no need to explore, given Codère's admission regarding the 'nature' of his deed, the test was objective, that of the reasonable man. In other words, it was not a question whether Codère believed that the quality of his deed was 'moral' but whether the reasonable man would do so. Otherwise, political assassins might have been able to escape the gallows by claiming insanity on the basis that they did not 'know' '(i.e., acknowledge) the immoral quality of their act, and therefore did not know the 'wrongness' of their homicidal deeds. We may also presume that this supposed objective test would likewise apply to the 'nature' of the accused's act, it being assumed that there was no *separate* proof, apart from his legal burden of proof that what he was doing was not 'morally' wrong, that he was suffering delusions (that he was dead-heading flowers, as distinct from slitting his victim's throat?) similar to McNaghten's himself. And, of course, being based in the United Kingdom, he would not have experienced the traumatic sights or have experienced incessant shelling that had reduced others to poor gibbering souls who had lost their human qualities. Yet for a man long dubbed 'Fou Codère', it is surprising that compelling evidence for the presence of delusions was not established. Again, like True, military service seemed almost incidental to his personality disorder, unlike the case with Rutherford. And in respect of Redfern, Parry, Lucas and, indeed, Rouse, there were, surely, sufficient grounds to mount at least a *prima facie* case linking post-war conduct to wartime trauma.[724]

> discrimination was alleged and shortly after a committee, chaired by Lord Justice Atkin, met to consider whether to advise a defence of diminished responsibility in murder cases where the criteria for a finding of insanity had not been met. The committee recommended such a change but the government refused to act (until the Homicide Act 1957) despite the doctrine applying in Scots law. For the Insanity Committee, see Geoffrey Lewis, *Lord Atkin*, Butterworths, 1983, pp. 158-62.

724 Actually, there was no warrant for this 'reasonable man', or objective, definition of 'quality' in the McNaghten Rules themselves. But despite the inevitable application of the rules to individual

The problem for shell-shocked soldiers (indeed, for any murderers) committing murder in England and Wales before the Homicide Act 1957 was that there was no halfway house between insanity and sanity as legally conceived under the McNaghten Rules. The prisoner was either wholly responsible for his actions (if of the age of criminal responsibility, while the plea of 'duress' by a third party, available as a defence for most crimes, did not apply to homicide prosecutions), or he was not responsible on the ground of insanity (in which case the disposal of killers would be to the lunatic asylum rather than to the gallows). The concept of 'diminished' (or lesser) responsibility for a criminal act, in particular, for murder, did not apply to questions of guilt, irrespective of the basis for that diminished responsibility. But after 1957 in some but not all cases, depending on severity and on what was considered 'abnormal', a prisoner suffering from paranoid psychosis, or from alcoholism or drug dependency as a disease (and not just someone 'hopelessly' drunk or 'high'), or from an irresistible impulse (as seen above), from (nowadays) post-natal depression or pre-menstrual tension, or from 'battered wives' syndrome', or from severe or chronic clinical depression or anxiety, could seek to invoke a diminished responsibility partial defence to murder. Indeed the critical wording of the 1957 Act, section 2, before it was tweaked in the Coroners and Justice Act 2009 stated that,

> Where a person kills or is party to the killing of another, he shall not be convicted of murder if he was suffering from such abnormality of mind (whether arising from a condition of arrested or retarded development of mind or any inherent causes or induced by disease or injury) as substantially impaired his mental responsibility for his acts.

Had that provision been applied retrospectively, might it have saved the syphilitic George Lucas and Frederick Holt from the gallows, in that they might have been suffering from an abnormality of mind induced by disease? Might it have saved Timothy Evans and Derek Bentley, both of whom were said to have possessed the IQ of a child? That is, might they not have been clear examples of abnormality of mind due to arrested or retarded development of mind? Then there is the case of the Yorkshire Ripper who spoke of 'voices' telling him to murder prostitutes. Since, arguably, he knew the nature and quality of his acts and recognized that they were (legally) wrong, he could not fall into the McNaghten insanity category. And this was despite modern psychiatrists finding him suffering from a personality disorder such as to render him, by their lights, not responsible for his actions. Yet would he not have qualified for the diminished responsibility defence on the ground that he was suffering from an abnormality of mind arising from an inherent cause, his paranoid schizophrenia? In the event the judge controversially refused to admit this plea despite the agreement of both Crown and the defence to its submission to the jury. Predictably, after his conviction in 1981 of numerous murders, Sutcliffe spent the first few weeks in a conventional,

cases, general (even if misguided) rules are surely critical to the retention of whatever credibility they possess today (and the credibility reposed by the legal system in the Rules' simplistic formula is wafer-thin, given present-day knowledge of psychiatric conditions). See Walker, *op. cit.*, pp. 113-4; *R v Codère* (1917) 12 Cr. App. Rep. 21. Codère was reprieved. In *R v Windle* [1952] 2 QB 826, the simple formula was confirmed that if the accused knew that his actions were *legally wrong*, then despite the Rules' more expansive wording regarding the quality of the act, he was not McNaghten insane. When arrested for murdering his wife, Windle told the arresting officer, 'I suppose they'll hang me for this'.

high-security prison before sense kicked in on the part of the authorities and he was then transferred to Broadmoor prison hospital where he remained until 2016 before being transferred to Frankland Prison in Durham.

Which brings us to cases of shell shock such as that of Henry Parry (alias Beckett), discussed previously, who had suffered a shrapnel wound in his head and had been blown up by high explosive. Was he not suffering an abnormality of mind induced by injury? Such a question, although on the surface a medical one, would in fact have been for the jury to decide on the basis of evidence submitted, had there been scope in the then current law in 1919 (which there was not), to permit its introduction. By the same token one could identify a number of cases of soldiers being tried for capital offences during the Great War, both civil and military offences (such as desertion), where the mental condition of the soldier was not adequately assessed. Thus if the defence were to argue that the soldier had been suffering from shell shock when the offence had been committed, the plea could not affect the verdict unless the prisoner had been rendered McNaghten insane by his experience. And if the prisoner had run away from the front line, or had slept on post, or had fired a rifle at a hated sergeant-major, it is unlikely, except in the most extreme of cases, that he would have been unaware of the nature and quality of the act, or that it was (legally) wrong. In any event scepticism among senior line officers regarding the concept of shell shock may have permeated many courts martial. As Corns and Hughes-Wilson have written,[725]

....by 1916 men often claimed shell shock as a defence at courts martial, these claims frequently having no foundation. This led, inevitably, to some men who were genuinely suffering from a mental breakdown being convicted of offences for which they were not truly responsible, and in some cases being shot.

The following capital courts martial cases from the Great War, focusing on the civilian offence of murder and not on military offences, illustrate some of the difficulties in having shell shock recognized as an excusatory defence.[726] Private Charles Knight of the 10th Battalion, Royal Welch Fusiliers, for example, had been in the front line at Sanctuary Wood and Ploegstraat in Flanders in late 1915. After his battalion had been withdrawn for rest at the village of Eecke where they occupied a barn as their billet, he was sitting having a coffee in a house when he experienced,

...an unfunny [sic] turn; he became mentally very disturbed and began to wander about in a restless, distracted fashion. The mental commotion persisted, Knight felt completely unable to relax but he managed to eat some supper at the barn and then went to find some friends in a near-by alehouse.

Returning to the barn he picked up a rifle and waved it around as if attacking an imaginary enemy. He initially resisted efforts to disarm him and managed to fire two to three dozen shots before he was overpowered. By then, in the confined

---

725 Cathryn Corns and John Hughes-Wilson, *Blindfold and Alone: British Military Executions in the Great War*, Cassell, 2001, p. 79.
726 Julian Putkowski and Mark Dunning, *Murderous Tommies*, Pen & Sword, Barnsley, 2012, Ch. 4, for this and following examples.

space, one soldier was dead and another severely wounded. At his subsequent court martial, the battalion medical officer, Captain Bernard Grellier, told the court that when he examined Knight after the incident, the prisoner seemed to be in a semi-conscious state, not fully appreciating his surroundings. He answered lucidly to most questions put to him but, crucially,

> ....his breath was of the alcoholic type and his breath was tainted with liquor: I examined him to see if there was anything that could account for his medical condition and found nothing beyond the signs of alcohol: his eyes were constantly wandering and he was moving his hands about as if to feel something: I do not consider his mental condition was normal at that time and I consider that it was due to drink.

The next morning the medical officer saw Knight again and 'found him quite sensible'. Yet although the soldier recalled speaking with Grellier the previous night, he could not remember any of the events in the barn. The court martial asked one question of Grellier: 'When you saw the accused on the morning of November 4, do you consider his mental condition was normal?' To this Grellier replied, 'Yes, except that he seemed to be depressed'. It is plain that little account was taken of that part of Grellier's testimony that spoke to Knight's vacant and wandering appearance and to his restless hand movements. His vexed mental state, it was reasoned, had been due to drink and the next day he was 'sensible'. As he was sane, not insane, the verdict was a foregone conclusion. At the review stage, that is, before the issue of confirmation of the finding and sentence was placed before the commander-in-chief, it fell to the brigade deputy judge advocate (DJAG) to advise the Director of Personal Services (an appointment subordinate to the Adjutant-General), Brigadier-General Gilbert Mellor, that,

> The substantial question for the Court to decide was whether the accused was in a state of mind to intend to kill or to inflict grievous bodily harm or to know that what he was doing would reasonably and probably cause that result, and in law it rested, it this case, upon the accused to show that he was not legally responsible for his actions.[727]

Though the matter is not free from doubt, it is possible that the above statement confused two separate issues. The first interpretation of the passage is that the DJAG was addressing the issue of insanity by referring to the accused's 'state of mind'. Was Knight insane, whether deriving from combat stress or not, under the McNaghten Rules (and therefore not legally responsible for his actions)? That is, did he not know the nature and quality of his act or, if he did know its nature and quality, did he not know that it was (legally) wrong? If this were the issue then the burden of proof was indeed upon the accused, albeit on the balance of probabilities (though how he was expected to commission his own independent medical opinion in the field was surely insurmountable).

But it is arguable that the DJAG was addressing not the question of insanity where no guilty mind (*mens rea)* would exist, but rather which *particular* guilty mind might have been present when the victim was shot. Thus if Knight had

---

727 Cited in Corns and Hughes-Wilson, *op. cit.*, p. 363.

intended to kill or cause serious harm (or even if his action in shooting rapidly and randomly made a death virtually inevitable), he was guilty of murder. If he lacked that intent, then if he had been 'reckless' regarding the discharge of the weapon, he would be guilty of manslaughter. Indeed if a previously undetected mechanical defect had caused the weapon to discharge, fatally wounding a third party, then an acquittal might follow. Moreover the reference to whether Knight was in a state of mind to know that what he was doing 'would reasonably and probably cause that result' could be perceived as referring to the question of the defendant's foresight of the consequences. And this issue bears on the above question of *mens rea*. But in respect of which category of *mens rea* was present in the mind of the accused, it was (and is) for the prosecution, not the defence, to establish the existence of that foresight and the relevant *mens rea*. The only non-statutory exceptions, that is, where there was a 'reverse burden of proof', were where the accused pleaded insanity (still the case) or admitted (this in 1915, before *Woolmington*, as noted previously) that he had caused the death but that it was an accident.

However, the matter was complicated by the issue of Knight's drunkenness. It is certainly the case that if he still intended to kill or cause serious harm while drunk, then he remained guilty of murder. In the modern adage, 'A drunken intent is still intent'. On the other hand had Knight claimed that he was so drunk that he did not know what he was doing when Private Edward was shot in the barn, he would still be 'blameworthy' for voluntarily becoming drunk. How the criminal law deals with this type of situation is by imposing on the defence what lawyers call an evidential burden to 'raise the issue' of his drunk-related lack of awareness, that is, to adduce prima facie evidence of his extreme state of insensate insobriety (perhaps not wholly impossible in Knight's case) and therefore lack of intent to kill or cause serious harm. Without more, this would result in a verdict of manslaughter. But if the prosecution still pursued a murder conviction despite the defendant's raising the issue of his drunkenness, then the Crown still bore the burden of proof beyond reasonable doubt that the accused, despite his claim to be drunk beyond reason, nonetheless intended to kill or cause serious harm. Thus whereas modern writers on the case have slightly inaccurately asserted that, '....although a man is innocent until proved guilty, it was up to the defendant to demonstrate that he was not responsible for his actions',[728] this implied reference to his possibly shell-shocked and deranged state of mind was not, strictly speaking, the issue in Knight's case, which was the level of his drunkenness.

Driver Thomas Moore of the 197th Company (Horse Transport), Army Service Corps, a unit with a poor disciplinary record, was serving in the Ypres Salient in February 1916. After a heavy enemy bombardment Moore shot a fellow-soldier in his billet. A week later he faced a court martial where he claimed insanity, stated that he was 'out of his mind at the time' and did not know what had happened. Such statements were very common at capital courts martial in the Great War. But when Moore also told the court that his mother had been detained in a lunatic asylum, the battalion medical officer testified that when he examined Moore, he could find nothing to indicate that the soldier was either sane or insane (which was not a very helpful diagnosis). He continued that the prisoner could only be woken by violent shaking, his pupils were dilated and did not react to the light,

---

728 *Ibid.*, pp. 363-4.

and he was only semi-conscious. The doctor did, however, add that, 'He gave me the impression of a man recovering from drunkenness. I do not consider that his condition could have been the result of shock'. Indeed an hour later Moore was talking rationally, albeit with slurred speech. A fellow-driver, testifying on behalf of the prisoner, said he knew Moore's family in Durham well. Apart from the mother in Durham Asylum (if she were still alive), Driver Lee added that the father was 'an eccentric sort of chap', while Moore's brother was a 'wild sort of chap'. Despite this testimony Moore was convicted and shot by firing squad eight days later.[729]

After shooting dead Lance-Sergeant Williams of the South Wales Borderers one morning in April 1918, following a dispute with him, Private John Skone, aged 38, was court-martialled for murder at Hersin-Coupigny, near Béthune. He had served in the Army since October 1914 and had previously completed 12 years of unblemished service as a stoker in the Royal Navy. Admitting to his 'client' being drunk at the time of the shooting, Skone's representative, Captain Louis Hoare, a qualified barrister, sought to rely on the prisoner's general good conduct and the adverse effect of both the malaria from which he had previously suffered while in the Navy, and the battle stress he had endured during heavy fighting throughout his time in the Army. Thus he had been wounded at Festubert in 1915 (where Rouse had also been blown up), and at both Loos in the same year, and at Passchendaele in 1917. In addition he was suffering depression due to family problems. Hoare, it seems, had had little time to prepare the defence. In any case he seems to have adopted a less-than-robust approach to his task, failing to press a manslaughter defence based on the accused's drunkenness (as we explained in respect of Knight, above), or suggesting that at the time of the shooting Skone might have been suffering from a malaria-induced illness, leading to McNaghten insanity. In particular, the issue of shell shock, given the extent of Skone's exposure to bloody conflict since early 1915, at least, was not raised by Hoare with the battalion medical officer who testified for the prosecution. For Hoare simply declined to cross-examine him (and by 1918 there was surely a greater awareness of the effects of shell shock than earlier in the war). Despite a recommendation for mercy by the court Skone was shot on May 10, 1918.[730]

Finally, the well-known case of Second Lieutenant John Paterson, who had been promoted from the ranks, was another instance in which evidence regarding possible shell shock was not raised at his capital court martial. As well as facing a number of other charges including desertion and forgery, he had been tried by general court martial (GCM) and convicted of murdering a military policeman, Sergeant Harold Collinson, who had arrested him near Calais after he had deserted from the Ypres Salient four months previously. Paterson had previously been wounded in the neck when fighting at Delville Wood. Also subjected to regular enemy artillery bombardment, he was diagnosed with shell shock and withdrawn from the front lines. On his return to combat after some months he suffered a further injury, receiving a head wound at an engagement prior to the Battle of the Somme. After this he was sent for officer training in Ayrshire before returning to France where his leadership qualities were in evidence. However

---

729   *Ibid.*, pp. 365-7; Putkowski and Dunning, *op. cit.*, Ch. 5.
730   *Ibid.*, Ch. 10.

during the German Spring Offensive of March 1918 the desertion that resulted in the death of Collinson occurred, which eventually led to Paterson's execution by firing squad on September 24, 1918.

It is notable that Paterson's court martial included a legally qualified judge advocate to advise the court on the law, as well as experienced officer-barristers for the prosecution and the defence (Captain Walter Blake Odgers, representing Paterson, was the son of a well-known King's Counsel and legal author). The focus of the trial investigation was on whether his revolver had gone off accidentally, killing Collinson, due to a faulty mechanism (which could, at best, result in an acquittal), or whether, when the shot rang out killing the military policeman, Paterson was not intending to escape arrest nor to shoot the victim (in which case a manslaughter verdict might be possible). Yet no question regarding Paterson's mental state, in the light of his lengthy military experience, which was accompanied by severe injury and shell shock, was raised at the trial. The probability is that in this instance it would have been difficult, if not impossible, for the court (or even the reviewing authorities up the chain of command to Field Marshal Haig) to accept that a man on the run for four months, living on his wits, passing dud cheques and forming a liaison with a young French woman in Calais, was so disordered in his mind that he lacked legal responsibility for his actions.[731]

Leaving aside Paterson's trial before a GCM characterized by the involvement of uniformed lawyers in the proceedings, field general courts martial (FGCM), before which Knight, Moore and Skone had been tried, were designed to permit more basic and rapid trial procedures than general courts martial (GCM), in view of the 'makeshift' situation in areas of military operations. But this did not mean that rules of evidence, as distinct from truncated rules of procedure, were permitted to be dispensed with. Yet in practical terms it was inevitable that strict adherence to the rules of evidence would be neglected. In particular the complex and detailed rules on admissibility of evidence, developed over the previous 150 years by the lawyers,[732] that is, rules of law with which even 'rude' FGCMs were obliged to comply, really fell into the domain of trained court advocates. Indeed as the 1914 edition of the War Office's *Manual of Military Law* stated, 'The rules of evidence to be followed by courts-martial are those to be adopted in courts of ordinary criminal jurisdiction in England'.[733] The layman, whether the officers forming the members of the court martial in the field, the battalion adjutant who would often conduct the prosecution, or the prisoner or his representative, might well be vaguely acquainted with doctrines such as the inadmissibility of the prisoner's previous convictions during the trial, or the outlines of the hearsay rule.[734] Perhaps the lay officer might also know the distinction between opinion and expert evidence, the relationship between hearsay and confessions, and the conditions under which confessions might be excluded. But he would not possess

---

731 Ibid., Ch 12; Corns and Hughes-Wilson, pp. 372-8.
732 John H. Langbein, *The Origins of Adversary Criminal Trial*, Oxford University Press, Oxford, 2003; Christopher Allen, *The Law of Evidence in Victorian England*, Cambridge University Press, Cambridge, 1997.
733 War Office, *Manual of Military Law*, HMSO, 1914, p. 56.
734 The 1914 *Manual* did contain a chapter on the law of evidence written by a distinguished parliamentary lawyer and draftsman, Sir Courtenay Ilbert. But it is surely unrealistic to believe that its contents would have been digested by those laymen, busy officers on active service, participating in the proceedings at an FGCM.

detailed knowledge of these doctrines, nor the then current exceptions to such exclusionary rules, nor even the exceptions to the exceptions (evidence law is riddled with rules subject to exceptions). Even less familiar would be evidential rules on such recondite matters as 'excited utterances' (known to lawyers as *res gestae*), the distinction between the evidential and the legal burden of proof, the admissibility or otherwise of documentary evidence, issues of 'credit', the status of prior consistent or inconsistent statements, and other more obscure points of evidence. As such, those rules would almost inevitably be neglected by both sides at trials. Indeed with few exceptions they were also generally overlooked by military lawyers at the post-conviction stage where the latter were tasked at headquarters with 'reviewing' the legality of proceedings before the final decision on confirmation by the commander-in-chief.[735]

This neglect of strict rules of evidence, perhaps understandable in the circumstances, was the structural flaw in trials before FGCM, and to a lesser extent before GCMs in theatres of war, where men's lives were at stake. The impracticability of convening such hearings miles behind the front lines or even back in Blighty, where criminal court-trained lawyers would be far more plentiful, was probably overwhelming in most cases. For witnesses, usually fellow-soldiers, commanders and medical officers, as well as relevant paperwork and exhibits, would also have to be transferred to the rear or back to Britain. Even if this would not seriously affect the operational effectiveness of units which needed all the manpower available, delays in conducting such trials might result in the loss through enemy action of crucial witnesses, possibly leading to the abandonment of some proceedings. It is misleading to claim that in general those British, Commonwealth and Chinese Labour Corps troops shot at dawn were tried and sentenced according to the robust standards of the day. It is not clear to which 'day' such a claim refers where the prisoner's life was at stake. The conduct of pre-war civilian capital trials, or even of pre-war courts martial, bore no relation to the haphazard processes in the wartime capital courts martial whose often scanty proceedings have been scrutinized in recent years. For in the latter the members of the court were usually not cognizant with the rules of evidence in criminal courts (of which courts martial were a species). Moreover wartime examiners-in-chief and cross-examiners at FGCMs were inexperienced in the techniques of determining 'matters in issue', and rules of evidence consequently received less focus than in a civilian criminal court. It is thus scarcely surprising that the late circuit court Judge Anthony Babington, who had lost an arm in combat in World War Two, and who was the first historian to be granted access to the Great War capital courts martial records, wrote in 1983 that,[736]

....few of the executed men received the most elemental [*sic*] form of justice. They were tried and sentenced by courts which often regarded themselves as mere components of the penal process and which, until the final year of the war, were asked to perform a complex judicial function without any sort of

735   See, for example, G. R. Rubin, "Military Law in World War One", *Journal of the Royal United Services Institute*, Vol. 143 (1), 1998, pp. 58-64; Gerry Rubin, "The Last Word on the Capital Courts Martial Controversy in Britain?", in Jean-Marc Berlière et al (eds.), *Military Justices and World Wars: Europe 1914-1950*, Presses Universitaires de Louvain, Louvain-la-Neuve, Belgium, 2013, pp. 39-56.
736   Babington, *op. cit.*, pp. ix-x.

legal guidance.

> The cases for the accused were scarcely presented adequately and sometimes were never presented at all. If crucial issues were raised which might have established their innocence they were rarely investigated by members of the court.

Of course a possible mitigatory or excusatory plea of battle shock might be wholly irrelevant in cases where the accused had not been exposed to combat. Moreover, to be fair to modern writers who insist that the accused *had* been tried according to the lights of the age, Babington did preface his damning judgment by stating, before the opening words of the above quote, 'Viewed by the standards of today'. However, as indicated previously, the present writers find it problematic to claim that the conduct of wartime courts martial merely reflected pre-war courts martial for serious offences, including capital offences, or even civilian trials before or during the Great War. It would, perhaps, be more accurate to compare the wartime trials in France and Flanders with the British Army proceedings held abroad during the Napoleonic, Crimean or Boer wars; and even then, it is a matter for investigation whether, for example, Wellington's contemptuous view of his soldiery, if not their fighting power, was reflected in their disposal at court martial.

Indeed, one of the greatest judges of the twentieth century, Craigie Aitchison, who subsequently became the second highest judge (Lord Justice-Clerk) in the Scottish legal system, and who delivered the devastating speech in 1928 for Oscar Slater at his successful appeal against his murder conviction, had little time for wartime court-martial processes. Writing in 1920, after serving as a Royal Artillery officer during the war, he observed that,[737]

> What matters are relevant to the issue, what questions can be competently asked and what are admissible, when and to what extent can surrounding circumstances be taken into account in judging of the fact or the quality of a crime.... These are questions which can only be answered by those who have received a proper legal training and are well grounded by the principles of the criminal law.

Thus lay historians unacquainted with the intricacies of court procedure and rules of evidence may well pass valid judgments on matters of justice and fairness at such hearings. But British criminal court procedure is not necessarily aimed at securing justice and fairness but at a verdict in accordance with complicated principles of relevancy and admissibility. One wartime academic lawyer was insistent that such courts martial were indeed an extended arm of Army discipline. Thus he considered them more as an inquiry than a court (though no British inquiry at the time, so far as is known, could order an execution!), and that the defending lawyer was 'an officer in the first place, an advocate only in second place'.[738] If this were the correct characterization of such tribunals, then lawyers' 'fiddle-faddle of legal technicalities', as the Victorian Army general, Sir Garnet

---

737 C. M. Aitchison, "Courts-Martial", *Juridical Review*, Vol. 32, 1920, pp. 147-58, at p. 154. His son, who shared the same name, became an internationally renowned painter. The son died in 2009.
738 Percy Winfield, "Courts Martial from the Lawyer's Point of View", *Law Quarterly Review*, Vol. 34, 1918, pp. 143-51, at p. 149. Winfield was an Oxford law don serving with the Army during the war.

(Later Viscount) Wolseley, described them,[739] might be dispensed with. But then one would have to admit honestly that neither courts martial nor military law had anything to do with law, but only with ensuring the commander's orders were obeyed. And if so, the mask would drop and rule of law principles would surely give way to something more totalitarian or, at least, more utilitarian as that term was understood by the state.[740]

Whether there was an alternative viable trial procedure for the Western Front, Gallipoli and Mesopotamia must remain problematic (leaving aside the separate question of whether the death penalty was either appropriate for so many military offences during the First World War, or whether it should have been carried out in the over 300 cases of soldiers executed for military offences). What seems clear is that of the executed British Army soldiers a defence plea of shell shock self-evidently was ignored or rejected. Yet since 89% of all death sentences by British Army courts martial in the Great War were commuted, and since the trial proceedings of those particular cases have not survived, we can only speculate on how many, if any, of the condemned men were reprieved from the firing squad by the commander-in-chief because of shell shock.

But what the cases discussed above, in which shell shock might have been relevant, have in common is that they were conducted during, or shortly after, the war. Rouse's trial, of course, took place 15 years after his wartime trauma. Could post-traumatic stress disorder (PTSD) manifest itself, or be triggered, for the first time many years after the traumatizing event so that, in theory at least, Rouse might have been suffering from shell shock, or from its more modern variant, a decade and a half later? Recent research into PTSD among armed forces personnel in the United Kingdom in the wake of the Falklands, Iraq and Afghanistan wars, buttressed by United States research into their own military veterans, suggests that delayed-onset PTSD does, indeed, exist. In one British study of soldiers returning from Iraq and Afghanistan which looked at 74 studies, researchers concluded that there were consistently high rates of delayed-onset military-related PTSD. Indeed it noted from other studies that in some cases Second World War and Korean War veterans did not manifest symptoms for 30 years, though there may have been signs of the condition in some of those cases that had simply not been picked up or recognized.[741] Other studies agree that delayed-onset PTSD is a problem but consider it a relatively rare occurrence, though this divergence

---

739 Cited in G. R. Rubin, "Parliament, Prerogative and Military Law: Who Had Legal Authority over the Army in the Later Nineteenth Century?" *Journal of Legal History*, Vol. 18 (1), 1997, pp. 45-84, at p. 72.

740 Those newspapers today which bemoan litigation against the Ministry of Defence (MOD) for alleged wrongdoing committed by military personnel against civilians in Iraq ('No end to the witch-hunt: now solicitors hounding heroes plan 1,100 Iraq War damages claims', *Daily Mail*, 11 January, 2016) perhaps seem to believe that the 'rule of law' and civil court proceedings (only some of which have been unsuccessful) should not apply to 'our boys'. Would they therefore also advocate the winding-up of the armed forces' Legal Services branches and the abolition of courts-martial? Would they turn a blind eye to the homicidal conduct and comments of Sergeant Blackman? What if an Iraqi civilian had committed an offence against a British soldier? That lawyers such as Phil Shiner of the now-disbanded Public Interest Lawyers firm might have committed wrongful acts in collecting alleged testimonies for proposed litigation by their Iraqi clients against the MOD is beside the point.

741 Bernice Andrews et al., "Delayed-Onset Post-traumatic Stress Disorder: A Systematic Review of the Evidence", *American Journal of Psychiatry*, Vol. 164, September 2007, pp. 1319-26. References are provided therein to the studies of the World War II and Korean War veterans where their PTSD was manifested decades later.

may simply be due to differences in definition.[742] Thus it may be common for sufferers not to recognize as PTSD their existing symptoms for many months or years after the traumatizing event. But it is rarer, though not unknown, for PTSD to manifest itself clearly some time after the patient experienced the wartime shocking events. This type of PTSD, howver, is more likely to occur within a year after the sufferer left the forces. The adverse psychological impact of battle shock might nonetheless remain latent in the sufferer's mind for many years after conflict has ceased, as his brain strives to repress the harsh and vivid memories of wartime shocks. Therefore when horrific incidents occur the mind may seek to neutralize the image by obliging the person to go into an unthinking, auto-pilot mode, either by his freezing on the spot, running away blindly or experiencing but not necessarily perceiving, his or her training 'kicking in'. Subsequently the brain will 'file away' the horrific experience as best it can. But that may not be a smooth process. For PTSD, in the shape of nightmares, flashbacks, panics, or disturbing hyper-vigilant behaviour may then manifest itself spontaneously when the brain can no longer keep the lid on the traumatic memories of the past, or perhaps following a related or unrelated, and otherwise innocuous, triggering event such as, ironically, a Guy Fawkes Night fireworks display. Thus the victim may experience frightening flashbacks, or begin to suffer nightmares, such as of his ship being blown up (as a number of Falklands naval veterans experienced). The recurring nightmare of a bayonet assault on Mount Tumbledown or elsewhere, depriving the sufferer of undisturbed sleep at night, and driving him to drink, recalcitrance and violent behaviour in a peacetime setting some years later, is also not an unfamiliar scenario.[743]

Such symptoms, as noted above, might possibly have applied to Rouse even though, unlike thousands of other Great War veterans, he neither manifested battle shock symptoms, nor was in receipt of a pension for neurasthenia, a payment that continued to be paid by the state to 120,000 veterans in 1939.[744] There is a suspicion that the image of the blazing car did trigger a mental reaction on Rouse's part as he embarked upon an irrational pattern of behaviour following the burning of his car. But whether fearful and repressed memories of the trenches, of exploding shells and bayonet attacks, and of flashbacks of the blazing aeroplane crashing to the ground near him on May 25, 1915 were triggered by the roaring noise as his car went up in flames is a moot point. Similarly, whether he actually suffered from delayed-onset battle shock in the run-up to the events of November 1930 may not be the only issue. For another question here is

742 See, for example, L. Goodwin et al, "Prevalence of Delayed-onset Post-traumatic Stress Disorder in Military Personnel: Is There Evidence for this Disorder? Results of a Prospective UK Cohort Study", *Journal of Nervous Mental Diseases*, Vol. 200 (5), May 2012, pp. 429-37; Bernice Andrews et al., "Comparison of Immediate Onset and Delayed Post Traumatic Stress Disorder in Military Veterans", *Journal of Abnormal Psychology*, Vol. 118 (4), 2009, pp. 767-77.

743 *Cf.*, the circumstances surrounding the court martial of Lance-Sergeant Alec Findlay, The Scots Guards. His case went to the European Court of Human Rights, the outcome of which obliged parliament to amend military law to render courts martial compatible with the Article 6 injunction in the European Convention on Human Rights that criminal courts be 'independent and impartial'. Yet the PTSD aspect of the defence was ignored. *Findlay v United Kingdom* [1997] 24 EHRR 221. A number of court-martial decisions have subsequently been challenged on Human Rights Act 1998 grounds. This is not the place to discuss these cases.

744 See, inter alia, Bogacz, *op. cit*; Bourke, *op. cit*; Peter Barham, *Forgotten Lunatics of the Great War*, Yale University Press, New Haven and London, 2004. Grogan notes that the Ministry of Pensions itself became paranoid about false claims. Ironic or what? See Suzie Grogan, *Shell Shocked Britain: The First World War's Legacy for Britain's Mental Health*, Pen & Sword, Barnsley, 2014, p. 146.

whether, without actually manifesting any obvious symptoms of delayed reaction to his wartime trauma, his mind was still wrestling to suppress those shocking memories 'filed away' since 1915. No answer can be offered to this question. But were there present less obvious symptoms that he had, indeed, been enduring mental struggles emanating from the war in the years prior to November 1930?

Let us remind ourselves of symptoms of PTSD.[745] They tend to fall into three clusters of re-experiencing the events, avoidance of thoughts and feelings concerning the traumas, and hyper-arousal symptoms which may cause relationship problems and stresses. The first, re-experiencing, group is associated with recalling unpleasant memories, suffering nightmares and flashbacks about the events, becoming upset at anything that might remind the sufferer of their trauma, and sensations of palpitations, sweating, tenseness and shaking when the events are recalled. The second cluster revolves around avoidance symptoms where the subject (obviously) avoids places and people associated with the trauma, where he loses interest in regular activities, socially isolates himself from those who 'do not understand' his situation, becoming devoid of emotional feeling, and feeling intense hopelessness. Finally, hyper-arousal symptoms refer to anger, short-temperedness, aggressiveness, sleeplessness, hyper-vigilance and seeing danger all around, and inability to concentrate.

In respect of Rouse we know that immediately after the blaze he claimed to have panicked when the flames shot up from his car, as he ran backwards and forwards for a short spell in an uncertain state. But that scarcely falls into any of the clusters of PTSD symptoms. Indeed the symptom of re-experiencing could obviously not have afflicted him before the early hours of November 6, 1930. However, there was the incident on the morning of Friday, November 7, when he was being driven from Gellygaer to Cardiff by Hendell Brownhill, a business acquaintance of Ivy Jenkins' father. It may be recalled that when Brownhill and Rouse stopped en route at the Cooper's Arms Hotel (which still exists), four miles from Gellygaer, Brownhill had told the landlord that Rouse's car had been lost but was then found burnt out. And at that point the butcher's boy, Idwal Morris, came into the bar to say that a woman's charred body had been found in the car, prompting Rouse to exclaim, 'Oh dear, oh dear. I cannot bear to hear any more of this' before he rushed out of the hotel. This could have been an example of one of the 'avoidance' symptoms of PTSD, but his escape from the bar could, alternatively, have been a ploy by him to avoid having to answer awkward questions.

There is nothing known about his war service that might point to his being of an especially nervous disposition compared to his fellow-soldiers. Yet Rouse's behaviour, fifteen years later, when sitting with Nellie Turner in the maternity hospital before he set off for Hardingstone, evinced a number of features listed as 'avoidance' symptoms of PTSD. In particular he really wanted to leave her bedside as soon as he had arrived. He was definitely distanced from her, perhaps even to the extent of 'Feeling detached and estranged from people, and feeling that nobody understands them', as the Combat Stress charity listing expresses it. Moreover its further identifying symptoms, 'Becoming emotionally numb, and

---

745 Basic information is available from various websites, including the NHS, Combat Stress organization, the Royal College of Psychiatry and the Unites States' Diagnostic and Statistical Manual (DSM). No claim is made here for an authoritative exposition.

having trouble experiencing...feelings', and 'A sense of futility in relation to their future....' can surely be perceived in Rouse's behaviour during that visit to the City Road Maternity Hospital. The problem is that Rouse's truculence, coldness and uncommunicative posture towards Nellie during that meeting could point to his preoccupation with his impending and momentous plan to bump off his passenger and build a new life, or even with thoughts of the sheer impracticability of what he had in mind. A diagnosis of delayed-onset PTSD seems a long shot by comparison. Consequently we would have to conclude that the more sympathetic view of Rouse's conduct probably has little traction. His wartime experience probably *did* alter the moral threshold of his sexual standards and of his post-war material behaviour as a man 'on the make', and with an eye to the main chance where it was easily grasped. However the shrapnel wound to his head on May 25, 1915 did not, in any clinical sense, bear on his criminality after the war.

Indeed the same might be said of a number of other murder cases after the war, involving ex-servicemen, where physical war wounds were not relied upon by the prisoners to excuse or mitigate their wrong-doing. Thus in August 1919 39-year old Hyman Perdovitch, a Russian-born machinist in a Manchester clothing factory, attacked and killed his foreman, 49-year old Solomon Franks. The two had maintained a state of animosity against each other over work practices, culminating in Perdovitch knifing Franks to death. It was discovered that the prisoner had joined the Army in 1916, transferring at some point from the Border Regiment to the Royal Irish Regiment, even though he had apparently not been naturalized British. At Ypres in 1917 he was severely wounded, was returned to hospital in England, and finally discharged from the Army in August 1918. Yet nothing medical connected with his wartime service was raised by his counsel, James Lustgarten, the father of Edgar Lustgarten, who later became known for his crime writing and for his television programmes on murder *causes célèbres*. Presumably the defence concluded that there was no mileage in pointing to Perdovitch's war wounds, except to demonstrate his 'good character'. It was to no avail. He was hanged at Strangeways on January 6, 1920.

Similarly Fred Wood, an upholsterer in Salford, was convicted of murdering a customer, Margaret White, in her home in December 1922. In Wood's case the injury he had suffered during the war, when a German bullet smashed his left forearm, was in fact invoked by defence counsel, not to raise an issue of mental instability as a result of war trauma, but to argue that the wound had rendered it impossible for the prisoner to have strangled Margaret White. Indeed this was a matter of disagreement among the expert medical witnesses who testified at Wood's trial. The jury, however, were evidently more impressed by the Crown's medical expert than by the defence's, and Wood was hanged at Liverpool's Walton Prison on April 10, 1923.[746]

Of course, given the depth of the footprint of the military within British society during the Great War, it is scarcely surprising that so many male prisoners after 1918 would have been in a position to raise the issue of their service in the trenches (and their exposure to horrific sights there) during the war. But even if

---

746 For both cases see John L. Eddleston, *Murderous Manchester: The Executed of the Twentieth Century*, Breedon Books, Derby, 1997, Chs. 10 and 13. A video account of the Perdovitch case is at www.salfordonline.com.

familiarity did not go so far as to breed contempt, it might nonetheless, except in especially troubling cases, have bred indifference if reference to war service had been made with a view to eliciting sympathy for the accused. The notorious killers of Irene Munro on the Crumbles at Eastbourne in August 1920 certainly derived no Brownie points from the jury as a result of their previous military service. In the older Gray's case, it was with the South African Heavy Artillery between 1915 and1917. And in 19-year old Field's case, it was with the Royal Navy (as was Freddie Bywaters' military service in the tragic Thompson-Bywaters case of 1922-23) from which he had been discharged the previous April. Both Field and Gray were hanged at Wandsworth in February 1921.[747]

What is therefore likely is that at most a handful of prisoners might have been so traumatized by their war service that their conduct touched the outer limits of non-responsibility for their post-military criminal actions, as determined by the narrow McNaghten Rules test for insanity. An indeterminate number of others might be placed in a category of diminished responsibility which at the time ought to have borne on sentencing in non-capital cases and disposal but not on technical guilt or innocence. Others might well have been displaying symptoms of unrecognized battle shock or PTSD in their behaviour while yet others, perhaps (or perhaps not) including Arthur Rouse, might have been harbouring delayed-onset but not yet manifested symptoms of PTSD. Mental health diagnosis of individual cases from 80 years ago is probably useless (though putting Hitler and Napoleon in the psychiatrist's chair is a well-trodden exploration), but so, too, from one obvious perspective at least, is resurrecting the cases of Timothy Evans, Derek Bentley, Mahmood Mattan, George Kelly, and Ruth Ellis, all of whom have had their cases considered by the Criminal Cases Review Commission decades after their executions (and in four of the cases the convictions were actually, or effectively, quashed years after their executions). On the other hand the reasons to re-open such cases, whether political, forensic, psychological or judicial, are far more compelling than 'letting sleeping dogs lie'. For miscarriages of justice (actually carriages of injustice) are a condemnation of democracy and of the 'rule of law'. There may be broader cultural and historical issues to explore in our analysis of the Rouse case (and they are a major aspect of this book), but where some observers raise considered and not spurious doubts and uncertainties

---

747 Winifred Duke (ed), *Trial of Field and Gray*, William Hodge & Co, Edinburgh, 1939. A non-exhaustive list of other ex-service executed prisoners after the Great War can be found at www.1914-1918.invisionzone.com. They include Eric Holt and Thomas Allaway, mentioned previously in this volume. Just as interesting would be the murder cases of ex-servicemen either acquitted or not hanged after the war. They would include the *cause célèbre* cases of Ronald Light (the 'Green Bicycle' case) and David Greenwood. Light, a former Army officer, was acquitted in 1920 of the murder of 21-year old Bella Wright the previous year while Greenwood was convicted of murdering Nellie Trew in February 1918. Greenwood had actually been discharged from the Army in November 1917 after having been buried alive by a shell burst at Ypres. He was suffering from a heart condition and, interestingly, from neurasthenia. So far as can be gathered, however, his post-military mental state was not raised by his counsel, Henry Slesser. Slesser is an interesting character. An early Fabian, his wartime activities involved offering *pro bono* legal advice to munitions workers and to poor tenants, often women, experiencing economic distress during the war. He later became Solicitor-General in the first Labour government in 1924. Appointed to the Court of Appeal in 1929, he faced anti-Labour prejudice from a few fellow-judges. He retired from the bench in 1940 due to 'ill health' but somehow managed to cling on to life for another 39 years, dying at the age of 96. Born Jewish (his early writings were under the name Schloesser), he eventually became a Benedictine Oblate, writing on theological, political, trade union and legal topics. See the present writer's entry on Slesser in A. W. B. Simpson (ed), *Biographical Dictionary of the Common Law*, Butterworths, 1984, pp. 475-6. For Light and Greenwood see, for example, Robin Odell, *Landmarks in 20th Century Murder*, Headline, 1995, pp. 92-4, 97-101.

about the convictions of executed prisoners, no matter how long ago the case, their resurrection, on those grounds of uncertainty, needs no further justification.

CHAPTER TWENTY-FIVE

WOULD YOU HAVE HANGED ALFRED ARTHUR ROUSE?

SUNDAY PICTORIAL, September, 1949

Conclusion: A Miscarriage of Justice and/or a Crisis of Masculinity?

The obvious question is whether Rouse had been properly convicted. It may indeed be the obvious one but it is not the only issue with which this book is concerned. For apart from exploring the 'whodunit', the 'howdunit' and the 'whydunit' that are characteristic of studies of famous murders,[748] our interest ranges more widely. To what extent was Rouse emblematic of his age, not in the sense of being a typical inter-war convicted murderer, but in respect of the social and cultural history of the age? Did this peripatetic commercial traveller, married though with no children from that marriage, owning (on mortgage) a semi-detached suburban London property, with Great War experience and its traumatic baggage, a proud owner of a succession of cars, a tinkerer in his suburban garage, a well-known presence in his local tennis club and a dapper dresser; did this man represent the 'rising thirties' which cocked a snook at the stories (true enough in much of the country) of inter-war economic depression? In a different sense, with his succession of women, extra-marital affairs and a number of illegitimate children to whose upbringing he was obliged to contribute, did his active polygamous sex life cast a spotlight on the darker realms of male/female relations or did it represent a not unfamiliar scenario during this period? Did it in fact reveal a more realistic and 'sordid' picture of inter-war sexual behaviour than that promulgated by establishment figures and institutions which preferred to pretend that respectable society did not possess the morals of the alley cat (or that if society did so, it was confined to the uncouth, the uneducated and the impoverished strata of that society)?

This book has therefore ranged over topics during the inter-war period such as consumerism, commercial travelling, the expansion of motor car ownership, and sexual behaviour. But since the point of departure was a criminal investigation, trial, conviction and execution of our principal protagonist, we have also explored the structure and organization of the criminal justice system during this period.

---

748   See, for example, J. H. H. Gaute and Robin Odell, *Murder 'Whatdunit': An Illustrated Account of the Methods of Murder*, Harrap, 1982; *ibid., Murder Whereabouts*, Harrap, 1986.

That being so, the original question posed at the start of this chapter still obtains. That is, was Rouse properly convicted or was he a victim of an irremediable miscarriage of justice? We know that, apart from the consequences of his sexual 'bad character' (revisited below), Rouse hardly helped his own case by his propensity to talkativeness throughout the saga. His other behaviour throughout most, if not all, of the process was frankly stupid. If only he had kept his trap shut, he would not have been hanged, Hastings reminded us. His arrogant performance in court most certainly would not have gone down well with those watching and assessing his performance in court. 'I think I have a little more brains than [crudely to dump the body across the seats]', the jury heard him boast. And the jury (unlike both us and Hewart's Court of Appeal), were present to see his every body movement, his tics, his demeanour, his shiftiness.

Yet, yet.......Juries have been notoriously wrong on the past (the trials of Adolph Beck, George Edalji. Oscar Slater, and more recent cases such as the Birmingham Six or Stefan Kiszko are obvious examples, most of them involving police cover-ups, corruption and improper undercover policing, planting of incriminating 'evidence' on suspects, withholding exculpatory evidence from the defence and so on). Recent research suggests that juries can be unreliable in a number of respects. In one experiment[749]volunteer members of the public attended a 'real-time mini rape trial re-enactment'. They were then divided into different jury groups of twelve. The researchers found that the jurors tended to make only the briefest reference to the judge's directions in his summing up about how they should come to their verdict, that is, to his legal directions, the weight of evidence, the credibility of witnesses and so on. Indeed they often misinterpreted his instructions about the law (the concept of 'consent' and its relationship to the drunkenness of the alleged victim are a common issue). The problem of inadequate foremen who failed to bring in all the jurors into discussion was also often observed, while logical flaws in reasoning and the focus on 'considerations informed by dubious socio-legal stereotypes' were common features.[750] In a follow-up study[751] the 160 members of the public who observed the same mock trial were, in addition, provided with the judge's written directions which they took with them into the jury room to reach their verdict. Again limited regard to the judge's, in this instance written, guidance was observed. The authors believe that this can be attributed to,

> fundamental tensions....between legal and lay imaginaries, such that jurors are reluctant to jettison their more natural inclinations to reach individual and collective verdicts on the basis of narrative constructions grounded in 'commonsense' and 'personal experience'.

It should be clear that we found little to criticize in Talbot J.'s summing up. Indeed

---

749 It is unlawful under the Criminal Justice and Courts Act 2015, section 74, which replaced section 8 of the Contempt of Court Act 1981, to question actual jurors on their decision-making in a case.
750 Louise Ellison and Vanessa E. Munro, "Getting to (Not) Guilty: Examining Jurors' Deliberative Processes in, and Beyond, the Context of a Mock Rape Trial", *Legal Studies*, Vol. 30 (1), 2010, pp. 74-97.
751 *Ibid.*, "'Telling Tales': Exploring Narratives of Life and Law Within the (Mock) Jury Room", *ibid.*, Vol. 35 (2), 2015, pp. 210-25. American research cited by the authors reinforces the belief that jurors are deterred from engaging with the judge's legal points due to their perceived complexity and to the legal jargon employed.

he might even have been more than fair to Rouse. But he was not the jury and it was the latter's 'lay imaginaries' that were sovereign on that day, Saturday January 31 1931 at Northamptonshire Assizes. So on the central question of his guilt or innocence of the offence charged as decided by those jurymen, we have to say that, irrespective of whether he had actually committed murder or manslaughter, let alone had acted in self-defence, we believe that no jury today would have convicted Rouse of murdering the unknown passenger. And even were we to be mistaken about a present-day jury's finding, our doubts regarding his conviction for murder were not magically erased as the caravan moved to the next, reprieve, stage of the process, after which there was no return for Rouse. At so many points the Crown's case, which required, it must not be forgotten, proof of guilt beyond reasonable doubt, fell short. Buckle's evidence, especially with regard to the loose petrol union nut, was demolished by public-spirited, concerned (and unpaid) experts, certainly post-trial, if not during the trial. Birkett posed an indefensible trick question to Isaacs which was ethically dubious, perhaps even in breach of Bar Council standards of conduct. The medical evidence was vanishingly thin. There was no forensic evidence against him (but did the jury, despite Talbot's strictures, still look at the mallet mentally and wonder?). Indeed the faecal stain on his shirt might have lent support to his story, had it been scientifically examined. The circumstantial evidence mainly turned on his eccentric behaviour and the inferences of guilt to be drawn from it were far from irresistible, to say the least. There was no eye-witness testimony. And then there was the prejudice. Even if the legality of Paling's revealing in the police court Rouse's own 'harem' speech remains moot, there are strong, albeit not overwhelming, grounds for believing that the subsequent trial had been tainted at the outset by prejudice against Rouse on account of the probably inadmissible disclosures at the same preliminary hearing regarding his extra-marital relationships with the 'indisposed' Ivy and with the mother of his two daughters, Nellie Tucker (Helen's situation as the 'mystery woman' was given full spotlight treatment by the intervention of her solicitor, Henry Flint, at the hearing and by the subsequent press coverage). And while what had already been said before the magistrates might, in Orwellian 1984-style, be later 'unsaid' (that is, not mentioned) at his trial, it could scarcely be forgotten. A legacy of perceived unfairness, expressed by Finnemore and by Hastings at the trial and appeal, could perhaps be said to have hovered over the subsequent proceedings.

General Principle of 'Legal' Prejudice

Regarding 'prejudice' and bad character which, despite their overlap, can be conceptually separated for analytical purposes, it has long been a principle of the law of evidence (though significantly amended in 2003) that a prisoner is obviously to be tried for the offence with which he is currently charged and not for his past criminal record. Consequently, unless a number of exceptions applied, the prosecution was forbidden from informing the jury of the prisoner's previous convictions or of his bad character more generally. This common law principle was enshrined in the Criminal Evidence Act 1898 which for the first time also permitted the accused to decide whether to remain silent (apart from making an unsworn statement from the dock, if he so chose) or to testify on oath on his own behalf. In view of the fate that befell Crippen, Seddon and Edith Thompson, who had all chosen to go into the witness box with disastrous consequences, perhaps the pre-twentieth century lawyers possessed more wisdom than that with which they might be credited. Even Rouse's trial judge, Talbot J., in his summing up, referred to what 'some may think is the cruel kindness of the law' in allowing the accused to testify. After 1898 the trial judge might pointedly remark to the jury that the accused chose not to enter the witness box, thereby no doubt encouraging the jury to ponder whether the prisoner had something to hide. But it is widely recognized that at least Seddon and Thompson, confident in their powers to persuade the jury of their innocence, probably talked themselves to the gallows.

Of course all evidence against (as distinct from 'for') an accused is prejudicial. After all, the purpose of adducing such evidence is to seek to establish guilt to the legal standard. So even before the issue of 'bad character' is addressed, the question is whether particular items of evidence are more prejudicial than probative. The latter refers to evidence that makes the 'matter in issue', such as the accused's presence at the scene of the crime, more or less probable. In contrast, where such evidence does not contribute to helping to resolve a 'matter in issue', then it is more prejudicial than probative and, consequently, inadmissible. Take some hypothetical examples. What of the clergyman charged with stealing church funds and who has been seen emerging from a massage parlour? Or what if it were known that the same defendant enjoyed a flutter on the horses and had been enduring a losing run? Are both pieces of evidence admissible in the theft charge? If so, for what purpose or purposes would they be admissible? Is it to show the clergyman's hypocrisy, or his propensity for wrong-doing, or (as in the Rouse claim) to show motive? Are some, all or none of these rationales for admissibility acceptable? Is only one of those examples of the defendant's conduct admissible and, if so, which one? Or is neither of them admissible? What if the defendant were a member of an extreme right-wing political party? Is that information admissible if he is charged with assault on a black man? Is it admissible if he is charged with burglary? In other words, is such information more prejudicial than probative, or vice-versa? Or suppose someone claims to be a devil-worshipper, or proclaims a fondness for viewing photographs of pre-pubescent girls or of extreme sexual violence (Graham Coutts, convicted in 2004 of the murder of the music teacher, Jane Longhurst, whose body had been deposited in the Big Yellow Storage Company premises in Brighton a year earlier, had images of the last category on his personal computer). As allegations touching on 'bad character' under the law as it stood in 1931, such information would scarcely be admissible in a case of, say, insurance fraud. But could it be admissible in the case of a middle-aged male charged with sexual assault on a young girl and where the attack took place on a makeshift altar dedicated to Aleister Crowley? Are we dealing with information that is more prejudicial than probative, or more probative than prejudicial? Were motive, hypocrisy and criminal propensity all grounds to admit bad character, or some or none of them in Rouse's time?

We have noted the general exclusionary principle above, now drastically modified in the Criminal Justice Act 2003 to allow in the defendant's bad character in various circumstances. (Crown witnesses' bad character is also less easy for the defence to attack than previously). But despite the general principle there were some well-recognised circumstances when bad character could be introduced by the Crown at a trial (though in Rouse's case it was only at the police court). First, for tactical reasons a prisoner might admit to his own previous theft convictions where they were so unlike the offence of violence with which he had been charged. The aim here would be the hope that the trier of fact might find it difficult to believe him guilty of a serious assault. Second, if the accused was charged with, say, assaulting a prison officer or driving while disqualified, then it is obvious that he had previous convictions. Third, if he (or his counsel) attacked the character of a Crown witness (the tit-for-tat rule where the accused 'lost his shield'), then his own previous convictions could be adduced against him, as Stinie Morrison discovered during his 'Clapham Common' murder trial in 1910 when his counsel, Edward Abinger, challenged the testimony of a Crown witness, Mrs. Deitch, whom he accused of living on immoral earnings and, effectively, of running a brothel in her house.[752] Fourth, if he claimed that his life mirrored that of a virtuous saint, then the Crown could rebut this assertion by adducing, for example, previous convictions. Thus under the Criminal Procedure Act 1865, section 6 (still in force), the prosecution could adduce a certificate of conviction from a previous court, as long, that is, as it does not relate to another person. For this was the gross failure by the Crown that led to the miscarriage of justice perpetrated over many years against the innocent Adolph Beck around the turn of the twentieth century. A similar situation to the rebuttal procedure, above, is where a witness insists that they are truthful. In such an event the other side can adduce their own witness to testify in examination-in-chief that the previous witness has a reputation for dishonesty. Generally, however, this questioning of one's own witness should not seek to elicit chapter and verse for such a belief, as this would move the trial into possibly wasteful 'collateral' territory. But the second rebutting witness may be cross-examined by the other side on the details to show, for example, that he is mistaken in believing the former's reputation for untruthfulness. These points were elucidated during one of the trials involving the notorious South London Richardson gang in the 1960s and 1970s.[753]

But there is a fifth, somewhat complex, situation where previous bad character, and not necessarily convictions, might be revealed to the jury. However, the principle governing this exception is that the antecedents are revealed not to prove the guilt of the accused on the current charge but for other purposes. The main exception to permit the introduction of bad character here is for the purpose of endeavouring to *disprove* the defence put forward by the defendant, rather than to prove his criminal liability. Thus if the defendant claims the victim's death was an accident, the prosecution can introduce evidence showing striking similarities with the present case and where the same defence of accident is

---

752 Andrew Rose, *Stinie: Murder on the Common*, Penguin, 1989; Eric Linklater, *The Corpse on Clapham Common*, Macmillan, 1971; Edward Abinger, *Forty Years at the Bar*, Hutchinson, n.d., pp. 26-73. Mr. Justice Darling had warned Abinger, Morrison's counsel, of the dangers to his client of attacking the character of a prosecution witness. He did not heed the warning and Stinie's previous convictions, including for violence, soon came out.

753 *Richardson and Longman* (1968) 52 Cr. App. Rep. 317. For the Richardsons, see James Morton, *Gangland*, Warner Books, 1993, Ch. 4; Donald Thomas, *Villains' Paradise: Britain's Underworld from the Spivs to the Krays*, John Murray, 2006, Ch. 17; Eddie Richardson, *The Last Word: My Life as a Gangland Boss*, Headline, 2006. If a witness denies bias (as distinct from, say, an unimpeachable character), rebuttal evidence can be adduced. For example when a witness denies knowing the accused and places him elsewhere than at the scene of the crime, the Crown can show that the two were in a relationship. See the old case of *Thomas v David* (1836) 7 C & P 350.

claimed. The most notorious example is the Brides in the Bath case where Sir Edward Marshall Hall, defending George Joseph Smith in 1915 for the murder by drowning of Bessie Munday in 1912, vainly sought to prevent the prosecution from introducing evidence regarding the similar deaths of newly-wed and recently insured Alice Burnham and Margaret Lofty, also attributed by Smith to accidental drowning in the bath. To paraphrase Oscar Wilde's Lady Bracknell, to lose one's new wife by drowning in the bath might be unfortunate. To lose two might look like carelessness. But to lose *three* looks decidedly suspicious.[754]

In her introduction to the Notable British Trials volume on the Rouse case, the editor, Helena Normanton, cited the earlier case of *Makin* v *Attorney-General for New South Wales* [1894] A C 57 (though she cited it for an unrelated reason). This was a Privy Council appeal against the conviction of 'baby farmers' for the murder of one of the foster children whom they had taken into their 'care' for financial reasons. The Privy Council (the House of Lords judges sitting as a final appeal court from the Dominions and colonies) upheld the trial judge's decision to admit evidence regarding the deaths of numerous other babies found buried on the prisoners' farm. For whereas the defendants had pleaded accident in respect of the one murder charge they were facing (it was then the practice to charge only one murder at a time), the prosecution were inviting the jury to treat the couple's explanation with disdain or even with derision, in view of the discovery of numerous other fostered babies found dead and buried in a similar fashion on the farm. Thus the prosecution's reliance on 'system' was not aimed at proving that the couple had murdered the baby named in the indictment (the prosecution would have to offer positive evidence for this), but that the defendants' innocent explanation for the death was incredible and not worthy of belief.

Similar rationales to admit this strain of 'bad character' evidence (whether of significance or not in the Rouse trial) would apply where, in a case of selling fake jewellery, the prosecution adduced evidence that the defendant had previous convictions involving the same item, or even that he had been acquitted on the ground that he had been previously unaware that the item was paste. In other words, if he were trying the same trick twice and hoping to get away with it, the prosecution was permitted to adduce his previous bad record where he had attempted a similar fraud. The disclosure would thereby show that he was aware that the stone or bracelet was a cheap replica that he had previously attempted to sell as genuine.[755] A further situation would be where bad character is adduced to establish or confirm identity where there were striking features in the case (the late second Lord Hailsham hypothesizing in 1978 the case of the burglar charged with gaining entry to properties while wearing an Indian head-dress, and whose previous convictions revealed a similar attire and *modus operandi*).[756] Thus in one case in 1918 the prisoner had been convicted of indecently assaulting a young boy. In the accused's possession were found indecent photographs and a powder puff. However he denied that he was the attacker. In response the prosecution

754 For Smith see *Smith* (1915) 11 Crim. App Rep 229. Major Armstrong's attempt to poison his fellow-solicitor and business rival could be adduced by the Crown when trying him for the murder by poisoning of his wife. See *R v Armstrong* (1922) 2 K B 555. For differing accounts of the case see Robin Odell, *Exhumation of a Murder: The Life and Trial of Major Armstrong*, Souvenir Press, 1988; Martin Beales, *Dead Not Buried: Herbert Rowse Armstrong*, Robert Hale, 1995.
755 *R v Francis* (1874) L. R. 2 CCR 128.
756 *Boardman v DPP* [1975] A C 421.

was permitted to adduce evidence of other sexual assaults on young boys by a man whose description was not unlike the defendant's and who, according to the complainants, was also in possession of homosexual pornographic photographs and a powder puff. The evidence from the other incidents, clearly suggesting a repeated course of unlawful behaviour by the accused, could therefore be conceived as a backdoor entry for bad character inasmuch as it cast doubt on his denial that he was the attacker while at the same time reinforcing the prosecution witness's testimony.[757]

The case of the psychopath, John Straffen, in 1952 is another example where bad character was admitted for identification purposes. In this case he had escaped from Broadmoor for a few hours where he had been permanently detained for the brutal killing of a young girl. Her body had been placed quite openly where it could easily be discovered but there had been no signs of sexual assault. However in the short duration of his escape from Broadmoor he had managed to carry out a similar killing, again without any evidence of sexual interference. The decision to admit the evidence of his first conviction, revealing his distinctive *modus operandi*, was upheld on appeal.[758] Similarly in a murder case in Twickenham in 1960, the defendant, Arthur Albert Jones, offered up a story that he had told his wife that he had been with a prostitute at the time of the attack on the victim, a young Girl Guide. The prosecution was, however, permitted to introduce evidence that he had given the same account to a different court some weeks previously when he had had some further 'difficulties'. Thus while the court did not permit the future DPP, Sir Norman Skelhorn, to adduce the defendant's previous conviction for rape on another Girl Guide, the strikingly similar alibi, rejected by the jury on the previous occasion, was admitted.[759]

It can be seen, therefore, that until a change of direction authorized by the Criminal Justice Act 2003, previous convictions could not, in principle, be introduced by the prosecution at the trial if the aim was to demonstrate a positive, that is, that since the accused had committed identical or similar kinds of crimes in the past, therefore it was likely that he was guilty of the present charge. Similarly, evidence tending to show that the accused possessed an immoral character or was of a lying disposition was *usually* inadmissible. However, as we have seen, the defendant's bad character could be introduced by a side wind, as 'tit-for-tat' (as with Stinie Morrison), or to seek to discredit the adduction of a 'negative' defence of, say, accident or mistaken identity, but only where the rebutting bad character evidence could loosely be called similar fact evidence suggestive of the defendant's 'system'. Evidence of the prisoner's immorality or previous untruthfulness could likewise be adduced by the Crown where the defendant in the instant case sought to paint his own character as saintly or upright. But it is significant that the cases upholding the Crown's adduction of 'bad character' to rebut a defence claim of accident, had involved the presentation of 'similar fact evidence' (or 'system') in the trials of the Australian baby farmers, the 'Brides in the Bath' killer, and the nineteenth century fake jewellery salesman, Francis.

---

757 *Thompson v R* [1918] A C 221. See also Matt Houlbrook, "'The Man with the Powder Puff' in Interwar Britain", *Historical Journal*, Vol. 50, 2007, pp. 145-71.
758 *Straffen* [1952] 2 QB 911.
759 Sir Norman Skelhorn, *Public Prosecutor: The Memoirs of Sir Norman Skelhorn, Director of Public Prosecutions, 1964-1977*, Harrap, 1981, pp. 51-53; *Jones* [1962] A C 635.

However a justification for the introduction of Rouse's immoral bad character at the police court, that it could be adduced in order to rebut Rouse's claim that the unknown passenger had died by accident, simply did not fall into the recognized category laid down in *Makin*, *Smith* and *Francis*, for there had been no previous 'system' or 'similar fact evidence' regarding previous burnt victims in Rouse's car to justify adducing evidence of his immoral bad character as a rebuttal. And he was not on trial for immorality. But that is not to say that the 'motive' justification to introduce his immoral character was invalid beyond all dispute. For whether the evidence regarding Rouse's situation (his harem speech and the police court testimony of Helen and Nellie) would fall within the class of admissible exceptions or not (above) might be arguable either way as to whether it made the 'matter-in-issue' (the alleged murder) more or less probable. That is, whereas the DPP had insisted that Rouse's immorality had been relevant to the murder charge in terms of the motive to disappear, the meaning of 'relevant' comes back to whether the link between immorality and guilt, assuming it existed, was more probative than prejudicial. There cannot, of course, be a mathematically precise answer to the question. Experience, common sense and logical thinking all come into the equation, and the experience of counsel and judge is critical. And presumably a High Court judge (and a King's Counsel, Norman Birkett) at the assizes enjoyed greater experience in such matters than did a magistrates' clerk and a DPP solicitor at the police court, which perhaps explains the divergence of approach adopted by the Crown in the different courts. One can only infer that experience told those more senior practitioners that the adduction of bad character was not permitted to establish a defendant's *motive* (unless possibly tied in, in some way, with the exceptions such as 'system' or the defendant's claims to sainthood, noted previously; exceptions which were surely inapplicable to Rouse's case).

Alternatively, if adduction of his immorality *was* permissible, in principle, to show motive, that latter (probative) object was arguably overwhelmed by the prejudicial nature of the evidence and would therefore probably be inadmissible for *that* reason. In other words the central issue of the trial involved the events surrounding a fatal fire that consumed an unknown man in a remote Northamptonshire B-road. However the relevance of the albatross of Rouse's sexual liaisons as a motive for murder seems distant from, and not at all necessary to, the Crown's principal task at the trial of establishing Rouse's specific guilty act (*actus reus)* and intent (*mens rea*) in respect of what had occurred in Hardingstone Lane. After all, it was not as if Rouse had been charged with murdering a prostitute or a lover or the husband of a lover where there might be a close link between his sexual appetite and a killing by him. It seems reasonable, therefore, to infer from those circumstances that Rouse did suffer unfairness so far, at least, as the police court hearing was concerned and, possibly, because his reputation had preceded him, also at his trial. And this would be especially so if it had been legally improper of the magistrates (which was more likely to be the case than not) to permit Paling to rake up Rouse's immorality. Certainly in Rouse's time, and for decades thereafter, there was an absence of clear legal authority *for* the proposition to allow bad character to be adduced by the Crown to establish the defendant's motive as against 'system' or sainthood claims etc. Indeed it was a grey area of legal interpretation, as some legal journals discussing the Rouse case at the time had suggested. But on the question of balance, it was surely then in favour of *inadmissibility*.

Yet even if the Court of Appeal had been minded, which it was not, to quash Rouse's conviction because of the probably wrongful adduction of his bad character at the police court (which Hewart had dismissed simply as 'unfortunate'), the position, so far as legal proceedings were concerned, was not straightforward. Granted there was no question of the Crown needing to rebut a Rouse assertion of moral probity. Nor had he attacked Crown witnesses' honesty, leading to 'tit-for-tat' response by Birkett. However complexities still remained, not least because Rouse himself had blurted out about his 'harem' which Paling, unrestrained by the magistrates' clerk (and by his own zeal), then sought to exploit at the police court by suggesting that Rouse had a financial motive (though insurance was not mentioned) to be assumed dead. Yet the comments by Hewart in the Appeal Court might be taken as suggesting that Birkett had been wise to eschew this information at the trial itself.

The magistrates' professional magazine, the *Justice of the Peace*, was itself clear that the Northampton magistrates had been misdirected by their clerk. In an article entitled, 'The Questionable Evidence in the Rouse Case', it concluded that, 'On the whole, we think it [the women's testimony raising the prisoner's bad character] was inadmissible'.[760] It noted that 'there was a tendency to break down the bad character rule', by which it meant that the rule was now suffering from such encroachments by exceptions that its 'sovereignty' was becoming attenuated. This was regrettable since, by undermining the exclusionary rule, there emerged a risk that juries might not be sharp enough to recognise that 'a man's character is no guide to his actions'. In concluding that in the Rouse case, 'We think that the danger here was too great', we may infer that the *Justice of the Peace* was either bemoaning the unfairness of the police court hearing, was criticising the Court of Appeal for inaction, or was insisting that it was impossible for Rouse to have had a fair trial; in which event, the Crown ought not to have proceeded to trial or ought not to have opposed Rouse's appeal, in much the same way that the Crown Prosecution Service today might drop a prosecution 'in the public interest' where evidence emerges of improper police conduct such as tampering with evidence, or not disclosing evidence to the other side, using improper means to obtain evidence or a confession, or using *agents provocateurs*.

The bottom line was that,

> With all our elaborate machinery of justice and with all the will of everyone concerned to secure impartiality and fairness, it is not too much to say that in this matter Rouse's trial fell painfully short of our ideals. This falling short was avoidable, and could have been avoided by right action on the part of any one of several people.

It added that since the proposed sexual misconduct evidence was 'of such doubtful value to the prosecution', which presumably related to its remoteness from directly shining a light on events in Hardingstone and to the absence of necessity to prove a motive, and since it was 'so near the line' (that is, was it not more prejudicial than probative?), then at the very least, the evidence at the police court could have been heard *in camera* after informal discussion on

760 *Justice of the Peace*, February 28, 1931, p. 131.

the matter, which was not uncommon, between counsel.[761] Indeed the magazine posited two potentially contradictory principles cited in a classic later nineteenth work by James Fitzjames Stephen (who, as the ailing Mr. Justice Stephen, had sentenced Florence Maybrick to death in 1889 for the poisoning of her husband, the Liverpool cotton broker, James Maybrick; the last-named being yet another Jack the Ripper suspect).[762]

'When there is a question whether any act was done by any person, the following facts are deemed to be relevant, that is to say—any fact which supplies a motive for the act.....' *Stephen's Digest of the Law of Evidence*, Art. 7.

'In criminal proceedings, the fact that the person accused....has a bad character is deemed to be irrelevant', *ibid.*, Art 56.

Patently the two observations could conflict with one another so that in Rouse's case there could be immorality per se (doctrinally usually inadmissible as irrelevant), *or* immorality causing financial problems which in turn might offer a suggested motive for murder. There was no clear legal guidance on the specific question and the point was not tested as a question of law because of Birkett's tactical 'withdrawal' at the trial and the Attorney-General's refusal to certify that a point of law of general public importance was at stake, when he refused to sanction Rouse's appeal to the House of Lords. Instead there is less-than-satisfactory broader guidance to be derived from judicial passages elsewhere, not least from the *Makin* case cited previously where the Privy Council had acknowledged that 'it may be often very difficult to draw the line and to decide whether a particular piece of [bad character] evidence is on the one side or the other'. Yet all the leading cases cited above (*Smith, Francis*; *Straffen* etc) were concerned with the negative implications for a prisoner's defence of 'similar fact evidence', adduced as 'bad character', and not with immorality as 'motive' per se. The principle at the time, though rough round the edges, was clear. Rouse was not to be tried on his past record of behaviour (his 'bad character'), and though he himself had disclosed to Skelly his sexual liaisons, any subsequent adduction by the Crown was more likely to have been inadmissible than not. But did not an atmosphere of prejudice (in the sense of pre-judgment) against a dissolute Rouse still pervade the trial, spurred on by a sensationalist press that ensured that his immoral character was a matter of widespread public knowledge? Unfortunately that was an occupational hazard for Rouse, with the jury being enjoined to dismiss such matters from their minds. The conundrum was whether Paling's performance in the police court exacerbated the prejudice against the prisoner to such an extent that it crossed a legal line. The point was never fully tested before Rouse was hanged.

761 Technically, the Crown could have decided not to use the 'harem' evidence if in doubt as to its admissibility but the DPP could have passed it to Finnemore for him to decide whether to ask Birkett to adduce it. Finnemore could then have sought to rebut it in cross-examination of Lawrence or in his examination-in-chief of Rouse. It would have been high risk for either side at the trial.

762 For Florence Maybrick, see, for example, Mary S. Hartman, *Victorian Murderesses*, Robson Books, 1985, Ch. 6; Richard D. Altick, *Victorian Studies in Scarlet*, J. M. Dent, 1970, Ch. 15; Victoria Blake, *Mrs Maybrick*, National Archives, 2008; Kate Colquhoun, *Did She Kill Him? A Victorian Tale of Deception, Adultery and Arsenic*, Little Brown, 2014. For the alleged link to Jack the Ripper, see Anne E. Graham and Carol Emmas, *The Last Victim: The Extraordinary Life of Florence Maybrick, the Wife of Jack the Ripper*, Headline, 1999; Shirley Harrison, *The Diary of Jack the Ripper: The Chilling Confessions of James Maybrick*, Smith Gryphon, 1994.

Blackwell harboured no doubts following the rejection of Rouse's appeal. 'Just as in a case of murder, for robbery evidence is constantly given of financial stress on the part of the prisoner in order to show motive, [and] in this case it was necessary to show motive, namely the embarrassed [financial] position in which the prisoner was placed by his relations and obligations to these women....' Here was a point of law of general public importance that the Attorney-General, Sir William Jowitt, ought to have recognized when deciding upon the grant or refusal of his *fiat* in respect of Rouse's application to take his appeal to the House of Lords. But it was easy to hide behind the reasoning that the challenged evidence had only been adduced at the police court and not, in terms, at the trial.

The stance of the *Justice of the Peace* towards the verdict and appeal outcome was perhaps surprising for a periodical expected to be on the side of 'law and order'. But the Home Office had its own explanation as to why the journal considered that 'the case will undoubtedly be cited for many years as an example of dubious guilt'. The reason was because the publication had 'become 'abolitionist' since it became the Local Govt. Review as well as the JP' (though whether the predominant view within local government circles nationally, as distinct from within certain authorities, favoured a campaign to abolish capital punishment, is open to debate).

But in this welter of criticism of the State's tactics, have we not tipped the balance of criticism too unfairly against the Crown? First, it is simply unprovable whether this particular jury was, indeed, improperly influenced in reaching its decision by its assumed knowledge of Rouse's reputation as an opportunist Lothario. Instead of being a commercial traveller, suppose he had been a sailor 'with a girl in every port'.[763] Perhaps such a character would attract both admiration and disgust in equal measure. Indeed public attitudes towards sexual scandal between the wars were often complex and contradictory, as we have seen in chapter 20. Certainly, at a simplistic level, it is possible to defend Blackwell's view, expressed in an internal Home Office note, that,

> Mere immorality with women wd. not prejudice any jury (and there were no women on this one) [the defence, at the start of the trial, having successfully objected to the presence of two jury women] to the extent of thinking that such a man wd. be likely to commit this sort of murder. The fact that he was financially embarrassed owing to his intrigues was material on the theory that his motive was to escape from that embarrassment.

And Tindal Atkinson also observed to Blackwell that juries in capital cases tended to be 'rightly impressed with the gravity of the occasion' rather than on 'extraneous prejudice'. In fact this is a proposition that has come under intense scrutiny in recent years by historians examining a number of *causes célèbres* of the nineteenth and twentieth centuries, such as the cases of Madeleine Smith, William Palmer, Florence Maybrick, Neill Cream, Edith Thompson, Marguerite Fahmy, Patrick Mahon, Norman Thorne, Guy Browne (and Kennedy), Mrs. Pace, Elvira Barney, Alma Rattenbury, Charlotte Bryant and Ruth Ellis, cases mostly cited elsewhere in this book. The interesting thing is that some of the most scandalous

---

763   At least one, more recent, author drew this analogy. See John Sanders, *Forensic Casebook of Crime*, True Crime Library, 2005, p. 116.

of defendants, as depicted by the prosecution, such as Madeleine Smith, Elvira Barney and Alma Rattenbury, were acquitted or else benefited, as in Smith's case, from the 'Scotch verdict' of 'not proven'.[764] Subliminal prejudice might yet have pervaded the jury's thought processes in Rouse's case when assessing the circumstantial evidence and the prisoner's own succession of unnecessary lies, which the DPP had recognized when he referred (chapter 14) to the possibility that 'some bent might not be given to the minds of some of them [the jury] by prior information to the prisoner's prejudice'.[765] Did Rouse's jurors leave behind them their own unspoken prejudices regarding sexual mores (even without hearing the litany of Rouse's sexual liaisons), rendering them saintly? Maybe they did, but they still convicted. The law of evidence must, in the end, seek to balance the principles of protectionism and paternalism in favour of the accused, in order to avoid prejudice, against the principle of individual responsibility where everyone must answer for his or her criminal conduct.

While complaints of prejudice and unfairness were one of the main planks of Rouse's appeal against conviction and of his subsequent plea for mercy, the problem is the elusiveness of the concept of prejudice (and of unfairness) when applied to the jury at Rouse's trial. Even bias can be more precisely pinned down; whether in terms of previous friendships or enmities, or financial or political influences, or moral or religious views (whether on capital punishment, abortion, single-sex marriage etc). Lord Hewart's 1924 dictum that 'Justice must not only be done but should manifestly and undoubtedly be seen to be done' has previously been noted. Yet without entering the detailed realms of the psychologist, Gordon Allport's, famous work, *The Nature of Prejudice*,[766] and the academic progress in understanding the concept since the book's publication,[767] it is perhaps widely accepted that prejudice may emanate from unspoken values not necessarily associated with political beliefs or vested interests and which, to others, remain hidden in the mind of the opinion-holder. Yet further research has suggested that well-crafted judicial instructions, including information which encourages jurors to set aside questionable stereotypes regarding the behaviour (or dress) of, in this case, the 'typical' rape victim enabled a more open and balanced consideration of whether the facts alleged at a rape trial crossed the threshold of illegality.[768]

As we noted previously Talbot J.'s conduct of Rouse's trial was, in our opinion and based only on the written record, fair to the accused. He did not seek to play on, or even allude to, Rouse's 'immoral' character, and legal-doctrinal issues were of marginal significance given the absence of submissions regarding insanity or manslaughter (and Birkett had sought to pre-empt legal disputes over admissibility). But as the research cited at the beginning of this chapter suggests, and despite the somewhat conflicting research findings on juries noted above in the previous paragraph, jurors might be inclined to carry on regardless within

764 See also Lillian Faderman, *Scotch Verdict: Miss Pirie and Miss Woods v Dame Cumming Gordon,*, Quartet, 1983, on an early nineteenth century Scottish *cause célèbre*.
765 As noted previously, nowadays juries should be issued with a *Lucas* direction [1981] Q B 720, instructing them that because it has been shown that the prisoner has lied on any specific matters, it does not follow that all his testimony is composed of lies.
766 Gordon W. Allport, *The Nature of Prejudice*, Doubleday, Garden City, NY., USA, 1958.
767 We have already noted the research of Rachel J. Cahill-O'Callaghan, "Reframing the Judicial Diversity Debate: Personal Values and Tacit Diversity", *Legal Studies*, Vol. 35 (1), 2015, pp. 1-29. .
768 *Ibid.*, "Turning Mirrors into Windows? Assessing the Impact of (Mock) Juror Education in Rape Trials", *British Journal of Criminology*, Vol. 49 (3), 2009, pp. 363-83.

their own comfort zone and their familiar frame of reference. Stereotypical images may be hard to dispense with in the jurors' own minds unless the judge and foreman strike a firm pose to ensure that evidence is assessed in the jury room logically and forensically against the sole test with which the jury is charged. That is, and without regard to the character, personality, habits, occupation, behaviour (sexual or other), beliefs or previous record of the accused, have the Crown proved to the jury's satisfaction his guilt *beyond reasonable doubt* in the light of the direct, circumstantial or expert evidence adduced? We are not convinced that the authorities 'got the wrong man' in executing Rouse (there was no 'other man', of course). We simply claim that the prosecution had failed to prove their case of wilful murder to the legal standard and that the jury had probably also been diverted from their proper task by Rouse's lurid reputation. *Ergo* the execution of Arthur Rouse was a miscarriage of justice and Rouse became yet another victim of a capital punishment system that could 'never make mistakes'. Rouse, of course, was never charged with involuntary manslaughter of the reckless or gross negligence variety, nor was the alternative option of finding him guilty of 'voluntary' manslaughter on the ground of provocation put to the jury. And, of course, the 'Scotch verdict' of not proven was unavailable, though possibly it might otherwise have been an apt outcome.[769]

Cecil Baines and Rouse

But to change the focus, there was another sense in which Rouse had been 'framed' and this idea derived from a social critic whom we have previously met. This was Cecil Baines whose contempt for the DPP solicitor, Gerald Paling, considered by Baines to be a prosecutor 'hard-wired' to get convictions at all costs, we have previously noted. His radical viewpoint was, in short, that Rouse, far from being a villain, was in fact a victim of a criminal justice system weighted heavily against the poor (within which grouping, albeit only with great imagination, one could just about include the non-working-class Rouse). Baines' attack on the trial verdict was informed by his belief that Rouse had been a victim of the ruling authorities who wished to maintain the hegemony of the criminal justice system against the interests of a prisoner who represented the common man. Baines was general secretary of an organisation called the Prison Reform Society (a body that seems to have had no connection with today's Prison Reform Trust. Nor did it appear to have links with the well-known Howard League for Penal Reform, active both then and now in supporting the condition of prisoners and ex-prisoners.). The society, whose president at some stage appeared on its letter-headed notepaper to have been Viscount Astor and whose vice-presidents were claimed to include the Mayor of Westminster and the prominent menswear manufacturer, Montague Burton, had offices near parliament.

The remit of Baines' society is well captured in a letter written by him to the London press in 1930.[770] In the letter he referred to a speech by the governor of Dartmoor Prison, Captain G. F. Clayton, reported in the paper a few days

---

769 Famous 'not proven' verdicts in Scotland include those of Madeleine Smith (1857), Alfred John Monson (the Ardlamont Mystery, 1893) and Helen McDougal in the Burke and Hare trial (1828). The cases are all discussed at length in William Roughead, *Classic Crimes: A Selection from the Works of William Roughead* (intro. by Luc Santé), New York Review of Books, New York, 2000. See also Faderman, *op. cit*, though technically a civil, not criminal, case.

770 *Evening Standard*, June 18, 1930.

previously. Baines had approved of Clayton's (apparent) endorsement of the view that 'most criminals are manufactured by the State', that 'Brother Criminal is sometimes a little better than some people outside' and that 'quite a proportion of them' are 'real white men'. The hardened criminal, claimed Baines, was frequently the victim of unfortunate circumstances and the hardening had been brought about by unjust treatment by society. Perhaps the timing of Clayton's speech (and of Baines' favourable approval of it) was significant. For, following the replacement in 1931 of Clayton by Governor Roberts, the latter considered to be a strict disciplinarian who had enjoyed long service in the Army and the prison service, the notorious Dartmoor Prison mutiny broke out in January 1932. Like most armed forces mutinies it had trivial beginnings (over the quality of the prison food),[771] but exploded like a pressure cooker when all the animosities and frustrations of the prisoners under the less benign regime of Governor Roberts than that experienced in the past boiled to the surface. With 440 uncontrolled convicts engaged on a rampage of destruction, looting and arson, it took large numbers of well-armed police to suppress the uprising, leaving about 70 prisoners with head wounds. Thirty prisoners were tried for various offences in May 1932, of whom 21 were convicted and sentenced by Mr. Justice Finlay to terms ranging from 12 years to six months.[772] Baines' diagnosis of what was transforming poor people into criminals would scarcely have been relevant to Rouse who, after all, had had no previous convictions. However we know that he did have a track record of vehicle insurance fraud. Notwithstanding, the campaigner's aim was to draw attention to the paucity of provision for criminal legal aid for the poor undefended prisoner, despite his acknowledging that there would be improvements in this regard in view of new arrangements proposed in the Poor Prisoners' Defence Bill going through parliament at that time (see chapter five). What his society desired was that in every large town there should be a 'competent solicitor' to offer 'free and absolutely unbiased [sic] legal advice' to poor persons arrested on a serious charge and who would have the 'privilege of a free consultation in prison'. Technically speaking it remains unclear whether his proposal applied to those being questioned by police after arrest and to advise them regarding their answers (whether 'no comment' or otherwise), or whether it referred to free legal consultation and advice after the arrestee had been charged, in which case further questioning by the police would normally be disallowed under the Judges' Rules which preceded the present-day provisions on questioning contained in the Police and Criminal Evidence Act 1984. In any case, apart from the measures in the Poor Prisoners' Defence Bill, the poorest of prisoners on trial on a serious charge could seek to invoke the 'dock brief' procedure if they could succeed in raising just over one guinea to pay for (usually young and inexperienced) counsel waiting in the 'taxi cab rank' to offer their services to clients in need. So why not provide the prisoner with free legal advice which would offer him a 'sporting chance to have his case fairly represented'? If subsequently convicted then the

---

771   Cf., Gerry R. Rubin, *Durban 1942: A British Troopship Revolt*, Hambledon, 1992, Ch. 7 on armed forces mutinies.
772   There are many accounts of the riot. See, eg, Philip Priestley, *Jail Journeys: The English Prison Experience Since 1918*, Routledge, 1989, pp. 104-13, and sources cited therein; Alyson Brown, *Inter-War Penal Policy and Crime in England: The Dartmoor Convict Prison Riots, 1932*, Palgrave Macmillan, 2013.

prisoner with the 'sporting instinct' might well feel that the ensuing sentence was 'all in the game'. Indeed this terminology was part of Rouse's own lexicon. For we saw previously that Rouse had soon overcome his depression following his arrest and detention awaiting trial when he concluded that he still had a 'sporting chance' of the jury acquitting him.[773]

So much was clear. But lurking behind Baines' campaign was a belief that '....we are up against a hard and fast tradition that the under dog [sic] is always in the wrong'. The poor prisoner, after yielding to temptation due to his unfavourable upbringing, now 'finds himself at the mercy of a well organised group of officials who do more or less as they like with him'. Unable to afford legal advice he is only encouraged 'to make a statement' to the police, with incriminating words being invariably put into his mouth 'by a none-too-friendly official who deems him guilty in advance'. The detainee's statement thus provides proof of guilt, resulting in a sentence 'quite out of proportion to the relevant guilt of the prisoner, who inevitably nurses a grievance against the law'. Recidivism would necessarily follow. In other words Baines was apparently adhering to a conspiracy theory of criminal justice. And this came out in his view of how the Rouse prosecution had been conducted.

That much becomes clear in the note he sent to Tindal Atkinson, the DPP, on July 1, 1931, after Rouse's execution, in which he inveighed against Paling as one of the 'dregs of the legal profession', as we saw in chapter five, a complaint that accompanied his (Baines') prepared summary of the case involving Rouse that he sent to the DPP. The summary was also sent to the Lord Chancellor, the Lord Chief Justice, members of parliament and to the Home Secretary, Clynes. To the latter he explained that he had in the past refrained from contacting him directly on any subject. However he was very dissatisfied with the 'methods adopted by the Home Office' which tended to elicit the same replies whenever his Prison Reform Society wrote to the department. Ever since Clynes' appointment as Home Secretary (in the Labour government under Ramsay MacDonald), Baines had 'expected great things of you'. So that was the reason that, although Rouse was now dead, he had still decided to write to him and to seek an interview with him on the Rouse affair.[774] For while he condemned Paling's police court tactics in revealing Rouse's bad character as a blatant abuse of power by prosecutors, he also sought to link his specific complaint regarding the Blazing Car case to the more general criticism, mentioned above, that the criminal justice authorities habitually colluded in creating criminality on the part of poor prisoners denied adequate legal representation. As he wrote to Clynes, this is what he was telling his weekly audiences throughout the country in his lectures on 'How the State Manufactures Crime'.

At one level his claim was a blinding glimpse of the obvious in that the contours of the criminal law and the behaviour that is labelled criminal at any point in time are determined by the legal sovereign, that is, by the state. And the latter can criminalise or decriminalise through proper legal procedures. Think of the

---

773   J. C. Cannell, *New Light on the Rouse Case*, John Long, c. 1931, p. 181.
774   In the following month MacDonald's Labour government resigned and was replaced by a National Coalition government which MacDonald had succeeded in forming. Clynes lost office and was replaced by the Liberal, Sir Herbert Samuel, as Home Secretary.

former criminal status of homosexual conduct or of the former non-criminal behaviour of driving without a seat belt or of company insider dealing. To that extent Baines was correct in asserting that the state manufactured crime until formal 'decriminalisation' occurred. Indeed that such an analysis was one that would be shared in the 1970s and 1980s by academics describing themselves as radical or critical criminologists would surely have given Baines some pleasure and a sense of vindication.[775]

But here Baines' complaint began to confuse two separate critiques. Thus his original point was that the state itself was creating criminality. For in stark contrast to what he perceived as a 'golden age' of DPP integrity when the office had been occupied by Sir Charles Mathews (which was between 1908 and 1920), '....immediately Sir Archibald Bodkin took charge [from 1920 to 1930], they [the DPP's office, presumably including Paling] deluded themselves that they were free to act as they choose, whereas they are merely the servants of the Public, and whenever officials exceed their powers, we intend to expose them'. Whether he had in mind the DPP's pursuit of criminal convictions for such behaviour as publishing Radclyffe Hall's lesbian novel, *The Well of Loneliness*, or for men engaging in consensual homosexual acts, or for working-class activities such as off-course cash betting which was unlawful, is not clear. However he also sought to claim that the state, through the instrumentality of Paling and the magistrates, was at the same time conspiring to 'fit up' innocent prisoners such as Rouse in order to secure convictions. This, to Baines, was not a case of broadening the scope of the criminal law to ensnare literature deemed obscene by Bodkin and Paling but not by contemporary literary luminaries, but of forcing, by corrupt proceedings, innocent citizens into finding themselves nailed down within the forbidden (and existing) territory of the criminal law.

We are not surprised that the DPP failed to oblige Baines with a response. However the Home Office was initially prepared to put up an official, probably Blackwell, to see Baines (he had, it will be recalled, sought a meeting with Clynes), though why the department took him seriously enough as a social commentator to issue an invitation is puzzling. But it soon saw the light (as perceived within its social world). Thus in preparation for Baines' arrival at the Home Office the department did some homework on him. First the assistant commissioner at Scotland Yard, Norman Kendal, confirmed to Blackwell that Baines was also known as William Jackson, that the Criminal Records Office had recorded convictions under both names (Baines had a previous conviction in 1924), and that CRO photographs confirmed that they were one and the same man since the subject in question had two distinct moles on his face.[776] The Home Office was also provided with a memorandum from an accountant, J. Kilpatrick, of Deloitte, Plender, Griffiths & Co.[777] It explained that in late August 1930 Baines had requested that Deloittes should become the honorary auditors of the Prison

---

775 See, for example, Ian Taylor, Paul Walton and Jock Young (eds), *Critical Criminology*, Routledge & Kegan Paul, 1975; Mike Fitzgerald, Gregor McLennan and Jennie Pawson, *Crime and Society: Readings in History and Theory*, Routledge, 1981.

776 HO144/19182. Kendal annotated that 'I think he would be a very good witness to call before the Persistent Offenders Committee!'

777 Kilpatrick had worked for Deloittes in pre-revolutionary Russia in 1913-14. See the 16-page pamphlet by James Kilpatrick, *Russian Interlude*, published by Deloittes in 1943; copy in Brotherton Library, Leeds University.

Reform Society. Kilpatrick was 'not impressed with the fellow', and declined the position. Baines (assuming it was he) had explained the society's objects and its hopes for the widespread availability of free or inexpensive legal advice throughout the country. Baines then 'entered into a diatribe against the police and police methods in general', which was rather unfortunate since 'I remembered we were Auditors to the National Police Fund'. However if the society were to put together a list of sponsors and a copy of its soon-to-be-prepared printed rules and objects, bankers and legal advisers (the society had not yet been incorporated), then his firm would be pleased to receive them. Needless to say, concluded Kilpatrick, no more was heard from Baines.

Further research would have uncovered a career in music hall promotion and a string of bankruptcies suffered by Baines in earlier years. For example in May 1911 the impresario and promoter, Oswald Stoll, owner of eight theatres including the London Coliseum, challenged a local magistrates' ruling in Bristol to refuse him permission to build a new Bristol Hippodrome.[778] At the appeal he was represented by George Elliott KC who had featured in the notorious George Chapman poisoning case in 1903 (Chapman being yet another Jack the Ripper suspect), the Moat Farm murder case involving the eccentric Samuel Dougal in 1903 and the Devereux trunk murder case of 1905. However opposition to Stoll's application was lodged by local residents, local theatre owners including the Theatre Royal, and the owners of the two existing music halls in Bristol, the Palace in Baldwin Street and the Empire in Old Market Street. But there was also a third music hall opponent, Cecil Baines. He claimed an (unspecified) interest in the nearby Bedminster Hippodrome which was due to open the following August in the capable hands of Mr. Lauri de Frece, a 'smarter businessman than Mr. Stoll (laughter)'. In the event Stoll's appeal succeeded enabling him to re-apply for a licence, which he did successfully. The Hippodrome opened in December 1912 while the Bedminster struggled financially until, in 1915, Stoll bought it to convert into a cinema. It was destroyed by enemy action in January 1941.

That the Bedminster faced financial difficulties no doubt partly explains Baines' bankruptcy petition in January 1912.[779] But the petition also revealed that he had lately been carrying on business as manager of the Theatre Royal in Cardiff. Moreover when the trustees in bankruptcy were released from their responsibilities in respect of Baines' creditors in February 1913, the debtor was listed as 'William Francis Jackson, otherwise known as Cecil Hamilton Baines'.[780] It may therefore have been from this time that he began to use both names interchangeably. Certainly by the time he was made bankrupt again in 1922 he was back using the name Baines and describing himself as a director of public companies and carrying on business at the Theatre Royal, Bristol which, as noted previously, had sought to resist Stoll's expanding empire into Bristol in 1911.[781]

Clearly Baines was a colourful character with an interesting hinterland of smoke and mirrors (a trait shared with Rouse). How much of this additional detail was known to the Home Office or to the police is unclear before the Home Office

778 *Bristol Times and Herald*, May 2, 1911.
779 *Edinburgh Gazette*, Jan 19, 1912, p. 70.
780 *London Gazette*, February 1913, p. 1526.
781 *Edinburgh Gazette*, February 10, 1922, p. 286; www.hippodromebristol.co.uk/Court.html.

meeting in 1931 was considered. Similarly, why he was especially exercised by the Rouse case is also slightly puzzling for there is nothing to indicate that he was acquainted with him either personally or professionally. As noted previously the society had on other occasions been in touch with the Home Office on penal matters, though whether it was its habit to take up the cudgels and to claim a conspiratorial injustice visited on every hanged murderer may be doubted. In any event he remained something of a man of mystery. Invited to call the Home Office to arrange a visit, he never did. So a ruling class conspiracy against Rouse might have been difficult to substantiate, especially if the advocates of this theory were as enigmatic as Baines.

Rouse's Masculinity

To conclude this study of Rouse and his place in inter-war British society, we wish to highlight one more feature of his character. This is the matter of his sense of masculinity. We have referred in chapter 20 to the emergence of the independent-minded New Woman from around the 1880s, a change linked to the drive for the franchise, separate property rights, equal divorce entitlements, better education, employment opportunities and companionate, in place of patriarchal, marriage. We have also noted that the public image of demure and 'respectable' womanhood, entailing sexual fidelity to one's lawful spouse, still prevailed (as Edith Thompson, Charlotte Bryant and Ruth Ellis, allegedly displaying the opposite when they faced trial for murder, found to their cost), and that this might be contrasted with both a desire in some predominantly middle-class circles for individual sexual identity and sexual choice, and also with changing female sexual behaviour and with non-establishment views on single motherhood, especially in working-class and more rural environments. On top of this, and despite 'respectable' opinion, the public retained an insatiable appetite to read about sexual shenanigans in the popular press.[782] Indeed it is, perhaps, obvious that a newspaper magnate's dictum instructing his journalists to 'Get Me a Murder a Day!'[783] was probably more likely to be appreciated by that publication's readers when a dollop of scandal and sex was poured into the homicide story.

But what can we say about Rouse and his identity as an inter-war male of the human species? Was his fate ultimately a result of his failure as a man to come to terms with ongoing changes in gender relations around him and to temper his predatory sexual habits when the idea of the roving 'silverback' was a throwback to a bygone age of male sexual licence, indeed licentiousness (if, in fact, there had ever been such an age)? Was he, in effect, a victim of his own outdated masculinity in a world where men had 'changed'? For his reference to harems scarcely conjured up an enlightened image of progressive masculinity to complement the New Woman. The long nineteenth century had begun to witness a more

782   Adrian Bingham, *Family Newspapers? Sex, Private Life, and the British Popular Press, 1918-1978*, Oxford University Press, Oxford, 2009; *ibid.* and Martin Conboy, *Tabloid Century: The Popular Press in Britain, 1896 to the Present*, Peter Lang Ltd, 2015; Chris Horrie, *Tabloid Nation: From the Birth of the Daily Mirror to the Death of the Tabloid*, Andre Deutsch, 2003, esp. Ch. 7 on the 1928 Ruth Snyder case in New York; Judith Rowbotham, Kim Stevenson and Samantha Pegg, *Crime News in Modern Britain: Press Reporting and Responsibility, 1820- 2010*, Palgrave Macmillan, 2013; cf., Duncan Campbell, *We'll All Be Murdered in Our Beds! The Shocking History of Crime Reporting in Britain*, Elliott & Thompson, 2016.

783   Kevin Williams, *'Get Me a Murder a Day!' A History of Mass Communication in Britain*, Arnold, 2004.

'civilising' process regarding men whereby their physical aggression and violent natures were gradually being curbed (unless, perhaps, they were the leaders of 'Great Powers' at the outbreak of the First World War) and where, following the intervention of the criminal justice system, husbands could no longer be fully indulged by the courts when the 'head of the household' meted out physical violence, on the basis of some self-serving 'unwritten law', to their allegedly errant wives.[784] A crisis of heterosexual masculinity has tended to include such issues as male domestic violence, gang activities, alcoholism, persistent unemployment and the degradation imposed by dole rituals, with unrest and disturbance on the flanks of the political spectrum, indicating that the 'civilising' process was never complete.

And, of course, the First World War was itself scarcely a 'civilising' experience for young men, though it did offer an opportunity to celebrate patriotic martial values, as distinct from abusive domestic violence. But what happened when the resilient domestic violence of the pre-war period which the magistrates could not wholly suppress began to rear its ugly head again after World War One? Newspaper accounts would now present a more nuanced picture of the war veteran husband standing in the dock before the magistrates and charged with wife beating. And the reason for this was that the image of the male changed to take account of the 'Tommy's' fighting experience. The post-war male defendant committing domestic violence may no longer have been simply a brutal wife beater and therefore beyond the pale of 'civilised' humanity. For as a former soldier he had displayed the requisite admirable qualities of masculinity in fighting for King and Country, while at the same time his wife was no shrinking violet. During the war she herself had been a munitions worker or a cart driver or a tram conductress, and not just the domestic angel or, more likely, domestic drudge. She had 'roughed' it with the men not called up. Her femininity was itself compromised while her husband's masculinity had attracted praise, not criticism. She was no longer depicted incontrovertibly as the victim tormented by the villain, her husband. So the picture of domestic violence after 1918 was perceived by the courts as more nuanced than before 1914. But how could one explain this apparent post-war male regression from the 'civilising' process where men's martial qualities, obviously embracing resort to controlled aggression, had been properly channelled to combat the enemy abroad? To answer this question attention was re-directed towards violent husbands as *psychological* victims of the war, those war veterans mentally haunted by the horrors of the trenches. It was to this mental breakdown that was attributed the resort to domestic violence

---

784 Clive Emsley, *'Hard Men': The English and Violence since 1750*, Hambledon and London, 2005; Martin J. Wiener, *Men of Blood: Violence, Manliness and Criminal Justice in Victorian England*, Cambridge University Press, Cambridge, 2004; Shani D'Cruze, "Sex, Violence and Local Courts: Working-Class Respectability in a Mid-Nineteenth Century Lancashire Town", *British Journal of Criminology*, Vol. 39 (1), 1999, pp. 328-45. It should not be thought that all young women at the time were timid, submissive and withdrawn. See Andrew Davies, "'These Viragoes are no Less Cruel than the Lads': Young Women, Gangs and Violence in Late Victorian Manchester and Salford", *ibid.*, pp. 72-89; Wiener, *op. cit.*, Ch. 4. Not all female killers resorted to poison. Some, such as Constance Kent and Mrs. Pearcey, used physical violence, as did baby farming killers. See Judith Flanders, *The Invention of Murder: How the Victorians Revelled in Death and Detection and Created Modern Crime*, Harper Press, 2011, *passim*. Nor should it be thought that domestic violence against women is a thing of the past. For recent research see End Violence Against Women (Holly Dustin, author), *Where Are We Now? 10 Year Review of Westminster Government Action to End Violence Against Women and Girls*, End Violence Against Women Coalition, November 2015. Progress is welcomed by the author while she insists that problems remain.

by the returned soldier. In short, it was not his fault.[785] Could this have applied to Rouse? Was his 'civilised' masculinity now brutalized by his frightening war experiences? In the narrow sense of a resort to domestic violence his record (till Hardingstone Lane) is clean, apart from one or two allegations vis-à-vis Helen. Of course the spectacle of witnessing his car going up in flames, *assuming he bore no culpability for the blaze*, may well have triggered dreadful wartime memories and flash-backs which might in turn have accounted for his subsequent bizarre and irrational behaviour as he sought to put distance between himself and Hardingstone Lane. But self-evidently, if he had indeed been blameless over the victim's death, then any traumatic psychological connection in his mind between burning aeroplane and blazing car must have occurred after or simultaneous with the demise of the unknown man. On this footing if he had been 'brutalised' by his war experiences, making him (more) prone to violence *after* the war, that process could not be causally linked to the death of the passenger.

On the other hand were his wartime physical wounds compounded by war-induced mental ones that might have unbalanced him if provoked by his allegedly blackmailer of a passenger? Did the psychological legacy of the trenches more generally, and not just the spectacle of the burning aeroplane and his near-death experience, remove from him those normative constraints against murdering other human beings so that, now brutalized by his war experiences, he readily contemplated bumping off his passenger? In this respect was he now located at the more extreme and violent end of the masculinity continuum so that one could 'understand' and 'explain' his violent behaviour without condoning it?

But varieties of masculinity might also address sexual behaviour and not just aggressive or martial conduct. This, of course, was more familiar territory vis-à-vis Rouse. Did the war alter his sexual behaviour, so that his sexual drive was 'normal' before he set out for France but became 'abnormal' thereafter as a result of his wartime experiences, in particular, of his shattering injuries? Helena Normanton certainly considered Rouse to have been a victim of the conflict on the Western Front, 'a war product and a war tragedy'.[786] Rather than the war acting as a moral purifier, she continued, 'it markedly helped his moral ruin'. Indeed '... his wound broke his mental power and shattered his controls without lessening his conceit'. His equilibrium suffered and his judgment on appropriate behaviour lost its moral compass.

Are we making too much of this aspect? Certainly one aim in life after the Armistice that drove Arthur Rouse was his pursuit of sexual thrills with other women, and his appetite in that regard was enormous. So his 'masculinity' continued to reflect the simple and uncomplicated model of a bygone age of a roving Casanova, not the more sophisticated and 'civilised' model of husbands who embraced equal and companionate marriage. But there was another driver in his life, the not especially abnormal craving to wear the mask of *petit-bourgeois* respectability and to dupe others into believing that he was respectable. Numerous examples have previously been quoted. There was his 'schmoozing' among his

785 Rebecca Crites, '"Brutes, Whores, and Shell-shocked Wretches': The Impact of the First World War upon News Media Representations of the Wife Beater in Britain, 1914-1929", unpublished paper at Open University Day Conference, May 2, 2014.
786 Helena Normanton (ed.), *Trial of Alfred Arthur Rouse*, Notable British Trials Series, William Hodge & Co., Edinburgh, 1931, p. xliv.

tennis club associates in Friern Barnet, his absurd promotion of himself as an Eton- and Cambridge-educated former Army officer, his expression of disgust to Ivy when she pointed out to him the two villagers in Gellygaer engaged in an affair (heaven forefend that Arthur would contemplate something as immoral as that), his bitter complaint at the police court hearing that he had been compelled to wear someone else's ill-fitting suit for his court appearance because his own clothes were being forensically examined, his discomfiture at occasionally being pulled up by Ivy for wearing a tatty jumper and, by way of contrast, his immaculate turn out at the assizes trial when he insisted on wearing spats.

In the examples above it was only the incident in Gellygaer that bore directly on his expressing 'respectable' views with regard to sexual morality. But it merely reinforced the fact that Rouse found no contradiction in projecting moral uprightness while at the same time living in a world of sexual deception and licentiousness. After all did not powerful and older ideas of masculinity (and for Rouse those older ideas surely remained current) embrace such duality in terms of 'real men' and of the acknowledgment that 'boys will be boys'?[787] And as for the opposite sex the despairing conclusion that '[and] women must weep', is surely part of Rouse's same theme. But he simply could not keep up the contradictions, that is, to appear (sexually) 'respectable' but to live the life of a two-timing liar; to epitomize inter-war consumerism and suburban smugness, but being unable to keep up the payments necessary to maintain the image. The 'perfect storm' erupted in Hardingstone Lane and, more importantly, it erupted for Rouse whether or not he was a murderer, guilty of manslaughter, or was otherwise a victim of a miscarriage of justice.

We have explored in chapter three Rouse's upbringing from childhood and also, in a later chapter, the confession he had 'written' in the *News of the World* on February 1, 1931, following the rejection of his appeal. In fact his own distinctly non-Proustian *à la recherche du temps perdu* was repeated in the pages of *Peg's Paper* on May 26 and June 2, 1931 more than two months after his execution, that is, after Lily and Nellie had published their own accounts of life with Rouse and just before Helen would have her say. Assuming, that is, that the words were his own genuine reflections and not (which may be just as plausible) the product of the feverish imagination of journalists happy to pay him (or his lawyer) for the loan of his name at the head of a piece which did, of course, bear *some* relation to Rouse's life story.

That his initial printed remarks, 'What a mess I have made of my life!' were intended as a theatrical opener may be acknowledged. But they verge more on the banal than on the dramatic, and perhaps unconsciously stress that this little suburban commercial traveller became famous because of, rather than despite, his own personal insignificance. Like Forrest Gump or Peter Sellers' eponymous gardener, Chance, in *Being There*, it was not just Rouse's personality, as Sydney Tremayne in his account of the trial explained, but it was also the context, circumstances, mystery and ingenuity that made the 'Blazing Car Murder' so

---

787   Recent cultural and criminological studies of masculinity include Antony Easthope, *What a Man's Gotta Do: The Masculine Myth in Popular Culture*. Paladin, 1986; Rosalind Miles, *The Rites of Man: Love, Sex and Death in the Making of the Male*, Paladin, 1992; and Tim Newburn and Elizabeth A. Stanko (eds.), *Just Boys Doing Business? Men, Masculinities and Crime*, Routledge, 1995. The titles indicate the ambiguity of the concept.

appealing and enduring (see chapter two).

Rouse seemed to go out of his way to risk being cast aside by society when he wrote before his execution of his 'couldn't care less' attitude towards his women. *Je ne regrette rien.* Was he thus a hard, unfeeling character or, alternatively, a brave one? Or was he possibly both? It is suggested that these particular newspaper 'memoirs' of his upbringing, of his marriage to Lily, and of his affairs reveal little more than a basic understanding of Rouse's character. For they admit only to his sense of a life wasted on the transient pleasures of the flesh, on recklessness, and on lack of forethought. They admit, also, to his social immaturity and shallowness and of his lack of appreciation of one of the fundaments (though not the only one) of a stable society glued together by the institution of the long-lasting (perhaps life-long) social partnership of two persons (whether bringing up children or not, but possibly in a stronger relationship in Rouse's and Lily's case had they had their own children). What emerges is his lack of that conceptual awareness of the building blocks of society. He preferred to play fast and loose and to ignore responsibility; and thereby paid a price which, admittedly, few others would pay for similar failings.

We have observed previously that while economic recession and mass unemployment from 1921, in particular, might destroy lives in the industrial areas of Britain, domestic consumer growth, including car purchases, characterized other areas of the country, especially the south-east. Contrast the title of Martin Pugh's inter-war social history, *'We Danced All Night'* with John Stevenson and Chris Cook's *The Slump*.[788] Such growth also corresponded to a new vision of family life (which also occurred after the Second World War where the family man cum-architect, re-designing and re-building Britain, was lauded as a hero).[789] Masculinity in this version (or vision) was now the suburban experience where the husband would respect his wife, provide her with an up-to-date kitchen, bedroom furniture and modern conveniences such as a vacuum cleaner, a new-fangled washing machine, wireless and gramophone. On his return from work each day he would interest himself in his children's activities and schooling, and at weekends take part in 'am-dram' and play tennis or go to the theatre and cinema, or take his son away on fishing trips and perhaps induct him into the mysteries of do-it-yourself in his workshop and of gardening.

Fatherhood was necessarily central to this 'modern' concept of masculinity among thirty-something lower middle-class suburban married men in white-collar employment between the wars. In one obvious sense Rouse deviated from the pattern since for most of the time his children did not live with him, his marriage had produced no children and Lily was not in employment until her husband was imprisoned. He seemed distant from Nellie's infants, Pamelita and (understandably) the newly arrived Patricia. Indeed, on his only visit to see his new-born daughter, he scarcely looked at her in her cot. But for Arthur Jnr., it was a different case. There is evidence that he doted on him and spoilt him when

788 Martin Pugh, *'We Danced All Night': A Social History of Britain Between the Wars*, Vintage, 2009; John Stevenson and Chris Cook, *The Slump: Society and Politics During the Depression*, Quartet, 1979.
789 Richard Hornsey, *The Spiv and the Architect: Unruly Life in Postwar London*, University of Minnesota Press, Minneapolis, Minnesota, USA, 2010. See, especially, the cartoon depiction of serious domestic bliss on p. 18.

he could. Is it because the child was a boy, and was named after his father? In other words was a chauvinistic streak to Arthur that his paternal pride stretched to sons but not to daughters? Was that an old-fashioned view to which Arthur remained resolutely committed? What about bringing up the boy? We know that Arthur Jnr. was fostered to his dad and to 'Aunt Lil' for some time before the fatal incident, though we do not know how much of a 'hands-on' father he was, or was able to be. Did he cook the boy's meals, did he read him stories, did he walk with him to school? Did Arthur *want* to do these things but simply did not have the time both because of his job and of his commitments to his other women? Or did the idea never occur to him on account of such tasks in 1930 being assumed to be the exclusive province of the woman of the house? We can perhaps give credit to Arthur for his apparent devotion to his young son (also reflected in his correspondence to Helen as he awaited trial and execution). But it was a devotion with strings attached, born either of the assumptions of the day regarding women's responsibility for child-rearing or because he was too busy seeking sexual pleasure elsewhere.

The late radio presenter and psychiatrist, Dr. Anthony Clare, once advised men seeking fulfilment and meaning in life to place a 'greater value on love, family and personal relationships and less on power, possessions and achievements'.[790] But for a man like Rouse who seemed to glory in reflecting upon his harem (when he spoke *ex tempore* to Inspector Lawrence of the Northamptonshire Constabulary), Dr. Clare's advice would presumably have been futile. For his 'harem' neatly brought together the trinity of power, possessions and achievements, while the former trio cited by Clare merely amounted, at most, to 'noises off' in Rouse's life.

An important insight into this debate is that, as one author has noted,[791]

> ....male responses to domesticity remained complex and ambivalent ....and that it was possible simultaneously to both embrace and reject the attributes of domestic manliness. Men constantly travelled back and forward across the frontiers of domesticity, if only in the realm of imagination, attracted by the responsibilities of marriage or fatherhood, but also enchanted by fantasies of the energetic life....

In short masculinity could be confusing and contradictory. Should it be strong and powerful and dispense with the need for women at all, as with the adventurers such as Allan Quartermain in H. Rider Haggard's *King Solomon's Mines*, or real-life characters such as Kitchener or Gordon of Khartoum or Lawrence of Arabia? Should it be guided towards the version of morally upright masculinity promoted by Baden-Powell and his Boy Scouts movement, or by the earlier public school 'muscular Christianity' adherents where women were absent from such restricted 'homo-social' environments (with their undertones of heroic homo-erotic love, and with women presumably continuing to play a traditional subservient family role in bringing their husbands' children into the world)? But if a more sensitive masculinity were to evolve, there were many who believed that it must avoid the

---

790 Anthony W. Clare, *On Men: Masculinity in Crisis*, Chatto & Windus, 2000.
791 Martin Francis, "The Domestication of the Male? Recent Research on Nineteenth and Twentieth Century British Masculinity", *Historical Journal*, Vol. 45 (3), 2002, pp. 637-52, at p. 643 for this and the following.

negative and weak images of manhood associated with comfortable and inward-looking suburbia (chapter 18).

The single male 'empire builders' and heroes of the late Victorian period could have their counterparts in the inter-war novels of John Buchan, in the activities of emboldened mountaineers and aviators, in E. M. Hull's fictional character of the beguiling 'Arab' sheik (which desert romance, as previously observed, played a controversial role in the trials of Edith Thompson and Mme. Fahmy), and even in the real-life intellectual recruits to the International Brigades during the Spanish Civil War. Indeed it might be added that despite the post-1918 'dismembering of the male',[792] not all ex-servicemen wished to forget the 'masculinity' of the experience and to move on as, indeed, social activities within the British Legion and 'remembrance day' reunions and commemorations in the 1920s might suggest.[793] It was not so much that these visions competed with domesticated masculinity by the inter-war period so much as they complemented it. Rouse could, therefore, 'travel...back and forward across the frontiers of domesticity', with his *faux* respectability, a stalwart of the local tennis club, comfortably providing for Lily, and cherishing and housing Arthur Jnr. as if the latter were the couple's; while simultaneously pursuing his numerous alter-lives, spinning yarns about his background, increasingly panicking as his rampant sexual masculinity inevitably leads to a calling in of his debts and as it begins to suffocate him mentally and emotionally. Rouse is not so much 'enchanted by the fantasies of the energetic life' as plunged into a crisis of masculinity when the fantasies prove to be real enough.

The fundamental point of Rouse's masculinity is that it was regressive, not progressive, and decidedly not domesticated. He was a restless soul but was clearly not the sort who was searching for something profound or spiritual to be located beyond the narrow confines of W. B. Martin & Co and 14 Buxted Road. He presumably got a 'buzz' from his sexual forays and reckless predations, with an appeal that could only draw contempt, not admiration. He was not shy in flaunting his muscular strength referring, in his confession, to his powerful grip with just one hand, sufficient to render unconscious his victim. But while showing an interest in engaging in sport, thus loosely endorsing the practices of 'muscular Christianity', it was with 'respectable' sport, and not with the popular variety reflected on the football pitch (or even on the cricket square, so far as we can tell), that his interest was to be found. He was proud of his table tennis skills and, even while incarcerated at Bedford, enthusiastically followed the fortunes of the top tennis players in the country. His involvement in the social and community aspects of his local tennis club might be reflective of the gentler suburban masculinity emerging in inter-war Britain, but it was more likely to have been camouflage as he strove for false respectability.

It is possible that Rouse felt a sense of inadequacy in his profession as he endeavoured, in his noticeably high-pitched voice, to persuade gentlemen's retail outfitters to buy in supplies of men's buckles, belts and suspenders. Perhaps it

---

792 Joanna Bourke, *Dismembering the Male: Men's Bodies, Britain and the Great War*, Reaktion Books, 1999.

793 For differing attitudes see the ex-service personnel described in the novel by Spencer Jordan, *Journeys in the Dead Season*, Pan, 2005.

was not the most demanding or intellectually challenging of work, or work where men might seek dignity in hard labour such as mining where the physical effort expended in cutting coal and operating the winding gear (Ivy had ironically done the latter at the Gellygaer colliery) testified to their manliness. His masculinity might therefore have taken a battering as he tootled from one coastal town to another with his wares and samples on the back seat. But he certainly compensated by exploiting the 'masculinity' that accompanied him at the wheel of his car as he drove through busy parts of London, contriving 'accidental' encounters with pretty and impressionable young women. And his elaborate garage workshop containing a vast array of tools and small engineering equipment might also speak to creative manliness. Yes, he could carry out repairs on his car and knew broadly how its moving parts worked, as he told his interlocutor at his trial (though contrary to expectations he modestly admitted to limitations regarding his motor engineering knowledge).

Rouse was a rather unpleasant, almost spiv-like character, full of his own self-importance, with a tendency to 'bull-shit', to seek immediate gratification and to refuse, until it was too late, to think through the consequences of his actions (perhaps he was not sufficiently clever to do so). His feelings of tenderness were rare and were crowded out by a stronger urge to amorality and a lack of empathy and affect. It is hard, therefore, to sympathise with him in the manner in which one might with other executed killers such as Dr. Crippen or Freddie Bywaters. Indeed he could not be compared with his fictitious alter ego, Arthur Parker. For the latter was cleverly crafted by Dennis Potter in *Pennies from Heaven* as a man who eventually came back from the dead as an act of redemption in order to be reunited with the West Country-accented and emotionally beguiling Eileen, with whom his musical dreams and his choice of a refashioned selfhood are reflected, *post mortem*, in the message of 'Roll on Prairie Moon' and other 1930s musical lyrics. Rouse was too material (if not materialist) to be romantic and, though he was musical, did not give the impression of one who dwelt on abstract concepts such as love, beauty or nature. He perhaps shared with Arthur Parker the frustrations of a salesman on the road during the Depression, though he did not give the impression that he was dealing with the equivalent of the music shop owners in Gloucester at whom Potter's Arthur was raging when they failed to appreciate the beauty in the music scores that he (Parker) was trying, without great success, to supply to them. Rouse's buckles, braces and men's suspenders, courtesy of W. B. Martin & Son, Leicester, and sold to Herne Bay drapers, were decidedly unromantic by comparison.

In Aldous Huxley's *Brave New World* the Director of Hatcheries and Conditioning advised his young students that sex should be perceived as a game that even young children should be encouraged to engage in, and that for adults it was a wholesome activity for the purpose of securing happiness. For, far from any recognition of the concepts of motherhood, fatherhood and families, within which copulation bred population, babies emerged from the laboratory via test tubes (and their futures would be mapped out, whether as 'proles' or as higher beings, in accordance with whether they were classed as Alphas, Gammas or Epsilons etc.). Clearly the sexual aspect of this 'brave new world' resonated with Rouse, even if the utopian/dystopian vista was unimaginable to him. For if he was at all conscious of population experts' injunctions to re-stock society after the carnage of the Great War, he did so not in terms of 'respectable behaviour', citizenship and physical culture, as alluded to previously, but in terms of, for him, a sexual free-for-all. His fecund masculinity, in short, scarcely applied to the new, post-war fertile generation. Was he a victim of the Great War? Of course he was, in a physical sense. But like 19 year-old Madeleine Smith, whose advanced sexual thoughts, revealed at her trial in 1857 for the murder of her lover, shocked her contemporaries,[794] perhaps Rouse was born at the wrong time (though most people in Britain would presumably consider it preposterous to believe that there could be any 'right' time for anyone, whether a struggling commercial traveller or not, to maintain a 'harem').

Last Words

'Nothing is ever settled until it is settled right' (Kipling). We raised at the start of this chapter the question whether there had been a miscarriage of justice. In doing so we pointed to the controversies surrounding the Crown's technical evidence as to how the fire had started. We then addressed the question whether the evidence and depositions regarding Helen, Ivy and Nellie and Rouse's own admission regarding his 'harem' were admissible at the police court and, if so, whether the revelations had prevented him from obtaining a fair trial. We next observed the arguably ambiguous nature of the circumstantial evidence against him and whether it was weighty enough to persuade the jury to find him guilty beyond reasonable doubt. The possibility that he had been suffering from late-onset shell shock was also floated, but if that had indeed been the case, could it explain his acknowledged criminality in Hardingstone Lane and his subsequent aberrant behaviour? We also noted the maverick opinion of Cecil Baines that Rouse had been a victim of class law, though our conclusion on this point is that the claim was as dubious as the person promulgating the idea.

We also considered whether his post-war experiences and conduct were emblematic of the age. His efforts to project an image of middle-class style through house and possessions and of middle-class monogamous respectability vied with the financial realities of his situation and with his insatiable sexual appetite outside marriage. Although the 'civilising' process virtually (but perhaps not quite) precluded any propensity to domestic violence on his part, he was not a 'modern' companionate husband, but one seized of a predatory and negative brand of sexual masculinity. He was clearly not alone in that regard, but the point is that unlike himself, Patrick Mahon, John Robinson and others, most such Casanovas had not been caught in flagrante delicto. He was also stupid, selfish, hypocritical, socially immature and emotionally blind and it was of no consequence that his sexual behaviour was not as deviant as respectable society, with its own dose of double standards, would prefer to believe (think of the unattractive fictional establishment figures peppered throughout the social commentary plays of Oscar Wilde, or the Birling family in J. B. Priestley's An Inspector Calls, set before the Great War, while immoral sexual revelations involving royalty, aristocracy, bishops and parliamentarians of the past would in due course come thick and fast).

794   See the comments about Smith in F. Tennyson Jesse's 'Introduction' to the Notable British Trials volume on Trial of Madeleine Smith, William Hodge & Co, Edinburgh, 1929.

Those who have read up to this point will be acutely conscious that our study is not simply a whodunit, nor a narrowly focused 'why did he do it?', nor an *exposé* into 'why the authorities got the wrong man'. If any readers believe that these were our objectives, then we make no apology in stating that they have misunderstood what this book is 'about'. For it is offered as a study in the social *history* of a criminal justice episode and, consequently, is not overly concerned with whether Rouse was properly convicted and hanged for murder, or was innocent of the murder of the unknown man, whether he was only guilty of manslaughter, or whether any of his different confessions were credible. That judgment is left to any reader who cares to consider those questions which, we acknowledge, remain tantalizing and teasing.

As a minimal justification for our study we note that one major publisher's crime editor, Tricia Jackson, has recently observed that "stories of criminality 'create a psychologically safe space that lets us dare to wrap our minds around otherwise unfathomable emotion'". Indeed true crime podcasts and television series such as 'Serial' and 'The Murder Detectives' in 2015 attracted a huge following. As the commentator and critic, Mark Kermode, notes, such programmes,[795]

> ....represent....another of the intermittent bids for respectability of a genre that has frequently been dismissed since its association with Victorian 'penny dreadfuls'. But an almost universal fascination with the extremities of human behaviour means the loftier parts of the arts also push through the police tape at crime scenes.

'Loftier' aims would be to raise the issue of Rouse as 'victim'. This would not be in the narrow sense of a man 'victimised' by a vengeful criminal justice system that had been driven by repulsion at his immoral behaviour, but in the sense of his being 'victimised' by his own almost uncontrollable sexual drive, whether attributable to his war experiences or otherwise.

> People think it's all about misery and desperation and death and all that shite, which is not to be ignored, but what they forget [*Spud is shooting up*] is the pleasure of it. Otherwise we wouldn't do it. At least we're not that fucking stupid. Take the best orgasm you ever had, multiply it by a thousand and you're still nowhere near it. When you are on junk you have only one worry: scoring. When you're off it you are suddenly obliged to worry about all sorts of other shite.....You have to worry about bills, about food, about some football team that never fucking wins, about human relationships and all the things that really don't matter when you've got a sincere and truthful junk habit.[796]

Whether the analogy between sex and Renton's drugs 'trip' in Irving Welsh's *Trainspotting* is apposite is for the reader to decide, though we believe that Rouse's 'habit' carried him along for many years before self-awareness of his predicament, leading to retribution, finally closed in on him. Clearly far from being the first to fail to keep it inside his trousers, he at least conceded that, 'I've

---

795 *Guardian*, December 12, 2015.
796 John Hodge, *Trainspotting*, Faber and Faber, 1996, p. 5. This is the screenplay version of Irving Welsh's novel published in 1993. 'Some football team that never fucking wins' presumably alludes to Welsh's favourite team, Hibernian FC, the city rival to the unsurpassable Heart of Midlothian FC.

been a dirty dog', and would await his punishment.[797] Don Giovanni, by contrast, was resistant to the end as the demons dragged him to Hades on the instructions of the statue of the Commendatore whom he, Don Giovanni, had killed in a duel following his attempt to rape or seduce the Commendatore's daughter. *"Questo e il fin di chi fa mal, e de' perfidi la morte alla vita e sempre ugual"* ("Such is the end of the evildoer: the death of a sinner always reflects his life").[798]

For obvious reasons we cannot interview Rouse (or any of the protagonists) in our pursuit of non-fiction crime. So we had a choice. One was whether we should write a narrowly focussed re-hash of the case, while still asking the pertinent question, guilty or not. That possibility held no appeal for us and, anyway, there are much better authors than us who write within this *genre*. Should we then seek to emulate those masters of fictional writing, such as Dorothy L. Sayers, P. D. James, Dennis Potter and Alan Moore, who employed the Rouse case as their inspiration and point of departure? While one of us possesses the requisite skill in creative fictional writing as well as in 'true crime' writing, the other sadly lacks an aptitude for producing fictional literature. *Faute de mieux* we chose the path of linking what to us appeared to be an astonishing and fascinating episode in true crime to the social history of the period, permitting us to establish Tricia Jackson's 'safe space' for our musings on an historically informed 'habitus' (as sociologists would say), an aim that we can only trust we have gone some way in meeting.

It should therefore be clear that the $64,000 question was not the essential purpose of this study. Consequently that and the subordinate matter of which other homicide act or acts, if any, Rouse had committed did not feature prominently in our account. Nonetheless we are conscious that some readers might well wish to be apprised of our final judgment on the central question, that is, on our 'theory of the case' as lawyers (and detectives?) would express it. We have already asserted that no reasonable jury today, properly guided by the trial judge, would have convicted on the evidence adduced. To that extent we hold that the execution of Rouse represented a miscarriage of justice. Indeed Sir Patrick Hastings' observation of 1949, noted previously, that 'If Alfred Arthur Rouse had only kept his mouth shut, he would never have been hanged', only serves to reinforce this point. But the relevant question here is not whether the Crown had proved their case to the legal standard of proof beyond reasonable doubt, but whether Rouse had actually killed the victim with the requisite *mens rea* to justify being hanged for murder. And on that question, our answer is that he definitely.......[799]

---

797 In other cases the sexually incontinent might become the murder victim themselves, such as the Suffolk farmer, William Murfitt, in 1938. See David Williams, *Poison Farm: A Murderer Unmasked after 60 Years*, Thorogood, 1994.

798 Had Rouse been acquainted with Dante's *Inferno* he might have observed too many uncomfortable reminders of his own impending fate in the 35-year old narrator, Dante's, account of his travels through Hell. The three beasts in the epic poem whom Dante cannot evade could even be likened to the two cousins and to the police driving him, like Dante, into a 'deep place' ('basso loco') where the sun stays silent ('I sol tace').

799 Annoyingly our keyboard and printer chose this very moment to pack up and no amount of tinkering using Rouse's vast range of garage tools or his mallet could fix them.

BIBLIOGRAPHY

Archives

National Archives, Kew
The following classes were consulted
ADM196/101/178; BT372/118/109; CAB21/5949; CAB23/30/2; HO45/19921; HO45/25052; HO144/19178-19185; HO324; HO336/10; MEPO3/1656; MEPO3/1660; MEPO3/2970; PCOM9/289; PCOM9/290/1; PIN26/9842; WO95/2744/2; WO98; WO339/23310.

Nottingham Galleries of Justice
Rouse Trial papers.

Northamptonshire Police Archives
Rouse murder investigation papers.

Newspapers and contemporary journals

Bedford & District Circular; Bedfordshire Times; Birmingham Evening News; Brisbane Courier; Bristol Times & Herald; Daily Express; Daily Mail; Daily Mirror; Daily Sketch; Daily Telegraph; Daily Worker; Edinburgh Gazette; Evening News; Evening Standard; Glasgow Herald; Guardian; Independent; Herald [Glasgow]; *John Bull; Justice of the Peace; Lancet; London Gazette; Light Car and Cyclecar; Manchester Guardian; News Chronicle; News of the World; New Scientist; Northampton Daily Chronicle; Northampton Herald; Pearson's Weekly; Peg's Paper; People; Straits Times* [Singapore]; *Sunday Dispatch; Sunday Pictorial; Sunday Times; The Times; Thompson's Weekly News.*

Books

Place of publication London or Harmondsworth unless otherwise indicated.
Edward Abinger, *Forty Years at the Bar*, Hutchinson, n.d., c. 1930
Rev. Michael Adler, *British Jewry Book of Honour, 1914-1918*, Naval and Military Press, 2007; first published 1922
Christopher Allen, *The Law of Evidence in Victorian England*, Cambridge University Press, Cambridge, 1997
Gordon W. Allport, *The Nature of Prejudice*, Doubleday, Garden City, NY, 1958
Richard D. Altick, *Victorian Studies in Scarlet*, J. M. Dent, 1970

Christopher Andrew, *Her Majesty's Secret Service: The Making of the British Intelligence Community*, Penguin, 1987

Id., *The Defence of the Realm: The Authorized History of MI5*, Penguin, 2010

Allen Andrews, *The Prosecutor: The Life of M. P. Pugh*, Harrap, 1968

Anon., *Diary of a Nursing Sister*, Amberley Books, Stroud, 2014

Id., *The Random Recollections of a Commercial Traveller*, Sherratt & Hughes, Manchester, 1909

Id., *The Strange Case of Adolph Beck*, The Stationery Office, 1999

John E. Archer, *The Monster Evil: Policing and Violence in Victorian Liverpool*, Liverpool University Press, Liverpool, 2011

David Ascoli, *The Queen's Peace: The Origins and Development of the Metropolitan Police, 1829-1979*, Hamish Hamilton, 1979

E. H. Tindal Atkinson, *Obscene Literature in Law and Practice*, Christophers, 1936

Automobile Association, *Handbook Supplement 1933*, 1933

Anthony Babington, *For the Sake of Example: Capital Courts Martial, 1914-1918, the Truth*, Paladin, 1985

Brian Bailey, *Hangman: From Ketch to Pierrepoint*, True Crime, 1993

Anette Ballinger, *Dead Woman Walking: Executed Women in England and Wales, 1900-1955*, Ashgate, Aldershot, 2000

George Pleydell Bancroft, *Stage and Bar: Recollections of George Pleydell Bancroft*, Faber and Faber, 1939

Dennis Bardens, *Famous Cases of Norman Birkett KC*, Robert Hale, 1963

Id., *Lord Justice Birkett*, Robert Hale, 1962

Peter Barham, *Forgotten Lunatics of the Great War*, Yale University Press, New Haven and London, 2004

'Barrister', *Justice in England*, Gollancz, 1938

Ronald Bartle, *The Telephone Murder: The Mysterious Death of Julia Wallace*, Wildly, Simmonds and Hill Publishing, 2012

Peter Batchelor and Chris Matson, *VCs of the First World War: The Western Front 1915*, Sutton Publishing, Stroud, 2015

Martin Beales, *Dead Not Buried: Herbert Rowse Armstrong*, Robert Hale, 1995

John Beattie, *Crime and the Courts in England, 1660-1800*, Clarendon Press, Oxford, 1986

Dierdre Beddoe, *Back to Home and Duty: Women Between the Wars, 1918-1939*, Pandora, 1989

John Benson and Laura Ugolini (eds.), *A Nation of Shopkeepers: Five Centuries of British Retailing*, I. B. Tauris, 2003

Christopher Berry-Dee and Robin Odell, *The Long Drop: Two Were Hanged—One Was Innocent*, True Crime, 1993

Adrian Bingham, *Family Newspapers? Sex, Private Life, and the British Popular Press, 1918-1978*, Oxford University Press, Oxford, 2009

Id., and Martin Conboy, *Tabloid Century: The Popular Press in Britain, 1896 to the Present*, Peter Lang Ltd, Oxford, 2015

Jon Birger, *Date-onomics: How Dating Became a Lopsided Numbers Game*, Workman Publishing, New York, 2015

Lord Birkett, *Six Great Advocates*, Penguin, 1961

Cecil Bishop, *From Information Received: The Reminiscences of Cecil Bishop*, Hutchinson, 1932

Lucy Bland, *Banishing the Beast: English Feminism and Sexual Morality, 1885-1914*, Penguin, 1995

Id., *Modern Women on Trial: Sexual Transgression in the Age of the Flapper*, Manchester University Press, Manchester, 2013

Louis Blom-Cooper, *The A6 Murder, Regina v James Hanratty: The Semblance of Truth*, Penguin, 1963

Thomas L. Bohan, *Crashes and Collapses*, Checkmark Books, New York, 2009

Joanna Bourke, *Dismembering the Male: Men's Bodies, Britain and the Great War*, Reaktion Books, 1999

Gavin Bowd, *Fascist Scotland: Caledonia and the Far Right*, Birlinn, Edinburgh, 2013

Ruth Brandon, *The New Women and the Old Men: Love, Sex and the Woman Question*, W. W. Norton, New York, 1990

Noreen Branson and Margot Heinemann, *Britain in the Nineteen Thirties*, Panther, 1973

Fenton Bresler, *Reprieve: A Study of a System*, Harrap, 1965

Christopher Breward, *The Hidden Consumer: Masculinities, Fashion and City Life, 1860-1914*, Manchester University Press, Manchester, 1999

Alyson Brown, *Inter-War Penal Policy and Crime in England: The Dartmoor Convict Prison Riots, 1932*, Palgrave Macmillan, 2013

Douglas G. Browne, *Sir Travers Humphreys: A Biography*, Harrap, 1960

Id., and Tom Tullett, *Bernard Spilsbury: His Life and Cases*, Reprint Society, 1952

Shan Bullock, *Robert Thorne*, T. Werner Laurie, 1907

Abraham Buschke and Friedrich Jacobsohn, *Introduction to Social Hygiene*, Routledge, 1932

Duncan Campbell, *We'll All Be Murdered in Our Beds! The Shocking History of Crime Reporting in Britain*, Elliott & Thompson, 2016

John Campbell, *F.E: The First Lord Birkenhead*, Random House, 1992

Sidney R. Campion, *Only the Stars Remain*, Rich & Cowan, 1946

J. C. Cannell, *New Light on the Rouse Case*, John Long, c. 1931

Id., *The Master Book of Magic*, Quaker Oats, 1935

Id., *The Secrets of Houdini*, Dover Publications, USA, 1973

Id., *When Fleet Street Calls*, Jarrolds, 1932

Donald Carswell (ed), *Trial of Ronald True*, William Hodge & Co., Edinburgh, 1950

Manfred Cassirer, *Medium on Trial: The Story of Helen Duncan and the Witchcraft Act*, PN Publishing, Stansted, Essex, 1997

J. D. Casswell QC, *A Lance for Liberty*, Harrap, 1961

Roger Chadwick, *Bureaucratic Mercy: The Home Office and Capital Cases in Victorian Britain*, Garland, 1982

Raymond Chandler, *Farewell My Lovely*, Penguin, 2005 (first published 1940)

Terry Charman, *The First World War on the Home Front*, Andre Deutsch, 2014

Sir Wyndham Childs, *Episodes and Reflections*, Cassell, 1930

Robert Church, *Accidents of Murder: Ten Cases Re-examined*, Robert Hale, 1989

Anthony W. Clare, *On Men: Masculinity in Crisis*, Chatto & Windus, 2000

David Clark, *Victor Grayson: Labour's Lost Leader*, Quartet, 1985

Neil Clark, *Stranger Than Fiction: The Life of Edgar Wallace; the Man Who Created King Kong*, History Press, Stroud, 2015

J. R. Clynes, *Memoirs, 1924-1937*, Hutchinson, 1937

Belton Cobb, *Murdered on Duty*, W. H. Allen, 1961

H. G. Cocks, *Classified: The Secret History of the Personal Column*, Arrow Books, 2010

Frank Coleman, *A Brief History of the 6th London Field Ambulance (47th London Division) During the War*, John Bale and Danielsson, 1924

Kate Colquhoun, *Did She Kill Him? A Victorian Tale of Deception, Adultery and Arsenic*, Little Brown, 2014

Id., *Mr Briggs' Hat: A Sensational Account of Britain's First Railway Murder*, Little Brown, 2011

Nicholas Connell, *Doctor Crippen: The Infamous London Cellar Murder of 1910*, Amberley Books, Stroud, 2013

Mark Connelly, *The Great War, Modern Memory and Ritual: Commemoration in the City and East London, 1916-1939*, Boydell and Brewer/Royal Historical Society, 2015

T. D. Cook and E. W. Cooper, *Drapery and Boot Management*, Cooperative Union Ltd, Manchester, 1925

Duff Cooper (Lord Norwich), *Operation Heartbreak*, Rupert Hart-Davis, 1950

Cathryn Corns and John Hughes-Wilson, *Blindfold and Alone: British Military Executions in the Great War*, Cassell, 2001

Peter Cotes (ed), *Trial of Elvira Barney*, David & Charles, Newton Abbott, 1976

Richard Crewdon (ed), *Dorothea's War: The Diary of a First World War Nurse*, Weidenfeld & Nicolson, 2013

William Crocker, *Far From Humdrum*, Hutchinson, 1967

Harry Daley, *This Small Cloud: A Personal Memoir*, Weidenfeld & Nicolson, 1986

Neil Darbyshire and Brian Hilliard, *The Flying Squad*, Headline, 1994

Harold Dearden, *The Fire-Raisers*, Ellis and Buckle, 1986 (first published 1934)

Id., *Some Cases of Sir Bernard Spilsbury and Others*, Hutchinson, 1948 (first published 1934)

Diana de Marly, *Fashion for Men: An Illustrated History*, Batsford, 1985

Charles Dickens, *Nicholas Nickleby*, Penguin, 1999 (first published 1838-39)

Hasia Diner, *Roads Taken: The Great Jewish Migration to the New World and the Peddlers Who Forged the Way*, Yale University Press, New Haven, 2015

Richard Du Cann, *The Art of the Advocate*, Penguin, 1964

Ernest Dudley, *Bywaters and Mrs Thompson*, Odhams Press, 1953

Winifred Duke (ed), *The Trial of Field and Gray*, William Hodge & Co., Edinburgh, 1939

John du Rose, *Murder Was My Business*, Mayflower, 1973

Neil Duxbury, *Lord Kilmuir: A Vignette*, Bloomsbury, 2015

Geoff Dyer, *The Missing of the Somme*, Phoenix, 2009

Antony Easthope, *What a Man's Gotta Do: The Masculine Myth in Popular Culture*, Paladin, 1986

John J. Eddleston, *Murderous Manchester: The Executed of the Twentieth Century*, Breedon Books, Derby, 1997

Id., The Encyclopaedia of Executions, John Blake, 2004

J. L. J. Edwards, *The Attorney-General, Politics and the Public Interest*, Carswell, Canada, 1984

Id., The Law Officers of the Crown: A Study of the Offices of the Attorney-General and Solicitor-General of England, Sweet & Maxwell, 1964

Russell Edwards, *Naming Jack the Ripper*, Sidgwick & Jackson, 2014.

Tim Edwards, *Men in the Mirror: Men's Fashions, Masculinity and Consumer Society*, Cassell, 1997

R. Edynbury, *Real Life Problems and Their Solutions*, Odhams, 1938

T. Ellison and A. N. Hill, *Salesmanship in the Drapery Department*, Cooperative Union Ltd., Manchester, c. 1935

Clive Emsley, *'Hard Men': The English and Violence Since 1750*, Hambledon and London, 2005

Id., 'Soldier, Sailor, Beggarman, Thief': Crime and the British Armed Forces Since 1914, Oxford University Press, Oxford, 2013

Id., The English Police: A Social and Political History, Longman, 1996

Id., The Great British Bobby, Quercus, 2010

End Violence Against Women, (Holly Dustin ed.), *Where Are We Now? 10 Year Review of Westminster Government Action to End Violence Against Women and Girls*, End Violence Against Women Coalition, 2015

David Englander, *Landlord and Tenant in Britain, 1838-1918*, Clarendon Press, Oxford, 1983

Howard Engel, *Crimes of Passion*, Robson Books, 2002

Frederick Engels, *The Condition of the Working Class in England*, Panther, 1969 (first published in Britain, 1892)

Colin Evans, *The Father of Forensics: How Sir Bernard Spilsbury Invented Modern CSI*, Icon Books, 2007

Letitia Fairfield (ed), *The Trial of Peter Barnes and Others*, William Hodge & Co., Edinburgh, 1953

Lillian Faderman, *Scotch Verdict: Miss Pirie and Miss Woods v Dame Cumming Gordon*, Quartet, 1983

Quentin Falk, *The Musical Milkman Murder*, John Blake, 2012

E. S. Fay, *The Life of Mr Justice Rigby Swift*, Methuen, 1939

S. T. Felstead, *Sir Richard Muir: The Memoirs of a Public Prosecutor*, John Lane, The Bodley Head, 1926

M. Ferguson, *Forever Feminine: Women's Magazines and the Cult of Femininity*, Heinemann, 1983

Martin Fido and Keith Skinner (eds), *The Official Encyclopedia of Scotland Yard*, Virgin, 1999

Henry Fielding (Arthur Murphy, ed.), *The Works of Henry Fielding, Esq: Miscellaneous: Covent-Garden Journal, Essays on Nothing, Charge Delivered to the Grand Jury, 29th June, 1749...* , Nabu Press, Charleston, South Carolina, 2014 (first published 1749)

Steve Fielding, *Pierrepoint: A Family of Executioners*, John Blake, 2008

Mike Fitzgerald, Gregor McLennan and Jennie Pawson, *Crime and Society: Readings in History and Theory*, Routledge, 1981

Judith Flanders, *The Invention of Murder: How the Victorians Revelled in Death and Detection and Created Modern Crime*, Harper Press, 2011

David Foxton, *The Life of Thomas E. Scrutton*, Cambridge University Press, 2013

Donald M. Fraser, *The Book of Glasgow Murders*, Neil Wilson Publishing, Glasgow, 2009

W. Hamish Fraser, *The Coming of the Mass Market, 1850-1914*, Palgrave Macmillan, 1982

Martin L. Friedland, *The Trials of Israel Lipski*, Macmillan, 1984

Helen Fry, *The King's Most Loyal Enemy Aliens: Germans Who Fought for Britain in the Second World War*, Sutton Publishing, Stroud, 2007

Rupert Furneaux, *Famous Criminal Cases 5*, Allen Wingate, 1958

Dorothy Gardiner and Katherine Sorley Walker (eds), *Raymond Chandler Speaking*, University of California Press, Oakland, CA, 1997

Juliet Gardiner, *The Thirties: An Intimate History*, Harper Press, 2010

Malcolm Gaskill, *Hellish Nell: Last of Britain's Witches*, Fourth Estate, 2001

Charles Neilson Gattey, *The Incredible Mrs Van Der Elst*, Leslie Frewin, 1972

J. H. H. Gaute and Robin Odell, *Murder 'Whatdunit': An Illustrated Account of the Methods of Murder*, Harrap, 1982

Id., *Murder Whereabouts*, Harrap, 1986

Barry S. Godfrey, Chris A. Williams and Paul Lawrence, *Crime and Justice, 1750-1950*, Willan, Cullompton, Devon, 2005

Jonathan Goodman, *The Burning of Evelyn Foster*, Headline, 1977

Id (ed)., *Masterpieces of Murder*, Magpie Books, 2004

Eleanor Gordon and Gwyneth Nair, *Murder and Morality in Victorian Britain: The Story of Madeleine Smith*, Manchester University Press, Manchester, 2009

Anne E. Graham and Carol Emmas, *The Last Victim: The Extraordinary Life of Florence Maybrick, the Wife of Jack the Ripper*, Headline, 1999

Robert Graves and Alan Hodge, *The Long Weekend: A Social History of Great Britain, 1918-1939*, Hutchinson, 1985 (first published 1940)

Frank Gray, *The Tramp*, Dent, 1931

Adrian Gregory, *The Last Great War: British Society and the Great War*, Cambridge University Press, 2008

Leonard Gribble, *Famous Judges and Their Trials: A Century of Justice*, John Long, 1957

Id., Notorious Crimes, Robert Hale, 1985

Edward Grice, *Great Cases of Sir Henry Curtis-Bennett*, Hutchinson, 1937

J. A. G. Griffith, *The Politics of the Judiciary*, 5th ed., Fontana, 1997

Richard Griffiths, *Fellow-Travellers of the Right: British Enthusiasts for Nazi Germany, 1933-39*, Oxford University Press, Oxford, 1983

Mary Grigg, *The Challenor Case*, Penguin, 1965

Suzie Grogan, *Shell Shocked Britain: The First World War's Legacy for Britain's Mental Health*, Pen & Sword, Barnsley, 2014

Hans Gross, *Criminal Investigation: A Practical Textbook*, Sweet & Maxwell, 1924 (first published in English in 1906)

Radclyffe Hall, *The Well of Loneliness*, Jonathan Cape, 1928

Halsbury's Laws of England, Volume 8(2), (ed. Lord Mackay of Clashfern), Butterworths, 1996

Cecily Hamilton (introduction by Jane Lewis), *Marriage as a Trade*, Women's Press, 1981 (first published 1909)

Neil Hanson, *The Unknown Soldier: The Missing of the Great War*, Corgi, 2007

Phillip Harding, *The British Shell Shortage of the First World War*, Fonthill, 2015

Shirley Harrison, *The Diary of Jack the Ripper: The Chilling Confessions of James Maybrick*, Smith Gryphon, 1994

Mary S. Hartman, *Victorian Murderesses*, Robson Books, 1985

Cate Haste, *Rules of Desire: Sex in Britain, World War 1 to the Present*, Pimlico, 1994

Macdonald Hastings, *The Other Mr Churchill*, Harrap, 1963

Sir Patrick Hastings, *Cases in Court*, Pan Books, 1953

Id., The Autobiography of Sir Patrick Hastings, Heinemann, 1948

George Hatherill, *A Detective's Story*, Andre Deutsch, 1971

The Rt. Hon. The Lord Havers, Peter Shankland and Anthony Barrett, *The Rattenbury Case*, Penguin, 1989

Mike Hepworth, *Blackmail: Publicity and Secrecy in Everyday Life*, Routledge & Kegan Paul, 1975

Denis Herbstein, *The Porthole Murder Case*, Hodder & Stoughton, 1991

Didi Herman, *'An Unfortunate Coincidence': Jews, Jewishness and English Law*, Oxford University Press, Oxford, 2011

Sir Thomas Hetherington, *Prosecution and the Public Interest*, Waterlow Publications, 1989

R. F. V. Heuston, *Lives of the Lord Chancellors, 1885-1940*, Oxford University Press, Oxford, 1964

James H. Hodge (ed), *Famous Trials 8*, Penguin, 1963

John Hodge, *Trainspotting*, Faber and Faber, 1996

Wendy Holden, *Shell Shock*, Channel 4 Books, 1998

Richard Holmes, *Tommy: The British Soldier on the Western Front*, Harper Perennial, 2005

Gordon Honeycombe, *The Murders in the Black Museum, 1870-1970*, Arrow Books, 1991

Nina Warner Hooke and Gil Thomas, *Marshall Hall: A Biography*, Arthur Barker, 1966

Pamela Horn, *Women in the 1920s*, Amberley Books, Stroud, 2010

Richard Hornsey, *The Spiv and the Architect: Unruly Life in Postwar London*, University of Minnesota Press, Minneapolis, 2010

Chris Horrie, *Tabloid Nation: From the Birth of the Daily Mirror to the Death of the Tabloid*, Andre Deutsch, 2003

Matt Houlbrook, *Queer London: Perils and Pleasures in the Sexual Metropolis, 1918-1957*, University of Chicago Press, Chicago, 2005

D. L. Howard, *John Howard: Prison Reformer*, Christopher Johnson, 1958

Elizabeth Jane Howard, *Slipstream: a Memoir*, Pan, 2002

Michael Howard (ed), *British Intelligence in the Second World War*, Volume 5, HMSO, 1980

Pendleton Howard, *Criminal Justice in England*, Macmillan, 1931

Sir Travers Humphreys, *A Book of Trials*, Heinemann, 1953

Steve Humphries and Pamela Gordon, *Forbidden Britain: Our Secret Past, 1900-1960*, BBC Books, 1994

Steve Humphries, *A Secret World of Sex: Forbidden Fruit, the British Experience, 1900-1950*, Sidgwick & Jackson, 1988

'Mrs Humphry' ('Madge' of 'Truth'), *Manners for Women*, Pryor Publications, Whitstable, 1993 (first published 1897)

H. Montgomery Hyde, *Norman Birkett: The Life of Lord Birkett of Ulverston*, Reprint Society ed., 1964

Id., Famous Trials 9: Roger Casement, Penguin, 1964

Id., A Tangled Web: Sex Scandals in British Politics and Society, Constable, 1986

Brian Inglis, *Roger Casement*, Coronet, 1974

Robert Jackson, *Case for the Prosecution: A Biography of Sir Archibald Bodkin*, Arthur Barker, 1962

Id., Coroner: The Biography of Sir Bentley Purchase, Harrap, 1963

Id., The Chief: The Biography of Gordon Hewart, Lord Chief Justice of England, 1922-1940, Harrap, 1959

Stanley Jackson, *Mr Justice Avory*, Gollancz, 1935

Id., Rufus Isaacs: First Marquis of Reading, Cassell, 1936

Pat Jalland, *Death in the Victorian Family*, Oxfoed University Press, Oxford, 1996

Id., Death in War and Peace: A History of Loss and Grief in England, 1914-1970, Oxford University Press, Oxford, 2010

Lawrence James, *The Middle Class: A History*, Abacus, 2008

H. Paul Jeffers, *Bloody Business: An Anecdotal History of Scotland Yard*, Pharos Books, New York, 1992

Keith Jeffrey, *MI6: The History of the Secret Intelligence Service, 1909-1949*, Bloomsbury, 2011

Sheila Jeffreys, *The Spinster and Her Enemies: Feminism and Sexuality, 1880-1930*, Pandora, 1985

Elizabeth Jenkins, *Harriet*, Persephone Press, 2014

F. Tennyson Jesse (ed), *The Trial of Madeleine Smith*, William Hodge & Co., Edinburgh, 1927

Paul B. Johnson, *Land Fit for Heroes: The Planning of British Reconstruction, 1916-1919*, University of Chicago Press, Chicago, 1968

Owen Jones, *Chavs: The Demonization of the Working Class*, Verso, 2012

Spencer Jordan, *Journeys in the Dead Season*, Pan, 2005

Courtney Stanhope Kenny, *Outlines of Criminal Law*, 4th ed, Cambridge University Press, Cambridge, 1909

Kenny's Outlines of Criminal Law, 15th ed., (by G. Godfrey Phillips), Cambridge University Press, Cambridge, 1936

Kathleen Kiernan, Hilary Land and Jane Lewis, *Lone Motherhood in Twentieth-Century Britain*, Clarendon Press, Oxford, 1998

P. J. R. King, *Crime, Justice and Discretion: Law and Social Relations in England, 1740-1820*, Clarendon Press, Oxford, 2000

Dick Kirby, *The Scourge of Soho: The Controversial Career of SAS Hero, Detective Sergeant Harry Challenor MM*, Pen & Sword, Barnsley, 2013

Arthur Koestler and C. H. Rolph, *Hanged by the Neck*, Penguin, 1961

Marek Kohn, *Dope Girls: The Birth of the British Drug Underground*, Granta, 1992

Brian Lake, *The Murder Book of Days*, Headline, 1995

Margaret Lane, *Edgar Wallace: The Biography of a Phenomenon*, Hamish Hamilton, 1964 (first published 1938)

Gordon Lang, *Mr Justice Avory*, Jenkins, 1935

John H. Langbein, *The Origins of Adversary Criminal Trial*, Oxford University Press, Oxford, 2003

Michael John Law, *The Experience of Suburban Modernity: How Private Transport Changed Interwar London*, Manchester University Press, Manchester, 2014

D. H. Lawrence, *England, My England*, Penguin, 1966 (first published 1922)

G. A. Leask, *VC Heroes of the Great War*, Harrap, 1916

Carol Ann Lee, *A Fine Day for a Hanging: The Real Ruth Ellis Story*, Mainstream, Edinburgh, 2012

J. Lee (ed), *From House of Lords to Supreme Court: Judges, Jurists and the Process of Judging*, Hart Publishing, Oxford, 2011

Molly Lefebure, *Murder on the Home Front: The Unique Wartime Memoirs of a Pathologist's Secretary*, Grafton, 1990

Jean-Yves Le Naour, *The Living Unknown Soldier*, Heinemann, 2005

David Leslie, *Bible John's Secret Daughter*, Mainstream, Edinburgh, 2007

Geoffrey Lewis, *Lord Atkin*, Butterworths, 1983

Jane Lewis, *Women in England, 1870-1950*, Wheatsheaf, Brighton, 1984

Philippa Lewis, *Everyman's Castle: The Story of Our Cottages, Country Houses, Terraces, Flats, Semis and Bungalows*, Frances Lincoln, 2014

June Lewis-Jones (ed), *The Secret Diary of Sarah Thomas: Life in a Cotswold Market Town, 1860-1865*, Nonsuch Publishing, Stroud, 2007

Peter Linebaugh, *The London Hanged: Crime and Civil Society in the Eighteenth Century*, Penguin, 1991

Anne Logan, *Feminism and Criminal Justice: A Historical Perspective*, Palgrave Macmillan, 2008

Anthony Ludovici, *Woman: A Vindication*, Constable, 1923

Edgar Lustgarten, *The Judges and the Judged*, Odhams Press, 1951

Rebecca Lee McCarthy, *Origins of the Magdalene Laundries: An Analytical History*, McFarland & Co., Inc., Jefferson, NC, USA, 2010

James McClure, *Killers*, Fontana, 1976

Ben McIntyre, *Operation Mincemeat*, Bloomsbury, 2010

Sir Frank MacKinnon, *On Circuit, 1924-1937*, Cambridge University Press, Cambridge, 1940

Angus McLaren, *A Prescription for Murder: The Victorian Serial Killings of Dr. Thomas Neill Cream*, Chicago University Press, Chicago, 1995

Hector MacLeod and Malcolm McLeod, *Peter Manuel: Serial Killer*, Mainstream, Edinburgh, 2009

Alan Mansfield and Phillis Cunnington, *Handbook of English Costume in the Twentieth Century, 1900-1950*, Faber and Faber, 1973

Edward Marjoribanks, *Famous Trials of Marshall Hall*, Penguin, 1951

Brian Marriner, *Forensic Clues to Murder*, Arrow Books, 1991

Arthur Marwick, *The Deluge: British Society and the First World War*, Macmillan, 1973

Emily Mayhew, *Wounded: The Long Journey Home from the Great War*, Vintage, 2014

Robert Meadley, *Classics in Murder*, Xanadu, 1984

Elizabeth Melling (ed.), *Kentish Sources: VI, Crime and Punishment*, Kent County Council, Maidstone, 1969

Rosalind Miles, *The Rites of Man: Love, Sex and Death in the Making of the Male*, Paladin, 1992

Nancy Mitford, *Wigs on the Green*, Penguin, 2010 (first published 1935)

John Montgomery, *The Twenties*, Allen & Unwin, 1970

Peter Moorey, *Who Was the Sailor Murdered at Hindhead 1786? A Search for His Identity*, Blackdown Press, Haslemere, Surrey, 2000

Lord Moran, *The Anatomy of Courage*, Constable, 1945

Blake Morrison, *And When Did You Last See Your Father?*, Penguin, 1994

Lord Morrison of Lambeth, *Herbert Morrison: An Autobiography*, Odhams Press, 1960

Frank Mort, *Capital Affairs: London and the Making of the Permissive Society*, Yale University Press, New Haven and London, 2010

John Mortimer, *Rumpole and the Penge Bungalow Murders*, Penguin, 2007

James Morton, *Bent Coppers*, Warner Books, 1994

Id., *Gangland*, Warner Books, 1993

Alan Moss and Keith Skinner, *The Scotland Yard Files: Milestones in Crime Detection*, National Archives, 2006

Roderick Munday, *Evidence*, 5th ed., Oxford University Press, Oxford, 2009

William S. Murphy (ed), *Modern Drapery and Allied Trades, Wholesale and Retail*, Gresham Publishing, 1914

Sir David Napley, *Murder at the Villa Madeira: The Rattenbury Affair*, Souvenir Press/Weidenfeld & Nicolson, 1990

Id., *The Camden Town Murder*, Weidenfeld & Nicolson, 1987

Tim Newburn and Elizabeth Stanko (eds), *Just Boys Doing Business? Men, Masculinities and Crime*, Routledge, 1995

Juliet Nicholson, *The Great Silence 1918-1920: Living in the Shadow of the Great War*, John Murray, 2009

Helena Normanton (ed), *Trial of Alfred Arthur Rouse*, William Hodge & Co., Edinburgh, 1931 (republished 1952)

Jonathan Oates, *John George Haigh: The Acid-Bath Murderer*, Pen & Sword, Barnsley, 2014

Sean O'Connell, *The Car and British Society: Class, Gender, and Motoring, 1896-1939*, Manchester University Press, Manchester, 1998

Robin Odell, *Exhumation of a Murder: The Life and Trial of Major Armstrong*, Souvenir Press, 1988

Id., *Landmarks in 20th Century Murder*, Headline, 1995

Avner Offer, *The First World War: An Agrarian Interpretation*, Oxford University Press, Oxford, 1989

Andrew O'Hagan, *The Missing*, Picador, 1995

Paul Oldfield, *Victoria Crosses on the Western Front, April 1915-June 1916*, Pen & Sword, Barnsley, 2015

M. W. Oldridge (ed), *Trial of Israel Lipski*, Mango Books, 2017

Gerard Oram, *Worthless Men: Race, Eugenics and the Death Penalty in the British Army During the First World War*, Francis Boutle Publishers, 1998

George Orwell, *The Decline of the English Murder and Other Essays*, Penguin, 1965 (first published 1946)

Richard Overy, *The Twilight Years: The Paradox of Britain Between the Wars*, Viking, 2009

Andy Owens and Chris Ellis, *Killer Catchers*, John Blake, 2008

Geoffrey de C. Parmiter, *Reasonable Doubt*, Arthur Barker, 1938

John Parris, *Most of My Murders*, Frederick Muller, 1960

J. M. Parrish and John R. Crossland (eds), *The Fifty Most Amazing Crimes of the Last 100 Years*, Odhams Press, 1936

Alan Paterson, *Final Judgment: The Last Law Lords and the Supreme Court*, Hart Publishing, Oxford, 2013

Angela Patrick and Lynne Barrett-Lee, *The Baby Laundry for Unmarried Mothers*, Simon & Schuster Ltd, 2012

Alyson Pendlebury, *Portraying 'the Jew' in First World War Britain*, Oxford University Press, Oxford, 2011

Conrad Phillips, *Murderer's Moon*, Arthur Barker, 1956

Melanie Phillips, *The Ascent of Woman: A History of the Suffragette Movement and the Ideas Behind It*, Abacus, 2003

Bernard Picton, *Murder, Suicide or Accident: The Forensic Pathologist at Work*, Robert Hale, 1971

George Pollock, *Mr Justice McCardie, A Biography*, John Lane, The Bodley Head, 1934

Harry Potter, *Hanging in Judgment: Religion and the Death Penalty in England*, SCM Press, 1993

Phillip Priestley, *Jail Journeys: The English Prison Experience Since 1918*, Routledge, 1989

Harry Procter, *The Street of Disillusion*, Revel Barker Publishing, Brighton, 2010

Martin Pugh, *Hurrah for the Blackshirts! Fascists and Fascism in Britain Between the Wars*, Pimlico, 2006

Id., *'We Danced All Night': A Social History of Britain Between the Wars*, Vintage, 2009

Julian Putkowski and Mark Dunning, *Murderous Tommies*, Pen & Sword, Barnsley, 2012

Ian Rankin, *Knots and Crosses*, Orion, 1998 (first published 1987)

William Rawlings, *A Case for the Yard*, John Long, 1961

Maud Pember Reeves, *Round About a Pound a Week*, Virago, 1979 (first published 1913)

Terry Reksten, *Rattenbury*, 2nd ed., Sono Nis Press, Vancouver, 1998

Elaine A. Reynolds, *Before the Bobbies: The Night Watch and Police Reform in Metropolitan London, 1720-1830*, Macmillan, 1998

Margery Spring Rice, *Working-Class Wives: Their Health and Conditions*, Virago, 1981 (first published 1939)

Eddie Richardson, *The Last Word: My Life as a Gangland Boss*, Headline, 2006

C. E. Bechhofer Roberts (ed), *The Trial of Mrs Duncan*, Jarrolds, 1945

Elizabeth Roberts, *A Woman's Place: An Oral History of Working-Class Women, 1890-1940*, Blackwell, Oxford, 1984

Id., *The Trial of Jones and Hulten*, Jarrolds, 1945

G. D. Roberts QC, *Law and Life*, W. H. Allen, 1964

Robert Roberts, *The Classic Slum: Salford Life in the First Quarter of the Century*, Penguin, 1971

Geoffrey Robertson, *Stephen Ward Was Innocent OK*, Biteback, 2013

Jane Robins, *The Magnificent Spilsbury and the Case of the Brides in the Bath*, John Murray, 2010

Jane Robinson, *In the Family Way: Illegitimacy Between the Great War and the Swinging Sixties*, Viking, 2016

Katie Roiphe, *Uncommon Arrangements: Seven Portraits of Married Life in London Literary Circles, 1910-1939*, Virago, 2008

Mark Roodhouse, *Black Market Britain, 1939-1955*, Oxford University Press, Oxford, 2014

Neil Root, *Frenzy: Heath, Haigh and Christie: The First Great Tabloid Murderers*, Preface Publishing, 2011

Andrew Rose, *Lethal Witness: Sir Bernard Spilsbury, Honorary Pathologist*, Sutton Publishing, Stroud, 2007

Id., Stinie: Murder on the Common, Penguin, 1989

Id., The *Prince, the Princess and the Perfect Murder*, Coronet, 2013 (first published as *Scandal at the Savoy: The Infamous 1920s Murder Case*, Bloomsbury, 1991)

June Rose, *Marie Stopes and the Sexual Revolution*, Faber, 1992

William Roughead, *Classic Crimes: A Selection from the Works of William Roughead*, New York Review of Books, New York, 2000

Id., Trial of Oscar Slater, William Hodge & Co., Edinburgh, 1910

Jo Rowbotham, Kim Stevenson and Samantha Pegg, *Crime News in Modern Britain: Press Reporting and Responsibility, 1820-2010*, Palgrave Macmillan, 2013

Sheila Rowbotham, *Hidden from History: 300 Years of Women's Oppression and the Fight Against It*, Pluto Press, 1974

Joshua Rozenberg, *The Case for the Crown: The Inside Story of the Director of Public Prosecutions*, Equation, 1978

Gerry R. Rubin, *Durban 1942: A British Troopship Revolt*, Hambledon Books, 1992

Id., Murder, Mutiny and the Military: British Court-Martial Cases, 1940-1966, Francis Boutle Publishers, 2005

George Rudé, *The Crowd in History: A Study of Popular Disturbances in France and England, 1730-1848*, John Wiley & Son, 1964

John Sanders, *Forensic Casebook of Crime*, True Crime Library, 2005

Dorothy L. Sayers and Others, *Great Unsolved Crimes*, Hutchinson, 1938

Sir Harold Scott, *Scotland Yard*, Penguin, 1957

Helen J. Self, *Prostitution, Women and Misuse of the Law: The Fallen Daughters of Eve*, Frank Cass, 2003

Graham Seton, *The W Plan*, Thornton Butterworth, 1929

Nina Shandley, *The Strange Case of Hellish Nell: The Story of Helen Duncan and the Witch of World War II*, Da Capo Press, Boston, USA, 2007

Ben Shephard, *A War of Nerves: Soldiers and Psychiatry, 1914-1994*, Jonathan Cape, 2000

R. C. Sherriff, *Greengates*, Persephone Press, 2015 (first published 1936)

N. W. Sibley, *Criminal Appeal and Evidence*, T. Fisher Unwin, 1908

A. W. B. Simpson (ed.), *A Biographical Dictionary of the Common Law*, Butterworths, 1984

Id., In the Highest Degree Odious: Detention Without Trial in Wartime Britain, Clarendon Press, Oxford, 1992

Sir Norman Skelton, *Public Prosecutor: The Memoirs of Sir Norman Skelton, Director of Public Prosecutions, 1964-1977*, Harrap, 1981

K. J. M. Smith, *Lawyers, Legislators and Theorists: Developments in English Criminal Jurisprudence, 1800-1957*, Clarendon Press, Oxford, 1998

Sally Smith, *Marshall Hall: A Law unto Himself*, Wildy & Sons, 2016

Denis Smyth, *Deathly Deception: The Real Story of Operation Mincemeat*, Oxford University Press, Oxford, 2010

'Solicitor', *English Justice*, Penguin, 1941 (first published 1933)

Diana Souhami, *The Trials of Radclyffe Hall*, Weidenfeld & Nicolson, 1998

Gerald Sparrow, *Vintage Victorian and Edwardian Murder*, Victorian (and Modern History) Book Club, Newton Abbott, 1972

Martin Spence, *The Making of a London Suburb: Capital Comes to Penge*, Merlin Press, 2007

John and Noreen Steele, *HMS Dasher*, Argyll Publishing, Glandaruel, Argyll, 2004

Dorothy M. Stetson, *A Woman's Issue: The Politics of Family Law Reform in England*, Greenwood Press, New York, 1982

John Stevenson, *British Society, 1914-45*, Penguin, 1990

Id., and Chris Cook, *The Slump: Society and Politics During the Depression*, Quartet, 1979

Joseph Stone (ed), *Stone's Justices' Manual*, numerous eds., Shaw & Sons/ Butterworths

Neil R. Storey, *The Dracula Secrets: Jack the Ripper and the Darkest Sources of Bram Stoker*, History Press, Stroud, 2012

Nicholas Storey, *History of Men's Fashions: What the Well Dressed Man Is Wearing*, Remember When/Pen & Sword, Barnsley, 2015

Kate Summerscale, *The Suspicions of Mr Whicher: or The Murder at Road Hill House*, Bloomsbury, 2008

D. J. Taylor, *The Prose Factory: Literary Life in England Since 1918*, Chatto, 2016

Ian Taylor, Paul Walton and Jock Young (eds), *Critical Criminology*, Routledge & Kegan Paul, 1975

John Terraine, *The Great War, 1914-18*, Arrow Books, 1967

Donald Thomas, *Villains' Paradise: Britain's Underworld From the Spivs to the Krays*, John Murray, 2006

David Thorns, *Suburbia*, Paladin, 1973

Sheila Tofield, *The Unmarried Mother*, Penguin, 2013

Thomas Toughill, *Oscar Slater: the 'Immortal' Case of Sir Arthur Conan Doyle*, Sutton Publishing, Stroud, 2006

Sydney Tremayne, *The Trial of Alfred Arthur Rouse*, Geoffrey Bles, 1931

Frank Trentmann, *The Empire of Things: How We Became a World of Consumers, From the Fifteenth Century to the Twenty-First*, Penguin, 2016

Sir Edward Troup, *The Home Office*, Putnam's, 1925

Tom Tullett, *Murder Squad: Famous Cases of Scotland Yard's Murder Squad*, Grafton, 1996

Violet Van der Elst, *On the Gallows*, 2nd ed., The Doge Press, 1939 (first published 1937)

Adrian Vincent, *A Gallery of Poisoners*, Warner Books, 1993

Stephen Wade, *Tracing Your Criminal Ancestors*, Pen & Sword, Barnsley, 2009

Nigel Walker, *Crime and Insanity in England, One: Historical Perspectives*,

Edinburgh University Press, Edinburgh, 1968

Derek Walker-Smith, *Lord Reading and His Cases: The Study of a Great Career*, Chapman & Hall, 1934

War Office, *Manual of Military Law*, HMSO, 1914

Bernard Wasserstein, *The Secret Lives of Trebisch Lincoln*, Penguin, 1989

Colin Watson, *Snobbery with Violence: English Crime Stories and Their Audience*, Eyre Methuen, 1971

Duncan Webb, *Deadline for Crime*, Frederick Muller, 1955

Jeffrey Weeks, *Sex, Politics and Society: The Regulation of Sexuality Since 1800*, 1st ed., Longman, 1981

Rene J. A. Weis, *Criminal Justice: The True Story of Edith Thompson*, Hamish Hamilton, 1988

Tom Welsh and Walter Greenwood, *McNae's Essential Law for Journalists*, 16th ed., Butterworths, 2001

Cynthia L. White, *Women's Magazines, 1693-1968*, Michael Joseph, 1970

Richard Whittington-Egan, *The Riddle of Birdhurst Rise: The Croydon Poisoning Mystery*, Penguin, 1988

Martin J. Wiener, *Men of Blood: Violence, Manliness and Criminal Justice in Victorian England*, Cambridge University Press, Cambridge, 2004

Roland Wild, *Crimes & Cases of 1933*, Rich & Cowan, Ltd., 1934

Id., and Derek Curtis-Bennett, *'Curtis': The Life of Sir Henry Curtis-Bennett*, Hutchinson, 1937

Roger Wilkes, *Wallace: The Final Verdict*, Grafton, 1985

Paul Willetts, *North Soho 999: A True Story of Gangs and Gun-Crime in 1940s London*, Dewi Lewis Publishing, Stockport, 2007

David Williams, *Poison Farm: A Murderer Unmasked After 60 Years*, Thorogood, 1994

Guy R. Williams, *The Hidden World of Scotland Yard*, Hutchinson, 1972

Kevin Williams, *'Get Me a Murder a Day!' A History of Mass Communication in Britain*, Edward Arnold, 2004

Colin Wilson, *World Famous Murders*, Magpie Books, 2005

Damon and Rowan Wilson, *Murder Spree: Real-Life Stories of Twentieth Century Crime*, Magpie Books, 2011

David Wilson and Paul Harrison, *The Last British Serial Killer: Closing the Case on Peter Tobin and Bible John*, Sphere, 2010

Jean Moorcroft Wilson, *Siegfried Sassoon: The Making of a War Poet, a Biography, 1886-1918*, Duckworth, 1998

Denis Winter, *Death's Men: Soldiers of the Great War*. Penguin, 1979

Jay Winter, *Sites of Memory, Sites of Mourning: The Great War in European Cultural History*, Cambridge University Press, Cambridge, 1995

Bob Woffinden, *Hanratty: The Final Verdict*, Macmillan, 1997

Id., Miscarriages of Justice, Coronet Books, 1988

John Carter Wood, *'The Most Remarkable Woman in England': Poison, Celebrity and the Trials of Beatrice Pace*, Manchester University Press, Manchester, 2012

Filson Young (ed), *The Trial of Hawley Harvey Crippen*, 2nd ed., William Hodge & Co., Edinburgh, 1950 (first published 1920)

Hugh Young, *My Forty Years at the Yard*, W. H. Allen, 1955

Thom Young, with Martin Kettle, *Incitement to Disaffection*, Cobden Trust, 1976

Articles in Books

Pat Ayres and Jan Lambertz, "Marriage Relations, Money and Domestic Violence in Working-Class Liverpool, 1919-39", in Jane Lewis (ed.), *Labour and Love: Women's Experience of Home and Family, 1850-1940*, Blackwell, Oxford, 1986, pp. 195-216

Anette Ballinger, "The Guilt of the Innocent and the Innocence of the Guilty: The Cases of Marie Fahmy and Ruth Ellis", in Alice Myers and Sarah Wright (eds.), *No Angels: Women Who Commit Violence*, Pandora Press, 1996, pp. 1-28

F. A Beaumont, "Men Hunters: The 'German Rouse Cases'", in J. M. Parrish and John R. Crossland (eds.), *The Fifty Most Amazing Crimes of the Last 100 Years*, Odhams Press, 1936, pp. 624-34

Sue Bowden, "The New Consumerism", in Paul Johnson (ed), *Twentieth Century Britain: Economic, Social and Cultural Change*, Longman, 1996, Ch. 14

Lucy Bland, "'In the Name of Protection': The Policing of Women in the First World War", in Julia Brophy and Carol Smart (eds.), *Women-in-Law: Explorations in Law, Family and Sexuality*, Routledge, 1985, Ch. 2

Alyson Brown, "The Bobbed-Haired Bandit and the Smash-and-Grab Raider", in David S. Nash and Anne-Marie KIlday (eds.), *Fair and Unfair Trials During the Age of Public Criticism*, Bloomsbury, forthcoming

John Burnett, "Introduction" to Margaret Penn, *Manchester Fourteen Miles*, Futura, 1982 (book first published 1947)

Simon Dentith, "From William Morris to Morris Minor: An Alternative Suburban History", in Roger Webster (ed.), *Expanding Suburbia: Reviewing Suburban Narratives*, Berghahn, Oxford, 2001

Julie English Early, "A New Man for a New Century: Dr Crippen and the Principles of Masculinity", in George Robb and Nancy Erber (eds.), *Disorder in the Court: Trials and Sexual Conflict at the Turn of the Century*, Macmillan, 1999, Ch. 11

Id., "Keeping Ourselves to Ourselves: Violence in the Edwardian Suburb", in Shani D'Cruze (ed.), *Everyday Violence in Britain, 1850-1950*, Pearson, 2000, p. 175

Lindsay Farmer, "Notable Trials and the Criminal Law in Scotland and England, 1750-1950", in Philippe Chassaigne and Jean-Philippe Genet (eds.), *Droit et Société en France et en Grande-Bretagne (XIIe-XXe Siècles)*, Publications de la Sorbonne, Paris, 2003, pp. 149-70

Margot C. Finn, "Scotch Drapers and the Politics of Modernity: Gender, Class and National Identity in the Victorian Tally Trade", in Martin Daunton and M. Hilton (eds.), *The Politics of Consumption: Material Culture and Citizenship in Europe and America*, Berg Publishers, Oxford, 2001

Kate Flint, "Introduction", in George and Weedon Grossmith, *Diary of a Nobody*, Oxford Classics series, Oxford University Press, Oxford, 2008 (first published in book form 1892)

E. J. Hobsbawm, "The Tramping Artisan", in E. J. Hobsbawm, *Labouring Men*, Weidenfeld & Nicolson, 1964

Paul Lawrence, "'Scoundrels and Scallywags and Some Honest Men', Memoirs and the Self-Image of French and English Policemen, c. 1870-1939", in Barry Godfrey, Clive Emsley and Graeme Dunstall (eds.), *Comparative Histories of Crime*, Willan Publishing, Cullompton, Devon, 2003, Ch. 7

Phillipa Levine, "'Walking the Streets in a Way No Decent Woman Should': Women Police in World War I", in Chris A. Williams (ed.), *Police and Policing in the Twentieth Century*, Ashgate, Aldershot, 2011

Joseph Melling, "Introduction", in Joseph Melling (ed.), *Housing, Social Policy and the State*, Croom Helm, 1980, pp. 9-36

Russell Miller, "The Obsession with the Black Dahlia", in Roger Wilkes (ed.), *The Mammoth Book of Unsolved Crimes*, Robinson, 1999, p. 179

John Mortimer, "Introduction", in John Mortimer (ed.), *Famous Trials*, Penguin, 1984

Katherine O'Donovan, "*Enfants Trouvés*, Anonymous Mothers and Children's Identity Rights", in Katherine O'Donovan and Gerry R. Rubin (eds.), *Human Rights and Legal History: Essays in Honour of Brian Simpson*, Oxford University Press, Oxford, 2000, Ch. 3

Ex-Superintendent John Prothero, "The Blazing Car Murder", in Dorothy L. Sayers and Others, *Great Unsolved Crimes*, Hutchinson, 1938, pp. 173-79

Nicholas Rance, "'Jonathan's Great Knife': Dracula Meets Jack the Ripper", in Alexandra Warwick and Martin Willis (eds.), *Jack the Ripper: Media, Culture, History*, Manchester University Press, Manchester, 2007, Ch. 8

Phillip Rawlings, "True Crime", in Jon Vagg and Tim Newburn (eds.), *The British Criminological Conferences: Selected Proceedings, Vol. 1: Emerging Themes in Criminology*, Loughborough University, Loughborough, 1998

Gerry Rubin, "The Last Word on the Capital Courts Martial Controversy in Britain?", in Jean-Marc Berlière et al. (eds.), *Military Justices and World Wars: Europe 1914-1950*, Presses Universitaires de Louvain, Louvain-la-Neuve, Belgium, 2013. pp. 39-56

G. R. Rubin, "The County Courts and the Tally Trade, 1846-1914", in G. R. Rubin and David Sugarman (eds.), *Law, Economy and Society: Essays in the History of English Law, 1750-1914*, Professional Books, Abingdon, 1984, pp. 321-48

Luc Santé, "Introduction", In William Roughead, *Classic Crimes: A Selection from the Works of William Roughead*, New York Review of Books, New York, 2000

Gail Savage, "'The Magistrates Are Men': Working-Class Marital Conflict and Appeals from the Magistrates' Court to the Divorce Court After 1895", in George Robb and Nancy Erber (eds.), *Disorder in Court: Trials and Sexual Conflict at the Turn of the Century*, Macmillan, 1999, Ch. 2

W. Teignmouth Shore , "Browne and Kennedy, 1928", in James H. Hodge, *Famous Trials III*, Penguin, 1950, pp. 13-42

Joe Sim and Tony Ward, "The Magistrate of the Poor? Coroners and Deaths in Custody in Nineteenth Century England", in Michael Clark and Catherine Crawford (eds.), *Legal Medicine in History*, Cambridge University Press, Cambridge, 1994, pp. 245-67

Laura Ugolini, "Men, Masculinities and Menswear Advertising, c. 1890-1914", in John Benson and Laura Ugolini (eds.), *A Nation of Shopkeepers: Five Centuries of British Retailing*, I. B. Tauris, 2003, pp. 80-104

Filson Young, "Introduction", in Filson Young (ed.), *The Trial of Hawley Harvey Crippen*, 2nd ed., William Hodge & Co., Edinburgh, 1950 (first edition 1920)

Articles in Journals etc

C. M. Aitchison, "Courts Martial", *Juridical Review*, Vol. 32, 1920, pp. 147-58

Bernice Andrews et al, "Delayed-Onset Post-Traumatic Stress Disorder: A Systematic Review of the Evidence", *American Journal of Psychiatry*, Vol. 164, September 2007, pp. 1319-26

Id., "Comparison of Immediate Onset and Delayed Post Traumatic Stress Disorder in Military Veterans", *Journal of Abnormal Psychology*, Vol. 118 (4), 2009, pp. 767-77

Roy Bainton, "Battle of the Airwaves", *Saga Magazine*, February 2000, pp. 64-5

Christine Barter, "Safeguarding Teenage Intimate Relationships: Connecting Online and Offline Contexts and Risks", *Policy Hub Scotland*, November 30, 2015

P. W. J. Bartrip, "Pedestrians, Motorists, and No-Fault Compensation for Road Accidents in 1930s Britain", *Journal of Legal History*, Vol. 31(1), April 2010, pp. 45-60

George Behlmer, "'A Whiff of Stale Debauch': Summary Justice and Working-Class Marriage in England, 1870-1940", *Law and History Review*, Vol. 12, 1994, pp. 229-75

Leslie Blake, "The Tricks of the Trade: The Lot of an Expert Witness under Cross-Examination Is Not a Happy One", *Estates Gazette*, January 27, 2001, pp. 136-8

Ted Bogacz, "War Neurosis and Cultural Change in England, 1914-22: The Work of the War Office Committee of Enquiry into Shell-Shock", *Journal of Contemporary History*, Vol. 24, 1989, pp. 227-56

Joanna Bourke, "Effeminacy, Ethnicity and the End of Trauma: The Sufferings of 'Shell-shocked' Men in Great Britain and Ireland, 1914-39", *Ibid.*, pp. 57-69

Ben Braber, "The Trial of Oscar Slater (1909) and Anti-Jewish Prejudices in Edwardian Glasgow", *History*, Vol. 88, 2003, pp. 262-79

Neil Bright, "A Lad from Lincoln", 2005, in www.londonwfa.org.uk

Alyson Brown, "Crime, Criminal Mobility and Serial Offenders in Early Twentieth Century Britain", *Contemporary British History*, Vol. 25 (4), December 2011, pp. 551-68

Rachel J. Cahill-O'Callaghan, "Reframing the Judicial Diversity Debate: Personal Values and Tacit Diversity", *Legal Studies*, Vol. 35 (1), 2015, pp. 1-29

Id., "Turning Mirrors into Windows? Assessing the Impact of (Mock) Juror Education in Rape Trials", *British Journal of Criminology*, Vol. 49 (3), 2009, pp. 363-83

Duncan Campbell, "The Man in the Mac", *Guardian Weekend*, September 5, 2009

David Cesarani, "The Anti-Jewish Career of Sir William Joynson-Hicks, Cabinet Minister", *Journal of Contemporary History*, Vol. 24 (3), 1989, pp. 461-82

Karen Chow, "Popular Sexual Knowledge and Women's Agency in 1920s England",

Feminist Review, No. 63, Autumn 1999, pp. 64-87

Cathryn Corns, "'Shot at Dawn': Military Executions in the Great War", *Journal of the Royal United Services Institute*, Vol. 143 (1), 1998, pp. 53-55

Andrew Davies, "'These Viragoes Are No Less Cruel Than the Lads': Young Women, Gangs and Violence in Late Victorian Manchester and Salford", *British Journal of Criminology*, Vol. 39 (1), 1999, pp. 72-89

Shani D'Cruze, "Intimacy, Professionalism and Domestic Homicide in Interwar Britain: The Case of Dr Buck Ruxton", *Women's History Review*, Vol. 16 (5), 2007, pp. 701-22

Id., "Sex, Violence and Local Courts: Working-Class Respectability in a Mid-Nineteenth Century Lancashire Town", *British Journal of Criminology*, Vol. 39 (1), 1999, pp. 328-45

Id., "'The Damn'd Place Was Haunted': The Gothic, Middlebrow Culture and Inter-War 'Notable British Trials'", *Literature and History*, Vol. 15 (1), 2006, pp. 37-58

P. E. Dewey, "Food Production and Policy in the United Kingdom, 1914-1918", *Transactions of the Royal Historical Society*, 5th Series, Vol. 30, 1980, pp. 71-89

Louise Ellison and Vanessa E. Munro, "Getting to (Not) Guilty: Examining Jurors' Deliberative Processes in, and Beyond, the Context of a Mock Rape Trial", *Legal Studies*, Vol. 30 (1), 2010, pp. 74-97

Id., "'Telling Tales': Exploring Narratives of Life and Law Within the (Mock) Jury Room", *ibid.*, Vol. 35 (2), 2015, pp. 210-25

Mary Beth Emmerichs, "Getting Away With Murder? Homicide and the Coroners in Nineteenth Century London", *Social Science History*, Vol. 25 (1), Spring 2001, pp. 93-100

Clive Emsley, "Violent Crime in England in 1919: Post-war Anxieties and Press Narratives", *Continuity and Change*, Vol. 23, 2008, pp. 173-95

Janet Fink, "Natural Mothers, Putative Fathers and Innocent Children: The Definition and Regulation of Parental Relationships Outside Marriage in England, 1945-1959", *Journal of Family History*, Vol. 25 (2), 2000, pp. 178-95

David R. Foran et al., "The Conviction of Dr Crippen: New Forensic Findings in a Century-Old Murder", *Journal of Forensic Sciences*, Vol. 56 (1), January 2011, pp. 233-40

Martin Francis, "The Domestication of the Male? Recent Research on Nineteenth and Twentieth Century British Masculinity", *Historical Journal*, Vol. 45 (3), 2002, pp. 637-52

Ginger Frost, "'She is But a Woman': Kitty Byron and the Edwardian Criminal Justice System", *Gender and History*, Vol. 16 (3), 2004, pp. 538-60

Id., "'The Black Lamb of the Black Sheep': Illegitimacy in the English Working Class, 1850-1939", *Journal of Social History*, Vol. 37 (2), 2003, pp. 293-322

Judy Giles, "'Playing Hard to Get': Working-Class Women, Sexuality and Respectability in Britain, 1918-1940", *Women's History Review*, Vol. 1 (2), 1992, pp. 239-55

L. Goodwin et al., "Prevalence of Delayed-onset Post-traumatic Stress Disorder in Military Personnel: Is There Evidence for this Disorder? Results of a Prospective UK Cohort Study", *Journal of Nervous Mental Diseases*, Vol. 200 (5), May 2012, pp. 429-37

B. V. Harris, "Judicial Review of the Prerogative of Mercy", *Public Law*, 1991, p. 386

Christopher Hilliard, "'Is it a Book That You Would Even Wish Your Wife or Your Servants to Read?' Obscenity Law and the Politics of Reading in Modern England", *American Historical Review*, Vol. 118 (3), 2013, pp. 653-78

James Hitchcock, "Murder as One of the Liberal Arts", *American Scholar*, Vol. 63 (1), March 1994, pp. 277-85

Matt Houlbrook, "A Pin to See the Peepshow: Culture, Fiction and Selfhood in Edith Thompson's Letters, 1921-1922", *Past and Present*, No. 207, 2010, pp. 215-49

Id., "'The Man with the Powder Puff' in Interwar Britain", *Historical Journal*, Vol. 50 (1), 2007, pp. 145-71

P. J. R. King, "Decision-makers and Decision-making in the English Criminal Law, 1750-1800", *ibid.*, Vol. 27 (1), 1984, pp. 25-58

Nicola Lacey, "Unspeakable Subjects, Impossible Rights: Sexuality, Integrity and the Criminal Law", *Canadian Journal of Law and Jurisprudence*, Vol. 11 (1), 1998, pp. 47-68

Jon Lawrence, "Forging a Peaceable Kingdom: Violence and Fear of Brutalization in Post-First World War Britain", *Journal of Modern History*, Vol. 75 (3), 2003, pp. 557-89

Diana Leat, "The Rise and Role of the Poor Man's Lawyer", *British Journal of Law and Society*, Vol. 2 (2), 1975, pp. 166-81

Deirdre McManus et al., "Violent Offending by UK Military Personnel Deployed to Iraq and Afghanistan: A Data Linkage Cohort Study", *Lancet*, Vol. 381, No. 9870, March 16, 2013, pp. 907-17

David Mills, "A Murderer Visits Gelligaer", *Gelligaer*, Vol. 14, 2004, pp. 47-8

Colin R. Moore and Gerry R. Rubin, "Civilian Detective Doctrine in the 1930s and Its Transmission to the Military Police in 1940-42", *Law, Crime and History*, Vol. 4 (3), 2014, pp. 1-30

W. T. Murphy and R. W. Rawlings, "After the *Ancien Régime*: The Writing of Judgments in the House of Lords, 1979/80", *Modern Law Review*, Vol. 44 (6), 1981, pp. 617-59

F. H. Newark, "The Campbell Case and the First Labour Government", *Northern Ireland Legal Quarterly*, Vol. 20, 1969, pp. 19-42

Sean O'Connell, "From Toad of Toad Hall to the 'Death Drivers' of Belfast", *British Journal of Criminology*, Vol. 46 (3), 2006, pp. 455-69

Christopher Pollnitz, "The Censorship and Transmission of D. H. Lawrence's *Pansies*: The Home Office and the 'Foul-Mouthed Fellow'", *Journal of Modern Literature*, Vol. 28 (3), 2005, pp. 44-71

Fiona Reid, "Distinguishing Between Shell-Shocked Veterans and Pauper Lunatics: The Ex-Services' Welfare Society and Mentally Wounded Veterans after the Great War", *War In History*, Vol. 14 (3), 2007, pp. 347-71

Gerry R. Rubin, "Calling in the Met: Serious Crime Investigation Involving Scotland Yard and Provincial Forces in England and Wales, 1906-1939", *Legal Studies*, Vol. 31 (3), pp. 411-41

Id., "Dennis, Alan and Arthur x 3: Literary Legacies of the 'Blazing Car Murder' of 1930", *Law and Humanities*, Vol. 9 (2), 2015, pp. 1-34

Id., "From Packmen, Tallymen and 'Perambulating Scotchmen' to Credit Drapers' Associations, c. 1840-1914", *Business History*, Vol. 28 (2), 1986, pp. 206-25

Id., "Judicial Free Speech versus Judicial Neutrality in Mid-Twentieth Century England: The Last Hurrah for the *Ancien Régimé?*" *Law and History Review*, Vol. 27 (2), 2009, pp. 373-412

Id., "Law as a Bargaining Weapon: British Labour and the Restoration of Pre-War Practices Act 1919", *Historical Journal*, Vol. 32 (4), 1989, pp. 925-45

Id., "Military Law in World War One", *Journal of the Royal United Services Institute*, Vol. 143 (1), 1998, pp. 58-64

Id., "Parliament, Prerogative and Military Law: Who Had Legal Authority over the Army in the Later Nineteenth Century?" *Journal of Legal History*, Vol. 18 (1), 1997, pp. 45-84

Id., "Posthumous Pardons, the Home Office and the Timothy Evans Case", *Criminal Law Review*, No. 1, January 2007, pp. 41-59

Id., "Pre-Dating Vicky Pryce: The *Peel* Case (1922) and the Origins of the Marital Coercion Statutory Defence", *Legal Studies*, Vol. 34 (4), 2014, pp. 631-59

Id., "Seddon, Dell and Rock 'n' Roll: Investigating Alleged Breaches of the Ban on Publishing Photographs Taken Within the Courts or Their Precincts, 1925-1967", *Criminal Law Review*, No. 11, November 2008, pp. 874-87

Id., "Some Immediate Consequences of the *Woolmington* Ruling (1935): British Colonies and Irish Cattle", *Journal of Commonwealth Law and Legal Education*, Vol. 7, 2009, pp. 76-86

H. Thornton Rutter, "The Chronicle of the Car", *Illustrated London News*, September 13, 1930

Gail Savage, "Erotic Stories and Public Decency: Newspaper Reporting of Divorce Proceedings in England", *Historical Journal*, Vol. 41(2), 1998, pp. 511-28

T. E. Scrutton, "The War and the Law", *Law Quarterly Review*, Vol. 34, 1918, pp. 116-33

Lizzie Seal, "Ruth Ellis in the Condemned Cell", *Prison Service Journal*, No. 199, January 2012, pp. 17-19

Id., "Violet van der Elst's Use of Spectacle and Militancy in her Campaign Against the Death Penalty", *Law, Crime and History*, Vol. 3 (3), 2013, pp. 25-41

N. D. Siederer, "The Campbell Case", *Journal of Contemporary History*, Vol. 9 (2), 1974, pp. 143-62

Stefan Slater, "Containment: Managing Street Prostitution in London, 1918-1939", *Journal of British Studies*, Vol. 49 (2), 2010, pp. 332-57

Nicky Stanley, Christine Barter et al, "Pornography, Sexual Coercion and Abuse and Sexting in Young People's Intimate Relationships: A European Study", *Journal of Interpersonal Violence*, Vol. 33 , No. 19, 2018, pp. 2919-44

Lord Thomas, "Expert Evidence: The Future of Forensic Science in Criminal Trials", www.judiciary.gov.uk, October 14, 2014

Sara E. Thomas, "'What Should I Do?' Young Women's Reported Dilemmas with Nude Photographs", *Sexuality Research Social Policy*, Vol. 15, 2018, pp. 192-207

Sir Edward Troup, "Police Administration, Local and National", *Police Journal*, Vol. 1, 1928

Sue Tweg, "Not the Full Story: Representing Ruth Ellis", *Biography*, Vol. 23 (1), 2000, pp. 1-28

Martin J. Wiener, "The Sad Story of George Hall: Adultery, Murder and the Politics of Mercy in Mid-Victorian England", *Social History*, Vol. 24 (2), 1999, pp. 176-95

Percy Winfield, "Courts Martial from the Lawyer's Point of View", *Law Quarterly Review*, Vol. 34, 1918, pp. 143-51

Jay Winter, "Shell-shock and the Cultural History of the Great War", *Journal of Contemporary History*, Vol. 35 (1), 2000, pp. 7-11

John Carter Wood, "'Those Who Have Trouble Can Sympathise With You': Press Writing, Reader Responses and a Murder Trial in Interwar Britain", *Journal of Social History*, Vol. 43 (2), 2009, pp. 439-62

Alison Woodeson, "The First Women Police: A Force for Equality or Infringement?" *Women's History Review*, Vol. 2 (2), 1993, pp. 217-32

Parliamentary Papers etc

House of Commons Debates

House of Lords Debates

Report of the Committee on Proceedings Before Examining Magistrates (chair, Mr Justice Tucker), Cmnd. 479, 1958

Report of the Departmental Committee on Detective Work and Procedure (1938), Vol. 2, HMSO, 1938

Report of an Inquiry by Mr. A. E. James QC...., Cmnd. 2735, 1965 (the Harold Challenor Inquiry)

Report of an Inquiry by Mr. W. L. Mars-Jones QC.... Cmnd. 2526, 1964 (the Grosvenor Hotel Inquiry)

Report of Royal Commission on Capital Punishment 1949-1953 (chair, Sir Ernest Gowers), Cmd. 8932, HMSO, 1953

Report of the War Office Committee of Enquiry into 'Shell-Shock'' (Southborough Committee), Cmd. 1734, 1922

Case Law

Alphabetical according to the prisoner's or litigant's name.

Armstrong (1922) 2 K B 555

DPP v Beard [1920] A C 479

Bentley (Deceased) [1998] EWCA (Crim) 2516

R v Secretary of State for the Home Department, ex parte Bentley [1994] Q B 349

Bingham [1991] Crim L. R. 433

Boardman v DPP [1975] A C 421

Byrne [1960] 3 All E R 1

Re Callaway; Callaway v Treasury Solicitor [1956] 3 W L R 257

Cleaver v Mutual Reserve Fund Life Association [1892] 1 Q B 147

Codère (1917) 12 Cr. App. Rep. 21

In Re the Estate of Crippen [1911] P. 108

Dallagher [2003] 1 Cr. App. Rep. 195
Findlay v *United Kingdom* [1997] 24 EHRR 221
Foster [1985] Q B 115
Francis (1874) L. R. 2 Cox C. C. Rep. 128
Ibrahim [1914] A C 599
Jones v *DPP* [1962] A C 635
Lucas [1981] Q B 720
Mancini v *DPP* [1942] A C 1
National Justice Compania Naviera SA v *Prudential Assurance Co. Ltd.* [1993] Lloyd's Rep. 68
Peace [1976] Crim. L. R. 119
Richardson and Longman (1968) 52 Cr. App. Rep. 317
Scranton (1921) 15 Cr. App. Rep. 104
Scranton's Trustee v *Pearse* [1922] 2 Ch. 87
DPP v *Shannon* (1979) 59 Cr. App. Rep. 250
Silverlock (1894) 2 Q B 766
George Joseph Smith (1915) 11 Crim. App. Rep. 229
Straffen [1952] 2 Q B 911
Sullivan [1984] 1 A C 156
R. v *Sussex Justices, ex parte McCarthy* [1924] 1 K B 256
Thomas v *David* (1836) 7 C & P 350
Thompson [1918] A C 221
Windle [1952] 2 Q B 826
Woolmington v *DPP* [1935] A C 435

Unpublished Papers and Theses

Rebecca Crites, "Brutes, Whores, and Shell-shocked Wretches: The Impact of the First World War upon News Media Representations of the Wife Beater in Britain, 1914-1929" (unpublished; Open University, 2014)

Douglas Commaille, "An Assessment of Causes, Responses and Attitudes to Insanity in Capital Cases in Post-World War One England", LL.M. extended essay, Kent University, 2014

Jo Pearman, "The Tribe of Ogres that Fatten on Little Children: Legal Responses to Baby Farming in the Late Nineteenth Century", Ph.D. thesis, Kent University, 2017

Websites

www.1914-1918.net/hospitals_uk.htm
www.1914-1918.invisionzone.com
www.ancestry.co.uk
www.bbc.co.uk/news/magazine-10802059
www.bbc.co.uk/news/uk-england-northamptonshire-17899027
www.cgsc.edu/CARL/nafziger/915BXAC.pdf

www.epsomandewellhistoryexplorer.org.uk/Kesson.html
www.fomphc.org.uk
www.gov.uk/government/collections/vehicles-statistics
www.gracesguide.co.uk
www.hendersonchambers.co.uk
www.historyofwar.org/battles_festubert.html
www.itsaboutlincoln.co.uk
www.jfklibrary.org
www.lockhatters.co.uk/men/fedors-homburgs.html
www.nilfisk.co.uk
www.northants.police.uk/default.aspx?id=9655&datewant=yes
www.northfinchley.townwalk.co.uk/local/history
www.oldbaileyonline.org/browse.jsp?path=sessionswPapers%2F18770917.xml
www.patent.ipex1.com/assignee/henry_snowden_rowell_1.html
www.ramc-ww1.com/chain_of_evacuation.html
www.sabre-roads.co.uk
www.stockport.gov.uk/hatworks
www.victoriacross.org

INDEX

9/11 attacks: victim identification, 124–5
24th London Regiment, 353–6, 358–62,
    363, 367

Abdication crisis (1936), 398n, 402
Abinger, Edward, 511 & n
abortion, 440 & n
accountancy fraud, 458
Achew, James, 89
'Acid-Bath Murders', 27, 51, 104, 199, 377
Acland, T. W. G., 318
actus reus, 457
adultery, 398–9, 401–5, 412
advocacy: defending guilty clients, 76;
    pre-trial meetings with clients, 76–7,
    255; golden rules, 77–8; styles of, 79,
    81–2, 83–5, 249; status of the advocate,
    85–7; in wartime courts martial,
    498–501
Agate, James, 81
Agility scheme, 64, 381
Aherne, Brian, 476
Aitchison, Craigie, 500
Alien Pioneer Corps, 422n
Allan, John, 394
Allaway, Thomas, 329–30, 347, 505n
Alliston & Co., London, 37, 353
Allport, Gordon, 518
Alphon, Peter, 308
Anderson, Sir John, 340
Andrews, Detective Inspector, 47, 48
Andrews, Mrs. (of Oxford), 387
Angel Lane police station, Northampton:
    closed on night of murder, 4, 54–5;
    Rouse detained at, 19, 63, 91; his
    'harem' speech, 19–20, 138, 396; Rouse
    charged at, 20, 131; allowed to see Lily,
    20, 424, 465; debris of Morris Minor
    removed to, 91, 171
anti-Semitism, 77–8, 332n, 473n
appeal hearing, Rouse case: appeal
    judges, 243–6; counsel for the defence,
    247–9; Rouse appears in dock, 243;
    grounds for appeal, 250–1; Rouse's
    memorandum, 252–4; case for the

defence, 254–9; damaging prejudice
    argument, 254–6, 261; conviction by
    grave suspicion argument, 256–9; no
    case to answer argument, 259; new
    scientific evidence rejected, 239, 242,
    257–8; case for the Crown, 259–61;
    appeal dismissed, 244, 252, 261–5,
    293; Rouse's reaction to decision,
    263–4; press coverage, 264; compared
    with Wallace appeal, 262–3
appeal in cases of wrongful admission of
    evidence, 349
Archer, John, *The Monster Evil: Policing
    and Violence in Victorian Liverpool,*
    23–4
Armstrong, Major Herbert Rowse, 72,
    243, 512n
Arthur, Keith, 308
Artois, Second Battle of (1915), 355, 357,
    358–62
Ashford, Arthur: photographs burnt-out
    vehicle, 6; interferes with wreckage,
    6–7, 56, 206, 257; evidence at trial,
    162, 163
Astill, Charles, 120
Atkin, Lord, 247, 492n
Atkinson, E. H. Tindal: background, 68; on
    DPP investigative role, 71n; and Rouse
    case, 128, 132, 272–3, 297–8, 305, 341;
    on limits of newspaper comment, 344;
    on conspiracy theory involving Lily
    Rouse, 466; on juries in capital cases,
    517
attainder, 281n
Attenborough, Walter Annis, 186–7
Attlee, Clem, 83
Aubers Ridge, Battle of (1915), 355, 357,
    358–9
Augustin, Ella, 473–5
Augustine Garage, Northampton, 241
Australian baby farming case (1894)
    (*Makin*), 512, 514, 516
Automobile Association (AA), 383
Avory, Horace (Mr. Justice): career and
    reputation as judge, 67, 89, 245–6, 269,

342n, 485–6; presides at Rouse appeal, 243, 244, 255, 257–8, 262

Babington, Judge Anthony, *For the Sake of Example: Capital Courts Martial, 1914–1918, The Truth*, 484, 499–500
'baby farming', 512, 525n
Bacon's Abridgement (legal text), 191
bad character evidence: general exclusionary principle, 73, 148n, 509–10; admissible exceptions, 511–13; and 'motive' justification, 514–15, 516; in Rouse case, 73–4, 142, 146–9, 148n, 152, 162–3, 169, 179–80, 254–5, 261, 271; Home Office stance, 293, 517
Bailey, George, 160
Bailey, Hedley, 3, 4, 54, 55n; removes body from wreckage, 56
Bailey, William: actions on night of murder, 3–4, 10, 34, 54, 55n; statement to police, 56–7; evidence at committal hearing, 133; photographed outside police court, 140; evidence at trial, 163; account disputed by Rouse, 190
Baines, Cecil: background and criminal record, 522–4; involvement with Prison Reform Society, 519–20; legal aid campaign, 520–1; criticises Bodkin, 68, 522; criticises Paling, 73, 519, 521, 522; attack on Rouse trial verdict, 519, 521–2
Baldock, Walter George (as Rouse's victim), 116
Bamber, Herbert William: credentials, 202–3; evidence at trial, 203–4, 221, 260; cross-examined, 204–7
Bancroft, George Pleydell, 79, 80, 160, 224; on Rouse's performance in witness box, 198
Bara, Theda, 403
Bardens, Dennis, *Lord Justice Birkett*, 87–8
bare-headedness, 1–2
Baring, Rupert, 4th Baron Revelstoke, 81
Barker, Stephen, 464
Barnes, Peter, 283, 309
Barnett, Herbert, 393
Barnett, Robert, 101n
Barney, Elvira: murder trial, 84, 86, 246, 255, 404, 412n, 518; demeanour in witness box, 411; sexual waywardness, 412
barristers: as 'celebrities', 85–7; immunity from being sued, 254
Barrow, Eliza, 68–9, 84, 371n, 468n
Barrowman, Mary, 71
Barry, Michael J. (as Rouse's victim), 116

Beck, Adolph, 245, 269, 508, 511
Bedford and District Daily Circular, 314, 316, 317
Bedford Prison: Rouse remanded at, 20; his prison photographs, 126–7, 128; examined by prison medical officers, 129–31; and Rouse's 'Own Life Story' article, 226, 230; mobbed by crowds outside, 264; awaiting execution, 298; history of executions at, 80, 308–9; as venue for Rouse's execution, 310–11; Rouse's last days and hours, 311–16; Nellie's last visit, 328; Rouse's alleged confession to prison warders, 336–7; his statement to Gwilliam, 335–6, 337–8; 'policy of silence' by prison authorities, 311, 318–19, 341; crowds outside, 316–18; execution of Rouse, 307, 317–18, 325–6; his alleged confession to prison chaplain, 325–7, 348; post-mortem and inquest, 307–8; prison burial ground, 308; Rouse's personal effects disposed, 309, 315; and *Daily Sketch* confession story, 335–6
Bedford railway station, 25–6, 367
Beerbohm, Max, 370
Bell, George, 13, 179, 181
Bellfield, Levi, 23
Benjamin, Elizabeth, 389n
Bennett, Keith, 118
Bentley, Derek: murder trial, 76–7, 246; and diminished responsibility, 493; campaign to re-open case, 200; posthumous pardon, 280n, 281, 283, 284; conviction quashed, 282, 505
Beron, Leon, 375
Berrett, Chief Detective Inspector James, 65n
Berry, James (hangman), 26
Berry, James (motor engineer), 26
Bible John (unidentified serial killer), 124
Biddle, Andrew, 458n
Bilby, Frederick, 39, 50
Bird, Reginald: complicity in Rouse's confession stories, 230, 322, 327, 331, 336
Birkett, Norman, 1st Baron: background, 79; early career as journalist, 87; legal career, 70n, 71n, 79–82, 83; qualities as defence advocate, 81–2; advocacy style, 79, 83, 85; as 'assassin', 83, 85, 165; William Reeve case, 79–80; appointed Rouse case, 68; opening address for prosecution, 160–2, 457; commutes to Commons to oppose Trade Disputes

Bill, 164–5; examines Spilsbury, 100–1; examines Nellie Tucker, 180; avoids 'bad character' evidence, 169, 179–80; cross-examines Rouse, 192–7; exhibits mallet in courtroom, 198; cross-examines Rae, 199; cross-examines Harvey-Wyatt, 99, 201; cross-examines Bamber, 204–7; cross-examines Isaacs, 209–11; trick question, 99, 207–8, 209, 210–11, 258, 289; cross-examines Cotton, 213; submission to recall Buckle, 214; closing speech, 217–18; raises indictment for bigamy, 224–5; relations with Campion, 87–8; appears for Crown at Rouse's appeal hearing, 243, 259–61; writes on Rouse case, 32; public service and committee work, 82; wartime BBC broadcasts, 82; judicial work, 82–3, 85; at Nuremberg trials, 83; on Patrick Hastings, 84; writes preface to Bancroft's autobiography, 80n
Birmingham Six trial (1975), 250, 324, 508
birth control, 117, 403, 404n, 448
Bishop, Cecil, *From Information Received*, 60
Bishop, Stanley, 234
Black, Ladbroke, 303
Black Dahlia murder (1947), 33, 324
Blackheath Road police station, 20, 48
Blackshirts (British Union of Fascists), 249n, 398, 475
Blackwell, Sir Ernley, 265; as *eminence grise* at Home Office, 269; legal adviser, 269–71; and Trebitsch Lincoln incident, 334; reviews evidence for Rouse's reprieve, 231, 241, 271–2, 273, 277, 288–90, 293–7; opinion on 'bad character' evidence, 293, 517; theory on joint insurance fraud, 191–2, 292, 294–6, 301, 340, 342, 348, 457, 458–9, 461, 463–7, 477; conference with Talbot and Clynes, 296; advises Rouse should hang, 286; dismisses Rouse's last-minute submissions, 339–41; disregards Ivy Jenkins newspaper story, 305; responds to letters from public, 300–1, 305, 316n; and Rouse's supposed confessions, 326–7, 346; general stance on prisoner confessions, 329–30; vets Rouse's last correspondence, 335; on conduct of newspapers, 341; and Cecil Baines, 522; memorandum on onus of proof, 269

Blazing Car Murder case: as *cause célèbre*, 25–6, 31–3, 229–30; chance v. fate, 33–4; literary legacy, 32, 168, 390, 399, 531; as unfinished business, 118
Bletchley Park Listening Station, 281
Bloom, Ursula, 229
Blue Anchor Hotel, Byfleet, 69
Blue Dahlia, The (film), 33
Blue Lamp, The (film), 386n
Bodkin, Sir Archibald: as state prosecutor, 68, 270, 522; and Vaquier case, 63, 69–71; prosecution of J. R. Campbell, 247–8; and Irene Savidge affair, 70n, 71; evidence to Royal Commission on Police Powers, 70–1; 'moral purity' prosecutions, 71; courtroom manner, 73
Bonati, Minnie: murder of (1927), 231
Bond, Dr. John, 122
Boocock & Son (Yorkshire solicitors), 120
Boodson & Woodford (Rouse's employer), 38
Booth, Charles, 410
Booth, Handel, 85
Booth, Mrs. Horace, 116
Boothby, Robert ('Bob'), Baron, 405
Bosworth, Arthur: reprieve for (1958), 284n
Bottomley, Horatio, 245, 246, 301, 348
Bow, Clara, 403, 416n
Bowmakers (finance company), 382
Brady, Hugh, 199
brass, coefficient of thermal expansion, 210–11, 232
Breen and Fitz murder case (1855), 24n
Brentford Canal murder (1935), 103, 105
Bresler, Fenton, *Reprieve: A Study of a System*, 129, 130–1, 270, 279, 280, 284–6
Bridgeman, William, 88, 270, 271, 285
Briggs, William Thomas (as Rouse's victim), 122
Briggs family, 96, 122
Bright, Harry, 119
Bright, Harry Jnr (as Rouse's victim), 119
Brighton police corruption case (1957), 72
Brighton taxi cab murder case (1923), 163, 270
Brighton Trunk Murder Number One (1934), 103
Brighton Trunk Murder Number Two (1934), 81, 103n, 264, 332
Bristol Hippodrome, 523
British Expeditionary Force (BEF), 356
British Medical Journal, 482–3

British Union of Fascists (Blackshirts), 249n, 398, 475

Brixton Prison, 310

Brown, Alfred: actions on night of murder, 3–4, 10, 34, 54; statement to police, 56–7; photographed outside police court, 140; evidence at trial, 163, 253; account disputed by Rouse, 190

Brown, Ernest, 233, 471

Browne, Guy Frederick: bowler hat photograph, 21; car insurance fraud, 468

Browne and Kennedy murder case (1927), 64–5, 65n, 245, 381, 468

Brownhill, Hendell, 15–16, 137, 503; evidence at committal hearing, 141; evidence at trial, 181–2

Brumby, Superintendent George: interviews Rouse and takes statement, 18–19; escorts Rouse to Northampton, 19; speaks to Lily, 464–5; charges Rouse with murder, 20, 131; requests assistance from Scotland Yard, 20, 62; requests second post-mortem, 93; searches crime scene for bullets, 93; searches for excrement, 166; enquiries into identity of victim, 106, 108, 110, 112, 133–4, 135, 140, 141; evidence at committal hearing, 133, 151, 152; relations with press, 133–4, 135; liaison with DPP, 132–3; evidence at trial, 165, 166–7; arrangements for burial of Rouse's victim, 93–4; attends burial, 94

Bryant, Charlotte, 72, 410, 524

Buckle, Colonel Cuthbert: background and experience as fire loss assessor, 171, 175; inspects remains of Morris Minor, 171; written report, 171–2, 173; evidence at trial, 172–4; cross-examined, 175–8; accused of misleading the jury, 202; re-evaluates evidence of carburettor tampering, 178, 213; recalled and disputes heat transfer theory, 214–15; evidence challenged after trial, 237–9, 240–1; weakness of testimony, 174–5, 267–8

Bulger, James, murder of, 23–4

burden of proof, 72–3, 80, 264, 269

Burke and Hare, 25, 519n

Burns, Simon, 270–1

Bushell's Case (1670), 233–4

Butterfill, John Charles, 121

Buxted Road (No. 14), Friern Barnet: name, 371; location, 46, 374–5; Rouse briefly returns to after murder, 11–12,

190–2, 195, 275n, 294–6, 295n, 321, 465; police enquiries at, 8–9, 10; sale of house and furniture, 74, 127, 138, 151, 374, 424

Byrne, Patrick: murder case (1961), 489n

Byron, Kitty, 30

Bywaters, Frederick, 285, 419, 505; see also Thompson–Bywaters case (1921–22)

Caine, Derwent Hall, 314, 330–1

Caine, Hall, 330

Camb, James, 102n, 118

Cameron-Waller, W. E., 463

Campbell, Helen: appearance, 45; background, 46, 445 & n; seduced by Rouse, 46, 425–6; first child by Rouse, 46, 426–7; boards in Islington, 44; bigamous marriage to Rouse, 35–7, 44, 158n, 427; second child by Rouse (Arthur Alfred), 44; moves to Lonsdale Square, Islington, 44–5; opens restaurant, 45; maintenance proceedings against Rouse, 45, 46; relationship with Rouse, 46–7, 346, 427–8; hands over Arthur Jnr to Lily, 47, 428; confrontation with Lily, 47, 423–4, 428; collects son from Lily and circle, 47; questioned over charred corpse story, 51; represented by Henry Flint, 88; name disclosed at committal hearing, 145–6, 150; evidence at committal hearing, 150; photograph in newspapers, 150, 229; and Arthur Jnr's alleged statement, 191, 463–4; not called as witness at trial, 162–3, 187; legal expenses covered by *Daily Sketch*, 187; reaction to jury verdict, 224; prison visits to see Rouse, 273, 336, 347, 419; at appeal hearing, 252; and Rouse's confession in *Daily Sketch*, 321, 324–5; correspondence with Home Office, 266, 275, 304–5; prison correspondence, 428–9; articles for *Peg's Paper*, 414–15, 425–9; payment for story, 416, 451

Campbell, J. R., 247–8

Campbell, William, 394

Campion, John B. E., 135, 141, 145

Campion, Sidney, 87–9, 187

Cannell, J. C.: role in Rouse case, 10, 199; on Lily Rouse's appeal to Mrs. Clynes, 235n, 303–4; and Rouse's 'confession', 319, 320, 322–3, 324–5, 334–5, 336; seeks Home Office meeting, 334–5; reproduces letter from Lily Rouse, 342;

investigates bigamous marriage, 36; and Arthur Jnr's alleged statement, 191, 295n, 463; arranges whip-round for Arthur Jnr, 450; on Rouse's performance in court, 197, 198; on Rouse's sexual immorality, 41, 427; on Helen Campbell, 445n; St Albans pub landlord story, 320n; charred corpse story, 51; and Agnes Kesson case, 471; investigates identity of Rouse's victim, 106, 109, 110–11; as practising magician, 319; *When Fleet Street Calls*, 319

capital punishment: opposition to, 235–6, 279, 517; parliamentary Select Committee on (1930), 300, 309; Gowers Committee (1949–53), 278, 291; abolition (1965), 280, 318; and insanity, 280–1, 491 & n; Pierrepoint's view on, 309; *see also* courts martial; executions

Cardiff, 16, 141
Carew, Horace, 239
Carman, George, 87
Carroll, Madeleine, 476
Carson, Sir Edward, 85
Carswell, Donald, 30; *Trial of Ronald True*, 489, 490–1
Casement, Sir Roger, 245, 269, 283
Casey, Mary Teresa: evidence at committal hearing, 141–2
Casswell, J. D., 72n
casualty clearing stations (CCS), 366
causes célèbres see murder *causes célèbres*
'celebrity barristers', 85–7
Challenor, Detective Sergeant Harold, 283
Chapman, George (Seweryn Kłosowski), 523
Chapman, John, 237
Chapman, Laura, 82
Charing Cross Bank collapse (1910), 68
Charlotte Street shooting (1947), 386n
Charteris brothers, 397 & n
chastity, female, 405, 406, 410
Chater, Mickey, 365
chequebook journalism, 199–200, 343
Cherrill, Superintendent Fred, 52
Chesser, Dr. Eustace, 407, 408
Chester & Cole Ltd (hire purchase firm), 183, 459, 468
Chesterton, G. K., 380
child-on-child murders, 23–4
children: testifying in court, 464
Childs, Sir Wyndham, 301–2
Chiozza Money, Sir Leo: and Irene Savidge affair, 70n, 71

Christie, Agatha, 376; *Hercule Poirot's Christmas*, 27; *Towards Zero*, 30
Christie, Reginald, 27, 32, 78, 283, 324, 406, 483; chased down by crime reporters, 199, 200
Churchill, Winston, 164–5, 243, 286n
circumstantial evidence, 161, 185, 257, 293–4, 396
City Road Maternity Hospital, 19, 20, 39, 44, 47, 141–2, 430, 503–4
Clare, Dr. Anthony, 529
Clarke, E. C. (as Rouse's victim), 113
Clarke, Kenneth, 280n
Clarke, Sir Reginald, 381
classified ads (personal columns), 400–1
Clayton, Captain G. F., 519–20
Cleft-chin murder case (1944), 28–9, 124, 286n, 372n
Clynes, Mrs., 235n, 303–4
Clynes, J. R.: ministerial career, 287; as Home Secretary, 235, 265, 287; role in reprieve process, 267; opposition to death penalty, 280, 286, 291, 309; William Podmore case, 286; considers Rouse case, 286–7; petitioned, 290–1; confers with Talbot and Blackwell, 296; responds to letter of appeal, 303; seeks private opinion from Hewart, 305; lack of political strength and character, 287, 298; rejects petition, 298; and newspaper reports of Rouse's last hours, 312–13; Commons statements, 326, 330–1, 332, 334, 345, 349; declines meeting with Cannell's informant, 334; Baines seeks interview with, 521, 522; succeeded by Herbert Samuel, 521n
Cobb, Richard, 29
Cockburn, Sir Alexander (Lord Chief Justice), 257
Cockerell (Bedford Prison officer), 315, 336–7
Codère, Georges, 492, 493n
coefficient of thermal expansion of brass, 210–11, 232
cold case investigations, 122, 123, 200, 458
Coles, Brian, 48
Collins, Inspector W.: Irene Savidge case, 71n; works Rouse case, 41, 44, 45, 50, 462; and 'Little Arthur' story, 191, 463–4; report on identity of blazing car victim, 111–12; enquiries into identity of victim, 114
Colney Hatch Lunatic Asylum, 123, 375
commercial travellers: little studied, 386,

388–9; and vacuum cleaner selling,
386–7, 388; and Harry Seymour
murder case (1931), 387–8; reputation
and public images of, 389–90,
412, 480; women as, 389; criminal
activities of, 390–1; associations and
representative trade bodies, 391, 392–
3; and hotels, 391; as absent voters,
392; involved in traffic accidents, 393,
394; as victims of crime, 393–4
Commercial Travellers' Benevolent
Institution, 392–3
Commercial Travellers' Benevolent
Society, 391
Commercial Travellers Society Trust
Fund, 391
committal proceedings, Rouse case:
primacy of prosecution, 132;
documents, 132; disclosure of
Crown evidence to the defence, 132;
courtroom, 131; attendance and
public interest, 135, 140, 145; Bench,
131, 133, 135, 141, 145; Rouse's first
appearance, 131; his requests for new
clothes, 133, 134, 136; his demeanour
in court, 141, 149–50; first hearing
(November 10 1930), 133; second
hearing (November 18 1930), 134;
Henry Flint intervention, 134; case
placed in hands of DPP, 134, 135; third
hearing (November 27 1930), 135–9;
Paling opens case for prosecution, 136–
9; second Hammersmith statement
read out in court, 137–8, 145; defence
objections, 137, 138; disclosures about
Rouse's private life, 137–8, 139, 153
& n; speculation as to motive, 139;
Rouse asks for aspirin, 139; moment of
levity, 139; fourth hearing (December
3 1930), 140; fifth hearing (December
9 1930), 141–4; evidence on Rouse's
journey to South Wales, 141, 142;
evidence on Rouse's hospital visit to
Nellie Tucker, 141–2; scene of crime
evidence, 143; evidence on mallet,
143, 149; testimony of Sergeant
Skelly, 143–4; defence objection to
Skelly's statement, 143–4; exchange
over Rouse's status at Hammersmith
station, 144; sixth hearing (December
15 1930), 145–50; Helen Campbell's
name disclosed, 145–6, 150;
automotive engineering evidence, 146;
medical evidence, 146; legal wrangle
over admissibility of 'bad character'
evidence, 142, 146–9; testimony of

Nellie Tucker, 149; Rouse besmirched
as philanderer and cad, 149; seventh
hearing (December 16 1930), 150–3;
testimony of Helen Campbell, 150;
testimony of Superintendent Brumby,
133, 151, 152; another legal wrangle,
151; Hammersmith statement
adduced, 151; testimony of Inspector
Lawrence, 152; defence again objects
to 'bad character' evidence, 152; final
appeal from defence counsel, 152–3;
Rouse committed for trial, 153; no
appeal mechanism, 153n; newspaper
coverage, 133, 134–5, 139–40, 141,
145, 150, 153; alleged prejudicial
evidence, 251, 264, 396, 514–16
common purpose, law of, 29
commutation, 280n
confessions: condemned cell, 328–30,
331–2, 335, 347; false, 116–17, 323–4;
death-bed, 324
Connelly, Peter ('Baby P'), 464
consumerism, 375, 382, 386, 388, 446
contempt of court, and press comment,
342–5, 349
contraception, 117, 403, 404n, 448
Cooper, Duff, *Operation Heartbreak,* 476n
Cooper, William, 298n, 308
Cooper's Arms Hotel, Ystrad Mynach,
15–16, 141, 503
Coote, Colonel Eyre, 134, 135, 145
Cope, Walter, 119
Copeland, R. B., 49
Copping, PC Harry: actions on night
of murder, 3, 4, 5, 54, 55n; takes
initial witness statements, 56–7;
incompetence and procedural failings,
57–8, 62; evidence at committal
hearing, 143; evidence at trial, 101,
163–4, 165, 167; attends burial of
Rouse's victim, 94
Corns, Cathryn, 483; *Blindfold and Alone:
British Military Executions in the Great
War* (with John Hughes-Wilson), 494,
495, 498
coroners: jurisdiction, 92; qualifications,
91
Coroners (Amendment) Act 1926, 91–2,
307
Coroners and Justice Act 2009, 285, 493
Cory, Divisional Detective (of Blackheath
Road police station), 48
Costs in Criminal Cases Act 1908, 128
cot death, 170, 250, 289
Cotton, Arthur, 208; credentials and
experience, 212; evidence at trial, 212,

213, 220, 267
Coulson, John, 309
Court of Criminal Appeal: created,
245; remit, 249, 261; grounds for
appeal, 249–50, 266; superficial
and unreasoning judgments, 262;
and 'judicial values', 263; Reeve case
(1915), 80; Beard case (1920), 264;
Scranton case (1921), 77–8; Rouse
case (1931) (*see* appeal hearing, Rouse
case); Wallace case (1931), 76n, 262–3;
Woolmington case (1935), 72–3, 264;
Bentley case (1998), 282
courts martial: and contempt of court,
343n; capital cases from the Great
War, 494–8, 499–500; and rules of
evidence, 498–9; questionable justice
and fairness, 499–501; shell-shock as
excusatory defence, 483, 494–8, 501;
and Human Rights law, 502n
Coutts, Graham, 510
Coventry IRA bombing (1939–40), 211,
283, 309
Covington, Arthur, 308
Cox, John H., 305
Cox, Thomas, 491n
Craig and Bentley case (1952–53), 76–7,
246; *see also* Bentley, Derek
Crawford and Shearon murder case
(1891), 23–4
Cream, Dr. Neill, 24, 25
credit drapers, 386, 389, 390
crime news reporting, post-war, 199–200,
320
crime wave, feared in post-First World
War Britain, 478–9, 485
Criminal Appeal Act 1907, 266, 288, 293
Criminal Cases Review Commission, 123,
283, 505
Criminal Evidence Act 1898, 222, 509–10
Criminal Justice Act 1925, 312, 313n
Criminal Justice Act 1967, 349
Criminal Justice Act 2003, 510, 513
criminal justice system: legal personnel,
66
Criminal Law Amendment Act 1922, 426
Criminal Lunatics Act 1884, 280, 285,
491n
Criminal Procedure Act 1865, 511
Criminal Procedure and Investigations
Act 1996, 132
Crippen, Cora, 26, 68, 374, 398, 467; DNA
testing of scar tissue, 103, 123; and the
suburban life, 370, 371, 373
Crippen, Dr. Hawley, 23, 24, 26, 68, 285,
373–4, 398, 467

Cripps, Alfred, 462–3
Crocker, William, 469
Crosland, T. W. H., 371
Crouch, Harriet, 81
Crown Inn, Hardingstone, 6, 56, 91, 93,
96, 98
Crown Prosecution Service, 55, 67, 515
Crown prosecutions, 67–8, 69
Crumbles murders: Irene Munro (1920),
117–18, 245, 505; Emily Kaye (1924),
20–1, 25, 41, 103
Cunnington, Arthur, 393–4
Curtis-Bennett, Sir Henry, 28, 77, 222,
271; advocacy style, 85

D. C. Thomson & Co, 433
da Costa, Sybil, 89
Dahl, Friedrich, 474, 475
Daily Express: on police organisation, 65;
coverage of Rouse case, 15, 234, 295;
contempt issue, 343, 344, 345; and
blazing car victim, 115–16; publishes
articles by Lily Rouse, 417–19
Daily Herald, 313, 485
Daily Mail: publishes 'Zinoviev letter', 248
& n; coverage of Rouse case, 6, 9, 10,
139–40, 150, 193, 194; Thomas Waite
story, 110; speculation on identity
of Rouse's victim, 122; commentary
and opinion pieces, 231 & n, 233–4;
on Rouse's final hours and execution,
313, 314, 316–17; attacks *Daily Sketch*
confession story, 321–2; deplores
disreputable newspapers, 343; 'Hurrah
for the Blackshirts' headline, 249n; on
Iraqi War damages claims, 501n
Daily Mirror, 202, 252, 304, 310
Daily Sketch: coverage of Rouse case,
10, 14–15, 17, 181; Phyllis Skinner
story, 41; reward offered, 106; pays
Helen Campbell's legal expenses,
187; publishes Rouse's murder
confession (11 March 1931), 311,
319–20, 327; reaction to confession
story, 320; further details published,
320–1, 325; reveals car frauds
perpetrated by Rouse, 322, 468–9;
reveals Agnes Kesson inspiration,
469–70; attacked by *Daily Mail,* 321–2;
Cannell's response, 322–3; veracity of
confession, 323, 324–5, 341; attacked
by *Sunday Dispatch,* 325; source of
confession, 322, 327, 328; Home Office
response, 331–2, 335; Cannell offers
corroboration for confession, 334–5,
342; view of prison authorities, 335–6;

John Bull seeks to discredit confession, 345–8; *see also* Cannell, J. C.
Daily Telegraph, 9, 10, 95, 264, 329, 332
Daily Worker, 235–6, 247
Daley, Harry, 12, 18
Damerel, Henry, 8
Dando, Jill, 23
Darling, Mr. Justice (*later* Baron Darling): flamboyant figure, 89; Steinie Morrison trial, 511n; Georges Codère trial, 492; Elizabeth Perfect trial, 390; George Lucas trial, 488; Lords debate on Rouse case, 343–4, 345
Darnell & Price (Northampton solicitors), 74, 129, 140, 254, 290, 320
Dartmoor Prison mutiny (1932), 520
Darwin, Mr. and Mrs. John, 458 & n
Davenport, Mrs. H., 121
Davenport, Tom, 121
Davies, C. H. (coroner), 91, 92
Davies, Dr. G. Meredith, 129, 131, 307, 317
Davies, Robert, 394
Dawson, Jill, *Fred & Edie,* 27
Day, Colonel Harry, 334
Day, Jack, 308
de Clifford, Lord, 459n
de Leon, Mr. and Mrs. (of Hendon), 48
de Wilde, H. (Dutch engineer), 237, 268
death and bereavement, attitudes towards, 96
death-bed confessions, 324
death penalty *see* capital punishment
Deats, Frederick, 470, 471
defence of provocation, 264–5
Deloittes, 522–3
Derham, John, 83
desertion, 483–4
detectives: formal training, 60–3, 64; on the job learning, 60; skills and qualities, 58–60; memoirs by, 12n, 59–60
detention without trial, 82
Diary of a Nursing Sister (Anon), 365
Dickens, Charles, 92, 103n, 159
Dickens, William, 178, 267
Dickey, Jacob, 270
Dickson, Robert: writes on Rouse case, 211
diet: civilian during Great War, 389n
diminished responsibility, 285, 328, 489n, 493–4
Director of Public Prosecutions (DPP): role and duties, 67–9; and Rouse case, 68, 132; poisoning cases, 70n; powers of investigation, 70–1, 71n; *see also* Atkinson, E. H. Tindal

dismemberment, 103–4; *see also* specific cases
divorce, 402, 421
divorce hearings, reporting of, 313n
Dixon Millar & Co., 49
DNA testing, 125, 170, 277, 308–9; blazing car victim, 96, 122; homicide cold cases, 103, 123, 308–9
Dobkin, Harry, 84n, 99n
Dobkin, Rachel, 99n, 103, 104
dock brief procedure, 80, 520
domestic violence, 432, 525–6
Dominion of Canada car insurance policy, 459, 460
'dope girls', 403
Dougal, Samuel, 26, 523
Dowler, Milly, 23
Doyle, Arthur Conan, 27
DPP v Beard [1920] AC 479, 264
drapery trade, 386, 389, 390
dressing stations, 365
drunkenness, factor in homicide, 24, 264, 279, 496, 497
Du Cann, Richard, *The Art of the Advocate,* 86
du Rose, John, 12n
Duffy, John ('railway rapist'), 375
Duncan, Helen, 118
Dunning, Mark, *Murderous Tommies* (with Julian Putkowski), 494, 495, 497
Durand-Deacon, Olive, 51, 104

Earl, Sergeant (of Northampton Borough Police), 55
Early, Julie, 370
earthquake, Tokyo (1923), 239
East Midland Forensic Science Laboratory, Nottingham, 121–2
Eastgate, Harold (as Rouse's victim), 116
Eastgate, Rhoda, 116
Eccles, David, 23
Eck, Captain, 86
Eclipse car insurance policy, 183, 459–60, 467–8, 477
Economic Motor Insurance Company, 460
Edalji, George, 508
Eddleston, John, *Murderous Manchester,* 23, 30 & n
Eddowes, Catherine: shawl, 123
Ede, James Chuter, 280
Edward VII, King, 13
Edward VIII, King *(earlier* Prince of Wales): and hat wearing, 2n; love affair with Marguerite Alibert (*later* Fahmy), 411; visit to South America, 392; in Abdication crisis, 398n, 402

Edwards, Russell, 123n
Eleanor crosses, 168
electricity: domestic supply, 382
Elliott, George, 523
Ellis, Havelock, 410
Ellis, Ruth: trial, 86; publicity and
newspaper coverage, 312; as 'tainted'
woman, 410, 412, 524; execution, 252,
318 & n; cold case examination, 200;
referred to Court of Appeal, 505
Ellis & Buckle Ltd (fire loss assessors),
171, 238; see also Buckle, Colonel
Cuthbert
Elmer, Netta Jean, 471
Elwes, Major Geoffrey, 145
Elwes, Polly, 87
Elwes, Richard, 68, 87, 145, 164, 180, 181
Emsley, Clive, 479, 486, 488
'Enery' (correspondent), 113–14
Engel, Howard, Crimes of Passion, 29
Engels, Frederick, 1–2
English Justice ('Solicitor'), 75, 76n, 287
English Mistery (fascist organisation),
475
Esler, Dr. M. S., 483
Estates of Deceased Persons (Forfeiture
Rules and Law of Succession) Act 2012,
468n
Evans, Aidan, 121
Evans, Inspector (of Glamorgan police),
150
Evans, Timothy, 109, 200, 280, 281, 283,
324, 480, 493, 505
Evening News, 5–6, 7, 9–10, 139, 141–2,
158, 185, 313, 314, 320
Evening Standard, 313, 471, 519
evidence: non-disclosure to defence, 132,
242
ex-servicemen: and crime, 478–9, 485–6,
485n, 487–92, 504–5; effects of First
World War on, 525
excreta: at crime scene, 126, 166, 200–1;
on shirt, 201, 253
executions: as morbid and corrupting
spectacles, 318; history of, at Bedford
Prison, 80, 308–9; of Alfred Rouse, 307,
316–18, 325–6; of Edith Thompson, 20,
440; of Henry Seymour, 388; of Maria
Manning, 159; of Ruth Ellis, 252, 318
& n; Koestler and Rolph's study, 279;
wartime, 281, 301, 304, 483–4, 501;
see also capital punishment
expert witnesses: role and rules of
evidence, 170–1, 203; qualifications,
207, 210n; fallibility, 233; fees and
expenses, 128

eyewitness identification evidence, 320n

Fahmy, Marguerite, 83, 227, 411, 468, 530
'faking own death', 458 & n
false confessions, 116–17, 323–4
Famous Trials series (Geoffrey Bles),
32–3, 479
Farmer, Eric, 12; evidence at trial, 179,
180–1
fashion, men's, 1–2
female chastity, 405, 406, 410
Ferguson, Major Robert, 485–6
Festubert, Battle of (1915), 355, 359, 361,
363, 365, 497
field ambulances, 365, 366
Field and Gray murder case (1920), 117–
18, 230, 245, 505
Fielding, Henry: on grand juries, 157n
Fields, Gracie, 402
Figg, Captain Douglas, 360, 363
Findlay, Lance-Sergeant Alec, 502n
fingerprint analysis, 52, 60n, 61, 277–8
Finlay, Mr. Justice, 98, 520
Finnemore, Donald: legal and political
career, 78; represents Rouse at police
court, 76, 132, 134, 137–8, 139, 142,
143–4, 146–7, 151, 152–3; defends
Rouse at trial, 76; challenges women
trial jurors, 160; cross-examinations,
57, 101, 165–7, 168, 175–7, 180,
182; legal objection to Nellie Tucker's
testimony, 148n, 179; submits 'no
case to answer' plea, 184–5, 186;
opening address for defence, 186, 187;
re-examines Rouse, 197; case for the
defence, 32, 202–4, 206–7, 208–9,
211–12, 213, 215n; closing speech,
178n, 216–17; disappointed at trial
verdict, 242; criticised by Rouse, 242,
254, 273–4, 288; immunity from being
sued, 254; receives fresh evidence
supporting defence case, 237–8,
240–1; drafts grounds for appeal, 266,
267–8, 271; petitions for clemency,
31–2; presides over Christie trial, 32
Firmin, Stanley, 199
First World War, 96; effects, 478–9, 485,
525; family loss and mourning, 107,
118; spiritualist belief in aftermath,
117
Fleeson, James: murder of, 24n
Flint, Henry: represents Helen Campbell,
88; retains Sidney Campion,
87; watching brief at committal
proceedings, 134, 135; names Helen
Campbell, 145–6, 150; represents

Phyllis Skinner, 41; photographed outside police court, 140; and Arthur Jnr's alleged statement, 463
Flying Squad, 381, 478–9
forensic science, 103–4, 105, 121–2, 123, 233, 277–8
Foster, Evelyn: murder of, 63, 233, 471
Foucault, Michel, 404–5
Fox, Sidney Harry, 391
France, war in 1915, 354–63
Francis (fake jewellery salesman), 512
Francis, Martin, 529
Franklin, W. B., 264
Fred (Helen Campbell's business partner), 44–5
Fremantle, Colonel F. E., 348–9
French, Gen. Sir John, 354, 357
Friern Barnet, 374–5; route to Hardingstone, 167–9; see also Buxted Road (No. 14)

Galbraith application, 183–4, 249
Galsworthy, John, The Man of Property, 2
Game, Mary, 48
Gardiner, A. G., 230, 300, 301
Gardiner, Juliet, The Thirties, 380
Gardner, James, 312, 326, 331
Gellygaer, Monmouthshire, 10, 13–15, 106, 150, 430, 434–6, 437, 527
George V, King, 2n, 21, 318
'German Rouse' cases, 32, 472–5
Gibbs, Sir Philip, 232, 370, 371, 372, 485; England Speaks, 378
Gibson, Gay: murder of, 102n, 118
Gilbert, Arthur Charles (as Rouse's victim), 121
Gilbert, Lucy, 304
Gilchrist, Marion, 24–5, 27, 397
Giles, Judy, 406–7, 409
Gillingham Street, Victoria, 20, 39 & n, 41, 43, 142, 434
Givenchy, Battle of (1915), 355, 359–62, 363
Gladstone, Herbert, 282–3
Glasgow CID, 108
Glasgow Herald, 323
Glasgow Weekly News, 'Rouse's Last Visit: My Escape from Poisoning', 305, 433
Goddard, Rayner (Lord Chief Justice), 246, 306, 333
Goodstein, Alexander, 391
Goodwin, PC, 23
'gothic' elements in classic murder cases, 24–5
Gowers Committee on Capital Punishment (1949–53), 278, 291

Graham, Alan, 302–3
Graham, John, 179, 182
grand jury system, 157–8
Grant, Duncan, 18
Grant, Lt Col Duncan, 476
Grattan-Doyle, Sir Nicholas, 345, 349
Gray, Frank, 108 & n
Grayson, Victor, 88n
'Great Arson Conspiracy', 469
Great Train Robbery (1963), 58, 103n, 211
Green, Moss, 38
'Green Bicycle' case (1919), 81, 83
Greenwood, David, 483n, 505n
Greenwood, Harold, 83
Greer, Mr. Justice, 488
Grellier, Captain Bernard, 495
Gribble, James, 187
Grierson, Dr. Hugh, 129–31
Griffith-Jones, Mervyn, 71n, 87
Gross, Hans, Criminal Investigation: A Practical Textbook, 233n
Grossmith, George and Weedon, The Diary of a Nobody, 370, 377
Guardian Weekend (magazine), 23
'Guildford Four', 324
Guildhall police court, 45
guilty clients, advocating for, 76
Gull, Sir William, 318n
Guthrie, Lord, 396–7
Gutteridge, PC George: murdered on duty, 64–5, 381, 468
Gwilliam, F. W.: and Rouse's 'Own Life Story' article, 127, 230; at Rouse's trial, 159; denies disturbances at prison in run up to execution, 310–11; Rouse confesses to, 335–6, 337–9; releases Rouse's final correspondence, 335; at Rouse's execution, 307, 317; testifies at Rouse's inquest, 307; refutes press stories, 313–14, 318; on Rouse's supposed confession to chaplain, 326; on Daily Sketch confession story, 335–6

Hadfield, Albert, 82
Haig, Sir Douglas, 354, 356
Haigh, John George, 27, 51, 104, 199, 377
Hall, Frank, 115
Hall, Radclyffe, The Well of Loneliness, 71, 522
Hall, Samantha, 122
Hamilton, Cicely, 419n
Hammersmith police station, 17–19
Hanratty, James, 24, 308–9
Hardingstone, Northamptonshire, 3
Hardingstone Church: burial of Rouse's

victim, 93–5; pilgrimages to gravesite, 112

Hardingstone Lane: crime scene, 1, 3–4, 5, 6, 10–11, 57, 325; excreta found, 126, 166, 200–1; location, 163; police search, 93

Hardman, Edward, 102–3

'harem' speech, 19–20, 138, 396, 415

Harewood House, near Leeds, 367

Harlesden police station, 115

Harris, Leopold, 469

Harris, Sergeant Joe: at crime scene, 6, 164; discovers mallet, 143; evidence at committal hearing, 149, 150; evidence at trial, 164; attends burial of Rouse's victim, 94

Hart, Charles (as Rouse's victim), 116

Harvey, Cyril, 78

Harvey-Wyatt, Dr. R. B.: examines excreta, 253; evidence at trial, 98–9, 201, 222; and Rachel Dobkin case, 99n

Hastings, Sir Patrick: early career as journalist, 87; legal and political career, 70n, 247–9; advocacy style, 84–5, 86; appointed Attorney-General, 247; and Campbell case (1924), 247–8; prosecutes Vaquier (1924), 249n; defends Rouse at Court of Criminal Appeal, 239, 243, 254–9, 261; on Norman Birkett, 81–2; writes on Hewart, 244; writes on Avory, 245; writes on Rouse case, 32; defends Elvira Barney, 411 & n

Hatherill, George, 58, 72, 103n

hats and hattedness, 1–2, 12–13, 12n, 20–1, 181, 197, 253

Hatton, Lily, 393

Hayman, Mr. (of Sale) (as Rouse's victim), 119

Healey, Denis, 2

heat transfer theory, 174–5, 202, 208, 210, 212, 237–9, 240; jury question on, 213; Buckle disputes, 215

Heath, Colonel E. C., 303

Heath, Neville, 26, 27, 72n, 199

Hendon Police College, 60n, 61, 64

Henry B. (as Rouse's victim), 113–14

Hermann, Marie, 83

Hertfordshire police, 106

Hewart, Sir Gordon (Lord Chief Justice): early career as journalist, 87; and Holt case, 488; reputation as appellate judge, 243–4, 244n, 262, 305–6; and Hobbs case (1925), 342n; presides at Rouse appeal, 239, 243, 259, 260, 261–2; judgment in Wallace case (1931),

262–3; declines to offer private opinion on jury verdict, 305; view on post-trial press coverage, 343–4, 345; biography of, 32, 243

Hichens, Robert, Bella Donna, 28, 226, 227

Hinton and Britton's (coach operator), Cardiff, 16

hire purchase, 382, 388

'history from below', 30

'hitch-hiker to Plymouth' (as Rouse's victim), 115

Hitchcock, James, 22

Hoare, Captain Louis, 497

Hoare, Sir Samuel, 280

Hobbs case (1925), 342 & n, 343, 344

Hobsbawm, Eric: on tramping, 105

Hodges, Inspector (of Cardiff police), 16

Hodgson, Herbert, 363

Hogg, Sir Douglas, 84n, 342n

Hogg, Quintin, 246

Holcroft, Leigh (as Rouse's victim), 116

Holden, Wendy, Shell Shock, 483

Holloway, Roland: evidence at trial, 215n

Holloway Prison, 304, 318; maternity ward, 235n

Holmes, Richard, Tommy: The British Soldier on the Western Front, 357

Holocaust victims, 293, 402n

Holt, Lieutenant Frederick, 488–9, 493

Home Office, Report of the Departmental Committee on Detective Work and Procedure, 60–2

Homicide Act 1957, 280, 285, 328, 489n, 493

homicide rates, 30, 32n

homosexuality, 269, 281, 284n, 337, 338, 390, 522

Hornsey, Richard, The Spiv and the Architect: Unruly Life in Postwar London, 386n, 528n

horror, and murder causes célèbres, 26

Horwell, Chief Inspector John, 387

Hosein, Arthur and Nizamodeen, 102n

Houlbrook, Matt, 124, 338n

Howard, Elizabeth Jane, 405

Howard, John, 310

Howard League for Penal Reform, 519

Hughes-Wilson, John, Blindfold and Alone: British Military Executions in the Great War (with Cathryn Corns), 494, 495, 498

Hull, E. M., The Sheik, 408, 530

Hulten, Karl, 28–9, 124, 286n, 372

Hume, Donald, 26, 52, 104, 489

Humphreys, Christmas, 246

Humphreys, Sir Travers (Mr. Justice): legal career and reputation as judge, 67, 71, 245–6; and Campbell case (1924), 248; presides at Rouse appeal, 243, 244; and Elvira Barney trial (1932), 255, 412n; writes on Avory, 245–6

Humphries, Steve, 401, 402, 406, 408

Humphry, Mrs., *Manners for Women,* 399

Hunter, Dr. Joseph, 300–1

Hurst, J. G., 79

Hutchison, Lt Col Graham Seton *see* Seton, Graham

Huxley, Aldous, *Brave New World,* 531

identity theft of dead children, 95n

illegitimacy, 397, 404, 405–6, 446–50

Incitement to Disaffection Act 1797, 248

Incorporated Sales Managers' Association, 392

Indictable Offences Act 1848, 264

infant witnesses, 191

infanticide, 92, 278

inquest on body of Rouse's victim, 91–3

inquests: criminal proceedings, adjournment for, 92

insanity: as factor in reprieve process, 285; and hanging, 280–1, 491n; and irresistible impulse, 488–9, 489n; legal definition, 486–7, 493 & n; *see also* diminished responsibility; McNaghten Rules

insurance: forfeiture rule in spousal killing cases, 467–8 & n

intoxication *see* drunkenness, factor in homicide

Iraq War: damages claims against MOD, 501n

irresistible impulse plea, 488–9, 489n

Irving, H. B., 30

Isaacs, Arthur: credentials and experience, 208, 213; offers his services *gratis,* 202; evidence at trial, 207–12; judge's censure of, 220; possibly Jewish, 212n

Isaacs, Rufus (Lord Reading), 77–8, 244, 488–9; advocacy style, 84, 85

Islington Gazette, 318

It Ain't Half Hot, Mum (TV programme), 260

Jack the Ripper: infamy, 23, 27; and hatred of prostitutes, 25; unknown identity and suspects, 26, 123, 318n, 330n, 375, 516, 523; as social reformer, 371

Jackson, Robert: writes on Hewart,

243, 244n; *Case for the Prosecution: A Biography of Sir Archibald Bodkin,* 69–70

Jackson, Tricia, 533

Jackson, William *see* Baines, Cecil

Jacoby, Henry, 270–1, 491n

James, Lawrence, *The Middle Class: A History,* 378–9

James, P. D., 32, 534

Janner, Greville, 69n

Jeffreys, Sheila, 409

Jenkins, Ivy ('Paddie'): early life in Gellygaer, 435–6; first meets Rouse, 433–4, 436; bogus marriage and pregnancy, 434; honeymoon, 435; love letter from Rouse, 436; cooling feelings, 436–7; Rouse visits after murder, 14, 437–8; statement to police, 14; ill-health and poisoning claim, 305, 433, 438, 439–40, 453, 454; and Rouse's plans to disappear, 52; still-born child, 53, 441n; possible miscarriage, 440; articles in *Thomson's Weekly News,* 433–4, 435–41, 453–4; forgets and erases Rouse, 53

Jenkins, Phyllis, 15, 435, 438, 439; evidence at committal hearing, 150; evidence at trial, 179

Jenkins, Roy, 281, 298

Jenkins, Trevor, 15

Jenkins, William, 13, 14, 15, 430; evidence at committal hearing, 150; evidence at trial, 179, 182

Jenner, Heather, 400

Jew as Criminal, The (anti-Semitic text), 473n

Jews and Jewishness, 212n, 423n; *see also* anti-Semitism

John Bull (journal), 301, 345–8

Johnson, Sergeant Bertie, 165n

Johnson, Fred, 44–5

Johnston, Dr. Ian, 210–11

joint criminal enterprise, 29

Jones, Mrs. (Alfred's wife), 70–1

Jones, Alfred, 69–70

Jones, Alfred William, 375

Jones, Arthur Albert, 513

Jones, Elizabeth, 28–9, 124, 286n, 372

Jones, Hattie, 42

Jones, Joan, 42–4

Jowitt, Sir William (Lord Chancellor), 83, 264, 342–3, 517

Joyce, William (Lord Haw-Haw), 27, 82

Joynson-Hicks, William, 235n, 392

judges: biographical studies of, 246–7; directions to juries, 223, 255–6, 297n,

508 & n, 518n; judicial values, 263; 'slumming' on circuit, 389; *see also* names of individual judges
Judges' Rules, 58, 61, 151, 520
juries: directions from Bench, 223, 255–6, 297n, 508 & n, 518n; fairness of trial by, 256; overnight adjournments, 272; recommendations for mercy, 285, 291; response to female defendants in murder cases, 410–12; trial by jury system, 249; women allowed to sit on, 160; wrong or ill-formed decision making, 508; *see also* grand juries
Juries Act 1974, 272n
jury in Rouse trial: peremptory challenges, 160, 397; list of juror names, 160n; and mallet evidence, 198; questions from, 214; witness factors influencing verdict, 212, 232–3; attitude to Rouse's immoral record, 396, 410, 412, 517; juror factors influencing verdict, 225, 396–7, 517–19; grasp of technical evidence, 232; directions from Bench, 255–6; deliberations, 224, 259; verdict, 224; exempted from future jury service, 224; independence of, 233–4; public debate over verdict, 231–5; present-day jury unlikely to convict, 509
Justice of the Peace (magazine), 344, 515–16, 517

Kabat, Wenzel, 104–5
Kaye, Emily: murder of (1924), 20–1, 25, 41, 103
Kaye, Violette, 81, 103n, 104
Kellie-MacCallum, Chief Constable James, 4–5, 10, 55, 65, 132
Kempson, Louisa: murder of (1931), 387–8
Kendal, Norman, 522
Kennedy, Denis, 183, 301n; evidence at trial, 460
Kennedy, Helena, 87
Kennedy, John F., 2n
Kennedy, Ludovic, 200
Kennedy, William *see* Browne and Kennedy murder case (1927)
Kent, Constance, 24, 64n, 371n, 525n
Kermode, Mark, 533
Kesson, Agnes: unsolved murder case (1930), 319, 469–70, 471
Keyworth, Lance-Corporal Leonard, 361–3
Kilpatrick, James, 522–3
Kingsley Long, H., 345

Kipling, Rudyard, 117, 429
Kipnik, Erich, 473, 474–5
Kiszko, Stefan, 324, 508
Knight, Private Charles, 494–6
Knott, Mirza, 429, 450, 451
Knutsford, Lord, 328–9, 332
Koestler, Arthur, *Hanged by the Neck* (with C. H. Rolph), 279
Kosminski, Aaron, 123, 375
Kürten, Peter, 13

Labour government (1924), 247–8
Lady Chatterley trial, 71n, 87
Lake, Madeleine, 323–4
Lanchester, Edith, 448
Land, Alfred, 323–4
Langford, William (as Rouse's victim), 116
Lansbury, George, 310
Larkin, Philip, 408
Law Journal, 292, 299, 302
Lawrence, D. H., 71 & n, 87; 'England, My England' (short story), 363–4
Lawrence, Inspector James: actions on night of murder, 4, 5, 6, 54, 56; fails to secure and preserve crime scene, 6–7, 56–8; incompetence and procedural failings, 57–8, 62; search for Rouse, 8; communication with Hammersmith police, 16–17; interviews Rouse, 18–19, 169; escorts Rouse to Northampton, 19; Rouse confides in, 19; charges Rouse with murder, 20; promoted Superintendent, 119; evidence at committal hearing, 152; evidence at trial, 57, 169; attends burial of Rouse's victim, 94
Lawrence, Lord Justice, 83
Le Neve, Ethel, 26, 229n, 373, 398
Lee-Roberts, George: appointed Rouse's solicitor, 21, 74, 126; views body and inspects blaze site, 126; and prison photographs of Rouse, 21 & n, 126–7, 128; authorised to sell Rouse's house and contents, 127; complains to Home Secretary, 128–9; briefs Finnemore, 134; photographed outside police court, 140; assisted by Darnell & Price, 140; last-minute interview with Rouse before trial, 159; denies knowledge of *News of the World* story, 230; conduct of defence, 254; prepares formal petition, 290, 299
Lee, Inspector, 119
Lee, Carol Ann, *A Fine Day for a Hanging: The Real Ruth Ellis Story*, 318 & n
Lee Doon, 309

legal aid, 74–6, 127n, 249, 402, 520–1
Legitimacy Act 1926, 450
Leicester University, 122
Lenny, William, 114
Lesage, Alain-René, 291
Lesser, Louis, 391
Lewis, Philippa, *Everyman's Castle,* 369
Ley, Thomas, 199
License, James, 393
Light, Ronald, 81, 83, 505n
Lilley, PC David, 18, 111, 141, 167;
    evidence at trial, 180–1, 197
limitation period for murder, 118
Lincoln, Trebitsch (John Lincoln), 333–4
Line, J. P., 238
Lipski, Israel, 332 & n
Liverpool: child-on-child murders, 23–4
Liverpool Road (No 284), Islington, 35,
    44, 144–5, 377, 427
Lloyd George, David, 357
Locke, A. (Home Office clerk), 331, 334,
    335, 341–2, 346
London: anti-German riots (1915), 360n
London Ambulance Column, 366–7
London Gazette, 361
Lord Mayor's Show: elephant stampede
    (1930), 133
Lovat-Fraser, James, 310
Lovelock (East Barnet bull-shitter),
    119–20
Lucas, Private (of Devonshire Regiment),
    364, 481–2
Lucas, George, 488, 493
Lucas direction, 223, 297n, 518n
Ludovici, Anthony, 475; *Woman: A
    Vindication,* 404
Lustgarten, Edgar, 504
Lustgarten, James, 504
Lyon, F. H., 318

MacDonald, Ramsay, 248, 303, 450, 521n
Machin, Sir Stanley, 392–3
MacKinnon, Sir Frank, 89
Macmillan, Dorothy, 405
MacRae, Andrew, 186–7
Macready, Sir Nevil, 486
Magdala Arms, Hampstead, 412 & n
Magdalene homes, 405, 449
'magical transformation' through
    homicide, 25
magistrates' court: legal aid provision,
    74–6
Mahon, Patrick, 20–1, 24, 25, 41, 103,
    245, 532
Maidstone Jail, 113
Makin case, 512, 514, 516

malice aforethought, 251, 339, 457 & n
mallet: owned by Rouse, 13, 143; as
    possible attack weapon, 97, 99, 187;
    found by Sergeant Harris, 143, 149;
    conflicting evidence about, 152–3, 189,
    194, 218; exhibited at trial, 198, 220;
    judge disregards as evidence, 194, 198;
    preserved after trial, 112n, 314
'Man Who Never Was, The' (Allied
    disinformation campaign), 301–2 & n,
    476 & n
Manchester: twentieth century murders
    in, 23, 30 & n
Manchester Guardian, 332
Mancini, Tony, 81, 103n, 332
Mancini, Tony 'Baby-face', 264–5
Mander, Geoffrey, 349
Mango Books, 24
Manning, Maria: execution of, 159
Mansfield, Michael, 87
Manual of Military Law, 498 & n
Manuel, Peter, 256n, 285
Margate: Hotel Metropole, 391
'marital coercion' defence, 458n, 459n
Marjoribanks, Edward, 84n, 331
Mark Green & Co. (tailors), 38
Markham, Major C. A., 133, 134, 135, 141,
    145
Marks, Laurence, 200
Marriner, Brian, *Forensic Clues to Murder,*
    25
Marshall, Archie Pellow: legal and
    political career, 78–9; defends Rouse at
    trial, 76, 187–8, 189–92; disappointed
    at trial verdict, 242; immunity from
    being sued, 254; receives fresh
    evidence supporting defence case, 238;
    drafts grounds for appeal, 266, 268;
    petitions for clemency, 31–2
Marshall Hall, Sir Edward: Camden Town
    Murder case (1907), 163; Brides
    in the Bath case (1915), 512; Holt
    case (1920), 488–9; 'Green Bicycle'
    case (1920), 81; Fahmy case (1923),
    227, 468; Vaquier case (1924), 70n;
    advocacy style, 83–4, 85
Martinez, Ancieto, 309
masculinity, 412–13, 524–32
Mason, Alexander Campbell, 270
Mass Observation, 407, 408
Massey, Rev. J. D., 94
Masterman, C. F. G., 374, 376
Mathew, Sir Theobald, 68
Mathews, Sir Charles, 68–9, 522
Maude, Captain G. C., 354, 355, 358,
    360–1, 363

Mawrey, Richard: on door-to-door
  salesmen, 386
Maxwell, Sir Alexander, 273, 297, 310,
  326
Maxwell-Fyfe, David, 246
Maybrick, Florence, 467, 516
Maybrick, James, 516
Mayhew, Henry, 159
Mayne, Ralph Mortimer, 116–17
McCardie, Henry (Mr. Justice): on
  demeanour of defendants, 225; on
  Horace Avory, 245
McCarthy, Michael, 104–5
McClure, James, *Killers,* 478
McKay, George, 247
McKay, Muriel, 102n, 118
McLaren, Angus, 29n
McNaghten, Daniel, 486
McNaghten Rules, 89, 285, 486–7, 488–9,
  492n, 505
Mead, Robert, 344
Meadley, Robert, *Classics in Murder,* 24, 27
Meadow, Professor Sir Roy, 170, 250, 289
Meads, H. C. (as Rouse's victim), 115
Meaney, T. C., 115–16
Meehan, Patrick, 200
Mellor, Brigadier-General Gilbert, 495
memoirs of detectives, 59–60
Memory, F. W., 233–4
men *see* masculinity
men's clothing styles, 1–2
mens rea, 457, 495–6
Mental Deficiency Act 1913, 405, 449
mental instability, as factor in reprieve
  process, 285
mercy, prerogative of, 66n, 267, 278,
  280–3
Merthyr Tydfil police station, 109
Messiter, Vivian, 235, 286
Metropolitan Police: enquiries at Buxted
  Road, 8–9, 10; Rouse intercepted at
  Hammersmith, 16–17, 62, 193; closed
  file related to Rouse case, 123; *see also*
  Scotland Yard
Michael, Glyndwr ('Major Martin'), 302n
middle classes: car ownership, 382;
  clothing and headgear, 2; consumer
  purchases, 375, 382, 388; home
  ownership, 376; and pre-marital sex,
  407–8
'Middlesbrough man' (as Rouse's victim),
  106, 110–11, 337, 340
military executions, wartime, 281, 301,
  304, 483–4, 501
Miller, Richard, 390, 391
Miller, Russell, 33

Mills, Herbert, 200n
Milne, A. A., 232
Milton, Mr. H. (husband of Harriet),
  345–6, 348
Milton, Harriet, 44–6
Ministry of Munitions, 207, 357
miscarriages of justice, 27, 82, 200, 242,
  505–6, 508; and Rouse case, 348, 508,
  519, 532, 534; *see also* Beck, Adolph;
  Bentley, Derek; Evans, Timothy; Slater,
  Oscar
missing persons: of Depression years,
  124; incidence, 105, 112
Mitford, Diana, 402
Mitford, Nancy, *Wigs on the Green,* 398,
  409
Mogford, Detective Constable (of Scotland
  Yard), 44
Molseed, Leslie, 324
Monjoin, Octave (and family), 107
Montgomery, John, *The Twenties,* 380
Montgomery Hyde, H., *Norman Birkett:
  The Life of Lord Birkett of Ulverston,* 80
Moore, Alan, 32; 'I Travel in Suspenders',
  168
Moore, Thomas, 496–7
Moorfield, S. H., 238–9
Moors Murders, 23, 118
'moral hygiene' movement, 401–2, 405,
  449
Moran, Lord, *The Anatomy of Courage,* 484
Mordechai, John, 393
Morgan, Frank, 391
Morris (motor manufacturer), 383
Morris, David, 15; evidence at committal
  hearing, 141
Morris, Idwal, 15–16, 503; evidence at
  committal hearing, 141
Morris Minor (car): launched (1928), 383
Morris Minor (MM 9043), 460 & n
Morris Minor (MU 1468): purchased
  by Rouse, 383; running costs, 460;
  insurance history, 459–60, 468, 477;
  repair work, 383–4; ablaze, 1, 3–4;
  scene of incident, 4, 5–7; tyre marks,
  5, 167, 198–9; corpse inside, 4, 5, 54;
  position of body, 5, 97–8, 100–1, 258–
  9, 287–8, 290; body removed from, 6,
  56, 91, 97–8; wreckage manhandled
  onto verge, 6, 56–8, 288; wreckage
  disturbed, 6–7, 56, 206, 215n, 257;
  items recovered from wreckage, 93,
  116, 287, 289, 290n; debris removed
  to Angel Lane station, 91, 171; traced
  to Rouse, 7; technical and mechanical
  evidence on fire, 170, 172–8, 189, 201–

13, 214–15, 220–1, 232, 237–9, 240–1, 268, 273–7, 287–8, 289; *see also* petrol union joint
Morrison, Blake, 23
Morrison, Herbert, 286 & n
Morrison, Stinie, 387n, 511 & n
Morriss, Hayley, 81
Mortimer, John: *Famous Trials,* 229; *Rumpole and the Penge Bungalow Murders,* 369 & n
Morton, Frederick, 471
Mosley, Oswald, 82, 402, 475
motive for killing, and homicide law, 294
motor bandits, 64, 381
motor cars and motoring: post-war appeal, 380; ownership, 380, 382–3; and motor bandits, 64, 381; insurance, 459; development and use, 382–3; repair and maintenance, 383; road traffic casualty statistics, 384–6, 393, 394; policing, 385
Moulton, John Fletcher, 1st Baron, 207
Muir, Sir Richard, 71, 85, 270
Müller, Franz, 332
Mullin, Chris, 200
Munro, Irene: murder of (1920), 117–18, 245, 505
murder *causes célèbres,* 22–31, 370, 488–92; Rouse case as, 25–6, 31–3, 229–30
'murder gang' (crime reporters), 167, 199
Murder on the Second Floor (play), 422n
murder rates, 30, 32n
Murfitt, William, 534n
Musgrave, Rev. Walter, 325–7, 339, 348
'Musical Milkman' trial (1920), 160
Myers, Charles: article on shell shock, 483n

National Coalition government, 521n
National Union of Commercial Travellers, 391, 392
Neasham (probationer constable), 4
Nelson, William Charles (as Rouse's victim), 116
neurasthenia: state pension payments, 502
Neuve Chapelle, Battle of (1915), 356–7, 365
New Dictionary of National Biography, 243, 245, 247
'New Man', 371, 412
'New Woman', 29, 371, 403, 524
Newport Pagnell police, 4
News Chronicle, 291
News of the World: coverage of sex and crime, 199, 229, 397, 401; coverage

of Rouse case, 91; buys copyright of Rouse prison photograph, 127; publishes 'Rouse's Own Life Story' (February 1 1930), 226, 227–9, 230, 441 & n, 527–8; reports confession by Rouse (March 8 1931), 320, 321; publishes Lily's supposed account of her husband's confession (March 15 1931), 327–8, 331, 335, 341–2, 347; Ruxton story, 200; Mancini article, 81, 103n, 332
Newsam, Sir Frank, 285, 329, 334
Nicholls, Superintendent (of Scotland Yard), 116
Nicholson, Elizabeth, 49
Nicholson, Otho, 49
'no case to answer' submission, 183–15
Nodder, Frederick, 82
Normanton, Helena: background, 33n; edits Helen Duncan trial for Jarrolds, 118n; *see also Trial of Alfred Arthur Rouse* (Normanton)
North Finchley, 374–5; *see also* Tally Ho Corner, Finchley
Northampton Borough Police, 4–5, 55, 119
Northampton Daily Chronicle, 131, 134, 140, 145
Northampton General Hospital, 91, 94
Northampton Herald, 94, 122
Northampton magistrates' court, 131
Northampton police station *see* Angel Lane police station, Northampton
Northamptonshire Assize court, 158–9
Northamptonshire County Police: territorial divisions and manpower, 55–6; at scene of blazing car incident, 4–6, 54–5, 56; operational and procedural shortcomings, 6–7, 8, 41, 56–8, 62; jurisdiction over Rouse enquiry, 62–3; Scotland Yard not called in, 7, 10, 62–3, 65; enquiries, 4, 7–8, 9; efforts to identify blazing car victim, 105–6; bombarded with unsolicited letters from public, 106–7; archives, 112n, 113, 314–15; sends Rouse file to forensics lab in Nottingham, 121–2; absorbs borough force, 55; approached by Briggs descendants, 122
Northamptonshire police archives: Rouse artefacts, 112n, 113, 314–15
Northamptonshire Regiment, 135, 354, 358
Northern General Hospital, Leeds, 367
'not proven' verdict in Scotland, 300, 518, 519 & n

Notable British Trials series (William Hodge & Co), 24 & n, 30, 32, 332n, 489, 532n; *see also Trial of Alfred Arthur Rouse* (Normanton)
Nuremberg trials, 83

O'Connor, Terence, 86
Odgers, Captain Walter Blake, 498
Odham's Press, 342 & n
O'Halloran, John (as Rouse's victim), 120-1
Oldridge, M. W., *Trial of Israel Lipski,* 332n
Once a Week broadcasts (Birkett), 82
Onions, Arthur, 119
Operation Mincemeat, 301-2 & n, 476 & n
Orwell, George: 'Decline of the English Murder', 229-30, 320, 370, 372n; *Coming Up for Air,* 377
Overy, Richard, 404n
Owen, Wilfred, 95
Oxford Prison, 388
Oxley, Frederick, 120

Pace, Beatrice, 72, 81, 124, 410-11 & n, 517
Paling, Gerald: background, 72; legal career, 71-3, 388; Vaquier case, 69-71; prosecutes Rouse at committal hearing, 19, 73-4, 135, 136-9, 141-2, 145, 147-8, 151, 515; requests copies of statements and reports, 132; photographed outside police court, 140; criticised by Baines, 73, 519, 521, 522; as malign influence, 144; reviews Rouse's petition for reprieve, 290; theory of joint insurance fraud, 459, 460-2, 465, 477; and Arthur Jnr's alleged statement, 463
Paling, Wilfred, 349
Palme, Olof, 324
Pankhurst, Emmeline, 397-8
Pankhurst, Sylvia, 397
pardons, 280-3, 284n; *see also* reprieve process
parish constables, 54
Parris, John, 76-7
Parry, Henry, 487, 488, 494
Parsons, Nicholas, 389-90
Paterson, Lieutenant John, 497-8
Paterson, Thomas (as Rouse's victim), 117
Peel House Training School, 60n
Peg's Paper: readership, 416; style and content, 407, 416-17; payment rates, 451; Lily Rouse's articles (April 1931), 419-25; Nellie Tucker's

articles (May 1931), 50, 429, 430-3; Helen Campbell's articles (June/July 1931), 414-15, 425-9; message and significance of articles, 417, 445, 450, 451-3; reprints Rouse story from *News of the World,* 441, 527
Peleus trial (1945), 86
Penguin Books, 24, 87
Penn, Margaret, *Manchester Fourteen Miles,* 406, 446
Penn, William, 234
Pennies from Heaven (TV drama serial), 390, 399, 412, 531
People (newspaper): and *Hobbs* case (1925), 342n; interview with Nellie Tucker (March 15 1931), 328, 341, 429-30; sexual behaviour survey, 407
Pepper, Mr. (as Rouse's victim), 96
Perdovitch, Hyman, 504
peremptory challenge, 160, 397
Perfect, Elizabeth, 390
Pethick-Lawrence, Emmeline, 303
Pethick-Lawrence, Frederick, 303
petitions for reprieve, 285
petrol union joint: unusual positioning in Morris Minor, 196; criminally loosened, 172-4; loosened through vibration, 203-4; loosened by heat transfer, 174-5, 202, 208, 210, 212, 213, 215, 237-9, 240; jury question on, 214; judge's summary of evidence, 221
Phillips, Alfred (as Rouse's victim), 120
Phillips, Conrad, 199, 200n
Phillips, Dr. E. L., 453
Phillips, Thomas, 307, 309, 314
photography of court proceedings, 312
Picton-Turbervill, Edith, 235n
Pierrepoint, Henry, 309
Pierrepoint, Thomas, 307, 309, 314
Pinner Royal Commercial Travellers' School for Orphans and Necessitous Children, 391
Pitt, Edwin: evidence at committal hearing, 139; evidence at trial, 179
Platz, Herr (furniture store owner), 473
Podmore, William, murder case (1930), 235, 286
Police and Criminal Evidence Act 1984, 520
police corruption, 72
policing: and inter-force cooperation, 64-6; and regulation of motor traffic, 385; *see also* Metropolitan Police; Northamptonshire County Police; Scotland Yard
policing memoirs, 59-60

Poor Laws, 405, 445
poor men's lawyers, 76, 520
Poor Prisoners' Defence Act 1903, 79, 128
Poor Prisoners' Defence Act 1930, 74–5,
80, 128–9, 520
Porthole Murder case (1947), 102n, 118
post-traumatic stress disorder (PTSD),
delayed-onset, 130, 481, 501–4, 505
Potter, Dennis: Pennies from Heaven, 390,
399, 412, 531
Praljak, Slobodan, 139
pre-marital sex, 399, 401, 404, 406–8,
409, 410, 417, 446
prejudice, 509, 510, 514, 515–16, 518
prerogative of justice, 281–2
prerogative of mercy, 66n, 267, 278, 280–
3; see also reprieve process
presumption of innocence, 73
Price, A. P., 320; see also Darnell & Price
Price, Fred, 237–8
Priest (Bedford Prison officer), 315,
336–7
Priestley, J. B.: An English Journey, 377; An
Inspector Calls, 31, 532
prison medical panels, and reprieve
process, 279, 280, 284, 285
Prison Reform Society, 519–20
prisoners: alleged confessions by, 328–30,
331–3, 335, 347; in condemned cell,
daily regime, 284; and confidentiality
of communications, 127, 334
Prisoners' Counsel Act 1836, 222
Pritchard, Annie, 186–7
private prosecutions, 66–7, 69
Procter, Harry, 199
procurator fiscal, 71
Prosecution of Offences Act 1879, 67
Prosecution of Offences Act 1908, 69
prosecutions, 67–8, 69
prostitution, 402
provocation, defence of, 264–5
Prudential Life Insurance Co., 462, 467,
468, 477
Pryce, Vicky, 458n
PTSD (post-traumatic stress disorder),
delayed-onset, 130, 481, 501–4, 505
Pudney, Frederick, 114
Pugh, Mervyn, 67
Purchase, Sir Bentley, 91–2, 98–9
Putkowski, Julian, Murderous Tommies
(with Mark Dunning), 494, 495, 497
Pye, Charlie, 38

quashing orders, 266, 281–2

Rae, Norman 'Jock': as crime reporter,

78n, 167, 199, 200 & n; 'flour of
Scotland' experiment, 199; evidence at
Rouse trial, 198–9; and Herbert Mills
case (1951), 200n
Ramsey, Ted, 323n
Rankin, Ian, Knots and Crosses, 200n
rape, last person hanged for, 309
Rattenbury and Stoner case (1935), 27–8,
72n, 86, 246, 411, 518
Rattigan, Terence, Cause Célèbre, 27–8
Rayner, Horace: reprieve of, 282
Reakes, Thomas, 14; evidence at
committal hearing, 142; in the
newspapers, 144; evidence at trial, 182
rebuttal procedure, 511 & n
Reck (chauffeur), 474
Redfern, Lieutenant, 487
Reeve, William, 308; murder trial (1915),
79–80
Regulation 18B, 82
Reid, Lord, 334
Report of the War Office Committee
of Enquiry into 'Shell-Shock'
(Southborough Committee), 484
Representation of the People Act 1918,
391–2
reprieve, Rouse case: Finnemore's
'Opinion' for Home Secretary, 266,
267–8, 271; formal petition, 266,
271–3, 290–1, 292; Rouse's own
petition, 266, 273–5, 287–8; letters of
appeal from the public, 266, 299–305;
letters from Helen Campbell to Clynes,
266; intimidating correspondence to
Home Office, 316n; public disquiet at
trial verdict, 267, 292; Home Office
response, 271–3, 277, 288–90, 291,
292, 293–8; Clynes agonises over,
286–7, 296; meeting between Clynes,
Blackwell and Talbot, 296; Rouse's last-
minute blackmail explanation, 339–40;
petition rejected, 298
reprieve process: grounds for
granting, 278, 288, 291; extenuating
circumstances, 278–9, 282–3, 291;
Home Office practice, 279–80, 282–3;
reprieves granted, statistics, 280;
legal principles, 280–2; procedure
for murderers facing death penalty,
284–6, 291; public opinion, role of,
285; insanity and mental instability
as factors, 285; intra-departmental
disagreement over reprieve decisions,
286
Reynolds, Mabel, 112
Reynolds, William Ernest (as Rouse's

victim), 112
Richards, James, 283, 309
Richardson, Major-General Frank, 483n, 484
Richardson gang, 511
Ridge, Chief Constable William, 72
Road Hill House murder (1860), 64n, 371n
Road Traffic Act 1930: indemnity requirements, 459 & n
road traffic casualty statistics, 384–6, 393, 394
Road Transport Act 1930, 385
Road Transport Act 1934, 386
Roberts (Governor of Dartmoor Prison), 520
Roberts, Alice, 121
Roberts, G. D., 77
Roberts, George, 113
Roberts, John, 435
Roberts, Robert, 1–2
Robertson, Geoffrey, 87
Robinson, Courtney, 113
Robinson, Jane, 405, 449
Robinson, John (commercial traveller), 393
Robinson, John (murderer), 231, 532
Rogers, Byron, 95
Rolph, C. H, Hanged by the Neck (with Arthur Koestler), 279
Rose, Andrew, 101
Rose, David, 200
Rothermere, Lord, 343
Roughead, William, 30, 397
Rouse, Alfred A. (no relation), 367n
ROUSE, ALFRED ARTHUR:
early life and military career: family background, 37, 129; birth, 37; childhood and upbringing, 37; office boy, 37; warehouseman, 37, 353; meets Lily Watkins, 37; enlists in Army, 38, 353; marriage to Lily, 36, 37–8, 353; deployed to France, 353–4, 357; with Territorial Force in Flanders, 354–6, 358–61; possibly fathers children while in France, 40, 355; wounded near Givenchy, 355, 360, 361, 363–5; evacuated as casualty, 365–6; taken back to England and hospitalised, 366–7; fatefully passes through Bedford station, 25–6, 367; recuperates at Harewood House, 367; at convalescent home in Clacton-on-Sea, 367; discharged from Army, 367; war injuries and disabilities, 367–8; further medical assessments, 368; disability

pension payments, 38, 368; effects of wartime experiences on, 328, 478, 479–81, 526; as sufferer of delayed-onset PTSD, 130, 481, 502–4, 505
commercial traveller and serial lover: speeding charge (November 11 1930), 384, 460; employed as commercial traveller, 38, 394; meets and seduces Helen Campbell, 46, 425–6; first child with Helen, 46, 426–7; bigamous marriage to Helen, 35–7, 44, 158n, 427; second child with Helen (Arthur), 47; maintenance and custody arrangements for Arthur, 45, 46, 47, 428; meets and courts Nellie Tucker, 47; first child with Nellie (Pamelita), 47–8, 49; Phyllis Skinner affair, 41; Hattie Jones incident, 42; affair with Ivy Jenkins, 433–7; second child with Nellie (Patricia Jean), 20, 39, 50, 136, 145; blags copy of false marriage certificate, 35–6, 39–40; visits Nellie in maternity hospital, 50, 142, 430–1, 503–4
murder and arrest: murky social and financial situation, 51; scheme to fake death and disappear, 51–3, 183, 232, 296, 348, 457, 458–9; leaves home, 188, 252; picks up victim, 19, 105, 111, 188, 252; journey to Hardingstone, 165n, 167–9, 252; his accounts of the 'murder', 319–20, 336–8, 339; movements after blaze, 1, 3, 325; encounter with Brown and Bailey, 3, 10, 190, 325; lift to Finchley, 10–11; description circulated by police, 4–5; car traced to, 7; police search for, 7–8; brief return to Buxted Road, 11–12, 190–2, 195, 275n, 294–6, 295n, 321, 465; flying visit to South Wales, 12–16; newspaper reports of blazing car, 7, 14–15; lift into Cardiff, 15–16; butcher's boy conversation at Cooper's Arms, 15–16; catches coach to Hammersmith, 16; intercepted by police, 16–17, 62, 193; 'I'm glad it is all over' comment, 17, 137, 143, 144, 165, 193; voluntary first statement, 17–18, 169; interviewed under caution, 18–19; detained at Angel Lane station, 19, 63, 91; 'my harem' speech, 19–20, 138, 396; charged with murder, 20, 131; visited by Lily, 20, 424, 465; police enquiries into his antecedents, 20, 41, 44, 108–9
legal proceedings and final days:

remanded at Bedford Prison, 20, 126; mental and physical condition assessed, 129–31; raises funds for defence, 74–5, 127–9, 249; police court hearing (see committal proceedings, Rouse case); prison visitors, 273, 328, 336, 347, 417–19; trial (see trial, Rouse case); life story published in News of The World, 227–9, 230, 441 & n, 527–8; date of execution fixed, 251–2; appeal (see appeal hearing, Rouse case); application to appeal to House of Lords refused, 264, 293; petition for clemency (see reprieve, Rouse case); alleged confession to Nellie, 328, 341, 429–30; alleged confession to Lily, 320, 321, 327–8, 341–2, 347; off-the-record confession to prison wardens, 311, 327, 336–7; confession to Gwilliam, 335–6, 337–9; last days and hours, 311–16; final letters vetted, 335; alleged confession to prison chaplain, 325–7, 348; execution, 307, 316–18, 325–6; post-mortem, 307; inquest on body, 307–8; burial, 308; personal effects disposed, 309, 315; murder confession published in Daily Sketch (11 March 1931), 311, 319–23, 324–5, 345–8
character and characteristics: car insurance fraud, 322, 468–9; cars, love of, 380; character, 41, 169, 222–3; earnings and finances, 182, 377–8, 391, 395; hats, 21, 181, 197, 253; joint insurance swindle with Lily, 53, 122, 183, 192, 232, 234, 294–6, 301, 340, 457, 458–9, 461–7; as 'knave of the road', 381–2; liar, 193, 218, 223, 297; masculinity, sense of, 413, 524, 526–32; mechanical expertise, 196, 273; memory loss, 130, 197, 363n, 368; motive for murder, 31, 139, 147–8, 161, 162, 184, 186, 217, 219, 292, 294, 457, 514; *petit-bourgeois* respectability, 526–7, 530; photographs of, 21 & n, 33n, 126–7, 128, 315; physical appearance, 397; as product of the suburbs, 377–9; service revolver, 45–6, 93, 144–5; sex appeal, 399; sexual immorality and promiscuity, 40–4, 149, 254–5, 263, 526, 533; triggers for murder, 319, 469–70, 471–7; verbosity and garrulousness, 188, 189, 198, 256, 508; as victim of miscarriage of justice, 348, 508, 519, 532, 534; voice, 37, 163
Rouse, Alice (*later* Dockree; sister), 37

Rouse, Arthur B. (no relation), 367n
Rouse, Arthur Jnr (son with Helen): birth and registration, 44; custody and maintenance arrangements, 44–5, 46, 47, 423, 428; father-son relationship, 46, 418, 427, 428–9, 528–9; stays with Lily, 9, 45, 47, 423, 428; and family photograph incident, 422; schooling altercation, 47, 423–4; alleged statement, 191, 234, 295n, 463–4; whip-round for, 450; illegitimate status, 183, 406, 450; possibly identified in closed MEPO file, 122
Rouse, Edith (sister), 37
Rouse, Elizabeth Alice (mother), 37, 304
Rouse, Lily (*née* Watkins; wife): meets Rouse, 37; marriage to Rouse, 36, 37–8, 353; looks after Arthur Jnr, 47, 428; confrontation with Helen Campbell, 47, 423–4, 428; takes out life insurance policy on husband, 296n, 462–3, 466; packs husband's belongings, 188, 252; and Rouse's return home after murder, 9, 190–2, 195, 294–6, 295n, 321, 465; wanted for questioning, 7; mistakenly notified of husband's death, 8–9; newspaper interviews, 9; travels to Northampton, 9, 91, 294–5, 424, 464–5; sees husband at Angel Lane station, 20, 424, 465; first statement to police about Rouse's whereabouts, 10; attends committal hearing, 135, 140, 151, 152; fetches aspirin, 139, 424–5; photographed outside police court, 140; attends auction sale, 145; not called as witness at trial, 158, 163; attends trial, 159, 160, 163, 164, 167, 190, 217; reaction to jury verdict, 224; prison visits, 417–19; joint insurance swindle with husband, 53, 122, 183, 192, 232, 234, 294–6, 301, 340, 457, 458–9, 461–7; writes to Home Office, 242; at appeal hearing, 252, 264; seeks intercession from Mrs. Clynes, 235n, 303–4; winds up Rouse's estate, 127n; last letter from Rouse, 346; requests return of Rouse's personal effects, 309, 315; insurance claim after Rouse's execution, 467; and husband's alleged confession, 320, 321, 327–8, 331, 335, 341–2, 347; depicted in press, 414, 415; articles for Daily Express, 417–19; articles for Peg's Paper, 419–25; payment for story, 416
Rouse, Pamelita (daughter with Nellie), 47–8, 49, 422, 430, 442

Rouse, Patricia Jean (daughter with Nellie), 20, 39, 50, 136, 145, 442
Rouse, W. (grandfather), 304
Rouse, Walter Edward (father), 37, 159, 164, 304, 336, 434
Rowell, Henry, 239–41, 268
Rowland, Walter, 23
Royal Commission on Police Powers and Procedure (1928), 70–1 & n
Rudé, George, 159
Ruebin, Harry, 393
Rumbelow, Donald, 123
Rumsey, Leonard George (as Rouse's victim), 121
Rutherford, Colonel, 486, 487 & n
Ruxton, Dr. Buck, 72, 81, 104, 200

Saffran, Fritz, 473–5
Salvation Army, 120–1, 449
Samuel, Sir Herbert, 521n
Sandwell, T. W., 484
Sankey, John, Viscount, 73, 269, 344, 345
Sassoon, Siegfried, 482
Saunders, Alison, 69n
Savidge, Irene, 70n, 71
Sayers, Dorothy L., 389
scaffold confessions, 324, 329
Schiller, Louis, 390–1
Schonberg, Joseph, 390–1
'Scotch drapers', 386, 391
Scotland Yard: training of officers, 60 & n; Flying Squad created, 478–9; and Browne and Kennedy case (1927), 65n; not called in by Northamptonshire Police, 7, 10, 62–3, 65; enquiries at Buxted Road, 8–9, 10; enquiries into Rouse's antecedents, 20, 41, 44, 108–9; enquiries into identity of blazing car victim, 116, 119, 121; provincial forces, relationship with, 63–5; and inter-force cooperation, 64–5; and Louisa Kempson murder case (1931), 387; investigation into police corruption at Brighton (1957), 72; see also Collins, Inspector W.; Metropolitan Police
Scott, Sir Harold, 60
Scranton case (1921), 77–8
Scrivener, Anthony, 87
Scrutton, Lord Justice, 389
Searle, Sister, 39
Seddon, Frederick, 68–9, 84, 94, 222, 256n, 371n, 468n, 510
Sentence of Death (Expectant Mothers) Bill 1931, 235n
Seton, Graham, 471, 475; The W Plan, 475–7

Setty, Stanley, 26, 52, 104
Sex Disqualification (Removal) Act 1919, 160
sex manuals, 408–9
sexology research, 407, 408, 410
Seymour, Henry, 387–8, 390n
shaken baby syndrome, 250n
sharia law, 468
Shaw, Dr. Eric: conducts post-mortems on blazing car victim, 8, 9, 93, 96–8, 99–100, 111, 138, 314; evidence at trial, 178, 179
Shearman, Sir Montague (Mr. Justice), 29, 80, 84, 271
Sheffield Mail, 485
shell-shock: as mental and physical condition, 481–2; breakdown symptoms, 130, 482–3; and military medical opinion, 483–4; Southborough Committee enquiry, 484; scepticism among senior line officers, 494; and link to criminality, 484–5; as defence in criminal trials, 483n, 486, 487–8; as defence in capital courts martial cases, 494–8, 501
Sheriffs Act 1887, 310
Sherriff, R. C., Greengates, 372–3
Sherwood, Arthur, 390
Shiner, Phil, 501n
Shipman, Dr. Harold, 23
Short, Elizabeth, 33, 324
Shortt, Edward, 491
Sidney, William, 394
Silvester, J. C. (prison officer), 113
'similar fact evidence', 512–14, 516
Simon, Sir John, 128
Simpson, Dr. Keith, 23
Simpson, Mrs. W. H., 113–14
Simpson, Wallis (later Duchess of Windsor): divorce petition, 81; and Abdication crisis, 398n, 402
single mothers see unmarried mothers
skeletal remains, identification of, 103–4
Skelhorn, Sir Norman, 513
Skelly, Detective Sergeant Robert: intercepts Rouse at Hammersmith Bridge, 16–17, 62, 193; voluntary first statement, 17–18; second statement, 18–19, 151, 188, 193–4; evidence at committal hearing, 143–4; evidence at trial, 165–6
Skinner, Phyllis, 41
Skone, Private John, 497, 498
Skuse, Dr. Frank, 250
Slater, Emma, 141
Slater, Oscar, 25, 27, 71, 320n, 396–7, 500,

508
Slater, Stefan, 402
Slesser, Henry, 505n
Smeaton, John, 171
Smethers, William: witness statement, 241–2; evidence withheld by Crown, 242
Smethwick rent strikes (1915), 80
Smith, Sergeant (of S Division), 47, 48
Smith, Detective Sergeant Clifford, 119–20
Smith, F. E. (later Lord Birkenhead), 85, 246
Smith, George, 12, 179, 181
Smith, George Joseph, 23, 24, 94, 128, 246, 324, 399–400, 435, 436, 512
Smith, Dr. Lisa, 122
Smith, Madeleine, 24, 403, 518, 519n, 532
Smith, May, 39n; evidence at committal hearing, 142
Social Purity and Hygiene Movement, 401–2, 405, 449
Somerset House, 40, 44, 108–9, 114
South London Press, 362
South Wales Echo, 14, 16
Southborough Committee enquiry, 484
Spectator (magazine), 308
Spendlove, Richard, 122
Spilsbury, Sir Bernard: Crippen case (1910), 123; Thorne case (1925), 26, 98; arrives in Northampton, 133; post-mortem report on blazing car victim, 96–7, 98–9, 111, 119, 121, 132, 138, 258–9, 297; supplementary report, 100; testifies at Rouse's trial, 100–1, 179, 185; 'Spilsburyism', 26, 98, 101, 146; and Brentford Canal murder case (1935), 103; testifies at Carrie Whitehouse inquest, 470; testifies at Agnes Kesson inquest, 470
spiritualism/spiritualists, 112, 114, 117–18
Squier, Dr. Waney, 250n
St Mary's Church, Islington, 35–6, 39–40
St Saviour Church, St Albans, 36, 37, 353
Stableford, Annie May, 37–8
Stableford, Phyllis (later Barnes), 37–8
Staunton, Harriet, 369n
Steel, Jack Fulton (as Rouse's victim), 108
Steer, David, 394
Stephen, James Fitzjames, Stephen's Digest of the Law of Evidence, 516
Stetson hats, 13
Stevens, Nellie (née Tucker; Nellie Tucker's mother), 20, 48
Stevens, Robert: writes on Hewart, 243
Stevenson, John, British Society, 1914–45,

376
Stevenson, Melford, 86
Stewart, Mamie, 103
Stewart & Ardern Ltd (Tottenham car repairers), 383, 459
Stileman-Gibbard, Leonard, 311
Stoll, Oswald, 523
Stoner, George see Rattenbury and Stoner case (1935)
Stone's Justices' Manual, 154n
Stopes, Dr. Marie, 29, 117, 247, 448; Married Love, 398, 403, 408
Stops, J. Faulkner, 133, 148, 151, 251–2, 307; at Rouse's execution, 317
Straffen, John, 513
strangulation, 323
stretcher bearers, 365, 366
suburbia: associated with murder and dark deeds, 369–70, 373–4; and growth of private transport, 372; expansion in London, 26, 374, 376; Friern Barnet, 374–5; housing and home ownership, 376, 378; snobbery, 376–7; mocking voices, 370–1, 374, 377; debt and social status, 378–9; Rouse as product of the suburbs, 377–9; scandalized by Rouse, 409, 410, 412
suicide by poisoning in courtroom, 139
Sullivan, Serjeant, 85
Summary Procedure (Domestic Proceedings) Act 1937, 344
Summerscale, Kate, The Suspicions of Mr Whicher, 24, 64n, 371n
Sumner, T. J., 394
Sunday Dispatch: 'My Doubts about Rouse Conviction' (February 8 1931), 231–2, 343; proposes blackmail theory, 106; change of clothes suggestion, 275n; on Rouse as 'expert engineer', 273; attacks Daily Sketch, 325; publishes prison chaplain story, 325–6
Sunday Express, 346
Sunday News, 330
surveillance work, 61–2
Sutcliffe, Peter (Yorkshire Ripper), 23, 25, 493–4
Swan and Pyramids (public house), Whetstone, 19, 111, 319, 320
Swetman, James, 12
Swift, Mr. Justice Rigby, 76, 390n, 459 & n

Talbot, Mr. Justice: qualities as judge, 76, 89; background and legal career, 89, 333; charge to grand jury, 157, 158; enters courtroom, 159–60; queries projected length of trial, 164; conduct of Rouse trial, 89, 180, 188, 251, 261, 508–9, 518; sharp exchanges with Rouse, 194, 195; rules on 'no case to answer' plea, 184–5; advises jury to disregard mallet evidence, 198; scathing of police failures, 7, 56, 62; questions from jury, 214; allows further examination of Buckle, 214–15; summing up, 218–24, 466; on technical evidence of car fire, 220–1; on character and admitted conduct of Rouse, 222–3; passes sentence of death, 224; trial notes, 186, 191–2, 197; reviews case with Clynes and Blackwell, 296; apprised of joint insurance fraud theory, 233, 296; on Rouse's blackmail explanation, 341; view on conduct of newspapers, 341

Tally Ho Corner, Finchley, 11, 110, 119, 165n, 188, 190, 374–5

Tapsell, Inspector, 120

Tarsh, Moey, 77–8

Tate, Reginald: evidence at trial, 163, 168

Taylor, D. J., *The Prose Factory: Literary Life in England Since 1918,* 372

Taylor, Superintendent (of Brighton CID), 109

Tebbey, Superintendent: search of crime scene, 93; on identity of blazing car victim, 122; proceedings at police court, 132, 133, 134, 140, 151; meeting with DPP, 132

Telling, Dr. Aubrey, 126, 130, 166; evidence at trial, 200–1

Tellus vacuum cleaner, 388

Tennyson Jesse, F., 30, 403, 532n; *A Pin to See the Peep Show,* 27

Tetzner, Kurt Erich, 472–3

Thames Transport Company: Villiers Street ticket office, 12, 181

thermal expansion of brass, 210–11, 232

Third Parties (Rights against Insurers) Act 1930, 459

Thomas, Roger, Baron Thomas of Cwmgiedd, 277

Thomas, Sarah, 435

Thompson, E. P., 30

Thompson, Edith *see* Thompson–Bywaters case (1921–22)

Thompson, Percy, 20, 28, 440

Thompson, Robert, 23

Thompson, W. S., 238

Thompson–Bywaters case (1921–22): Frederick's military service, 505; Edith's character and search for selfhood, 28–9, 226–7, 376, 403; death

by accident theory, 440; trial, 77, 222, 510; appeals against death sentence, 285, 305–6, 419; Edith sedated, 313; executions, 20, 440; in literature, film and theatre, 27, 422n

Thomson's Weekly News: Ivy Jenkins's articles (February 1931), 418, 433–4, 435–41, 453–4

Thorne, Norman, 25, 26, 98, 215

Thorne, Thomas (as Rouse's victim), 116

Thornton, F. H. (magistrate), 131, 133, 134, 135, 145

Tickler, Mr. (parish councillor), 93–4

Times, The, 257, 264, 313n, 318, 369, 407n, 485; on tramps, 93; coverage of Rouse case, 145, 153

Tindal Atkinson, E. H. *see* Atkinson, E. H. Tindal

Tingey, Superintendent R., 307

Tinsley, Mona: abduction and murder of, 82

Tipplestone, Edgar, 6–7, 163

Tobin, Peter, 124

Tokyo earthquake (1923), 239

Tolley, Cyril, 81

Trade Disputes and Trade Unions Act 1927, 164–5

Trade Disputes Bill, 164–5

tramps and tramping, 93, 105, 108

travelling salesmen *see* commercial travellers

Treasury counsel, 67

Tremayne, Sydney, *The Trial of Alfred Arthur Rouse,* 33 & n, 202, 295n, 479–80, 527

trench warfare, 357, 358, 364

trial, Rouse case: funding for defence, 74–6, 258; charge to grand jury and indictment, 157–8; attendance and public interest, 158–9, 167, 179, 186, 198, 213–14; Mr. Justice Talbot enters courtroom, 159–60; Rouse brought up from cells, 160; his appearance and demeanour, 160, 163, 169, 179, 217, 508; arraignment and plea, 160; jury, 160 & n; opening address by the prosecution, 160–2; proposed motive for murder, 161, 162; case for the prosecution, 162–85; bad character evidence not adduced, 162–3, 169, 179–80, 514; crime scene evidence, 163; police witnesses, 163–4, 165–7, 169, 180–1; projected duration of trial, 164; evidence of Inspector Lawrence, 169; technical evidence on car fire, 170, 172–8; Colonel Buckle's evidence,

172–4; cross-examination of Buckle, 175–8; medical evidence, 178, 179; objection to Nellie Tucker's testimony, 179–80; Nellie Tucker's evidence, 180; lorry and coach company witnesses, 181; South Wales witnesses, 181–2; evidence on Rouse's employment and financial difficulties, 182–3; defence application of no case to answer, 183–5; opening speech for the defence, 186, 187; case for the defence, 187–215; Rouse gives evidence, 187–97; breaks down in witness box, 189–90; admits brief return home, 190–2, 195; Rouse cross-examined, 192–7; his performance in witness box, 190, 191, 192–3, 197–8, 256; sharp exchanges with Mr. Justice Talbot, 194, 195; black cat omen, 194; Rouse questioned on technical aspects of Crown's case, 196; shocking statement, 196–7; re-examined by Finnemore, 197; irreparable self-inflicted damage, 197–8; jury examines mallet, 198; tyre mark evidence, 198–9; defence medical evidence, 200–1; defence mechanical evidence on car fire, 201–13, 214–15, 220–1, 232; sensational letter, 202; flawed questioning by Birkett, 207–8, 209, 210–11; questions from jury, 214; Buckle recalled, 214–15; closing speech for defence, 216–17; closing speech for prosecution, 217–18; judge's summing up, 218–24; jury deliberations and verdict, 224; Rouse's reaction to verdict, 224; sentence, 224; bigamy indictment remains on file, 224–5; judge's notes, 186, 191–2, 197; newspaper coverage, 185; post-trial newspaper coverage, 226, 227–9, 230–5; defence strategy criticised by Rouse, 242, 254, 273–4, 288; prejudice and unfairness, 509, 514, 515–16, 518
trial by jury system, 249
Trial of Alfred Arthur Rouse (Normanton): publication history, 32, 33n; transcription anomalies, 161n, 209n; incomplete, 202, 295n; photograph of burnt car, 288; on Rouse as war invalid, 367, 478, 479, 526; on incident at Bedford, 25–6; on technical and mechanical evidence, 172–3, 178; on Rouse's performance in dock, 190; on prejudicial revelations, 254–5; on the defence experts, 208; on Rouse fathering child with Helen Campbell,

426 & n; on triggers and parallel murders, 471–2, 473, 476; on *Makin* case, 512; *see also* Normanton, Helena
True, Ronald, 27, 243, 270, 489–92
true bill, 157, 158
Tucker, Frederick, 48
Tucker, Nellie: meets and courted by Rouse, 47; first child by Rouse (Pamelita), 47–8, 49; obtains affiliation order, 48; employment history, 48, 49; pregnant for second time, 48; second child by Rouse (Patricia Jean), 20, 39, 50, 136, 145; forged marriage certificate, 39, 50; Rouse visits Nellie in maternity hospital, 50, 142, 430–1, 503–4; discharged, 50; interviewed by police and gives statement, 47; legal wrangle over admissibility of her testimony at committal hearing, 146–8; evidence at committal hearing, 149; called as witness at trial, 162–3; legal objection to her anticipated testimony, 179–80; evidence at trial, 180; reaction to jury verdict, 224; photographed for *News of the World* story, 229; at appeal hearing, 252; prison visits, 328, 336; interviewed in *People* about Rouse's apparent confession, 328, 341, 429–30; articles in *Peg's Paper*, 50, 414–15, 429, 430–3; payment for story, 416, 451; marriage to Mirza Knott, 429, 450, 451
Tucker Committee report (1958), 344, 349
Tumblety, Francis, 330n
Turing, Alan, 281, 284n
Turner, Henry, 11, 179, 190, 195
Turner, Walter, 35–6, 39–40

Ugolini, Laura, 2
unidentified victims, convictions for murder of, 31–2, 102–3, 105
United Commercial Travellers' Association, 392
United Dominions Trust (UDT) (finance company), 382
Unknown Man: picked up by Rouse, 19, 105, 111, 188, 252; Rouse's accounts of 'murder', 319–20, 336–8, 339; charred remains found in car, 4, 5, 54; position of body, 5, 97–8, 100–1, 258–9, 287–8, 290; body moved to Crown Inn, 6, 56, 91, 98; post-mortem findings, 8, 9, 93, 96–101; cause of death, 9, 96; age determination, 99, 111; burn-related injuries, 97; carbon monoxide inhalation, 97, 99–100; coal deposit

inhalation, 119; dental features, 99, 108, 111, 140; physical description, 99, 111; sex determination, 93, 96–7; remains preserved at Northampton General Hospital, 91; inquest, 91–3; burial, 93–5, 96; gravesite today, 95; pilgrimages to gravesite, 112; comparison with Unknown Warrior of the Great War, 95–6, 118; enduring vitality of his story, 96; artefacts, 112 & n; remembrance and closure on grief, 118–19

Unknown Man: identity of: police and journalists enquiries, 105–7, 108–11, 112, 133–4, 135; letters from public, 106–7, 112, 117; names, suspects and dead-ends, 113–17, 119–22; Briggs family claim, 96, 122; 'Middlesbrough man', 106, 110–11, 337, 340; Welsh miner theory (Thomas Waite), 106, 109–10, 140, 141; Rouse's claims, 106, 110, 188–9, 252, 319, 337, 340; as tramp, 108; conspiracy theories, 122; false confessions, 116–17; spirit messages, 112, 114; DNA profiling, 122, 123

Unknown Sailor (Hindhead murder victim, 1786), 32, 102–3

Unknown Warrior, tomb of, 95–6, 107

unmarried males and females in 1911 (statistics), 400

unmarried mothers: in eighteenth century, 445–6; popular attitudes to in inter-war period, 446, 448–9, 450–1; condemnatory views in modern period, 443–4; illegitimate birth statistics, 446–8; and illegitimacy, 397, 404, 405–6, 446–50

vacuum cleaners, 386–7, 388

Valentine, PC Robert: actions on night of murder, 4, 5, 6, 55, 56–8; incompetence and procedural failings, 57–8, 62; takes statement from William Smethers, 241; evidence at committal hearing, 150–1; evidence at trial, 164; attends burial of Rouse's victim, 94

van der Elst, Violet, 310n, 316

Vaquier, Jean-Pierre, 63, 69–71, 249n

Vardon, Thomas, 120

Vaughan-Morgan, Colonel, 392

Venables, Jon, 23

venereal disease, 402

veterans: and crime, 478–9, 485–6, 485n, 487–92, 504–5; effects of First World War on, 525

victim identification, and homicide law, 293

voting rights, 391–2

W. B. Martin Ltd, Leicester (menswear manufacturers), 51, 127, 182, 394–5 & n

W. G. Ward (Northampton Undertakers), 94

Waddingham, Dorothea, 82

Wagstaffe, John, 458

Wainwright, Henry and Thomas, 257

Waite, Thomas (as Rouse's victim), 106, 109–10, 140, 141

Wakley, Dr. Thomas, 92

Wallace, Edgar, 231 & n, 302

Wallace, Julia: murder of, 27n, 76n, 263, 445

Wallace, William, 27n, 76n, 262–3, 379, 462

Walls, Inspector Arthur: murdered on duty, 247

Walters, Harold, 309

Walton Street police station, 49

war fervour, 353 & n, 357–8

Ward, Stephen: trial of (1963), 78–9

wartime trauma evoked as defence by veterans, 485–6, 487–9, 504–5

Watkins, Irene, 330

Watkins, Iris, 63

Watkins, Leonard, 37

Watkins, Lily see Rouse, Lily

Watson, Colin, Snobbery With Violence, 376–7

Webb, Duncan, 78n, 199

Weir, Detective Sergeant Douglas, 42, 43

Welby, Inspector, 169

Wells, H. G., 374n; The History of Mr Polly, 457–8

Welsh, Irving, Trainspotting, 533

Welsh miner see Waite, Thomas

Wensley, Superintendent Frederick, 381, 387n

West, Rosemary, 23, 297

Westbrooke, Bowen: evidence at committal hearing, 143

Whetstone: Price of Wales (public house), 119–20; Swan and Pyramids (public house), 19, 111, 319, 320

Whetstone police station, 7, 10, 20, 119

Whicher, Jonathan, 64n

White, Joan, 115

White, S. P., 462

Whitehouse, Carrie, 470–1

Whiteley, William, 282

Whyley, G. J. M., 307

Widgery, Lord, 306
wife-murder, 24
Wigram, Sir Clive, 318
Wild, Sir Ernest, 77–8
Wilkinson, Francis, 285
Williams, Kenneth, 390
Williamson, Chief Constable John, 5, 55
Windle case, 493n
Winfield, Percy, 500 & n
Wise, Olive, 235 & n, 304
Withers (London solicitors), 81
Woffinden, Bob, 200
women: allowed to sit on juries, 160; and
  chastity, 405, 406, 410; 'coerced' into
  sex, 407n; as commercial travellers,
  389; as domestic goddesses, 444;
  'New Women', 29, 371, 403, 524; and
  offers to marry Rouse if reprieved,
  286n; respectability and femininity,
  406–7, 409, 410, 524; right to vote,
  391–2; Sentence of Death (Expectant
  Mothers) Bill 1931, 235n; sexual
  liberation, 403, 408–9; singleness and
  sex ratio imbalance after Great War,
  400–1; as spectators at murder trials,
  159, 179; wartime employment, 485,
  525; and working class domestic life,
  444; *see also* adultery; pre-marital sex;
  unmarried mothers
women's magazines, 226, 407, 444, 453;
  see also Peg's Paper
Wood, Fred, 504

Wood, John Carter, 22, 124
Wood, Robert, 83, 163
Woolmington v DPP [1935] AC 462, 72–3,
  80, 264, 269
'working-class killings', 24, 30–1
working classes: clothing and headgear, 1,
  2; and domestic life, 444; and domestic
  violence, 432; home ownership, 376;
  and inter-war affairs and marriage,
  403, 409, 417, 421–2; reading material
  for, 416, 445; respectability and
  femininity, 406–7; taboos against sex
  outside marriage, 405, 410
Wormwood Scrubs, 310
Worth, Anthony, 337n
Worthington, Walter, 308
Wright, Whitaker, 84, 139
'Wullie' (Glaswegian down-and-out),
  120n

Yallop, David, 200
Yates (newspaper reporter), 16
Yates, Gertrude: murder of (1922), 489,
  490–1
Yorkshire Ripper (Peter Sutcliffe), 23, 25,
  493–4
Ypres, 357
Ystrad Mynach, 15–16, 141, 453, 503

'Zinoviev letter' forgery, 248 & n